# ITALY FROM LIBERALISM
## TO FASCISM: 1870–1925

CHRISTOPHER SETON-WATSON

# Italy from Liberalism to Fascism

## 1870-1925

METHUEN & CO LTD

*First published in 1967 by*
*Methuen & Co Ltd, 11 New Fetter Lane, EC4*
© *1967 Christopher Seton-Watson*
*Printed in Great Britain by*
*Butler & Tanner Ltd, Frome and London*

TO THE MEMORY OF
MY FATHER

Distributed in USA by Barnes and Noble Inc.

# CONTENTS

# Part II: Stresses and Strains 1887–1901

# Part III: Expansion 1901–14

# Part IV: Crisis 1914–25

# MAPS

# PREFACE

This book has been a long time in the making. It could perhaps be said to have started with the purchase at Blackwells in the autumn of 1943 of Cecil Sprigge's *Development of Modern Italy*, which had then just appeared. Sprigge's volume subsequently travelled with me from Cassino to Bologna during the final fifteen months of the Italian campaign. At that time there seemed little connexion between the pre-fascist Italy that Sprigge described and the prostrate and devastated Italy that confronted the wartime British soldier. Only later, during the visits which took me to every region of Italy in the first ten post-war years, did I come to understand that connexion and to appreciate the continuity in Italy's modern history.

In 1946, when I began to teach in Oxford, I found that Italy constituted a serious gap in the English historical literature on Europe since 1870. Neither Croce nor Sprigge satisfied the needs of the enterprising under-graduate who had no knowledge of the Italian language. It was primarily for such a person that this book was written. Since it was started, Dennis Mack Smith's *Italy* and John A. Thayer's *Italy and the Great War* have appeared. These two studies cover much of the ground but do not wholly fill the gap. I believe there is still room for a different interpretation, with different emphases, different partialities and, doubtless, different prejudices.

One third of the first draft was written in 1953 during a sabbatical term at the Institute for Advanced Study, Princeton. My debt to the Institute, and in particular to the late Edward M. Earle, at that time director of its History Department, is very great. From 1959 to 1964 I held a Special Lecturership in the Faculty of Social Studies in Oxford. I am most grateful to my colleagues on the Faculty Board for appointing me to this post which, by reducing my tutorial load, allowed me to make substantial progress with my writing.

This is a political history. The economic and social sections make no pretence to comprehensiveness; they are intended merely to provide the minimum framework within which political events become intelligible. Cultural history receives scant attention. Croce and Labriola, D'Annunzio and Gentile, Gramsci and Salvemini appear in these pages in their political roles or as commentators on political events, not as scholars, poets or philosophers. Such limitations were essential if fifty-five years of political history were to be treated in substantial depth within the confines of a single volume.

Few historians concerned with recent times can escape moments of despair at the volume of material that threatens to swamp them. In Italy since 1945 the flow of publication and documentation on the post-Risorgimento period, pent up for twenty years by the constraints of fascism, has been especially formidable. It shows no sign of slackening and is already too great for one individual to master. With the exception of certain Foreign Office files on the years 1890–8, consulted in the Public Record Office, I have relied wholly on published material, much of it still little known outside Italy. My indebtedness to fellow historians is, I hope, fully documented. What cannot be documented is what I have learnt from my travels in Italy, from observation of its physical and human landscape, and from much talking with patient Italian colleagues and friends. To this must be added my debt to those fellow students and lovers of Italy with whom I have argued and exchanged ideas over the years in Oxford, in London and in many other places. Without their encouragement this book could never have been written.

MARCH 1967

ORIEL COLLEGE
OXFORD

# PROLOGUE

# UNIFICATION
## 1859–70

# The Makers of Italy

The unification of Italy was the joint achievement of the liberal monarchist moderates and the revolutionary democrats: two political groupings differing widely in programme and temperament which emerged from the confused failure of 1848 and worked together uneasily for the same end. Both drew their leaders, like other national movements in nineteenth-century Europe, predominantly from the propertied and professional middle class. There were few working-men, and fewer aristocrats, among the makers of Italy. The contribution of the peasantry was negligible. National sentiment was perhaps strongest among students and young university graduates, who were prominent in the rank and file of Garibaldi's volunteers. Lawyers, doctors, journalists and teachers were fired by the vision of a united Italy which would free them from their intellectual frustrations and provide new, more rewarding outlets for their constructive energy. Their idealism was powerfully reinforced by the more calculating ambitions of merchants, bankers and manufacturers, who looked forward impatiently to the prosperity which they believed an Italian customs union would bring. An essential role was played by the Piedmontese House of Savoy, for which the plains of northern Italy were the traditional target of dynastic ambition. To all these must be added the foreign patrons of Italy's Risorgimento: Napoleon III, who provided the military force which Italians did not possess, and the British Liberal statesmen without whose moral support Italy might have been born not independent, but a satellite of imperial France. Without foreign assistance unification could never have been achieved so rapidly and at such an astonishingly low cost in human life.[1]

Among the democrats Mazzini was the outstanding figure. He was the prophet who in the dark days kept faith in the future alive and made national unity a religion. He so influenced a whole generation that compromise schemes for confederations, or for a peninsula divided between several kingdoms, never found sufficient supporters. His teaching is summed up in his own famous phrase, 'God and the People', and in his conception of the proletariat as 'a tide moved by the divine breath'. His faith in the People, in its revolutionary possibilities and its capacity for self-government, was fundamental. From it followed logically his republicanism and his anti-clericalism, for both monarchy and the church were institutions that came between God and the People and restricted the

---

[1] The total casualties of the regular and volunteer forces between 1848 and 1870 have been estimated at 6,000 dead and 20,000 wounded.

latter's freedom. For Mazzini the triumph of the national principle and the redemption of the proletariat were inseparably linked. Further, the creation of a united Italy, with the Third Rome of the People as its capital, would, by liberating the Italian people for its mission, be but the first step towards a new fraternal world of democratic nations.

Mazzini lived most of his life in exile and conspiracy, among political abstractions. As a politician and man of action, except for the brief glory of the Roman Republic of 1849, he was an utter failure. Few of his followers understood him and none could rise to his philosophic and religious heights. He died in 1872, a lonely and embittered old man, abandoned by all his prominent disciples.

Mazzini nevertheless left a permanent mark on the Italian democratic tradition. Faith in popular initiative and enthusiasm did not fade, and throughout modern Italian history there recurs, in successive programmes of the left, the hope that a wholly new Italy could be fashioned by a great upsurge of the People. Enthusiasm as a substitute for organisation, amateurishness and a consistent underestimating of obstacles remained characteristic of many politicians of the left. This naivety showed clearly in their taste for conspiracy, their exaltation of the voluntary spirit and their distrust of diplomacy. Conspiracy was in their blood and too often was considered sufficient preparation for a revolution. A voluntary citizen militia was the only safe form of military organisation, because regular armies were dynastic and militarist institutions. Red shirts and picturesque hats, high ideals and reckless personal bravery could achieve more than military training and discipline. Diplomacy, too, was dynastic, aristocratic and therefore suspect. As the name they gave their party implies – the Party of Action – they believed in deeds, not words, in battle, not negotiation. The many concessions that had to be made to international reality in the course of the Risorgimento seemed to Italian democrats just plain treachery to the national cause. In later years one of the bitterest accusations that they hurled against Cavour and his successors was that of 'diplomatising the revolution'.

The moderates became an effective political force after 1848, in the reaction against the disunity and regional rivalries, the unskilled leadership and unplanned enthusiasm which had ruined the Italian cause in that year. They were the party of caution, with a well-developed sense of the practicable. Monarchist because the monarchy was a bulwark of social stability, they insisted that Italy should be unified by respectable methods, without disorder and with at least an appearance of legality. This meant setting clear limits to the national revolution and killing such dangerous ideas as land reform. On the other hand they were modern in their outlook, with a high respect for efficiency and a keen interest in agricultural improvement, railways and trade. The essential tools of unification seemed to them to be a strong regular army, an efficient bureaucracy and a well-organised police force able to keep popular enthusiasm within bounds. Most important of all, their European contacts had given them a realistic vision of the international situation. Being aware of the smallness of Piedmont and the military weakness of the Italian unitary movement, they saw the necessity for diplomacy and foreign aid.

Cavour dominated the moderates to an even greater extent than Mazzini dominated the democrats. He became Piedmontese Prime Minister in 1852, and with only one short break remained in power continuously until his death in June 1861, becoming in March of that year the first Premier of united Italy. In his zeal for modernisation, his faith in constitutional monarchy and his understanding of the diplomatic game he had no rival. His study of British and French politics had made him a free trader and a strong admirer of Peel. He realised that among the first needs of the future Italy would be schools, roads, canals and railways, and in the years 1850-9 he did his utmost, with the help of French and other foreign capital, to equip Piedmont with them. Cavour never shrank from paying the price of this development, in the shape of high taxation, budgetary strain and a mounting national debt. His political programme was reform, not revolution. He abhorred the very word revolution and did not hesitate to repress the republican movement, even at the cost of straining the constitution. His liberalism was that of post-1832 Britain and Louis Philippe's France: he saw his task as the progressive liberalisation of the 1848 Piedmontese constitution and its defence against the two extremes of clerical conservatism and revolutionary democracy. His diplomatic task was to win the respect of western Europe and convince his potential allies that Piedmont was a reliable, progressive state. In his speeches and diplomatic notes Cavour repeatedly stressed the contrast between the efficiency and orderly constitutional development of his country and the dangers of disorder and revolution inherent in Austrian repression and papal misgovernment. Such arguments were well designed to appeal to British opinion, and when the time came Cavour was able to successfully represent unification as a conservative process.

By 1859 he had made Piedmont a going concern and the pet of western Europe. Though tucked away in the far north-west, with only five million inhabitants against Austria's thirty-two, and with a population which to a Neapolitan seemed half French, it had yet securely won the leadership of the Italian national movement. Turin was already in some sense the capital of Italy, to which exiles flocked from Venice, from the Papal States, from Naples and from Sicily. The moderates had been in origin Piedmontese and were always predominantly northern: but Cavour, who refused to admit a clash between Piedmontese and Italian interests, had greatly weakened Piedmontese particularism. By winning the respect and colla- boration of men such as Minghetti at Bologna and Ricasoli in Tuscany, he had transformed his group into the nucleus of a truly Italian party. Grow- ing numbers of republicans were acknowledging his leadership and that of monarchical Piedmont, the only part of Italy where liberal institutions had been tried and proved.

Cavour's diplomatic achievement will always rank beside Bismarck's as a masterpiece of the nineteenth century. Probably it should rank higher, for Cavour had far slenderer material resources than Bismarck's to back his diplomacy. Italy could not be unified against both Austrian and French opposition, still less against a combination of Austria, France and Britain. The first step was therefore the French alliance. Cavour understood Napoleon III as did few foreigners: he saw how the Emperor was torn between Napoleonic ambition, romantic attachment to the principle of nationality and the need to appease French Catholics. Napoleon III was a half-hearted friend of Italy, but Cavour saw that his army was necessary to break the tough crust of Austrian power. In 1859 the French, with Piedmontese help, expelled the Austrians from Lombardy. For this, and for Napoleon III's grudging consent to the annexation of central Italy, Cavour was prepared in 1860 to pay a stiff price – the cession to France of Nice and Savoy, and renunciation for the time being of Venice and Rome. With the north and centre secured, all eyes in Italy turned south. Cavour now found himself squeezed between Napoleon III and the Party of Action led by Garibaldi. If he tried to suppress the democratic movement and left the Kingdom of Naples in peace, leadership of the Italian cause would pass out of the hands of the monarchy and the moderates; the threat of revolution, not for the first or last time, spurred the House of Savoy into action. If on the other hand he openly supported the democrats, who were straining at the leash to get at the Bourbons and the Pope, he might create just that hostile combination of all the conservative powers of Europe that would be fatal to his further plans. After months of doubt and danger, Cavour succeeded in mastering the situation and harnessing the revolu- tionary movement to his purpose.

Garibaldi was the key to the problem. He and Cavour were never on better than speaking terms. Cavour could not forget Garibaldi's association with Mazzini in Rome in 1849; Garibaldi could not forgive the cession of his birthplace, Nice, to France. From the conflict between them, Italy was created, each playing an essential part in the process which the other was incapable of playing. Fortunately Garibaldi and King Victor Emmanuel II had learnt to respect each other. By adopting the slogan 'Italy and Victor Emmanuel' in 1857, Garibaldi became the link between the Party of Action and the moderates, and his example reconciled many republicans to serving a king. He and the Thousand sailed from Genoa in May 1860 against the wishes of Cavour, to whom the expedition seemed reckless folly. But as first Sicily, then the Neapolitan mainland, went down before the redshirts like the walls of Jericho before Joshua, Cavour saw and brilliantly seized his opportunity. He was determined to put the brake on the forces of revolution and keep them away from Rome, guarded by a French garrison; at the same time he was resolved to secure the fruits of Garibaldi's triumphs. In September 1860, after all other expedients had failed, the King issued a proclamation, addressed as much to France and Britain as to Italians, on the need to restore the principles of moral order and preserve Europe from the continual dangers of revolution and war; then the Piedmontese army marched down the whole length of the peninsula, occupied the south and brought the revolution to an end. Cavour thus won, at the cost of the bitter enmity of Garibaldi and the Party of Action. With the annexation of Sicily, Naples and more than half the Papal States, the Kingdom of Italy was born.

Cavour died on 6 June 1861 with unification still incomplete. For the next nine years the need to win Venice and Rome overshadowed all other problems. Their acquisition was regarded by the makers of Italy as essential, for historical and sentimental reasons. Venetia was also necessary to give the new kingdom military security from the north-east. Moreover, when Cavour proclaimed Rome as the capital of Italy in March 1861 in the first Italian parliament, more than sentiment lay behind his action: he saw that only the acquisition of Rome could quell the growing antagonisms between Turin and Milan and Florence and Naples, which threatened to undermine Italian unity.

Cavour and his successors insisted that Italy could reach Rome only with French consent. They put their trust in peaceful methods, in *mezzi morali*, believing that, given time and patience, papal Rome could not indefinitely resist the attraction of liberal Italy. But an essential first step was to have the French garrison removed. The September Convention of 1864 achieved this object, at a price: Napoleon III undertook to withdraw his troops within two years on condition that Italy guaranteed the frontiers of the reduced Papal State and moved the Italian capital from Turin to Florence, as a proof that the renunciation of Rome was in earnest. In this agreement there was a fatal ambiguity. The Italian government signed because it looked on Florence as a step on the road from Turin to Rome. Napoleon III signed in the belief that Florence would block the road to Rome. There was only one solution to this situation that could satisfy both sides – a genuinely spontaneous revolution inside Rome and a vote for union with Italy, which would have made it possible for the Emperor to abandon the Pope in spite of the rage of his clerical supporters. But this *deus ex machina* was never to appear.

To the Party of Action this deference to the French Emperor seemed treachery. Garibaldi's veterans were itching to repeat their exploits of 1860: they could not pack away their red shirts and settle down to civilian life while Rome was still unredeemed. Garibaldi's popularity was such that he overshadowed the governments which succeeded Cavour's. They, like Cavour in 1860, were squeezed between Napoleon III and the Party of Action, and not all of them had the skill or courage to keep Garibaldi under control. Rattazzi in particular, who was Prime Minister in 1862 and 1867, lowered Italy in the eyes of Europe by his indecision and weakness. Hoping to repeat Cavour's triumph of 1860, he twice turned a blind eye to Garibaldi's preparations for invading the Papal State, intending later to intervene in the name of order and annex Rome with European consent. Such weakness at the top affected the army and all levels of the state administration: officers and civil servants gave help to the volunteers in the belief that the government wished its hands to be forced and would condone any *fait accompli*. On both occasions the weakness of toleration was followed by the weakness of repression. In 1862 Garibaldi's expedition ended in a clash with Italian troops on Aspromonte in southern Calabria. In 1867 his invasion of the Papal State ended in the rout of his redshirts by French and papal forces at Mentana, twenty miles north of Rome. Order was restored by the Italian army and for the next two years Italy was ruled by authoritarian, military methods that were hard to reconcile with Cavour's constitutional liberalism.

The years 1866–70 were an unhappy contrast to the glorious years 1859–61. In 1866 Venice was won, but thanks only to a Prussian victory in Bohemia, after the Italian army and navy had suffered humiliating defeats by the Austrians at Custoza and Lissa. In 1867 the fiasco of Mentana brought a French garrison back to Rome less than a year after it had been evacuated. In 1870 Italy reached Rome at last, not through the triumph of *mezzi morali* nor by a rising of the Roman People, nor even through an invasion by Garibaldi's veterans, but thanks once again to Prussian victories, this time on the Rhine and in the Ardennes.

### The Church

The makers of Italy were forced into anti-clericalism by the Papacy's unrelenting opposition to national unification. The democrats were anti-clerical by conviction and few of them shared even Mazzini's deistic faith. Atheism and Darwinian materialism flourished among them; many were freemasons and fought the spiritual authority of the church as resolutely as they fought its temporal power. But the majority of the moderates were devout Catholics. For them Article I of the Piedmontese constitution, which declared that Catholicism was 'the sole religion of the State', was no empty formula. But they drew a distinction between the Catholic faith and the temporal power of the Papacy, and refused to accept the church's official claim that the latter was a necessary guarantee of spiritual independence.

Early hopes of papal leadership of the Italian cause had foundered with Pius IX's allocution of 29 April 1848, which condemned the idea of a national war against Austria. But Cavour dreamed of achieving harmony between the church and Italy on different lines. His formula 'A free church in a free state'[1] summed up his hopes of reconciling the church and liberty, Catholicism and the nineteenth century, the rights of the nation and the freedom of the Pope, while simultaneously disarming the hostility of foreign Catholics to Italy. The Pope, in his view, could safely abandon his temporal power, for his independence would be better guarded by the love and respect of 22 million Italians than by 25,000 bayonets; and the spiritual strength of the church could only grow if the Pope were freed from the incubus of temporal power and so made immune to criticism for short-comings as a secular ruler. When the church had renounced political power, then the state could safely renounce its controls over the church and allow it to order its own affairs without either the privileges or the restrictions of a Concordat. Cavour believed that 'the era of Concordats' was over. He saw that the solution of the problem of church and state, and the Italian acquisition of Rome, were two parts of a single question. He dreamed of signing, 'from the heights of the Campidoglio . . . a new religious peace, a treaty which will have a greater effect upon the future of human society than the Peace of Westphalia'.[2] But in his optimism he overestimated the strength of Liberal Catholicism and of the clergy with nationalist sympathies. Neither the Papacy nor the anti-clerical patriots were in the mood for compromise and his dream of reconciling church and state came to nothing. On his deathbed in June 1861 almost his last words, spoken in delirium, were 'A free church in a free state'. Three months earlier his negotiations with the Papacy had broken down.

The democrats denounced the formula 'free church in a free state' as a dangerous illusion, which in practice would mean a state within the state, 'a church free to attack the free state'. Instead they demanded the retention and tightening of existing controls over the church. Inevitably this view gained supporters among the moderates also, as clerical opposition

[1] He borrowed it from the French Liberal Catholic writer, Montalembert.
[2] Quoted in S. W. Halperin, *The Separation of Church and State in Italian Thought from Cavour to Mussolini* (Chicago 1937), p. 11. The Campidoglio is the Capitoline Hill.

to the constitution and the national movement grew more bitter. It was under the guidance of Cavour himself that a long series of secularist laws was passed in Piedmont between 1850 and 1859. The clergy lost most of their ancient privileges, religious orders were suppressed or deprived of their property, monasteries and convents were closed, civil marriage was introduced and church schools subjected to state control. This legislation was extended to the rest of Italy after 1860 and made more rigorous. In 1866 part of the revenue from confiscated church property was paid into a special Ecclesiastical Fund, administered by laymen, which equalised the stipends of the clergy and enabled the state to end its direct subsidy to the church. Further, religious orders were forbidden to acquire real property in the future. There was nothing novel about such legislation in western Europe; but the tension it created between the church and the 'persecutor' Italian state was such that in 1865 nearly half the sees of Italy were without bishops (though a partial understanding on this point was reached in the following year). Cavour did not have time to resolve this ambiguity between the political sovereignty of the state and the independence of the church, nor to work out the implications of separation, which, to be effective, required a mutual limitation of freedom by both sides. His successors continued to work for a settlement. In 1867 Bettino Ricasoli, Cavour's disciple in ecclesiastical matters, presented parliament with a Free Church Bill which would have gone far towards separating church and state; but the outcry was such that he fell from power. This killed all hope of reconciliation. It is unlikely that even Cavour, had he lived, could have persuaded Italian patriots to renounce voluntarily their control over an institution which proclaimed itself the implacable enemy of liberalism and of Italy. Few even of the moderates were prepared to concede more than freedom within limits strictly defined by the state.

The seizure of half the Papal States by Piedmont in 1860, and the Italian threat to the remainder of his temporal kingdom, turned Pius IX finally against every manifestation of the liberal spirit and against every new idea. His resistance to Italian unification was only one aspect on the political plane of the far deeper struggle between the Catholic church and the 'revolution', between Catholic doctrine and 'the errors of the century', between faith and reason. The Risorgimento appeared to Pius IX no more than the advance guard of militant liberalism, a synthesis of all current heresies, 'the triumph of disorder and the victory of the most perfidious revolution'.[1] The Syllabus of Errors of 1864, reinforced by the proclamation of papal infallibility in 1870, was both a direct challenge to the Italian

---

[1] Spadolini, *L'opposizione cattolica*, pp. 38, 121–4. For an able and reasoned exposition by an English Catholic historian of the motives behind the Syllabus, see E. E. Y. Hales, *Pio Nono* (London 1954), pp. 257–62.

state and a declaration of war on nineteenth-century liberalism. The Syllabus rejected reconciliation or compromise 'with progress, with liberalism and with modern civilisation'. It condemned freedom of conscience and worship, the sovereignty of the secular state and the latter's claims to a monopoly of education and jurisdiction in matrimonial matters, and reaffirmed the intangibility of the temporal power. The infallibility decree was the culminating step in a long process of defining doctrine, centralising authority and enforcing discipline within the church. The influence of Liberal Catholics and of the clergy with national sympathies, among whom were six cardinals, was systematically destroyed. The Syllabus confronted every Catholic with a clear choice, 'either liberal or Catholic, either Catholic or liberal'; for to profess Liberal Catholicism was, in Pius IX's own words, 'to embrace simultaneously God and the devil'.[1]

The church fought back with every weapon at its disposal. Victor Emmanuel, his ministers and all who shared responsibility for secularist legislation were excommunicated. Pius IX refused to recognise the new state, even to the extent of never referring to the Italian Kingdom, but always to the 'Subalpine usurper'.[2] In 1857 a Piedmontese priest-journalist, Don Giacomo Margotti, had devised the formula 'Neither elected nor electors' and urged abstention from the polls. Many Catholics followed his advice after 1861, believing that to vote would constitute recognition of the Italian state. In 1866 the Holy Penitentiary declared that Catholics might sit in parliament only if they took the oath with the reservation *salvis legibus divinis et ecclesiasticis*. This reservation the chamber of deputies refused to accept. In the years 1860–70 the Papacy encouraged and sought the help of every enemy of Italy, both internal and external. In the disordered south the Bourbon cause was upheld against the Piedmontese usurpers.[3] In the north, especially in Emilia, opportunities were found for agitation among peasants exasperated by taxation.[4] The priest, who before 1860 had been a supporter of peace and order in the countryside, now became a disturbing and subversive element. In towns such as Milan and Florence, too, where social unrest was growing, there were priests and agitators and clerical journalists who propounded revolutionary slogans so similar to those of the extreme left that frightened liberals suspected a secret alliance between the socialists and the Vatican, between the Red and Black Internationals.[5]

But internal allies were insufficient. Pius IX never wavered in his claim to the temporal power, right down to its destruction on 20 September 1870.

[1] Spadolini, *L'opposizione cattolica*, p. 124.
[2] Only in Piedmont, and in Lombardy and Venetia, which had been legally ceded by treaty, was the government recognised as legitimate.
[3] See below, p. 26.        [4] See below, p. 27.        [5] Chabod, *Storia*, p. 404.

He believed that without it the Pope would become merely 'the Grand Chaplain of the House of Savoy'; and for the sake of his spiritual independence, the renunciation by the population of Rome of its political liberty and national aspirations seemed a small sacrifice to ask. But the temporal power survived for ten years after 1860 only because France was its protector. Fortunately for Italy, the Papacy in 1870 was more isolated than at any time since the first stirrings of Italian nationalism. The proclamation of papal infallibility had made even Catholic governments anxious. Austria-Hungary had a liberal, Protestant foreign minister and had recently denounced the Concordat of 1855. Spain, a republic since 1868, was friendly to Italy. When the French Empire collapsed under Prussia's battering and the French garrison was finally withdrawn from Rome, there was no European Power prepared to take effective steps to halt the march of the Italian army.[1]

## The Institutions

It was in the decade 1860–70 that the framework of the modern Italian state was constructed, with little publicity and little discussion, even in parliament. Public opinion was concerned with the immediate problems of Venice and Rome and the Pope; it was little interested in constitutional and administrative questions which, it was argued, would have to await solution until unification was complete. But there were innumerable problems which could not wait, on which quick decisions were necessary. These decisions, at the time that they were made, in an atmosphere of internal strain and international tension, might be regarded as provisional: but, as so often happens, the provisional became permanent. By the time Rome had been won and the excitement was over, the Italian state had been moulded in its essential outlines and politicians, administrators and private citizens were already settling down into that mould. Very few voices were raised after 1870 to demand a re-examination of the foundations on which the new kingdom had been constructed.

Inevitably in such circumstances the state was built from above by Cavour's party, the Right, which was then in power.[2] Inevitably, also, the Piedmontese undertook a major share of the work and Italy was fashioned on Piedmontese lines. It would have been folly to neglect the working model which lay ready to hand and launch out on risky experiments in govern-

[1] The only government to break off relations with Italy in 1870 was that of Ecuador. Spadolini, *L'opposizione cattolica*, p. 627.

[2] After 1861 the moderates became generally known as the Right, the democrats or Party of Action as the Left; but the conventional categories of 'conservative' and 'progressive' fitted neither exactly.

ment. What Mazzini and the democrats had feared, did to a large extent occur. Italy was 'Piedmontised', not built by the People on new foundations. Lombardy, central and southern Italy, and later Venice and Rome, were annexed before elections were held, so that there was no chance for constituent assemblies to lay down terms for unification, as the Left had so ardently desired. It is true that in each case annexation was confirmed by plebiscites and universal suffrage. This was the Right's concession to democratic sentiment, a compromise which later received constitutional sanction in the new royal title assumed by Victor Emmanuel – 'King by the grace of God and by the will of the Nation'. But plebiscites for or against 'Italy and Victor Emmanuel', held in the flush of victory, were no substitute for elections and gave no guidance as to the feelings of the public with regard to the future organisation of Italy. And though Victor Emmanuel consented to be called King by the will of the Nation, it was significant that he insisted on remaining Victor Emmanuel II, even though he was the first King of Italy.

Massimo D'Azeglio's much quoted epigram of 1860, 'Italy is made; now we must make Italians', drew attention to what many of the makers of Italy had overlooked. Italy had been transformed from a geographical expression into a political entity, but the work of fusing its heterogeneous regions and populations had hardly begun. Parochialism and provincialism were deepseated, reinforced by the still living traditions of the Renaissance Communes. Few outside the restricted educated class thought of themselves as primarily Italians. Among the people there was not even a common language. Piedmont and Lombardy were divided from Naples and Sicily not only by physical space but by the space of centuries. Even inside the former political units there were fierce rivalries: Genoa against Turin, Leghorn against Florence, traditionally separatist Sicily against the Neapolitan mainland. Close beneath the enthusiasm for unity had always lain important regional differences of outlook. Many Tuscans among the moderates feared that their duchy, rich and pleasantly stagnant, would lose by unification with the hustling, hard-headed Piedmontese. Lombards, accustomed under Austrian rule, whatever its shortcomings, to an efficient administration and the beginnings of commercial prosperity, might well ask themselves how fusion with the papal and Bourbon south would affect them. The Piedmontese, too, had their doubts. Many foresaw with apprehension the loss of their national individuality and the family atmosphere of their ruling class; and after a glorious decade in which they had occupied the centre of the Italian stage, the future seemed to promise only an insignificant minor role far from the centre of national life and political power.

With the creation of the Italian Kingdom in 1861 these regional rivalries, which had paralysed Italy in 1848, once again came to the surface. The

first important political realignment after 1860 appeared inside the Right
and split it along regional lines, between the Piedmontese Permanente and
the Lombard-Tuscan Consorteria. The Permanente watched jealously
over Piedmontese interests, in 'permanent' opposition to any government
which attempted to transfer the capital anywhere but to Rome. In 1864 the
September Convention was signed by a government which contained not
a single Piedmontese; and the news of the transfer of the capital to Florence
was greeted by bloody riots and clashes with the police and army in the
streets of Turin. Twelve years later it was the turn of the Tuscans who,
resentful at the losses incurred by Florence when the capital moved on to
Rome, once again disrupted the Right and brought about its final downfall
in 1876. Italian politics from the start took on a sectional character which
has not disappeared even today.

It was in the south that the protests against Piedmontisation were
loudest. A horde of Piedmontese administrators and policemen and soldiers
had descended upon Naples in 1860 to restore order out of the Bourbon
collapse. What they found there appalled them. With northern energy and
thoroughness, with little tact and all the paternalism characteristic of the
Right, they set about bringing modern civilisation to a 'medieval' land of
barbarism and corruption. The Neapolitan and Sicilian liberals who returned
at the same time, after twelve or more years of exile, were scarcely more
tactful or closer in touch with southern feelings. Cavour recognised that to
harmonise north and south was as difficult a task as to wage war on Austria
or overcome the hostility of the church. His prescription was strong honest
government, not martial law. 'Anyone can govern by martial law', he repeated on his deathbed; 'I will govern them with liberty'. His lieutenants
and successors were not always so scrupulous and the brigands were suppressed by the army with a savagery that is still remembered in peasant
legend. The south was treated as a semi-colonial territory. It was not surprising that, like many semi-colonial peoples, southerners were soon contrasting unfavourably the efficiency of a 'foreign' administration with their
former government, which, though inefficient and arbitrary, had at least
been 'native'.

The rulers of Italy, for forty years to come, were to be obssessed with
the precariousness of their position. They realised only too well that
unification had been the work of an enlightened minority; the masses,
particularly in the countryside, remained 'outside' the state. Every act of
government was seen as an episode in a continuous war of defence on two
fronts: on the right against the church with its allies abroad; on the left
against republicanism and the forces of social revolution. Fear of these
enemies explains the extreme centralisation which was introduced. The
Piedmontese system of local government had been modelled on that of

Napoleonic France. The country had been divided into provinces of roughly equal size (the equivalent of the French *département*), each with its prefect, and communes of widely differing size but identical powers and organisation, each with its mayor (*sindaco*). Both prefect and *sindaco* were appointed and controlled by the Minister of Interior. In 1859 this system was hurriedly extended to Lombardy. The many protests and grumblings forced the government to set up a special commission to reconsider the whole question of local government. In February 1861 the Minister of Interior, Minghetti, presented to parliament a bill which in its main outlines had received the approval of Cavour. It provided for the creation of a new unit of government, the region, between the central government and the province, subject, in the wide spheres of activity delegated to it, to only general supervision by the central government. Minghetti's view was that by thus providing outlets for local energy and patriotism, the unity of Italy would be exposed to fewer strains than if an attempt was made to stifle all separatist forces by rigid centralisation. It was significant that Minghetti was a native of Bologna and a future leader of the non-Piedmontese Consorteria. But parliament, appalled by reports of southern corruption and depravity, and fearing that regional assemblies would perpetuate the internal feuds of old Italy, rejected the bill by a huge majority. In September 1861 a standardised system of local government was introduced which divided Italy into 59 provinces[1] governed by prefects. In later years schemes of decentralisation repeatedly found their place in programmes of democratic reform, but never reached the statute book. The explanation is the same as that for the rejection of Minghetti's scheme in 1861 – fear of undermining the fragile unity of the nation.[2]

The Piedmontese constitution of 1848, which in 1861 became the constitution of Italy, was modelled on that of France of 1830: 'a constitution', said its critics, 'imported from England in a bad French translation'. It established a limited constitutional monarchy in which executive power lay in the hands of the King. The elementary political liberties were guaranteed, a senate appointed by the crown had powers equal to those of the chamber of deputies, and the franchise was restricted by a stiff property or income qualification. The preamble stated that it was 'perpetual and irrevocable'; but Cavour's opinion that it could, and should, be improved was that of the majority of liberals. In fact, like most of the liberal constitutions of western Europe, it evolved slowly but surely in the direction of parliamentary and cabinet government.

[1] 69 after the acquisition of Venetia and Rome.
[2] Since 1948 the regional reorganisation of Italy has been enshrined in the new republican constitution, but in 1967, for the same reasons, has only in part been carried out.

The crown was no constitutional cypher. Victor Emmanuel II came from a long line of stubborn, paternal despots; he attached much importance to the traditions of his House and intended to rule. But although he had the strongest reservations about 'the constitutional system' and greatly disliked the lawyers, journalists and parliamentary orators who had come to the fore in 1848, he also had a shrewd understanding of the times in which he lived. Louis Philippe, not Charles X, was his model. The constitution gave him ample powers. His choice of prime minister was never a formality, and he was free to grant or refuse a dissolution. The atmosphere of his court was military and in times of crisis he tended to turn to Piedmontese generals.[1] The early years of the constitution abound in instances of the free use of the royal power. During the climax of the Risorgimento he conducted a personal foreign policy which was not always that of Cavour, and in 1870 he again resorted to dynastic diplomacy, behind the backs of his ministers. His religious scruples and his personal regard for Pius IX, with whom he corresponded throughout his reign, made him a moderating influence in problems of church and state. While Cavour was alive and master of parliament, the King's freedom was limited; but he chafed at control and his actions after 1861 showed that what he was forced to tolerate in Cavour, he was not disposed to tolerate in Cavour's less forceful successors. After 1870 the power of parliament grew at the expense of the crown; but right down to the fascist conquest of power the King continued to play an active political role, especially in foreign and military matters. Few prime ministers chose their foreign or service ministers without first making sure of the royal approval.

Under the electoral law inherited from Piedmont, only 529,000 adult males, less than 2% of the total population, had the right to vote in 1870.[2] In many constituencies, until the extension of the franchise in 1882, the total poll amounted to only a few hundreds. For many years after unification over one-third of the electorate habitually abstained. The voters in the small towns, especially in the south, were well known and easily influenced by the local magnates, who acted as 'grand electors'.[3] But the man who really counted at election time was the prefect. He had many weapons at his disposal. Votes could be won by the promise of political preferment, a decoration, a job in the administration, or money for public works in the

[1] He appointed General La Marmora in 1864 to carry out the September Convention and General Menabrea in 1867 to restore order after Mentana.

[2] To qualify for the vote it was necessary (with a few exceptions) to be over 25, to be able to read and write, and to pay a minimum of 40 lire a year in direct taxes. In 1877–80 26·9% of the population had the vote in France, 20·6% in Germany and 8·8% in the United Kingdom. *Compendio*, I, pp. 68–70.

[3] Until 1919, with the exception of the years 1882–91, the electoral system was that of single-member constituencies, with the second ballot, as in France.

constituency; and the government's enemies could be discouraged by judicious use of the police, by banning political meetings or censoring electoral propaganda. Governments in Italy never lost elections, though an electoral victory rarely guaranteed them a stable parliamentary majority. Centralisation meant that the government, through the Minister of Interior or the Minister of Public Works, had the last word in even trivial local affairs and was the arbiter of parochial politics. Political life became concentrated in parliament and the only means by which local interests could get a hearing was by forcing their deputy to act as their spokesman and protector. Deputies gave or withheld their support from governments according as they were satisfied or dissatisfied with the favours they received for themselves or their constituents. No party in the modern sense, with a nation-wide organisation, existed in Italy before the foundation of the Socialist party in 1892. Prime ministers were therefore forced, in order to maintain themselves in power, to create their majority in parliament by patronage and by ceaseless negotiations with the leaders of the fluctuating regional or personal groupings of deputies. In so far as they had a national policy, it was built up from a jigsaw of disconnected sectional policies.[1]

Cavour set the future pattern of Italian parliamentary life with his famous *connubio*[2] which brought him to power in 1852. This was a coalition between his own Right Centre and the Left Centre under Urbano Rattazzi. It gave him a solid majority for five years until Rattazzi, partly under the influence of the King, abandoned the partnership. Subsequent prime ministers looked back on the *connubio* with envy and were always attempting to repeat the manœuvre. In the Italian parliament, as in Piedmont before 1860, majorities were created by governments, not governments by parliamentary majorities; and the electorate had little say in the choice of a prime minister and none in the composition of the government. In 1852 Cavour's motive was to free himself from dependence on the Piedmontese anti-Italian conservatives on his right and to free Rattazzi from dependence on the democrats and republicans on his left; their combined forces were then able to pursue the 'middle way' against the two extremes. These successful tactics of dividing the opposition and absorbing part of it into the governmental coalition became an accepted part of the parliamentary game.

The emergence of the Permanente and the Consorteria in 1864 marked the final disintegration of the Cavourian majority. Regional discords ushered in a period of parliamentary confusion which gave the King a commanding position for five years. In 1869 the appointment of Lanza as

---

[1] There are obvious points of similarity between politics in nineteenth-century Italy and eighteenth-century Britain. Depretis at the height of his power was nicknamed by some of his critics 'the Italian Walpole'. See below, p. 91.

[2] Literally, marriage.

Prime Minister ended General Menabrea's two years of authoritarian rule, tolerated by parliament only because, after the fiasco of Mentana, it seemed preferable to mis-government by the Left. Lanza reverted to Cavourian liberalism but failed to build a solid majority. Instability continued for another twelve years until Depretis succeeded in forming a coalition which was another *connubio* in all but name.

## The Economy

Italy at its unification was a predominantly agricultural country. Nearly one-third of its area was uncultivated mountain or swamp, one-third hill pasture and forest, and slightly more than one-third under crops. In spite of the poverty of so much of its soil, its population in 1861 was 21·8 millions,[1] living at a higher density than that of either France or Germany. The new state contained a bewildering variety of climate, soil and crop, of standard of living and social structure, from the central European character of Lombardy to the north African squalor of rural Sicily and Calabria. Its economic backwardness was only too apparent. In the whole kingdom there were less than 2,200 kilometres of railways, 1,600 of them in Piedmont and the Po valley. Roads were few and bad, and even the leading ports of Genoa and Naples were primitive. Only 25% of the population over five years of age could read and write, and in the more remote provinces of the south illiteracy was virtually universal. Large areas of the interior lived in primitive isolation and a pre-capitalist, self-sufficient rural economy which had remained unaltered for centuries. Italy had the highest wheat acreage in Europe, in proportion to size, and the lowest wheat yield per acre outside Russia. Except in Piedmont, Lombardy and Tuscany, a class of improving landlords, ready to invest capital in their land, was conspicuously lacking.

Apart from agriculture, natural sources of wealth were few. The mining of Sardinian lead and zinc and Sicilian sulphur was attracting foreign capital, but Italy had virtually no coal and little iron ore. The agricultural population outnumbered the non-agricultural by three to one. Most of those engaged in manufacture worked not in factories but in their own homes, retaining close links with the land, and a high proportion of them were women. In silk production Lombardy and Piedmont led the world; but four-fifths of it was exported raw and only in Piedmont had silk manufacturing begun to take root. There were the beginnings of a cotton industry in Lombardy and of wool manufacturing in eastern Piedmont. But an engineering industry was non-existent outside Milan, Genoa and

[1] 25 millions within the post-1870 frontiers (i.e. with Venetia and Rome included).

Naples, where a handful of arsenals, shipyards and railway workshops had been created and protected, from non-economic motives, by the Austrian administration and the Piedmontese and Neapolitan governments. In industrial production Italy lagged behind not only Britain and France, but also Austria, Belgium and Switzerland. Its industrial revolution was still far in the future.

The young kingdom started its career under the threat of bankruptcy. The cost of war and independence had now to be paid and money raised to provide the essential apparatus of a modern state – a unified army and navy, public works and an efficient administration. In 1862, the first year in which a unified Italian budget was presented, the state's revenue of 450 million lire was less than half its expenditure. For more than ten years the country lived financially from hand to mouth. In such circumstances the post of Minister of Finance was an unenviable one. But Italy was fortunate in the remarkable succession of men who held it during the first fifteen years. The greatest of them was Quintino Sella, the chief hero of 'the heroic period of Italian finance'. He regarded the balancing of the budget as essential for national survival. The new state had to prove that it was not merely the fragile creation of romantic nationalism and foreign patronage, but could hold its own in a competitive, industrial world. If it failed, the fate of Egypt or Tunis awaited it, and effective sovereignty would pass into the hands of foreign bankers and investors.[1] So, with grim determination, Sella and his colleagues of the first decade set about paring down expenditure to a minimum and squeezing the maximum revenue out of a poor country. 'Economy to the bone' was Sella's motto, and he boasted of examining all requests for expenditure 'through a miser's spectacles'. But there was a limit to the economies that could be made. The bureaucracy, however humbly paid and overworked, was bound to grow and to cost more. Heavy expenditure on communications was inevitable, for overriding political and economic reasons. Appropriations for the army and navy were cut down, even in 1865 and 1869, on the eve of the struggle with Austria and the Franco-Prussian war. Even so the war of 1866 sent the deficit soaring to its peak of 740 million lire.

To meet current expenses it was necessary to borrow lavishly, sell state property and pile on the taxes. Borrowing was especially heavy in the years 1861–5, and in a decade the national debt quadrupled and the annual burden of interest payments almost trebled, rising from 21% of total expenditure in 1861–5 to 31% in 1866–70. A substantial proportion of these loans was subscribed from abroad, particularly from France, with the result that Italian financial stability became uncomfortably dependent on foreign

---

[1] Chabod, *Storia,* pp. 489 ff.

confidence and the state of the Paris Bourse.[1] Italian credit started high in
1861 but by 1865 was becoming exhausted; in 1866 it collapsed. The
expectation of war between Italy and Austria, a general European depression, bank failures in Germany and Austria and panic on the stock exchanges, set foreign bondholders clamouring for repayment and Italian
bonds tumbling. Faced with financial disaster, the government was compelled to issue a depreciated, non-convertible paper currency. The year
1866 was black for Italy, militarily, politically and financially. Borrowing
now became for a time impossible. But the country, thrown back on its own
resources, survived the shock, and finance ministers grimly turned elsewhere for the revenue they required.

Part of this was obtained from the disposal of state property. Certain
canals and railways built or owned by the state were temporarily handed
over to private companies and in 1868 the state tobacco monopoly was
farmed out, on terms which brought immediate relief to the exchequer.[2]
More important was the sale of expropriated church property and of the
demesne lands inherited from the old states, which were thrown on the
market, often at depressed prices, to the delight of speculators and the
landowning class. It was a shortsighted policy which not even the terrible
need for cash could fully excuse.

Taxation however provided most of the funds. In a poor country without
industrial and commercial wealth the main burden was inevitably borne by
land and by the consumer. Landowners had good reason to protest that
'land was being martyred' when on an average they paid 25% of their
income, and sometimes as much as 50%, in government and local taxes.
The pocket of the consumer was squeezed even harder. The list of indirect
taxes was a long one; among the most severe were those on alcohol, salt and
tobacco, the last two being state monopolies. The most hated of all was the
grist (*macinato*) tax, levied on all grain ground at the mill and calculated by
a mechanical meter attached to the mill wheel. Introduced by Sella in 1868,
its virtue from the point of view of a Minister of Finance was that it was
simple and easily collected. But it brought more odium upon the country's
rulers than all the other taxes combined. Several parts of Italy had suffered
from it before unification and its abolition in Sicily in 1860 had been one
of Garibaldi's most popular acts. In the north a tax on bread was an innovation and it drove the peasants of Emilia to insurrection.[3] Sella became,
in popular legend, 'the starver of the people'. Well might a taxpayer write in
1868 that 'Italy, famous in past ages as a museum of the *beaux arts*, has

[1] Between 1861 and 1870 about one-third of the interest payments on the
national debt were made to foreign bondholders.
[2] It returned to direct state administration in 1883.
[3] See below, p. 27.

now become a museum of taxes'. But the heroic effort was not in vain. After 1867 the financial situation gradually improved and by the end of the decade solvency seemed at last within reach.

The continuous financial crisis and the sucking up of savings by taxation and government borrowing starved both agriculture and industry of sorely needed capital. Yet by 1870 Italy had made much progress. Trade was stimulated by the sweeping away of internal customs barriers and by the building of the railways, which continued even in the periods of greatest financial stringency. In the first five years the essential trunk lines were completed and railway mileage was doubled; by the end of 1870 the 2,175 kilometres of January 1861 had grown to 6,208. The leaders of the Right were not dogmatic believers in *laisser faire* and from the first the state played the leading part in railway construction. Foreign capital and foreign contractors had often to be attracted on terms most onerous to the Italian taxpayer, and many lines were uneconomic. But railways were necessary, whatever the cost, to 'stitch the boot of Italy' and bring a breath of modern fresh air into the stagnant south.

Improved communications allowed Italy's foreign trade to expand. The Suez Canal was opened in 1869 and the first Alpine railway tunnel, under Mont Cenis, in 1871. In commercial policy Italy followed the example set by Piedmont under Cavour and adopted tariffs lower than those of any European state except Britain and Belgium. A series of free trade treaties was concluded, the most important of them with France in 1863, which secured for the French one-third of Italy's total foreign trade. In the four years 1867–70 exports were 30% greater, and the excess of imports over exports 60% smaller, than in the previous four years. The south benefited from expanding exports of wine, olive oil, fruit and Sicilian sulphur. Silk increased in importance as the main pillar of Italian foreign trade, accounting in 1867–70 for one-third of both imports and exports. In 1869 the introduction of the first mechanical looms started a process which was soon to turn north Italy into the silk factory of Europe. British-made machinery also laid the foundations of the future cotton and wool manufacturing industries. Imports of coal doubled between 1862 and 1870, and cheaper imported food relieved the Italian consumer. Italy was finding a place in the world economy.

Economic growth, however, brought much dislocation and suffering. A flood of manufactured goods from Britain and France killed old-established domestic handicrafts and deprived the peasant of an important source of income. There was no social legislation to alleviate the resulting misery and emigration, unregulated by the state, was often the only alternative to destitution. The south, being economically weaker, suffered most heavily. The few industries which had been established before unification, behind protective tariffs, were ruined by foreign and north Italian competition. Carpetbaggers descended from Piedmont and Lombardy to 'reconstruct' the south; northern contractors and speculators snapped up church lands, felled the mountain forests and grew rich from the construction of roads and public works. Naples, with its huge parasitical *lumpenproletariat*, lost the bread and circuses which the Bourbon court had provided and sank to the level of an overgrown provincial city. Mounting taxation brought bitter protests from Neapolitans and Sicilians (and Tuscans), whose former governments may have signally failed to provide the services expected of a modern state, but whose taxes at least had been low. After 1861 they resented being forced to pay for the 'financial extravagance' of the Piedmontese, who had been responsible for over half the initial total of the unified national debt. Southerners had some reason, too, for lamenting that too much of the money they paid out in taxes found its way into the pockets of northern bondholders, contractors and business men. The state's financial policy unintentionally contributed to the draining of wealth from the south.

The decade 1860–70 was one of crisis and struggle, overshadowed by the gradual realisation of Italy's backwardness and natural poverty. During the Risorgimento many northerners had pictured the south as a land of milk and honey, 'the garden of Europe'. Disenchantment came quickly. Soon discouraged voices were heard regretting unification which, it was said, had attached a leaden weight to the feet of the progressive north. The gap between north and south was bridgeable in 1861, if the task had been taken energetically in hand. Cavour had seen that the key to the south's regeneration lay in its economic development and he recognised that special legislation might be necessary for this purpose. But most of his party put their faith in the long-term effects of political and economic liberty, and deprecated the very idea of discrimination by the state in favour of one region. So the gap was allowed to grow ever wider until, in the next century, the full significance of 'the Southern question' was recognised.

Yet the dark side of the picture can be overdrawn. When a fair balance is struck, the first decade appears as one of solid achievement, modest in relation to what still remained to be done, but impressive when the starting-point of 1861 is borne in mind. The privations and sacrifices of 1861–70 bore fruit in the following fifteen years.

## The People

The condition of the peasantry varied greatly from region to region. The most prosperous and secure were the tenant farmers of Lombardy and the sharecroppers (*mezzadri*) of Tuscany. Less happy were the small peasant proprietors, numerous in the Alpine foothills, all down the Apennine backbone and in the rich plains around Naples and Palermo. The most depressed section were the casual landless labourers (*braccianti*) who were found in every part of the country, but particularly in the lower Po valley, the Roman Campagna and the interior of Sicily and the Neapolitan provinces. They made up well over half Italy's agricultural population. Living close to the destitution line, they found work for 100, perhaps 200 days in the year. Among them malaria and pellagra[1] were rife and even in the wheat-growing areas of Emilia they could seldom afford to eat white bread.

The most wretched part of Italy was of course the south.[2] The economy of the interior was dominated by the *latifondi*: great estates devoted mainly to cereals and pasture, owned often by absentee landlords, managed by profit-making middlemen and worked in small units by peasant tenants on annual leases. Great tracts of country were without roads or houses or water; many of the plains were swampy and malaria-ridden. The peasants lived far from their work, clustered in great villages which might have many thousands of inhabitants but lacked all the amenities of a town. Legal feudalism had been abolished, but the peasant was still frequently in a position of moral servitude and personal dependence on his landlord, owing him services in labour or payments in kind. The economy of the *latifondo* was insulated from the outside world and almost self-sufficient; tools, clothes and building materials would be produced on the estate and little of its produce would reach the market. The pressure of population was such that labourers were forced to accept desperation wages, and small tenants to agree to terms of lease so onerous that they lived permanently in debt and totally without security.

The political and social consequences were disastrous. Bitter class hatred lay close below the surface of the southern countryside. A sharp cleavage divided the privileged from the disinherited; on the one side were the landowners and the *signori*, with their agents and dependents, the lawyers and merchants, the bureaucrats and petty intellectuals of the towns; on the other side the peasantry. Even where they lived side by side in the same village, there were few contacts between them. A middle class of the type common to all north-western Europe did not exist outside the handful of large towns. The disappearance of the Bourbons did nothing to alter this. The makers of united Italy shrank from upsetting the social structure

---

[1] Pellagra is a disease of malnutrition, found mainly in maize-eating areas. In its late stages it causes insanity and finally death.

[2] Unless otherwise stated, the term 'the south' will in future be used to describe the mainland provinces of the former Neapolitan kingdom, together with Sicily and Sardinia.

of the countryside and saw in the landowning class the one element of stability on which they could rely against counter-revolution and social upheaval. If some had reservations about the reliability of these eleventh-hour patriots, so recently the pillars of Bourbon rule, their doubts were resolved by their conviction that the opening up of the south to trade, and the introduction of modern institutions and honest government, would transform the old society and destroy the relics of feudalism and poverty. But the introduction of liberal institutions, framed on the assumption of the existence of a numerous middle class as in the north, in fact had the opposite effect when superimposed on social conditions belonging to another stage of civilisation. Liberty in the south after 1860 meant only too often the liberty of the powerful to rob the weak. The propertied classes enjoyed absolute economic power; in addition, local government, justice and the administration of charity were in their hands. They decided local taxation which was frequently of an unashamedly class character. Only they possessed the vote. The deputy was their creature, and to secure his support in parliament, governments were prepared to turn a blind eye to the grievances of the peasantry, putting their electoral interest before their duty to the nation as a whole. The prefect was reduced to the status of 'a diplomatic agent' accredited by a 'foreign' government to the local potentates.[1] The national revolution of 1860 did not bring freedom and prosperity to the southern peasant; though 'declared a citizen by the law, he remained an oppressed serf'.[2]

With the exception of Sicily, where a large-scale peasant revolt preceded Garibaldi's landing, there were few places where the peasantry played a positive part in the unification of Italy. The countryside in general had remained passive; if it stirred itself, it had usually been on the side of the old order. Governments in peasant eyes are unnecessary evils. The new Italian government was specially odious because it had been imposed by the *signori* and the towns, because it persecuted the church, increased the taxes and enforced conscription; but above all because it was efficient.[3] Though Garibaldi had played with the idea of land reform on his first arrival at Naples, neither moderates nor democrats subsequently made much effort to win support among the peasantry. Indeed it was Garibaldi's

[1] Franchetti, *Mezzogiorno e colonie*, pp. 23–5, 44–6, 204.
[2] Franchetti and Sonnino, *La Sicilia*, II, p. 133. Franchetti and Sonnino were wealthy Tuscan conservatives who in the years 1873–5 conducted extensive private enquiries into the social and administrative conditions of the Neapolitan mainland and Sicily.
[3] Sonnino remarked in 1880 that 'the tax gatherer and the policeman are the only propagators of the religion of patriotism amongst the brutalised masses of our peasantry'. 'Victor Emmanuel is robbing us of everything', a Calabrian peasant woman told Franchetti in 1874. Franchetti, *Mezzogiorno e colonie*, p. 140.

lieutenants who put down the Sicilian peasant revolt with extreme severity when it showed signs of getting out of hand. Most of the makers of Italy shared Mazzini's view, for which there was much justification, that the countryside was 'the reservoir of anti-national reaction'. A great chance was lost when the church lands were sold. It is true that some of the legislation contained provisions to encourage the growth of small peasant properties. But the state was in too great a hurry for cash to worry overmuch about land distribution. The auctions were often rigged, especially in the south, by the large landowners; and a majority of the peasants who did buy plots for themselves were soon forced through lack of capital or skill to resell. Most of the church lands found their way into the hands of the wealthy and powerful.

Southern land hunger was intensified by large-scale misappropriation of the common lands (*demani*) controlled by the local authorities. Despite constant pressure from the peasants for their distribution to the landless, the *signori* who filled the local councils frequently divided the *demani* amongst themselves or sold them illegally and enjoyed the proceeds. The peasants were thus deprived not only of the prospect of land of their own, but also of common grazing and other ancient rights. This was one of the few grievances that 'exhausted the inexhaustible patience of the peasants' and drove them to desperate action; it was perhaps the most important single cause of class hatred in the southern countryside. Again and again in succeeding decades the peasants would try to seize and squat on these common lands which had been stolen from them by 'an act of brigandage', with the connivance of the state, and which they still regarded as rightfully theirs.[1]

Even in the north and centre of Italy a great gulf separated the social classes in the countryside, isolating the peasantry from the main stream of national life and leaving it outside the state to which it did not seem to belong. The distinction often drawn between 'real' and 'legal' Italy was no literary fantasy.[2] 'Legal' Italy was the King and parliament, the politicians and bureaucrats, concentrated in a distant capital: 'real' Italy was the mass of the peasant population. Communication between the two was rare and unfriendly. After 1860 land hunger and rural overpopulation were the two main features of the Italian countryside and were responsible for a steadily growing social tension. This did not quickly become apparent to 'legal'

[1] ibid., pp. 119, 206. 'The *questione demaniale* is the real social question of southern Italy', declared Fortunato (see below, p. 87) in 1880. *Il Mezzogiorno e lo stato italiano*, I, p. 72.
[2] The terms were first used by a conservative, Jacini, and occur again and again in the polemical literature of the time. Both the Catholic opposition and the extreme left championed 'real' against 'legal' Italy.

Italy because the peasantry was illiterate, politically inarticulate and for the most part still passively resigned to a life of poverty, toil and subjection, broken by sporadic outbursts of desperate violence.

But even in the decade 1861–70 there were two significant signs of stirring: southern brigandage and the northern revolt against the *macinato* tax. Brigandage was the southern peasant's traditional method of protest against misgovernment and inhuman social conditions. Young men would take to the mountains because they could not find work or pay their taxes, or to evade the police, or perhaps just in search of adventure. They lived in bands named after chieftains with high-sounding titles and made their living by robbery, assassination and blackmail. Some became legendary Robin Hoods who plundered the *signori* and distributed the loot to the poor. But in the years 1861–5, when over large parts of the south the authority of the central government existed in little more than name, brigandage assumed greater political and social significance. The brigand bands were swollen by demobilised N.C.O.s and soldiers of the Bourbon army and by many who had lost jobs or power with the destruction of the Neapolitan kingdom. The peasants supported them because they were their only allies against the *signori* in league with a 'foreign' government. Land hunger, protests against Piedmontisation, devotion to the church and Neapolitan separatism all helped to provoke a confused and savage insurrection. Many country priests and secret committees in the towns gave the brigands active support. From Rome, the seat of the exiled Bourbon court and headquarters of the counter-revolution, came spiritual encouragement and material aid. For four years the south was in a state of civil war and 100,000 troops and Piedmont's best generals were required to pacify it by systematic military conquest and police repression. More lives were lost in this grim war than in all the military campaigns of the Risorgimento. Though Sicily suffered less than the mainland from political brigandage, its condition was little happier. After the imposition of conscription in 1861, for the first time in the island's history, 25,000 young men took to the hills to evade the law. Troops were used on a massive scale to round them up, but with very limited success. In 1866 insurrection broke out in Palermo. It was led by many of the same men who had organised the popular rising against the Bourbons six years before, and it had the support of the church, Bourbon loyalists, Mazzinian republicans and regional separatists. For seven days the city was in the hands of the rebels. Casualties were higher than in 1860. Martial law and stern repression followed. By 1870 the south was exhausted and the government had regained control. The collapse of the temporal power and the flight of the Bourbons from Italian soil ended the possibility of organised counter-revolution. Brigandage has survived into our times in parts of Sicily (and Sardinia), but without political significance.[1] Elsewhere it has not outlived the coming of roads and railways and the provision of a more effective safety valve for the countryside in the shape of emigration.[2]

The riots of 1869–70 against the *macinato* tax were the northern counterpart to southern brigandage. Desperate peasants all over Emilia attacked the mills, sacked local government offices and burnt the tax registers, and set on the police with cries of 'Down with the rich' and 'Long live the Pope'. What most worried the authorities was that the disturbances were not just another of the spontaneous, unplanned explosions with which they were familiar; this time the peasants were showing the first elements of organisation and discipline. But the movement ended, like southern brigandage, in repression and exhaustion, after causing 250 deaths. The towns of Emilia were strongholds of political extremism, and in a few isolated cases young republican leaders saw in the rioting peasants useful allies against the monarchist state. But most of them, like Mazzini, scorned a movement in which the handiwork of the church seemed so evident. The towns held aloof and unaided the peasants could achieve nothing.[3]

In 1860 there was still no industrial proletariat in Italy. But in some of the northern cities, notably Turin, Genoa and Milan, the skilled artisans and craftsmen had begun to organise, and in Piedmont there was already a network of mutual benefit and friendly societies, under the paternalist direction of philanthropic moderates like Sella. These men hoped to redeem the lower classes from poverty and ignorance by teaching them thrift, self-reliance and respect for property, and by discouraging strikes and political agitation. After 1860, under the leadership of a young Venetian economist and social reformer, Luigi Luzzatti, the movement spread throughout northern Italy.[4] But as these working-class societies multiplied, they grew more political and militant, to the dismay of their former conservative patrons. Outside Piedmont, which remained a stronghold of the moderates, a substantial minority fell under Mazzini's influence and

[1] Except in the years 1943–8, when banditry thrived after another collapse of the central authority and for a time had connexions with Sicilian separatist movements.

[2] Yet the heroic days of brigand resistance are still remembered in legend. Carlo Levi, in *Christ Stopped at Eboli*, tells how in 1935, in the remote interior of Basilicata, when peasants talked to him of 'the war', they were referring not to Mussolini's invasion of Ethiopia, then in progress, nor to the 1915–18 war, but to the brigands' war of 1860–5.

[3] Rosselli, pp. 230–48.

[4] In 1862 there were approximately 400, with 100,000 members; sixteen years later there were over 2,000, with 330,000 members. Luzzatti's special interest was People's Banks for the provision of cheap credit on a local, cooperative basis. He founded the first at Lodi in 1864 and by 1876 there were 112. In Luzzatti's own words (*Memorie*, I, p. 148), 'The care of the people was regarded as a mystic vocation, an essential way of loving and serving one's country.'

adopted a republican programme. In 1864 a congress was held in Naples at which representatives of 57 societies signed a Mazzinian Pact of Fraternity. But in his social doctrine Mazzini, the revolutionary republican, was little less conservative than the moderates. He believed that the future revolution would have to be made in the interests of the proletariat, just as past revolutions had been made in the interests of the middle classes; the proletariat would be liberated from the tyranny of capital by the creation of cooperatives, a wide distribution of property and the substitution of free association for unrestricted competition. But all depended on the prior establishment of a republic, the only form of government which could achieve social justice. This political rigidity cost Mazzini much support, as did his deistic, moralistic preaching and his austere prescription of education, hard work, thrift, sacrifice and virtue. 'Bread, not words', was the refrain of the working-class critics who attacked him with growing bitterness towards the end of the decade. He and his lieutenants failed to grapple with concrete questions such as wages, hours of work and unemployment; and their insistence on class collaboration and private property left them vulnerable to outbidding on their left by the socialists and anarchists of the First International.

Early in 1864 the notorious Russian revolutionary, Bakunin, paid his first visit to Italy, the country which was to occupy much of his time and energy during the last years of his life. Bakunin was a true internationalist and at once felt at home in Italian democratic and revolutionary circles. His romantic and childlike personality, his fantastic energy and his love of the most theatrical forms of conspiracy made an immediate impression. He was soon working hard, with Marx's approval, to undermine Mazzini's influence and win over the revolutionary wing of the Italian democratic movement to the cause of social revolution. Progress was slow. Six years after Marx founded the First International in London in September 1864, its strength in Italy was still limited to half a dozen secret sections, all in the south; the largest, in Naples, had 3,700 due-paying members. Its organisation was rudimentary and the police had no difficulty in disrupting it in February 1870.[1] In that year Italian socialism was still in the embryo stage, chaotic and 'populist',[2] and socialists were still hard to distinguish from republicans or democrats or militant anti-clericals. To the disgust of Bakunin, several of his most trusted collaborators dashed off in 1866 to volunteer in the patriotic war against Austria, and again next year to join Garibaldi at

[1] Hostetter, pp. 130–6.
[2] Populism is usually regarded as a Russian or east European phenomenon, but the word may fairly be applied to Italian socialism. Italy, with its primitive economy and predominantly peasant society, was something between a 'western' and an 'eastern' country in 1870.

Mentana. Only when nationalist fervour had been assuaged by the acquisition of Rome did the ideal of social revolution begin to make headway
in Italy.

Mazzini, though worried by the threat from his left, pursued his old
programme unchanged. In 1866 he founded a new revolutionary and conspiratorial organisation, the Universal Republican Alliance. It made many
recruits in Emilia, in some of the larger cities of northern and central Italy,
and in Sicily where it thrived on resentment against Piedmontisation. In
March 1870 a mutiny occurred in the Pavia garrison; the execution of its
ringleader, a young republican corporal named Pietro Barsanti, provided
the movement with a martyr. Barsanti Associations sprang up all over
Emilia and were responsible for several disturbances over the next five
years, usually in the form of protests against the cost of living. But police
spies kept the government well informed and republican conspiracies were
never a serious threat to public order. When Mazzini landed at Palermo in
August 1870, to rouse Sicily against the government and prevent Italy
being dragged into war on the side of France, he was at once arrested and
the island hardly stirred. This fiasco marked the end of Mazzini's political
career. The occupation of Rome next month by the hated monarchist
government of the Right dealt what proved to be a mortal blow to the
revolutionary republican cause.

## Italy in Europe

In 1871 Italy, with 26·8 million inhabitants, came sixth in order of population among the nations of Europe.[1] But its economic and military weakness,
revealed to the outside world by the struggle against bankruptcy and the
defeats of 1866, reduced its diplomatic weight far below what the population
figures suggested. At least for the remainder of the century Italy was
nearer a second-class than a first-class power. This fact alone, which so
many Italians were loath to recognise, accounts for much of the frustration
which apparent failures in foreign policy caused in later years. Liberal
Italy had been born into an illiberal world, where Mazzinian dreams of
national missions in the service of humanity counted for little beside modern
armies and industrial power. The creation of Italy was distasteful to most
of Europe, but especially to its land neighbours, Austria-Hungary and
France. Both had for centuries regarded the Italian peninsula as a free field
for diplomatic and military manœuvre, in which the feelings of the native
population could be safely ignored. Now Italy's 'international servitude'

[1] The populations of the Great Powers in 1871 were as follows: Russia 78
millions, Germany 41, France 36, Austria–Hungary 35, United Kingdom 32.

was over and room had to be found for an unwelcome intruder in the councils of Europe. France also feared a rival for power and influence in the Mediterranean. Catholic Europe hated the impious usurper, and this hostility was only in part balanced by the sympathy of British liberals. In general Europe noted the new kingdom's weakness with satisfaction and hoped that its financial difficulties and its quarrel with the church would continue to keep it in a subordinate position.

Italy's foreign policy can be explained largely in terms of strategic necessity. The Alpine boundary with France gave military security. But when the northern and north-eastern frontiers were drawn after the war of 1866, Austria-Hungary, thanks to Bismarck's support, retained possession of the Trentino bulge and the mountains on the west bank of the Isonzo, which together dominated the Lombard and Venetian plains. Italy was therefore at a serious military disadvantage. Inability to defend both land frontiers simultaneously made it imperative to avoid quarrelling with more than one neighbour at the same time. To this insecurity on land was added naval inferiority in the Adriatic. Italy's east coast contained only four un-satisfactory ports – Venice, Ancona, Bari and Brindisi: facing it were the Dalmatian coast and islands, amongst which all the navies of the world could safely shelter, while at the northern end of the Adriatic the Austrians had, beside the commercial ports of Trieste and Fiume, a fine naval base at Pola. This position of inferiority made Italy hyper-sensitive to Austrian designs for expansion into the Balkans, particularly towards Albania. For Albania was to Italy what the Low Countries were to Britain; if the Austrians ever established themselves only forty-five miles across the Straits of Otranto from the Apulian heel, Italy would face encirclement and the Adriatic would become an Austrian lake.

This strategic aspect of Italo-Austrian relations was closely connected with irredentism, which was born from the Italian failure to win Trieste and the Trentino in 1866. These two 'unredeemed' lands played in Italian foreign policy a role similar to that played by Alsace-Lorraine in France. The number of active irredentists, as of active French *revanchards*, might at times be small. But the two questions lay close beneath the surface of international relations. Dissatisfaction that Italian unity was incomplete was common to all parties and classes, especially in the north which had known the *tedeschi* and Austrian rule at first hand. Salandra, the con-servative Prime Minister who took Italy into the Great War, wrote many years later that there was a 'a germ of irredentism in every Italian heart'. Though conservative governments might repress the irredentist movement, none could openly repudiate its aims. Italy had been built on the principle of nationality and lasting friendship was difficult with the multi-national, anti-national Habsburg Monarchy. Andrássy, the Austro-Hungarian Foreign

Minister, lucidly summed up the position in 1874 in a despatch to his ambassador in Rome:

> The very day on which we were to consent to a modification (of the Austro-Italian frontier) on the basis of an ethnographic delimitation, similar claims could be raised by others and it would be almost impossible to refuse them. We could not in fact cede to Italy the populations which resemble her in language without artificially provoking a centrifugal movement among the nationalities placed on the frontiers of the Empire towards the sister nationalities bordering on our realms. This movement would face us with the alternative of resigning ourselves to the loss of these provinces or, always following the system of nationalities, incorporating the countries on our borders within the Monarchy.[1]

There was the further reason for intransigence that Trieste was a vital trade outlet, without which Austria-Hungary could hardly survive. In 1869 the Austrians had been prepared, during the abortive negotiations for a Franco-Austro-Italian alliance against Prussia, to discuss the cession of the Trentino in return for compensations in Germany. But the creation of the German Empire in 1871 destroyed such a possibility for ever. Not until the crisis of 1915, and then only under heavy German pressure, did an Austrian government again consent to discuss territorial concessions to Italy.

Outside the Adriatic a long vulnerable coastline made friendship with Britain, the leading sea power of the Mediterranean, a vital necessity. Moreover without British goodwill Italian influence in the Mediterranean could never grow in the face of French hostility. Italian eyes turned naturally to north Africa as a field for future activity. Only seventy miles separated Sicily from Cape Bon, and already by 1871 there were 6,000 Italian residents in Tunisia, who far outnumbered the French. Both Cavour and Mazzini believed that Italy must one day go to Tunis, if only to keep France out. Cavour also looked further afield, both to the Red Sea, where he established friendly relations with the rulers of Ethiopia, and to the eastern Mediterranean, where he was determined that Italy should have a say in the Eastern question. In 1855 he had declared, as one motive for the intervention of Piedmont in the Crimean War, that Russian control of the Straits and Russian domination of the Mediterranean would be fatal to the interests of Piedmont and Italy. Six years later his successors insisted that Italy should not be excluded from the European Concert's intervention in the Lebanon. For all these tentative aspirations British friendship was vital; and indeed friendship with Britain, however exasperating and aloof that country's governments might appear, was a dogma which remained unchallenged by any Italian foreign minister before Mussolini. Britain also

[1] Sandonà, I, pp. 104-13.

had strong motives for keeping Italian friendship. Italy almost cut the Mediterranean imperial highway in two; and though the Italian fleet by itself might be of secondary importance, the British position would have been uncomfortable if both that fleet and its bases at La Spezia and Taranto had been at the disposal of a hostile alliance.

The inescapable dilemma which confronted Italian foreign ministers was whether, in a divided Europe, their country needed allies or could safely remain neutral. Italy lay in an uncomfortable strategic position between east and west, controlling in the Po valley one of the great military highways of Europe and jutting far out into the great maritime highway of the Mediterranean. There was good cause to fear involvement in disputes between more powerful neighbours, who might try to force Italy into their own combination or at least keep it out of that of their rivals. Alliance with one side could increase that danger. On the other hand neutrality, unless armed to the teeth, might merely mean incurring the dislike of both sides and suffering the revenge of the victor.[1] The debate between alliance and neutrality runs through modern Italian history and has not ended today. The aim of the ablest Italian statesmen has been to reduce the causes of tension, to mediate and to maintain a middle diplomatic position of equilibrium. But in periods when Europe has been divided into two blocs so equally balanced that Italy's weight seemed sufficient to tip the scale, the temptation to turn to the highest bidder has sometimes proved irresistible. Italy, in inheriting Piedmont's strategical position, also inherited the Piedmontese tradition of oscillating between rival great powers in order to avoid vassalage to any single one of them.[2] Such a policy can without difficulty be represented as cynical, unheroic machiavellianism; but it is highly questionable if any other foreign policy between 1871 and 1915 could have served Italy's basic interests so well.

By 1870 two broad views of Italy's foreign relations had emerged. These were but the application to international questions of the ideals and habits of mind of the Risorgimento. Thus the Right, with its diplomatic experience, its caution and realism, had a saner understanding of Italy's true weight in Europe and of what could and could not be done. Its leaders saw that irredentist demonstrations and press abuse of Austria-Hungary were luxuries which a weak Italy could not afford. Cavour had said that Trieste and the Trentino would have to wait for a generation. His successors believed that if they were ever to be won, it would be by negotiation backed

---

[1] In the parliamentary debate of February 1855 on the Crimean alliance, Cavour quoted Machiavelli's opinion that in war the neutral state is bound to be 'sempre la preda di chi vince, con piacere e satisfazione di colui che è stato vinto'. Cilibrizzi, I, p. 166.

[2] Morandi, pp. 74–6.

by military strength. As early as 1844 Cesare Balbo, in his book *Delle speranze d'Italia*, had expressed the idea that Italian independence would come through Austria's 'easternisation'; eastward expansion would shift the Empire's centre of gravity into the Balkans and reconcile its rulers to losing the hegemony of the Italian peninsula. This idea persisted long after unification. With an easternised Austria-Hungary, stripped of its Italian provinces, the leaders of the Right would have had no quarrel. On the contrary, they believed that the survival of Austria-Hungary was essential if the equilibrium of Europe was to be preserved, Russia kept out of the Balkans and the Slav tide held back from Italy's frontiers.

For Mazzini's followers the principle of nationality was sacred and irredentism an article of faith. Solidarity with oppressed peoples, whether Poles or Greeks, Bulgars, Egyptians or Boers, remained for many decades an essential part of the Italian democratic ideal. Both Tsarist Russia and Turkey were detested as oppressors; but most odious of all was Austria. At the first rumour of an Austrian advance into eastern Europe, the democrats would organise support for the Balkan peoples and pass stirring irredentist resolutions. Mazzini had preached a holy war of the oppressed nations, with *Delenda Austria* as its slogan; he saw Italy as the natural leader of this crusade and the Austrian Slavs as natural allies. Before 1870 Prussia was the nation which the Left most admired, while imperial France was the object of dark suspicion. Bismarck's struggle to unite Germany commanded the sympathy of all who believed in the national principle and it was understandable that many looked to Protestant Prussia as Italy's natural ally against the Pope. It was not until much later that Italian democrats became disillusioned with Prussian militarism and Bismarck's 'blood and iron'. Napoleon III, on the other hand, seemed to Mazzini's disciples a truly satanic figure. He was the 'man of December 1851' who had destroyed the Second French Republic, the protector of the Pope and the patron of the Right which had frustrated the democratic revolution. In 1859 he had preserved Austrian rule in Venice; in 1860 he had stolen Nice and Savoy; in 1864 he had forced a servile Italian government to renounce Rome and thereby 'made Victor Emmanuel his prefect'; and in 1867, by sending troops to fire on Garibaldi at Mentana, he had finally cancelled Italy's debt to France for the alliance of 1859. More than dislike of a tyrant lay behind this antagonism to France; it was also inspired by resentment of French patronage and national jealousy of a more powerful rival, and it survived long after the disappearance of Napoleon III.

The leaders of the Right, by contrast, acknowledged Italy's debt to Napoleon III. They felt themselves to be 'sons of Magenta and Solferino', and the very thought of fighting France was abhorrent to them, even for the sake of recovering Nice and Savoy, which were 'the price freely paid for blood shed for us'.[1] They could also understand the feelings of Catholic Europe and were prepared to make an effort to soothe them. They believed that if they showed patience and self-restraint, time would work in Italy's favour. The men of the Left disagreed. They were haunted by the fear that Italy might arrive too late and clamoured for it to be accepted immediately into the European community, not as a Cinderella among the nations, but as an equal.[2] In helping Italy to fulfil its regenerating mission and to contribute to the building of a better world, they hoped to find as much excitement and adventure, as many outlets for idealistic self-sacrifice, as they had found in the Risorgimento. When these naive but generous hopes were disappointed, many allowed their idealism to turn sour; visions of Italian greatness degenerated into rhetorical nationalism and Italy's 'civilising mission' into pseudo-Roman imperialism.

The man who did most, after Cavour, to mould Italy's foreign policy was Emilio Visconti Venosta. He was a member of a Lombard noble family who in his youth had been a disciple of Mazzini, but by 1859 had become one of Cavour's staunchest supporters in Lombardy. In 1863 he was made Foreign Minister at the age of thirty-four and he held that office five times over the next forty years.[3] In 1906 he led the Italian delegation to the Algeciras Conference and he died only in 1914. His active life therefore coincides almost exactly with that of liberal Italy. He was a true disciple of Cavour. Though he lacked Cavour's unscrupulous audacity, parliamentary brilliance and ability to dominate events, he possessed to the full those qualities of realism, adaptability, patience and common sense which were characteristic of the best representatives of the Right. Like Cavour, he hated revolution and distrusted the masses; but he was a conservative, not a reactionary, with a profound belief in liberty and in the parliamentary régime as liberty's surest bulwark.[4] In 1863 he decided that Italy should remain uncommitted and summed up his policy in the phrase 'Always independent, never isolated'. His aim was to be on good terms with all his neighbours, above all with France. The September Convention was his work. The temporary alliance with Prussia in 1866, concluded while he was out of office, did not conflict with his long-term aim, for it brought Italy closer to Prussia without alienating France; and very soon after the war was over, Italo-Austrian relations were friendlier than ever before.

The first major test of Visconti Venosta's policy came with the Franco-Prussian war. For two years before it broke out, Napoleon III had been

---

[1] Chabod, *Storia*, p. 113. Magenta and Solferino were the French victories which led to the expulsion of the Austrians from Lombardy in 1859.

[2] ibid., p. 286.

[3] In 1863–4, 1866–7, 1869–76, 1896–8 and 1899–1901.

[4] Chabod, *Storia*, pp. 563–7, 585–7.

pressing for a Franco-Austro-Italian alliance against the growing Prussian menace. The negotiations failed because France refused to abandon Rome. 'Better the Prussians in Paris than the Italians in Rome', the Empress Eugénie was alleged to have declared. When war broke out on 19 July 1870, Italian public opinion was divided. In Visconti Venosta's words, 'the government was French and the country was Prussian'.[1] The Left was enthusiastic for Prussia, and Mazzini was eager, with Bismarck's encouragement, to launch a revolution, should Lanza's government go to Napoleon III's aid. Many would gladly have acted on Bismarck's pressing invitation to seize Nice. But the proclamation of a republic in Paris and the shattering Prussian victories turned France into an oppressed democratic nation and, once again, the champion of the ideals of 1789. Garibaldi rushed to defend it with a handful of faithful volunteers and won a minor victory over the invader at Dijon. The Right also was divided. Several prominent ministers shared the belief of Victor Emmanuel and his generals that Italy had a debt of honour to France to fulfil; they also feared the fate of a neutral Italy in a Europe dominated by Prussia. Another section of the cabinet, led by Sella, held out stubbornly for neutrality. Fortunately for Italy the war went so fast that intervention was soon impossible.

Meanwhile there was Rome to tackle. Visconti Venosta clung to Cavour's belief that Italy must go to Rome by *mezzi morali* only, and resisted the employment of force until the last moment. As late as 16 August he re-affirmed Italy's loyalty to the September Convention, hoping for a peaceful solution in the form of an international guarantee of the Pope's independence in an Italian Rome. But Pius IX refused to negotiate. At the end of August the last French troops evacuated Rome, leaving the gunboat *Orénoque* at Civitavecchia to take the Pope on board in case of need. On 2 September Napoleon III surrendered to the Prussians at Sedan and two days later the Third Republic was proclaimed. Continued loyalty to the September Convention now became impossible. Inside the cabinet Sella was pressing for immediate occupation. Even Visconti Venosta became convinced that if the government did not seize Rome in an orderly fashion, volunteers of the left would soon seize it in revolutionary disorder; Rome could not be left to its own devices, for 'it would inevitably have become the Roman Republic'.[2] Once again, as in 1860–1, the Italians sought and obtained European approval for 'a conservative action', in defence of order and the monarchical principle. Victor Emmanuel, on whose solemn protestations of devotion to the church Pius IX still counted,[3] was reluctantly stirred into action by fear of revolution. Two days after the proclamation of the French Republic the government made its decision. On

[1] ibid., p. 121.    [2] ibid., pp. 330–2.    [3] Pirri, XXIV, pp. 292, 303.

12 September the Italian army crossed the papal frontier and on the 20th entered Rome.

The foundation of the German Empire meant the end of the old Europe. Visconti Venosta spoke for many of the Right when he lamented its passing. The future seemed uncertain and comfortless. The spirit of force and conquest was abroad. Rome had been won, but Napoleon III, on whom the Right had leant so heavily, had vanished. Catholics throughout the world felt outraged; and in France not only Catholics but liberals and republicans were embittered by Italian ingratitude. Europe's equilibrium had been shattered and the continent seemed to be at the mercy of the two giants, Germany and Russia. The Slav menace loomed larger; the power of the new Germany might soon be felt at Trent and Trieste.[1] The Paris Commune had unleashed the forces of revolution and anarchy. The values and institutions on which the Right set so great store – moderation, tolerance, liberty and order, parliamentary monarchy, a balance of power in Europe – were now at a discount.

But many Italians, especially on the left, rejoiced at the upheaval, and saw fascinating prospects for their country in a new world dominated no longer by tradition but by science and power. The future lay with the young, vigorous, virile nations, Germany and Italy, whose aspirations ran parallel and whose interests coincided. Italy could now assert itself, achieve real independence, and show that the Risorgimento had been as great a revolution as that of 1789. The forces of Italian nationalism and liberalism, barely distinguishable since 1815, now began to diverge. It was not only on the left that there was talk of wiping out the humiliation of 1866 and cementing national unity by a victorious war. Victor Emmanuel fully shared such hopes. The possession of Rome generated dreams of an imperial mission in Africa, of making the Mediterranean *mare nostrum,* of showing that the Roman warrior mentality was not dead. Even Mazzini, in his later writings, admitted colonial expansion as a legitimate part of Italy's national mission. Some of his former followers, notably Crispi, went much further, till energy and action, power and prestige became ends in themselves.

Italian sympathies continued to be divided after 1870 between France and Germany, both of which had their passionate admirers. Those who were impatient to see Italy great, looked to Germany; those who thought Italy needed time and calm, worked for friendship with France. But there was no clean division between Right and Left on problems of foreign policy. As France evolved from clericalism and monarchism to republicanism, and Germany from the militant anti-clericalism of the *Kulturkampf*

---

[1] Chabod, *Storia,* pp. 113 ff., 140 ff., 465 ff.

to solidarity with reactionary Austria-Hungary and Russia, many Italians transferred their affections. Both Right and Left contained Francophils and Francophobes, Germanophils and Germanophobes. The real difference between them was rather one of style and temperament than long-term aim. The men of the Left, whether they believed in democracy or national greatness, in the principle of nationality or an imperial mission, were in a hurry to see results and to put Italy on the map. The Right was cautious; liberty must be tempered by order, the principle of nationality by the maintenance of equilibrium in Europe; Italy was young and immature, and must move forward step by step. Thus the clash of method and temperament, which had divided Cavour and Garibaldi, persisted long after unification had been achieved.[1]

[1] ibid., pp. 545–62.

# PART I

# CONSOLIDATION
## 1870–87

# 1

# Right and Left

## The Parliamentary Revolution

On 20 September 1870 Italian Bersaglieri troops under General Raffaele Cadorna breached the walls of Rome near the Porta Pia and against resistance that, by express order of Pius IX, was purely token, entered the city. On 2 October the population voted by an overwhelming majority in a plebiscite for union with Italy, and on 27 November 1871 the Italian parliament met for the first time in Rome. In his speech from the throne Victor Emmanuel spoke of the political *risorgimento* that was ended and of the economic *risorgimento* that would follow close behind. In declaring that prose had succeeded to poetry, he echoed the feelings of all Italians that the year 1870 had been a turning-point. The problem which for ten years had obsessed them was now solved. A deadweight had been lifted from Italian foreign policy, and at home energies could be turned into new and more constructive channels.

But the years after 1870 seemed to many who lived through them a period of disillusionment and anticlimax.[1] The Italians are not a prosaic people. Nostalgia for the poetry of the Risorgimento, for the battles and conspiracies and heroism, tortured the Garibaldini. Mazzini reviled the new Italy as 'a great lie', created by dynastic egoism and humiliating diplomatic compromises. No golden age followed unification, but instead an arduous national struggle for existence and countless private struggles for bread and butter and jobs. Big issues were replaced by small issues, great men by little men. Giosuè Carducci, Italy's greatest lyrical poet of modern times, expressed in an extreme form this bitterness and nostalgia, these merciless criticisms of his own generation, which did so much to create the atmosphere of those early years. 'Oh for the days of sun, of liberty and glory in 1860!' he declaimed in 1886; 'oh for the struggles of titans between Cavour and Garibaldi in 1861! What have we become!'

[1] See Croce, pp. 1–4, a fine passage very characteristic of the author.

41

The occupation of Rome, by removing the main point of difference between the parliamentary parties, ushered in a period of political uncertainty. It became increasingly difficult as time passed to say what Right and Left stood for. The Left, it was true, was more fiercely anti-clerical than the Right, believed more staunchly in *laisser faire* principles, and was in a greater hurry for greater reforms. But what chiefly separated them, apart from personal antagonisms and memories of the past, was the fact that for the first ten years of Italy's existence the Right had provided the governments and the Left the opposition: that the one was 'in' and the other 'out'. The leaders of the Right looked upon themselves as the true makers of Italy and the trustees of its future. They had no illusions about the political immaturity of the people and were convinced that many years of strong honest government would be necessary before political liberties could be widened or the suffrage extended. This attitude of moral superiority embittered members of the Left. It seemed to them that Garibaldi's contribution to unification had been systematically underrated. Veterans of the Thousand writhed under the barely concealed contempt with which Piedmontese generals greeted their incorporation in the regular army.[1] The new jobs in diplomacy, in the judiciary and the administration had with few exceptions been given to supporters of the Right. A further cause of bitterness arose from the Right's treatment of the south. Ruthless repression of brigandage and prolonged martial law gave the Left its chance to brand the government as the oppressor of the people. Garibaldi, whose achievements had already passed into legend, now became the poor man's king, whose portrait hung beside the Madonna's over peasant fireplaces. He was the symbol round which the conflicting discontents of the south focussed. And so, ironically, the crusader who had dealt the Bourbon kingdom its deathblow became in the space of a few years the patron of a political opposition in which barely concealed Bourbon sympathisers found their place; a situation which provided plenty of opportunities for self-righteous sarcasm by the Right. By 1870 the Left had become the champion of all the injured classes and depressed areas which were demanding political recognition. In its manifestos it continued to speak in the name of the people and the disinherited. But by now many of its leaders had moved far from Mazzini's intransigence or Garibaldi's mania for opposition. They were impatient and greedy for power, and prepared to combine with discontented sections of the Right in order to obtain it.

The Right was exhausted and in visible decline. The rift between the

[1] Only 1,584 out of Garibaldi's 7,000 officers were given commissions in the army after 1860; the remainder were dismissed with a small pension. Cilibrizzi, I, pp. 371-2.

Piedmontese Permanente and the anti-Piedmontese Consorteria had not been healed, and regional antagonisms persisted. There were also personal divisions within its ranks. Of its three leading figures, Giovanni Lanza, Marco Minghetti and Quintino Sella, the latter two never consented to serve in the same government. Lanza, who became Prime Minister in 1869, was a Piedmontese of modest origins and simple tastes: son of a blacksmith, graduate in medicine and self-made man, he showed to a conspicuous degree the stubborn integrity and devotion to the public service which marked so many of the leaders of the Right. Sella, his Minister of Finance, also Piedmontese, was a member of the family which had created the woollen industry of his native Biella. A geologist, mathematician and mining engineer by training, he believed in science and technical progress, and was deeply interested in social problems. Like Lanza, he was austere and simple in his private life; with his rough country clothes and mountaineer's boots he seemed 'even in his appearance to personify Italy's necessity for economy'.[1] Above all he was an outstanding administrator. Minghetti by contrast was a polished, cultured Romagnole from Bologna, with little of the austerity and stiffness of the Piedmontese, a wide knowledge of Europe and a gift for oratory which had earned him the name of 'the siren'. In politics he showed more subtlety and flexibility than most of his party, and in 1870 he was the acknowledged leader of the 'dissident Right'.

These men disagreed on major questions of policy. In religious affairs Lanza and Minghetti were the heirs of Cavour's liberalism; Sella, who in 1870 had been the Right's most impatient advocate of immediate occupation of Rome, believed in stricter control of the church. In finance Sella was uncompromising in his fight to balance the budget and cared nothing for unpopularity; Minghetti was more sensitive to pressure for less rigorous taxation. The Piedmontese Sella was an unrepentant centraliser; the Romagnole Minghetti sympathised with the Left's demands for decentralisation. A small section of the Right, of which the Neapolitan Silvio Spaventa was the intellectual leader, was influenced by Hegelian ideas. Spaventa confessed himself 'an adorer of the state', which he regarded as the directing conscience of the nation, and whose all-powerful authority he believed would be not a threat to individual liberty, but its essential guarantee. Sella and Minghetti, without being 'adorers', wished to extend the functions of the state to embrace social legislation, post office savings banks and the direct management of railways, hoping by such means to control capitalist speculation, both Italian and foreign, and limit the power of 'financial feudalism'. Such ideas were abhorrent to *laisser faire*

[1] Underwood, pp. 9–10.

liberals, and especially to the Tuscan Right under Ricasoli's successor, Ubaldino Peruzzi.[1]

These internal differences of the Right made the position of Lanza's government precarious after 1870. Minghetti's group combined on many occasions with the most moderate section of the Left under Depretis, and in June 1873 Lanza fell on a question of finance. Attempts to form a coalition broke down and Minghetti formed a new ministry of the Right, no more secure than Lanza's. In the general election of November 1874 the Left made striking gains, especially in the south, and returned 232 strong in a chamber of 508. The Right's achievements were remarkable. A tolerable solution of the problem of church and state was reached in the Law of Guarantees of 1871.[2] In foreign policy Visconti Venosta successfully pursued his aims of conciliation and independence.[3] Public order was maintained throughout the country, though often by strong-handed methods.[4] Sella and Minghetti continued to practise 'economy to the bone', and in March 1876 the latter was able to announce that the state was at last solvent.[5] But these successes did not prevent the Left from exploiting the rising discontent over taxation, restrictions on freedom and a 'weak' foreign policy. The Right was pilloried as a closed oligarchical caste, which claimed a monopoly of patriotism and a semi-divine right to rule. Cavour's successors have been fairly described as a 'spiritual aristocracy', for whom affairs of state were a religion.[6] Their scrupulous personal honesty caused them to die poor. They wished to educate Italy to their own high ideals of government and were deaf to what seemed sordid demands for favours from those whom their policies injured. This failure to unbend was their downfall.[7]

The Right finally fell from power in the 'parliamentary revolution' of 18 March 1876. Minghetti's announcement of a budget surplus two days before had helped to precipitate his fall, by giving tax-conscious deputies the feeling that 'economy to the bone' could now be dispensed with. But two other issues helped to bring about the decisive vote in the chamber: Florence's demand for financial help and the organisation of the railways.

[1] Carocci, pp. 53–4. Luzzatti, the Right's most prominent recruit from the post-Risorgimento generation and a close collaborator of Minghetti, referred to Peruzzi and his friends as 'Smithiani arrabbiati'. *Memorie*, I, p. 507.
[2] See below, pp. 55–6.        [3] ibid., pp. 98–102.        [4] ibid., pp. 66 ff.
[5] ibid., p. 62.
[6] Croce, pp. 4–5.
[7] Most of the leaders of the Right recognised this fault after their defeat. Ruggero Bonghi, the party's leading intellectual and publicist, and ex-Minister of Education, wrote in 1876: 'Noi partiti moderati attendevamo a fare le cose, e l'Opposizione ha atteso a far le coselle.' R. Bonghi, *Come cadde la Destra* (2nd ed., Milan 1929), p. 222.

Florence's claim was based on the fact that its selection as the capital of Italy in 1865 had involved the municipality in a costly programme of building and embellishment. Tuscan deputies were unanimous that the city was entitled to compensation from the nation for the sudden move of the capital to Rome, but the government was unsympathetic. The railway question roused even stronger feelings. In pre-industrial Italy the railways offered the greatest opportunities for capital investment. When the Minister for Public Works, Spaventa, introduced a bill for state ownership and management of the whole railway system, powerful financial interests felt threatened and mobilised their political spokesmen, both on the Left and among the *laisser faire* Lombards and Tuscans of the Right. On 18 March Peruzzi and the Tuscan Right voted with the Left and defeated the government. Minghetti resigned and the King commissioned Agostino Depretis, the leader of the moderate Left, to form a new ministry.

At the time this change of government seemed more important than it appears in retrospect. Republicans hailed it as the first step towards a republic and prophesied that the monarchy would not survive Victor Emmanuel. The excitement on the Left was intense. At last it had won effective power, a just reward for its achievements in the Risorgimento and for the long years of waiting. The south, too, felt elated. By including a substantial number of southerners in his cabinet, Depretis fulfilled the hopes of the southern middle class which had looked to him to rescue it from the frustration it had felt under the Right.[1] In the election of November 1876 the Right was routed. Giovanni Nicotera, the new Minister of Interior, changed almost every prefect throughout the kingdom and subjected voters, local authorities and the press to greater electoral pressure than Italy had yet known. Well might Spaventa lament 'administrative terror' and the 'reduction of the State to a monstrous electoral machine'. The Left won 414 seats and the opposition 94. Of the 194 deputies representing the south, only 9 belonged to the Right.

The King chose Depretis as his Prime Minister because he was a northerner, from Stradella on the boundary between Piedmont and Lombardy, and because he belonged to the most moderate section of the Left. He had been elected to the first Piedmontese parliament in 1848 and he remained a deputy continuously until his death in 1887. At first he had sat with the democratic opposition, declining in 1852 to support Rattazzi's *connubio* with Cavour. But by 1876 his democratic fervour had cooled, his republicanism had long since vanished and he had grown into a cautious, realistic, hard-working politician. He was a good administrator, a brilliant judge of character and a sober, effective speaker; he never lost his head or took too much to heart the vicious personal attacks from which he suffered,

[1] Carocci, pp. 65–9.

and preferred to appease rather than antagonise or excite passion. On
occasions he carried his preference for procrastination to lengths which,
especially in foreign affairs, did his country harm. But, though there were
few ready to admit it, Italy owed Depretis a great debt. He was Prime
Minister for over eight of the eleven years from March 1876 to July 1887,
and Minister of Interior for a further eighteen months in the same period.[1]
It was in large part due to his guidance and sure judgement that Italy had
time to consolidate its unity.

The new government's programme had been foreshadowed by Depretis
in a famous speech at Stradella in October 1875. Its chief points were
devotion to the monarchy, unrestricted constitutional liberties and electoral freedom,[2] a cautious foreign policy and a series of major reforms
– extension of the suffrage, decentralisation of the administration, abolition
of the *macinato* tax and free, secular, primary education.[3] It was a moderate
programme, and it soon became clear that Depretis was in no hurry to put
it into effect. His ministers, some of whom had stormy republican pasts,
disappointed all hopes of revolutionary change. On Nicotera, the Minister
of Interior, for instance, the responsibilities of office had a sensational
effect. This Calabrian disciple of Mazzini now put his Jacobin tempestu-
ousness and delight in personal vendetta at the service of the monarchy and
the cause of law and order. Depretis himself set the tone of his administration by declaring that he was ready to accept the collaboration of all
honest, loyal and competent men, to whatever party they belonged. This
overture did not remain without response. In October 1876 Sella praised
the new government and parts of its programme, and said he would not
oppose merely for the sake of opposition. Minghetti associated himself
with these views. Soon Lanza was claiming that Depretis's programme was
that of the Right, and Spaventa, not without bitterness, was describing the
government as 'a government of the Right, but not so good'.[4]

This moderation was most displeasing to a vocal section of the Left and
almost at once the heterogeneous majority returned in the 1876 election
began to break up. Within it ex-Mazzinians and Garibaldini sat side by
side with former supporters of the Right and recently converted Bourbon
sympathisers. Many of the deputies elected for the first time, who constituted one-third of the total, were men new to politics, to whom the old
slogans and ideals meant little. The biggest triumph of the Left had been

[1] He was Prime Minister from March 1876 to March 1878, December 1878 to
July 1879 and May 1881 to July 1887; and Minister of Interior from November
1879 to May 1881 under Cairoli.

[2] Nicotera's management of the November 1876 election was an ironic com-
mentary on this part of the programme.

[3] Cilibrizzi, II, pp. 92–3.

[4] P. Romano, *Silvio Spaventa* (Bari 1942), p. 226.

in the south, which had been least influenced politically by Mazzini and Garibaldi. Quite rapidly two main sections of the Left became distinguishable: the moderates under Depretis, and the 'progressives' or 'pure' Left. The latter demanded immediate, sweeping reforms and regarded Depretis's gradualism as a betrayal of the Left's ideals. But the two groups overlapped and there was constant passing from one to the other and back again, often from purely personal motives.

The three leading personalities of the 'pure' Left were Francesco Crispi, Benedetto Cairoli and Giuseppe Zanardelli.[1] Crispi was a Sicilian, of mixed Italian and Albanian descent. As a young and fervent Mazzinian he had been a leading organiser of the Sicilian revolution of 1848. Long years of exile had followed in Malta, France and London. In 1860 he sailed with the Thousand as Garibaldi's political secretary and became dictator of Sicily, then secretary of state in Naples. Next year he was elected to the first Italian parliament. At first he sat on the extreme left. No one denounced the Right more scathingly for 'diplomatising the revolution'. But personal ambition and restlessness made him a difficult colleague and soon earned him the name of 'Il Solitario'.[2] In 1864 he finally deserted Mazzini, declaring that 'the monarchy unites us, the republic would divide us'. This was his first step towards power. Depretis omitted him from his first cabinet, but in December 1877 he succeeded Nicotera as Minister of Interior. He was a man of violent temper and enormous energy, whose whole life, public and private, was turbulent, dramatic and marked by a succession of bitter enmities. He abhorred compromise, was incapable of tact or conciliation, and had a craving for bigness, both for himself and for his country. His first term of office could hardly have been stormier. In February 1878 a Neapolitan newspaper, inspired by Nicotera, accused him of bigamy. A judicial investigation subsequently cleared him of the charge: but his defence was not edifying,[3] and he was meanwhile forced to resign after only three months in the government. For nine years after 1878 he remained a leader of the 'progressive' opposition.

Cairoli's political past was similar to Crispi's, but he was a man of very different character: the Bayard of democracy, the knight-errant in politics,

[1] Zanardelli became Depretis's Minister of Public Works in March 1876, but resigned in November 1877. This move led immediately to the formation of the 'pure' Left, with about eighty members.

[2] F. Petrucelli della Gattina, in *I moribondi del Palazzo Carignano* (2nd ed., Bari 1913), p. 153, describes how he once asked Crispi whether he was a Mazzinian. 'No,' he replied. 'Are you a Garibaldian, then?' 'Certainly not,' he replied. 'And what are you then?' 'I am Crispi.'

[3] In December 1854 Crispi had been married by an itinerant Jesuit priest in Malta to Rosalia Montmasson, who later accompanied him on the expedition of the Thousand to Sicily. In 1875 he left her in order to legitimise his daughter by Lina Barbagallo, with whom he went through a religious marriage ceremony. As

'in whom all was tolerated, even romantic naivety and political incompetence'.[1] Four of his brothers had lost their lives in the Risorgimento. He himself had fought the Austrians in his native Lombardy in 1848–9, then served with Garibaldi in Sicily and again in 1867 outside Rome. He remained devoted to Garibaldi as long as his hero lived and often acted as his political mouthpiece; but his democratic leanings, his sympathy with irredentism and his passionate belief in liberty proved an embarrassment when he succeeded Depretis as Prime Minister. He himself pronounced the fairest judgement on his statesmanship, during his first term of office in 1878. 'We will not be clever', he said, 'but we wish to be honest.' He fully lived up to his promise.[2] Zanardelli, another Lombard, was a distinguished jurist and an eloquent orator, who fully shared Cairoli's belief in liberty. Even the slightest restriction caused him pain, and throughout his long career he was the most ardent advocate in Italian politics of free trade and *laisser faire*, of freedom of conscience and divorce.

Further to the left again was the small but growing Extreme Left, which numbered about a dozen deputies after 1876. At first it had been intransigently republican and swore undying enmity not only to the monarchy, but to parliament and the whole political system. But successive waves of republicans overcame their scruples to the extent of swearing loyalty to King and Constitution, with mental reservations, and taking their seats as deputies. Their republicanism was slowly reduced to lip service to a noble but remote ideal, which they felt little bound to transform into reality. Typical of this evolution was the career of Agostino Bertani, who had organised Garibaldi's Sicilian expedition in 1860 and remained a militant Mazzinian long after most of his companions had accepted the monarchy. On Mazzini's death he became leader of the Republican party. But in 1878 he too compromised and founded the Radical party, which preached an advanced democratic programme within the framework of the monarchist state. Bertani died in 1886 and was succeeded as leader of the Extreme Left by Felice Cavallotti. Chivalrous, dashing and romantic, Cavallotti had joined Garibaldi in 1860 at the age of eighteen and later achieved fame as poet, dramatist, journalist and demagogue. His love affairs were discussed throughout Italy. He was an inveterate dueller and met his death in his thirty-third duel in 1898.[3] Known as 'the bard of democracy', he soon became one of the outstanding political figures of his time.

this was not legally binding, the charge of bigamy did not arise until January 1878, when they celebrated a civil marriage. Crispi's defence was that the marriage with Rosalia Montmasson had been invalid.

[1] Bonomi, *La politica italiana da Porta Pia a Vittorio Veneto*, p. 56.
[2] M. Rosi, *I Cairoli* (Bologna 1929), I, p. 321; Cilibrizzi, II, pp. 162–3.
[3] He and a friend once challenged all the officers of a Milan cavalry regiment.

After 1876 this Extreme Left, with its radical nucleus and socialist and republican fringes, performed the same function of criticism as the Left had performed before 1876. Its patron was Garibaldi, who since 1867 had rarely left Caprera, his island retreat off the north coast of Sardinia. In 1879 he emerged from his retirement and came to Rome. There under his benevolent eye was founded the League of Democracy, with a programme that was to be the prototype of all the democratic programmes of the next forty years. It included universal suffrage, democratic reform of the constitution, decentralisation, redistribution of the tax burden and large-scale land reclamation. As was to be expected, it was fiercely anti-clerical; it was also both pacifist[1] and irredentist. Garibaldi was elected deputy for Rome in 1880 but resigned his seat soon afterwards, refusing to be a legislator 'in a country where freedom is trampled on, and where the law is applied only to guarantee the liberty of Jesuits and the enemies of Italian unity'.[2] His death in 1882 strengthened the more moderate radicals who wished to play a positive role in parliament and obtain reform by constitutional methods.

After the Left came to power there was a decline in the stability of governments. Crispi's involvement in a charge of bigamy and subsequent resignation brought down the whole government in March 1878. Depretis was succeeded by Cairoli, who formed a government of a more pronounced democratic flavour, with Zanardelli as his Minister of Interior. Cairoli drew his main support from the radical middle class of Milan and the north, and his cabinet was overwhelmingly northern in composition. Garibaldi and the progressives expected great things of him, but he soon disappointed them. Shaken by diplomatic defeat at the Congress of Berlin,[3] he fell in December 1878 after an anarchist attempt on the life of the King, for which his lax police measures were held responsible.[4] Depretis returned to power with a more conservative team and programme. For the next two and a half years abolition of the *macinato* tax was the dominant political issue.[5] Cairoli was given a second term of office in July 1879, but made no attempt to repeat the democratic experiment of the previous year. After five months, as if to emphasise his new moderation, he took Depretis as his Minister of Interior, a choice that earned him denunciation by the 'pure' Left (led this time by Crispi, Zanardelli and Nicotera) for abandoning his principles and contracting an immoral *connubio*. In the election of May 1880

---

[1] The military panacea of the Extreme Left was the 'armed nation', i.e. a popular militia instead of regular troops. Garibaldi wanted two million healthy volunteers instead of 200,000 soldiers rotting and 'ruining the race' in barracks.

[2] Cilibrizzi, II, p. 201. The chamber refused to accept his resignation.

[3] See below, pp. 104–6.      [4] ibid., p. 77.      [5] ibid., p. 64.

the Right recovered ground. The government's supporters dropped from over 400 in 1876 to 218; the Right increased its representation from 94 seats to 171 (only 33 from the south) and the 'pure' Left won 119 (95 from the south). In May 1881 Cairoli was swept away by the storm which followed the French occupation of Tunis.[1] The King sent for Sella; but the threat of the Right's return, under the 'starver of the people', reunited the squabbling Left. Depretis resumed power for six unbroken years.

The first five years of rule by the Left brought no fundamental changes. Compulsory elementary education was introduced in 1877 for all children between the ages of six and nine, but many years passed before it could be effectively enforced. Anti-clericalism was given a freer hand, but the Law of Guarantees remained intact.[2] The *macinato* tax disappeared, but taxation continued to press inequitably on the poor.[3] After experimenting with milder police restrictions on political freedom, the Left reverted to the stern methods for which they had previously attacked the Right.[4] The drastic change in foreign policy, for which the Mazzinians and Garibaldians longed, never came.[5] By 1882 the phrase 'parliamentary revolution', as a description of the change of government in 1876, sounded strangely stale.

One major reform did, however, take place: in 1882 the suffrage was extended. This had figured prominently in the Left's programme even before 1870 and a minority, including Cairoli, supported the demand of Garibaldi and the League of Democracy for universal suffrage. On this point they had strange allies in a few conservatives like Sidney Sonnino, who wished to neutralise the votes of the radical towns by those of the peasantry. But Depretis, Crispi and the majority of the Left opposed the enfranchisement of the peasantry, just because it would strengthen the forces of reaction and the political power of the church. They therefore insisted on literacy as a minimum qualification. The Right, with its fear of the masses and of revolutionaries, whether red or black, wished to retain a high property qualification; it believed that a wide suffrage would lower the quality of both voter and deputy, and wither the fragile plant of liberty, so precariously planted in Italian soil. After nearly two years of debate the suffrage bill became law in January 1882. It retained a literacy test, but reduced the minimum voting age from twenty-five to twenty-one, lowered the property qualification[6] and added as an alternative to the latter a certi-

---

[1] See below, pp. 108-9.   [2] ibid., pp. 57-8.   [3] ibid., pp. 63 ff.   [4] ibid., pp. 76-7.   [5] ibid., pp. 102 ff.

[6] The following possessed the minimum property qualification: taxpayers contributing 19·8 lire a year in direct taxes; agricultural tenants paying 500 lire annually in rent; sharecroppers on farms taxed at 80 lire a year; and householders paying an annual rent of 150 lire. *Compendio*, I, pp. 71, 83. There were also a number of fancy franchises.

ficate of primary education. Its effect was to increase the electorate from 600,000 to over 2 million, from 2% to 7% of the total population. It thus set the seal on the 'parliamentary revolution' of 1876, by broadening the base from which the ruling class was drawn. One consequence, which the Right did not fail to deplore, was a lowering of political tone and a decline in administrative standards. This was the inevitable price of an extension of power from an élite to new groups more representative of an immature people; it was the price of progress towards democracy.[1]

After 1882 personal antagonisms and memories of past conflicts could still rouse deep feeling in parliament, but they could not disguise the fact that the differences between Right and Left, already small in 1876, were now rapidly vanishing. This process was aided by the disappearance of most of the great figures of the Risorgimento.[2] The Left was growing fat and satisfied in power, and had few critics to fear on its right. Successive waves of conversion from republicanism had removed the monarchy from party controversy. Anti-clericalism was becoming stale and no longer sufficient by itself as a political battle-cry. By 1882 there was agreement in most sectors of parliament and public opinion on the main lines of financial, religious and foreign policy, and on the need for prudent restrictions on freedom in the interests of public order. Individuals differed on technical questions rather than questions of principle. Right and Left were becoming conscious of what they had in common. The two in fact constituted a broad liberal party of the centre, which monopolised political and public life. Its task was the defence of the monarchy, the constitution and the unity of Italy against the subversive forces of clerical reaction and social revolution.

Depretis understood this situation. In the autumn of 1882 he dissolved the chamber and in an electoral speech at Stradella on 8 October outlined a new programme of conciliation and administrative progress. Criticising those who harped on the differences between Right and Left, and wished to 'crystallize and fossilize the parties', he declared: 'We are a progressive government, and if anyone wishes to transform himself and become progressive, if he wishes to accept my very moderate programme, can I reject him?'[3] The election was a triumph for the government. Six weeks later the King's speech from the throne called for less political dissension and better administration. Finance, public works and railway reorganisation, tariff reform and adjustment of the nation's economy to industrialisation and agricultural crisis – these were the problems that occupied parliament's

[1] C. Morandi, *La Sinistra al potere* (Florence 1944), pp. 116–19; Carocci, pp. 72–3.
[2] Victor Emmanuel II and Pius IX died in 1878, Garibaldi and Lanza in 1882, Sella in 1884, Minghetti in 1886, Depretis and Cairoli in 1887. Of front-rank personalities only Crispi survived after 1887.
[3] Cilibrizzi, II, pp. 263–4.

attention over the years 1882–7. Neither foreign nor church affairs provided excitements equal to those of the previous decade. Through the many cabinet reshuffles there was a large measure of ministerial continuity, particularly in finance and foreign policy. Depretis himself controlled the Ministry of Interior without a break from November 1879 until April 1887. His calm, anti-demagogic temperament was admirably suited to a period in which technical and administrative problems were predominant.

In appealing to his opponents to 'transform themselves' and contribute to the creation of 'a great new national party' of the centre, Depretis was returning to the parliamentary tradition of Cavour's *connubio*. To describe his manœuvre a new word – *trasformismo* – was coined from his own phrase. The intransigents of both Right and Left soon made it a term of political abuse. Nevertheless his appeal was not left unanswered. Minghetti, Luzzatti and about seventy members of the Right gave him their support, admitting that the old divisions had lost their meaning. Both moderate Right and moderate Left felt uneasy after the adventure of electoral reform; it seemed that only the solidarity of all supporters of liberal institutions could save Italy from the republican and socialist abyss.[1]

In May 1883 Zanardelli and Alfredo Baccarini resigned from the government, disgusted with Depretis's growing conservatism and his indifference to the Left's traditions and ideals. Together with Crispi, Cairoli and Nicotera they formed a Pentarchy with the purpose of intensifying the opposition which the dissident 'pure' Left had provided since 1876. In October 1884 General Cesare Ricotti, who had been the Right's Minister for War before 1876, resumed his old post in Depretis's cabinet, in order to give greater cohesion to the 'transformed' majority of moderate Left and moderate Right. Depretis's relations with the latter were not always easy, for he had no intention of becoming its prisoner. Luzzatti lamented the Prime Minister's coolness and 'the bitter pills' which the government forced the Right to swallow; nevertheless, he felt 'compelled to support it, for fear of worse'.[2] Depretis maintained his majority for five years after 1882 by playing on such fears, sometimes cajoling, sometimes bullying the fluid groups in the chamber, but always opposing radical change. In spite of advancing age and growing irresolution he remained in control, the indispensable conciliator between clashing pressure groups and a master of the art of parliamentary government.

---

[1] Chabod, *Storia*, pp. 384–6; Cilibrizzi, II, pp. 269–71; Carocci, pp. 262–78. Among those who remained in varying degrees intransigent and declined to follow Minghetti's lead were Bonghi, Spaventa, Visconti Venosta and the Right's future leader, Rudinì.

[2] Luzzatti to Minghetti, July 1884. Luzzatti, *Memorie*, II, p. 183.

## The Church and the Law of Guarantees

Relations with the church and the Papacy overshadowed all other problems at the end of 1870. Even after 20 September Lanza's government hoped it would be possible to come to an agreement. The terms of surrender negotiated between the two commanding generals on that day excluded the Leonine City[1] from the area to be occupied by the Italian army. Though it was taken over next day in the interests of order, at the express request of the papal authorities, the government attempted to exclude it from the plebiscite on 2 October; but its population insisted on going to the polls with the rest of Rome. This was the end of attempts to prepare the way for an agreement which would have given the Papacy a less symbolic degree of temporal power than that which it finally accepted in 1929. Pius IX refused to negotiate in the face of violence and agreement was impossible without mutual confidence on both sides, which grew only with the passage of many years. In 1870 Pius insisted that the temporal power had been 'granted by divine Providence to the Apostolic See, in order that the successors of St Peter might freely and with full security exercise their spiritual powers'.[2] He neither hoped nor wished to recover the whole of his former kingdom; but restitution of 'a little corner of land', where he would be master, was an essential preliminary to negotiation.[3]

Every successive action of the government in taking over the city drew a fresh protest and fresh appeals for help from Catholics abroad. All who had been concerned with the occupation were excommunicated. Pius IX declared he would not leave the Vatican until the usurper had retired, and for over fifty-eight years no Pope set foot outside the palace precincts, choosing to remain voluntary, 'moral prisoners'. Pius IX's aim was to boycott Italy in Rome and to prevent even the most trivial act that might imply recognition.[4] He failed to persuade Catholic governments to instruct their ambassadors to remain in Florence: but the ban on visits of heads of Catholic states to Rome was effective for thirty-four years and was not

[1] The Leonine City, named after the ninth-century Pope Leo IV who had built its original walls, included St Peter's, the Vatican, the Castel Sant' Angelo and a large part of the Trastevere district, all on the west bank of the Tiber. It had a population of 15,000 in 1870.

[2] Encyclical *Respicientes ea omnis*, 1 November 1870.

[3] R. Aubert, *Le pontificat de Pie IX* (Paris 1952), p. 369.

[4] The importance attached to this withholding of recognition is shown by a petty incident described in Underwood, pp. 249–50. For a short period in 1871 Crown Prince Humbert and Princess Margherita used to attend mass in S. Maria Maggiore. When the sacristan put out red cushions for their use, he was reproved for thus acknowledging the sovereignty of the House of Savoy. It was therefore arranged that a footman should carry two cushions from the royal palace to the church every Sunday before mass.

finally lifted until 1920. Roman society split into the black nobility, which remained loyal to the Pope, and the white nobility, which acknowledged allegiance to the King of liberal Italy. For many years the two factions were not even on speaking terms. To Pius IX and to millions of Catholics all over the world, it was not only the destruction of the temporal power that seemed intolerable; there was also the desecration and violation of the Universal City. In the wake of the Italian army came the freethinkers, with visions of striking a deathblow to the very heart of Christianity; the freemasons; the worshippers of the 'golden calf' of material progress who hoped that Rome would become a centre of science instead of superstition; the Protestants, taking full advantage of the freedom guaranteed by the constitution; and, most galling of all, the anti-clerical press and theatre, the blasphemous pamphlets and periodicals which flourished on the borders of legality with the tolerance of the government. The bitterness of Catholics was summed up in the comment of the Archbishop of Paris in 1874, that Rome had become 'the vulgar capital of a modern state'.

In such circumstances the Italian government was anxious to give Pius IX as few opportunities as possible for protest and to avoid all appearance of limiting papal independence. Only by moderation, it seemed to Lanza and Visconti Venosta, could foreign intervention be averted. They gladly returned to the *mezzi morali* which they had abandoned with reluctance in September 1870. It was particularly necessary to dissuade Pius IX from leaving Rome. There was a party at the Vatican, in which the Jesuits were prominent, which was urging him to go. But the historical precedents were unpromising, and Pius was frail and old and not a man to run away from danger. All the major Powers, including Austria-Hungary, advised him to stay, while simultaneously urging restraint upon the Italian government. For a few weeks Pius nursed hopes of Prussia, the only power which had the strength, and possibly the inclination, to intervene in his defence. On 10 October he appealed personally to William I to 'aid a just cause' and 'uphold a principle which is the foundation of the social order'. But the King's reply was vague and evasive.[1] A last attempt was made in November when Cardinal Ledochowski, Archbishop of Posen, pleaded Pius IX's case before William I and Bismarck at the Prussian G.H.Q. at Versailles. The latter seems for a moment to have played with the idea of posing as the champion of the Catholic church against Italy and offering Pius IX asylum at Cologne or Fulda; but William I would not hear of it.[2] The Prussian

[1] Pirri, XXIV, pp. 320–4; XXV, pp. 238–44.

[2] Bismarck's arguments were characteristic: the Pope would have to be politically useful to Prussia in return for asylum; and the Pope's unpopularity in Rome suggested that his presence in Prussia would soon cure German Catholics of their ultramontane illusions. Halperin, pp. 85–8; Salata, *Per la storia diplomatica della questione romana*, pp. 261–8.

refusal to intervene relieved Italy of all immediate anxiety. Before 20 September Visconti Venosta had expressed readiness to accept an international guarantee of the Pope's spiritual independence. But the suggestion had met with a chilly reception from all governments except the Belgian, and the Vatican showed no enthusiasm for a scheme which would have sanctioned the destruction of the temporal power. By the end of 1870 it was clear that Italy would be left free to work out its own solution of the Roman question and of relations between church and state.

This solution took the shape of the Law of Guarantees of 13 May 1871. Its main authors, Lanza and Visconti Venosta, were both disciples of Cavour, but realised that it was impossible in 1871 to return to the 1861 formula of a 'free church in a free state'. In its final form the Law was a compromise between Cavour's liberal vision and the illiberal demands of the Left. It fell into two parts: the first dealing with the status of the Pope, the second with the relations of the church with the Italian state. The Pope was given the rank and privileges of a sovereign within Italy. Free communication with Catholics abroad, freedom of the conclave and the immunity of three papal residences[1] were guaranteed. Foreign envoys accredited to the Vatican were given full diplomatic status and special privileges were granted to the papal press. The Pope was to receive an annuity of $3\frac{1}{4}$ million lire (£130,000) from the Italian state, a sum calculated from the expenses of the papal court and Curia as published in the budget of the former Papal States. As regards the second part, Lanza and Visconti Venosta wished to abolish state jurisdiction over church affairs. Under the Law the state did in fact surrender its right to nominate bishops, and the royal *exequatur* and *placet* were no longer to be required for the execution of decisions of the church authorities. But the government was forced to make important concessions to the Left: the state's right of nomination was retained for the many episcopal sees and benefices in the patronage of the crown of Savoy and of the old monarchies whose privileges the Italian crown had taken over in 1861;[2] and abolition of the *exequatur* for the allocation of benefices was made conditional on the redistribution of ecclesiastical property and revenues. Since a redistribution law was in fact never passed, the state retained, even under the Law of Guarantees, the power to prevent new bishops from taking over the temporalities of their sees until their appointment had been approved by royal decree. Later Italian governments did not hesitate to make use of this formidable political weapon.

[1] These were the Vatican and Lateran palaces and the papal summer villa at Castel Gandolfo in the Alban Hills. The Quirinal had already been appropriated by the Italian government as the royal residence.
[2] These included all the episcopal sees in Sardinia and Sicily, over 60 of the Neapolitan sees, 4 in Emilia and the patriarchate of Venice. Binchy, pp. 377–8.

The Law was a compromise and, like all compromises, disliked by the extremists on both sides. Parliamentary orators of the Left thundered against the alleged clerical sympathies of the government. The Italian nation, they argued, was 'an advanced sentinel of progress', standing for liberty of conscience against the spiritual tyranny of the church; reconciliation was unthinkable. Mancini, a learned and eloquent Neapolitan jurist, pleaded for the retention of state controls, to protect Italy from the menace of its clerical enemies at home and abroad. Sella supported him from the benches of the Right. Pius IX on his side attacked the Law even more violently. In his encyclical of 15 May he spoke of an 'indecent mockery', 'the monstrous outcome of revolutionary jurisprudence', and referred scathingly to the 'Subalpine government' which had fabricated 'some futile privileges and immunities which are commonly called guarantees'. He made no distinction between the moderation of the Right and the militant anti-clericalism of the Left. The annuity from the Italian state was rejected and the Papacy relied instead for its essential needs on Peter's Pence, the voluntary offerings of Catholics throughout the world. In November 1871 Pius IX once again declared that 'no conciliation will ever be possible between Christ and Belial, between light and darkness, between truth and falsehood'.

Visconti Venosta and the Right regarded the Law as a temporary, unilateral solution, to be followed soon by a permanent, bilateral agreement. In this they were disappointed. But they had built more solidly than they ever imagined. The main motive behind Pius IX's intransigence was the need to prove his independence to the outside world. If he had accepted even part of the Law of Guarantees, his acceptance could have been interpreted abroad as an admission of dependence on the Italian government, and used as a pretext for obstructing the exercise of his spiritual authority over non-Italian Catholics. As time passed it became clear that the Law of Guarantees did effectively ensure the Pope's independence. Long before it disappeared in 1929, it had proved the temporal power unnecessary. This, its greatest achievement, was in the 1870s still in the future. The immediate service it rendered both church and state was to soothe the apprehensions of moderate Catholic opinion and reduce the danger of intervention which the policy of the Left would have merely aggravated.

In spite of much goodwill on the part of ministers, tension between church and state increased after 1871. This was due partly to alarm at the threats and diatribes of French clerics, partly to the concessions to anti-clerical sentiment which both the Lanza and Minghetti governments felt compelled to make. In 1872 theological faculties were suppressed in all universities, and seminaries were subjected to government inspection. Next year the existing legislation for the suppression of religious corporations and the confiscation of their property was extended to Rome. Under pressure from the Left even the buildings occupied by the generals of forty world-wide Catholic orders were included, though the government was given, and exercised, discretionary power to exempt them from the full rigour of the law.[1] After 1873 Minghetti was less tolerant than Lanza. The Colosseum was deconsecrated, as if to symbolise the sovereignty of the secular power over Rome.[2] Religious gatherings were banned or broken up, nominally for reasons of public health; priests were conscripted; and while clerics were continually taken to task for disobeying the law, abuse of Pius IX and blasphemous attacks on the Catholic faith, though contrary to the Law of Guarantees, were conspicuously tolerated. In 1875 the Left's campaign for an Italian *Kulturkampf* grew fiercer. In answer to accusations of weakness, Minghetti promised that the Law of Guarantees would be enforced. The promise was kept, and thirty-three bishops were expelled from the temporalities of their sees because they had refused to apply for the *exequatur*.

The coming to power of the Left in 1876 raised expectations of yet greater severity. Depretis himself was a freemason. The previous year, while proclaiming his belief in freedom of worship, he had issued a warning that 'when religious sentiment turns against the political organisation of the state, then it is time to sound the alarm and see to the state's defence. The war has begun and it will be necessary to wage it *à outrance*.' The Ministry of Justice, which was responsible for church affairs, was given to Mancini, the most eloquent advocate of state control. The prospect of persecution was not displeasing to some clericals, who hoped that it would finally disillusion moderate Catholics and hasten foreign intervention. 'We prefer the clear language of Depretis to the fictions and hypocrisies of his predecessor', wrote a leading Catholic newspaper.[3] Pius IX himself compared Right and Left to cholera and earthquake, with the implication that he preferred the latter.[4]

At first it seemed that these expectations would not be disappointed. In November 1876 Mancini presented a Clerical Abuses Bill which prescribed heavy penalties for the exercise of political pressure from the pulpit or in the confessional, or by withholding the sacraments. Its approval by the chamber drew from Pius IX his bitterest protest yet, and clerical agitation in France in response to the Pope's appeal added to the tension. But the senate rejected the bill as untimely and tyrannical, arguing that the existing

---

[1] The general of the Jesuits was specifically excluded from the benefits of exemption.
[2] Spadolini, *L'opposizione cattolica*, p. 77.     [3] Halperin, p. 403.
[4] Spadolini, *L'opposizione cattolica*, p. 125.

penal code was sufficient to prevent abuses. The Education Act of 1877 abolished compulsory religious instruction in elementary schools, though voluntary instruction could be arranged at the request of parents in school buildings after teaching hours. The state school, 'the church of modern times', as Depretis described it, was the favourite weapon of the anti-clericals for fighting the church's hold over the masses[1] and equipping Italy for life in the nineteenth century. But the Left's anti-clerical fervour soon abated. In 1879 a bill to penalise the celebration of religious marriage, unless it had been preceded by civil marriage, was passed by the chamber but shelved in the senate. The Left became slowly reconciled to the Law of Guarantees, which was declared a fundamental law by the Council of State, and the period of greatest danger for the church was over.

The fault of the leaders of the Left was to harp on the disagreements and smile tolerantly on the hotheads in their own ranks, rather than try, like the Right, to damp down passions and help time to heal the breach. Anti-clerical demonstrations were allowed to fill the streets of Rome with clamour during these years, though on the whole ministers kept away from them. Depretis and Mancini, however, went further than Minghetti in insisting that bishops should apply for the *exequatur*. Instructions were issued that, if they refused, they were to be deprived of their spiritual prerogatives as well as the temporalities of their office. The threat was effective and the Vatican yielded: after 1877 the *exequatur* clause of the Law of Guarantees caused little further trouble.[2] It was thus in administrative practice rather than in legislation that the rule of the Left differed from that of the Right. For many supporters of the government the Law of Guarantees was a maximum concession, and their pressure often caused its spirit, and sometimes its letter, to be violated.

From the side of the Papacy there were occasional gestures which gladdened the hearts of patriotic Italian Catholics and quickened their hopes of a better future. One such occurred during the last illness of Victor Emmanuel II. Before he died on 9 January 1878, the King sent a message to the Pope, regretting the personal displeasure he had caused him in the past but denying any intention of harming religion. Pius IX was greatly moved and rejoiced that Victor Emmanuel, though formally ex-communicated, received the sacraments and died a good Catholic. Though no bishop or high dignitary of the church attended the funeral, a few priests were permitted to walk in the procession to the Pantheon and requiem masses were held in northern Italy.[3]

[1] Chabod, *Storia*, p. 265. Compulsory religious instruction had been instituted by the Piedmontese Lex Casati of 1859.

[2] Halperin, p. 407.

[3] Pirri, XXV, pp. 427–32, 439; G. Massari, *La vita ed il regno di Vittorio Emanuele II di Savoia* (3rd ed., Milan 1880), p. 591; Halperin, pp. 465–9.

A month later, on 7 February, Pius IX died at the age of eighty-six, after the longest papal reign in history. The conduct of the next conclave had been a matter of concern to foreign and Italian statesmen ever since 1870. Some cardinals, notably Manning, now urged that it be held outside Italy; but the leading Catholic governments strongly opposed such a course.[1] In Italy both Right and Left acknowledged the obligation to ensure a free election, as a matter of national honour. Demonstrations were banned in Rome, parliament was kept adjourned and public order strictly enforced. Crispi, the newly-appointed Minister of Interior, warned the cardinals, with characteristic brutality, that if they decided to leave Italy, they would be escorted to the frontiers with the full honours due to them by the Law of Guarantees, but that the Vatican would be occupied and they would never be allowed to return. On 20 February Gioacchino Pecci, Archbishop of Perugia, was elected in one of the freest conclaves in the church's history and took the title of Leo XIII. The Law of Guarantees had triumphantly survived its first great test. But hopes of a conciliatory gesture from the new Pope were quickly disappointed. As a first symbolic act of protest the papal benediction, customary after election, was pronounced inside St Peter's, not from the external loggia overlooking the piazza. There would be no provocation, no challenges, declared the new Secretary of State in March, 'but a firm stand on principles'.[2] Soon afterwards the claim to the temporal power was reasserted and there was no interruption in the flow of remonstrations from the Vatican.

The gulf between church and state thus showed no signs of narrowing, and all attempts to bridge it were wrecked by the intransigents on either side. The church defined its views on abstention from the polls more precisely. In 1871 the Holy Penitentiary declared that it was 'not expedient' (*non expedit*) for Catholics to vote in parliamentary elections, a ruling that Pius IX himself confirmed just before the election of 1874. Three years later, to remove any remaining uncertainty, the Holy Penitentiary changed the *non expedit* to a categorical *non licet*.[3] Catholics obedient to papal wishes were thus forced to withdraw from the political life of the nation into a closed life of their own and became 'internal émigrés'.[4] But they were by no means inactive. The aim of the church was to keep the faithful separate from the rest of the nation, free from the contamination of liberalism. For this purpose it set out to organise the laity in a network of associations soon to become known as Catholic Action. A start had been

---

[1] Engel-Jánosi, I, pp. 200–6.
[2] ibid., p. 214.
[3] Chabod, *Storia*, p. 516, note 2: Spadolini, *L'opposizione cattolica*, pp. 150–1.
[4] Vercesi, *Tre papi*, p. 109.

made in 1865, but all that had been achieved was destroyed by the government's repressive action during the war with Austria. In 1867 the Society of Italian Catholic Youth was founded, with the motto 'Prayer, Action, Sacrifice'. From its ranks four years later came the initiative for the creation of a single national organisation which would embrace and coordinate the activities of all militant Catholics throughout Italy. This was achieved in June 1874 when the first Catholic congress assembled at Venice.

The aim of Catholic Action was to defend Catholic dogma and morals, the liberty of the church and the independence of the Pope against the tyranny of the state. It was built on the assumption that the 'revolution' had triumphed, at least in the short run, and that liberal Italy would not just wither away. In the recent past many Catholics had trusted in Providence to punish the church's enemies; 'protest and wait' was all they could do.[1] But now 'the era of illusions' was over, and action was required. 'Catholics', urged a leading orator at the Venice congress, 'let us pray to God that the revolution die to-morrow, but then let us work as if it must live for ever'.[2] The movement was not reactionary; it looked forward. From the outset it denied any link with legitimism and threw over the Bourbon cause. Nor would it have been satisfied with restoration of the temporal power. Its aims were much vaster: the reconquest of Italy for Christianity, the re-linking of Italy and the Papacy, the launching of a general counter-offensive against 'the sons of Belial' and the spirit of the nineteenth century. Its members, in the words of Meda, a leading Catholic politician of the future, were 'neither liberal Catholics, nor national Catholics, nor legitimist Catholics, nor Catholics of any other kind: but just Catholics'.[3] The Syllabus was their inspiration. Their leaders demanded unquestioning devotion to the Pope and total submission to ecclesiastical authority. The Risorgimento and the 'revolution' were to be fought without quarter, not by conspiracy or violent rebellion, but with the 'revolution's' own weapons – freedom of the press, freedom of association, freedom of thought and speech. Every legal means would be used to undermine and destroy the law.[4]

From small beginnings Catholic Action expanded steadily. The second congress, held at Florence in 1875, set up a permanent organisation called the Opera dei Congressi, with a central executive and committees in every region, diocese and parish. Nicotera dissolved the third congress in 1876, for reasons of 'public order'; but thereafter, for nearly thirty years, con-

[1] The phrase was that of Cardinal Giacomo Antonelli, the papal Secretary of State, in October 1870. De Rosa, *L'Azione Cattolica*, I, p. 54.
[2] Fonzi, pp. 32–3; De Rosa, *L'Azione Cattolica*, I, p. 93.
[3] Fonzi, p. 55.
[4] De Rosa, *L'Azione Cattolica*, I, pp. 99–100; Spadolini, *L'opposizione cattolica*, pp. 105–6.

gresses were held at frequent intervals. A Catholic press grew up in close association with the movement. Education was its constant care, and great efforts were made to found Catholic schools, free from the grip of the secular state, which would form 'a dam against the murky torrent of corruption and impiety' that threatened Christian society.[1] The congresses also concerned themselves with religious observance, with celebrations and pilgrimages, and with the expansion of the missionary Marian Congregations. The committees of the Opera collected Peter's Pence and organised demonstrations of loyalty to the Pope. Catholics were also urged to be active in local government, which was regarded as non-political and therefore not affected by the *non expedit*. It was not easy for an obedient Catholic to occupy a position of responsibility, even in a small commune, when he might be involved in the organisation of secular education or the enforcement of laws such as that on civil marriage, which the Pope had condemned. But an essential part of the Catholic Action programme was to penetrate local administration and thus prepare a secure base on the periphery from which eventually to move inwards to the conquest of the state.[2]

There thus grew up among the Catholic laity a militant and fanatical generation. Many clergy at first looked with suspicion on the new phenomenon. Bishops disliked the intrusion of laymen into ecclesiastical affairs and felt their own authority threatened by a centralised movement so blindly obedient to the Vatican.[3] But as one intransigent after another was appointed to the sees that fell vacant, the number of doubters in positions of influence declined. Squeezed between the militants of Catholic Action and the aggressive anti-clericals, first the liberal Catholics, then the more cautious advocates of conciliation were silenced.[4] The church, deliberately cutting itself off from non-Catholic society, continued to centralise and tighten its discipline over clergy and laity alike, and so 'prepared in abstention' for the decisive battle of the future.[5]

[1] De Rosa, *L'Azione Cattolica*, I, pp. 75–6.
[2] ibid., pp. 81–2; Spadolini, *L'opposizione cattolica*, p. 95.
[3] Fonzi, pp. 56–9.
[4] Notable conciliators were a Jesuit priest, Curci, founder of the great Jesuit review, *Civiltà Cattolica*, whose declaration in 1877 that Rome now 'belonged to the Italian people' led to his expulsion from his order; and Don Giovanni Bosco, founder of the Salesian teaching order (canonised as St John Bosco in 1934), who had many friends among Italian politicians and often acted as unofficial intermediary between church and government.
[5] Chabod, *Storia*, pp. 258–9. The formula 'Preparation in abstention' was first used in 1880 and never condemned by Leo XIII.

## Finance and Administration

The grim financial struggle continued for five years after 1870. Sella and Minghetti[1] retained the hated *macinato* tax and made no concessions. When taxation failed to fill the gap between revenue and expenditure, they preferred to print new paper money rather than resort to further borrowing. Expenditure which the Left regarded as essential was refused. In April 1873 it was decided not to enlarge the Taranto naval arsenal, to meet the supposed threat from clerical France. Next year compulsory primary education was shelved. The Left's gains in the election of 1874 revealed growing impatience with what Sella himself called the status of 'the most heavily taxed people in Europe'. But Minghetti exhorted parliament to one final effort, and on 16 March 1876 he was able to announce that, after fifteen arduous years, the budget had been balanced.[2] This was the Right's last triumph, and one of its greatest.

At the time the magnitude of the achievement was less apparent than the sufferings it involved. Critics of the Right, conservative as well as radical, accused Sella and Minghetti of sacrificing economic development to the dogma of a balanced budget. As Depretis observed, economy to the bone maimed vital muscles and nerves. The Left also denounced the class character of the Right's fiscal policy, as exemplified in the high proportion of revenue drawn from indirect taxes, and claimed that it was deepening the gulf between 'real' and 'legal' Italy.[3] There was indeed a disturbing growth of social unrest in these years. The financial crash of 1873, which affected all Europe, ended a period of inflationary prosperity and depression set in. Italian credit was again shaken and the lira reached a record low level.[4] The Right was nevertheless able to complete the administrative structure of the Italian state. Among its most notable achievements were the unification of the seven separate fiscal systems of the old states and the reconstruction of the armed forces. The reform of the army was the work of Ricotti, a tough single-minded Piedmontese general who served

[1] Sella was Lanza's Minister of Finance from 1869 to 1873; Minghetti was his own Minister of Finance from 1873 to 1876.

[2] Minghetti, like all Italian Ministers of Finance of the period, excluded from his calculations expenditure on railway construction, which was classed as 'extraordinary'. If this is included, the surpluses for 1875 and 1876 become deficits of 33 and 28 millions, and the budget remained unbalanced until 1898. From 1862 to 1875 revenue increased from 450 million to 1,058 million lire, expenditure from 906 million to 1,091 million. Coppola d'Anna, p. 85.

[3] In fact the proportion of tax revenue drawn from consumption taxes had fallen from 47·4% in 1861–5 to 46·9% in 1866–70 and 44·4% in 1871–5; it rose again steadily after 1876 under governments of the Left. Coppola d'Anna, p. 102.

[4] In May 1873 it was quoted at 17·6% below the French franc. The pre-1914 rate of exchange at par was 25 lire = 25 French francs = $5 = £1.

as Minister for War. Though always short of funds, he created a modern force of ten army corps and twenty divisions, with a peace-time strength of 224,000 which could be increased to 350,000 by mobilising the first-line reserve. By 1873 the worst gaps in Italy's defences had been filled and the essential fortifications and strategic railways had been built. The army was also designed to perform a wider function than mere defence: it was to be a 'school of national education'. Conscription, normally for a term of three years, was enforced on a national, not regional, basis. Each regiment was recruited from two distinct regions, speaking different dialects, and was stationed in a third; and its location was changed roughly every four years.[1] This reform was not popular, least of all in Sicily where there had been no conscription before 1861. But over the years the barracks, like the school, played a major part in fusing regional loyalties and fostering Italian patriotism. The navy, too, was transformed. In 1861 the small Piedmontese and Neapolitan fleets were still built entirely of wood and one-quarter of their ships were powered by sail. The humiliating defeat of Lissa was followed by a period of demoralisation and inaction. But after 1870 an ambitious building programme was devised by Benedetto Brin, a brilliant naval engineer, and in May 1876 the *Duilio* was launched, the first of several ironclads which rivalled the greatest ships of the British navy in size and power.

The advent of the Left brought no immediate change of fiscal policy. While in opposition it had clamoured in the same breath for lower taxation and increased expenditure, an infallible receipt for political popularity. Once in office, Depretis flatly declared that he would not 'yield a single lira of the revenues' and would defend the solvency of the budget. Plans for basic tax reform dwindled to minor reliefs for the worst-hit taxpayers. But though the Left resisted the temptation to destroy the work of sixteen years for the sake of immediate popularity,[2] it soon showed that it lacked the toughness of the Right. In December 1877 Agostino Magliani took over the Ministry of Finance from Depretis and retained it, with only two short breaks, for eleven years. Magliani was a brilliant Neapolitan who had served in the Bourbon financial administration. Personally honest but politically weak and accommodating, he was the perfect instrument for a parliamentary majority which wished to give politics precedence over finance. His acceptance of office coincided with the end of the economic

---

[1] Rochat, pp. 299–300. The only exception to the rule was the creation in 1873 of regiments of Alpini, recruited entirely from the Alpine districts. As Rochat points out, the system also had a more specific political purpose: 'Units composed of soldiers from different regions would be more efficient and disciplined instruments for the repression of popular insurrections of a regional or social character.'

[2] Corbino, II, pp. 291–3. In 1880 the state absorbed 11·38% of the national income, compared with 6·96% in 1862. Romeo, p. 32.

depression and he initiated a decade of 'lively finance', marked by high expenditure on armaments and public works and heavy borrowing. This was accompanied by minor cuts in direct taxation, designed to attract foreign capital and stimulate the 'productive forces' of the nation.[1] His critics accused him of jugglery and illusionism, and of concealing budget deficits by ingenuity in accounting. But his persuasive oratory exuded confidence and he was adept at soothing deputies who longed to be convinced, against their better judgement, of the rosiness of the financial situation.[2]

Magliani was responsible for two important fiscal reforms: the abolition of the *macinato* tax and the restoration of convertibility. Between 1871 and 1880 the *macinato* tax yielded an average of 69 million sorely needed lire every year. The chamber of deputies was very ready to vote its abolition, but reluctant to authorise the new taxes which the more cautious senate insisted should replace it. Cairoli made the first attempt at abolition in July 1878. Over the next two years the tax was the main issue in Italian politics. It caused a constitutional clash between the senate and the chamber, dominated the 1880 election and became 'the devourer of ministries'. At last, in July 1880, the senate reluctantly approved Magliani's new plan to abolish it in stages over four years, thus acknowledging that the removal of a major political grievance must take precedence over purely financial considerations.[3]

The restoration of convertibility meant much to the Left because it regarded a depreciated currency as a national humiliation. In 1880 Magliani set about finding the necessary financial backing abroad. The growing tension with France over Tunis hampered him[4] and the Rothschilds in Paris refused their help; but in November he was able to tell parliament that the non-convertible paper currency would disappear by the spring of 1883. A syndicate of British, French and Italian bankers was formed to float a loan of 644 million lire. This was sufficient to reduce the note circulation by one-third and more than double the metallic currency. The immediate results were excellent. The lira appreciated by over 10% in 1880 and three years later reached parity with the French gold franc for the first time since 1866. Between 1881 and 1887 there was a further great influx of foreign capital, directed mainly to transport and public utilities, and Italian bonds rose to unprecedented heights on the Paris Bourse.

In the years that followed, however, Italy's financial position deterior-

[1] Carocci, pp. 79 ff., 337–8. On Depretis's favourable attitude to foreign capital and contacts with foreign bankers, see Carocci, pp. 52, 98 ff., 169 ff.
[2] Corbino, III, pp. 40–2.
[3] ibid., II, pp. 297–306; Cilibrizzi, II, pp. 182–7, 200–1.
[4] See below, pp. 107 ff.

ated rapidly. The agricultural crisis, which grew acute soon after 1880, should have warned the government that difficult times lay ahead. But industrial development and buoyant revenue generated the illusion of permanent prosperity. The pace of inflation quickened. Between January 1882 and December 1886 the issue banks increased their note circulation from 732 to 1,032 million lire[1] and reduced the metallic coverage from 51% to 38%. The government borrowed freely and spent lavishly. In the nine years after 1880 expenditure increased by 58%, revenue by only 18%.[2] Railways and roads were constructed on a grand scale, ports were improved, slums were cleared in Naples and speculative building schemes launched in Rome. In 1882 eight new infantry brigades were formed and the number of army corps was increased from ten to twelve. Under the direction of Brin, who served as Minister for the Navy from 1876 to 1878 and from 1884 to 1891, heavy naval building continued, with special emphasis on expensive large ships. The acquisition of a colony further increased the strain. In 1885 the lira once again dropped below the gold franc. Next March Magliani, after postponing the day of reckoning for years by evasion and artifice, was forced to admit a budget deficit, and in June 1886 the speech from the throne called for 'severe parsimony'.

A substantial proportion of the state's expenditure was absorbed by the railways. Their future was already a burning issue when the Left took over in 1876. The Right had advocated state management. Depretis and a majority of his followers believed that the state was unfit to run an industry and supported the principle of private enterprise. The government's proposals were savagely attacked by the Extreme Left as a sell-out to bankers, speculators and monopoly capitalists. An important section of the Left agreed with this criticism, notably two of the Pentarchs, Zanardelli[3] and Baccarini. After nine years of heated debate, complicated by the manœuvres of rival financial and banking groups, Depretis finally got his way. By the conventions of 1885 the operation of the railways was entrusted to two reconstructed companies. These were to share profits with the state, whose property the railways remained. With the intention of stimulating traffic between north and south and wiping out the last traces of regional antagonism, the companies were organised longitudinally down the whole length of Italy, one on the Adriatic, the other on the Tyrrhenian

---

[1] *Sommario*, p. 163; Corbino, III, p. 437.

[2] Coppola d'Anna, p. 87. The national debt grew from 8,447 million lire in January 1876 to 9,833 million in January 1881 and 11,503 million in the middle of 1887. Corbino, II, p. 321, III, p. 376.

[3] On two occasions, in 1877 and 1883, Zanardelli resigned office rather than support proposals for what he regarded as a monopolistic railway system.

coast, both meeting in Rome. Depretis declared they would be 'like in-flexible girders reinforcing the unity of the fatherland'.[1]

Railway construction meanwhile continued. In spite of the Right's economy to the bone, nearly 1,500 kilometres had been built between 1871 and 1875. The Left was more ambitious. By resorting to the issue of large quantities of railway bonds, most of which were subscribed from abroad, it extended the railway system by 50%, from 8,700 to 13,100 kilometres, within the decade 1881–90.[2] Railway construction in the period of *tras-formismo* had its political uses, for it helped Depretis to consolidate his majority by the sale of railways for votes. A new motive was also beginning to appear: the need to provide work to immunise the unemployed against revolutionary propaganda. At the same time the new railways brought real economic and social benefits, both in the south where secondary lines opened up the remote interior, and in the north, where they created the essential infrastructure for industrialisation.

There was therefore a credit side to the financial record of the Left. The beneficial effects of cheaper money and heavy capital investment long outlasted the pricking of the speculative bubble. Nevertheless the long-term prospect was doubtful and by 1887 there were clear signs of strain. The Italian state had taken on too many commitments and indulged too freely in prestige spending. The armed forces were a conspicuous example: their cost rose between 1871–5 and 1886–90 from 204 to 424 million lire (from 18·7% to 25·2% of total expenditure).[3] The heaviest burden fell upon the consumer. In spite of the abolition of the *macinato* tax, consumption taxes remained crushing, and indeed contributed a larger share of total tax revenue than before 1876.[4] The contrast between Magliani and his predecessors, Sella and Minghetti, was not comforting. The Left had inherited a sound budget and turned it into a growing deficit. During the period of prosperity it failed to build up reserves for more difficult times, and as the long years of Depretis's rule came to an end, Italy plunged again into economic and financial crisis.

## Law and Order

The maintenance of law and order was the constant preoccupation of the leaders of the Right. Their aim, now that the revolution had ended with

[1] Sereni, p. 27. Two separate companies were formed, on the same terms, to operate the railways of Sicily and Sardinia.

[2] *ASI 1919–1921*, p. 507; Corbino, II, p. 271, III, p. 316.

[3] Coppola d'Anna, p. 108. By contrast the cost of education rose from 1·9% to 2·4% of total expenditure between 1873 and 1889–90. Neufeld, p. 128.

[4] 44·4% in 1871–5, 46·6% in 1878–80, 48·3% in 1881–5 and 49·5% in 1886–90. Coppola d'Anna, p. 102.

the capture of Rome, was to make Italy an element of order, liberty and peace in Europe.[1] Conscious of the frightening gap between rulers and people, they realised that their Italy was a fragile creation, with many internal enemies: clericals, republicans, the International and the endemic forces of disorder in the south. All these had to be watched and controlled.

The government was inclined at first to regard republicanism as the biggest danger. In fact, though momentarily encouraged by the fall of the Second Empire, it dwindled steadily in strength after the occupation of Rome. Many who had been republican now came to believe that only a king could hold the capital against the Pope. As new problems arose, the old constitutional controversy lost its passion and began to seem just a sterile conflict of abstract formulae. That section of the population which was drawn to violence found satisfaction elsewhere, and Mazzini was soon fighting a rearguard action against the rising forces of social revolution on his left.

In March 1871 the eruption of the Paris Commune threw all sections of the Italian revolutionary movement into confusion. Bakunin, Marx and Engels acclaimed it as a socialist enterprise, the entry of the proletariat upon the stage of world history. Mazzini condemned it for its materialism, its exaltation of the class struggle and its contempt for national and patriotic feelings. To the bewilderment of young republicans, Mazzini, the arch-revolutionary, was heard to denounce a revolution. His attacks on Marx's International provoked a counter-attack from Bakunin, who denounced him as the ally of all the reactionaries of Europe and ridiculed his social theories as 'bourgeois soporifics'. These polemics split the old Party of Action. Many young radicals, thirsty for excitement, followed the example of Garibaldi who, unlike Mazzini, gave the Commune his blessing. Garibaldi was no political theorist, and the only form of government which appealed to him was 'honest dictatorship'; but his instinct was to have no enemies on his left. From praise of the Commune he went on to hail socialism as 'the sun of the future' and proclaim himself an Internationalist. Massimo D'Azeglio had said of him many years before that he had 'a heart of gold but the brains of an ox'; even his right-hand man of 1860, Crispi, once admitted that he 'was unfit to govern a village'. But he was the incomparable man of action, 'the hero of two worlds'. His example was sufficient for thousands of his admirers to embrace 'socialism', seeing in it merely the continuation of the Risorgimento. Marx, Engels and Bakunin exploited his name and prestige, with contemptuous amusement, to break Mazzini's grip over the extreme left. Their tactics bore fruit. After 1871 the International became for the first time a serious political

[1] Chabod, *Storia*, pp. 328–9.

force, and in April 1874 the police estimated its Italian membership at 32,000.[1]

Mazzini fought back desperately. In November 1871 he summoned a working-class congress in Rome, to revive the Pact of Fraternity of 1864. It was a failure. Garibaldi urged the workers to stay away. Only 135 of the 900 working-class societies sent delegates, and the anti-socialist front, based on Mazzinian social principles, was stillborn.[2] Next year Mazzini died, knowing that he had lost control of the working-class. His cooperatives and mutual benefit societies survived him in many parts of north and central Italy, but he had failed to capture the People for his ideas. 'Better the return of the Austrians than the planting in Italy of these false and perverse doctrines, which would divide the Italians themselves into oppressors and oppressed', he wrote to a friend in 1871.[3] Such words express the full bitterness of spirit in which he died.

Garibaldi continued for a time to patronise the International, and to confuse socialism with justice, the brotherhood of man and the march of reason. In 1871 he decided to summon a national congress of his own, to rival Mazzini's and to consolidate the unity of the democratic movement under himself. His main support came from Emilia, where a group of workers' associations grew up under his patronage, starting with the foundation of a Fascio Operaio in Bologna.[4] But gradually Garibaldi became disillusioned, as the anarchist character of the International in Italy became apparent and as he realised that he himself was being used as a tool by 'doctrinaires and exaggerators' whose ideals were totally different from his.[5] The democratic congress never met, and during 1872 the Emilian associations went over one by one to Bakunin. In November of that year a republican rally was planned at the Colosseum in Rome, but banned by the government; but republican leaders gathered on the Capitol and signed the Pact of Rome, an anti-monarchist and anti-parliamentary manifesto with a socialist tinge. Garibaldi gave it his warm approval, finding its language more to his taste than Bakunin's appeals for social revolution. After 1872 he drifted further from socialism and abandoned his attempts to unify the extreme left.

The International had barely time to enjoy its victory over Mazzini when it was rent by the quarrel between Marx and Bakunin. This was in

[1] Hostetter, p. 322. The largest concentrations were in Tuscany (8,000 members), Romagna (6,000), Naples (4,500), Sicily (4,000) and the Marche (4,000).

[2] Hostetter, p. 194.

[3] Rosselli, p. 421.

[4] The word *fascio*, meaning 'group' or 'association' (literally 'bundle'), was in common use in Italian politics, particularly on the left, long before Mussolini adopted it and gave it a special meaning.

[5] Hostetter, p. 334.

part personal, in part ideological, and had been brewing for a long time. Marx and Engels had disapproved of many of Bakunin's activities in Italy since 1864, particularly his persistent failure to carry out the decisions, on both doctrine and tactics, of the General Council of the International in London. They suspected, with reason, that he was trying to build up a solid base of power for himself, from which he could make a bid for the leadership of the international socialist movement. The ideological controversy centred round the rival 'authoritarian' and 'libertarian' concepts of socialism. Marx was determined to create a disciplined, centralised movement, based on exclusively working-class parties and obeying a uniform set of tactics in every country; its aim would be the seizure of political power and the transformation of the bourgeois state into the collectivist dictatorship of the proletariat. Bakunin, by contrast, demanded a minimum of organisation, and believed that the first duty of the proletariat after the triumph of the revolution would be to destroy all political power; he wished not to transform the state but to abolish it, and to replace it by a loose federation of autonomous communes and workers' associations. He also differed fundamentally from Marx in the tactics he wished to employ. Instead of methodical political preparation, he called for direct action and immediate social revolution; instead of restricting the International to genuine proletarians, he welcomed the help of all men of goodwill who were ready to join in the work of destruction. Unshaken by the disasters of 1848, he still dreamt of a vast conflagration, an almost miraculous explosion, in which states, governments, churches, property and all classes but one would be destroyed.

Bakunin's anarchist programme found eager supporters in Italy, as also in Spain and French Switzerland, and the rift within the International assumed the form of a clash between northern love of disciplined organisation and southern individualism and ebullience. The Latin world was 'federating, organising and rising up in the name of liberty against the dictatorship of the Pangermans of London', Bakunin wrote in December 1871.[1] His condemnation of the centralised state had a special appeal in those parts of Italy that were smarting under Piedmontisation. Bakunin argued that revolution depended on the support of both urban and rural proletariats; both were 'instinctively socialist', but so far the countryside had supported reaction throughout Europe. The main question, therefore, was 'how to revolutionise the peasants'.[2] In Italy he saw his best chance. Marx and Engels regarded the Italians as 'a backward people of peasants' and expected as little from them as from the Russians.[3] It was this very backwardness that appealed to Bakunin. He was convinced that the

[1] ibid., p. 232.        [2] ibid., pp. 254–5.
[3] Letter of Engels, 10 July 1872. Rosselli, p. 431; Hostetter, p. 272.

inflammable material lay ready to hand; the peasant was 'a natural federal-
ist', whose spontaneous rebelliousness mattered far more than his lack of
discipline and class consciousness. Only a handful of energetic leaders was
required to apply the spark, and these were to be found in the young
intellectuals and students who joined him after 1871. Many were former
militants of the Party of Action who discovered in the new movement, in
an extreme form, the optimism and amateurishness, the conspiratorial
atmosphere and thirst for action which was so characteristic of the Italian
left. In April 1872 Bakunin declared: 'Italy, after Spain, and with Spain,
is perhaps the most revolutionary country of the present moment. It has
what other countries lack: a youth that is ardent, energetic, completely
uprooted, unemployed . . .'[1]

Marx and Engels watched their rival's progress with envy and disgust,
but also with a feeling of impotence which goes far to explain the ferocity
of their attacks upon him. For the propagation of their own views in Italy
they had to rely on the newspaper *La Plebe* of Lodi, a small Lombard
manufacturing town, whose editor, Enrico Bignami, was a socialist of
dubious doctrinal reliability. Bakunin had the great advantage of being a
familiar, much loved figure in Italy, whereas Marx was only a name.[2]
This fact was more important than any of their doctrinal disputations,
which meant little to Italian Internationalists. Engels was convinced that
'the authentic workers' of Milan and the north were on the side of the
General Council, but communication with them was blocked by 'those
damned Bakuninist doctrinaires, lawyers, doctors, etc'.[3] Marx's well-
known description of Bakunin's disciples, though cruel, was not wholly
off the mark:[4]

The Alliance in Italy is not a working-class group, but a gang of *déclassés*. All

---

[1] Rosselli, pp. 427–8; Michels, p. 28. Bakunin saw many similarities between
the conditions of the Italian and Russian peoples, and believed that the revolutionary tactics that he had worked out for Russia were equally applicable to Italy.
In 1869 he wrote: 'The brigand is always the hero, the defender, the avenger of
the people, the irreconcilable enemy of the entire State regime . . . The brigand
in Russia is the true and only revolutionary.' Some of his Italian disciples were
equally impressed by the revolutionary potentialities of the brigands of southern
Italy. F. Venturi, *Roots of Revolution* (London 1960), p. 369. See also F. Della
Peruta, 'La Banda del Matese', in *Movimento Operaio*, vol. 3 (1954), pp. 337–84.

[2] When a tall blond foreigner turned up at the secret meeting in Naples at which
the first Italian section of the International was founded, some of those present at
once assumed, from his Teutonic appearance, that he must be Marx. B. Croce,
*Materialismo storico ed economia marxistica* (8th ed., Bari 1946), p. 54.

[3] Hostetter, p. 272.

[4] *L'Alliance de la Démocratie Socialiste et l'Association Internationale des Travail-
leurs* (London 1873), p. 48. Bakunin founded his International Alliance of Socialist
Democracy in 1868. Its sections were incorporated in the International next year,
with many misgivings on Marx's part.

the so-called sections of the Italian International are directed by lawyers without clients, by doctors without patients or medical knowledge, by students expert at billiards, by commercial travellers and clerks, and especially by journalists of the minor press, of more or less dubious reputations.

Carlo Cafiero was the best-known of these young men. He was an Apulian of good family who threw up a diplomatic career and sold all his estates, presenting the proceeds to Bakunin for the cause. Kropotkin, Bakunin's successor as leader of the international anarchist movement, described him as 'an idealist of the highest and purest type, . . . a thinker plunged in philosophical speculation, a man who never would harm anyone'.[1] For a time he had been Engels's most trusted Italian agent, but in 1872 he went over heart and soul to Bakunin. This defection was a bitter blow to Marx and Engels. In August of the same year the first Italian socialist congress was held at Rimini. Thirty-five delegates, representing twenty-one sections, attended and Cafiero presided. It decided to break away from Marx's International and found an autonomous, loosely organised Italian Federation. The decisive motion, drafted by Cafiero, attacked the General Council in London for trying to force on all members of the International 'a special authoritarian doctrine . . . that of the German Communist party'.[2] Bakunin's triumph seemed complete.

The congress was the prelude to a vigorous attempt to build up the scattered underground sections of the International into a nation-wide organisation. These efforts were helped by the economic crisis of 1873, which provoked strikes in the north and riotous demonstrations for bread and work in the Romagna and Tuscany. Bakunin had 'full confidence in the instincts of the popular multitudes'[3] and the efficacy of 'propaganda by deed'. His plan was to stage a number of local insurrections, in the belief that they would develop into a general conflagration. In 1874 he decided that the hour of revolution had come. One of his young lieutenants from the Romagna, Andrea Costa, proclaimed in a manifesto, 'We want the destruction of the state in all its economic, political and religious manifestations.'[4] The insurrection was to start in the Romagna and spread rapidly to Tuscany, Apulia and Sicily.

Bakunin's illusions were soon shattered. The government was well informed and carried out a series of preventive arrests throughout the country. On 2 August a group of twenty-eight radical and republican leaders, including Aurelio Saffi, the Roman triumvir of 1849 and Alessandro Fortis, a future Prime Minister, were surprised by the police in

[1] P. Kropotkin, *Memoirs of a Revolutionist* (2nd ed., London 1906), pp. 367–8.
[2] Michels, p. 40; Hostetter, p. 284.
[3] Hostetter, p. 312.
[4] ibid.p. 331.

conference at the Villa Ruffi near Rimini. Their arrest[1] effectively destroyed the slender possibility of republican support and left the Internationalists isolated.[2] On 7 August a handful of conspirators mustered 150 peasants at Imola and set out to march on Bologna, where Bakunin himself was waiting with a few hundred more supporters, ready to attack the arsenal. At the first encounter with the police the insurrection collapsed. Costa had been arrested even before the action began; Bakunin now escaped to Switzerland disguised as a priest, to die there disillusioned two years later. The conspirators nevertheless set to work again and reconstructed their organisation. Two events gave them momentary encouragement: the advent to power of the Left in 1876, and the acquittal of their arrested comrades by sympathetic juries or their release after serving sentences of astonishing leniency. In 1877 Cafiero, a young disciple, Errico Malatesta, and a Russian revolutionary, Stepniak, made a second attempt to spark off the conflagration, this time forty miles north of Naples in the mountains of the Matese, an old brigand stronghold. Inflammatory speeches roused the peasants of two villages to seize the municipal buildings in the name of social revolution. Primitive arms were distributed, the tax registers were burnt and the *macinato* tax meters smashed. One village priest gave his blessing and presented the revolutionaries to his flock as apostles preaching the true gospel. Once again the government was fully prepared. Troops were dispatched, the little armed band of twenty-six was arrested and order was restored. Hopes of greater leniency from the new government were soon dispelled. The International was proscribed, its newspapers suppressed and its members arrested or driven into exile.

The ignominious failure of these infantile proceedings led to much heart-searching among the Internationalists. In Costa's case the Imola fiasco had already been enough to shatter his Bakuninist faith, and in 1877 he made no attempt to join Cafiero in the south. In November 1878 King Humbert narrowly escaped assassination in Naples. Though the would-be assassin had no connexion with the International, another wave of arrests followed, and the public execration of anarchism completed the disillusionment of the Internationalists. After 1878 Marx's programme began for the first time to make converts in Italy, starting in Milan. Impressed by the example of the German Social Democratic party, Italian socialists turned their thoughts to the formation of a working-class party pledged to contest elections, send its spokesmen to parliament and prepare for the conquest of power by legal means. In 1879 Costa announced his conversion

---

[1] They were kept in prison for five months before the judicial authorities decided there was no case against them. Their release was hailed by democrats as a triumph over arbitrary persecution.

[2] Hostetter, pp. 334–6.

in an open letter to his friends in Romagna, written from exile in Lugano. In the past, he said, they had been too concerned with ideas and programmes, and had never seriously studied the conditions and needs of the people; the result was that 'when, impelled by a generous impulse, we tried to raise the banner of revolt, the people did not understand us, they let us alone. Let us profit from the lesson of experience.'[1] In December 1880 the Italian International[2] held a congress across the Swiss border at Chiasso, at which the anarchists obtained a majority for the last time. Next year Costa, now back in Italy, took the first step towards legal political activity by founding the Romagna Revolutionary Socialist party. With the exception of Malatesta, who remained an impenitent advocate of insurrection throughout his long life, one after another of Bakunin's disciples followed Costa's example. During the next two decades Italian anarchism acquired an unenviable notoriety. 'Propaganda by deed' degenerated into terrorism and many assassins of kings and presidents were Italian. The anarchist faith did not die out. On many occasions over the next forty years, at times of extreme social tension, the anarchist call to insurrection met with a ready response. Groups of anarchists continued to flourish in areas like the Romagna, the Marche and the Carrara marble quarries, and in some of the great cities. Nevertheless, as a political movement, anarchism in Italy was never again after 1880 of more than peripheral importance.

Socialism at no time constituted a serious threat to law and order, even during the years of Bakunin's ascendency. Governments faced a far more baffling problem in Sicily, where persistent crime and violence magnified the already formidable task of governing the south. In 1860, wrote Sonnino, Sicily found itself 'with modern laws and with medieval customs and traditions'.[3] The former were powerless against the latter. The central administration was 'as it were encamped in the middle of a society, all of whose ordinances were founded on the assumption that no public order existed'. The social prestige of the individual depended on the exercise of private power and private justice, and a sense of the public interest was totally lacking. The law was respected only by those not strong enough to violate it.[4] Deeply rooted in the society of western Sicily was the Mafia, a network of small criminal organisations, mainly operating independently

---

[1] Michels, p. 75; Hostetter, p. 154. Costa returned to the same theme in December 1880 in a letter to Anna Kuliscioff: 'We treat the workers like imbeciles. But the imbeciles are we ourselves, who in the arrogance of our theories raise ourselves above the people and want to appear to it like Moses . . .' Lipparini, p. 165.

[2] The First International was formally dissolved in 1876, but the socialist movement in Italy continued for some years to be known as 'the International'.

[3] Franchetti and Sonnino, II, p. 338.

[4] ibid., I, pp. 12, 65.

of each other, which enforced their own laws by terror or violence. Its
leaders were drawn from the largely parasitical rural middle class – the
tenants of absentee landlords who ran the *latifondi* and sub-let them in
small plots for rack rents, the merchants who bought the grain and lent at
exorbitant rates of interest, and the lawyers and 'intellectuals' who filled
the municipal councils. The rank and file was recruited partly from
criminals and the unemployed, partly from the peasants, rural policemen
(*guardie campestri*), traders and minor officials at the bottom of the social
hierarchy of the *latifondo*. The main stronghold was the province of
Palermo, where the population was comparatively prosperous, but dominated by a primitive code of honour and a long tradition of vendetta and
private violence. Property owners, if they were wise, came to terms with
the Mafia and paid to be 'protected' by it; if not, their orchards might be
stripped or their cattle disappear, their crops be set alight in a waterless
countryside or they themselves receive a knife in the back on a dark night.
Those who controlled the Mafia had great power; the more clients they
could bring under their protection, the greater that power, even if those
clients were criminals. The organisation penetrated the civil service, the
police and even the prisons; it could be used to manipulate elections,
dictate agricultural wages and rents, maintain order in the countryside, or
even to provide an insurrectionary movement with manpower in the form
of armed *squadre*, as the Palermo rising of 1866 had shown.

The government was confronted with almost insuperable difficulties in
dealing with this situation. The police and administrators sent over from
the mainland to enforce the rule of law were faced by a conspiracy of
silence when they started to investigate a crime. Because normal legal
procedures proved useless, the state authorities felt compelled, like the
Bourbons before them, to resort to arbitrary arrests, imprisonment without
trial and many minor restrictions on personal freedom. After the insurrection of 1866, these illegal methods were extended to political offenders,
and over the next fifteen years thousands of alleged clericals, republicans,
Internationalists and Bourbon sympathisers were 'detained at the dis-
position of the political authority'. The consequences were deplorable. As
the prefect of Palermo, General Giacomo Medici, pointed out to the
Minister of Interior in May 1871, 'The law itself suffers a loss of prestige
when those entrusted with its enforcement are the first to violate it.'[1]
But though the judicial authorities put up a fight in defence of legality, the
practices continued, with the tacit, and sometimes even explicit, approval
of the government in Rome.[2] This was not the only practice of the *ancien*

[1] Alatri, *Lotte politiche*, p. 359.
[2] For well-documented examples from the years 1866–71, see Alatri, *Lotte
politiche*, pp. 151–7, 181–6, 219–22.

*régime* to survive unification. The Bourbons had ruled Sicily by compromising with those who possessed the real power and by buying the Mafia into their service. Many of the agents of liberal Italy did the same, believing that the alternative was to remain powerless.[1] The poison then spread outwards from Sicily and affected even parliament in Rome. The island's deputies were elected not to make new laws, but to secure exemption from the existing laws for their constituents;[2] all too often they sold their votes to the government of the day for a tacit promise not to interfere in Sicilian affairs.

The far-sighted saw that police repression by itself would not solve Sicily's problems. General Medici, during his prefecture from 1868 to 1873, called repeatedly (but with only limited effect) for massive expenditure on public works, as the essential condition of economic development and political and social progress. Sonnino was convinced that long-term improvement depended on raising the mass of the population from its economic and social serfdom and reducing the power of the exploiting ruling class. For this purpose he demanded legislation to enforce fair rents and decent wages and to encourage peasant unions. But governments were loath to admit that Sicilian lawlessness had social origins. They preferred to strengthen the police and military garrison, and to employ, in a milder form, the same methods as had been used on the mainland to suppress brigandage. In 1875 Minghetti's government obtained parliamentary approval, by a small majority, for an exceptional law which legalised for a period of one year many of the well-used arbitrary practices. The police were given extended powers of admonition (*ammonizione*),[3] house search

[1] This aspect of the Sicilian situation was brought before the public by a *cause célèbre* of 1871. The procurator-general of the Palermo court of appeal, Diego Tajani, instituted the prosecution of the city's chief of police, Giuseppe Albanese, on charges of conniving at crime (including murder), faking political conspiracy and enlisting criminals and members of the Mafia in his police force. The government did its best to hush up the affair; Albanese was transferred and the charges were dropped. Tajani resigned his post, was elected as an opposition deputy in 1874 and played a big part in a debate on Sicilian affairs in June 1875. On that occasion the Minister of Interior, Girolamo Cantelli, admitted that many of Tajani's accusations were true, but claimed that every government since 1860 had tried to eradicate such abuses. For details see Alatri, *Lotte politiche*, ch. 6 and pp. 590–611.

[2] Franchetti and Sonnino, I, p. 274. This was true not only of Sicily but of the whole south. Franchetti observed in 1911 that every government after 1860 'saw in the south not a country to govern but a group of deputies to be wooed'. Franchetti, *Mezzogiorno e colonie*, p. 224.

[3] A person subject to *ammonizione* was bound over to stay in his home town, report weekly to the police, observe a curfew from dusk to dawn, obtain regular employment, possess no arms and avoid all contact with criminals. One violation of these restrictions was punishable by a term of imprisonment, the third by deportation to a penal island.

and preventive arrest of suspects and false or reticent witnesses; the Minister of Interior was given authority to impose sentences of deportation (*domicilio coatto*)[1] for one to five years on the advice of a local committee of which the prefect was chairman.[2] But the habits and way of life of a whole island could not be changed in a few years. Lawlessness continued, the Mafia still flourished and the authority of the central government remained precarious.

While the Left was in opposition, it denounced every police measure against republicans or Internationalists as a tyrannical violation of the constitution. The Villa Ruffi arrests caused an outcry. Garibaldi thundered against the 'system of depravation' by which the south was governed, and Crispi protested in 1875 that Sicily had been subjected to fifteen years of martial law and practices more cruel than those of the Bourbons. Lanza and Minghetti acted upon the formula 'Prevention, not Repression' (*prevenire, non reprimere*), which meant anticipating disorder by preventive arrests and restrictions on freedom of meeting and movement. A large section of the Left advocated the opposite method of 'Repression, not Prevention'. Among a people which revelled in mass meetings in the *piazza* and was easily swayed by rhetoric and incited to violence, the Left's formula meant waiting until passions had risen to fever heat and the mob was out of control, then restoring order by the lavish use of excitable soldiers only too ready to press the trigger. The leaders of the Right preferred timely use of the police to risking bloodshed through dogmatic devotion to the concept of liberty. Yet though they feared the masses and tended to see some sinister hand behind every explosion of popular discontent, there were limits which they felt bound to observe. Visconti Venosta responded coolly to suggestions from abroad for a Holy Alliance against the International, the new barbarism threatening Europe from below. He and his colleagues preferred enforcement of the law, however severe, to blind repression, and never quite forgot that they were heirs of Cavour.[3]

When the Left came to power, most of its leaders forgot their previous criticisms. The exceptional law of 1875 was allowed to lapse, but the authorities in Sicily continued, with the government's approval, to practise most of the illegalities for which the Right had been denounced. The power of the Mafia did not diminish. Nicotera, the Left's first Minister of Interior, far outdid his predecessors in ruthlessness. He made himself the

---

[1] A person subject to *domicilio coatto* was banished from home and had to reside in a named locality under police supervision. In its severest form this meant deportation to the Lipari or other small, remote islands.

[2] Alatri, *Lotte politiche*, pp. 590–1, 609–10.

[3] Chabod, *Storia*, pp. 401 ff., 428–37.

terror of the clericals, reinforced the police in Sicily, filled the Lipari Islands with suspects, suppressed Barsanti clubs and demonstrations against the *macinato* tax in Emilia and Apulia, used troops to break strikes and hunted down what remained of the International, declaring it to be a criminal organisation. This devotion to the principle of 'Prevention, not Repression' made large sections of the Left unhappy. In December 1877 Nicotera overreached himself with a blatant violation of the secrecy of the telegraph and resigned. Crispi succeeded him and applied his methods to ensuring order during the papal conclave in February 1878. But when Cairoli became Prime Minister in March and chose Zanardelli as his Minister of Interior, there was a sudden change. Both believed dogmatically in 'Repression, not Prevention' and refused to betray the ideals of the Risorgimento by restricting freedom. 'We will be inexorable in repression, not arbitrary in prevention', said Cairoli, and promised to guarantee 'liberty within the law'.[1] In November 1878, as King Humbert and Queen Margherita were driving on a state visit through the streets of Naples, an anarchist named Passanante made an attempt on the King's life. Cairoli, who was sitting in the same carriage, threw himself in front of the King to protect him, and Passanante's dagger wounded him in the thigh. Cairoli's reputation for personal bravery was enhanced, and commentators made much of the happy symbolism of the event: the King's life had been saved by a man who but a few years before had been seen on republican platforms. But in parliament Cairoli was attacked by both Right and Left for inexcusable laxity. His government fell and the policy of 'Repression, not Prevention' was finally discredited.

From December 1878 to April 1887 Depretis held the Ministry of Interior continuously except for one break of four months. His period of office was not without incident. Irredentist demonstrations and anti-clerical rowdyism on occasions caused a stir far beyond the frontiers of Italy. Anarchists were watched with special care and harassed continually by the police. In his dealings with strikes and working-class organisations Depretis was little less stern than Nicotera. But his firm hand gave Italy much-needed quiet and the preservation of law and order ceased to be a major topic of controversy.

[1] Cilibrizzi, II, pp. 162–7. One immediate result of the change in government was an outbreak of anti-clerical and irredentist agitation which caused diplomatic embarrassment. See below, pp. 102–3.

# 2

# Italy under Depretis

## Industrial Development and Agricultural Crisis

Italy's material progress in the ten years after the occupation of Rome was substantial. Though the pace of industrialisation was slow, there were many signs of healthy growth: expanding trade, improved land and sea communications and public utilities, the restoration of financial credit abroad, the development of banking and the steady commercialisation of the economy.[1] The population grew from 26·8 millions in 1871 to 28·5 millions in 1881, and was to reach 32·6 millions at the next census in 1901. After many years of stagnation the towns began to expand and the amenities of life to spread even into the countryside. As Rome grew into a modern capital, with bustling streets, residential suburbs and massive, ugly government buildings, it attracted people from every province and became a crucible of national unity. By 1880 common institutions, a standard education, conscription, railways and economic development had created a national consciousness and greatly reduced separatist and anti-Piedmontese sentiment. In this process the monarchy played an important part. In the summer of 1878 King Humbert and Queen Margherita toured northern Italy and won the hearts of thousands of republicans in Romagna. Humbert's pardon of Passanante after the attempt on his life, and his visit six years later to cholera-stricken Naples, struck the popular imagination.[2] The crown had ceased to be a factor of discord and was becoming the symbol of national unity.

Some parts of Italy progressed much faster than others. The south, geographically more remote from western Europe, starved of capital and handicapped by a social structure which discouraged innovation, lagged far behind the north. The uneven rate of progress is clearly demonstrated by the illiteracy figures which, in Minghetti's words, continued to be 'a

[1] Between 1861–5 and 1876–80 agriculture's share of the gross internal product fell from 56·7% to 55·5% and industry's from 20·3% to 18·8%, while that of tertiary activities rose from 23·0% to 25·7%. Romeo, pp. 36–7; *Indagine*, p. 36; Neufeld, p. 539.

[2] Volpe, I, pp. 197–201.

78

disgrace to a civilised nation'. Compulsory primary education was introduced on paper in 1877, but the poverty of many communes prevented its effective application. In 1881–2 only 57% of children between the ages of six and twelve attended school. The proportion of illiterates therefore fell slowly, from 74% of the population over six years of age in 1861 to 69% in 1871 and 62% in 1881. But whereas between 1861 and 1881 the rate for the north fell from 54% to 41%, the rate for the centre fell only from 78% to 65%, for the southern mainland from 86% to 79%, and for Sicily and Sardinia from 89% to 81%.[1]

Until 1880 agriculture dominated the economy. Its condition varied greatly but some sectors prospered. Rising prices stimulated production; exports rose and imports declined, in spite of the increase in population.[2] There were also notable examples of technical progress. In 1878 parliament approved a first timid scheme for land reclamation in the Roman Campagna, inspired in part by Garibaldi. By this law the state accepted financial responsibility for agricultural development. Later legislation introduced the principle of compulsion for proprietors who refused to improve derelict or poorly cultivated estates. Land reclamation received its share of the spate of expenditure on public works. But there was much resistance to state activity in this field, and far more was achieved by private enterprise. The most notable results were obtained between 1870 and 1890 in Emilia, where in the plains round Ravenna and Ferrara great tracts of waste land and marsh were reclaimed. Here wheat, sugar beet, hemp and other industrial crops were produced by modern capitalist methods on a scale hitherto unknown in Italy. Much land passed into the hands of a new rural middle class, or into those of banks and even industrial companies.[3] In the same period lower Lombardy was being transformed by irrigation into a region of dairy and stock farms capable of competing with the most efficient in western Europe.[4]

In the south a different kind of transformation occurred. All down the Adriatic shore of Apulia, round the southern tip of Calabria and along the eastern and northern coasts of Sicily, thousands of bare acres were transformed into an intensively cultivated garden, and the south began to take on the physical aspect it wears today, of sudden startling contrasts between

[1] Neufeld, pp. 126, 523; Vöchting, p. 92; *ASI 1886*, p. 954.
[2] The index of the gross saleable product of agriculture (1938 = 100) rose from 46·0 in 1861–5 to 62·1 in 1876–80. *Indagine*, p. 204; Romeo, pp. 25–8, 159.
[3] Sereni, pp. 290–312, 338–55. Sereni estimates that 13% of Italy's area accounted for 30% of its total agricultural production.
[4] Other notable examples of land reclamation were the Fucino marshes in the Abruzzi, drained by their owner, Prince Torlonia, and the Apulian plain round Foggia.

the crowded, tree-covered coastal areas and the barren, treeless, extensively farmed *latifondi* of the interior. Landowners and peasants hastened to take advantage of the growing export market for wine, olive oil and fruit which low tariffs and favourable commercial treaties had opened up over most of Europe. In 1879 an even greater opportunity was presented when phylloxera destroyed the vines of France. In Italy the 2 million hectares under vines in 1874 grew to 3·2 millions in 1883, while the area under oranges, lemons and other citrus fruits more than quadrupled between 1860 and 1880.[1] This increasing specialisation showed that large sections of Italian agriculture were very far from stagnation.

This progress was abruptly halted by the agricultural crisis which hit most of Europe in the mid-1870s and reached Italy at the end of the decade. Improved land communications in the new world and fast steamships brought cheap transatlantic grain and Far Eastern rice and silk to undercut Italian producers. Imports of wheat, which had averaged under 300,000 tons a year between 1871 and 1884, rose steeply in 1885 and reached a peak of 1,000,000 tons in 1887.[2] The fall in cereal prices of over one-third between 1877 and 1884 supplied a further powerful inducement to southern proprietors and sharecroppers to turn their land over to vines and fruit, with the result that they too were soon suffering from overproduction. No part of the countryside escaped the depression. By contrast the same decade 1881–90 saw the birth of Italian heavy industry. This was a turning-point in Italy's development. Agriculture now began to lag behind and lose its commanding position in the nation's economy.[3]

Industrialisation proceeded rapidly[4] after 1880 in the area between Turin, Milan and Genoa, which in these years became Italy's 'industrial triangle'. Coal imports rose from under 1 million tons a year in 1871–5 to 2·4 million tons in 1881–5:[5] figures which, though they revealed the smallness of Italy's industrial consumption, showed also that the pace of industrialisation was gathering speed. The greatest expansion was in textiles, steel and mechanical engineering. Silk held its place as Italy's largest industry, but by 1887 cotton was not far behind. Imports of raw cotton more than trebled between 1871–5 and 1886–90, and the number

[1] Corbino, II, p. 76, III, pp. 101–3.

[2] *Sommario*, p. 159; Preti, pp. 77–8.

[3] Agriculture's share of the gross internal product fell from 57·4% in 1871–5 to 49·5% in 1886–90. *Indagine*, p. 36; Neufeld, p. 539. The proportion of the economically active population engaged in agriculture remained roughly constant at 60%. Neufeld, p. 138.

[4] Gerschenkron, pp. 361–4, calculates the annual average rate of growth of Italian industrial production in the years 1881–8 (which he calls 'a period of modern growth') at 4·6%.

[5] *Sommario*, p. 160.

of spindles rose from 700,000 in 1878 to 1,200,000 in 1887.[1] Both silk and cotton manufacturing were becoming mechanised and concentrated in new factories, while domestic handicrafts were dying out. By 1881 Italy was able to supply all its own railway equipment except locomotives, and many of the looms and other machines required by the textile manufacturers. During the boom years 1882–6 railway construction and speculative building gave a great stimulus to the steel and engineering industries. In 1884 the government took the initiative in promoting and financing a large steelworks at Terni. Brin was its chief political patron and a self-made industrialist, Breda, was its technical creator. Its primary purpose was to free the navy and the railways from dependence upon foreign supplies. The national output of steel, which had been under 4,000 tons in 1881, reached 158,000 tons in 1889.[2]

Industrial development and agricultural crisis changed the pattern of Italy's foreign trade. Silk remained the largest single item, producing a handsome and growing export surplus. Agriculture, too, still contributed a surplus, in spite of heavier cereal imports, thanks to rising exports of cattle, olive oil, wine and fruit, mainly to France. The situation worsened, however, after 1883. Imports continued to increase, in response to the needs of expanding industry, but exports declined. The appreciation of the lira after 1880 put exporters at a disadvantage. Italy's adverse balance of trade grew from 91 million lire a year in 1878–82 to 374 million in 1883–7.[3]

These difficulties contributed to the abandonment of Cavour's policy of free trade. Industrialists clamoured for protection of their infant industries, pleading the need for military security and economic independence, and pointed to the example of other European states: to France, where the protectionist movement had got under way as early as 1872, and to Germany, which adopted both industrial and agricultural tariffs in 1879. It was argued that free trade was only 'the economic appendix of political liberty', not an essential part of the liberal creed, and that the commercial treaties of the 1860s had been based on excessive confidence in Italy's economic strength. There were also fiscal arguments for a change: it was anomalous that so many foreign goods should be exempt from taxation when virtually no form of domestic wealth or economic activity had been spared.[4] The most vocal and energetic tariff reformer was Alessandro

---

[1] ibid., p. 159; Corbino, III, p. 142.

[2] *Sommario*, p. 129; Corbino, III, pp. 124–30; Luzzatto, II, p. 408; Romeo, p. 170.

[3] *Sommario*, p. 152.

[4] Luzzatti, *Memorie*, I, pp. 435, 450, 461.

Rossi, creator of Italy's most modern wool manufacturing firm at Schio in Venetia, and an outstanding figure of the industrial world. Rossi was an expansionist who believed that 'a great state could not be managed like a family, by economies to the bone'. Appointed to the senate in 1870, he treated that body to persistent repetition of his 'Catonian *Caeterum censeo*: defend the nation's production'.[1]

Protectionist views had already been popularised by a commission of enquiry into the state of industry, which reported in 1874. Next year, to the distress of Peruzzi and the free traders, Minghetti's government decided, from primarily fiscal motives, not to renew the current commercial treaties with France, Austria-Hungary and Switzerland. Minghetti put the young Luzzatti in charge of the consequent negotiations, which were still in progress when the Right fell. Depretis, whose concern for agriculture made him a more convinced free trader than Minghetti, nevertheless accepted his predecessor's policy. Satisfactory agreements were reached with Austria and Switzerland, after tough and prolonged bargaining. The negotiations with France ran a stormier course. A new treaty was ratified by the Italian parliament in April 1878 but rejected next month by the French chamber. This strengthened the hand of Rossi and his supporters and in July a higher general tariff was introduced. Because of the opposition to abandonment of the principle of free trade, it was presented as a fiscal, not economic, measure. In fact it had a mildly protectionist effect and proved particularly favourable to the cotton industry over the next ten years  In May 1881 the French protectionists secured the adoption of the highest general tariff in Europe. Yet in spite of the clamour in both countries and the political tension caused by the French occupation of Tunis, a new and mutually beneficial treaty was signed in November 1881 and passed against fierce opposition through both parliaments. It was a triumph for Depretis and his Foreign Minister, Mancini, who were struggling to keep the antagonism within bounds. But Depretis was forced in 1883 to appoint a new commission to examine the whole tariff question. It produced a moderately protectionist report. In June 1886 the French chamber, repeating its action of 1878, rejected a shipping treaty which the Italian parliament had approved. After this the pressure in Italy became irresistible and in December Depretis's government denounced the 1881 treaty. In the following July, with reckless over-confidence in the Italian economy, a new general tariff, the second highest in Europe, was introduced. It was intended to be the prelude to new negotiations from strength with France, but this proved a miscalculation.

The 1887 tariff was the outcome of years of agitation by powerful pressure groups which the pliant Depretis grew less and less able or willing to

[1] Carocci, pp. 150–1.

resist. The industries which led the campaign were cotton and wool, steel and engineering. For all these the tariff produced the results they desired. Imports of finished goods dwindled; imports of raw materials, exempt from duty, continued to increase. The most immediate beneficiaries were the cotton manufacturers, who happily exploited the protected home market, and the infant steel industry, which enjoyed a brief but glorious boom.

Agricultural interests had been anxious and suspicious in the early stages of the protectionist agitation. The collapse of cereal prices brought a changed outlook and demands for increasing the import duty on wheat. Depretis argued on behalf of the consumer that such a step would make nonsense of the abolition of the *macinato* tax, and Sonnino attacked even the current small duty as 'a tax on hunger'.[1] But the example of the rest of Europe was infectious and few Italians were capable of considering the problem coolly. Rossi spoke for many industrialists when he called for agricultural protection in the interests of national unity and equity between town and country. By 1887 the principle of protection for agriculture had been decided and the new tariff included the raising of the wheat import duty from 1·4 to 3 lire per quintal.

The political and nationalist motives behind the 1887 tariff are obvious, and it cannot be understood except in the context of Franco-Italian relations. Trade with France greatly exceeded that with any other country, and it was therefore on France that the protectionists concentrated. In both countries the necessary goodwill was lacking; political differences, which did not disturb the concurrent negotiations with Austria-Hungary, Germany and Switzerland, prevented agreement. The protectionists were delighted and looked forward with relish to a tariff war. Free trade, declared Rossi, was accepted only by weak and fearful peoples; 'economic autonomy' gave a nation strength.[2]

The adoption of protection profoundly influenced Italy's future development. From 1887 dates the tacit alliance between heavy industry and wheat-growing landowners which was to dominate the Italian economy for sixty years. The duty on foreign wheat was the bribe which made higher industrial prices acceptable to one section of agriculture. Though the most vocal partisans of the agricultural tariff were to be found among the capitalist landowners of the north, the chief beneficiaries were the southern *latifondisti*. The price was paid by the consumer, particularly in the south. Reduced manufactured imports from abroad meant reduced agricultural exports from Italy. In 1887 the south was overruled by the

[1] Since 1864 imported wheat had been subject to a small revenue duty which was raised in 1871 to 1·4 lire per quintal. Corbino, II, pp. 180–1.

[2] Carocci, p. 455.

north and became its economic tributary. The natural differences between north and south were magnified by state policy and the Southern question grew more acute. At the same time ruthless pressure groups, often more interested in speculation than in production, were granted special favours by governments for the sake of short-term political advantage. Opposition was disarmed by a camouflage of patriotic language. Modern steelworks, an armaments industry and a large merchant navy,[1] however dubious the economic arguments in their favour, were status symbols which no nation aspiring to be a Great Power could do without. But the links so forged between the state and privileged industrial and financial groups were not healthy. In the long run the distortion of the natural course of economic development proved a source of both internal and international weakness.[2]

## The Social Question

Between 1861 and 1880 the national income rose slowly and painfully by 22%; the increase in consumption (10%) was smaller than the increase in population (13%). The agricultural depression caused a sharp fall in *per capita* national income and in 1881-5 *per capita* consumption reached the lowest level in the history of united Italy.[3] As a leading Italian economist of the time, Maffeo Pantaleoni, observed in 1890, the private *per capita* wealth of even the richest regions of Italy was less than half that of France as a whole.[4]

[1] The tariff reform campaign was accompanied by a campaign for state subsidies to the merchant navy and the shipbuilding industry, in order to strengthen them against French competition and accelerate conversion from sail to steam. Certain shipping services had been subsidised since 1862. In 1885 parliament greatly increased the subsidy and voted special tax exemptions for shipbuilding. Champions of a large merchant navy usually also supported tariffs, a big naval building programme and colonial expansion. Carocci, pp. 380-95.

[2] Gerschenkron, pp. 367-70, points out that the post-1887 tariff system, by favouring the industries which consumed coal (which Italy did not possess), hindered rather than promoted healthy industrial growth. By contrast the mechanical engineering industry, in which Italy's traditional artisan skills might have proved a decisive advantage, was left largely to itself and the chemical industry was totally neglected.

[3] Romeo, pp. 31, 39. A recent calculation by the Istituto Centrale di Statistica (see *Indagine*, p. 42; Neufeld, p. 538; Romeo, p. 149) gives the following figures for *per capita* national income in lire (1938 prices):

| 1861-65 | 1,851 | 1881-85 | 1,884 |
| 1866-70 | 1,875 | 1886-90 | 1,885 |
| 1871-75 | 1,895 | 1891-95 | 1,888 |
| 1876-80 | 1,919 | 1896-1900 | 1,938 |

[4] Pantaleoni calculated the *per capita* wealth at 2,411 lire (£96) in northern Italy, 1,961 lire in the centre and 1,372 lire in the south, compared with 6,600 lire in France. Corbino, III, pp. 17-19.

The mass of the rural population was the most depressed. Bertani's words of 1872 remained true fifteen years later: 'In Italy one can distinguish two races of men; the race that eats white bread and the race that eats coloured bread.' The benefits of agricultural improvement and rising prices in the first twenty years after unification went not to the peasants but to the propertied class.[1] Money wages rose little if at all, while food prices and taxation rose steeply. The transformation of the economy after 1880 brought the rural masses little net improvement. In the north industrialisation drew labour into the towns and helped to relieve rural unemployment, but south of the Apennines there was no such outlet. Though the fall in food prices after 1877 brought a rise, sometimes substantial, in the labourer's real wage, this gain was often outweighed by loss of income from domestic spinning, weaving and handicrafts. The life of the peasant was particularly grim in the mountains. Between 1860 and 1880 over two million hectares of forest were cut, either by landowners greedy for quick profits or by land-hungry peasants remorselessly extending their patches of cultivation up the mountain sides. Poor land was soon exhausted by this 'robber economy' and soil erosion set in. The number of peasants who owned their own land had fallen even before 1880.[2] The agricultural depression accelerated the decline and many of the smallest proprietors, crushed by debts and taxation, sank into the rural proletariat. The absence of a stable class of landowning peasants, such as was to be found in France and most countries of north-western Europe, continued to be an unhappily distinctive feature of Italian society.

The fiscal policy of the state aggravated the distress of the countryside. Land and agriculture provided the bulk of the revenue that was needed for capital investment in railways and public works, for building up the armed services and for modernising the structure of the state. Little public spending took place in the countryside, least of all in the south. To a large extent this process was the necessary condition of economic growth. Nevertheless a high price was paid in rigorous compression of consumption by the rural non-propertied classes, which constituted the majority of the nation's population.[3] The suffering was great, and it was understandable that those who spoke for the countryside should lament that the government was killing the goose that laid the golden eggs.

In 1878 parliament appointed a commission of enquiry into the state of Italian agriculture, under the chairmanship of a conservative senator and Lombard landowner, Count Stefano Jacini. Its report, which was published in fifteen volumes over the next eight years, revealed for the first time the size and nature of Italy's agrarian problem. After unification,

[1] Romeo, pp. 28–30.
[2] Sereni, pp. 277–81; Preti, pp. 184–7.        [3] Romeo, pp. 30–3.

Jacini declared, 'political Italy had sacked agricultural Italy'. Taxation
had destroyed many of the sources of income in the countryside and the
rural classes had been exploited for the benefit of the towns. The remedy
lay in the state's hands. Jacini insisted that the social and technical problems of agriculture were inseparable and must be solved together. His
views were those of an English Tory; he believed in class collaboration and
the social responsibility of owners of property, and dismissed land reform
as an irrelevant, impracticable solution which could appeal only to ignorant
demagogues. His recommendations included legislation to improve public
health and technical education, the provision of cheap credit, more expenditure on irrigation and land reclamation, and tax reform to reduce
the burden on land. By acting along these lines, the state could create the
conditions in which private enterprise could carry through an economic
*risorgimento*. But time was pressing. Jacini warned parliament that new
ideas were reaching the countryside and the peasant was ceasing to be
apathetic and resigned.

> Undeniably [he wrote], the population of the countryside is worse off today
> than in the past, not because in fact conditions have deteriorated, but because
> thirty or forty years ago the population did not look forward to any change,
> while today, in various ways hard to define, it aspires to a change equivalent
> to the profound political transformation which has taken place in Italy.[1]

Very similar views were held by the remarkable group of writers whose
mouthpiece in the years 1878–82 was *La Rassegna Settimanale* of Florence.
Its most distinguished members were Sidney Sonnino, Leopoldo Franchetti, Pasquale Villari and Giustino Fortunato, four pioneers in the study
of the problems of the south. Sonnino and Franchetti had made their
name in 1873–6 by their sociological investigations in Tuscany, the
Neapolitan provinces and Sicily. In their writings they fiercely criticised
the absenteeism of landlords, the misappropriation of common land and
the harsh iniquity of the leases which tenants and sharecroppers were
forced to accept. Both they and Jacini admired Gladstone's Irish agrarian
legislation and wished to see the Italian peasant similarly protected. Their
ideal system was the Tuscan *mezzadria*,[2] which gave the tenant security
and an incentive to improve his land. Villari, the Neapolitan historian of
Renaissance Florence, tried in his *Lettere meridionali*, published in 1875,
to put the stark reality of the south before the Italian public. He, like
Sonnino, pleaded for legislation to protect the weak and admired the state

---

[1] Quoted in Preti, p. 74. Jacini noted that it was usually in the districts where
conditions had improved most that the greatest unrest was to be found.

[2] *Mezzadria* (*métayage*) is the form of sharecropping by which owner and tenant
divide expenses and profit equally between them.

emigration, believing that a reduction of surplus rural labour would stimulate technical progress and force proprietors to improve wages and working conditions. On one point most students of the question were agreed: that the state should protect ignorant peasant emigrants from exploitation by the shipping companies and the recruiting agents of North American industrialists. But parliament and governments remained for many years indifferent to the need.

The growth of industry and the birth of an industrial proletariat introduced Italy to the social problems which had long been familiar in north-western Europe. The factory worker lost his country roots and developed a new psychology. During the 1870s trade unions spread slowly over Lombardy and Piedmont. The first two nation-wide unions were formed by the printers in 1872 and the railwaymen in 1885. Industrial strikes, which had averaged only 13 a year in the decade 1861–70, became much more frequent after 1871, and in 1885 reached what was considered the alarming total of 89, involving 34,000 workers.[1] The most notable were the strikes of 1877 in the Biella woollen industry, which lasted for three and a half months. Nicotera dealt with them with characteristic energy; the strike leaders were arrested or deported, and mutual benefit societies and other workers' associations dissolved. It took ten years for the Biella working-class movement to recover. But the interest aroused by the affair led in 1878 to the appointment by Crispi, Nicotera's successor, of a commission of enquiry. The position of trade unions was still regulated by the 1859 Piedmontese penal code, which discouraged combinations of both employers and workers and penalised strikes as illegal unless there was 'reasonable cause', a phrase which magistrates usually interpreted in favour of employers. The enquiry proved that the notorious International had played no part at Biella; those workers who were interested in politics were radical and Mazzinian in sympathy, and the strikes had been economic, not political, in aim.[2] The commission recommended that the right of workers and employers to combine should be recognised by law, subject to safeguards against violence and intimidation. Depretis accepted its recommendations, which even Sella, a member of the family that ruled industrial Biella, approved. But parliament, unable to overcome its fear of collective working-class action, rejected the proposal. Trade unions continued to be dependent on the arbitrary tolerance of employers and police.[3]

In 1886 Crispi told a large audience at Palermo that the social problem

[1] Corbino, II, pp. 5–6, III, p. 3; *ASI 1919–1921*, p. 512; Neufeld, p. 547.
[2] Rigola, *Il movimento operaio nel Biellese*, pp. 1–15, 67–89.
[3] Rigola, *Storia*, pp. 146–52.

would be solved in Italy without danger because 'the workman in our
country, with a few exceptions, has great common sense and the virtue of
knowing how to wait'.[1] This complacency, from which Crispi suffered
much less than the average politician, goes far to explain why Italy lagged
behind the rest of western Europe in social legislation. This had sturdy
advocates in Minghetti and Luzzatti from the Right, Cairoli from the
Left, Bertani from the Extreme Left and independent conservatives like
Franchetti and Sonnino. But the deputies of the majority continued to
obstruct long after they had swallowed the principle of state intervention
in the form of tariffs. While Depretis was in power, only two measures of
social legislation were passed. In 1883 an industrial workmen's compensation scheme was introduced, on a voluntary basis, after the defeat of a
more radical measure which would have enforced employers' liability.
A more important law regulated the employment of children. In 1876
Sonnino had revealed the inhuman conditions in the Sicilian sulphur
mines, where young boys worked cruelly long hours as the slaves of the
more privileged adult miners. For ten years Luzzatti conducted a passionate
campaign for state intervention.[2] At last, in 1886 parliament limited the
working day of children under twelve to eight hours, and forbade the
employment of children less than nine years of age in industry, less than
ten years underground and less than fifteen years in dangerous or unhealthy
occupations. Very slowly views on social problems changed. An outbreak
of cholera in Naples in 1884 killed 8,000, and statistics showed that the
death rate was eight to ten times as heavy in the slum *bassi* as in the upper-
class districts. Cavallotti ¡brought a squad of voluntary relief workers
down from the north, the King and Depretis and the Archbishop of
Naples toured the stricken city, press correspondents filled their papers
with descriptions of the living conditions of the poor. When the epidemic
ended, an ambitious scheme of slum clearance was launched, half the cost
of which was borne by the state.[3] Such jolts to the Italian conscience
encouraged serious study of the problem of public health and led to a
greater flow of social legislation in the next decade.

[1] Crispi, *Scritti e discorsi politici*, p. 553.
[2] Franchetti and Sonnino, II, pp. 345–58; Luzzatti, *Memorie*, II, pp. 30–41.
Luzzatti's chief antagonist was Alessandro Rossi, the protectionist leader, who
argued with passion that state intervention in the form of factory inspectors would
'sterilise the field of human charity'.
[3] Corbino, III, pp. 272–4; *ASI 1886*, p. 158. Cholera caused 55,000 deaths
between 1884 and 1887. Corbino, III, pp. 10–11. For a description of the Naples
epidemic, see Axel Munthe, *Letters from a Mourning City* (London 1887).

## The Political System and its Critics

Against the background of economic ferment and change, the daily chronicle of parliamentary and administrative routine seems uneventful. It was this very contrast that in the years 1882–7 caused growing dissatisfaction with the political system. Depretis's rule was unheroic and prosaic, and those who yearned for poetry felt suffocated by it. Italy seemed to be living from day to day, with no direction, no sense of mission and no national vision; mediocrity was at a premium. The frustrated and disillusioned found an outlet for their emotions in attacks upon Depretis, *trasformismo*,[1] the parliamentary system and the whole structure of 'legal Italy'. The rich polemical literature of the time gives an impression of universal failure, and *trasformismo* became a synonym for corruption and degradation.[2]

The attacks concentrated on two aspects of Italian politics: the absence of parties and the spoils system. It was felt to be a disgrace that the British two-party system had never taken root in Italy. Instead of the healthy 'cut and thrust of debate' and the clash of great ideals, Italians had to be content with puny manœuvres for private or sectional advantage between shifting, shapeless parliamentary groups. Writers, politicians and political theorists searched desperately for 'a great idea, a great principle, round which a majority and a minority could form'. Depretis became a legend: the incorruptible arch-corrupter, the Italian Walpole, who maintained himself in power by cynical bargains and intrigues, and prevented the growth of parties founded on principle. He was accused of parliamentary dictatorship and caricatured as the white-bearded magician of Stradella, who made the deputies dance like puppets to his invisible strings. As Minister of Interior he used the prefects and mayors of communes, all of whom he nominated, to bind the electoral cliques of the south to the government by a judicious mixture of threats and favours.[3] Parliament became the market-place for the distribution of spoils. The government was regarded as a milch-cow, to be milked of a job or a decoration, a new railway or a tariff, in return for votes to swell its majority. 'They made

---

[1] See above, p. 52.

[2] Enemies of parliament and democracy made good use of this literature in later years. Most of the criticisms were re-hashed by nationalist writers in the early twentieth century and by fascists after the Great War. *Trasformismo* is still used as a term of political abuse. A useful summary of the polemics may be found in R. De Mattei, *Dal trasformismo al socialismo* (Florence 1940), ch. I.

[3] For examples of Depretis's use of prefects for this purpose, see Carocci, pp. 307, 475–9, 605–7. 'It's all right to wish to do without political prefects, except in the smallest quantities: but the wish is one thing, the deed is another,' Depretis said in the senate in 1879.

Italy to devour her', said the cynics. Deputies had ceased to be the representatives of principles and become the mere tools of local interests, lamented Minghetti. In 1886 Crispi told his electors at Palermo:

> You should see the pandemonium at Montecitorio[1] when the moment approaches for an important division. The agents of the government run through the rooms and corridors, to gather votes. Subsidies, decorations, canals, bridges, roads, everything is promised; and sometimes an act of justice, long denied, is the price of a parliamentary vote.[2]

Many directed their wrath against Rome, the least Italian and most cosmopolitan of Italian cities, the home of corruption, bureaucracy and rhetoric, indifferent to the problems of either the suffering countryside or the struggling industrial pioneers of the north. In Milan and Genoa, cities of enterprise and productive achievement, the decline in political standards was freely attributed to the shift of the capital to parasitical Rome and to the increasingly 'southern' atmosphere of government.[3]

There was some truth in most of these accusations. Italian liberalism had unquestionably lost its revolutionary fire. Drift and compromise were only too characteristic of the years of Depretis's supremacy. But the political system within which Depretis had to work did not allow him a wide choice of method. The rulers of Italy were still recruited from a single, though broadening, class of the population. There was no conservative party in the British sense, because the social bases for such a party were lacking. Most of the surviving nobility remained aloof, looking backward to the *anciens régimes*; industry, still in its infancy, had not yet created a political business class; the church's hostility further narrowed the ruling class and, reinforced by illiteracy, kept the peasantry out of politics. Nor was there yet a sufficiently mature and organised proletariat to give birth to a coherent left-wing party. It was thus inevitable that political life should be monopolised by an amorphous liberal party whose members were united by little more than a negative, conservative creed of opposition to political extremes, whether of the right or left.

The critics of the system may be divided into four main groups: the conservative Centre (*Centro tecnico*), the Pentarchy, the National Conservatives and the Extreme Left. The opposition of the first two was one of tactics rather than principle; the last two were the advance guard of new forces whose entry into politics would eventually rejuvenate the whole system.

The Centre sprang from dissatisfaction with Magliani's finance. It was

[1] The chamber of deputies sat, as it does today, in the Palace of Montecitorio.
[2] Crispi, *Scritti e discorsi politici*, p. 575.
[3] Chabod, *Storia*, pp. 179 ff., 316–23.

a loosely organised group of independent-minded men from both Right and Left, with a majority from the former. Of its forty-five members, four were future Prime Ministers: Rudinì, Giolitti, Pelloux and Sonnino. While refusing to be 'transformed', they tried to keep out of sterile political controversy. Instead they concentrated on filling the financial and other technical committees of parliament, and on acquiring a mastery of facts and figures with which to attack Magliani's extravagance. The Centre thus became a nucleus round which the government's critics gathered, and played a big part in whittling down Depretis's majority between 1883 and 1887.

The Pentarchy was formed in 1883 by five nostalgic survivors of the old Left, Baccarini, Cairoli, Crispi, Nicotera and Zanardelli. Its aim was to protest against Depretis's betrayal of the ideals of the Left and to maintain contact with the radicals and republicans of the Extreme Left.[1] The partnership between the northern liberalism of Zanardelli and Cairoli, and the southern authoritarianism of Crispi and Nicotera, was never harmonious or coherent. Nevertheless the Pentarchy had by 1887 built up a following of about 100 deputies. Its southern elements were the more powerful and from the first it was dominated by Crispi, who led the attacks on both the foreign and internal policies of the government.[2] Crispi condemned *trasformismo* as 'parliamentary incest' and upbraided Depretis for putting the clock back to 1876 and pursuing a policy indistinguishable from that of the Right. His remedy for Italy's problems was thus a return to the antagonisms of the previous decade. In 1886 he declared:[3]

> After 1878 there were no more political parties, only politicians . . . I deplored this state of affairs and stood aloof with a few faithful friends. Not being able to be on the side of men, I remained on the side of ideas, which are immortal, awaiting the day of their triumph. (*Applausi.*) I kept alight the sacred flame of my convictions, which have been the patrimony of my political life. (*Benissimo.*)

This fine talk of sacred convictions was unconvincing, for the Pentarchy was quite ready to engineer a rival *trasformismo* of its own. Nicotera made overtures to the Right for a Nicotera–Sella coalition. In 1886 the Pentarchy reached an agreement for concerted opposition with the Centre, itself a 'transformed' group with members from both Right and Left. Crispi, who by this agreement became leader of a combined opposition, showed the strength of his sacred convictions in April 1887 when he accepted office as Minister of Interior under Depretis, and thus himself became 'transformed'.

Among the National Conservatives the clearest thinker was Jacini. In

[1] Carocci, pp. 515–23, 583–7.
[2] ibid., pp. 330–7.　　　[3] Crispi, *Scritti e discorsi politici*, p. 567.

his view the most serious weakness of the Italian system of government was the exclusion from national political life of the Catholic organisations and the peasantry, and the consequent absence of a conservative party. Reconciliation between Italy and the Papacy was therefore the essential condition of healthy political progress. If the *non expedit* were cancelled, he believed that a great number of patriotic Catholics would quickly find a common interest with the old Right in the preservation of order and social peace, and so create the conservative party that was required. He also wished to strengthen the political influence of the countryside by two constitutional reforms, decentralisation and indirect universal suffrage. Decentralisation would break 'the monstrous *connubio*' between a parliamentary system imitated from that of Britain and extreme centralisation on the French model. Strong local self-government would reduce the paralysing interference of the central government in local affairs and limit the spoils system. It would also provide an opportunity for the peasants, whom Jacini considered too backward to be given a direct vote, to acquire political experience. New life would thus be infused into the stale, inbred parliamentary system. The change of atmosphere in the Vatican, following on the election of Leo XIII in 1878, spurred the National Conservatives into greater activity. Meetings to discuss their programme were held in Rome early in 1879 between prominent Catholic conciliators, leading members of the Unione Romana, the organisation which promoted the Catholic interest in local elections, and sympathetic liberal conservatives, of whom Tommaso Tittoni, the future Foreign Minister, was one. Outside Rome the response was greatest in Milan,[1] where Jacini found sympathisers in leading members of the rising industrial class. But the intransigents on both sides were too powerful and blocked all progress. While church and state remained at loggerheads, the National Conservatives could be no more than a handful of far-sighted individuals whose political influence was small.[2]

The Extreme Left, like the National Conservatives, had its main centre in Milan, where its great daily newspaper, the *Secolo*, was published. In the general election of 1882, which immediately followed the electoral reform, it increased its parliamentary strength to sixteen and acquired a socialist wing. The extension of the suffrage, by offering the working-class

---

[1] A programme of decentralisation had a special appeal for the Milanese, who prided themselves on being in the vanguard of progress and were always lamenting their frustration at the hands of Rome. Milan liked to be known as the moral, as opposed to political, capital of Italy.

[2] De Rosa, *I conservatori nazionali*, pp. 32–43; Jacini, *Un conservatore rurale*, II, pp. 21–4, 104–8; Tittoni, 'Ricordi personali di politica interna', pp. 306–11; Fonzi, pp. 38–44. For the views of the National Conservatives on the Roman question, see also below, pp. 219–21.

a prospect of peaceful political advancement, quickened the conversion of the Internationalists from revolutionary to constitutional forms of agitation. In 1882 even Cafiero, Bakunin's closest disciple, became a whole-hearted advocate of 'the parliamentary tactic in the German social demo-cratic sense'. Costa stood at Ravenna, with Cafiero's blessing, as candidate of the Romagna Democratic Union and was elected to parliament as Italy's first socialist deputy. Many still felt the need to apologise for these new tactics. The task of socialist candidates, said Bignami, 'must be above all a task of demolition'. Yet Costa took the deputy's oath without reser-vation and quickly settled down on the parliamentary benches of the Extreme Left.[1]

Meanwhile the organised workmen of Lombardy were making an inde-pendent entry into politics. The first working-class deputies to sit in the Italian parliament had been elected under the patronage of the Milan democratic organisations, at a time when the distinction between radical, republican and socialist was still far from clear. In 1882 the Partito Operaio Italiano[2] was founded in Milan, in a spirit of revolt against both the patronising middle-class democrats and the International, which it re-garded as a crazy organisation led by semi-deranged intellectuals. To belong to the Partito Operaio it was necessary to be a real worker, 'with blistered hands'. The party sprang directly from the workmen's unions and was led by a tough, intransigent, largely self-educated printer named Costantino Lazzari. The main emphasis of its programme was on specific-ally working-class demands: the right to strike, the formation of trade union federations, and measures to reduce unemployment and promote working-class housing and cooperatives. Its keynote was the fight against capital. Initially the government treated it with a good deal of favour, see-ing in it a useful tool for weakening the Milanese democrats. In 1886 the party put up independent parliamentary candidates of its own at Milan to the disgust of Cavallotti who accused it of accepting money from the government and of collusion with the police. A serious breach between radicals and socialists resulted, to the government's satisfaction. But Depretis's benevolence did not last long. The Partito Operaio soon turned its attention to the countryside, made contact with the embryonic peasant unions of the Po valley and helped to finance and organise the agricultural strikes of 1882–6.[3] Depretis recognised that the peasants had real griev-ances, but found it impossible to resist for long the landowners' clamour for stern measures. In 1885 troops were sent to Mantua and Parma to

---

[1] Hostetter, pp. 424–5, 429–31; Lipparini, pp. 186 ff.

[2] The word *operaio* is used in Italian to describe the factory worker, whereas the wider term *lavoratore* covers workers of all kinds.

[3] Carocci, pp. 534–7; Preti, pp. 97–102. See also above, p. 88.

break the strikes and bring in the harvest, and in June 1886 the Partito Operaio was suppressed as a criminal organisation and its leaders arrested.[1] Over the next five years it led an uneasy existence of sporadic persecution, which helped to break down its working-class exclusiveness. Sympathetic contacts between it and the legalitarian socialists prepared the way for the formation of a united socialist party.

In spite of its gains from the extension of the suffrage, the Extreme Left remained numerically weak in parliament. It was led by men of arresting personalities, but its criticism was rarely constructive and it never spoke with one voice. In 1883 the radical Felice Cavallotti, the republican Giovanni Bovio and the socialist Andrea Costa formed the Fascio della Democrazia, to revive the waning inspiration of the League of Democracy of 1879 and intensify opposition to Depretis both in parliament and in the constituencies. Much of its energy went into denouncing the government's foreign policy.[2] In attacking *trasformismo* it claimed to speak for 'real Italy', in whose name it demanded a policy inspired by democratic faith. A growing minority of radicals looked forward to the formation of an efficient party, 'living in the present', with a practical programme of political and social reform.[3] But the majority of radicals and republicans still lived in the romantic, Garibaldian past; they were incapable of reconciling themselves to the constitution and regarded parliament as 'a filthy pigsty' which would corrupt honest men.[4] The impetuous, emotional Cavallotti was torn between these conflicting pressures. At times he worked constructively for democratic reform; at others he relapsed into denouncing the immorality of the whole political system and appealed eloquently for honesty, purity and idealism in public life. These things, he declared in 1883, were not to be found in parliament, where politics consisted only of 'acrobatics, optical tricks, petty transactions and transformations'.[5] His displays of sterile invective and nostalgia for the heroic past secured him an admiring audience, but did nothing to advance the democratic cause.

In these years of deepening pessimism, one theme often recurs: the need for a strong executive and a strong man to lift Italy out of the slough. Disillusioned leaders of the Right like Bonghi and Spaventa looked to the King, reminding him in speeches and writings of his duty to ensure good government and avoid excessive 'constitutionalism'. Others hoped that

---

[1] Carocci, pp. 569–75.

[2] See below, pp. 115–16.

[3] See for example letter of 20 July 1887 to Cavallotti from Comandini, a right-wing radical, in *L'Italia radicale*, pp. 103–4.

[4] See for example the efforts of Bizzoni, an intransigent radical, to dissuade Cavallotti from entering parliament in 1873, in *L'Italia radicale*, p. 38.

[5] Cilibrizzi, II, p. 273.

the great man would appear in parliament. Similar sentiments were expressed by supporters of the Pentarchy, whose criticisms often coincided with those of the Right. In March 1886 Crispi ended a long speech on the evils of Depretis's system by turning to the government benches and crying 'Put a man of energy there'. The man he had in mind was himself.[1]

The years of Depretis's rule were a period of gestation. His achievement, in spite of drift, indecision and opportunism, was to hold Italy together and provide a stable framework within which growth could take place. By 1886 new and more vigorous forces were stirring and making ready to play their part in the life of the nation. Depretis, had he lived longer, would have been a soothing, cool-headed guide. But he was now an old man, whose grip over parliament and the political machine was weakening. In March 1886 he narrowly escaped defeat at the end of a long debate on Magliani's finance, which developed into a searching inquest on the shortcomings of *trasformismo*. His reply was to dissolve and hold an election in May, fighting on an unashamedly conservative programme. The result was a triumph for the government, which won as many seats as in 1882. Minghetti's moderate Right, thanks to official benevolence, almost doubled its strength. All sections of the opposition, the dissident Right, the Pentarchy and the Extreme Left, lost ground. Nevertheless in the new chamber Depretis's decline was apparent and change and uncertainty were in the air. The government's resignation on a colonial issue in February 1887 was followed by the longest cabinet crisis Italy had yet known. Depretis formed one more government but died in office in July. With his death the long period of consolidation came to an end and Italy moved out of a dull but secure haven into stormy seas.

[1] Volpe, I, pp. 262–3; Chabod, *Storia*, pp. 638 ff.; P. Romano, *Silvio Spaventa*, pp. 248 ff.; Carocci, pp. 613–20; Cilibrizzi, II, p. 288.

# 3

# From Isolation to the Triple Alliance

## The Roman Question

The Roman question dominated Italian foreign relations for twelve years after 1870 and the defence of Rome was Italy's main preoccupation. The fury of Catholics abroad, particularly in France, was indeed alarming. In February 1871 the French elected a National Assembly with a royalist and ardently Catholic majority. In a series of manifestos the Comte de Chambord, who seemed likely soon to become King Henri V, stressed his belief that the restoration of his royal House and the restoration of papal independence were inseparable; the protection of the Holy See had been in past centuries 'the most incontrovertible cause of France's greatness among the nations'.[1] French bishops organised petitions to the National Assembly, urging the government to rescue the Pope from 'imprisonment' and restore the temporal power.[2] Fortunately for Italy, the strength of the monarchist cause in France declined steadily after 1871. Thiers, who became provisional President of the French Republic in July 1871, had no thought of a crusade to liberate the Pope. But, though a republican, he was no great friend of Italy, which he described in public as a nation 'created by the unhappy blindness' of Napoleon III. Many besides clericals and monarchists regarded the seizure of Rome as an insult to Gallic pride and accused the Italians of base ingratitude. Nor could Thiers and his prime ministers, even had they so wished, entirely ignore the pressure of their Catholic supporters. Italian fears seemed to be confirmed by Thiers's refusal to withdraw the *Orénoque* from Civitavecchia, where it remained to wound Italian feelings, waiting to take Pius IX aboard should he decide to leave Rome. In May 1873 the fall of Thiers and his replacement as President by MacMahon, a devout Catholic with monarchist sympathies,

[1] Halperin, p. 198.
[2] 'God will know how to take his revenge', had written the clerical *Monde* on 30 September 1870: 'May He deign to do so by the sword of a purified and regenerated France.' Halperin, p. 71.

were followed by a new outbreak of bellicose clerical demonstrations and a sharp increase of tension between the two countries.

French hostility strengthened the influence of the Italian Francophobes, most of whom belonged to the Left. They assiduously exaggerated the clerical danger and pressed for bigger armaments and a German alliance. The more irresponsible among them dreamt of recovering Nice and annexing Corsica, with German assistance. They greeted the beginning of the German *Kulturkampf* in May 1873 with fierce joy and contrasted Bismarck's enlightened crusade against the powers of darkness with their own government's servility to France and the Pope. In September 1873 the tension with France forced Italy to move closer to Germany. Victor Emmanuel visited first Vienna, then Berlin, accompanied by his Prime Minister and Foreign Minister, Minghetti and Visconti Venosta. No commitments were entered into, but both Austria-Hungary and Germany assured the Italians of their disapproval of French clerical agitation, and the Germans of their support if France should attack Italy. The tension of 1873 subsided in 1874. MacMahon was not a hothead. When told of Italian anxieties, he was shocked and exclaimed: 'I will write to Victor Emmanuel; he knows me, we have fought side by side; whatever I say, he will believe.'[1] The French government was uncomfortably aware of its isolation and ready to make a gesture to Italy. In July 1874 the Archbishop of Paris was publicly rebuked by his Foreign Minister for provocative references to the Roman question in a pastoral letter, and in October the *Orénoque* was withdrawn, with Pius IX's consent, from Civitavecchia to Toulon.[2]

Visconti Venosta was Foreign Minister continuously from 1869 to 1876. Both the royal visits of 1873 and the reduction of tension with France in 1874 were part of his policy of friendship with all countries. He saw that Italy's main need was time for consolidation. His aims were therefore negative: first, to contribute to the preservation of peace, especially between France and Germany, because Italy could only lose by a war, whoever might be the victor; second, to preserve the *status quo* in eastern Europe and the Mediterranean, at least until Italy was strong enough to insist on an equal slice when the 'Turkish cake' was cut.[3] His greatest fear was another German onslaught on France, which would leave Europe divided between a German-dominated west and a Russian-dominated east. By keeping Italy uncommitted and as little talked about as possible, he

[1] Duke de Broglie, *An Ambassador of the Vanquished* (London 1896), p. 131. MacMahon had been Napoleon III's most successful commander in the Italian campaign of 1859.

[2] Another warship, however, was sent to Ajaccio in Corsica, where it was to remain at the disposal of the Pope.

[3] Chabod, *Storia*, p. 543.

hoped to contribute towards the preservation of peace, liberty and equilibrium in Europe.[1]

If there was a bias in Visconti Venosta's policy, it was towards France rather than Germany. This was in the Francophil tradition of so many of the northern leaders of the Right. He did his utmost to play down the antics of French clericals, pinning his hopes on the growing strength of the liberal republicans. His relations with Bismarck were not cordial. The latter in the years 1873–5 was eager for an alliance with Italy, to strengthen his hand in the fight against Catholic ultramontanism and to deprive France of a possible ally. But Visconti Venosta was cautious. He had no wish to involve Italy in a Franco-German dispute or to risk his country becoming a diplomatic satellite of Germany. In any case he was confident that Germany could never allow Italy to be overwhelmed by France, whether there was a formal alliance or not. From his visit to Berlin he brought back the impression that Bismarck was 'a travelling companion whom I should not like to have with me always'.[2] The distrust was mutual. Bismarck disliked those who declined to fall in with his plans.

With Austria-Hungary relations were satisfactory. Visconti Venosta never publicly renounced Italy's irredentist aspirations; but in private he assured the Austrians that since 1866 Italian governments had given up all thought of further annexations, realising in particular that Trieste would never belong to Italy.[3] On the Austrian side, Francis Joseph made no secret of his wish to forget the past. In April 1875 he impressed his good-will on all Europe by paying an official visit to Venice, which had been his less than ten years before. This gesture greatly moved Victor Emmanuel, who assured him, without consulting his ministers, that there would be no war between their two countries. With dynastic relations so cordial, Andrássy had no wish to make trouble for Italy over Rome, provided the Italians refrained from making trouble on the Austrian frontier. On the other hand, the Austrian government, assured of Russian benevolence after 1872 through the League of the Three Emperors, could and did talk firmly to Italy and make it clear that it would stand no nonsense.[4]

The year 1875 was stormy. In February Pius IX took the grave step of declaring Bismarck's anti-clerical May Laws null and void and releasing German Catholics from their normal obedience to the secular power. During Minghetti's visit to Berlin in 1873, Bismarck had lamented that it was no longer possible to send a warship to Civitavecchia to bring the Pope

[1] Chabod, *Storia*, pp. 120 ff., 531–4, 582 ff.
[2] Sandonà, I, p. 104; Chabod, *Storia*, pp. 587–8.
[3] Sandonà, I, p. 112.
[4] Chabod, *Storia*, pp. 663–8. See above, p. 31, for Andrássy's note on irredentism, the language of which Victor Emmanuel entirely approved.

to his senses. He now told the Italian government that he would hold it responsible for papal actions, and urged it to modify the Law of Guarantees which allowed the Pope to attack foreign states with impunity. Visconti Venosta, in a dignified refusal, argued that the Pope was sovereign, not just an Italian bishop to be hauled before the Italian courts. The episode was a striking demonstration of the effectiveness of the Law of Guarantees.[1] But it angered Bismarck who at this time saw clerical plots everywhere. This Italian deference to the Pope, followed by Francis Joseph's visit to Venice, seemed to him the prelude to a monstrous Franco-Austro-Italian clerical combination directed against an isolated Germany. Such fears helped to create the war scare of April 1875, when a German preventive attack upon France was thought imminent, and both Russia and Britain made representations in favour of peace in Berlin. Visconti Venosta did not join in these, but unofficially made his desire for peace known. Bismarck, who in later years regarded April 1875 as his greatest diplomatic humiliation, did not forget. Already in January he had made the first of many suggestions to the French that they should occupy Tunis. As relations between Germany and France improved after April 1875, Bismarck's contempt for Italy grew. When William I visited Milan in October 1875, to return Victor Emmanuel's visit to Berlin, he took with him Moltke, his Chief of General Staff: but Bismarck stayed at home.

## The Congress of Berlin

In the same year of 1875 the Eastern question erupted, far too soon for Visconti Venosta's liking. The Bosnian insurrection of July and rumours of Austrian plans for Balkan expansion revived old hopes in Italy of an 'easternisation' of Austria-Hungary. Count Carlo di Robilant, Italian ambassador in Vienna, hoped that Austria would indeed annex Bosnia, because this would give Italy a perhaps unique opportunity to improve its frontiers in the Trentino or on the Isonzo, and he advocated an Italo-German alliance to enlist support for Italian claims.[2] The immediate reaction of the Left to the news from the Balkans was to organise irredentist meetings and enrol volunteers for the cause of Slav liberation in Dalmatia. The press was full of indiscreet discussions of compensations. High hopes were held that the Trentino had been discussed during William I's visit to Milan, and an enthusiastic crowd greeted the Emperor at Trent where he passed a night on his way back to Berlin.[3] Visconti Venosta, who did not

[1] Bismarck in 1877 complained to Crispi of the immunity which the Law of Guarantees had given the Pope: 'Vous l'avez emboîté dans le coton, et personne peut l'atteindre.' Crispi, *Memoirs*, II, p. 61.
[2] Albertini, *Origins*, I, pp. 23–4; Chabod, *Storia*, p. 690.
[3] Sandonà, I, p. 114.

share Robilant's optimism, was struggling to prevent a worsening of relations with Austria-Hungary when he fell from power with the Right in March 1876.

Italian public opinion, largely uninformed in foreign questions, was far from appreciating the skill with which Visconti Venosta had weathered successive storms. Critics on the left were disgusted by his apparent servility to France or Francis Joseph, by his indifference to the irredentist cause and his refusal to imitate Bismarck in his dealings with the church. His policy of equilibrium was not understood. Many Italians had hoped for more excitement and satisfaction to national prestige, not realising that big ambitions go ill with small means. They counted on great changes when the Left came to power. But very soon, as over domestic questions, they were disappointed. The Left was deeply divided on foreign policy and before long the 'progressives' were criticising Depretis as fiercely as they had ever criticised Visconti Venosta. Depretis, once faced with the responsibilities of power, had no wish to break with the past. Victor Emmanuel, too, intervened effectively to ensure continuity; he assured the Austrians that his promise to Francis Joseph at Venice still held good, and that he would make his ministers do what he wanted.[1] Depretis was a Francophil and welcomed the prospect of cordial relations with France, where the first elections since 1871 had brought the republicans into power only a month before the Left in Italy. As regards the Eastern question, he had little sympathy for irredentists or oppressed Slavs, and regarded Austria-Hungary as a bulwark against the Russian drive towards the Mediterranean. His interests lay at home and he regarded foreign policy as a necessary evil. 'One wants as little of it as possible', he once said; 'it's enough, on the occasions when storm clouds appear on the horizon, to put one's back to the wall and open one's umbrella.'[2] The main consequence of Visconti Venosta's departure was the removal of a firm guiding hand; his consistent policy was replaced by erratic oscillation between the policies of rival personalities at home and abroad.

The change of government did, however, encourage the irredentists to intensify their agitation, and in October 1876 Garibaldi addressed an open letter to his friends in the Trentino, bidding them hold themselves ready for action in the spring.[3] Next year an Italia Irredenta Association was founded by Matteo Renato Imbriani, a fiery, eloquent and irrepressible republican from Naples, who had fought with Garibaldi in 1860.[4] The

[1] Chabod, *Storia*, pp. 668–78.
[2] Cilibrizzi, II, p. 339.
[3] Sandonà, I, pp. 131–2.
[4] Imbriani coined the term 'irredentism' at his father's funeral in 1877, when in the presence of delegates from Trieste he dedicated himself to the cause of

government, responding to this pressure, drew the attention of the Great Powers to the dangers to European equilibrium that would result from Austrian expansion in the Balkans. Andrássy did not miss the implication and retorted that 'at the first sign of an annexationist policy (on the part of Italy), Austria would not limit itself to self-defence, but would proceed to the attack'. Andrássy had reached an agreement on the Balkans with Russia, and so could talk toughly to the Italians. In July 1877, worried by Italian interest in Montenegro and Albania, he made it clear that Italian expansion across the Adriatic would be opposed just as fiercely as expansion over the Austrian frontier.[1]

Relations with Austria-Hungary were thus deteriorating when on 16 May 1877 MacMahon, the French President, replaced his republican Prime Minister by a royalist and dissolved the chamber of deputies with ts republican majority. The French clericals at once renewed their anti-Italian demonstrations and the critics of Depretis, led by Crispi, redoubled their clamour for bigger armaments and a German alliance. Depretis, reassured by the French, tried to calm anxieties: 'Governments pass away', he said, 'but nations remain.'[2] But even Depretis saw that with the threat of two unfriendly neighbours, inertia was becoming dangerous. He consented to a strengthening of the defences of Rome and started to look about for diplomatic support.

Three possibilities suggested themselves: Russia, Germany and Britain. A few persons in Rome favoured an approach to Russia for joint resistance to Austria-Hungary in the Balkans. But the certainty of British opposition, the risk of a rupture with Austria, Russian indifference and anti-Russian popular prejudice never allowed this plan to get beyond the talking stage.[3] Support from Germany seemed more probable. In September 1877 Crispi, then President of the chamber of deputies, was sent by Depretis on a tour of the European capitals, with the secret mission of enlisting Bismarck's help against both France and Austria-Hungary. Victor Emmanuel, suddenly forgetting his protestations of friendship for Francis Joseph, gave his warm approval.[4] Depretis hoped for a defensive Italo-German alliance,

---

'the unredeemed lands'. The phrase quickly passed into common use. Imbriani served the cause with fanatical single-mindedness for the rest of his life.

[1] Sandonà, I, pp. 141, 165–9; Albertini, Origins, I, p. 25.

[2] Chiala, Pagine, I, p. 245.

[3] In November 1876 Lord Salisbury, passing through Rome on his way to Constantinople, reported that 'the Ministers here are very peaceful . . . The Court, on the contrary, i.e. the Prince Humbert and the King, are for war – and are Russian.' Cecil, II, p. 106.

[4] Chabod, Storia, pp. 680–92. According to Crispi's own account, in Memoirs, II, p. 9, 'The King feels the need of crowning his life-work with a victory which shall give our army the power and prestige it now lacks in the eyes of the world.'

in which the price for Italian military aid against France would be a German veto on Austria's annexation of Bosnia, or compensations in the Trentino if Bosnia was annexed.[1] Bismarck refused to discuss an anti-Austrian alliance, or even German diplomatic pressure on Austria, but proposed an offensive and defensive alliance against France. Crispi, who immediately fell under Bismarck's spell, welcomed the idea with enthusiasm. But on returning to Rome he found that Depretis's eagerness had evaporated. The French election of October 1877 had resulted in a republican victory and there seemed no point in taking up Bismarck's offer. Crispi's mission therefore led to nothing. The third possibility, a closer association between Italy and Britain, was first suggested in February 1878 by Disraeli, who had conceived the idea of a Mediterranean League of Britain, Austria-Hungary and Italy against Russia, whose army was then at the gates of Constantinople. Depretis responded favourably, but in the middle of March, just as the British draft for the League arrived in Rome, his government fell and Cairoli came to power.[2]

In the negotiations in which Italy engaged during the Eastern crisis of 1875–8, the subject of compensations figured prominently. The solution which Bismarck favoured was that all the Great Powers should satisfy themselves, by mutual agreement, with pieces of Turkish territory. Tunis, Tripoli and Albania were the morsels intermittently dangled before Italy by the various governments. The diplomatic difficulties were not insuperable, though Austria-Hungary had vetoed Albania and France would certainly veto Tunis. But more important than foreign opposition was the fact that the Italians were indifferent. 'We don't want to hear anything about African territories', Robilant had told Andrássy in 1876,[3] and he expressed the general view. Crispi himself told Bismarck that Albania did not interest Italy. Italian eyes were turned northwards: the only compensation acceptable to public opinion would have been the Trentino.

Cairoli's appointment as Prime Minister worried the Austrians. As late as November 1877 he had reiterated Italy's right to Trieste and the Trentino (and Nice) at a public banquet.[4] His hostility to Austria-Hungary was notorious and his wife was a native of Trent. But, to their relief and surprise, his Foreign Minister turned out to be Count Luigi Corti, a courteous, old-fashioned Lombard aristocrat from the diplomatic service.

[1] Depretis, like Visconti Venosta (see p. 100, above), was confident that Germany could never allow France to attack and crush Italy, even in the absence of an Italo-German alliance. It was therefore reasonable to ask Germany to pay for Italian aid against France.

[2] Dwight E. Lee, 'The Proposed Mediterranean League of 1878', in *Journal of Modern History*, vol. 3 (1931), pp. 33–45.

[3] Chiala, *Pagine*, II, p. 107.

[4] Cilibrizzi, II, p. 162.

Corti accepted office only on the condition that collaboration with Austria-Hungary should be the keystone of the government's policy. Peace and equilibrium were his aims, and above all no adventures. He refused to see any threat to Italy in Austrian expansion in the Balkans. The whole idea of compensations seemed ridiculous to him: African colonies would mean expense and diplomatic complications, and public opinion was hostile; the Trentino could be obtained only by war.[1] He immediately rejected Disraeli's scheme for an anti-Russian League, not wishing to involve Italy with a bellicose, jingoistic Britain, and in April 1878 he allowed the talks with Austria-Hungary on Mediterranean compensations to peter out. On 6 June, after threatening to resign, he extracted from his colleagues the instructions that he wanted as delegate to the Congress of Berlin: he was to press for as limited and temporary an Austrian occupation of Bosnia as possible, and to consider sounding other Powers about compensations only if Andrássy insisted on annexation.[2] He arrived at the Congress resolved to cause no trouble. At the critical session of 28 June he gave his approval to Austria's occupation. Bismarck was delighted with him. But on 8 July even Corti was shaken when he learnt from the newspapers that the British had acquired their share of the loot from the Turks in the shape of Cyprus. He hurried to Bülow, the German second delegate, who suggested that Italy should take Tunis. 'So you want to embroil us with the French?', was Corti's reply, and he let the subject drop. Nor did he follow up Salisbury's guarded hints that there might be room in north Africa for both France at Tunis and Italy at Tripoli.[3] Disregarding Cairoli's agitated telegrams, he returned a few days later to Rome with hands that were both 'clean' and empty, as he had always intended.

[1] 'A thing that surprises me', he told the Austrian ambassador in Rome on 1 April, 'is that everyone is offering us something, even Prince Bismarck.' Albertini, *Origins*, I, p. 26; Sandonà, I, pp. 216–17.

[2] E. C. Corti, 'Il conte Corti al Congresso di Berlino', in *Nuova Antologia*, vol. 318 (April 1925), pp. 353–4.

[3] On 7 July Bismarck had promised Tunis to the French. Whether Bülow was aware of this, and whether Bismarck knew of Bülow's suggestion to Corti of 8 July, is uncertain. Chiala, *Pagine*, II, pp. 107–17; Salvatorelli, pp. 41–2; Albertini, *Origins*, I, pp. 28–30; W. L. Langer, 'The European Powers and the French Occupation of Tunis', in *American Historical Review*, vol. 31 (1925–6), pp. 65–71. The best comment on proceedings at the Congress is that of Corti, made several years later to Dilke: 'At that time everyone was promising everyone something that belonged to someone else.' S. Gwynn and G. Tuckwell, *Life of Sir Charles Dilke* (London 1917), I, p. 334. Corti wrote to Luzzatti in 1884: 'They wanted to tear me to pieces in 1878 because during the few weeks I spent in the jungle I was unable to get Italy a piece of Turkey, or even something nearer home, and contented myself with saving her from disgrace and war.' Luzzatti, *Memorie*, II, p. 92, note 2.

I L F—E

## Tunis

Italian interests suffered no immediate or irreparable damage at Berlin. Yet the results of the Congress were greeted in Italy by explosions of indignation. Corti was stoned in Milan. Crispi talked of national humiliation. Cairoli made the most of the fact that Bosnia had been occupied, not annexed;[1] but great expectations had been aroused and an excited public was in no mood to be reassured. In October Corti and the Ministers for War and the Navy resigned in protest against Cairoli's refusal to suppress anti-Austrian demonstrations. Resentment at Austria's triumph and Italy's failure found expression in intense irredentist agitation over the next two years. The Austrians showed great forbearance, realising that irredentism was a republican programme of which the King and most Italian statesmen disapproved; but they feared that Cairoli and Depretis were too weak to hold the wild men in check. In December 1879 the state funeral of General Giuseppe Avezzana, who had been Garibaldi's Minister for War in Rome in 1849 and organiser of the invasion of the Papal States in 1867, developed into an irredentist riot. A major diplomatic incident followed the revelation that members of the government had discussed the funeral arrangements with officials of the Italia Irredenta Association, of which Avezzana had been chairman. After this the government, prompted by Depretis as Minister of Interior, took more energetic action, and the following March Cairoli calmed relations between the two countries by declaring in the chamber that friendship with Austria meant far more to Italy than any frontier rectification.[2] Nevertheless in the spring of 1880 the Austrians reinforced their garrison in the Trentino and for a few weeks the tension seemed near breaking point.

During the winter of 1880–1 attempts were made on both sides to improve relations. Haymerlé, Andrássy's successor as Austro-Hungarian Foreign Minister, distrusted the Russians and would have welcomed an understanding with Italy. A possible basis might have been an Italian promise of neutrality in a war between Austria-Hungary and Russia, and an Austrian promise of support for Italian aspirations in north Africa. In their mood of frustration after the Congress of Berlin, many Italians who had contemptuously rejected the idea of compensation in Tunis now began to show interest in that country. But Haymerlé's overtures came to nothing for two reasons: first, because the Italians, particularly Depretis, still

---

[1] Andrássy told Corti that he had consented to occupation rather than annexation in order to please Italy. This was no doubt true, but he had the stronger motives of not wishing to provoke the Turks to resistance, nor to offend his Magyar compatriots by formally adding to Austria-Hungary's Slav subjects.

[2] Chiala, *Pagine*, II, p. 51.

hoped for friendship with France and were reluctant to commit themselves; second, because Bismarck had no desire to see Austro-Italian relations grow too friendly. The latter's policy at this time was to push Austria-Hungary towards Russia and revive the Three Emperors' League, which had been disrupted by the Eastern crisis of 1877–8. He therefore treated the Austrians throughout 1880 to apocalyptic pictures of an Italy on the brink of republicanism and disintegration. Obsessed by his *cauchemar des coalitions*, he imagined the Italians flirting with the Russians or, with less fantasy, making advances to his *bête noire*, Gladstone. When tension between Italy and Austria was at its height, he urged the latter to be tough. 'These Italians,' he said, 'have such a big appetite and such bad teeth'; they deserved a severe and humiliating warning.[1] Haymerlé rejected Bismarck's advice and worked successfully for a reduction of the tension. But such clear expressions of disapproval from his ally[2] ruined the chances of agreement with Italy. Thus in the spring of 1881, when the crisis came in Tunis, the Italians were isolated and friendless.

There were good reasons for Italy's growing interest in Tunis. Strategically it was most desirable to keep the fine potential naval base of Bizerta out of the hands of the French, who already possessed Corsica and Toulon. No country offered more promising prospects for emigration and trade. Its Italian community now numbered 11,000, while its French residents had still to be counted in hundreds. But the diplomatic situation was most unfavourable to Italy. Cairoli did not know that both Salisbury and Bismarck had promised at the Congress of Berlin not to oppose a French occupation; nor that Bismarck, eager to develop his *entente* with France and divert French attention from Alsace-Lorraine, was repeatedly inciting Jules Ferry's government to 'pluck the ripe Tunisian pear'. What should have been clear to Cairoli, for he received repeated warnings, was that the French intended to secure a controlling position in Tunis and would not tolerate an Italian challenge. They were, however, willing to discuss guarantees for existing Italian interests and compensation in Tripoli or elsewhere if they themselves occupied Tunis.

The last thing that Cairoli wanted was a quarrel with France. But after the excitement over the Treaty of Berlin, he saw that another 'humiliation' must be avoided. A French occupation of Tunis would not be acceptable even if accompanied by the promise of Tripoli for Italy. The only alternative was to work to preserve the existing situation, in which both French and Italian interests could have free play in Tunis. This was indeed

[1] Langer, 'The European Powers and the French Occupation of Tunis', in *American Historical Review*, vol. 31, p. 253; Pribram, II, p. 6.

[2] The Dual Alliance between Germany and Austria–Hungary was signed in October 1879. The Three Emperors' League was renewed in June 1881.

Cairoli's policy, as it had been that of the Right. But the French could be forgiven for otherwise interpreting some of Italy's actions. Cairoli's weak grip gave dangerous power to Macciò, the Italian consul in Tunis. For two and a half years a war of prestige and economic concessions was waged between him and his French colleague, Roustan.[1] In July 1880 the Italian Rubattino shipping company, backed by a financial guarantee from the government, bought up the Tunis–La Goulette railway at a huge price from its British owners, outbidding a French company. Next January a delegation of Italian settlers, led by Macciò and accompanied by a relative of the Bey, crossed to Sicily to present a provocative address of loyalty to King Humbert, and their return to Tunis was made the occasion for excited displays of Italian patriotism.

These incidents discredited Cairoli's repeated declarations of fraternal feelings towards France and played into the hands of the French colonialists. Until then important sections of French opinion had been opposed to African expansion. Gambetta, France's outstanding political figure, attached great importance to friendship with Italy and had many personal friends among the leaders of the Italian Left. Bismarck's incitements made French statesmen suspicious, and the replacement of the British Conservatives by the Italophil Gladstone in April 1880 made them hesitate further. But in the spring of 1881 the clamour in the French press, inspired by powerful economic interests, grew louder. Even Gambetta was converted to the view that the Italians were threatening the French position; believing that Trieste and the Trentino would always keep Italy and Austria apart, he gave his support to Ferry's plans.[2] On 24 April French troops from Algeria crossed the Tunisian frontier, on the pretext of punishing a raid by local Krumir tribesmen.[3] Cairoli, optimist to the end, believed their assurances that the occupation would be temporary. But on 12 May,

[1] The disastrous influence which Roustan and Macciò exercised over their governments emphasised the good sense of Visconti Venosta's remarks to the French representative in 1872, on the tendency of consuls *grossir les questions* in order to increase their own personal importance. Chabod, *Storia*, p. 597.

[2] Chiala, *Pagine*, II, p. 346.

[3] This pretext had been thought up as early as January by Roustan, who was even accused by his enemies of organising the raid. There had been 2,365 Krumir raids into Algeria in the previous ten years without any necessity for a punitive expedition. Rochefort, the French radical journalist, remarked in his paper *L'Intransigeant* that the government would pay 30,000 francs to anyone who could produce a Krumir to be shown to the troops. In fact the Krumirs either laid down their arms or fled or took employment with the invading army as porters for five francs a day. A. Giaccardi, *La conquista di Tunisi* (Milan 1940), pp. 207–9, 281–3; A. M. Broadley, *The Last Punic War* (Edinburgh 1882), I, pp. 204 ff., 344–5; Langer, 'The European Powers and the French Occupation of Tunis', in *American Historical Review*, vol. 31, p. 253, note; C. A. Julien, *Jules Ferry*, in *Les politiques d'expansion impérialiste* (Paris 1949), pp. 26–35.

by the Treaty of Bardo, what was virtually a French protectorate was established over the whole of Tunisia. Bismarck saw to it that there were no diplomatic complications. Gladstone's government, on which Cairoli had relied, showed displeasure but did nothing. The Italians were helpless.

## The Making of the Alliance

Italian fury over the Treaty of Bardo swept Cairoli out of power and brought back Depretis, with Pasquale Stanislao Mancini as his Foreign Minister. Italy had had enough for the moment of romantic heroes. But the French seizure of Tunis had more lasting effects. Like Mentana fourteen years before, it caused an emotional revulsion against France and brought to the surface, in their most virulent form, all the mutual suspicions that have so persistently divided the two Latin nations. In June a rumour that Italians in Marseilles had hissed French troops returning from Tunis started a *chasse aux Italiens* through the streets of the city – the first of many anti-Italian riots in southern France. In reply crowds shouted 'Down with France!' in the cities of northern Italy. Even Garibaldi, in the last year of his life, gave way to bitter contempt for the French republic for which he had fought in 1870. Depretis was urged by both Right and Left to repair the damage by drawing closer to Germany and Austria-Hungary. Among those who pleaded most insistently was Sonnino. 'Isolation', he argued, 'means for us annihilation'; Italy must forget Trieste, which was vital to Austria, and the Trentino, which was less valuable than Austrian friendship. 'Friendship with Austria', he wrote, 'is for us an indispensable condition for a conclusive and effective policy.'[1] After May 1881 Italian opinion swung decisively against the policy of neutrality which Visconti Venosta, Depretis and Cairoli had followed. Italy had decided it wanted allies.

In every section of political opinion there was a minority that resisted the clamour. Three leaders of the Right, Lanza, Peruzzi and Ruggero Bonghi, bravely blamed the Italian government more than the French for the Tunis affair, and remained faithful to the Cavourian tradition of collaboration with France. Bonghi was also one of the first to warn Italy against the perils of Bismarckian 'blood and iron'. On the Left, neither Depretis nor Mancini believed that Italy had suffered any great loss at Tunis, or wished to widen the breach with France.[2] Cavallotti, Imbriani and most of the Extreme Left still kept their eyes on Trent and Trieste, and retained their admiration for the French Republic. Six years before,

[1] Article in the *Rassegna Settimanale* of 29 May 1881, quoted in Chiala, *Pagine*, III, pp. 20–4.
[2] Chiala, *Pagine*, III, pp. 10–14.

at the height of the *Kulturkampf*, Bismarck had been their hero and a German alliance against clerical France their aim; now, with the French republicans firmly in power and the *Kulturkampf* over, it was the conservatives who wanted Bismarck's friendship, while the radicals and democrats looked once again to France as the champion of the Rights of Man. Thus, though individuals reversed their positions, the old cleavage between partisans of France and Germany persisted. But Tunis killed much of the Left's sympathy with France. To all except incorrigible Francophils it seemed that the French republicans had proved as hostile to Italian aspirations as Napoleon III and the clericals. The sharp pain of Tunis obscured the old ache of Trent and Trieste, and made Austria-Hungary acceptable as an ally even to old militants like Crispi. Even before Tunis, Crispi had reached the conclusion that

> the Austro-Hungarian Empire is a necessity for us. It and the Swiss Confederation keep us at a reasonable distance from other nations which we wish to be our friends, which must be our friends, as they were once our allies, but whose territory it is as well should not be in immediate contact with Italy.[1]

Thus Garibaldi's lieutenant of 1860, who as late as 1877 had suggested to Bismarck that German unity was incomplete without German-Austria,[2] moved one step further from the ideals of Mazzini and the principle of nationality, and became, like Visconti Venosta, Sonnino and Robilant, a disciple of Cesare Balbo and an apologist for Austria-Hungary as an indispensable buffer.[3] Crispi, thirsting for action, power and greatness, attributed all Italy's setbacks since 1870 to flabby, mediocre governments. He now felt sure that the way to national greatness was alliance with Germany and Austria-Hungary.

There were further motives for seeking alliance with the central Empires. Many conservatives believed that the Tunisian fiasco had shaken the prestige, not only of government and parliament, but also of the monarchy. Humbert could not command the same devotion and loyalty as Victor Emmanuel, 'the Father of the Fatherland'. Militant republicanism, irredentism, anti-clericalism and the forces of social disorder seemed to be lifting their heads again, subsidised, it was widely believed, by French extremists bent on the creation of a subservient Italian republic. In 1881 the Extreme Left was also campaigning for a repeal of the Law of Guarantees, and on 12 July occurred an incident which brought Italy into

---

[1] Speech of 23 March 1880, in ibid., II, p. 58; Cilibrizzi, II, p. 195.

[2] Crispi, *Memoirs*, II, p. 34; Chabod, *Storia*, pp. 75 ff.

[3] In March 1878 even Cavallotti demanded friendship with Austria – but an Austria shorn of Trieste and the Trentino. In his case hatred of Tsarist Russia, at that moment almost master of the Balkans, had eclipsed the old hatred of Austria – but only for a time.

universal disrepute. The remains of Pius IX were being carried from St Peter's to their final resting place in the Basilica of San Lorenzo when a hostile mob attacked the procession as it crossed the Tiber and attempted to throw the coffin into the river. Leo XIII, believing an attack on the Vatican was imminent, appealed for help to Francis Joseph and prepared to leave Rome. This recrudescence of the Roman question was one more reason for Italy to find allies quickly.

Yet a whole year passed between the occupation of Tunis and the signing of the Triple Alliance. Depretis and Mancini shrank from a painful decision. Magliani, engaged in his operations to restore convertibility of the lira, hoped to retain the goodwill of French bankers and investors. In November 1881 a favourable commercial treaty with France was signed.[1] French governments, now that Tunis was safe, went out of their way to be conciliatory. But probably Depretis's main motive for caution was his reluctance to risk strengthening conservative and clerical forces in Italy by alliance with Germany and Austria-Hungary. Friendship with republican France still seemed to him essential for Italy's healthy development. A further argument for delay was put forward by Robilant in Vienna; he saw how little his country would gain from an alliance if it threw itself into the arms of Germany and Austria when its bargaining position was at its weakest. After the renewal of the Three Emperors' League in June 1881, neither Bismarck nor the Austrians had much need of Italy.

Nevertheless, under the pressure of public opinion, Depretis and Mancini moved step by step towards an alliance. The King, too, played an important part, and in October 1881 insisted on paying a state visit to Vienna.[2] At the end of November Bismarck referred pointedly in the Reichstag to Germany's friendly relations with the Vatican, and the German press, inspired from above, began to discuss the Pope's insecurity. The threat of a revival of the Roman question[3] induced the Italian government to make its first definite request for an alliance in December. The Austrians were encouraging. Bismarck at first laid down stiff conditions, but he dropped them in February when rumours of talks between France and Russia once again gave him bad dreams, this time of a coalition between France, Russia and a republican Italy. On 20 May 1882 the treaty of the Triple Alliance was signed in Vienna.[4]

[1] See above, pp. 64, 82.
[2] In later years Humbert liked to speak of the Triple Alliance as his own idea and creation. Finali, pp. 407, 689.
[3] Bismarck's motives were primarily domestic. The German Catholic Centre party had won many seats in the election of October 1881 and he needed its votes in the Reichstag.
[4] The best summary of the negotiations is in Langer, *European Alliances and Alignments*, ch. 7. For text of the treaty, see Pribram, I, pp. 64–73.

Under its terms Germany and Austria-Hungary undertook to assist Italy, and Italy to assist Germany, if either was attacked by France. It also bound all three allies to assist each other, if one or two of them were attacked by two or more Great Powers. Though Bismarck forbade any mention of Russia in the text, this second clause was clearly framed to deal with aggression by a Franco-Russian combination. A further clause provided for the benevolent neutrality of two of the allies, if the third started a preventive war: which meant Italian neutrality if Germany attacked France or Austria attacked Russia. The treaty contained no territorial guarantees: neither did Italy renounce Trieste and the Trentino, nor did Austria abandon the Pope. Nevertheless it ended the acutest phase of the Roman question, which now became largely a domestic matter. No longer would the Italians be embarrassed by German or Austrian intrigues with the Vatican, and they could deal confidently with French threats when they had two allies behind them. This was their greatest gain from the Alliance. Italy was no longer isolated, with hostile neighbours on both frontiers.

It was a conservative, limited, defensive treaty. Its conservative character was made plain in the preamble, which stated the intention of the three sovereigns 'to fortify the monarchical principle' and so strengthen European peace and the political and social order. The formula sounded sweet to Humbert and his advisers, with their exaggerated fears of republicanism, and closely reflected the views of Kálnoky, Austro-Hungarian Foreign Minister since October 1881. Kálnoky believed that to bolster up the Italian monarchy was to bolster up the Papacy. At this time Francis Joseph and he did their utmost to promote reconciliation between Italy and the Vatican. They warned Leo XIII of the risks of leaving Rome and tried to persuade him that the Italian monarchy was a bulwark against the Papacy's most dangerous enemy, revolution. Though Leo listened to these counsels of caution, he was never convinced by the argument. The formation of the Triple Alliance was a bitter blow to him, softened only in part by Francis Joseph's promise that he would never visit the King of Italy in Rome.[1] Kálnoky nevertheless persisted in looking upon the Alliance as an organisation of the forces of Catholicism and order against the three subversive forces of atheistic republicanism, irredentist nationalism and Panslavism.[2] This ideological inspiration of the Alliance in great part explains its later decline. Italy's internal development before and after 1882 resembled that of the French Third Republic. The latent conflict between liberal progress at home and collaboration with two illiberal empires abroad subjected the Alliance to increasing strain as the years passed.[3]

[1] See further below, pp. 215–16.
[2] Chabod, 'Kulturkampf e Triplice Alleanza', pp. 261–4, 272–8.
[3] Chabod, *Storia*, p. 463.

Article I defined the limited character of the treaty. The three states undertook to exchange ideas 'on political and economic questions of a general nature which may arise' and promised each other 'mutual support within the limits of their own interests'. The Triple Alliance was thus not a treaty of unlimited solidarity: it was a system of restricted pledges in defined areas. It contained no mention of the Balkans: firstly, because Kálnoky did not want to give the Italians an excuse for interfering there; secondly, because Bismarck wished to minimise its anti-Russian aspect. What was even more serious for Italy was that it contained no mention of the Mediterranean. Popular enthusiasm for friendship with Germany was based on the assumption that, with the help of allies, it would be possible, if not to force the French out of Tunis, then at least to obtain satisfaction elsewhere for wounded national pride. After 1881 Italian interest in north and east Africa grew steadily. But from the first both Bismarck and Kálnoky insisted on a restrictive interpretation of Article I: they had signed a conservative treaty which could not be distorted to cover Italian Mediterranean or colonial adventures. The guarantee against France was thus reduced to very little, for there was no likelihood, except in the imagination of the wilder Italians, of a French attack on Italy in Europe.

On the whole these limitations worked to the disadvantage of the Italians. But they themselves insisted upon one most important limitation. Three identical declarations were appended to the treaty in which the allies stated that it 'cannot, as has been previously agreed, in any circumstances be regarded as being directed against England'. This was a matter essential to Italian security. Italy felt comfortable in the Triple Alliance only as long as Germany and Britain were on friendly terms.

The Italians did not enter the Alliance as equals; negotiating from weakness, they joined a well-established Austro-German partnership. Never did they enjoy such intimacy with their allies as Austria-Hungary and Germany enjoyed with each other. Germany was always the dominant partner, who looked with jealousy on too much cordiality between Austria and Italy, and tried to ensure that the only road from Rome to Vienna ran through Berlin. Neither Bismarck nor his successors set much value on Italian military aid. Many years later Bismarck said that he would be content if, during a war in which Germany and Austria were involved, 'one Italian corporal with the Italian flag and a drummer at his side should take the field on the western front against France and not on the eastern front against Austria'.[1] Bismarck's main gain from the Alliance

[1] The Emperor William I did not share this view. In January 1882 he reminded Bismarck that the 130,000 troops which the Austrians sent against Italy in 1866 might have changed Sadowa from a Prussian to an Austrian victory. Albertini,

was that it removed all fears of a combination between Russia, France and an Italian republic which might be too strong for Austria-Hungary and Germany. After 1882 it was no longer Austria, but France, which was faced with the threat of a war on two fronts.

## The Founding of an Empire

By Article VI of the treaty, not only its contents but also its existence were to be kept secret. In fact it became known in the spring of 1883 that an Alliance had been signed, though its exact terms were revealed only in 1920. Throughout the rest of 1882 there was no obvious sign of a change in Italy's position. During the Egyptian crisis of July, Italy received no backing from Germany or Austria-Hungary, and in September another grave incident occurred in Italo-Austrian relations.

Of the many European communities in Egypt, the Italian was the second largest, being outnumbered only by the Greeks. Italian commercial and financial interests were not negligible. But all requests to Britain and France for a share in the administration of the country had met with rebuffs. In the summer of 1882, when Arabi Pasha's nationalist movement began to threaten the whole system of European control in Egypt, Mancini fought hard to prevent an exclusive Anglo-French condominium and to establish the principle of joint intervention by the European Concert. When the British, having quarrelled with the French, suddenly asked Italy on 26 July to intervene with them to restore order, Mancini had irrevocably committed himself to international action and felt bound to decline. He had other reasons as well: fear of the French reaction, lack of military preparation and apprehension about the cost and difficulty of the enterprise. Public opinion was mostly sympathetic to Arabi, in whom it saw an Egyptian Garibaldi leading a struggle for national liberation. Mancini was also uncomfortably aware of Bismarck's disapproval: Egypt was not covered by the Triple Alliance and no help could be expected if trouble with the French occurred. It was a situation that required a Cavour: Mancini was wise to refuse.[1] But as the facts became known, and the ease with which the British pacified Egypt was observed, a reaction set in which was comparable to that which followed the Congress of Berlin. Crispi, who was in London at the time, was furious. Sonnino and Minghetti joined in the laments of a lost opportunity. The episode left feelings of frustration and humiliation behind it.[2]

---

*Origins*, I, p. 42. One of the Italian government's first actions after concluding the Alliance was to increase the strength of the army from 10 to 12 army corps (20 to 25 divisions).          [1] Morandi, p. 118.

[2] Lucien E. Roberts, 'Italy and the Egyptian Question 1878–82', in *Journal of Modern History*, vol. 18 (1946), pp. 314–32.

Two months later a young Trieste student named Guglielmo Oberdan was betrayed to the Austrian police and arrested. On him were found two bombs with which he had planned to assassinate Francis Joseph during a visit to Trieste. Oberdan had deserted from the Austrian army in 1878 and gone to Rome University. There he soon made his mark in irredentist circles and decided that 'the cause of Trieste had need of the blood of a Trieste martyr'. Francis Joseph refused to reprieve him and on 20 December 1882 he was hanged, his last words on the scaffold being 'Long live Italy! Long live free Trieste!' At once he became a national martyr. Oberdan associations sprang up all over Italy. Carducci invoked justice against the hangman emperor. Cavallotti declared that 'beside the pale martyr's corpse, Italy's honour swung in the noose'.[1] The government did its best to calm the storm, confiscated irredentist newspapers and broke up a protest meeting in Piazza Sciarra in Rome. But Oberdan's death left a permanent mark on Austro-Italian relations.

Bad feeling also arose from Francis Joseph's failure to visit Rome.

[1] Cilibrizzi, II, p. 259.

Humbert's visit to Vienna in October 1881 was never returned because successive Italian governments insisted that a visit to any other city but Rome would be a national insult. As the years passed, Italian resentment over this issue became a serious weakness in the Triple Alliance. The Italians were still further disillusioned when they discovered that the Alliance gave them no say in the Balkans. In March 1884 they were neither consulted nor informed when the Three Emperors' League was renewed. In September the three emperors met at Skiernewice to discuss Balkan affairs. When Mancini, taking his stand on Article I of the Triple Alliance, asked to be informed of the outcome of the discussions, he was told that the Balkans concerned only Russia and Austria-Hungary.[1]

The Oberdan affair caused satisfaction in France, where it was interpreted as proof that Italy and Austria could never be friends. Many leading Frenchmen had believed in May 1881 that, with the Tunisian irritation out of the way, cordiality could quickly be restored between the two Latin nations. Depretis shared their hopes and never intended the Triple Alliance to preclude friendship with France. But when the existence of the Alliance became known in the spring of 1883,[2] the French reacted strongly. It took them fifteen years to forgive Italy for becoming the ally of Germany, and one of the main aims of their foreign policy now became to force Italy out of the Alliance.

Mancini soon realised that in such a situation Bismarck could not be relied upon. In the years 1882–5 the latter set a higher value on his *entente* with France than his alliance with Italy. The Italians, whose anger over Tunis had driven them into Bismarck's arms, now found their ally pressing them to abandon their African hopes. In the spring of 1884 France appeared to be contemplating seizure of part of Morocco. Mancini shared the common view that this would alter the Mediterranean equilibrium to Italy's disadvantage and he was determined to prevent it. To renounce Italian aspirations in north Africa would, he had declared in 1883, be 'a policy of suicide, a treasonable crime'.[3] But when he appealed to Bismarck for diplomatic support, he was brusquely advised not to cause complications with France just because of vague alarms over largely imaginary Italian interests all over the Mediterranean.[4] Undeterred, the Italian government felt bound to take precautions. In October 1884 General

[1] Chiala, *Pagine*, III, pp. 368–72, 401.

[2] Mancini made the first public reference in his parliamentary speech of 15 March, with the intention of showing that his foreign policy had not been as sterile as his critics claimed. Salvatorelli, pp. 74–5; Chiala, *Pagine*, III, pp. 333–9.

[3] Zaghi, pp. 25–6.

[4] GP, III, 678–9; Zaghi, pp. 28–9, 141–3, 147–8. Mancini also appealed to Austria and received an equally unhelpful, though courteous, reply. Zaghi, pp. 139–41.

Ricotti, a leading figure of the Right, entered the cabinet as Minister for War. Next month he was authorised to prepare in secrecy an expeditionary force of 30,000 men, to be held at ten days' notice to sail to Tripoli and Benghazi if the French moved into Morocco.[1] Fortunately the Moroccan scare subsided at the end of the year and Italy was spared a risky enterprise. Mancini achieved his aim of maintaining the Mediterranean *status quo*. But the incident showed that Italy was almost as friendless and impotent as four years before. The Three Emperors' League and the Franco-German *entente* formed a loose continental bloc from which Italy was excluded. The one consolation was British friendship, which found its expression in continuous collaboration in Egypt and in 1882-5 led to the creation of a modest Italian empire, not in north Africa but far away on the Red Sea.

The opening of the Suez Canal in 1869 had stimulated Italian interest in the Red Sea coast of Africa and its hinterland. Backed by geographical societies and chambers of commerce in Genoa, Florence and Milan, explorers penetrated first the Somali coast, then Ethiopia, then the remote interior. Some of these men were private adventurers, others were missionaries or scientists; many, convinced that Suez should be 'the highway of the Italians', were inspired by a passionate longing to take civilisation to darkest Africa and to hear the name of Italy on native lips.[2] Victor Emmanuel was personally interested, and it was thanks to his intervention that in 1870 the Rubattino shipping company bought the port of Assab from a local sultan. Its early history only encouraged the pessimists who felt that colonies were useless for Italy. Britain under Disraeli showed extreme sensitiveness to the presence of a European power on the route to India, and did its utmost between 1874 and 1880 to stir up the Egyptians, who claimed sovereignty over the area, to resist Italian encroachments.[3] Assab remained a sun-parched desert port with little trade, a tiny hinterland and, owing to Egyptian opposition, no Italian garrison or administration.

After 1880 the situation changed. Gladstone's government, with its more cautious imperial policy, attached less importance to exclusive control of the Red Sea, and even encouraged Italy to consolidate its position. In March 1882 the Italian government bought Assab from the Rubattino

[1] Zaghi, pp. 55-6, 69-72, 151-3; Battaglia, pp. 166-7.
[2] Volpe, I, pp. 93-105, 163-8; Ciasca, pp. 39-56; Battaglia, pp. 146 ff.
[3] A. Ramm, 'Great Britain and the Planting of Italian Power in the Red Sea', in *English Historical Review*, vol. 59 (1944), pp. 216-21; Chiala, *La spedizione di Massawa*, pp. 8 ff.; Ciasca, pp. 70 ff. The Red Sea littoral had been in Turkish possession since the sixteenth century. The Egyptians took over Massawa in 1865 and in the course of the next ten years extended their occupation both inland and down the coast as far as Harrar.

company and in June, with British approval, it became Italy's first colony. In July the Italians rejected the British invitation to intervene in Egypt. But soon the victories of the Mahdi in the Sudan began to threaten the whole Egyptian position down the Red Sea coast, and it became necessary to withdraw the Egyptian garrisons. The French had been established since 1862 at Obock, on the Somali coast, and now showed signs of preparing to fill the vacuum. To forestall them, the British occupied Zeila in August and Berbera in October 1884, in what was later to become British Somaliland; but they were unwilling to plunge into Harrar and the hinterland, which were in a state of anarchy. Italian collaboration thus became important to them, and Italy seized the opportunity, with British benevolence, to found an east African empire of its own.

There had been a great change in Italian opinion since the French seizure of Tunis. Some conservatives were still anti-colonialist, believing that Italy was too young and poor for African adventures. On the Left and Extreme Left, too, there were many who, like Carducci, condemned colonial expansion as a betrayal of the Risorgimento's ideals of freedom and self-determination. But even the Extreme Left was divided, with Bovio, the republican, arguing that African natives had no right to barbarism. The desire to prevent further French aggrandisement, and the example of the Germans, who in 1884 made their first bid for colonies, stimulated colonialist agitation. The greatest enthusiasm was to be found in the south, where agrarian misery and the pressure of overpopulation made emigration to an overseas territory under the Italian flag attractive. But Italy, with its infant industry, adverse trade balance and lack of capital, did not have the same economic urge towards empire as more advanced European nations. Italian colonialism was largely imitative.

In October 1883 the murder of the explorer Gustavo Bianchi by natives in the hinterland of Assab provided a welcome element of drama in the monotony of life under Depretis. Mancini, like Depretis, had hitherto been interested solely in the Mediterranean and had rejected colonial conquest further afield as productive only of unwelcome expense and diplomatic complications. But he was a Neapolitan and Italy's first southern Foreign Minister. He was also reluctant, after the Egyptian incident of 1882, to expose himself a second time to the charge of 'renunciation'. Under the pressure of public opinion his views changed, and in the autumn of 1884 he too was caught by the imperialist fever. When the plan for occupying Tripoli was abandoned in December, he turned his eyes decisively towards the Red Sea and began to dream not only of replacing the Egyptians at Harrar and on the coast north and south of Assab, but of establishing Italian power on the Indian Ocean, as far south as the fertile Juba valley, and making Italy predominant in Ethiopia and the Sudan.

For such plans British approval was essential; but Granville, the British Foreign Secretary, after being the first to broach the subject unofficially in October 1884, later became 'evasive and dilatory', not wishing to offend the Egyptians or the Turks. Much pestering was needed to extract from him a declaration that he would raise no objection to an Italian occupation of Massawa.[1] At last, on 17 January 1885, a battalion of Bersaglieri sailed from Naples, amid great popular enthusiasm and evocations of Garibaldi's embarkation at Genoa in 1860, and three weeks later Massawa was occupied. The British were pleased, the French were forestalled, Italian prestige was satisfied and Bianchi's death was avenged.

Mancini meant Massawa to be only the first step. On 27 January he had turned on the parliamentary critics of the expedition with the words, 'Why won't you recognise that in the Red Sea, the closest to the Mediter-ranean, we may find the key of the latter, the road that will lead us to effective security from new disturbance of its equilibrium?'[2] His eyes were on the Sudan, where joint action with the British against the Mahdi might wipe out the Egyptian failure of 1882 and, by creating bonds of common African interests, prepare the way for that British alliance in the Mediterranean which every Italian statesman desired. The concept did not lack courage and grandeur. But the dreams quickly evaporated with the death of Gordon in Khartoum in January.[3] The British declined a pressing offer of Italian military help, first made on 9 February and repeated in March, and soon afterwards decided not to reconquer the Sudan.[4] The Anglo-Italian alliance and the key of the Mediterranean vanished, and Italy was left isolated and 'chained to a rock in the Red Sea'.[5] Mancini had roused big expectations and now his critics set upon him. In Italy, as elsewhere, colonial expansion was popular only when success was quick and cheap. In March 1885 the Egyptians evacuated Harrar. Mancini offered to occupy it and to take over Zeila, Harrar's port, from the British. Granville gave a cautious assent, but with the return to

[1] Zaghi, pp. 89–91, 156–63; C. Giglio, 'L'Inghilterra e l'impresa di Massawa', in *Nuova Antologia*, vol. 456 (November 1952), pp. 251–77. Granville gave no encouragement to Mancini's suggestion that Italy should also occupy Harrar. C. Giglio, 'Il primo tentativo di Mancini per Zeila e l'Harar', in *Il Risorgimento*, October 1954.

[2] Chiala, *Massawa*, p. 171; Battaglia, p. 180.

[3] The news of the fall of Khartoum reached Rome on the same day as Massawa was occupied. Chiala, *Massawa*, p. 191.

[4] Zaghi, pp. 92–4, 104–6, 166–74, 178–80. The only form of help agreeable to Granville was an Italian expedition to relieve the besieged Egyptian garrison at Kassala, to be undertaken as 'une œuvre d'humanité', without any commitment on Britain's part. Mancini not unreasonably declined this suggestion of 'le rôle d'un chevalier d'aventure'.

[5] Chiala, *Massawa*, p. 247.

power of the Conservatives under Salisbury in June the scheme had to be abandoned.[1] Mancini was attacked both for doing too much and for doing too little. Sonnino accused him of straining the Triple Alliance by going to Massawa without consulting his allies.[2] Crispi poured scorn on his puny achievement and lamented that since 1882 Depretis's *Italietta* had missed every opportunity of becoming a truly great nation. On 17 June, discredited and discouraged, Mancini resigned.

## The Transformation of the Alliance

Mancini's successor was Count Carlo di Robilant, who had been ambassador in Vienna since 1871. There he had acquired a mastery of European diplomacy and a knowledge of the Eastern question that was unrivalled in Italy. He came of a Piedmontese noble family and was well connected in the European aristocracy. Before 1871 he had had a distinguished military career, losing a hand in action in 1849 and rising to the rank of general. As a diplomatist he soon proved a worthy disciple of Cavour. He was a man of strong character, accustomed to action, and had no use for sentiment or emotion in foreign policy; his motto was *Faire sans dire*. As Foreign Minister he was handicapped by his lack of oratorical skill and his impatience with parliamentary niceties. But his courage, experience and clarity of vision enabled him to give Italy a purposeful and coherent foreign policy for the first time since 1876.[3]

Robilant disapproved of Mancini's colonial policy. Compared with Italy's European and Mediterranean interests, expansion on the Red Sea seemed a futile and possibly dangerous diversion. But Massawa could not be abandoned, so he set about consolidating the colony. Its Egyptian garrison was ejected, Italian troops were pushed a limited distance into the interior and efforts were made to establish friendly relations with the two main powers of the region, the Emperor John IV of Ethiopia and Ras Menelik of Shoa.[4] British opposition made him deaf to all suggestions that Italy should occupy Harrar and he took no action when Menelik captured and sacked it.[5] Robilant was determined that there should be no further Italian conquests. The task he set himself was to improve Italy's position

---

[1] C. Zaghi, 'Perchè l'Italia non occupò Zeila e Harar nel 1885', in *Nuova Antologia*, vol. 411 (September 1940), pp. 42–9; Salata, *Il nodo di Gibuti*, pp. 12–16.

[2] Mancini had not in fact informed Germany and Austria-Hungary beforehand.

[3] Chiala, *Pagine*, III, pp. 400, 417, 472; Chabod, *Storia*, pp. 625 ff.

[4] Chiala, *Massawa*, pp. 290 ff.; Battaglia, p. 215 ff. Ras Menelik was the Emperor's most powerful, and largely nominal, vassal, and a grandson of one of his predecessors. Shoa is the central region of Ethiopia, in which Addis Ababa, the present capital, is situated.

[5] Salata, *Il nodo di Gibuti*, pp. 16–17.

in Europe. He saw only too clearly the shortcomings of the Triple Alliance which, as one of Mancini's critics had said in June, made Italy and the central empires 'allies but not friends' and Italy a mere auxiliary. If it was to be renewed before it expired in May 1887, he intended it to be on a very different basis. He was not going to be rushed like Depretis and Mancini in 1882, or overawed by Bismarck, 'the *pro tempore* master of the world'.[1] 'Italy is weary of this sterile alliance', he wrote in June 1886 to his ambassador in Berlin, who was urging him to open negotiations at once, 'and I have no desire to force her to renew it, for I feel too deeply that it will always be unproductive for us . . . I shall not fall into the error committed by my predecessor.' He refused to meet Bismarck and gave instructions that the Germans or Austrians were to be left to make the first move.[2]

This confident and independent attitude was justified by the international situation, which Robilant saw was rapidly changing to Germany's disadvantage. In March 1885 Jules Ferry's fall from power had killed the Franco-German *entente*. In September the union of Bulgaria with Eastern Rumelia, in defiance of the Treaty of Berlin, had reopened the Eastern question. The tortuous struggle for predominance in Bulgaria, into which Austria-Hungary and Russia plunged, disrupted the Three Emperors' League. A wave of Panslavism in Russia coincided with the rise of General Boulanger in France, and in the autumn of 1886 the two countries seemed to be drawing closer. These events enormously increased Italy's value to Germany. With great skill Robilant pressed home his advantage. He warned Kálnoky that the Italians would no longer tolerate exclusion from the Balkans and pressed for the Bulgarian crisis to be handled by the European Concert, of which Italy must be a full and equal member. When the French made overtures for a Mediterranean agreement which would have involved their renunciation of Tripoli, provided Italy abandoned the Triple Alliance, Robilant went out of his way to express friendly feelings, at the same time keeping Germany informed of the talks. Thus he strengthened his bargaining position and played upon Bismarck's old fear of a Franco-Russo-Italian combination.

By October 1886 Bismarck realised that concessions would have to be made and he took the initiative in opening negotiations that Robilant had confidently awaited. The latter now demanded the extension of the Triple Alliance to both the Mediterranean and the Balkans. The Mediterranean,

---

[1] Chabod, *Storia*, p. 634.
[2] Chiala, *Pagine*, III, pp. 465–78. It is unlikely that Robilant would in fact ever have refused to renew the Alliance. As Costantino Nigra, the veteran ambassador in Vienna, pointed out to him, 'After ending an alliance, it is difficult to remain friends as before, however explicitly one may say so. Something will have changed, perhaps more in appearance than reality, but it will have changed, or at least people will think it has. And here lies the danger.'

he argued, was as important to Italy as were the Balkans to Austria or Alsace-Lorraine to Germany: an alliance which failed to guarantee Italy's Mediterranean interests was therefore worthless. Kálnoky struggled to keep Italy out of the Balkans and to avoid Austrian commitments in the Mediterranean. But Robilant stood firm. Under relentless pressure from Bismarck, Kálnoky was forced step by step to yield, and on 20 February 1887 the second treaty of the Triple Alliance was signed in Berlin. It gave Robilant almost all that he had asked for.[1]

In form it was somewhat complicated. The 1882 text was renewed unchanged for five years, but to it were added separate German-Italian and Austro-Italian treaties. A protocol stressed the common spirit behind all three. As regards the Mediterranean, Bismarck agreed that if the French threatened Morocco or Tripoli, and Italy felt it necessary to oppose them, Germany would come to the latter's assistance. It was further agreed that if Italy required 'territorial guarantees' from France after victory in such a war, Germany would 'in a measure compatible with circumstances' support Italian demands. Nice, and perhaps Corsica, were probably in Robilant's mind. The Austrians took on no Mediterranean commitments, arguing with justification that they were too weak to do so. In the Balkans Italy and Austria-Hungary agreed to preserve the *status quo* and to exchange information on their own and other governments' plans. If, however, either Austria or Italy should be compelled to modify the *status quo* 'in the regions of the Balkans or of the Ottoman coasts and islands in the Adriatic and the Aegean Sea' by a temporary or permanent occupation, this could only take place

after a previous agreement between the two said Powers, based upon the principle of a reciprocal compensation for every advantage, territorial or other, which each of them might obtain beyond the present *status quo*, and giving satisfaction to the interests and well-founded claims of the two Parties.[2]

Germany also undertook to support the *status quo* 'on the Ottoman coasts and islands in the Adriatic and Aegean Seas'; the general phrase 'regions of the Balkans' was deliberately omitted from the German-Italian treaty in order not to commit Germany to opposing Russia in Bulgaria or at the Straits. Bismarck still refused to allow the Triple Alliance to be aimed directly at Russia.

Robilant thus obtained for Italy, at last, a foothold in the Balkans. By the

[1] The best summary of the negotiations is in Langer, *European Alliances and Alignments*, pp. 388–95.

[2] This Article I of the Austro–Italian treaty became Article VII of the revised Triple Alliance of 1891 and regulated relations between the two countries up to 1915. See below, p. 149. For text of treaty, see Pribram, I, pp. 104–15.

new treaty he hoped it would be possible to limit Austria's *Drang nach Osten* by compromise and cooperation, and at the same time to create a solid Austro-Italian front against Panslavism and the expansion of Russia which, in the tradition of Cesare Balbo, he considered the greater danger.[1] If the Austrians could not be restrained, Italy would at least be entitled to compensation; henceforth they could not move down towards Salonika without at least conceding Albania to Italy. Kálnoky saw very clearly the dangers of the compensation clause. In vain he attempted to have inserted an agreement that Austro-Hungarian territories could not be demanded as compensation, and that Italy would be entitled to nothing if Austria-Hungary in the future annexed Bosnia. The Italians noted Austrian reservations on these two points, but made no official renunciation of Trieste and the Trentino.[2]

Robilant did not ask for a renewal of the 1882 declaration that the Alliance could never be directed against Britain. It seemed to him unnecessary because eight days previously the British and Italian governments had agreed in an exchange of notes to cooperate for the maintenance of the *status quo* in the Mediterranean, the Adriatic, the Aegean and Black Seas. The Italian note further stated that Italy would support Britain in Egypt, while Britain was 'disposed, in case of encroachments on the part of a third Power, to support the action of Italy at every other point whatsoever of the North African coast districts, and especially in Tripolitania and Cyrenaica'. Salisbury's reply was much more cautious, and stated that 'the character of the cooperation' between the two governments 'must be decided by them, when the occasion for it arises, according to the circumstances of the case'.[3] This understanding, now known as the First Mediterranean Agreement, owed much to Bismarck's efforts. Bismarck needed Britain to bolster up Austria-Hungary in the Balkans and provide the extra strength against Russia which he himself was not prepared to give at the risk of a German-Russian rupture. Italy was the link between Austria and Britain; hence the increased value to Germany of the Triple Alliance. Both Bismarck and Robilant tried hard to tie Salisbury closer; but the latter refused to commit his country in advance to any course of action in an undefined situation. The exchange of notes bound only his government, did not require parliamentary sanction and was known only to his cabinet and the Queen. It was, he reported to her, 'as close an alliance as the parliamentary character of our institutions will permit'. Its value to Italy was therefore limited. On the British side it was never intended to

[1] As Chabod, *Storia*, pp. 472–3, points out, Article VII was the diplomatic application of Cesare Balbo's doctrines.
[2] Albertini, *Origins*, I, pp. 54–5.
[3] Texts in Pribram, I, pp. 94–7.

lead to action.[1] Yet it was a great gain that Britain was now associated, however loosely, with the Triple Alliance. On 24 March Austria-Hungary adhered to the agreement and in May Spain was brought in. Italy thus became the centre of a defensive Mediterranean system.[2]

The second Triple Alliance and the First Mediterranean Agreement together gave Italy security on land and on sea.[3] Without undertaking any extra commitments against either France or Russia, Robilant had obtained insurance against a 'Tunisification' of Morocco or Tripoli, and had taken the first of the many diplomatic steps which were to lead up to the conquest of Tripoli in 1911. He had also asserted Italy's right to an equal say in the affairs of the Balkans. The Alliance remained limited: Egypt and the Red Sea were still outside its provisions, Austria was not directly involved in the Mediterranean, and Germany was only partially committed in eastern Europe. It also remained defensive, since the Italians could not call on German support in either Europe or north Africa unless their interests were threatened by France. From Italy's viewpoint the 1887 system of alliances and agreements rested on four pillars: good relations between Britain and the central empires, and friction between Britain and France; a French threat of renewed expansion in north Africa; the menace of international exploitation of the Roman question; and Italian confidence in Austria's readiness to collaborate in the Balkans.[4] While these four pillars stood firm, Italian loyalty to the Triple Alliance remained unshakeable.

It was ironic that a fortnight before the treaty was signed, its chief architect should have decided to leave office. East Africa was Robilant's

---

[1] In February 1896 Salisbury made this comment on the agreement to the Austrian ambassador: 'Je Vous l'avouerai franchement, c'est que cet accord ne m'engage pas à grand chose, car il ne nous oblige pas à faire la guerre.' E. Walters, 'Lord Salisbury's Refusal to Revise and Renew the Mediterranean Agreements', in *The Slavonic Review*, vol. 29 (1950–1), p. 283. On the other hand, in order to reassure the Italians, Salisbury had stated in February 1887 that an exchange of notes 'would have the same effect for England as if they were to make a treaty'. Lowe, p. 17.

[2] Langer, *European Alliances*, pp. 395–405; Lowe, pp. 12–18. By the Italo-Spanish agreement of 4 May 1887 Spain undertook, from the desire to fortify the monarchical principle and strengthen peace, to support the Mediterranean *status quo* and to make no agreement with France with respect to north Africa that was directed against any member of the Triple Alliance. Austria–Hungary and Germany acceded to the agreement and its text was communicated to Salisbury. For details of the negotiations, which started in September 1886 with an unsuccessful request from Spain to be allowed to adhere to the Triple Alliance, see F. Curato, *La questione marocchina e gli accordi mediterranei italo-spagnoli del 1887 e del 1891*, I (Milan 1961). Text in Pribram, I, pp. 116-23.

[3] As Depretis told his cabinet. Chiala, *Pagine*, III, p. 703.

[4] Salvemini, *La politica estera dell' Italia*, p. 80.

downfall. In the course of 1886 it became clear that Italy's efforts to establish friendly relations with the Emperor John had not overcome Ethiopian resentment at Italian encroachment. Robilant duly reinforced the Massawa garrison. But at a time when he was engaged in the most delicate negotiations in Europe, he could not conceal his view that east Africa was an insignificant sideshow. On 24 January 1887, on being questioned in the chamber about the Ethiopian threat to Massawa, he protested against so much importance being attached to a handful of African bandits.[1] One week later news reached Rome that a column of 500 Italian troops had been wiped out by several thousand Ethiopians at Dogali, after fighting almost to the last man and last round. This 'Italian Thermopylae' caught the public imagination.[2] Even Cavallotti and all but five deputies of the Extreme Left were swept away by patriotic fervour and forgot their anti-colonialist principles.[3] Robilant apologised handsomely for his unhappy phrase, but on 4 February, after a big drop in the government's majority, he announced his intention to resign. Four days later the whole government followed his example. The Triple Alliance was thus renewed while Italy was in the throes of a cabinet crisis. Robilant was appointed ambassador in London, where he died a few months later. 'We leave Italy in an iron boot', he remarked on leaving the Foreign Ministry. Though the magnitude of his achievement was not appreciated outside a tiny circle, his clear-sightedness, diplomatic skill and strength of character entitle him to be regarded as one of Italy's greatest Foreign Ministers.

[1] Chiala, *Massawa*, p. 338; *Pagine*, III, p. 479.

[2] It created much the same stir in Italy as Gordon's death had created in Britain two years before. The square in front of the main railway station in Rome is still called Piazza dei Cinquecento after the heroes of Dogali. For the popular mythology which the disaster subsequently generated (for instance, the legend that the dead were found dressed by the right, as if on the parade ground, and that the last survivors presented arms as they awaited death), see Battaglia, pp. 236–42.

[3] Carocci, p. 597. Costa was one of the five. He had been an unwavering opponent of colonial expansion since 1882, his slogan being 'Not a man, not a penny' for Africa. Battaglia, pp. 203–4, 246–9.

# PART II

# STRESSES AND STRAINS

## 1887–1901

# 4

# Crispi and the
# Heyday of the Triple Alliance
## 1887-93

### Crispi the Reformer

Depretis's resignation on 8 February 1887 was followed by the longest cabinet crisis in Italian experience. Two solutions presented themselves: either a new edition of the previous government, under Depretis, Robilant or a younger colleague, in which Minghetti's moderate Right would be more strongly represented;[1] or a coalition of the critics of *trasformismo*, the Pentarchy, the Centre and the intransigent Right, under the leadership of the strong man, Crispi. After a month of fruitless negotiations Depretis was persuaded by the King to stay in office, and on 11 March he extracted a grudging vote of confidence from parliament. Three weeks later, to the disgust of Minghetti's party, he took a decisive step to the left and offered seats in his cabinet to Crispi and his fellow-Pentarch, Zanardelli, who both accepted. Thus Crispi, the champion of political principle, who had branded *trasformismo* as parliamentary incest, entered the system and was himself 'transformed'. As a counterweight to the two ex-Pentarchs Depretis gave the Ministry for War to a representative of the Right and the Ministry of Public Works to one of the Left's most able administrators, Senator Giuseppe Saracco, who ever since his strenuous defence of the *macinato* tax before 1880 had enjoyed the reputation of watchdog of the budget. Nevertheless Crispi as Minister of Interior was from the first the cabinet's dominant figure. When Depretis died at the end of July he became Prime Minister, at the age of sixty-eight.

Crispi's coming to power opened a new phase in Italian politics. He was the first southern Prime Minister of Italy. He was also a true representative of Garibaldi's generation, a man of big ideas, boundless self-confidence and restless energy, in revolt against mediocrity and longing for excitement and colourful achievement. Like most of the Left, he believed in an Italian

[1] Minghetti himself had died in December 1886.

129

'mission', but his former Mazzinian ideals had been watered down into self-assertive nationalism. A Jacobin by temperament, he believed no means illegitimate in the pursuit of the one end that was the passion of his life – the preservation of Italian unity.

In character he was the opposite of Depretis. For that reason he came to power with the goodwill of all the disillusioned and frustrated. 'Incipit vita nova', wrote his fellow-Pentarch, Baccarini, hailing the end of *trasformismo*. He offered no programme beyond a determination to get things done and to make Italy respected in the outside world. Italian morale was low and Crispi, 'the man of destiny', seemed just the leader to produce the desired miracle.[1] He decided to be his own Minister of Interior and Foreign Minister. He also elevated the office of Prime Minister by creating a new secretariat for it, thus reducing his colleagues, so the critics declared, to mere departmental managers. His intention was to strengthen the executive and put an end to the practice under Depretis, by which 'parliament had become a tyrant and the cabinet a slave'. His parliamentary position was strong. He had inherited Depretis's majority and could in addition count on the support of the Centre, most of the followers of the Pentarchy and, at first, even the Extreme Left. But he never created the great party of principle for which he had pleaded so eloquently in opposition. On the contrary, he merely operated a new edition of *trasformismo*, drawing his ministers indifferently from the old Right and the old Left, and even giving a junior post to Fortis, one of the republicans arrested at Villa Ruffi in 1874. After a year of power Crispi himself was almost the only person who failed to recognise that, though Depretis was dead, Depretis's system of government lived on. Very soon he too had to answer the familiar accusations of 'parliamentary dictatorship'. While never concealing his belief in authority and the concentration of power, he always denied he was a dictator and pointed to Cavour's strong methods of government as a precedent. 'Italy', he said in 1887, 'is a country too much made for liberty to be able to tolerate dictatorships.' But though his theoretical devotion to liberty was unquestioned, his authoritarian practice was often hard to reconcile with the spirit of parliamentary government. In this he differed profoundly from Depretis.

His record of practical achievement was impressive. In an onslaught of reforming ardour he set out to reinvigorate the machinery of state. A law of 1888 revised the powers of the police over public meetings and defined more clearly the penalties of preventive arrest and banishment. In the same year local government was reformed: the franchise was extended to all literate male citizens who paid five lire a year in taxation, and the communal councils in the larger towns were given the power of electing their

[1] For a vivid description of the political atmosphere in 1887, see Croce, pp. 163–9.

*sindaco.* In 1889 the creation of a special judicial section of the Council of State laid the foundation of a system of administrative law on the French model.[1] Crispi was also responsible, in the years 1888–90, for prison reform, for the first timid measures to protect the emigrant and for the first effective public health legislation, designed to prevent further outbreaks of cholera. He reorganised the private charitable institutions (Opere Pie), many of which were badly administered or misused for non-charitable purposes, taking them out of the hands of the church and placing them under public, lay control. Another major reform was the introduction by Zanardelli in 1890 of a new penal code, which for the first time unified penal legislation throughout Italy. It abolished capital punishment, recognised the freedom to strike together with the freedom to work, and prescribed penalties for the exercise of political pressure by clergy in the course of their spiritual duties.

These were solid achievements. But it was to foreign policy that Crispi devoted most of his energy in his first three and a half years of power.

## The Foreign Policy of Prestige

In September 1887 Bismarck told the Italian ambassador in Berlin that 'if some favourable breeze should waft Crispi' to Germany, he would be delighted to see him.[2] Crispi lost no time. On 1 October he arrived at Bismarck's country seat, Friedrichsruh, and once again, as in 1877, fell under the Chancellor's spell. Their talks ranged over all the European questions of the day. The only decision taken, at Crispi's suggestion, was to strengthen the Triple Alliance by an Italo-German military convention. On his return Crispi proclaimed to the world at a Turin banquet that he and Bismarck had 'conspired for peace' and had thus 'rendered Europe a great service.[3] Next summer Crispi paid a second visit to Friedrichsruh. In October 1888 William II visited Rome, and in the following spring Crispi had more talks with Bismarck when he accompanied King Humbert to Berlin. Bismarck flattered Crispi and played upon his vanity, thus making him a willing instrument of his policy.[4] These visits, and the intimate relations which they appeared to have established between the rulers

[1] Since 1876 the leading advocates of this reform had been two statesmen of the Right, Minghetti and Spaventa. Crispi appointed the latter the first president of the new judicial section in 1889.

[2] Crispi, *Memoirs*, II, p. 208.

[3] Chiala, *Pagine*, III, p. 504; Crispi, *Memoirs*, II, pp. 227–8.

[4] In October 1887 Crispi noted in his diary that, during a drive through the forest, Princess Bismarck, 'fearing my overcoat was thin, put over my shoulders her husband's great military cloak'. In 1888 Bismarck arranged a special fireworks display in his guest's honour and himself led the cheers of 'Viva Crispi', standing bareheaded among the crowd. Crispi, *Memoirs*, II, pp. 221, 327.

of the two countries, were given lavish publicity. They made Italians feel
that Italy was now an equal in the Triple Alliance. Crispi, with characteristic lack of modesty, described his achievement at the end of 1888 in these
words: 'There are some who for twenty-seven years were inclined to
believe that Italy was forced to wait upon a word from Paris or Berlin. But
the day came when the man arose who believed that Italy was the equal of
all nations, and who intended to make Italy's words heard and respected.'[1]

Crispi's intention was to display unwavering loyalty to the Triple
Alliance and extract the last ounce of power and prestige from the diplomatic system which he had inherited from Robilant. He thrust Italy into
the forefront of the Balkan crisis, angering the Russians by his enthusiastic
support for Prince Ferdinand of Bulgaria, and took the lead in strengthening the Mediterranean coalition. With Bismarck's approval the Second
Mediterranean Agreement was made in December 1887.[2] Britain, Austria-
Hungary and Italy again agreed in a secret exchange of notes to work for
the preservation of the Mediterranean *status quo*, but this time with particular reference to Turkish integrity and independence. Their aim was to
prevent the Turks from conceding territory or influence to Russia, either
at the Straits or on the Caucasus or in Bulgaria; if necessary the three
Powers would consult each other on measures such as the occupation of
points of Turkish territory, in order to block a Russian advance. Crispi,
not yet satisfied, bombarded Salisbury and the Austrians with proposals
for military conventions, but to no avail.[3] However, in February 1888 the
Italo-German military convention was signed, under which Italy undertook, if the Triple Alliance was at war with France and Russia, to make its
main effort on the Alps but to send five army corps and three cavalry
divisions to fight on the Rhine. These new commitments meant bigger
armaments. Already in June 1887, while Depretis was still Prime Minister,
Brin had launched a new naval building programme, directed against
France, and a large expansion of the cavalry, artillery and engineers, to
match the infantry increase of 1882, had been approved. In December
1888, following the example of Bismarck, extraordinary military credits
were again voted, Italy rose to the position of third naval power in the

[1] Cilibrizzi, II, p. 599.

[2] For details of the negotiations, see Langer, *European Alliances*, pp. 434–41;
Lowe, pp. 20–5. Text also in Pribram, I, pp. 124–33. In May 1888 Crispi also
adhered to the Austro–Rumanian treaty of 1883. He used Mazzinian arguments
to justify these commitments against Russia: Italy had both a duty and an interest
in defending the right of the Rumanian and Bulgarian peoples to independence.

[3] The Austrians wanted no Italian help against Russia, for they feared that Italy
might claim compensation for military services rendered. The British, however,
did consent at the end of 1887 to a secret exchange of information on the results of
the British and Italian naval manœuvres of that year. Marder, pp. 128–9, note.

world, with ten first-class ironclads built or building, including five which for size, speed, range and armament had no equal.[1]

The new tone of confidence and self-assertion in Italian foreign policy soon convinced the French that the Triple Alliance had been transformed in 1887 into an aggresive instrument. They had had great hopes of Crispi, ex-republican and ex-revolutionary, when he first came to power, but they were rapidly disillusioned.[2] Crispi had no wish for war with France. Culturally a child of the French Revolution, he sincerely believed that such a war would be a civil war and a disaster to both nations, whichever won.[3] But, like Mazzini and many of the Left, he regarded France, whether monarchist, imperial or republican, as Italy's evil genius. Stronger than racial and sentimental links was the conflict of national interest over the Mediterranean and the Papacy. Before France and Italy could be friends, the French must forgo their ambition of turning the Mediterranean into a French lake. His predecessors had been weak and 'servile'. He, on the contrary, was determined to unmask and defeat all the plots of French revolutionaries and imperialists and Jesuits which, with his conspirator's complex, he imagined being hatched on every side against united Italy. Challenge, not conciliation, was his method, and he believed that bluntness was the only language which the French would understand.

French hostility was not merely a product of Crispi's imagination. France was in an ebulliently nationalist mood, and not until the eclipse of Boulanger in April 1889 did fears of a militarist *coup d'état* lose reality. A major aim of French diplomacy after 1887 was to break the Triple Alliance and force Italy out of it. To this purpose the commercial and financial weapons were used to the full. Encouragement was given to the irredentists of the Italian Extreme Left in the hope of damaging Italo-Austrian relations. Simultaneously the French responded favourably to overtures from the Vatican when papal diplomacy swung decisively in their favour after 1887. In November 1890 Leo XIII urged French Catholics to 'rally' to the Third Republic and began to encourage a Franco-Russian alliance.[4] The

[1] Marder, p. 141. The total tonnage of the Italian navy increased from 158,000 tons in 1880 to 312,000 in 1890. The new ships were designed to operate in the western Mediterranean. Brin recognised that naval superiority over France was unattainable; but by giving high priority to speed and range, he was able to construct a fleet that presented a serious though limited challenge to France's control of the Mediterranean. *La marina italiana*, I, pp. 257–9. The French had 14 ironclads in the Mediterranean in 1888, 20 in 1891. Lowe, p. 34.

[2] For the same reason Bismarck had been displeased by the inclusion of Crispi and Zanardelli in Depretis's last government, believing that 'it was a step towards the republic'. Chiala, *Pagine*, III, pp. 497–8.

[3] Crispi, *Memoirs*, II, p. 226; Cilibrizzi, II, p. 346; Chiala, *Pagine*, III, pp. 483, 503.

[4] See further below, pp. 217–18.

French never made the restoration of the temporal power an object of their diplomacy; but the Vatican hoped that if a European congress were ever summoned to avert war, or if a European war were to break out and end in Italy's defeat, restoration would follow.[1] Leo XIII therefore wooed France and the French used their influence at the Vatican to embarrass and weaken Italy.

While Crispi remained in power, tension between France and Italy rarely relaxed. Commercial relations were the first to suffer. Although the trade treaty, which had been denounced in December 1886,[2] was due to lapse at the end of 1887, Crispi delayed sending negotiators to Paris until September. His visit to Bismarck next month created a strained political atmosphere and the talks ran into difficulties. Powerful interests in Italy opposed any treaty at all, fearing to lose all they had gained by protection. The French government, too, was overawed by a fanatically protectionist chamber. The existing treaty was prolonged by agreement for two months beyond 31 December 1887, but the Italians refused to consider a further extension. The negotiations were resumed at the end of the year in Rome. In February 1888 an indiscretion at the Italian court revealed the existence of the Italo-German military convention to the French and their commercial delegation abruptly left Rome, declaring that no treaty would be possible while Italy remained in the Triple Alliance. On 1 March the French introduced their discriminatory tariff, the Italians raised their duties on French goods by 50% and a full-scale tariff war began.

Throughout the years 1887–90 Crispi made a major contribution to the nervous tension of Europe. At the first rumour of a French move in north Africa, at the first hint of a French threat or imagined insult, he tried to set the whole machinery of the Triple Alliance and Mediterranean Agreements in motion. In February 1888 the Germans started a war scare by informing Britain and Italy, correctly, that the French had concentrated their fleet of ironclads at Toulon. Crispi needed no reminder of the vulnerability of Italy's coasts to naval bombardment. On this occasion Rome was full of reports that an attack on La Spezia was imminent, and only the arrival of the reinforced British Channel squadron at Genoa restored calm.[3] In July 1889, at a moment of extreme tension between Italy and the Papacy,[4] Crispi again decided, on the strength of a story from an informant

---

[1] Engel-Jánosi, I, pp. 265–6; see also article in *Revue des Deux Mondes* of 15 July 1889, quoted by Langer, *European Alliances and Alignments*, p. 472.

[2] See above, p. 82.

[3] Lowe, pp. 35–7; Langer, pp. 475–6; Marder, pp. 126–9. The Italians believed that the British squadron 'saved the day', and that only its arrival deterred the French from attacking. The squadron was again ordered to Genoa, at German instigation, at the end of March.

[4] See below, p. 222.

in the Vatican, that a French invasion was imminent; but this time Bismarck listened to the message of a special Italian emissary with polite incredulity. In the summer of 1890 Crispi received reports that the French were transforming Bizerta into a naval base, had signed a treaty with the Bey for the annexation of Tunis on his death, and were planning to move east into Tripoli. Once again Crispi appealed for help to his allies and to Britain. Another source of tension was Morocco, where Crispi tried to build up Italian influence through expansion of trade and the supply of arms. He saw these plans threatened by French designs on the Saharan oasis of Tuat, which lay between Algeria and Morocco, and by alleged conspiracies between France and Spain to partition Morocco between them.[1] These, too, formed the subject of repeated diplomatic alarms.

By these tactics Crispi soon succeeded in wearying his friends and allies. The Germans were not sorry to see friction between France and Italy. By nourishing Italy's aspirations in north Africa, they hoped to prevent it from falling into the arms of France and to bind it to the Triple Alliance. But they had no intention of allowing Crispi to involve them in war irresponsibly over some trifling African complaint. Thus while applying diplomatic pressure to the French, in response to Crispi's appeals, they tried to cool him down.

Salisbury was even less sympathetic, realising that Crispi's 'conspirator's temper leads him to political gambling, which, in the present state of men's feelings, is full of danger to the world's peace.'[2] He suspected that both Italy and Germany were exaggerating the French danger in the hope of extracting from him a more binding British commitment, and he discounted Italian alarms even when, as in the case of Bizerta, they were well founded.[3] His inclination was to mediate, reduce the tension and himself negotiate piecemeal colonial agreements with France. But even at the height of his personal exasperation with Crispi, he recognised that a too callous attitude might throw Italy into the arms of the French, destroy the Triple Alliance and the balance of power, and dangerously weaken Britain's ability to keep

---

[1] Taylor, p. 347. Tuat is 600 miles south of Oran. The French disputed the Moroccan claim to ownership and maintained it was part of the hitherto unoccupied hinterland of Algeria.

[2] Salisbury to his ambassador in Rome, December 1888. Cecil, IV, p. 105. On another occasion he complained that Crispi was 'the Randolph Churchill of Italy'.

[3] Salisbury was inclined to believe French denials that they were fortifying Bizerta. In any case he shared the British Admiralty's scepticism about its importance, and told the Italians that the French fleet would be weaker, not stronger, if divided between African and French bases. Sir A. Lyall, *Life of Marquis of Dufferin and Ava* (London 1905), II, pp. 247–8; Crispi, *Memoirs*, III, pp. 85 ff.; Marder, pp. 149–52; Lowe, p. 65. Crispi disagreed, though his successor accepted the British view (see below, p. 148).

France and Russia in check in the Mediterranean. In March 1888 he therefore committed himself to stating that the British fleet would come to the aid of Italy if subjected to a completely unprovoked French attack, an eventuality that Salisbury regarded as virtually inconceivable. Crispi made the most of this promise, persuading himself that it amounted to an Anglo-Italian naval alliance. Again in the summer of 1890, when Crispi's alarm over Bizerta and Tripoli was at its peak, Salisbury stated his view that if changes in the Mediterranean *status quo* became unavoidable, Italy's special claim to Tripoli should be recognised. But his advice 'to act with the utmost circumspection and patience' was followed, and the idea of a military expedition to Tripoli was dropped. On this as on many other occasions Salisbury's policy was to concede the minimum, to give no written guarantee and 'to make words do as much work as can be got out of them'.[1] By these methods he succeeded in part in calming Crispi and moderating his fear, by no means groundless, of a British colonial deal with France or Germany at Italy's expense.[2]

In the intervals between crises, Crispi was prepared to negotiate with the French. The economic and financial situation, which by the end of 1889 had become alarming, forced him to make conciliatory gestures. In October 1889 he announced the unilateral abolition of the differential tariff on French goods, and in April 1890 an Italian squadron paid a visit to Toulon to greet the French President. But further talks during the summer on Tripoli and east African frontiers broke down because the French insisted on too high a price: recognition of their protectorate in Tunis and convincing proof of the defensive character of the Triple Alliance. There was a pathological element in Franco-Italian relations during these years. French governments were often conciliatory; but the antics of the protectionists and the press polemics embittered popular feeling in both countries. Crispi's delight in creating a conspiratorial atmosphere and his demagogic, brutally 'frank' speeches, which made him a pioneer of open diplomacy, might have been deliberately designed to offend French *amour propre*. It became virtually impossible for any French government to make concessions while Crispi remained in power.

Meanwhile relations with Austria-Hungary were not always cordial. The Russian menace was the constant theme of Crispi's speeches and despatches. 'I consider Austria's existence necessary for the maintenance

[1] Crispi, *Memoirs*, II, pp. 448–61; Cecil, IV, pp. 372–6; Lowe, pp. 36–40, 46–51, 65–72, 81–2.

[2] The Anglo–French colonial agreement of August 1890 recognised a French zone of influence south of Tunisia. This, in the Italian view, deprived Tripoli of much of its value as a future colony by encroaching on its hinterland and cutting it off commercially from central Africa.

of the balance of power in Europe', he told Bismarck in 1887, and promised that Italy 'will prove herself a faithful ally to the neighbouring empire'.[1] The rising tension with France made Austrian friendship indispensable. Crispi was therefore prepared to suppress irredentism with greater energy than any prime minister before or after. In May 1889 Imbriani, the irredentist leader, entered parliament as deputy for Bari and declared in his maiden speech that he represented 'the entire nation', the unredeemed provinces of Trent and Trieste no less than Apulia. In July Crispi dissolved the Trent-Trieste Committee, over which Imbriani presided, for organising protests against the arrest of an Italian citizen in Trieste. Next year the Austrians dissolved the Italian Pro Patria Association in Trent. Ignoring the public outcry, Crispi suppressed all Barsanti and Oberdan societies and dismissed his Minister of Finance, Federico Seismit-Doda,[2] for listening without protest to an irredentist speech at a public banquet. During the electoral campaign in October 1890 Crispi declared at Florence that, 'surrounded as it appears to be by the ardent poetry of patriotism, irredentism is the most dangerous of those errors by which Italy is today distracted'. Why, he asked, were the irredentists interested only in Italy's eastern frontier, not in Nice or the west? This was sufficient proof for him that Imbriani was 'sold' to France and that the aim of the agitation, secretly encouraged by the clericals, was to drive Italy to a rupture with Austria-Hungary and so pave the way for a Franco-Austro-Papal combination to recover Rome.[3]

Crispi, however, was not deaf to the grievances of Italians across the frontier. While publicly rebuking the irredentists, in private he protested with great energy to the Austrians and appealed for German support. To Bismarck and William II he confided his fears of Taaffe's clerical, anti-Italian and pro-Slav policy.[4] German intervention helped to secure permission for the Pro Patria Association to reform, as a non-political, cultural organisation, under the new name of the Lega Nazionale. The Germans were not displeased to be asked to mediate between their allies, who thus made Berlin the pivot of the Alliance. Kálnoky, on the other hand, was apprehensive: in 1888 he already foresaw that one day German pressure

---

[1] Crispi, *Memoirs*, II, pp. 217–18.

[2] A Dalmatian by origin, who had fought the Austrians at Venice in 1848.

[3] Crispi, *Scritti e discorsi politici*, pp. 750–4; Cilibrizzi, II, pp. 390–6; Volpe, I, pp. 306–14. Before the 1890 election funds were raised in Paris for the Italian Extreme Left. Crispi, *Politica interna*, p. 258. In the same election a native of Trieste, Salvatore Barzilai, became one of the deputies for Rome.

[4] Taaffe was Austrian Prime Minister from 1879 to 1893. Crispi saw the hand of the Vatican behind every anti-Italian act of the Austrian government. 'I beseech you', wrote Nigra, his ambassador in Vienna in August 1890, 'not to see Jesuits where in fact there are none.' Crispi, *Memoirs*, III, p. 156.

might be exerted on Austria to cede the Trentino, in the higher interests of the Alliance. Though this did not in fact occur until 1915, its menace already overhung Austro-Italian relations.

For the moment, however, greatly to the relief of the Austrians, Africa had become Crispi's chief concern. He had disapproved of the Massawa expedition in 1885; but in spite of its disappointments he had opposed withdrawal because, he said, 'I do not understand modest policies'. On becoming Prime Minister he decided that Dogali must be avenged. In October 1887 an expeditionary corps was dispatched to Massawa. It re-occupied the areas evacuated after Dogali, overawed the Ethiopians by a show of force and withdrew. Crispi declared it would be madness to think of the conquest of Ethiopia, but he believed that Italy must stay in Africa in order to win the respect of savages, and because colonies were 'a necessity of modern life'. This conservative policy was endorsed by a majority of 302 to 40 in the chamber in May 1888.

In the years that followed Crispi slowly changed his mind. Under the inspiration of military and colonial enthusiasts, a programme of piecemeal expansion was planned and carried out. The experts were divided between two schools of thought. One, led by Count Pietro Antonelli, nephew of the cardinal, hoped to make Italy master of all Ethopia by patronising Ras Menelik of Shoa, supplying him with arms and strengthening him against his rivals. The other, less ambitious school, to which the military commander, General Antonio Baldissera, and many other soldiers on the spot belonged, distrusted Menelik and preferred to secure the safety of the colony through friendship with the rulers of the neighbouring Ethiopian province of Tigré. In practice Italian policy wavered dangerously between these so-called Shoa and Tigré programmes.

At first Antonelli seemed to be winning. In March 1889 the Emperor John of Ethiopia was killed in battle against the Mahdist dervishes. Menelik at once proclaimed himself John's successor, ignoring the rival claim of Ras Mangasha of Tigré, John's illegitimate son and designated heir. These events fired Crispi's imagination with visions of imperial conquest. They also stirred the King, for whom Africa, the army and the Triple Alliance were the three concerns closest to his heart.[1] But there was opposition within the government, notably from the Minister for War, General Bertolè-Viale, who supported Baldissera's pleas for caution. On 5 April 1889 Crispi's proposal to order Baldissera to occupy Asmara was defeated in the cabinet, on one of the few occasions on which a colonial matter was

[1] Finali, pp. 412, 644, 688. Senator Finali belonged to the Right, had sat in Minghetti's cabinet before 1876 and succeeded Saracco as Crispi's Minister for Public Works from March 1889 to 1891.

brought before it. Crispi took this rebuff hard. 'I am still a Garibaldian', he wrote to Bertolè-Viale, 'and in spite of my sixty-nine years I see things differently from the tacticians educated in military academies.' Bertolè-Viale replied, 'You see things with the daring of the old Garibaldian . . . Daring counts for much: but in Africa, even more than elsewhere, daring must be accompanied by prudence and foresight.' For the moment Crispi had to submit.[1]

After this the pace of events quickened. On 2 May Menelik and Antonelli signed the Treaty of Uccialli, which seemed to give the latter all he had ever hoped for. In return for Italy's friendship and a loan of 2 million lire, Menelik agreed to the extension of Italian rule to the highlands west of Massawa and consented to conduct his foreign relations through Italian diplomatic representatives. In October the Great Powers were informed of this last provision and all except Russia acknowledged the establishment of an Italian protectorate.[2] Crispi talked triumphantly of wiping Ethiopia off the map.[3] Meanwhile Baldissera, having completed his preparations, decided it was safe to advance. Keren was occupied in June 1889 and Asmara two months later, and Italian authority was extended southwards towards the river Mareb.[4] In the same year the establishment of a protectorate over a long stretch of the Indian Ocean coast laid the foundations of what was later to become Italian Somaliland. In 1890 the northern colony was reorganised and named Eritrea.[5]

Trouble soon followed. Menelik grew alarmed by the Italian army's persistent encroachments in Tigré. Tiring of Italian patronage, he refused to accept the Mareb as the frontier between Ethiopia and Eritrea and announced that, according to the Amharic text of the Treaty of Uccialli, Italy had no right to claim a protectorate.[6] At the end of 1890 Antonelli

[1] As Battaglia points out, the contrast in temperament between Crispi and Baldissera (and Bertolè-Viale) was only a new edition of the old contrast between Right and Left during the Risorgimento. Baldissera was a cautious, methodical professional soldier, with a sure understanding of the realities of the Ethiopian situation and a marked capacity for colonial administration. Paduan by birth, he had learnt his trade in the Austrian army, with which he fought in Bohemia in 1866. He was therefore totally free of the romantic memories and prejudices of the Risorgimento by which Crispi was ruled all his life. He resisted Crispi's clamour for glory and believed that Italy's interest would be better served by waiting till the Ethiopians had exhausted themselves in civil war and were forced to ask for help. Then the Italian forces would advance not as conquerors but as liberators. Crispi had little use for so undramatic a policy. Battaglia, pp. 339–45, 361–6.

[2] The French in later years maintained that they had merely acknowledged receipt of the Italian communication, not recognised the protectorate.

[3] Finali, pp. 411, 559.

[4] On these occasions the cabinet was not consulted. Finali, pp. 411, 588, 644–5.

[5] After the Roman name for the Red Sea (Mare Erythraeum).

[6] Menelik asserted that the treaty enabled him, but did not oblige him, to conduct his foreign relations through Italy.

was sent on a special mission to his court but failed to retrieve the situation. Having with Italian help firmly established his position as Emperor over all former rivals, Menelik was now beginning to look to the French and Russians as protectors of his independence.

Meanwhile the extension of Eritrea had led to friction with Britain. Salisbury thought Italy too weak to become a major colonial power and disapproved of Crispi's 'misplaced and suicidal African ambitions',[1] particularly when directed westwards towards the Nile and the Sudan. A sharp quarrel blew up over the town of Kassala which had been since 1885 in the hands of the Mahdi. Crispi wished to annex it. The British insisted that it was part of the Sudan and would consent only to a temporary Italian occupation until Egyptian rule could be restored. In October 1890, after fruitless talks with Sir Evelyn Baring at Naples, Crispi advertised the quarrel to the world in a bitter communique.[2] Italian reproaches of British frigidity in east Africa were now added to the laments about Salisbury's indifference to the Mediterranean danger.[3]

Crispi thus drifted into a policy of expansion. In his speeches he dilated on the commercial value of colonies and on 'the vast areas of land' that they would provide for emigrants; themes to which the south and his own Sicily did not fail to respond.[4] In Tunis, Egypt and the eastern Mediterranean he created a network of Italian schools to combat French influence. 'Italy is on the march', he boasted; from the furthest oceans rose the cry of 'Italy!', restoring meaning to the ancient phrase *Civis Romanus*

---

[1] Cecil, IV, pp. 325–6.

[2] Crispi, *La prima guerra d'Africa*, p. 234. Sir Evelyn Baring (later Lord Cromer) was British Resident in Cairo. In March 1890 he wrote to Salisbury: 'I have no hesitation in saying that I should prefer to see the Dervishes in possession of Kassala and Khartoum' rather than the Italians. Salisbury agreed. The Italian alliance, he told Baring, 'is desirable; but it is not worth a very great price even in African square miles'. Lowe, pp. 62–3. Kassala was the richest province of the Sudan.

[3] 'Crispi reproaches me like a neglected lover; Tornielli [the Italian ambassador in London] scolds me like an injured wife', wrote Salisbury in January 1891. There had also been friction two years earlier on the Somali coast, where only the presence of the British navy stopped Crispi from bombarding Zanzibar. Cecil, IV, pp. 234–7, 325–32, 377–8.

[4] In 1891 Franchetti visited Eritrea as commissioner for colonisation. He found the climate of the highlands not unlike that of parts of Italy and decided they were suitable for settlement by Italian peasants. His aim was systematic, state-financed colonisation on the democratic Australian or New Zealand model and he hoped to 'transform the penniless, proletarian emigrant into a peasant proprietor', to give a decent livelihood to the disinherited classes 'for whom the land of Italy does not provide sufficient work and bread', and eventually to make Eritrea both financially and militarily self-sufficient. His scheme ran into many difficulties, but by 1895 fifteen pilot families had been established. For details see Franchetti, *Mezzogiorno e colonie*; also Battaglia, pp. 517–26.

*sum.*[1] In his day-to-day handling of foreign and colonial policy he was often prudent and even hesitant. But his public utterances were those of the man of energy, the believer in the old poetry of the Left, the advocate of action and 'activism' – in what direction mattered little. By 1891 Crispi had come to stand in the public eye for imperial expansion.

## Crispi's first Fall

The tariff war hit Italy harder than France. Before the rupture the French were Italy's best customer, taking 41% of Italian exports in 1881–7. In 1888–90 they fell to fourth place and took 18%. In the same period the value of Italian exports to France dropped by 63%, that of imports from France by 47%.[2] Some compensation was provided by higher exports to Switzerland and central Europe, but over the years 1888–90 these gains were less than one-third of the loss. Crispi at first gloried in the rupture, declaring in February 1888:[3] 'Having won our national independence, having become politically a great state, sure of its destiny, we must also strengthen ourselves economically and financially, to make ourselves independent of other nations.' He repeatedly proclaimed himself 'an impenitent free trader'; but, knowing little of economics, he was at the mercy of the protectionists, who complacently convinced themselves and the public that France could not do without Italian products.

Disillusionment came quickly. Agriculture was the chief sufferer. The agricultural balance of trade, which had shown a surplus of 455 million lire in 1881–5, turned to a deficit of 315 millions in 1886–90.[4] Both north and south were affected. In the north a collapse of raw silk prices inflicted great loss, and there was a sudden increase in transatlantic emigration, particularly from the silk, rice and dairy-farming regions of Lombardy and Venetia. For the south the heaviest blow was the slump in the price of wine and the collapse of wine exports which occurred in 1888.[5] The landowners and peasants who had recently turned with such enthusiasm from cereals to vines now had to face the loss of the French market on which they so largely depended. Simultaneously phylloxera began to devastate Italian vines just as French vines were recovering. The government's only remedy for agricultural distress was an increase in the duty on imported grain. Under the pressure of the agrarian lobby in the chamber, the wheat duty

---

[1] Speech at Palermo, 14 October 1889. Crispi, *Scritti e discorsi politici*, pp. 737–8.

[2] *Sommario*, pp. 152, 155, 157; Corbino, III, pp. 188–90; Luzzatto, II, p. 403.

[3] Cilibrizzi, II, p. 355.

[4] Corbino, III, p. 186.

[5] Exports of wine dropped from 3·6 million hectolitres in 1887 to 1·8 in 1888 and reached a minimum of 0·9 in 1890. *Sommario*, p. 161.

was raised from 3 to 5 lire per quintal in February 1888 and the duty on other grains by comparable amounts. Once again the impact of the depression was softened for one section of Italian agriculture at the expense of the consumer, the landless labourer and the southern producer of wine, olive oil and fruit.

The state of industry was almost as gloomy, even though certain interests, notably cotton manufacturing,[1] thrived on the trade war. Crispi's first term of office coincided with a period of depression throughout Europe and no tariff could insulate Italy from its effects. In 1888 a slump in speculative building in Rome caused sudden unemployment, followed by mass protest meetings and violence. Next year the iron and steel boom burst. In a country so dependent on agriculture for its prosperity, the fall in the purchasing power of the peasant inevitably put a brake on industrial development.[2] The slow but steady progress which Italy had been making since 1861 came to an abrupt end and from 1888 to 1896 the Italian economy stagnated.[3]

Economic depression aggravated the unhealthy financial situation which Crispi inherited from Depretis. Magliani retained the Ministry of Finance for sixteen months after Depretis's death because Crispi, no less than his predecessor, wished to give politics precedence over finance. State expenditure continued to rise and in 1890 was one-third greater than in 1881. Rearmament raised the armed forces' share of the total to 30% in 1888–9. The budget deficits crept up from 213 million lire in 1885–6 to 386 million in 1887–8 and 488 million in 1888–9, the highest figure since 1866.[4] Crispi defied the chamber to show him where economies could be made, while Magliani, in his search for extra revenue, squeezed the consumer yet harder.[5] But by 1888 Magliani's optimism and financial conjuring tricks had worn thin and in December of that year he resigned. Finance began to create serious difficulties for Crispi who used up four ministers of finance in two years. As his parliamentary majority wavered he began to talk of economies. But there was hardly one politician prepared to put the dilemma in plain language: either a radical change in foreign and

[1] Average annual imports of raw cotton rose from 647,000 quintals in 1881–5 to over 1 million in 1891–5. *Sommario*, p. 159.

[2] The growth in the national income barely kept pace with the increase in population. Romeo, p. 49; see also above, p. 84, note 3.

[3] According to Gerschenkron's calculations (pp. 362–4), the index of industrial output (100 = 1900) fell from 74 in 1888 to 64 in 1892, and did not again reach the 1888 figure until 1896. The annual average rate of growth of industrial production was 0·3% in 1888–96, compared with 4·6% in 1881–8.

[4] Coppola d'Anna, pp. 85–7, 106–8. In 1888–9 revenue covered only 74% of expenditure.

[5] The proportion of total revenue provided by consumption taxes reached a peak of 42·8% in the years 1886–90. Coppola d'Anna, p. 95.

colonial policy and an end to reckless spending on public works, or continuing deficits. Little was done but drift, in the hope that time would solve the difficulty.

The political tension with France made things worse. On the Paris Bourse organised attacks were made on Italian securities, contemptuously referred to as 'macaroni'. French bankers, with their large holdings of Italian government bonds, could effectively undermine Italian credit. Twice Crispi appealed to Bismarck for relief 'from the tyranny of the French market'. The German banker Bleichröder, at Bismarck's urgent request, reluctantly formed a financial syndicate which by systematic buying halted the collapse.[1] But German help alone could not save the situation and Crispi was forced to recognise the need to come to terms with France. In October 1889 he swallowed his pride and announced that the differential tariffs on French goods would be lifted at the beginning of the next year. However hard he might try to disguise the fact, this was unconditional surrender. In vain he awaited a friendly response from the French, who continued to enforce their discriminatory tariffs until February 1892, then replaced them by a new and equally prohibitive general tariff. Crispi was no more successful in his efforts to obtain French financial help. In October 1890 he sounded the Rothschild Bank for a loan, but the proposal was vetoed by the French government; there were to be no concessions while Italy's foreign policy remained unchanged.[2]

These economic and financial difficulties, added to the burden of armaments, anxiety about Africa and the strain of prolonged international tension, rapidly swelled the ranks of Crispi's critics. His majority was not immune from the process of disintegration which had undermined every prime minister from Cavour to Depretis. Personal antagonisms reinforced nostalgia for the peace and quiet of the Depretis era. Nicotera, Crispi's old rival from the pre-Pentarchy years of 1877–8, who had a large personal following in the south, tried during 1890 to promote a coalition of all the opposition groups and negotiated with both the remnants of the Right and the Extreme Left. The latter was reluctant to break with Crispi. It was in sorrow more than anger that the republicans lamented the corruption of a good man by the court and monarchical institutions.[3] Cavallotti retained

[1] Crispi, *Memoirs*, III, pp. 209–18. As a consequence of the influx of foreign capital in the years 1881–8, the proportion of Italian government bonds in foreign hands rose from 26·2% in 1881 to 48·8% in 1891–2. Nitti, *Il bilancio dello stato*, p. 361. The sum of interest payments to French, British and German bondholders rose from 62 million lire in 1881 to 163 million (of which 96 million to French) in 1892–3. Nitti, *Il capitale straniero*, pp. 71–3.

[2] DDF (1), VIII, 176, 181, 183, 185, 217.

[3] See, for example, Pantano to Colajanni, 25 March 1888, in *Democrazia e socialismo*, pp. 52–5.

his personal reverence for the hero of 1860 and still hoped he would fulfil the role of democratic reformer. Nevertheless the two old friends began to draw apart. In May 1890 the Extreme Left published a Pact of Rome, signed by Cavallotti, Bovio, Imbriani, Costa and many other radicals, republicans and socialists. It demanded the strengthening of parliament against the executive, an end to the concentration of ministries in one man's hands, a drastic reduction in expenditure on armaments and the replacement of the Triple Alliance, the militaristic *pactum sceleris*, by a democratic Latin Union. With its emphasis on political liberty and social reform, it was intended to serve as an immediate programme for a constructively democratic party. Cavallotti was under pressure to go much further. Emilio Giampietro, a leading member of the reformist wing of his party, urged him to join Nicotera and accept full membership of a coalition that could become the government when Crispi fell.[1] But though Cavallotti met and talked with Nicotera, he would not commit himself the whole way. As he later told Giampietro, at the age of forty-eight he was too old to change, and it would be moral suicide for him to take office.[2] Cavallotti's indecisiveness thus persisted and the coalition against Crispi hung fire.

On the other side the Right was recovering confidence. The split which Depretis had caused in its ranks by inviting it to 'transform itself' was ended by Crispi's advent to power. On the death of Minghetti in 1886, Marquis Antonio Di Rudinì had assumed the leadership. Rudinì was a Sicilian, but of a very different type to Crispi: a sceptical aristocrat with Norman blood in his veins, impressive in his monocle and white beard, but a man of indecision and weak character. At the age of twenty-seven he had found himself Mayor of Palermo during the 1866 rebellion and had acquired a national reputation by his handling of the situation. Nicknamed 'the infant prodigy', he became Minister of Interior when he was only thirty; but as the years passed by, 'the prodigy vanished, the infant remained'.[3] After 1882 he resisted Depretis's blandishments and declined to follow Minghetti, becoming instead a leading critic of Magliani's finance which he foretold would end in national bankruptcy. Under his leadership his party's relations with Crispi's government oscillated between wary support and exasperated criticism. The Right approved of many of Crispi's

[1] Giampietro, a business man with banking and mining experience, was known as 'the financier of the Extreme Left'. He made the perfect complement to Cavallotti, the glamorous popular tribune. Giampietro greatly admired the heroic and 'manly figure' of Nicotera, whom he 'loved as a father', and despised the extremists of his own party who 'wanted to eat a king for lunch and an emperor for supper'. Giampietro, *Ricordi e riforme*, p. 81; *L'Italia radicale*, p. 205.

[2] Giampietro, p. 62.

[3] An epigram of Francesco de Sanctis, the historian of Italian literature and the leading educationalist of his time.

domestic reforms and of his energy in keeping the radicals and irredentists in check. On the other hand it deplored his 'personal government', his scant respect for parliament, his financial recklessness and his vast expenditure on armaments. The Right did not demand, like the Extreme Left, that Italy should abandon the Triple Alliance; but it did demand an end to Crispi's excessive *triplicismo*, a brake on African adventures and relief from the continuous tension for which it held Crispi responsible.

These views met with a special response from the National Conservatives, from many members of the rising industrial class in the north and from independent spokesmen for agriculture and the south. Practical men of business such as Giuseppe Colombo, a prominent Milanese engineer, and Giulio Prinetti, a manufacturer of bicycles, wanted retrenchment, tax reductions, time to build up their adolescent industries and a peaceful world in which to trade. Realists like Jacini and Fortunato, who were familiar with the distress of agriculture and conscious of the smallness of Italian resources, noted bitterly the great sums devoted to armaments or Africa which could be better spent in revitalising the countryside. Italy, argued Fortunato, should be content to be first among the second-class nations.[1] Jacini summed up their criticism of Crispi's policy in one word: megalomania. With scathing contempt Crispi rounded on these timid doubters and reminded them that megalomaniacs created Italy.[2]

In the autumn of 1890 financial difficulties drove him to dissolve parliament. The election was fought apathetically in November on a programme of budget economies, opposition to irredentism and defence of the monarchy and the social order. These were issues on which the Right was glad to offer its support and Crispi arranged that many of its candidates should be unopposed. The only effective opposition came from the Extreme Left, which suffered severe disappointment, even though it slightly increased its strength. The government won 402 seats out of 508. But this overwhelming triumph was short-lived. In a financial debate at the end of January 1891, Bonghi upbraided Crispi and his colleagues for failing to repeat the heroic achievement of Sella and Minghetti before 1876. Crispi's temper flared up: when Bonghi was in power, he declared, it was not hard to balance the budget, for in those days there was neither army nor navy owing to the Right's 'servile policy towards the foreigner'. At this affront to 'sacred memories',[3] many of Crispi's supporters joined Rudinì's Right, Nicotera's dissidents and the Extreme Left and brought the government down.

The King let Crispi go with mingled relief and regret and called upon

---

[1] Fortunato, *Il Mezzogiorno e lo stato italiano*, II, pp. 211–12.

[2] Volpe, I, pp. 321–30; Crispi, *Scritti e discorsi politici*, pp. 735–7.

[3] The phrase was Luzzatti's. *Memorie*, II, p. 301.

Rudinì, who formed an uneasy coalition with the dissident Left. The Right thus insecurely returned to power after fifteen years. Nicotera became Minister of Interior and Colombo, the Milanese critic of megalomania, Minister of Finance. At the outset Rudinì was supported not only by all Crispi's opponents, but also by many who owed their election two months before to Crispi's patronage and now passively accepted his successor. But the new government's career was brief and troubled. The Right found Nicotera, the architect of its humiliation in 1876, an embarrassing and not always loyal partner. Rudinì lost support by taking up the cause of decentralisation and proposing to revive Minghetti's scheme of 1861; the prospect pleased Colombo and his conservative friends in Milan, but alarmed all those who, like Crispi, feared for Italy's unity.[1] The anti-clericals were meanwhile offended by Rudinì's appeasement of the Vatican[2] and the Extreme Left by his foreign policy. Cavallotti's most ardent wish was to prevent renewal of the Triple Alliance. For this purpose he counted on Nicotera, who in March 1891 was confident of success. But in May Rudinì authorised the signature of a new treaty in Berlin without even consulting his cabinet.[3] When he informed parliament next month, Imbriani denounced him as 'an Austrian minister'. Cavallotti, who at first had persuaded his followers to vote for the government, now felt betrayed. Nicotera's heavy-handed restriction of public liberties, under pretext of suppressing anarchism, was a further cause of disillusionment. The anarchists were indeed active and finding responsive listeners among the urban unemployed. In October 1891 one of their best-known leaders, Amilcare Cipriani, a Romagnole who had fought for the Paris Commune, was sentenced to two years' imprisonment for incitement to violence. But Nicotera's police also harassed many who were not anarchists, so adding to the government's enemies. By the end of 1891 the entire Extreme Left had reverted to opposition.

The government's most serious failure was in finance. Rudinì promised to arrest the drift towards bankruptcy by a return to the example of Sella, to a miser's programme of economy to the bone. For this he relied upon Luzzatti, his Minister of the Treasury and closest collaborator. Luzzatti by now enjoyed an international reputation as economist, public financier and social reformer. Even the government's critics admitted that he was 'the right man in the right place'.[4] In a vigorous attack on the deficit he announced that he would authorise no new expenditure that was not covered

---

[1] See above, pp. 15, 92, 94.

[2] See below, pp. 222–4.

[3] Giampietro, p. 89; Farini, I, pp. 27–8. For the renewal of the Triple Alliance, see below, pp. 149–50.

[4] A. Plebano, *Storia della finanza italiana* (Turin 1899–1902), III, p. 169, where the English phrase is used.

by new revenue. In December 1891 he claimed that his budget was the soundest and most honest in the kingdom's history, and that solvency was within sight. The extravagant hopes which such statements inspired soon turned to disillusion. Rudinì and Luzzatti lacked Sella's toughness and the deficit, though smaller, persisted.[1]

Among the government's fiercest critics was the small but brilliant group of free traders who in 1890 took over the *Giornale degli Economisti* as their mouthpiece. Its best-known members were the economists Maffeo Pantaleoni and Vilfredo Pareto. They continued the tradition of Peruzzi's Florentine Adam Smith Society and preached *laisser faire* in its purest form. Wherever the state had touched it, the economy had suffered, Pareto declared. After denouncing Crispi's protectionism, with its inevitable concomitants, megalomania, militarism and reckless spending, the free traders refused to disarm when the opposition came to power; no good could be expected of Rudinì and Luzzatti because they defended the 1887 tariff, the creature of corrupt banks and industrial racketeers. If Italy was to prosper, they argued, the fiscal system must be radically transformed, the Triple Alliance ended and the burden of armaments reduced. They therefore backed the Extreme Left, the only party that had the courage to 'tell certain truths' and to 'call robbers robbers to their face'.[2] Pareto told Cavallotti that he was the true leader of the Italian Liberal party; if he failed, it would be *finis Italiae*.[3] In numbers the free traders were few and their political influence was limited. Nevertheless they gave the Extreme Left valuable intellectual reinforcement.

By the spring of 1892 it seemed clear that the budget could be balanced in only one of two ways: by higher taxation or by savings on the army. There was growing support for the second alternative, in the form of a proposal to suppress the two additional army corps created in 1882 and revert to Ricotti's original establishment of ten. Its keenest advocates, beside Ricotti himself, were the Extreme Left, the Milanese industrialists and National Conservatives, represented in the cabinet by Colombo, and a vigorous group of senators led by Crispi's former colleague, Saracco. A bitter controversy flared up. Crispi's admirers argued with passion that to reduce the army would shatter the confidence of Italy's allies, disrupt the Triple Alliance and lead to national disintegration. 'They are planning to unmake Italy', lamented Domenico Farini, President of the senate and one of the King's most trusted advisers; 'poor Italy is plunging to its end in dishonour'.[4] The King, too, believed that to mutilate the army would be

---

[1] It fell from 206 million lire in 1890–1 to 129 million in 1891–2 and 47 million in 1892–3. Coppola d'Anna, p. 85.

[2] Pareto, *Lettere a Maffeo Pantaleoni*, I, pp. 185–90, 240.

[3] Pareto to Cavallotti, 30 June 1892, in *L'Italia radicale*, p. 285.

[4] Farini, I, pp. 67, 73.

a sign of Italian decadence, and talked of abdicating rather than consent to it.[1] Luzzatti exactly shared this view[2] and carried Rudinì and the majority of the cabinet with him, but Colombo resigned. In May, on being invited to vote new taxes, the chamber revolted. Rudinì asked the King for a dissolution; on his request being refused, he resigned.

## The Second Renewal of the Triple Alliance

Rudinì's record in foreign policy was more positive. The statesmen of Europe had sighed with relief at Crispi's fall and welcomed the lull which at once descended upon the Italian Foreign Ministry. Salisbury was impressed by Rudinì's moderation and political sense. The alarms over Bizerta ceased, and in March and April 1891 Anglo-Italian friction in Africa was eliminated by the signature of two conventions defining Italy's colonial frontiers with the Sudan and British Somaliland. Rudinì, conceding what Crispi had refused, agreed that any future Italian occupation of Kassala should be temporary. He would gladly have abandoned the role of 'sentinel' in Africa and evacuated Eritrea altogether. So extreme a step was politically impossible, but he pleased the Extreme Left by promising to reorganise Eritrea as a civil colony. In December, with a sudden swing away from Crispi's Shoa policy and in defiance of Menelik, a treaty was signed with Ras Mangasha of Tigré which virtually recognised the latter's independence in return for the concession of Italy's claim to the Mareb frontier. Plans for further southward expansion were dropped.

Rudinì tried to revert to the elastic policy of Visconti Venosta and Depretis by improving relations with France. He hoped 'to lead France to appreciate the real nature of the (Triple) Alliance and remove all unjust suspicions and minor asperities'.[3] His main motive was financial, as was shown by a new appeal in February 1891 to the Rothschild Bank for a loan of 140 million lire. He was quickly disappointed. National passions still ran high and the French demanded as stiff a political price from him as from Crispi: before financial help, a trade agreement or concessions in east Africa could be arranged, the Italians must prove they had no aggressive intentions by disclosing the terms of the Triple Alliance. To consent to such a demand would have undermined the Alliance and this, in spite of

[1] Farini, I, pp. 87, 100; Finali, p. 690.
[2] 'Disorganisation of our army and navy would signify the beginning of our decadence in the world', he had told the chamber in June 1891. Luzzatti, *Memorie*, II, p. 309. Savings were in fact made by General Pelloux, the Minister for War, not by reducing the number of army corps but by shortening the training period of conscripts and allowing each basic unit to fall below strength. The opposition argued with some force that this gave Italy twelve weak instead of ten strong corps.
[3] Rudinì to Austrian ambassador, February 1891. Lowe, p. 78.

pressure from Nicotera and the Extreme Left, Rudinì had no intention of doing. His repeated assurances of friendship failed to satisfy the French. The tactless approaches of Padoa, Rothschild's agent, made him indignant: his first impulse, he told the King, had been 'to take the dirty Jew by the neck and kick him downstairs', but he had restrained himself by remembering that such conduct 'would have been unbecoming in a Marquis Di Rudinì'.[1] He gave up his attempts to obtain a French loan and turned to his allies, urging them to renew the Triple Alliance at once, a year before it was due to lapse.[2]

Both Kálnoky and Caprivi, Bismarck's successor, greeted this suggestion favourably but were disturbed by Rudinì's proposed modifications. The most important of these were that the Germans should take on extra commitments in the Balkans and north Africa, and that the new treaty should contain the promise of German-Italian and Austro-Italian commercial agreements. Italy was never satisfied, Caprivi complained, and wondered whether the Triple Alliance was really worth the risk of being 'dragged into a war of life and death for the sake of some African oasis'.[3] But in an uneasy international situation Italy's bargaining position was strong, and Caprivi conceded. The new treaty, signed on 6 May 1891, was to last for twelve years unless denounced before May 1896. At Rudinì's request it was redrafted as a single document, the Austro-Italian compensation clause of 1887 being renumbered Article VII. Rudinì's intention was to emphasise the interdependence of the separate German-Italian and Austro-Italian treaties of 1887, though at the same time Kálnoky was assured that the Italians expected no Austrian help in north Africa. The Germans declined new commitments in the Balkans. They also rejected some of Rudinì's demands for north Africa and vetoed any specific reference to Morocco in the text. But a new article provided for German-Italian cooperation, should the two countries decide the African *status quo* had become untenable; which meant that an Italian occupation of Tripoli was no longer dependent on a French threat, but on a decision by Germany and Italy. This was one step nearer an Italian Tripoli. Two protocols were added: one expressing the desirability of commercial treaties to consolidate the Alliance, the other stating that the three Powers would exert themselves to secure British accession to the clauses affecting the western Mediterranean.[4] These

---

[1] GP, VII, 1418; DDF (1), VIII, 256 ff., 290, 334 ff.
[2] This had already been suggested by Crispi in talks with Caprivi at Milan in November 1890. Rudinì also adopted Crispi's suggestions regarding the new form of the treaty and its transformation into an 'economic league'.
[3] GP, VII, 1412.
[4] The Italians were satisfied with the Second Mediterranean Agreement as regards the eastern half of the sea, but wanted to 'fill the gap' in the 1887 system by a more specific British commitment in the western Mediterranean.

modfications did not alter the general character of the Alliance, which remained conservative, limited and defensive.[1]

Rudinì, aided by the Germans, strove hard during May and June 1891 to extract more binding commitments from Britain. But Salisbury, under pressure from the Liberal opposition, would consider neither an Anglo-Italian exchange of notes nor a stiffening of the First Mediterranean Agreement. He was ready to collaborate with Italy to defend the *status quo* and indeed regarded close Anglo-Italian cooperation as 'the key of the present situation in Europe'. Once again he declared that 'in case of a French attack upon the Italian coasts, . . . Italy can count on British support whether or not there is any previous agreement'. Beyond that he would not or could not go.[2] In October the Germans once again tried to stir him into action by reviving the scare of a French seizure of Tuat, on the borders of Morocco. Salisbury refused to be rattled by what he regarded as a 'trifling question'. This British passivity caused Rudinì much anxiety. But he had to be satisfied with reassuring words.[3]

Italy's situation in the summer of 1891 was therefore much the same as in 1887. But many in the outside world believed a significant change had taken place. Anglo-German relations at this time were cordial. In July 1891 the British fleet visited the Adriatic and was welcomed by Humbert at Venice and Francis Joseph at Fiume. On 29 June Rudinì announced the renewal of the Triple Alliance in the senate, and after referring to an Anglo-Italian exchange of views on the peace and *status quo* of the Mediterranean, added that he could 'conceive of no question in which Italy's way of looking at it would not be identical with England's'. The statement was clearly designed to give the impression that the British were more closely committed than was in fact the case, and rumours circulated that they had joined the Triple Alliance.[4] The French, who had hoped for a change in Italian policy with the fall of Crispi, felt angry and humiliated; but they still believed that economic, financial and diplomatic pressure would break down Italian resistance. Negotiations on east African frontiers, which had made good progress, were abruptly broken off. Large-scale selling of

---

[1] On 4 May the Italo–Spanish Agreement of 1887 was also renewed for four years. Germany and Austria again acceded; Salisbury was informed and expressed satisfaction. BD, VIII, pp. 17–18.

[2] Lowe, pp. 82–4, 90; Cecil, IV, pp. 404–5.

[3] Taylor, pp. 350–3. Salisbury still refused to do more than 'make words do as much work as can be got out of them' (see above, p. 136). In November 1891 he instructed his ambassador in Rome to 'press the note of mutual interest, esteem and affection, without, of course, entering into any definite engagements'. Lowe, p. 85.

[4] In private conversation with Farini on 19 June, Rudinì spoke as if 'the adhesion of England' had been secured. Farini, I, p. 32.

Italian securities on the Paris Bourse began again, and all through the summer Luzzatti had to fight hard to prevent a collapse of Italian credit abroad.[1] In July the French fleet visited Kronstadt and next month occurred the first military talks which were soon to lead to the Franco-Russian Alliance.

Rudinì thus failed to break the vicious circle in Italian relations with France. Italy would not weaken the Triple Alliance until sure of French financial and economic help; France would not make financial or economic concessions until sure that Italy would not abet German aggression. Both countries suffered from this deadlock, but Italy, the weaker of the two, suffered the more. Italian commercial difficulties were, however, greatly relieved by treaties with Germany, Austria-Hungary and Switzerland, which came into effect in the spring of 1892 for twelve years. Important concessions were won for Italian agricultural products and Austria-Hungary, whose vineyards were now in their turn afflicted by phylloxera, opened a valuable market for Italian wine.[2] No major alterations were made to the 1887 industrial tariffs and the small band of free traders remained scornfully critical. Nevertheless within the framework of the tariff system adjustments could be made, and in 1892 agriculture received partial compensation for the blows it had suffered in 1887. The new treaties introduced a long period of commercial stability and a fairer economic balance between north and south. Even so, while the quarrel with France persisted, Italy's financial and economic position remained insecure, and this in its turn weakened its international standing.[3]

## Giolitti and the Bank Scandal

When Rudinì resigned in May 1892, Crispi expected to return to power. Summoned by the King for consultation, he painted a catastrophic picture of the slough into which Italy had fallen and declared that only a big man could save the situation.[4] But Humbert ignored his hints and turned to

[1] Luzzatti, *Memorie*, II, pp. 313–18.

[2] Italian wine exports to Austria–Hungary increased from an annual average of 26,000 hectolitres in 1887–91 to 956,000 in 1892–1900. Corbino, IV, p. 171.

[3] Italy's financial difficulties, and the extent to which they were being attributed by Italians to the Triple Alliance, caused Italy's allies much concern. Though William II appears to have approved a temporary reduction of the Italian army in the spring of 1892, both the German and Austrian governments were understandably reluctant to get involved in Italian domestic politics by offering advice on so delicate a matter. GP, VII, 1435–41; Farini, I, pp. 107–9, 175, 436, 467–8. The King was particularly sensitive to any suggestion of foreign intervention or patronage. Luzzatti, *Opere*, I, p. 7.

[4] T. Palamenghi-Crispi, *Giovanni Giolitti* (Rome 1913), pp. 18–24; Farini, I, pp. 89–90, 102–3.

Giovanni Giolitti, a relative newcomer in parliament, whom he and his politically influential adviser, Urbano Rattazzi,[1] had for some time marked down as the Prime Minister of the future.

Giolitti was a Piedmontese from Dronero at the foot of the Alps. This fact in itself commended him to the King and to Rattazzi, who also was Piedmontese. By political sympathy he was a man of the Left but, like all the Piedmontese Left, an unswerving monarchist. He came of solid middle-class stock; both his father's and his mother's families had long records of public service as magistrates, soldiers and administrators. The young Giolitti took no part in the wars of the Risorgimento. Instead of rushing off to volunteer like so many of his contemporaries in other parts of Italy, he stayed at home and with Piedmontese common sense continued his study of law at Turin University. In 1862, at the age of twenty, he entered the civil service and after a career of twenty years, during which he worked directly under Sella and Minghetti in the Ministry of Finance, reached the top of his profession as secretary of the Court of Accounts and a member of the Council of State. This qualified him for election to parliament and in 1882, on the suggestion of friends, he somewhat reluctantly became deputy for Dronero. Politics in rural Piedmont were still patriarchal, and the patronage of the retiring deputy made even an electoral speech unnecessary.[2] He represented Dronero continuously from 1882 until his death in 1928.

In the chamber Giolitti made a quiet start, concerning himself mainly with technical and financial questions, and continuing to talk like a civil servant. His natural instinct was to support the King's government, whether led by Depretis or by Crispi, and on most issues he voted contentedly with the majority. On finance, however, he had views of his own. In February 1886 disgust with the government's failure to limit expenditure drove him to join the Centre[3] as one of Magliani's sternest critics. In May 1889, within five months of Magliani's resignation, he became Crispi's Minister of the Treasury. In that post he strengthened his reputation as a sound financier and champion of economy. His resignation in December 1890, after a disagreement with his colleagues over the public works esti-

[1] Rattazzi, known familiarly as Urbanino, was the nephew of his namesake Urbano, Cavour's partner in the *connubio* of 1852. As Secretary-General, and later 'Minister', of the Royal Household, he was the King's chief personal and financial adviser.

[2] After the election of 1886 the mayor of a commune in Giolitti's constituency apologised to him for the fact that two votes in the commune had been cast against him. 'We have found out whose those two votes were', he said, 'and they have been given such a time of it that they have decided to emigrate to France' – so it would not happen again. Giolitti replied that 'this was really too much'. Giolitti, *Memorie*, p. 42.

[3] See above, p. 93.

mates, was regarded by many as a shrewd desertion of a sinking ship and proved a severe blow to Crispi. Rudinì would have been delighted to have him as a colleague, but Giolitti refused all his offers, partly because he thought his cabinet too heavily weighted towards the right, partly from aversion to Nicotera's methods of government. At first he supported Rudinì's programme of economies, then played a leading part in bringing him down.

Giolitti had much in common with Depretis, whom he had greatly admired: the same calm temperament and appearance of inertia, the same understanding of human frailties, the same Piedmontese sense of government and respect for order. He had a clear head, a mastery of facts and figures, and the knack of reducing complex problems to simple intelligible phrases. From his Piedmontese background and from his teachers Sella and Minghetti he had learnt to regard a balanced budget as something almost sacred. His approach to politics was empirical; as a schoolboy he had acquired a distaste for speculative philosophy and all his life he avoided rhetorical appeals to emotion. 'When I have said what I have to say', he once told Cavallotti, 'it is impossible for me to go on speaking.' He was an unrelenting hard worker to whom social distinction meant nothing. In Rome he lived in modest bourgeois style in the ugly new Esquiline quarter. But Rome was no more than his place of work; his Piedmontese roots were deep, and even at the height of his fame and power it was to long country walks and family holidays in the Alpine valleys that he returned for refreshment.[1]

Giolitti's cabinet was drawn predominantly from the Left and was the nearest approach to a single-party government that Italy had known since 1882. In forming it he relied heavily on Zanardelli, as he lacked a personal following of his own. His parliamentary début was inauspicious. Giolitti was still thought of as a bureaucrat, and the appointment of such a man as Prime Minister was greeted with a storm of incredulous disapproval. Crispi had told the King that Giolitti was 'incapable of ruling the country' as he was a mere novice in the art of government. This was the general opinion. Not only was he distrusted as a parliamentary *arriviste* and a creature of the King; he was also the first Prime Minister who could boast of no part, however modest, in the Risorgimento. To many this seemed unnatural and almost indecent. Right, Left and Extreme Left deplored the absence of 'patriots' in his cabinet. The programme he offered was retrenchment,[2] financial and administrative reorganisation, a quiet foreign

---

[1] Ansaldo, pp. 51–4.
[2] Giolitti intended to freeze military expenditure, but he promised the King that there would be no cuts in the armed services. As security for this promise he retained Rudinì's Ministers for War and Navy in his cabinet. Farini, I, p. 87.

policy and measures to stimulate 'the economic *risorgimento* of the country'. Its matter-of-fact style and prosaic content shocked the chamber. 'In mediocre times, mediocre princes appoint mediocre ministers', commented Imbriani, quoting from Cesare Balbo. On 26 May Giolitti was given a majority of only nine on his first vote of confidence. He kept his head, secured the King's consent to a dissolution which had been refused to Rudinì, asked parliament for six months' supplies and on 11 June obtained a majority of 72.

The election which followed in November became in later years a byword for governmental pressure and corruption. Giolitti's weak parliamentary position forced him to make a more thorough use of the weapons at his disposal than any of his predecessors. He dismissed or transferred 46 out of 69 prefects, dissolved many local authorities and made a mass of more than usually partisan nominations to the senate. His Under-Secretary of Interior, the Neapolitan Pietro Rosano, directed a fierce campaign against Nicotera's supporters in the south. Nineteen elections were later annulled for irregularities, a record number. Even though the Extreme Left increased its strength despite great pressure, Giolitti obtained the results he desired. At the cost of alienating many of the established political leaders, he created a nucleus of loyal Giolittians on whom he could thenceforth rely. The new chamber gave him a majority of 214.

A prominent item in the government's programme was the improvement of working-class conditions. Giolitti saw that the social question was becoming dominant. Already as Minister of the Treasury in 1889 he had made a minor but important innovation by deciding that public works contracts could be assigned to workmen's cooperatives. In 1892, as Prime Minister, he startled the old-fashioned by addressing a working-class association at Turin. Next year he adopted the cause of fiscal justice and announced his intention of making the rich shoulder a fairer share of the burden in the form of higher death duties and a more steeply graduated income-tax. But long before he had had time to achieve any fiscal or social reform, he had become involved in a great banking scandal which soon reduced Italy to nervous hysteria.

The scandal had been brewing for several years. Under Magliani's regime of inflation and easy credit the six issue banks[1] had steadily increased their note circulation, until by 1887 five of them had exceeded their legal limit. This was well known to the government and in banking and

---

[1] The failure to create a single national bank with a monopoly of note issue had been a strange exception to the policy of centralisation carried out after 1861. The Left had consistently favoured the regional issue banks, particularly the Banco di Napoli.

financial circles, but restriction of credit in a period of speculative boom
was considered politically impossible. In 1889 the boom burst. Three
Turin banks, heavily involved in building speculation in Rome, suspended
payments. The issue banks were persuaded by the government to intervene,
in order to avert a major disaster, and so themselves became dangerously
involved in the crisis. In June 1889 an inspection of one of them, the
Banca Romana, revealed grave irregularities in its administration and
accounts. Crispi feared that publicity might further undermine public confidence and suppressed the report. Over the next three years there was
much talk of the need for a single issue bank and for a reduction in the note
circulation. But neither Crispi nor his successors, Rudinì and Luzzatti,
had the courage to face the revelations and political storms which any
serious attempt at banking reform was bound to precipitate. In preferring
to trust to time, they made a tragic miscalculation.

The facts about the Banca Romana soon leaked out. A copy of the suppressed report came into the hands of Pantaleoni, who passed it on to
Napoleone Colajanni, the independent socialist deputy from Sicily.[1] On
20 December 1892 Colajanni read out long extracts in the chamber. Amid
much excitement Giolitti was forced to appoint an expert commission,
under the chairmanship of Gaspare Finali, to investigate the issue banks.
Its report, published on 18 January 1893, confirmed a serious state of
affairs in the Banca Romana: a deficiency of cash, cooked accounts, a note
circulation of 135 million lire instead of the 75 million permitted by law,
a great quantity of bad debts due to speculation in building, and 40 million
lire in a duplicated series of notes which had been printed in Britain but
not issued owing to the honesty of minor officials of the bank.[2] Next day
the governor of the bank, Bernardo Tanlongo, and several of his subordinates were arrested. Early in February it became known that a militant
journalist and deputy of the Right, Rocco De Zerbi, was under investigation for receiving 425,000 lire from the Banca Romana in return for services
rendered in parliament. A fortnight later he died of a heart attack. This
strong whiff of corruption roused parliament, press and public to frenzy.
Italy seemed determined not to lag behind France where the Panama
scandal was then raging.

[1] Colajanni, a doctor by training and journalist by profession, was the author of
numerous works on anthropology, criminology and sociology. In the 1880s he
abandoned republicanism for socialism, a subject upon which he was for a time
Italy's leading theoretical writer. After 1890 he became a collaborator of the free
traders and often acted as their spokesman in parliament. At the time of the 1892
election, Pareto and Pantaleoni helped to pay his deputy's expenses in order to
prevent him from resigning from parliament.
[2] Despatched from London to Rome 'just as if it were a barrel of beer', was
Giolitti's comment. *Memorie*, p. 78.

With the technical side of the problem Giolitti was well fitted to deal, and he acted with energy, even if belatedly. His Bank Act of August 1893 liquidated the Banca Romana and reformed the whole system of note issue, restricting the privilege to a new and powerful Banca d'Italia and to the Banco di Napoli and Banco di Sicilia, and providing for stricter state control. Though it did not immediately restore confidence nor, owing to southern obstruction, achieve the single bank of issue, it was nevertheless a sound reform of lasting value. Giolitti received no credit for it because by now the affair of the Banca Romana had become a burning political issue. An irresponsible press spread wild rumours of corrupt dealings between bankers and politicians, of interference with the course of justice, of financial crooks with protection in high places. The good names of parliament and the whole state machine became involved. Some of these suspicions were confirmed when the facts were revealed. Leading bankers had resorted to criminal acts in order to stave off disaster. Many politicians had had unwise dealings with the banking world and a few had been indisputably venal. Successive governments had been culpably negligent, though not corrupt, in their control of credit and note issue. At every level there had been repeated attempts to cover up shortcomings rather than tackle the basic need for reform. Nevertheless there is a striking disproportion between the extent of the irregularities and the political storm which followed. The explanation lies partly in the nervous tension created by financial crisis, partly in the avidity with which rival politicians seized upon every scandalous allegation, 'each hoping', in Farini's words, 'to catch his own particular enemy with his fingers in the till'.[1]

Giolitti became the favourite target. He was indeed vulnerable to attack. He had been Minister of the Treasury in the government that had suppressed the original report of 1889. As Prime Minister he had borrowed from the Banca Romana through the Treasury, for governmental purposes, in August 1892 and had nominated the bank's governor, Tanlongo, to the senate just after the election in November.[2] He had resisted a parliamentary enquiry, thus encouraging suspicions that he had something to hide. He had, in short, acted unwisely and carelessly. But in the hands of his enemies these actions were so twisted that he was presented to the public as a monster of corruption. Tanlongo and the Banca Romana's political friends did their utmost to defame him, in the calculation that a change of government would lead to the release of the arrested culprits. Some of the mud thrown by the scandalmongers stuck, and the resentments which

---

[1] Farini, I, p. 151.

[2] The accusation that he had obtained money from the bank for electoral purposes was false. The loan of August 1892 was repaid after six months. Natale, pp. 181, 219–22; Giolitti, *Memorie*, pp. 94–5.

had burst out on Giolitti's appointment as Prime Minister were now given free rein. Both Right and Extreme Left joined in the fray. Nicotera was implacably hostile. Cavallotti eloquently denounced corruption in high places. The free traders, who explained both political corruption and banking irregularities by governmental interference with what should be private business, attacked Giolitti even more vehemently than they had attacked his predecessors. Rudinì, still smarting from his defeat in May 1892 and the King's refusal to grant him a dissolution, hoped by discrediting Giolitti to hasten the return of the Right to power. Formidable opposition developed in the senate, where Giolitti had made many enemies by his mass creation of senators and his inclusion of only one member of the upper chamber in his cabinet. Bonghi wrote an article entitled 'The Function of the Sovereign in a Free State' which could be interpreted only as a censure upon the King for protecting Giolitti and ignoring his duty to exercise 'a moral surveillance over the state'. Villari deplored the reduction of Italy to moral chaos by the survival of a suspect government in power. Less reputable critics pointed to the deaths of four of Giolitti's ministers within a year as proof that he possessed the evil eye.[1] The government lost ground throughout 1893. Giolitti was forced to yield to the demands for a parliamentary enquiry and only the King's refusal to accept his resignation kept him in office. By autumn, when parliament reassembled, his position had been further undermined by an explosion of social discontent in Sicily, which frightened conservatives into believing that revolution was imminent.

## The Rise of Socialism

The years 1887–93 were critical for the Italian socialist and working-class movements. In 1889 the Second International was founded during a meeting of working-class delegates to the great Paris Exhibition. One result of this gathering was the decision to proclaim May 1st as Labour Day. Orderly demonstrations in the great cities on 1 May 1890 gave the Italian public its first indication of a rising working-class movement;[2] on the same occasion next year, anarchist-inspired riots created a far less favourable image. Among the Italian delegates at Paris was Osvaldo Gnocchi-Viani, one of the earliest Italian Marxists, who returned full of admiration for the French *bourses de travail* and on their model founded a *camera di lavoro* in Milan in the same year. By 1893 there were fourteen,

[1] The possessor of the evil eye in Italian is a *jettatore*, and the Prime Minister figured in hostile newspapers and cartoons as *Gioljettatore*.

[2] Another indication was the increase in the average number of industrial strikes per year from 67 in 1881–5 to 106 in 1886–90. *ASI 1919–1921*, p. 512; Neufeld. p. 547.

linked in a national organisation. These institutions were soon to play a key role in the Italian working-class movement, exercising more power and commanding more devotion than the federations of trade unions which were later created on the British and German models. The federations appealed mainly to the more skilled and prosperous, and therefore more conservative, elements of the industrial working-class, which were primarily interested in improving wages and conditions in their particular trade. The chambers of labour, on the other hand, were more aggressively political and appealed to the less sophisticated, especially in the rural areas. They provided a central organisation for all the unions and working-class institutions of a commune or province, developed a wide range of welfare activities, and planned and directed the local class struggle.[1]

By 1891 the working-class exclusiveness of the Partito Operaio had broken down and its leaders were ready to combine with the middle-class intellectuals of the Milan Socialist League. This collaboration led to the founding of a united Workers' party at a congress in Genoa in August 1892. Almost as soon as the congress opened, the anarchist minority broke with the legalitarian majority and founded a party of its own. This was a turning-point in the history of Italian socialism. In September 1893 a congress at Reggio Emilia confirmed the party programme: class war, organised resistance to capital, socialisation, independent political action at elections and in parliament and no collaboration with bourgeois parties. In the course of 1892–3 the agricultural unions of the Po valley, under their middle-class leaders, came over to the party in mass, and the congress at Reggio Emilia ended with a march-past of 10,000 peasants, with banners flying in the style of a religious procession. In the same year the party included the word 'Socialist' in its official title.[2]

The three elements which made up the new party were thus the legalitarian socialists, the Partito Operaio and the agricultural unions of the Po valley. From the first it was dominated by the intellectuals. To the youth of the middle class graduating from the universities in the decade after 1880, socialism came as a revelation. Brought up in the intellectually fashionable rationalism of the time, they had accepted the Darwinian concepts of evolution and scientific progress with little questioning. From Darwin's vision of the world it seemed but a short step to socialism. Thousands of young men, already instinctively leftist in their politics, came to believe, like Prampolini, that 'there is a historical and psychological relation, of cause and effect, between modern science and socialism', and

---

[1] Rigola, *Storia*, pp. 159–62; Neufeld, pp. 319–21.
[2] The party was known by three successive names in its first four years of existence: the *Partito dei Lavoratori Italiani* until 1893, the *Partito Socialista dei Lavoratori Italiani* from 1893 to 1895, and the *Partito Socialista Italiano* after 1895.

to identify the latter with inevitable progress towards a higher civilisation.[1]

Outstanding in this generation of socialist intellectuals was Filippo Turati. Son of a conservative, devoutly Catholic prefect, he acquired an interest in criminology while studying law at Bologna University and on graduation plunged into the radical-democratic politics of Milan. In 1885 he met a Russian revolutionary exile, Anna Kuliscioff,[2] who became his wife in all but name and the inseparable companion of his long political career. Her influence accelerated his conversion to socialism. Soon he was well known as 'the socialist poet' and author of the Workers' Hymn. When the rupture between the Milanese democrats and the Partito Operaio occurred in 1886, Turati passionately took the side of the latter. Three years later he helped to found the Milan Socialist League and subsequently played a leading part in the formation of the united socialist party. In 1891 he founded in Milan a fortnightly review, *Critica Sociale*, which has been called 'the heart and brain of Italian socialism' and the guide of an entire generation. Physically delicate, intellectually brilliant, humane and sensitive, Turati was eclectic in his ideals and never swallowed the Marxist dogma in its full rigour. His heart, more than his head, was converted. Throughout the next thirty years he fought for two things: the strengthening of socialist unity and the advancement of democracy. From these goals he never wavered, in spite of constant conflict between them. While hating violence and the revolutionary demagogy in which so many of his fellow-socialists indulged, he always acknowledged the ties of party loyalty and put unity above differences of programme or temperament. At the same time, though conscious of the party's immaturity and its need of a long education for its predestined role, Turati never lost faith in the processes of democracy which one day, he was convinced, would bring the proletariat to power.

A very different, but equally important, contribution to the intellectual development of Italian socialism was made by the eminent Neapolitan philosopher, Antonio Labriola, who in 1874 became professor at Rome. Labriola's approach to socialism was through Hegel, not Darwin. About 1890 he discovered Marx, then published the first Italian translation of the *Communist Manifesto*. For the rest of his life he regarded it as his mission to popularise 'scientific' Marxism. He was a brilliant scholar and teacher who found it difficult to forgive the failings of humbler men. No Italian socialist escaped his sarcasm, for all except himself were charlatans. 'I am

[1] See Prampolini's letter to Colajanni, November 1883, in *Democrazia e socialismo*, pp. 285–90.

[2] Anna Kuliscioff first became interested in Italy through Andrea Costa, whom she met in 1877 at Lugano and by whom she later had a child. In 1878 she was tried for conspiracy with other Bakuninists in Florence but acquitted. Costa's conversion to legalitarian socialism was in part due to her.

just a lone German lost in Italy', he wrote half-seriously to Engels in 1893.[1] Labriola was the first Italian to present socialism not as the natural off-spring of the leftism of the Risorgimento but as a philosophical system, and after his death his orthodoxy earned him a high reputation amongst Marxist intellectuals.

Yet, great though Labriola's influence has subsequently been, it was Turati's socialism that after 1890 made the sensational conquests of what has been called 'the decade of Marx'. Socialism spread like a fashionable new gospel amongst the younger generation. Middle-class youths went out to preach in the factories and the countryside, crusading for the material and moral elevation of the masses with a simple, evangelical fervour that recalled the followers of St Francis. In Italy socialism won the students and intellectuals before it won the working-class, and so acquired a distinctive flavour which it has never lost. The Socialist party became the party of youth, in revolt against *trasformismo*, parliamentary corruption and an effete ruling class. Benedetto Croce, himself at this time attracted by the new doctrine, paid this tribute thirty years later, as an elder statesman, philosopher and historian, to his own generation in its youth:

> If one passes in review the intellectual world of those days . . . one is forced to conclude . . . that socialism won over all, or almost all, the flower of the younger generation; and that to remain uninfluenced by and indifferent to it, or to assume, as some did, an attitude of unreasoning hostility towards it, was a sure sign of inferiority.[2]

Italian socialism was in origin a popular rather than a working-class movement. Though the German social democrats enjoyed enormous prestige in Italy, attempts to imitate their discipline and massive organisation never met with success. The socialist movement which most closely resembled the Italian was that of France. Middle-class intellectual leadership, Latin ebullience and the restricted size of the industrial proletariat made the party peculiarly liable to heresies and deviations. These characteristics, which were later to disrupt the movement, were assets in its turbulent early years. The foundation of the party coincided with economic depression, the trade war with France, financial disorder and the bank scandals. Crude messianic socialist propaganda kept ignorant workmen and peasants in feverish excitement and in 1893 led to a major explosion.

In August of that year violent anti-Italian riots occurred at Aigues Mortes, in the Camargue sixty miles west of Marseilles. They were not the first instance of attacks by French workmen on Italian immigrant labourers who were prepared to accept work at cut-rate wages. But at Aigues Mortes

---

[1] Antonio Labriola, *Lettere a Engels*, p. 118.     [2] Croce, pp. 148–9.

the violence was such that thirty Italians were killed. As soon as the news reached Italy, demonstrations took place in Naples and other cities. In Rome the windows of the French Embassy were smashed and for a time the mob seemed likely to get out of hand. The incident revealed an alarming ferment of revolt close beneath the surface.[1]

At the end of the year Sicily was the scene of a far more serious upheaval. Depression and the trade war with France had dealt a heavy blow to the island's main sources of wealth – wine, fruit and sulphur.[2] The dominant landowning class had been able to throw most of the economic burden on to the peasantry, in the form of higher rents and discriminatory local taxation. As social tension rose to breaking-point, a handful of socialist intellectuals saw and seized their opportunity. In 1891 a Fascio dei Lavoratori was founded at Catania by Giuseppe De Felice Giuffrida, the local leader of the Extreme Left. The fascio's rapid success as a combination of trade union and mutual benefit society led during 1892 to the foundation of similar fasci in Palermo and other Sicilian towns. Loosely linked among themselves, they constituted the first organised mass movement in Sicilian history. Their leaders, many of them recent graduates of Palermo University, were mostly very young and hitherto quite unknown. The keenest socialist among them was Garibaldi Bosco, founder of the Palermo fascio. In August 1892 he attended the Socialist party's congress at Genoa and on his return obediently purged his fascio of its anarchist, Mazzinian and other non-socialist members. De Felice by contrast resisted dictation from the mainland and preferred to keep membership of his Catania fascio open to all sections of the extreme left. His ideal of a united democratic front was shared by the father of Sicilian socialism, Colajanni. De Felice also maintained contact with leading anarchists like Cipriani, now a French citizen living in France.[3] On these and other important issues there was much friction between Catania and Palermo. Nevertheless the leaders successfully drafted a socialist programme and secured its adoption in May 1893 by a congress of 500 delegates. Two months later candidates sponsored by the fasci scored striking successes in the local elections. This, said Bosco, was the first independent battle fought by socialists in Sicily. 'Our

[1] In a letter to Engels, Antonio Labriola described the demonstrations as 'a remarkable case of spontaneous anarchy', which ended in 'rousing the revolutionary instincts of the people'. *Lettere a Engels*, p. 119.

[2] The price of sulphur, on the production of which about 50,000 Sicilian families depended for their livelihood, fell from 141 lire per ton in 1874–5 to 113 in 1891 and 55 in the first half of 1894. The price of wine fell from 40·5 lire per hectolitre in 1887 to 10·2 in 1890–3, that of citrus fruits by between one-third and one-half in the same period. Romano, *Fasci*, p. 89; Colajanni, pp. 85–6.

[3] Romano, *Fasci*, pp. 385–7, 392–4. Cipriani and the anarchists had been looking to Sicily since 1890 as the most promising field for insurrectionary action.

programme', he wrote in October, 'is that of the Italian Workers' Socialist party, the programme of the Marxist school.'[1]

In the spring of 1893 the leaders of the movement decided to carry their propaganda to the peasants and miners of the countryside. Their success, like that of their northern comrades in the Po valley, was sensational. Between March and October the number of fasci grew from 35 to 162.[2] Few of these new recruits were true socialists. The peasants who flocked into the fasci were impatient for social justice and convinced that a new world was about to be born. In many of their meeting-places a crucifix hung beside the red flag, or portraits of the King and Queen beside those of Garibaldi, Mazzini and Marx, and cheers for the King were often heard in their quasi-religious processions.[3] Their immediate demands were not unreasonable: fair rents, higher wages, lower local taxes and distribution of misappropriated common land. In July a peasant conference at Corleone drafted model agrarian contracts for labourers, sharecroppers and tenants and presented them to the landowners. When the latter refused to negotiate, the *braccianti* and *mezzadri* struck over a large part of western Sicily. In September the state authorities intervened and some of the landowners were persuaded to capitulate. Elsewhere the strike continued until November. The success of the peasants was infectious. During the autumn the railwaymen of Catania and Palermo, the sulphur miners and many other smaller groups of workers followed their example and won higher wages or better working conditions. The aim of the leaders of the fasci, like that of the socialists of northern Italy, was to inculcate discipline, teach the elements of organisation, discourage blind violence and so elevate the peasants and workers both materially and morally. But in the autumn of 1893 they lost control and the popular agitation got out of hand. Land was seized by peasant squatters, violent crowds demonstrated for work and against local misgovernment, tax offices were burnt down and clashes with the police grew more frequent and bloody. The old peasant fatalism seemed to have vanished[4] and the whole island to be on the verge of revolution.

The Sicilian ruling class was seized by panic. Prefects and frightened

---

[1] Romano, *Fasci*, pp. 216, 222–5.

[2] ibid., pp. 185, 225–6. Bosco and De Felice claimed at the Socialist party's congress at Reggio Emilia in September 1893 to speak for 300,000 Sicilian socialists. This was certainly a wild exaggeration.

[3] The primitive character of much of their 'socialism' is demonstrated by such statements by peasants as 'In the fascio is to be found the truth of Christ', and 'Jesus was a true socialist and wanted just what the fasci were demanding'. Nicola Barbato, leader of the fascio of Piana dei Greci, was known as 'the workers' apostle'. Romano, *Fasci*, pp. 231–6; Colajanni, pp. 15, 186.

[4] It is significant that in the areas where the fasci were best organised and most consciously socialist, the grip of the Mafia over the peasants was substantially, and sometimes permanently, weakened.

local councils bombarded Rome with requests for the immediate suppression of the fasci. Landlords, astonished by their peasants' presumption in bargaining over rents and wages, demanded the closing of all schools to halt the spread of subversive doctrines. Giolitti recognised the need to suppress sedition. Sporadic arrests of leaders of the fasci took place from May 1893 onwards, and police and military reinforcements were sent to the island. But in spite of heavy pressure from the King, the army and conservative circles in Rome, he would neither treat strikes as a crime nor dissolve the fasci nor authorise the use of firearms against popular demonstrations. His policy was 'to allow these economic struggles to resolve themselves through an amelioration of the condition of the workers' and not to interfere in the process.[1] This inertia encouraged both sides to resort to extreme measures: the peasants, intoxicated by their new sense of organised power, to bolder demands and demonstrations, and the ruling class to blind resistance.

Giolitti's reluctance to deal firmly with what many conservatives believed to be imminent revolution shook even the King's confidence in him[2] and sealed the fate of his government, already undermined by the banking scandal. On 23 November 1893 the report of the parliamentary enquiry into the Banca Romana was read out, for three and a half hours, in a wildly excited chamber. It 'deplored' or 'disapproved' of the actions of a number of ex-ministers, deputies, civil servants and journalists in accepting loans from the Banca Romana which they had made no attempts to repay, or for using their political influence to obtain favours from the bank for their friends; and it 'disapproved' of the conduct of Crispi, Giolitti, Luzzatti, Nicotera and other members of Crispi's and Rudini's governments in concealing and failing to act on the original report of 1889. While recognising that Giolitti's personal rectitude was beyond question, it nevertheless censured him for his nomination of Tanlongo to the senate and returned an open verdict on several of the allegations against him that were freely circulating.[3] Grave doubts were therefore still left in the public mind, and political passions and personal hatreds prevented any critical consideration of the disclosures. Howls of abuse greeted the Prime Minister when the reading of the report was completed, and from the Extreme Left came roars of 'Robber! To prison!' Giolitti was caught unprepared and

[1] Romano, *Fasci*, pp. 349–60, 434–7; Farini, I, pp. 379, 385; Giolitti, *Memorie*, p. 88; Crispi, *Politica interna*, pp. 284–7.
[2] Romano, *Fasci*, pp. 375–6; Natale, pp. 243–4; *Quarant' anni di politica italiana*, I, 225, 229.
[3] The two most important were that he had obtained money from the bank for corrupt electoral purposes, and had abstracted documents incriminating himself from Tanlongo's house.

lost his nerve. Deciding that he must defend himself as a simple deputy, he weakly abandoned his majority and resigned.[1] This was taken as proof of guilt and it was widely assumed that his inglorious political career had come to an end.[2]

[1] Natale, pp. 277–8.

[2] One of Rudinì's friends commented that Giolitti was like 'a Bologna sausage: half ass and half swine'. Bülow, II, p. 56. Even the King, who knew that the allegations against Giolitti were false, blamed him for 'running away from the chamber', and told Farini in 1895 that he had been mistaken in thinking Giolitti a great man. Farini, I, pp. 333–5, 540, 668.

# 5

# The Crisis of the Liberal State
## 1894–1901

### Crispi's Second Term

After a prolonged ministerial crisis, Crispi took office again as the saviour of his country. It was a grim moment. As if the Banca Romana scandal and the threat of anarchy in Sicily were not enough, one of Italy's leading banks, the Credito Mobiliare, closed its doors at the end of November 1893. The ensuing financial crisis, the most severe since 1866, heightened the atmosphere of impending catastrophe. Convinced that Italy was on the brink of ruin, the Prime Minister appealed dramatically for 'a truce of God' in party politics[1] and turned at once to the crisis in Sicily. Crispi was now seventy-five years of age and beginning to show signs of physical failing: his speech was often confused, he tired easily and was prone to bouts of extreme discouragement and tearful melancholy.[2] Nevertheless much of his old energy survived and his admirers were not disappointed. The King, though wryly admitting he was difficult to work with, recognised him as 'the man for the situation' and bowed to his insistence that Giolitti's patron and admirer, Rattazzi, should resign from his dominant position at court. Farini told Crispi that he was the last remaining moral force capable of saving Italy; if he failed, there would be no alternative to naked force.[3] The fact that Crispi, like Giolitti, had been censured by the Banca Romana enquiry was forgotten. His return to power was a return to the Risorgimento, the replacement of a dubious prosaic *arriviste* by the strong man of the heroic generation.

Crispi was not blind to the existence of misery. 'I love the people; I too am a worker', he liked to say. On many occasions since 1887 he had stressed his sympathy with the poor and his awareness of the need for social reform. Before 1891 he had been the patron of the Sicilian working-class and many

---

[1] Crispi, *Politica interna*, pp. 294–7.
[2] Farini, I, pp. 407, 477, 487–8, 518.
[3] ibid., pp. 339, 383, 388.

of their associations had been named after him.[1] Now one of his first acts was to circulate all prefects in the island on the need to reform local taxation. Important measures of land reform were promised for the near future. Colajanni, the chief architect of Giolitti's fall, was first offered the Ministry of Agriculture, which he refused, then sent to Sicily on a mission of appeasement. In spite of bitter reproaches from the socialists, Cavallotti, Imbriani and most of the non-socialist Extreme Left promised Crispi their support.[2]

Crispi's good intentions were soon drowned in the clamour for strong measures. Giolitti's fall had aggravated the situation in Sicily. In the three weeks of uncertainty before the new government was formed, the rapid spread of violence and arson drove many local authorities to defy Giolitti's ban on the use of firearms. During December ninety-two peasants lost their lives in clashes with the police and army. These disorders were not the product of a revolutionary plot. The leaders of the fasci were in fact undecided about what to do. Though De Felice, counting on the anarchists,[3] urged immediate insurrection if the government tried to dissolve the fasci, the majority recognised the futility of barricades and favoured calm and prudence. But in Rome disaster seemed imminent. On the strength of dubious documents and reports, Crispi decided there was an organised conspiracy to detach his own Sicily from Italy; the leaders of the fasci were in league with the clericals and financed by French gold, and war and invasion were imminent.[4] The slightest hesitation, he told Farini two months later, would have meant the loss of Sicily, and 'it would have been necessary

---

[1] Romano, *Fasci*, pp. 350–3, 367–8. Romano plausibly explains Crispi's animosity towards the leaders of the fasci by resentment at being supplanted by new, unknown men from the position of Sicily's most popular politician.

[2] Colajanni, pp. 252–5; Romano, *Fasci*, pp. 509–10; Crispi, *Politica interna*, pp. 296, 302; Giampietro, pp. 97–9. This support led to a rupture between the parliamentary Extreme Left and the leaders of the fasci. Colajanni, disillusioned by the spread of violence in Sicily, to which he believed the Socialist party's preaching of the class war had contributed, reverted in 1894 to his original republicanism. Within a few days of the declaration of martial law, however, he broke with Crispi and later in 1894 wrote his book on the events in Sicily which placed the main blame on Crispi. *Democrazia e socialismo*, pp. 1–lix.

[3] Romano, *Fasci*, pp. 394–8, 410–13. De Felice and Cipriani met at Marseilles in late December and discussed plans for the latter to go to Sicily, procure arms and assume command of the revolution. Malatesta, with whom Cipriani was in contact, had issued an appeal from London in November for immediate insurrection throughout Italy in support of the fasci. ibid., pp. 404–5, 424–5.

[4] Though he told the chamber he had 'overwhelming proof', no evidence of revolutionary conspiracy was produced at the subsequent trials. The allegation of clerical complicity was wholly false. The story of French gold was given a minimum of credence by De Felice's contacts with Cipriani. Romano, *Fasci*, pp. 476–9, 511–12.

to reconquer it'.[1] On 3 January 1894, only four days after Crispi had promised Colajanni there would be no state of siege, martial law was declared
in the island. Army reservists were recalled and General Morra was despatched with 40,000 troops to restore order. The next fortnight saw mass
arrests, the establishment of courts-martial and the deportation of 1,000
persons to the penal islands without trial.[2] All working-class societies and
cooperatives were dissolved and freedom of the press, meeting and association was suspended. On 13 January the anarchists of the Carrara marble
quarries rose in sympathy and martial law was proclaimed there also.
Crispi confessed that the use of the army to hold down Sicily was repugnant to him, but 'pillage, arson and plunder could not be dealt with by
acts of benevolence'. 'I have done today what I did in 1860', he replied
to a critic; strong measures had been needed then to create Italy, they
were needed now to preserve it.[3]

In May 1894 eleven leaders of the fasci, seven of them under thirty and
none over forty, were tried by court-martial. In spite of an eloquent defence, which turned the court into a political platform and thrilled every
socialist in the country, they were condemned to savage terms of imprisonment. De Felice was given eighteen years. Further acts of repression were
justified by a series of anarchist outrages. There were bomb explosions in
the capital in the spring of 1894. In June an Italian anarchist killed President Carnot of France at Lyon and Crispi himself narrowly escaped
assassination in Rome. Before terminating the state of siege in Sicily in
August, he drove through parliament two emergency laws 'for the repression of anarchism', which prescribed heavy penalties for 'incitement
to class hatred' in the press and gave the police extended powers of preventive arrest and deportation. As a further measure to curb subversion,
parliament authorised an extraordinary revision of the electoral register, as
a result of which 847,000 voters were disfranchised.[4] In September, with
a characteristic impetuosity which pained his anti-clerical supporters, he
appealed to the church for its help in the fight against the forces of disorder.[5] Next month he dissolved the Socialist party, together with 248 other
'subversive organisations', and had its deputies placed under arrest. Huge

---

[1] Farini, I, p. 416.
[2] Colajanni, pp. 271–2; Romano, *Fasci*, pp. 471–5.
[3] Farini, I, p. 454; Romano, *Fasci*, p. 516. The reference was to the suppression
of the Sicilian peasant revolt in the summer of 1860, for which Crispi, as Garibaldi's Secretary of Interior in the island, was in large part responsible.
[4] The enfranchised percentage of the population had increased from 7·4 in 1882
to 9·8 in 1892; Crispi's revision reduced it to 6·9. *Compendio*, I, pp. 71–3, 84. There
is little doubt that the register had been inflated between 1882 and 1892 by the
addition of many electors who lacked the necessary educational qualifications.
[5] See further below, pp. 223–4.

majorities in parliament showed that for the moment 'legal' Italy stood solidly behind him.

Persecution united and invigorated the Socialist party. Its first reaction to the events in Sicily had been embarrassment. Most northern socialists were suspicious of a movement whose members cheered the King and whose leaders consorted with anarchists. Seen from Milan, the Sicilian disorders seemed a mere 'hunger revolt', neither proletarian in character nor socialist in inspiration. Harassed members of the fasci had good reason to complain of their northern comrades' indifference.[1] But not all remained silent. Turati, while deploring their anarchistic errors and condemning insurrection, declared that the fasci showed a socialist spirit and deserved the solidarity of all Italian socialists. 'Their conspiracy is ours', he wrote in his *Critica Sociale*. Antonio Labriola, too, after dismissing the fasci with contempt in their early stages,[2] was by December 1893 writing to Engels, 'The proletariat is moving towards the front of the stage', and expressing the hope that the Sicilian movement would give birth to a true socialist conscience and party.[3] This evolution was typical of many thinking socialists. All remaining doubts were resolved by Crispi's repression. The party now eagerly took up the cause of the fasci and basked in their leaders' heroism. Socialists courted martyrdom and thrived on it when it came.

The sensational spread of socialism since 1892 had not been greeted with enthusiasm by the democrats of the old Extreme Left. Before the Sicilian upheaval they had collaborated cordially with socialists of the older generation like Costa and Colajanni. But now a new generation was coming to the fore, impatient, confident and dogmatic. Its members tended to harp on 'the abyss of private property'[4] which separated them from radicals and republicans, and to reject cherished items in the latter's programme such as irredentism, which socialists despised as outmoded nationalism. The young Socialist party intended to stand on its own feet and tolerated no democratic patronage, while at the same time upbraiding democrats for lack of solidarity. This behaviour increased the reluctance of the more moderate radicals like Giampietro to abandon faith in Crispi.

---

[1] Romano, *Fasci*, pp. 528–33. Some of De Felice's followers referred to the Socialist party as 'la camorra milanista'; Colajanni called it 'the church of Milan'. ibid., pp. 402–3; *Democrazia e socialismo*, p. lii.

[2] On 1 July 1893 he wrote to Engels, 'Tutta questa roba siciliana è del romagnolismo peggiorato' and described the Sicilian agitation as a mixture of 'socialistico, anarchico, affaristico e maffioso'. *Lettere a Engels*, p. 108.

[3] Labriola, ibid., p. 137. See also Labriola's letters on the same theme to the Austrian socialist, Ellenbogen, in E. Ragionieri, *Socialdemocrazia tedesca e socialisti italiani 1875–1895* (Milan 1961), pp. 339–40, 400–2.

[4] The phrase was Bosco's, in an open letter to Colajanni, December 1893. *Democrazia e socialismo*, pp. 370–1.

In July 1894 Giampietro tried to negotiate an understanding between Crispi and Cavallotti whereby the latter would support the government in return for a toning down of the emergency laws. But after a promising start to the negotiations, Crispi was once again stampeded into repression by what Cavallotti called a *pronunciamento* of 'the pretorians' of his majority.[1] Crispi's excesses now began to stir non-socialist consciences. The sentences of the Sicilian courts-martial revived memories of Austrian and Bourbon courts before 1860 and recalled Cavour's observation that 'anyone can govern by martial law'. The dissolution of the Socialist party destroyed the last of the democratic Extreme Left's illusions and broke down many of the barriers between it and the socialists. From October 1894 the idea gained ground of a coalition between Cavallotti, Zanardelli and Rudinì in defence of the constitution and political liberty. To growing numbers not only of democrats but of liberals, Crispi's arbitrary methods of government seemed a betrayal of the Risorgimento.[2]

Of all Crispi's projected reforms for Sicily, only one reached even the stage of parliamentary debate. In July 1894 he introduced a land reform bill to compel large landowners to divide their estates into plots and hand them over to small tenants on long leases. Crispi's intention was to break up the *latifondi* and create a socially conservative class of peasants attached to the land. The bill nevertheless roused the wrath of men of property throughout Italy. Rudinì, himself a Sicilian landowner, wrote scathingly to Luzzatti of 'a revolutionary socialist government which threatens the deepest and solidest foundations of the present social order'.[3] There was bitter opposition in parliament and the bill made no progress.

The financial situation remained critical throughout 1894. The crash of the Credito Mobiliare in November 1893 was followed two months later by that of the Banca Generale. These two banks between them had financed most of Italy's foreign trade and much of its industry.[4] Their failure severely shook Italian credit abroad. The lira dropped 16% below

[1] ibid., pp. 152–4; Giampietro, pp. 100–3; *L'Italia radicale*, p. 193.

[2] See for example Zanardelli's letters to Cavallotti, September–November 1894, in *L'Italia radicale*, pp. 365–70.

[3] Luzzatti, *Memorie*, II, p. 413; also Farini, I, pp. 573–6. See also Rudinì's article, 'Terre incolte e latifondi', in *Giornale degli Economisti*, February 1895, where he deplored the bill's tendency towards nationalisation of the land and argued convincingly that it would do nothing to solve the essentially technical problem of the *latifondo*. 'The bill', he wrote (p. 197), 'is a socialist bill because it injures and represses, if it does not extinguish, individual liberty.'

[4] The Italian banking system resembled that of Germany rather than Britain. The acute shortage of capital led Italian banks to play an active role in directing savings into industry, and often to become permanent shareholders and obtain seats on boards of directors. The Credito Mobiliare and Banca Generale between them had by 1893 acquired a substantial interest in almost every major industrial

the French franc and there was a massive flight of foreign capital.[1] Crispi's return to power provoked a new wave of selling of Italian securities on the Paris Bourse. Once again Crispi was forced to appeal to Germany and in 1894 the Banca Commerciale Italiana was founded in Milan, on the model of a German mixed bank, with German directors and mainly German capital.[2] Besides taking action to counter foreign speculation, it took over the industrial assets of the two crashed banks. Its creation was the prelude to an influx of German capital into Italian industry and commerce which in later years was to assume substantial proportions.

Sonnino, Crispi's Minister of Finance and the Treasury, bravely accepted the challenge of the falling lira, the persistent budget deficit and the disarray of the banking world, and made the most comprehensive attempt since 1876 to set Italy's finances in order. Sonnino was a unique figure among politicians. Son of a Tuscan Jew who had made his fortune in Egypt and a Scottish Presbyterian mother, brought up as a Protestant and almost bilingual in Italian and English, he had the outward appearance of a Nordic professor. He was an austere, silent, hard-working man, with a self-imposed mission of public service and, thanks to his travels in the 1870s, a knowledge of rural Italy and the south which was shared by few politicians of his time. Crispi in December 1893 called for sacrifices; Sonnino was the right man to enforce them. In February 1894 he treated the chamber to one of the most complete and gloomy financial surveys that it had ever heard, and prescribed a cheerless cure of higher taxes and lower expenditure. His sternness made him much disliked and led to the government's resignation in June. In the reshuffled cabinet Sonnino kept only the Ministry of the Treasury, but his influence was little diminished. Over the next eighteen months income-tax was raised, the dividends of state bonds were subjected to taxation for the first time,[3] the duties on salt,

---

enterprise. The depression caught them with a high proportion of unrealisable assets. Romeo, pp. 43–5, 51–2. See also Pantaleoni's essay, 'La caduta della Società Generale di Credito Mobiliare Italiano', in *Giornale degli Economisti*, April, May and November 1895. Among the bank's major interests Pantaleoni listed railways, shipping, the Terni and other steelworks and slum clearance schemes in Naples. 'No great enterprise could have been founded without the collaboration of the Mobiliare', he summed up (April 1895, p. 359).

[1] The percentage of Italian government bonds in foreign hands fell from 48·8 in 1891–2 to 22·8 in 1897–8. Nitti, *Il bilancio dello stato*, p. 361.

[2] Crispi, *Memoirs*, III, pp. 218–23; Romeo, pp. 56–8. The German mixed banks combined the financing of short-term commercial operations with long-term industrial investment. A second bank, the Credito Italiano, was founded in Genoa in 1895, also with German capital.

[3] This measure reduced the net rate of interest on government securities from 5% to 4%. Because it applied to foreign as well as Italian bondholders, it was criticised for 'damaging the nation's dignity'.

sugar and alcohol were increased, new taxes on matches and the consumption of gas and electricity were introduced and the wheat import duty was raised from 5 to $7\frac{1}{2}$ lire per quintal.[1] Sonnino also reorganised the public debt, modified Giolitti's Bank Act by imposing further controls over note issue, introduced a new nickel coinage and cleared up almost every department of the national finance. Such energy and administrative severity had not been seen since the day of Sella. Parliamentary opposition was by-passed by frequent use of the royal decree. The results were that the budget deficit was kept under control,[2] the lira recovered and Italian bonds appreciated steadily throughout 1895. By 1896 the worst was over. The stronger financial structure created by Giolitti's and Sonnino's reforms provided monetary stability and a solid basis for industrial expansion.[3] Revenue, savings, foreign trade and the balance of payments showed an upward trend for the first time since 1887. The banking crisis had prolonged and intensified the economic depression, but now Italy began to share in the general recovery which had already set in over most of Europe.

Sonnino's task was complicated by renewed controversy over the armed forces. Ricotti's plan for a reduction in the number of army corps was again canvassed and secured the backing, as in 1891-2, of the Extreme Left, part of the Right and leading members of the Left such as Zanardelli and Giolitti. In resisting the plan, Crispi had the support of a united cabinet, the King, court circles and the great majority of conservatives. The army, Farini believed, was 'the only cement holding Italy together'; while the soldiers 'held steady', there was no need to fear clericals or radicals or external enemies, but without the army the nation would disintegrate.[4] Crispi reassured him: 'While I am here, there need be no fear of military cuts.'[5] Sonnino agreed that any formal reduction in the size of the army would damage Italian prestige and undermine the Triple Alliance. Though he was able to secure minor economies, the twelve corps remained intact on paper and he failed to achieve a balanced budget.

The bank scandal meanwhile continued to envenom public life. During the summer of 1894 it developed into a merciless duel between Crispi and Giolitti, in spite of attempts by the King, Rattazzi, Zanardelli and others

---

[1] This was the result of strong pressure from the agrarian lobby, which also forced Sonnino to abandon his original proposal for increasing land tax. As late as 1887 Sonnino had attacked the wheat duty as a hunger tax. Between 1891 and 1894, however, the price of foreign wheat had fallen from 23 to $13\frac{1}{2}$ lire per quintal.

[2] The budget deficit fell from 175 million lire in 1893-4 to just under 100 million in 1894-5 and 1895-6. Coppola d'Anna, p. 85.

[3] Romeo, pp. 51-3.

[4] Farini, I, pp. 368, 395, 400, 465, 711, 727, 733.

[5] ibid., pp. 534, 557.

to bring about a reconciliation in the national interest. Crispi, who was as reckless in his private as in his political life, and rarely free from pecuniary embarrassment, was, unlike Giolitti, personally compromised in his relations with the Banca Romana. Nevertheless he led the attack and appeared set on Giolitti's political destruction. In July 1894 Tanlongo and his accomplices were acquitted, on the grounds that 'the major criminals are elsewhere'; a plain reference to Giolitti, and a verdict in striking contrast to the sentences passed on Sicilian socialists. It was widely assumed that the acquittal was the result of political pressure upon the judges. In September Crispi ordered the prosecution of a number of police officials for abstracting documents, alleged to incriminate Giolitti, from Tanlongo's house. This gave Giolitti his chance to counter-attack. In answer to the accused's appeal for help, he revealed that he had indeed acquired a packet (*plico*) of compromising documents, but from an independent source, not through the police. In fact the *plico* compromised not himself but Crispi, and contained evidence of certain transactions of the latter with the Banca Romana which he had concealed from the parliamentary enquiry. Giolitti's revelation rekindled the passion and hysteria of the previous year and there was a clamour for immediate publication of the documents. On 11 December Giolitti handed the *plico* to the President of the chamber and amid huge excitement a committee of five was appointed to examine it.

Cavallotti was one of the five. Until then, in spite of growing political differences, he had preserved his personal reverence for Crispi, the hero and patriot. Now, as he sat on the committee with the evidence of Crispi's shortcomings before him, he was overcome with anger and disgust. Never, he wrote afterwards, would he forget that terrible night. In November 1893 he had shouted to Giolitti, 'Never will I shake hands with you again'; now he realised that Giolitti had been misjudged. Cavallotti's emotional revulsion marked the beginning of a political transformation by which Giolitti, hitherto the butt of the Extreme Left, was to become within five years its champion and ally.

On 15 December the committee's report was published, giving details of debts contracted by Crispi, his family and friends with the Banca Romana. The opposition demanded an immediate debate. Crispi, with ruthless disregard for both the forms and the spirit of parliamentary government, muzzled his critics by proroguing the chamber that same evening. Giolitti's friends, fearing his arrest and trial by a suitably prepared court, urged him to leave the country. He took their advice and departed on a visit to a married daughter in Berlin. Next day, on the initiative of four leading politicians, Rudinì from the Right, Zanardelli and Brin from the Left and Cavallotti from the Extreme Left, a large gathering of deputies passed a motion deploring the prorogation on the ground that it had prevented the chamber from 'clearing up doubts concerning the honour and dignity of the Prime Minister'. This was the beginning of a passionate 'moral campaign'. The opposition gathered momentum and the alliance of 1891 between Right and Extreme Left assumed new vigour. Rudinì talked excitedly of defending King and constitution, liberty and the honour of parliament; either he would destroy Crispi or Crispi would destroy him.[1] Even within the government there was disquiet. In January 1895 Saracco, Minister for Public Works, told Farini that he could no longer remain in 'a government of violence'.[2]

Crispi fought back with an arrogant, dictatorial self-confidence that revealed how far he had lost faith in parliamentary government. His defence was that there was 'an eternal law above the constitution' which justified his ruthlessness. 'Parliamentary government in Italy is not possible', he told Farini.[3] After keeping the chamber prorogued for five consecutive months, an unprecedented length of time, he went to the country in May 1895 to demand a personal vote of confidence. The only alternative to his government, he declared, was 'political nihilism'.[4] The election was a personal triumph, especially in the south, where the opposition's moral campaign was widely regarded as a Milanese plot. The government won 334 out of 508 seats and he himself was elected in eight constituencies. The Right and the supporters of Giolitti and Zanardelli lost many seats, and the radicals and republicans barely held their own. The socialists by contrast polled three times as many votes as in 1892 and returned fifteen deputies instead of five, among whom were three of the imprisoned leaders of the fasci.[5] But this success weighed little beside the clear verdict of the polls. In spite of his dubious record in the Banca Romana affair and his contemptuous treatment of parliament, the electorate held Crispi's merits to outweigh his moral lapses. Even those who, like Farini, regarded 'monarchy, national unity and parliament as three inseparable terms'[6] and deplored Crispi's authoritarianism, nevertheless believed that only he could master the *piazza* and keep the radicals out of power. The mood which dominated the old ruling class in 1894–5 was one of black despair, relieved only by the hope that Crispi's energy and prestige would save the established order.

Crispi's position nevertheless weakened in the second half of 1895.

---

[1] Farini, I, pp. 609, 612; Luzzatti, *Memorie*, II, pp. pp. 415–20.

[2] The King appears to have dissuaded Saracco from resigning. Farini, I, pp. 614, 627–8.

[3] ibid., pp. 594, 611–12. Crispi added, 'I shall not be the one to act against parliament, but my successor will be unable to govern with it.'

[4] Crispi, *Politica interna*, p. 337.

[5] *Compendio*, II, p. 129.

[6] Farini, I, pp. 598, 615, 657.

Giolitti returned to Italy in February to face a criminal charge of mis-appropriating documents and a libel suit brought by Crispi. In April the Court of Cassation quashed both proceedings and Giolitti at last gained his point that the charges against him, being political, were a matter for parliament alone. In June Cavallotti published a *Letter to the Honest Men in All Parties*, which sold 300,000 copies in a few weeks. In it he repeated the old charge of bigamy,[1] attacked Crispi for using his political influence to procure favours for his friends from the Banca Romana, and accused him of concealing his own debts, lying to the investigating judges and violating the constitution.[2] He called upon Italy to demand the whole truth, for a people that was lax about honour had no right to survive. The bank scandal, which Crispi had done so much to inflate, had now recoiled upon himself. When the chamber at last had a chance in December to debate responsibilities, Giolitti made a calm, factual statement which did much to revive his political credit at Crispi's expense. The whole affair was then hurriedly buried, amid general weariness and disgust. Three years of scandalmongering had badly shaken the reputations of parliament and 'legal' Italy. It was, nevertheless, some consolation that when all the dirty linen had been displayed, most of the shortcomings were shown to be political, not criminal. Governments had been weak and negligent, but the rumours of deep-seated corruption in Italian public life were proved false. Beneath the morbid hysteria lay a healthy conviction that corruption must not be tolerated.[3]

The Extreme Left proved to be the ultimate beneficiary. Cavallotti rose on the wave of the moral campaign to heights of popularity such as he had never enjoyed before. The King summoned him for consultation and con-servatives like Farini gloomily contemplated the prospect of seeing him one day reach the cabinet.[4] In pursuing his aim of a democratic united front which would attract the more liberal sections of the Left, he was greatly helped by the fact that the socialists had been forced by persecution to change their tactics. It was impossible to maintain that all bourgeois politicians were equally the enemies of the proletariat when some of them, not without risk, were holding out the hand of friendship. Though a section of the party still maintained a rigid isolation, cooperation between social-

[1] See above, p. 47.
[2] Another of Cavallotti's accusations was that Crispi had accepted 50,000 lire from Herz, one of the villains of the French Panama scandal, for services in pro-curing him a high Italian decoration.
[3] 'The scandals ceased to be scandalous just because they were stigmatised and dealt with as such', writes Croce, pp. 183–4, with perhaps excessive complacence.
[4] Farini, I, p. 579. Rudinì's supporters were undismayed by the prospect, believing that cabinet office would have the same moderating effect upon Caval-lotti as upon his fellow-radical in Britain, Joseph Chamberlain.

ists, radicals and liberals became more frequent, especially in parliament. At the end of 1894 Turati joined Cavallotti in founding in Milan a League for the Defence of Liberty. This venture had the enthusiastic approval of Pareto, Pantaleoni and the free traders who, while sceptical of the usefulness of the moral campaign, saw in a democratic-socialist alliance the only hope of radically changing the political and economic system.[1] Next year a semi-clandestine congress at Parma decided that socialists might vote at the second ballot for non-socialist candidates who could be trusted to fight for political liberty. This was recognition of the fact that isolation meant impotence. By the end of 1895, when the emergency laws lapsed, it was clear that the socialists were successfully building up the first mass party in Italy and that some at least of its leaders were prepared to use it in partnership with non-socialists in the fight for democracy.

Fortunately for Crispi the opposition, though growing in numbers, remained divided. Groups of the Right, Left and Extreme Left could combine to press for cuts in the army, to promote the moral campaign or to defend the constitution; but on other issues they fell apart. Rudinì led the campaign against Crispi's land reform bill, while Cavallotti welcomed it. The Extreme Left, in attacking the army, was also attacking the Triple Alliance, which neither Rudinì nor Zanardelli, for all their reservations about Crispi's excessive *triplicismo*, were ready to destroy. Cavallotti fought for democracy, with socialist support and Zanardelli's sympathy; Rudinì, like most conservatives, feared democracy and so felt unable to condemn all Crispi's acts of repression.[2] In their advocacy of decentralisation, Rudinì and the Milanese conservatives found common ground with the Extreme Left, while disagreeing with Giolitti and Zarnardelli. Financial problems, too, were a source of complex parliamentary discord and helped to prevent a combination capable of overthrowing the government. The cement necessary to unite the opposition was lacking until Crispi himself supplied it by plunging his country into a disastrous adventure in Africa.

[1] Pareto and Pantaleoni abhorred socialism in principle but were prepared to accept socialists, whose political effectiveness they valued highly, as temporary allies in the cause of liberty. Their friend Colajanni was a leading advocate of the democratic-socialist alliance. On the moral campaign, Pareto commented to Colajanni in July 1895: 'It's useless to prove Crispi a scoundrel. Everyone knows it, but the more of a scoundrel he is, the better he is liked.' *Democrazia e socialismo*, pp. 318, 331, 345–6, 354, 358–9.

[2] There were times when Rudinì, too, thought Crispi indispensable. In January 1895 he wrote to Luzzatti, 'We must be extremely gentle to Crispi . . . who, after all, holds aloft the banner of order and national unity.' Luzzatti, *Memorie*, II, pp. 406, 416.

### The Road to Adowa

On his return to power Crispi found the international situation much less favourable to Italy than when he went out of office in January 1891. The 1887 system was breaking up fast. The first shock had come in August 1892 when a British Liberal government under Gladstone replaced that of Salisbury. Gladstone was known to disapprove of Italy's military commitments and to be sceptical of the value of Britain's association with the Triple Alliance. Rosebery, the new Foreign Secretary, told the Italians that the Mediterranean Agreements had only been arrangements between governments, by which the Liberals were not bound, and he refused even to look at their texts. The most he would do, when pressed, was to give his personal opinion that Britain was likely to support Italy if groundlessly attacked.[1] The Siamese crisis of July 1893 revived hopes in Rome; if Britain and France went to war, as seemed likely, then Britain was bound to turn to the Triple Alliance. But Rosebery quickly settled the dispute by negotiation, to the Italian government's intense disappointment. Later that year, as the Franco-Russian alliance took shape, Rosebery thawed slightly. In October, when the Russian fleet made its dramatic visit to Toulon, a British squadron was sent to Taranto and La Spezia as a counter-demonstration. But though there were long discussions between the British and the Austrians, the Mediterranean Agreements were never renewed.

The Italians were most dissatisfied. Benedetto Brin, Giolitti's Foreign Minister, who was a strong Anglophil, declared he personally regretted the renewal of the Triple Alliance and would have preferred an Anglo-Italian alliance.[2] Baron Alberto Blanc, the career diplomat who succeeded him as Foreign Minister under Crispi, was equally insistent. In January 1894 he made what the British Foreign Office took to be yet another 'bid for an English alliance'.[3] Blanc was especially keen to secure British help in preventing French penetration of Morocco or its partition between France and Spain. But the British wouldn't commit themselves. The Admiralty thought poorly of the Italian navy, which by the mid-1890s was no longer the third largest in the world, but smaller than that of Russia and only the equal of the infant German fleet.[4] Rosebery was no less keen than Salisbury that the *status quo* in the Mediterranean should be preserved, and

---

[1] BD, VIII, pp. 4, 7, 13; GP, VIII, 1737–42; Temperley and Penson, pp. 475–6.
[2] PRO, FO 45/683, 99, 159 (despatches from Rome dated 1 June and 2 August 1892).
[3] PRO, FO 45/716, 26–33 (despatch and memoranda from Rome dated 31 January 1894).
[4] Marder, pp. 172–3.

that Italy should be kept out of the Franco-Russian camp;[1] on the other hand, like Salisbury, he was afraid of increasing the risk of a European war by making the Italians too confident. To their disgust he even seemed to prefer to flirt with France and Russia rather than show loyalty to Britain's 'true friends'. British policy was 'short-sighted, petty and full of contradictions', Blanc declared,[2] and longed for the return to power of the more understanding Salisbury.

When Salisbury did return in June 1895, there was no change for the better. In the previous year Rosebery had abandoned Britain's traditional policy of cooperation with Austria-Hungary against Russia. Instead, under the pressure of British public opinion stirred by the Armenian massacres, he had tried to collaborate with France and Russia in pressing reforms upon Turkey. Salisbury accepted this reversal of policy, turned down renewed Italian and Austrian requests to revise and strengthen the Mediterranean Agreements,[3] rejected Italian offers of naval support against Russia at Constantinople, and began to think of Italy as a liability rather than an asset to Britain. Another new factor which embarrassed the Italians was the antagonism between Britain and Germany, which became alarming during the Congo dispute in the summer of 1894 and reached its climax in January 1896 with William II's telegram to Kruger. Talk in Berlin of an anti-British Continental League, and ostentatious German collaboration with France and Russia in Africa and the Far East, made the Italians feel the world was tumbling about their ears. 'If Germany and England were to quarrel', Blanc told Bülow, the German ambassador in Rome, in December 1895, 'Italy would be in the position of a child whose parents were coming to blows.'[4]

This fluidity in European alignments complicated Italy's relations with France. Giolitti and Brin had tried, like Rudinì, to combine loyalty to the Triple Alliance with friendship with all other nations. In September 1892 they were rewarded by the visit of a French squadron to Genoa for the celebrations of the 400th anniversary of Columbus's discovery of America. But the Aigues Mortes riots next year revived much of the tension and passion of 1887-91.[5]

[1] See Rosebery's statements to the Austrian ambassador in December 1893 and January 1894, in Temperley and Penson, pp. 478-9. There was in fact no significant change in British foreign policy for the first two years of the Liberal government's period of office, as Brin for instance recognised. Lowe, pp. 91-3.

[2] GP, VIII, 1771.

[3] E. Walters, 'Lord Salisbury's Refusal to Revise and Renew the Mediterranean Agreements', in The Slavonic Review, vol. 29 (1950-1), pp. 267-86; Serra, L'intesa, pp. 10-16; Lowe, pp. 101-2, 108-11.          [4] GP, X, 2556.

[5] See above, pp. 160-1. Giolitti dismissed the prefects of Rome and Naples for tolerating anti-French riots and did his utmost to conciliate the French. His moderation earned him attacks for failing to safeguard the nation's dignity.

Crispi's return to power, though displeasing to the French, was not accompanied by showy displays of German-Italian solidarity as in 1887. It was part of Germany's 'new course' in foreign policy to damp down quarrels between Italy and France; and Italy's economic and financial troubles were acute enough to make even Crispi see the advantages of amicable relations. He therefore made overtures for a commercial treaty in April 1894 but once again failed to break the deadlock, being unwilling to pay the political price that France demanded.[1] The prospects of success had not been improved a month earlier when the French admitted what Crispi had long suspected, that Bizerta was being fortified as a naval base. Further incidents occurred over the next two years to keep the two countries apart. In June 1894 the French President was assassinated by an Italian anarchist. Next January Crispi brusquely recalled his ambassador from Paris on the ground that he was too Francophil, without consulting even his own cabinet. In August 1895 the French denounced the 1868 treaty of commerce between Italy and Tunis, on which the privileged status of the Italian settlers in Tunisia depended. In their dealings with France, the Italians felt isolated and friendless. The French, still working to disrupt the Triple Alliance, saw in Italian weakness welcome proof that their tough policy was showing diplomatic results.[2]

It was above all in east Africa that the dangers of Italy's isolation became apparent. In February 1893 Menelik had formally denounced the Treaty of Uccialli. The French and the Russians encouraged him to defy Italy and sent him military and religious missions, personal gifts and arms. In 1894 a French company, with the backing of the French government, began to build a railway from Djibouti to Addis Ababa, in order to provide Ethiopia with an outlet independent of Italy. The French were already contemplating an expedition eastward from the Congo to the Nile, and Ethiopia was cast for an important secondary role in the grand design of creating an ocean-to-ocean French African empire.

Giolitti and Brin, for whom east Africa had no appeal, had tried to combine a Shoa and a Tigré policy,[3] and to be friendly with everyone. The result had been to give an impression of weakness and confusion. Even so staunch an ally as Ras Mangasha of Tigré was alienated and made his peace with Menelik. Crispi, though he too lacked a clear aim, was not the man to be content with a passive policy. In December 1893 an Italian

---

[1] Farini, one of the staunchest partisans of the Triple Alliance, feared that a commercial treaty would prove 'the first step towards a future Latin League'. Farini, I, p. 450.

[2] DDF (1), X, 424; XI, 45, 88, 89.

[3] See above, p. 138.

force under Colonel Giuseppe Arimondi won a resounding victory over 10,000 dervishes at Agordat. This was united Italy's first authentic military success. Next July the Governor of Eritrea, General Oreste Baratieri, a veteran of Garibaldi's Thousand, led a column to the borders of the Sudan and at long last occupied Kassala. At the end of 1894 the rebellion of a hitherto trusted Eritrean chieftain, and the invasion of Eritrea by Ras Mangasha, provided the occasion for a new advance. Baratieri crossed the Mareb, defeated Mangasha's army, overran Adowa, established a forward base at Adigrat and pushed a column eighty-five miles further south to Makalle. The annexation of a large region to Eritrea now irrevocably committed Italy to enmity with Menelik.

The army's victorious advance filled the King,[1] the soldiers and the colonialists with pride, but it also stirred opposition. Inside the cabinet Sonnino opposed African adventures on financial grounds; Saracco too grew apprehensive, grumbled at Crispi's recklessness and talked of resignation. Impressed by the opposition even among his own followers, Crispi urged caution on Baratieri. If Eritrea were to be saved in parliament, he wrote in April 1895, Adigrat must be the limit of the Italian advance. When Baratieri appealed for more troops and supplies, Crispi replied, 'Find your own way of solving the problem, with the resources that the colony offers. Napoleon I made war with the money of the vanquished.'[2]

In July Baratieri returned to Italy for consultations. He was greeted as a national hero. Two weeks of speeches and banquets followed. At a reunion of veterans of the Thousand, Garibaldi's son, Menotti, toasted the man who had 'renewed in Africa the splendour of Garibaldi's victories'; in reply Baratieri, reminiscing with deep emotion, paid tribute to his old comrade, Crispi, 'the instigator and organiser of the expedition of the Thousand'. In the enthusiasm that the visit generated, no serious discussion on Africa took place. Crispi promised a small increase in the Eritrean budget and authorised the recruitment of more native troops; but no clear decisions on policy or objectives were made.[3] On his return to Africa in September, Baratieri found the situation had gravely deteriorated. His advance had united every chieftain of Ethiopia under Menelik, who was mustering a large army and marching northwards. Baratieri allowed his forces to become dangerously extended. On 7 December Amba Alagi, his

[1] Farini, I, pp. 403–4, 617; Battaglia, pp. 576–7. The capture of Kassala was 'a new triumph for civilisation', the King wired to Baratieri; Baratieri wrote to Crispi of 'feeling the Garibaldian blood in my veins'.

[2] Crispi, *La prima guerra d'Africa*, pp. 300–3; Ciasca, p. 221; Battaglia, pp. 609–10.

[3] Battaglia, pp. 618–23. Baratieri seriously underestimated the danger from Menelik. With much bigger reinforcements than he in fact asked for, his position south of the Mareb would still have been precarious.

southernmost position forty miles beyond Makalle, was attacked by an army of 30,000 and overwhelmed; all but 300 of its 2,000 defenders were killed. On 21 January 1896 the 1,500 men of the Makalle garrison surrendered to Menelik after a dramatic three weeks' siege. Italian power in the Tigré crumbled. Dreams of glittering conquests evaporated and the discomforts of diplomatic isolation became acute.

The only country to which Italy could turn was Britain. The capture of Kassala, by which Italy became 'a co-occupant with Great Britain of Egyptian territory', had greatly excited Blanc, who saw in it, as Mancini had seen in Massawa nine years before, 'une base d'alliance anglo-italienne' of great promise.[1] But this could only be a dream for the future. As the position in Ethiopia grew critical, immediate help was required. The only way of saving the situation appeared to be to invade Harrar and attack Menelik's rear. Harrar had been recognised as an Italian sphere of influence by an Anglo-Italian convention of May 1894. The British were therefore requested in January 1895, and again after the defeat at Amba Alagi in December, to allow Italian troops to land at Zeila and move inland to Harrar through British Somaliland. Both Rosebery and Salisbury impressed upon the Italians the risks of an Ethiopian adventure, and urged them first to square the French. But negotiations with France once again came to nothing, even though this time Crispi and Blanc were prepared to pay a stiff price in concessions over Tunis.[2] In February 1896 the idea of the Harrar expedition was abandoned. Blanc commented bitterly to the British ambassador, 'Italy can no longer count on the friendship of England'.[3]

This situation brought home to Crispi in the most painful fashion the limitations of the Triple Alliance. It was not just an Italo-Ethiopian war with which they were faced, he and Blanc argued; it was a war between the Triple Alliance on one side, France and Russia on the other. It was the Italians' very loyalty to the Triple Alliance that had made them the target first of economic and financial pressure and revolutionary propaganda, and now of military attack in Africa. 'Our position is intolerable', Crispi told Bülow in February 1896; 'for us the Triple Alliance means war.'[4] Yet the Germans refused to bully the French as in Bismarck's day. They merely reminded their allies of what the latter could not deny: that east Africa had never been brought within the scope of the Triple Alliance. The Alliance was 'a conservative pact, not a profit-making society', declared Hohenlohe, the German Chancellor, and the Germans had no intention of

[1] GP, VIII, 1996; PRO, FO 45/717, 151.
[2] DDF (1) XII, 240, 242, 245, 260; DDI (3), I, 6, 136.
[3] Serra, L'intesa, pp. 8–9.
[4] Crispi, Memoirs, III, p. 337.

supporting Italy at the cost of offending France. The Italians were advised
to moderate their African ambitions. Italy, said Bülow to Blanc, was like
a child being carried across the waters in its father's arms; it was quite
safe provided it didn't wriggle too hard and make its father drop it. As for
Italian hints of abandoning the Alliance, Hohenlohe pointed out that
Germany might then be forced to come to terms with the Vatican, and the
Austrians with Russia, so that Italy would be compelled to disgorge Rome
and restore Austria's pre-1860 frontiers. Such talk between allies showed
that Italy's stock stood lower than at any time since 1882–4.[1]

By the end of 1895 Crispi had made a host of enemies who were only
waiting for the opportunity to drag him down. The African crisis coincided
with, and intensified, the crisis in his political situation at home. Crispi
was torn between hope of a glorious victory over Menelik, which would
silence his critics, and fear of another defeat. After capturing Makalle,
Menelik was anxious for peace. But Crispi was prepared neither to abandon
the newly annexed territory nor to renounce the protectorate which he
still claimed by the Treaty of Uccialli. Peace on such terms was unobtain-
able. After Amba Alagi, parliament voted another 20 million lire for the
war, and in response to Baratieri's increasingly urgent appeals, 20,000
troops were dispatched from Italy between mid-December and mid-
February. But the purpose for which they were to be used was never
clearly defined, and in any case they arrived too late. In the new year
Crispi's need of success became desperate. To gain time, the reopening
of parliament after the Christmas recess was postponed from 20 January
to 5 March; but Saracco and his fellow-critics within the cabinet were
growing dangerously importunate. 'The country expects another victory
and I expect a complete victory', Crispi wired to Baratieri on 7 January.
A month later he told him, 'In your hands lie the honour of Italy and that
of the monarchy.'[2]

On 28 February Baratieri held a confused conference with his commanders at his headquarters north of Adowa. The general feeling of the
meeting was in favour of attack. Baratieri himself would have preferred
to retreat behind the Mareb, but he decided to compromise: a short
advance would be made southwards towards Adowa in order to provoke
the Ethiopians into attacking well-prepared Italian positions; but because
supplies were short, the whole force would withdraw after twenty-four
hours if Menelik failed to attack. It was to be an offensive demonstration

---

[1] GP, X, 2564, XI, 2658, 2766.
[2] Crispi, *La prima guerra d'Africa*, p. 394; Ciasca, p. 224; Battaglia, pp. 716–20.
Yet Crispi could assure Farini on 19 February that he had never 'incited Baratieri,
never spurred him to action'. Farini, II, p. 851.

preliminary to retreat.[1] The plan went wrong. Bad reconnaissance and
incompetent generalship dispersed the three columns during a confused
night march and exposed them next morning to piecemeal attack by a
vastly superior, well-armed force of 100,000 men. By the evening of
1 March Baratieri's army was in precipitate, disorderly retreat. Of its
16,500 men, 6,000 were dead (as many as in the whole Risorgimento)
and 1,900 Italians were Menelik's prisoners.[2]

When the news reached Italy there was an explosion. In Rome, Milan,
Naples and other cities crowds demonstrated in the streets against 'Crispi's
war' and there were cries of *Via dall' Africa!* and even *Viva Menelik!*
Crispi had staked all on victory in Africa. Defeat gave his enemies the
chance they had awaited and for a brief moment united the conservative
critics of megalomania, the anti-colonialists, the democrats of the League
for the Defence of Liberty, the champions of economy to the bone, the
supporters of the moral campaign, the timid and the opportunists who
liked to be on the winning side. Under the impact of the disaster his
majority melted away. On 5 March he faced the howls of abuse in the
chamber and announced his resignation without waiting for a vote. He
was never to hold office again.[3]

Adowa left a lasting mark on modern Italy. Other nations had suffered
colonial disasters almost as dramatic and complete. The army was not
dishonoured, for officers and men, both Italian and native, had fought
bravely against great odds. But in later years nationalists and fascists
looked upon 1896 as a second 1866; a 'year of shame', the disgrace of
which could be wiped out only by a victorious war. More humiliating than
the military defeat was the 'moral collapse' which followed, the execration

[1] Battaglia, pp. 727–37. Had Baratieri retreated or waited a few more days,
Menelik's army, itself critically short of supplies, might well have broken up and
left Ethiopia open to Italian penetration. G. F. Berkeley, *The Campaign of Adowa
and the Rise of Menelik* (2nd ed., London 1935), p. 259; Battaglia, pp. 722–6.

[2] Approximately two-thirds of Baratieri's troops were Italian and one-third
Eritrean *askaris*. Of the dead, 4,900 were Italian, 1,000 *askaris*. 5,000 Italians and
4,000 *askaris* got away. The figures given by the various authorities differ greatly.
Those given here are taken from C. Conti Rossini, *Italia ed Etiopia* (Rome 1935),
pp. 340, 447–8, 701–2, and accepted by Battaglia, pp. 785, 789, as the most reliable. The Ethiopian numbers are variously estimated at between 70,000 and
120,000, and their dead between 4,000 and 7,000.

[3] Crispi lived until 1901, a lonely, poverty-stricken, embittered old man to
whose advice and warnings no one listened. In December 1897 a committee of five
deputies was appointed to investigate charges that Crispi had borrowed from the
Banco di Napoli for electoral purposes in 1895, and had subsequently tried to hush
up an enquiry into irregularities in the bank's administration. The report of the
committee, accepted by the chamber in March 1898, pronounced a verdict of
'political censure' on Crispi, who resigned his seat and was triumphantly re-elected.
This was the final end of the moral campaign.

of Crispi and the revulsion from Italy's mission in Africa. After Adowa, Humbert 'never knew happiness again'.[1] As Farini justly observed, the disaster could easily have been repaired if the Italian people had been unanimous and resolute; but it lacked 'unity of heart and purpose' and failed to rise to the challenge of adversity.[2] Yet the real lesson of 1896 was a warning against impulsive, irresponsible improvisation in foreign and colonial affairs, and against overstraining Italy's slender resources in the pursuit of glory and greatness. Unhappily for Italy that warning was later forgotten.

## The Threat of Anarchy

The King's first choice to form the new government was Saracco, who found his past association with Crispi too great a handicap and suggested that the crisis demanded a general. The only one likely to succeed was Ricotti, who insisted on army reform. To preserve the army was at that moment the King's chief concern, and with Farini's help he tried without success to extract a promise that it should not be touched.[3] Ricotti preferred to hand the premiership to Rudinì and himself serve as Minister for War. Rudinì therefore succeeded Crispi for the second time. Part of Crispi's majority abandoned its fallen idol, as in 1891, and transferred itself to the new government. But even with the support of liberals of the left like Zanardelli and Giolitti, Rudinì's position was precarious and he had no option but to renew the tacit alliance of 1891 with the Extreme Left. Cavallotti's misgivings were overcome by Colajanni, an enthusiastic advocate of collaboration, and by Giampietro, who admired Rudinì as a true liberal and modern parliamentarian. In May the government survived by three votes, thanks to the support of the Extreme Left.[4]

Rudinì's first task was to take urgent decisions on Africa. Eritrea was threatened in the south by the Ethiopians, in the west by the Mahdist dervishes who were besieging Kassala. Eleven days after Adowa the British decided, partly in order to relieve the pressure on the Italians, to begin the reconquest of the Sudan. Rudinì authorised Baldissera, who had returned to Africa as Baratieri's successor, to abandon Kassala if it became militarily untenable, but urged him to hold on to it if he could, in the interests of Anglo-Italian friendship.[5] In April 1896 it was relieved by an Italian force

---

[1] Finali, p. 690.
[2] Farini, II, pp. 865–6 (diary entry for 3 March).
[3] ibid., pp. 871–82, 972.
[4] *L'Italia radicale*, pp. 195, 213; Giampietro, pp. 119–23, 133.
[5] DDI (3), I, 16, 71, 352; PRO, FO 45/748, 41, 78, 45/749, 114, 119. The replacement of Baratieri by Baldissera, who had been military commander in Eritrea in 1888–90, had been decided by Crispi before Adowa.

which inflicted a sharp defeat on the Mahdist army. The reinforcements despatched from Italy before Adowa had by now reached Baldissera and the army in Eritrea had more men, guns, transport and supplies than ever before. So strengthened, Baldissera turned southwards with confidence, rescued the besieged garrison of Adigrat, won some minor skirmishes and finally withdrew all his troops north of the river Mareb. Menelik's main force had already disappeared to the south. Eritrea was now safe and the repatriation of Italian troops began.

Rudinì's African programme was peace with honour and renunciation of further conquest. He steered a middle course between the demands of Crispi's supporters for revenge and those of the Extreme Left for total evacuation. Though he privately agreed with the latter,[1] he saw that so extreme a course was politically impracticable. The King stubbornly opposed the cession of even a single fortress and the soldiers and colonialists were still formidable enough to dictate caution. In October 1896 the protracted peace negotiations ended with the signature of the Treaty of Addis Ababa, which annulled the Treaty of Uccialli and recognised the independence of Ethiopia. For Humbert it was a bitter humiliation 'to yield before a horde of barbarians' and forgo revenge.[2] Yet much was saved from the wreck. The Somali coast protectorate was preserved and the Mareb was provisionally recognised as Eritrea's southern frontier.[3] In November 1897 Ferdinando Martini, a distinguished writer and one of Zanardelli's political lieutenants, was appointed civil governor of Eritrea. No further attempts were made to settle Italian peasants on the land.[4] Nevertheless under Martini's nine years' rule the colony, though always starved of funds, was developed with much success. Eritrea dropped out of

[1] In May 1896 King Leopold II of Belgium, who was then dreaming of expanding his Congo State northwards to Egypt and the Red Sea, suggested to the Italian government that he should lease Eritrea. Secret negotiations followed next year. It appears that Rudinì and Luzzatti were attracted by the idea, but Visconti Venosta was hostile. Nothing came of it, partly because of domestic opposition, partly because of British objections. Th. Simar, 'Léopold II et l'Erythrée', in *Congo*, vol. 2 (1924), pp. 319–26; DDI (3), I, 335, 399, 407, II, 141, 148, 154, 211, 258.

[2] Luzzatti, *Opere*, I, pp. 5–6; Finali, pp. 563, 690; Farini, II, pp. 1041, 1064, 1235–6, 1285–6. According to Farini, Humbert took a long time to forgive Rudinì for forcing him, 'the descendant of a glorious line with eight centuries of military renown, to be the first European king to sign, after a defeat, a treaty of peace with an African ape'.

[3] Final agreement on the frontier, which followed the Mareb and its tributaries, the Belesa and Muna, was not reached until the Italo–Ethiopian convention of July 1900. For all but a few days in the year the Mareb was a waterless river bed.

[4] Franchetti's colonisation scheme (see above, p. 140, note 4) had collapsed in the demoralisation that followed Adowa. Franchetti, *Mezzogiorno e colonie*, pp. lxxvii–lxxviii, 403–7.

the news and was hardly noticed again by the outside world until 1934. In Martini's own words, 'Blessed are the colonies which nobody talks about.'

Next to Africa, finance was Rudinì's most pressing problem. He scored an initial success when a war loan of 140 million lire was oversubscribed. But the old issue of army expenditure soon caused trouble. Ricotti was convinced of the need for a smaller, more efficient army which would not overstrain Italy's resources. Backed by the Minister of the Treasury, Colombo, he pressed for drastic economies.[1] The King resisted, arguing that to reduce the army at so critical a moment would shatter all that was left of Italian prestige. In July the disagreement came to a head in the cabinet and Rudinì resigned. He at once formed a new government with General Luigi Pelloux in place of Ricotti. Luzzatti replaced Colombo, taking over the Ministry of the Treasury for the second time. The pro-clerical conservative, Prinetti, became Minister for Public Works and Visconti Venosta returned to the Foreign Ministry after an absence of twenty years. This decisive shift to the right worried the Extreme Left and Rudinì's more liberal supporters like Zanardelli and Giolitti,[2] but it ended the deadlock over the army. Pelloux found the necessary savings, as in 1891-2, by concentrating the service of conscripts in seven months of the year and allowing each basic unit to fall below strength. Parliament regularised this system in an act of June 1897, which preserved the twelve army corps and brought the long controversy to an end. Luzzatti meanwhile continued Sonnino's 'miserly' policy and battled with his colleagues for economies in every department. This time he achieved the success which had eluded him in 1891-2. Taxation remained unaltered, yet the budget deficit dropped steadily, until in the financial year of 1898-9 the first genuine surplus since unification was achieved.[3] In 1896 the economy entered upon a period of rapid growth which was to last for twelve years.

In domestic affairs, Rudinì pursued a policy of appeasement. Reacting against Crispi's authoritarian practice, he showed great deference to parliament. Although he refused to permit any reconstitution of the fasci, a

---

[1] Ricotti had dropped his plan to reduce the number of army corps from 12 to 10, but wished to make an equivalent total reduction by suppressing one-quarter of all basic units (companies, squadrons, etc.) and bringing the remainder up to full strength. The controversy was once again worrying Italy's allies. In March 1896 William II expressed to Goluchowski a strong preference for 10 good Italian corps rather than 12 bad. He appears to have repeated this view to the King through the Italian ambassador in Berlin in July. Walters, 'Austro–Russian Relations', II, pp. 507–8; Farini, II, pp. 995, 1001.

[2] *Quarant' anni di politica italiana*, I, 303 ff.

[3] Coppola d'Anna, p. 85.

political amnesty was declared in March 1896 and the last socialists, including the deputy De Felice, were released from prison. In 1898, largely
through the efforts of Luzzatti, two substantial measures of social legislation were passed: the industrial workmen's compensation scheme, which
dated from 1883, was made obligatory, with the employer bearing the
whole cost; and a fund for contributory disability and old age pensions
was created on a voluntary basis. A further measure of local government
reform extended the power to elect a *sindaco* to all communes.

Rudinì wished to go much further than this. For the past five years he
and Luzzatti had been advocating the grouping of provinces into units
which would have resembled the regions proposed by Minghetti thirty
years before.[1] In the atmosphere created by Crispi's fall these ideas found
many supporters. Regionalist sentiment had changed in character since
1870. *Ancien régime* separatism, founded on sentimental attachment to the
old historical divisions, had vanished and been replaced by a new regionalism of a predominantly economic nature. Southern free traders resented
the sacrifice of their agriculture in order to line the pockets of the industrial
barons of the north.[2] The rich northern cities, especially Milan, with their
new, thrusting capitalist class, lamented their subordination to the 'Roman
octopus' and to the dead hand of a bureaucracy largely recruited from the
south. Radicals and republicans preached the virtues of local self-government as a step towards direct democracy, and socialists looked forward to
the day when wider municipal autonomy would accelerate the growth of
socialism in the great cities. But the opposition was as effective in 1896 as
in 1861. Decentralisation, it was argued, would strengthen the clerical and
revolutionary enemies of national unity and lead inevitably to disintegration.[3] In April 1896 Rudinì appointed a temporary civil commissioner for
Sicily with a seat in the cabinet. Armed with extensive powers over prefects
and local authorities, he was given the mission of remedying fiscal injustice
and 'closing the gap between the administration and the people' of the
island. This one innovation was a failure. The commissioner soon grew
discouraged by obstruction and indifference, and Rudinì allowed his

[1] See above, p. 15.
[2] Not all the champions of the south believed in decentralisation. Fortunato
warned the reformers that they would only tighten the grip of the parasitical
southern ruling class over the peasantry.
[3] One of the most fanatical opponents of decentralisation was Domenico Farini,
son of Luigi Carlo Farini, co-author with Minghetti of the 1861 scheme. Domenico
insisted that his father intended regionalism to be merely a step on the road to full
unification. Farini, I, pp. 407, 473, 480. He also opposed reorganisation of the
army on a territorial basis, which Crispi at one time favoured for financial reasons,
on the ground that it too would mean 'the end of national unity'. 'Romagnole
territorial regiments would proclaim the republic within six months', he told the
King in 1895. Farini, I, pp. 4–5, 272–3, 790–1.

powers to lapse at the end of one year. The schemes for wider decentralisation came to nothing.

Rudinì's irresolute handling of the Sicilian problem typified his government's failure to devise a policy. He survived mainly because his supporters, however disillusioned, realised that his fall would mean the return of Crispi. The Extreme Left was the first to lose patience. For a year after March 1896 it clamoured for an immediate election. Cavallotti was obsessed by the need to destroy Crispi. Italy 'must renew herself or perish', he declared. He yearned to cleanse Italian political life, to sweep away the corrupt chamber which had been Crispi's creature and so to finish the moral campaign, still only half-won.[1] But the King and Rudinì procrastinated. The Extreme Left was shocked by the entry of so many conservatives into the reconstructed cabinet of July 1896, and in September it went back into opposition. The election came at last in March 1897. The radicals and republicans, fighting on a revised Pact of Rome, won 51 seats and hailed the result as a democratic revolution. On the left the socialists maintained their position and increased their representation from 15 to 16. Rudinì eliminated many of Crispi's henchmen and strengthened his own position. But he failed to make good use of his success. At times he appeared to be working towards the creation of a united conservative party, based on the remnants of the old Right; at other times he seemed determined to maintain a coalition of the centre, in the tradition of Cavour and Depretis, and to keep both right and left split. Repeated re-shufflings of the cabinet satisfied neither conservatives nor democrats, and a dangerous impression was created of weakness and aimlessness at the top.

Rudinì was under constant pressure from the right. His vacillation seemed suicidal to those conservatives who had panicked over the Sicilian fasci in 1893–4 and now saw Crispi's firm hand removed at a critical moment. Their most lucid spokesman was Sonnino, in whom Crispi's followers saw their fallen leader's political heir. In January 1897 Sonnino wrote a famous article entitled 'Return to the Constitution'.[2] In it he argued that the last ten years had proved democracy unsuited to the Italians, because liberty in Italy was bound to degenerate into licence. The solution was to rearm the liberal state against its socialist and clerical enemies, abandon the attempt to imitate the British political system and return from parliamentary to representative government. This could most simply be done by restoring the executive powers of the sovereign and enforcing the article of the constitution which laid down that ministers should be responsible

[1] Cavallotti to Giampietro, September 1896, in Giampietro, p. 136; Cavallotti to Colajanni, January 1897, in *Democrazia e socialismo*, pp. 158–60.
[2] 'Torniamo allo Statuto'. Published in *Nuova Antologia* on 15 January 1897. Reprinted in N. Valeri, *La lotta politica in Italia* (Florence 1946), pp. 257–75.

solely to the crown. Thus endowed with authority, the monarchy could rally the masses by bold paternalist social reform. Such a programme, reactionary and pessimist, appealed to many veteran liberals, including Visconti Venosta. But not all conservatives were as coldly logical as Sonnino. The King himself was displeased and affronted by the article.[1] To the commercial and industrial class of the north, Sonnino's programme sounded academic and archaic. Rudinì too rejected it and maintained his distance from Sonnino, preferring to preserve his freedom of manœuvre by keeping contact with the forces of the left.

This situation confronted the democratic Extreme Left, in the acutest possible form, with the agonising choice which had plagued it for twenty years. Should it wash its hands of the monarchy and the liberal constitution and revert to intransigent opposition? Or should it persevere, in the face of rebuffs and disappointments, in rescuing Rudinì from the reactionaries, and shoulder all the responsibilities of a constitutional party, even to the extent of accepting office in a monarchist government? The first course implied breaking down the last barriers between democrats and socialists, at the risk of seeing the latter submerge the former; the second implied isolating the socialists and driving them into a lonely intransigence. There were advocates of both among Cavallotti's followers. On the one side Giampietro worked tirelessly to keep Cavallotti and Rudinì in touch; on the other there was a growing number of exasperated republicans who thirsted for a complete break. Rudinì never fully trusted Cavallotti but maintained good relations with him, believing that his thirst for office was growing and that this made him a valuable 'new card in the constitutional game'. Cavallotti still hesitated, but by the end of 1897 he was nearer than ever before to accepting the full logic of a constructive democratic programme.[2]

Rudinì's chief preoccupation was the persistent social unrest. Even though the depression was over by 1896, there was still a timelag before economic revival could be translated into political and social stability. The continuing distress of the countryside was revealed by a rise in the number of emigrants from 222,000 per year in 1886–90 to 310,000 in 1896–1900. Significantly, the share of the south in this movement was growing.[3] Yet

[1] Farini (II, pp. 1102–3, 1133, 1185) described the article as 'lunacy', 'a Germanically abstruse sociologist's bee in the bonnet'. He believed that Sonnino's proposals, if carried out, 'would destroy a tradition of fifty years that gave power and glory to Victor Emmanuel' and would prove fatal to the monarchy.

[2] Giampietro, pp. 133–64; L'Italia radicale, pp. 215–23; Farini, II, pp. 1013, 1022, 1278.

[3] ASI 1913, p. 429; Arias, I, tables 1 and 3; Coletti, p. 32. In the years 1876–86 68% of emigrants came from the north, 11% from the centre and 21% from the south; in the years 1887–1900 the figures were 56%, 12% and 32%. Coletti, p. 39.

even this great volume was insufficient to act as a safety valve. Almost every week the peasants of some southern commune revolted in protest against taxes or the price of grain or lack of land. Fortunato vividly described the recurrent violence:

> An assault on the town hall, devastation and destruction of the tax registers; then the arrival of police or soldiers, volleys of stones from the crowd, opening of fire by the troops. The crowd retreats cursing, leaving its dead and wounded on the ground. Then questions in the chamber, transfers of officials, resignation of the mayor, trial and conviction of the arrested, and quiet returns. A few weeks or months pass, and suddenly in another commune the story repeats itself.[1]

In the north revolt took a different form: strikes, a ten-hour movement in the textile factories, the election of republican or socialist deputies and local councillors. There was no revolutionary design, but rather a widespread turbulence and exasperation. After the explosion of March 1896 rebellion remained in the air.

In these troubled waters many were fishing. The anarchists were still active. Early in 1897 Malatesta arrived in Ancona, after twelve years' exile from Italy. For ten months he preached insurrection and campaigned vigorously against the Socialist party's legalitarian degeneration.[2] In the same year the King narrowly escaped assassination. In 1898, after the assassination by an Italian of the Austrian Empress Elizabeth at Geneva, the Italian government convened an international anti-anarchist conference in Rome, though with few practical results. Of more importance than anarchism was a revival of republicanism in the north, stimulated by the discredit which Humbert's association with Crispi had brought upon the monarchy. After Adowa there were rumours that Humbert would abdicate, as his grandfather Charles Albert had abdicated after defeat in 1849. The socialists, taking advantage of the greater freedom which followed Crispi's fall, found a ready hearing in the mushroom factory towns of the north. They also thrived in Sicily and began to penetrate areas such as Piedmont and Apulia which had hitherto been untouched.[3] On Christmas Day 1896 the first number of *Avanti!*, the party's daily newspaper, appeared in Rome and under Bissolati's editorship quickly reached the front rank of Italian journalism.

The Catholics, too, were active. In the local elections of 1895 they had made big gains. Though the idea of collaboration with liberals in defence

---

[1] Fortunato, *Il Mezzogiorno e lo stato italiano*, II, p. 183.

[2] Malatesta was arrested in January 1898. In May 1899 he escaped from *confino* on the island of Lampedusa and departed once again into exile.

[3] Apulia, where the agrarian situation resembled that of Emilia, was the first area of the southern mainland, with the exception of the city of Naples, to offer socialism a foothold.

of the social order had its supporters,[1] the Opera was still controlled by the intransigents. Its congress of 1897 resounded with attacks on the liberal state, whose progeny were bank scandals, anarchy in Sicily and African megalomania. Adowa was depicted as a lesson administered by Providence and Menelik as the plague sent to punish Pharaoh.[2] 'Let the liberal house burn down', said the intransigents: Catholics were not to be mere tools of social conservatism, and if the liberals wished to be saved from socialism, let them pay a stiff price and dismantle the secular state.[3]

Angered by such demagogy, Rudinì fell back on repressive anti-clericalism, to act as an ideological cement for the hard-pressed liberal state. In September 1897 he warned prefects against the clerical danger. The Catholic movement was to be diligently watched and the Opera's subversive activities curbed.[4] In December the government was defeated on a minor measure of army reform and Pelloux resigned. In the reshuffle that followed, the pro-clerical Prinetti was dropped and Zanardelli was brought in as Minister of Justice, to intensify the anti-clerical campaign. At the same time Visconti Venosta's continued presence did something to reassure those who regarded socialism as the greater menace. Rudinì's aim was to construct a coalition broad and strong enough to fight subversion on both fronts. But no effective action followed. Long-discussed proposals for strengthening the powers of the police, for restricting the suffrage and for introducing plural or compulsory voting, remained, thanks to Zanardelli's liberal scruples, at the talking stage. Rudinì's experiment in neo-transformism failed. By the beginning of 1898 his government was discredited and the situation in the country was drifting out of control.

In May 1897 Fortunato had noted the rumbling of the volcano in the south and warned the chamber: 'In the air down there, there's something of the sultriness which precedes the hurricane, a kind of hushed storm of hatreds and rancours; and those who, like myself, abhor violence, cannot help fearing and foreseeing danger.'[5] The harvest of 1897 was disastrous in Italy and throughout Europe. Next April the Spanish-American war sent sea freight charges soaring. The price of wheat rose from 22·6 lire per quintal in 1896 to 37 lire in May 1898. The government failed to act in time. The wheat import duty was reduced from $7\frac{1}{2}$ to 5 lire per quintal in January 1898, against bitter opposition from the agrarian lobby, and on 5 May it was necessary to suspend it altogether for two months.[6] By then

---

[1] See further below, pp. 224–5.
[2] Spadolini, *L'opposizione cattolica*, p. 375.
[3] De Rosa, *L'Azione Cattolica*, I, pp. 162–8.
[4] Fonzi, p. 84; Spadolini, *L'opposizione cattolica*, pp. 439–45.
[5] Fortunato, *Il Mezzogiorno e lo stato italiano*, II, p. 69.
[6] The full duty of $7\frac{1}{2}$ lire was restored on 15 August 1898 and remained unaltered until 1914.

it was too late. A wave of violence and disorder had already spread north-wards up the whole length of Italy. Riots, strikes and demonstrations for 'bread and work', followed by clashes with the police, arrests and often martial law, occurred first in Bari, then in Naples, Florence and Emilia. The climax came in May in Milan, the city which had become 'a crucible where all the discontent, all the rancours, all the class hatred scattered through the peninsula accumulated'.[1]

The causes of the southern disturbances were economic; those of the Milan rising were more complex. Two months before, Cavallotti had been killed by a fellow-deputy in his thirty-third duel. His funeral drew vast crowds and was the occasion for inflammatory calls to action. The celebration of the fiftieth anniversary of the 1848 revolution revived memories of barricades and contributed to the excitement. The working-class of the city, after years of socialist propaganda, was more ready than in 1893 to respond to the news of disorders in the south. Minor incidents precipitated the explosion: the death of the student son of a popular radical deputy in a clash with the police at Pavia and the arrest at the Pirelli rubber works of three workmen who were distributing a socialist manifesto. Violent demonstrations and a general strike followed. In the absence of Cavallotti, who might have calmed the storm, Turati worked hard but in vain to restrain his followers. The authorities lost their heads and called for the army. From 7 to 10 May the streets of Milan were filled with barricades and shooting.

When the news reached Rome, Rudinì and Zanardelli became prey to fears as exaggerated as those of Crispi in 1894.[2] General Bava-Beccaris proclaimed martial law and pacified Milan, at the cost of 80 civilians and 2 policemen killed and 450 wounded.[3] Thousands of indiscriminate arrests followed, including Turati, Anna Kuliscioff, Bissolati, Costa, Lazzari, the republican deputy Luigi De Andreis, the radical leader Carlo Romussi and Don Davide Albertario, editor of the Milan *Osservatore Cattolico*. Turati and De Andreis were sentenced to twelve years' imprisonment and scores to shorter terms. Over 100 newspapers were suppressed, including the *Secolo*. Trade unions, cooperatives and chambers of

[1] Michels, p. 201.

[2] See for example Rudinì's alarm at rumours of an anarchist invasion from Switzerland, in DDI (3), II, 442–54. About 200 Italian workmen did in fact try to march across the Simplon into Italy, but were arrested by the Swiss authorities and handed over to the Italian army on the frontier.

[3] These were the official figures. A contemporary socialist estimate was 118 civilians killed. The military authorities were clearly affected by the hysteria which had overcome the wealthy citizens. The most ludicrous incident was the storming, with the support of artillery, of a monastery inhabited only by monks, in the belief that it was a nest of revolutionaries. The ladies of Milan brought out cakes and marsala to encourage the gunners.

labour were dissolved, together with 70 diocesan and 2,500 parochial committees and hundreds of other Catholic institutions. So disproportionate a reaction at once created martyrs, as in 1894, and when the King publicly congratulated General Bava-Beccaris on the service he had rendered 'to our institutions and to civilisation', and honoured him with a high military decoration, the monarchy and army became dangerously associated with blind reaction.

The events of May 1898 sealed Rudinì's fate. His instable coalition split over a demand from Zanardelli for further repressive measures against the church. At the end of the month first Visconti Venosta, then Zanardelli, then the rest of the government resigned. The attempt to rally liberals to the traditional offensive on two fronts had failed, and would never be made again.[1] Rudinì formed a new government and drafted a comprehensive programme of repressive legislation to end disorder and subversion. Should parliament withhold its confidence, Rudinì counted on the King to grant him a dissolution and, if necessary, to promulgate the budget by royal decree. On 16 June the new government was greeted in the chamber by almost universal hostility. Crispi's supporters exulted in its discomfiture and Rudinì's overtures to Sonnino met with no response. On the left Zanardelli and Giolitti joined the radicals and socialists in opposition. Rudinì's final humiliation came when Humbert once again, as in 1892, refused him a dissolution. On 18 June he resigned without awaiting an adverse vote.[2]

## The Failure of Reaction

Under the shock of the catastrophe in Milan and in a political situation of extreme confusion, the weak and bewildered King had for a moment been tempted to depart from constitutional practice. Only at the last moment, and after half committing himself to a dissolution, did he decide to abandon Rudinì. He then considered appointing a prime minister from outside parliament to govern by decree. But his advisers, notably Farini, begged him not to 'leave the broad path of the constitution' and allow himself to be dragged down 'the slippery slope'. Their warnings were effective and the King turned on their advice to the senate.[3] After unsuccessful attempts

[1] 'We wish to defend the Italian idea against all enemies', wrote Rudinì to Luzzatti in May 1898: 'the fainthearted . . . wish to capitulate to the clericals'. Luzzatti, *Memorie*, II, p. 513.

[2] Farini, II, pp. 1302–11.

[3] ibid., pp. 1311–16, 1320–5, 1375. According to the evidence of Farini's diary, the King was very near to sanctioning a violation of the constitutional conventions that would have amounted to a *coup d'état*. On 15 June he had told Finali, 'Questa volta facciamo bum!' Pelloux later told Farini that on the eve of Rudinì's resignation, 'a *coup d'état* was in preparation'. ibid., pp. 1308, 1346.

by Finali and Visconti Venosta, General Luigi Pelloux was commissioned to form a government. Pelloux had fought with distinction in the campaign of 1859-60 and commanded the artillery that breached the walls of Rome in 1870. Elected to the chamber in 1880, he had served as Minister for War under both Rudinì and Giolitti and been elevated to the senate in 1896. This made him the first senator since 1869 to form a government. In the previous month, while military commander of the Bari area, he had maintained order without resorting to martial law. For this reason he was popular with the Left, representatives of which filled a majority of the seats in his cabinet. His programme was progressive and his first acts were conciliatory. Economic and financial reforms to relieve the distressed sections of the population were promised. The repressive measures against the Catholics were cancelled and by the autumn of 1898 Catholic Action and the Opera were again flourishing. Martial law ended in August, the press was allowed to reappear without restriction and a partial amnesty was declared in January 1899. In the following June, after they had been re-elected to parliament while in prison, Turati and De Andreis were released.

Pelloux immediately ran into trouble when he tackled the problem which had perplexed every Italian government since 1861: the reconciliation of liberty and order. In February 1899 he presented to parliament a comprehensive coercion bill which closely resembled the proposals put forward by Rudinì in his last month of office. It made strikes by state employees illegal, gave the executive wider powers to ban public meetings and dissolve subversive organisations, revived the penalties of banishment (*domicilio coatto*) and preventive arrest for political offences, and tightened control of the press by making authors responsible for their articles and declaring incitement to violence a crime. Though it had clearly been inspired by the school of thought of Sonnino, the bill was not as tyrannical as orators of the Extreme Left chose to represent.[1] It passed its first reading by a handsome majority.

In May 1899 the political situation was suddenly transformed. Pelloux resigned, to avoid defeat on his Chinese policy,[2] and formed a new government, the most decisively conservative since 1876, in which six representatives of the Left were replaced by six of the Right. Sonnino, though not a minister, was acknowledged as its *éminence grise*. Pelloux now committed a long series of blunders. Though the country was now calm and economic recovery under way, the coercion bill was amended in committee and made more repressive. The Extreme Left, believing that it was only a first

[1] Many of the powers it conferred had in fact been exercised, with doubtful legality, by preceding governments.
[2] See below, pp. 210-11.

instalment of systematic 'liberticide', decided on 1 June to obstruct its passage through parliament, imitating the example of the Irish in the British House of Commons. Radicals, republicans and socialists forgot their differences and achieved a unity they had never known before. The hero of the battle was a socialist named Enrico Ferri, whose unquenchable oratory and brazen vocal chords allowed him to speak continuously for the whole sitting of 7 June. Sonnino then proposed the introduction of a closure on the British model of 1881. Discussion of this proposal also was obstructed. Pelloux replied by proroguing the chamber for six days and promulgating the coercion bill by royal decree. This procedure was deplored as unconstitutional even by members of Pelloux's majority, which began to lose its nerve. On 30 June, when the President of the chamber attempted to enforce the closure, the deputies of the Extreme Left surged forward and overturned the ballot boxes, to cries of 'Long live the Constituent Assembly!' The sitting ended in chaos and parliament adjourned until the autumn.

The political issue was now no longer a particular bill or form of procedure, the merits of which had indeed never been calmly debated. The cleavage in the country went deeper. Pelloux and Sonnino represented the conservatives who believed that only a reactionary, authoritarian method of government could hold Italy together. Against them were ranged, with growing unanimity, liberal and democratic opinion, the press, the universities and the intellectuals, the chambers of commerce and the business world. The extra-constitutional parties became the defenders of constitutional progress, the organisers of parliamentary obstruction became the champions of political liberty. The spirit and slogans of the Risorgimento were revived. For the first time since 1870 Italy was confronted by a clear choice between progress and reaction.

Giolitti and Zanardelli played a leading part in this crystallisation of opinion. Giolitti had returned to active politics when Crispi fell. At first he supported Rudinì; but as the latter moved rightwards and revealed his incompetence, Giolitti grew impatient and critical. During 1897 he made a series of speeches on the theme that reaction was a greater menace than socialism to liberal Italy. Fiscal and social reform, not coercion, was his remedy for the country's ills, and he looked to a concentration of all the forces of the left to carry his programme through. Although this plan was temporarily frustrated by Zanardelli's desertion to Rudinì in December 1897, Giolitti's progressive views, and his refusal to follow Zanardelli's example,[1] won him the sympathy of the Extreme Left. Cavallotti was moving fast towards alliance with him when death cut short his career. In June 1898 Giolitti played a leading part in the formation of Pelloux's first

[1] *Quarant' anni di politica italiana*, I, 361 ff.

THE FAILURE OF REACTION

government. Several of his political friends sat in the cabinet and his relations with the Prime Minister were close and cordial.[1] Hoping to reinforce Pelloux's liberal intentions and to neutralise reactionary pressure from Sonnino, he gave the government all the support he could. In spite of doubts and reservations, he and Zanardelli voted in favour of the original coercion bill. But when Pelloux formed his second, conservative government in May 1899, he broke with Giolitti who went into opposition. Zanardelli, who had by now lived down his responsibility for the repression of May 1898, joined him. Giolitti and Zanardelli now acquired a following of about fifty deputies of the 'constitutional Left'. They neither approved of nor took part in systematic obstruction, but they regarded Pelloux's drift into unconstitutional action as the greater danger. The Extreme Left noted Giolitti's position. 'On the other side there's a man who has understood us', said Turati. Giolitti was thus carried back into political prominence on the rising democratic tide.

When parliament reassembled in November 1899, Pelloux announced a new programme of conciliation and reform. But it was too late for gestures to liberal opinion. The government's position had weakened during the summer and it had failed to gain the support even of Rudinì, Luzzatti and the rump Right. In February 1900 the Court of Cassation declared the promulgation of the coercion bill by decree to be legally null and void. Pelloux was forced to reintroduce it, together with the proposals for procedural reform, and obstruction began again. On 3 April, after two months of passionate excitement, the new procedure was approved by the majority without discussion, but only after the whole of the Extreme Left and constitutional Left, 160 strong, had marched out of the chamber.

Pelloux and Sonnino now made their final blunder. Faced with a refusal on the part of the President of the chamber to enforce the closure against one-third of the deputies, they dissolved. This action did credit to their constitutional scruples but resulted in a crushing moral defeat. They retained a majority in the new chamber, with 296 supporters; but the constitutional Left won 116 seats and the Extreme Left, fighting as a coalition, increased its strength from 67 to 96. Of the votes cast, the government obtained only a minority of 663,000, against 272,000 to the constitutional Left and 334,000 to the Extreme Left.[2] Pelloux lost heart and on 18 June he resigned. This was the most decisive date in Italian politics since the parliamentary revolution of 1876.

[1] ibid., 383, 386, 390, 400, 402, 415.

[2] *Compendio*, II, pp. 117, 129. The 96 deputies of the Extreme Left consisted of 29 republicans, 34 radicals and 33 (compared with 16 in 1897) socialists. The voting revealed a sharp division between north and south. The government won a minority of the seats in the north (106 out of 226), a small majority in the centre (46 out of 81) and a large majority in the south (144 out of 201).

## The New Reign

By June 1900 the economy was buoyant and pessimism had turned to confidence. The country was weary of politics and of living from one state of emergency to the next. The King found the Prime Minister that suited this mood in Saracco, Farini's successor as President of the senate. Saracco, now seventy-eight years of age, was a venerable survivor from the old Piedmontese parliament, who had twice accepted cabinet office from Crispi without damaging a reputation for integrity, common sense and financial wisdom. By including in his government representatives of all groups except the Extreme Left, he won the wary tolerance of both Sonnino and Giolitti, each of whom hoped soon to be his heir. His first act of pacification was to appoint a committee, on which the Extreme Left was well represented, to study the question of parliamentary procedure. It agreed on a compromise which, though it failed to close the door to future obstruction, satisfied the wish of the majority that freedom of debate should not be too severely restricted. On 1 July the chamber approved its recommendations, Sonnino's group abstaining, and after a year of paralysis parliament resumed its work.

Saracco's government was little more than a month old when, on 29 July, an anarchist named Gaetano Bresci fired on and killed the King at Monza near Milan. Bresci was a skilled, educated workman, aged thirty, who returned to Italy from Paterson, New Jersey,[1] specially in order to execute justice on the King who had honoured Bava-Beccaris, 'the butcher of Milan'. The reaction of all classes to the crime showed how the political climate had changed in two years. This time the government did not panic. No martial law, no mass arrests, no repression followed. Outside the anarchist ranks not one voice was raised in defence of the deed. *Avanti!* called Bresci 'a criminal lunatic'. Bovio, the veteran republican, declared that the crime had robbed a king of a few years of life, but added centuries to the life of the monarchy. Humbert had never been a blind reactionary and on several occasions he had moderated the zeal of Crispi, Pelloux and Sonnino. The realisation that he had been a scapegoat created a sense of shame and led to a searching of the national conscience.

Victor Emmanuel III thus started his reign at the age of thirty in a glow of sympathy, loyalty and hope. Little was known of him. After completing a rigorous, solitary education under the supervision of a military

---

[1] The textile manufacturing town of Paterson was a centre of anarchism at this time, and Malatesta spent some time there in 1899–1900 as editor of an anarchist paper, *Questione Sociale*. Malatesta, who was a friend of Bresci, never himself advocated assassination but never agreed to condemn it. A. Borghi, *Errico Malatesta* (New York 1933), pp. 86–93, 134–44.

tutor, he had for three years commanded the Naples garrison. In 1896 he married Elena, the daughter of Prince Nicholas of Montenegro. By 1900 he had acquired a well-deserved reputation for modesty and lack of ostentation, but otherwise he was an unknown quantity. The first politicians to discuss public affairs with him after his accession were surprised and delighted to find a serious-minded, well-informed, progressive young man.[1] In public he immediately struck the right note. In his accession proclamation and his first speech to parliament he declared his determination to protect Italy's free institutions, 'precious inheritance from our ancestors', and to defend liberty and the monarchy, 'both linked by an indissoluble bond to the supreme interests of our country'.[2] These words thrilled his audience and created a myth of youth, modernity and devotion to liberty which clung to Victor Emmanuel for many years to come.

In December 1900 the political calm ended. The prefect of Genoa dissolved his local chamber of labour on the grounds that it was a subversive organisation and so revived the old controversy over the freedom of the working-class movement. Twenty thousand workmen in Genoa struck in protest. Saracco, after personally negotiating with a working-class delegation, overruled the prefect. This pleased no one. Giolitti, Zanardelli and the Extreme Left attacked him for violating the right of association and reverting to the repressive methods of 1894-9; Sonnino attacked him for capitulating to violence. On 4 February 1901 Giolitti delivered in the chamber what turned out to be the keynote speech for the next four years. Its theme was that the state should remain neutral in disputes between capital and labour, and intervene only when the law was broken. Deploring the tendency to regard chambers of labour as illegal and dangerous, a tendency which only turned the working-classes into enemies of the state, he declared:

> The upward movement of the popular classes is accelerating day by day, and it is an invincible movement, because it is common to all civilised countries and based on the principle of the equality of all men. Let no one delude himself that he can prevent the popular classes from conquering their share of political and economic influence . . . It depends chiefly on us, on the attitude of the constitutional parties in their relations with the popular classes, whether the emergence of these shall be a new conservative force, a new element of prosperity and greatness, or whether instead it shall be a whirlwind that will be the ruin of our country's fortunes.[3]

Shaken by attacks from both flanks, Saracco tried to save himself by inviting Sonnino and Luzzatti into the government. Sonnino, believing he

---

[1] *Quarant' anni*, I, 463-4, 466, 481. See also Barrère's first impression, in DDF (1), XVI, 374.

[2] Cilibrizzi, III, pp. 143-5.

[3] Giolitti, *Discorsi parlamentari*, II, p. 633.

had a majority behind him and need only wait to become Saracco's successor, declined. Two days after Giolitti's speech the government was brought down by the combined votes of the Right, Left and Extreme Left. The King, instead of summoning Sonnino, chose Zanardelli, who formed a government in partnership with Giolitti. With the new century a new phase in Italian politics had begun.

Saracco had served his country well. During his eight months of office passions had calmed and the extremists on both sides had lost ground. The leaders of the Socialist party had received a shock in 1898. The aimless, eruptive Milan rising had shown the uselessness of barricades and the dangers of inflammatory propaganda. Turati in particular was confirmed in his view that premature attempts at revolution would only provoke reaction, and that a long period of education would be necessary before the working-class was fit for political power; the first step towards socialism must be the creation of 'a new, modern, bourgeois Italy'.[1] From this realisation the reformist programme was born. The party had begun in 1895 to discuss maximum and minimum programmes, but it was not until its Rome congress of September 1900 that these were finally drawn up. The maximum programme proclaimed the class struggle, nationalisation of land and the means of production, the political and economic expropriation of the ruling class. It was 'the compass by which the party should keep its direction'. The minimum programme contained a long list of reforms designed to extend liberty and social justice. It was a democratic programme, suited to the conditions of 1900, with which all radicals and many liberals could agree.[2]

The Socialist party was thus ready by 1901 to play a more constructive political role. Its deputies in parliament were putting more argument and less dogma and denunciation into their speeches, even on such subjects as foreign and colonial policy which they had previously spurned. The party's opposition to the monarchy was also wavering. Turati was prepared to argue that the institutional question of monarchy versus republic was of little importance: a republic could be as reactionary as a monarchy, and the latter was not necessarily an obstacle to democratic progress towards

---

[1] Bonomi, *La politica italiana da Porta Pia a Vittorio Veneto*, p. 190.

[2] Its main points were universal suffrage for both sexes, proportional representation, freedom for the working-class movement, neutrality of the state in labour disputes, social and factory legislation, decentralisation and municipal autonomy, abolition of indirect taxation, reduction of armaments, extension of compulsory, free, secular education, nationalisation of transport and mines. The nationalisation of land was omitted in the hope of winning support from peasant proprietors and sharecroppers. Preti, p. 169. For the texts of both programmes, which remained unchanged until 1919, see Michels, pp. 212–22.

socialism. A growing interest in immediate reforms led naturally to closer
cooperation with non-socialists. The events of 1898–9 had weakened the
party's electoral isolationism; the triumph of radical-republican-socialist
'popular blocs' in the June 1900 election killed it. At the Rome congress
local party organisations were given freedom to form electoral alliances in
their constituencies with other groups of the Extreme Left. Socialists had
learnt the value of political liberty during the persecution of 1898; they
now shared the optimism of the new reign and the new century. 'Every
paragraph of the constitution', declared Turati, 'is a safety-valve, opening
in one direction only', that of greater liberty. The twentieth century would
be the century of the working-class, he told the chamber, and he himself
would feel happy and proud to have acted as a pioneer, to have fulfilled in
history the modest function of an usher announcing the arrival of Labour.
When Pietro Chiesa, one of the two workmen elected to parliament in 1900,
rose to speak in the debate on the Genoa strike, his fellow-socialists greeted
him as the voice of the future and shouted 'Silence for Labour'.[1]

Republicanism had undergone a similar transformation. The old Mazzinian groups had fought a losing battle since 1882 with the radicals on their
right and the Partito Operaio and the socialists on their left. But republicanism survived, with new leaders, new tactics and a revised programme.
Its strength lay in a puritanical attitude of protest, inherited from Mazzini,
against corruption and the abuse of power. Unlike socialists and radicals,
republicans identified the source of corruption in the monarchy, under
which they argued, no lasting social reform, no truly democratic reconstruction of the Italian state were possible. In 1895 an organised Republican
party was founded, which thrived in the favourable atmosphere created by
Adowa. The younger republicans now attempted to modernise their appeal
by enlarging the target of their attack from the monarchy, with its associated 'fortresses of privilege', the court, the army, diplomacy and the senate,
to industrial and plutocratic privilege, tariff-protected profiteering,
colonialism and bureaucratic centralisation. Local self-government, to
provide training in democracy and prepare the emancipation of the People,
became the central point of republican propaganda. This new emphasis
won sympathy for the party among free traders and *meridionalisti*. Its
membership was restricted mainly to the north, where opposition to Crispi
and Pelloux had been strongest. Though it made vigorous efforts to woo
the working-class, it never secured mass support except in Romagna,
where romantic, insurrectionist republicanism of the Mazzinian type
lingered. Nevertheless republicans played a leading part in organising
parliamentary obstruction against Pelloux, and in June 1900 they won only
three fewer seats than the socialists. Many of the new generation rejected

[1] Cilibrizzi, III, p. 131.

the old leadership of the Extreme Left and condemned Colajanni, Cavallotti and his successors for rallying to the monarchy. Even so, the Republican party still had its reformists and continued to suffer, as in the past, from a steady trickle of desertions by those who preferred to join the radicals and accept the monarchy.

The radicals also thrived on northern discontent with Crispi and Pelloux, drawing their support from the 'leftist' professional and lower middle classes. Their programme was largely identical with the socialist minimum programme, which, indeed, they declared was plagiarised from their own Pact of Rome. Had Cavallotti lived, he would almost certainly have taken office with Zanardelli and Giolitti. His successor, Ettore Sacchi, leader of the radical right wing, shared his views. The left wing, led by Giuseppe Marcora, was more sensitive to the republican argument that the reaction of 1898 had shown the failure of Cavallotti's policy of compromise. But success in the 1900 election encouraged the moderates, and by 1901 the radicals were on the way to becoming a government party and a bridge between liberalism and socialism.

All sections of the Extreme Left seemed thus to have turned their energies into constructive channels. On the right, too, moderate views prevailed and it was recognised that repression had merely strengthened socialism. In Crispi's day every strike or riot had been interpreted as a challenge to the social order and to Italy's very existence. In 1901 many agreed with Giolitti that the state could be defended without committing it to the support of employers in every labour dispute. The alternative to repression was stated by the conservative Villari in 1899. Italian liberals, he wrote, should imitate British conservatives, who had defeated socialism by adopting social reform; conciliation was not only a sacred duty, it was also political wisdom.[1] Zanardelli and Giolitti agreed with this diagnosis. Prosperity was growing and the time was ripe for economic and social reforms.

There were still differences of outlook among liberals. Sonnino, accepting the verdict of the 1900 election, abandoned his idea of a 'return to the constitution' and declared himself reconciled to parliamentary government. But he deplored the flouting of the will of the majority by the organisers of obstruction and regarded the compromise of July 1900 on parliamentary procedure as a capitulation to unconstitutional violence.[2] Sonnino still believed that liberty was a precious gift, to be bestowed sparingly, and

[1] Michels, pp. 237–8.
[2] This point of view is elaborated at length by Albertini in his *Venti anni di politica italiana*. Albertini argued that in 1900 began 'that policy of acquiescence on the part of the government towards the extreme parties that lasted for twenty years and led to fascism'. *Venti anni*, I, p. 26.

doubted whether the masses, now thrusting their way into politics, would ever accept the liberal Italy which he loved.[1] Zanardelli and Giolitti, more optimistic, wished to bring the hitherto subversive forces within the pale of the constitution by giving them a share in political power. They were prepared to take risks, in the belief that only through the exercise of liberty would the masses learn responsibility.

A revival of parliament's prestige accompanied the easing of tension. That prestige had been brought low by the Banca Romana scandal and the battle over obstruction. The democratic electoral triumph of 1900 had been won at the expense of the old parliamentary groups and was in spirit an anti-parliamentary victory. Parliament, in the eyes of 'real' Italy, had all too often been identified with reaction. Fortunato, travelling round Italy in 1900, heard 'only one cry, "Down with the deputies" '.[2] Yet Saracco's term of office and the formation of Zanardelli's government showed that liberty could be effectively defended inside parliament. When the leaders of both the opposing factions of 1898–1900 declared their loyalty to parliamentary institutions, faith in their future revived. In the words of one radical observer, 'Something like the ferment of spring is at work in our political life . . . The indifferent and the sceptics are out of fashion. The public is aware that at last a breath of new life has entered the chamber.'[3]

## The New Course in Foreign Policy

Rudinì's foreign policy was the same in 1896 as it had been in 1891: loyalty to the Triple Alliance and good relations with other countries, particularly Britain. In May 1896 he told the chamber that he was proud of being accused of 'excessive tenderness towards Russia and France'. His private view was that the Triple Alliance had become 'a pretty anodyne affair' which would die a natural death and not be renewed at the end of its present term.[4] But to abandon the Alliance, as the Extreme Left demanded, would have been madness after Adowa when Italy's standing was at its lowest. For the moment Rudinì wished rather to 'perfect' the Alliance and strengthen Italy's position inside it.[5] During the previous five years it had been subjected to two strains: Crispi's attempt to transform it into a full-scale colonial alliance, and the tension between Britain and Germany. Rudinì's abandonment of the Ethiopian dream removed one source of strain; but Anglo-German relations did not improve.

[1] See Sonnino's article 'Quid Agendum?' in *Nuova Antologia* of 16 September 1900. Reprinted in part in N. Valeri, *La lotta politica in Italia* (Florence 1946), pp. 287–8.
[2] Volpe, I, p. 481.          [3] Papafava, I, p. 152.
[4] Farini, II, p. 923 (diary entry for 18 April).
[5] Chiala, *Pagine*, III, pp. 626, 633.

The Triple Alliance had been renewed in May 1891 for twelve years, unless one of the allies gave notice of a wish to modify or terminate it before May 1896. Rudinì used this opportunity to request a renewal of the 1882 declaration, which had lapsed in 1887, that the Alliance could in no circumstances be directed against Britain. He was worried by the possibility, however remote, that in a war between France and Germany, British sympathies might lie with France. Italy, he explained to his allies, could never fight both Britain and France, 'the two greatest naval powers in the world; no Italian government could undertake the responsibility of dragging its country into such a war'.[1] The Austrians were sympathetic. The Germans, however, argued that to declare that the Alliance was not directed against Britain would imply that it was directed against Russia, an implication to which Germany would not subscribe; and in any case, joint Anglo-Russian or Anglo-French action was inconceivable within any predictable period of time.[2] Rudinì, having made his point, did not press it, and in May 1896 the Alliance was automatically prolonged until 1903. His failure was to have far-reaching consequences. At the very moment when Italy had returned to a restrictive interpretation of the Alliance as a defensive, conservative, limited instrument, the Germans were insisting on leaving the door open to an extensive interpretation, in Germany's interest, against Britain. But British friendship was for Italy an essential complement to the Alliance, and not many years were to pass before Rudinì's fears of an Anglo-French *entente* were realised. When that occurred, Italy's loyalty to the Alliance was, as he had foreseen, subjected to intolerable strain.

The liquidation of the quarrel with France did not prove easy. The commercial treaty of 1868 between Italy and Tunis had been denounced by France in 1895 and was due to lapse in September 1896. The French insistence that negotiations for a new treaty should be conducted with themselves, not the Tunisian government, amounted to a demand for Italian recognition of their protectorate. For fifteen years Italy had refused this concession. Rudinì was prepared to risk the unpopularity involved, provided the French agreed to a new Franco-Italian commercial treaty. Hanotaux, the French Foreign Minister, replied that the virulence of French protectionist sentiment made this impossible.[3] No progress had been made by July when Visconti Venosta returned to the post which he had last held in 1876.

He soon found that over Tunis he could count on diplomatic support from no one. The Germans, who in Crispi's day had often bullied France

[1] GP, XI, 2807; DDI (3), I, 40, 53, 87.
[2] GP, XI, 2802; DDI (3), I, 92.
[3] DDF (1), XII, 368, 395 ff., 412 ff.; DDI (3), I, 95, 105 ff., 136.

at Italy's request, showed no interest. The Austrians recognised the
French protectorate in July without even informing Italy. The British
made it clear that they, too, intended to make their own terms. Italy was
left to face France alone.[1] Visconti Venosta realised that 'the fork in the
road' had been reached[2] and decided, unlike Crispi before him, that better
relations with France were worth a stiff price. On 1 October, after hard
bargaining, he signed a series of conventions regulating commerce, shipping and the legal status of the 20,000 Italians in Tunis. The latter were
to retain for the next nine years their Italian citizenship, their own schools
and institutions, and many economic privileges. Visconti Venosta thus
saved all that could be saved from the wreck, at the same time abandoning
an untenable position and removing 'the corpse' of Tunis from Italian
diplomacy.[3] In the previous fifteen years Italy could have bartered recognition of the French position in Tunis against a commercial treaty or concessions in east Africa or acquiescence in the Italian claim to Tripoli. In
1896, only seven months after Adowa, there were no compensations.
Nevertheless it was a first step towards ending what Visconti Venosta
considered a pointless and dangerous quarrel. With the elimination of
Tunis from international diplomacy, one of the roots of the Triple Alliance
began to wither.[4] In his own phrase, Visconti Venosta had given a decisive
thrust to the helm of Italian foreign policy.[5]

The year 1896 also brought a new crisis in the eastern Mediterranean.
Throughout 1895 the fate of the Armenians had preoccupied the Great

[1] DDI (3), I, 136, 139, 142. Rudinì told Farini on 31 July: 'He [Visconti Ven-
osta] is upset. He thought the French would concede him everything, just because
he was Visconti Venosta; and instead they give him nothing.' Farini, II, p. 1019.

[2] Luzzatti, *Memorie*, II, p. 476.

[3] DDF (1), XIV, 219. The *Enciclopedia Italiana* (XXXIV, p. 491) gives the
following figures for the Italian and French populations of Tunisia (out of a total
population of approximately 2 million):

|      | Italian | French |
|------|---------|--------|
| 1871 | 6,000   | —      |
| 1881 | 11,500  | less than 1,000 |
| 1891 | 21,000  | 18,000 |
| 1901 | 72,000  | 24,000 |

After 1881 the Italian immigrants were mainly Sicilian and predominantly working-class. The great increase between 1891 and 1901 was due at least in part to the
security offered by the 1896 agreement.

[4] Salvemini, *La politica estera dell' Italia*, p. 112. 'Now the French have realised',
commented Rudinì, 'that by conceding to us they can make the Triple Alliance
unnecessary.' Farini, II, p. 1045.

[5] Luzzatti, *Memorie*, II, pp. 525–6. Hanotaux commented in December 1896
to the Italian ambassador in Paris, 'On a senti, dès que le Marquis Visconti est
rentré au Gouvernement, que Vous aviez enfin un Ministre des Affaires étrangères.'
DDI (3), I, 321.

Powers. In May 1896 the Greeks of Crete revolted against the Turks, and Crete soon eclipsed Armenia as a centre of international tension. When Greece proclaimed the annexation of the island in February 1897 and sent ships and volunteers, the Great Powers established an international naval blockade and landed detachments of marines. The following April Greek provocation led to war with Turkey, in which the latter won a crushing victory in less than a month. The Powers then intervened to save Greece from the consequences. It was not until the end of 1898 that a settlement was reached whereby the Turks withdrew their troops from Crete and the island was granted autonomy under a Greek governor and Turkish suzerainty.

The Italians had played only a minor part in the affairs of Armenia, but in Crete they felt vitally concerned. Throughout the long crisis Visconti Venosta's main aim was to keep the creaking machinery of the European Concert in motion and to play an active part in that Concert. He was under constant pressure from philhellenes at home. Cavallotti, the irredentists and Bissolati, the Socialist party's expert on foreign affairs, urged action against 'the barbarous Turk' in the name of national self-determination. Inside the cabinet Luzzatti was their spokesman.[1] Italians were also beginning to show interest in Macedonian and Albanian aspirations. Crispi in his retirement took up the idea of Balkan federation and talked of chasing the Turk out of Europe. In 1896 the marriage of the heir to the throne to the daughter of the Prince of Montenegro heightened interest in the Slavs. Next year Italian socialist, anarchist and republican volunteers under Ricciotti Garibaldi fought the Turks beside the Greeks at the battle of Domokos. The whole of the Italian Left and Extreme Left deplored their government's passivity.

The reopening of the Eastern question, with the possibility of a partition of Turkey, greatly excited Rudinì. 'I want war', he told Farini in February 1897; 'the dynasty, the monarchy need one . . . I am an irredentist; Austria must be pushed east . . . I aspire to Trieste in the event of a large share-out.'[2] Such sentiments were in the best tradition of Cesare Balbo and the old Right. Visconti Venosta, however, was forced to face diplomatic realities. By 1896 there was nothing left of the Mediterranean coalition of 1887. His German and Austrian allies were unsympathetic to Greece, and he dared not risk estrangement from them while Italian ties with Britain remained so loose and vague. An effective European Concert was the only solution to his dilemma. While, therefore, he pressed for reforms in Crete and opposed the extreme forms of coercion which his allies wished to apply to Greece, Visconti Venosta supported the international blockade of the island. A large Italian squadron took part and an Italian admiral, Canevaro, was placed in command of the whole force. European peace and

[1] Luzzatti, *Memorie*, II, p. 474.          [2] Farini, II, pp. 1132, 1138, 1151.

the Concert were more important than the nationality principle.[1] Yet when the Concert threatened to disintegrate, it was to Britain and France rather than to Germany or Austria-Hungary that Visconti Venosta tended to turn. In March 1898 Germany and Austria withdrew their squadrons from the Cretan blockade, but the Italian ships remained, together with those of Britain, France and Russia. Visconti Venosta's main concern was to see that Italy, as a Mediterranean power, did not lose its voice in Cretan affairs. But he also welcomed the opportunity of showing, even at the risk of weakening the Triple Alliance, that Italy and France could collaborate in the Mediterranean.[2]

Nevertheless Italy's relations with Austria-Hungary were amicable. One danger of the troubles in Crete was that unrest might spread to the Balkans. In March 1897, on the eve of the Greco-Turkish war, Visconti Venosta exchanged views by letter with Goluchowski, Kálnoky's successor as Austro-Hungarian Foreign Minister. Goluchowski declared he had no secret Balkan plans and promised he would take independent action only in the last resort and after consulting Italy in accordance with Article VII of the Triple Alliance. Visconti Venosta likewise disclaimed any intention of upsetting the Balkans.[3] In May the Austrians finally despaired of reviving the Mediterranean Agreements and under German pressure came to terms with Russia. The two governments agreed to 'discard in advance all idea of conquest' in the Balkans and to cooperate in preserving the Turkish *status quo*. This agreement, of which Rudinì and Visconti Venosta were informed in general terms, inevitably revived Italian fears of the old bogey, the Three Emperors' League. Visconti Venosta himself was not worried. As he remarked to Bülow, German ambassador in Rome, Italy desired to expand neither in the Balkans nor in Africa, for it was incapable of 'digesting' any acquisitions.[4] When Prince Nicholas of Montenegro, emboldened by his new link with the Italian royal house, proposed a partition of Albania between Italy and Montenegro, to forestall alleged Austrian designs, Visconti Venosta dismissed the Prince's fears as groundless.[5] In November 1897 he and Rudinì met Goluchowski at Monza.

[1] DDI (3), I, 367, 371, 374, II, 366, 373–6; DDF (1), XIII, 111, 118, 130.
[2] DDI (3), II, 400–1; DDF (1), XIV, 150, 219. The French ambassador, Barrère, was wrong, however, in deducing that Visconti Venosta's aim at that time was to abandon the Triple Alliance. But Rudinì, less cautious than his Foreign Minister, remarked to Farini that events could in time bring a new Italo–Franco–British orientation. Farini, II, p. 1148.
[3] DDI (3), I, 379, 383–4, 391; GP, XII, 3129.
[4] Walters, 'Austro–Russian Relations', III, pp. 187–8; DDI (3), II, 8, 13, 20.
[5] DDI (3), I, 298–9, 384, 390, II, 111. When Nicholas visited Rome for the marriage of his daughter in October 1896, Rudinì told him 'curtly, even harshly' that Italy could not alter its foreign policy to please Montenegro. Farini, II, pp. 1060–1.

Goluchowski disclosed his proposal, which he had discussed with the
Russians, that if Turkish rule in Albania collapsed, a neutral and indepen-
dent Albanian state should be created. Visconti Venosta readily gave his
approval. This agreement suited both countries well and lasted until 1914.
It was the complement of the Austro-Russian agreement of the previous
May, which put the Balkans 'on ice' for ten years.[1]

A further consequence of the Eastern crisis was to revive both French
and Italian interest in Tripoli. Throughout 1896–7 troop concentrations in
the south of Tunisia suggested that the French might be preparing to forestall an Italian move, should the European Concert break up or Turkey
disintegrate. Visconti Venosta was inclined to believe the repeated French
denials of any such intention. Even so, he was not going to be taken by
surprise. 'For Tripoli', he told an English friend, 'even I would put a
match to the powder barrel.'[2] He recognised that at the moment Italians
were in no mood for colonial conquest, but he was also convinced that
'after Tunis, Italy could not tolerate a French occupation of Tripoli as
well'.[3] Salisbury, on being approached in April 1896, had replied that he
was opposed to any French advance, but refused to commit himself 'until
the contingency arose'.[4] Visconti Venosta was therefore left with two
alternatives: either to try to deter the French by revealing to them the
terms of the German guarantee under the Triple Alliance, or to discuss
the problem amicably with them and even negotiate a direct understanding.
The first alternative might merely exasperate the French, and would
require German consent; the second might arouse German suspicions and,
if it led to an agreement, would weaken the Triple Alliance.[5] In March
1897 he cautiously sounded the Germans and concluded from their obvious
embarrassment that no help could be expected from them.[6] He then decided that, sooner or later, he would have to negotiate with France over
Tripoli, as he had negotiated over Tunis in the previous year. When
Hanotaux proposed talks in May 1897, he at once agreed. With his usual
clarity he summed up the implications of this decision for the benefit of
his ambassador in Paris as follows:

> You know that, for us, the *status quo* at Tripoli is protected by a formal pledge
> in our treaty with Germany. Therefore, a protocol on the same subject

[1] Goluchowski's account of the discussions is printed in Walters, 'Austro–
Russian Relations', III, pp. 190–3. See also DDI (3), II, 286, 479. But relations
between the Austrian and Italian agents on the spot were never as harmonious as
those between the two governments. For examples of alarmist reports from Italian
consuls in Albania, who tended to suffer from what Nigra called the *morbus
consolaris*, see DDI (3), II, 9, 56, 265, 379, 385, III, 40.

[2] Steed, I, p. 150.         [3] DDI (3), II, 51.          [4] Serra, *L'intesa*, pp. 18–19.
[5] DDI (3), I, 386.                    [6] DDI (3), I, 396, 403–4.

between Italy and France might resemble those separate, secret reinsurance agreements *alla Bismarck* which, if not contrary to the letter, are nevertheless contrary to the spirit and good faith of existing alliances.[1]

On the other hand the Germans had repeatedly pointed out that they were not vitally interested in the Mediterranean, and had encouraged the Italians to go ahead and 'look outside the Triple Alliance for a grouping suitable for the protection of Italy's eastern and Mediterranean interests'.[2] Visconti Venosta therefore felt justified in drafting, not a protocol, but a less formal Franco-Italian declaration of mutual disinterest in Tripoli. But the French were after bigger game. Hanotaux denied all designs on Tripoli, but would not put it into writing until solutions had been found to other matters in dispute between the two countries. The talks on Tripoli therefore petered out in June 1897.[3]

It was not until 1898 that a decisive change occurred. In February Barrère took over the French embassy in Rome, a post which he was to hold until 1924, and in the following June the ultra-protectionist government of Méline fell. Delcassé, the new Foreign Minister, was less handicapped than his predecessor by conservative, protectionist colleagues, and he made rapid progress in creating a new basis for Franco-Italian relations. He and Barrère saw that Italy was the weak link in the Triple Alliance, which French rigidity in the past had strengthened. Instead of refusing concessions to Italy while it remained Germany's ally, they planned to make concessions in matters of minor importance to France and so, by corrosion from within, to make the German-Italian Alliance innocuous. They calculated that if their fears of France could be removed, Italians would soon find the weight of the Alliance uncomfortable. During a visit to Rome in March 1898 Delcassé had told Visconti Venosta, 'It is the Mediterranean that must reconcile us.' Many years later he declared his aim had been 'to make Italy a friend in the Mediterranean, in order to have her as a friend in Europe'.[4] The undermining of Italy's loyalty to Germany was now to be the consequence, not the condition, of Franco-

---

[1] DDI (3), II, 51.
[2] See Bülow's memorandum of 21 April 1898 to William II, in GP, XII (ii), 3295. In January 1897 Humbert assured the anxious Farini that he need not worry about Rudinì's Francophil tendencies: Bülow's initial doubts had been cleared up and 'Germany actually encouraged us to move closer to France'. Farini, II, p. 1119. The Austrians gave similar advice. In his talks with Visconti Venosta at Monza in November 1897, Goluchowski expressed satisfaction with Italy's efforts to improve relations with France and offered to help in any way he could. Walters, 'Austro–Russian Relations', III, pp. 192–3.
[3] DDF (1), XIII, 255; Serra, *Camille Barrère*, pp. 60–1; DDI (3), II, 30, 45, 51, 55, 87–96.
[4] Serra, *Camille Barrère*, p. 73.

Italian friendship. To build up that friendship was the life's work which awaited Barrère. Cautiously, thread by thread, he wove his intricate web from his embassy, flattering the men and encouraging the interests favourable to France, and establishing a position of such authority in Rome that he came to wield almost as much influence over Italian foreign policy as some Italian foreign ministers themselves.

His first success was a commercial treaty. The Italians had been pressing for this ever since Adowa and very secret, unofficial talks had begun in May 1897.[1] One of the keenest was Luzzatti, who hoped a treaty would prepare the way to conversion of the national debt with the help of a French loan.[2] By June 1898, when Rudinì was succeeded by Pelloux, with Admiral Canevaro as his Foreign Minister, the commercial talks had made much progress and the protectionist frenzy was subsiding in both countries. After being assured by the King, Pelloux and Canevaro that Visconti Venosta's policy would be continued,[3] Luzzatti, no longer a minister but by now indispensable as a foreign trade negotiator, secretly took charge of the final phase of the discussions in Paris. On 21 November the treaty was signed. The two countries granted each other, with the important exceptions of cattle and silk, their most favourable tariff. Mutual trade expanded rapidly over the next few years, though it never recovered the dominant position it had occupied in the Italian economy before 1888.[4] But the treaty's commercial importance was eclipsed by its political implications. Though foreign policy was never mentioned during the negotiations, both sides recognised that one more obstacle to Franco-Italian friendship had been removed. The treaty was intended to be, in Pelloux's words, 'a new point of departure'.[5]

The announcement of its signature caused great surprise in Italy, but in spite of the hostility of Crispi's followers it was generally welcomed. Many liberals had come to share the Extreme Left's disapproval of the militaristic Triple Alliance, which forced Italy to waste its resources on armaments. All through their own domestic battles of 1898–1900, Italian champions of liberty followed with admiration the parallel struggle of the Dreyfusards against reaction and dreamt of a Latin League with radical France.

[1] DDI (3), II, 21, 32.
[2] Luzzatti, *Memorie*, II, pp. 542–3; DDF (1), XIII, 18, 151, XIV, 120; Farini, II, p. 1430; DDI (3), III, 122.
[3] DDF (1), XIV, 253.
[4] See below, p. 291.
[5] Luzzatti, *Memorie*, II, p. 540; DDF (1), XIV, 527, 529, XV, 53. As the Italian ambassador in Paris, Tornielli, pointed out six months later, the political significance of the treaty derived from the unanimity with which the French press and parliament welcomed it. DDI (3), III, 163.

Further progress, however, was interrupted by the Fashoda crisis.[1] Canevaro, though an Anglophil monarchist of the old school, was appalled by the prospect of naval war between France and Britain in the Mediterranean, and his assurances that Italy would remain neutral were certainly sincere. But it would be a neutrality benevolent to Britain and, as he warned Barrère, Italy would resolutely defend it. Certain naval precautions were therefore taken, which caused alarm in Berlin.[2] There was a further anxiety. While Canevaro exerted such influence as Italy possessed in favour of peace, he was afraid that Britain and France might resolve their African quarrel at the expense of Italian aspirations. This anxiety was clearly conveyed to Britain. Any further encroachment on Tripoli's hinterland, Canevaro declared, would be 'so ruinous to our interests that no government in Italy could tolerate it'.[3] The Anglo-French convention of 21 March 1899 seemed to confirm his fears: the French renounced their designs on the Nile, but in return were guaranteed a free hand in a vast area north and north-east of Lake Chad. Canevaro expressed his pained surprise. From Britain his protests brought no satisfaction. Salisbury denied that the agreement in any way affected Tripolitania proper; but while 'ready to give any explanation the Italian Government desired with regard to our present intentions', he refused to promise that Britain 'would under no circumstances occupy any part of Tripoli' in the future.[4] The French were more conciliatory. Though Delcassé resisted Barrère's pressure for a public declaration of disinterest, he agreed to give Canevaro details of recent French assurances to Turkey with regard to the integrity of Tripolitania.[5] This satisfied Canevaro for the moment and enabled him to stand up to his critics at home. But there seemed to be but one conclusion to be drawn from the affair: Italy's interests in Tripoli could be guaranteed only by direct agreement with France.

Anglo-Italian relations had been unsatisfactory ever since Adowa. The

[1] The commercial treaty was signed at the height of the tension between Britain and France, which dragged on through the winter of 1898–9.

[2] BD, I, 217, 229; DDF (1), XIV, 497, 508, 512, XV, 174; DDI (3), III, 124.

[3] BD, I, 236; DDF (1), XV, 25, 35–6, 41–2; DDI (3), III, 205. Italian interests had already in the Italian view been damaged by the Anglo–French agreement of 1890 (see above, p. 136, n. 2). Successive Italian governments had argued that their special interest in Tripoli extended far south across the Sahara, even into territories not under effective Turkish control. Other governments resisted this extensive interpretation of 'hinterland' and limited their commitments as regards Italy to the Turkish *vilayet* of Tripoli along the Mediterranean coast.

[4] BD, I, 246–9, 251–2; DDI (3), III, 212, 225–6, 247, 254. 'Who can answer for the future?', Salisbury said to the Italian ambassador in London; 'Anything is possible . . .'

[5] DDF (1), XV, 129 ff., 148, 152; DDI (3), III, 241. Delcassé told Luzzatti in Paris that if Visconti Venosta returned to power, he would give him the written declaration that he had refused to Canevaro. DDF (1), XVI, 74.

hasty Italian withdrawal from Ethiopia had threatened to leave a vacuum which France might fill.[1] In particular Italy's impatience to abandon Kassala seemed likely to encourage an alliance between the Mahdists and Menelik, which would endanger the left flank of the British advance into the Sudan. 'I have often been pestered by people who wanted to get something', said Salisbury in September 1897, 'but never before have I seen people in such a hurry to give up something.'[2] The question was finally solved satisfactorily when an Anglo-Egyptian force relieved the Italian garrison of Kassala on Christmas Day 1897.

Friction also arose over Malta and China. A British decision of March 1899 to eliminate the Italian language from the Maltese courts within fifteen years aroused much resentment in Italy. In China the Italians had fewer interests than any other Great Power. They were, however, reluctant to be excluded if China should disintegrate or be partitioned, as seemed likely in 1898–9. Rudinì and Visconti Venosta favoured strictly commercial penetration. Pelloux and Canevaro, with the encouragement of the King, decided, largely for reasons of prestige, to imitate the Russians, Germans and British in a more dramatic policy. In March 1899 the Chinese government was presented with a demand for a naval base in the bay of San Mun, south of Shanghai, and a large sphere of influence in the province of Chekiang. The Chinese, to the general astonishment, replied with a curt, undiplomatic refusal, and remained unmoved by either a four-day ultimatum or the despatch of three Italian warships to San Mun. The use of force, to which China would doubtless have capitulated, was vetoed by Britain, whose support Canevaro had from the outset regarded as indispensable. The Chinese, who were aware of this, concluded that they had nothing to fear and made Italy, the last of the European nations to appear on the scene, the target of all their pent-up xenophobia. Canevaro, embittered by what he regarded as Salisbury's double dealing,[3] demonstrated by a series of diplomatic blunders his incompetence as Foreign Minister. In May Pelloux resigned in order to avoid defeat in parliament and formed a new cabinet. Canevaro was replaced by Visconti Venosta who had disapproved of the whole Chinese venture. Realising that public opinion and parliament were 'absolutely opposed to a policy of territorial or military

[1] The French did in fact make strenuous efforts to win Menelik as an ally and to strengthen Ethiopia against both Britain and Italy. Menelik was urged to extend his rule to the right bank of the Nile and there link up with Marchand's expedition from the west. The French capitulation after Fashoda ended these schemes.

[2] Steed, I, pp. 122–3.

[3] Salisbury, while irritated by Italian pretensions, was anxious to keep on good terms with both Italy and China. He therefore gave the Italians purely diplomatic support and vetoed the use of force, in the full knowledge that it was only to force that the Chinese would yield. This was equivalent to a refusal of any effective help. Borsa, pp. 87–92, 115–18; BD, I, 60; DDI (3), III, 156, 162, 200.

occupations', he concentrated all his efforts on finding a way out that did not involve humiliation.[1] But even though he reduced his demands by stages to minor commercial concessions, he was totally unsuccessful. In December he was forced to announce that the Chinese question was closed, with nothing gained. It was a major diplomatic fiasco, relieved only in part during the Boxer rebellion next year, when Italy took part in the international military expedition to Peking and subsequently acquired a concession at Tientsin.

Delcassé and Barrère missed no chance of contrasting France's sympathy with Salisbury's coldness,[2] and in October 1899 the negotiations over Tripoli were resumed.[3] It was now the French government that was the more eager for agreement. Encouraged by Britain's humiliations at the hands of the Boers, it was making ambitious plans for southward expansion from Algeria. These were certain to cause alarm in Morocco, and Italy's acquiescence was important. Delcassé therefore suggested not the negative, unilateral French undertaking to respect the Tripoli *status quo*, which had been under discussion since 1896, but a positive, bilateral agreement anticipating changes in the *status quo* both in Tripolitania and in Morocco. Visconti Venosta regretted the introduction of this new complication and took time to make up his mind. He regarded Tuat and the Saharan oases as in themselves of secondary importance to Italy.[4] Nevertheless he feared that a 'Tunisification' of Morocco, without compensation for Italy, would cause such an explosion that not only the Triple Alliance but the Italian monarchy would be in danger. As he told his ambassador in Berlin in January 1900:[5]

> You know that I have no love of adventures for our country, and believe that it needs a few years of calm at home and abroad. . . . But after Tunis, after the fortification of Bizerta and the Anglo-French agreement of last year, if another alteration occurred in the Mediterranean position, Italy could not remain passive.

In Berlin Italy's growing friendliness with France had been watched with concern. Already in December 1898, after the signature of the commercial treaty, Bülow, now Foreign Secretary, had warned that Germany would be worried

> if Franco-Italian relations became, or only appeared to become, too intimate. . . . Germany is like a husband who loves, respects and trusts his beautiful

---

[1] Borsa, pp. 161, 174–5; DDF (1), XV, 166, 181; DDI (3), III, 259, 262, 264.
[2] Of all the Great Powers, France was much the most sympathetic to Italy in its Chinese troubles. Borsa, pp. 119–21, 180–1; DDI (3), III, 185, 260.
[3] DDF (1), XV, 298, XVI, 3; DDI (3), III, 336, 344.
[4] DDI (3), I, 163, 282.
[5] GP, XVII, 5156; DDI (3), III, 353, 387, 402.

wife, is pleased to see her courted and doesn't take offence even if she dances
with other men, but becomes jealous and suspicious if he discerns too accentuated a 'flirt'.[1]

In the following April, when a French naval squadron greeted Humbert
and his queen at Cagliari during their state visit to Sardinia, the warmth
of the toasts and exuberance of the celebrations revived German suspicions.
Canevaro affirmed on repeated occasions, and with convincing sincerity,
that Italian foreign policy remained 'rigorously unchanged'.[2] But of
Visconti Venosta the Germans felt less sure. In July 1896 Bülow, then
ambassador in Rome, had protested to the King and Rudinì against his
appointment to the Foreign Ministry.[3] Again in May 1899 William II
and Bülow tried to persuade the King and Pelloux to appoint Sonnino
rather than Visconti Venosta, as a public demonstration of loyalty to old
allies.[4] Their failure increased their apprehension.

Before committing himself to Barrère, Visconti Venosta tried in the
spring of 1900 to have with Bülow a full and frank discussion of the Mediterranean situation, making no secret of his intention to 'find compensation
for what could not be prevented (i.e. a French advance in Morocco) where
that compensation could be found (i.e. at Tripoli)'. Having discovered that
neither Britain nor Germany intended to oppose France over Morocco,[5]
he felt justified in taking the plunge. Already in February he and Barrère
had reached agreement in principle that Italian disinterest in Morocco
should be bartered against French disinterest in Tripoli.[6] In the course of
the next six months the French occupied Tuat and several other southern
oases, unopposed by Germany or Britain as Visconti Venosta had foreseen.
An exchange of notes dated 14 and 16 December 1900 constituted the
final agreement. Barrère confirmed the verbal assurance of the previous
year that France had no designs on Tripoli; Visconti Venosta recognised
that French action in Morocco designed 'to exercise and safeguard the

[1] DDI (3), III, 129.

[2] DDI (3), III, 129, 219, 234; BD, I, 347.

[3] Farini, II, pp. 1006, 1042.

[4] According to Barrère's uncorroborated account of this episode, Luzzatti and
Rattazzi were mainly responsible for persuading the King and Pelloux to appoint
Visconti Venosta, after Sonnino had declined Pelloux's offer. DDF (1), XV, 180,
196.

[5] GP, XVII, 5152 ff.; BD, I, 288; DDI (3), III, 361, 387, 391, 397, 399, 401-2;
Taylor, pp. 364-6. Between 1887 and 1895 Italy had tried to keep France out of
Morocco by collaboration with Britain and Spain. Britain now no longer wished
to try. An attempt had been made in April 1896, with Austrian support, to revive
the Italo-Spanish agreement which had lapsed in 1895; it failed because Spain
demanded a guarantee against the U.S.A. of its possession of Cuba. DDI (3), I,
85, 90-1, 100, 135.

[6] DDI (3), III, 372; DDF (1), XVI, 51, 55, 72.

rights resulting from the contiguity of her territory' did not injure Italian interests in the Mediterranean, while reserving Italy's right, should the French alter the political and territorial status of Morocco, to extend its own influence in Tripolitania and Cyrenaica.[1]

It was thus a strictly limited agreement. French consent to Italy's occupation of Tripoli was dependent on a previous French move in Morocco. Visconti Venosta had attempted to extract a more positive French commitment, but Delcassé would concede no more while Italy refused to give France assurances in Europe.[2] Visconti Venosta for his part had no intention of abandoning his allies. In the same month of December 1900 he signed a naval convention with Austria-Hungary and confirmed in writing the verbal agreement of 1897 on Albania. Even so, his understanding with Barrère was a blow to the Triple Alliance, for it removed that fear of France in Africa which had driven Italy to seek allies in 1881–2. Both men, in resolving to 'close a bad chapter' in Franco-Italian relations and eliminate Mediterranean discords, had the further aim of rendering superfluous the anti-French clauses of the Triple Alliance and removing all *raison d'être* for an Anglo-Italian coalition directed against France.[3] Barrère was more than satisfied with the results of his eighteen months' effort.[4] Visconti Venosta, too, was well aware of the significance of what he had done. In spite of the scruples he had felt in May 1897,[5] he had agreed with Barrère that the two notes should remain secret and had still informed neither Germany nor Austria-Hungary when he left office for the last time in February 1901.

On that occasion he could look back on five years of solid achievement. After Adowa Italian prestige had been at its lowest. As Visconti Venosta himself complained, Salisbury had treated Italy as 'a negligible quantity'.[6] The British Admiralty considered that the advantages of an Italian alliance would be outweighed by the obligation to defend Italy's ports and coasts, which the Italian navy was incapable of defending alone.[7] Theories of Latin decadence were fashionable in northern Europe and in 1898 Italy was believed to be on the brink of revolution. Yet, in spite of internal turmoil, Visconti Venosta by patience, skill and attention to detail had gained time for Italy to recover strength and confidence, and had laid the foundations of its future diplomatic security. The tribute which Bülow paid him many years later was well-deserved: 'I do not think', he wrote in his *Memoirs*, 'that he ever did a stupid thing in any sphere during the whole of his life.'[8]

---

[1] Texts in DDF (2), I, 17.
[2] Serra, *Camille Barrère*, pp. 91–2; DDF (1), XVI, 136, 148.
[3] DDF (1), XVI, 72, 79, 136, 148.     [4] DDF (1), XVI, 415; DDF (2), I, 17.
[5] See above, p. 206.     [6] BD, I, 355.     [7] Marder, pp. 270–2, 575–7.
[8] Bülow, IV, p. 339.

# 6

# The Church under Leo XIII

## Papal Diplomacy

Leo XIII was almost sixty-eight years of age when elected Pope in 1878. He was a complete contrast, in character and experience, to his predecessor. Though he had been Bishop of Perugia since 1846, his early training had been in papal administration and diplomacy. Being less simple and warm-hearted, less Italian in his outlook than Pius IX, he had disapproved both of the latter's nationalist phase in 1846–8 and of his intransigence towards the Italian state since 1861. For this reason Leo had been out of favour at the Vatican and distrusted by Antonelli, the Secretary of State. The cardinals who secured his election were aware of this. In view of his age, his pontificate was expected to be short; but it was hoped that, with his greater flexibility and understanding of the modern world, he would find new paths out of the *impasse* into which Pius IX seemed to have led the Papacy.

Leo believed that the church's mission was to save not only souls but human society.[1] He was inspired by 'the great dream of Catholic imperialism', through which his greatest predecessors had made the Papacy a dominant power in Europe.[2] His ambition was to restore the authority of the church throughout the world; to influence governments and sway peoples, to be an arbiter in international conflict and the defender of peace. He also dreamt of reunification with the Eastern churches and looked far beyond Europe to the expanding Catholic communities overseas.[3] The essential preliminary task was to end the dangerous isolation in which he found the church in 1878. Anti-clerical republicans were in power in France and in Germany the *Kulturkampf* was still raging. Leo XIII from the first adopted the language of moderation. Instead of harping on principles he showed himself ready to concede in secondary matters, in order more effectively to pursue his greater aim.

Towards Italy he was outwardly unyielding. He had even less desire

[1] King and Okey, p. 34.    [2] Crispolti and Aureli, pp. 18–19.
[3] Spadolini, *L'opposizione cattolica*, pp. 630–1.

214

than Pius IX to recover the Papal States and on occasions seemed almost to admit the need for reconciliation; yet in the course of his pontificate he issued sixty-two formal protests against the destruction of the temporal power. The main aim of his diplomacy was to convince the outside world of the perils of his position and to win its support against Italy. For twenty-five years, by sheer persistence, he kept the Roman question alive. It was a losing battle. He never succeeded in creating a diplomatic situation in which a friendless Italy would be forced to negotiate from weakness with the Papacy. Yet, in spite of many failures, Leo enormously increased the church's international prestige. The impression he made on contemporaries was striking. His keen sense of sovereignty and the regal pomp of his court, his intellect and vision, his enigmatic personality, his marble-like pallor and frailty that in extreme old age gave him the appearance of a wraith – these won him admiration and devotion even from Protestants and unbelievers. 'The Pope complains, he pretends to be a prisoner', said Humbert to a French diplomat in 1886; 'but he is far more popular with Italians and foreigners than I am. They come here to see him far more than me . . . It is he who still rules in Rome; I have only the edge of the throne to sit on.'[1]

The diplomacy of Leo XIII's pontificate falls into two periods. In the first ten years, during which the directing hand was his own, it was on Germany that he pinned his hopes of papal resurgence. Though his first soundings for an end to the *Kulturkampf* proved unfruitful, he refused to be discouraged. By 1881 the international situation looked brighter. Bismarck made no secret of his contempt for Italy, whose impotence and isolation had been revealed in the Tunisian crisis, and in his Reichstag speech in November he went out of his way to stress Germany's cordial relations with the Papacy. On the other hand, Humbert's visit to Vienna and the clamour in Italy for a German alliance were disquieting. The mood of the Vatican oscillated between extravagant hopes and black despair.

After the brawl over Pius IX's coffin in July 1881,[2] Leo XIII felt more than ever encompassed about with enemies in Rome. The anti-clerical tempest was rising and his friends abroad were failing him. In March 1882 Francis Joseph sent a veteran diplomat, Baron Hübner, to Rome on a special mission, 'to inject a drop of balm in Leo's tortured and excited soul'. All his hopes, his love, his trust were concentrated, after God, on Francis Joseph, the Pope told Hübner, and if the Emperor failed him, his heart would burst.[3] Yet Francis Joseph's response brought cold comfort.

---

[1] *Mémoires d'Auguste Gérard* (Paris 1928), p. 118.
[2] See above, pp. 110–11.
[3] Salata, *Per la storia diplomatica della questione romana*, p. 172; Engel-Jánosi, I, p. 232.

Though he promised asylum in Austria in extreme need, he urged Leo to stay in Rome rather than move to 'a cold Alpine land'. Leo agreed, provided there was no war, no armed attack on the Vatican, and no abolition of the Law of Guarantees by a radical majority in the Italian parliament.[1] A more solid consolation was Francis Joseph's personal promise that he would never visit the King of Italy in Rome.

In March 1883 the existence of the Triple Alliance became known. It was a bitter blow to Leo XIII. Francis Joseph hastened to assure him that it contained no written guarantee of Italy's possession of Rome. Yet, as Leo wrote to him in reply, its very existence strengthened Italy and, so he argued, weakened his own position. He never accepted the German and Austrian contention that the Alliance was a bulwark of conservatism which, by strengthening the Italian monarchy, also strengthened the Papacy. Leo looked upon the monarchy as the tool of the secret atheist 'sects' and the child of revolution; it could never arrest the 'inevitable drift towards the time when Italy would be ruled by men whose aim would be the destruction of the Papacy'.[2]

The years 1887–8 were the turning-point in Leo XIII's pontificate. In March 1887, after nine years of hard bargaining, the *Kulturkampf* was brought to an end. In the same month Cardinal Luigi Galimberti was sent on a special mission to Berlin to attend the celebrations of William I's ninetieth birthday. Galimberti was a forceful advocate of the policy of winning Bismarck's friendship. He may also have shared the hopes of many Italians that the ending of the *Kulturkampf* and the renewal of the Triple Alliance[3] might together lead to a *modus vivendi* between Italy and the Papacy.[4] Galimberti received an impressively cordial reception in Berlin. But when he broached the Roman question to Bismarck, the latter replied non-committally, 'Chaque jour a son travail.'[5] This rebuff strengthened the party in the Vatican which condemned the concessions that had ended the *Kulturkampf* as a capitulation. Leo himself was for a long time undecided; but in June 1887 he appointed Cardinal Mariano Rampolla, the chief opponent of Galimberti's policy, as his Secretary of State.

Six months after the optimism of spring 1887, Leo was again plunged into despair by Crispi's much-publicised journey to Friedrichsruh.[6] The

---

[1] Salata, *Per la storia*, pp. 156–7.
[2] ibid., pp. 110–15; Chabod, 'Kulturkampf e Triplice Alleanza', pp. 278–80; Engel-Jánosi, I, pp. 233–4, 240.
[3] On 20 February 1887. See above, p. 122.
[4] De Rosa, *L'Azione Cattolica*, I, p. 123; Engel-Jánosi, I, pp. 244–6. The summer of 1887 did in fact see the first serious attempt at reconciliation since 1870. See below, p. 220.
[5] Crispolti and Aureli, p. 134; Soderini, III, p. 351.
[6] See above, p. 131.

Powers had abandoned and betrayed him, he lamented.[1] In March 1888 Galimberti revisited Berlin, this time to attend William I's funeral. For the second time he raised the Roman question with Bismarck and received an unhelpful reply – 'Il faut savoir attendre.'[2] In August Leo was again thinking of leaving Rome and Hübner was dispatched from Vienna on a second soothing mission. Kálnoky, much alarmed, extracted from Crispi a promise that he would not touch the Law of Guarantees. Leo's final disillusionment with Germany came in October 1888 when William II visited Humbert in Rome. This was the first visit of a sovereign of a Great Power to the capital since 1870. The Pope, making the best of a painful occasion, invited the Emperor to the Vatican. The visit was paid, but no frank discussion of the Roman question took place, and William II's tactlessness and brash indifference to protocol left sore feelings behind.[3] After this the star of Galimberti, now nunzio at Vienna, declined and papal diplomacy, in the resolute hands of Rampolla, launched out on a new path.

Rampolla was an administrator and diplomatist by training, like Leo, and a Sicilian as proud and stubborn as his fellow-Sicilian, Crispi. From the day of his appointment he worked for an *entente cordiale* with a strengthened and re-Christianised France,[4] to which he dreamt, with more fantasy than realism, of uniting an Austria enticed out of the Triple Alliance; the two great Catholic nations, flanked by Spain, might then use their united strength to impose upon Italy a settlement acceptable to the Papacy. The first step was to win the confidence of French governments by persuading French Catholics to abandon their monarchist prejudices and 'rally' to the Third Republic. In November 1890 Cardinal Lavigerie, Archbishop of Algiers and Primate of Africa, made the first public move. With the Pope's approval he declared at a banquet of naval and civilian dignitaries in Algiers that the supreme need was for all good citizens to accept the republican form of government. In February 1892 Leo himself urged French Catholics to respect the established constitution, while continuing to fight against irreligious laws 'by all honest and legal means'.[5] At the end of that year he explained his views with startling clarity to a leading French diplomatist.[6] Britain, Austria and Germany were all unreliable, he

[1] Engel-Jánosi, I, p. 251.
[2] Crispolti and Aureli, pp. 236–7; Soderini, III, p. 389.
[3] Crispolti and Aureli, pp. 252–79; Soderini, III, pp. 393–404.
[4] Engel-Jánosi, I, pp. 252–3; DDF (1), VI (ii), 56, 58, 71. In December 1887 Leo himself assured the French *chargé d'affaires* of his 'true affection for the nation which is still, in spite of everything, *ma fille privilégiée*'.
[5] D. W. Brogan, *The Development of Modern France* (London 1940), pp. 257–67.
[6] To Paul Cambon, French ambassador in Constantinople, who was passing through Rome. DDF (1), X, 62.

said, and only France, with a well-governed, conservative republic, had a future; if France and the Papacy worked together in harmony, 'we would dominate the world'.

French republicans, however lukewarm their Catholic faith, had at least one inducement to respond to Leo XIII's advances. Anti-clericalism, Gambetta had declared, was not an article for export, and French governments, however anti-clerical, had continued to value their old-established protectorate over the Catholics in Asiatic Turkey. Since the advent of Crispi, Italy was showing unwelcome interest in Italian Catholic communities abroad, seeing in them a means of extending its political influence. The French had little to fear from their rival while their relations with the Papacy remained cordial. They hardly required Rampolla's reminder that 'the Roman question gives France great strength – against Italy'.[1]

Russia, too, had a place in Leo XIII's grand design. He hoped, by improving relations and by making concessions to Slav sentiment in questions of liturgy and ecclesiastical organisation, to win converts and even pave the way for the return of the Orthodox churches to the Roman fold. In vain Kálnoky warned him that his concessions, far from preparing reunion, would merely encourage Panslavism and strengthen the influence of Russia over the western Slavs.[2] After 1890 all the Vatican's influence was exerted in favour of the nascent Franco-Russian alliance and against the reconciliation of France with Italy. In the months after Adowa, Leo XIII was so cheered by the discredit which had fallen on the Italian monarchy, and by the strength of the Franco-Russian counterweight to the Triple Alliance, that he was talking of the partition of Italy and his recovery of a portion of Rome.[3]

For more than ten years after 1887 French influence was paramount at the Vatican. For the Papacy this dependence upon France proved unwise. In 1899 Italy's veto, supported by Germany, prevented Leo XIII from sending a delegate to the disarmament conference at The Hague. Leo protested in vain that an international peace congress at which the Catholic church was unrepresented would be a farce. France and Italy meanwhile drew closer, to the Vatican's growing alarm.[4] Then came the victory of the Dreyfusards and a new wave of anti-clericalism in France. The *ralliement* proved an illusion and Rampolla's policy seemed bankrupt. Must he be forced to reverse the political trend of his whole pontificate, to the delight of France's enemies, Leo bitterly asked the French ambassador

[1] Engel-Jánosi, I, p. 253.
[2] Crispolti and Aureli, pp. 280–94; Chabod, 'Kulturkampf e Triplice Alleanza', pp. 272–80.
[3] DDF (1), XII, 387, XIII, 312, 330.
[4] DDF (1), XIV, 570, XV, 149, 165, 194.

in March 1900? In the last years of his life, while still protesting his love of France, he was reluctantly turning again to Germany and Austria-Hungary.[1] When he died in 1903, the Papacy was diplomatically almost as isolated as when he was elected in 1878.

## Church and State

Many patriotic Italian Catholics hoped in 1878 that the new Pope would bring about that reconciliation between Italy and the Papacy for which they longed. Over the next four years the National Conservatives were busy behind the scenes.[2] They believed that the best way of defending the church's interests was to bring the Catholic masses into national politics. To solve the Roman question they proposed an international guarantee, not restoration of a papal kingdom, calculating that the Pope's independence would be better protected by the moral force of Catholic opinion throughout the world than by the material force of the temporal power. Among the supporters of this programme were Bishops Geremia Bonomelli of Cremona and Giovan Battista Scalabrini of Piacenza. In Bonomelli's prophetic words to Leo XIII,[3]

> Today, with the changed state of affairs, with liberal forms of government, territorial dominion is worth very little, and is perhaps a handicap. . . . With the diplomatic corps by your side, with the telegraph, with unlimited means of communication, with the moral power which you possess, with the eyes of the world always upon you, with ears always stretched to hear your words, with that illimitable, invincible publicity which accompanies your every action, you are the freest of monarchs.

The electoral reform of 1882, which reinforced the anti-clerical left in parliament, strengthened the arguments of the conciliators for an abandonment of the *non expedit*. They had sympathisers in high positions in the Vatican and Leo XIII himself was ready to listen to their arguments. Depretis had his contacts with them through Minghetti and Scalabrini, and would have welcomed an electoral arrangement as part of his *trasformismo*.[4] But in the end all their efforts came to nothing. In 1886 the Holy Office reaffirmed the ban on voting with a declaration that 'Non expedit prohibitionem importat'. The intransigent clericals who controlled the Opera launched a savage and successful campaign to discredit the conciliators: bourgeois institutions were to be destroyed, not preserved, and no distinction was to be made between obedience to the Pope in

[1] DDF (1), XVI, 9, 12, 97, 369; Engel-Jánosi, I, pp. 303–7.
[2] See above, p. 94.
[3] Jacini, *Un conservatore rurale*, II, pp. 185–6.
[4] Carocci, pp. 321–4.

matters of faith and obedience in politics.[1] On the other side the fanatical
anti-clericals were equally successful in keeping passions high, while even
sane men like Sella deprecated the smallest concession to clericalism.
Though its ideas survived in the 'clerical-moderate' programme of the
next two decades, the National Conservative party was stillborn.

In 1887, however, for a few excited weeks, it seemed that reconciliation
was within reach. The *Kulturkampf* had just ended and peacemaking was
in the air. The tragedy of Dogali provided the occasion. High clerics
expressed patriotic sentiments and the Archbishop of Florence celebrated
a requiem mass for the fallen in his cathedral, in the presence of the King
and Queen. On 23 May Leo XIII gave an allocution in which he spoke
affectionately of Italy and referred to his wish to end 'the lamentable
quarrel', without once mentioning the temporal power. A few days later
the Benedictine Father Luigi Tosti, Abbot of Montecassino, published a
pamphlet entitled *La Conciliazione*. Tosti was a warm-hearted old man
who had never shed the illusions of 1848 and still dreamt of a liberal
Papacy at peace with a united Italy. Pleading for recognition by Leo XIII
that Rome was now the possession of the Italian nation, and that the
surest protection for the Papacy would be a unanimous and devoted
people, he declared that 1888, the year of Leo's sacerdotal jubilee, could
also be the year of conciliation and peace.

Four days before the publication of his pamphlet Tosti had discussed
the prospect of conciliation with Crispi, then Minister of Interior, and
told him, incorrectly but in good faith, that his proposals accorded with
the wishes of the Pope.[2] Crispi's Sicilian temperament responded to
Tosti's enthusiasm. Though an anti-clerical and freemason, Crispi was
fascinated by the church's spiritual power and its deep roots in Roman
and Italian history. He may have seen himself in the role of conciliator,
succeeding where even Cavour had failed. He certainly saw the advantages
to Italy of solving the Roman question: French diplomacy would lose a
weapon and the church's blessing would open up new horizons for Italy
in world politics. Whatever his motives, he was ready to transform secret
negotiations on finance and church property, which were then in progress
between the Vatican and the Italian government, into discussion of a
general settlement of problems of church and state.

The dream was short-lived. Rumours of negotiation roused generous
hopes, but they also rallied the opposition which Tosti had underestimated.
On 10 June the government was interpellated on its religious policy. Bovio
from the Extreme Left glorified the 'clash of civilisations' between the
church's dogma and the intellectual adventurousness of the modern world,

[1] De Rosa, *L'Azione Cattolica*, I, pp. 136 ff.; Dalla Torre, pp. 30–9.
[2] Crispi, *Politica interna*, pp. 101–4.

from which Rome drew greatness and true progress was born. Reconciliation, he argued, would be stagnation. Crispi, embarrassed and irritated, denied the rumours and declared that 'Italy had no wish or need for conciliations'.[1] On the other side Rampolla, the newly appointed Secretary of State, and the intransigent party in the Vatican bestirred themselves. Alarmed protests came from Catholics in France, Belgium and Spain. At the end of July Leo published a letter to Rampolla in which he 'interpreted' and amplified his May allocution: a 'real, effective sovereignty' for the Papacy was the essential condition of a settlement, and no alternative to the temporal power could be considered. Rampolla reassured foreign governments and on 28 July a recantation by Tosti was published.[2] Once again the unconscious alliance of the clerical and anti-clerical fanatics had triumphed.

Even then some of the conciliators continued stubbornly to hope. In 1889 Bonomelli published an article suggesting the creation of a 'miniature' Vatican State on the right bank of the Tiber. The article was placed on the Index and Bonomelli was forced to retract from his own pulpit. Jacini continued to work for conciliation until his death in 1891 and his younger associates achieved some influence in Rudinì's two governments. But conciliation on terms acceptable to the majority of Italians was irreconcilable with Rampolla's policy of leaning on France. The *ralliement* was welcomed by French governments just because it prevented that extension of Italian influence in the world which would have followed on Italy's reconciliation with the Papacy. Crispi had good reason for regarding Cardinal Lavigerie, the architect of the *ralliement*, as one of his country's most effective political agents in Africa.[3] Only one form of conciliation could have been acceptable to France: that between a Papacy firmly attached to France and an Italian democratic, Francophil republic. There was a small current of Italian democratic opinion which dreamt of such an event. Led by one of Nicotera's supporters, the deputy Achille Fazzari, who had fought as a colonel under Garibaldi in 1860, and enjoying the sympathy of Garibaldi's son, Ricciotti, it achieved a brief moment of importance in the years 1886–8. Contact was made with Rampolla, who himself had several meetings with Fazzari.[4] The Vatican's readiness to flirt with democracy and its apparent prejudice in favour of the republican

[1] Cilibrizzi, II, p. 330; Jemolo, pp. 414–17.

[2] Crispi, *Politica interna*, pp. 116–18. Tosti wrote his recantation at the Pope's request; its publication, which he had not expected, humiliated and embittered him.

[3] Lavigerie had been conspicuous for his anti-Italian activity in Tunis before 1881. Vercesi, *Tre papi*, pp. 57–60.

[4] Crispolti and Aureli, pp. 175–7; Soderini, II, pp. 121–6. Interest was also shown by Flourens, French Foreign Minister from December 1886 to March 1888.

222

form of government caused conservative Catholics like Kálnoky much anxiety. Rampolla never concealed his main motive: it would be easier to come to terms with an Italian republic than with the present pseudo-kingdom, and with only one crowned head within its walls, Rome would once again become the capital not just of a few million Italians but of many hundreds of millions of Catholics.[1] This dream did not survive the collapse of the *ralliement* at the end of the century.

The disappointments of 1887 were followed by ten stormy years. Crispi, now Prime Minister, abruptly abandoned the role of peacemaker and fell back into his old habits of thought and language. For three years crises in relations between Italy and the Papacy coincided with the recurring international crises. In December 1887 Crispi dismissed the Mayor of Rome for presuming to convey to the Vatican the good wishes of the people of the city for Leo XIII's sacerdotal jubilee. Sacramental tithes were abolished, begging for alms in the open air was forbidden and stricter regulations against clerical abuses were introduced. On Whit Monday in June 1889, at a moment of acute tension between France and Italy, a statue of Giordano Bruno was unveiled in the Campo dei Fiori, on the spot where he was burnt for heresy in 1600. Amid grandiloquent tributes to the 'patron saint of free thought', Bovio and his friends proclaimed the beginning of the end of the Papacy's spiritual power. Leo XIII summoned a secret consistory and talked of leaving Rome; Crispi sent Cardinal Hohenlohe to him with a message that he was free to leave, but that once he had gone he would never return. Second thoughts prevailed and Leo XIII stayed.[2] Four months later, in a speech at Palermo, Crispi poured scorn on the Papacy's claim to Rome and declared, 'Our task is to fight for Reason, and to see that the Italian state is the evident expression of Reason.' This was too much for Kálnoky, who described it as 'beyond comment'. The more solid the Triple Alliance, he complained, the more anti-clerical Crispi became, and the harder his own job of making the Alliance popular in Austria.[3] In 1890 the church's charitable trusts were reorganised according to what Crispi called 'the great principle of secularisation of civil institutions', and priests were excluded from their administration. All these provocative measures and demonstrations were accompanied by strong protests from Leo XIII.

Rudinì was more conciliatory. He announced that the Law of Guarantees

[1] Engel-Jánosi, I, pp. 258, 265, II, pp. 18–19; Fonzi, pp. 46–7. Bismarck revealed the same thought when he remarked to Galimberti in 1888 that restoration of the temporal power would lead to an Italian republic and a Franco–Italian alliance. Soderini, III, p. 389.      [2] Crispi, *Memoirs*, II, pp. 399–407.
[3] Salata, *Per la storia diplomatica della questione romana*, pp. 231–4.

would be regarded as a permanent law of the state and in private showed readiness to discuss a wider settlement.[1] But goodwill on his part was not enough. In October 1891 French working-class pilgrims demonstrated in favour of 'le Pape-roi' at the Pantheon, where Victor Emmanuel II lay buried. Anti-clerical riots broke out in Rome, the freemasons mobilised their forces and Leo XIII once again talked of departing.

Crispi's return to office in December 1893 brought a change in atmosphere which, though short-lived, was of great significance. To deal with the socialist threat and the spread of violence in Sicily, Crispi called for 'a truce of God' in party strife. New contacts were made with the Vatican and Crispi had a secret but inconclusive talk with the Bishop of Perugia on the improvement of relations between church and state. In a private message to Leo XIII, Crispi denied all feelings of enmity; on the contrary, he declared, the Papacy was for him 'an Italian institution' and one of Italy's glories.[2] Next September, in the presence of the Archbishop of Naples, he proclaimed the slogan 'With God, with the King, with the Fatherland', to combat 'the infamous sect' which had 'Neither God nor authority' inscribed on its banner. In the same year he made concessions over many long-delayed church appointments,[3] and a separate apostolic prefecture was created in Eritrea which soon led to the replacement in the colony of French Lazzarist missionaries by Italian Franciscans.

This precarious harmony was soon broken. On 20 September 1895, the twenty-fifth anniversary of the occupation of Rome, Crispi, in the King's presence, unveiled the monument to Garibaldi which still overlooks the Vatican from the Janiculum. Earlier in the year September 20th had been declared an annual public holiday. Leo XIII retaliated by reaffirming the *non expedit* in a more rigid form than ever before. In October he forced King Carlos of Portugal to cancel a publicly announced visit to his cousin Humbert in Rome, and Crispi broke off diplomatic relations with Portugal in protest. A settlement seemed as far off as ever.

Crispi's oscillations typified those of many liberals. As early as 1880 Luzzatti had confessed to Sella his admiration for Leo XIII and his disgust with demagogic anticlericalism. How long, he asked himself, could liberals continue to evade the choice between the priest's holy water and the anarchist's petrol-bomb?[4] That dilemma had become more acute

[1] A. Luzio, 'Il Cardinale Rampolla e il Marchese di Rudinì', in *Nuova Antologia*, vol. 397 (1938), pp. 19–26. The tentative project was for Italy to recognise papal sovereignty over the Vatican and for the Pope to raise the ban on visits by Catholic heads of state to the King of Italy in Rome.

[2] Crispi, *Politica interna*, pp. 134–6.

[3] The most important were those of Cardinal Sarto, the future Pope Pius X, as Patriarch of Venice, and Cardinal Ferrari as Archbishop of Milan.

[4] 'Il dilemma dell' acqua santa o del petrolio'. Luzzatti, *Memorie*, II, p. 118.

with the rise of socialism, which few yet distinguished from anarchism. An important part of the liberal ruling-class began to doubt the viability of the secular, de-Christianised state and to dream of enlisting 'holy water' as an ally. The blessing of the priest was needed to reinforce the social order and the fabric of the Italian state.[1] These apprehensions explain the sporadic efforts of Crispi and Rudinì between 1891 and 1897 to secure an easing of the *non expedit* and win new voters for the constitutional cause. If Catholics continued to boycott the polls, socialism might triumph.

Many liberals, however, remained unshaken in their resolve to continue the traditional war on two fronts, against both red and black subversion. One of the severest critics of Crispi's and Rudinì's oscillations was Farini. Crispi did not understand the papal question, he complained; no reconciliation was possible without restoring Rome to the Pope, and 'the embrace of the Vatican would suffocate the monarchy'. To Crispi's 'Better the clericals than the socialists', Farini replied 'Neither.'[2] Both Crispi and Rudinì soon tired of their desire for an understanding with the church. When their overtures were rebuffed, they relapsed into their old anti-clerical attitudes.

The Catholics were as divided as the liberals in their response to the socialist challenge. The militants who controlled the Opera and Catholic Action interpreted liberal overtures as heartening proof of the enemy's weakness, and redoubled their efforts to 'prepare in abstention' for total victory.[3] Outside the Opera, however, many Catholics were sufficiently alarmed to welcome Crispi's appeal for a 'truce of God'. After 1894 the idea of a 'clerical-moderate' coalition made many converts. In local government there was no difficulty. Leo XIII had no patience with his own diehards who wished to abstain from local as well as national politics. By collaborating with sympathetic liberals, Catholics could hope to challenge anti-clerical control of schools, hospitals and charitable trusts, to keep freemasons off local councils and bring an element of religion back into official municipal life. In return the liberals could hope for sufficient Catholic votes to defeat the radicals and socialists. The clerical-moderate alliance developed most rapidly in Milan, where the Archbishop, Cardinal Andrea Ferrari, was an enthusiastic supporter and where conservative sympathisers like Colombo and Prinetti had great influence. In the local elections of 1895 clerical-moderate pacts were common, and in many towns of Lombardy and Venetia, in Rome, Turin and Genoa, the Catholics made striking gains.[4] Such alliances at the periphery could not fail in the end to

[1] Fonzi, p. 75, describes the attitude of these frightened liberals as 'atheistic clericalism'.
[2] 'Nè petrolio nè acqua santa'. Farini, I, pp. 563–6, 642–6,   8, 739.
[3] See above, p. 61.
[4] Spadolini, *L'opposizione cattolica*, pp. 351–4, 388–9.

influence the centre. But time was needed. The 'clerical revival' frightened many liberals and stimulated resistance.[1] Another nine years were to pass before open collaboration between church and state became possible in national politics.

Crispi's fall brought hopes of a new atmosphere. In July 1896 Prinetti, the friend of Cardinal Ferrari, entered Rudinì's cabinet as Minister for Public Works. At the end of the year Leo XIII, with the King's and Prime Minister's approval, sent an envoy to Addis Ababa to plead with Menelik for the early release of his Italian prisoners. Rudinì conferred secretly with Rampolla, whom he had already met in connexion with the Crown Prince's marriage in October, and once again there seemed a chance of far-reaching negotiations. But Rudinì was as prone as Crispi to oscillation. When the mission to Menelik failed, anti-clericals accused the Vatican of exploiting Italy's misfortunes in order to win diplomatic prestige. Rudinì promptly reversed his policy.[2] The next two years saw restrictions on the Catholic movement, Zanardelli's appointment as Minister of Justice and wholesale repression after the Milan rising.[3] Leo XIII protested forcefully that to weaken the church was to encourage, not prevent, revolution. The last years of his life were further saddened by the appointment of Zanardelli as Prime Minister and by the abortive divorce bill of 1902.[4]

Yet, beneath the surface of tension, a *modus vivendi* had been reached. By 1887 it had already become clear that Italian unity was not the fragile, transitory thing that champions of the temporal power had hoped between 1861 and 1870. Church and state might officially not be on speaking terms; but they had to live together, and intermediaries could always be found for the unavoidable negotiations.[5] While preserving its intransigence on the question of principle, the church was prepared and compelled to make concessions on a thousand matters of day-to-day practice. It was a situation which gave full scope to the genius of both Italians and the Catholic

[1] In July 1895 Bovio warned the chamber that the Catholic conquest of local government was only preparation for an assault on the centre, and prophesied a new period of tension ahead. Fonzi, p. 79.

[2] Rudinì tried to withdraw his original consent to the papal mission. Leo was disgusted and expressed his regret that Crispi was no longer there; things would have gone differently with him, because 'Quello era un uomo'. Soderini, II, pp. 208–19; Bülow, IV, pp. 671–2. Farini believed that the liberation of the prisoners by the Pope 'would be a mortal blow' to Italy and the monarchy. Farini, II, pp. 941, 947, 969, 1026.

[3] See above, pp. 190–2.

[4] See below, pp. 241–2.

[5] 'The secret threads between Vatican and Quirinal were never completely snapped', writes Binchy, p. 51. Binchy's discussion of the problem is by far the best available in English.

church for *combinazioni*. As the bitterest passions faded, the number of those who wanted either permanent reconciliation or permanent separation declined. Anomalies, such as the dependence of priests upon the state for part of their stipends, were accepted by both sides. Even in the delicate question of state approval of church appointments, though sees might be left unfilled for long periods, *ad hoc* agreements were in the end always reached, while all the time the church refused to recognise the governments with which it was negotiating and denied in principle their right to any say in the matter under discussion.[1]

After 1890 the church had little cause to complain of legislation. Anti-clerical bills were introduced from time to time in parliament but rarely reached even the stage of debate. More important, existing laws were not strictly enforced. Catholic schools and charitable and monastic foundations, though legally suppressed, soon revived. The law turned a blind eye to the church's acquisition of property through trusts and holding companies. The church on its side showed similar tolerance. Humbert, like his father, was given a religious funeral, in spite of the sentence of excommunication of 1870. The gulf between the black and white nobility narrowed and papal families even bought their share of confiscated church land from the state. Religious bodies invested in state bonds and house property, and thus acquired a stake in the economic stability of Italy.

The *non expedit* was made more emphatic in each successive pronouncement of the Vatican. But as time passed, the number of voters who defied it increased. In the 1870 election the abstention rate had been strikingly high and it fell only very slowly in later years.[2] But this was due as much to indifference or to republicanism as to clerical boycotts. Abstention was most widespread in the great cities where anti-clericalism flourished. In the south, where the power of the church was less seriously challenged, the percentage of voters remained consistently higher.[3] With the rise of socialism the temptation for Catholics to defy the ban increased. One Turin cleric in 1900 declared that 'no papal veto could prevent him from carrying water when the house was on fire'.[4] As early as 1886 a priest in Giolitti's constituency told his flock, 'Go and vote, all of you, because this

[1] Binchy, pp. 356–7.

[2] In 1870 only 1·97% of the total population was entitled to vote; of these 55% abstained. Figures for 1874 were 44%, for 1876 41%, for 1895, 1897 and 1900 between 41% and 42%. Chabod, *Storia*, pp. 512–20; *Compendio*, II, pp. 8–9.

[3] In 1870 64% of voters abstained in Milan, 72% in Bologna, 84% in Leghorn; only 38% in Sicily. Until 1909 the highest percentage of voters was always to be found in the mainland south, where it rose steadily from 54% in 1870 to 72% in 1882, and in Sicily, where it rose from 62% to 68% in the same period. Chabod, *Storia*, p. 514; Spadolini, *L'opposizione cattolica*, p. 217, note; Fonzi, p. 81; *Compendio*, II, pp. 6–9.

[4] King and Okey, p. 48.

slogan "Neither elected nor electors" is all nonsense.'[1] The shock of 1898
swelled the ranks of the clerical-moderates. Many militant Catholics were
quick to disassociate themselves from the Extreme Left, with which they
had shared the rigours of persecution. They proclaimed themselves, in
contrast with the socialists, to be law-abiding men who wished to be 'free
citizens under the shadow of the constitution'.[2] Pelloux's government
acknowledged the distinction and after 1898 the Catholic movement was
never again treated by the liberal state as an enemy. In 1900 liberals and
Catholics were drawn yet closer by Humbert's assassination and the
celebration of the Holy Year.[3] By the end of Leo XIII's pontificate the
*non expedit* had become little more than symbolic. Leo himself recognised
this and was not unduly disturbed. But though the ban kept few Catholics
from the polls, it did prevent the formation of a Catholic party. This
became possible only with the cancellation of the *non expedit* in 1919.

The church unquestionably suffered at the hands of the Italian state.
The removal of crucifixes from schools symbolised the absence of religion
in state education. Careers in the public service could be precarious for
Catholics who attended mass too often. Though responsible statesmen
seldom indulged in the more virulent forms of anti-clericalism, scurrility
and blasphemy were little discouraged. Article I of the constitution became
an empty formula, for the state, by avoiding all religious functions,
eliminated any opportunity of demonstrating that Catholicism was its 'sole
religion'. At the same time Italian statesmen, however liberal, clung to
the weapons of state control and restricted the church's freedom. The
church suffered all the disadvantages and none of the advantages of being
tied to the state.[4]

Yet there was far less persecution of the church in Italy than in France.
Events proved Cavour right in his prophecy that the Papacy, relieved of
the burden of temporal government, would grow in prestige and influence.
The noisy quarrel with Italy served the essential purpose of demonstrating
the church's independence of any secular authority. It also gave Italy
time for consolidation. 'The irreconcilability of the Curia is fortunate for
Italy', Humbert once said, 'because it allows the maturing of a system
which will conduce to the healing of the quarrel.' That, too, was a wise
prophecy. Meanwhile the wrangling affected the mass of the people very
little. The Italians might be sceptical or anti-clerical, but they remained
unshakeably Catholic.[5] Garibaldi's portrait hung beside the Madonna in
countless peasant homes, and millions of Catholics found it possible to

[1] Giolitti, *Memorie*, pp. 41–2.
[2] Spadolini, *L'opposizione cattolica*, pp. 508–12.
[3] Fonzi, pp. 84–5.                                    [4] Binchy, pp. 45–6, 355–6.
[5] ibid., pp. 46–7; Jemolo, pp. 389–94.

remain both Catholic and Italian, patiently waiting for the day when the quarrel would end. By the end of the century that day seemed nearer. Social questions were beginning to eclipse religious controversies, as elsewhere in Europe. The fervour which had coloured the quarrel between church and state during the Risorgimento had died away, and hardly one statesman of importance was interested in ecclesiastical problems. A basis for 'reconciliation in indifference' was slowly taking shape.[1]

## Christian Democracy

Militant Catholics reacted to the rise of socialism in two very different ways. Some turned to the conservative clerical-moderate programme and tried to enter politics. Others, soon to become known as Christian democrats, preferred social to political action and set out to capture the masses by democratic methods and challenge the socialists on their own ground.

The Christian democratic programme grew naturally out of the social activities of the Opera, which in their turn were the natural consequence of the Opera's self-exclusion from national politics. Its leaders championed 'real' Italy against 'legal' Italy, the masses against the oppressive, egotistical, 'revolutionary' minority. In 1880 the first rural credit bank was founded in Venetia by a priest, Don Luigi Cerutti, who later became known as 'the apostle of the rural banks'. In the same year the Banco di Roma was created, under the control of the Vatican, mainly in order to provide capital at low rates of interest for Catholic organisations. Another Catholic venture was an association for the protection of emigrants, in which Bishops Bonomelli and Scalabrini played a leading part. Slowly the traditional Catholic view, that social misery could be alleviated by charity alone, was discarded. The section of the Opera which dealt with social questions changed its title in 1879 from 'Charity' to 'Charity and Christian Economy', and in 1887 dropped 'Charity' altogether. Under its energetic chairman, Stanislao Medolago Albani, it quickly expanded its activities. Between 1890 and 1897 it concentrated mainly on the countryside, where a network of cooperatives, peasant unions, friendly societies, insurance and rural credit institutions was built up. After 1897 it turned its attention to the urban working-class. In spite of greater resistance than among the peasants, there were over 600 working-class societies by 1897. In that year the Opera reached its peak.[2]

---

[1] Jemolo, pp. 489–93.

[2] In 1897 the Opera controlled 190 diocesan and 4,036 parochial committees, with a total membership of 115,000. In addition, 7,672 associations, some of a religious, some of an economic or social character, were affiliated to it (including 691 rural banks and 653 workers' societies). The great majority of these institu-

This movement, strongly paternalist in spirit, was greatly influenced by Catholic corporatist theory, the leading Italian exponent of which was Giuseppe Toniolo, Professor of Political Economy at Pisa University. Toniolo condemned both capitalism and socialism on religious and moral grounds, and equated the liberal state with materialistic plutocracy, social oppression, usury and centralised, 'absolutist caesarism'. The social institutions of the Catholic movement appeared to him to be the modern equivalent of the medieval guilds and corporations of Tuscany, which he had studied and idealised. He believed that on their foundation a modern Christian society could be built, inspired by a spirit of mutual solidarity between landlord and peasant, employer and employee, and freely organised in mixed corporations defying class divisions. If the Catholic movement continued to expand, it could become the framework, prefabricated and tested by experience, of a new Catholic state, rising from the ruins of liberalism.[1]

This growing preoccupation with social problems alarmed the conservative leaders of the Opera, who feared that the Roman question and the political grievances of the church might be forgotten. In the words of Count Giambattista Paganuzzi, the masterful organiser who became President of the Opera in 1889, 'For us the papal question is the alpha and the omega.'[2] Leo XIII took a less rigid view. He shared the opinion of his predecessor on liberalism and its offspring, socialism, but, like many Catholic thinkers, saw that the negations of the Syllabus were no longer enough. Nor was he afraid of democracy. As he remarked to a close friend, 'the Church has baptised other barbarians no less dangerous' in the course of its long history.[3] In his encyclicals he made it clear that all forms of government were legitimate, provided they respected religious principles; there was no Christian objection to democracy, but only to secular, Jacobin democracy.[4] 'If your democracy is Christian', he told a French Catholic in 1890, 'it will give your country a future of peace, prosperity and glory.'[5]

The growing interest of Catholics in social questions gave Leo XIII his opportunity for a positive step forward. In northern Europe the

---

tions were to be found in the north, particularly Lombardy and Venetia. In central Italy the Opera was always weak and in the south it hardly existed. Gambasin, pp. 317 ff., 454 ff.

[1] This long-term political aim explains the Catholic rejection of Luzzatti's overtures in 1894–5 for collaboration between liberal and Catholic cooperatives, savings banks and mutual benefit institutions. Luzzatti, *Memorie*, II, pp. 382–4.

[2] Gambasin, pp. 313, 491.

[3] Vercesi, *Il movimento cattolico*, p. 9.

[4] Spadolini, *L'opposizione cattolica*, pp. 191–2, 640–1.

[5] Vercesi, *Il movimento cattolico*, p. 76.

Christian social movement, led by men like de Mun, Cardinal Manning
and Bishop Ketteler of Mainz, was far more advanced than in Italy. In 188.
the Union de Fribourg, an international Catholic organisation for the
study of social and labour questions, was founded in Switzerland. Five
years later an Italian Catholic Union for Social Studies was created by
Toniolo and Medolago Albani, with the active support of Rampolla, and
soon became so influential that it aroused the jealousy of the Opera itself
Meanwhile in 1887 the first workers' pilgrimage to Rome took place. In
the words of one of its organisers, de Mun, the Pope 'abandoned himsel
to men of the people in working dress'. In his allocution to the pilgrimage
of 1889, Leo XIII warned governments that 'to remove the peril tha
threatens, neither repression nor armed soldiers will be enough'. Next
year he gave his warm support to the international labour conference
held under William II's patronage in Berlin. Two years before a delegation
from the Union de Fribourg had told Leo that 'all eyes are turned to the
Vatican', and asked for a papal pronouncement on the problems of
labour.[1] On 15 March 1891 appeared the encyclical *Rerum Novarum* on
the 'Condition of the Working Classes'.

In the first flush of enthusiasm *Rerum Novarum* seemed the beginning
of a new world. Leo XIII was hailed as 'the economist Pope', 'the Father
of the Workers', and the encyclical as 'the Magna Carta of Labour'.
Though extravagant, such excitement among Catholics was understandable. *Rerum Novarum* was the positive complement to the negative
Syllabus and the anti-socialist encyclicals. Its language was cautious and
nebulous. Free Christian trade unions and mixed corporations of employers
and employees were the prescribed instruments for achieving social justice;
the strike weapon was to be used only in the last resort; limited state intervention was legitimate where the working-class was too weak to resist
injustice unaided, but class collaboration must always be the aim. In spite
of its ambiguities, by condemning *laisser faire* capitalism *Rerum Novarum*
ranged the church on the side of social reform and offered an alternative
to traditional conservatism for the reclamation of the proletariat from
socialism.[2] Nor, as has recently been pointed out, was it a coincidence that
a great encyclical 'on the relations between the church and the modern
state should have come from the pen of the first Pope for centuries who
had no state to govern'.[3]

In Italy its immediate effect was to give a new stimulus to the Catholic
social movement. Hundreds of new institutions were founded and the
Opera's congresses were dominated by discussion of social problems. In

[1] A. De Gasperi, *I tempi e gli uomini che prepararono la 'Rerum Novarum'* (3rd
ed., Milan 1945), pp. 135–9.
[2] Jemolo, pp. 379–80.                          [3] Binchy, p. 13.

1896 the Catholic University Federation, from which the future leaders of Italian Christian democracy were to come, was formed.[1] By then the term 'Christian Democracy' was in common use. It was a concept which appealed above all to the new generation which, though deeply influenced by Toniolo's teaching, demanded a less academic approach to contemporary problems than Toniolo's romantic corporatism. Toniolo, and still more the intransigents who controlled the Opera, looked back to a golden medieval age, idealising rural life and deploring urbanisation, the seedbed of the 'revolution'.[2] They still dreamt of a return to a 'papal Italy', based on the loyal peasantry and a paternalist, aristocratic élite. The young Christian democrats, on the contrary, looked forward. Their horizon was not limited by visions of a revived medieval order nor by nostalgia for the pre-1860 world; their ideal was not the old papal Italy, but an entirely new, Christian Italy.[3] They were weary of the isolation in which Catholics had wrapped themselves since 1870. Papal independence was important to them, but they protested against making it the sole aim of the Catholic movement. Instead of their elders' negative strictures on the liberal state and their prudent submission to ecclesiastical control, they demanded an independent, aggressive initiative. Neither the urban masses nor the techniques of democracy frightened them. They had no use for mixed corporations of employers and workers, which even Toniolo was forced to admit were impracticable in the existing social tension.[4] Instead they were prepared to organise strikes and trade unions, even to plagiarise the socialist programme and colour their propaganda with the language of class conflict. Their eventual aim was to create a modern, popular Catholic party which would capture the masses for the church. In the apparent bankruptcy of the liberal state after Adowa they saw signs of the dawning of their new world. It was this offensive, missionary spirit that filled Rudinì, Sonnino, Farini and the guardians of the heritage of the Risorgimento with alarm.

From the first, two schools of thought were distinguishable among these young Christian democrats. The more extreme was led by Don Romolo Murri, a young, headstrong priest from a poor family of the Marche. Murri was a disciple of another priest, Albertario, who as editor of the Milan *Osservatore Cattolico* had mercilessly attacked Tosti, Bonomelli and all conciliators, and earned the names of 'Don Belligero' and 'hammer of the liberals'. Albertario by 1896 had greatly moderated his views, but Murri never mellowed. Like Bovio and the philosophical anti-clericals,

[1] Spadolini, *L'opposizione cattolica*, pp. 337–8, 393–6.
[2] De Rosa, *L'Azione Cattolica*, I, pp. 87–90.
[3] Spadolini, *L'opposizione cattolica*, pp. 358–60.
[4] Gambasin, pp. 430–1, 520–2.

he regarded the Roman question as a clash of civilisations; he wished to widen the gulf between the church and the heretical 'monster', the liberal state, and to substitute for the latter a theocratic society dominated by a church restored to its ancient glory.[1] The more moderate school of thought was led by Filippo Meda, a Milanese lawyer and journalist with a large following in Lombardy. Meda was more conservative than Murri in social questions but more adventurous in politics. He believed that a Christian society would be built most quickly by the reconciliation of church and state and by Catholic participation in every aspect of the nation's life. Abstention from the polls was a duty while the Pope demanded it; but to Meda it was a purely negative act and a painful sacrifice. His Christian democracy was reformist and his tactics were in practice very close to those of the clerical-moderates. Meda wished to conquer the liberal state by gradual penetration, Murri by disruption. For Meda it was 'a sinner to save', for Murri 'an enemy to destroy'.[2]

There were therefore deep differences of temperament and tactical method, if not of final aim, between Murri and Meda. Nevertheless in the years 1893–1903 they found much common ground. Both differed from the old guard of the Opera in accepting the *fait accompli* of 1870; their quarrel was with Italian liberalism, not with Italian unity. Both believed that the best instrument for achieving their final aim was a democratic mass party. Meda hoped that this party would be created by a transformation of the Opera; Murri preferred to build up his own Christian democratic fasci as the nucleus of a party outside the Opera. Both believed that the political and ecclesiastical spheres must be distinct, and that an effective party must be autonomous, so that its mistakes and failures would not compromise the church and the Papacy. This belief, hard to follow in practice, was to recur persistently in Christian democratic programmes.

The growth of Christian democracy was sharply checked in 1898.[3] The hand of General Bava-Beccaris fell heavily on Milan, one of Christian democracy's strongholds, and Albertario was sent to prison for a year. Throughout Italy the Catholic movement was disrupted. When the storm had passed a marked change of tone was audible among Catholics. The spectre of anarchy had frightened them as much as it had frightened liberals. From Leo XIII downwards, some relaxation of the old intransigence was seen to be desirable, and the conciliators within the Opera gained influence. Murri still refused to compromise. In 1899–1900 he approved of parliamentary obstruction and welcomed the Extreme Left's call for a constituent assembly, and during the 1900 election he opposed

---

[1] De Rosa, *L'Azione Cattolica*, I, pp. 213–18, II, pp. 5–10.
[2] Fonzi, p. 88.                              [3] See above, pp. 191–2.

any alliance with the conservative bourgeoisie. But the current was against him, particularly in Milan, which had suffered most in 1898 and where both Meda and the clerical-moderates were strong. Meanwhile in 1899 a detailed Christian democratic programme was drawn up at Turin. It called for constitutional reform, bold social legislation, freedom for trade unions and state encouragement for the reorganisation of society into cooperative associations.[1] It was the equivalent of a full-fledged party programme, though the party, while the *non expedit* lasted, could not yet be born. Christian democracy was ceasing to be a theoretical abstraction.

Leo XIII smiled benevolently on the eager young men and publicly praised them. 'Let us come forth from the sacristy', he wrote, 'and go among the people.'[2] In his encyclical *Graves de communi* of January 1901 he gave official sanction to the term Christian Democracy which thereby, in Meda's words, 'came of age'.[3] Dismayed by such encouragement of ideas which shocked his conservative convictions, and by the mounting pressure for a democratic reconstruction of the Opera, Paganuzzi resigned from the presidency in 1902. In his place Leo XIII appointed Count Giovanni Grosoli, a man of moderate and conciliatory views. His attempts to pacify internal dissension failed. The young men were in no mood to compromise. Meda and Murri combined their forces and in November 1903 won a majority over the old oligarchy at the Bologna congress of the Opera. Though they fell apart almost immediately, at the time their triumph seemed complete.

The more cautious, such as Toniolo, by now the elder statesman of Italian Christian democracy, began to grow alarmed and to ask themselves if these young Christian democrats were not becoming too democratic and too little Christian. Leo XIII was aware of this danger. Indeed, *Graves de communi* had been intended as a warning as well as an encouragement. Christian democracy, it stressed, was non-political and did not aim at establishing any particular form of government, nor at encouraging insubordination to lawful authority. The church had a duty to the upper classes also, and the Christian ideal was class collaboration and a share in government for all, for the benefit of all. Too much emphasis must not be laid on rights and too little on duties. Above all, unity and harmony among Catholics must be preserved. Later in 1901 the Opera was reorganised

---

[1] Specific items included proportional representation, decentralisation, statutory minimum wages and maximum working hours, aid for cooperatives and small proprietors, a progressive income tax and the abolition of consumption taxes, disarmament and legal recognition of trade unions. The full text is printed in M. P. Fogarty, *Christian Democracy in Western Europe 1820–1953* (London 1957), pp. 319–20. See also Howard, pp. 51–65.

[2] Vercesi, *Il movimento cattolico*, p. 93.

[3] Gambasin, p. 525; Soderini, I, p. 442.

and the Vatican's control strengthened. Next year Leo XIII forced Murri's autonomous fasci to submit to the authority of the Opera, and in a public letter to Rampolla warned against excessive enthusiasm for 'novelties' and 'new ideas'.[1] In the last year of his life Leo XIII was thus clearly applying the brake. Under his successor Christian democracy at once passed under a cloud. But the pioneering of Toniolo, Meda and Murri had not been in vain; the seeds they had sown bore vigorous fruit twenty years later.

Leo XIII died on 30 August 1903 at the age of ninety-four. Diplomatically his twenty-five-year reign appeared to have ended in failure, with anti-clericalism rampant in France, the Triple Alliance unbroken and Italian prestige rising in the world. The Roman question had become 'a fossil of international politics'.[2] Rome was now a modern capital city whose divorce from Italy was unthinkable. No foreign government had any intention of adopting restoration of the temporal power as an object of its peace-time diplomacy, nor of including it amongst its hypothetical war aims. Leo's formal protests against the restriction of his freedom had been sounding more unreal with the passage of every year. In Italy a new generation of Catholics had grown up which had never known the temporal power and, in so far as it thought of it at all, regarded it as an historical accident rather than as an institution essential to the life of the church. Nevertheless the church's prestige and spiritual influence were greater in 1903 than at any time since 1848. In Italy Leo had so governed and restored it through his long reign that his successor could safely sanction a relaxation of the *non expedit* from strength, not weakness. Outside Italy the church was no longer, as in 1878, at loggerheads with almost every government in Europe. No longer could it be represented by its enemies as an archaic, reactionary survival, with no function in modern society and no message for the coming industrial mass age. This was Leo XIII's greatest and lasting achievement.

[1] Soderini, I, pp. 434–45; De Rosa, *L'Azione Cattolica*, I, pp. 230–41.
[2] Salvemini, *La politica estera dell' Italia*, p. 117.

# PART III

# EXPANSION
## 1901–14

# 7

# The New Liberalism
## 1901-11

### The Rise of Giolitti 1901–4

The appointment of Zanardelli as Prime Minister in February 1901 brought into power those who had sympathised with the parliamentary obstructors in 1899–1900. This relieved the tension and transformed the political atmosphere. Zanardelli at once proclaimed his devotion to 'the principles of liberty' and his determination to defend both the letter and the spirit of the constitution. His parliamentary position, however, was precarious. The radicals declined his invitation to accept office, though their more moderate leaders were severely tempted; the obstacle was their demand for cuts in military expenditure which Zanardelli, bound by a contrary undertaking to the King, could not concede. Neither the conservative majority nor the Extreme Left were prepared for the moment to do more than tolerate the new government. Its dominant personality was Giolitti. After seven years' exclusion from office, he had so far reestablished his position that no one but he could fill the Ministry of Interior.[1] He at once put into effect the policy he had advocated while in opposition and instructed prefects that the state must in future remain neutral in labour disputes.

The consequences were startling. All over Italy peasants and industrial workers sprang into action. The number of strikes leapt from 410 (involving 43,000 persons) in 1900 to 1,671 (involving 420,000) in 1901.[2] A brief calm descended in the autumn, but early in 1902 strikes broke out again in an infectious rash. To strike, in Fortunato's phrase, became 'a national hallucination'. Sheer exuberance and the exhilaration of freedom, after ten years of restraint, go far to explain the outburst. But basically its motives were economic. They were prosperity strikes, and peasants and

[1] 'Giolitti – I found him already at the Palazzo Braschi' (the Ministry of Interior), was Zanardelli's own comment. Ansaldo, p. 133.
[2] Corbino, V, p. 466; Rigola, *Storia*, pp. 214 ff.; *ASI 1919–1921*, p. 512; Neufeld, p. 547.

workmen were out to secure their share of the new wealth that economic expansion was creating. Landowners and industrialists, taken unawares, were repeatedly forced to concede higher wages or shorter working hours. Throughout the north trade unions, peasant leagues and chambers of labour multiplied in their hundreds. In one branch of industry after another, disciplined workers' organisations were established, and with the spread of the movement to the agricultural labourers, the whole northern countryside seemed suddenly to come to life.[1] Besides these regular associations, which were socialist in allegiance, innumerable other mushroom organisations sprang up, often with no political or social aim beyond striking for the sake of striking. Yet, with amazingly few exceptions, the strikes were orderly and ended in agreement. Italian democrats felt both proud and surprised at these signs of discipline in an inexperienced working-class. 'We must conclude', said Giolitti, 'that the Italian people is mature for liberty.'[2]

Bewildered and frightened, the conservatives turned upon Giolitti and accused him of bowing to the *piazza* and undermining the authority of the state. The alarm was greatest in the countryside. Landlords from the Po valley declared that a 'socialist state within the state', a fortress of sedition, was being created under their noses. Sonnino, who in 1876 had commended peasant leagues as the only way of relieving rural misery, now urged Giolitti to take drastic action against a movement whose ultimate aim was political subversion. But Giolitti stood firm. Troops were used to maintain order, but never to break strikes or bring in the harvest. Low wages might be in the employers' interest, but he refused to admit that they benefited the state or the nation's economy. There were only two policies, he declared, repression or liberty; and the past had proved repression a failure. It was his 'profound conviction that only on the field of liberty is it possible to fight socialism'.[3]

Giolitti hoped by such methods to break down the old barrier between the state and the masses, between 'legal' and 'real' Italy. In part he succeeded, a fact to which many liberals might be blind but which the King, for one, appreciated.[4] Peasants in the north shouted *Viva Giolitti!* at their meetings. The radicals were enthusiastic, seeing in Giolitti the democratic prime minister of the future. Many socialists, too, fell under his spell.

[1] On the organisation of the labour movement, see further below, pp. 297 ff.
[2] Giolitti, *Discorsi parlamentari*, II, p. 667.
[3] ibid., p. 673.
[4] Giolitti 'understood how to treat the masses' and would reconcile them with the dynasty, Victor Emmanuel told Bülow in May 1903. A year later he expressed to William II complete satisfaction with 'his own system of government' and with 'the excellent functioning of the parliamentary machine'. Bülow, II, pp. 598-9; GP, XX (i), 6399.

The pioneers of the 1890s had believed that to organise was also to civilise and educate; now they found the Minister of Interior himself was their ally. Giolitti made himself accessible to deputations, listened to complaints of repressive or provocative action by provincial officials, made use of socialist deputies as mediators in labour disputes and helped responsible working-class leaders to strengthen trade union discipline and eliminate violence. Bissolati, with whom he had frequent meetings, worked hard behind the scenes for pacification and indulged in the minimum of public criticism, realising that interpellations in parliament would merely bring discredit on Giolitti's liberal policies.[1] Turati could truthfully claim that he and his friends were 'acting the policeman gratis'.[2] Giolitti's common sense, the 'modernity of his thought', his civil servant's lack of sympathy with landowners and industrialists, his refusal to be flustered by the conservatives, won him their lasting admiration. Turati welcomed an era of 'consolidation of liberty and respect for the law', in which insurrections and barricades could be relegated to the museum.[3] The years 1901–3 were the heyday of reformist socialism in Italy, and several times the socialists voted with the rest of the Extreme Left to save Zanardelli's government in a hostile chamber.

This harmony was soon subjected to strain. By the end of 1902 the working-class movement was running into difficulties. Industrialists and landowners began to organise resistance, the number of successful strikes declined and trade union membership fell. It was now the turn of the working-class to feel helpless and, like the industrialists and landowners in 1901–2, to find its scapegoat in the government. Giolitti indeed soon showed that his benevolence towards working-class agitation had its limits. His approach to this, as to all political problems, was empirical. He insisted on three things: the maintenance of essential public services, the preservation of law and order, and the right to work.[4] The first major test came with the threat of a railway strike in February 1902. Where a vital public service was concerned, neutrality was impossible. Giolitti combined the stick with the carrot. The railwaymen, who had well-found grievances over pay and conditions of service, were first coerced by the call-up of the army reservists among them, then granted part of their demands, largely at the expense of the taxpayer. The leaders of the

[1] Natale, pp. 430 ff., 520 ff.; *Quarant' anni*, II, 66, 78, 94, 393, 496.
[2] Salomone, p. 51.
[3] ibid., pp. 46, 66.
[4] See for example Giolitti's telegram to the prefect of Genoa, 16 April 1901: 'While the government rigorously respects the freedom to strike, I intend with equal vigour to protect the freedom of those who do not wish to take part in the strike.' *Quarant' anni*, II, 32. 'Freedom to work, no less sacred than freedom to strike', he wrote many years later in his *Memorie*, p. 166.

Extreme Left contributed much to the final settlement. It was at their prompting that Giolitti persuaded the cabinet to make the gesture of inviting a deputation of railwaymen to Rome and to sanction negotiations with it. Responsible socialists and radicals like Turati, Sacchi and the editor of the *Secolo*, Romussi,[1] saw that a railway strike would discredit Giolitti's methods and might even set back the cause of liberty to 1898. On his side Giolitti was anxious to strengthen the influence of the moderates over the working-class movement and to prevent damage to the national economy. The settlement was therefore a victory for common sense.[2] It angered the extremists on both sides. The conservatives denounced it as capitulation to blackmail and foretold (with some truth, as the future was to show) that it would constitute an unhappy precedent for every section of the public service. The irreconcilable socialists deplored it for removing an opportunity for agitation and violence. As Giolitti wired to Romussi, 'It is very difficult to govern with liberty when even many intelligent people believe that to have liberty it is necessary to fall into anarchy.'[3]

It was Giolitti's insistence on the maintenance of law and order that led to his first breach with the socialists. Liberal government was not weak government, he once reminded an erring prefect.[4] His maxim was that 'insufficient strength can encourage disorders'.[5] His prefects were therefore urged repeatedly to arrest and bring promptly to justice all who incited to violence, and to ask for reinforcements of police in good time; to be taken by surprise was unforgivable. If the situation demanded it, Giolitti ensured that troops and even warships were at hand. But in spite of his vigilance, disorder could not always be prevented. On several occasions, mostly in the south, strikers were fired upon by the police. These 'proletarian massacres', as the socialists liked to call them, caused forty deaths between June 1901 and September 1904.[6] In the excitement that such tragedies aroused, most socialists held Giolitti personally responsible for his subordinates' actions.[7] Giolitti, on his side, had the civil servant's respect for the state. Very rarely did he publicly admit that in these incidents the police

---

[1] *Quarant' anni*, II, 245, 304. Romussi had become Giolitti's devoted admirer during his imprisonment in May 1898, when Giolitti gave him encouragement and help. ibid., I, 374.

[2] ibid., II, 294, 296–7, 304–5; Natale, pp. 494–8.

[3] *Quarant' anni*, II, 279; Natale, p. 504.

[4] Telegram to prefect of Foggia, 2 June 1902. *Quarant' anni*, II, 399.

[5] Telegram to prefect of Bari, 20 May 1901. A year later he telegraphed, again to Bari: 'Always act on the principle of having more force than is necessary when there is a threat of disorder.' *Quarant' anni*, II, 69, 375.

[6] Rigola, *Storia*, p. 267.

[7] Bissolati was one of the few prepared to take a more generous view. *Quarant' anni*, II, 66.

could have been in the wrong. Turati continued to defend the government, but found it increasingly hard to justify his attitude to the extremists of his own party. At the Socialist party congress at Imola in September 1902 the reformists came under heavy attack. Led by the eloquent Ferri, hero of parliamentary obstruction, and a young Neapolitan syndicalist, Arturo Labriola,[1] the militants warned the party against 'the fatal downward slope of ministerialism', and clamoured for a fight to the bitter end against parliament and the bourgeois state. The split was temporarily healed by a shelving motion but beneath the surface deep dissension persisted. The moderates steadily lost ground. In the spring of 1903 another 'proletarian massacre' roused the party agitators to fever point. On 23 March the socialist deputies decided formally to go into opposition.

The labour question, though it dominated politics for more than two years, was not the only difficulty which the government had to face. Zanardelli's programme gave a prominent place to tax reform and social legislation. In taxation he failed. In July 1901 his Minister of Finance, Leone Wollemborg, a leading social reformer, presented radical proposals for shifting the burden from indirect to direct taxation. The cabinet, faced by a major split in its majority, rejected the proposals and Wollemborg resigned.[2] His successor prudently avoided controversy by limiting himself to minor changes. In social legislation, to the principle of which there was now little opposition, Zanardelli was more successful. A commission was appointed to supervise emigration, the minimum age for industrial employment was raised and legislative protection was extended to women workers.[3] A Labour Council for the study of labour questions was set up, on which parliament, industry, commerce and agriculture, employers and organised labour were represented. The south also received attention. In September 1902 Zanardelli himself visited Basilicata. Deeply moved by its misery and desolation, he returned to Rome convinced that political action was required. His voyage marked the first step towards recognition that the state of the south was the responsibility of the whole nation, and led directly, though belatedly, to special legislation on southern problems in subsequent years.[4]

In 1902 Zanardelli was defeated in a field very near to his heart, that of divorce. A freemason and an impenitent anti-clerical, he had presented a divorce bill as Depretis's Minister of Justice as long ago as 1883. His bill of 1902 only followed the lines of legislation already in force in most of

---

[1] No relation of his namesake and fellow-Neapolitan, Professor Antonio Labriola.

[2] See below, p. 293. Tariff reform was another cause which suffered a decisive reverse in 1901-2. See below, pp. 320-1.

[3] ibid., p. 296.                          [4] ibid., pp. 309-10.

western Europe, but it raised a storm. Leo XIII protested; petitions, organised by priests, poured into parliament. The popular demand for divorce was in fact negligible and the proposal offended not only Catholics but many liberals. Only the radicals and socialists supported it with enthusiasm. Zanardelli was deserted by part of his majority and had to drop the bill.

Shaken by this defeat, the cabinet was further weakened by setbacks in foreign policy[1] and by friction between the Prime Minister and Giolitti. The latter's studious indifference to the fate of the divorce bill led Zanardelli to suspect him of excessive tenderness towards the church. A more serious cause of friction was Giolitti's administrative energy and his interference in the departments of his colleagues. 'That man is shaking my whole government', Zanardelli complained. Nor was the Prime Minister happy at Giolitti's intimacy with the socialists.[2]

In the spring of 1903 there was a wave of anti-Austrian demonstrations,[3] mainly in the universities and schools. Giolitti believed that displays of irredentism harmed both Italy and Austria's Italian subjects. He therefore took strong police action and sharply criticised the Minister of Education, Nunzio Nasi, for weakness in handling the school disturbances.[4] This caused further strain in the cabinet. On 10 June, on a motion for an investigation of the Ministry for the Navy,[5] the government was deserted by many of its more liberal supporters and saved from defeat only by conservative votes. Giolitti urged his colleagues to resign and allow the conservatives to take office. When his proposal was defeated, he resigned by himself. It was a shrewd move. His skill in deserting a sinking ship had already been shown in 1890. Zanardelli lingered on ineffectually in office, his health failing, until October. The King, ignoring the conservative candidates, Rudinì and Sonnino, chose Giolitti as his successor.

Giolitti's intention was to form a liberal-labour government in which the radicals and socialists would be represented. He at once appealed through Romussi for 'the open, sincere support of the extreme left'[6] and began negotiations with Marcora, Sacchi, Turati and Bissolati. The two socialists, though gratified by Giolitti's proposal and personally anxious to support a democratic government, knew they could not carry their colleagues and declined. Socialists throughout Europe were still arguing over Millerand's acceptance of office in the French government of 1899. To imitate his example would have invited immediate condemnation by

---

[1] The Tsar cancelled a state visit to Italy after Italian socialists announced they would hiss him out of the country. See below, p. 334.

[2] Natale, pp. 543–56.      [3] See below, p. 335.      [4] *Quarant' anni*, II, 519–39.
[5] See below, pp. 265, 358–9.                [6] *Quarant' anni*, II, 563.

the left wing and probably a split in the Italian party. Giolitti's negotiations
with Marcora and Sacchi were equally unfruitful. The radicals demanded
a government that would be, in Romussi's words, 'all of one colour, all of
one piece', which would make a clean break with the old systems and
personalities and carry out a boldly democratic programme.[1] Giolitti
accepted the need for a sharp break and decided to include no member of
Zanardelli's last cabinet in his. But he was prepared neither to swallow
the whole radical programme[2] nor to exclude all liberals right of centre
from his government. He also wanted a safe Foreign Minister and techni-
cally competent colleagues to handle pressing problems like finance, foreign
trade negotiations and the railways. His choice fell upon Tommaso Tittoni,
a Roman conservative with clerical connexions, as Foreign Minister, and
Luzzatti, till recently an intimate colleague of Rudinì, as Minister of the
Treasury. Luzzatti was the only minister beside himself who had held
office before. An important new recruit was Vittorio Emanuele Orlando,
a young barrister and professor of law from Palermo, who was given the
Ministry of Education. Giolitti's democratic admirers were sadly disillusioned by the final shape of the government, which in its combination
of right centre and left centre closely conformed to the tradition of Cavour
and Depretis. Romussi spoke for them all when he lamented the presence,
in the shape of Luzzatti, of 'a gnawing cancer', a 'Trojan horse', and
begged him to 'throw out the ballast'. Their faith in Giolitti's person survived, but they deplored his refusal, at a moment when he was master of
the political situation, to commit himself unreservedly to the democratic
cause.[3]

Giolitti made almost as unpromising a start as on his first appearance
as Prime Minister in 1892. Two of his colleagues, Tittoni and Rosano,
the Minister of Finance, became the victims of virulent attacks. Tittoni,
denounced by the left-wing socialist press as a reactionary crypto-clerical
who, while prefect of Naples, had had shady relations with the Camorra,
successfully fought back.[4] Rosano, a leading criminal lawyer and one of
Giolitti's most trusted collaborators, was accused of using his political

[1] ibid., 560, 566.
[2] A new divorce bill, cuts in the armed forces and an immediate election to
liquidate Pelloux's chamber were the three most important items which he
rejected.
[3] *Quarant' anni*, II, 574.
[4] Tittoni's conservatism and clerical connexions were indeed well known (see
above, p. 94). As prefect of Perugia during the repression of May 1898, he had
declined to suppress the Catholic movement. His shady relations with the Camorra,
the secret politico-criminal association of the Neapolitan underworld, were a
myth. It was in fact his energy in cleaning up the local politics of Naples that first
brought him to the notice of Giolitti as a potential cabinet minister.

influence to distort the course of justice.[1] Too sensitive to face the barrage of abuse to which socialist demagogues, moralistic democrats and reactionary enemies of the new government all contributed, he committed suicide. For a few weeks it seemed that a 'moral campaign' like that of 1893 was under way. Some of the Banca Romana mud still stuck after ten years. But in those ten years Giolitti had learnt much. This time there was no premature resignation. Though momentarily shaken by the tragedy of Rosano, who had been a personal friend, by the spring of 1904 he had got the chamber under control. For the next ten years Giolitti ruled Italy as Depretis had ruled it from 1881 to 1887. Between 1903 and 1914 there were only 219 days on which an opponent of his was in power.[2]

The relations between the government and the socialists were the burning issue of the first year of Giolitti's premiership. Open dissension broke out within the Socialist party in 1903 and next year the reformist leadership lost control. At the party congress at Bologna in April 1904 the revolutionary syndicalists and Ferri's left centre together won a clear majority.[3] During the summer several fatal clashes between strikers and police caused mounting tension. When the news of 'massacres' at Castelluzzo in Sicily and at Buggerru, a Sardinian mining village, reached Milan, the syndicalist leaders called a general strike. It began in Milan on 16 September and spread quickly through north Italy and down to the main cities of the centre and south. The railways were paralysed. For four days Milan was a dead city. The chamber of labour virtually took over its government, red guards were posted to protect property and the police kept tactfully out of sight. But the strike was a failure. Many workmen in key industries remained at work. The strike leaders had no plan beyond that of striking terror into bourgeois hearts. By the fourth day it had begun to peter out. Giolitti had been waiting for that moment. During the strike he had taken precautions against a serious attempt at revolution and had concentrated troops to deal with violence. But he told his prefects not to worry: it was 'an ephemeral affair, a crazy movement', which could not last.[4] Men of order were appalled to see the state 'abdicate' and deliver cities like Milan over to mob rule. 'Until a few years ago', said Pelloux in the senate, 'there were two contrasted methods of government: prevention and repression.

[1] Rosano himself seems to have been innocent of the charge, though some of his relatives and professional colleagues were not. Rosano's career at the bar had not infrequently caused him political embarrassment. Two of his most notorious clients had been Raffaele Palizzolo, the Mafia leader, and Alberto Casale, the political boss of Naples (see below, p. 309). Natale, pp. 567–82.

[2] Giolitti was Prime Minister from October 1903 to March 1905, from May 1906 to December 1909 and from March 1911 to March 1914. Of the three other prime ministers who held office during this time – Fortis, Luzzatti and Sonnino – only the last could claim to be independent of Giolitti.        [3] See below, pp. 264–6.

[4] Giolitti, *Discorsi parlamentari*, III, p. 1371; Natale, p. 635.

The present ministry has found a third – neither repression nor prevention.'[1] The Prime Minister ignored his critics and saw his patience rewarded.

Nevertheless, though he kept his head, Giolitti was intensely angered by the strike, and especially by the weakness of the socialist and trade union leaders with whom, only a year before, he had been collaborating to such good purpose. Even the mildest of the reformists had felt compelled to declare their solidarity with the strikers. The socialist deputies demanded the immediate recall of parliament and legislation to outlaw firing by the police on 'peaceful demonstrations'. They threatened obstruction if their demands were refused. Giolitti decided that the Extreme Left must be taught a lesson: the working-class movement was becoming a menace and the balance must be redressed. Instead of recalling parliament he dissolved it. His answer to illegality was a legal appeal to the electorate. The 1904 election is notable in Italian history for the fact that it saw, for the first time since 1870, Catholics going to the polls with the church's blessing. This was one result of the change of popes on Leo XIII's death in the previous year. Pius X was a strong conservative who, in order to buttress the social order, was willing to temper the church's hostility to the Italian state and give cautious support to the clerical-moderate programme. In November 1904, accordingly, Catholics were authorised by their bishops to vote in certain constituencies where it seemed possible to prevent a socialist victory. Four Catholics stood for election and three were elected.[2] This first step towards reconciliation of church and state was cordially welcomed by Giolitti who, from 1904 onwards, always included the Catholic group in his majority.

Giolitti's slogan during the election was 'Neither revolution nor reaction'. He hoped to reduce the power of both the socialists and the conservative right wing. The electors reacted sharply, as he had hoped. The general strike had been staged in cold blood, without any of the provocation which had seemed to justify the disturbances of 1894 and 1898. The commercial and professional middle class, the shopkeepers, intellectuals and black-coated workers, many of whom in their desire to be progressive had sympathised with socialism in the days of Crispi and Pelloux, now swung sharply towards the right.[3] 'The Italian people',

[1] Cilibrizzi, III, pp. 294–5; Albertini, *Venti anni*, I, p. 159. For a description of the strike in Milan, see ibid., pp. 143–6.     [2] See further below, p. 274.

[3] *Compendio*, II, pp. 128–9, gives the following figures for the 1900 and 1904 elections:

|                           | 1900 | 1904 |
|---------------------------|------|------|
| Ministerial               | 296  | 339  |
| Constitutional opposition | 116  | 76   |
| Radical                   | 34   | 37   |
| Socialist                 | 33   | 29   |
| Republican                | 29   | 24   |
| Catholic                  | —    | 3    |

commented Giolitti, 'did not intend to permit certain limits to be exceeded by any side.'[1] The socialists received a sharp check and lost four seats, while their relations with the radicals and republicans deteriorated. The old Cavallottian concept of a united Extreme Left suffered a blow from which it never fully recovered. Giolitti exploited his advantage. At the same time he demonstrated that he did not wish the pendulum to swing too far by having Marcora, leader of the more extreme radicals, elected as president of the chamber. The majority that Giolitti now created remained faithful to him until 1914 and enabled him to perfect the political system which came to be known as *Giolittismo*.

## Giolittismo and its Critics

*Giolittismo* was a new edition of Depretis's *trasformismo*, based on the intimate links between governments and individual deputies which the single-member constituency favoured. The liberals had no permanent organisation, no party newspaper, no central funds, no party whip. In the words of one contemporary, the Liberal party was the 'great absentee' of Italian political life.[2] The terms 'liberal' and 'party' were indeed antipathetic. In parliament Crispi and Giolitti, Rudinì and Zanardelli, Sonnino and Pelloux – all except the Extreme Left and the Catholics – called themselves liberals; but by 1906 the word meant little more than a general loyalty to the monarchy, the constitution and the unity of the nation. The parliamentary battle was fought not primarily between liberals and non-liberals, but between the many liberal factions, some personal, some regional, some doctrinaire in basis. In the constituencies the liberals were the local notables: the landlords, the industrialists and business men with a taste for politics, the lawyers and professional men, with all their dependents and hangers-on. They usually belonged to a loose 'constitutional' association or club which came to political life only at elections, in order to promote the candidature of their chosen man. This system produced deputies whose main function was to act as agents for local interests. They constituted the raw material from which Giolitti fashioned his majority. Their support was bought by the judicious distribution of state patronage and expenditure, or by the negative favours of a blind eye to local abuses or the transfer of an awkward official. Nor was it only the liberal notables whose loyalty could be thus secured. Socialists could be wooed by a land reclamation scheme in the Po valley, by a subsidy to a cooperative or a public works contract to a peasants' union. When the Catholics entered parliament, they too received satisfaction, in the form of state favours for their cooperatives, or a local relaxation of anti-clerical regulations, or

---

[1] Salomone, p. 51; Giolitti, *Memorie*, p. 215.          [2] Salomone, p. 30.

facilities for church schools or a charitable foundation. These favours were the dividend which every member of the majority received for the investment of his vote in the service of the government.

This personalisation of politics, so marked in the days of Depretis, remained a notable characteristic of Giolitti's Italy. The needs of the country were satisfied, not through the clash of organised parties, but through individual deals. Politics became a series of business transactions with a recognised technique that could be learnt. To handle these deals, a certain type of deputy was required: probably a provincial lawyer, well versed in local problems and well connected with the notables, without roots in Rome, with no political ambitions, who perhaps never spoke in the chamber except on an issue that specially concerned his constituency.[1] The government needed his vote; he needed the government's patronage, to satisfy his constituents and secure his own re-election. This system suited Giolitti. He was not interested in political theory and never tried to found a 'party of principle'. Like Depretis, he accepted the political situation as he found it. In 1882 Depretis had offered *trasformismo* when the old differences between Right and Left had vanished; in 1904 Giolitti offered *Giolittismo* at a moment when the issue which had dominated the previous decade, that of political liberty, seemed to have been resolved. His majority included former supporters both of Depretis and of Crispi, besides those who had followed himself and Zanardelli. He was not interested in keeping old passions alive. Like Depretis, he tried to lower the temperature of public life and to satisfy the reasonable requests of those who relied upon him.

Giolitti's hold over his majority was not due solely to his skill in distributing the spoils; he could also be ruthless when need arose. Throughout his years of power he kept the Ministry of Interior for himself. His mastery of elections had been proved in 1892 and in 1904, 1909 and 1913 he improved his technique. In 1892 he had overplayed his hand in favouring his friends and fighting his opponents. In subsequent elections his system was to employ only the minimum of pressure necessary to secure the minimum number of reliable supporters. Distinguished opponents, who might make dangerous enemies, could often be left to enjoy their seats in peace. Two hundred deputies from the south provided a nucleus round which he could build up his majority, leaning sometimes to the right, at other times to the left. These placemen were known as Giolitti's *askaris*: politically neutral, dumb and unambitious, their reason for being there was to give the government their votes.

Giolitti always maintained that elections are won by convincing declarations of policy and that this was the secret of his success. The stories of

[1] Ansaldo, pp. 281–2.

violence and corruption he attributed to the chagrin of candidates who lost their seats.[1] This was part of the truth. In fact he varied his electoral tactics with local conditions. In the north, where political education was advanced and the middle and working-classes well organised, declarations of policy, appealing to the ideals or interests of a wide public, were both necessary and effective. In the south, where the electorate was small and society unorganised, it was to the real rulers, not the masses, that Giolitti looked for support. Southern politics often amounted to no more than the feuds of a 'municipal jungle', inside which rival oligarchies fought for a monopoly of power. Giolitti would back one faction against another and, as the reward for its votes, allow one section of the local ruling-class to tighten its grip over the peasantry. If his clients proved rebellious or unreliable, he could bring them to heel by use of the state's authority, which included the power to dissolve local councils.[2] He did not order corruption or violence from Rome. But if it suited him, he would turn a blind eye to the methods his followers used, and allow prefects and notables to employ the local Camorra or gangs of toughs in order to secure his candidate's election. It was these malpractices that the socialist deputy, Salvemini, exposed in 1909 in a book entitled *Il ministro della malavita*.[3]

Once elected, with five years of the legislature to run, the Giolittian deputy might feel adventurous and resent the master's rein. Giolitti's method for dealing with a young and restive chamber was to resign, enjoy the respite from office and wait. In March 1905, in December 1909 and again in March 1914, he resigned within a few months of overwhelming victories at the polls. On the first two occasions he was back in power within fifteen months. Giolitti knew how to make himself wanted and never had to stoop to the corridor intrigues in which lesser politicians indulged. His henchmen, left to themselves and leaderless, soon felt unhappy.[4] As the life of the legislature wore on, they grew more docile. It was the general belief in these years that the King would never grant a

[1] Natale, pp. 91–2.

[2] The Naples municipal council was dissolved fourteen times between 1861 and 1906 for a variety of malpractices and temporarily replaced by a royal commissioner. Volpe, II, p. 441.

[3] 'The Government of the Underworld'. It is a sign of the benevolence with which Giolitti is regarded in post-fascist Italy that one of his biographers, Ansaldo, has given his book the title *Il ministro della buonavita*. Salvemini himself wrote in 1945: 'My knowledge of the men who came after Giolitti in Italy as well as of countries in which I have lived during the last twenty years, has convinced me that if Giolitti was not better neither was he worse than many non-Italian politicians, and he was certainly less reprehensible than the Italian politicians who followed him.' Introduction to Salomone, p. xv.

[4] See, for example, the worried letter of 25 July 1905 from the deputy De Tilla to Giolitti (who was then out of office), requesting instructions as to how to vote in the chamber: 'For me, a soldier who obeys his orders, a mere nod from my

dissolution to anyone but Giolitti. Whatever the King's intentions or wishes, it remains true that all three elections between 1903 and 1914 were managed by Giolitti. Fear of losing their seats powerfully reinforced the loyalty of his dependants as an election approached.

The crown played an essential and not always passive part in the development of the Giolittian system. Victor Emmanuel was an enigma. Shy, modest and virtuous, he soon earned the nickname of bourgeois monarch. His tastes and instincts were scholarly; it was among his books and coins that he felt most at home. Nevertheless he performed his constitutional duties with scrupulous care, even if his concept of the constitution was mechanical and pedantic. In later years he showed clear signs of a psychological sense of inferiority, which probably arose from his short stature and delicate physique. But during the first decade of his reign, if he inspired little devotion, his critics were few. His relations with Giolitti were marked by little affection but much mutual respect. While playing the active part which pertained to his office at that time, especially in foreign, military and naval affairs, Victor Emmanuel gave his Prime Minister unstinted support.

Giolitti has been described by an admirer and colleague as 'an English-style premier'.[1] The description is apt as regards his temperament and empirical approach to politics. Many found his studied calm, his almost casual style of dealing with a crisis and his deflation of emotional appeals both mysterious and maddening. They wondered whether there was any warmth in him at all. To all except his few intimate friends he seemed distant and inscrutable. He habitually spoke and acted 'in a minor key', believing that 'rhetoric never did any good to anyone'.[2] No stirring manifestos came from his pen and he launched no crusades. The many reforms for which he was responsible were carried out, not for the sake of any high principle, but because he believed they were 'mature' and therefore unavoidable. Politicians must not be precursors, he once declared.[3] In 1892 Cavallotti had accused him of the sin of empiricism, the failing common to 'practical men who think they can solve big questions by small methods'. Giolitti acknowledged the sin. 'I confess', he told Turati in 1902, 'that my policy is indeed empirical, if by empiricism is meant taking account of facts, taking account of the real conditions of the country and of the populations among whom we have to carry out our policy.'[4]

---

Chief will be sufficient for me to understand his intention and faithfully execute his wish.' *Quarant' anni*, II, 637.

[1] Soleri, p. 38.                    [2] Natale, p. 18.

[3] Giolitti, *Discorsi parlamentari*, III, p. 1371 (speech of 8 April 1911).

[4] ibid., II, p. 725; Valeri, introduction to Giolitti, *Discorsi extraparlamentari*, pp. 23, 27.

The inability of the Italian parliament to provide stable government except under Giolitti is the outstanding feature of the politics of 1903–14. Giolitti dominated the scene as completely as Cavour and Depretis in their prime. Like them he was a masterful manager of men, who never neglected those upon whom he depended. He selected colleagues of the most varied temperament and experience, and liked to have every part of Italy represented in his cabinet. By avoiding controversy, particularly at elections, he offended as few potential allies as possible and kept open every door by which his parliamentary base might be broadened. Giolitti believed, with Bagehot, that parliament's main duty was not to legislate, but to elect and maintain an executive. As long as his majority remained stable and contented, the chamber could be given long vacations and the work of government carried on with a minimum of disturbance. Inevitably, like Cavour and Depretis, he was accused of parliamentary dictatorship. Like them, he denied the charge. So far from depreciating parliament, he counted upon it to moderate extremism, to resolve the conflicts of opposing sectional interests and to preserve Italy from irrational passions and violent minorities. It was his basic faith in reason and common sense that made Giolitti a great parliamentarian.

Giolitti's vision was not bounded by parliament. He was conscious of the stirring of 'real' Italy and wanted to bring it within the pale of the constitution. Crispi and Zanardelli had been frightened by the rise of a socialist movement, as was Sonnino in his own day. Giolitti on the contrary welcomed it, believing that organised forces were more easily influenced and restrained than unorganised, and therefore less to be feared.[1] He rejected the class struggle but was quite content to plagiarise the Socialist party's programme. It always gave him pleasure épater le bourgeois.[2] If he had bothered to rationalise his empirical programmes, he would probably have attempted some synthesis of liberalism and socialism;[3] his political outlook was 'lib-lab' and he would have felt at home in the welfare state. But he did not underestimate the Catholics, now beginning to reach for political power. If they, as well as radicals and moderate socialists, could be attracted into his majority, then he had achieved his object. Anyone prepared to be friendly, whatever his views, would receive a helping hand. Giolittismo rested on a broader base than Depretis's trasformismo, which had been confined to the minority of the nation that was represented in parliament. Giolitti aimed at a wider partnership with forces whose main strength lay outside parliament, in the hope of disarming their hostility and reconciling them to a democratic compromise.

[1] Giolitti, Discorsi parlamentari, II, p. 628 (speech of 4 February 1901).
[2] Soleri, p. 39.
[3] Valeri, introduction to Giolitti, Discorsi extraparlamentari, pp. 31–3.

By balancing conservatives against democrats, Catholics against socialists, he checked extremes and navigated a centre course. This was possible because he had few personal ties. He was bound by no family tradition, he owned no great estates, he had no interests in industry or business, he possessed no newspaper or journalistic ambitions.[1] He could thus, within the limits of the monarchical constitution, indulge in pure politics and enjoy to the full the exercise of power.

Giolitti was by temperament and experience an administrator. As Minister of Interior he was outstanding. Having himself served in the civil service for twenty years, he knew its ways. His subordinates liked and respected him. They could expect no mercy if they disobeyed his orders or failed in the task he set them,[2] but they also knew that efficiency and loyalty would be rewarded. Giolitti trained a whole generation of prefects and senior administrators of a type not known before.[3] The prefect's function was extended. No longer was he merely the enforcer of law and order and the government's electoral agent; now he was plunged into the social question and ordered to study wages and conditions of employment in his province, to mediate in labour disputes and interview trade union leaders.[4] When a strike or riot occurred, Giolitti might call for reports three times a day.[5] His correspondence with his prefects shows an astonishing mastery of detail. Under his untiring supervision the administrative machine ruled Italy, subject only to parliamentary ratification, and acquired sufficient solidity to face and survive a world war. Within the framework which Giolitti constructed, Italy prospered and expanded. Economics were given priority over politics, efficiency and technical skill

[1] Ansaldo, pp. 232–3, suggests that, with the possible exception of Pelloux, Giolitti was the one Italian Prime Minister who never wrote a newspaper article. See also Natale, pp. 7–8, 79–80. But he never lacked friends prepared to ensure that his views found public expression.

[2] Giolitti's papers abound in examples of his ruthlessness as a disciplinarian. See for example his telegrams to prefects in *Quarant' anni*, II, 158, 226 ('I repeat I will punish inexorably any disobedience of the orders I have given'), 280, 307, 318, 399 ('I warn you that if other similar incidents occur, your career will come to an unseemly end'), 431, 487 ('You had an order; carry it out, otherwise I shall relieve you of your functions within twenty-four hours'); also 533–4.

[3] Natale, pp. 47 ff., 104; Ansaldo, pp. 227–32. Natale writes: 'Cavour created the constitutional state, Giolitti created the liberal administrative state.'

[4] See for example his telegram to the prefect of Vicenza, 10 May 1901: 'Your main duty is to maintain order and protect the freedom of labour. But that is not enough; wherever a strike breaks out or threatens to do so, the prefecture must undertake the task of conciliation between proprietors and peasants . . .' In a circular of 1 June 1906 he exhorted all prefects and officials of the Ministry of Interior to show 'the most sympathetic concern for the legitimate aspirations of the working classes' and to 'undertake a real apostolate of social peace'. *Quarant' anni*, II, 58, 669; Natale, p. 673.

[5] Natale, p. 447.

over reforming ardour or doctrinal intransigence. Behind the façade were many shortcomings. Giolitti did not pretend that all was well. He merely believed it was unwise to turn up the stones to see what lay underneath.

Such an Italy, though dull, pleased the generation that had lived under Crispi and through 1898. Even at the peak of Giolitti's power, however, there was a critical minority of liberals who refused to enter his system. Its leader was Sonnino, the anti-Giolitti of the Giolittian era. In 1900 he had been the heir of Crispi and Pelloux, and leader of the parliamentary majority. Three years later he turned his back on reaction and recognised that there was no alternative to a generously liberal domestic policy. By 1904, being no match for Giolitti in parliamentary management, he had sunk to the leadership of a handful of 'incorruptibles'. The most distinguished of his collaborators in parliament was Antonio Salandra. Outside he had the support of Luigi Albertini, editor of Italy's most influential newspaper, the Milanese *Corriere della Sera*. These men attacked Giolitti for lack of political principle, lack of vision and failure to uphold the authority of the state. Like the critics of Depretis twenty years before, they craved for a clash of great ideals, for a new liberal party based on 'pure', coherent liberal principles, with which the socialist, Catholic and reactionary oppositions could do battle in the name of their own doctrinal convictions.

Sonnino had a puritanical loathing of political intrigue and of the personal bargains which were the basis of Giolitti's power.[1] *Giolittismo* was *affarismo*, the anti-Giolittians declared; political differences had vanished, only shady business deals (*affari*) remained.[2] Giolitti had smudged party lines, flirted with socialism and clericalism, and demoralised public life through a system of 'oriental personalism'. Under his rule the idea had taken root that government by the 'constitutional' majority was impossible and that repeated concessions to the socialist and Catholic minorities must be made. Thus, so the argument ran, liberal principles were betrayed, effective opposition vanished and parliament was reduced to a rubber stamp.[3]

Sonnino's approach to politics was that of the professor, not the ad-

---

[1] One of his severest critics, Sforza, has written of Sonnino's 'puritan and, seemingly, pharisaical mania to thank God that he was not as other men'. His motto was *Quod aliis licet non tibi*. Sforza, *Makers of Modern Europe* (London 1930), p. 288, and *Contemporary Italy*, p. 159.

[2] Ansaldo, pp. 150–1.

[3] Albertini, *Venti anni*, I, pp. 133 ff., 318 ff., II, p. 66; Volpe, III, pp. 269–71.

ministrator.[1] Much of the ardour of his youthful years had survived. He wanted to cleanse the whole structure of the state and use its power to reform society. The liberal party, in his view, must serve no sectional interests but only the general interest of the whole nation. His concept of the statesman's task was paternalist and authoritarian; a strong leader, indifferent to popularity, was needed. In the words of his admirer, Albertini, Sonnino was 'a bold reformer and a strict governor'.[2] Giolitti, by contrast, seemed to his critics to have no vision, no long-term programme; his reforms appeared to be designed solely to catch votes in the chamber. Giolitti's aim, Sonnino declared, was 'merely to repair day by day the leaks of the moment and to silence whoever shouts loudest'; he did not worry if the partial remedy of today intensified the problems of tomorrow or obstructed radical reform of the whole. Thus, beneath the deceptively smiling surface, Italy's basic problems were allowed to fester till they became insoluble.

Giolitti was further accused of undermining the authority of the state. In September 1904 the government had 'abdicated' to the forces of disorder; again and again in later years it seemed to these critics that the state capitulated to importunate pressure groups or to threats from subversive minorities. Instead of governing boldly on liberal principles, Giolitti preferred to appease; rather than stand up to the extreme left, he tried to smother it with kindness. Many years later Albertini contended that this deference to minorities led directly to the triumph of fascism in 1922; the abdication of the state favoured not the reformists but the revolutionaries.[3] Giolitti dug the grave of liberalism by allowing it to sink from a high ideal to a mere day-to-day practice of government. It became no more than a myth for banquets and ceremonial occasions.[4]

Besides Sonnino's austere band, Giolitti had eloquent critics on the left. In the philippics of radicals, republicans and socialists, all the rhetorical phrases which were hurled at Depretis reappear: dictatorship, debauching of the parties, destruction of the national soul. He 'works upon the vices rather than upon the virtues of men', declared the republican Salvatore Barzilai. He had reduced parliament, cried Ferri, 'to an intellectual and moral morass'.[5]

Giolitti listened to his critics and went on his way unmoved. But he was not unaware of the defects of *Giolittismo*. His defence amounted to

[1] One of Sonnino's most loyal collaborators, Bergamini, records that after a meeting between Sonnino and Giolitti in 1900, in the former's house, to discuss the possibility of a joint government, Giolitti's only comment was 'Too many books, too many books.' *L'Osservatorio politico letterario*, vol. 4 (1958), p. 7.

[2] Albertini, *Venti anni*, I, p. 212.

[3] ibid., pp. 26 ff.

[4] Einaudi, p. 402.        [5] Salomone, p. 108; Natale, p. 700.

this: Italy was young and sometimes required crude methods of government; 'a tailor who has to cut a suit for a hunchback is obliged to make a hunchback suit'.[1] This was in essence the argument that Cavour had used to defend his management of elections. 'Political education', Giolitti told the chamber in 1902, 'comes only with very long experience of public liberties. Certainly what is possible in England today was not possible a century and a half ago'; to which he added his hope that Italy's progress would be so rapid that soon Ministers of Interior would be spared the need to shoulder painful responsibilities. A few months later he returned to the theme. In reply to a demand from Colajanni for the same liberty for public meetings and demonstrations as the British enjoyed, Giolitti declared that when Italians had enjoyed freedom for two hundred years, they too would be able to indulge in such things.[2] It is not true that Giolitti revelled in corruption or encouraged malpractices. On the contrary, he made persistent efforts to clean up the abuses of southern politics and local government, and made many enemies in the process. Nevertheless it is a fair criticism of his record that he took the Italians too much as he found them, exploiting both their virtues and their vices, and too readily accepted his country's shortcomings. Both Cavour and Giolitti had to deal with hunchbacks; but Giolitti could have shown more energy in reducing their number.[3]

With the passage of time, Giolitti's critics multiplied. A new generation entered politics that held him responsible for all that was wrong. As memories of Crispi and 1898 faded, the lack of poetry in contemporary Italy became oppressive. In ten years of power Giolitti had failed 'to make a single chord of the nation vibrate'.[4] Even his two most dramatic achievements, the conquest of Libya and the introduction of universal suffrage, were carried out 'in a minor key', as if he were afraid of exciting dangerous emotion. Idealists and perfectionists, no less than demagogues, now began to shrink from him as the personification of 'legal' Italy – stagnant, sordid and small-minded. New forces, more violent and impatient, claiming to speak for the 'real' nation, were breaking surface. In the Great War, which destroyed Giolitti's Italy, their poetry eclipsed his prose.

In the perspective of today, Giolitti occupies a place in history that would have astonished his contemporaries. Personally incorruptible, though

[1] Giolitti, *Memorie*, p. 319.

[2] Giolitti, *Discorsi parlamentari*, II, pp. 725–6, 749 (speeches of 12 June, 15 December 1902).

[3] 'Cavour left fewer hunchbacks behind him than he had found, while Giolitti increased their number', declared Salvemini in 1950. Valeri, introduction to Giolitti, *Discorsi extraparlamentari*, p. 69.

[4] A phrase of the radical Papafava, in *Giornale degli Economisti*, October 1904. Papafava, II, p. 441.

his system might tolerate corruption, he worked for no one party or interest and so discontented all a little. He loved power and the mastery of men; but beneath his apparent coldness there lay genuine sympathy with the underprivileged. He was not an innovator or a heroic leader. His gifts were common sense and clarity of vision. These enabled him to see the direction in which the current was flowing and show his skill as a navigator, never trying to fight upstream but successfully avoiding the shoals and rapids. He thus gave Italy a decade of greater stability and contentment than it had ever known or would know again for forty years.

## Parliamentary Politics 1905–10

In the years 1905–10 the questions which occupied the attention of parliament and government were mainly technical; reorganisation of the railways and the merchant marine, conversion of the national debt, education, the problem of the south, social legislation, reform of the civil service, modernisation of the armed forces. Some of these stirred controversy and caused changes of government, but on the whole a lull descended on Italian politics. Giolitti's dominance was unchallenged. The lack of success of those who from time to time replaced him in power only emphasised his supremacy.

In spite of his overwhelming victory in the election of November 1904, Giolitti did not remain Prime Minister for long. His immediate difficulties arose over the railways. The conventions of 1885[1] were due to expire in 1905 and the choice between private and state enterprise had again to be made. In addition the railwaymen were still discontented. Encouraged by the precedent of 1902, when Zanardelli's government had bought them off, they presented a long list of new demands early in 1905, backed by syndicalist threats of direct action. In February the government published a bill for the complete nationalisation of the railways, which also provided for compulsory arbitration and made railway strikes punishable by imprisonment or dismissal. The railwaymen angrily decided to work to rule in protest. On 4 March Giolitti resigned, giving ill-health as his reason. His critics assumed the illness was diplomatic. In fact it was genuine; he was not just shirking a difficult problem. The new chamber was, however, proving troublesome. By resigning before he was defeated, he lost no face and remained free to return to power on an issue of his own choosing. This tactic later became a recognised part of the Giolittian technique.

Alessandro Fortis, the new Prime Minister, was Giolitti's nominee and depended upon his patron's majority. A native of Romagna, he had started his career as a republican and was among those arrested at Villa Ruffi in

[1] See above, p. 65.

1874.[1] Since then he had moved steadily towards the right, fallen under the spell of Crispi and served in Pelloux's government. His chief assets were brilliance in debate and the wide range of friends which this varied political past had given him.

The only success of his ten months in office was the settlement of the railway problem. The railwaymen's union had exulted in the fall of Giolitti's 'liberticide government, under the blows of our energetic and dignified action'.[2] On 16 April it gave the order to strike, but less than half the railwaymen obeyed. Fortis stood firm and after four days the strikers drifted back to work. The union was forced to capitulate. On the 22nd the railway bill became law: the state took over operation of the railway system and the principle that strikes in the public services were illegal, which Pelloux had preached in vain, was established.[3] In spite of this achievement, Fortis now began to lose ground. He failed to inspire confidence in Giolitti's askaris, who resented being handed over, unconsulted by their master, to a locum tenens. Piedmont and the south were offended by a commercial arrangement with Spain which lowered the tariff on Spanish wines. More 'proletarian massacres' embittered the socialists. The terms on which Fortis agreed to take over the railways were so generous to the former companies that the extreme left was able to start a new moral campaign and denounce him for subservience to big business. In response to Fortis's appeals, Giolitti did his best from his Piedmontese retreat to calm his friends and dissuade them from abandoning the government.[4] For a time he was successful, but by the end of the year he could no longer hold them. In February 1906 part of the Giolittian majority deserted Fortis, in spite of Giolitti's wishes, and combined with the conservatives and extreme left to bring him down. Sonnino came to power at the head of the first anti-Giolittian government of the Giolittian decade.

Sonnino had for some time begun to find favour on the extreme left, in spite of his past devotion to Crispi and Pelloux. The radicals, having rejected Giolitti's overtures in 1903, were now greedy for power and thought they had found the ally they needed in Sonnino. Even socialists, after the 1904 election, were in a mood for experiment. Turati could not be shaken from his attachment to Giolitti, but Turati's rival, Enrico Ferri,

---

[1] See above, pp. 71–2.

[2] Albertini, Venti anni, I, p. 194.

[3] During the bill's passage through parliament, imprisonment as a penalty for striking was eliminated but dismissal was retained. This last provision was enforced for the first time in July 1907 when 500 railwaymen were dismissed for taking part in a general strike in Milan and the north.

[4] Quarant' anni, II, 643–7.

was more adaptable. In 1905 he had launched a new party programme of economic, fiscal and educational reform, with special emphasis on the south.[1] This 'new reformism' had notable points of resemblance to Sonnino's programme. Support grew for the idea of a conservative-radical coalition, enjoying socialist benevolence, which would break the grip of the 'parliamentary Tammany'[2] and 'bring honesty and sincerity into political life'. Sonnino therefore became Prime Minister amid the enthusiasm of the two political extremes, who thus avenged their defeat of 1904, and radicals took office for the first time. There was talk of a breath of fresh air entering politics, of 'a new Italy' being born.[3]

The new government was strong in experience and administrative ability but politically instable. Its most striking feature was the inclusion of men who had been on opposite sides during the struggle of 1898-1900: former colleagues of Pelloux like Sonnino and Salandra, together with leading organisers of parliamentary obstruction like the radical Ettore Sacchi and the recently republican Edoardo Pantano. Sonnino's programme made a remarkable contrast in style to those of Giolitti. Instead of colourless generalities about improving the condition of the masses, it contained a long list of specific reforms. The Southern question, it declared, was Italy's fundamental problem, and must be tackled by tax reduction, fiscal relief for agriculture, credit for peasant proprietors and 'internal colonisation' of uncultivated land. Sonnino also proposed to strengthen the freedom of the press by abolishing preventive sequestration of newspapers, and to limit the government's power to dissolve municipal councils. This last proposal was designed to weaken the links between the Ministry of Interior, the prefects and local government, and to prevent the use of local power for electoral purposes. It would have destroyed the foundations of the Giolittian system in the south.

Sonnino's reforming ardour won him respect but not a majority. His cabinet of radicals and conservatives was hard to keep together. Aloof, silent, difficult to approach and indifferent to popularity, he refused to stoop to Giolitti's bargaining methods and remained wrapped in statistics and blue books. He lacked the human touch which was Giolitti's greatest asset in managing the chamber. Giolitti had welcomed Sonnino's government and even helped it in its first difficulties, believing that his conservative antagonist should be given a chance to show his capacity in office.[4] This apparent generosity was based on confidence that the experiment

---

[1] See below, p. 267.

[2] The phrase was Turati's. Albertini, *Venti anni*, I, p. 209.

[3] L. Lodi, *Venticinque anni di vita parlamentare* (Florence 1923), p. 91; Volpe, II, pp. 425-6; Albertini, *Venti anni*, I, p. 212.

[4] He had expressed this opinion on several occasions over the past three years. *Quarant' anni*, II, 540, 542, 560, 638, 659-60.

would be short-lived and that Sonnino's failure would consolidate his own position. In 1906 this calculation proved correct. Very soon the Giolittian *askaris* who had voted for Sonnino began to feel the breath of fresh air turn chilly. The censorious talk of regeneration and honest administration grew tedious. Men who owed their election to the old system were hardly likely to help Sonnino to destroy it. They began to think regretfully of the past when they were comforted by the master's guiding hand. As feelings of this kind took hold of the chamber, Sonnino's government was doomed.

A breach with the socialists precipitated its fall. The socialists, under Ferri's influence, had at first given Sonnino their votes, just as under Turati's leadership they had supported Zanardelli and Giolitti in 1901–3. In April 1906 there was another 'massacre' in Apulia and in May a cotton strike in Turin led to more loss of life and a general strike of twenty-four hours over most of northern Italy. Sonnino acted much as Giolitti had acted two years before; the police were instructed to avoid incidents and keep out of the way. This passivity led to an ominous development in Bologna: the formation of middle-class 'volunteers of order' who patrolled the streets in defence of property.[1] Turati reintroduced his bill of 1904 to forbid firing on unarmed demonstrations and to enforce punishment of officials responsible for 'massacres'. When it was rejected by the chamber, the socialist deputies resigned their seats in a body. On 17 May the government was defeated on a question of procedure and abandoned office.

Sonnino had tried to destroy the Giolittian system in a hundred days, but had soon learnt that the task of government required more than honest intentions. His failure showed that Giolitti's methods were the more effective.[2] This was a depressing conclusion for the idealists who thought that the salvation of Italy depended on the birth of a 'pure' liberal party. It was ironic that Sonnino's first step towards this goal should have been to confuse political alignments still further by forming a coalition that easily outclassed Giolitti at the game of *trasformismo*. In May 1906 men as far apart in politics as Albertini and Bissolati saw that the only chance of a new deal was for Sonnino to dissolve and create his own majority. But the King refused his consent. The chamber was only eighteen months old; the last election had given Giolitti a huge majority and Sonnino's following was exiguous by comparison. On constitutional grounds the King was clearly justified. The immediate effect of his refusal was to

[1] Albertini, *Venti anni*, I, p. 218.

[2] In his *Memorie*, pp. 277–8, Giolitti comments: 'If he [Sonnino] was familiar with problems, he was never sufficiently familiar with men . . . He found himself little at his ease in assemblies that wish to be dominated, though by means of a wise persuasiveness which takes account of all their humours and knows how to turn them to its own ends.'

consolidate the Giolittian bloc and end the doubts of the waverers. Giolitti returned to power for three and a half years, the longest term of office, with one exception, of any Prime Minister between Cavour and Mussolini.

Giolitti's third ministry was slightly more conservative than his second. It rested on the centre majority that the 1904 election had created. This time Giolitti made no offers to the extreme left. Once again Romussi sorrowfully conveyed to him the disappointment of his democratic admirers, and warned him of the danger from his clerical colleagues.[1] But Giolitti's placemen hurried back with relief into the security of the familiar fold, and on 12 June he was given an overwhelming vote of confidence.[2] There followed a lull of three years during which *Giolittismo* was perfected. It was a period rich in useful reforms, many of them based on Sonnino's or radical or socialist proposals. 'Neither reaction nor revolution' was still the motto. The economy steadily expanded. The armed forces were modernised[3] and the administrative machine toned up. Giolitti's undramatic but solid legislative achievement[4] pleased his supporters and won him the toleration of both conservatives and extreme left, neither of which wished to drive him into the arms of their enemies by pressing their hostility too far.

The government's most notable success was the conversion of the national debt. This was the result of long preparation, to which Luzzatti, while Sonnino's Minister of the Treasury, had made a decisive contribution. On 29 June 1906 the chamber passed the conversion bill in a scene highly charged with patriotic emotion. The real hero of the operation, declared Luzzatti, was the Italian taxpayer.[5] Conversion seemed to close Italy's dismal financial past and open a bright future. For the next three years Ministers of Finance had a comfortable surplus with which to satisfy appetites that had been starved for decades. It was characteristic of the limitations of *Giolittismo* that much of this surplus was used to appease the most vocal pressure groups, rather than to carry out the far-reaching fiscal reform of which Giolitti himself had talked for so many years.[6]

[1] *Quarant' anni*, II, 668. The 'clericals' whom Romussi and the radicals particularly distrusted were Tittoni, who returned to the Foreign Ministry, and Emanuele Gianturco, the Minister for Public Works, who was well known as an opponent of divorce.

[2] Symbolic of the return to *Giolittismo* was Giolitti's abandonment of Sonnino's bill for limiting the government's power over local authorities, and his dissolution of the Naples city council in September 1906. Volpe, II, pp. 440-1.

[3] See below, pp. 358-60.

[4] For details of social legislation in this period, see below, p. 296; for legislation on southern problems, see pp. 310-13.

[5] Natale, p. 682.          [6] See further below, pp. 293-4.

In February 1909 Giolitti dissolved. Following the precedent of 1904, Catholics were authorised to vote in a limited number of constituencies and sixteen Catholic deputies entered the new chamber.[1] In spite of their intervention the extreme left increased its strength from 90 to 110[2] and Bissolati became the first socialist deputy for Rome. Nevertheless the government's majority was overwhelming. Giolitti had characteristically chosen a quiet moment for the election. To the new chamber he offered merely the continuation of his old policies which, he claimed, had contributed much to Italy's progress since 1900. Once again he found the newly elected deputies less docile than their predecessors. Only nine months after his victory he resigned.

In 1905 the troubles of the railways had shaken his parliamentary position; in 1909 it was the troubles of the merchant navy. The latter owed its size and prosperity, and virtually its existence, to a system of state subsidies designed to keep freight charges low and stimulate building in Italian shipyards. The state also financed regular services to the Italian islands and to Mediterranean, oriental and South American ports. Most of these services had recently been maintained by the Società Generale di Navigazione Italiana, a company controlled by the Banca Commerciale Italiana. Its contract with the state being due to expire in 1910, it announced it would renew it only on more favourable terms. Giolitti and his Minister for Posts, Carlo Schanzer, believed that other arrangements could be made which would give better services at less cost. This proved difficult to achieve, mainly because the Società Generale, thanks to its previous acquisition of several minor shipping lines, occupied a dominant position. The placidity of parliament was soon disturbed by the manœuvres of rival banking and industrial groups, each seeking support for its own shipping companies. Regional rivalries also flared up. Genoa and Venice fought each other for state favours, while Naples and the Sicilian ports protested that their interests were being forgotten in the clash between the commercial mammoths of the north. Sonnino's attacks on the government for failure to safeguard the interests of the state turned a technical problem into an explosive political issue. Radicals and socialists eagerly denounced the hidden power of high finance. Giolitti himself attacked the plutocracy of Italian capitalism. During the debates on the government's proposals in the summer of 1909, the turbulence of the chamber and the virulence of the press almost brought back the atmosphere of the Banca Romana scandal.[3]

[1] See further below, p. 278.
[2] The socialists increased their seats from 29 to 41 and the radicals from 37 to 45, while the republicans remained steady with 24. *Compendio*, II, pp. 128–9.
[3] Corbino, V, pp. 292–302.

On the reassembly of parliament in the autumn, Giolitti presented new proposals. When they, too, failed to win support, he decided to resign, recognising that his government and programme had grown stale.[1] Preferring not to be defeated on the merchant navy issue, he presented without warning a proposal for higher income-tax and death duties. This was a deliberate act of political suicide. But Giolitti was looking ahead. By courting defeat on a motion with a democratic appeal, he freed himself from what had become an embarrassing dependence on conservative support and prepared the way for a return to power with the benevolence of the extreme left.[2] The opposition to his proposal was as fierce as he had anticipated and on 2 December he resigned. Sonnino succeeded him for a second term of a hundred days.

Sonnino's position was weaker than in 1906. No section of the extreme left was now willing to collaborate with him and he was entirely dependent on Giolitti's majority. His government, built round a nucleus of personal friends such as Salandra, was the most conservative since 1901. Indifferent to the lessons of past experience, he presented parliament with another detailed programme of reform. Giolitti repeated his tactics of 1905–6. After urging his supporters to give Sonnino a fair chance, he disappeared to Piedmont to rest, confident that in due course 'nature would do its work'. The interlude was even briefer than he expected. Once again Sonnino's aloofness and inflexibility proved his undoing. In their master's absence, the Giolittians grew restive, being loath to save Sonnino by their votes, yet fearful for their seats should he be granted a dissolution. After three months Giolitti's lieutenants decided, against Giolitti's wishes, that they could do no more to stave off the crisis: the alternative would be to risk a serious schism in the Giolittian majority.[3] In March 1910 Sonnino's proposals for the merchant navy ran into heavy difficulties. On the 22nd he resigned without waiting for a vote. For the second time the King refused him a dissolution. Never again did he become Prime Minister. For years his tiny band of faithful supporters had been dependent on Giolitti's tolerance at elections.[4] Now, after his second failure, several abandoned him and even Salandra made his peace with Giolitti.

The King selected Luigi Luzzatti as next Prime Minister, at the sugges-

---

[1] Besides the discontent over the merchant marine, there was also pent-up dissatisfaction with Tittoni's handling of the Bosnian crisis (see below, pp. 343–6).

[2] Tittoni, 'Ricordi personali di politica interna', pp. 461–2.

[3] *Quarant' anni*, III, 4–12.

[4] Bonomi, *La politica italiana da Porta Pia a Vittorio Veneto*, p. 262, writes unkindly that they had been treated during the elections of 1904 and 1909 'with the same scrupulous care that is shown towards rare game, preserved for the future enjoyment of sportsmen'.

tion of Giolitti who was himself not yet ready to return to power. Luzzatti was by 1910 the most distinguished of Italian elder statesmen and enjoyed almost universal respect. Throughout his long career he had tried to remain loyal to the traditions of Sella and Minghetti, from whom he had learnt his first lessons in politics. His reputation rested on his success as negotiator of every major commercial treaty since 1875 and as Minister of the Treasury in successive governments of Rudinì, Giolitti and Sonnino. He was unlike both Giolitti and Sonnino in temperament: a verbose and emotional orator, tolerant and humane, vain but not ambitious. He had a huge circle of friends, both in Italy and abroad, which included scholars and social reformers as well as politicians, and Catholics and socialists as well as liberals.[1] With Giolitti's help he formed a wide coalition of Giolittians, Sonninians, conservatives and radicals, leaving only the Catholics, republicans and socialists unrepresented. His programme contained two items of a highly political nature: reform of the senate and extension of the suffrage. These proposals brought the radicals into his government and won him the socialists' benevolence. So marked a radical note made the Catholics nervous, but Luzzatti set their fears at rest by proclaiming his belief in the formula 'Free religions in the sovereign state' and promising strict observance of the Law of Guarantees.[2] Thus Luzzatti, though dependent on Giolitti's benevolence and much scoffed at for holding a mere 'regent's sceptre', started with goodwill on all sides.

At the outset he scored two great successes. The first was the settlement of the problem of the shipping subsidies. Passions had cooled after a year's wrangling and a new company was formed to take over the subsidised services for three years, while a permanent solution was worked out.[3] The second success was the most sweeping educational reform since 1877, drafted by the radical minister, Luigi Credaro, but largely inspired by Sonnino. Its aim was to improve elementary education, especially in the rural south, by increasing the state's responsibilities at the expense of the communes, many of which had evaded their obligations under the existing laws.[4] The Catholics fiercely opposed centralisation and defended communal autonomy. Liberals, radicals and socialists were almost unani-

[1] When Gladstone died in 1898, Luzzatti was elected to the French Academy in his place.

[2] Luzzatti's formula, which had been submitted to Giolitti for his approval (*Quarant' anni*, III, 15), was a deliberate modification of Cavour's 'Free church in the free state'. Luzzatti was a Jew.

[3] The definitive reorganisation of the subsidised shipping services took effect from July 1913. Long before that the politicians had lost interest in the question.

[4] The ultimate aim of the law was to establish a uniform school-leaving age of twelve in primary education. In the towns it had been raised (on paper) to twelve in 1904, but in many parts of the countryside, not only in the south, it had remained since 1877 at nine.

mous in their support, believing that with stricter state inspection and more money for better teachers and new schools, an effective attack on illiteracy could at last be made. Though their hopes were only in part fulfilled, owing to a persistent shortage of funds, Credaro's law did prove a landmark in Italian education.

Luzzatti was less successful with reform of the senate. Since 1882 that body had steadily declined in importance owing to the absence of a limit on its membership, its high age qualification of forty and persistent absenteeism.[1] Many leading statesmen, including Cavour himself and Crispi, had talked of transforming it into an elected chamber. Luzzatti was anxious to strengthen it as a check on the chamber of deputies, shortly to be reformed by extending the suffrage. But in 1910 there was little interest in the subject. Giolitti disapproved of any change. The senators themselves appointed a commission, then came to the conclusion that nothing need be done. Luzzatti did not press the matter and the senate was left undisturbed.[2]

In November 1910 Luzzatti presented his proposals for suffrage reform. Literacy was in future to be the only qualification and voting was to be compulsory, under penalty of a fine. The consequence would be to increase the electorate from 2·9 to 4·5 millions, rising to 12 millions when illiteracy disappeared. The bill was attacked from all sides. The socialists pressed for universal male suffrage. Compulsory voting pleased the conservatives but alarmed the extreme left, both assuming that it would favour the clerical-conservatives by forcing the apathetic countryside to the polls. The Giolittian majority, increasingly bewildered in its leader's absence, saw its own security threatened and tried to shelve the bill. By January 1911 it was clear that Luzzatti could not last much longer. Giolitti's friends became more insistent in their demands that he should return, in spite of poor health, and 'put a little order into the ranks'.[3] It was the 'sincere and ardent wish' of Luzzatti himself that his patron should take over.[4] There was a general feeling that a new sense of purpose and a new programme were needed, which only Giolitti could provide. In March he at last made up his mind and returned to Rome for the reopening of parliament. On the 18th he spoke on the suffrage question, accepting the need for delay but advocating an even bolder reform. The extreme left, realising

[1] Since 1869 the senate had provided only two prime ministers, Pelloux and Saracco.
[2] In 1918-19 reform of the senate was again discussed. The only change made was in the office of president, who after 1919 was elected by the senators instead of being appointed by the King. Under the republican constitution of 1948 the senate is an elected body.
[3] *Quarant' anni*, III, 39.
[4] Luzzatti to Giolitti, 4 January 1911. ibid., 32.

that they would get more from Giolitti than from Luzzatti, voted against the government, whereupon the radical ministers resigned and brought Luzzatti down. Giolitti was the only possible successor.

## The Socialists 1903-11

At the 1900 congress of the Second International, Andrea Costa had com-placently rebuked the French socialists for their disunity and urged them to look to Italy for a model. A few months later the Italian party, too, was in the throes of dissension and it became clear that only persecution had kept it united hitherto. The first split was caused by the parliamentary socialists' decision to vote for Zanardelli's government.[1] Thereafter the party's biennial congresses resounded to passionate and eloquent debates between reformists and revolutionaries.[2]

In 1903 the protagonists were Turati and Bissolati on the one side, Enrico Ferri on the other. Turati and his friends believed that excitability and a tendency to violence were weaknesses in the Italian people which socialists should try to eradicate. Violence, in their view, was a weapon to be used only when the working-class found all doors closed. In 1900 Turati had written:[3]

> Every school that is opened, every mind that is enlightened, every spine that is straightened, every gangrenous abuse that is rooted out, every rise in the standard of life of the wretched, every law to protect labour – every one of these . . . is an atom of revolution added to the mass. The day will come when the snowflakes form an avalanche. It is by increasing these latent forces, by working every day to that end, that one performs a daily revolutionary task, far more than by shouting from the rooftops about the inevitable revolution which can never make up its mind to break out.

It was precisely in shouting from the rooftops that Ferri excelled. Ferri was a bizarre figure who typified the worse in Italian socialism. His influence upon his party was disastrous. By training a criminologist of the positivist school, he had entered politics as a radical and helped to draft the Pact of Rome of 1890. He then drifted into Marxism, like so many intellectuals of his generation, and joined the Socialist party in 1893. His prowess as a parliamentary filibuster in 1899–1900 had won him national

---

[1] See above, p. 239.

[2] The leaders of the Italian Socialist party were of course much influenced by the intellectual debate over revisionism which Bernstein initiated in 1896 and which preoccupied the international socialist movement throughout the subsequent decade. Both Bernstein and his antagonist Kautsky had their admirers in Italy. But practical issues of national tactics and policy were more important than doc-trinal disputation in provoking dissension in the Italian party.

[3] *Critica Sociale*, 1 January 1900. Cilibrizzi, III, p. 181.

renown. He was brilliant, ambitious, eloquent, irresponsible and extremely handsome: his flowing hair, wide-brimmed hat and theatrical poses fascinated adoring audiences.[1] No one could more eloquently denounce the sins of Giolitti after a 'proletarian massacre'. Ferri believed that the Italian people was apathetic by nature and that Turati's reformism would lull it to sleep; constant agitation was needed to create 'a socialist conscience'. His alternative to reformism was not revolution but revolutionary oratory.

In May 1903 Ferri displaced Bissolati as editor of *Avanti!* He soon showed how he intended to create a socialist conscience by launching a virulent attack on Admiral Giovanni Bettolo, Minister for the Navy, whom he accused of corrupt dealings with industry over naval contracts. Why was it, he asked, that the shares of the Terni steelworks always soared as soon as Bettolo took office? Though Bettolo sued him for libel and won his case, Ferri's facts were not all wrong.[2] The main significance of his attack, however, was to revive the Cavallottian tradition of 'moral campaigns' and to stimulate the taste of socialists for bourgeois scandals. Later in 1903 Ferri helped to hound Rosano to suicide,[3] and in 1905 he denounced Fortis's whole government as a pack of racketeers.[4] Turati and the moderates fought a losing battle against this demagogy, to which they found themselves forced again and again to make concessions. There seemed no other way of preserving party unity and keeping in touch with the rank and file.

Ferri was soon ousted from the pleasurable position of wild man of the party by the syndicalists, who far surpassed him in the vigour of their denunciation. Reformism, they declared, meant acceptance of capitalist society, ministerialism, humanitarianism, pacifism, Christian meekness and 'degeneration into the democratic abyss'. But the syndicalists were not content with revolutionary oratory. Socialism, they believed, was something to be willed, to be achieved by direct action and physical violence. No reform was worth having unless extracted by force, as 'booty of war'. By constant agitation and exacerbation of the class struggle, they hoped to train and temper a heroic élite for the final epic battle, the revolutionary general strike which would culminate in the expropriation of the bourgeoisie and the destruction of the capitalist state. They would then build a new society based not, as the reformists wished, on existing state institutions, suitably adapted, but on the one distinctively proletarian organism, the syndicate or trade union. The latter would thus play a dual role, as an instrument of revolution and as a model for the future. Their fiercest hatred was reserved for the lawyers and professors of the Socialist

---

[1] Michels, pp. 144–6.     [2] See below, pp. 358–9.     [3] See above, pp. 243–4.
[4] Fortis had been Bettolo's counsel in the libel action against Ferri.

party,[1] and for the fat, sleek bureaucrats and organisers who had 'castrated' the trade unions. The syndicalist programme had a strong appeal for those anarchistic sections of the working-class, both industrial and agricultural, which still clung to Bakunin's insurrectionist tradition. It also attracted the extremist minority of the Socialist party which under the leadership of Costantino Lazzari, a veteran of the old Partito Operaio, had never succumbed to reformism.[2]

For all their hatred of intellectuals, there were few working men among the syndicalist leaders. Many came from the south, where socialism and trade unionism were weakest. Their outstanding personality, Arturo Labriola, was born and bred in Naples, where he had made his mark while still very young as an economist, university lecturer and journalist. His fulminations against the working-class oligarchies spawned by reformism had much in common with the attacks of the *meridionalisti* on northern privilege and tariff-protected parasites.[3] In 1902 Labriola moved to Milan, Turati's city, and took that fortress of reformism by storm. His *L'Avanguardia Socialista* soon eclipsed the official *Avanti!* The restless proletariat of industrial Milan and the Po valley gave him a ready hearing. By preaching uncompromising anti-monarchism and anti-militarism, he also won the sympathy of important anarchist and extreme republican groups in Milan. His success forced Turati and his friends, who described their youthful rivals as 'anarchists disguised as socialists', to resign from the Milan section of the party and found autonomous groups to safeguard the principles of true socialism.

In April 1904 the socialists held their party congress at Bologna. Both reformists and syndicalists lost their motions; but Labriola then joined Ferri in sponsoring the winning 'left centre' resolution, which condemned support of any capitalist government. Thus in the two years since the Imola congress the relative strengths of moderates and extremists had been reversed; the reformists were now the minority. The general strike followed in September,[4] organised by the syndicalists and supported with enthusiasm by their anarchist and republican allies. Labriola hailed it as the entry of the Italian proletariat on to the national stage and boasted that it had shown the masses that 'five minutes of direct action were worth as

[1] In 1903 28 of the 33 socialist deputies were of middle-class origin.

[2] Syndicalism was French in origin. The writings of Georges Sorel, the philosopher of syndicalism, were as well known in Italy as in France and much discussed in Italian intellectual circles. But it was not the intellectual content of syndicalism that appealed to the Italian working-class.

[3] Compare the communist analysis of Gramsci (see below, p. 526) in *La questione meridionale*, p. 23: 'In a certain sense syndicalism was a weak attempt of the peasants of the south, represented by their most advanced intellectuals, to seize the leadership of the proletariat.'

[4] See above, pp. 244–5.

many years of parliamentary chatter'.[1] It was also claimed to have demonstrated the solidarity of the northern workers with the peasants of the south. In fact, despite syndicalist exultation, it was a crushing defeat which took the heart out of the working-class movement. The fiasco of the railway strike followed next spring.[2] The conflict between syndicalists and reformists split the labour movement from top to bottom. The ranks of the trade unions thinned out and only the tougher chambers of labour survived.[3] The Socialist party, rent by internal wrangling, sank into the sorry condition of impotence and demoralisation which was to be endemic for twenty years.

Ferri now set himself up as mediator. His contribution to the restoration of party unity was a programme of 'new reformism', inspired by the 'integralist' formula of 'Neither to right nor to left, but straight ahead'. This was an attempt at compromise between the anarchistic deviation of syndicalism and the radical-democratic deviation of reformism. Direct action was approved, but only as a weapon to be used sparingly and in the last resort; support of bourgeois governments was to be permitted in special circumstances, but 'systematic' support was condemned. This programme was the basis of Ferri's support for Sonnino's government in 1906, but the experiment was short-lived.[4] The syndicalists treated the new reformism with as much contempt as they dismissed the old. At the Rome congress in October 1906, Ferri's integralist motion again triumphed. 'We are for reforms and against reformism', he declared; 'We are for the syndicate and against syndicalism.'[5] 'Integralist thought', said one of his supporters, Oddino Morgari, 'affirms that there is no antithesis between the concept of violence as such and that of the gradual development of socialism within the very bosom of bourgeois society.'[6] But whereas in 1904 the integralists had combined with the syndicalists, now Ferri won with the votes of the reformists; in 1904 he was on the left of the party, now he found himself on the right. Ferri had been disillusioned by the general strike of 1904 and it was now little more than personal rivalry and the clash of temperament that kept him and Turati apart. Both went on devising compromise formulae for unity which served merely to prolong ambiguity and dissension.[7]

Revolutionary syndicalism reached its peak in the years 1907–8, during which the number of strikes exceeded the previous record of 1901–2. In May 1906 a dispute in the Turin cotton industry led to a general strike

[1] Michels, p. 319.          [2] See above, p. 256.
[3] See further below, pp. 299–300.     [4] See above, pp. 256–7.
[5] Cilibrizzi, III, p. 351.     [6] Salomone, p. 67.
[7] Ferri's acrobatic formulae may be compared with Turati's masterpiece of 1902, 'I am a reformist because I am a revolutionary, and a revolutionary because I am a reformist.'

throughout the north. There was some disorder, but most workers treated it lightheartedly as an extra holiday. Much grimmer were the agricultural labourers' strikes round Ferrara in the summer of 1907, led by a young syndicalist organiser named Michele Bianchi. In October another general strike in the north started with the gasworkers of Milan and spread to the railways. Most of these ended in defeat for the unions and none were clear victories. Most famous of all was the agricultural strike of May 1908 in Parma province, which lasted over two months. For a long time the proprietors and the unions, under syndicalist leadership, had been spoiling for a fight. It was to be a decisive trial of strength. There was much violence. Blacklegs were hired from neighbouring provinces, armed with cudgels and organised in squads. Barricades were erected in the working-class district of Parma city. Children of the strikers were moved to other provinces where sympathisers cared for them, and 200,000 lire were subscribed to the cause. After many weeks of tension the police stormed the chamber of labour and made 150 arrests. Alceste De Ambris, the strike leader, escaped under a load of hay and left Italy for Lugano. By the middle of July spirits were flagging and the landowners had got most of the harvest in. The reformists then stepped in to mediate and end the struggle. All the heroism and proletarian solidarity was powerless to avert defeat.[1]

The main reason for the repeated failures of the syndicalists was the resistance of landlords and industrial employers, who began to organise themselves and oppose violence by violence.[2] But the syndicalists also contributed directly to their own failure. General strike 'gymnastics', instead of tempering 'the heroic will' of the proletariat, merely wearied the workers, strained the unions beyond breaking-point and dissipated their limited funds to no purpose. Such tactics appealed chiefly to the least educated section of the working-class, which could most easily be roused by revolutionary promises of utopia. 'We are returning', wrote a syndicalist paper during the Parma strike, 'after a long and necessary parenthesis to the tactics of that Workers' International, the memory of which is still living in Italy.'[3] The appeal to Bakunin was thus deliberate. Turati called syndicalism 'the stone age of socialism': the syndicalists were 'mystics, messianics, who await a kind of apocalypse' in which they would lead 'an army of underfed, hungry, uncouth and coarse people, an army of slaves, to realise the complete liberty of the world'.[4] Syndicalist intellectuals might argue to themselves that defeat in any one battle was more useful

[1] The best account is in Riguzzi, pp. 110 ff. See also Preti, pp. 294–8.
[2] See further below, pp. 298–9.
[3] L'Internazionale of Bologna, 23 May 1907. Quoted in Michels, p. 340; Riguzzi, p. 134.
[4] Speech to Socialist party congress, October 1906. Salomone, p. 68.

than victory, because it widened the gulf between the classes and so hastened revolution. But even the intellectuals grew disillusioned when the masses failed to live up to their heroic ideal. As doubt crept in at the top, the movement began to disintegrate. Labriola moved nearer the reformists; others cut themselves off from the Socialist party and joined forces with the anarchists or extremist republicans. Syndicalism remained an important element in the Italian working-class movement but it never again was dominant.

While the syndicalist fever was raging, the reformists felt bewildered and impotent. 'We cannot separate ourselves from the proletariat, even in its aberrations', said Turati.[1] Though they disapproved in principle of strikes in the public services, they protested against the dismissal of striking railwaymen. They deplored mob violence, yet repeatedly demanded limitation of the power of the police to suppress it. Even the Parma strike won their grudging sympathy, though they intervened and stopped it at the first opportunity. The role of firemen trying to put out the blaze was an ungrateful one. They therefore watched the decline of syndicalism with unconcealed relief. Their position was strengthened by the foundation in 1906, under moderate leadership, of the General Confederation of Labour (C.G.L.), embracing chambers of labour and trade union federations in a single organisation.[2] At the party congress at Florence in September 1908 they triumphed. The syndicalists stayed away. Ferri had disappeared on a protracted lecture tour of South America, leaving the integralists dispirited and leaderless. The congress declared that revolutionary syndicalism was incompatible with the principles and methods of the party as laid down in 1892, and agreed that collaboration with the C.G.L. should be the foundation of its future policy. General strikes and strikes in the public services were condemned except as a last resort. Constructive action in parliament was approved and a list of immediate reforms drawn up: universal suffrage, proportional representation, a graduated income tax, reduction of military expenditure, more education and social legislation. The congress also restored Bissolati to his old position of editor of *Avanti!* The reformist victory was complete.

The years 1908–10 were the second golden age of the reformists. As if to symbolise their triumph, the veteran Costa was elected a vice-president of the chamber in 1908. The party fought the 1909 election united and confident and increased its parliamentary strength from 29 to 41. With the blessing of the C.G.L. the reformists seemed to be turning their party into something not unlike the British Labour party. Many of its leaders discarded their republican prejudices. Turati argued that the monarchy

[1] Albertini, *Venti anni*, I, p. 303.          [2] See below, p. 299.

should be tolerated as long as it did not obstruct popular aspirations; socialists had more urgent problems on their hands, and to substitute a president for a king might mean no more than changing the coats of arms on public buildings. Meanwhile socialist cooperatives, savings banks and municipal enterprises received their share of the state's favours and substantial instalments of social legislation passed through parliament. In spite of the bitter memory of 1904, the socialist deputies were reconciled with Giolitti. 'To us, his adversaries, he gives positive facts', said Turati in 1908;[1] and to Anna Kuliscioff he wrote, 'I remain more than ever faithful to my former opinion: Giolitti is the only serious statesman we have in the chamber, the only real radical in temperament whom it was our enormous folly to abandon and oppose, instead of holding him to us and urging him forward.'[2] Giolitti on his side was content. His faith in the working-class seemed at last to have been justified. 'Karl Marx has been relegated to the attic', he announced in 1911. Events had shown that his liberal system of government, 'in appearance semi-revolutionary, was the only truly conservative system'.[3]

The 'liberal-labour' trend within the Socialist party might reveal a growing statesmanship in its leaders, but it also showed that the party had lost the fire and enthusiasm of its youth. 'It is suffering from a precocious old age', wrote Anna Kuliscioff in 1910.[4] Socialism, now that it was respectable, had as little appeal as *Giolittismo* for the younger generation. The intellectuals and the universities were turning elsewhere and the days of crusading evangelism were gone for ever. The party's growing complacency reflected the outlook of its most influential members, the black-coated workers, the railwaymen, the state employees and the skilled industrial workmen of the north. These groups, being better organised and enjoying easier access to the centre of political power, could claim wages and conditions of employment far superior to those of the mass of the population. In making the satisfaction of their demands one of its main purposes, the party was in danger of becoming the instrument of a privileged minority of the working-class.

This situation roused protest within the party itself. The angriest of the critics was Gaetano Salvemini, native of Apulia and champion of the south, who had won fame by his attacks on Giolitti's *malavita*.[5] Salvemini was shocked to see northern reformists complacently feeding from the hand of the very man whom he regarded as the arch-corrupter of the south. 'Even in the Socialist party there are two Italys', he declared in

[1] Salomone, p. 58.
[2] Valeri, introduction to Giolitti, *Discorsi extraparlamentari*, pp. 57–8.
[3] Giolitti, *Discorsi parlamentari*, III, pp. 1370–5 (speech of 8 April 1911).
[4] G. Mariotti, *Filippo Turati* (Florence 1946), p. 150.
[5] See above, p. 248.

1908, and begged his colleagues to care 'not only for that part of the proletariat which is most developed and powerful, but also for the more backward part, that which is most in need of your help.'[1] According to Salvemini, what the south required was political reforms, above all universal suffrage, without which the illiterate peasant masses could never hope to secure a fair share of the nation's wealth and opportunities.[2] But he made little impression. The reformist leaders continued to concentrate on the needs of the organised labour aristocracy of the north and to look at Italy through northern eyes. It was unreasonable, argued Turati, with what Salvemini regarded as arrogant complacency, to expect the pace of advance to be dictated by the most backward. Where the north had blazed the trail, the south would follow, and the privileges of northern workers would contribute in time to the south's redemption. Salvemini could not agree. At the Milan party congress in October 1910, when electoral reform was already in the air, he fervently approved the party's demand for universal suffrage, but added that it must be conquered by the people, not bestowed from above, because everything that Giolitti touched was corrupt. Turati replied that he 'would accept it not only from Giolitti but, if necessary, from the Pope himself'.[3] Soon after the congress, saddened by the lack of sympathy he had found, Salvemini left the party to carry on his fight for the south outside its ranks.

The reformists dominated the Milan congress, but Salvemini was not the only critic. Lazzari's revolutionary left was more lively than for many years. Its resolution secured 6,000 votes against 13,000 for Turati's motion confirming the 1908 reformist programme. One of Lazzari's supporters at Milan was a hitherto unknown young man named Benito Mussolini who, in 'a telegraphic' and 'heretical' speech, denounced parliament, patriotism and the 'cardboard reformists' of the party leadership.[4] Other voices were raised against the lawyers and intellectuals who dominated the party, and against the freemasons who symbolised its corruption by bourgeois-democratic, humanitarian heresies. Beneath the surface of unity, rancours continued to smoulder. The revolutionaries had less long than they realised to wait; next year the Libyan war gave them their chance.

[1] Speech at the Florence party congress, October 1908. Salomone, p. 56. The syndicalists, in Salvemini's view, were as guilty as the reformists of promoting the interests of minorities at the expense of the working-class as a whole. Salvemini, *Scritti*, pp. 564–8.
[2] See further below, pp. 321–2.
[3] Salomone, p. 70; Valeri, introduction to Giolitti, *Discorsi extraparlamentari*, p. 56.
[4] Mussolini, III, pp. 256–8.

## The Catholics 1903–11

On 4 August 1903 Cardinal Giuseppe Sarto, Patriarch of Venice, was elected Pope. He took the title of Pius X. The choice was a surprise, for Rampolla had been the favourite; but Rampolla's chances vanished when Cardinal Puzyna, Bishop of Cracow, made it known that Francis Joseph was opposed to his election.[1] Pius X was a startling contrast to Leo XIII. He came of peasant stock and was kindly, simple and austere by nature. His career in the church had been wholly pastoral and he had no taste for pomp, diplomacy or political manœuvre. He soon showed that he intended to be a 'religious', not a 'political' pope, interested in matters of faith and dogma, in church reform and the welfare of the clergy, not in international power.[2]

The major task he set himself was the curbing of modernism. The modernists wished to reconcile the church with the modern world, to reform its structure and revise its dogma in the light of modern science and biblical criticism. Pius X, a deeply conservative man of authoritarian temperament, stamped out these perilous tendencies as ruthlessly as Pius IX had stamped out liberal Catholicism forty years before. In this task he had the enthusiastic support of the integralist party, as the ultra-conservative clericals who had been out of favour during Leo XIII's pontificate now came to be known. Ecclesiastics suspected of 'modern' views were subjected to investigation,[3] the organisation of the church was further centralised, and the authority of bishops was strengthened while at the same time their independence was curtailed. In July 1907 an anti-modernist Syllabus was issued, followed in September by the encyclical *Pascendi*, which required the clergy to submit to the direction of their bishops in almost every field of human activity. The works of many well-known writers, including some of the liberal Catholic novelist, Antonio

---

[1] Since the sixteenth century the sovereigns of France, Spain and the Holy Roman Empire (to which Austria–Hungary was the successor) had claimed the right of veto in papal elections. It was tacitly accepted but never formally recognised by the church. In 1889 Leo XIII expressed the opinion that it was obsolete. Engel-Jánosi, II, p. 43. Since 1823 it had been the policy of Austrian governments to exercise the right only in the last resort, and no veto was pronounced in 1878; but the decision to exclude Rampolla, if necessary, had been taken in 1897. Engel-Jánosi, II, pp. 16 ff. Goluchowski wired confirmation of that decision to his ambassador at the Vatican within half an hour of receiving the news of Leo's death. In view of Rampolla's notorious partiality for France and Russia, Puzyna's action was not unexpected. Engel-Jánosi, I, p. 323, II, pp. 25, 33–5. In January 1904 Pius X issued a papal bull suppressing the right and forbidding any cardinal to pronounce a veto, under pain of excommunication.

[2] Pius X was canonised in 1954.

[3] For a time the future Pope John XXIII was under suspicion.

Fogazzaro, were placed on the Index. Under such pressure most Italian modernists within the church submitted.

This crusade against religious unorthodoxy had its political implications, both internationally and inside Italy. Papal diplomacy under the Spanish-born Raffaele Merry del Val, the first non-Italian Secretary of State in papal history, leant once again towards the monarchist defenders of order. As Pius X reminded the Austrian ambassador, he himself was a Venetian and had been for thirty-two years 'a loyal Austrian subject'.[1] His desire to draw closer to Austria-Hungary was reinforced by his distrust of Russia, 'the greatest enemy of the church', and of all Slavs.[2] Leo XIII's dream of reuniting the eastern and western churches was abruptly abandoned. The Vatican's attitude towards France also underwent a dramatic change. Pius X shared none of his predecessor's tenderness for the democratic republic. In May 1904, after President Loubet's state visit to Rome,[3] diplomatic relations were broken off. Next year the separation of church and state in France proved the final, fatal blow to the *ralliement*.

For a time Italian Christian democracy passed under a cloud. Even had a few Christian democrats not discredited the movement by drifting into modernism, Pius X would still have distrusted its leaders' claim to independence in politics and their evident desire to turn the Opera into a democratic political party. When they won a majority at the Bologna congress in the autumn of 1903, a clash with the Pope became inevitable. The Vatican publicly demonstrated its loss of confidence in the president of the Opera, Grosoli, whose sympathies lay with the Christian democrats, and in July 1904 he resigned. Ten days later Pius X dissolved the central organisation of the Opera and all but one of its constituent sections,[4] transferring their powers to regional and diocesan bodies under the direct control of bishops. There were to be no more national congresses unless the Pope himself summoned them. Bishops were charged with the duty of purging the Catholic movement of any 'element of discord' and of 'propagators of unhealthy novelties'. 'It is preferable', stated Merry del Val's directive, 'that a task should not be carried out at all, rather than be carried out independently of, or against the will of, the bishop.'[5]

---

[1] Engel-Jánosi, II, pp. 45, 54.

[2] ibid., pp. 123–5. In 1913 Pius X referred to the Balkan nations, at that moment engaged in war with Turkey, as 'a mob of savages' (*sono tutti quanti barbari*).

[3] See below, p. 332.

[4] The section concerned with the economic and social organisations was permitted to survive.

[5] De Rosa, *L'Azione Cattolica*, I, pp. 270–2. Most bishops shared Scalabrini's satisfaction at the curbing of the power of Catholic Action's lay 'bishops in top hats'. Fonzi, p. 94.

This was the end, for the time being, of attempts to construct a Catholic party. Pius X had another political aim in view. He believed that in the face of militant materialism, freemasonry and socialism, it was wiser for the church to have the state as a friend than an enemy. He was totally free of nostalgia for temporal power. As the Austrian ambassador observed, while Rampolla had believed that the collapse of the Italian monarchy would restore Rome to the Pope, the new rulers in the Vatican feared it would give birth to a radical republic.[1] Pius X's Venetia was the region where liberal-Catholic collaboration in local politics had developed furthest and it had enjoyed his full support as archbishop. As Pope he extended that policy to the national sphere and gave official encouragement to the clerical-moderates against the Christian democrats. Once the Catholic laity had been brought under effective ecclesiastical control, a bold initiative was possible.

The election which followed the general strike of September 1904 provided the occasion.[2] The initiative came from Tittoni, who had advocated a conservative-Catholic alliance ever since his youthful association with the National Conservatives in 1879.[3] At his suggestion the liberal deputy for Bergamo, Gianforte Suardi, who was a personal friend, appealed to the Catholics of his native city to support the government against the forces of subversion. Bergamo was not a chance choice: it was a fortress of Catholicism, where the rate of electoral abstention had always been the highest in Italy and where the Catholics, with liberal support, had long controlled the city council. Suardi warned them that failure to rally to the government would mean the end of this clerical-moderate coalition in Bergamo. The threat was not taken lightly. Within a few days a delegation of Bergamo Catholics was received by Pius X. The latter had only just rejected one more plea from Bonomelli for conciliation.[4] Now, after hearing the case of the Bergamo deputation and reflecting for a few moments, he replied, 'Do what your conscience tells you', and promised his silent approval.[5] Two months later Catholics voted openly in constituencies where their support was needed to defeat subversive candidates. Four Catholics stood for election and three, all clerical-moderates from Lombardy, were elected. The Vatican made no objection, though it was careful to point out that the successful candidates were deputies only in their own right, not members of a Catholic party nor in any way representatives

[1] Engel-Jánosi, II, p. 110.

[2] See above, p. 245.

[3] Tittoni, 'Ricordi personali di politica interna', pp. 306 ff.

[4] G. Astori, 'S. Pio X ed il Vescovo Geremia Bonomelli', in *Rivista di storia della chiesa in Italia*, vol. 10 (1956), pp. 223–35.

[5] G. Suardi, 'Quando e come i cattolici poterono partecipare alle elezioni politiche', in *Nuova Antologia*, vol. 334 (1927), pp. 118–23.

of the church.[1] In June 1905 the relaxation of the *non expedit* was officially confirmed in the encyclical *Il Fermo Proposito*, which gave bishops power to authorise voting where it appeared to them to be necessary in the interests of the church. It also stated that it was the duty of Catholics to prepare themselves 'prudently and earnestly' for the day when they might be called to take part in political life. This first cautious step made the 1904 election a landmark in Italian history.

*Il Fermo Proposito* also outlined the new form to be given to Catholic Action. The main organisation was to be an Unione Popolare, modelled on the German Volksverein, the purpose of which would be 'the union of Catholics of all social classes, but especially the great masses of the people, round one single, common centre of doctrine, propaganda and social organisation'. The details were worked out by a commission of three, one of whom was Toniolo, and ratified at a small congress at Florence early in 1906. The most striking feature of the reorganisation was that the Catholic movement was deliberately left without a central directing body. In addition to the Unione Popolare, there were to be an Unione Economico-Sociale, which took over the functions of the one surviving section of the Opera, and an Unione Elettorale, which would organise Catholics in local politics and relieve the bishops of the unwelcome responsibility for electoral tactics.[2] These unions were to be mutually independent, subject only to loose coordination of their activities by periodic meetings of their presidents. The Unione Popolare was designed to promote and stimulate organisation, but not to direct it; the concentration of power which had proved so dangerous in the Opera was to be avoided. The basis of the new organisation was diocesan. All its leaders were safe conservatives, strictly subordinate to the clergy. Internal dissension was to cease, even at the cost of muzzling the Catholic movement.[3]

The new policy dismayed many Catholics, but virtually all accepted it. The clerical-moderates were naturally jubilant. The ultra-conservatives of the older generation and the integralists were more pleased by the discomfiture of the Christian democrats than distressed by the church's rallying to the liberal state. Of the Christian democrats, a few opportunists like Filippo Meda declared that Catholics had 'deserved' the relaxation

[1] The official formula was 'Deputati Cattolici, no; Cattolici deputati, si'.

[2] In 1908 a Union of Catholic Women was added. The youth organisation (Gioventù Cattolica Italiana), which had existed since 1867 independently of, and often on bad terms with, the Opera, was reorganised and given a status equal to that of the new unions. On the Catholic workers' and peasants' organisations, see further below, pp. 301-2.

[3] M. Vaussard, *L'intelligence catholique dans l'Italie du XX<sup>e</sup> siècle* (Paris 1921), pp. 53-5; De Rosa, *L'Azione Cattolica*, II, pp. 28-31, 142-9.

of the *non expedit* and urged that full advantage be taken of it. Many of the keenest, however, lost heart and lapsed into disillusioned apathy.

A few actively rebelled. The most prominent was Murri. He was convinced that the Pope's adoption of the clerical-moderate programme would identify the church with the propertied classes and lose it the devotion of the masses. The creation of a mass Christian party, independent of the Vatican, was still his aim and in 1905, defying all warnings, he founded a National Democratic League. Within one year priests had been forbidden to join it and within two Murri himself had been unfrocked. Step by step he cut himself off. Because the church had rejected reform and turned its back on liberty and democracy, he decided that it must be forced by outside pressure to reform itself. Murri and his League therefore began to look towards the extreme left for help and to demand total separation of church and state, in order to save both from mutual contamination. In growing frustration and personal bitterness, Murri drifted into a kind of militant anti-clericalism that sprang from religious conviction. In 1909 he was elected to parliament as a radical in his native Marche, on a programme of church reform and with socialist and republican support. In the chamber he sat with the extreme left, dressed as a priest – a sight which had not been seen for over forty years, and which provoked Giolitti to enquire whether the extreme left had acquired a chaplain. But few followed him. The National Democratic League became entangled in modernism and broke up.[1] Murri was excommunicated and his writings placed on the Index.[2] Once again it was shown that Italy is not fruitful soil for revolts within the church.

Murri's extremism did much to discredit the Christian democratic idea; yet it survived, thanks in large part to another priest, Don Luigi Sturzo. Originally one of Murri's disciples, Sturzo declined to follow him into active rebellion and never dabbled in modernism. Born of the minor nobility of Sicily, he became an energetic organiser of Catholic Action in the island after 1898 and made local government his special field. In 1905 he became deputy mayor of his native town, Caltagirone, and later achieved prominence in the non-party National Association of Communes, of which he was elected vice-president in 1910. Sturzo also attracted attention by his writings on a variety of philosophical and sociological subjects. Local government was not the limit of his ambition. Like Murri, he desired a national, democratic Catholic party which would be independent of the Vatican, the disaster to the Opera having in his view demonstrated that it

---

[1] Its maximum membership had been 1,600 in 1906. Four years before there had been 6,000 active members of Christian democratic groups.

[2] In 1912 he married the daughter of a Swedish senator, who subsequently gave him a son. In 1943, in his very old age, he was received back into the church.

was fatal for a body under ecclesiastical control to mix religion and politics. Sturzo also shared Murri's disgust at Pius X's acquiescence in the political demands of secular conservatism.[1] On this point he differed from the more complacent Meda. Sturzo, familiar from his Sicilian experience with the nature of *Giolittismo* in the south, foresaw that the consequences of the clerical-moderate policy would be to dilute and distort the Catholic political programme and turn Catholic deputies into Giolittian *askaris*. But he differed from Murri, too, in having no sympathy with the latter's theocratic aim of committing a 'modernised' church to a particular political and social programme. Sturzo accepted the secular state without reservations. The aims of the autonomous, non-confessional, lay party which he envisaged would therefore be neither the restoration of the temporal power nor the clerical reconquest of the state, but the fullest development of the secular unitary state and of democratic liberties, amongst which Catholic liberties would find their place. Sturzo hoped to satisfy the democratic aspirations of large sections of the Italian people in a party inspired by Christian principles.[2]

These ideas were to bear fruit in the creation of the Popular party after the war, but for the moment they were suspect and could make no headway. Sturzo, unlike Murri, never rebelled against Pius X, but carried on with his work in local government. He knew how to wait and was not embittered by successive rebuffs. Though excluded from the leadership of the Unione Popolare, he did provide a rallying point for the Christian democratic opposition within the Catholic movement, and so helped a little to check the ultra-conservative influences then dominant in the Vatican. The very fact that he and his young supporters bore no responsibility for the direction of the Catholic movement before 1914 proved an advantage to them when at the end of the war the ban on the formation of a Catholic party was at last removed.

Meanwhile Pius X deliberately played down the Roman question. Protests against the loss of Rome became increasingly formal and the church reconciled itself to tolerating, rather than rejecting, the *fait accompli*. Hope of foreign intervention to restore Rome to the Papacy was abandoned for ever.[3] Nor did the church any longer, as in the days of the Syllabus, regard all liberals as germ-carriers of atheism and revolution; on the contrary, some were now looked upon as at least potential germ-carriers of

[1] Sturzo developed his ideas in a speech delivered at Caltagirone in December 1905, which is reprinted in Sturzo, *I discorsi politici*, pp. 351–80. See also De Rosa, *L'Azione Cattolica*, I, pp. 308–12.
[2] Sturzo, *I discorsi politici*, pp. 357–60; De Rosa, *L'Azione Cattolica*, II, pp. 151–60.
[3] De Rosa, *L'Azione Cattolica*, I, p. 326.

Christian restoration. Catholics could be loyal citizens and many were soon to become nationalists. On the other side most liberals lost their fear of clericalism when they saw how the church could be politically useful to them in combating subversion.

There were many outward signs of a new cordiality and mutual respect between church and state. Prefects began to look to the Catholic movement as an ally in maintaining the social order. Members of the Curia could be seen in the company of members of the government on public occasions and the Italian tricolour flew over the Vatican on national holidays. Orlando, on becoming Minister of Justice in 1907, established more direct contact with the Vatican, through a trusted clerical intermediary, instead of relying like his predecessors on Roman lawyers with clerical connexions.[1] In 1906 the generals of Catholic orders resident in Rome accepted from the government the compensation for their expropriated property which they had refused for thirty-five years. Next year military honours were paid to the Bishop of Lucca on his nomination as cardinal, and three warships visited Calabria for the celebration of the fourth centenary of the death of St Francis of Paola. Catholic-conservative coalitions flourished in local government, and the general election of 1909 brought a further relaxation of the *non expedit* under the supervision of the Unione Elettorale. Catholics were allowed to vote in seventy-two constituencies, either for Catholic candidates or for liberals who gave explicit assurances that they would oppose any measures harmful to religion. The sixteen[2] Catholic deputies who entered the new chamber included both clerical-moderates and Christian democrats. The most prominent of the latter was Meda, who in his election address accepted the constitution without reservation and referred to Rome as the city 'where beats the heart of Italy, risen again to nationhood'.[3] In 1911 Cardinal Bourne told a Catholic congress in England that there was 'no desire on the part of the Papacy for territorial dominion as such'. His declaration drew no rebuke from the Vatican. The Roman question seemed dead indeed.

These developments did not pass without protest. The inevitable reaction came in the form of an anti-clerical revival. Popular Blocs were formed between radicals, republicans and socialists to fight the clerical-moderates in local elections. The old passions over divorce and the secularisation of schools, hospitals and charitable trusts flared up again. The separation of church and state in France provided a further stimulus. In 1907 liberal dissensions gave the Popular Bloc control of the Rome

[1] Orlando, *Miei rapporti*, pp. 15–26.
[2] This is the figure given in *Compendio*, II, pp. 128–9. Other authorities calculate the number as over 20.
[3] De Rosa, *L'Azione Cattolica*, II, pp. 234–5.

municipal council and Ernesto Nathan, ex-republican, Jew, freethinker and former masonic Grand Master, became mayor of the city. One of the new council's first acts was to pass a resolution deprecating religious instruction. Nathan tried in 1911 to turn the celebration of the fiftieth anniversary of Italian unity into an anti-clerical occasion. The attempt failed, but the consequent polemics helped to keep the clerical issue in the public eye.

It was not only on the extreme left that the Catholic *ralliement* caused anxiety. Liberals of the old school like Sonnino, Salandra and Albertini feared that one of the basic achievements of the Risorgimento, the secularisation of the state, was in danger of being undone. If Giolitti, as seemed all too likely, was ready to pay this price for Catholic votes, then liberalism would be fatally corrupted; the institutions of the liberal state might be saved, but its *raison d'être* would be sacrificed. There were shocked protests in 1907 when it was discovered that the ministries for the armed services had been interrogating officers about their masonic connexions, a practice which seemed to confirm fears of hidden clerical power. Nor were all liberals, however anti-socialist they might be, satisfied with even the short-term results of the relaxation of the *non expedit*. Catholic seats were won from liberals more often than from socialists; and the questions which the Unione Elettorale submitted to liberal candidates, before pronouncing them worthy of Catholic votes, savoured too much of religious tests to be tolerable to men of strong liberal convictions.[1]

Giolitti deprecated the fuss. He himself was typical of the Piedmontese middle class in the reserve behind which he concealed his personal religious views.[2] A sincere but not devout Catholic, he avoided religious controversy and never promoted anti-clerical legislation. On becoming Prime Minister in 1903, he had made no attempt to revive Zanardelli's abortive divorce bill, having no sympathy with his predecessor's old-fashioned convictions.[3] His lack of interest in ecclesiastical matters, and indeed in the whole modernist controversy, reflected the indifference of the twentieth-century liberal,[4] which contrasted so sharply with the passionate interest of liberal leaders of an earlier generation like Ricasoli.

---

[1] Albertini, *Venti anni*, I, pp. 154–7, II, pp. 10–13; De Rosa, *L'Azione Cattolica*, II, pp. 227 ff.

[2] The evidence with regard to Giolitti's religious views is scarce. One of his daughters told Sforza in 1942 that her father used to read a few pages of the New Testament almost every night before going to sleep. Sforza, *Italy and the Italians* (London 1948), pp. 73–4. In a letter of 1923 to a close friend, Giolitti wrote, 'I believe in the immortality of the soul.' Frassati, p. 55. See also Jemolo, pp. 503–7. Giolitti was never a freemason.

[3] Spadolini, *Giolitti e i cattolici*, pp. 26–8; Giolitti, *Memorie*, p. 173.

[4] Sonnino was one of the few exceptions. His interest in modernism, added to the fact that he was a Protestant, made him an object of suspicion to the Vatican. De Rosa, *L'Azione Cattolica*, II, pp. 68–73.

Giolitti was content with the Law of Guarantees, which had worked well for thirty years, and believed in letting well alone. In the spring of 1904, in the excitement generated by Catholic protests against the French President's visit, Giolitti responded to pressure for an authoritative pronouncement by declaring, 'Our principle is this – the state and the church are two parallels which should never meet.' This formula, which he repeated in later years, nicely expressed his mildly sceptical optimism and his dislike of sectarian intolerance.

Education was the one sphere where the parallels did threaten to meet and where Catholics and anti-clericals clashed fiercely. In 1908 Bissolati introduced a motion in the chamber for the elimination of religious instruction from state schools. There followed a long passionate debate, ending with victory for the government's motion which left the compromise of 1877 substantially unchanged: local authorities were to decide, and where their decision was negative, parents would be allowed to make their own arrangements for religious instruction. In 1911 Credaro's educational reform[1] provoked a storm of protests and petitions from the Catholics, who feared that closer state control would undermine the influence of commune, teacher and family. The reform nevertheless went through with little opposition.

These debates showed that, in spite of the noisy activity of Popular Blocs in local government, anti-clericalism on the national level was a declining force. The stale rhetorical clichés about miracles, superstition and the Inquisition, the scurrilities about convents and Jesuits, were losing their appeal to the post-Risorgimento generation. Even the Socialist party, though anti-clerical by instinct and containing many fanatics within its ranks, was more interested in the social question than in divorce or even education.[2] The majority of liberals were content with Giolitti's acceptance of Catholic support. Giolitti welcomed the strength the Catholics brought to the forces of order and encouraged their integration in the life of the nation, just as he had encouraged the integration of the working-class movement since 1901. In 1908 he told the chamber, 'The Italian regards the clerical and the anti-clerical alike as the enemies of his peace and of his country.'[3] His policy was to discourage excessive zeal on either side. He believed the past was dead and the church no longer a threat to Italy's unity and progress. His cure for the inevitable friction was to talk about it as little as possible. This was his contribution to the slow reconciliation of Italy with the Papacy.

[1] See above, pp. 262–3.
[2] Jemolo, pp. 544–7, 556–62; Spadolini, *L'opposizione cattolica*, pp. 544–53; *Giolitti e i cattolici*, pp. 165–77.
[3] In March 1912 he returned to the theme: 'We have had no religious wars in our history.' Giolitti, *Discorsi parlamentari*, II, p. 1018, III, p. 1446.

## Giolitti's New Deal 1911

When he returned to power in March 1911, Giolitti made a determined bid for socialist support and invited Bissolati to join his government. Amid shocked protests from conservatives and from the left wing of his own party, Bissolati drove to the Quirinal in answer to the King's summons, wearing a soft hat and lounge suit in order to show a decent minimum of contempt for bourgeois etiquette. He was tempted to accept Giolitti's offer. But Turati warned him that if he did so, he would be isolated not only from his own party but from the conservative majority in the chamber: his appointment would be the King's alone, and would amount to a *coup d'état* by himself and Giolitti against parliament.[1] This advice carried weight, and in the end Bissolati declined. Giolitti therefore had to content himself with recruiting Francesco Saverio Nitti, a young radical economist and student of southern problems. With Sacchi and Credaro, Nitti made the third radical in the cabinet. Giolitti nevertheless still intended to secure socialist support and framed his 'liberal-labour' programme accordingly. Its main items were a state monopoly of life insurance and almost universal male suffrage.

Giolitti's opponents attacked him for pure opportunism. They recalled his scornful rejection of universal suffrage only seven years before on the ground that it would be the 'apotheosis of ignorance', which 'was never the friend of liberty and progress'.[2] Not even to his closest friends had he given any hint of a change of mind. His conversion, the critics argued, must be entirely cynical, with the object of bringing Luzzatti down and returning to power. Giolitti denied this. Luzzatti, he said, had thrust the suffrage question on parliament; it was now 'mature' and could be disposed of only by a radical solution. Probably, too, he hoped to neutralise Salvemini and other anti-Giolittians in the Socialist party by stealing their programme. Whatever his motives, his tactics were successful. On 8 April he was given a vote of 340 to 88. As in 1906, the anti-Giolittian liberals seemed to have evaporated. A conservative chamber, which had been hostile to Luzzatti's reform because it was too radical, now swallowed a programme twice as radical. The Giolittian sheep returned to the fold. Rarely had Giolitti's power over parliament seemed so formidable.

The suffrage bill was presented in June 1911.[3] Few except the socialists were enthusiastic, but few resisted. Giolitti's supporters had one powerful motive for obedience: the extension of the suffrage would make their

---

[1] Albertini, *Venti anni*, II, pp. 61–2. In a letter to Giolitti, Bissolati also pleaded his attachment to the 'simple life' and his invincible repugnance to the exterior trappings of office. Natale, p. 727.

[2] Albertini, *Venti anni*, II, p. 57.

[3] Owing to the interruption of the Libyan war, it became law only in June 1912.

political survival more than ever dependent on his patronage. The bill gave the vote to all male literates at the age of twenty-one, and to illiterates on completing their military service or on reaching the age of thirty. Experience of life, said Giolitti, was a better qualification than literacy. Provision was also made for the payment of deputies. The effect of the reform would be to increase the electorate from 3·3 million (9·4% of the population) to 8·6 million (24%), at least 3 million of whom would be illiterate.[1] Some conservatives, notably Sonnino, supported the measure in the hope that it would hasten the birth of genuine parties of principle. This optimism was not widely shared. Most liberals feared the irruption into politics of the uneducated masses. It was truly a leap in the dark. But even Austria had adopted universal male suffrage in 1907 and Giolitti probably felt that Italy could not lag behind. Had the calm of June 1911 lasted, the impact of the change could have been softened and the new energies that it unleashed could have been absorbed. The Libyan war and the upheavals that followed allowed no time. In the debate on the bill, Bissolati predicted that universal suffrage would destroy *Giolittismo*.[2] Though few realised it so soon, Giolitti had indeed dug the grave of the political system he had created.

The nationalisation of life insurance was clearly designed to win socialist approval. Giolitti had no love of capitalism or high finance, nor any prejudice against state socialism. Nearly half the life insurance business in Italy was in foreign hands and this was a further motive for nationalisation. Giolitti's original intention was to devote the profits from the state monopoly to workers' old age and sickness pensions, which otherwise would require new taxation. During stormy discussions in parliament and in the press, and under the critical scrutiny of financial experts like Luigi Einaudi, many illusions were destroyed. When the details of the scheme were worked out, it was found necessary to postpone pensions indefinitely and Giolitti was forced to admit that the state monopoly would be a burden, not a source of profit, for some years to come. Salandra, spokesman of the conservatives, warned against 'the paternalist, employer state' and the suffocation of the economic life of the country by state capitalism.[3] In spite of the opposition, including that of foreign governments, the bill passed comfortably.[4] The subsequent career of the National Insurance Institute was satisfactory and today it is one of the most powerful financial concerns in Italy.[5]

[1] *Compendio*, I, pp. 68–9.                              [2] Salomone, p. 59.
[3] Albertini, *Venti anni*, II, p. 75.
[4] Like the suffrage bill, it was delayed by the Libyan war and did not become law until April 1912.
[5] The monopoly of the Istituto Nazionale delle Assicurazioni was cancelled in 1923.

In the summer of 1911 it seemed that a stable political equilibrium had been established. Giolitti's new deal leant heavily towards the left. Bissolati was working indefatigably to win it socialist support. Yet Giolitti's essential aims were unchanged. He still claimed that his was the only truly conservative policy; there was no inconsistency between the new deal and his programmes of the last ten years. On both right and left he had determined opponents and he was not loved; but he seemed to have the situation under control. This happy equilibrium was shattered in September 1911 by the Italian declaration of war on Turkey which, though it temporarily consolidated Giolitti's position, nevertheless heralded the end of the Giolittian era.

# 8

# Italy under Giolitti

## Economic and Financial Progress

Between 1901 and 1910 Italy made the greatest relative material progress of any major European country.[1] The trough of the depression had been reached in 1896. Recovery started in manufacturing industry and spread rapidly through the whole economy as soon as the crisis of 1898 was over. For the next ten years industry boomed. In 1907–8 came a financial crisis and a sharp recession. This time effective action was taken to prevent banking disasters and there were no scandals, riots or political upheavals. In 1909 the economy entered a new, though less sensational period of growth, characterised by a high degree of industrial cartellisation and a significant level of unemployment. The war with Turkey in 1911–12 brought new strains. Yet on the eve of the World War Italy had acquired a degree of stability and solidity which made an astonishing contrast with its weakness of twenty years before.

The population grew from 28·5 millions in 1881 to 32·6 in 1901 and 34·9 in 1911, in spite of the drain of emigration. The fall in the death rate was mainly responsible. The birth rate was by 1914 beginning to decline especially in the cities of the north-west. The population density rose from 101 persons per square kilometre in 1881 to 125 in 1911,[2] a figure exceeded in Europe only by industrialised Britain and Belgium, and by flat, fertile Holland. The increase in population was accompanied by a steady movement from the countryside into the towns, and from the mountains into the plains. By 1911 not much more than half the Italian nation depended upon the land for its livelihood.[3]

---

[1] According to Romeo, p. 82, industrial production increased between 1901 and 1913 in Italy by 87%, in Europe as a whole by only 56%. But as Gerschenkron points out (p. 366), Italy's rate of growth was still not as high as that of Germany and Russia in the 1870s, or Sweden between 1888 and 1896, or Japan between 1907 and 1913.

[2] *Sommario*, p. 39.

[3] In 1911 57% of the population drew their livelihood from the land (compared with 75% in 1862) and about 28% from industrial occupations. Einaudi, pp. 4–5;

284

The years 1896–1908 were a period of very rapid industrial growth.[1] One clear index is the rise in coal imports: from 4·1 million tons in 1896 to 8·3 in 1907 and 10·8 in 1913.[2] The relative importance of agriculture in the national economy suffered a sharp decline.[3] Italian industry was still characterised by the very small firm. Of the 244,000 industrial establishments in existence in 1911, 160,000 employed five persons or less.[4] But in these years modern large-scale industry won a firm foothold. The output of textiles and steel, already substantial in 1900, made further great strides, and to these were added new products such as machine tools, electrical equipment, chemicals and motor-cars. It was in these new sectors of industry that the highest rates of growth were achieved.

Textiles continued to hold a commanding place in the economy, second only to agriculture. In 1911 they employed 11% of the men and 73% of the women in industrial occupations.[5] The silk industry made a rapid recovery from the depression of the early 1890s and after extensive modernisation and mechanisation reached its peak in 1906–7. Then came the recession and a 40% drop in silk prices in three months. From this the industry never fully recovered, and in 1911 it was employing many fewer persons than thirty years before.[6] But while silk declined, cotton boomed. From 1898 to 1905 were the years of the 'cotton fever', especially in Lombardy. Between 1900 and 1914 the number of spindles and looms more than doubled, imports of raw cotton rose by more than 50% and the number of workers from 135,000 to 220,000. But the cotton industry, too, was hit

---

Chabod, *L'Italie contemporaine*, pp. 20–1. For different estimates, see Serpieri, p. 3; Coppola d'Anna, pp. 30–4; Romeo, p. 75. Chabod gives comparable figures for other countries (in 1911) as follows: France, agriculture 43%, industry 32%; Germany, 35% and 40%; Britain, 12% and 44%.

[1] Gerschenkron, p. 364, calculates the annual average rate of growth of industrial production, based on six leading industries, as follows (per cent):

| | |
|---|---|
| 1881–8 | 4·6 |
| 1888–96 | 0·3 |
| 1896–1908 | 6·7 |
| 1908–13 | 2·4 |

The index of industrial production (1896–1900 = 100) rose to 167 in 1906–10 and 183 in 1911–15. Neufeld, p. 529.

[2] *Sommario*, p. 160.

[3] Between 1896–1900 and 1911–15 agriculture's share of the gross internal product fell from 50% to 44%, while that of industry rose from 19·4% to 25·6%. *Indagine*, p. 36; Neufeld, p. 539.

[4] Einaudi, p. 6; *ASI 1913*, pp. 150–1.

[5] Corbino, V, p. 147.

[6] But Italy continued to be the greatest silk producer outside the Far East, and Milan remained the leading silk market of Europe. Raw and manufactured silk together earned Italy a larger net export surplus (300 million lire annually) than any other commodity. Corbino, V, pp. 156–63, 200–1; Romeo, pp. 69–70.

by the depression of 1907–8, which brought short-time working and rationalisation. Export prices were drastically cut and new markets developed in the Balkans, western Asia and South America. In 1913 the cotton spinners set up their own central organisation, the Istituto Cotoniero, to regulate prices, limit production and challenge foreign competition.[1]

The iron and steel industry expanded vastly. In 1899 the first integrated plant was built at Portoferraio in Elba, to exploit the island's state-owned deposits of iron ore. Over the next six years it became the nucleus of a giant steel combine, Ilva, which absorbed the old-established Terni steelworks and built a more efficient plant at Bagnoli, near Naples, as part of the effort to industrialise the south. Ilva also acquired important interests in shipbuilding and armaments production. It was closely linked with the Banca Commerciale Italiana which provided the major part of the capital for its expansion. Meanwhile a rival company built another modern plant at Piombino, on the mainland opposite Elba. The Piombino and Bagnoli establishments remained the two giants of the Italian steel industry up to the World War. After 1902 the government prohibited the export of iron ore from Elba and in effect subsidised its sale to Italian industry. As a consequence between 1896 and 1913 the extraction of ore trebled and steel production increased twelvefold.[2] Thanks to a high tariff and the deliberate reliance of the navy upon home-produced steel, big profits were made. The industry, however, did not escape the consequences of excessive expansion. In 1907 it had to be rescued from an acute crisis by a banking consortium led by the Banca d'Italia. Though collapse was averted, foreign competition, and especially German dumping, began to create serious embarrassment. In 1911 the five biggest steel companies took a further step towards combination. A cartel was formed for the purpose of limiting internal competition, restricting production and arranging joint sales, and Ilva was entrusted with the management of all the companies' plants for twelve years. In 1913 Ilva negotiated a price and quota agreement with German exporters which effectively stopped dumping. On the eve of the war the Italian iron and steel industry supplied 73% of national consumption. Its costs of production were inflated, its financial position was not happy and no plant was working at full capacity. The nation had received a poor economic return on the large sums of capital invested. Against this must be set the gain in war potential and military security.[3]

[1] Corbino, V, pp. 148–54; Romeo, pp. 68–9.
[2] *Sommario*, pp. 121, 129. Annual average in thousands of tons:

|                     | 1896–1900 | 1909–13 |
|---------------------|-----------|---------|
| Iron ore extracted  | 216       | 523     |
| Steel produced      | 88        | 796     |

[3] Corbino, V, pp. 119–30; Romeo, pp. 60–3.

The engineering industry made great progress, even though handicapped by foreign competition, the high price of tariff-protected steel and an initial lack of skilled labour. An important stimulus came from the big orders for railway equipment which followed on nationalisation of the railways in 1905. Beside the old-established firms catering for the railways, shipbuilding and the armed forces, which before 1900 comprised virtually the whole of the engineering industry, new firms now appeared which supplied a much wider range of machinery and machine tools. Between 1900 and 1913 the number of firms grew from 43, employing under 100,000 workers, to 207, employing over 200,000.[1] Even so, in 1913 Italian production was very far from satisfying home demand.

Of particular significance for the future were the rise of the motor-car industry, concentrated mainly in Piedmont, and the development of electrical power. The former dates from 1899, when the Fiat company was founded in Turin. In 1904 there were seven firms in existence with a total capital of 8 million lire; three years later there were 70 with a capital of almost 100 millions. Then came the slump, in which the industry suffered huge capital losses.[2] By 1914, after a painful period of concentration and retrenchment, it had regained stability, with 44 firms, 12,000 employees and capital assets of 67 million lire. In that year there were 21,000 motor-vehicles on the roads of Italy, nearly three times as many as in 1910, and over 3,000 a year were being exported.[3]

The development of electric power – the 'white coal' in which Italy was potentially so rich – was slower. The first power station in Europe had been opened in 1884, to give electric light to Milan. Ten years later Colombo prophesied that electricity would emancipate Italy from dependence on British coal 'and make us one of the most flourishing industrial nations'.[4] His optimism was premature. Yet between 1898 and 1914 the output of electric energy increased from 100 million kilowatt-hours to 2,575 million (of which 2,325 million were produced by water-power).[5] Many of the Alpine rivers were harnessed and even in the south a few hydro-electric plants were constructed. But it was only during the war and immediate post-war years that, under the stimulus of shrinking coal imports, the foundations of a second industrial revolution were laid.

[1] Corbino, V, pp. 130–5.
[2] Fiat shares, which were of a nominal value of 25 lire, reached a peak quotation during the boom of 1,885 lire; they fell from 445 to 17 between January and September 1907. Romeo, p. 72. The title Fiat stands for Fabbrica Italiana Automobili Torino.
[3] Corbino, V, pp. 135–9; Romeo, p. 66.
[4] Volpe, II, p. 156.
[5] *Sommario*, p. 135; Romeo, pp. 66–7. In production of electricity, Italy came third in Europe, after France and Norway.

The close association of banks with industry continued to be a leading feature of the Italian economy. Some of the consequences were dangerous. Financial considerations too often took precedence over technical and managerial needs; dividends often came before sound development. Both the steel and motor-car industries suffered in this respect. Grave political problems were also created by the high degree of financial concentration and by the formation of giant industrial combines, backed by rival banks. These combines sometimes owned their own newspapers and never lacked spokesmen in parliament. The extent of their political power became apparent in 1909–10 during the debates on the merchant navy.[1] The dependence of industry upon the banks had a further important consequence. A slump in a major sector of industry was almost bound to precipitate a crisis in one or more major banks, followed by appeals for help which governments found it hard to resist. By 1914 there had been numerous instances of rescue operations by the state, mainly through the Banca d'Italia. In this way many of the risks and losses of industrialisation were thrust on to the shoulders of the long-suffering taxpayer.[2]

The progress of agriculture, while not insignificant, was modest by comparison with that of industry. Agricultural prices rose by 50% between 1896 and 1914, interest rates fell and the burden of debt and taxation upon land diminished. The rising standard of living, the growth of the cities and the improvement of transport all stimulated demand and production.[3] Notable technical progress was made on the dairy farms of Lombardy and Emilia, and in the development of specialised crops such as fruit, vegetables, flowers, rice, sugar beet, wine and hemp. There was a great increase in the use of chemical fertilisers and agricultural machinery. Effective labour organisation and higher wages supplied an additional spur to progress, at least in the north, and private capital began to be attracted to the land. Progress would have been greater if Giolitti's governments had recognised the need for a more positive and coherent agricultural policy. Apart from the maintenance of existing tariffs, little was done except increase the piecemeal allocation of funds for technical education, agricultural credit, cooperatives and land improvement. Luzzatti and Sonnino were exceptional among politicians in sharing a passion for the problems of the land, and their tenure of office was too short to achieve results. As a consequence of this neglect, poverty, low consumption, over-

[1] See above, p. 260.
[2] Romeo, pp. 80–2.
[3] The index of the gross saleable product of agriculture (1938 = 100), after remaining almost stationary since 1871, rose from 63·2 in 1896–1900 to 83·3 in 1909–13, a rise unequalled in western Europe in the same period. *Indagine*, p. 204; Romeo, p. 159.

population and technical stagnation were still the dominant features of large sectors of Italian agriculture in 1914 and constituted a serious drag on the nation's economy.

The fortunes of different branches of agriculture varied and progress was uneven. Wheat was the most important crop, covering in 1909–14 about 18% of the total cultivated area. Production was stimulated, often in unsuitable areas, by the import duty of $7\frac{1}{2}$ lire per quintal, which remained unchanged from 1898 to 1914. In 1913 the average yield was only 10·5 quintals per hectare.[1] As grain prices rose, socialists, radicals and free traders redoubled their protests against this exploitation of the consumer by a minority of big landowners, but they never won sufficient support to reduce, still less to abolish, the duty. Fear of the dislocation that any change of policy would cause and the argument of national security prevailed. Even with the tariff, home production could not keep pace with demand, and wheat imports increased steadily.[2]

Sugar beet attracted even greater political attention than wheat. Production of sugar grew from 6,000 tons in 1898 to over 300,000 in 1913, and the area under beet from 1,300 hectares to 62,000, mostly in northern Emilia and southern Venetia. This expansion was the result of a tariff four times the wholesale price of imported sugar. At the same time sugar consumption per head in Italy was startlingly low, about one-twelfth of that of Britain and one-fifth of that of France, owing to a heavy tax which accounted for two-thirds of its retail price. The refiners were organised in a powerful trust, the Unione Zuccheri, and made handsome profits by boosting exports. It was a situation that justified the impassioned protests of free traders, who placed the 'sugar barons' beside the steel and armaments kings as their favourite targets. The tariff, however, remained unchanged and the tax was only slightly reduced. As in the case of the import duty on wheat, governments needed the revenue and shrank from alienating powerful interests.[3]

Wine and fruit, on which the south increasingly depended, held their own. Between 1890 and 1910 many thousand hectares of new vines were planted, mainly in Apulia and Sicily, and the number of citrus trees grew from $4\frac{1}{2}$ to nearly 8 million. The consequence was overproduction and a

[1] Corbino, V, pp. 78–81. But one-third of this area (mainly in the Po valley) gave a yield of 19 quintals, which was not much below that in countries like Germany and Britain, where the total area under wheat was much smaller than in Italy. See also Valenti, pp. 61–6.

[2] Between 1896–1900 and 1909–13 home wheat production increased from 35·7 to 48·6 million quintals and imports from 6·7 to 15·5 million (annual averages). *Sommario*, pp. 106, 159.

[3] Corbino, IV, pp. 156–9, V, pp. 177–9; Fossati, pp. 447–8; Romeo, pp. 67–8; *Sommario*, p. 126.

price collapse in 1908, which forced the government to intervene with subsidies and other first-aid measures. After 1910 prices recovered and exports at least did not decline, but the area under vines diminished.[1] Champions of the south called in vain for the saner policy of lowering industrial tariffs and so opening up large new export markets for southern produce. The voice of northern industry continued to prevail.

Though the improvement in the condition of the rural classes was substantially greater in the fifteen years after 1900 than in the previous forty, the social problems of the countryside remained acute. Almost half the peasant population consisted of landless labourers,[2] and unemployment and underemployment were rife among them. In spite of the indifference of all governments except Luzzatti's, the number of peasant proprietors increased faster after 1900 than before, especially in the Po valley. But only in Piedmont and Liguria could a rural, property-owning democracy like that of France be found. Elsewhere the Italian peasant was still hungry for more land or for any land at all.[3]

A popular solution for this problem was reclamation of marsh and waste land. Wonders had indeed been performed in the northern plains, where in the province of Ferrara alone the cultivated area had been doubled by drainage in thirty years.[4] By contrast, in the Roman Campagna, on the doorstep of the capital, the traveller was still greeted in 1914 by a melancholy mixture of semi-desert and swamp, untouched since papal days. Further south the record was even more dismal. But even had the state spent far more on reclamation, the quantity of uncultivated land on which peasants could be settled would still have been extremely limited – enough, perhaps, to absorb half a million persons, or fewer than were emigrating in a single year. The real need was less to increase the cultivated area than to make more intensive use of the land already under cultivation. Except in the north, the possibilities of irrigation were still largely unexplored. Most neglected of all were the mountains and forests. Between 1860 and 1910 500,000 hectares of forest had been cut and only 30,000 replanted.[5] A terrible price was paid in floods and soil erosion. The peasant in the mountains, even though he owned his land more frequently than the

[1] Corbino, V, pp. 83–92; Volpe, II, pp. 143–4.

[2] Serpieri, p. 8, calculates that in 1911 the number of peasants (i.e. persons who performed manual labour on the land) above the age of ten was a little over 10 million. Of these 4·4 million were labourers, 3·2 tenant farmers and sharecroppers, and 1·8 proprietors.

[3] Einaudi, p. 5. Luzzatti attempted while Prime Minister in 1910 to legislate in favour of small proprietors, but none of his measures reached the statute book. As Preti observes (pp. 335–7), Giolitti was surprisingly indifferent to the social significance of peasant ownership, even though he came from the province of Cuneo, one of the few where peasant proprietors flourished.

[4] Corbino, V, pp. 62–3.                                        [5] Volpe, II, p. 136.

peasant in the plains, led as grim a life as any Italian. In fifty years parliament passed over twenty laws dealing with land improvement and as many again dealing with reafforestation, but their effect was small. Funds were inadequate, landowners were given too little incentive to take part in improvement schemes, and governments were reluctant to use the ultimate weapon of expropriation.[1] Luzzatti was responsible, while Prime Minister in 1910, for a series of laws which might have inaugurated a new deal for the mountain economy, but the war came before significant results had been achieved.[2]

Italy's progress was reflected in its foreign trade. In the years 1891–5 this had sunk to the lowest level since 1870, but in 1898 the pre-depression peak of 1887 was left behind. The combined value of imports and exports rose from an average of 2,600 million lire in 1896–1900 to 4,800 million in 1906–10 and 5,900 million in 1911–13, a rate of expansion which only Germany among European nations could rival. The trade deficit, however, increased steadily. Exports paid for 83% of imports in 1901–5, but only 64% in 1909–13.[3] Large increases in the import of coal, machinery, wheat, cotton and other raw materials for industry were responsible. The main increase in exports was in manufactured goods. The foreign trade deficit was made up by the earnings of the merchant navy, by the expenditure of foreign tourists in Italy and above all by the remittances of emigrants from abroad.[4]

By 1910 Germany had a clear lead over every other country both as a customer of Italy and as a supplier of its needs. Trade with France recovered after the signing of the commercial treaty in 1898, but it never again assumed the same importance as before the rupture of 1887. In 1910 Germany, Austria-Hungary and Switzerland between then bought one-third of Italy's exports and supplied one-quarter of its imports.[5] Commercial relations with these countries, however, were not without their difficulties. The treaties of 1892 lapsed at the end of 1903, and it required all Luzzatti's skill to prevent serious damage to Italy from the agrarian protectionists of Germany and Austria-Hungary. In the new treaties which came into force in the spring of 1906, Italy had to make concessions to

[1] Corbino, V, pp. 60–4; Valenti, pp. 112–21.

[2] Volpe, III, pp. 236–7; Corbino, V, pp. 66–9.

[3] *Sommario*, p. 152; Romeo, pp. 180–1; Luzzatto, II, p. 475.

[4] Over the years 1901–13 the merchant navy earned a total of 1,200 million lire, tourists spent 4,900 million and emigrants remitted 6,200 million, totalling 12,300 million; the trade deficit in the same period was 10,200 million. Corbino, V, pp. 215–16.

[5] In 1887 France took 44·4% of Italy's exports and supplied 20·2% of its imports; for 1911–13 the figures were 9·3% and 8·4%. Corbino, V, p. 210; Stringher, pp. 58–9, 108.

German and Swiss industry, and failed to overcome the opposition of the wine producers of Hungary to a renewal of the very favourable duty of 1892 on Italian wine.[1] Luzzatti was, however, able to secure compensating concessions for other agricultural exports, particularly fruit.

The trade figures do not reveal the full measure of the German stake in the Italian economy. German influence in the banking and insurance world was considerable and Italian banks often had Germans among their directors. The Banca Commerciale Italiana and the Credito Italiano, both founded with German capital and maintaining close links with Germany, held big stakes in shipping, steel and electricity. Much of Italian industry depended on Germany for its machine tools and on German technicians to instal and maintain them. A large part of Italy's foreign trade was handled by German shipping and commercial agencies. German capital investment, on the other hand, was small and far outweighed by that of Belgium, France and Britain.[2] The alarm over Italy's economic dependence, which was shrilly expressed at the outbreak of war in 1914, was less the product of serious analysis than of partisan political agitation. In fact Italy's foreign indebtedness decreased between 1901 and 1913, and by that date Italian investment abroad, in the Balkans, Turkey and north Africa, though still far smaller than foreign investment in Italy, was nevertheless beginning to acquire importance.[3]

One further economic link between Italy and its northern neighbours must be mentioned. A growing number of Italians chose to seek their livelihood abroad and Italian emigrants were becoming the navvies of western Europe. Italian labourers built the Alpine tunnels, the harbours of Marseilles and Calais, and flocked into the mines and steelworks of the Ruhr and Lorraine. But here too there was no exclusive dependence on one country; France took as many emigrants as Germany, and Switzerland more than either.[4]

[1] Italian wine exports to Austria–Hungary were 991,000 hectolitres in 1903; with the lapse of the 1892 treaty came a catastrophic fall to 8,000 in 1905. Total wine exports were 813,000 hectolitres in 1906, the lowest since 1878, but recovered to 1,400,000 in 1911–13. Vöchting, p. 210; Corbino, V, p. 195; *Sommario*, p. 161.

[2] Nitti, *Il capitale straniero in Italia*, ch. 3.

[3] Corbino, V, pp. 218–23. For a less optimistic view, see Volpe, III, pp. 638–40.

[4] Foerster, pp. 8–9 (see also *Sommario*, p. 66) gives the following figures for Italian emigration to Europe (annual averages in thousands):

|           | Austria–Hungary | France | Germany | Switzerland |
|-----------|-----------------|--------|---------|-------------|
| 1896–1900 | 46              | 25     | 31      | 26          |
| 1901–1905 | 54              | 54     | 56      | 54          |
| 1906–1910 | 37              | 60     | 62      | 77          |
| 1911      | 35              | 63     | 65      | 89          |
| 1912      | 42              | 74     | 76      | 89          |

Financially the years 1898–1907 were Italy's golden decade. Never had the nation enjoyed such confidence and stability. Thanks to Giolitti, Sonnino and their successors at the Treasury, and a national effort almost as 'heroic' as that of 1869–76, Italy rose from the depths of 1893–4 to achieve its first genuine budget surplus five years later.[1] The brake on expenditure maintained by successive governments and the firmness of Bonaldo Stringher, director-general of the Banca d'Italia, prevented a repetition of the inflation of Italy's last period of prosperity in 1882–7. No big loans were contracted abroad. Metallic reserves rose from 50% of the note issue in 1900 to 72% in 1913.[2] After 1902 the lira remained virtually at par with the French franc and Italian credit stood high abroad. Large numbers of Italian securities were repurchased from foreigners and Italy's financial independence was correspondingly strengthened.[3]

This healthy situation made possible a major financial operation, the conversion of the national debt. For this the support of French bankers was essential.[4] Negotiations started in 1903, but were interrupted by the demands on French financial resources of Russia's war with Japan. Luzzatti made decisive progress during his brief tenure of the Ministry of the Treasury in Sonnino's government and Stringher concluded the deal at Paris in June 1906. With the backing of an international syndicate with 400 million lire at its disposal, the national debt, totalling 8,000 million lire, was converted from 5% to $3\frac{3}{4}\%$, to be further reduced to $3\frac{1}{2}\%$ after five years. The operation was an outstanding success and the number of demands for repayment was negligible, even from foreign bondholders. The financial crisis of 1907 left the credit of the Italian state unshaken. The contrast with 1893 was comforting.

There were few changes in taxation, though politicians had been talking of reform for decades. In 1901 Zanardelli's Minister of Finance, Wollemborg, proposed a comprehensive reform of both national and local taxation. It involved a large and immediate reduction in the duties on the most essential articles of consumption, the abolition of many local *octrois* and a decisive shift of the burden on to the wealthy through an increase in income-tax and a new tax on industrial companies. But the opposition was

[1] Coppola d'Anna, p. 85.

[2] Corbino, V, p. 410.

[3] Between 1900–1 and 1907–8 the total of government bonds in foreign hands fell from 1,900 million to 720 million lire, and the interest paid to foreign holders from 76 million to 27 million lire. Giolitti, *Memorie*, p. 251. After 1908–9 this trend was reversed. Nevertheless by 1914 Italians probably held as many foreign government bonds as foreigners held Italian. Nitti, *Il capitale straniero*, pp. 18, 51–2, 71–5.

[4] The winning of French financial support for the conversion had been a major motive behind the *entente* with France which developed between 1896 and 1902. See below, ch. 9.

too great. The most radical step that parliament would tolerate was the abolition of the national (but not local) tax on bread, flour and *pasta*. Many, including Giolitti, had regarded conversion of the national debt as the essential first step. But after 1906, though conversion relieved the exchequer of 20 million lire annually in interest payments, rising after five years to 40 million, expenditure kept on growing and left little room for experiment. The armed forces absorbed nearly one-quarter of revenue throughout the period.[1] Besides armaments, there were the growing needs of education, the post office, public works and the civil service.[2] The budget surpluses trickled away and fiscal reform remained a vague aspiration. In 1907 the duty on paraffin was halved and postage rates were lowered, and in 1910 the tax on sugar was slightly reduced. But Giolitti's proposal of 1909 for a steep rise in income-tax and death duties was stillborn. The taxes on salt, tobacco, coffee and many other widely consumed articles remained extremely high. Indeed the proportion of tax revenue obtained from consumption taxes (53.7%) was greater than ever in the years 1906–10.[3] The basic structure of the fiscal system remained unchanged and the burden on the poorer taxpayer, tolerable while prosperity lasted, again became an acute political problem when less easy times returned.

Public works absorbed growing sums, though a smaller proportion of total expenditure than in previous decades. After nationalisation in 1905, the railways received much attention. Equipment was modernised and the total length of the system increased from 15,670 kilometres in 1901 to over 18,000 in 1914. The electrification of some of the lines leading out of Genoa and Milan marked the beginning of a new era in the history of Italian railways, and the opening of the Simplon tunnel in 1906 brought new traffic from north-western Europe. Between 1896 and 1909 the tonnage of freight carried more than doubled. Though the railways barely succeeded in covering running costs, they reached a high degree of efficiency and made a vital contribution to the expansion of the economy.[4] The ports also received long overdue attention, under legislation of 1907. The number of ships arriving in Italian ports doubled between 1900 and 1913, and Genoa rose to third place, after Marseilles and Barcelona, among the ports of the Mediterranean.[5]

[1] Coppola d'Anna, p. 108.

[2] The number of civil servants increased from 98,000 in 1882 to 166,000 in 1914, and in spite of poor pay their cost more than doubled. Corbino, V, pp. 249, 375.

[3] After falling from 49.5% in 1886–90 to 46.5% in 1896–1900. Coppola d'Anna, p. 102.

[4] Corbino, V, pp. 325–31; *ASI 1919–1921*, p. 507. In later years it became a cliché of admirers of fascism that 'Mussolini made the trains run to time'. With the chaotic conditions of 1918–22 fresh in mind, few remembered that trains had run to time in Giolitti's day.

[5] Corbino, V, pp. 282–3.

After 1908 the financial situation deteriorated. Eleven years of budget surplus ended with a deficit in 1909–10 and the lira lost its parity with gold. The world recession was the main cause. An additional strain arose from the Messina earthquake of 1908,[1] which in six years cost the state 107 million lire in reconstruction, as much as had been spent on land reclamation in forty. In 1911 a new and greater strain was imposed by the conquest of Libya, and before the country had had time to recover its breath, its financial structure had been engulfed by the World War. Not until 1924–5 was the budget again balanced.

Industrial development, limited agricultural progress and financial stability brought greater wealth and greatly improved living conditions for most Italians. *Per capita* national income rose by 28% between 1896–1900 and 1911–15.[2] In many parts of the north, at least, the rural population shared the amelioration which the towns enjoyed. The death rate fell from 26·7 per thousand in 1887–91 to 19·2 in 1910–14;[3] expectation of life at birth (which had been seven years in 1871–5) rose from twenty to thirty-one in the same period.[4] Energetic state action reduced deaths from pellagra from 3,788 in 1900 to 731 in 1914, and those from malaria from 15,865 to 2,042.[5] The consumption of wheat rose from 117 kilograms per head per year in 1896–1900 to 164 in 1909–13, and there was a steep rise in the proportion of income spent on non-essentials, even by the peasantry.[6] Savings banks deposits more than doubled between 1900 and 1913.[7] Illiteracy declined as the number of schools and teachers increased and attendance at school improved. National expenditure on education trebled between 1900 and 1913, though it still represented only 4% of the total. In 1911 only 37·6% of the population over six years of age was unable to read or write, compared with 48·5% in 1901 and 68·8% in 1871.[8] Wages,

[1] See below, p. 323.
[2] *Per capita* national income (in lire, 1938 prices) was:

| 1896–1900 | 1,938 |
| 1901–5 | 2,169 |
| 1906–10 | 2,365 |
| 1911–15 | 2,478 |

*Indagine*, p. 42; Neufeld, p. 538; Romeo, pp. 149–50.
[3] *Sommario*, p. 69.
[4] ibid., p. 54.
[5] *ASI 1904*, pp. 129–31; *ASI 1915*, p. 44. The most effective anti-malaria measures were the provision of cheap quinine and mosquito netting. Pellagra was reduced by the provision of facilities for the proper drying and storage of maize.
[6] Volpe, II, p. 280; Corbino, V, p. 81; Einaudi, p. 12; *ASI 1904*, p. 391; *ASI 1914*, p. 217.
[7] *ASI 1915*, p. 387; *Sommario*, p. 164.
[8] Corbino, V, pp. 7, 375; *ASI 1911*, p. 51; *ASI 1914*, p. 107; Neufeld, p. 523.

which had remained almost stationary since 1880, began to rise after 1900, markedly in industry and slightly also in agriculture. In spite of the rise in prices between 1898 and 1901, and the much more severe rise in 1907–9, real wages increased as a whole over the years from 1899 to 1914. Hours of work were reduced at the same time. Whereas in 1870 a working day of thirteen to fourteen hours was not uncommon, by 1914 ten hours was normal.[1]

In the field of social legislation there was respectable achievement. In 1901 a commission was set up, thanks chiefly to Luzzatti, to protect emigrants. In 1902, and again in 1907, further restrictions were placed on the employment of children in industry and the first regulations for the protection of women were introduced. As a consequence, female industrial labour dropped from 54% of the total in 1903 to 23% in 1911, and juvenile labour from 14% to 10%.[2] Special legislation was passed to protect workers in the tobacco industry and to improve the appalling physical conditions under which 50,000 migrant peasants of both sexes worked annually in the rice fields of Piedmont and Lombardy.[3] The voluntary old age and disability insurance schemes, which dated from 1896, received state assistance. Night baking was made illegal and a weekly holiday of twenty-four consecutive hours, normally on Sunday, was imposed on industry. Some modest public housing schemes were started. Extensive prison reform was carried out. None of this legislation was sensational, but its total effect was not negligible.

Italy was a far happier country in which to live in 1914 than in 1900. It now ranked as one of the industrial nations of Europe. A decade of progress and prosperity generated an uninhibited national pride which found expression in the celebrations of the first fifty years of unity in 1911. Yet Nitti did well to warn his countrymen against the illusion of national greatness. Italy had started so far behind the nations of northern and western Europe that the gap between it and them was still formidable. Its death rate had fallen, but was still the highest in Europe except Spain, Hungary and Russia. *Per capita* income in 1911–13 was still only just over half that of Germany and under one-third that of Britain. The average

[1] Fossati, pp. 422–4, 630–4; Neufeld, p. 540. The index of industrial real wages rose from 76 in 1899 to 100 in 1909 and, after a slight fall, again reached 100 in 1913. Preti (p. 334) estimates that the money wage of the agricultural day labourer in the Po valley, after remaining stationary since 1880, increased by one-third between 1900 and 1915.

[2] Einaudi, p. 6. After 1907 minimum ages were 12 for employment in a factory, 14 for night work and 15 in certain dangerous or unhealthy occupations. Hours of work for children between 12 and 15 were limited to eleven. Night work for women was prohibited and their working day was limited to twelve hours. But there were far too few inspectors to enforce these regulations. Corbino, V, p. 474.

[3] Preti, pp. 286–90.

Italian's daily diet contained 20% fewer calories than that of the average Englishman.[1] Industrially, Italy had still not caught up with even Austria-Hungary, which in 1912 had more cotton spindles in operation, consumed twice as much coal per head of population and produced three times as much steel.[2] Agriculture occupied a far more important place in the national economy of Italy than in that of France, yet France enjoyed an income from agriculture almost double that of Italy. The emigration figures were the clearest index of lack of balance in the economy, while the illiteracy rate, though greatly reduced, gave a dramatic measure of backwardness. Yet with such a fragile material basis, Italy was determined to rank as a Great Power. Within a few years the nation was to conquer a new African colony and plunge into a world war.

## Social Tensions and Organised Labour

As prosperity increased and standards of living rose, the labour movement flourished. Its growth, however, was irregular. After the exuberant expansion of 1901–2, the pace for a time slackened. The resistance of employers stiffened, the unions' successes were fewer and the general strike of 1904 was followed by a period of weary demoralisation. There was a revival in 1906, with a wave of strikes as extensive as in 1901–2, a lull during the depression of 1908–9 and two more lively years in 1911 and 1913.[3] Before 1901 organisation on more than a local level had been confined to the printers, railwaymen and workers in the iron and steel industry, the building trade and state-owned establishments. After 1901 trade unionism took root in most sectors of industry and among the agricultural labourers of the north, while the scale of organisation greatly increased. By the end of 1902 there were 24 national federations of trade unions with a combined membership of 480,000. The main strength of the working-class movement, however, continued to lie in the chambers of labour,

---

[1] Chabod, *L'Italie contemporaine*, p. 16; Coppola d'Anna, p. 67.
[2] The following figures are taken from *The Statesman's Year Book 1914*:
Coal consumption per head of population, 1912, in tons: Russia 0·17, *Italy* 0·28, Austria–Hungary 0·52, France 1·48, Germany 2·12, Belgium 3·35, United Kingdom 3·83.
Number of cotton spindles in operation, 1913, in millions: Belgium 1·5, *Italy* 4·3, Austria–Hungary 4·9, Russia 7·1, France 7·2, Germany 10·4, United Kingdom 49·8.
Steel production, 1912, in millions of tons: *Italy* 0·9, Belgium 2·5, Austria–Hungary 2·6, Russia 3·9, France 4·3, United Kingdom 6·9, Germany and Luxemburg 17·0.
[3] The peak years were 1901 (1,671 strikes and 420,000 strikers), 1907 (2,258 and 576,000), 1911 (1,255 and 386,000) and 1913 (907 and 465,000). Corbino, V, p. 466; *ASI 1919–1921*, p. 512; Neufeld, p. 547.

which increased in number from 19 in July 1900 to 90 in 1904.[1] In 1902 a Central Resistance Secretariat was set up in Milan to coordinate the activities of the two branches of the labour movement. Total membership of labour organisations reached 678,000 in 1907, 817,000 in 1910 and 962,000 in 1914. Yet, impressive though this growth might appear, over 7,000,000 potential members still remained unorganised.[2] Furthermore, nearly two-thirds of the actual membership was concentrated in a small area, within the Turin–Milan–Genoa triangle and among the agricultural population of Piedmont, Lombardy and Emilia.

Powerful agricultural unions were a distinctive feature of the Italian working-class movement. In November 1901 a socialist National Federation of Land Workers (Federterra) was formed at Bologna from 70 provincial and district federations. Within a year it claimed 240,000 members. Though its subsequent career was chequered, its creation was one of the most remarkable feats of organisation in the history of the Italian labour movement.[3] After 1910 the agricultural unions expanded faster than the industrial and by 1913 they had very nearly as many members (469,000). Two-thirds of these were *braccianti*, who stood to gain most from organisation. Collective bargaining, to which employers were obliged to submit, brought higher wages and shorter hours, and narrowed the gap in status and living conditions between the labourer and the rest of the rural population. Agricultural unionism achieved its greatest successes in Lombardy and Emilia. Membership of a mass movement changed the mentality of the *bracciante*, who ceased to feel a pariah at the bottom of the social scale.[4] When, during the syndicalist strike at Parma in 1908, the strikers refused to feed their employers' beasts, it became painfully clear that the *bracciante* was losing his peasant mentality and beginning to think of himself as a worker.

The militancy and success of trade unions forced industrialists and landowners to imitate their example and turn to organisation. A Piedmontese Industrial League was founded in 1906 and four years later a national organisation, the General Confederation of Industry (Confindustria), came into existence. Its aim was to form a united front against the unions, bargain from collective strength, concert counter-strike action and arrange mutual financial assistance among its members. The landowners of the Po valley meanwhile founded a regional association with its headquarters

---

[1] Rigola, *Storia*, pp. 220–1, 228–30; Neufeld, pp. 325 ff.

[2] Einaudi, p. 15; Salomone, p. 54; Salvemini, *Scritti*, pp. 545–6; *ASI 1911*, p. 212; *ASI 1914*, p. 296; Neufeld, p. 351. The highest percentages of organised workers were to be found in the smaller industries. In 1907 only 4·7% of the 503,000 textile workers were organised.

[3] Neufeld, pp. 328–9; Rigola, *Storia*, pp. 230–3; Preti, pp. 211–17.

[4] Serpieri, p. 11.

in Bologna. Among its activities were the drafting of model wage agreements, the provision of help to its members in negotiating with and resisting the unions, the creation of a system of insurance against strike damage, the blacklisting of union leaders and the financing of 'free labour' to be imported from strike-free areas.[1] These efforts bore fruit and the unions had to fight hard for even the most modest gains.

The labour movement was greatly weakened in its struggle by disunity. In addition to the split between socialists, Catholics and independents,[2] the socialist unions were themselves divided between syndicalists and reformists, whose concept of trade unionism had little in common. The syndicalists regarded unions as instruments of direct action for the revolutionary destruction of capitalism; the reformists saw their purpose as the piecemeal improvement of the lot of the worker through disciplined organisation, collective bargaining and controlled strike action. After 1904 the socialist labour movement was rent by internecine conflict. Action at the national level was paralysed, while few local chambers of labour escaped a disruptive struggle for power between passionately hostile factions.

These dissensions had by 1906 reduced the Central Resistance Secretariat to impotence and caused a serious decline in membership. Responsible trade union leaders came to the reluctant conclusion that a formal schism was inevitable. In that year the General Confederation of Labour (C.G.L.) was founded. It embraced both chambers of labour and trade union federations, but found its main strength in the latter. In theory it was non-political, and radicals and republicans as well as socialists gave it their blessing. In practice its politics were those of the moderate socialists and its first secretary, Rinaldo Rigola, was a reformist. It slowly overcame the demoralisation of the years of dissension and increased its membership from 190,000 in 1907 to a peak of 384,000 in 1911.[3] At the height of its power it controlled about one-half of all organised workers. Its leaders concentrated on building up a disciplined, financially sound, central organisation, strong enough to coordinate the policies and actions of its member associations. The C.G.L. reserved to itself the power to call a general strike. It was to be wholly concerned with the economic action of the working-class, political action being the province of the Socialist party. This division of labour, hard to observe in practice, conformed with the

[1] Preti, pp. 218–23. In 1911 a National Confederation of Agriculture was formed, but it failed to operate effectively on a national scale.

[2] In 1914 the distribution of membership was: socialists (reformists and syndicalists) 682,000; Catholics 103,000; independents 176,000. *ASI 1914*, p. 296. Some of the independent unions were truly non-political, others had Mazzinian-republican or anarchist leanings.

[3] Rigola, *Storia*, pp. 332, 367, 410; Salomone, p. 53, note.

decision of the Stuttgart congress of the Second International in 1907. In spite of occasional friction, relations between the C.G.L. and the party remained close and usually cordial.

At the constituent congress of the C.G.L., a minority of syndicalists, anarchists and extreme republicans withheld their support, thus bringing about a formal rupture in the socialist working-class movement. The syndicalists set up their headquarters in Parma and in 1912 formed the Italian Syndicalist Union (U.S.I.), with about 100,000 members. Its leaders believed in a minimum of administration, low membership dues and strike pay, and an almost anarchist reliance upon revolutionary spontaneity. They directed their appeal to the least sophisticated workers and preferred to operate through autonomous chambers of labour, where agitation could produce quick results, rather than through the bureaucratic, slower-moving national federations. While disliking all organisation, they preferred a horizontal pattern to the vertical which the C.G.L. had adopted. The main strength of the U.S.I. lay among the lowest-paid agricultural workers of Emilia, who had been responsible for the bitterest syndicalist strikes in the years 1906–8. It also had a big following among the railwaymen, who in 1913 split into rival reformist and syndicalist unions, and among the merchant seamen of Genoa. The latter were led by an ambitious, demagogic officer of the merchant navy named Giuseppe Giulietti, who succeeded in organising all ranks, from captain to cabin boy, in a single union. In 1913 he won a famous fight for higher wages from the subsidised shipping companies, who then recovered the extra cost from the state.[1] This was only one instance of the syndicalists beating the reformists at their own game by cruder, more forceful methods. The rivalry between C.G.L. and U.S.I. was as a consequence bitter and frequently accompanied by violence.

The concentration of the working-class movement in the north led to a dangerous preoccupation on the part of its leaders with the interests of privileged minorities. This was specially true of the C.G.L. which, as its southern[2] and syndicalist critics pointed out, had become the organ of a labour aristocracy—the workmen in the sheltered industries of Piedmont, Lombardy and Liguria, the *braccianti* of Emilia, the railwaymen and the black-coated workers of the ever-expanding state bureaucracy. The railwaymen obtained a 28% wage increase between 1902 and 1908, and extracted yet another rise in 1911. Schoolteachers, the police, customs officials, post-office employees, workers in the state arsenals, one after another threatened to strike. Their claims were invariably supported by the Socialist party, inside which the black-coated workers exerted growing

---

[1] Einaudi, pp. 22–3; Corbino, V, p. 465.

[2] See above, pp. 270–1, for Salvemini's attack on the reformist leadership.

influence. The Railways Act of 1905 and Giolitti's civil service reform of 1908, which prohibited strikes by state employees under pain of dismissal, limited the powers of the unions. But there were other equally effective ways of exerting pressure. Reformist trade union leaders and socialist deputies were constantly to be seen in ministers' ante-rooms. Just as capitalists fought for subsidies, tariffs, contracts and toleration by the state of monopolistic prices and profits, so the unions fought for social legislation, subsidised employment or toleration of monopolistic wages. Both competed for a share of the pork barrel, or even combined in tacit alliance to support each other's claims. In either case it was the taxpayer and the unorganised, unprivileged consumer who paid the price.

To the syndicalists, the most heinous feature of this situation was the undermining of class solidarity. The privileged minority developed a bourgeois mentality and a vested interest in capitalism, and the humble mass of the working-class was betrayed. The facts on which they based these denunciations could hardly be denied. Governments gladly appeased the most vocal and best-organised sections of the working-class. Nothing pleased Giolitti more than to see workers and peasants acquiring a stake in society. Northern socialists and trade unionists were therefore encouraged to cultivate their own little gardens, rather than worry about ideals and principles. Reformist collusion with both employers and the state was open and continuous. Sometimes governments even forced concessions on employers in the interest of public order. In 1913, for instance, the government threatened the Turin Industrial League with the deportation of its president, a French citizen, if it refused to concede a shorter working day in the motor-car industry.[1] Sometimes the cost of such concessions was paid by the state. Firms in their turn might dismiss workmen and create unemployment merely in order to extract favours from the government. Such manœuvres became in time an accepted part of the political game.

The Catholic labour movement developed more slowly than either the socialist or syndicalist, and along distinctive lines of its own. Its growth was hindered by prolonged controversy within the Opera as to whether unions that did not contain both employers and employees could be recognised. Inter-class cooperation was at the heart of Catholic social teaching and it was not until after 1900 that pure workers' organisations were reluctantly accepted by the leadership. But 'white' peasants' and workers' associations multiplied in spite of official discouragement. Their most militant champion was a young man named Guido Miglioli, who wished to imitate socialist organisation and tactics and to abandon all inhibition against use of the strike. Sturzo, too, favoured the development

[1] Einaudi, pp. 22–3; Corbino, V, p. 465.

of a vigorous trade union movement. But in 1904 Pius X imposed a sharp check. A confessional test of membership was enforced, Catholics were enjoined to keep out of chambers of labour, and all association between Catholic and non-Catholic organisations was forbidden. In spite of discouragement from above, the movement had by 1914 won a foothold beside the C.G.L. and the syndicalists, both in agriculture and in industry, and claimed about 100,000 members, roughly one-eighth of all organised workers.[1] Officially the Catholics professed class collaboration and renounced violence, though they did not rule out the strike as a last resort. Occasionally they worked in tacit collaboration with the socialists, but were more often distrusted, sometimes with justification, as blacklegs and tools of the landowners.[2] It was their persistent grievance that they received less favourable treatment from the state than the C.G.L., and one of their main aims was to win parity of status.

The keenest supporters of the Catholic social movement were artisans rather than factory workers, and small proprietors, peasant tenants and sharecroppers rather than agricultural labourers. Catholic doctrine, with its advocacy of fair rents and just wages, its emphasis on both the blessings and the responsibilities of property, and its condemnation of usury, appealed most to those who had a modest stake in society and wished to improve it. The Catholic organisations did excellent work in securing less onerous leases for tenants and sharecroppers, and in protecting the small farmer against pressure from both his landlord above and the organised labourers below. They built up a network of insurance and mutual benefit societies, cooperatives, local savings banks providing cheap credit and farmers' unions for the purchase of tools, materials and fertilisers. This complex of institutions, together with the peasants' and trade unions, was closely controlled by the Economic and Social Union of Catholic Action, and priests played a leading part in all of them. In 1912 they claimed a joint membership of 346,000, of whom 70% were to be found in Lombardy and Venetia. In the south only Sicily made a significant contribution.[3]

The socialists, by contrast, found their rural supporters among the labourers, the only section of the agricultural population to which the idea of land nationalisation appealed. This item of the party's maximum programme, though supported by economic arguments against splitting the land into small holdings, sprang primarily from dogmatic conviction. The

---

[1] In 1914 about three-fifths of the 100,000 were peasants (mainly in Lombardy and Venetia) and two-fifths industrial workers (railwaymen and textile workers in particular). Neufeld, p. 358.

[2] Preti, p. 225.

[3] C. Torricelli, 'Le organizzazioni dei cattolici in Italia', in *Nuova Antologia*, vol. 69 (January 1914), pp. 129-37; Vercesi, *Il movimento cattolico*, pp. 250-3.

peasant proprietor was a class enemy. His mere existence obstructed the proletarianisation of the peasantry which Marxists believed was both inevitable and necessary for progress. Sharecropping was equally an object of suspicion, particularly in Tuscany and Emilia, where its most successful variety, *mezzadria*, was to be found. The *bracciante* resented the *mezzadro*'s reliance upon his own family and his reluctance to employ paid labour. The fact that he had a stake in his farm and felt affection for his house and animals made him chary of risking eviction by quarrelling with his landlord. Even when he could be persuaded to strike, he would often work secretly by night, thus sabotaging proletarian solidarity. In theory, therefore, socialists marked down both *mezzadro* and peasant proprietor for ultimate destruction.

In practice the socialists were constantly driven to compromise. Nationalisation of the land remained in the maximum programme, but defence of the interests of sharecroppers, small tenants and even peasant proprietors became an acceptable part of the democratic minimum programme. In areas where the socialist unions were weak, they found it tactically necessary to woo the *mezzadro*. The motive might be to win extra socialist votes in local elections, or to intimidate the landlords by presenting a united front. Often they succeeded in persuading the *mezzadro* that he too was exploited, and were able to extract concessions from proprietors on his behalf. After 1906 it was the official policy of the reformist Federterra to sponsor sharecroppers' organisations, integrate them with the labourers' unions and jointly promote the demands of both. Over large parts of the Po valley this policy was successful.[1]

It was not always easy, however, to resolve the conflicts of interest within the peasant community. Friction arose from the fact that the *mezzadri* who were initially better off than the *braccianti*, tended to gain the major share of the benefits of collaboration. Moreover, though the socialist unions might reconcile themselves to the existence of *mezzadria* and peasant proprietorship, they were determined to prevent the spread of these institutions. There was, indeed, danger of this. The individual *bracciante* rarely lost his yearning for a piece of land of his own. Catholics, republicans and conservatives talked much of satisfying this aspiration and turning the labourer, the most explosive element in the countryside, into a contented member of society. The growing power of the unions forced some proprietors to translate their social theories into practice. In the hope of stemming the socialist tide, they put more capital into their estates, built roads and houses to facilitate the settlement of *mezzadri* and tenants, and even helped peasants to buy small plots of land. This development threatened the *braccianti* collectively because it reduced the demand for paid

[1] Preti, pp. 248–55, 263–72.

casual labour. The reformist unions reacted to the challenge by redoubling their efforts at integration. The syndicalists, by contrast, tended to adopt an intransigent 'proletarian' line and emphasise the clash of interest. Sometimes the latent hostility and suspicion erupted in open warfare.

The most important conflict between *mezzadri* and *braccianti* occurred in the Romagna in 1910, when a bitter quarrel broke out over the ownership and control of threshing machines. The ambition of the labourers' unions was to establish a monopoly of threshing throughout the region for the machines owned by their cooperatives. The *mezzadri* resisted, being determined to keep their own machines and man them by reciprocal exchange of labour amongst themselves. This was no dispute arising out of economic misery, but a struggle between two relatively privileged sections of the agricultural community. The hot tempers of the Romagna added to the bitterness and there was much violence. The proprietors backed the *mezzadri*, while the *braccianti* enjoyed the support not only of all the revolutionaries of Romagna, anarchist, socialist and syndicalist, but also of the whole Socialist party which passed a resolution of solidarity at its congress in October. The struggle ended in victory for the *mezzadri*, who kept their machines, but not before Luzzatti's government had been forced to send in troops to suppress the violence. As a result of this conflict the *mezzadri*, whose political loyalties had always been republican, broke away entirely from the socialist unions, taking with them a substantial minority of *braccianti*. From 1910 the working-class movement in the Romagna was split between mutually hostile 'red' and 'yellow' unions, cooperatives and chambers of labour.[1] This antagonism had important political consequences in the post-war years.

Emilia was the region of Italy where class organisation was furthest developed and where political and social tension was sharpest. Nowhere else had organised labour acquired such power; indeed it dominated the economic life of many parts of the region. The bases of this power were tightly organised unions, a network of consumers' and producers' cooperatives, both industrial and agricultural, labour exchanges which controlled the supply of casual labour, and a growing number of local councils with socialist majorities. Emilia contained centres of syndicalism like Parma and Ferrara, and towns with a revolutionary tradition like Forlì, where Mussolini began his political career. But Reggio Emilia and Molinella were more typical: two reformist strongholds which had risen to prominence under gifted leaders, Prampolini and Massarenti, who combined idealism with practical business sense and organising ability. Their success constituted a formidable threat to private enterprise. Perhaps most remarkable of all were the labour cooperatives. The first had been founded in 1886 by

[1] Preti, pp. 255–63.

another reformist, Nullo Baldini, at Ravenna. After 1900 they spread to many parts of the Po valley. These cooperatives bought or leased derelict land, drained and improved it, then cultivated it as a business enterprise, sometimes subletting plots to their members, sometimes managing a large estate as a collective farm. Their organisers felt justifiably proud of their success in turning unskilled *braccianti* into intelligent, enterprising co-operators. Ravenna became a socialist showpiece and gave birth to a powerful mystique of cooperation.

The main task of the Emilian working-class movement was to fight unemployment. The schemes of land reclamation round Mantua, Ferrara and Ravenna were mostly finished by 1905. Even though the area of cultivation had been greatly extended, there was no hope of finding full-time employment on the land for all the thousands of labourers whom these schemes had attracted into the region, particularly from the mountains. It was therefore necessary both to create jobs and to distribute them as fairly as possible. Jobs were created by constant pressure upon the government to finance public works, to be carried out if possible by labour cooperatives. The socialist party and C.G.L. pursued this policy with much success, particularly after 1911 when unemployment became a threat to public order. In 1913 the government promoted through the Banca d'Italia an institution, originally inspired by Luzzatti, for the supply of credit to cooperatives. In the same year a large sum was allocated to public works with the motive, officially avowed for the first time, of relieving unemployment.[1] The fair distribution of work was enforced through the unions' labour exchanges. They kept records of every hour's work by each of their members, and forced proprietors or *mezzadri* who applied for casual labour to accept the next man on their roster. This system, known as the *turno di lavoro*, was intended to destroy the employer's freedom to select his own labour and dictate his own price.[2] The extent to which this monopolistic control could be enforced varied greatly from province to province, but by 1914 there were large areas of Emilia and lower Lombardy where, with the tolerance of the government, the labour movement had created oases of socialism within capitalist society.

The landowners did not accept so humiliating a position without protest. Following the example of industrialists, they improved their own organisation, developed effective methods of united resistance[3] and after 1911 counter-attacked vigorously. Renewed attempts were made to weaken the unions by transforming *braccianti* into more docile tenants or *mezzadri*. Strikes grew more bitter and prolonged. The use of blacklegs, often escorted by police or troops, led to much violence, and in parts of Emilia

[1] Einaudi, p. 23; Volpe, III, pp. 515–16.     [2] Preti, pp. 231–5.
[3] See above, pp. 298–9.

unofficial 'volunteers for the freedom of labour' made their appearance.
They were the precursors of agrarian fascism.[1] High unemployment, which
reached 50% to 80% in some places, aided the counter-offensive. But Red
Week in June 1914[2] showed both the power of the organised working-class
and the spirit of rebellion that lay below the surface. Emilia was destined
to play an unhappy role in the post-war years.

## The South

The opening years of the century saw the beginning of the great debate on
the Southern question, which sixty years later shows no sign of ending.
The basic facts about the south had been known to a restricted circle for
over twenty years,[3] but they now began to reach a wider public. Geog-
raphers and anthropologists, historians and sociologists, economists and
agrarian experts all produced their diagnoses: climate, lack of water, racial
inferiority, centuries of misgovernment, exploitation by northern industry
or small-minded politicians. The remedies they proposed were no less
various: irrigation, public works, tax relief, abolition of industrial tariffs,
regional autonomy, local self-government, universal suffrage. The variety
of their recommendations was in itself a true reflection of the complexity
of the south's problems.

One of the most widely read writers was Francesco Saverio Nitti, a
young radical economist of Naples University and a native of Basilicata.
His ambition was to strengthen Italian unity by bringing into the open
facts about the south whose suppression had already done great harm. He
did not deny that the south had made huge progress since 1861. But he
claimed to prove that, if the south had progressed, the north had progressed
much more, and the gap between them had widened. Indeed, he argued,
the progress of the north was founded in part on the sacrifices and 'colonial'
exploitation of the south, which had not only contributed more to the
state, proportionately to its wealth, than the north but had also received
less in the form of state expenditure.[4] Though his statistics have been

---

[1] 'The blackleg was the father of the *squadrista*, or the *squadrista* himself',
justly observes Ansaldo, p. 242.

[2] See below, pp. 393–4.                    [3] See above, p. 87.

[4] Nitti, *Nord e Sud, passim*, but especially pp. 2–13, 81–3; and *L'Italia all' alba
del secolo XX*, pp. 107–8, 124. In *La ricchezza dell' Italia*, p. 130, Nitti gives the
following figures (in lire) for (*a*) per capita tax contribution and (*b*) per capita expenditure by the state, in selected regions about 1900:

|                     | (*a*)  | (*b*)  |
|---------------------|--------|--------|
| Piedmont            | 34·99  | 29·71  |
| Liguria             | 52·71  | 71·15  |
| Basilicata          | 18·55  | 8·77   |
| Calabria            | 18·54  | 11·26  |
| Abruzzi and Molise  | 17·92  | 8·64   |

criticised and many of his conclusions shown to be exaggerated, the substance of his argument has long since won wide acceptance. The achievement of Nitti and his generation of *meridionalisti* was to make the nation
aware of the regional maldistribution of the nation's wealth, just at the
moment when, under the impact of the nascent labour movement, it was
becoming aware of the maldistribution between classes. The problem of
the south was recognised as only one part of the economic and social
problem of the whole nation.

The relative poverty of the south was easily demonstrated. Its *per capita*
income in 1900 was just under one-half that of the north. It contained 40%
of the population of Italy, yet in 1911 its total consumption of industrial
power was only just larger than Piedmont's.[1] In most branches of agriculture, too, it lagged far behind. Wheat yields of 3 to 5 quintals per hectare
were common, and even in the best years the national average of 10·5 was
rarely achieved. Mortality and housing statistics tell the same story. In
1910–14 the national death rate was 19·2 per thousand inhabitants; but for
the south the lowest rate was 19·7 in Calabria, the highest 22·6 in Basilicata.[2] Whereas in 1911 less than 1% of the population of Genoa, Florence
and Leghorn lived in one room, in Bari the figure was 42% (with an average
of 4·7 persons per room) and in Foggia 70·5% (six inhabitants per room).[3]

The illiteracy rate increased steadily from north to south. In 1911 it was
11% in Piedmont, 37% in Tuscany, 54% in Campania, 65% in Basilicata
and 70% in Calabria, Sicily showing some improvement with 58%. The
national average was 37·6%.[4] The remoter communes of the south could
show rates of up to 90%. The shortage of schools was scandalous. In
1907–8 Piedmont with 3·4 million inhabitants had 9,000 schools, Sicily
with 3·6 millions had 5,000.[5] Many of the southern schools that did exist
were insanitary hovels without heat or light, and huge numbers of children
of school age stayed away. In 1907–8 Sicily had the best attendance rate
in the south (57%) and Calabria the worst (40%), compared with the
national average of 75%.[6] In education, as in agricultural and industrial
development, the south was slipping behind.

It was the contention of the *meridionalisti* that the state's policy since
unification had aggravated the disparity. Since 1887 the tariff system had
forced the south to buy its manufactures dear and sell its agricultural

---

[1] Arias, II, p. 199; *ASI 1913*, pp. 156–9. One half of the south's industrial power
was concentrated in one region, Campania.

[2] Arias, I, p. 335; *ASI 1916*, p. 32.                           [3] Arias, II, pp. 147–8.

[4] Corbino, V, p. 7; Arias, II, p. 512; Neufeld, p. 523; *ASI 1913*, pp. 74–5. The
illiteracy rate here given is the percentage of the population over six years of age
which was unable to read or write.

[5] Salvemini, *Scritti*, pp. 443–4, 490; *ASI 1911*, p. 54.

[6] Corbino, V, p. 6; Arias, I, pp. 455–6, II, pp. 493–7.

produce cheap. A system of taxation which had been framed to fit northern conditions had been extended to the rest of Italy indiscriminately after 1861. For instance, before 1906 the exemption from tax of agricultural buildings did not apply to most of the south, where the peasantry lived in villages and towns, not scattered over the countryside. As a consequence, in 1900 15% of the population paid the buildings tax in the south, compared with 6% in the north and centre.[1] Indirect taxes hit the poorest hardest, and therefore the poorer south harder than the richer north. Moreover, tax evasion was easier and more frequent in the north, where a smaller proportion of income came from real property. A striking index of the harshness of the fiscal system is provided by the statistics for the seizure of property for non-payment of taxes. Between 1885 and 1897 there was one expropriation per 27,416 inhabitants in Lombardy, one per 5,435 in Emilia, one per 900 in Apulia and one per 114 in Calabria.[2] Fortunato was not exaggerating when he condemned the system of taxation as 'regionally progressive in reverse'.

And yet the state spent more freely in the richer north. To a great extent this was inevitable. Defence expenditure, for example, which included much road, railway and port construction, had to be directed towards the northern frontiers. But the south had a just grievance over land reclamation and improvement. The southern taxpayer had helped to pay for the reclamation schemes of Lombardy and Emilia, while the south had been shamefully neglected. In education there was an even greater anomaly. Because the state did not build new schools, but subsidised those that were built by local authorities, it was the richer communes, which could afford to build, that got most of the money. Between 1889 and 1898 Apulia, the richest of the southern regions, received less than half the *per capita* educational subsidy that went to Piedmont, and substantially less than any northern region; the poorer parts of the south received even less.[3] As Nitti put it, over much of the south the state was as absentee as the landlords;[4] yet the south had deserved more attention just because it was poorer and more deficient in private initiative, and could offer a smaller return on capital investment. Action had been inhibited in the past by the stubborn belief that special treatment for the south would undermine national unity.[5] In the new century opinion changed. Under the influence of Nitti

[1] Nitti, *Nord e Sud*, pp. 60–5; Vöchting, pp. 124–5.

[2] Nitti, *Nord e Sud*, pp. 192–5, *L'Italia all' alba*, p. 143, and *La ricchezza*, p. 205; G. Carano-Donvito, *L'economia meridionale prima e dopo il Risorgimento* (Florence 1928), p. 158.

[3] Nitti, *Nord e Sud*, pp. 104–7; Salvemini, *Scritti*, pp. 74, 446–7.

[4] Nitti, *Nord e Sud*, p. 8.

[5] For instance Crispi, who carried his belief in unity to fanatical lengths, declared in 1890, 'We cannot do more for one province than we are doing and can do for the others.' Zingali, I, p. 184.

and the *meridionalisti*, there was a growing demand that the state should intervene.

Popular interest in the south at the turn of the century was further stimulated by a series of scandals and trials, two of which deserve mention. In 1902 a Sicilian deputy, Raffaele Palizzolo, who was notoriously connected with the Mafia, was sentenced to thirty years' imprisonment for ordering the murder seven years previously of a senator, former Mayor of Palermo and director of the Bank of Sicily, Emanuele Notarbartolo, who had proved a fearless enemy of corruption in both banking and municipal politics. A sensation was caused by the evidence which emerged during the trial of the Mafia's power to terrorise, obstruct justice and penetrate the state machine. The second trial concerned Alberto Casale, who had been returned unopposed for eight years by a Neapolitan constituency. In 1900 he was denounced by Arturo Labriola's newspaper, *La Propaganda*, for being a leader of the city's Camorra and for living on the proceeds of municipal corruption. Casale sued *La Propaganda* for libel, lost his case and resigned his seat in parliament and on the city council. Once again public opinion was amazed by the picture of a great city riddled with corruption and ruled by organised intimidation, often with the connivance of agents of the government.

The Casale trial led to the appointment of a royal commission on Naples. Its chairman, Giuseppe Saredo, a Ligurian senator and president of the Council of State, soon discovered that 'almost all the communes of the province of Naples . . . are in the grip of associations of delinquents'.[1] The revelations of his report, which Giolitti insisted should be published in full, provoked the first thorough parliamentary debate on the south since unification. Zanardelli's speech of 13 December 1901, which promised special legislation, marked the official recognition that Italy was confronted with a national, not a regional, problem, which neither time nor inaction would solve. Indeed, as Luzzatti pointed out, Italy's future depended upon the future of the south; unless its problems were solved, it would impoverish the rest of the nation. In September 1902 Zanardelli at the age of seventy-six made a two weeks' voyage of exploration to Basilicata, 'Italy's Ireland'. He returned appalled by what he had seen – depopulation, deforestation, malaria, illiteracy, misery. Twenty-one communes in Basilicata, he discovered, had no road fit for wheels. At the small town of Moliterno he was greeted by the mayor in the name of eight thousand citizens, 'three thousand of whom are in America and the other five thousand are preparing

---

[1] *Quarant' anni*, II, 1. As a result of the enquiry, Casale and twenty-six others were put on trial for corruption and sentenced to periods of imprisonment of up to three years.

to follow them'.[1] The mere sight of a Prime Minister in that abandoned land created a sensation. On his return Zanardelli appealed eloquently for moral unity and fraternal cooperation to redeem the south.[2] This time speeches were not all; action, however inadequate, was soon to follow.

Zanardelli did not live to see his promises translated into action, but Giolitti took over his programme. 'To raise the economic conditions of the southern provinces is not only a political necessity, but a national duty', he declared in his first parliamentary speech as Prime Minister in December 1903.[3] Next year parliament passed special laws for Basilicata and Naples, and similar measures for Calabria and Sardinia followed a few years later. The purpose of this special legislation was to encourage industrialisation and agricultural improvement, mainly by reducing taxation and increasing expenditure on public works. Meanwhile Sonnino, during his first hundred days of power in 1906, introduced a more ambitious bill, which applied not to a single region but to the whole south. It was concerned less with public works than with raising the standard of agriculture and remedying the grosser forms of fiscal injustice. He fell before his bill became law, but Giolitti incorporated large parts of it in a bill of his own which passed through parliament in July 1906.

The attempts at industrialisation concentrated on Naples. A special zone was created east of the city in which new industry enjoyed ten years' exemption from taxation and customs duties. Funds were allocated for the improvement of the port and the city was given a monopoly of hydro-electric power from the river Volturno. These measures were not without effect. By 1910 the industrial zone contained 88 new factories, including important engineering works and two modern cotton mills which thrived on exports to the Balkans and the Levant. Between 1903 and 1910 goods traffic through the port of Naples grew by 63%, a rate of increase greater than that of any northern port. Even so, though Naples benefited from the influx of capital and the creation of new employment, industrialisation proved more difficult than the optimists had forecast. The big firms that established themselves did not supply the necessary stimulus to general industrial growth. Lack of skilled labour and managerial ability, distance from markets and sources of supply, and the absence of an enterprising commercial middle class, largely outweighed the special privileges. The gap between north and south continued to widen. In 1911 the southern mainland, with 25·6% of the population of Italy, still contained only

---

[1] Sereni, p. 394.

[2] Cilibrizzi, III, pp. 193–203.

[3] Giolitti, *Discorsi parlamentari*, II, p. 759. In November 1903 Giolitti wrote to Nitti, who had appealed to him to tackle 'the resurrection of the south': 'I believe it [the Southern question] is a national question, perhaps the greatest of all.' *Quarant' anni*, II, 581–2.

9·8% of those working in factories with more than ten employees, while over 65% of the factories employing more than 100 persons were concentrated in four regions of the north. Southern industry remained on a small scale and tied to artisan labour. The economic life of the south had hardly been touched.[1]

The public works programme included roads and minor railways, village water supplies, inland waterways, flood control, reafforestation, and the building of schools and houses. The two largest projects were a direct main railway line along the coast from Rome to Naples[2] and the Apulian aqueduct. The latter, after being discussed since 1869, was at last started in 1906. The plan was to bring drinking water from the source of the river Sele, high on the western slope of the Apennines, to a population of two and a half millions in waterless Apulia. This involved building 150 miles of main aqueduct, two long tunnels through the Apennines and another 1,500 miles of subsidiary pipes and channels. By 1915 the water had reached Bari and the main towns, though the network was not completed until fifteen years later. The aqueduct was one of the most beneficial projects undertaken in Italy between unification and fascism.[3]

Another successful enterprise, of incalculable benefit to the south, was the campaign against malaria. Under a law of 1901, cheap quinine was provided and funds were allocated for making houses mosquito-proof in areas classified as malarial. The effect was remarkable. In 1900–2 the annual death rate from malaria was 183·7 per 100,000 inhabitants in Basilicata, the most malarial region of Italy, and 26·5 in Campania, the least malarial region of the south; in 1912–14 the respective death rates had fallen to 25·6 and 3·3.[4] The record with regard to another scourge of the south, illiteracy, was less creditable. The Credaro law of 1911 established the principle that the state should pay for the building and maintenance of all new schools, including teachers' salaries; but the funds it set aside for the purpose were too meagre to bring about any rapid improvement.[5]

The rehabilitation of agriculture was a task as formidable as the conquest of illiteracy. Giolitti's bill of 1906, which was based on Sonnino's proposals, gave the south substantial tax relief. The land tax on assessments below

---

[1] Arias, I, pp. 206–11, II, pp. 200–3; Vöchting, pp. 220–3; Corbino, V, p. 100; Romeo, pp. 78–80; Neufeld, pp. 307–8, 534. Piedmont, Liguria and Lombardy together possessed 35·4% of Italy's industrial population in 1901, 38·9% in 1911. The south's share of labour employed in the iron and steel and engineering industries fell from 22·1% in 1903 to 18·4% in 1911.

[2] Completed only in 1927.

[3] Vöchting, pp. 198–202; Corbino, V, pp. 261–3; article in *Enciclopedia Italiana*, I, pp. 407–10.

[4] Vöchting, p. 31. The rate for the whole country fell from 40·3 to 7·4. The final elimination of malaria had to await the discovery of DDT in the 1940s.

[5] Arias, II, p. 497; Salvemini, *Scritti*, pp. xxi–xxii, 448–51.

6,000 lire a year was reduced by 30%, agricultural buildings were exempted even where located in towns, and concessions were made to reafforested or reclaimed land. Much of the benefit went to landowners rather than to the peasantry;[1] yet the fact remains that over a decade the south's share of direct taxation dropped from 21·4% to 16·5%.[2] Another beneficial measure was the reduction in 1903 of railway freight charges for southern wine and agricultural produce. But most of the hopes of agricultural improvement were disappointed. The funds for providing cheap credit were too limited to free the peasant from the tyranny of the usurer. Technical education never took root. A negligible amount of land was irrigated, reclaimed or improved. Legislation proved incapable of increasing the number of small peasant proprietors. Sonnino had intended to give protection to tenants and sharecroppers by state regulation of rents and leases, but Giolitti shelved this part of his bill. Instead, a parliamentary commission was appointed to enquire into the conditions of the southern peasant. Its report, published in 1910–11 in sixteen volumes, contained a wealth of information; but like Jacini's enquiry of thirty years before, it was read by few except experts and research students, and acted upon by none.

Of all the varied phenomena which made up the Southern question, few attracted more public attention or showed greater resistance to change than the *latifondo*. There was no mystery about what was wrong. Great areas of the south were devoted to low-grade cereals and pasture, cultivated extensively by the most primitive methods. Most of the proprietors of the *latifondi* were absentees. With the demand for land far exceeding supply, the landowner or his agent could impose almost any terms they fancied on peasant tenants, in annual or very short leases. All the risks of production were thrust downwards. The owner had no incentive to invest capital or raise productivity: he could just sit back and collect the rents. The import duty on wheat was a further disincentive to innovation or improvement. But it was an illusion that the *latifondo* could be abolished by legislation. It needed more than paper restrictions on the size of estates, or even the provision of credit for the purchase of small plots of land, to create a mass of new peasant proprietors and transform the desolate *latifondi* into smiling orchards and vineyards.[3] Such transformations did indeed occur in the immediate neighbourhood of towns. But in a desolate countryside lacking roads, houses and water, the small proprietor without capital was helpless. He soon gave up the fight and the *latifondo*, the natural economic

[1] Salvemini condemned Sonnino's programme as one of 'political and social conservatism in favour of the great southern landowners' and 'a ruinous programme for the southern proletariat'. *Scritti*, p. 191.

[2] Zingali, I, pp. 315–16.

[3] Crispi's abortive bill of 1894 (see above, p. 169), was a good example of this superficial approach to the problem.

unit, reasserted itself. The first modest change in these conditions occurred with the return of emigrants from America with savings in their pockets.[1] But they only touched the fringes of the problem. Until a massive supply of capital could be found and poured into the south, the *latifondo* remained, in Fortunato's words, 'an almost irreducible economic and technical necessity'.[2]

Lack of capital was, indeed, the main reason for the persistence of a Southern question. The south had no enterprising urban middle class which was prepared to invest in land. There were few attractions for foreign capital. The burden therefore fell upon the limited resources of the state. The exigencies of the national budget made it necessary to spread expenditure over many years, so that quick results were impossible. At a conservative estimate, investment ten times as great was required to make an impact. But even within the limits set by orthodox finance, funds were not always well spent. Progress was hampered by shortage of skilled technicians, by bureaucratic obstruction and by the bankruptcy of many of the local authorities which were required to share the financial burden. Some public works schemes were started from political motives: those who shouted loudest and had most electoral influence got the money. The executive machinery was often deficient, and the experiment of appointing a regional commissioner for Basilicata was not pursued with enough courage. After twenty years, less than one-third of the public works authorised for Basilicata had been completed. It was not surprising that champions of the south like Fortunato condemned the special laws as intermittent philanthropy, 'a niggardly, breadcrumb policy'. Sonnino compared them to a glass of water offered to a feverish man: they merely relieved some of the symptoms of the underlying disease.[3]

If the condition of the rural south did nevertheless improve between 1900 and 1914, this was due much less to action by governments than to emigration, a phenomenon for which governments could claim no credit. Year by year the number of emigrants from Italy grew, checked only momentarily by the slump of 1907–8 and the Libyan war of 1911, until in 1913 the peak of 873,000 was reached.[4] No other country except Ireland could show an exodus on so dramatic a scale. The south's share grew steadily from one-quarter of the total in the 1880s to just under one-half

[1] See below, pp. 316–17.
[2] Caizzi, pp. 62–8; Arias, II, pp. 99–104; Valenti, *Il latifondo* (1895), reprinted in Romano, *Storia della questione meridionale*, pp. 383–8.
[3] U. Zanotti-Bianco, *Un esperimento di decentramento amministrativo*, reprinted in Caizzi, pp. 447–62; Fortunato, *Pagine e ricordi parlamentari*, II, p. 10.
[4] The following figures are taken from *Sommario*, p. 65; *ASI 1911*, p. 22; *ASI 1913*, pp. 40, 429. See also Arias, I, tables at end of volume; Zingali, I, pp. 114–15;

between 1905 and 1913. With this shift to the south came a change in the character of the movement. Emigration from the north and centre was mostly of a short-term, even seasonal, character and directed chiefly to northern Europe; emigration from the south was of a long-term, sometimes permanent character and directed across the Atlantic.[1] After 1898 North America replaced Brazil and the Argentine as the most popular destination, and over three of the eight millions who left Italy between 1901 and 1913 went to the U.S.A. Even in the case of transatlantic emigrants, however, the proportion of those who left for good was falling. Out of every 100 emigrants, 40 returned in the years 1897–1901 and 68 in 1911–13.[2] It has been calculated that between 1862 and 1913 the net permanent loss to Italy was 4·5 million persons.[3]

The exodus from the south had started in Basilicata, Calabria and Campania in the 1880s, and spread to the Abruzzi soon afterwards. At the turn of the century the stream became a flood. Sicily joined in later, but took the lead in total numbers after 1904. The only region of the south with a rate lower than the national average was Apulia.[4] Southern emigration was a truly proletarian phenomenon, a spontaneous act of protest against intolerable conditions. It started in the plains and along the coasts, where contact with the outside world was easier, then spread inland, reaching a peak of intensity in the remoter, mountainous areas where poverty

---

Foerster, pp. 7–10; Coletti, pp. 32–48. The official figures are certainly underestimates. On this point see Foerster, pp. 10–21, and Coletti, pp. 1–19.

*Number of emigrants in thousands:*

|  | (i) To Europe and Mediterranean | (ii) Overseas | (iii) Total (i) & (ii) | (iv) Percentage of (iii) from south | (v) Percentage of (ii) from south |
|---|---|---|---|---|---|
| 1891–1900 ⎫ annual | 129 | 154 | 283 | 32% (1887–1900) | 54% |
| 1901–5 ⎬ averages | 245 | 309 | 554 ⎫ 47% | 74% |
| 1906–10 ⎭ | 258 | 394 | 651 ⎭ | 71% |
| 1911 | 271 | 263 | 534 | 38% ⎫ | |
| 1912 | 308 | 403 | 711 | — ⎬ | 69% |
| 1913 | 313 | 560 | 873 | 47% ⎭ | (1911–14) |

[1] In 1913 64% of all Italian emigrants, but 90% of southern emigrants, went across the Atlantic.

[2] Foerster, pp. 28, 32, 42; Coletti, pp. 74–7. Foerster estimated that about two-thirds of the total emigration (and at least nine-tenths of emigration to Europe) was temporary, and that from 1901 to 1913 between 300,000 and 400,000 emigrants returned annually to Italy.

[3] Coppola d'Anna, pp. 20–1; Foerster, p. 42.

[4] In 1909–13 1·96% of the total population of Italy emigrated annually. Percentages for the regions of the south were: Abruzzi 3·3%, Calabria 3·3%, Basilicata 2·9%, Sicily 2·6%, Campania 2%, Apulia 1·4%. Vöchting, p. 246; *ASI 1914*, p. 68.

was greatest. The larger towns were affected relatively little.[1] A few emigrants were artisans, but the vast majority were peasants and unskilled labourers. Those who owned property or enjoyed security of tenure were more reluctant to go. Four-fifths of the emigrants were males, mainly between the ages of twenty and fifty. Villages could be found in the remoter districts which were inhabited almost entirely by old men, women and children. It was this drain of youthful energy to foreign lands that embittered the nationalists and inspired their concept of Italy as the proletarian nation.[2]

The state was slow to recognise its responsibility to emigrants, preferring for many decades to leave their welfare to private organisations or to the church. But in 1901 this *laisser faire* attitude was abandoned. Legislation was passed to protect credulous peasants from speculators, shipping companies or the recruiting agents of foreign industry. A commissariat was created under the Foreign Ministry to provide inspectors in the ports and on the emigrant ships, to regulate fares and keep an eye on labour contracts. In later years extra consular officials were appointed overseas to provide information about employment. Special facilities were provided in the Banco di Napoli for the transmission to Italy of emigrants' remittances. Even so, the lot of the emigrant in the new world was usually grim. The labour treaties that were negotiated with the governments of receiving countries, to ensure minimum standards of employment, made little practical difference. The vast majority of Italians in the Americas found work in building, in road and railway construction and as unskilled factory labourers.[3] New York and the great cities were the Meccas that attracted them; but once there, most would live in ghettos, hardly mixing with non-Italians, spending little and saving and remitting as much as was humanly possible. About half would return within five years, and a slump like that of 1907 caused a stampede back to Italy. Such behaviour earned them little respect in their adopted country, where they were regarded as temporary birds of passage and second-class citizens. This situation, too, provided ammunition for the nationalists.

Emigration, however, brought undoubted blessings to the south. It provided a safety valve by drawing off surplus labour from the land, thus performing the function which in the north was performed by industrialisation. In spite of a rising population and a stagnant rural economy, emigration saved the south from a recurrence of the explosions of 1893 and 1898.[4]

---

[1] Coletti, pp. 205–13.       [2] See below, p. 352.

[3] In 1908–13 76% of the emigrants returning from the U.S.A. were still unskilled labourers. Foerster, p. 41.

[4] It is significant that the syndicalist leaders, many of whom were southerners, had to move north to find an audience responsive to their preaching of violence.

Wages rose, by very varying amounts according to local conditions.[1] Landowners were given an incentive to mechanise or to switch from grain to
more profitable crops. Some sold land to small proprietors who cultivated
it more intensively. In these ways the standard of agriculture rose. The
peasants who stayed were able to force down rents or obtain sharecropping
leases on more favourable terms. It is true that marginal land went out of
cultivation, especially in Basilicata, the population of which declined between 1881 and 1911.[2] It is also true that the landowners, and particularly
the middle class which depended on rents from land for its livelihood,
suffered severely. It can hardly be denied, however, that in terms of social
justice, the balance-sheet of emigration was positive. Education, too, was
stimulated as knowledge spread of the extent to which illiteracy handicapped an emigrant in the U.S.A.

By far the greatest benefit, however, was the influx of new wealth into
even the most impoverished corners of the south, in the form of remittances
and the savings of returning emigrants. In 1911 it was calculated that
emigrants transmitted about 500 million lire to Italy every year, of which
350 million went to the south.[3] The impact of the returning emigrants, the
*americani*, was also substantial. Most who could afford it fulfilled the dream
which had sent them to America by building a house and buying a piece
of land of their own.[4] They often dissipated their savings in extending
their holdings, to acquire social prestige, rather than in improving what
they already possessed. Debts and bankruptcies were all too frequent. Too
many put their money into the post office savings bank, which benefited
the north much more than the south.[5] But on balance the *americani* raised
agricultural standards.[6] The area under intensive cultivation increased and

[1] Arias, I, pp. 371 ff.; Vöchting, pp. 249–50. Between 1900 and 1913 the money
wages of day labourers increased by 50% in many areas, and sometimes by as much
as 200%. The rise in real wages was probably not very significant over the south
as a whole.

[2] From 525,000 in 1881 to 474,000 in 1911. The population also fell between
1901 and 1911 in two of the four provinces of the Abruzzi and in three of the five
provinces of Campania. Arias, I, pp. 294–8; *ASI 1913*, p. 15.

[3] Arias, I, p. 399; Vöchting, p. 258; Corbino, V, pp. 215–16; Coletti, pp. 238–48.
Serpieri, pp. 20–1, estimates the total amount earned by peasant manual labour in
the south at only 1,066 million lire per annum, and calculates that the 350 million
lire of remittances raised the annual *per capita* income of the south from 178 to
236 lire.

[4] But the number of proprietors of land did not increase significantly, except
perhaps in Sicily, because the *americani* tended to buy from existing small proprietors. Zingali, I, pp. 86–7; Vöchting, pp. 255–6.

[5] The south's share of the total of savings banks deposits increased from 24%
to 29% between 1906 and 1913. Corbino, V, pp. 416–17; Arias, II, pp. 237–40.

[6] For instance, by introducing American vines which were immune to phylloxera.

erosion of the *latifondi* at their outer edges gathered speed. Emigration did something to relieve the shortage of capital which was the south's main affliction. Debts were reduced, the stranglehold of the usurer was weakened and interest rates fell.[1] The *americani* also brought many intangible benefits. They returned as men of the modern world, with a higher sense of personal dignity and higher standards of dress, hygiene and education. Some had acquired technical skill. By 1914 there were few villages without at least one house, more solidly constructed and more brightly painted, and providing comforts unknown to its neighbours, which revealed the presence of an *americano*. No doubt they also brought back some of the bad features of American city life.[2] But on balance they were a civilising, modernising force which gave a salutary shock to the stagnant south. 'I pray to God', said Fortunato in 1908, 'that nothing induces the United States to close its doors.'[3]

Emigration, however, like special legislation, provided relief for the south, not a solution of its problems. The *meridionalisti* located the causes of southern backwardness in the very nature of southern society and the very structure of the Italian state. Their diagnosis began with the southern middle class which monopolised political power and local government. It was not a rich class; there were no fortunes to be made, as in the north, in commerce or industry. It drew its income from possession of land which others cultivated and from exploitation of the peasantry.[4] Its outlook was coloured by a classical and literary education, which produced a surplus of lawyers. The successful minority made careers, often in the north, in politics or teaching, at the bar or in the public service; the unsuccessful majority returned from the universities to their home towns to form an underemployed intellectual proletariat, whose chief occupation was to indulge in the passionate faction fights which passed for politics in the south.[5]

[1] In Molfetta, Salvemini's home town, interest rates fell from 25% to between 4% and 5% in fifteen years. But so great a reduction was not general. Salvemini, *Scritti*, p. 250.

[2] For instance, tuberculosis. But the evil effects of emigration were grossly exaggerated in later years by nationalist writers. Coletti, pp. 248–55; Arias, II, pp. 427–38.

[3] Fortunato, *Pagine e ricordi parlamentari*, II, p. 35.

[4] Although they were not physically absentee, these middle-class *galantuomini* were in spirit as absentee from the land as the big proprietors who lived in Naples or Rome. Vöchting, pp. 84–5.

[5] For a brilliant analysis of the southern landed and 'intellectual' bourgeoisie, see G. Dorso, *La classe dirigente meridionale*, in Caizzi, pp. 377 ff. Also Salvemini, *Scritti, passim*; Mosca, *Uomini e cose di Sicilia* (1905), reprinted in *Partiti e sindacati*, pp. 185–94. Nitti, *L'Italia all' alba*, pp. 200–9, gives figures for the formation of an 'academic proletariat' through the overproduction of graduates in law, medicine, etc.

The main objective of these contending factions was to win control of the local councils and so of the jobs and privileges which were the spoils of victory. The material benefits of power could be very great. Local taxation could be manipulated to the detriment of defeated opponents, and always at the expense of the peasant; the common lands owned in trust by the municipalities could be appropriated, or the income from charities diverted to improper purposes; contracts could be assigned, or superfluous jobs created, for the benefit of relatives or supporters; extravagant expenditure could be authorised on luxuries such as theatres and budget deficits covered up. For immunity from the law or from interference by higher authority, the faction in power depended upon their deputy, who would often be one of Giolitti's placemen. His job was to secure a blind eye to local abuses on the part of the prefect and the government, and to obtain jobs, decorations and public funds for the members of the narrow class which he represented.[1]

Over most of the south, politics in the northern sense were unknown. Marxists such as Arturo Labriola lamented the absence of the class war which in Emilia and the northern cities had been 'the motor of progress'.[2] Lack of industry, absence of a commercial middle class, primitive agriculture and an illiterate, voteless peasantry had bred political stagnation. Salvemini calculated in 1899 that in the average southern town of 20,000 inhabitants only fifty newspapers would be sold daily, compared with 2,000 in a northern town of the same size.[3] Local factions might appropriate national party labels, but southern elections were fought on local or personal, not national, issues. Modern party organisation was confined to Naples and certain parts of Apulia and Sicily because elsewhere its essential mass basis was lacking. In such conditions neither Catholics nor socialists could make much headway.

The Opera and Catholic Action were conspicuously weak in the south. Only in Sicily, where there was a tradition of organisation, could Sturzo and his followers create a popular movement. Elsewhere the peasantry passively resisted efforts to organise them, whether in cooperatives or agricultural unions or political associations. In the north the Catholic social movement drew its organisers from the prosperous upper strata of the peasantry or from the urban professional class. In the south such persons were very few. Moreover the priest, who in the north was usually of peasant or artisan stock and a man of the people, belonged in the south

---

[1] Salvemini, *Scritti, passim*, but especially pp. 42–50, 412–26; Nitti, *Nord e Sud*, pp. 9–10; Mosca, pp. 196–203.

[2] Arturo Labriola, *Il segreto di Napoli e la leggenda della camorra* (Naples 1911), pp. 49–55.

[3] Salvemini, *Scritti*, p. 60.

to the ruling oligarchy. Often he was related to the local landowner or
grand elector, or owned land from which he supplemented his modest
stipend. He was on the side of the *galantuomini* and his leadership was
therefore suspect to the peasant.

Similar difficulties confronted the socialists. They were strongest in
Apulia, where a mass of underemployed *braccianti* offered opportunities
resembling those of Emilia. The fact that the Apulian *braccianti* lived in
towns and large villages, not dispersed over the countryside as in Emilia,
made the organisation of trade unions all the easier. It was no coincidence
that Apulia provided fewer emigrants than any other region of the south;
the labour movement was a partial substitute. In Sicily, too, where the
tradition of the fasci lived on, the socialists had a foothold, particularly
among the *braccianti* of the Catanian plain. Emigration, however, greatly
weakened the Sicilian labour movement in later years. Apart from Apulia
and Sicily, the most promising field for proselytism was in the cities such
as Naples and Bari. In Naples Arturo Labriola's *La Propaganda* led the
fight against the Camorra and the tradition of government by cliques and
corruption, and won much sympathy from non-socialists for its moral
campaign. Similar motives led Bari industrialists in 1902 to support Enrico
Ferri at a by-election, as the representative of a 'modern' party which
stood for progress against 'feudal' stagnation.[1] But these were exceptional
episodes. Only 4 of the 33 socialist deputies elected in 1900 came from the
south; in 1909 only 2 out of 41.[2] Over most of the south the old-established
oligarchies still retained control.

It was the contention of the *meridionalisti* that governments were chiefly
to blame. Ever since 1861, they argued, the rulers of Italy had used their
power, not to protect the masses from exploitation, but to preserve the
privileges of a parasitical minority in exchange for safe seats and steady
votes in parliament. Governments thus sacrificed the south's long-term
interests to their own short-term political advantage. The southern deputies, in their turn, voted the laws, taxes and tariffs that the government
wanted even when the south was cruelly injured. In most cases they did
so not because they were dishonest or corrupt men, but because they were
the victims of a situation in which neither the government nor the electorate
provided any incentive to do otherwise.[3] Willingly or unwillingly, they had
become the tools of northern capitalism, which guaranteed the survival of
their class in return for their support of a national economic policy which
systematically sacrificed the south to the north.

[1] Michels, pp. 337-9.                          [2] *Compendio*, II, pp. 128-9.
[3] But not all the *meridionalisti* took such a charitable view. Salvemini described
the southern petty bourgeoisie as delinquent, putrefied and morally rotten, and
the southern deputies as 'the dregs (*bassi fondi*) of the chamber'.

The *meridionalisti* had two major remedies for this dismal situation: a reversal of tariff policy and universal suffrage. In their struggle for the first, they found allies in the northern free traders, who championed the consumer and the unprotected producer against the tariff-protected minority. Their headquarters were in Turin, where an Anti-Protection League was founded in 1904. It was clear to most *meridionalisti* that in attacking 'the hierarchy of privilege' in the nation, the free traders were also fighting the south's battle. Most southern producers were unprotected and the whole south was a quasi-colonial consumer of industrial products. It was therefore natural that a leading part in the campaign against tariffs should have been played by southerners such as Nitti, Antonio De Viti De Marco, Salvemini and Fortunato.

Tariffs were not their only target; they attacked the whole basis of the collectivist state. Special laws for Naples or Basilicata were condemned as fiercely as tariffs for northern steel barons or subsidies for socialist cooperatives in the Po valley.[1] What the south required was not more sops from a state that was ceaselessly increasing its functions, but a dismantling of the state and a reduction of its functions; lower taxes and tariffs, which would benefit all, not higher expenditure in order to add to the ranks of the privileged; a smaller bureaucracy and more modest armed forces, not diplomatic and colonial megalomania. If this programme could be carried out, the free traders claimed, the south would be able to save, invest and attend to its own regeneration.

The free traders, however, were fighting a losing battle. They could claim some credit for the commercial treaties of 1904–6 which, though they did not lower industrial tariffs, at least prevented further restriction of markets for southern exports. But the rejection by parliament in 1905 of a commercial agreement with Spain, owing to an outcry from southern wine interests, showed that wheat-growing *latifondisti* were not now the only protectionists in the south. Sectional interests usually proved stronger, or were more easily understood, than the general interest. When Bissolati's Reformist Socialist party[2] came out against all tariffs in 1913, it was significant that its Sicilian representatives pleaded for the retention of the import duty on wheat. Likewise many northern socialists were keen to abolish the wheat duty but wanted to retain tariffs for the particular industries from which they earned their living.[3] It was on this issue that the veteran free trader, Pantaleoni, quarrelled with his former political friends.

---

[1] But on this point Nitti differed. Though he agreed that the south would benefit from a reduction rather than an increase in state activity, he was also a leading advocate of special legislation on the ground that the south was entitled to its fair share of privilege.

[2] See below, p. 385.

[3] Romano, *Storia della questione meridionale*, pp. 59–60.

When elected to parliament as a democrat in 1900, he had hoped to make free trade a main plank of the campaign against Pelloux. Two years later, disgusted by the preoccupation of the socialists with class and sectional interests, he broke with the Extreme Left and set out on a road which was eventually to carry him to the opposite political extreme.[1] Though a small band of free traders remained vocal up till 1914, in both press and parliament, they failed utterly to reverse the trend (not confined to Italy) towards protection and collectivism. In the short run their defeat was the defeat of the south, because in a collectivist state run by conflicting pressure groups, the south was at a disadvantage. In the long run, however, it was to be massive state action and foreign assistance, not a reversion to *laisser'faire*, that would offer the south its first solid hope of redemption.

The campaign for universal suffrage, coupled with decentralisation and municipal autonomy, was led by Salvemini. He placed his faith in the southern proletariat, in its potential energy, intelligence and creativeness. Like Sonnino in 1876, he argued that the south would have found its own way to salvation after 1860, but for the intervention of 'foreign' governments.[2] If the proletariat were given the vote, the power of the oligarchies would crumble, Giolitti would lose his *askaris* and the monstrous alliance of northern capitalists and southern *latifondisti* would be shattered. Southern politics would assume the form long familiar in the north, and democrats and socialists would be able to fight effectively for the interests of the whole south. The superficial 'revolution of the *galantuomini*' in 1860 had been sterile; universal suffrage would bring the fruitful 'revolution of the peasantry'.[3]

Sturzo and his Sicilian Christian democrats had certain points in common with Salvemini. They too blamed the central government for many of the south's miseries and detested Giolitti as the personification of an evil system. Sturzo himself was almost a *meridionalista*, who saw the Southern question in Christian democratic terms. He wanted stronger local government and new regional authorities for education, industry and agriculture. By such means the south would develop a healthy democratic life and produce a new governing class.[4]

The pessimists, many of them sincere friends of the south, dismissed such ideas as illusion. Fortunato believed that to weaken the central gov-

---

[1] Pareto, *Lettere a Maffeo Pantaleoni*, II, pp. 405, 416–17. Pantaleoni's fellow-free trader of the 1890s, Pareto, dropped out of active Italian politics soon after his appointment to the chair of economics at Lausanne in 1893, and became progressively disillusioned with Italy, liberalism, parliamentary government and politics in general.

[2] Salvemini, *Scritti*, pp. 86–94.

[3] ibid., pp. 396–8.

[4] De Rosa, *L'Azione Cattolica*, II, pp. 161–7.

ernment would merely tighten the oppressive grip of local oligarchies. Nitti, too, looked to the power of the Italian state to rescue the south. Even within the Socialist party, there was little enthusiasm for Salvemini's ideas. Turati expected little from the southern proletariat and Salvemini never convinced him that universal suffrage would bring a miraculous transformation.[1] Events justified his doubts. When the first election under the extended suffrage was held in 1913, sceptics like Turati were proved more right than the optimists. In later years Salvemini himself sadly admitted that his faith in the southern proletariat's capacity for independent action had been misplaced, or at least that democracy in the south would be a slower growth than he had believed as a young man.[2]

In any analysis of the Southern question, the psychological factor cannot be omitted. The two Italys were separated by both a material and psychological gulf, and the latter was perhaps the harder to bridge. The myth of the south as a garden of Eden was dead, as was the theory that southerners were racially degenerate. Yet most northerners still regarded the south as idle, parasitical and a drag on progress, and lamented the pouring of good northern money into the bottomless southern swamp. The sins of the bureaucracy were freely attributed to the southerners who filled an increasing proportion of its lower ranks, and every visit to a dirty post office strengthened this prejudice. Democrats talked of the southern Vendée, a reservoir of reaction, militarism and corruption. Southerners in their turn still accused the north of crippling the southern economy and squeezing fat profits and high wages out of southern misery. If southerners were now invading the civil service, because they had few outlets in commerce or the free professions, this 'conquest of the north' seemed but a fair revenge for the 'liberation' of 1861 and years of colonial exploitation.

But when the north tried to help, the reaction of the south could be disconcerting. A government that tried to check corruption could be accused of victimisation, as Giolitti had frequent reason to know. At the time of the Palizzolo trial many southerners reacted to expressions of northern disgust by making a martyr of the condemned man. Palizzolo cleverly played upon such feelings, declaring 'We must keep united, as this is a war of northern Italy against Sicily.'[3] A similar reaction was provoked by the downfall of Nunzio Nasi, the liberal democratic deputy for Trapani in western Sicily. Nasi, a freemason and staunch anti-clerical,

---

[1] Salvemini, Scritti, pp. 159–82. See also above, p. 270, for Salvemini's attacks on the Socialist party leadership.

[2] See his prefaces to Caizzi, Antologia della questione meridionale, pp. 9–13, written in 1949, and to his own Scritti sulla questione meridionale, pp. xxxvi–xxxix, written in 1955.

[3] Underwood, p. 180.

was the idol of his constituents and one of the ablest southern politicians of his day; he had even been spoken of as a future prime minister. In 1904 the socialists, led by Bissolati, accused him of embezzlement of public funds during his tenure of the Ministry of Education under Zanardelli. After three years of dramatic controversy, he was impeached before the senate and sentenced to eleven months' imprisonment and four years' exclusion from public life. Violent demonstrations of protest were held in the towns of Sicily and there was loss of life in Palermo. Nasi was twice re-elected at Trapani, in 1909 and 1913, and twice the chamber annulled his election, readmitting him only in 1914 when all hope of political advancement had vanished. Many southerners, above all Sicilians, bitterly contrasted the penalty exacted from Nasi for trifling misdemeanours with the immunity of crooked northern financiers and the 'northern Mafia' of sugar and steel barons. Once again Sicily had been the victim of persecution by the hypocritical north or, in another popular version, of the machinations of Giolitti who had seen in Nasi a rival.[1] Such polemics revealed the depth of the psychological gulf.

The divisions can, however, be exaggerated. Moments of mutual exasperation alternated with moments of generosity and solidarity. One such followed the earthquake of December 1908, which destroyed Messina and Reggio di Calabria. 77,000 lives were lost and the material damage was appalling. As soon as the extent of the disaster was known, Giolitti put the devastated area under martial law and sent all available troops to assist in the task of relief. He even broke the habit of a lifetime by holding a cabinet meeting after dark and arriving in his office long before his usual hour next morning.[2] Many years passed before the damage was repaired and the state machine responded sluggishly to a crisis which was a major test of its efficiency. But money, gifts and teams of relief workers poured down from the north, and the nation's conscience was deeply stirred. For many northerners, who saw the south for the first time, it was a shattering experience, and a few devoted the rest of their lives to its cause.[3]

In 1914, after fifteen years of enquiry and debate, good intentions and timid action, the Southern question seemed no nearer solution. Excessive pessimism had replaced the excessive optimism of the Risorgimento. But

[1] Cilibrizzi, III, pp. 360–7; Albertini, *Venti anni*, I, pp. 137–8. Albertini's *Corriere della Sera* played an important part in securing Nasi's conviction.

[2] Ansaldo, pp. 244–5. But it is significant that Giolitti did not think it necessary to pay a personal visit to the scene of the disaster. The reluctance of Giolitti and other northern statesmen to visit the south, even when out of office, may be compared to the reluctance of British nineteenth-century statesmen to visit Ireland.

[3] Notably Umberto Zanotti-Bianco, one of the founders of the Associazione Nazionale per gli interessi del Mezzogiorno. Other examples in more recent times of northerners whose lives have been profoundly affected by contact with the south have been Carlo Levi and Danilo Dolci.

at least it was a step forward that the complexity of the problem, with all its regional variations,[1] was now widely understood, and that the need for simultaneous action on many interconnected fronts – education, health, transport, land reform, taxation, industrial and agricultural development – was recognised. The basic mistake of the newly created Italian state had been to ignore the differences between north and south. Its rulers, with what they believed was impartiality, had applied the same laws to the whole nation, 'not realising that a law useful in one part of it can be damaging to another'.[2] The British had made the same mistake in Ireland, with which, indeed, *meridionalisti* often compared the Italian south. Just as British governments, starting with Gladstone, were forced, against all their national instincts and *laisser faire* prejudices, to legislate specially for Irish conditions, so were Italian governments forced to make special provision for the south and accept its redemption as a national responsibility. But the resources of Italy were not those of Britain, and therefore the national effort was feebler. Today, when the needs of underdeveloped societies are so much better understood, the achievement of the Giolittian era seems puny. But the special legislation of 1904–14 was a first step on the right road. For a decisive advance the south had to await the era of planning and massive foreign aid forty years later.

[1] It was a fault of many *meridionalisti* that they saw the Southern question too exclusively in terms of their own region's problems. Fortunato, for instance, never visited Sicily. But clearly Sardinia and Basilicata, with population densities in 1911 of 35 and 47 to the square kilometre, had very different needs to those of Sicily with 143 and Campania with 205.

[2] A. Niceforo, *L'Italia barbara contemporanea* (Milan 1898), p. 20. Compare Sonnino's speech on the same theme in 1902, quoted in Zingali, I, pp. 226–8.

# 9

# The Decline of the Triple Alliance
## 1901–11

### Prinetti and the Entente with France

The accession of Victor Emmanuel III and the appointment of Giuseppe Zanardelli as Prime Minister brought a new orientation in foreign as well as in domestic policy. Zanardelli had fought the Austrians in his native Brescia in 1848. Fifty years later he was still, in Barrère's words, 'an impenitent irredentist, who could never resist the pleasure of displeasing Austria'.[1] These sentiments made him anxious for friendship with France. Giolitti, too, though he irritated Zanardelli by restraining irredentist exuberance, desired better relations with France and less dependence upon the Triple Alliance.

Giulio Prinetti, the new Foreign Minister, had no previous experience of diplomacy. Like many of his fellow-industrialists in Milan, he had opposed Crispi's 'megalomania', and in 1891 he made an outspoken speech in the chamber against renewal of the Triple Alliance. He regarded himself as a man of the Right, standing close to Rudinì and Luzzatti; he was also a friend of Cardinal Ferrari and had clerical-moderate sympathies.[2] Though by 1901 he had toned down his views on the Triple Alliance, he shared Rudinì's anxiety that Italy might be dragged into Germany's quarrels with France or Britain. East Africa did not interest him, but he believed in Italy's right to Tripoli. As a business man he wished to see a growth of Italy's influence not only in the Balkans, where Austria's activity alarmed him, but also in Turkey and the eastern Mediterranean. Ambitious and hot-tempered, with some of the instincts of a gambler, he craved for

---

[1] DDF (2), V, 441. Zanardelli had been Minister of Interior in 1878 at the time of the irredentist outbursts after the Congress of Berlin.
[2] He had been a member of Rudinì's government in 1896–7, but resigned when Zanardelli entered the cabinet to carry out an anti-clerical policy. See above, p. 190. Many conservatives never forgave Prinetti for accepting office from Zanardelli only three years later.

personal success and hoped to bring off a brilliant stroke.[1] The task he
set himself was to develop Visconti Venosta's *entente* with France and
at the same time strengthen Italy's position within the Triple Alliance.
Between a defensive Triple Alliance and a defensive Franco-Italian *entente*
there could in his view be no conflict.

Victor Emmanuel had no intention of being a cypher in foreign policy
and Prinetti's diplomatic inexperience allowed him to play an active role.
According to a British ambassador who became his close friend, he 'regarded himself somewhat in the relation of a permanent Under-Secretary
to succeeding Governments'.[2] All foreign observers were impressed by
his industry and intelligence, his lack of prejudice, his sound judgement
and wide knowledge. William II and Bülow distrusted him, believing him
to be an irredentist at heart and unhealthily influenced by his Montenegrin
queen and her Russian connexions. Though their fears were exaggerated,
Victor Emmanuel's personal dislike of William II was well known and
reciprocated,[3] and Barrère was to find the Russian and Montenegrin
courts a useful channel for pressure upon Italy. Victor Emmanuel had the
dignity and prestige of his dynasty much at heart. For this reason he refused
to visit Vienna unless Francis Joseph promised to come to Rome, a promise
that could never be given. He was not, however, a man of sentimental
likes or dislikes, nor was he either anti-German or pro-Russian. If he was
pro-French in 1901, it was from calculation, because he wished to see Italy
extricated from the narrow limits of its past alliances.[4]

The consequences of the change of King and government quickly
became apparent. Zanardelli declared to the *New York Herald* in March
1901 that if the treaties of the Triple Alliance were renewed, they would
have to be divested 'of all suspicion, which unfortunately has several times
arisen, of animosity towards France'.[5] In April the King's cousin, the Duke
of Genoa, took a naval squadron to Toulon and invested the French
President with Italy's highest decoration, the Collar of the Annunciation.
Barrère was delighted with the change and already inclined to believe that
Italian public opinion would not tolerate war against France even in the
defensive circumstances envisaged by the Triple Alliance.[6] In December,
in a statement drafted with the help of Delcassé and Barrère, Prinetti
revealed the existence of the Visconti Venosta–Barrère agreement on
Tripoli, and added that France and Italy were in full accord on all Medi-

---

[1] In his private letters he lamented that his achievements were not receiving the
credit due to them. Serra, *Camille Barrère*, pp. 106–7, and *L'intesa*, pp. 69–71.
[2] Rodd, III, p. 25.
[3] Albertini, *Origins*, I, pp. 118–19.
[4] Morandi, pp. 176–7; Serra, *Camille Barrère*, pp. 103–5; DDF (1), XVI, 374.
[5] Albertini, *Origins*, I, p. 119.
[6] DDF (2), I, 201.

terranean questions. Public statements by Delcassé and Barrère shortly afterwards reiterated the cordiality and wide range of Franco-Italian friendship.

Italy's allies grew uneasy. Within three weeks of choosing Zanardelli as his Prime Minister, Victor Emmanuel had asked the Germans, in the greatest secrecy, to allow the Italo-German military convention of 1888 to lapse.[1] In April 1901 Bülow, now Chancellor of Germany, told his mother-in-law, Donna Laura Minghetti, that 'Italy will have to decide soon to make her choice between matrimony and concubinage'. Prinetti's statement on Franco-Italian relations provoked him to a public reply in the Reichstag on 8 January 1902. Taking up again the metaphor he had used in private three years before, he declared:[2] 'In a happy marriage the husband must not get violent if his wife ventures to dance an innocent *extratour* with another. The main thing is that she doesn't run away from him, and she won't do that as long as she is better off with him than with anyone else.' His irony concealed irritation, and he added the warning that the Triple Alliance was useful but not essential to Germany. Prinetti assured him that Italy put the Alliance before any *entente* with France and offered to negotiate its renewal. But this did not remove German distrust.

The change in Franco-Italian relations caused anxiety in Britain also. The breakdown in May 1901 of Joseph Chamberlain's negotiations for an Anglo-German alliance had brought home the dangers of isolation, and therefore the value of Italian friendship. Prinetti lost no chance of dilating upon British ingratitude and indifference, and contrasting it with French sympathy. At the end of 1901 he recklessly worked up a number of petty incidents into a major diplomatic issue, hoping to shock Britain into concessions.[3] The gamble came off and negotiations started. In January 1902, in a speech full of friendly references to Italy, Chamberlain announced the withdrawal of the Maltese language decree.[4] This was followed in the middle of March by a formal exchange of notes on Tripoli. The British

---

[1] For a discussion of this obscure episode, see Albertini, *Origins*, I, pp. 125–7; Salvatorelli, pp. 239–40. The King's motive appears to have been to put himself and his government in a position to tell the French with a clear conscience that the Triple Alliance contained no offensive clauses aimed against France. The Germans agreed to the Italian request in March 1901. Yet in September 1902 Saletta, the Italian Chief of Staff, was talking to his German colleague as if the convention was still in full force. In 1908 Tittoni told the Russian ambassador in Rome that the convention had been allowed to lapse when the Triple Alliance was renewed in 1902. DDF (2), XI, 560.

[2] Bülow, II, p. 571; Albertini, *Origins*, I, p. 120. For the previous occasion, 23 December 1898, see above, pp. 211–12.

[3] Serra, *L'intesa*, ch. 3.

[4] See above, p. 210; also J. L. Garvin and J. Amery, *Life of Joseph Chamberlain*, IV (London 1951), pp. 176–8.

THE DECLINE OF THE TRIPLE ALLIANCE

note disclaimed all 'aggressive or ambitious designs' in regard to Tripoli and Benghazi, and declared that, while 'H.B.M. Government continue to be sincerely desirous of the maintenance of the *status quo* there', it would be their object, should there be any alteration in the *status quo*, that 'such alteration should be in conformity with Italian interests'. This assurance was given 'on the understanding and in full confidence that Italy on her part has not entered, and will not enter, into arrangements with other Powers in regard to this or other portions of the coast of the Mediterranean of a nature inimical to British interests'. In reply Prinetti gave assurances of the Italian government's full and solemn agreement 'with regard to the entire contents' of the British note. He also allowed the British ambassador to take a copy of Barrère's note to Visconti Venosta of December 1900.[1]

This was a substantial success for Prinetti. It was true that Salisbury and his Foreign Secretary, Lansdowne, promised no support for Italian aggression at Tripoli, and indeed had shown some nervousness during the negotiations about Italy's immediate intentions. But for the moment, whatever Prinetti's personal inclinations, aggression was ruled out by opposition at home, notably on the part of Zanardelli.[2] The importance of the agreement lay in the future. After March 1902 cordiality quickly returned to Anglo-Italian relations, and as the two countries drew closer, it became progressively more certain that Britain would not in the end object to Italy taking Tripoli. In its wider diplomatic aspects the Anglo-Italian agreement, together with the Visconti Venosta-Barrère agreement, formed a loose substitute for the obsolete Mediterranean system of 1887. It marked an important stage in the process by which the three Mediterranean Powers were to come together over the next ten years.

Prinetti had meanwhile been negotiating for a revision of the Triple Alliance, which was due to expire in 1903, in the hope that Italy's reviving friendship with France would force his allies to make concessions. He proposed three additions to the treaty: a new statement on the defensive character of the Alliance, which would be put in a preamble and published for France's benefit; stronger guarantees of the Italian claim to Tripoli and Italian interests in the Balkans; and a promise of new commercial treaties.[3] 'Without a treaty of commerce, no alliance', he declared. Bülow, understanding Prinetti's game, refused. He believed Germany's dominant position in Europe was unassailable and saw no need to humour the Italians,

---

[1] Serra, *L'intesa*, pp. 179–85; BD, I, 360–1. Serra's account fills the gaps in the published British documents.

[2] Serra, *L'intesa*, pp. 118, 150, 193–201.

[3] The commercial treaties of 1892 (see above, p. 151) were due to lapse at the end of 1903.

still less to help the schemings of Delcassé and Barrère. Italy needed Germany more than Germany needed Italy. He therefore agreed to renew the Triple Alliance, out of a feeling of friendship to Italy and a sense of *pietas* towards an old institution, but renew it unaltered. Some of Prinetti's suggestions were, he admitted, reasonable, but 'the better is the enemy of the good'.[1] The Austrians, enjoying the security of their *entente* with Russia, agreed. Prinetti knew that Italy was too weak to risk isolation. On 3 May, with feelings of bitter frustration, he agreed to renew the Alliance as it stood, and on 28 June the new treaty was signed. It was to last for twelve years, unless denounced before July 1907. Prinetti obtained only two concessions: Bülow consented to renew the protocol of 1891 on the desirability of commercial treaties[2] and of a closer British connexion with the Alliance; and Goluchowski pledged Austria-Hungary not to interfere with any Italian move at Tripoli.

On 8 May, five days after resentfully submitting to Bülow's terms, Prinetti told Barrère he was ready to discuss a Franco-Italian agreement that would harmonise with the Triple Alliance. During 1901 Barrère had argued that a renewal of the Alliance unchanged would violate his agreement with Visconti Venosta; he wanted all pledges against France removed from the text. In May 1902, in spite of Delcassé's initial disapproval, he realistically contented himself with a more limited aim and employed all his skill and influence to achieve it. Prinetti's injured pride was played upon; the press in both countries was influenced; the support of Luzzatti, Visconti Venosta, Rudinì and Rattazzi was enlisted, together with that of the Russian ambassador and the Montenegrin court; hints of French support for a new Italian loan were dropped. His reward was the secret exchange of notes of 30 June, which has since been known as the Prinetti–Barrère Agreement.

Prinetti's note extended the 1900 agreement on Morocco and Tripoli-Cyrenaica, so that either country could go ahead in its own sphere without waiting for the other's consent. Italy promised neutrality if France were attacked by one or two powers; and further, if France, 'in consequence of direct provocation,[3] were forced to take the initiative of a declaration of war to defend its honour or security', Italy would remain neutral provided it was previously informed and satisfied as to the provocation. Barrère in his note promised reciprocal French neutrality in similar circumstances.

[1] Albertini, *Origins*, pp. 121–3.

[2] New commercial treaties with Germany and Austria–Hungary were concluded after prolonged negotiations and came into force in 1906. See above, pp. 291–2.

[3] 'Direct provocation' was afterwards defined as concerning only direct relations between the provoker and the provoked. The Ems telegram of 1870, the Schnaebele affair of 1887 and 'certain episodes in the Fashoda incident' were quoted as examples.

France's gains from this agreement were immense. No longer could Italy become the tool of German aggression, as so many Frenchmen had feared in Crispi's day. In Prinetti's words, 'a veritable act of madness on France's part' would now be necessary to bring Italy into a war against it.[1] The French could confidently denude their Alpine frontier of troops and concentrate them in Alsace. Italy's gains also were substantial. Closer friendship with France carried the promise of commercial and financial benefits. Tripoli was at last safe, and the prospects of increasing Italian influence in the Mediterranean without incurring French hostility became much brighter. But the agreement's chief importance for Italy lay in its potentialities as a reinsurance treaty. There was now the possibility of French support in the Adriatic and the Balkans, should the Triple Alliance fail to hold Austria-Hungary in check; while the Triple Alliance remained in reserve as a check on France, should opinion change in that country. Italy for the first time since 1878 could enjoy a measure of diplomatic freedom. Such a situation also had its dangers. It was scarcely realistic to expect that if France and Germany went to war, there would ever be general agreement as to whether there had or had not been 'direct provocation' on the German side. The Italians would offend either France or Germany, whether they stayed neutral or fought beside their German ally. Worse still, in a crisis they might estrange both parties to a dispute, just because they were committed to both. Bismarck in 1887 had tried to solve the same problem by similarly attributing to himself an arbiter's decision on 'direct provocation' between Russia and Austria-Hungary. But Prinetti was no Bismarck, nor had Italy the industrial and military strength of Germany to back the arbiter. Within three years an Italian government was faced with a crisis of this very nature, which it was lucky to survive with nothing worse than embarrassment.

An improvement in Franco-Italian relations was not in itself a danger to the Triple Alliance. In the past both Austria-Hungary and Germany had pressed the Italians to make that improvement, as Bülow himself admitted in his Reichstag speech in January 1902. In May Goluchowski had declared publicly that 'the present cordial relations between Italy and France are one of the most hopeful phenomena of recent times'. Prinetti had never concealed his wish to reinsure by removing French doubts; in this respect he had been franker than Bismarck in 1887. Since 1882 both Germany and Austria-Hungary had taken advantage of the elasticity of the Alliance to make special agreements with other countries outside its limited sphere. Germany had always maintained that it was not concerned with the Mediterranean, except in circumstances carefully defined in 1887 and 1891, and in 1897 Bülow had encouraged Visconti Venosta to look elsewhere for

[1] DDF (2), II, 194.

guarantees of Italy's Mediterranean interests. Yet the agreement of 1902 clearly violated the spirit of the Triple Alliance,[1] which required full frankness between allies. The Italians were well aware of this, as their anxiety for secrecy shows. Moreover, at the request of Prinetti and the King, the two notes bore the false date of November. They wished to conceal the fact that they had been signed only two days after the renewal of the Triple Alliance. Such scruples betray a guilty conscience.[2]

The Alliance and the *entente* were not necessarily incompatible. But the desire to reinsure implies distrust, and after 1902 distrust continued to weaken the alliance. All four of the pillars upon which it rested[3] were beginning to give way. Relations between Britain and Germany were strained, tension between Britain and France was subsiding; the French threat in north Africa had been brought under control; the Roman question had ceased to count in international diplomacy; and Italian confidence in Austria-Hungary's Balkan intentions had greatly diminished since 1897. The establishment of good relations with France turned Italian eyes away from Tripoli, Tunis and Morocco to Trieste and the Trentino, and made more Italians conscious of the price that had to be paid for the Triple Alliance.

In July 1902 Victor Emmanuel chose for the first visit of his reign not an allied capital but St Petersburg. On his way home he stayed in Berlin but ostentatiously avoided Vienna. In April 1903 Edward VII visited Rome and at a state banquet toasted the Crimean alliance. In return Victor Emmanuel went to London in the autumn. On the way he visited Paris, after extracting from the French President a promise to return the visit in Rome: a promise he was reluctant to give, for fear of complications with the Vatican. On 8 April 1904 the Entente Cordiale, the very Anglo-French combination which Rudinì had postulated in 1896 and Bülow had dismissed as inconceivable, came into being. Too late, Bülow saw the danger and wired to William II: 'The force of attraction of the Anglo-French Entente over Italy will be much stronger than was that of each of the two Western

---

[1] As did the renewal of the Three Emperors' League in 1884 (see above, p. 116), the German–Russian Reinsurance Treaty of 1887 and, to a much smaller degree, the Austro–Russian Agreement of 1897 (see above, p. 205).

[2] The existence of the agreement soon became generally known, but its content long remained the subject of speculation. The text was published only in 1920. The Italians kept the secret until then, the French did not. The French Foreign Minister informed his Russian colleague verbally of its content during the Bosnian crisis of 1908 (see below, p. 347). The British Foreign Secretary, Grey, was informed, also verbally, during the Agadir crisis of 1911 and showed 'agreeable surprise'. DDF (2), XIV, 205.

[3] See above, p. 124, and Salvemini, *La politica estera dell' Italia*, p. 80.

powers separately.'[1] A fortnight after signing the agreements with Britain, President Loubet and Delcassé arrived in Rome. Demonstrations of goodwill throughout Italy set the stamp of popular approval on the new relationship with France. As Loubet had foreseen, his visit precipitated a rupture with the Vatican, soon to be followed by the separation of church and state in France. This readiness on the part of the head of a Catholic state to defy the Pope's wishes added to the significance of the occasion and removed the last Italian fears of French interference in the Roman question. Italians now felt towards France as they had felt on the morrow of unification, declared Barrère.[2] The Germans had vainly pressed the Italians to restrict the scale of Loubet's reception and their failure rankled. William II retorted with bellicose speeches glorifying the German army. The warning was intended for Italy as much as for France.

In spite of the *entente*, France and Italy still had many conflicting interests in the Mediterranean. Over the next seven years both countries attempted to minimise their importance. In August 1905 the French abandoned their claim to be sole protectors of all Catholics in Asiatic Turkey[3] and allowed Italian Catholic communities to apply for Italian consular protection. In Tunis, where immigration from Sicily had swollen the Italian population to 80,000, Visconti Venosta's convention of 1896 expired in 1905. It was allowed to remain in force and in 1906 Bourgeois, the French Foreign Minister, privately promised not to denounce it, though he said he could not make that promise official.[4] In Ethiopia, too, it was possible to reach agreement. In December 1906, after more than four years of difficult negotiation, Britain, France and Italy signed a tripartite treaty which staked out their respective spheres of influence and ended the old struggle for predominance at Menelik's court.[5]

The change in Italian feelings towards France had a basis much firmer than mere political or diplomatic convenience. In the early years of the century French culture dominated educated Italians. The younger generation was soaked in French literature; Paris was its Mecca. Italian democrats looked with admiration to the triumphant Dreyfusards, and the French quarrel with the Papacy, culminating in the separation of church

[1] Albertini, *Origins*, I, pp. 149–50.

[2] DDF (2), V, 117.

[3] This claim, which dated from the sixteenth century, had in fact already been modified by the Treaty of Berlin, but the French conceded nothing without great pressure. Tommasini, II, pp. 191 ff. The French feared that the Italians would take advantage of the rupture between themselves and the Papacy. DDF (2), X, 261, 289. Tittoni, with his clerical sympathies, took a personal interest in the problems of Italian Catholic communities overseas.

[4] Tommasini, III, pp. 15–16.

[5] See further below, p. 362.

and state, strengthened the mutual sympathy between anti-clericals in the two countries. Clericalism, militarism and autocracy were common enemies, and Germany and Austria-Hungary stood for these things. Barrère, with his journalist's flair for publicity, made good use of these sentiments. Eminent French writers, artists and professors descended upon Italy; no anniversary of an event significant for Franco-Italian friendship was overlooked. Friends of France societies were organised all over Italy. Prominent freemasons and politicians of the extreme left were welcomed to the French embassy. Barrère's brilliance, personal charm and lavish hospitality won many friends for France in Roman society. Italian conservatives might be disgusted by his patronising propaganda, his subsidies to the democratic press and his promises of financial and commercial favours for good behaviour. But their effectiveness was beyond dispute.[1]

Already in May 1903 Barrère had reported to Delcassé: 'Without doubt, Italy is at the start of a road which will take her, if she continues to follow it, to a rupture with Austria'.[2] In February 1904 he wrote: 'I have the clearest impression that, in this psychological moment, it depends on us whether Italy is definitely separated from Germany'.[3] Barrère was always an optimist. But the German reading of the situation was little different. In December 1903 the German ambassador in Rome lamented the estrangement of cultured Italians, especially the young, from Germany and Austria. 'For the youth', he wrote, 'patriotism and irredentism are the same thing ... He who has youth on his side, has the future.'[4]

## Italy, Austria and the Balkans 1901-6

Italy's drift towards France and Britain was quickened by events in eastern Europe. Insurrection against the Turks broke out in Macedonia in the autumn of 1902 and in Albania next spring. Neither Austria-Hungary nor Russia wished to see Turkey disintegrate. Their negative agreement of 1897 therefore developed into the more positive policy of imposing reforms upon the Turks and keeping the Balkan peoples quiet under their joint supervision. The details of this policy were worked out in a series of meetings between the Foreign Ministers, Lamsdorff and Goluchowski, culminating in that of Mürzsteg in October 1903. Two 'civil agents', one Austrian and one Russian, and European police officers were installed in Macedonia. Austria-Hungary and Russia took it upon themselves to preserve the settlement of 1878, acting as agents for the European Concert and treating the Balkans as their closed preserve.

In all this Italy had no part. Prinetti was greatly alarmed. When he

---

[1] Serra, *Camille Barrère*, pp. 217-23, 230-1.     [2] DDF (2), III, 270.
[3] DDF (2), IV, 304.                              [4] GP, XVIII, 5789.

asked for information, Goluchowski grew angry and evasive. This strengthened his suspicion that, behind the fine talk of reform in the interest of civilisation, lay Austrian designs for the peaceful penetration of Macedonia and Albania. One of Prinetti's main ambitions was to recover the effective voice in Balkan affairs which Italy had enjoyed for a few years after 1887. At first he had hoped to achieve this by a revision of the Triple Alliance. Frustrated in his efforts by Bülow, he decided that, to keep Austria-Hungary in check, an *entente* with Russia must be added to the *entente* with France. In July 1902 he accompanied the King to St Petersburg and returned with vague promises of collaboration. Nothing came of these. Italy could indeed offer Russia little that would compensate the latter for quarrelling with Austria-Hungary. Prinetti hoped for much from the Tsar's return visit to Rome. The Italian socialists frustrated him by announcing they would declare a general strike and greet the 'Cossack butcher' with organised boos and catcalls, from the moment he set foot on Italian soil. Thousands of whistles, carved with the Tsar's effigy, were distributed for the purpose.[1] Russian police experts advised that the visit would be too risky and in October 1903, the same month as the Mürzsteg meeting, it was indefinitely postponed.[2] This public humiliation, which hurt Victor Emmanuel most of all, ended Italian efforts for an *entente*. When the Russo-Japanese war broke out next year, the greater part of the Italian press sympathised with the Japanese.

Prinetti's health collapsed early in 1903 and he resigned in March, a dying man. When Giolitti succeeded Zanardelli in November, he made Tommaso Tittoni his Foreign Minister. A novice in diplomacy, like Prinetti in 1901, Tittoni owed his appointment to the good impression he had made as prefect of Naples on both Giolitti and Victor Emmanuel. He was an intelligent man, but vain and irresolute, with a Roman's liking for *combinazioni*. No one expected him to survive long: in fact he remained at the Foreign Ministry, with one break of five months, until December 1909. His intention was to pursue the traditional aims of Italian foreign policy: European equilibrium, no adventures, no territorial changes except with the approval of the European Concert, a balance between allies and friends, and good relations with all. Though he thought that Prinetti had committed Italy dangerously far to France, he attached great value to French and British friendship. Barrère disliked him because he was less amenable than his predecessor, and encouraged the left to attack his clerical and

---

[1] Angelica Balabanoff, *My Life as a Rebel* (London 1938), p. 77.

[2] Salvatorelli, p. 272, suggests that reluctance to allow Russian relations with Austria–Hungary to be compromised by commitments to Italy, and fear of complications with the Papacy, may have been the real reasons for the postponement, and that socialist threats were used as an excuse.

conservative connexions. Yet this gave him little credit in the eyes of his allies. He worked hard to make relations with Germany and Austria-Hungary more intimate, but was trusted in neither country and perpetually hampered by the hostility of Italian opinion.

The year 1903 had added a new source of friction with Austria-Hungary. In May and again in November, German-Austrian and Italian-Austrian students came to blows at Innsbruck University. The Italian press printed dramatic accounts, and students and schoolchildren in Italy reacted by crowding to irredentist meetings and smashing the windows of Austrian consulates.[1] The Innsbruck incidents, the product of mounting racial tension inside the Dual Monarchy, revived an old demand for an Italian university at Trieste. This the Austrian government refused to consider, on the ground that it would enrage not only Germans but Slavs and merely increase racial violence. In November 1904 an Italian Law Faculty was opened at Innsbruck, but more riots, this time on a serious scale, in which citizens of the town joined in, forced the authorities to close it on the very first day. The Austrian government then introduced a bill for the establishment of a Law Faculty at Rovereto in the Trentino; but the business of the Vienna parliament was paralysed by racial wrangles and obstruction, and early in 1906 the bill was withdrawn, the government pleading helplessness. Agitation amongst the Austrian Italians continued, with the slogan 'Trieste or nothing', and the university question became a major source of bad feeling between Italy and Austria-Hungary.

Two serious irredentist incidents increased the strain of these years. In August 1903, during summer manœuvres near the Austrian frontier, Italians from Trieste paraded with flags draped in black in front of the King's hotel, unmolested by the authorities. Goluchowski told the Germans he would never have renewed the Triple Alliance, had he foreseen such incidents. 'One thing is certain', he said, 'one can't go on like this with Italy.'[2] In July 1905 Marcora, the radical President of the chamber of deputies, referred in a public speech to 'our Trentino'. Furious protests came from Vienna and Tittoni had to give satisfaction in an official communique which stated, untruthfully, that Marcora's words had no irredentist significance.

This revival of old-fashioned irredentism, after its quenching by Crispi, was a natural consequence of the decline of the Triple Alliance. The irredentists enjoyed the sympathy of Zanardelli and, at least in popular belief, of the King, but they never recovered the dominant position on the left which they had enjoyed before 1890. The reason for this was the rise

---

[1] It was Zanardelli's failure to deal firmly with these demonstrations that led to Giolitti's resignation as Minister of Interior in June. See above, p. 242.

[2] Tommasini, I, p. 208; Albertini, *Origins*, I, p. 135, and *Venti anni*, I, p. 122.

of the Socialist party which, though it detested the reactionary, clerical, militarist Habsburg Monarchy, had no desire to provoke war for its destruction. Socialists were anti-irredentist because irredentism encouraged militarism and jingoism at home. Bissolati, the party's expert on foreign affairs, believed that the grievances of the unredeemed Italians could be removed by the transformation of Austria-Hungary into a democratic, genuinely multi-national empire. To achieve this he counted on the Austrian socialist movement. In May 1905 he attended a meeting of Italian and Austrian socialists at Trieste, at which the Austrians agreed to support autonomy for the Trentino and an Italian university at Trieste. Bissolati and Adler, the Austrian socialist leader, both denounced militarism and imperialist expansion. Bissolati returned encouraged, though he regretted the absence of the German socialists; for only with their help, he wrote, 'will the official Triple Alliance be replaced by the socialist Triple Alliance, a peaceful barrier against warlike provocations'.[1]

Though the influence of Mazzinian irredentism was now limited, national aspirations of a new kind, equally disturbing to Austria-Hungary, were taking shape in Italy. Economic development stimulated the search for markets and fields for Italian enterprise in the Balkans. Italian shipping was subsidised in the Adriatic to compete with Austrian companies. In Montenegro, Italian firms secured mining, timber and tobacco concessions and contracts for the construction of a modern seaport and railway. Italian schools were founded and subsidised in Albania and Italian democrats began to show interest in the Albanian nationalist movement. After successfully challenging the French claim to protect all Catholics in Asiatic Turkey, Italian governments now challenged the similar Austrian claim in Turkey-in-Europe. Albania and Montenegro seemed promising bases for the spread of Italian economic and cultural influence throughout the Balkans. In his efforts to erect barriers against Austrian expansion, Tittoni also cultivated good relations with the Balkan states and encouraged them, particularly Serbia and Bulgaria, to collaborate amongst themselves.[2] In 1906 the King of Greece paid a state visit to Rome, which Victor Emmanuel returned in Athens the following year. This 'mania for being everywhere' infuriated the Austrians. Italian interest in Montenegro was taken as a deliberate challenge to the virtual protectorate which Austria-Hungary had enjoyed there since 1878 – a challenge made more serious by the fact that it was welcomed by Prince Nicholas, Victor Emmanuel's father-in-law. Goluchowski accused the Italians of 'inventing the Albanian question'[3] and William II complained that Victor Emmanuel was 'hypnotised' by

[1] Bissolati, *La politica estera dell' Italia*, p. 112.
[2] Tommasini, II, pp. 107 ff., III, pp. 262, 319–20.
[3] ibid., II, p. 19.

Albania, knew all about every man, rifle and cartridge in the country, and could 'quote the names of all the Albanian brigand chiefs'.[1]

Goluchowski's irritation was increased by Tittoni's persistent attempts to interfere in Macedonia. In January 1904 he pleased the Italians by forcing Turkey to accept an Italian general as commander of the reorganised Macedonian *gendarmerie*. But Tittoni was determined to break much further into the Austro-Russian preserve, either by establishing Italy as a third and equal partner or by reviving the active European Concert of 1896-8 in which Italy would have an equal voice. The plan for an *entente* with Russia having failed, he fell back on the Concert. Neither Germany nor France, tied to their respective allies, gave him any encouragement, but he found the British more responsive. Tittoni's special anxiety was that the Austrians might resume their advance towards Salonika by annexing the Sanjak of Novibazar, the strip of Turkish territory between Serbia and Montenegro which the Treaty of Berlin had given Austria-Hungary the right to garrison. Goluchowski assured him in February 1904 that he had no designs on either Macedonia or Albania; but he insisted that the Sanjak concerned Austria-Hungary and Turkey alone. Tittoni made overtures to the French for support, then suggested to the British a joint occupation of part of Turkey's Adriatic coastline, should Austria-Hungary make a move in the Balkans. The reactions were discouraging.[2] Next month, however, when zones of Macedonia were allotted to the Great Powers for the supervision of law and order, it was largely British support that enabled Italy, in spite of strong Austrian objections, to secure the zone nearest Albania. On 9 April Tittoni met Goluchowski at Abbazia and was assured that Austria-Hungary would annex the Sanjak only in the last resort and after giving due warning. Tittoni on his side agreed that if Austria-Hungary did eventually take over the Sanjak, or converted occupation of Bosnia into annexation, Italy would have no claim to compensations under Article VII.

The French President's visit to Rome followed and tension persisted. The Austro-Hungarian Delegations voted large credits for fortifications and heavy guns on the Italian frontier. In September 1904 Giolitti felt it necessary to pay a sudden visit to Bülow in Germany. He tried to convince

[1] DDF (2), X, 440. Austro-Italian rivalry in Albania at a somewhat later date was described by a British observer as follows: 'In Scutari in 1908 Austria and Italy were both working strenuously to obtain influence over Albania. Austria had had a long start. Italy was now a good second. One made a hospital, the other replied with a home for the aged. One played a dispensary, the other an infant school, and so on, regardless of expense.' M. E. Durham, *Twenty Years of Balkan Tangle* (London 1920), p. 180.

[2] Salvatorelli, pp. 279-84; Tommasini, I, pp. 304-13. The immediate cause of Tittoni's anxiety was the outbreak of the Russo-Japanese war on 8 February, which seemed to give Austria-Hungary an opportunity for action at Russia's expense in the Balkans.

his host of Italy's loyalty to the Triple Alliance and of the innocence of Italian interest in Albania, and boasted of his energy in suppressing irredentism. Bülow was not convinced. In spite of Tittoni's sincere efforts to improve relations, the Austrians remained nervous. On 15 October, with German approval, they signed a secret reinsurance treaty with Russia which secured Russian neutrality in a war with Italy.[1] It was followed by minor Austrian troop movements to the Italian frontier, which forced the Italians in their turn to reinforce their frontier garrisons. Next month saw the recrudescence of the university question. Tittoni, greatly discouraged, wrote to his ambassador in Berlin at the end of the year: 'We find ourselves today in this situation: it is from the policy of an allied state that we fear the major surprises, and it is against an ally that we feel the special need of safeguarding ourselves.'[2] In 1905 Austria's annual military manœuvres were held in Tirol and attended by Francis Joseph in person, and next year Dalmatia was the scene of a combined military and naval exercise which Austrian officers openly described as a rehearsal for war with Italy.

Nevertheless 1905 did at last bring some relaxation of the tension. Goluchowski had amicable talks with Tittoni at Venice in April. In the same month a six-Power commission was set up to supervise the finances of Macedonia, giving Italy an equal share of responsibility and influence, and marking a further stage in the transition from control by Austria-Hungary and Russia to control by the Concert. But diplomacy was not enough. Tittoni's position as the most conservative member of the government was uncomfortable and his efforts to win Austria-Hungary's confidence were in themselves sufficient to make him unpopular. What little cordiality he had been able to infuse into the Triple Alliance rapidly vanished in 1906 when Italy's relations with the other ally, Germany, suddenly deteriorated.

### The Moroccan Crisis

In March 1905 William II landed at Tangier to assert Germany's right to a voice in Moroccan affairs. This direct challenge to France, at a moment when the latter was diplomatically weakened by Russia's defeat by Japan, was designed to show up the hollowness of the Anglo-French and Franco-Italian *ententes*. Not content with forcing the resignation of Delcassé, the Germans insisted on an international conference at which France should be publicly humiliated and isolated. The major European crisis which followed put Tittoni in a position of acute embarrassment. Italy had

---

[1] Tittoni first learnt of the existence of this treaty from the Russians in 1909. See below, p. 348.
[2] Tommasini, I, p. 462.

abandoned Morocco to France in 1900–2 and could not now back Germany without losing French support over Tripoli. Moreover, William II's escapade at Tangier could certainly be claimed by France to fall within the definition of 'direct provocation' agreed by Prinetti and Barrère. If the French felt bound to go to war to protect their interests in Morocco, they would certainly expect Italian neutrality; yet Germany would demand Italian help against a French attack, according to the terms of the Triple Alliance. Tittoni thus had to try to reconcile commitments which the first test showed to be irreconcilable.

The Germans at first demanded unconditional solidarity and declared that 'the mere passive attendance of Italy at the conference would amount to a *reductio ad absurdum* of the Alliance'.[1] Bülow was thus demanding just that extensive interpretation of the Alliance which had always been refused to Italy, in spite of the fact that Morocco, on German insistence, had been expressly omitted from the text of the treaty in 1891. Tittoni took refuge in evasive assurances to both sides and optimistically tried to mediate. Bülow soon guessed the extent of Italy's commitments to France and realised that Italian support could not be counted on at the conference. As the crisis developed, Tittoni's embarrassment was increased by the rapid consolidation of the Anglo-French Entente. Open friction between Germany and Britain found Italy unprotected by the declaration of 1882, which Rudinì had failed to revive in 1896 and which Prinetti had not even attempted to revive in 1902.

Tittoni decided that Italy's role at the conference must be to conciliate and to refrain from public support of either France or Germany; by showing vague benevolence to German views wherever possible, the face of the Triple Alliance could be saved without offence to France. He rejected Barrère's suggestion that, 'as a mark of Italian friendliness to France', he should appoint Visconti Venosta as Italy's delegate, and instead nominated his ambassador in Madrid, an undistinguished diplomat who would attract no notice.[2] But in December 1905 Fortis, who had succeeded Giolitti in March, replaced Tittoni by Marquis Antonio Di San Giuliano. Barrère tried again, this time with success, and persuaded Visconti Venosta to accept the appointment. Of all Barrère's achievements, none shows so clearly the extent of his influence in Italy.[3]

Visconti Venosta, now seventy-seven years of age, was inevitably a leading figure at the conference which opened at Algeciras on 16 January 1906. His intention was that Italy should emerge from the conference with

[1] Albertini, *Origins*, I, p. 162.
[2] He was also Tittoni's cousin and had the reputation of a keen partisan of the Triple Alliance.
[3] DDF (2), VIII, 151, 182, 301, 322–5, 359; Tommasini, II, pp. 229–31, 253–6.

its international position unchanged[1] and he insisted, as a condition of his appointment, on being left independent and unhampered by instructions from Rome. This enabled him to play a major part in negotiating the final agreement of 7 April, which defined the status and rights of the Great Powers in Morocco. His impartiality pleased neither side. Barrère complained that the office of mediator didn't exempt Visconti Venosta from fulfilling obligations and threatened to withhold French financial help for the conversion of the national debt, then in the last stages of preparation.[2] The Germans also complained[3] and put great pressure on San Giuliano and his successor Francesco Guicciardini, who came into office with Sonnino in February 1906. San Giuliano made a good impression by speaking with enthusiasm of the Triple Alliance and showing positive interest in the Italo-German military convention. Sonnino and Guicciardini were even more satisfactory: Sonnino, reported the German ambassador, was the most Germanophil statesman of the first rank in Italy.[4] Visconti Venosta nevertheless retained his independence. If he departed from the role of mediator, he leant towards France. Though he tried to avoid voting on matters of substance, on 3 March he did side with Britain and France on a question of procedure, leaving Germany and Austria-Hungary, with Morocco, in a minority of three. For a moment the alignment of 1915 emerged with frightening clarity.

The Algeciras agreement was a sensible compromise by which Germany forestalled the 'Tunisification' of Morocco. But the weakness of the Triple Alliance had been revealed and a false impression given of a German diplomatic defeat. The Germans found a scapegoat in Italy, which was publicly abused for treachery. William II saw the reality of the situation: 'Italy', he commented, 'remains with us only so long as we are friends with England. If that doesn't happen again, she will leave the Triple Alliance'. Such was his fury that he told the Austrians he would be delighted, if the opportunity should arise, to join them 'in administering a salutary lesson to Italy, perhaps even with sword in hand'. On 13 April 1906 a telegram from the Emperor to Goluchowski was published in which he thanked his 'faithful ally and brilliant second'.[5] He couldn't have more ostentatiously drawn attention to Italian faithlessness.[6]

---

[1] Albertini, *Origins*, I, pp. 170–1.

[2] DDF (2), IX, 24; X, 58, 69.

[3] The German delegate at Algeciras, however, was pleased with Visconti Venosta. Salvatorelli, p. 305; Tommasini, II, pp. 276–80.

[4] Albertini, *Origins*, I, p. 169.

[5] The telegram, with its implication that Austria–Hungary was Germany's satellite, destroyed the position of Goluchowski, who was replaced by Aehrenthal later in the year.

[6] Albertini, *Origins*, I, p. 175; Pribran, II, p. 138.

The French did not miss their opportunity. 'France is trying to compromise us with her protestations of love', Sonnino complained.[1] When he asked Barrère for permission to pacify the Germans by showing them the text of the 1902 agreements, Barrère refused. But the storm slowly subsided. Bülow calmed his Emperor and convinced him of the need to conceal Germany's isolation by preserving at least a facade of Triple Alliance solidarity. In June 1906 William II and Francis Joseph sent a cordial joint telegram to Victor Emmanuel from Vienna: 'Reunited the two of us, we send to our third and faithful ally the expression of our unshakeable friendship.'[2] Tittoni, who returned to office under Giolitti in May, made frequent reassuring statements. On the surface there was a deceptive calm.

The Alliance had been renewed in 1902 for twelve years, unless one of the allies gave notice of a wish to modify or terminate it before July 1907. There were doubts in all three countries. Many Germans thought that Italy's drift towards France and Britain had long since deprived the Alliance of meaning. In Austria-Hungary there was growing distrust of Italian ambitions in the Adriatic and Balkans. In Italy men as far apart politically as Bissolati and Visconti Venosta believed that a direct Italo-Austrian agreement was necessary, either to replace the Alliance or transform it into a league of peace: only thus could Austria-Hungary and Italy put an end to Germany's 'dictatorship' and avoid being engulfed in Germany's quarrel with Britain.[3] But in governing circles there was no desire for risky experiment. Francis Joseph and his ministers were pacific and conservative, preferring to leave things as they were. Bülow, though forced to admit that the Alliance was now only of negative value, held that Germany could not afford to lose an ally when no replacement was in sight. Tittoni was not the man to initiate a new and delicate policy, nor did he even try to revive the declaration of 1882 regarding Britain. In May 1907 the Alliance was therefore automatically renewed until July 1914 because, as Tittoni put it, 'no one cares to denounce it'.[4]

Calm descended upon Italian diplomacy for a time. Never since 1900 had relations with Austria-Hungary been so cordial. The power of attraction of the Entente Cordiale was increased in August 1907 when the Anglo-Russian agreement transformed it into the Triple Entente; yet Italy atoned for Algeciras by voting solidly with Germany at the second Hague Peace Conference. The year 1908 thus opened in an atmosphere of hopefulness. It was to prove stormier than 1906.

[1] Tommasini, II, p. 324.
[2] Albertini, *Origins*, I, p. 179.
[3] Bissolati, *La politica estera dell' Italia*, pp. 119 ff.; Steed, I, pp. 188–90; DDF (2), X, 396, 480.
[4] Pribram, II, p. 141.

## The Annexation of Bosnia

In October 1906 Aehrenthal became Austria-Hungary's Foreign Minister. Next month Conrad von Hötzendorf became Chief of the Austro-Hungarian General Staff. The two appointments were generally supposed to strengthen the influence of Francis Ferdinand, the nephew of Francis Joseph and heir to the Habsburg throne. Francis Ferdinand was well known for his clerical sympathies, his hatred of Italy and his desire to replace the Triple Alliance by a revived Three Emperors' League. Aehrenthal, too, had the reputation of an extreme conservative and Russophil, and as ambassador in St Petersburg had been a principal architect of the Mürzsteg programme. Conrad far surpassed Francis Ferdinand in the violence of his views on Italy. He was tortured by the threat to his country from the principle of nationality. The two champions of that principle were Italy and the Southern Slavs whom, like Mazzini, he considered to be natural allies. Believing that war was inevitable, he wished to save his country by destroying Italy and Serbia in time. In April 1907 he submitted to his Emperor the first of many memoranda advocating a preventive war before Italy became dangerously strong.

Francis Ferdinand agreed with much of Conrad's analysis, but he opposed war because of Austria-Hungary's internal weakness. His solution for the Southern Slav question, which had begun to dominate Austrian home and foreign policy, was to convert the dual Austro-Hungarian monarchy into a trial monarchy, in which the Slavs would have an equal place. By thus winning the loyalty of Austria's Slavs, the threat from Serbia, 'the South Slav Piedmont', could be neutralised. Aehrenthal substantially agreed. As a first step he advocated the formal annexation of Bosnia. The second stage would be to draw Serbia within Austria's orbit. Only if Serbia resisted would Conrad's plan of destruction have to be adopted.

During 1907 Aehrenthal went out of his way to calm Italian apprehension. He and Tittoni exchanged visits and the latter was delighted with his extreme friendliness. But in January 1908 Tittoni received a first shock. Aehrenthal suddenly announced Austria's intention of building the long-projected Sanjak railway, which would open up a new route, avoiding Serbian territory, from Vienna to the Aegean. The announcement caused a stir throughout Europe. Austria-Hungary, it seemed, was again on the march in the Balkans. It was also assumed that Aehrenthal had agreed, as the price of Turkish consent to the building of the railway, to wreck the Concert's programme of Macedonian reform. Izvolsky, the Russian Foreign Minister, was the most directly affected. He retaliated by adopting the rival Serbian scheme, also long-projected, for an east-to-west railway from the Danube through Macedonia to an Adriatic port in Albania. He also proposed new reforms for Macedonia under direct control of the Concert, which meant the end of the Mürzsteg policy. Tittoni, too, felt aggrieved, having received no previous warning such as he belie¬ed an ally had the right to expect. He therefore gave his enthusiastic support both to Izvolsky's Macedonian proposals and to the Danube–Adriatic railway.[1] The elusive Italo-Russian *entente* seemed within his grasp; it might be the first step towards a triple partnership of Italy, Russia and Austria-Hungary in the Balkans.

Tittoni was wrong, however, in supposing that the Mürzsteg spirit was quite dead. Izvolsky did not want a rupture with Austria-Hungary and his opinion of Italy was as low as that of his predecessors. He knew that Aehrenthal wished to annex Bosnia and was prepared to support him, provided he helped to get the Straits opened to Russian warships. In July 1908 the Young Turks seized power in Turkey. Aehrenthal saw that he must act quickly, before they attempted to make a reality of the nominal Turkish sovereignty over Bosnia which had been preserved in 1878.[2] To appease the Great Powers, he decided to renounce the right to garrison the Sanjak. This concession would cost little, for he knew that the Sanjak was militarily worthless; nor would the loss of the short cut to Salonika matter, for the best route lay through Serbia, which he intended should soon be Austria-Hungary's satellite. Izvolsky would be squared by the offer of a deal over the Straits. As for Italy, Tittoni had agreed at Abbazia in 1904 that the annexation of Bosnia would justify no claim to compensation; there would be 'a bit of fuss', but it would soon die down.[3]

During September 1908 Tittoni met Aehrenthal at Salzburg, Aehrenthal met Izvolsky at Buchlau and Izvolsky met Tittoni at Desio. What exactly was said at these meetings will probably never be known. Two things are certain. Firstly, Aehrenthal talked of annexation, but did not specify how or when. Secondly, Tittoni raised no objection in principle to annexation, even though it would involve a unilateral breach of the Treaty of Berlin. Izvolsky looked forward eagerly to gaining control of the Straits. Tittoni was delighted by Aehrenthal's promise, not only to evacuate the Sanjak, but also to renounce all special privileges in Montenegro.[4] Once again he saw a tripartite understanding on the Balkans taking shape. Both

[1] The Banca d'Italia joined the international financial syndicate formed to build the railway, providing 35% of the capital. The railway promised to be a channel of Italian influence in the Balkans. Giolitti, *Memorie*, pp. 261–6; Tommasini, IV, pp. 102–6. Neither it nor the Sanjak railway have been built to this day.

[2] The Young Turk revolution also led to the precipitate abandonment of European control in Macedonia.          [3] Albertini, *Origins*, I, p. 201.

[4] In 1878 Montenegro's sovereignty had been restricted under Article 29 of the Treaty of Berlin, which forbade the building of a Montenegrin navy and the

he and Izvolsky thought they had been clever. But Aehrenthal was cleverer than either.

On 6 October Tittoni spoke at Carate Brianza on the international situation. After strong hints of imminent changes in the Balkans and contemptuous references to 'the mere fictions' of the Treaty of Berlin, he declared: 'Italy can calmly await events, for however they may develop, they will not take her by surprise nor find her unprepared and isolated.'[1] A few hours later Aehrenthal announced the annexation of Bosnia. Its hopes raised by the tone of Tittoni's speech, the Italian public waited for the announcement of big compensations for Italy. When it was realised that these consisted merely in the evacuation of the Sanjak and the grant of full sovereignty to Montenegro, there was an explosion of protest. Tittoni had forgotten the lesson of 1878 and found himself with hands nearly as empty as Corti's. The press was almost unanimously critical. Scipio Sighele, an irredentist from Trentino, called him 'the unconscious satellite of Austria and secretary of Aehrenthal'; Bissolati in *Avanti!* demanded his resignation. His dilemma was this: either he knew beforehand and was therefore Aehrenthal's accomplice; or he didn't know, and was incompetent.[2] On the whole he preferred to be thought incompetent and begged Aehrenthal, in the interests of the Triple Alliance, to say as little as possible about Austro-Italian agreement. Both his own position and Italian faith in the Alliance had been shaken; to save both, he looked desperately to Austria-Hungary for concessions. He got nothing.

His first suggestion arose out of the proposal for a conference to legalise revision of the Treaty of Berlin, for which the British in particular were pressing. Before the crisis he had given the matter no thought, and he now found British protests against Austria's violation of the treaty embarrassing. He therefore pleaded with Aehrenthal for the conference to be held in an Italian city, as 'moral compensation' for Italy. But Aehrenthal disliked the idea of a conference and Bülow was determined not to have one at all. Tittoni also begged for an Italian university at Trent, as 'a spontaneous act of enlightened generosity' on the part of the Emperor; then for the cession to Italy, as token compensation, of the town of Aquileia, to which Aehrenthal's only reply was to rebuke his ambassador for consenting even to listen to such a proposal.[3] At the end of November Italian

---

fortification of Montenegrin ports, and empowered Austria–Hungary to police Montenegrin waters. The cancellation of Article 29 was suggested by Izvolsky at Buchlau and agreed to by Aehrenthal.     [1] Albertini, *Origins*, I, pp. 219–20.

[2] ibid., p. 234. The phrase is that of the Austrian ambassador in Rome. See also DDF (2), XI, 485.

[3] Albertini, *Origins*, I, pp. 241–2; Tommasini, IV, pp. 459–63. Aquileia lies on the coast twenty-five miles west of Trieste. Its cession to Italy had been discussed in 1866 when the frontier was settled.

and German students again came to blows, this time in Vienna, and feeling ran high in Italy. Tittoni told Aehrenthal that the university question had now eclipsed Bosnia in Italian eyes, and that upon the foundation of a university at Trieste depended the future of the Italian government and the Triple Alliance. Aehrenthal replied that neither he nor the Emperor had the power to meet Tittoni's wishes, but only the Vienna parliament.[1] Thus, when the debate on foreign affairs opened on 1 December 1908, Tittoni went down to the chamber with empty hands. He was attacked from all sides, by conservatives as fiercely as by the extreme left. The most damaging speech was that of Fortis, champion of the Triple Alliance, ex-Prime Minister and a leading member of the government's majority. He and his friends, he said, wished in spite of everything to remain loyal to the Triple Alliance, but their loyalty was made daily more difficult, above all by the scale of Austrian armaments. 'May we', he concluded, 'see the end of this most abnormal state of affairs, in which Italy has to fear war only from an ally.' His words were greeted with a storm of patriotic applause and Giolitti himself rose to shake him by the hand, leaving Tittoni sitting alone on the government benches.[2] Tittoni defended himself by admitting the blunders in his Carate Brianza speech and making the most of Austria's withdrawal from the Sanjak and Montenegro. But it was only the speech of Giolitti, who knew that elections were not far ahead, that rallied the majority and saved both Tittoni and the government.

In the following months relations with Austria-Hungary did not improve. After the Messina earthquake on 28 December a military periodical in Vienna, believed to reflect Conrad's views, urged an immediate settling of accounts with Italy while its army was engaged on relief work in the south. Italian indignation would have been even greater had it been known that Conrad was in fact at that moment pressing the Emperor for his consent to a preventive war. On 20 January 1909 the Austrian government introduced a bill to establish an Italian Law Faculty in Vienna, thus once again refusing a university at Trieste.[3] Tittoni, who had optimistically told the chamber in December that the Austrian government had responded favourably to his representations for a university, was dissuaded from resigning only by Giolitti, who pointed out that demonstrations of impotent wrath served no purpose. The only alternative, he argued, to patching up the Triple Alliance was war, for which Italy was unready. Tittoni told the German ambassador that Aehrenthal had been his ruin

---

[1] Albertini, *Origins*, I, pp. 235, 244–6; Tommasini, IV, p. 482.
[2] Albertini, *Origins*, I, p. 258, and *Venti anni*, I, p. 452; Cilibrizzi, III, pp. 393 ff.
[3] Even the Vienna scheme proved abortive as the bill failed to secure parliamentary approval.

and instructed his ambassador in Vienna to confine his contacts with the Foreign Minister to a cold, official minimum.[1]

The international crisis dragged on into the spring. Izvolsky's position was even more uncomfortable than Tittoni's. He could find no support for his plans for the Straits and was fiercely attacked at home for being the dupe of Aehrenthal. The latter, with full German backing, was determined to extract recognition of the annexation from the Great Powers and to obtain declarations of good neighbourliness from the Serbs and the Montenegrins who, in a fever of nationalist protest, were demanding territorial compensations. Aehrenthal got his way. By the end of May all the Great Powers had consented, without a conference, to revision of the Treaty of Berlin as regards Bosnia, the Sanjak and Montenegro. The Russians had capitulated to a German ultimatum. The Serbs made their declaration of good neighbourliness and renounced compensations. Tittoni's attempts, with British support, to mediate on behalf of the Montenegrins and spare them a similar submission were unsuccessful. The diplomatic triumph of Germany and Austria-Hungary was almost complete; the price of that triumph was paid in 1914.

The Bosnian crisis destroyed all hope of making the Triple Alliance popular in Italy and set in motion a dangerous armaments race with Austria-Hungary.[2] The whole world now knew that inside the Alliance there was a solid Austro-German partnership, based on an intimacy which was denied to Italy and prepared to override Italian interests.[3] Aehrenthal grudgingly admitted that Italy had acted correctly, but he contrasted Italian hesitations with the blank cheque Germany had gladly signed. Tittoni's confidence in Aehrenthal having been shattered, he started searching with redoubled energy for independent safeguards for Italy's Balkan interests. His particular fear, for which in fact there was no foundation, was that the Austrians might reoccupy the Sanjak and so set off another explosion of anti-Austrian sentiment in Italy. His ideal was still a tripartite understanding with Austria-Hungary and Russia; failing that, an agreement with Russia or, as a last resort, a further understanding with Austria-Hungary to strengthen Article VII of the Triple Alliance. What above all he dreaded was a revival of Austro-Russian cooperation, which would ex-

[1] Albertini, *Origins*, I, p. 267; Tommasini, IV, pp. 639 ff.
[2] See below, pp. 359–60.
[3] The German and Austro-Hungarian general staffs had secretly agreed in the spring of 1909 that, if Austria-Hungary attacked Serbia and became involved in war with Russia, Germany would back its ally and immediately invade France. This agreement, of which no hint was given to Italy, was totally irreconcilable with the defensive Triple Alliance as conceived by Bismarck and interpreted by Italy since Crispi. Albertini, *Origins*, I, pp. 268–73.

clude Italy from the Balkans. Another Mürzsteg, he told Germany in June 1909, would mean his resignation within twenty-four hours and the end of the Triple Alliance.[1]

At first he had great hopes of Izvolsky, his fellow-sufferer at Aehrenthal's hands. In December 1908 he and Muraviev, the Russian ambassador in Rome, drafted an agreement for collaboration in the Balkans, but Muraviev's sudden death held up further progress.[2] Izvolsky, in spite of his personal resentment towards Aehrenthal, was dilatory and unenthusiastic. He was sceptical of Italy's value as an ally, disliked Tittoni's patronage of the Montenegrins, and in spite of everything still vaguely hoped for an understanding with Austria-Hungary. He and Tittoni both made public statements on the intimacy of Italo-Russian relations, but that was all.[3] In March 1909 a new Russian ambassador was appointed. His immediate task was to arrange a visit by the Tsar to Italy, another postponement of which, Tittoni declared, would end cordial relations between the two countries.[4] The visit was fixed for October. But in July Tittoni lost patience and asked for the return of the Tittoni–Muraviev draft.[5] He decided to fall back on his third method, that of preventing Austrian expansion by agreement with Aehrenthal himself.

Aehrenthal, like the Germans, still thought the Triple Alliance worth preserving and agreed to negotiate; but he asked for and received assurances that there was no secret Italo-Russian pact, written or verbal, in existence. On 20 October agreement was reached in principle that reoccupation of the Sanjak would entitle Italy to compensations under Article VII, and that neither Italy nor Austria-Hungary would make exclusive agreements on the Balkans with a third Power.

On 23 October the Tsar, accompanied by Izvolsky, arrived at Racconigi, Victor Emmanuel's country palace near Turin. His route was carefully planned to avoid Austrian territory. The visit had a good press in Italy. Even the socialists contented themselves with protest meetings and there were no catcalls. The King disarmed the left by inviting Nathan, the anti-clerical Mayor of Rome, so that, though the Tsar refused to visit the capital, Rome 'was present at Racconigi'. To Tittoni's embarrassment, Izvolsky, almost as soon as he arrived, produced a draft Italo-Russian agreement which could not be harmonised with the provisional under-

---

[1] ibid., p. 303.    [2] ibid., p. 261; Tommasini, IV, pp. 531–2.

[3] Izvolsky's lack of enthusiasm may also have been due to the fact that in November 1908 he had been informed verbally by the French of the content of the Prinetti–Barrère agreement. He could well have concluded that Italy was already so far committed to Russia's ally that Russian concessions in the Balkans were superfluous. The French Foreign Minister did not tell Tittoni what he had done because of 'le désarroi de son (Tittoni's) esprit'. DDF (2), XI, 560, 563, 565, 571.

[4] Tommasini, V, p. 479.    [5] ibid., p. 370.

standing Tittoni had just reached with Aehrenthal. To overcome his hesitations, Izvolsky read out the text of the secret Austro-Russian reinsurance treaty of October 1904. Faced with this proof of Austrian 'duplicity', Tittoni assented. On 24 October the two ministers exchanged the notes which have subsequently been known as the Racconigi Agreement. They promised to maintain the Balkan *status quo*, but if this became impossible, to work for modifications according to the principle of nationality; to undertake joint diplomatic action against any major Power that disturbed the *status quo* or violated the principle of nationality (which meant Austria-Hungary); and to make no agreements on the Balkans with a third Power unless the other participated (which ruled out both a revival of Mürzsteg and a new Italo-Austrian understanding). Italy promised benevolent support of Russian aims at the Straits, and Russia of Italy's aims in Tripoli. The agreement was to be kept secret and only the Tsar, Victor Emmanuel and Giolitti were informed.[1] The notes were written in the two ministers' own hands.

Tittoni was now faced with the embarrassing problem of his relations with Austria-Hungary. Not daring to break off negotiations, he lied hard to Aehrenthal, saying that no more than an exchange of views with Izvolsky had taken place. Aehrenthal was almost sure he was lying, but on 19 December the Italo-Austrian agreement was signed. By its terms reoccupation of the Sanjak became subject to Article VII, and both parties undertook to make no Balkan agreement with a third Power without participation of the other and to exchange information on any proposals made to them. The agreement was to last as long as the Triple Alliance and only Germany was to be informed. This last clause was in direct violation of the Racconigi pact.

The agreement was signed not by Tittoni, who had left office with Giolitti on 2 December, but by his successor, Guicciardini. The latter disliked Tittoni's double dealing with Izvolsky and Aehrenthal, and he saw the danger in being simultaneously committed to two Great Powers which were in open conflict. It required much ingenuity to reconcile a promise to Russia to preserve the *status quo* or, failing that, to favour the principle of nationality, with an agreement with Austria-Hungary which condoned in advance the violation of both the *status quo* and the national principle. Guicciardini signed in spite of his misgivings because he dared not risk a rupture.[2] It was fear of Austrian military strength that now kept Italy in the Triple Alliance, and very little else.

<hr />

[1] The secret was kept until December 1912, when Izvolsky, then Russian ambassador in Paris, read out the text to Poincaré, the French President.

[2] F. Guicciardini, *Cento giorni alla Consulta* (Florence 1943), pp. 18–20; Tommasini, V, pp. 563–4. Guicciardini argued that concealment from Russia was not

NATIONALISM, IRREDENTISM AND IMPERIALISM

Tittoni did not return to office for nearly ten years after December 1909. His achievements had been modest. Italy's international position had improved during 1909, but at the cost of distrust all round. After Racconigi there was a general inclination in Europe to believe that Italy had joined the Triple Entente camp. Italian statesmen might argue that friendship with France, Britain and Russia was compatible with membership of the Triple Alliance; but to most outsiders the Alliance appeared moribund. The truth was less simple. Tittoni had failed to make the Alliance more intimate or more popular in Italy, but neither he nor his successors wished it to disappear. 'We shall come out one day, but it will be to go to war', Tittoni remarked to Izvolsky at Racconigi.[1] The statesmen of the Triple Entente realised this and had no desire to seduce Italy completely from the Alliance, believing that it was of more use to them as a dead weight inside.[2] Italian policy remained pacific, its chief aim being the maintenance of the *status quo* both in the Mediterranean and the Balkans. Article VII was kept in reserve but Italy's object was to prevent the need for its application. For the success of such a policy of checks and balances a calm and patient public opinion was essential. It was just this that was now lacking.

## Nationalism, Irredentism and Imperialism

Adowa had discredited but not destroyed the imperialist idea in Italy. A nationalist school of thought survived, at first confined to literary and inintellectual circles, but steadily gaining adherents in the changed climate of the twentieth century. After the Bosnian crisis it acquired political significance. The nationalists claimed inspiration from the Risorgimento but despised the Risorgimento's liberal tradition. In their writings nationalism completed its renunciation of Mazzini; the 'idea of Rome' became identified with domination, the 'mission' of the Third Italy with colonial conquest. They claimed to be in harmony with the times. The U.S.A. had seized an empire from Spain, the British had crushed the Boers, the young and virile Japanese had defeated Russia, the French were quietly absorbing Morocco. Imperial expansion was the fashion. Meanwhile *Italietta* was

---

a violation of the Racconigi pact because the Italo–Austrian agreement was not a new agreement, but merely an 'interpretation, development and corollary' of Article VII of the Triple Alliance. It is also significant that at Racconigi Tittoni concealed the existence of Article VII from Izvolsky and tried to give him the impression that the Triple Alliance was concerned only with Albania in the Balkans. See DDF (2), XII, 338, 340.

[1] Albertini, *Origins*, I, p. 317. The Alliance was now like 'a fly entangled in a spider's web; either the fly broke the web or the web paralysed the fly', writes Salvemini, *La politica estera dell' Italia*, p. 163.

[2] BD, IX (i), 72; DDF (2), XI, 577, 589, also XIII, 43.

being left behind, engrossed since 1896 in a humdrum, vulgar, domestic routine, devoid of heroism or sense of mission. So it seemed to Alfredo Oriani, one of the precursors of modern Italian nationalism, a prophet without honour in his own lifetime. His hero was Crispi, whose rejection after Adowa he regarded as a stain on Italy's honour far greater than military defeat by Ethiopians. For Oriani expansion was a national duty. He believed that only conquest in Africa and domination of the Adriatic and Mediterranean could complete the Risorgimento, only war could toughen the fabric of the nation; only 'in greatness' could Italy's social divisions and economic problems be resolved. Greatness was the end, heroism was the means.

Oriani died in 1909. By that year his ideas had begun to arouse interest, particularly among the young. Rationalism, positivism, humanitarianism, even socialism were losing their appeal; Mazzini and Marx were being eclipsed by Gabriele D'Annunzio, who won an astonishing ascendancy over the educated youth in the first decade of the new century.[1] D'Annunzio the poet, novelist, dramatist and aesthete, lived for sensations, gloried in violence, revelled in speed, power and adventure. Theatrical and flamboyant in both his private and public life, he offered his public fascinating tales of brutality, voluptuousness and Nietzschean supermen. Often he took as his themes the martial tradition of Rome and the maritime power of Venice. Though he dabbled in politics only fitfully and ineffectually, he educated a whole generation to despise *Italietta*, 'the art museum and servile boarding-house keeper for the spendthrifts of Europe', and to dream of a new Italy, assertive, masterful and imperial. This mood of energy and revolt found its extreme expression in the futurists, who despised traditional art and literature, preached the beauties of abstract painting, ferro-concrete, sport and flying and sang the praises of war, 'the awakener of the weak' and 'the hygiene of the world'. To such men Giolitti's moderation and empiricism were repellent, and D'Annunzio was soon to become the most passionate of anti-Giolittians. D'Annunzio and Giolitti reflected the two extremes of the Italian character. 'In the

---

[1] For a description of the 'idealist renaissance' which transformed the intellectual climate of Italy in the new century, see Croce, ch. 10; also Volpe, II, pp. 325–40; H. Stuart Hughes, *Consciousness and Society* (London 1959), pp. 62–3, 200 ff., 339–40. Croce himself played a leading part in that transformation, having by 1900 'burnt through' and discarded Marxism. As Hughes observes, in Croce's case the idealist reaction against nineteenth-century positivism took 'a rational and measured form'; but on many of the younger generation it had the effect of a 'spiritual explosion' which swept them to the extreme limits of irrationalism in philosophy and political doctrine. For a useful anthology of articles from the *avant-garde* Florentine reviews of the decade, which did so much to mould the new generation of nationalist intellectuals, see the series *La cultura del '900 attraverso le riviste* (Turin 1960–).

former', wrote a shrewd observer with nationalist sympathies, 'the Italian enjoys the pleasures of poetry, while in the latter he feels the solidity and satisfaction of prose.'[1] Their mutual antipathy symbolised the rift in the nation which was to contribute so much to the destruction of liberal Italy.

The second great figure of the nationalist movement was Enrico Corradini, a brilliant writer and journalist who had been converted to patriotism by the 'shame' of Adowa and later fell under D'Annunzio's spell. In November 1903 he founded the first nationalist review, *Il Regno*, to be 'a voice of protest against the cowardice of the present time, and above all against that of ignoble socialism'. Its aim was to stir the Italian bourgeoisie, 'decadent, but not irremediably decadent', from its torpor; to mould an élite that would create wealth, cultivate self-discipline and aspire to power and conquest. The Italian bourgeoisie required its Joseph Chamberlain or, better still, a second Crispi.[2] For years Corradini and his friends seemed to be crying in the wilderness. Nevertheless, very slowly, nationalist groups and publications began to multiply. Industrial and commercial expansion gave the movement a more solid basis and turned the attention of its leaders to exports and markets, investment and technical progress. The old habits of thinking in foreign policy – monarchical solidarity with Germany or democratic solidarity with France, friendship with Britain, support for small nations, preservation of peace – were challenged. Talk of ruthless egoism, the struggle for existence and the rewards of force became fashionable far beyond the narrow circles of intellectual nationalism.

Corradini made an exhaustive study of emigration and visited the Italian communities of Tunis, the U.S.A. and South America. He returned disillusioned, having found his countrymen exploited, assimilated and impotent in lands dominated by foreign capital. Italians built the railways and roads of the new world and reclaimed its swamps and forests, yet were lost to Italy. Worse still, Italians boasted of this perpetual haemorrhage, thereby revealing the mentality of slaves. Emigration, he asserted, was 'a phenomenon, if not of an inferior people, at least of a people at an inferior stage of existence'; it was 'beneficent like death'.[3] The remedy lay in Africa, where soil must be conquered and Italians settled under the Italian flag. Only when the emigrating spirit had been converted into the spirit of colonialism and imperialism would the Italians be a great people.[4]

[1] Salomone, p. 89 note, quoting G. Prezzolini. For the futurists, see the study of their leader, Filippo Tommaso Marinetti, in Joll, *Intellectuals in Politics*. They first forced themselves on public attention through the publication of the Futurist Manifesto in February 1909.
[2] Corradini, *Discorsi politici*, pp. 8 ff.; also Salomone, pp. 89–91; Volpe, II, pp. 360–3; Cilibrizzi, IV, pp. 123–4.
[3] Corradini, *Il volere d'Italia*, pp. 52, 60.
[4] ibid., pp. 71–2.

Corradini's special contribution to the theory of nationalism was the concept of 'the proletarian nation'. He appropriated the language of Marxism and transferred the class struggle to the international sphere. The French and British, he declared, built their power on capital; the Italians could build theirs only on labour, the one resource in which they were rich. In a world dominated by plutocracies,[1] Italy was the proletarian nation. Nationalism would be Italy's socialism in the world, her method of redemption, which would rouse a warlike spirit in the nation as socialism roused it in the working class. War, too, would put an end to internal wrangles, create a national conscience and bring greater riches for all. 'Italy', he wrote, 'must have her war, or she will never be a nation.'[2]

This language appealed not only to colonial enthusiasts but to part of the extreme left, and especially to the syndicalists. Corradini recognised the kinship between syndicalism and nationalism. They had common enemies in pacifism and humanitarianism, in the parliamentary spirit and reformist socialism. Both proclaimed inequality, the one of classes, the other of nations, and nurtured the 'will to power'. Syndicalism was 'working-class imperialism'; it fought the bourgeoisie at home while nationalism fought the plutocratic bourgeoisie of foreign lands. Both were 'schools of solidarity', rejecting 'Christian individualism' and signifying the return of 'the religion of collective man'.[3] The aim of nationalists, Corradini asserted, must be to weld Italians into a real nation, a collective unit with an individuality of its own. Then it would be possible to expel from Italy the survivals of two foreign revolutions, 'the bourgeois French revolution and the socialist German revolution', and 'sow in our soil the seeds of our future civilisation, that will take the road of the world'.[4]

The nationalists were not all agreed on the direction in which that road should run. Some thought Italy's future lay in Africa, others looked up and across the Adriatic. Many of them despised the traditional sentiment for Trieste and the Trentino, and proclaimed instead the opportunities that awaited Italy in the big world outside. But the student riots at Innsbruck in 1903–4, the growth of Austrian military and naval power, Austrian jealousy of Italian activity in the Balkans, and above all the Bosnian crisis forced nationalists to reconsider the problem of irredentism and to study the situation of the Italians inside Austria-Hungary. Before 1859 they had been one of the privileged races of the Austrian Empire. Italian had been the language of the administration, the press and the schools, not only in

[1] The greatest plutocracy of all was Britain, 'the nation of five meals a day' as D'Annunzio was to describe it in 1919.
[2] Corradini, *Il volere d'Italia*, pp. 205–7; *Il nazionalismo italiano*, pp. 34, 47–9, 67–8.          [3] Corradini, *Il volere d'Italia*, pp. 29 ff.
[4] Corradini, *Il nazionalismo italiano*, pp. vi–vii.

Lombardy and Venetia, but also in Trieste, Istria and Dalmatia; it was also the language of command in the Austrian navy. The educated and professional classes of the coastal provinces, if they wished to rise in the world, became 'Italians', thereby acquiring a higher social standing and distinguishing themselves from the mass of the Slav peasantry. Their sons went to Pavia or Padua universities and many entered the imperial bureaucracy or armed forces. With the loss to Italy of Lombardy and Venetia, the Italian subjects of Austria Hungary shrank from 5 millions to an insignificant minority; in 1910 they numbered under 800,000 in a total population of 51 millions.[1] No university remained for them within the Dual Monarchy. Their cultural assimilation of the Slavs ceased and they found themselves distrusted and debarred from positions of responsibility in the administration. In the years after 1866 they lost their privileges one by one and became immersed in a bitter racial struggle for survival, under growing pressure from the Germans, Magyars and Southern Slavs.[2]

German pressure was greatest in the Trentino. In 1910 361,000 of its 374,000 inhabitants were Italian, but it was jointly administered as one province with German Tirol. Italians held only one third of the seats in the provincial Diet, which sat at Innsbruck, the capital. The university riots were only one sign of mounting racial tension. In 1905 the Tiroler Volksbund was founded to combat Italian culture and promote loyalty to the Habsburgs. A Deutsches Schulverein and Pangerman associations, powerfully backed from the Reich, were created for 'national defence', to finance German schools, spread Germanism south of the Brenner and buy land from Italians on which to build German villages. These activities attracted sufficient attention for Tittoni and Aehrenthal to discuss them at their meeting at Semmering in August 1907.[3] German pressure was also

[1] The following figures are taken from the Austro–Hungarian census of 1910 which classified the population, often ambiguously, by 'habitual language':

|  | Total population | Italian population | Italians as % of total |
|---|---|---|---|
| Trentino | 374,000 | 361,000 | 97 |
| South Tirol (Alto Adige) | 238,000 | 22,000 | 9 |
| Trieste and district | 230,000 | 119,000 | 62 |
| Gorizia–Gradisca | 261,000 | 90,000 | 36 |
| Istria | 404,000 | 147,000 | 38 |
| Dalmatia | 646,000 | 18,000 | 2·8 |
| Fiume | 49,000 | 24,000 | 49 |
| Total in Austria (i.e. excluding Fiume) | — | 768,000 | 2·7 |

In addition to the 119,000 Austrian–Italians of Trieste, 30,000 of the 38,000 'foreigners' who appear in the census were Italians from the Kingdom.

[2] Maranelli and Salvemini, pp. 98 ff.

[3] Tommasini, III, pp. 390–2. Aehrenthal declared himself as hostile to Pangermanism as to Italian irredentism.

felt in Trieste. German nationalists had claimed the city for the German Confederation in 1848 and it had sent representatives to the Frankfurt Diet. The port was 'Austria's lung' and its prosperity depended upon its links with central Europe. As German industry and commerce expanded, German merchant houses, shipping and insurance companies established themselves in the city. Control of Trieste became a vital part of the German imperialist *Drang nach Osten*.[1]

A much greater threat to the Italian communities on the Austrian Adriatic coast came from the 'rising Slav tide'. Southern Slav nationalism rapidly gathered momentum after 1890. Urbanisation and industrialisation brought Slav peasants into the Italian towns; they obtained jobs on the railways and in the merchant navy, in the police, local administrations and state bureaucracy. A Slav professional and commercial middle class grew up; Slav banks and shipping lines,[2] a theatre and press were founded. The Croats and Slovenes acquired their own schools and ceased to be ignorant peasants. Italian-owned estates dwindled as tenants bought their own land. As the status of Italian declined, Italianised Slavs became 'renegades' and proudly reverted to being Croats or Slovenes. The old Italian oligarchies were dispossessed by democratic pressure from below.

The situation was gravest in Dalmatia, where Italians formed only 3% of the population.[3] One after another of the 82 communes fell into Slav hands, until in 1910 only Zara retained an Italian majority.[4] In 1861 the Dalmatian Diet had contained 26 Italians and 15 Slavs; in 1910 the Italians were only 6. By 1914 all 11 Dalmatian deputies in the Vienna parliament were Slavs. North of Dalmatia, in Fiume, Istria, Trieste and Gorizia, the Italians still retained much of their influence and security. Fiume had been since 1779 a *corpus separatum* of the Hungarian crown, outside Croatia and ruled by a governor directly responsible to Budapest. Though the Croat population was growing, the Italians were still the most numerous national group[5] and could count on the Hungarian government's support in maintaining control of the port, which was Hungary's 'lung'. In Istria the west coast had an Italian majority, the interior and east coast were over-

[1] Even Bismarck, the 'little German', once referred to Trieste as 'Germany's only port on the southern seas'. DDF (1), III, 307.

[2] Many of them with Czech capital. Gayda, *L'Italia d'oltre confine*, pp. 97 ff., 346 ff.

[3] The Austro–Hungarian census of 1910 certainly discriminated against the Italians. Moderate Italian writers have estimated the Italian population at 40,000, or 6% of the total. Maranelli and Salvemini, pp. 83–9.

[4] Nearly half of the whole Italian population of Dalmatia lived in Zara, the provincial capital.

[5] If the population of Sušak, separated from Fiume by a narrow river, was added, the Italians became a minority; but Sušak was part of Croatia, not of the *corpus separatum*.

whelmingly Slav. In 1911 the Italians still controlled 33 of the 46 communes and polled 48% of the votes in the general election of that year, though they constituted only 38% of the population. Their position in Trieste was strengthened by the presence of 30,000 citizens of the Kingdom of Italy (*regnicoli*) and by an important Jewish element which was entirely Italian-ised. But even at Trieste Croats and Slovenes were slowly infiltrating towards the centre of the city from the suburbs and surrounding countryside.

This decline of the Italian communities was inevitable, even if it was accelerated by action of the Vienna government.[1] Racial antagonism, which found expression after 1900 in frequent disturbances down the Adriatic coastline, was not unwelcome to the authorities, who saw the uses of *divide et impera* as a method of government. The Italians were regarded as less reliable citizens than the Slavs. The former looked to a united Italy just across the frontier, while until 1905 few Croats or Slovenes felt attracted to a weak and primitive Serbia, separated from them by religion, culture and centuries of history. The Austrian government hoped its benevolence would reinforce Slav attachment to church and throne. It therefore financed Slav schools at the expense of Italian, and promoted Croat and Slovene as official languages. The proposal for an Italian university at Trieste was sacrificed to Slav (and German) resistance. Even after 1905, when the Serbs and Croats of Austria-Hungary formed a political coalition and the Yugoslav movement[2] began to make headway, the position of the Italians improved little. In January 1906 the municipal autonomy of Trieste was curtailed. In 1907 the introduction of universal male suffrage in Austria sealed the fate of the Italians in Dalmatia and many parts of Istria.[3] Even in Trieste the Italian liberal-national parties were heavily defeated in the 1907 election. In the local elections of 1909 and the general election of 1911 they sank their petty differences and recovered ground; but unceasing effort was required to hold their own. In 1909 a new compromise on the language question in Dalmatia struck a further blow at the superior status enjoyed by Italian over Serbo-Croat in the administration and courts of law.

This growing insecurity increased the numbers of those who looked to Italy for salvation and many chose voluntary exile in order to further the

[1] With the exception of Fiume, all the Italian-inhabited regions were in the Austrian half of the Dual Monarchy and governed from Vienna.

[2] The Yugoslav movement aimed at the fusion of Serbia, Montenegro, Bosnia and the Southern Slav provinces of Austria–Hungary in a united Yugoslav state. One of the immediate aims of the Serbo–Croat coalition of 1905 was the administrative union of Austrian Dalmatia with Hungarian Croatia.

[3] Although the Italians obtained more parliamentary seats in proportion to their numbers than any other nationality. R. A. Kann, *The Multinational Empire* (New York 1950), I, pp. 266, 424.

irredentist cause. Italy, however, was Austria-Hungary's ally and Italian governments could give no official encouragement. Among the Italians who remained in Austria, irredentism was not a powerful force. In the Trentino the majority of the population remained passive and reasonably content. Austrian rule was mild, the Italians enjoyed many privileges and their political leaders practised a wary opportunism. The stronger of the two main parties, the Christian Socialist, while demanding the administrative separation of the Trentino from Tirol, felt pride in Tirol's history as a fortress of Catholicism and retained its devotion to the Habsburgs. [1] The rival Socialist party campaigned against Austrian clericalism and 'feudalism' and accused the Christian socialists of servility to Vienna. Its leading personality, Cesare Battisti, was an unorthodox socialist, a Garibaldian in spirit, passionately proud of the Italian traditions and culture of the Trentino. In public he too demanded no more than local autonomy; in private he was an irredentist and union with Italy was his ultimate aim. But on this point few of his followers shared his views.

In Dalmatia irredentism was negligible. The Italian party, which until 1890 had called itself Autonomist, was chiefly concerned in preventing the union of Dalmatia with Croatia and Bosnia, in order to escape total submersion in the Slav sea. Dalmatia had never figured in the traditional irredentist programme. The same was true of Fiume, where the Italians concentrated on preserving the town's autonomy against Budapest's policy of centralisation and Magyarisation, and on holding the Croats in check. Only among the younger generation was there any irredentist sympathy. In 1905 a secret Giovane Fiume society was founded, with a Mazzinian programme, but its influence was very small. Irredentism was strongest in Trieste and Istria. Yet even here it was powerfully combated by the church and the socialists. The church was anti-Italian because the Italian middle class of the towns was anti-clerical and the Slav countryside was devout. The socialists were anti-Italian because they subordinated national to social questions and championed the largely Slav proletariat against the largely Italian bourgeoisie. Both socialists and Christian socialists tried to be multi-national parties and looked to Vienna.

The militant irredentists and nationalists of Italy were deeply disturbed by this state of affairs. Drastic action seemed necessary to ensure the survival of *italianità* across the frontier. Inside Austria the Lega Nazionale, founded in 1890 in place of the suppressed Pro Patria Society,[2] tried to combat German and Slav encroachment by financing schools, libraries and

---

[1] One of its leaders was Alcide De Gasperi, who represented a constituency of the Trentino in the Vienna parliament from 1911 to 1918 and ended his life as Prime Minister of the Italian Republic from 1945 to 1953.

[2] See above, p. 137.

lecture tours, granting scholarships at Italian universities and buying property in the Trentino to keep it in Italian hands. From Italy the Dante Alighieri Society gave it encouragement and a little financial help. The militants despised such legal, highbrow activities. In 1903 a Trent and Trieste Society was founded to revive irredentist sentiment. In the excitement caused by the Innsbruck incidents it won rapid support, particularly in the universities and in Lombardy and Venetia, the two most irredentist regions of Italy. Corradini had at first despised 'the Adriatic pond', but a visit to Istria and Dalmatia changed his mind. He found inspiration in Dalmatia's 'Venetian construction and Roman foundation', and in the heroism of its Italian inhabitants who 'stand fighting alone, advanced sentinels of *italianità* cut off in the thick mass of the Slav population', inspired by a collective spirit so deplorably absent in parliamentary Italy.[1] This theme soon dominated nationalist writing. In 1908 D'Annunzio published his verse play, *La Nave*, glorifying the traditions and achievements of Venice, once mistress of what had now become for Italy 'the bitter, bitter Adriatic'. 'Arm the prow and set sail towards the world', cried one of the play's characters.[2] Irredentism and nationalism began to merge. A myth grew up that the whole eastern shore of the Adriatic was essentially Italian and that only a hostile Austrian government had contrived its denationalisation.[3] Brawls between Italians and Croats were written up by the Italian press as officially instigated brutalities.[4] The claims of the Slavs to a Risorgimento of their own were dismissed as unworthy of consideration; the Croats were branded as the Habsburgs' traditional instrument for the oppression of Italy, an inferior race, incurably clerical and faithful to the Dual Monarchy – in short, *austriaci*. Italian nationalists convinced themselves that the Slav intellectuals of Dalmatia were an insignificant handful and that 'their mentality is Italian'. 'The Italian population seems to be in a minority [in Dalmatia] compared with the Slavs', wrote Virginio Gayda, a nationalist journalist, in 1914; 'but the country's past has been wholly Italian, as its soul is even now.'[5] These illusions were soon to cost Italy dear.

The Bosnian crisis and the consequent disillusionment with the Triple Alliance accelerated the fusion of nationalism and irredentism. The latter

[1] Corradini, *Il volere d'Italia*, pp. 80, 84, 95.

[2] Salomone, p. 89.

[3] 'The history of Dalmatia in the last hundred years . . . is the massacre of a nation.' Gayda, *L'Italia d'oltre confine*, p. 259.

[4] One of these incidents, at Sušak in 1906, was even compared by Tittoni to the Aigues Mortes incident of 1893 (see above, pp. 160–1). Tommasini, III, pp. 78 ff., 95 ff.

[5] Gayda, *Modern Austria*, p. 38. These arguments were used to support Italian claims at the Peace Conference in 1919.

ceased to be the monopoly of the left and began to penetrate conservative, monarchist and even military circles. In November 1909 General Asinari, commander of the Brescia military district and veteran of the 1866 war, made an irredentist speech which Giolitti described as 'a veritable declaration of war'. Giolitti insisted, against initial resistance from the King, on Asinari's immediate dismissal from the army.[1] In the same year a young journalist, Luigi Federzoni, launched a passionate newspaper campaign against the de-Italianisation of Lake Garda by German tourists, German-owned hotels and German *Kultur*, aided by a 'servile' local population.[2] The new irredentists were no Mazzinians and looked far beyond Trent and Trieste. They dreamt of naval domination of the Adriatic, secure military frontiers, hegemony of the Balkans and expansion to the east: of a Greater Italy to be achieved by *Realpolitik* and force. More and more they counted on war to satisfy Italy's aspirations and wipe out the shame of 1866 and 1896.

The possibility of war was meanwhile being forced upon the attention of Italian statesmen by the growing military and naval strength of Austria-Hungary and by the violent tone of the Austrian military press, widely believed to owe its inspiration to Conrad himself. An expensive six-year programme for the army and navy had been approved in 1901–2, but by 1905 it had already proved inadequate. Successive Italian governments tried to evade the issue. Giolitti was primarily interested in domestic reform and reluctant to add to the nation's financial burden. Tittoni appreciated the need for military strength from which to bargain, but deprecated public agitation. Both realised the folly of provoking Austria-Hungary. The result of this neglect was a serious decline in the army's efficiency and morale. The officer corps was disgruntled with low pay and onerous conditions of service. Shortage of funds meant that less than half of each annual class of conscripts could be called up. The peace-time structure of twelve army corps looked impressive on paper but almost every unit was under strength. In 1908 a commission of enquiry discovered a grave shortage of modern artillery and revealed that the 650 kilometres of frontier with Austria contained only one modern armed fort. The railways of Venetia were so inadequate that the general staff planned on mobilisation to concentrate the army behind the Piave and so abandon eastern Venetia to the enemy after no more than a delaying action.

The state of the navy was healthier, though it too had its anxieties. Ferri's allegations of corruption against Admiral Bettolo[3] had led to the appointment of a parliamentary commission of enquiry, with Franchetti as *rapporteur*. Its report was published in 1906. Some of Ferri's accusations were proved true: the navy had established undesirable links with the

[1] *Quarant' anni*, II, 702–5.    [2] Cilibrizzi, IV, pp. 126–9.    [3] See above, p. 265.

shipyards and steel manufacturers, and had paid excessive prices for inferior products. In spite of these shortcomings the service achieved a high
standard of efficiency. It was fortunate in having a single minister, Admiral
Carlo Mirabello, for six unbroken years from December 1903. Mirabello's
task was made easier by the fact that even the extreme left regarded the
navy as a less reactionary and militaristic institution than the army. While
expenditure on the latter was hotly contested and rose by only 3·5% between 1893–4 and 1906–7, expenditure on the former increased by 42% in
the same period.[1]

Until 1900 Austria-Hungary had shown little interest in naval power.
Its ships were designed for coastal defence and caused Italy no anxiety.
But in the new century there came a change. The new ships that were built
were clearly designed for offensive operations. This was acknowledged in
1906 by Francis Ferdinand himself, who declared: 'The fleet must become
sufficiently strong to carry out its tasks in the Adriatic, not just limiting itself to passive defence of the coasts, but putting to sea to seek out
and destroy the enemy.' After 1902 Austria-Hungary replaced France
as Italy's chief naval rival. Mirabello's policy was to maintain decisive
superiority in the Adriatic. In order to achieve this, Italy was by 1908
spending twice as much as Austria-Hungary on its navy (and less than
half as much on its army). Even so, the margin of superiority was shrinking,
particularly in large ships. Between 1899 and 1903 Italy and Austria-
Hungary each laid down six battleships, and in 1905–7 Italy also laid down
four smaller battle-cruisers. The Austrians replied with a new class of
three ships of 14,500 tons, due for unprecedently rapid completion in
1909–10, which were larger and more formidably armed than any unit of
the Italian fleet.[2] This was the most serious threat to Italian security in
the Adriatic for over thirty years.

The Bosnian crisis intensified Italian fears and set off an armaments race
with Austria-Hungary on both land and sea. On 31 March 1909 the Minister for War, Senator Severino Casana, the first civilian ever to hold that
post, resigned in protest against the cabinet's refusal to agree to an increase
in military expenditure. Earlier that month Mirabello had with difficulty
been dissuaded from doing the same.[3] Giolitti was forced to make concessions. During the summer Casana's successor, General Paolo Spingardi,
obtained extra credits for the army. With his backing General Alberto
Pollio, Chief of Staff since 1908, was able to take the problems of land

---

[1] Albertini, *Venti anni*, I, pp. 312–15. The figures are Sonnino's, from a parliamentary speech of March 1908. Nevertheless over the whole period 1862–1913,
three times as much was spent on the army as on the navy. Rochat, p. 297.

[2] *Jane's Fighting Ships 1915*, pp. 285–8, 336–8; *La marina italiana*, I, pp. 277–
285 and Appendix 3, pp. 454–9.

*Quarant' anni*, II, 685–90.

defence in hand. Mobilisation plans for the eventuality of an Austro-Hungarian attack, which had existed on paper since 1885, were overhauled and brought up to date. Over the next two years artillery and fortifications were modernised, railway tracks towards the frontier were doubled, the period of military service was reduced from three to two years and a higher percentage of each annual class was called up, more realistic manœuvres were held and experiments were made with motorisation and military aviation. Exaggerated nervousness on both sides of the Austro-Italian frontier led to frequent incidents and mutual accusations of espionage. The Italians transferred the bulk of their garrisons from the French to the Austrian Alps, while the Austrians built up the Trentino into what seemed to Italians 'a great entrenched camp in the heart of Lombardy and Venetia threatening the valley of the Po'.[1]

The naval rivalry generated even greater tension. In 1908 the Italian naval general staff called for a fleet twice the size of Austria-Hungary's in order to compensate for the latter's geographical advantage in possessing secure bases. The attainment of a 2:1 ratio was of course far beyond the bounds of political possibility. Italy's first dreadnought, the *Dante Alighieri*, of 18,400 tons and armed with twelve 12-inch guns, was laid down in June 1909. But by then Austria-Hungary had already announced its intention of building four equally well-armed dreadnoughts of 20,000 tons, the first to be completed by the autumn of 1912. While France and Britain speculated whether the Italian and Austrian programmes signified a bid, with Germany's blessing, for naval supremacy in the Mediterranean, most Italians assumed that the purpose of the Austrian ships was to be used against Italy. The reaction was spirited. Between January 1910 and April 1912 five more dreadnoughts, each of 22,000 tons, were laid down, to make a total of six to Austria-Hungary's four by 1915.[2] The cost of this programme was frightening, but the determination to meet it strengthened as the years passed. In January 1911 the Prime Minister, Luzzatti, declared to the British ambassador, 'When the Italians had nothing left but their shirts to wear, they would if need be sacrifice them also for the national defence.'[3] Luzzatti spoke for the majority of the nation.

Even the pacifists became less vocal after 1909. Anti-militarist resolutions were still a feature of every socialist congress, but they now mostly

---

[1] Gayda, *Modern Austria*, p. 15. Giolitti had assured Barrère in November 1907 that no fortifications had been built on the French frontier for a long time, and that such limited funds as were available would be used on the Austrian frontier. DDF (2), XI, 213.

[2] *Jane's Fighting Ships 1915*, pp. 281–4, 335; *La marina italiana*, I, pp. 260–1, 285–6 and Appendix 3, pp. 454–5. For the French reaction, see DDF (2), XII, 199, XIII, 150.

[3] BD, VI, 426.

called for a reduction in armaments, not their total suppression. Bissolati in particular, shaken by the failure of Austrian socialists to protest against mobilisation and the threat to invade Serbia, turned to constructive criticism of the army's organisation and efficiency. His reformist colleague, Ivanoe Bonomi, argued that while German and Austrian socialists remained so susceptible to patriotic appeals, pacifism in Italy was merely 'patriotism in reverse' which could be fatal to democratic progress.[1] Even socialists could no longer ignore the danger of war with Austria-Hungary.

A determined effort to remove the causes of tension was made by Marquis Antonio Di San Giuliano, who became Foreign Minister for the second time in March 1910 and retained that post without a break until his death in October 1914. San Giuliano was a Sicilian aristocrat from Catania, of which he had been mayor at the age of twenty-seven. A deputy since 1882, he had stuck to Crispi, held cabinet office under Pelloux, became Fortis's Foreign Minister in 1905, then served as ambassador in London and Paris. Ambitious, hard-working and much-travelled,[2] he felt more sympathy than either Giolitti or Tittoni with the nationalist programme. He had studied emigration, served on an Eritrean commission in 1891 and visited Tripoli, Albania and Macedonia. Italy's future, he believed, lay in the Mediterranean and Africa, and in economic expansion to the east. 'To us falls the duty', he wrote to his Prime Minister, Luzzatti, in October 1910, 'of thinking of that greater Italy which, with different methods but, we trust, not dissimilar results, will emulate ancient Rome, spread through all the regions of the world and enrich them with her own labour.'[3]

San Giuliano's policy was to revive the Triple Alliance and transform it into an instrument of expansion. He was neither pro-French nor pro-Austrian, but he respected German military strength, distrusted Russia and the Slavs, and had many doubts about the fibre of democratic France and liberal Britain. He was anxious to collaborate with Austria-Hungary, provided Italy was not frustrated in its attempts to extend its influence in the Balkans, Asia Minor and the Levant. At the same time he was alive to the danger of Austrian expansion, particularly in Albania. He therefore supported substantial armaments, believing that only a strong Italy could ensure that its interests were not neglected inside the Alliance. These ideas were touched upon at meetings between San Giuliano, Aehrenthal and the German Chancellor, Bethmann Hollweg, between March and October 1910. San Giuliano stressed his indifference to the Trentino and his anxiety for a strong Austria-Hungary, whose disappearance would lead to

---

[1] Michels, pp. 411 ff.
[2] In 1906 he became President of the Italian Royal Geographical Society.
[3] Volpe, III, p. 322.

unification of the Southern Slavs and create grave danger for Italy. He assured his allies that irredentism would die if Austria's Italian subjects did in fact receive the enlightened treatment that the Vienna government had promised. At the same time he gave warning that further Austrian advances in the Balkans, without compensation for Italy, would cause a violent revulsion of Italian opinion. Bethmann Hollweg and Aehrenthal were pleased with him and calm returned to the Triple Alliance in 1910–11; the French were correspondingly worried.[1] San Giuliano's success, however, was limited and his optimism was not shared even by his Prime Minister, Luzzatti.[2] He never secured German help in pressing the Austrian government to treat its Italian subjects better;[3] and, like Tittoni, he was constantly hampered by public opinion at home, which soothing official communiqués failed to satisfy.

Interest in Africa was meanwhile reviving. The ten years since Adowa had seen modest but solid progress in Eritrea and Somaliland, thanks to the unpublicised devotion and enterprise of a few administrators and soldiers who received little support from Rome. Under Ferdinando Martini's long governorship from 1897 to 1907, Eritrea acquired secure frontiers, an efficient administration, good roads, a railway and an adequate capital at Asmara. The abandonment of all idea of settling Italian peasants on the land ensured good relations with the native population. Trade expanded and the towns grew.[4] Martini scrupulously refrained from interference in the affairs of Ethiopia and Menelik began to turn to the Italians, as the least dangerous Europeans, for support against Britain and France. This period of non-interference ended with the Anglo-Franco-Italian treaty of December 1906, which, at the price of reviving Ethiopian fears of Italy, guaranteed Italian interests against the day when Menelik, now very old, should die.[5] The Somali coast had been administered since 1892 by private capitalist companies. Public interest was awakened in 1902

[1] DDF (2), XIII, 43, 58.

[2] The British ambassador reported on 12 January 1911 that in the course of a long conversation, mainly concerned with Austrian hostility to Italy, Luzzatti 'spoke throughout as though Italy were the ally of Great Britain and France, and not of Austria and Germany'. BD, VI, 426.

[3] In February 1911 yet another project was launched for the solution of the university problem, this time for an Italian Law Faculty in Vienna, to be transferred to an Italian town within four years. It never materialised.

[4] The population of Eritrea in 1908 was about 450,000, of whom under 3,000 were Italians (exclusive of soldiers).

[5] The treaty recognised the hinterlands of Eritrea and Italian Somaliland as Italian spheres of influence and acknowledged Italy's right to connect the two colonies by a strip of territory west of Addis Ababa. It was a common opinion that Ethiopia would disintegrate on Menelik's death.

when joint operations were undertaken with the British against the 'Mad Mullah'. The fighting lasted for three years and the Italian authorities played a leading part in the negotiations that led to the temporary restoration of peace.[1] In 1905 the government bought the sovereign rights over the Somali coast from the Sultan of Zanzibar and created the colony of Italian Somaliland. In the same year the British agreed to lease part of the Kenyan port of Kismayu, which Italy had claimed in vain since 1888. Pacification and frontier delimitation were followed by appreciable economic development.

The nationalists despised these modest achievements. Their hero was Crispi, whom *Italietta* had rejected, and they revived his dreams of imperial greatness. As in Crispi's day, the keenest support for overseas expansion came from southerners who still longed for land where emigrants could settle under the Italian flag.[2] They were not interested in Somali deserts or Eritrean mountains, but in Tripoli, Italy's 'fourth shore'. William II's escapade at Tangier in 1905 put Tripoli back into Italian minds. 'There are signs of a revival of a policy of African expansion', wrote Barrère in May.[3] Successive governments were nevertheless cautious. Diplomatic recognition of Italy's 'right of pre-emption' had been secured, but no responsible politician was anxious to hurry the day when Tripoli should become Italian. To upset the *status quo* in North Africa might well encourage others to upset it in the Balkans. Tripoli would be occupied 'only when circumstances made it absolutely indispensable', said Tittoni during the Moroccan crisis.[4] Five years later San Giuliano's policy was the same: Italy wished Tripoli to remain Turkish.[5] The immediate task was to develop an economic stake in the country and keep other nations out. The Turks were to be required to hold on to Tripoli until Italy felt strong enough to take over.

Italian fears of foreign encroachment were not unreasonable. The French continued to nibble away on the Tunisian and Algerian frontiers. The British occupied Sollum bay in 1909 and were popularly believed to have designs for a coaling station at Bomba, another 150 miles further west. The Germans were suspiciously active in Tripoli, establishing banks and shipping services, contracting for public works and buying land. A more

[1] J. L. Glanville, *Italy's Relations with England 1896–1905* (Baltimore 1934), pp. 127–34; Ciasca, pp. 276–9. The Mad Mullah continued to make the British uncomfortable in British Somaliland until 1920.

[2] In 1909 5·5 million Italians resided abroad. Of these 4·4 million were in America, 836,000 in Europe and 192,000 in Africa (less than 5,000 under Italian rule). Coletti, p. 80.

[3] DDF (2), VI, 417.

[4] Tommasini II, p. 60.

[5] Speech of 2 December 1910. Cilibrizzi, IV, p. 156; Askew, p. 32.

serious source of anxiety was Turkish obstruction of Italian enterprise. In 1907 the Banco di Roma[1] established an agency in Tripoli and began to finance Italian commerce, shipping lines and small-scale industry. The Turks had every reason to be suspicious of the agency, which was virtually a government department. Its investments totalled a mere £1,000,000 and most of its allegedly economic activities were cover for political penetration.[2] By 1910 Italy occupied second place in Tripoli's foreign trade and Italian residents numbered about a thousand. The greater their influence became, the more obstructive the Turkish authorities grew, while Italian consuls and press correspondents systematically magnified every petty incident. In April 1908 a request to open five additional Italian post offices within the Turkish Empire was refused.[3] Tittoni lost patience and a naval squadron was ordered to the Aegean. The Turks then promptly conceded all that was asked of them. Later that year the Young Turk revolution intensified Turkish nationalism and xenophobia, and the Bosnian crisis exasperated nationalist feeling in Italy. Friction increased at Tripoli and the diplomatic protests at Constantinople multiplied. A growing section of the Italian press began to agitate for an end to temporisation and a drastic assertion of Italian 'rights'.

In December 1910 the first nationalist congress met in Florence. It was a heterogeneous gathering of imperialists and irredentists, republicans and monarchists, democrats and ex-syndicalists, ex-socialists and reactionaries. Its tone was authoritarian and its themes were the creation of a forceful, united nation and its education for war. 'It is time to resume the heroic task, it is time to reconquer Italy for Italy', wrote the ex-socialist poet Giovanni Pascoli in a message of greeting.[4] On 1 March 1911, the fifteenth anniversary of Adowa, Corradini published the first number of a weekly, L'Idea Nazionale. It glorified Crispi and bewailed the flabbiness and degeneracy of the decade that followed Adowa. The same year saw the celebration of the fiftieth anniversary of unification. It was the occasion of a great display of national unity, shared by all except the Catholics. A congress of Italians resident abroad was held in Rome. Pride in Italy's progress, vitality and prosperity was the keynote of the year.[5] 'The harsh

[1] The Banco di Roma had close connexions with the Vatican. Its President was Ernesto Pacelli, member of one of the most influential 'black' families and uncle of the future Pope Pius XII. Tittoni's brother was a vice-president.

[2] E. Staley, War and the Private Investor (Chicago 1935), pp. 62–70; Askew, pp. 11, 29.

[3] All the Great Powers had their own post offices in Turkey and a similar request had never before been refused.

[4] Salomone, pp. 93–4.

[5] As part of the celebrations the grandiose monument to Victor Emmanuel II was unveiled at the foot of the Capitol.

winter has ended', declared Nitti, 'and already the tree is in flower.'[1] Italy had come of age.

All through the spring and summer of 1911 the nationalist press hammered away on the theme of Tripoli. Corradini paid a visit for *L'Idea Nazionale* and reprinted his despatches in a book entitled *Tripoli's Hour*. 'Over there in Tripoli', he wrote, 'millions of men could live happily';[2] only Turkish barbarism and obstruction withheld from Italy the Promised Land which would solve the problem of the south and end the haemorrhage of emigration.[3] In the mood of national pride and exaltation which the celebrations of 1911 generated, such ideas caught on. Italy was preparing psychologically for action.

[1] Volpe, II, p. 349.

[2] Corradini, *L'ora di Tripoli*, p. 14.

[3] ibid., p. 227; G. Bevione, *Come siamo andati a Tripoli* (Turin 1912), pp. 162, 190.

# 10
# From Tripoli to Sarajevo
## 1911–14

## The Conquest of Libya

On 1 July 1911 the German cruiser *Panther* dropped anchor in the Moroccan port of Agadir. The international crisis which followed thrust Tripoli upon Italy's attention even more forcibly than William II's landing at Tangier in 1905. Only three weeks earlier, San Giuliano had repeated in the chamber that Italy's policy was 'the maintenance of the territorial *status quo* and the integrity of the Ottoman Empire'.[1] Now, after hearing the news from Agadir, he told his subordinates in the Foreign Ministry, 'The hour of Tripoli draws near for Italy', and instructed the newly appointed consul to be prepared 'to be the last consul at Tripoli'.[2] There was one powerful argument against action: an attack on Tripoli might precipitate attacks on Turkey by the Balkan states, with consequent risk of a European war and inevitable damage to Italy's relations with Austria. On the other hand San Giuliano realised that the Moroccan crisis, the state of Italian opinion and Turkey's continued obstructiveness at Tripoli would probably force Italy to act within a few months. He therefore urged rapid and intensive military preparations. These might intimidate the Turks and induce them to be more conciliatory. If not, Italy would be in a position to strike a crushing blow and present Europe with a *fait accompli*. Giolitti did not disagree in substance, but he insisted on waiting until the storm over Agadir had subsided.[3] The nationalists meanwhile intensified their agitation. Even the moderate press called for action and the public was soon in no mood for half measures. 'Tripoli must be ours or we will suffocate', wrote the nationalist Bevione on 1 August.[4] By the middle of September an agreement between France and Germany seemed

[1] Cilibrizzi, IV, p. 150; Volpe, III, p. 337.
[2] Askew, p. 48; Rodd, III, p. 141; Galli, p. 46.
[3] San Giuliano's memorandum of 28 July to Giolitti, in *Quarant' anni*, III, 49; Giolitti, *Memorie*, pp. 333–8.
[4] Askew, p. 51.

likely, whereby Morocco would become a French protectorate and Germany receive compensation in west Africa. The government decided to act without delay.

Giolitti had no thirst for African glory nor did he dream of reclaiming vast deserts for civilisation. His motives were sober and realistic. It was clear to him that no Italian prime minister could afford to repeat the misadventures of 1881–2 by missing a chance to acquire a north African colony. He hoped by a short, limited war to remove Tripoli from international diplomacy,[1] strengthen Italy's position in the Mediterranean and at the same time consolidate his own position at home. The socialists had been given nationalised insurance and universal suffrage; now it was the nationalists' turn. Speed, however, was essential. The navy advised that October was the latest month of the year in which landings could be made with safety. To wait for the spring would be politically too risky. There were also disquieting signs of German activity in Tripoli. The Banco di Roma was threatening to sell out to a group of Austro-German bankers,[2] and some Italians feared that the *Panther*, frustrated at Agadir, might turn up at Tobruk and stake a German claim to Cyrenaica. Most important of all, Italy's agreement with France made action necessary. Since 1900 Morocco and Tripoli had been diplomatically linked. If France now acquired Morocco and Italy failed to acquire Tripoli, it was unlikely that the French would continue to show concern for Italian aspirations. The alternative was, in Giolitti's words, 'either to assert our rights or to renounce them'.[3]

The military preparations were made in great haste. Pollio, the Chief of Staff, estimated in August that 22,000 men would be needed. Giolitti instructed him to prepare a force of 40,000.[4] On 17 September the King gave his consent in principle to war, but only on the 24th was the final decision taken. On the 28th a twenty-four-hour ultimatum was handed to the Turkish government. Consent to an immediate military occupation of Tripoli was demanded, on the ground that it had been allowed to fall into a 'state of neglect and disorder' which endangered Italian lives and interests. The Turks rejected the demand and war was declared next day. Giolitti did not bother to recall parliament. Without waiting for the expeditionary corps, which was still not ready, the fleet sailed for Tripoli and bombarded the town. The Turkish garrison withdrew inland and on 5 October 1600 marines landed under command of Admiral Umberto

[1] Once Italy had occupied Tripoli, it could no longer be offered under Article VII as compensation for Austrian acquisitions in the Balkans.

[2] Giolitti, *Memorie*, pp. 338–9; *Quarant' anni*, III, 50.

[3] Giolitti, *Memorie*, p. 334; *Discorsi parlamentari*, III, p. 1667.

[4] Giolitti, *Memorie*, pp. 357–8.

Cagni. For a week these 'Garibaldini of the sea' held the town by bluff until the first troops arrived. By 22 October Homs and the main ports of Cyrenaica – Benghazi, Derna and Tobruk – had also been occupied.

The Italian attack received a bad press throughout Europe. Liberal and left-wing opinion was shocked by the naked aggression and moved by sympathy for the Young Turks. Governments were more cautious, not wishing to push Italy into the camp of their opponents. All the Great Powers had by 1911 given their consent, in varying degrees, to Italy's acquisition of Tripoli; but all had hoped it would never happen, and found the present moment highly inconvenient. There was risk of their economic and financial interests in Turkey being upset. War might spread to the Balkans and precipitate another major Eastern crisis, a possibility which particularly disturbed Austria-Hungary. Britain feared the war would rouse anti-European feeling among Indian Moslems. The French were reluctant to have the Italians, allied to Germany, as their neighbours in Africa. Austria-Hungary and Germany, especially William II, were afraid that their ally's behaviour would destroy their own influence in Turkey and revive that of Britain. There was therefore general approval of the attempts at mediation which were made, principally by Germany, during October 1911, on the basis of Italian occupation under Turkish suzerainty. To cut short any such endeavours Giolitti, overruling San Giuliano, proclaimed the annexation of Libya[1] and the abolition of Turkish sovereignty on 5 November. He had judged Italy's mood correctly. When the annexation decree was submitted to the chamber next February for ratification, only 38 deputies out of 470 opposed it. Italy's action ended the possibility of mediation, for no Turkish government could cede Libya outright to an enemy which had so far done no more than establish a few precarious coastal footholds.[2] The annexation decree in fact stimulated Arab resistance and Moslem fanaticism, prolonged the war by making it popular in Turkey and thus dangerously increased international tension.[3]

The declaration of war and the first landings roused huge enthusiasm in Italy. The nationalists were exultant. 'We are no longer a people of

[1] Libya was the name adopted for the new colony which comprised Tripolitania and Cyrenaica.

[2] The Turks pointed out, correctly, that Italy's act of annexation violated both the Treaty of Paris of 1856 and the Treaty of Berlin; but no one took any notice. San Giuliano, in excusing Italy's action to his allies, used the old argument: if Libya were not annexed, the monarchy would be in danger.

[3] Most foreign observers expected Turkey to submit after a show of resistance, but they were wrong. Jules Cambon, for instance, wrote on 4 October: 'En réalité, toute cette guerre n'est pas une guerre; c'est une négotiation diplomatique, précédée d'une prise de gage violente.' This was undoubtedly what Giolitti had hoped it would be. DDF (2), XIV, 398.

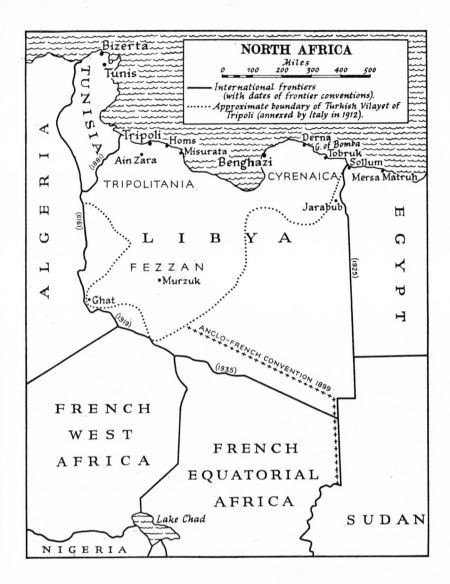

**NORTH AFRICA**

Miles

0    100    200    300    400    500

——— International frontiers
(with dates of frontier conventions).

·········· Approximate boundary of Turkish Vilayet of
Tripoli (annexed by Italy in 1912).

Bizerta

Tunis

TUNISIA

ALGERIA

(1881)

(1919)

Tripoli    Homs

Ain Zara    Misurata    Benghazi

TRIPOLITANIA    CYRENAICA

Derna
G. of Bomba
Tobruk
Sollum
Mersa Matruh

L  I  B  Y  A

Jarabub

EGYPT

(1925)

FEZZAN

•Murzuk

•Ghat

(1919)

ANGLO-FRENCH CONVENTION 1899

(1935)

FRENCH

WEST

AFRICA

FRENCH

EQUATORIAL

AFRICA

SUDAN

Lake Chad

NIGERIA

emigrants, but of free workers', wrote Corradini; 'We Italians breathe the first air of spring after the gloomy winter.' Marinetti, the futurist leader, revelled in 'the warlike fervour' that had swept Italy and invited the government, 'which had finally become Futurist, to magnify all the nation's ambitions'.[1] Thousands of southerners applied for passports to go to Tripoli and help restore the granary of ancient Rome. Liberals like Luzzatti and Martini rejoiced in the proof that Italy could, in spite of Adowa, prepare and carry through a war like other nations. Even the cautious Fortunato approved. 'Who more than I', he wrote to a friend serving in the army overseas, 'is convinced that Tripoli will be a fruitless and perilous enterprise?' And yet having seen, for the first time in his life, that the peasants of his Basilicata were at last 'conscious of being Italians', he joyfully gave thanks to the war for proving 'that fifty years of national life have not passed in vain, that something new and fine and promising has appeared in our Italy'.[2] Catholics, too, in Meda's words, were deeply stirred by 'the nationalist wind that blew from the coasts of Africa'. 'Italian Catholics yield to no one in the ardour with which they defend the interests and grandeur of their country', wrote one of their leading newspapers. Many Catholics praised the army for its military virtues, its discipline and its defence of religious values. 'Today Italy completes her mission of civilization, for she plants the cross in Tripoli where the crescent once waved', declared Cardinal Vincenzo Vannutelli.[3] The Cardinal was promptly disavowed by the Vatican, which remained scrupulously neutral, but leading Catholic laymen, priests and even bishops joined in the popular rejoicing and gave their blessing to the war. D'Annunzio, from his retreat on the French Atlantic coast, composed his *Canzoni delle gesta d'oltre mare*, full of evocations of ancient glories to be regained. Poetry had burst into the grey routine of Giolitti's Italy.

The war split all the parties of the left. Some radicals welcomed it as an act not of conquest but of redemption, and talked of Italy's civilising mission. Many others, like the pacifist, anti-imperialist *Secolo* of Milan, depicted the attack on Turkey as an intrigue of the Banco di Roma to put money in the pockets of clerical plutocrats. The republicans were no less divided. At their Bologna congress in October the opponents of war secured a majority, whereupon the pro-war minority led by Barzilai left the party. Both socialists and syndicalists suffered from the same clash of opinions. The executives of the Socialist party and the C.G.L. met jointly on 25 September and announced a protest general strike of twenty-

[1] Volpe, III, p. 371; Joll, p. 151.
[2] Fortunato, *Pagine e ricordi*, II, pp. 57–60.
[3] Askew, p. 53; De Rosa, *L'Azione Cattolica*, II, pp. 328–31; Spadolini, *Giolitti e i cattolici*, pp. 232–7, 249–52.

four hours. Similar instructions were issued by the syndicalist Action Committee at Parma. The unions responded half-heartedly and the strike had no influence on events whatsoever. The only incident of note occurred at Forlì, where two young extremists, the socialist Benito Mussolini and the republican Pietro Nenni, incited a mob to tear up tramlines and block the passage of troop trains to the south. Elsewhere the protests were only verbal. All over Italy the opponents of war were conscious that majority sentiment was against them.

In October 1911 a special Socialist party congress assembled at Modena. Its purpose was to discuss Bissolati's visit to the King[1] and future relations with the government. The ultra-reformist right wing seized the opportunity to declare its support for the war. Bissolati and Bonomi even acknowledged the claims of patriotism and argued that colonial expansion was in the interest not of one class but the whole nation.[2] In any case, they pointed out, the war was a *fait accompli* which socialists were powerless to reverse. Unless the party shouldered responsibility in a national crisis, it would lose all right to influence; only by supporting Giolitti could it make sure of universal suffrage. 'You may break me', declared Bissolati, 'before I will pass to the opposition against the government of Giolitti.'[3] These arguments failed to move the bulk of the party, the C.G.L. or even a majority of the reformists. Turati described the Italian ultimatum to Turkey as 'a cynically barbaric document of hypocrisy', and secured the approval of the congress for his motion which condemned both socialist membership of any bourgeois government and 'systematic' support of Giolitti. The congress revealed an unhappy party. Turati and his friends were stunned by what they regarded as Giolitti's betrayal. The enchanted decade of progress towards democracy was over and they felt the revolutionary currents gathering strength around them.

The syndicalists also spoke with two voices. De Ambris denounced Giolitti's 'colonial brigandage'. Arturo Labriola welcomed war as 'a school of character, virility and courage' and declared that 'A people that does not know how to make war, will never make a revolution.' Italians had ranged themselves against plutocracy and foreign capital, he wrote; 'Behind Turkey is the Europe of money, which desires its prey . . . We are really combating Mammon.'[4] Such language differed little from that of the nationalists. It appealed, too, to many socialists. 'The great prole-

---

[1] See above, p. 281.

[2] Italian socialists who supported the war could quote Antonio Labriola, who in 1902 had expressed the hope that Tripoli would one day become the colony of the Italian proletariat. Cilibrizzi, IV, p. 169; Michels, p. 407.

[3] Salomone, p. 74. But even Bissolati voted against the proclamation of Italian sovereignty, on the ground that it would prolong the war.

[4] Volpe, III, pp. 355–6.

tarian nation has stirred herself', cried the poet Giovanni Pascoli, for many years a romantic sympathiser with socialism. De Felice, champion of the Sicilian fasci, went over to Tripoli as a war correspondent. 'We have visited the desert', he wrote back with naive enthusiasm, 'and it is all most cultivable soil.'[1] The Italian proletariat was about to take possession of the promised land.

The course of the war soon damped these flights of enthusiasm. The conquest of Tripoli proved not to be the walkover that everyone had expected. Faulty generalship added to the difficulties. The landing of the marines on 5 October, though dramatic and pleasing for the Italian press, had allowed the Turkish garrison to withdraw intact. Its resistance in the interior proved surprisingly resilient. Much store had been laid upon Arab hatred of their Turkish rulers and General Carlo Caneva, the commander-in-chief, duly proclaimed that the Italian army came as a liberator.[2] This policy bore fruit in the town of Tripoli, where Hassuna Pasha, head of the Karamanli family, went over to the Italians and was made mayor.[3] But the Arabs of the interior did not follow his example.[4] Roused by two ardent Tripolitanian deputies in the Turkish parliament, they flocked in, some from as far as the southern oases of Fezzan, to enrol in irregular formations and fight the infidel invader. On 23 October, while the Turks staged an attack to the east of Tripoli, some hundreds of Arabs infiltrated the Italian lines and attacked from the rear. In the town itself there was some isolated sniping and the Italians lost their heads, believing a full-scale rising was in progress.[5] Arab atrocities were followed by stern reprisals. The whole population of the oasis within the Italian lines was forcibly moved into the town and 2,500 persons were transported to Ustica and other Italian islands. All Arabs found with arms were shot and in the panic many innocent civilians were executed or maltreated.[6] These

---

[1] Quoted in E. N. Bennett, *With the Turks in Tripoli* (London 1912), pp. 7–10; F. McCullagh, *Italy's War for a Desert* (London 1912), p. xxvii.

[2] Cilibrizzi, IV, p. 164.

[3] The Karamanlis had ruled Tripoli under nominal Turkish sovereignty from 1711 to 1835, when direct Turkish rule was restored. Hassuna Pasha had been sounded by Crispi in 1890 and, according to a report from the Italian consul, had said he would welcome an Italian occupation, with himself in a similar position to that of the Bey of Tunis under the French. Crispi, *Memoirs*, II, pp. 474–5. In recent years both the Banco di Roma and the government had renewed the attempts to win him over, not without success. Giolitti, *Memorie*, p. 343; Askew, p. 28; *Quarant' anni*, III, 50, note 3.

[4] Giolitti's earlier attempts to stir up disaffection among the Senussi of Cyrenaica (Giolitti, *Memorie*, pp. 329–30) proved unsuccessful.

[5] Galli, pp. 116–21.

[6] Arab casualties in these reprisals have been variously estimated between 400

incidents, which were greatly magnified by the friends of Turkey and the European left-wing press, destroyed Italy's chances of winning Arab support.[1]

Military operations were marked by extreme caution. The shadow of Adowa lay heavy over the army and General Caneva was determined that Italian arms must suffer no reverse, however slight. No move was to be undertaken except with overwhelming strength. The first expeditionary force numbered 35,000 men, well equipped and supplied. A further 50,000 had been despatched by the end of 1911 and a total of 100,000 were landed n Libya before the war was won. A high proportion of these were conscripts, contrary to the normal European practice of using only professional soldiers for colonial campaigns.[2] On 4 December a large force advanced to the oasis of Ain Zara, ten miles south of Tripoli, where the Turks had established their H.Q. The oasis was captured but the Turkish H.Q. got away. Thereafter the war stagnated. The Italians sat in their entrenched camps, bored, frustrated and plagued by cholera. The Turks and Arabs harassed their lines and disappeared again into the desert before they could be methodically engaged. The Italian army, whose only previous experience had been of Ethiopian massed attacks, had arrived in Libya with no conception of the problems of a desert war. Its position was particularly precarious in Cyrenaica, where the enemy was led by an inspiring commander, Enver Bey, with the Bedouin and the powerful religious order of the Senussi behind him.[3] Contraband supplies, arms and a few reinforcements began to reach the Turks through Tunisia. Plentiful money and food, religious fanaticism and contempt for Italian inaction swelled the ranks of the Arab guerilla forces until by March 1912 they numbered 25,000, four times the size of the original Turkish garrison. Turkish morale rose, both at home and in Libya. The Italians, by contrast, saw a great army encamped in the desert and a great fleet patrolling the Mediterranean, and wondered whether it had all been worth while for five small footholds on African soil. By December 1911 it was clear that if the war was to be won, Turkey must be hit in a vulnerable place far from Tripoli. Before that could be done, great diplomatic obstacles had to be overcome.

The main opposition to an extension of operations outside Africa came

---

and 4,000. They probably included some women and children. The accounts of war correspondents, who claimed to have been eye-witnesses, differ wildly.

[1] The impetuous De Felice was rapidly disillusioned. 'I supported this war because I thought it was a work of civilization', he wrote in December, 'but I now see that this work is carried on by means of the gallows.' F. McCullagh, *Italy's War for a Desert*, p. 149.

[2] Albertini, *Venti anni*, II, p. 126; *L'esercito italiano*, I, pp. 57–8; Rochat, pp. 311–12.          [3] Evans-Pritchard, pp. 109–12.

from the Austrians. They did not trust Italy not to use the opportunity to seize some vantage point in the Balkans or Aegean. Even if Italy had no such designs, operations in Europe would unsettle the Balkans and possibly precipitate a general war. When, therefore, within a few hours of the declaration of war in September, an Italian naval squadron sank two Turkish torpedo-boats in the harbour of Preveza in Epirus, Aehrenthal made a strong protest. San Giuliano had to promise there would be no more operations in the Adriatic, no bombardment of ports in Albania or Epirus, no attack on the Straits or in the Aegean and, finally, no operations outside African waters. He also assured Aehrenthal, quite truthfully, that Italian policy was to respect Turkey's integrity in Europe and give no encouragement to Balkan warmongers.

Relations between the two allies were showing many signs of strain. The critical and sometimes abusive comments of the Austrian press provoked Italian newspapers to write of 'the swan song of the Triple Alliance'.[1] Though San Giuliano had never concealed Italy's determination to get its way over Tripoli, he had given Austria-Hungary no hint that war was imminent until it was too late to protest. This was certainly a breach of the letter and spirit of the Alliance. Aehrenthal found himself being treated by San Giuliano as he himself had treated Tittoni in 1908, and felt understandably resentful. Nevertheless on balance he saw profit rather than loss for Austria in the war, provided it could be kept to Africa. The Italians would work off their surplus energy in Tripoli, far from the Adriatic; it was also likely they would have trouble with France, from which the Triple Alliance would gain.[2] Conrad's view was very different. He warned Francis Joseph against the danger of a stab in the back from an Italy strengthened, not weakened, by the acquisition of Libya. The only remedy was to crush her now, which Italian treachery in the past gave Austria a perfect moral right to do. In equally forceful language Aehrenthal demanded sole control of foreign policy. The pacific Francis Joseph took his side and on 30 November dismissed Conrad from his post of Chief of Staff. There was jubilation in Italy. Aehrenthal however maintained his veto on operations outside African waters and threatened, as he was fully entitled to do, that should the Italians break their promises, he would either claim compensation under Article VII or request the elimination of that article from the treaty. All these protests and warnings were kept carefully concealed from the Italian public.

The Italians were still trying to overcome this obstacle when relations with the French suddenly worsened. France had been the friendliest of all the Great Powers at the outbreak of the war. Before long, however, protests were heard in Italy against the passage through Tunisia of men,

[1] Volpe, III, p. 380.　　[2] Albertini, *Origins*, I, pp. 342, 350.

arms and supplies for the Turks. These protests were not unfounded, though French laxity was less to blame than the difficulty of guarding a long desert frontier, on both sides of which the population unanimously favoured the Turks. On 16 January 1912 an Italian destroyer stopped the French mail-boat *Carthage* off the Sardinian coast and took her to Cagliari to be searched. Two days later a second French ship, the *Manouba*, was similarly intercepted. On board her were twenty-nine officials of the Turkish Red Crescent whom the Italians detained, claiming they were combatant officers in disguise.

A few days before these incidents a new French government had been formed by Poincaré, a tough patriot from Lorraine with few diplomatic graces. French nationalist sentiment had been wounded by the concessions extracted by Germany as a price for France's free hand in Morocco.[1] Now that Morocco was safe and Italian friendship no longer so important, Italy was a convenient scapegoat. On 22 January Poincaré peremptorily demanded the release of the *Manouba's* passengers. In the debate that followed, chauvinist deputies waxed eloquent on the honour of the French flag. The French press, in Tittoni's words, 'exhausted the whole vocabulary of vilification'.[2] Barrère worked hard to prevent the destruction of all that he had achieved by twelve years' patient diplomacy. Poincaré himself realised he had gone too far and tried to conciliate Italian feelings.[3] On 25 January Italy agreed to release the Turks, twenty-seven of whom were found to be genuine members of the Red Crescent, and the dispute was referred to the Hague Court. That same day a third ship, the *Tavignano*, was seized off the coast of Tunis and taken to Tripoli, where it was found she carried no contraband. Tension rose again. Giolitti kept his head, calmed San Giuliano and informed Barrère that he had secretly ordered the Italian navy to cease interference with French ships. By the end of the first week in February the crisis was over. In May 1913 the Hague Court ruled that Italy had been entitled to search the ships but wrong to detain them, that no affront to the French flag had been intended and no deliberate hostility shown. With the payment of £6,600 to France as indemnity, the affair was at last settled.

The incidents had meanwhile caused an Italian revulsion against France that on a smaller scale recalled that of 1881. Italians, nervous and hypersensitive, found in Poincaré and Tunisian contrabanders a scapegoat for frustration in Libya. The Triple Alliance suddenly became more popular

---

[1] By the Franco–German agreement of 4 November 1911, France ceded part of the French Congo to Germany and Germany renounced all claim to political influence in Morocco.

[2] Volpe, III, p. 393. Tittoni was ambassador in Paris at the time.

[3] J. Laroche, *Quinze ans à Rome avec Camille Barrère* (Paris 1948), pp. 261–6.

than it had been for twenty years. To San Giuliano the main significance of the affair was that it had revealed the fragility of the 1902 *entente*. Strengthened in his view that, with Libya won, Italy would need to flirt no more with Britain and France,[1] he decided to lean heavily on the Triple Alliance. By impressing his allies with Italy's loyalty, he hoped to secure their help in forcing Turkey to renounce Libya and end the war.

San Giuliano had made proposals for a premature renewal of the Alliance as early as July 1911, probably wishing to make sure of his allies' support should war for Tripoli prove necessary. In December, irritated by Aehrenthal's obstructiveness and his refusal to recognise the annexation of Libya, he dropped the negotiations, thus adding to Aehrenthal's annoyance. On 25 March 1912 Victor Emmanuel and William II met at Venice. The King repeated Italian complaints against Austria-Hungary, but stressed the growing popularity of the Alliance in Italy since France had 'dropped her mask' in the *Manouba* affair.[2] William II was impressed. His Turcophilia of the previous autumn had by now quite vanished and he at once set about persuading the Austrians to welcome the errant sheep back to the fold of the Alliance. Aehrenthal had died in February. His successor, Berchtold, though less friendly to Italy, was also weaker and more amenable to German pressure. In April he most reluctantly accepted San Giuliano's contention that the islands of the eastern Aegean were Asiatic, and therefore not covered by Article VII, and agreed to allow a temporary Italian occupation of three of them.

While the Germans were trying to get Austria's consent to an Italian attack in the Aegean, San Giuliano was using the threat of operations outside Africa to blackmail the Great Powers into forcing Turkey to come to terms. No European government was keen to risk its influence over the Turks by offering unpalatable advice, yet none wished to see the war spread and its economic interests suffer. The one exception was Russia, which from December 1911 onwards acted as 'Italy's solicitor with the Powers'.[3] Enthusiastically loyal to the Racconigi programme, the Russian Foreign Minister, Sazonov, urged the Italians to act and other governments to bring the Turks to their senses. But all efforts to obtain a diplomatic

---

[1] On the other hand Giolitti had expressed the contrary opinion in November 1911 that 'henceforward Italy would have to be very careful not to alienate the goodwill of the two great Maritime powers in the Mediterranean, France and England, on which her position in Tripoli would make her much more dependent'. BD, IX (i), 302.

[2] Albertini, *Origins*, I, p. 358.

[3] In the first two months of the war the Russian government had been most hostile to Italy and acted as Turkey's protector, hoping to secure Turkish and European consent to the opening of the Straits to Russian warships. When this failed it abruptly reversed its policy.

solution favourable to Italy were frustrated by Turkey's refusal to recognise Italian sovereignty in Libya.

On 18 April the Italian fleet forced the issue by sailing into the Dardanelles, without specific authorisation from Rome. The enemy forts were bombarded and the fleet withdrew under heavy fire. The Turkish government retaliated by starting to expel its resident Italian citizens, who numbered 70,000. They also closed the Straits to all shipping, to the dismay of British traders, but reopened them a fortnight later under pressure from the Russians. At the beginning of May the Italians occupied not three but thirteen Aegean islands, the chief of which was Rhodes.[1] This strained Austrian tolerance to the limit. Admiral Millo attacked the Dardanelles a second time in July, again without his government's authorisation, and penetrated over ten miles as far as Chanak; but plans for occupying Chios or landing at Smyrna had to be dropped in the face of unanimous disapproval in Europe.

The occupation of the so-called Dodecanese created a new source of tension in the Mediterranean. Encouraged by Italian promises of autonomy and protection for their religion and traditions, the islanders soon began to demand union with Greece. The Italian authorities then turned to repression.[2] In Italy the nationalists, their appetites whetted, acclaimed 'the first act of Italian imperialism in the Levant'.[3] Tripoli, they declared, was only a starting-point; now Italy could look eastwards from an Aegean base to new fields of conquest in Asia Minor. Neither Britain nor France nor Italy's allies viewed these prospects with favour. Berchtold realised that Greece and the Balkan states would be encouraged to commit similar acts of plunder, and he attached little importance to official Italian assurances that the occupation would be temporary.[4] Britain and France saw a threat to their positions in the Middle East in the possibility that the Triple Alliance might build naval bases in the Aegean as well as in Libya. Grey, the British Foreign Secretary, told the Italian ambassador in August 1912 that he hoped that his government 'would not pass any Decree about the Islands, or commit themselves in any way with regard to them'.[5] Next month most of the British Mediterranean fleet moved into the North Sea to face the Germans, while the French Atlantic fleet was transferred to the Mediterranean. This dramatic consolidation of the Entente Cordiale provoked immediate agitation in Italy for a counter-agreement among the navies of the Triple Alliance.

---

[1] They were, in order of occupation: Astypalaea (Stampalia), Rhodes, Chalki, Karpathos (Scarpanto), Casos, Telos (Piscopi), Nisyros, Calymnos, Leros, Patmos, Lipsos, Symi, Cos.

[2] Sertoli Salis, pp. 15–20, 47–51.   [3] Volpe, III, pp. 406–7.
[4] It lasted until 1943.   [5] BD, IX (i), 439.

Military operations in Libya had meanwhile made progress. The Italian army was reinforced until close on 100,000 men, including *askaris* from Eritrea, faced an enemy about one-third as numerous. A Turkish-Arab force was defeated in a sharp encounter outside Benghazi in March and during the summer the whole coastline of Tripolitania was occupied. But these limited successes did not bring victory. Had it not been for events in the Balkans, the war might have dragged on indefinitely. The seizure of the Dodecanese, however, had been a telling blow. The Turks feared a political landslide among the Greek inhabitants of their other Aegean islands; they also realised by midsummer of 1912 that something serious was afoot in the Balkans. The secret Balkan League had in fact been formed and Serbia, Montenegro, Bulgaria and Greece were awaiting a favourable moment to fall upon Turkey. Though Italy's attack created their opportunity, they received little Italian encouragement. Giolitti and San Giuliano had one very good reason for keeping the war out of Europe: the desire to rob Austria-Hungary of all pretext for demanding compensations under Article VII. When the Italophil Prime Minister of Bulgaria, Gueshov, offered an alliance, he was urged to cultivate Austria's friendship, advice that ran exactly counter to the ambitions of the Balkan League. Montenegrin and Greek proposals for concerted attacks on Turkey were given an equally cool reception.[1] Nevertheless it was the Balkan menace that in the end forced the Turks to accept the loss of Libya and open negotiations for peace.

The first contacts were made soon after the occupation of the Dodecanese through a leading Italian financier, Giuseppe Volpi,[2] who in his capacity of Serbian consul in Venice was able to travel to Turkey during the war. Official talks opened in Switzerland in July, with Volpi as one of the Italian delegates. Progress was slow. The Turks feared Arab accusations of betrayal if they abandoned Libya, and hoped to be saved by the Great Powers at the eleventh hour from attack in Europe. They therefore procrastinated all through the summer. On 30 September the Balkan states mobilised. San Giuliano took fright, both at the prospect of being dragged into a European war and at the risk that Italy might be excluded as a belligerent from the Balkan deliberations of the Great Powers. For the sake of immediate peace he was ready to confine Italian sovereignty to the coastal areas and leave the status of the Libyan interior undefined. Giolitti

[1] Helmreich, pp. 65–6, 84–5, 106; Giolitti, *Memorie*, pp. 480–1; De Bosdari, pp. 64–8.

[2] Volpi, whose financial empire was based on electric power in his native Venetia, had achieved international status as founder and director of several companies with interests in Montenegro, Serbia and the Turkish Empire, and played a leading part in financing loans to Montenegro and negotiating over the Danube–Adriatic railway.

knew such a settlement would never satisfy Italian opinion; instead he calmly accepted the risk of delay and negotiated with consummate skill.[1] On 2 October he delivered an eight-day ultimatum. The Great Powers, particularly Germany and Austria, urged Turkey to concede. On the 8th the Montenegrins attacked and started the Balkan war. On the 11th a second Italian ultimatum demanded immediate peace, while preparations were made for landings at Smyrna and in Thrace.[2] On 17 October Serbia, Bulgaria and Greece joined Montenegro at war. Next day the signature of the Treaty of Ouchy brought the Italo-Turkish war to an end.

The terms of the treaty were moderate. Turkey renounced sovereignty over Libya, but the Sultan's religious authority as Caliph was to be preserved under Italian rule. Italy undertook to evacuate the Dodecanese as soon as the Turkish forces had left Libya, subject to guarantees for the future autonomy of the islands. Turkey also received an indemnity. Recognition of Italian sovereignty by the Great Powers followed quickly. The great majority of Italians greeted peace with joy and relief, but not all were satisfied. The nationalists were offended by the indemnity and the undertaking to evacuate the Dodecanese. Democrats and irredentists protested that to make peace just at that moment was to betray the cause of civilisation in the Balkans and abandon the very peoples whom Mazzini had declared to be Italy's natural allies. Those who knew the Moslem world pointed out that it was impossible to allow the Sultan-Caliph to be officially represented in Libya, and to authorise public prayers for him in the mosques, without creating in Arab minds the impression of an Italo-Turkish condominium.[3] This was indeed the impression that was created, and it helped to prolong resistance to Italian authority, especially in still unconquered Cyrenaica.

The Treaty of Ouchy was not the end of Italy's troubles in Libya. In October 1912 only the coastal areas were secure. Enver Bey refused to recognise the treaty and went on fighting in Cyrenaica with a few Turkish troops and solid Arab support. When most of the Turks were recalled to fight in the Balkans, Sayid Ahmed el-Sherif, head of the Senussi order, took over command in the name of the Sultan. The Italians extended their control inland from Benghazi and Derna, but their resources were stretched to the limit by guerilla operations against the Bedouin, in which superior numbers and equipment were of small advantage.[4] The pacification of Tripolitania was less difficult. The fertile *jebel* south of Tripoli was occupied without much opposition in March 1913. Next year an Italian column penetrated deep into the south. Murzuk, chief city of the Fezzan, was occupied in March and Ghat, 500 miles from the Mediterranean, in

[1] Giolitti, *Memorie*, pp. 430–9.      [2] ibid., pp. 460–2.
[3] Evans-Pritchard, pp. 114–15.        [4] ibid., pp. 115 ff.

August. But the harassing of the army's lines of communication by the Senussi made its hold on these outposts precarious. In spite of the formation of a permanent colonial force of 24,000 men, there were still over 60,000 metropolitan troops tied down in Libya in the summer of 1914.[1]

While these campaigns proceeded, the foundations of the Libyan administration and economy were laid. A Ministry of Colonies was created with Pietro Bertolini, one of the peace delegates, as its first head. The latter, visiting Libya in December 1912, promised to respect the Moslem religion and customs and appealed for Arab cooperation in government. Italian rule was to rest on political consent, not military force. In Tripolitania this policy met with growing success. The colony's resources were meanwhile scientifically studied. Nitti dispatched an agricultural commission and the indefatigable Franchetti, undeterred by his Eritrean disappointments, went over to search for land for southern peasants.[2] The opportunities for settlement were found to be limited. The government wisely restricted immigration and there was no immediate diversion of the flow of transatlantic emigrants. In time, however, with much sacrifice of capital and labour, parts of Libya were transformed – the desert was driven back by irrigation, olives, vines and fruit trees replaced the waste sand and the Italians were able to indulge to the full their genius for public works. Even though the money and effort could have been better employed in southern Italy, the civilisation and redemption of Libya inspired many beside the imperialist demagogues with pride.

Nevertheless a high price had been paid for victory and its material rewards were meagre. Casualties had been light,[3] but the cost was admitted in the spring of 1914 to have been over 1,300 million lire, more than twice the provisional estimate of 1913. Arsenals and supply depots had been emptied, home formations weakened and the army rendered incapable of mobilisation at the very time when the threat of war in Europe was acute. Italian morale, too, had been strained. As in many other colonial campaigns undertaken in expectation of easy triumphs, the war had brought little glory and much disillusion. Victory was due as much to diplomacy and to events outside Italy's control as to success in battle. Yet victory had been won and for the first time since 1860 Italy had a successful war to its credit. Italians felt they had achieved something which merited, and was gaining, the respect of other nations. In Villari's words, 'the new

[1] Ciasca, pp. 339–46; Volpe, III, pp. 610–14; L'esercito italiano, I, p. 59; Rochat, p. 312.

[2] Ciasca, pp. 337–9; Volpe, III, pp. 429–39; Cilibrizzi, IV, pp. 216–18.

[3] The figures were 1,432 killed in action and 4,250 wounded; 1,948 died from sickness. Askew, p. 249.

great Italy' had become a reality recognised by all and national unity, 'cemented by blood shed in common, has become truly indissoluble'.[1]

The history of Libya as an Italian colony was to prove short and unhappy. The outbreak of war in Europe made it imperative to reduce commitments in Africa. The Senussi forced the evacuation of the Fezzan at the end of 1914. When Italy declared war on Turkey in August 1915, the Grand Senusso proclaimed a holy war in Libya. The Arab revolt spread until by the end of 1915 the Italians held only Tripoli, Homs and a handful of fortified points in Cyrenaica. Libya was not fully under their control till 1931. In 1935 large-scale settlement of Italians began in the fertile *jebel* of Cyrenaica; but by then Italian rule had only seven more years to run.

## Post-War Unrest

When the war ended, Giolitti's position seemed unassailable. Italy owed him a great debt. He had played for high stakes, both in precipitating war at such short notice and in proclaiming annexation in defiance of all Europe. His gamble had come off.[2] He never lost his nerve and kept a tight control of operations. The performance of the High Command did not impress him: 'Thirty generals against one lieutenant-colonel', he is alleged to have remarked.[3] It was due to him at least as much as to San Giuliano that a way was found through the maze of diplomatic obstacles. According to the German ambassador, he had autocratically dominated his Foreign Minister, who had done no more than carry out his instructions.[4] Giolitti also directed the peace negotiations and with a fine sense of timing obtained better terms than many of his colleagues believed possible. Many mistakes had been made; but in comparison with Italy's previous African campaigns, the war had been a masterpiece of organisation. The King had good reason to offer him a dukedom on the signing of peace. It was characteristic of Giolitti to refuse it.[5]

The war had disarmed the constitutional opposition. Sonnino and Salandra continued to criticise, but their criticisms were little more than formal. In the spring of 1911 they had opposed Giolitti when he was wooing the socialists; a year later they were defending him against socialist attacks. Parliament met in February 1912 for the first time since the start of the war and ratified the annexation decree. In the course of the next

---

[1] Albertini, *Venti anni*, II, pp. 203–4.

[2] Giolitti had remarked to a friend at the time of the annexation decree, 'I am in a powder-magazine with a lighted match between my fingers. I have to solve the problem of not burning my finger and not sending up the magazine.' Frassati, p. 4.

[3] Volpe, III, p. 501. The lieutenant-colonel was Enver Bey.

[4] GP, XXX, 10917, 10928.

[5] Soleri, pp. 40–1.

three months the suffrage and insurance bills went through smoothly with hardly an echo of the previous year's controversy. This lack of opposition, declared Giolitti complacently, revealed the nation's maturity.

But the war also stimulated the spirit of revolt. The nationalists were not satisfied with Giolitti, whom they patronisingly described as 'the last convert' to nationalism. He had failed to 'vibrate'. 'I did not undertake the conquest of Libya out of enthusiasm – quite the contrary', he declared in December 1913.[1] Wars in his view were matters for the King's ministers and soldiers, not for romantic journalists and nationalist demagogues. This unheroic, matter-of-fact attitude left many whose national pride had been stirred with the feeling that something vital was missing. Instead of taming the nationalists, as Giolitti had intended, the war turned them into a restless, disruptive political force. Though he presented them with a new colony, he failed to draw their sting.[2]

A second nationalist congress met in December 1912. Resolutions were adopted in favour of protection, autarky, anti-strike legislation and bigger armaments. 'Let us have the courage to call ourselves conservatives', urged Corradini. The tone of nationalist writing became authoritarian. The ideals of equality, democracy, the rights of man and internationalism were dismissed as sentimental nonsense; the state was all, the individual nothing. Liberty, it was argued, was a concession which could be revoked at will, and must never be permitted to hamper the toughening of the nation for war and imperial expansion.[3]

Such language alienated the nationalists with democratic sympathies, but it pleased those members of the propertied classes who had never wholly accepted Giolittian liberalism. While the economy continued to expand and Giolitti seemed to have the working-class under control, they had remained passive; but when the rate of expansion slowed down and universal suffrage threatened to open the flood-gates of revolution, their attitude changed. The nationalists were urging the middle class to assert itself and make Italy prosperous through world power. They seemed to offer the alternative to Giolitti which had been lacking since 1901. This was the basis of the alliance between the nationalist movement and heavy industry which now began to take shape. At the same time the bonds of mutual sympathy between the nationalists and the pro-war syndicalists,

[1] Giolitti, Discorsi parlamentari, III, p. 1667.

[2] In October 1913 Giolitti told Barrère that he would always fight the Italian nationalists 'because nationalism seemed to him a dangerous caricature of patriotism'. DDF (3), VIII, 339.

[3] Volpe, III, pp. 528, 617; Cilibrizzi, IV, p. 139. The futurists shared this contempt for liberty. In the second Futurist Manifesto, issued on the outbreak of the Tripoli war, Marinetti launched the slogan, 'The Word Italy must prevail over the Word Freedom'. Joll, p. 158.

which was based on a common taste for violence and action, grew closer.[1] Even more significant for the future was the influence of nationalism over the young. Thanks to the intoxication induced by war, it was becoming as dominant in the universities as socialism twenty years before. This boded no good for either Giolitti or Italian democracy.

The nationalists were also beginning to recruit admirers in a quite different quarter. Many conservative Catholics were attracted by their emphasis on order, authority and discipline and their hostility to socialism and freemasonry. The nationalists on their side, now that they were becoming a respectable force in politics, abandoned the literary paganism in which Corradini had earlier indulged[2] and began to patronise the church. It was the 'Roman element' in Catholicism that they admired. 'Nationalism', wrote one sympathiser, Mario Missiroli, 'will have to be Catholic if it truly wishes to draw inspiration from Italian tradition.' 'Catholicism', wrote another, Papini, 'is authority, domination, organisation, stability, security.'[3] Nationalism of this brand was anathema to the Christian democrats, but it appealed powerfully to the ultra-conservative clericals who enjoyed Pius X's favour.

While Giolitti's critics on the right were multiplying, the opposition on the left presented a more immediate threat. Even before the war ended, many of its liberal and democratic supporters had begun to react against nationalist excesses. In their sober second thoughts the debit side of the Libyan balance-sheet assumed larger proportions. With post-war disillusionment came a revival of the polemics against *Giolittismo*. The free traders revived the Anti-Protection League and intensified their attacks on the parasites of big business and high finance, who were pressing for yet higher tariffs. Salvemini and the *meridionalisti* renewed their moral campaign against the *malavita*. In the spring of 1913 this democratic discontent found a point of focus in a new parliamentary scandal. Plans had been approved in 1883 for the building of central law courts[4] in Rome. Thirty years later they were still unfinished, even though five times the original estimate had been spent. In April 1913 a parliamentary enquiry uncovered a long succession of frauds and corrupt transactions on the part of contractors and civil servants. The republicans led the attack in the name of morality and after passionate debates four compromised deputies

---

[1] The nationalist and subsequently fascist 'philosophy of action', with its glorification of the will and force, owed much to syndicalism.

[2] De Rosa, *L'Azione Cattolica*, II, p. 304 ff.

[3] Quoted in De Rosa, *L'Azione Cattolica*, II, pp. 313, 324. The Catholic spirit was essentially different from the Christian spirit, Corradini claimed. Fonzi, p. 100

[4] The Palazzo di Giustizia.

resigned their seats. Indirectly the reputation of Giolitti and his system suffered.

The socialists took full advantage of the restless post-war mood. No opportunity was lost of denouncing colonialism and militarism as the causes of Italy's present discontents. The war had given the party a push towards the left. New leaders were now emerging who proclaimed their scorn for 'a liberal party with a socialist banner' and their disgust with the feeble show of opposition provided by their deputies in parliament. There were renewed signs of turbulence among the rank and file. Giolitti, it seemed, had been premature in consigning Marxism to the attic. On 14 March 1912 an anarchist named D'Alba attempted to assassinate the King. The chamber of deputies decided almost unanimously to go in a body to the palace to express their sympathy and congratulations. Three socialists, Bissolati, Bonomi and Angelo Cabrini, accompanied their colleagues. Their action precipitated a crisis which came to a head at the party congress at Reggio Emilia in July.

Its proceedings were stormy. The attack on the parliamentary party was led by Mussolini, the irrepressible revolutionary from the Romagna. He gave the delegates an uninhibited display of the rebelliousness and violence of temperament that characterise that region. Mussolini was still not twenty-nine years of age. In earliest boyhood he had imbibed a primitive romantic socialism from his father, an unrepentant Bakuninist. Soon after leaving school in 1902 he spent two years in Switzerland, earning a precarious living as journalist, socialist agitator and organiser of Italian emigrant labourers. The next five years were occupied in military service,[1] schoolteaching, journalism and provincial politics. In this period he professed himself a revolutionary syndicalist. In 1909 he again left Italy to become secretary of the Trent chamber of labour and the collaborator of Cesare Battisti. After eight months he was expelled by the Austrians and returned to his native Forlì. There he threw himself into local revolutionary politics and edited the weekly *Lotta di Classe*, which he made his private mouthpiece. It faithfully reflected his republicanism, anti-militarism and anti-clericalism, his hatred of the bourgeoisie and his almost anarchist contempt for parliament, democracy and moderation in any form.[2] In 1910,

---

[1] He received his call-up papers in Switzerland, ignored them and was posted as a deserter. In 1904 an amnesty was declared on the birth of an heir to the throne. Mussolini took advantage of it to return to Italy and do his military service.

[2] Mussolini's early journalistic writings, including the *Lotta di Classe*, reveal him as the intellectual jackdaw that he always remained. A voracious reader, he absorbed the latest ideas with facile enthusiasm, provided they were extreme or shocking. As De Felice observes (p. 42), 'his socialism was above all a state of mind'. His Marxism never went deep. Among the writers who influenced him in these years were Blanqui, Nietzsche, Stirner and Sorel.

when the Romagna was convulsed by agrarian conflict, Mussolini passionately supported the *braccianti* in their struggle with the *mezzadri*.[1] After the reformist victory at the Milan congress of that year, he persuaded the Forlì branch of the party, of which he was secretary, to secede in protest. His attempt to rouse the local proletariat to revolution on the outbreak of war in September 1911 earned him five months in prison. This incident gave him a national reputation among socialists. On being released he rejoined the party in order to be present at Reggio Emilia and help to purge it of the reformist traitors.

At the congress his chief supporters were Lazzari, the revolutionary veteran who had been his patron, Giacinto Menotti Serrati and Giovanni Lerda, self-made men of similar views and backgrounds, and Angelica Balabanoff, a Russian exile who had chosen Italy as her adopted country. Mussolini treated the congress to a brutal denunciation of kings, reformists and 'parliamentary cretinism' and demanded that socialist deputies obey their party or be expelled.[2] Turati deprecated expulsion and fought for party unity. 'There is not room in Italy today for two socialist parties', he pleaded. When it came to voting, he ranged himself on the left. Bissolati, Bonomi, Cabrini and Podrecca were expelled from the party by 12,556 to 8,883 votes. The same day they founded a Reformist Socialist Party. Its aim was to win power for the proletariat, not by the class struggle, but by peaceful reconciliation of the interests of the working-class with those of the rest of the nation in a new, classless society. Bissolati hoped to secure the support of the C.G.L. and base his party, like the British Labour party, on the trade unions. The C.G.L.'s leaders were sympathetic. Its secretary, Rigola, had defended reformism at the Modena congress in 1911. 'The time has passed', he declared, 'when Marx could say that the workers had nothing to lose but their chains; today they have something to defend and do not intend to imperil it by thoughtless, ill-timed agitations.'[3] But the furthest the C.G.L. would go was to declare itself autonomous of the Socialist party. Most reformists felt unable to follow Bissolati to the logical conclusion of reformism.[4] His party found more support among non-socialists than socialists, particularly in the south. Before long it was barely distinguishable from other democratic groups of the left.

Having expelled the heretics the Socialist party laid down its new directive: class struggle, republicanism, expulsion of all who favoured class collaboration or socialist participation in government, absolute

[1] See above, p. 304.

[2] Mussolini, IV, pp. 161–70. The King, Mussolini said, 'is the useless citizen by definition'; attempted assassination should be regarded as merely 'an accident of the trade of kings'.                     [3] Michels, p. 404; Cilibrizzi, IV, p. 250.

[4] In addition to the four who were expelled, nine socialist deputies, including De Felice, joined the new party.

obedience to the resolutions of the congress by all members, including deputies, absolute intransigence and isolation at elections. Changes in personnel reinforced this directive. Lazzari was made secretary of the party. Mussolini was elected to the executive and in December took over the editorship of *Avanti!* He ran it as he had run the *Lotta di Classe*, making it his personal mouthpiece and showing scant respect for Marxist orthodoxy.[1] The Libyan war and its supporters were his favourite targets. Another recurrent theme was the need to transform the party into a militant revolutionary élite, 'an aristocracy of the intellect and will', capable of achieving the violent conquest of power. His pithy, hard-hitting, inflammatory style doubled the paper's circulation in a few months and made him the idol of the youngest socialist generation.

The socialist swing to the left coincided with a revival of revolutionary syndicalism, inspired in part by the anarchists. In the summer of 1913 Malatesta returned to Italy from fourteen years of exile, taking advantage of a recent amnesty on the occasion of a royal birth. In December he attended the congress of the Italian Syndicalist Union (U.S.I.) in order to preach the necessity of transforming the syndicalist general strike into anarchist insurrection. He received an enthusiastic welcome and there were cries of 'Long live Bresci!', Humbert's anarchist assassin. The congress decided to intensify the assault on reformist strongholds, extend boycott and sabotage against *mezzadri* and proprietors, and prepare for an agricultural general strike.[2] During 1913 the syndicalists fought one of the longest and bitterest labour battles Italy had yet known in the province of Ferrara. The industrial workers, too, were in a militant and turbulent mood, particularly in the Lombard engineering industry and the motor-car works of Turin. Economic recession intensified unrest and strikes were numerous and bitter.[3]

[1] De Felice, pp. 115–23, 136–43, 185–7. Croce (pp. 266–7) writes: 'Having been alive in his youth to contemporary currents of thought, he [Mussolini] succeeded in investing socialism with a new spirit, bringing to it Sorel's theory of violence, the Bergsonian idea of intuition, pragmatism, the mysticism of action, and all the one-sided emphasis upon "will" which had filled the intellectual atmosphere for some years past.' Mussolini had hoped at Reggio Emilia to initiate an 'idealist renaissance' of the party. Many of his pronouncements at this time show the influence of Pareto's recently propounded theory of élites. During his stay in the Trentino, Mussolini had made contact with Prezzolini, editor of the nationalist Florentine review, *La Voce*, which subsequently published his pamphlet, *Il Trentino veduto da un socialista*. After 1912 Mussolini opened the columns of *Avanti!* to many non-socialists, including syndicalists, anarchists, republicans, *meridionalisti* (e.g. Salvemini) and members of the *Voce* group.

[2] Preti, pp. 270–1; Neufeld, pp. 353–4; Borghi, pp. 138–44.

[3] In 1913 there were 810 industrial strikes involving 385,000 persons. These figures were the highest yet reached in a single year. *ASI 1919–1921*, p. 512; Neufeld, p. 547.

In Milan the syndicalists found a new leader in Filippo Corridoni, a firebrand of twenty-five whose impassioned oratory and devotion to the revolutionary cause earned him the title among his fellows of 'poet of the masses'. In the summer of 1913 he won national fame by organising in the city two general strikes, accompanied by much violence, within three months. The C.G.L. and most of the socialist leaders deplored his misdirected enthusiasm, but Mussolini came out in support of the strikers, arguing that it would be suicide for *Avanti!* 'to abandon the workers' at a time of trial. Though the syndicalists resented this competition for the leadership of the industrial workers, their common love of violence began to draw Corridoni and Mussolini together. In December the latter supported the candidature of the veteran anarchist and communard, Amilcare Cipriani, in a Milan by-election, in order to demonstrate his 'unshakeable faith in revolution'. A new wave of violence seemed to have submerged the reformist citadel, and with it the whole Socialist party. Turati and Claudio Treves, Rigola and the sober trade union leaders watched with dismay while Mussolini, 'the Duce', as his admirers were already beginning to call him, pursued the task he had set himself in 1912, 'the psychological preparation of the proletariat for the use of violence'.[1]

In September 1913 Giolitti dissolved. By then the chamber was four and a half years old and the war had been over for eleven months. A general election under the new suffrage law could not be delayed any longer. Following his usual tactics, Giolitti tried to fight the election on a non-controversial programme, in order to facilitate the formation of a broad majority. To ensure success in an electorate almost trebled in size, the old techniques had to be applied on a more massive scale than ever before. Giolitti's opponents were hounded out of their seats, especially in the south. Salvemini, campaigning as the opposition candidate at Molfetta in Apulia, fearlessly exposed Giolitti's methods; he had pinned his faith on universal suffrage and now saw as its first fruits, not a cleansing of political life, but cruder, more shameless corruption and intimidation. It was small consolation that Turati now agreed with the view Salvemini had expressed in 1910, that universal suffrage must be conquered, not bestowed from above by a tainted hand. The main issue of the election was the Libyan war, over which the conservative-liberal 'national' forces

---

[1] Mussolini, IV, p. 147. For Mussolini's support of Cipriani (after whom his father had named him Amilcare), see VI, pp. 43–7, 57–66. 'This man [Mussolini] pleases me very much', Cipriani had written in a French newspaper after the Reggio Emilia congress. De Felice, pp. 127–8. Mussolini extolled Cipriani's electoral victory as 'the apotheosis of the Commune'. Cipriani however remained in Paris and never took his seat.

ranged themselves against the 'anti-national' forces of socialism. The former enjoyed massive Catholic support. The results were a victory for the government, but a qualified victory. In 1904 and 1909 Giolitti had increased his majority; this time it fell. Only little more than half the electorate voted. The liberals dropped from 382 to 310, while the Catholics rose from 16 to 29, the radicals from 45 to 73 and the socialists from 25 to 52.[1] Six nationalists were elected, including Federzoni whose nationalist-Catholic-conservative coalition defeated Nathan's Popular Bloc in Rome. One-third of the deputies entered the chamber for the first time. Universal suffrage had given the spirit of revolt parliamentary expression.

Five days after the second ballot Count Vincenzo Gentiloni, president of the Unione Elettorale Cattolica, revealed the extent of organised Catholic support for Giolitti. The *non expedit*, he announced, had been raised in 330 constituencies, two-thirds of the total, and 228 deputies had been elected with the aid of Catholic votes. The price they had paid was a promise to fight divorce, to oppose discrimination against private (i.e. Catholic) schools, to defend the right of parents to obtain religious instruction for their children in state schools, and to support parity of treatment by the state of Catholic and non-Catholic social and economic organisations.[2] There was no formal agreement on a national scale, as the Vatican was quick to point out, while admitting the substance of the guarantees demanded. The Gentiloni Pact, as it at once came to be known, was only an elaboration of the clerical-moderate directives laid down for Catholics in 1909. Even so, it marked a decisive step towards the creation of a Catholic party.

Gentiloni's revelations revived old fears of the priest-ridden masses and infuriated supporters of the Popular Blocs. Albertini deplored one more stage in the progressive demoralisation of the Liberal party under Giolitti's 'dictatorship'. It was less the substance of the pact than its secrecy and inquisitorial style that gave offence. There were heated debates in parliament and the press on church–state relations and the political aims of Catholics. Giolitti, too, showed irritation. Whatever promises his followers might have made, he himself remained uncommitted. He still believed that church and state should move on parallel lines and never clash. His acceptance of Catholic support since 1904 did not mean that he was now prepared to submit to Catholic dictation. Gentiloni's boasts

[1] *Compendio*, II, pp. 128–31. In addition to the 52 deputies of the Socialist party, 8 independent socialists and syndicalists (including De Ambris, secretary of the U.S.I.), and 19 members of Bissolati's Reformist Socialist party, were elected. The total strength of the extreme left rose from 110 to 169 (73 radicals, 17 republicans and 79 assorted socialists).

[2] Salomone, p. 40; De Rosa, *L'Azione Cattolica*, II, pp. 341–2; Cilibrizzi, IV, p. 291.

and conqueror's airs convinced him that the balance needed to be re-dressed.[1] He therefore inserted in the King's speech a statement that no infringement of the state's sovereignty would be tolerated. He also introduced a bill to enforce the precedence of civil over religious marriage, but dropped it as soon as it had served its purpose of appeasing his anti-clerical supporters. More significant than the anti-clerical protests was the passivity with which the majority of liberals accepted the Gentiloni Pact. This showed how greatly opinion had changed in twenty years.

The massive entry of Catholics into Italian political life could not fail to affect relations between Italy and the Papacy. In December 1913 Agostino Cameroni, one of the Catholic deputies, declared that he and his colleagues were 'Italian deputies like all the others, wholly and loyally constitutional', and even drank a toast to 'Rome, capital of Italy'.[2] Almost simultaneously Monsignor Anastasio Rossi, Archbishop of Udine, was telling a Catholic gathering in Milan that the freedom of the Pope, on which depended the freedom of the church, would be better ensured by some form of inter-national guarantee than by a restoration of the temporal power. At the same gathering Count Giuseppe Dalla Torre, president of the Unione Popolare, expressed the belief of Catholic citizens that 'peace between the state and the church can be made by the constitutional will of the country, by the action of the state, without any infringement of the latter's civil sovereignty'.[3]

Such declarations, though not official statements of Vatican policy, accurately reflected the trend of thought among Pius X's closest advisers. In November 1912 Merry del Val had privately remarked to a foreign diplomat that it would be a cause of extreme embarrassment to the Vatican to have to govern even the Leonine City.[4] A year later, after the Archbishop of Udine's statement, he admitted to the Austro-Hungarian ambassador the Vatican's interest in having the question of an inter-national guarantee publicly discussed, and even threw out the suggestion that Italy could act as mandatory of the Great Powers.[5] Such talk showed how far the Vatican had moved since the days of Rampolla. On the Italian side there were still liberals of the old school like Luzzatti and Albertini who bridled at the first hint that the Law of Guarantees was not perfect

[1] Spadolini, *Giolitti e i cattolici*, pp. 335–44. Anyone who had sacrificed his independence by signing the Gentiloni Pact 'cannot, as far as I am concerned, be regarded as a liberal', Giolitti told the chamber. *Discorsi parlamentari*, III, p. 1675.
[2] Cilibrizzi, IV, pp. 300–1.
[3] ibid., pp. 294–5; Dalla Torre, pp. 53–4; De Rosa, *L'Azione Cattolica*, II, pp. 350–1. [4] Engel-Jánosi, II, p. 134.
[5] ibid., pp. 135–6. The Vatican's interest in an international guarantee was prompted mainly by awareness of the danger of a European war and of the diffi-culties that would confront the Papacy if Italy became involved.

or eternal. But Giolitti's instinctive recognition that the old antagonism
between Italy and the Papacy was dying was widely shared. Thirty Catholics sat in parliament, a party in all but name, symbolising the loyalty of
Catholic citizens to the Third Italy. The majority of Italians were content
that this should be so.

The new chamber of deputies, like its predecessors in 1905 and 1909,
grew restive within a few weeks of its election. The radicals, their numbers
swollen by success at the polls, split into two groups. One stayed loyal
to Giolitti. The other, strongly influenced by freemasonry, professed disgust at Giolitti's 'monstrous, underhand *connubio* between the *malavita*
and the sacristy',[1] and redoubled its anti-clerical and reforming fervour.
The socialists, too, were ebullient. At the opening session of parliament
they sang the Workers' Hymn and taunted the Prime Minister with shouts
of *Banca Romana!* Karl Marx had been brought back from the attic to the
ground floor, declared the *Critica Sociale*. Among democrats there was
much disillusion: in the south nothing had changed, while in the north
Giolitti seemed, with Gentiloni's help, to have deliberately stifled democratic aspirations.[2] Even Bissolati, his faith shaken, argued that, with the
extension of the suffrage, Giolitti had exhausted his function.[3] One of the
most effective attacks on his personal 'dictatorship' that the chamber had
ever heard was delivered by an independent socialist, Orazio Raimondo.

The truth is that under a democratic banner we have imperceptibly arrived
at a dictatorial regime. The Honourable Giolitti has four times conducted
elections, in 1892, 1904, 1909 and 1913. Moreover, in his long parliamentary
career he has nominated practically all the senators, practically all the councillors of state, all the prefects and all the high officials in our administrative,
judicial, political and military hierarchy. With this formidable power of his,
he has drawn parties together by means of reforms, and individuals together
by means of personal attentions. Now, Honourable Giolitti, when parties
forget their programmes, when those who arrive at the threshold of the
chamber discard the rags of their political convictions at the door, it is necessary to create a majority by other means ... with trickery and corruption. In
this way parliamentary institutions are annulled, parties are annihilated, and
*trasformismo* ... is achieved.

---

[1] A phrase of the independent socialist deputy, Carlo Altobelli. Cilibrizzi, IV,
p. 247.
[2] The 1913 election has been called 'the peasant revolution'. The communist
Gramsci later described Giolitti's change of tactics as 'the replacement of the
alliance between the bourgeoisie and the [northern] working class by an alliance
between the bourgeoisie and the Catholics, who represent the peasant masses of
the north and centre'. Gramsci, *La questione meridionale*, p. 25.
[3] Volpe, III, p. 582.

'You are only a man,' cried the republican Innocenzo Cappa, 'but you must go, for the regeneration of Italy.'[1]

In spite of these philippics Giolitti obtained a majority of 362 votes to 90 in December. But this was only a respite. In February 1914 his Minister of Finance, Luigi Facta, revealed the full cost of the Libyan war and proposed new, 'ultra-democratic' taxation to wipe out the budget deficit. The socialists and anti-colonialists seized the chance to press home their attack. At the same time the government was accused from the right of financial dishonesty[2] and failure to restore the armed forces to their pre-war strength. While his colleagues confidently denied the charge and declared there was no need for alarm, Giolitti rebuked the socialists for their pacifism, warning them that 'the proletariat of a conquered people will never be a happy proletariat'.[3] His position, however, deteriorated rapidly after a Radical party congress at which the militant left wing, which wished to break with the government, won control. On 7 March the party's deputies went into opposition and its ministers decided to resign. Giolitti still had a majority in the chamber; but seeing that a left coalition had become unworkable and the chamber was in a rebellious mood, he too resigned. Sonnino declined to form a government unless the King allowed him to dissolve and free himself from dependence on Giolitti's majority. The King refused his consent, as in 1906 and 1910, and turned to Antonio Salandra who accepted without conditions. As on previous occasions, Giolitti was expected to return to power within a few months.[4]

Salandra was a striking contrast to Giolitti in political style and temperament. He came from the landowning middle class of the south and had chosen an academic career, culminating in his appointment as professor of administrative law at Rome in 1902. Elected deputy for his native Foggia in 1886, he held his first cabinet post under Pelloux in 1899 and became Sonnino's most prominent follower. After the Libyan war Salandra moved closer to Giolitti, though he never became a Giolittian. In the 1913 election he abandoned Sonnino, whose group was almost wiped out, and

[1] Salomone, p. 113; Cilibrizzi, IV, pp. 299, 305. For similar sentiments, see also Albertini, *Venti anni*, II, pp. 279–80.
[2] Giolitti and his colleagues had been studiously optimistic in their financial pronouncements during and after the war, and in December 1913 a budget surplus of 114 million lire had been announced for 1912–13. In fact, as the corrected budget statistics show, a deficit had reappeared in 1909–10. The Libyan war increased it to 340 million lire in 1911–12 and 556 million (20% of expenditure) in 1912–13. The latter was the largest deficit since 1866. The total cost of the war was calculated at 1,276 million lire, most of which was met by borrowing. Coppola d'Anna, pp. 85–8.
[3] Giolitti, *Discorsi parlamentari*, III, p. 1676.
[4] This was Salandra's own opinion. See his *Memorie politiche*, p. 2.

stood as a supporter of the government. Like Sonnino, he was a learned man with a doctrinaire approach to politics; a cold though polished speaker, he rarely moved his audiences and inspired respect rather than devotion. He proclaimed himself a liberal of the classical school of Cavour. Parliamentary government, he asserted, had degenerated under Depretis and Giolitti into compromise and bureaucratic appeasement. Believing that liberalism and democracy were antithetical terms, he dedicated himself to the task of creating a party in the image of the old Right, that would carry out the austere, paternalist, patriotic mission of true liberalism, untainted by either clericalism or socialism.

The new government was composed chiefly of Salandra's own conservative friends, with a few representatives of the left. The most distinguished of the latter was the Minister for Colonies, Ferdinando Martini, former governor of Eritrea, whose political past had been Zanardellian. San Giuliano reluctantly remained Foreign Minister, at Giolitti's insistence.[1] Salandra secured Catholic and nationalist support by announcing that the civil marriage bill would not be reintroduced. The cabinet contained no strict Giolittians or radicals or Catholics, and thus resembled Sonnino's team of December 1909. Though it owed its birth to rebellion against Giolitti, it was formed with his assistance, depended upon his majority and inherited his enmities. It was not expected to live long.

At the outset it scored a success by averting a railway strike through a combination of firmness and conciliation. Less tractable were the closely connected problems of finance and the armed forces. Salandra frankly admitted a budget deficit and announced that he would ask for an increase in income-tax in the autumn. The financial stringency meanwhile slowed down the rearmament programme. A comprehensive four-year plan had been worked out in the spring of 1913 by the Chief of Staff, Pollio, and Giolitti's Minister for War, Spingardi. Giolitti accepted it, but a year later its execution had still not begun. The naval building programme also was cut down. Salandra had criticised Giolitti for neglecting the army and intended to remedy its deficiencies. For this purpose he had originally selected General Carlo Porro, a soldier with a reputation for energy, as his Minister for War. But Giulio Rubini, the Minister of the Treasury, proud of his loyalty to the Sella tradition, demanded that the balancing of the budget take first priority. Porro's request for an extra 600 million lire over four years was turned down and after a few days in office he resigned. His successor, General Domenico Grandi, contented himself with 200 millions, and the task of replenishing stocks and making good the losses in Libya went ahead only slowly.[2]

[1] *Quarant' anni*, III, 118–20; Giolitti, *Memorie*, p. 511.
[2] Salandra, *La neutralità*, pp. 254–9. Porro's intention was to carry out Pollio's

Salandra's real test came in the summer with an outburst of revolutionary unrest. In April 1914 the socialists held their congress at Ancona. It was dominated by Mussolini, who imposed upon it the theme of freemasonry. Distrust of the latter had always been strong in the party.[1] Freemasons stood for many of the things that Mussolini hated most: democracy, class collaboration and humanitarian internationalism. His motion for their expulsion was passed by a huge majority and one of the last links between socialism and the remainder of the old Extreme Left was broken. The congress reaffirmed its faith in the class struggle and the intransigent, revolutionary methods that had been approved at Reggio Emilia, and the ban on cooperation with bourgeois parties was extended to local elections. 'Italian democracy can never be sufficiently combated', Mussolini declared.[2]

Six weeks later on 7 June, Constitution Day, an anti-militarist, anti-nationalist, anti-capitalist demonstration at Ancona led to clashes with the police and three deaths. Its chief organisers were Nenni, the extremist republican, and Malatesta, who had operated from Ancona since his return to Italy in the previous year.[3] The revolutionary socialists had been waiting for some such incident for eighteen months. The shooting of seven *braccianti* in January 1913 at Roccagorga in Lazio had roused passionate resentment throughout the working-class movement. Mussolini had devoted a whole inflammatory number of *Avanti!* to 'proletarian massacres', and the party and the C.G.L. had resolved that if another occurred, they would call a general strike. Now, in protest against what Mussolini called

---

maximum programme. This included artillery re-equipment and modernisation; more fortifications on the Austrian frontier, in addition to those just completed under the 1909 programme, and also a few on the French; an increase in the quota of conscripts called up; the development of aviation; and the military re-organisation of Libya to make it self-sufficient. Grandi's 200 million lire were insufficient to carry out even Pollio's 'ultra-minimum' programme. Nevertheless the peace-time strength of the army increased from 205,000 in 1907–8 to 250,000 in 1912–13 and 275,000 in 1913–14, an achievement for which Giolitti was justified in later claiming credit. *L'esercito italiano*, I, pp. 61–6, 71–2; Rochat, pp. 313–316.

[1] At the Milan congress of 1910 Salvemini had denounced freemasonry as one of the occult forces from which the south had to be freed, and carried a motion, which was not enforced, that membership of a masonic order was incompatible with membership of the party. Salomone, pp. 81–3.

[2] Mussolini, VI, p. 165.

[3] The demonstration was one of many held to protest against the relegation to penal companies of 'subversive' conscripts, and to display solidarity with Masetti, a soldier who to the cry of 'Long live Anarchy' had shot his colonel in the shoulder in barracks at Bologna while the latter was haranguing troops about to leave for Libya. This act had made Masetti the hero of the anarchists and of all revolutionaries. Borghi, p. 116.

'a premeditated assassination', the general strike was duly declared. A wave
of disorder spread across Italy. The revolt had no leader or plan. Socialists,
syndicalists, anarchists and republicans, in sudden and unprecedented
harmony, plunged into the fray for sheer love of rebellion, and Italy seemed
to have reverted to the age of Bakunin. There were riotous demonstrations
and barricades in Rome and the great cities. The climax was reached in
Emilia and the Marche where authority virtually collapsed. Local dictators
proclaimed republics, the red flag was hoisted above town halls, taxes were
abolished and prices reduced by decree, churches were attacked, railways
and telegraph lines damaged, landlords' villas sacked, troops disarmed and
even a general captured. Ancona itself was held by the rebels for a week. In
Milan the syndicalists rioted under Corridoni. Mussolini in *Avanti!* praised
the aggressive character of the general strike, 'the most serious popular
uprising that has shaken the Third Italy between 1870 and today', and
surveyed the scene 'with something of that legitimate joy with which the
craftsman contemplates his creation'.[1]

After two days the C.G.L. called off the general strike and most of Italy
returned to normal. But Salandra took no chances. Ten thousand troops
were deployed in Emilia, where the restoration of order took ten days.
Corridoni, Nenni and other leading rebels were arrested, while Malatesta
escaped once again to exile in London. Red Week, as it was immediately
named, had lasting consequences and led to much heart-searching. The
optimists had prophesied that socialism would civilise the masses and
time would tame the socialists. It was a sobering experience to see large
sections of the population of Emilia behaving as irresponsibly in 1914 as
in 1874, and indulging in violence on a vastly greater scale. Such a spectacle
was bound to discredit the policy of internal appeasement to which
Giolitti had committed Italy since 1901. Even more shocking was the fact
that the state had been forced to abdicate its authority over a large area
and had only by a major effort regained control. Red Week had revealed
the growth over the past decade, under authority's complacent eye, of
socialist 'states within the state', of local centres of almost despotic
socialist power. For this, too, Giolitti and his system were blamed, and
the whole structure of Giolittian Italy was brought into question.

Even the Socialist party was shaken by the week of frenzy. The reformists
resolved to make a stand and the party's deputies passed a motion, presented by Turati, that 'the emancipation of the proletariat is not to be
achieved by outbursts of disorganised mobs'. In the *Critica Sociale* Claudio

---

[1] *Avanti!*, 12 June 1914. 'Workers, I am not a poet', he told a meeting of strikers
in Milan, 'but I would like to be one, in order to hymn your magnificent movement . . . I would like to be the poet of the general strike.' Mussolini, VI, pp.
217–21.

Treves attacked hooliganism and 'the divine right of the *piazza*'.[1] Rigola carried the C.G.L. with him in rejecting Mussolini's accusations of treachery. But the exponents of violence still controlled the party. Even its representatives in parliament felt bound to prove their revolutionary spirit. When the budget was introduced, they resorted for several weeks to systematic obstruction against Salandra, the 'assassin' and 'modern Pelloux'. In the middle of July the renewed threat of a railway strike led Salandra to call up a class of reservists. The threat of disorder thus persisted and the revolutionary trend within the Socialist party showed little sign of weakening.

Signs of reaction from the right were not lacking. In Bologna and other cities 'volunteers for the defence of order' again made their appearance, to supplement the police. The propertied class, not content with the inadequate security that the state provided, was beginning to think of taking the law into its own hands. The nationalists meanwhile turned their backs decisively upon liberalism and founded a party of their own. Great efforts were made at their congress in May 1914 to win Catholic sympathy by emphasising their respect for religion, the family and freedom in education. 'Anti-clericalism', said Federzoni, 'no longer has a right to exist.'[2] In June Corradini was given the support of Catholic Action when he contested a by-election in Venetia, though without success. In the same month, in the aftermath of Red Week, local elections were held. At Naples, Ancona, Verona and Bologna the extreme left won big victories; the socialists captured Milan and Mussolini won a seat on its municipal council. But the clerical-moderates were victorious at Turin and Genoa, while at Rome a nationalist-conservative-Catholic coalition defeated the Popular Bloc and made Prospero Colonna mayor in place of the freemason Nathan.

Thus on the one side the middle class, whose flabbiness the nationalists had so long derided, showed signs of stirring; on the other the working-class movement was led by revolutionaries. The extremists of both right and left regarded Giolitti with loathing or contempt. It seemed that the political balance which had lasted from 1904 to 1913 had been destroyed and that universal suffrage had ushered in a new era of strain and violent change. Given several years more of peace, Giolitti, though now growing old, might have found new techniques for guiding Italy through a period of confusion. But at the end of July Europe plunged into war and the world which Giolitti knew and understood began to crumble.

---

[1] Salomone, p. 61; Cilibrizzi, IV, p. 339; De Felice, pp. 209 ff. Treves rebuked Mussolini for his 'anarchistic' un-socialist language and 'Dionysiac prose'.

[2] De Rosa, *L'Azione Cattolica*, II, pp. 370–2. 'Nationalism has found the right road', commented a leading Catholic newspaper, *L'Avvenire d'Italia* of Bologna.

## The Revival of the Triple Alliance 1912–14

On 9 October 1912 San Giuliano remarked to the French chargé d'affaires that as soon as peace had been made with Turkey, 'we shall devote all our endeavours to protecting her territorial integrity against the attack that threatens it'.[1] Italy was for the moment sated with Libya and militarily disorganised. San Giuliano therefore reverted to a traditional policy of prudent conservatism, and would indeed have much preferred to see no change in the Balkan *status quo*. But the victories of the Balkan League soon put Turkey beyond the aid of Italy or anyone else. In the long international crisis that followed, Austria-Hungary's main concern was the creation of an independent Albania which would keep the victorious, ebullient Serbs away from the Adriatic. In December 1912 an Ambassadors' Conference in London approved the establishment of an autonomous, neutralised Albanian state under six-Power supervision, within frontiers to be delimited by the conference. This decision, which was entirely in line with the Austro-Italian agreements of 1897 and 1900, secured San Giuliano's wholehearted approval.

Meanwhile the negotiations for the renewal of the Triple Alliance, which had petered out during the Libyan war, were resumed. On 5 December a new treaty was signed in Vienna, nineteen months before the Alliance was due to expire, extending it until July 1926. Germany and Austria-Hungary rejected all Italy's proposed amendments and insisted on a public announcement that it had been renewed unaltered. An additional protocol, however, guaranteed Italian sovereignty over Libya and confirmed the Austro-Italian agreements of 1900 and 1909 on Albania and the Sanjak.

San Giuliano's long-term aim had always been to strengthen the Triple Alliance, and in the Balkan Wars he now saw his opportunity. The risk of estranging France did not worry him greatly, for he believed that the acquisition of Libya had removed the main motive of the *entente* of 1902. But the dangers of dependence upon Austria-Hungary were apparent even to San Giuliano, and still more to the King and Giolitti. They supported Austria mainly from fear and the desire for peace. San Giuliano might be afraid that a Serbian port on the Albanian coast would bring Russian naval power to the Adriatic; but he was even more afraid that it would give the Austrians a pretext for attacking and swallowing Serbia. It was to keep out the Austrians, far more than the Serbs, that he insisted upon a large, autonomous Albanian state. As a second best he envisaged the partition of Albania between an Austrian sphere in the north and an Italian sphere

[1] Albertini, *Origins*, I, p. 418.

in the south. In June 1913 he defined his policy: 'No one to enter Albania; but if someone else goes in, we go to Valona immediately.'[1] One of the chief functions of the Triple Alliance was still, in Italian eyes, the restraint of Austria-Hungary. Italo-Austrian collaboration continued to be the product of mutual distrust.

The opposition in Italy to the renewal of the Alliance had been less vocal than on any previous occasion. It was welcomed by the colonialists, whose eyes were now turning to Asia Minor and the east, by the Franco-phobes in the tradition of Crispi, by the industrialists and traders who had German connexions, and by those socialists and pacifists who had faith in it as an instrument of peace. But there was also uneasiness in well-informed circles. Visconti Venosta on the right, Barzilai and Bissolati on the left, continued to be preoccupied with the risk that Italy might become involved through the Triple Alliance in the naval rivalry between Germany and Britain. Others saw no object in preserving the Alliance now that Italian aims in north Africa had been realised. Democrats sympathised with the small nations of the Balkans, detested the very idea of backing Austria against the Serbs and kept up the traditional attacks on the Alliance as a breeder of militarism. Many nationalists and business men, too, regretted the loss of an opportunity to extend Italian influence and trade throughout the Balkans by patronising Serbia and Montenegro.[2] Visconti Venosta spoke the truth when he told Barrère that no Italian government could join Austria-Hungary in an aggressive war.[3] Suspicion of Austria revived when, two days after the signature of the new treaty, Conrad was reinstated as Chief of Staff. Berchtold assured San Giuliano that he need have no alarm. But Italian public opinion was still 'the Achilles heel of the Triple Alliance'.

Events in the Balkans soon tested the Alliance severely. With the collapse of Turkey, Albania sank into tribal chaos. A national congress proclaimed Albanian independence in November 1912 and set up a precarious government in the centre of the country. Serbian and Montenegrin troops penetrated deeply from the north and east. Greek forces, advancing up the coast from the south, threatened Valona and the neighbouring island of Saseno, the two points in which Italy was most interested. A major international crisis blew up in March 1913 when the Serbian and Montenegrin armies laid siege to Scutari, which the Ambassadors' Conference had assigned to Albania. Russia backed Serbia, and mobilised armies

---

[1] Galli, p. 167. Naval preparations for the occupation of Valona were made in May. *La marina italiana*, I, p. 43.

[2] A Serbian port on the Adriatic would clearly help Italian penetration of the Balkans and this was one of the reasons why Austria opposed it.

[3] Albertini, *Origins*, I, p. 420.

AUSTRIA-
HUNGARY

Aquileia
Trieste
Venice
Fiume
Pola
Krk
Rab

Croatia

Bosnia

Dalmatia

Zara
Sibenik
Split

Lagosta

Herzegovina

Belgrade

SERBIA

MONTENEGRO
Lovćen
Kotor
Scutari

Rome

Bari

Naples

Durazzo
Tirana

ALBANIA

Macedonia

GREECE

Valona

Corfu

**THE ADRIATIC·1915**

*Miles*

0      50      100      150      200      250

Territory demanded by Italy, March 1915
Territory demanded and granted by Treaty of London

faced each other across the Austro-Russian frontier. The Austrians, with German approval, clamoured for action to eject the Serbs and Montenegrins, and declared they would act alone if the Great Powers shrank from their duty. Conrad urged war, to cut the Gordian knot of the Southern Slav question.

The divergence of Italian and Austrian aims in the Balkans now became apparent. Even San Giuliano was unable to tolerate the independent use of force by Austria in the Adriatic, and he warned Berchtold that it would cause a crisis in the Triple Alliance and perhaps lead to war. His solution was that Italy and Austria-Hungary should jointly enforce the ambassadors' decision. Giolitti, clearer-sighted, overruled him, having realised that such an arrangement would 'bind us hand and foot to Austria' and might trap Italy in war against Russia and France. If the Serbs and Montenegrins were to be ejected from Scutari, he insisted that it should either be by all the Great Powers acting together, or at least by a combination which included one member of the Triple Entente, preferably Britain.[1] Happily for Italy, the Powers agreed. In April a multi-national naval squadron, including Italian ships, was despatched to the Montenegrin coast. It proved powerless to influence events ashore. The desired effect was, however, obtained by concerted diplomatic pressure. First the Serbs withdrew, then King Nicholas of Montenegro, to whom Scutari had meanwhile surrendered, submitted to the Great Powers' decision. In mid-May the town was occupied by an international force and tension subsided.

Two months later the Second Balkan War brought an even graver crisis. The Bulgars, after treacherously attacking their allies, were crushingly defeated by Serbia, Greece, Rumania and Turkey. Berchtold warned Germany and Italy on 4 July that Austria might have to intervene to save Bulgaria, as an act of national self-defence;[2] if so, and if war with Russia resulted, he argued that the *casus foederis* under the Triple Alliance would arise. San Giuliano was at that moment in Germany, after accompanying the King on a state visit to Sweden. He found his German colleagues anxious to prevent their ally from precipitating a European war, even though they declared they would in the last resort march with Austria. To San Giuliano it seemed clear that the Triple Alliance could not be invoked to support an Austrian attack on Serbia. Giolitti, consulted by telegram, fully agreed: 'If Austria intervenes against Serbia, it is evident that no *casus foederis* arises. She undertakes such an adventure purely on her own account; both because there is no question of defence, since no one is thinking of attacking her, and because it is a matter in which no

[1] Albertini, *Origins*, pp. 440-8, and *Venti anni*, II, pp. 368-80; Giolitti, *Memorie*, pp. 485-96; *Quarant' anni*, III, 91-7.
[2] Albertini, *Origins*, I, p. 455.

interest of either Italy or Germany is involved.'[1] On 11 July San Giuliano, now back in Rome, bluntly told the Austrian ambassador that an attack on Serbia would be 'an offensive act in the full sense of the word'. 'We will hold you back by your coat-tails if necessary', he declared.[2] Fortunately for Italy, Rumania's intervention on 10 July sealed Bulgaria's fate and the war ended in August with the moral defeat of Austria-Hungary.[3] But only Austrian indecision had saved Italy from a terrible dilemma, and the effectiveness of restraining the Austrians by collaboration had again proved highly doubtful.

Undismayed by these alarms, San Giuliano persisted in his attempts to strengthen and extend the Alliance. A new note of nationalist assertion appeared in his speeches. Panegyrics of the Triple Alliance, 'the cornerstone of our foreign policy', were combined with a vague, menacing insistence on equilibrium in the Mediterranean and on 'Italy's great interests in every part of the world'. The Mediterranean was no one's *mare nostrum*, San Giuliano declared, but a free highway for all nations, among whom Italy had a leading place; if territorial changes occurred, 'Italy could not remain a passive spectator and would have to ensure that her position as a Mediterranean Great Power was held in due respect by all.' At the end of 1913 he returned to the theme: 'For Italy the days of a submissive policy have gone for ever.'[4]

The revival of the Triple Alliance, combined with this new note of confidence in Italian foreign policy, strained Italy's relations with Britain and France. In October 1912, as soon as the Libyan war ended, Grey and Poincaré proposed a tripartite Mediterranean pact for the mutual guarantee of Britain's position in Egypt, Italy's in Libya and France's in Tunisia, Algeria and Morocco. Though Giolitti was encouraging, San Giuliano showed only polite interest. Mutual confidence was lacking, and Britain and France decided to wait until the Balkan crisis had subsided. On 20 November Tittoni, now ambassador in Paris, startled Poincaré by declaring that if war between Austria and Russia broke out over Albania, and France were subsequently involved, the Austro-Italian convention of 1900, being anterior to the Prinetti-Barrère and Racconigi agreements, would force Italy to take Austria's side.[5] Giolitti at once toned down Tittoni's statement, San Giuliano confirmed Italian loyalty to the 1902

[1] *Quarant' anni*, III, 109–10.                    [2] Albertini, *Origins*, I, pp. 458–9.
[3] Helmreich, pp. 378–9.

[4] Speeches in chamber of deputies, 18 December 1912, 22 February and 16 December 1913. Cilibrizzi, IV, pp. 237–40, 245.

[5] DDF (3), IV, 502; R. Poincaré, *Au service de la France*, II, *Les Balkans en feu* (Paris 1929), pp. 341–2. Giolitti had made substantially the same point to the British ambassador on 9 November, though without Tittoni's exaggerated emphasis. BD, IX (ii), 172.

agreement and Visconti Venosta, author of the 1900 convention on Albania, assured Barrère that it contained no military obligation. But distrust had been sown in both France and Russia.[1] When the Triple Alliance was prematurely renewed, the French concluded that it had been transformed into an aggressive Mediterranean alliance and refused to be impressed by assurances to the contrary. While Poincaré talked of France's determination to maintain preponderance over Italy, the French and Italian press revived the ill-tempered polemics which had broken out over the *Manouba* incident. Italian policy 'is as subordinated to the Triple Alliance as in the days of Crispi, and perhaps even more so', reported Izvolsky from Paris at the end of 1913, reflecting the official French view.[2]

The main source of British and French alarm was Italy's high-handed treatment of Greece. San Giuliano's struggle for a big Albania involved him in a quarrel with that country as well as with Serbia. The Greeks had occupied southern Albania (or, as they preferred to call it, northern Epirus), claiming that its population was Greek, and organised bands of irregulars to stir up trouble further inside Albania. They enjoyed warm French and cautious British sympathy. For this very reason San Giuliano was determined to check Greek expansion to the north. In particular he shared the fears of his naval advisers that if the coastline opposite the Greek island of Corfu were also to fall into Greek hands, the Corfu Channel might become a naval base for the Triple Entente, threatening free navigation in the Straits of Otranto. Giolitti was sceptical. He was prepared to treat a Greek occupation of Saseno as a *casus belli* but Corfu seemed to him no more worth a war than Scutari. Nevertheless San Giuliano, impressed by the strident anti-Greek campaign of Italian nationalists, imitated the Austrians in their dealings with the Serbs and even warned Greece that Italy would, if necessary, go to war to prevent Greece holding both sides of the channel.[3] In August 1913 the Ambassadors' Conference accepted Italy's proposals for the southern frontier of Albania,[4] subject to detailed

---

[1] DDF (3), IV, 560, 625; Poincaré, *Au service de la France*, II, pp. 363–4; Albertini, *Origins*, I, pp. 420–1. One consequence of Tittoni's statement was Sazonov's agreement to the French request to be given details of the Racconigi agreement. Izvolsky, now Russian ambassador in Paris, read out the text to Poincaré in December, on the understanding that no one else, not even members of the French cabinet or officials of the French Foreign Ministry, should be informed. In return Poincaré authorised the communication to Sazonov of the text of the Prinetti–Barrère agreement, of which Izvolsky personally had already been informed in November 1908 (see above, p. 347, note 3).

[2] Serra, *Camille Barrère*, p. 275.

[3] *La marina italiana*, I, pp. 389–96; *Quarant' anni*, III, 99; BD, IX (ii), 974; De Bosdari, pp. 74–7, 90 ff.; Giolitti, *Memorie*, p. 494; Salandra, *La neutralità*, pp. 38–9; Cataluccio, pp. 124–5.

[4] These gave Albania the disputed district of Koritza and the island of Saseno, as well as the coast opposite Corfu.

delimitation by an international boundary commission. But the Greeks remained in the disputed area. Italian goods were boycotted in Greece, the chauvinist press in both countries whipped up feeling and the dispute dragged on into 1914.

Rivalry in the Aegean increased the tension. Greece, its appetite whetted by seizure of most of the Aegean islands from Turkey, coveted the Dodecanese as well. By the terms of the Treaty of Ouchy, the latter were to be handed back to Turkey as soon as the Turks left Libya. San Giuliano's policy was to ensure that they remained Turkish when Italy withdrew, and did not subsequently find their way into the hands of Greece. Alarmed by Panhellene aspirations in Asia, he opposed the cession to the Greeks even of the islands they themselves had captured,[1] and fought Greek expansion in the Aegean as stubbornly as in Albania. By sheer persistence he achieved his aim. In August 1913 the Ambassadors' Conference decided that when the Dodecanese had been handed back to Turkey, the Great Powers, including Italy, should decide their final fate, together with that of the other Aegean islands. The decision remained on paper. At the end of the year Italy announced that 200 Turkish officers were still fighting with the Senussi in Cyrenaica. This convenient fact allowed the Italians to stay in the Dodecanese, with the tacit collusion of the Turks who regarded the Italian presence as the best protection against Greece. The Italian administration favoured the Turkish and Jewish minorities and suppressed demonstrations in Rhodes for union with Greece, provoking the Greek press into attacking General Giovanni Ameglio, the Italian governor, as a greater tyrant than the Turks.[2] When the European war broke out in July 1914, the fate of the Dodecanese and the other Aegean islands was still undecided.

It was in the Aegean that Italian policy clashed most directly with that of Britain and France. The latter were ready to make concessions over the southern frontier of Albania if the Italians would be conciliatory over the islands; but in spite of repeated assurances, they suspected that Italy had no intention of ever leaving the Aegean. Indeed many Italians frankly compared their situation with that of the British in Egypt, whose occupation, in spite of repeated promises of evacuation, had already lasted thirty years. As Grey himself remarked in July 1913, 'To make a thing dependent upon the fulfilment of a treaty by Turkey, though it was not exactly equivalent to a freehold, might almost be regarded as equivalent to a 999 years' lease.'[3] While the British cared little whether the Dodecanese

---

[1] Cataluccio, pp. 126–9.

[2] Sertoli Salis, pp. 85–6, 96–7; De Bosdari, p. 75.

[3] Rodd, III, p. 176; DDF (3), VIII, 315; BD, X (i), 144–9; Viscount Grey of Fallodon, *Twenty-Five Years* (London 1925), I, p. 271.

belonged to Greece or Turkey, the French backed Greece's claim. Both were determined not to allow the establishment of a naval base for the Triple Alliance in the Aegean. In the French view, not only the balance of power in the Mediterranean, but the security of France itself, were at stake. Pichon, the French Foreign Minister, said privately that France would oppose Italy's permanent establishment in the Dodecanese 'by every means', which implied even war.[1]

Another reason for French and British anxiety was Italy's growing interest in Asia Minor. Nationalist writers had long marked down Adalia to be an Italian sphere of interest,[2] where railways and public works could be constructed by Italian labour, mines exploited, new markets found and peasant colonists established on underdeveloped land. The intention was to secure a foothold in southern Anatolia against the day when the Turkish Empire finally collapsed. San Giuliano told his allies that only if the Triple Alliance were extended from the tense, enclosed Adriatic to the wider Mediterranean could it hope to survive. No one welcomed Italy's intrusion, but there was a great expansion of Italian financial and commercial interests in Asia Minor after 1912.[3] Germany was the first to recognise Italy's claims. Britain followed in May 1914 with a railway agreement which opened the door to Italian enterprise. The French and Austrians, who had designs of their own on Asia Minor, were more obstinate, and the Turks used their normal technique of procrastination. In July 1914 the Italian concession in Adalia still existed only on paper. But Italians were pleased at being accepted as equals among the protectors and exploiters of Turkey, and were confident that an extension of Italian trade, culture and prestige would follow.

During 1913-14 the military links of the Triple Alliance were strengthened. General Pollio, the Italian Chief of Staff since 1908, was an enthusiastic admirer of Germany. In November 1912 he found it necessary to inform his allies that, with 60,000 troops still tied down in Libya and mobilisation plans still disrupted, Italy could not provide the five army corps for the Rhine which the military convention of 1888 specified in the event of war; but he promised a maximum effort on the Alps and suggested an Italian landing in Provence. In March 1914 the convention was restored to life, though Italy's obligation was reduced from five to three

---

[1] Albertini, *Venti anni*, II, p. 409; Volpe III, p. 480. On 19 July 1913 Pichon minuted: 'Il nous est absolument impossible de ne pas opposer aux *manœuvres ultra-tripliciennes* de l'Italie *une résistance résolue* . . . Il s'agit de notre sécurité dans la Méditerranée.' DDF (3), VII, 498.

[2] In Italian, *una zona di lavoro e di interesse*.

[3] Cataluccio, pp. 138-42. Volpi's Società Commerciale d'Oriente was one of the most active institutions. In 1914 Italy obtained a mining concession in the coalfield of Eregli (Heraclea) on the Black Sea coast east of Constantinople.

corps. General Luigi Zuccari, designated as commander of the Italian force, went to Berlin to make detailed arrangements for its reception, and staff plans were worked out in Vienna to accelerate its transit across Austria so that it would be ready for battle in Alsace within four weeks of mobilisation.[1] In April Pollio went further and suggested unofficially to the German military attaché that Italian troops might fight beside Austria against Russia or Serbia; on hearing which, the German reported, 'I nearly fell off my chair.'[2] Meanwhile in June 1913, with the warm support of Moltke, the German Chief of Staff, the naval convention of 1900 was replaced by a new and far more binding convention, to come into force in November. It provided in detail for the concentration of the Italian and Austro-Hungarian navies on the outbreak of war, together with any German warships that might be in the Mediterranean.[3] Command of the joint fleets was to be given to the Austrian Admiral Haus, whose immediate task would be to destroy the French fleet before that of Russia arrived and to intercept north African troops on their way to France. The convention was a direct answer to the Anglo-French naval agreement of the previous year.

These military agreements were significant evidence of the new life that seemed to have been injected into the Triple Alliance. Nevertheless their importance can be exaggerated. The Italian general staff enjoyed the full confidence of the King, who was informed in detail of all staff conversations, but it had a negligible influence on foreign policy. In time of peace the Chief of Staff had only advisory powers and was subordinate to the Minister for War, through whom the cabinet controlled the army. There was moreover an astonishing mutual incomprehension and lack of contact between the soldiers and the civilian politicians, which was to cost Italy dear in war.[4] Pollio, the ardent Germanophil, was ignorant both of the text of the Triple Alliance and of the very existence of the Prinetti–Barrère agreement. As Conrad later wrote in his memoirs, 'General Pollio was not Italy'.[5] The appearance of military solidarity in the Triple Alliance was therefore to a large extent deceptive.

In spite of San Giuliano's ostentatious display of goodwill, the clash of

[1] Rochat, pp. 313, 317–18. At this time expenditure was also authorised, for the first time for many years, on fortifications on the French frontier.

[2] Albertini, Origins, I, p. 561, Venti anni, II, p. 431.

[3] A squadron of four German cruisers, headed by the Goeben, had been stationed in the Mediterranean since November 1912.

[4] Albertini, Origins, I, p. 564, Venti anni, II, pp. 434–5; Rochat, pp. 321–4. In 1906 the Chief of Staff was designated commander in time of war, with sole responsibility for military operations under the King as nominal commander-in-chief.

[5] Volpe, III, p. 473; Conrad von Hötzendorf, Aus meiner Dienstzeit (Vienna 1922), III, p. 433.

Italian and Austrian interests in the Adriatic persisted. The signing of the naval convention was immediately followed in July 1913 by Giolitti's refusal to acknowledge the *casus foederis* if Austria attacked Serbia. Yet another Balkan crisis occurred in October. The Serbs recrossed the provisional Albanian frontier under pretext of a revolt in the Albanian districts already ceded to them, hoping that the international boundary commission would accept the *fait accompli*. On 18 October Berchtold demanded evacuation within eight days. Conrad urged war while the situation was still favourable. Germany this time stood unreservedly behind Austria. To avoid a repetition of San Giuliano's plain words of July, Berchtold informed him of the ultimatum only six hours after it had reached the Serbs. San Giuliano protested sharply, though the form of his protest implied an admission that the *casus foederis* would arise if Austria's action led to general war. Without German encouragement he felt unable to speak out as in July.[1] On 20 October the Serbs submitted and for the third time within a single year the Triple Alliance was saved from almost intolerable strain.

Albania, however, still failed to settle down. Moslems and Christians were at each other's throats and the squabbles of petty chieftains tempted all Albania's neighbours to intervene. The Ambassadors' Conference had drawn up a constitution which provided for a sovereign prince, a Dutch-commanded police force, neutral status and a measure of international control for ten years. After lengthy negotiations the Italians accepted the Austrian candidate for the throne, the Prussian Prince William of Wied, who landed in Albania in March 1914. He had not been two months in his kingdom before a Moslem revolt broke out in the interior. The insurgents were soon threatening his capital, Durazzo. Italian and Austrian marines were landed to guard his palace and he himself was persuaded to take temporary refuge with his family on an Italian warship. In the middle of this crisis Essad Pasha, Prince William's Minister of Interior and Minister for War, was arrested for treason and sent to Italy, where he was given a hero's reception. Both Germany and Austria-Hungary suspected that there was Italian money behind Essad and deplored their ally's betrayal of the Prince of Wied.[2] An 'independent' republic of Epirus had meanwhile been proclaimed in southern Albania with Greek connivance. Under

---

[1] Albertini, *Origins*, I, pp. 480-2.

[2] Swire, pp. 206 ff. Essad Pasha was a feudal landed proprietor from the Tirana district of central Albania. In April 1913, when commander of the Turkish garrison in Scutari, he had surrendered the town to the Montenegrins. Subsequently he renounced all allegiance to Turkey and espoused the cause of Albanian independence. It was alleged that his secret motive for surrendering Scutari had been the hope of winning Serbian and Montenegrin support for his own candidature for the Albanian throne.

strong diplomatic pressure the Greek government reluctantly withdrew its troops from Albanian soil, but the Moslem insurrection in July provided a new opportunity for intervention. Savage fighting broke out again in Epirus. Against an external threat to Albania, Italy and Austria-Hungary could still cooperate. But inside Albania, in its Ruritanian atmosphere of corruption and intrigue, cooperation was virtually impossible. Both governments doubted the other's good faith. The suspicions of the Austrians were enhanced by Carlo Aliotti, the forceful Italian minister in Durazzo, who intrigued incessantly against them. Giolitti and San Giuliano officially deplored his activity and urged him to collaborate with his Austrian colleague; but they dared not disown or recall him because, as San Giuliano explained to the German ambassador, he had become a hero at home, 'the new Garibaldi'. San Giuliano genuinely wished to collaborate with Austria-Hungary on a basis of parity, but was forced to recognise that the growing antagonism arose 'from the force of circumstances'. By July 1914 he had been driven to the conclusion that 'we must restrict the [Italo-Austrian] *tête à tête* within the narrowest possible limits, in order to make it tolerable'. The attempt at joint control of Albania had led only to mutual exasperation.[1]

Further north there were other causes of friction. Victory over Turkey had given Serbia and Montenegro a common frontier, and champions of Yugoslav unity impatiently awaited union of the two kingdoms. The Austro-Hungarian government was inclined to permit this, provided the united kingdom were cut off from the Adriatic by the cession of the Montenegrin coastline to Albania. Conrad demanded in addition that Austria-Hungary be given Mount Lovčen, the 'black mountain' from which Montenegro takes its name. To San Giuliano such proposals were intolerable. A common frontier with Albania would have given Austria-Hungary predominance in that country. The cession of Lovčen, besides making Montenegro indefensible, would have allowed Austria-Hungary to create a first-class base in the gulf of Kotor and so destroy the balance of naval power in the Adriatic. In April 1914 he told the Germans that the acquisition of Lovčen by Austria would cause a grave crisis in the Triple Alliance and force him to turn to Russia for support.[2]

Most damaging of all for Italo-Austrian friendship was Austria's treatment of the unredeemed Italians. In August 1913 the Governor of Trieste, Prince Conrad Hohenlohe, decided to enforce a hitherto neglected law of 1867 and ordered the dismissal of all citizens of the Italian Kingdom from

[1] Albertini, *Origins*, I, pp. 525–6; Salandra, *La neutralità*, pp. 42–4; Aldrovandi, *Guerra diplomatica*, pp. 45–7; DDI (4), XII, 225. Even Aliotti's recall, San Giuliano observed, would be no more than 'a momentary palliative'.

[2] Albertini, *Origins*, I, pp. 518–19.

public employment in the city. The severity of the measure was increased by the fact that it had long been made difficult for the 20,000 *regnicoli* of Trieste to acquire Austro-Hungarian nationality. The Hohenlohe decrees were interpreted by public opinion in Italy as proof of 'systematic persecution of everything Italian'.[1] Irredentism at once revived. The Trent and Trieste Society, under an energetic new president, the nationalist Giovanni Giuriati, planned a congress of protest in Venice which Giolitti promptly banned. In November more student riots at Graz showed that the university question still rankled. These incidents reflected the rising racial tension in the Adriatic. The conquest of Libya had stimulated Italian national pride and irredentist sentiment among Austrian-Italians; after Turkey, they hoped, it would be Austria-Hungary's turn. Similarly Serbia's triumph over the Turks had roused the Croats and Slovenes of Istria and Dalmatia to paroxysms of Yugoslav ardour. Anti-Italian demonstrations occurred all down the Adriatic coast. The Slovenes approved of the Hohenlohe decrees and protested when, in deference to Italian feeling, they were slightly modified. Italians complained that the Austrian police showed anti-Italian bias. Arrests, confiscations of newspapers, restrictions on the Lega Nazionale's schools and harassing of distinguished visitors from Italy grew more frequent. Many Austrian-Italians began to feel desperate. 'Either we beat the Slavs or the Slavs beat us', wrote Scipio Slataper, an irredentist from Trieste; 'we must conquer to avoid being conquered.'[2]

As the points of friction with Austria-Hungary multiplied, San Giuliano felt compelled, like Prinetti and Tittoni before him, to reinsure. In October 1913, conscious of the danger of 'finding ourselves on bad terms with both our neighbours simultaneously', he took the initiative in reviving the long dormant negotiations with Britain and France for a tripartite Mediterranean pact. They did not go smoothly. The Dodecanese and Italian ambitions in Asia Minor proved major irritants. At the end of the year the French obtained the key to the Italian diplomatic cypher and so got wind of the recent Italo-Austro-German naval convention. This discovery confirmed their belief that the Triple Alliance had been extended to the Mediterranean. San Giuliano deepened their suspicion by insisting, from fear of German reproaches for any new 1902-style flirtation, that the text of any Mediterranean pact must, unlike the Prinetti–Barrère agree-

---

[1] Giolitti to San Giuliano, 7 November 1913. *Quarant' anni*, III, 113. Eight months later San Giuliano observed that in the summer of 1913, 'thanks to my efforts supported by Giolitti, Italian feelings towards Austria had become friendlier than ever before'; but the Hohenlohe decrees destroyed this amity and regrettably revived popular pressure in Italy for closer relations with France. DDI (4), XII, 225.

[2] Volpe, III, p. 562.

ment, be communicated to Germany.[1] Nevertheless slow progress was made. The press polemics in France and Italy died down. Giolitti and San Giuliano encouraged France and Britain to play a more active part in Albanian affairs, showing a growing preference for international control of that country rather than the exclusive Austro-Italian condominium which they had hitherto favoured. In January 1914 the Greek Prime Minister, Venizelos, visited Rome, where San Giuliano assured him that Italy had no intention of retaining 'a single stone of the Dodecanese'.[2] In April San Giuliano once again injected new life into the Mediterranean negotiations and showed a keen desire to reach agreement. Next month France and Italy signed a convention on the international status of their Tunisian and Libyan subjects, in itself of little importance but politically significant as the first written agreement between them since the *Carthage* and *Manouba* incidents.

Meanwhile another attempt was made to reduce friction with Austria-Hungary. When William II visited Victor Emmanuel at Venice in March 1914, he was able to listen happily to his host's attacks on France, his praise for the naval convention and his assurance that Italian relations with Austria were 'completely normal and satisfactory'.[3] The Hohenlohe decrees had forced San Giuliano to postpone a visit he had planned to pay Berchtold in the autumn of 1913, but on 14 April 1914 the two Foreign Ministers met at Abbazia. San Giuliano made every effort to be friendly, even declaring his belief that, in view of the danger of the *marée slave*, 'a strong Austria was a necessity for Italy'.[4] But no frank exchange of views occurred. On Serbian-Montenegrin union, on Lovčen, on spheres of influence in Asia Minor, on the university question[5] and the treatment of Italians in Austria, Berchtold was evasive. Officially San Giuliano exuded optimism; in private he lamented that his great sacrifices for Austro-Italian friendship had brought no response from the other side. Ten days later the Austro-Hungarian delegations voted credits for four more dread-

---

[1] *Quarant' anni*, III, 111–12; DDF (3), VIII, 223, 333, 377, 408; BD, X (i), 151–2. San Giuliano wrote to Giolitti on 28 October: 'In any case I agree with you that it would be a grave error to indulge in flirtation (*far giri di waltzer*).' The reference is to Bülow's comment of 1902 on Italy's *extratour* (see above, p. 327). It is not clear from the published documents who took the initiative in reopening negotiations. San Giuliano in his letter to Giolitti speaks of French and British *avances*; but from DDF (3), VIII, 223 it would appear that the Italian chargé d'affaires in Paris made the first move, perhaps without direct instructions from San Giuliano.

[2] DDF (3), IX, 38.

[3] Albertini, *Venti anni*, II, pp. 463–4.

[4] Albertini, *Origins*, I, pp. 519–20.

[5] In March 1914 the Austrian parliament once again shelved a project for an Italian Law Faculty at Trieste.

noughts, causing as much anxiety in Italy as among the navies of the Triple Entente.[1] On 1 May riots broke out in Trieste between Italians and Slovenes. In dispersing the crowds the police set upon Italian demonstrators. Students in Italy rioted in protest and the Austrian consulate in Naples was attacked. Salandra dismissed the prefect and closed down Rome university for several days. In the chamber Federzoni interpellated the government on these 'first fruits of Abbazia'.[2]

By the spring of 1914 the Italians' dislike of Austria had once again eclipsed their suspicion of France, as had happened between 1901 and 1911. Even devotees of the Triple Alliance were discouraged. 'I am now almost the only person to believe in the good faith of the Austro-Hungarian government', wrote San Giuliano to his ambassadors in Berlin and Vienna, Riccardo Bollati and Giuseppe Avarna, on 4 July.[3] Bollati regretfully agreed: 'There is perhaps not one single question in which the interests of Italy are not in conflict, or thought to be in conflict, with those of Austria-Hungary'; San Giuliano's struggle over the last four years to harmonise the necessities of Italy's international situation with Italian popular sentiment 'had been, alas, a labour of Sisyphus'.[4] On 14 July San Giuliano told Bollati: 'All our policy must aim at preventing Austria-Hungary's territorial aggrandisement' and preserving equilibrium in the Adriatic. Any acquisition of territory by Austria in Albania or elsewhere in the Balkans, and even the establishment of a common Austrian-Albanian frontier, would be tolerable to Italy only if accompanied by compensation in the form of the Trentino or, failing that, southern Albania.[5] Four days earlier he had warned the German ambassador in Rome that Austria's acquisition of Lovčen, unaccompanied by cession of the Trentino, 'would mean not

---

[1] At the beginning of 1914 Italy had one dreadnought completed and five building; Austria–Hungary had two completed and two building. Austria's extra four were in fact never built; but the voting of the money for them spurred the Italians into laying down four heavily armed super-dreadnoughts of 30,000 tons in 1914–15. *Jane's Fighting Ships 1919*, pp. 337–40. Since the appointment of Admiral Thaon di Revel as naval Chief of Staff in 1913, a radical reconstruction of the Italian navy had been taken in hand. Special attention was paid to light craft, in which Austria–Hungary had a clear superiority, and to the development of submarines and naval aviation. Thaon di Revel's building programme was designed to give Italy a ratio of naval strength of 1 : 0·8 in relation to Austria and 1 : 1·8 in relation to France. *La marina italiana*, I, pp. 262–3, 269 ff.

[2] Irredentists and nationalists were particularly incensed with San Giuliano for consenting to meet Berchtold at Abbazia, an unredeemed Italian town on the Gulf of Fiume.

[3] DDI (4), XII, 77.

[4] Bollati to San Giuliano, 8 July 1914. DDI (4), XII, 120; Salandra, *La neutralità*, pp. 50–6; Albertini, *Origins*, II, p. 219.

[5] San Giuliano to Bollati, 14 July 1914. DDI (4), XII, 225.

only the end of the Triple Alliance but war between Italy and Austria'.[1]
Such was the feeling in official circles of the Triple Alliance in the days
following Francis Ferdinand's assassination at Sarajevo on 28 June.

[1] Despatch to Berlin of 10 July from German ambassador, in Albertini, *Origins*,
I, p. 523. See also DDI (4), XII, 124.

# PART IV

# CRISIS
## 1914–1925

# 11

# The Great War

## Neutrality

The significance of the Sarajevo assassination was no more clearly under-stood in Italy than elsewhere in western Europe. The government was engrossed with the aftermath of Red Week and the sudden European crisis took it unawares. 'I had only modest proposals', wrote Salandra a few weeks later, 'for putting the state, weakened by ten years of disastrous policies, back on the rails; and here I am entering history.'[1]

San Giuliano knew well that another Balkan crisis would do serious damage to Italo-Austrian relations, already dangerously strained over Albania. It was therefore with growing concern that he watched the tension mounting between Austria-Hungary and Serbia during the first half of July. On the 14th he set out his thoughts and fears in a long letter to Bollati. 'I think it possible, and perhaps even probable,' he wrote, 'that in the perhaps not distant future it will suit us to leave the Triple Alliance'; but for the moment all three allied countries were governed by men who were loyal to the Alliance and 'convinced of the need to ensure its solidarity and efficiency'. In the immediate future the military strength of Germany and Austria-Hungary, and the impossibility of reaching a satisfactory under-standing with France from a position of isolation, made a reversal of policy impracticable. The most urgent task, then, was to eliminate friction within the Alliance, and in particular to make sure of territorial compensation for Italy if Austria made any forward move in the Balkans.[2]

The Austro-Hungarian government, with German approval, went to great lengths to conceal from Italy its intention to crush Serbia. Fearing that San Giuliano might react as in July 1913, Berchtold decided to present him with a *fait accompli*. This would eliminate the risk of an Italian veto on military operations and delay the inevitable demand for compensation. In the middle of July San Giuliano became aware from German indiscretions

---

[1] Salandra to Sonnino, 7 August 1914, in Salandra, *La neutralità*, p. 198; Salandra–Sonnino, *Carteggio*, p. 487.

[2] DDI (4), XII, 225.

of what was being planned. From his information he correctly concluded that the Austrians were set upon a course that was likely to precipitate a European war.[1] When similar circumstances had arisen in the previous year, San Giuliano had played his part in pulling the Austrians back from the brink. But now not only did he ignore the precedent of July 1913; he did not even disclose the facts about it to Salandra, who was to learn of it for the first time in December from a speech by Giolitti in parliament. For nearly a month after Sarajevo San Giuliano remained passive, if not acquiescent, hoping there would be no war but making only half-hearted attempts to avert it. His diplomatic activity consisted mainly in exhortations to the Serbs to yield to Austria's demands, and in attempts to stir other governments, notably the Rumanian, into making the pleas for moderation in Vienna which he felt unable to make himself.[2]

There were three main reasons for San Giuliano's passivity. First, he was aware of Italy's military weakness and feared Germany, which seemed certain to win a European war. Second, he realised that the Germans were now backing Austria-Hungary unreservedly, whereas in 1913 they had applied the brake, a fact which seemed to make the precedent worthless. Third, he shrank from plain speaking to the Austrians from fear that it might prejudice Italy's chance of compensation. This last was indeed the question that dominated his and Salandra's thoughts. Both were desperately anxious, if war occurred and Austria-Hungary made gains in the Balkans, to acquire the Trentino or, if all else failed, Valona and southern Albania. Both foresaw danger to the monarchy if Italy emerged from the crisis 'with clean hands'. Clearly compensation could best be secured by whole-hearted support of Austria-Hungary, but this was ruled out by the state of Italian opinion. As San Giuliano told the Germans, it was in Italy's interest that 'Serbia should not be crushed'; nor could Italy ever support demands upon Serbia that conflicted with 'the liberal principles of our public law'.[3] Direct negotiations with Austria-Hungary were ruled out on the ground that they would merely bring latent discord perilously into the open. The only course left was to turn to the Germans and press them, with growing urgency, to extract from Berchtold the formal confirmation of Article VII that Italy required.[4] San Giuliano therefore 'muttered grumbles, expressed doubts, asked for compensation' in his talks with the

[1] DDI (4), XII, 272, 311; Albertini, Origins, II, pp. 225-6.
[2] DDI (4), XII, 89, 90, 201, 311, 393, 424, 621, 644, 657, 682; Albertini, Origins, II, pp. 226-7, 239. 'The only hope of peace', he declared on 28 July, 'lies in the immediate and total acceptance by Serbia of Austria's demands.'
[3] DDI (4), XII, 225, 272, 413, 424; Albertini, Origins, II, pp. 227-8. As an example of demands which Italian opinion would find intolerable, San Giuliano mentioned limitation of freedom of the press and association.
[4] DDI (4), XII, 124, 225, 334, 413.

German ambassador; but he never gave the Austrians a clear direct warning.[1]

The Austro-Hungarian ultimatum was despatched to Serbia at 6 p.m. on 23 July. It was not until midday on the 24th that San Giuliano received the full text. He now spoke out: the Vienna government's action was provocative and aggressive; its concealment of its intentions in concert with Germany was a violation of the Triple Alliance and the *casus foederis* did not therefore arise. Avarna was instructed to demand recognition of Italy's right to compensation, but in such a way as to give Berchtold 'an impression of friendliness, not of threats or blackmail'. This implied that if Italy were satisfied, diplomatic support and even military intervention might be forthcoming.[2]

San Giuliano was probably relieved that his allies had kept him in the dark. He was now able to exploit to the full the free hand that the Austrian *fait accompli* had given him. On 26 July he defined his policy in a letter to Salandra: 'No immediate decisions are required, indeed they would be extremely dangerous. We must for the moment leave everyone, at home and abroad, in doubt as to our attitude and our decisions, and in this way try to obtain some positive advantage.' His recommendation was to 'work in silence, say little, not be hurried and stay away from Rome as much as possible'.[3] Reports that Italy intended to remain neutral were emphatically denied. As late as 1 August San Giuliano was saying that though the *casus foederis* did not arise, Italy might still intervene on the side of its allies if its interests were safeguarded by 'previous and precise agreements'.[4] This deliberate vagueness was designed to extract guarantees from Austria-Hungary before the war started. San Giuliano required an agreed interpretation of Article VII that would cover every possible form of Austrian aggrandisement, from permanent territorial annexation to temporary military occupation. Without such an agreement, he warned, Italy would be forced to adopt an anti-Austrian policy and obstruct Austria's expansion by every means, including diplomatic cooperation with its enemies.

---

[1] Albertini, *Origins*, II, pp. 241–53, 311–18. In spite of its over-severe strictures on San Giuliano's 'super-diplomacy', this work contains the most reliable analysis of Italian diplomacy in July 1914 and corrects Salandra's own, not always accurate, account in *La neutralità*. See also, for greater detail, Albertini, *Venti anni*, III, pp. 40–73, 91–101, 157–252. The recently published documents (DDI (4), XII) substantially confirm Albertini's analysis.

[2] DDI (4), XII, 468, 470, 488; Albertini, *Origins*, II, pp. 315–20; Salandra, *La neutralità*, pp. 76–80.

[3] DDI (4), XII, 560. San Giuliano was suffering acutely from the gout from which he died three months later, and tried to spend as much time as possible at Fiuggi away from the heat of Rome which he found intolerable. DDI (4), XII, 42, 119, 525, 552; Salandra, *La neutralità*, pp. 74–5.

[4] DDI (4), XII, 644, 661, 673, 778, 829, 839; Albertini, *Origins*, II, pp. 243–4.

The occupation of Lovčen in particular, he declared, would shatter the Triple Alliance. But all his efforts were in vain. Berchtold gave unofficial assurances that no permanent territorial acquisitions were contemplated and that Lovčen would not be occupied provided Montenegro remained neutral. But in spite of German prompting to be more conciliatory, he refused all promise of compensation until Italy did its full duty as an ally.[1] On 28 July Austria-Hungary declared war on Serbia. Within a week Russia, Germany, France, Belgium and Britain had been drawn in. In the face of Austrian obstinacy, Italy had only one possible course of action. Salandra and San Giuliano decided on neutrality on 31 July. The cabinet agreed next day and the decision was announced to the world on the morning of 2 August.

The first reaction of all but a tiny minority of Italians was unreserved approval. The exceptions were some nationalists, who had preached the glories of war for ten years and were now disgusted by the government's cowardice; and a number of conservative politicians, soldiers and diplomats who included Sonnino,[2] Bollati and Avarna. These conservatives respected and feared Germany and had no doubt it would win. They distrusted republican France, retained their faith in the Triple Alliance as a bulwark of monarchism and believed that to abandon two allies of thirty years' standing in their hour of need was to violate both the honour and the interests of their country.[3] But most Italians were in no mood for adventures. The socialists and trade unions were aggressively pacifist. Mussolini threatened revolution if the government dared to declare war. The democrats and irredentists had for years dreaded involvement through the Triple Alliance in a dynastic, militaristic war; the declaration of neutrality ended their nightmare. The Catholics, too, were content. The Vatican was instinctively on the side of Austria-Hungary, the strongest bulwark

---

[1] DDI (4), XII, 672, 713, 721–2, 754, 778, 797, 804, 848. Berchtold required Italy not merely 'not to create difficulties' for its ally, but to give 'constant support'. He also argued, unconvincingly, that Article VII was concerned only with Turkey, so that Italy would not be entitled to compensation if Austria occupied or annexed non-Turkish, i.e. Serbian or Montenegrin, territory. Jagow, the German Foreign Secretary, after examining the text of the Triple Alliance, agreed with the Italian interpretation of Article VII. On 26 July San Giuliano remarked to Salandra, 'For the first time since the Kingdom of Italy has been in existence, a German Foreign Minister has declared that the moment is favourable for us to have the Trentino.' DDI (4), XII, 483, 550, 560; Albertini, *Origins*, II, pp. 229–30, 236–7.

[2] But in a matter of days Sonnino became convinced that neutrality was the correct policy. By 4 September he was already considering the possibility of intervention on the side of the Entente. Valiani, p. 130 note 26.

[3] San Giuliano himself felt unhappy on the point of honour, but pleaded *force majeure*. Malagodi, I, pp. 16–17.

of the Catholic faith against Russia. Merry del Val approved the ultimatum to Serbia 'unreservedly'. Pius X, though appalled at the catastrophe that had engulfed Europe, nevertheless told the Austro-Hungarian ambassador just before his death on 20 August that he could not intervene with Francis Joseph in the cause of peace because Austria's war against Serbia was 'wholly just'.[1] While some Italian Catholics shared the clerical partiality for the Habsburgs, none advocated intervention. The great majority believed, like Meda, that the peaceful mission of a neutral would bestow far more glory upon Italy than any military victory.[2] Thus, for the moment, there was almost unanimity throughout the country.

Many thoughtful Italians, however, perceived that neutrality, too, had its dangers. If the Entente won, Italy could expect from it little consideration in the Adriatic and Mediterranean. If Germany and Austria-Hungary won, Italy would at best become the despised satellite of former allies who felt betrayed. As in Cavour's day and the years of isolation before 1882, the neutral risked becoming 'the prey of the victor, to the delight and satisfaction of the vanquished'.[3] Such thoughts were constantly in the minds of Salandra and San Giuliano. On the very day that neutrality was declared, Salandra remarked in private that a victory of the central Powers would mean servitude for Italy.[4] One thing was clear from the start: once the decision to stay neutral had been taken, intervention in cold blood on the side of Germany and Austria-Hungary, and against Britain, became unthinkable. The Triple Alliance, as Salandra himself admitted, was morally dead.[5] The problem was henceforth whether Italy should remain neutral or intervene on the side of the Entente.

Italy's decision had an immediate influence on the course of the war. By allowing the French to denude their Alpine frontier of ten divisions and bring their troops across from north Africa unmolested, it contributed directly to the defensive victory on the Marne in September. The Germans and Austrians were the first to appreciate this. San Giuliano's failure to speak out in time and his harping on compensations robbed the declaration of neutrality of all dignity and at once exposed Italy to the charge of treachery. But whatever the statesmen and soldiers of Germany and Austria-Hungary might say in private, they suppressed their feelings in public. The Triple Alliance still stood. The important thing now was to prevent Italy from abandoning its neutrality in favour of the Entente. On

[1] Engel-Jánosi, II, pp. 149–52; Albertini, *Venti anni*, III, pp. 256–63; Sforza, *Contemporary Italy*, pp. 153–5. Rampolla, by contrast, had believed that Austria–Hungary was 'a state doomed to destruction'.

[2] Cilibrizzi, IV, p. 510.

[3] See above, p. 32.

[4] Malagodi, I, pp. 18, 23.

[5] ibid., p. 22.

4 August the Austrians removed one of Italy's acutest anxieties by a promise not to occupy Lovčen even if Montenegro entered the war. At the end of the month Berchtold, dropping his previous condition, accepted the Italian interpretation of Article VII and undertook to negotiate compensations when the situation clarified.[1] He probably had Albania in mind, certainly not the Trentino. Nevertheless it was a substantial concession. The need for more such gestures of appeasement to Italy became apparent as German and Austrian hopes of rapid victory faded.

The Italian government meanwhile faced a difficult military problem. Pollio had died on 1 July. More than three weeks lapsed before his successor, Luigi Cadorna, took over as Chief of Staff. Cadorna immediately demanded reinforcement of the French Alpine frontier and rapid preparation of the expeditionary force for the Rhine.[2] During the critical last week of July, the government made no attempt to keep him informed, with the result that the declaration of neutrality took him by surprise. He at once saw its military implications. On 3 August he urged immediate mobilisation to forestall an Austrian attack. He also argued that speedy armed intervention, before the issue of the war had been settled, might win Italy a decisive voice in the future of Europe. Salandra and San Giuliano refused his request. They did not share his optimism about the effect of Italian intervention, and believed that general mobilisation 'meant war' and might precipitate just that attack which Cadorna feared. It would be a delicate operation requiring twenty-three days, during which the Italian army would be at the mercy of an invader. The Minister for War, General Grandi, instead wanted partial mobilisation, which Cadorna opposed because it would disrupt existing staff plans. Thus at the very outset of the European war, the consequences of long-standing mutual incomprehension between soldiers and civilians became apparent.[3] But by mid-August the worst danger had passed. All the belligerent armies were now fully engaged and Cadorna agreed to postpone general mobilisation. Instead two classes were called up, a few troops and artillery were moved to the Austrian frontier and urgent attempts were made to fill

[1] DDI (5), I, 49, 448; Albertini, *Venti anni*, III, pp. 229, 329; Salandra, *La neutralità*, pp. 167–8.

[2] Cadorna, *Altre pagine*, pp. 15–23; Salandra, *La neutralità*, p. 264; Rochat, pp. 324–6.

[3] Rochat, pp. 326–33; Salandra, *La neutralità*, pp. 261–8; Cadorna, *La guerra*, I, pp. 41–3. 'It is not an exaggeration', wrote Cadorna after the war, 'to say that if Austria had attacked us at the moment that we declared our neutrality, we would have found ourselves almost defenceless.' Cadorna, *La guerra*, I, p. 162. At that moment Italy had 350,000 men under arms (the normal peace-time force of 275,000, supplemented by 75,000 reservists called up in July after Red Week). On the 'extreme complexity and rigidity' of Italian mobilisation plans, see Rochat, pp. 319–21.

the worst gaps in officers, N.C.O.s, arms, ammunition, equipment and clothing which the emergency had revealed.[1]

For the first two months of the war San Giuliano's policy swayed with the fortunes of battle. The Entente was diplomatically most active and far from satisfied with Italian neutrality. The Russians pressed hardest. During August San Giuliano received offers of Valona, the Trentino, Trieste, even Dalmatia. Already on the 9th he foresaw 'if not the probability, at least the possibility' of intervention against Austria, but only 'when there is a certainty, or almost certainty, of victory'. Two days later he made a first draft for Grey of the terms on which Italy might consider intervention.[2] But while the French and British were in headlong retreat in the west, 'prudence, reserve, secrecy' were essential; relations with Germany and Austria-Hungary had to be improved and 'a cold douche' administered to over-eager ambassadors in London and St Petersburg.[3] At the end of August, assailed by 'truly agonising doubts'[4] and pressures on every side, Salandra and San Giuliano informed all governments that Italy intended to remain neutral.

On 5 September the French retreat ended and a week later the Germans were withdrawing from the Marne. In the east, Conrad's Galician offensive came to a halt and the Austrian army began a general retreat. Lwow, the Galician capital, was captured by the Russians and the fortress of Przemysl besieged. Salandra and San Giuliano decided that a rapid German-Austrian victory was now impossible and that Italy's intervention would probably be necessary; that if Italy was to complete its unification, it was 'now or never'.[5] Rumours that Austria-Hungary was anxious for a separate

---

[1] Salandra had been informed by the Minister for War in March 1914 that mobilisation stocks, depleted by the Libyan war, had been fully replaced by the end of 1913, and he had publicly stated this on 2 April when presenting his government to parliament. At the end of July he discovered, to his intense irritation, that he had been misled. If general mobilisation had been carried out at the beginning of August, only 732,000 of the planned total of 1,260,000 men could have been fully equipped (though some of the deficiencies, for instance in clothing, were relatively trivial). Salandra, *La neutralità*, pp. 260–1, 268–83; *L'esercito italiano*, I, pp. 139 ff.; Rochat, pp. 336–40.

[2] These included the Trentino 'up to the main Alpine watershed', i.e. the Brenner. DDI (5), I, 151, 201; Trevelyan, *Grey of Fallodon*, pp. 291–2.

[3] San Giuliano to Salandra, 13, 25 and 28 August. DDI (5), I, 230, 440, 479. In a letter to Cadorna on 26 August, San Giuliano repeated his view that there must be a 99% probability of victory before Italy intervened, because another 1866 would mean the end of the monarchy. Rochat, p. 331.

[4] Salandra to Sonnino, 28 August. Salandra–Sonnino, *Carteggio*, p. 489; Vigezzi, *I problemi della neutralità*, p. 11.

[5] Salandra later wrote, 'In September, after the Marne, I had a clear vision of the road we had to follow.' *La neutralità*, pp. 174, 190. But his clarity was, at least in part, retrospective.

peace with Russia made them wonder whether they might not have to hurry to be in time. San Giuliano therefore resumed discussions with Grey on 16 September, and in an effort to strengthen Italy's diplomatic position, negotiated an understanding with Rumania.[1] The latter had followed Italy's example and declared its neutrality on 3 August. Both governments realised the advantages of threatening the Austrians with a concerted attack on two fronts, and on 23 September they bound themselves to give each other eight days' notice before abandoning neutrality.[2] On the 25th San Giuliano sent Grey a new, detailed draft of Italy's conditions.[3] Four days later he was in favour of intervention, 'if our military position permits it'.[4] But he insisted, as an essential preliminary, on offensive action by the British and French fleets in the Adriatic, in the form, perhaps, of a landing at Trieste followed by a plebiscite of its population. Not only, he argued, would this weaken Austria; it would also shock Italian opinion into recognition of the need to defend vital Italian interests.[5] But the British and French seemed reluctant to fight Austria-Hungary. In the end Salandra and San Giuliano could not bring themselves to take the plunge. By the end of September the war in both east and west had reached a temporary stalemate. Cadorna, who had previously been ready to go to war on the assumption that it would soon be over, now changed his mind. The army, he emphasised, was short of heavy clothing and unable to face a long winter campaign.[6] With obvious relief the government decided to wait, if possible until the spring.[7]

Public opinion was meanwhile crystallising and the great debate between the advocates of neutrality and intervention had begun. The first to take a

[1] The positions of Italy and Rumania were strikingly similar. Both were allies of Germany and Austria–Hungary; both had claims against the latter – Italy in the Trentino and at Trieste, Rumania in Transylvania; both had potential quarrels with the Entente – Italy in the Mediterranean and Africa, Rumania over Bukovina and Bessarabia.

[2] Aldrovandi, *Nuovi ricordi*, pp. 193–5; DDI (5), I, 705, 712, 763, 773.

[3] DDI (5), I, 703, 803.

[4] San Giuliano to Salandra, DDI (5), I, 842.

[5] Vigezzi, *I problemi della neutralità*, pp. 13–16. Salandra disliked the idea; so did Sonnino, whom he consulted on this and other matters with growing frequency during September and October.

[6] Cadorna, *La guerra*, I, pp. 46–8. But Rochat (pp. 342–6) shows conclusively that the decision not to intervene in September was political, and much less determined by the army's shortcomings than Salandra's own account in *La neutralità* suggests.

[7] Recent research has confirmed Albertini's view (*Venti anni*, III, pp. 359, 490) that the most favourable opportunity was thus lost. The arguments for and against intervention in September 1914 rather than May 1915 resemble the arguments as to whether Britain's military situation was or was not more favourable in October 1938 than in September 1939.

stand for intervention were the democrats, freemasons and republicans. They could not let Italy stand aside when France, the country of the Rights of Man, was in danger. Volunteers rushed off as in 1870, and by December 4,000 Garibaldini under command of Garibaldi's grandson, Peppino, were in action with the French Foreign Legion in the Argonne. Four of Peppino's brothers fought with him and two of them soon lost their lives in action. Destrée, a Belgian deputy, toured Italy and won thousands of converts by passionate speeches on the martyrdom of his country. The radicals, reformist socialists and many liberals were soon swept into the movement. Bissolati became its chief spokesman. Although he approved of the declaration of neutrality as a first step, already on 2 August he had written to Bonomi:[1] 'Very different trials await us. Our task (I have already begun and you will help me) will be to prepare the spirit of the Italian proletariat for war . . . Let us so hope to make of our Italy a solid instrument for bringing to birth, out of international crisis, the new world whose dawn you, too, foresee.' Mazzini might have written those words. The interventionist movement was in origin democratic, idealist and internationalist. The Mazzinian programme had been raised 'from the grave in which it seemed to have lain for fifty years'.[2]

Three other groups, who had no respect for Mazzini and no love of democracy, soon became prominent in the movement for intervention: the futurists, the nationalists and the revolutionaries. The futurists responded as in 1911 to the stimulus of war. 'March, not rot (*marciare non marcire*)' was Marinetti's slogan. Their emotional and intellectual ties with France made them thirst to take part in 'a war not only of guns and ships, but also of culture and civilisation'.[3] The nationalists quickly forgot their ardour on behalf of Germany and Austria-Hungary in July. What they wanted was war, on whose side mattered little: war not for ideals or sentiment but 'in order to be great'. They looked far beyond Trent and Trieste and dreamt of Italian domination of the Balkans, Africa and the Levant. Italy, they declared, 'must fight the Entente's war, but fight it for Italy'; it must be not Italy's last war of unification, but Italy's first war as a Great Power.[4]

The irredentists were divided in sympathy between the democrats and the nationalists. Hundreds of 'unredeemed' Italians came across the frontier to escape military service in the Austrian army. Cesare Battisti,

---

[1] Bonomi, *Leonida Bissolati*, pp. 145–6.

[2] Salvemini, *Dal patto di Londra*, p. xxi. By the end of August Bonomi was writing of 'a war of liberation' and Salvemini of 'a war to end war'. De Felice, pp. 229–32.

[3] Joll, pp. 162–3.

[4] Corradini, *Discorsi politici*, p. 303; Cilibrizzi, V, pp. 146–9; G. Perticone, *La politica italiana nell' ultimo trentennio* (Rome 1945), pp. 55–63.

the socialist from Trent, denounced Habsburg feudalism and militarism before enraptured audiences and preached an uncompromising democratic programme. Austria-Hungary, he asserted, was beyond redemption; it must be destroyed. This soon became the programme of Bissolati, Salvemini and all democratic interventionists. Another refugee from Trent, the fanatical Ettore Tolomei, preached the irredentist cause in a very different spirit. His single-minded aim was to plant the Italian flag on the Brenner, 'the summit of Italy', and redeem the 'Italian land' of south Tirol from German occupation.[1] Similarly Giuriati, nationalist president of the Trent and Trieste Society, while echoing the cry for a war of liberation, talked also of establishing Italy at Fiume and on the Dalmatian coast in defiance of Slav aspirations. At the end of the year a Pro Dalmazia Society was founded to further these aims. It soon attracted the support of the militant irredentists from Istria and Dalmatia who cared nothing for the Mazzinian dream of Italo-Slav friendship. Their sole concern was to rescue the *italianità* of the unredeemed lands at the eleventh hour, and they regarded Austrians and Slavs alike as foes between whom no useful distinction could be made.

The revolutionaries, both socialist and syndicalist, were again split by the issue of war, just as in 1911, and the subversive coalition of Red Week disintegrated. The official Socialist party line was uncompromisingly pacifist. The U.S.I., with its influential anarchist elements, was equally pacifist, but a powerful minority broke away to found a new trade union organisation, the Unione Italiana di Lavoro (U.I.L.). Among its leaders were Michele Bianchi, Edmondo Rossoni and Alceste De Ambris, organisers of the syndicalist strikes in the Po valley in 1907–13, Giuseppe Giulietti, the boss of the Genoa seamen's union, and Filippo Corridoni, 'the poet of the masses', who was still in prison for his part in Red Week. Placing all their technique of agitation at the service of the interventionist cause, they embarked on the task of mobilising the working-class in support of war.

Of greater significance for the future of Italy was the conversion of Mussolini. In July he had been the most aggressive pacifist of them all. But once neutrality had been proclaimed by the government, it became respectable and there was little joy left in preaching it. Weeks of agonising indecision followed. Before the end of August he was already in private committing the heresy of justifying neutrality on national rather than socialist grounds, and declaring that he would fight the Austrians with enthusiasm if they attacked Italy. On 8 October he publicly confessed

---

[1] Herre, pp. 22–8, 35–9. Tolomei's 'natural' frontier coincided with the frontier claimed by San Giuliano (and later Sonnino) on strategic grounds; but it is not clear whether Tolomei directly influenced either foreign minister.

his sympathy for the cause of the Entente. Ten days later he launched the slogan 'From absolute to active neutrality'. Censured by the party, he resigned from the editorship of *Avanti!* and on 15 November launched his own daily paper, *Il Popolo d'Italia*, with the financial backing and technical assistance of a conservative newspaper of Bologna. Within a few weeks it had become the organ of the whole interventionist left, both democratic and revolutionary. Under its title Mussolini put quotations from Blanqui and Napoleon: 'He who has steel, has bread' and 'Revolution is an idea that has found bayonets'. His inaugural cry was 'a fearful and fascinating word: War'.[1] On 24 November he was expelled from the Socialist party. He promptly founded an 'autonomous fascio for revolutionary action', designed to appeal to 'all truly revolutionary socialists'. In December it fused with the Fasci di Azione Rivoluzionaria which Corridoni, Bianchi and the pro-war syndicalists had formed in Milan and other cities. The movement spread throughout northern and central Italy and claimed 5,000 members in fifty fasci by the end of the year.

The socialist leaders and the politically conscious working-class were never to forgive Mussolini for his 'betrayal'. His motives, like those of Corridoni, De Ambris and many others, were mixed. For an incorrigible journalist the temptation of owning his own newspaper was probably irresistible. His personal ambition to make history certainly played its part. So did disillusionment with the Second International and with the German proletariat, which had rallied so willingly to the war. The whole of the interventionist left felt sympathy for France, 'the cradle of a hundred revolutions',[2] where Hervé, the ultra-pacifist, had volunteered as an army private. Corridoni was moved by the sufferings of Belgium and Serbia, and saw the war as a continuation of the fight against oppression which he had fought all his life. De Ambris declared that a French victory would liquidate militarism and end all war. But the dominating motive was

---

[1] For a full analysis of Mussolini's personal crisis, in the context of the general crisis in the Socialist party, see De Felice, ch. 9. The technical assistance for *Il Popolo d'Italia* was provided by Filippo Naldi, editor of *Il Resto del Carlino*, who also secured funds (probably about one million lire) from industrial sources. Giulietti's union also made a small financial contribution. Mussolini broke with Naldi three months later, after discovering that he had connexions with the Foreign Ministry. ibid., pp. 271–7.

[2] Mussolini, VII, p. 118. Syndicalists, many socialists and even some anarchists were powerfully influenced by the patriotism of the French left. Prominent leaders of the international anarchist movement, including Kropotkin himself (but not Malatesta), were later to sign a manifesto in support of France. Jouhaux, secretary of the French trade union federation (C.G.T.), visited Milan in February 1915, with the approval of the French government, and appealed to a mass meeting organised by Corridoni to support the 'syndicalist, liberty-loving' French proletariat. The aged Cipriani also supported the war from Paris. Borghi, pp. 155–9.

thirst for action. From 'Revolution if war', Mussolini changed his slogan to 'Revolution if no war'. 'Neutrality is for the castrated', declared Corridoni. War offered the excitement and opportunities for heroism that had previously been sought in syndicalism. It also seemed the shortest road to social revolution at home.[1]

Mazzinian democrats, nationalists and revolutionaries made strange political bedfellows. As Mussolini's newspaper put it, they had got into the same train by accident and were bound for different destinations.[2] For the moment the interventionists were a small minority. But as the weeks passed, their ranks swelled and a growing number of sober liberals joined them. These included industrialists and financiers who wished to break Germany's grip on the Italian economy, or who predicted such dire economic consequences from the Entente blockade that intervention seemed the only way of escape. Others were obsessed, like Salandra himself, by the fear that the monarchy could not survive if peace came before Italy's national aspirations had been satisfied. Others again believed that permanent neutrality would be an ignoble evasion of responsibility. The most articulate of those who held this last view was Albertini, editor of the *Corriere della Sera*. 'Neutrality is merely a starting-point', he had written on 4 August.[3] In his opinion it was not just a matter of territorial aspirations, nor of the vengeance which a victorious Germany and Austria-Hungary might exact for Italy's 'betrayal'. It was a question of winning the honourable place to which Italy was entitled in the new Europe that would emerge from the war. Neutrality meant isolation; intervention meant an opportunity to rise above petty national self-interest and merge Italy's aspirations in the struggle for a better world.

The great majority of liberals, including Giolitti, remained unshaken by such arguments. Admiration of Germany, mingled with fear, persisted. The soldiers admired its military strength, the bankers and business men its industrial power and commercial efficiency, the intellectuals its culture,

---

[1] At the end of November Prezzolini and a group of *Voce* contributors telegraphed to Mussolini, 'The Socialist party expels you, Italy welcomes you.' Though Mussolini continued to think of himself as a socialist, he had, in De Felice's words (pp. 283–4), 'made his choice: he had chosen the élites' and crossed the class barrier. This was the beginning of the road that was to carry him from extreme left to extreme right within seven years. De Felice suggests (pp. 180, 217–20, 290–1) that even before August 1914 Mussolini had become disillusioned with the revolutionary capacity of his party and was psychologically prepared for a rupture with the socialism of the past. The war gave him the opportunity for which he had been searching. As Joll points out (pp. 164–5), already at the beginning of August he was using futurist language and displaying a most un-socialist fascination for war.

[2] *Il Popolo d'Italia*, 19 April 1915. Quoted in G. Volpe, *Il popolo italiano tra la pace e la guerra* (Milan 1940), p. 231.

[3] Albertini, *Venti anni*, III, p. 281.

science and learning. France seemed weak, if not decadent, in comparison and Russia hardly less menacing than Austria. As the neutralists pointed out, not only had Germany been Italy's natural ally since the days of the Risorgimento; it was also the only Great Power with which Italy had no direct conflict of interest. The economic arguments, too, were strong. Most industrial leaders were conscious of industry's need, after a decade of expansion, of a calm period in which to consolidate and reorganise. They therefore feared the dislocation that war would bring. Italy's best agricultural markets lay in central Europe and the severance of the close links with Germany would inevitably bring hardship, especially to the south. Disgust with the tactics of the war party also played its part in determining liberal attitudes. The stridency and inflammatory language of the interventionists seemed vulgar, ill-informed and reckless. Croce protested against the crude propaganda about German atrocities, Fortunato deplored the nationalists' demagogy. Many were appalled by the irruption of the *piazza* and the press into delicate questions of international diplomacy.[1] But perhaps the most persuasive argument for liberal neutralists was Italy's military weakness. They knew that the army was unprepared for an offensive against Austria and were pessimistic regarding the effect of Italian intervention upon the result of the war. To all who were troubled by such misgivings, the need for caution and delay seemed paramount. Neutrality was the only policy that a sane government could pursue.

In the autumn of 1914 the predominant feeling in political circles was bewilderment. The arguments for and against intervention, sooner or later, were debated, but few felt able to come to a decision. Salandra, like most liberals, was repelled by the irresponsibility of the interventionists. On 28 August, in a letter to Sonnino, he had deplored their crazy plans to embroil Italy with Austria by sending an expedition, 'a caricature of the Thousand', to Trieste, and commented, 'We are walking on a razor's edge.'[2] His intention was to keep the initiative with regard to peace and

---

[1] See, for example, Bollati, ambassador in Berlin, to Avarna, ambassador in Vienna, 9 October 1914: 'It is, as you say, downright monstrous to see, at a moment like this, foreign policy becoming the object of public discussion, meetings and party votes.' 'Carteggio Avarna-Bollati', in *Rivista storica italiana*, vol. 61 (1949), p. 265.

[2] Salandra–Sonnino, *Carteggio*, pp. 489–90; Vigezzi, *I problemi della neutralità*, p. 12. Between August 1914 and May 1915 a multitude of interventionist groups, both nationalist, democratic and revolutionary, were busy hatching conspiratorial projects of this kind. Many looked to the Garibaldi brothers for leadership. In some cases arms were procured and volunteers trained. Mussolini tried without success to obtain funds from an agent of the Russian government. Salandra was kept accurately informed of these activities and had the revolutionary groups watched with special care, rightly suspecting that their enthusiasm was as likely to be directed against his own government as against Austria. De Felice, pp. 303–9.

war firmly in the hands of the Liberal party, to which should be reserved the historic task of completing the work of the Risorgimento. But meanwhile Italy was militarily weak, politically divided and under pressure from both belligerent groups. The government was insecurely dependent on Giolitti's parliamentary goodwill. Inside the cabinet Martini, Minister for Colonies, led an interventionist faction while Rubini, Minister of the Treasury, insisted on 'finance as usual' and resisted all extra military expenditure. On 16 October San Giuliano died after a long and painful illness. Salandra himself temporarily took over the Foreign Ministry. A few days later he exhorted its staff to cast away every preconception, prejudice and sentiment 'except that of an exclusive and unlimited devotion to our country, a sacred egoism for Italy'.[1] This last phrase was later seized upon joyfully by foreign critics of Italy, in order to contrast Italy's selfish aims with the altruism of Britain, France and the U.S.A. At the time it amounted to no more than an appeal for restraint and unity while the government kept its hands free and played for time.

In the course of the autumn Salandra reconstructed his government. Giolitti's closest supporters were still excluded, but some liberals of the left were brought in, among them Orlando. A new and energetic Minister for War, General Vittorio Zupelli, of Istrian origin, took the job of military preparation systematically in hand, no longer obstructed by Rubini who resigned. Zupelli and Cadorna worked out a detailed and flexible plan for gradual mobilisation, to be carried out with a minimum of publicity. The intention was not so much to increase the ultimate size of the army as to ensure that when mobilisation had been completed, all fighting and service units would be at full strength and efficiency. High priority was also given to completion of the 1910 programme of artillery modernisation. By December mobilisation stocks had been replenished, most of the frontier fortifications required as cover for mobilisation had been built, and preparation of the first staff plans for an offensive against Austria-Hungary was well advanced. Thanks to the government's liberal provision of funds, the maximum four-year programme, drafted by Spingardi and Pollio in 1913 and rejected on financial grounds, was carried out by their successors under the pressure of war in the course of a few months.[2]

These measures had the wholehearted approval of Sonnino, who became Foreign Minister on 5 November. From early August he had been urging

[1] Salandra, La neutralità, pp. 376–81.
[2] L'esercito italiano, I, pp. 69–71. Military expenditure authorised by the government rose from 148 million lire in August–September to 602 million in October–November. L'esercito italiano, I bis, p. 28. Already by December stocks of equipment were sufficient to mobilise 1,404,000 men, compared with 732,000 in August. ibid., I, pp. 142, 191.

Salandra to arm.[1] Like Salandra, he had been impressed by Germany's defeat on the Marne, but he was less sure that Italy should intervene on the side of the Entente. His whole past was linked to the Triple Alliance and though he admired Britain, he felt deep distrust of France and the Slav nations. His and Salandra's plan was to use the breathing-space of the winter, while the army was being prepared, to resume the negotiations with Austria-Hungary which San Giuliano had dropped in August. If the Austrians, as was probable, refused to give Italy satisfaction, then intervention would be necessary; but 'whatever we decide to do, we will be wise to reveal our decision as late as possible'.[2] It was only by first exhausting the resources of diplomacy that a reckless gamble could be avoided and opinion at home united. This was the policy that Salandra and Sonnino pursued over the next five months. Working in the most intimate collaboration and consulting almost no one except the King, they decided the fate of Italy in apprehensive but proud isolation.

Sonnino could not have publicly formulated his intentions even had he been less secretive; but their general nature was easily divined by intelligent observers. Only the dedicated interventionist minority disapproved. Giolitti, who had been in Piedmontese seclusion since August, made no comment or criticism. His friends were less happy. The loyal Frassati vainly urged him to return to power.[3] In the absence of the master the Giolittian deputies began to feel uneasy, as in 1905 and 1909, and scrutinised Salandra's performance with less complacent eyes. Many were worried by the government's passivity. Nothing was being done, they complained, to educate opinion or curb the excesses of the interventionist press. In October a section of the latter attacked Giolitti for 'disarming Italy' over the previous ten years and declared him responsible for the country's present military weakness. The Giolittians, reacting sharply, had an authoritative article published to disprove the charge of neglect.[4] These polemics were renewed in parliament when it met, for the first time since the outbreak of war, on 3 December. Salandra presented his reconstructed government. A reference in his speech to Italy's 'just aspirations' stirred the deputies and drew the cry of *Viva Trieste!* from the veteran socialist, De Felice. Two days later Giolitti, who had come to Rome for the purpose, spoke in support of the government, pointedly praising the policy of neutrality. With all the authority of an elder states-

---

[1] Salandra–Sonnino, *Carteggio*, pp. 488, 491; Vigezzi, *I problemi della neutralità*, pp. 7–11, 18.

[2] Salandra to Sonnino, 5 November 1914. Vigezzi, *I problemi della neutralità*, pp. 23–4, 61.

[3] Frassati, pp. 10–11. Senator Alfredo Frassati was owner and editor of the Turin daily newspaper *La Stampa*, and a devoted admirer of Giolitti.

[4] *Quarant' anni*, III, 128–9; Giolitti, *Memorie*, pp. 525–8.

man he revealed the facts about the precedent of July 1913,[1] in order
to rebut German and Austrian accusations of betrayal and quieten uneasy
consciences. His was 'the voice of wisdom combined with patriotism',
Luzzatti told him.[2] The Giolittians voted solidly for the government,
which obtained a majority of 413 votes to 49. The senate passed a unanimous vote of confidence ten days later. Parliament then adjourned and
Giolitti returned to Piedmont.

Having secured their parliamentary position and obtained virtually unlimited freedom of action, Salandra and Sonnino turned with renewed
confidence to the tasks of diplomacy. One step towards increasing Italian
security could be taken immediately, without risk of war, in Albania.
That country had relapsed into chaos. International control had ended
in August when all the belligerent Great Powers withdrew their representatives, leaving the Italians in sole charge. In September Prince William of
Wied was rescued from Moslem insurgents in an Italian warship and left
his kingdom for ever. Albania was at the mercy of covetous neighbours –
Austrians, Serbs, Montenegrins and Greeks. Many Italians believed that
this was Italy's opportunity. San Giuliano had contemplated occupation
of the island of Saseno in September, but decided it would cause too many
diplomatic complications. Cadorna, too, opposed a diversion which would
weaken Italy's fighting strength against Austria.[3] Sonnino was less timid.
Ever since mid-September he had been urging Salandra to be bold and
quick, 'without any more asking permission from anyone'.[4] In fact none
of the belligerents wished to offend Italy by refusing consent. At the end
of October, a fortnight after San Giuliano's death, Italian marines landed
on Saseno to forestall Greek troops advancing northwards from Epirus.
On Christmas Day Valona was occupied. Sonnino announced that the
occupation was temporary; its purpose was to defend Albanian integrity
against Greek encroachment and enforce the 1913 convention, of which
Italy was now the only neutral signatory. But his secret intention was that
Italy should stay for good. Albania became an obsession with him as the
war progressed, and Cadorna's fears that more and more troops would be
sucked into Valona's rugged hinterland were to be amply fulfilled.

On 9 December Sonnino reopened negotiations with Austria-Hungary
on compensations under Article VII. His pretext was Austria's renewed

[1] See above, pp. 399, 414.
[2] *Quarant' anni*, III, 136. Giolitti's speech was probably also designed to demonstrate his continued mastery of the chamber and to cut Salandra down to size by
claiming his own share of credit for the policy of neutrality.
[3] DDI (5), I, 576 ff., 593; Cadorna, *Altre pagine*, pp. 104 ff.
[4] Sonnino to Salandra, 26 September. Salandra–Sonnino, *Carteggio*, pp. 490–5;
Vigezzi, *I problemi della neutralità*, pp. 17–20.

advance into Serbia, though by the 14th the Serbs had thrown the Austrians ignominiously back across their frontier. On the 17th Bülow arrived in Rome on a special mission to keep Italy neutral. Early in the new year he was joined by Erzberger, leader of the German Centre party, who in three successive visits put all his influence at the Vatican and in both Austrian and Italian Catholic circles at Bülow's disposal. Bülow was horrified to find how much the situation had deteriorated to Germany's disadvantage and he was eager to be generous, at Austria's expense. Unless Italy received in the near future an offer of the Trentino and the right bank of the Isonzo (but not Trieste, which was 'Austria's lung'), he foresaw that the neutralist party would be overwhelmed. 'Bis dat qui cito dat', was his urgent refrain.[1] Slowly Berchtold was driven to the conclusion that the Trentino would have to be ceded, and on 9 January he submitted his advice to that effect to Francis Joseph. Five days later he was forced to resign.[2] His successor as Austro-Hungarian Foreign Minister was Burian, a protégé of Tisza, the powerful Prime Minister of Hungary. That same day Sonnino told Bülow that the Trentino without Trieste was not enough. Burian's idea was to gain time. A major offensive was being planned in the Carpathians for the spring. If the Italians could be kept quiet until the Russians had been dealt a crushing blow, then they would not dare to make trouble. Burian despised the Italians. 'When I have an empty pistol pointed at my chest', he declared, 'I don't hurry to take out my wallet, but wait till the pistol is loaded before making up my mind.'[3] His resistance sprang not merely from reluctance to pay a blackmailer, nor from Francis Joseph's sentimental attachment to the royal *Erbland* of Tirol. He and Tisza saw that the cession of territory to Italy would encourage first the Rumanians, then the Czechs, Poles and Southern Slavs; logically it must lead to the partition of Hungary and the disintegration of the Dual Monarchy. Their conclusion was identical with Andrássy's of 1874.[4]

On 12 February Sonnino grew impatient and withdrew all his proposals. While he pressed Salandra for a rapid decision on the minimum Austrian concessions that would be acceptable,[5] he warned Burian that Italy would assume complete liberty of action if any military operations whatsoever took place in the Balkans before compensations were agreed.[6] Four days

[1] Salandra, *La neutralità*, p. 469; Bülow, III, p. 216; Erzberger, p. 28.
[2] Valiani, pp. 98, 110; H. Hantsch, *Leopold Graf Berchtold* (Graz 1963), II, pp. 705–30. Beside the Emperor, the two main opponents of cession were the Prime Ministers of Austria and Hungary, Stürgkh and Tisza.
[3] Albertini, *Venti anni*, III, p. 416.
[4] See above, p. 31.
[5] Vigezzi, *I problemi della neutralità*, pp. 28–34, 62–3.
[6] Sonnino was able to remind Burian of Aehrenthal's veto on Italian operations in the Balkans during the Libyan War. See above, p. 374.

later he dispatched to Marquis Guglielmo Imperiali, his ambassador in London, a memorandum setting out Italy's minimum terms for intervention on the side of the Entente. On the 19th the British and French fleets carried out their first bombardment of the Dardanelles. This irruption of the war into the Mediterranean, foreshadowing the involvement of Greece and Bulgaria, possibly even the rapid defeat and partition of Turkey, revived Salandra's and Sonnino's fears of arriving too late. On 3 March Salandra agreed that Imperiali should disclose Italy's terms to Grey. Negotiations with the Entente began.

## The Treaty of London

Sonnino's terms were stiff. They were designed to give Italy, in addition to Trent and Trieste, a defensible land frontier and domination of the Adriatic. These aims were to be achieved by expanding north to the Brenner and east to the crests of the Julian Alps, and by annexing the whole of Istria, three-quarters of the Austrian province of Dalmatia and the bay of Valona with its immediate hinterland. Those portions of the eastern Adriatic shore that were not claimed were to be demilitarised. Outside the Adriatic, Sonnino asked for equitable treatment in the Middle East and Africa. Strong opposition came at once from Russia. The Russians now felt confident of victory and were no longer ready, as in August 1914, to pay a high price for an Italian military contribution of dubious value. They neither wished to see Italian power replace Austrian in the Balkans nor wanted another claimant to the spoils at the peace conference. Dalmatia was the crux. Italy's pretensions, said Sazonov, were 'a challenge to the Slav conscience';[1] they would cost the Entente the sympathy of the oppressed nationalities of Austria-Hungary, alienate the Serbs and sow the seeds of a new war between Slavs and Italians. Britain and France set a much higher military value on Italy. Having begun to despair of a decision in the west, they were searching for new fronts and new manpower. Italy's intervention might be decisive in overcoming the hesitations of Rumania, Bulgaria and Greece, and create a solid Balkan front against hard-pressed Austria-Hungary. Grey believed that 'Italian cooperation will be the turning-point of the war.'[2]

On 22 March the Russians captured the Galician fortress of Przemysl and seemed about to invade Hungary. Italian fears of a separate Austro-Russian peace revived. Sonnino was determined that Italy should not

[1] M. Paléologue, *La Russie des Tsars pendant la grande guerre* (Paris 1921), I, p. 336.
[2] *L'intervento dell' Italia nei documenti segreti dell' Intesa* (Rome 1923), p. 113; Trevelyan, *Grey of Fallodon*, p. 297.

arrive too late and reduced his claims, renouncing Split and southern Dalmatia. But all through April the haggling continued, the Russians resisting every concession inch by inch.

Sonnino was meanwhile still negotiating with Austria-Hungary. On 9 March, with the Russians attacking in the east, Burian agreed under relentless German pressure to discuss the Trentino. At last, after three months, the negotiations had reached the crucial question. Both Sonnino and Salandra appreciated the risks of a rupture with the central Powers before agreement had been reached with the Entente. They had been warned by Cadorna and Zupelli that the army would not be ready before the end of April. It was therefore necessary to drag out the discussions.[1] Sonnino replied to Burian's concession with an uncompromising demand that all transfer of territory must take place immediately. In vain Bülow and Erzberger offered their country's guarantee that Austrian promises would be kept after the war. When Burian offered Trent, Sonnino raised his terms further, and on 8 April set out his demands in detail. He still asked for less for neutrality than he was asking from the Entente for intervention; but in addition to the Trentino[2] and the west bank of the Isonzo (with Gorizia on the east bank as well), he demanded autonomy for Trieste, the cession of the Curzolari islands off central Dalmatia and of Valona and its hinterland, and Austrian disinterest in the rest of Albania. In reply Burian offered a slightly larger slice of the Trentino, still substantially smaller than Sonnino had demanded and to be ceded only at the end of the war: otherwise nothing. Sonnino thereupon took the plunge. On 26 April the Treaty of London was signed,[3] committing Italy to enter the war on the side of the Entente within one month. On 4 May the Triple Alliance was denounced.

The treaty was a compromise which the Russians accepted only after last-minute appeals from Britain and France. It promised Italy the Brenner frontier, Istria, the line of the Julian Alps and central Dalmatia with its islands. This meant the transfer to Italian rule of 230,000 German-Austrians and 700,000 Slavs. The principle of nationality was further violated by the assignment to Italy of Valona and its hinterland,[4] and by

[1] Vigezzi, *I problemi della neutralità*, p. 37; Salandra, *L'intervento*, pp. 120–1.

[2] The frontier demanded by Sonnino was that of Napoleon's Kingdom of Italy of 1811, which ran south of the Brenner but north of the ethnic line dividing the Italian-speaking and German-speaking populations.

[3] The full text of the treaty is printed in Albrecht-Carrié, pp. 334–9, and in Temperley, V, pp. 384–91. The fullest account in English of the diplomatic negotiations is in W. W. Gottlieb, *Studies in Secret Diplomacy during the First World War* (London 1957).

[4] The treaty envisaged the partition of Albania between Italy on the coast, Serbia and Montenegro in the north, Greece in the south and 'a small autonomous

the recognition of the Italian claim to the Dodecanese which France and
Britain had contested since 1912. Salandra and Sonnino were not imperialist megolamaniacs. They wanted strong frontiers, Adriatic security
and a balance of power in the Mediterranean. They were proud of the
Treaty of London, believing it to be 'a working formula'.[1] Fiume, the
Hungarian coastline and southern Dalmatia were left to be 'assigned by
the four Allied Powers to Croatia, Serbia and Montenegro'.[2] There would
thus be room for all, whatever the future of Austria-Hungary and the
Southern Slavs. Cession of part of the Dalmatian coast and demilitarisation
of the rest would give Italy that exclusive domination of the Adriatic which
Sonnino considered the sole justification for plunging into war. Sonnino
did not desire the disruption of Austria-Hungary; on the contrary, he
relied on it as a buffer against the Slavs and thought a swollen Serbia,
backed by Russian military and naval power, might be a much less comfortable neighbour than 'an ancient state in decadence'.[3] He envisaged a
limited war for limited national aims, not a crusade to destroy the old
Europe which he loved. Once national unity was complete and Italy was
secure in the Adriatic, friendship with conservative Germany and an
easternised Austria-Hungary would be no less desirable than in 1882.[4]
These were the views to which Sonnino clung, a true disciple of Cesare
Balbo, throughout all the upheavals of the next four years.

Sonnino's outlook explains many features of the treaty which have
since been severely criticised. Preoccupied with the Adriatic, he paid little
attention to Turkey and colonial Africa. Unknown to him, Britain, France
and Russia had already agreed in March that Russia should acquire
Constantinople and the Straits. If Sonnino had known, he would have
been less content with the treaty's vague acknowledgement of Italy's
interest 'in the maintenance of the balance of power in the Mediterranean'

---

neutralised state' in the centre. This was a reversal of Italy's pre-1914 policy
which had aimed at a large, independent Albania.

[1] Salandra, *L'intervento*, pp. 190–6.

[2] Sonnino would have liked to add 'Hungary' to the list. He recognised the
traditional links of sentiment and interest between Hungary and Italy, which
dated from the Risorgimento, and agreed to have discussions, which proved
abortive, with unofficial Hungarian emissaries in March–May 1915 on the possibility, however remote, of an anti-German, anti-Slav Italo-Hungarian alliance. See
Valiani, pp. 213–20, 229–31.

[3] The phrase is Salandra's, in *L'intervento*, pp. 171–2. If Austria–Hungary was
to disappear, Sonnino would have much preferred a strong Hungary to a strong
Slav state.

[4] On this point Sonnino differed from San Giuliano who, in anticipation of a
war to the death with Austria–Hungary, had included in his draft terms of August–
September 1914 a permanent defensive alliance with the powers of the Entente
after the war. DDI (5), 151, 201, 803.

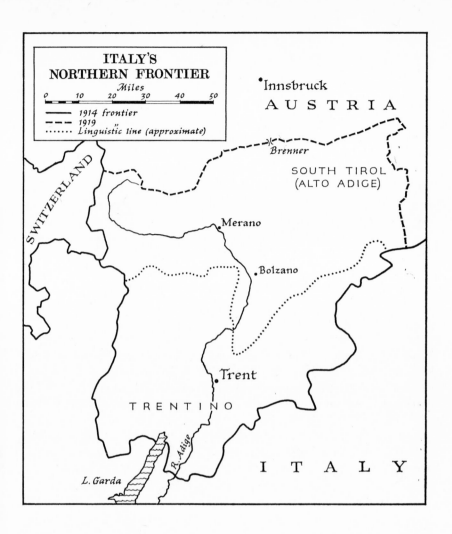

ITALY'S
NORTHERN FRONTIER

Miles

0    10    20    30    40    50

——— 1914 frontier
– – – 1919    "
········· Linguistic line (approximate)

SWITZERLAND

•Innsbruck

AUSTRIA

Brenner

SOUTH TIROL
(ALTO ADIGE)

•Merano

•Bolzano

•Trent

TRENTINO

R. Adige

L. Garda

ITALY

and its promise of 'a just share of the Mediterranean region adjacent to the
province of Adalia' in the event of a partition of Turkey-in-Asia (Article 9).
The formula on colonies (Article 13) was equally vague: Britain and
France agreed in principle, should they acquire German colonies, 'that
Italy may claim some equitable compensation, particularly as regards the
settlement in her favour of the questions relative to the frontiers' between
Italian and neighbouring colonies. Though Sonnino rejected a French
proposal to exclude Djibouti from the compensations that might be offered
to Italy, he showed little interest in the elaborate memoranda which
reached him from the Ministry of Colonies. He was presumably reluctant
to add British and French antagonism over Africa to Russian antagonism
over Dalmatia; and he may also have thought it unwise to press claims
against Germany whose military defeat he thought improbable. In any
case he believed that colonial details could safely be left till after the war.[1]
Only on the Trentino, Trieste and the Adriatic, where Austria-Hungary
was concerned, did he consider precision essential.

Sonnino's expectation of a short, limited war is further shown by the
absence of economic clauses and by his failure to secure the simultaneous
intervention of Rumania. Britain promised a loan of £50 million, a sum
which very soon proved pitifully inadequate. There was no mention of
coal, raw materials or munitions. Salandra later justified the omission on
the ground that Italy did not wish to enter the war as a mercenary;[2] but
it is clear that he and Sonnino totally misunderstood the type of war into
which they were plunging.

The Rumanians had tried throughout the winter to keep close to Italy,
and on 6 February a further secret agreement had been signed in Bucharest
whereby the two governments promised each other military help, should
the Austrians launch a preventive attack.[3] But though Bratianu, the
Rumanian Prime Minister, asked Sonnino in April not to commit Italy
to the Entente without informing him, his request was ignored and he
was presented with a *fait accompli*. Sonnino's advice to follow Italy's
example was not helpful. The Russians held out against Rumanian claims
much more obstinately than against Italy's claims in the Adriatic, and
having made excessive concessions to the latter, were in no mood to listen
to pleas for generosity to Rumania. Bratianu therefore achieved nothing
and Rumania remained neutral. The two armies, had they attacked
simultaneously, would, in Cadorna's words, have squeezed the enemy in a

---

[1] Salata, *Il nodo di Gibuti*, pp. 123–43; R. Albrecht-Carrié, 'Italian Colonial
Policy 1914–1918', in *Journal of Modern History*, vol. 18 (1946), pp. 127–35. Italy
was hardly in a strong position to bargain over colonies, having during the winter
of 1914–15 lost control of all Libya except the coastal oases.

[2] Salandra, *L'intervento*, p. 188; Malagodi, I, p. 93.

[3] Aldrovandi, *Nuovi ricordi*, pp. 200–1.

vice.[1] But Sonnino was probably relieved. He wished to win his war with as little help as possible, not to hasten the dissolution of the Habsburg monarchy and weaken Hungary by backing the Rumanian claim to Transylvania.

The most serious objection to the Treaty of London lay in its Adriatic clauses. It was intended to remain strictly secret, and in Italy only the King, Salandra, Sonnino and two senior officials of the Foreign Ministry had knowledge of its text. But rumours about the negotiations soon reached the Yugoslav leaders, Trumbić and Supilo, who like Battisti had escaped from Austria on the outbreak of war. At the end of March Supilo was in St Petersburg, where he found Sazonov in a bitter mood over Grey's 'capitulation' to Italy. By exercising the full force of his remarkable personality, Supilo was able to worm out of him the details of the Adriatic negotiations and inform the Serbs.[2] Early in May he and Trumbić founded a Yugoslav Committee in London. Its first manifesto claimed for the projected Serbo-Croat-Slovene state not only Dalmatia, but Istria and Trieste. This was the beginning of a long and bitter quarrel. Sonnino may be excused for ignoring this handful of émigrés who in May 1915 'represented nobody'. But there was little excuse for ignoring the Serbs. Pašić, the Serbian Prime Minister, was prepared to pay a big price for agreement with Italy, but Dalmatia was something that he could never concede. Every Yugoslav believed that it was, and must remain, Slav. San Giuliano had grasped this point and would probably have renounced Dalmatia for the sake of agreement with Serbia.[3] Sonnino was less far-sighted. With a passion for secrecy that was soon to become pathological, he turned down British and French suggestions that Pašić should be officially told of the Treaty of London. The Treaty was his bond and discussion could only weaken it. Better Dalmatia at the cost of enmity with the Yugoslavs than agreement with them on the basis of national self-determination and war against Austria-Hungary in its name.

Italy was to pay dearly for Sonnino's illusions. Dalmatia was not an Italian land, as Sonnino succeeded in persuading himself.[4] Its annexation

[1] Albertini, *Venti anni*, III, pp. 485–8; Aldrovandi, *Nuovi ricordi*, p. 204.

[2] Steed, II, pp. 64–5.

[3] DDI (5), I, 201, 803. Tittoni, too, opposed claiming any part of the Dalmatian mainland and regarded the nationalists' maximum programme as 'pure madness'. DDI (5), I, 834, 905. In January 1915 Sonnino sent Galli to Trieste, where he had been vice-consul in 1911–13, to make contact with the Slovene and Croat leaders. On his return he submitted a memorandum in favour of Italo–Yugoslav agreement, but Sonnino ignored it. Galli, pp. 240–54.

[4] In his reply to the Entente Powers' memorandum of 21 March, Sonnino wrote: 'The principal cities of Dalmatia have remained purely Italian notwithstanding sixty years of persistent Slavophil policy by Austria, and so have a good part of the islands facing the coast.' Salandra, *L'intervento*, p. 168.

would have imposed a major economic burden upon Italy. It would also
have been militarily defenceless against a hostile Slav state, as the general
staff would certainly have pointed out had Sonnino ever consulted it
during the treaty negotiations.[1] His greatest illusion was that Austria-
Hungary could be shorn of Trent, Trieste and Dalmatia, yet resist the
clamour of other nationalities and still survive. The damage the treaty
inflicted on the cause of the Entente was immediate. The call for resistance
to 'Italian imperialism' powerfully reinforced the loyalty of Austria-
Hungary's Slav subjects. Pašić was right when he declared that the
Yugoslavs would prefer Austria to Italy.[2] Crown Prince Alexander of
Serbia wrote to the Russian Commander-in-Chief, Grand Duke Nicholas,
on 5 May that it was impossible now to ask his soldiers to continue the
fight with their old devotion.[3] The Treaty of London became the cement
of the Austro-Hungarian army. In Albertini's words, it 'constituted a
serious obstacle to the success of our arms'.[4]

### Radiant May

While Sonnino negotiated in secret, the public debate over war and
neutrality grew fiercer. The socialists and the Catholics were the most
resolute against war, though even they were not united. Many young
socialists joined Corridoni and Mussolini. Emilio Caldara, the socialist
mayor of Milan, with his entire city council, rejected absolute neutrality
and declared his faith in democracy and the principle of nationality. Yet
the bulk of the organised working-class accepted the party's official view
that war was desired by the rich and would reinforce the monarchy,
capitalism and militarism. Because Italy was in no direct danger, no
conflict arose, as in France or Germany, between patriotic sentiment and
socialist duty. Italian socialists envisaged their party as the keystone of a
new Second International, refashioned after its betrayal in July 1914 by
their German and Austrian comrades. Emissaries from the German Social
Democratic party, led by the deputies Südekum and Haase, encouraged
them in these ideas. The Italian leaders grew more intransigent as time
passed. Party members were forbidden to belong to interventionist groups.
Insurrection was threatened if the government dared to order mobilisation.
No chance was lost of exploiting the distress caused by war: the food

[1] Cadorna, *La guerra*, I, p. 68; Valiani, p. 373; Sforza, *Contemporary Italy*,
p. 171. But on this point the Italian navy disagreed with the army and pressed for
Dalmatian bases.
[2] Pašić to Serbian minister at St Petersburg, 27 April 1915. Toscano, *La Serbia
e l'intervento in guerra dell' Italia*, p. 32.
[3] Toscano, *Il patto di Londra*, p. 131.
[4] Albertini, *Venti anni*, IV, p. 10.

shortages, the growth of unemployment, the rising cost of living and the sufferings of the 470,000 emigrants who had returned from Europe, often destitute, when war broke out.[1] On 21 February a 'day of socialist propaganda' was observed throughout the country. On the 25th demonstrating socialists clashed with interventionists and blood flowed in Milan and Reggio Emilia. Over the next three months there was recurrent violence.

Catholic support for neutrality was in part the reflection of the Vatican's anxieties. Pius X had died on 20 August 1914. At the conclave there was no outstanding candidate for the succession, Rampolla having died in 1913, but wide agreement that an integralist would not be acceptable. On 3 September Cardinal Giacomo Della Chiesa, Archbishop of Bologna, was elected at the fifteenth ballot and took the title of Benedict XV. In contrast to his predecessor, he was a member of one of the oldest families in Italy. Until 1907 his career had been purely diplomatic. So far from being an integralist, he had during his years at Bologna come under suspicion of modernist sympathies. He soon fulfilled expectations that he would be more of a 'political' than a 'religious' Pope. Although he had been one of Rampolla's closest collaborators, he shared none of Rampolla's political prejudices. His election and his choice of Cardinal Pietro Gasparri as Secretary of State pleased the German and Austrian governments, which were satisfied that both men were their friends.[2]

Benedict's first pronouncements were appeals to both sides to lay down their arms. All his influence was exerted to keep Italy neutral. Apart from his general desire to stop the war spreading, he had a special reason for wishing to keep Italy out of it. The Law of Guarantees was silent on the Pope's position in a belligerent Italy, but it was realistic to assume that his freedom to govern the supra-national church would be curtailed. Benedict also nursed the ambition of attending, perhaps presiding over, the peace conference and obtaining from it international guarantees of papal independence. Should Italy be a belligerent and a victor, that ambition was unlikely to be fulfilled.[3] There was therefore, as the Pope remarked to the Austro-Hungarian ambassador in January, 'an absolute identity of interest' between the Vatican and Austria. Discreet but determined pressure in favour of neutrality was applied behind the scenes, through con-

[1] The price of grain rose from 26 to 30 lire per quintal in August 1914, then dropped, but had reached 40 lire in April 1915. The wheat duty, which had stood at 7½ lire per quintal since August 1898, was reduced to 3 lire in October 1914 and suspended altogether next March.

[2] Engel-Jánosi, II, pp. 186–8.

[3] Salandra and Sonnino were aware of the Pope's ambition and successfully forestalled him. By Article 15 of the Treaty of London, Britain, France and Russia agreed to prevent the Vatican's representation at the peace conference. Salandra, La neutralità, pp. 426–8; L'intervento, pp. 203–8.

THE GREAT WAR

tacts with politicians, the press and even the royal family. 'We are doing everything we can', Gasparri assured the ambassador in February, 'first in our own interest, then in that of Catholic Austria-Hungary.'[1]

Italian Catholics could not remain uninfluenced by the Vatican's clear desire that Italy should remain neutral. They had, moreover, no love for anti-clerical France, Protestant Britain or Orthodox Russia, and were disgusted by the bellicose clamour of the freemasons, nationalists and revolutionaries. An ultra-conservative minority, which still dreamt of the temporal power, prayed for an Austrian victory. At the opposite extreme, Miglioli's peasant unions were aggressively pacifist. But the majority, unable to suppress all patriotic sentiment, remained undecided. Catholics had no wish to renounce their country, as in the years after 1870, and once again become 'internal exiles'. During the winter Catholic spokesmen like Meda and Dalla Torre, President of the Unione Popolare, expressed the view that neutrality must be conditional on the satisfaction of Italian interests. Thus, while continuing to oppose war, they left themselves a door open and showed that they would not blindly follow the Vatican's lead.

Liberal doubts persisted throughout the winter. In January the interventionists, their patience exhausted, launched a press campaign of denigration against Giolitti. He, they realised, was the key to the domestic situation; if he could be discredited, their chances of victory would be enhanced. Giolitti was therefore denounced as pro-Austrian (*austriacante*), depicted as Bülow's toady and accused of intriguing to overthrow the government and favouring neutrality even at the sacrifice of Italian interests.[2] To silence this disreputable campaign, the neutralist newspaper *La Tribuna* published on 1 February a letter from Giolitti to his supporter, Camillo Peano, which made his views clear. In it he denied that he was a pacifist: his record in 1911 proved that. But war, he argued, was a grim matter, which should not be undertaken out of sentimental enthusiasm. Moreover in the present situation 'quite a lot' (*parecchio*) could be obtained by Italy without war.[3] In other words, he counted on success in the

---

[1] Engel-Jánosi, II, pp. 203–4. Erzberger reported in April (Epstein, p. 126) that Benedict had told him that he had 'applied pressure upon Cadorna'. On 15 January the nunzio in Vienna delivered a personal letter from Benedict to Francis Joseph, pleading for concessions to Italy in the interests of both the Pope and 'the last Catholic Great Power'. To this general plea the nunzio added a specific reference to the Trentino. Burian promptly instructed his ambassador to remind the Pope that the preservation of Austria–Hungary's integrity was the motive and purpose of the war, and that the cession of the Trentino would be 'suicidal'. Engel-Jánosi, II, pp. 210–15.     [2] *Quarant' anni*, III, 137–9.

[3] ibid., 141–5; Giolitti, *Memorie*, pp. 529–31. The original letter, as addressed to his friend and supporter, the deputy Peano, on 24 January and reprinted by Giolitti in his *Memorie*, contained the word 'much' (*molto*); this was toned down to *parecchio* for publication. Malagodi, I, pp. 41–2.

negotiations with Austria-Hungary. What the letter did not reveal was his belief that Italy was too weak to prevent the Germans from reaching Milan and that war, even if perhaps it could not in the end be avoided, must at least be delayed as long as possible. Giolitti's motive for publishing the letter was not to attack the government, but rather to strengthen it against the interventionists and reinforce its diplomatic hand. Neither Salandra nor Sonnino gave any sign that his action was unwelcome.[1] Giolitti travelled to Rome soon after the reassembly of parliament on 18 February. Having sized up the political situation and had a talk with Salandra on 8 March, he returned to Piedmont in an optimistic mood. Salandra, he was satisfied, was following a policy of which he could approve.[2] On 22 March his followers in parliament again voted on his instructions for the government, in spite of misgivings. The chamber then adjourned until May.

Giolitti's optimism was misplaced, as his supporters very soon discovered. By 22 March the parallel negotiations with the Entente and the central Powers had entered the crucial stage. The government had in fact travelled far on the road to war; psychologically, at least, it was already committed. 'The Monarchy must be saved . . . Italy will march', Martini had told a visiting French deputy in February.[3] The private views of Salandra and Sonnino were little different. The *Parecchio* letter had been a turning-point. By publishing it, Giolitti unintentionally assumed the leadership of all the neutralist forces and turned the campaign for intervention into an anti-Giolitti crusade.[4] Giolitti still dominated parliament. But since the beginning of the war Salandra had enjoyed power and prestige such as could never have been his when Europe was at peace. He

---

[1] On 2 February Sonnino told Malagodi privately that he was in general agreement with Giolitti's letter, though he confessed to being more sceptical than Giolitti about the prospects of extracting adequate concessions from Austria–Hungary without war. Sonnino was clearly not revealing his whole mind. Malagodi, I, pp. 42–3; Orlando, *Memorie*, pp. 31–3. Early in March Facta, speaking on behalf of Giolitti, urged the Austro-Hungarian ambassador 'to hurry'; if Austria continued to be unyielding over compensations, Italy would be forced to go to war. Valiani, p. 114.

[2] Giolitti, *Memorie*, pp. 532–4. Giolitti was later to accuse Salandra, with extreme vehemence and bitterness, of deliberately lying to him on this occasion 'in Apulian fashion' (*da pugliese*). Malagodi, I, pp. 57, 64, 83–4.

[3] C. Benoist, *Souvenirs* (Paris 1932–4), III, pp. 246, 258, 293. This remark reflected liberal anxiety over the shrill republican note in the interventionist agitation. Mussolini wrote in his paper on 26 February that 'the days of the monarchy are numbered' if it failed to lead Italy into war, and he repeated this threat at intervals over the next two months. Mussolini, VII, pp. 220–1, 251, 314.

[4] As Salandra himself afterwards observed (*L'intervento*, p. 61), 'The *parecchio* letter acquired a significance which, I believe, its author neither foresaw nor intended.'

was forced by Giolitti's sponsorship of the neutralist cause into dependence upon the interventionists, if he was to emancipate himself from Giolitti's patronage. Thus the struggle between the war and peace parties merged in the older struggle between Giolittians and anti-Giolittians. As soon as parliament had dispersed, the attacks on Giolitti became more virulent. To the interventionists he was henceforth 'the anti-hero, the suffocator of the nation's energies', the man of dishonour, 'the *longa manus* of Bülow and Germany'. Only war could rescue Italy from the miseries of *Giolittismo*.[1]

If these attacks were not directly inspired by the government, as many neutralists suspected, they certainly received no official discouragement. The Giolittians, led in the master's absence by one of his most faithful lieutenants, Luigi Facta, became thoroughly alarmed. Was Salandra, they wondered, intending to plunge the country into war without even recalling parliament? The news that reached them through their many contacts with the German embassy only intensified their alarm. It seemed to them imperative that Giolitti should come to Rome, speak out and exert his full power against the 'feline', reckless, upstart Prime Minister.[2] But Giolitti ignored their appeals, not wishing to add to the nation's disunity. In keeping silent, he deluded himself. Not even his total abdication could have healed the deep and bitter schism by which the Italian ruling class was now divided.

During April the tension rose rapidly. Only a handful of people knew how Sonnino's negotiations were going, but it was clear to all that the crisis was approaching. Rival demonstrations clashed in the streets of the great cities and violence spread. On the 11th the police broke up mass meetings in both Milan and Rome; Mussolini and Marinetti were among the hundreds briefly detained. Salandra deplored all such attempts, whether neutralist or interventionist, to limit the government's freedom of action. He therefore reprimanded his prefects for laxity and ordered them to maintain public order at any cost.[3] Meanwhile the belligerents, too, stepped up their pressure. Unofficial German and Austrian intermediaries tried to stir Giolitti and the neutralists into action.[4] Lavish German propaganda, backed by generous press subsidies, proclaimed the

[1] Corradini, *Discorsi politici*, p. 267; Mussolini, VII, p. 241.

[2] *Quarant' anni*, III, 151–8.

[3] Salandra, *L'intervento*, pp. 45, 70–1; Vigezzi, *Le Radiose giornate*, pp. 329–335.

[4] Giolitti, *Memorie*, pp. 536–7; Frassati, pp. 12–13, 18–20; Valiani, pp. 120–3. In mid-April Frassati defined Giolitti's *parecchio* for the benefit of the Austrians as follows: cession of the Trentino and the west bank of the Isonzo, and the status of free cities under Austo-Hungarian sovereignty for Trieste and Fiume.

invincibility of the German army and confirmed the fearful in their conviction that war would bring defeat, economic disaster and revolution. Bülow exploited to the full his wife's connexions and his contacts in Roman society. Against him Barrère worked indefatigably for the consummation of seventeen years of diplomatic effort. French democrats and British liberals mobilised their Italian friends; encouragement and cash were sent through French socialist channels to Mussolini.[1] The very diversity of the interventionist groups increased their impact on Italian opinion. They also had a disproportionately large section of the press on their side, including two of the most influential newspapers in the country, the *Corriere della Sera* and the *Secolo*. 'Without the newspapers', Salandra was to write in retrospect, 'Italy's intervention would perhaps have been impossible.'[2]

Nevertheless, on the morrow of the signature of the Treaty of London, Salandra faced a truly formidable task. Italy's fate had been sealed on paper; he had one month to win the nation's consent. The interventionists had made much progress in recent weeks but they remained a minority. Against the government were ranged the church, organised labour and a majority in parliament. The mass of the rural population, especially in the south, was passive but more for peace than for war. Rome and central Italy were predominantly neutralist. Only in the north was the war party strong. Even there Piedmont was Giolittian and outside Venetia the interventionists could count with confidence only on Milan and the large towns.[3]

The final crisis began on 5 May. On that day, at Quarto near Genoa, a

---

[1] For a careful analysis of the evidence on this point, see De Felice, pp. 276–7, 285–7, 300–3; also Salvemini, *Mussolini diplomatico*, pp. 419–31, and Sir Ivone Kirkpatrick, *Mussolini, Study of a Demagogue* (London 1964), pp. 64–73. One of the chief intermediaries was Marcel Cachin, later to become a leading communist, who with the approval of the French government visited Italy in December 1914 and afterwards made himself responsible for contacts between French socialists and Italian interventionists of the left. For many years after 1914 Mussolini's detractors alleged that the payments began even before his public conversion and that *Il Popolo d'Italia* was financed from the start with 'French gold'. From the evidence presented by De Felice it is clear that after Mussolini's break with Naldi, the newspaper was for several months in financial difficulty. On 15 March Mussolini told Prezzolini, 'The future is most uncertain.' The French (and Belgian) subventions appear to have started only in May 1915, and to have consisted of an initial grant of 100,000 lire, followed by 10,000 lire monthly.

[2] Salandra, *La neutralità*, p. 228. Bollati wrote bitterly to Avarna on 9 March of the government's willingness 'to lose hundreds of thousands of men and hundreds of millions of money just because . . . they are afraid of the *Idea Nazionale* and the *Corriere della Sera*'. 'Carteggio Avarna-Bollati', in *Rivista storica italiana*, vol. 62 (1950), p. 82. The chief neutralist newspaper was Frassati's *Stampa*, published in Turin, with a circulation second only to that of the *Corriere della Sera*.

[3] Salandra had asked all prefects on 12 April for a special report on the state of public feeling in the event of war. The replies are summarised in A. Monticone,

monument was to be unveiled to Garibaldi on the spot from which he and his Thousand had sailed for Sicily exactly fifty-five years before. D'Annunzio had been invited to speak at the ceremony. At the last minute Salandra, having seen his script, decided to stay away and advised the King to do the same. D'Annunzio's theme, before an audience of 20,000, was not the past but the greater Italy that was being born, the glory and sacrifices that were to come. The speech was intended and understood as a call to arms.

But Germany and Austria-Hungary had not given up hope, even after Italy's denunciation of the Triple Alliance on 4 May. On the 2nd their long-prepared offensive against Russia began. Within a few days they had achieved a break-through at Gorlice and were rolling the Russian army back through Galicia. This success could not be exploited if Italy intervened. The German general staff declared that every day's delay was valuable. Conrad and Tisza were ready to go to the extreme limit of humiliation for the sake of a few weeks' respite, consoling themselves with the thought that promises extorted by threats were not binding and could be cancelled after victory.[1] Erzberger returned to Rome on the 2nd to act as honest broker. Next day, after an interview with Sonnino, he sent an urgent appeal to the German Chancellor, Bethmann-Hollweg: Austria must be 'decisively and, if necessary, ruthlessly' constrained to yield within three days.[2] Over the next fortnight he was feverishly busy. In his own words, 'Meetings in obscure churches, crypts, remote monasteries and alleys' alternated with high-level conferences at embassies. Once again he was able to mobilise the support of the Vatican, including that of the Pope himself, and sixty bishops were induced to sign a petition against war.[3] Meanwhile unofficial reports of further extensive concessions by Austria were passed into circulation. Bülow redoubled his efforts to stir the neutralists into action and sent a special message to Piedmont to inform

---

'Salandra e Sonnino verso la decisione dell' intervento', in *Rivista di studi politici internazionali*, vol. 24 (1957), pp. 72–89. They give a general impression of a country with little desire to go to war but unlikely to offer active opposition.

[1] Many other advocates of concession to Italy, including William II, Moltke, the German Chief of Staff, and Stürgkh, the Austrian Prime Minister, made the same mental reservation. Valiani, pp. 104, 115, 118–19.

[2] Erzberger, p. 31.

[3] Epstein, p. 130. For an attempt by a politically active monsignor to bring pressure upon the government through the Minister for Posts, Riccio, one of Salandra's closest colleagues, see C. de Biase, 'Il diario del ministro Vincenzo Riccio (1915)', in *Nuova Antologia*, vol. 465 (1955), pp. 539–41. Erzberger was also in touch with the Minister of Education, Pasquale Grippo, who informed him of the state of opinion in the cabinet. The Pope hoped that Grippo would resign and bring down the government, so that Giolitti could return to power. Epstein, pp. 132–3; Valiani, p. 124.

Giolitti that the Triple Alliance had been denounced.[1] This was closely followed by two appeals from Facta, informing Giolitti of the latest Austrian offer and begging him 'in the supreme interest of the country' to come to Rome and halt Italy's precipitate 'rush to ruin'.[2] There seemed to Bülow and Erzberger to be just a chance, if a few more concessions could be extracted from Austria, that Giolitti might overturn Salandra and keep Italy out of war.

Giolitti arrived at last on 9 May. In spite of boos at Turin the previous evening and another interventionist demonstration at Rome station, more than 300 deputies and 100 senators showed their loyalty by leaving cards at his house. Over the next week a flood of letters and telegrams reached him from all parts of Italy, from deputies and former ministerial colleagues, professors and journalists, mayors and civil servants, soldiers, business men, priests and humble private citizens. Only Giolitti could save Italy from disaster, was their recurrent refrain.[3] Giolitti's parliamentary supporters were meanwhile clamouring for him to be consulted before any final decision was made. Under the shock of this 'neutralist insurrection' many of Salandra's followers, even some of his cabinet colleagues, wavered. The King, too, grew seriously alarmed.[4]

On the same day that Giolitti reached the capital, Erzberger and the Austro-Hungarian ambassador, Macchio, prepared a new document setting out the concessions which had been circulating unofficially during the previous week. They were generous proposals: cession of the Italian-speaking districts of the Trentino, the right bank of the Isonzo and Valona; autonomy for Trieste within the Dual Monarchy, total Austrian disinterest in Albania and guarantees for all Italians still left under Habsburg rule. In addition, benevolent consideration was promised for Italy's claim to Gorizia and to certain Dalmatian islands. Execution of the agreement was to be guaranteed by Germany. Had this offer been made two months earlier, it might have proved conclusive. It in fact satisfied almost all the demands that Sonnino had listed on 8 April. Macchio still had no authority from Vienna to make it official. It was nevertheless communicated to the King, the Pope and a number of active neutralist deputies, with the intention of forcing the government's hand.

[1] The messenger was Count Giacomo Rattazzi, son of Urbano, Giolitti's friend and patron of the 1890s. Ansaldo, p. 422; Herbert von Hindenburg, *Am Rande zweier Jahrhunderte* (Berlin 1938), pp. 295–6.

[2] *Quarant' anni*, III, 162, 164; P. Bertolini, 'Diario (agosto 1914–maggio 1915)', in *Nuova Antologia*, vol. 306 (1923), p. 220.

[3] *Quarant' anni*, III, 148–69.

[4] Salandra, *L'intervento*, p. 260; De Biase, 'Il diario del ministro Vincenzo Riccio', in *Nuova Antologia*, vol. 467 (1956), pp. 514–17; Vigezzi, *Le Radiose giornate*, pp. 335–7.

On the evening of 9 May Giolitti received a visit on behalf of the cabinet from his friend and former colleague, Paolo Carcano, now Minister of the Treasury. Carcano explained to him, without revealing the precise content of the Treaty of London, that the decision to intervene had been made. Giolitti was by now in a highly excited state, having lost all his usual calm.[1] On the morning of the 10th he saw the King. Soon afterwards he was shown the text of the latest Austrian offer, which impressed him favourably. Later that same day he saw Salandra. Deeply pessimistic, he repeated to both King and Prime Minister his warning that the army was unreliable, the Austrians and Germans would reach Milan, the economic strain of war would be intolerable, revolution would follow. Instead he earnestly advised them to treat the latest Austrian proposal as a basis for further negotiation; if they would wait just a little longer, a new and better proposal would come that could be accepted. Giolitti even offered in that event to put his parliamentary strength at the government's disposal, thereby assuring it of a four-fifths majority in the chamber.[2] On return from his long talk with Salandra, Giolitti spoke hopefully to his friend Bertolini of the chances of avoiding war. Give Salandra time to reflect, he told him; meanwhile there was nothing to be done but wait.[3]

Late on the evening of 10 May, at Giolitti's suggestion, Bülow and Macchio put the latest Austrian offer into the form of an official note and dispatched it to Salandra and Sonnino, adding the suggestion that mixed Austro-Italian commissions should start immediately to delimit the new frontier. Macchio put his signature to it with the greatest reluctance, under extreme pressure from Bülow and Erzberger. The offer was published in full in the *Stampa* next morning. Sonnino rejected it on the ground that it did not include immediate transfer of territory. On the 12th Erzberger announced yet more minor concessions, together with William II's personal guarantee of Italy's permanent possession of the territories to be ceded.[4]

On the morning of 12 May the cabinet met for three hours. The neutralist pressure and the change in the military situation had shaken its confidence. The Austrian break-through in Galicia and the failure of the

[1] Malagodi, I, p. 56.                                    [2] Salandra, *L'intervento*, pp. 252–5.
[3] P. Bertolini, 'Diario (agosto 1914–maggio 1915)', in *Nuova Antologia*, vol. 306 (1923), pp. 221–3. A bitter controversy later arose as to whether Giolitti was told the facts about the Treaty of London or not. Salandra (*L'intervento*, pp. 255–6) maintained that, though he was not shown the text, he was told the substance. Giolitti in his *Memorie* (pp. 539–42) and on many other occasions, 'not once but a hundred times' (Frassati, pp. 14–15), denied that either Carcano or the King or Salandra told him of the existence of the treaty. To this day neither Salandra's nor Giolitti's partisans are willing to admit the possibility of a genuine misunderstanding.
[4] Erzberger, pp. 35–8; Epstein, p. 134.

British landings at the Dardanelles[1] were anxiously debated. Parliament
was due to meet on the 20th. Salandra and his colleagues recognised that
they could take their country into war only with an overwhelming majority
in parliament and the unanimous consent of 'the Constitutional party'.[2]
It was therefore agreed that Salandra should consult the leaders of the
various parliamentary groups. This proved a sobering experience. Bissolati
alone was in favour of war. When he and Salandra gloomily went through
the list of deputies, they found only 60 convinced interventionists and at
most 120 to 150 on whose votes they could rely. Martini and some other
ministers wished to face the chamber and fight out the issue in public
debate. Salandra refused, on the ground that it would expose the crown.[3]
Late on the evening of the 13th, after another long cabinet meeting, it
was announced that, owing to lack of the necessary agreement among the
constitutional parties on the government's conduct of international policy,
the government had resigned. 'Bright blue sky', telegraphed a foreign
journalist to Vienna.[4]

The government's resignation left a political void. Salandra himself had
no plan to meet the crisis. No attempt was made to enlighten the press
on the issues at stake and the government's lack of contact with public opinion became painfully apparent. The first reaction of many interventionists,
including Mussolini, was despair. Even the prefects were left in the dark.
Salandra and Sonnino became unapproachable and withdrew into a mysterious silence.[5] Depression and bewilderment reigned at the Ministry
of Interior. The government's abdication placed the fate of Italy in the
hands of the King and extra-parliamentary opinion.

[1] The landings had started on 25 April.
[2] De Biase, 'Il diario del ministro Vincenzo Riccio', in *Nuova Antologia*, vol.
470 (1957), p. 89; Vigezzi, *Le Radiose giornate*, pp. 339–40, quoting Martini's
diary; Salandra, *L'intervento*, p. 269.
[3] Though the King regarded himself as personally committed to the Treaty of
London, he nevertheless admitted that parliament had power to reject it. Vigezzi,
*Le Radiose giornate*, pp. 335–6. Giolitti believed (Malagodi, I, p. 61), and said so
to Victor Emmanuel on 10 May, that only Salandra's government was committed
and that the King was free to choose another prime minister who could, with the
support of parliament, reverse the decision for war. This was also the belief of
Salandra and Sonnino (Vigezzi, *Le Radiose giornate*, pp. 335–8), though according
to Orlando (*Memorie*, pp. 38–42) a minority of the cabinet, including Orlando
himself, disagreed. Salandra had in fact told the King on 9 May that he was ready
to resign if that would ease the King's task. Salandra, *L'intervento*, pp. 251–2.
[4] ibid., pp. 269–72.
[5] De Felice, p. 315; Albertini, *Venti anni*, III, pp. 531–4. One prefect learnt of
the government's resignation from his newspaper next morning. The only guidance
given to prefects was a circular authorising them in an emergency to hand over
maintenance of public order to the army. Vigezzi, *Le Radiose giornate*, pp. 342–3.

The essential issue, peace or war, was now clear to the whole country and the interventionists went into action. On its own initiative the *Corriere della Sera* revealed that the Triple Alliance had been denounced, in order to prove Giolitti's efforts useless. There was an explosion of manifestos and demonstrations. These varied in character in different parts of the country. In the south they were mainly orderly and conservative. In town after town the notables of the local ruling class turned out, often led by the mayor and accompanied by the town band, to demonstrate publicly their loyalty to the monarchy and to their fellow southerner and conservative, Salandra. In the cities respectable citizens flocked to meetings or formed processions in their thousands. The neutralists were conspicuously absent.[1]

In central and northern Italy passions ran higher and the demonstrations were on a greater scale. The universities, both professors and students, set the pace and the revolutionary interventionists were prominent. But the neutralists, too, were active. Some sections of the peasantry and urban working-class, less politically apathetic than in the south, were prepared to challenge the warmongers in the streets. In Florence, Bologna, Genoa and other cities, brawls between rival demonstrations brought bloodshed and thousands of arrests. Leading neutralists were threatened and Austrian consulates attacked.[2] Milan was especially agitated. Corridoni and Mussolini urged the people to occupy the streets and stay there in order to impose its will on the monarchy. 'War or revolution' was the cry: 'War on the frontier or war at home.' Mussolini warned the King once again that he would lose his throne if he refused to bow to the popular will.[3] The socialists called a general strike in the city for 15 May, in protest against the death of a neutralist demonstrator, but it proved a fiasco.[4] Throughout the north the interventionists, though still a minority, were the more aggressive and better organised. Everywhere except at Turin they created an impression of superior strength.

The excitement was greatest in Rome. Democrats, nationalists, conservatives and revolutionaries joined in denouncing Giolitti, 'the accomplice of the foreigner and enemy of his country'. On 12 May D'Annunzio had arrived in the capital. Nearly 100,000 people greeted him at the station. From the balcony of his hotel he lashed the crowd into passion. 'For three days a stink of treason has been suffocating us', he cried: 'Romans, sweep away all the filth, chuck all the garbage back into the sewer.' 'Friends, it is no longer time for talk but for action', he declared next day; 'If it is a crime to incite citizens to violence, I shall boast of this

---

[1] ibid., pp. 54–9.          [2] ibid., pp. 75 ff.
[3] Mussolini, VII, pp. 378, 386, 389–90.
[4] Vigezzi, *Le Radiose giornate*, pp. 87–92.

crime . . . Form platoons, form citizens' patrols.'[1] Many took him at his word. Students surged into the chamber of deputies' building and searched the streets for friends of Giolitti to assault. Peano and Bertolini were recognised and manhandled, and only a barrier of troops saved Giolitti's house from attack. Red shirts appeared on the streets, Garibaldian songs were sung and there were cries of 'Liberty or Death'. To Erzberger, who had the windows of his car smashed, Rome seemed a city in the grip of terror and revolution.[2]

The King meanwhile grappled with the ministerial crisis. Salandra recommended that Giolitti be asked to form a government. Giolitti refused, realising that his commitment to neutrality made him the person least able to extract further concessions from Austria. Instead he recommended Carcano or Marcora, the President of the chamber, either of whom, he thought, had a good chance of winning massive support in parliament and conducting the negotiations with Austria to a successful conclusion. But Marcora and Carcano both declined, as did the King's third choice, Paolo Boselli, the *doyen* of the chamber. The King's personal inclination was never in doubt. He regarded the crown's honour as at stake and talked of abdication if parliament overruled the decision for war. It was therefore with joy and relief that he felt able on 16 May to refuse to accept Salandra's resignation.

When the announcement was made, the war party let itself go in paroxysms of rejoicing. 'The King has saved Italy', declared the nationalist press. Mussolini hailed 'the victory of the people'. A crowd of 100,000 demonstrated before the royal palace and the Foreign Ministry, 200,000 in the Piazza del Popolo. Battisti urged 'To the frontier, all to the frontier'. On the 17th, at a huge gathering on the Capitol, D'Annunzio theatrically kissed the naked sword of Garibaldi's lieutenant, Nino Bixio. 'The honour of the country has been saved, Italy has been liberated', he declared:

---

[1] D'Annunzio, *Per la più grande Italia*, pp. 83–95.

[2] Erzberger, p. 38. The Giolittians attributed this 'undergraduate hooliganism' to the freemasons and to British and French gold, and were shocked by the tolerance shown by the police to 'the cowardly *canaille*' (*Quarant' anni*, III, 192, 194). Salandra (*L'intervento*, p. 277) observes, with excessive complacency, that the extent of the 'terror' has been exaggerated; no person was seriously hurt and not a single shop or house was damaged in Rome. He also denies (pp. 278–9) the allegation that the demonstrations were financed by the government or, to any significant extent, by foreign embassies. For an effective demolition of the myth (in part fostered by Salandra himself) that Salandra's resignation and the demonstrations of 'Radiant May' were a plot to overawe parliament and plunge Italy into war by a *coup d'état*, see Vigezzi, *Le Radiose giornate*, pp. 319 ff. Albertini is nearer the truth, though he too exaggerates, in observing (*Venti anni*, III, pp. 533–4) that Salandra and Sonnino could claim no credit whatsoever for 'the noble, burning, stirring passion' of the great cities which swept Italy into war.

'Our arms are in our hands.'[1] The same day Erzberger was escorted to the frontier and Giolitti, calm once again and resigned, left Rome for Piedmont, 'my mission at an end'.[2]

On the 18th Bülow handed Sonnino a draft Italo-Austrian treaty which had been intended for a neutralist government. It included one further concession: the transfer of Austrian territory was to take place within one month of ratification of the decisions of the mixed frontier commissions. On the same day Benedict XV conveyed to Salandra through Vincenzo Riccio, the Minister for Posts, his personal conviction that Austria would accept all Italy's requests and carry them into immediate effect. At the same time he vainly urged the Austro-Hungarian ambassador to obtain from Burian a written promise of immediate cession which Salandra could read out in the chamber of deputies.[3] Bethmann Hollweg commented on the generosity of Austria's concessions in the German Reichstag, adding his fervent hope that war would be avoided. Tisza spoke likewise in the Hungarian parliament. Yet further offers were being made on the 23rd. But with the resumption of office by Salandra, the die had been cast. Austria had once again indulged in 'her hereditary vice of arriving too late'.[4]

The country on the whole accepted its fate with resignation. Giolitti's followers deplored Salandra's 'abdication to the *piazza*', but acknowledged the King's right to exercise his prerogative. Now that the crown had made its decision, only a revolution could prevent war. 'We who believe in the constitution can only support the government's proposals and pray fervently for victory and the greatness of our country', wrote the Giolittian Carlo Schanzer to his chief on 16 May.[5] Giolitti himself decided to retire into silence. Believing that it was now every citizen's duty to do his utmost to assure victory, he resolved to utter no word 'that could cause discouragement or disturb the nation's unity'.[6] The neutralists seemed to have melted away. Only in Turin was there serious opposition. There on the 16th the Socialist party and C.G.L. called a general strike which brought nearly 100,000 industrial workers and sympathisers on to the streets. There was talk of answering mobilisation with revolution and barricades were built. The military authorities were obliged to take over, troops occupied the chamber of labour and 100 arrests were made.[7] But the national general

[1] D'Annunzio, *Per la più grande Italia*, p. 135; Mussolini, VII, p. 396.
[2] Giolitti, *Memorie*, p. 542; Malagodi, I, p. 63.
[3] Engel-Jánosi, II, pp. 245–6.
[4] The phrase was Bülow's. Salandra, *L'intervento*, p. 97; Bülow, III, p. 227.
[5] *Quarant' anni*, III, 195.
[6] Giolitti, *Memorie*, p. 544. See also *Quarant' anni*, III, 219; Natale, pp. 737–8.
[7] Spriano, *Torino operaia*, pp. 104–9; Vigezzi, *Le Radiose giornate*, pp. 97–100.

strike, called by the Socialist party and C.G.L. for the 19th, was hardly noticed. The crowds preferred to turn out to cheer the army and demonstrate their patriotism. Salandra reiterated his instructions to prefects to maintain public order at any cost. Demonstrations against war were rigorously suppressed and interventionist ebullience was damped down. Now was the time for discipline, restraint and silent preparation for the serious business of war.

Parliament met on 20 May. The government asked for full powers for war. Only Turati spoke against. Giolitti had abdicated and the 300 Giolittian deputies, shamefaced and bewildered, followed their instinct to rally to the government. Salandra won a vote of 407 to 74, with one abstention, in the chamber; the senate next day was unanimous. Salandra and Sonnino received ovations. On 22 May mobilisation was ordered. Next day Sonnino dispatched an ultimatum to Austria and on the 24th Italy was at war. Cadorna assumed command of the army and on the 25th the King left for the front, leaving behind his cousin, the Duke of Genoa, as his regent in Rome.

Italy thus entered the war with jubilation but in an atmosphere of civil war. Beneath the surface the country was deeply divided. The peasants answered their mobilisation summonses obediently, but to many it seemed a war manufactured by the *signori* and the towns. An ardent minority had imposed its will, just as fifty-five years before a minority had achieved unification. Parliament suffered dangerously in prestige. During the crisis the neutralists, especially the socialists, had denounced the *piazza* and praised Giolitti for defending parliamentary privileges. 'Parliament', wrote Mussolini, 'is Italy's bubonic plague which poisons the blood of the nation. It must be extirpated.'[1] After victory the nationalists exulted that a revolution of the national conscience had struck down the parliamentary tyrant. Turati deplored 'a general rout, a collective abdication'. 'The first effect of the war', he said, 'has been to destroy the vigour and dignity of our parliamentary institutions.'[2]

The political and constitutional crisis of May 1915 left a lasting mark on Italy. Italians have argued ever since over the actions of the King, Salandra and Giolitti. Some have criticised the King for abandoning the crown's impartiality, others have praised him for listening to the true 'will of the people'. Some have praised Giolitti's far-sightedness and dated 1915 as the beginning of Italy's later disasters;[3] others have gloried in

[1] *Il Popolo d'Italia*, 11 May. Mussolini, VII, p. 376.
[2] Turati, II, pp. 1366–7. Ferri talked of 'the South American days of May'.
[3] The Giolittian view was well expressed by Frassati in a review of Albertini's posthumous *Venti anni*: 'In 1915 began the disintegration of the work not only of Giolitti but of all the great men of the Risorgimento. It was precisely in 1915, dear Albertini, that fascism was born.' Frassati, p. 5.

Giolitti's defeat as a victory for youth over age, idealism over materialism, a heroic élite over the supine masses; a victory without which Italy would have been doomed to stagnation. The debate will continue. But few interventionists, whether liberal or revolutionary, democrat or nationalist ever doubted the wisdom of their choice: neutrality would have been the great abdication[1] and 'radiant May' was one of Italy's finest hours.

## The First Year of War

Italy went to war on 24 May along what was the most difficult front in Europe. Shaped like a huge 'S', it stretched for nearly 400 miles through hills or high mountains. Wherever the Italians attacked, they had to fight uphill. Large-scale operations were possible only in two sectors: against the Trentino bastion, northwards into the Tirol; and on the Isonzo, south-eastwards to Trieste and eastwards towards the Ljubljana Gap. Whichever sector was chosen, the attacking Italian army must expose an open flank to the enemy. The nightmate that haunted Italian soldiers throughout the war was a simultaneous enemy attack in both sectors.

The military situation in May was less promising for Italy and the Entente than at any time since the beginning of the year. In France and at Gallipoli there was stalemate. In the east the Germans and Austrians were triumphant. Przemysl was recaptured on 2 June, Lwow three weeks later, and the Russian retreat was to continue all summer from the Baltic to the Carpathians. The Austro-Hungarian army, in spite of huge losses in the previous ten months, was as strong in men and weapons as in July 1914. Italy's intervention came too late to bring about that 'turning-point of the war' on which Grey had counted. To prevent a knock-out blow against Italy before it was ready to defend itself, the Entente had agreed, in a series of military conventions, to subject Austria-Hungary to a threefold, simultaneous attack: by the Russians from the east, by the Serbs from the south-east and by the Italians from the south-west. In fact neither the Russians nor the Serbs were in a fit state to carry out their obligations. Within a month of declaring war, Salandra was writing to Sonnino in a torment of remorse at the thought that Italy's intervention might have been premature.[2]

By 24 May Cadorna had assembled 400,000 men in 35 divisions on the frontier. Against him the Austrians had 14 divisions and the Germans

---

[1] Salvemini, in *Dal patto di Londra*, pp. xii–xiii, argues that had intervention been delayed, Italy would have become the plaything of the belligerents and been reduced to the state of civil war and national humiliation which was the lot of Greece in 1915–17.

[2] Vigezzi, *I problemi della neutralità*, pp. 43–4, 65–6.

only one: about 100,000 men in all. Knowing that he had numerical superiority, though he did not appreciate its extent, Cadorna went into action immediately the Italian ultimatum expired, while three Austrian divisions were still on their way from the Galician front. But he achieved little. The enemy's defences were formidable, even if critically under-manned. Cadorna was all too conscious of the weaknesses of his own army. Officers and N.C.O.s were under strength and poorly trained, his artillery was inferior to the Austrian and machine-guns were in dangerously short supply. Only two of his seventeen corps were fully efficient. Such a situa-tion dictated caution, at least until mobilisation was complete.[1] In the first month's preliminary operations the Italians crossed the frontier, pushed in the Austrian outposts and reached the Isonzo everywhere except at Tolmino and Gorizia, where the Austrians retained bridgeheads. But nowhere were the enemy's main defences penetrated. Never again would the Italians have so great a numerical advantage. By the middle of June, when their mobilisation was completed, over twenty divisions had been assembled against them.

Cadorna nevertheless enjoyed a superiority of roughly two to one. Between 23 June and 5 December he launched four offensives on the Isonzo. The river was crossed near its mouth and Italian troops reached the edge of the Carso, a bare, waterless, limestone wilderness. North of Gorizia a small bridgehead was established east of the river at Plava. Many forts were stormed, many mountain tops were seized. The infantry fought with magnificent élan and pertinacity in what proved to be the toughest battles of the whole war.[2] Many leading interventionists dis-tinguished themselves. D'Annunzio at the age of fifty-two volunteered for active service in the trenches. Bissolati was wounded while serving, at the age of fifty-eight, as sergeant in an Alpine regiment. Corridoni died in action as a private on the Carso. Battisti too volunteered, only to be cap-tured a year later and executed as a traitor at Trent. The heaviest losses were borne by the young middle-class volunteers who provided the new officers and N.C.O.s. On the Isonzo, no less than on the battlefields of France, an entire generation was decapitated. But bravery and numbers were not enough. The Italian command had failed to absorb the tactical lessons of the Western front and it was the Italian infantryman, con-fronted for the first time by trenches, barbed wire and artillery barrages, who paid the price. The weight of Italian artillery was pitiful in com-parison with that employed in France. Ammunition had run short even before the first offensive began, and it was to limit every attack in the

---

[1] Cadorna, *La guerra*, I, p. 121.
[2] ibid., p. 156. The casualties in the first seven months were 66,000 killed and 190,000 wounded.

future. Rain and mist repeatedly halted operations. Cholera claimed many victims and almost the last reserves were thrown in. The reward for all these sacrifices was a few kilometres' advance. After seven months of war, Trent and Trieste were still a long way off.

Cadorna soon revealed his merits and shortcomings as commander. Aged sixty-five and member of a Piedmontese family with a long military tradition,[1] he had all the virtues and prejudices of an old-fashioned staff officer. Calm, stubborn, solitary and methodical, he was a fierce disciplinarian[2] and a bad psychologist, but a first-class organiser. In defending his apparent lack of success, he argued that to wear down the enemy was more important than to make territorial advances. But Cadorna's offensives wore down his own army too. For several months in the late winter of 1915–16 it was close to collapse.[3]

The war at sea was equally discouraging. The Italian plan was to harass and sink the enemy fleet. But the Austro-Hungarian navy lurked in its fortified bases, making only small and infrequent sorties. Offensive action was ruled out by the refusal of the heavily committed British and French to venture far into the Adriatic 'viper's nest'. By the spring of 1915 enemy submarines were already operating in the Mediterranean, making the use of large ships hazardous. The great Italian battleships, on which so much money had been lavished before 1914, proved almost useless, and construction of the four super-dreadnoughts was suspended in 1915.[4] The main role of the Italian navy became the enforcement of a blockade across the mouth of the Adriatic, an undramatic task for which it was necessary to construct large numbers of smaller craft. On the sea, therefore, it was as much a war of attrition as on land. Meanwhile on the home front economic hardships multiplied. Throughout the country, among soldiers and civilians alike, the illusion of quick victory vanished. At the end of 1915 Italian morale was low.

Dealings with the new Allies were far from happy. The first difficulty arose in relations with the Serbs, over which the Treaty of London cast an unhappy shadow. All through June the Serbian army remained inactive.

---

[1] His father Raffaele commanded the troops that breached the walls of Rome at Porta Pia in 1870; his son Raffaele commanded the Resistance forces behind the German lines in 1944–5.

[2] He dismissed 27 generals in the first two months of war and another 199 by November 1917. This ruthlessness made him many enemies.

[3] Cadorna, *La guerra*, I, pp. 167–8; Malagodi, I, p. 80. Cyril Falls, in *The First World War* (London 1960), pp. 205–6, describes Cadorna as 'the out and out attritionist of the war', surpassing all the commanders on the Western front, 'and one who always suffered more from attrition than his foe'.

[4] See above, pp. 360, 408 n. 4.

In July an inter-Allied staff conference at Chantilly called for concerted attacks to relieve the pressure on Russia. The Italians made their contribution on the Isonzo, and the British and French attacked in Artois and Champagne in September. But still the Serbs made no move. Their difficulties were great: typhus on the top of heavy battle casualties had reduced their strength by half, and after liberating all Serbian soil from the Austrians in December 1914, the temptation to conserve their strength to meet a likely Bulgarian attack in their rear was irresistible. But fear of Italian landings in Dalmatia also played its part. This Serbian passivity allowed the Austrians to move many thousands of war-hardened troops to the Italian front. Cadorna even suspected that Austria-Hungary and Serbia had reached some secret understanding.[1] Meanwhile the Serbs marched into Albania and seized Tirana, while the Montenegrins occupied Scutari. Sonnino exploded: 'The Serbs would not have acted differently, had they been the allies of Austria', he protested.[2] Combined Allied pressure stopped the Serbian advance, but Sonnino was left in a bitter, uncompromising mood.

The mutual suspicion of Italians and Serbs wrecked Allied attempts to create a solid front in the Balkans. This could be done only by persuading Serbia, Rumania and Greece to reconcile Bulgaria by disgorging some of their gains from the Balkan wars. The Serbs refused to cede territory to Bulgaria (or Rumania) without the promise of compensation in the Yugoslav provinces of Austria-Hungary. Here Sonnino's insistence on the Treaty of London proved decisive; he was ready to see Bosnia go to the Serbs, but refused to discuss Dalmatia or the future of Croatia.[3] The sequel was tragic. On 7 October the Germans and Austrians attacked Serbia. Four days later Bulgaria joined in. Cut off from Salonika, the Serbian army retreated, amidst appalling privations, through the Albanian mountains to the Adriatic. By the end of November all Serbia had been overrun. In January 1916 it was the turn of Montenegro; Lovčen and Scutari fell to the Austrians and northern Albania was occupied. The Greeks and the Rumanians stood by.

Cadorna was not blind to the advantages of inter-Allied solidarity. In the summer he had done his best to relieve the pressure on Russia. His third Isonzo offensive on 18 October was designed to aid the Serbs. At the same time he was ready to send 60,000 men to Salonika,[4] provided they were used for a major Allied offensive in the Balkans. This was

---

[1] Cadorna, *La guerra*, I, p. 107, note. See also Steed, II, pp. 67–8.
[2] Salandra, *L'intervento*, p. 325.
[3] Toscano, *La Serbia e l'intervento in guerra dell' Italia*, pp. 97 ff.
[4] Cadorna, *Altre pagine*, pp. 110–13. Two Allied divisions, evacuated from Gallipoli, had begun to land at Salonika on 5 October, too late to help Serbia.

vetoed by Salandra and Sonnino who, in spite of Allied appeals to help Serbia, opposed any reduction of strength on the Isonzo. But as the Serbian disaster developed and Cadorna's third offensive came to a halt, they changed their minds. When Barrère hinted that British and French troops might be sent to Albania, Sonnino demanded action 'in order that we shall be there as well, if the others go there'.[1] Energetic steps were taken, even though tardily and under Allied pressure, to save the Serbian army. Of the 185,000 troops rescued, 115,000 were evacuated in Italian ships, together with 150,000 civilian refugees, to Italy, Corfu and elsewhere.[2] At Sonnino's instigation, an Italian brigade was landed at Durazzo, but had to be evacuated in confusion at the end of February 1916 when the Austrians attacked. Valona, however, was successfully reinforced and built up into a strong armed camp.

A more serious cause of inter-Allied friction than these Balkan difficulties was Italy's failure to declare war on Germany. Salandra had never revealed that the Treaty of London bound Italy to fight all the enemies of the Entente. Parliament consequently gave its consent to war against Austria-Hungary alone, and on 24 May 1915 only diplomatic relations were severed with Germany. Three days earlier the Italian and German governments had signed a convention which guaranteed the safety of the persons and property of each other's citizens, allowing them to reside and travel freely except in special military zones. There was therefore no internment of Germans in Italy. On Sonnino's insistence, despite prolonged and anguished resistance from Salandra,[3] war was declared on Turkey in August 1915 and on Bulgaria in October; but still not on Germany.[4]

This policy was prompted mainly by fear that a declaration of war would bring large German formations to the Italian front. If there was to be a break, let it come from the other side, so that Germany could be represented to Italian opinion as the aggressor. But the diplomatic risks of this policy were very great. For Britain and France, Germany was the main enemy and the defeat of Austria-Hungary was only a subsidiary objective. Italy's attitude confirmed Allied suspicions that the Italian government wished to fight its own private war and strengthened their temptation to regard the Italian front as a sideshow. Events were soon to prove that British and French tenderness towards Austria was likely to hurt Italy far more than Italian tenderness towards Germany could hurt Britain and France.

[1] Sonnino to Salandra, 18 October. Vigezzi, *I problemi della neutralità*, pp. 49-52, 68-9.
[2] Albertini, *Venti anni*, IV, p. 145.
[3] Vigezzi, *I problemi della neutralità*, pp. 45-8, 66-8.
[4] The presence of German troops in the Trentino in the first months of the war was officially ignored, even though German prisoners were taken.

Many interventionists, notably Bissolati and Albertini, saw the danger and called for 'one war' of unlimited solidarity with the Allies. Towards the end of 1915 Sonnino, too, grew anxious and began to press Salandra to take the plunge. But a majority of the cabinet still shrank from a declaration of war. As a compromise it was decided gradually to increase financial and economic pressure, in the hope of provoking Germany to a rupture.[1] Meanwhile Sonnino himself aggravated Italy's diplomatic discomfort by avoiding too close contact with the Allies. British and French statesmen met frequently, but not until March 1916 could Salandra and Sonnino be persuaded to attend an inter-Allied conference in Paris. Sonnino's dislike of conferences and his pathological aversion to publicity did Italy's cause great harm. The Allies were given no chance to appreciate the magnitude of Italy's war effort[2] and showed little eagerness to provide precious food, supplies and munitions for so eccentric an ally.[3] The Italians in turn felt slighted and isolated.

By the end of the first grim Alpine winter, the striking power of the Italian army had grown greatly. Engineers worked miracles in building defences, roads and cable railways. The number of divisions rose from thirty-five to forty-three. The quantity of guns was doubled, that of lorries trebled and that of machine-guns multiplied sevenfold. The air force expanded, Ljubljana was bombed in retaliation for Austrian raids and D'Annunzio led dramatic flights over Trent and Trieste. But the campaigns of 1916 did not start well. The Germans forestalled coordinated Allied attacks by striking first at Verdun in February. In March Cadorna staged his fifth Isonzo offensive, with negligible results. Conrad had meanwhile been urging the Germans to concentrate on the elimination of Italy by a knockout attack from the Trentino. The German High Command disagreed and attacked at Verdun instead. But Conrad went ahead and planned his own *Strafexpedition*, the blow he had been longing to deliver since 1906.

Cadorna got wind of the enemy's preparations in March but did not attach great importance to them, thinking it unlikely that the Austrians would attack with the Russian menace in their rear. He was also reluctant to upset his own plans on the Isonzo. He did, however, reinforce the Trentino front, so that on the critical thirty-mile sector the opposing armies were roughly equal in numbers. But one-third of Conrad's force

[1] Charles-Roux, *Souvenirs diplomatiques, Rome-Quirinal*, pp. 88–92; Malagodi, I, p. 74.
[2] Albertini, *Venti anni*, IV, pp. 140–9.
[3] Italy was an ally *sui generis*, observed Runciman, President of the British Board of Trade, in May 1916. Albertini, *Venti anni*, IV, p. 302.

was formed of experienced divisions brought from the Eastern front; Cadorna's was largely untried. In many sectors of the line the Italian troops occupied exposed advanced positions which were incapable of resisting a major attack. The Austrians had 2,000 guns to Italy's 850.[1] The battle began on 15 May with an artillery bombardment comparable in weight to those of the Western front. It was the Italian army's first experience of such an ordeal and in the centre it gave way. The battle raged for over a fortnight and the Austrians advanced five to twelve miles. They reached the last crest above the Venetian plain, only eighteen miles from Vicenza, and seemed about to sweep down and roll up the Isonzo armies from behind.

Cadorna rose to the emergency and showed his calibre as a commander. To meet an enemy break-through into the plain, he moved ten divisions from the Isonzo in a fortnight, formed them into a new army and held them ready for a counter-attack. At the same time he threw all his remaining reserves (including two divisions from Albania) into the battle and made preparations for a general retreat behind the Piave. But stubborn resistance made so drastic a step unnecessary. On 3 June Cadorna was able to announce that the enemy advance had been halted all along the line. Next day the Russians, answering urgent Italian appeals, attacked in Bukovina and Galicia and smashed through the Austrian positions. Conrad was forced to abandon his Trentino offensive and transfer three divisions to the east. In the middle of June Cadorna counter-attacked and recovered much of the ground that had been lost. On 9 July he ordered a halt and turned back to the Isonzo.

The *Strafexpedition* shocked Italy into recognition of the true nature of the war. Invasion had become a reality. All the latent discontent boiled up and forced a political crisis, of which Salandra became the victim. Disappointment sharpened interventionist criticism of Salandra's 'limited' war: limited in its lack of solidarity with the Allies, limited in its failure to mobilise the nation's manpower and resources. Italy repeated all the mistakes that Britain and France had made a year earlier. Industrial mobilisation had been proclaimed in July 1915 but most imperfectly carried out. Munitions were still short, in spite of the energy and organising skill of General Alfredo Dallolio, Under-Secretary in the War Ministry. Shortage of ships, aggravated by submarine attacks, and soaring freight charges threatened the supply of food, raw materials and war equipment. Taxation had been raised, but not enough to satisfy the interventionists, and the government had preferred the easier course of borrowing. In short, the problems of a long war had been most inadequately foreseen. Ministers made few speeches and few efforts to inspire the country by

[1] Cadorna, *La guerra*, I, pp. 191–207; *Pagine polemiche*, pp. 130–3.

taking it into their confidence. Salandra had brought Barzilai into his cabinet in July 1915, but this was the only change in his government since declaring war. The censorship made little distinction between the neutralist and interventionist press. The military authorities continued to regard as subversive all soldiers with a republican or socialist past, even if they had volunteered for the front. Mussolini was refused a commission with Salandra's personal assent.[1] Such treatment made all interventionists feel frustrated and left out. On 2 February 1916 Salandra addressed a liberal-conservative meeting at Turin. His theme once again was the need to revive the 'liberal monarchist party, this great party that made Italy and must now complete her', to which the leadership of the country at that moment belonged. Non-liberal interventionists retorted that it was just the liberal mentality which was frustrating the war effort.[2] Nationalists and democrats alike urged an end to this liberal monopoly of the war and called for a national government.

It was also widely known that there was friction between the government and the High Command. Cadorna had a phobia of politicians. Not even the cabinet was informed of his military plans and he ruled the war zone as if it were his own exclusive kingdom. He made no allowances for the parliamentary difficulties with which the government had to contend and repeatedly quarrelled with Zupelli, the Minister for War. In particular he stubbornly opposed the occupation of Albania. After stormy scenes with Sonnino, Albania was removed from his command in December 1915 and placed directly under the War Ministry. Sonnino wanted Italian control extended into the Albanian interior, as a 'pledge' held against the future peace settlement; Cadorna argued that victory on the Isonzo, the vital front, was the only 'pledge' worth having, and sent an ultimatum to Salandra that either he or Zupelli must go. This raised a constitutional issue which was smoothed over only by the intervention of the King. After the forced evacuation of Durazzo, Albania was restored to Cadorna's command, and in April 1916 Zupelli resigned.[3] But during the *Straf-expedition* tempers flared again. Salandra was shaken by Conrad's initial success and appalled by Cadorna's plan to retreat, in the last resort, to the Piave. Such a decision, he maintained, being essentially political, could be taken by the government alone. When Salandra proposed a meeting of ministers and commanders, Cadorna bluntly declared he had no use for 'collective deliberations' or councils of war and insisted that, as long as he enjoyed the confidence of the government, the responsibility for decision was his. So serious did the friction become that the cabinet approved

[1] De Felice, pp. 318–20.
[2] Albertini, *Venti anni*, IV, pp. 62–5; Cilibrizzi, V, pp. 387–8.
[3] Albertini, *Venti anni*, IV, pp. 90–1, 156–68.

Cadorna's dismissal on 30 May; but Salandra could find no competent substitute and shrank from the responsibility.[1]

Parliamentary debates in March and April had shown that Salandra was losing ground. Though most Giolittians 'swallowed the pill' once again and voted for the government, with their absent master's approval, it was clear that the neutralists were growing bolder; the temptation to pay off the old grudge against Salandra would soon become irresistible.[2] When the chamber reassembled at the beginning of June, while the battle was still raging in the Trentino, he was assailed from all sides. A drastic reconstruction of the government might still have saved him. But Salandra had lost confidence. He lacked 'parliamentary spirit' and was proud, inflexible and weary of political wrangles. Moreover he distrusted the democratic interventionists, his most likely allies, fearing that their presence in the government might lead to the subordination of the Italian monarchy to the French republic.[3] In the end he provoked his own fall. In a statement on the Trentino battle, he declared that better prepared defences would have halted the enemy sooner.[4] This view was in fact exactly that of Cadorna; but Salandra's remark, in its context, appeared to be an attack on the high command. Cadorna was the hero of the interventionists, who now decided to be rid of Salandra's 'government of discord'. Many neutralists joined them, yielding at last to temptation, and on 10 June Salandra was defeated by 197 to 158 votes. Thus fell Italy's last purely liberal government.

## The Second Year: War Aims and War Diplomacy

The new Prime Minister was Paolo Boselli, aged seventy-eight, 'father' of the chamber of deputies, selected mainly because his age put him above party.[5] He formed a wide coalition of nineteen ministers: six conservative-liberals, five liberals of the left, two radicals (including Sacchi), two reformist socialists (Bissolati and Bonomi), one republican and one Catholic (Meda).[6] Sonnino remained at the Foreign Ministry, Orlando moved to

[1] ibid., pp. 221–4; Cadorna, La guerra, I, pp. 226–30; Pagine polemiche, pp. 136–41.

[2] Quarant' anni, III, 229–31.

[3] Salandra, Memorie politiche, pp. 5–11. The mutual distrust between Salandra and men like Bissolati was but a modern edition of the distrust between moderates and democrats during the Risorgimento.

[4] Cilibrizzi, V, p. 398; Albertini, Venti anni, IV, p. 240.

[5] Boselli, a Ligurian, had started his political career in 1870 as a deputy of the Right and subsequently held cabinet office under Crispi, Pelloux and Sonnino. His reputation rested on his competence in such matters as finance, foreign trade, education and the merchant navy.

[6] The remaining two were non-political ministers from the services.

the Ministry of Interior and Gaspare Colosimo became, with Giolitti's approval,[1] Minister for the Colonies. The inclusion of a Giolittian element displeased the interventionists, but they were comforted by the exclusion of the uncompromising neutralists and by Bissolati's presence as minister without portfolio. Boselli secured a huge vote of confidence for this 'ministry of concord, for war and for victory'.

At the outset of its career it was strengthened by military success. Between 27 July and 4 August Cadorna sent back to the Isonzo seven of the ten divisions he had removed in May. So rapid and so successfully concealed was this operation that he achieved complete surprise for his sixth Isonzo offensive. On 6 August seventeen divisions of the Duke of Aosta's Third Army attacked eight Austrian divisions in the Gorizia bridgehead. After three days' fighting the powerful fortresses of Monte Sabotino and Monte San Michele had been brilliantly captured, the bridgehead wiped out, the Isonzo crossed and Gorizia itself occupied. Then the pace slowed. The Austrians could not be dislodged from the hills dominating Gorizia from the east and hopes of a break-through died. Nevertheless a strip of ground three miles deep and fifteen miles long had been gained, in an advance which compared favourably with those on the Western front. The military importance of Gorizia was small, but the moral importance of its capture was enormous. It was 'the first great, *authentic* Italian victory', wrote Bissolati.[2] Italian prestige rose abroad and, for the moment, depression on the home front vanished.

During August two steps were taken which went far to reduce suspicion between Italy and the Allies. Firstly, a division was sent to Salonika to take part in the coming offensive which, it was hoped, would coincide with Rumania's long-delayed intervention and eliminate Bulgaria from the war. Sonnino remained unenthusiastic but deferred to Cadorna's opinion that it was unwise for Italy to be absent from a campaign that would settle the future of the Balkans. Secondly, on 28 August, the day following Rumania's intervention, Italy declared war on Germany. This act, for which Sonnino had so long pressed in vain against Salandra's obstruction, had only formal significance. The Italo-German convention of 21 May 1915 had long lost any meaning and commercial relations had been severed in January. Even so, there was still opposition within the cabinet to a complete break, particularly from Orlando and Meda. But Sonnino this time insisted, for he had by now become painfully aware of the perils to which nonconformity with the Allies exposed Italy.

The rest of 1916 was one long series of disappointments. Rumania's intervention, after an internal struggle reminiscent of Italy's 'radiant May',

[1] *Quarant' anni*, III, 232.
[2] Bissolati, *Diario di guerra*, p. 69.

came too late. Germany and Austria-Hungary hit back and by the end of
the year had overrun all but the northern quarter of the country. Bulgaria,
far from being knocked out, was stronger than ever. The offensive from
Salonika, in which the Italian division took part, captured Monastir in
Serbian Macedonia in November, but entirely failed to help the Rumanians.
The Russians were exhausted by their summer offensives and the British
attack on the Somme made little progress. Between 14 September and 3
November Cadorna launched his seventh, eighth and ninth Isonzo offensives on the Carso. Each lasted only a few days, till heavy losses, torrential
rain and ammunition shortage enforced a halt. The maximum advance at
any point was three miles.

The situation of the Allies was not in fact as depressing as it appeared to
be. The enemy also was exhausted. In November 1916 Francis Joseph died.
His successor, Charles, in his first proclamation expressed his longing to
save his empire by ending the war. Some Germans, too, were ready to consider a compromise peace which would leave them in possession of at least
some of their wartime gains. In December the German Chancellor made a
public offer to negotiate and President Wilson asked both sides to declare
their terms of peace. The Allies refused to negotiate with the enemy but
decided to publish a statement of their war aims in reply to Wilson. The
text was agreed at a meeting of the British, French and Italian leaders in
Rome early in January 1917. It included among the Allies' aims 'the liberation of the Italians, as also of the Slavs, Roumanes and Czecho-Slovaks
from foreign domination'.[1] This was a landmark in war diplomacy, even
though all three Allied governments subsequently denied that they had
committed themselves to dismembering Austria-Hungary.

The main purpose of the Rome meeting was to plan the knockout blow
for 1917. A few weeks earlier Bissolati had sounded the British government on a proposal for a major Allied offensive on the Italian front, in
which large numbers of British troops would take part. He argued that the
quickest way to victory over Germany was to knock Austria-Hungary out
of the war. Cadorna supported him, believing that the chances of reaching
points of vital importance to the enemy were greater on his front than
in the west. But Bissolati's motive was as much political as strategic: he
wanted to commit hitherto lukewarm allies to war to the death against

[1] Temperley, I, p. 172. The first draft mentioned only 'Italians, Slavs and
Roumanes'. The 'Czecho-Slovaks' were added later on French initiative, with
British approval. This made nonsense of the text. To talk of 'Slavs and Czecho-
Slovaks' was as absurd as to talk of 'Latins and Italians'. Sonnino, however, would
never have permitted a reference to 'Yugoslavs', so the text was approved at Rome
as it stood. Valiani, pp. 280–2.

Austria-Hungary and to give encouragement to all the subject nationalities of central Europe. Lloyd George, who had just become British Prime Minister, was horrified by mounting casualties on the Western front and was looking for another theatre of war where victory might be won at smaller cost. He came to much the same conclusion as Bissolati: that 'a combined Allied offensive', to which Britain and France would contribute guns and possibly also infantry, should be launched on the Italian front. But when he presented his proposal to the Rome conference, he was stubbornly opposed by the French government and by the British and French generals, who were fanatical 'westerners'. Cadorna vacillated. Sonnino, perhaps fearing the presence of Allied troops in Italy would compromise his aim of a limited 'Italian war', gave the proposal only lukewarm support. As a result it was referred to the military experts and shelved.[1]

This proved the most serious blunder that the Italians committed during the whole war; they threw away the chance of seizing the military initiative and thus forestalling Caporetto.[2] The conference made two minor decisions which assisted Italy: staff plans were prepared for moving troops to Italy from France, should an emergency occur, and a loan of French and British artillery units, 99 medium and heavy guns in all, was arranged. Both Cadorna and Bissolati soon realised what an opportunity had been lost. The latter, who had not been present at the conference, went to Paris and London in February and attended a meeting of the British war cabinet, to plead for the dispatch of Allied divisions to Italy. But Lloyd George explained he was now committed to support of Nivelle's spring offensive in France. Cadorna resigned himself to the inevitable and told Boselli, 'We must rely upon ourselves.'[3] The prospect was not encouraging. Ever since

[1] Colapietra, pp. 239–47; Malagodi, I, pp. 96–108, 163–4; Lloyd George, III, pp. 1432 ff.; Albertini, *Venti anni*, IV, pp. 397–401; Rodd, III, pp. 325–8. Lloyd George and the 'easterners', like their successors in the Second World War, were searching for 'the soft underbelly of Europe'. As Valiani (pp. 266–7) points out, the motives of Bissolati and Lloyd George did not exactly coincide; the latter hoped that victory on the Italian front would force Austria-Hungary into a compromise separate peace. Lloyd George explains Cadorna's coolness by a misguided feeling of professional solidarity with the British and French generals. When Hankey, secretary of the British War Cabinet, went to see Cadorna on Lloyd George's behalf to win his support, he found he had already been 'got at' by Robertson, British Chief of Staff. Hankey, II, p. 608.

[2] After Caporetto, Lloyd George said to Bissolati: 'Neither of us is guilty of this.' Salvemini, *Dal patto di Londra*, p. liii; Malagodi, I, p. 195.

[3] Bissolati, *Diario di guerra*, pp. 73–81; Colapietra, pp. 246–7; Malagodi, I, pp. 110–12, 130–2; Albertini, *Venti anni*, IV, pp. 397–406. After the failure of the Nivelle offensive, Lloyd George again pressed for an Allied offensive in Italy as an alternative to Passchendaele, but could not secure his generals' consent. The Italians vainly appealed for more guns later in the summer. Lloyd George, IV, pp. 2169 ff., 2275 ff.; Hankey, II, pp. 674–7.

the Rumanian collapse, Cadorna had feared that crack German divisions might be diverted to Italy for a second *Strafexpedition*. That possibility was greatly increased by the first Russian revolution of March and the disintegration of the Russian war effort during the summer. Nivelle's offensive meanwhile failed and was followed by mass mutinies in the French army, which remained on the defensive for the rest of the year. The intervention of the U.S.A. in April helped to revive confidence, but it was clear that there would be a long delay before America's weight was felt in Europe.

Allied misunderstandings in the military sphere were closely bound up with diplomatic differences. These covered almost the whole field of war diplomacy and peace aims: the future of Austria-Hungary, the Yugoslav question and the problems of Greece, the Balkans, Asia Minor and the Middle East. Asia Minor was the first to come to the fore. At the time of the signature of the Treaty of London, the British, French and Russian governments had decided not to reveal their recent agreement on Constantinople, but instead to present Italy with a *fait accompli* at the end of the war.[1] Further Anglo-French negotiations led in February 1916 to the Sykes–Picot Agreement, later approved by Russia, which precisely delimited spheres of influence in Asiatic Turkey, reserving Adalia for Italy in accordance with Article 9 of the Treaty of London. In spite of their extreme secrecy, Sonnino got wind of these negotiations and became seriously alarmed. He was determined that Italy should not be left out of any Middle Eastern settlement, as his declaration of war on Turkey in August 1915 had shown. But all his enquiries from the Allies received evasive replies. Full information could not be given, he was told, because Italy was not yet at war with Germany. Immediately after declaring war in August 1916, he enquired again. Further delays made him bitter and impatient. Italy wished to be a loyal ally but was not receiving 'fair play', he protested: 'a thousand times better to remain alone and isolated' than become a protected client. Sonnino warned the British ambassador that if Italy failed to secure the promised 'fair share' in the spoils of the Turkish Empire, he himself would resign and admit publicly that he had been wrong to trust his allies.[2] This threat had some effect. As Barrère pointed out, it was in the interests of the Allies to keep Sonnino, the stubborn interventionist, in power.[3] Grey therefore gave Imperiali the texts of the Constantinople and Sykes–Picot agreements. In December 1916 Sonnino

[1] See above, p. 432.

[2] Sonnino to Imperiali, 17 September 1916, in Aldrovandi, *Nuovi ricordi*, pp. 118–23.

[3] Toscano, *Gli accordi di San Giovanni di Moriana*, p. 139.

adhered to the former, on condition that equilibrium in the eastern Mediterranean was preserved by the satisfaction of Italy's claims. These, as defined by Sonnino in November, comprised the southern third of Asia Minor: not only Adalia, but Smyrna, Konia, Adana and Mersina as well. The claim to Smyrna alarmed the Russians who did not want Italy so close to the Straits; the claim to Mersina and Adana infuriated the French, in whose sphere they lay under the Sykes–Picot Agreement. At the beginning of 1917 the negotiations had reached deadlock.

These wrangles revealed a dangerous spirit of rivalry between Italy and France, which was intensified by friction in Greece. Ever since its formation in October 1915 the Salonika front had been paralysed by the refusal of the Greek King Constantine to enter the war. The leading Greek interventionist was Venizelos, who dreamed of winning a Greater Greece in Asia Minor by adherence to the Allied cause. In October 1916 he rebelled against the King and set up a provisional government at Salonika, which declared war on Germany. But the rear of the Salonika army was still endangered by Greek troops loyal to the King, and Britain and France were driven to the use of force to eliminate their resistance. Sonnino did not want the Greeks to intervene, fearing that Smyrna would be Venizelos's reward.[1] Like San Giuliano before 1914, he regarded Panhellenism, backed by the French, as a major obstacle to Italian expansion in the Mediterranean. He also considered that the ejection of Constantine by the troops of republican France would be an unpardonable offence to monarchical principles. He therefore opposed the use of force in Athens. Meanwhile, partly in order to forestall the Greeks, the Italian occupation of southern Albania was extended and an overland link from Valona to the Salonika front was established.

Asia Minor and Greece were questions of secondary importance for Italy; the future of Austria-Hungary was vital. Over this problem, too, deep differences with the Allies developed. At the end of January 1917 the Emperor Charles made an overture to the French for a separate peace through his brother-in-law, Prince Sixtus of Bourbon, a French subject serving in the Belgian army. He at first received a warm response, particularly from President Poincaré, Italy's old antagonist of 1912. Lloyd George was told in April and was enthusiastic, seeing a chance of eliminating Austria-Hungary by a process much less painful than an offensive on the Italian front. For six months negotiations continued, with Sixtus travelling to and fro between Paris, Switzerland and Vienna. The Austrian proposals were generous, at Germany's and Turkey's expense: Alsace-Lorraine to be restored, Belgium evacuated, Constantinople to be given to

[1] Grey had in fact offered Smyrna to Greece in January and April 1915 during abortive negotiations for Greek intervention.

Russia, even Serbia to have a port on the Adriatic; but no mention of Italy. The integrity of the Dual Monarchy was to be preserved. Poincaré and his Prime Minister, Briand, were inclined to regard the Italian side of the question as of little importance. But in March Briand fell from power. He was replaced by Ribot who saw, as did Barrère, that even to discuss peace on such terms violated the Treaty of London and involved the honour of France. Ribot and Lloyd George hopefully discussed an idea that Italy should accept Smyrna and Cilicia instead of Trent and Trieste. But both realised that loyalty to Italy must come first. On 19 April they met Boselli and Sonnino at St Jean de Maurienne in French Savoy. At the first hint of a compromise peace with Austria, Sonnino exploded. To ask him to give up even the least part of the Treaty of London, he said, was equivalent to asking himself to resign and his King to abdicate. The matter was hastily dropped and a communiqué issued on the inopportuneness of negotiations that might weaken Allied unity.[1] Sixtus was told that no proposal could be considered that did not take Italian views into account. Charles, however, continued sporadic discussions for another eleven months, and in certain French and British circles the illusion persisted that he was prepared to betray his German ally. But for the moment Sonnino's firmness had won. At the end of July Ribot told him the whole story and so cleared the air.[2]

The ostensible purpose of the meeting at St Jean de Maurienne had been to discuss Greece and Asia Minor. Here too, after stormy scenes, Sonnino triumphed. Though he had to renounce Adana and Mersina to France, he obtained the promise of Konia and Smyrna, in spite of tart observations by Lloyd George on the disproportion between Italy's ambitions and war effort. In return Sonnino recognised the Sykes–Picot Agreement and withdrew his opposition to the ejection of Constantine from his throne, provided that the Greek monarchy was preserved. 'We give them a King for Smyrna', remarked Boselli.[3] In June Constantine abdicated, Venizelos

[1] A. F. J. Ribot, *Letters to a Friend* (London 1925), pp. 251–2; Lloyd George, IV, pp. 2004–8.

[2] In order to break down French and British scruples over Italy, Charles alleged that an emissary from the Italian G.H.Q. had offered the German and Austrian ministers in Switzerland a separate peace on the sole condition of the cession of the Trentino and Aquileia. Lloyd George, IV, pp. 2008 ff.; Toscano, *Gli accordi di San Giovanni di Moriana*, pp. 280–3, note 109. The evidence with regard to this episode is still scanty. The Italians do appear to have put out feelers both in Madrid and in Switzerland during the first three months of 1917; but if Charles was referring to these, he was certainly exaggerating their significance. See Valiani, pp. 468–9.

[3] Aldrovandi, *Nuovi ricordi*, p. 159. The decisions reached at St Jean de Maurienne were formalised in the Franco–Italian and Anglo–Franco–Italian agreements of 26/27 July and 18/22 August 1917. For texts, see BFP, IV, pp. 21, note 9, 639–42; Toscano, *Gli accordi di San Giovanni di Moriana*, pp. 340–2.

became Prime Minister and Greece unreservedly entered the war. Sonnino, however, was taking no chances. For some months he had been alarmed at the political activities of General Sarrail, the Allied commander-in-chief at Salonika, who had established a puppet Albanian republic at Koritza under Essad Pasha. On 3 June General Giacinto Ferrero, the Italian commander, proclaimed at Argyrocastro the unity and independence of Albania under Italian protection. This act violated the Treaty of London. Sonnino was forced by British and French protests to explain, very lamely, that the word 'protection' should be interpreted in the dictionary, not the diplomatic, sense, and that Albania's future was still unprejudiced.[1] In the end Sonnino's stubborn defence of Italian interests in Asia Minor was to prove largely in vain. Russia's consent, without which the St Jean de Maurienne Agreement remained invalid, was never obtained. In November 1918, even though Russia had long since dropped out of the war, the British government took refuge behind this failure to declare that all its obligations towards Italy under the agreement had lapsed.[2]

The knowledge that important negotiations were in progress provoked heated debates on Italy's war aims during the spring and summer of 1917. These revealed grave divisions among the interventionists. As the war dragged on, the nationalists grew contemptuous of the limited aims of 1915. The colonialists, impressed by the Allied conquest of most of Germany's colonies, pressed upon Sonnino detailed maximum and minimum programmes for Africa. The maximum programme demanded the cancellation of the tripartite treaty of 1906,[3] in order to give Italy supremacy in Ethiopia; the cession to Italy of Djibouti, British Somaliland, Jubaland[4] and Kassala; and a vast extension of Libya to the south, by the cancellation of the Anglo-French treaty of 1899.[5] The minimum programme involved the cession of Djibouti by the French and Jubaland by the British, and smaller modifications to the boundaries of Libya. The Italian government had no illusions about the difficulties such programmes would cause when presented to the Allies. When Boselli had dropped hints about Djibouti at St Jean de Maurienne, Ribot had retorted that if the matter was mentioned

[1] A. Pingaud, *Histoire Diplomatique de la France pendant la Grande Guerre* (Paris 1937–47), III, pp. 309–12.
[2] Balfour to Imperiali, 26 November 1918, in BFP, VII, pp. 259–60, note 4; DDI (6), I, 451.
[3] See above, p. 362.
[4] The largely uninhabited north-eastern province of Kenya, which however contained a good port at Kismayu and good cotton-growing land in the Juba valley.
[5] See above, p. 209.

again, he would leave for Paris immediately.[1] Sonnino therefore rejected
the maximum programme and said he would attempt to secure the minimum only at the peace conference, 'neither before nor after'.[2]

Sonnino was more sympathetic to nationalist agitation over Asia Minor,
which strengthened his hand in negotiation. The nationalists upbraided
the Allies for their indifference to the needs of Italy, 'the prisoner of the
Mediterranean', and ridiculed their 'hypocritical' concern for the rights of
small nations. Among their most vocal spokesmen was the *meridionalista*
Franchetti, champion of emigration to Africa in Crispi's day. With the
surreptitious encouragement of the Minister for Colonies, Colosimo, he
now devoted his energy to popularising Asia Minor as the ideal outlet for
Italian settlement. In April 1917, just before the St Jean de Maurienne
meeting, he presented to Boselli and Sonnino a memorandum signed by
3,000 senators, deputies, mayors, writers and intellectuals. It set out what
should be Italy's minimum war aims: Trent and Trieste, Istria, Fiume,
Dalmatia and the exclusive military domination of the Adriatic; Djibouti, a
protectorate over Ethiopia and an enlargement of Libya; and all southern
Asia Minor from Smyrna to Alexandretta. Federzoni called it 'the fundamental charter of our rights in the Adriatic and Mediterranean'.[3]

The democrats were shocked by these grandiose proposals. Bissolati,
though he was Sonnino's colleague in the government, had publicly stated
his views in October 1916. The enemy, he declared, was not just Austria-
Hungary but German militarism and all imperialisms. Consistently with
this conviction, he urged Italy to renounce the Dodecanese and all claims
on Dalmatia,[4] in the name of national self-determination. The unlimited,
imperialist war of the nationalists disgusted him quite as much as the
limited, private war of Sonnino. The slogan he adopted was the Mazzinian
*Delenda Austria*; 'the many-headed monster' had to be killed in the
interests not only of Italy but of all the subject nationalities.[5] Three events

[1] A. F. J. Ribot, *Journal d'Alexandre Ribot* (Paris 1936), p. 72, note.
[2] Toscano, *Pagine di storia diplomatica contemporanea*, I, pp. 212–20; R. Albrecht-Carrié, 'Italian Colonial Policy 1914–1918', in *Journal of Modern History*,
vol. 18 (1946), pp. 135–41; Salata, *Il nodo di Gibuti*, pp. 144–56, 264–76. Sonnino's
reluctance to be importunate over colonies was presumably strengthened by the
disastrous situation in Libya. The Senussi, encouraged by German and Turkish
officers, had ardently joined in the *jihad* (holy war) proclaimed by Turkey in July
1915. In February 1916 they attempted to invade Egypt but were defeated by a
British force near Mersa Matruh. In July the British concluded a truce on the basis
of the *status quo*, without any commitment on their part to restore Italian rule in
Cyrenaica. Evans-Pritchard, pp. 134–45.
[3] Cilibrizzi, VI, p. 348.
[4] With the exception of the town of Zara, which was Italian.
[5] Cilibrizzi, VII, p. 8; Albertini, *Venti anni*, IV, p. 357; Colapietra, pp. 233–6.
Bissolati and Supilo had met in Rome in April 1916 and found themselves in com-

of 1917 strengthened his convictions: the Russian democratic revolution, the intervention of the U.S.A. and the growing strength of the Yugoslav movement. In their interpretation of all three Bissolati and the democrats differed fundamentally from Sonnino and from the nationalists; but they felt more certain than ever that the latter were out of step with the political forces which were already beginning to mould a new Europe and a new world.

President Wilson had declared war in April in the name of democracy and the rights and liberties of small nations. Soon afterwards the Russian democratic government called for a revision of Allied war aims and 'peace without annexations or indemnities'. Sonnino was suspicious and disapproving, Bissolati was enthusiastic, in spite of the fact that it was the revolutionary socialists who most eagerly took up the cry in Italy. In June the proclamation of an Albanian protectorate, authorised by Sonnino without reference to the cabinet, provoked the resignation of Bissolati and three democratic colleagues, and only Boselli's strenuous efforts brought about reconciliation and a 'fraternal embrace' between him and Sonnino.[1] Most serious of all was the growing cleavage among the interventionists over the Yugoslav question. The Russian revolution had forced Pašić, who had always leant heavily on Tsarist, Orthodox Russia, to draw closer to the Yugoslav exiles in the west, whose incessant propaganda since 1915 had been winning influential converts in both Britain and France. In July 1917 he and Trumbić signed the Pact of Corfu, the foundation stone of the future united Yugoslav state. Pašić, who in April 1916 had declared that 'Serbia understands and accepts the Italian demand for supremacy in the Adriatic', now repeated in public that 'a close and loyal understanding with Italy' was an essential objective of Serbian policy.[2] Bissolati, true to the concept of 'the last war of the Austrian succession', saw that only friendship between Italy and the Yugoslavs could neutralise the Austrophils in France and Britain. He also believed that after the war it would protect both peoples against resurgent Pangermanism, of which Austria-Hungary was now the mere tool, and give Italy the leadership of the Balkans. In this way Italian security in the Adriatic would be far more effectively ensured than by seizing a precarious foothold on the Dalmatian coast. But Sonnino was deaf to such ideas and boasted in secret sessions of

---

plete agreement. At that time Supilo was being denounced by the nationalists as an Austrian agent. Sonnino did not believe this; he nevertheless refused to see him. Valiani, pp. 258–63.

[1] Bonomi, *Leonida Bissolati*, pp. 180–2; Colapietra, pp. 249, 296; Malagodi, I, pp. 134–9.

[2] Salvemini, *Dal patto di Londra*, p. 70; Mamatey, p. 116; Albertini, *Venti anni*, IV, pp. 540, 544. See also Sforza, *Fifty Years of War and Diplomacy in the Balkans* (New York 1940), pp. 128–9.

the senate that he had refused to negotiate with the 'irresponsible' Serbs.[1]
The Allies were still swithering between nostalgic tenderness for Austria-
Hungary and sympathy for the Yugoslav cause. Whichever their final
decision, Sonnino had contrived that Italy would find itself isolated.

## The Second Year: The Home Front

By the summer of 1917 the home front was under severe strain. Unrestricted submarine warfare, which destroyed 312,000 tons of Italian shipping
during the year, caused acute shortages of vital supplies. Coal imports fell
to half the pre-1914 level and in June some districts of Calabria were
without bread for a week. In the north-west the feverish expansion of
industry attracted large numbers of inexperienced workers to the cities,
so creating intractable problems of health, housing and social welfare.
Sacrifices were inevitable, but the burden was spread unevenly. Attempts
were made in the autumn of 1916 to regulate prices and consumption, but
to little effect. The government was reluctant to introduce the thorough-
going austerity for which the interventionist leaders clamoured. War
profiteers flourished, in spite of higher taxation, and spent their new wealth
ostentatiously in the cities.[2] The industrial workers resented their long
hours (up to sixteen a day), the introduction of compulsory arbitration and
the military discipline and surveillance under which the factories were run.
In 1917 industrial real wages reached a level 27% below that of 1913.[3]
Inflation hit the professional and *rentier* middle class, and above all the
families of soldiers at the front. The peasantry, though less vocal, probably
suffered most. Requisitioning of grain and cattle for the army and the cities
was rigorous. Agricultural wages lagged even further behind the cost of
living than wages in industry. Mobilisation and the needs of industry had
reduced the number of men on the land from 4·8 to 2·2 million. Exemption or release from the armed forces were readily granted to skilled
workmen, but long delays and bureaucratic indifference kept peasant
soldiers far from the land even at harvest time. In spite of this, thanks to
women's efforts, agricultural production hardly fell below 90% of the pre-

[1] Albertini, *Venti anni*, IV, p. 528; Valiani, pp. 374–5. Sonnino and the Foreign
Ministry were still insisting, as in 1915, that Dalmatia was Italian. See, for instance,
Sonnino to Italian ambassador in Washington, 16 April 1917, in Monticone, p. 62,
note; Beneš, pp. 170–2.

[2] Average profits of industrial companies rose from 4·26% to 7·7% between
1914 and 1917. Romeo, p. 85.

[3] The index of industrial real wages (100 = 1913) dropped from 99·7 in 1914 to
93·4 in 1915, 85 in 1916, 73·1 in 1917 and 64·6 in 1918. Neufeld, pp. 363, 540;
Fossati, p. 634. The cost of living index (100 = 1913) rose to 133·9 in 1916, 189·4
in 1917 and 264·1 in 1918. Fossati, p. 631; *Sommario*, p. 172.

war total.[1] But enthusiasm for the war, which had never been great in the countryside, fell decisively during 1917. A steady shift of income from country to town strengthened the peasants' feeling that this was a war made for the exclusive benefit of the cities.

The most thorough in their exploitation of war weariness were the socialists. In 1915 Lazzari, the party's secretary, had coined the slogan 'Neither support nor sabotage'. This was sufficiently elastic to cover both extreme pacifism and humanitarian activity like that of Caldara, Mayor of Milan, on behalf of the Red Cross and soldiers' families. Turati and the moderates were prepared to give cautious approval to certain of the Allies' war aims and argued that if war was bad for the proletariat of any country, defeat would be worse.[2] They looked to victory to accelerate the advance towards democracy and social justice, and so bring partial compensation for the sufferings of the working-class.[3] But the majority of socialists dismissed Turati's arguments with contempt. They merely submitted to war and washed their hands of it, preferring to cut themselves off from the wartime life of the nation. 'Let the bourgeoisie fight its own war,' *Avanti!* declared.[4] As the war lengthened, the moderates lost ground. Strong Italian delegations attended the international socialist conferences at Zimmerwald in September 1915 and Kienthal in April 1916. These denounced the imperialist war, called for immediate peace 'without annexations or indemnities', urged the proletariat to resume the class struggle and proclaimed that only socialism could ensure a lasting peace. At Kienthal several of the Italians supported Lenin's demand for an untainted Third International, to replace the Second which was now 'in Allied pay'. Italian delegates to socialist meetings in Allied countries pressed for a truly international conference at which they could meet their German and Austrian comrades. In parliament no opportunity was lost for urging immediate peace negotiations.

[1] Einaudi, pp. 82–4; Serpieri, pp. 61–9, 94–107.

[2] Malatesta, pp. 111–12. As Turati explained to Orlando's *chef de cabinet*, Camillo Corradini, on 11 May 1917 in a letter of protest against the censorship, he and his friends were trying to convince their party and the working-class that 'this war has changed during its course from black to white . . . From a struggle between two imperialisms it has become, thanks to Russia and Wilson, a struggle against one single imperialism, on the part of one vast democracy.' De Rosa, *Giolitti e il fascismo*, p. 57.

[3] The reformists published their 'Peace and Post-War Programme' in May 1917. Its main items were a republic, abolition of the senate, guaranteed constitutional liberties, election of judges, social insurance, massive land reclamation and public works.

[4] Malatesta, pp. 64–6; De Felice, pp. 260–2, 317. As De Felice points out, this policy of 'clean hands' and waiting upon events, which excluded both the Mussolinian and revolutionary alternatives, amounted to abdication. Its continuation after the war was to cost the party dear.

The Russian revolution in March 1917 strengthened the Italian extremists, even though the Russian provisional government proclaimed its determination to continue the war. Peace seemed nearer, and it was the moderate Treves, Turati's collaborator, who on 12 July uttered the ominous phrase, 'Out of the trenches before next winter.' In September it became known that Lazzari had invited all socialist mayors to consider ways of ending the war by winter; among the methods suggested were mass resignations by socialist councils and the active encouragement of desertion from the armed forces.

Extremism was strongest in Turin, where war had feverishly accelerated the pace of industrialisation and the growth of the city's population.[1] The skilled and militant workers in its motor-car and engineering factories had long looked upon themselves as the élite of the Italian working-class. Before the war the engineering industry's leading trade union, F.I.O.M. (Federazione Italiana Operai Metallurgici), had fought and lost a battle for the recognition of elected workshop committees[2] for the discussion of grievances and working conditions with the management. Since 1915, however, the unceasing demands of the fighting fronts for higher output had strengthened the unions' bargaining power, so that they were able, as the price of their consent to more intensive production, to obtain unofficial recognition of these institutions by the state authorities, though not by the employers. Some of the committees soon came to be dominated by young shop stewards of revolutionary opinions and temperaments. Whereas the older trade union officials were content to use their power to pursue traditional economic objectives, these emergent leaders shared the political ideals of the socialist intransigents who had brought the workers into the streets of the city in May 1915. Inspired by events in Russia, the extremists intensified their militant peace campaign. All forms of participation in the war effort were condemned, even support for such organisations as the Red Cross which they denounced as 'oxygen for the war'. The signs of renewed revolutionary ferment were noted by the prefect of Turin. In November 1916 and again in May 1917 he urged the government to take repressive action; but Rome remained unmoved by his warnings.

The rising discontent caused by inflation, urban overcrowding and maldistribution of essential supplies gave the revolutionaries their chance. The spring of 1917 brought many disturbances, frequently led by women, in Milan, Emilia and other parts of northern Italy. They started as spontaneous protests against the cost of living, but often developed into anti-war demonstrations. 'We are living on a volcano', Turati reported from

---

[1] Between 1914 and 1918 the population of Turin rose from 456,000 to 525,000, and the number of its industrial workers from 75,000 to 150,000. Spriano, *Torino operaia*, p. 142.                              [2] *Commissioni interne.*

Milan on 4 May.[1] Turin was temporarily without bread on several occasions in the first half of 1917. On 13 August it was visited by a Menshevik and Social Revolutionary delegation from the Petrograd Soviet, which was touring Italy to mobilise support for Russia's continuing war effort. At the meeting which Orlando authorised to welcome the visitors, the city's first public meeting since 1915, the extremists among the crowd of 40,000 were able to turn the occasion into an anti-war demonstration, with cheers for Lenin and revolution.[2] In the tension created by this incident, another bread shortage occurred on 22 August. Bread was made available within a few hours, but too late to forestall large-scale public protests which developed spontaneously into peace demonstrations and revolutionary riots. By evening almost all factories had closed down and public transport was at a standstill. The socialist and trade union leaders, taken by surprise, appealed for calm, but never had any control over events. Anarchist groups joined in and added to the violence. Shops were sacked, police stations attacked, two churches burnt down and barricades erected in working-class districts. On the afternoon of the 23rd the army took over. Tanks and machine-guns were brought into action. All attempts by converging columns of workers to march on the city centre were repulsed and by the evening of the 24th order had been restored, at the cost of nearly fifty lives (including three soldiers) and over 800 arrests. Meanwhile the national leaders of the Socialist party and the C.G.L. ignored appeals from Turin to bring the whole country out on strike. Not even Milan stirred. Sporadic incidents occurred in Turin over the next few days, but on the 28th the city was back to normal.[3] The impact upon the country of this week of violence, unplanned though it had been, was enormous. It had revealed the extent of the ferment beneath the surface and seemed to prove that the socialists were capable of more than talk. The shadow of revolution had fallen on Italy.

The church, too, exerted its influence in favour of peace. The majority of Catholics had rallied to the national cause in 1915,[4] though often with reservations. The formula of Dalla Torre, President of the Unione Popo-

[1] R. De Felice, 'Ordine pubblico e orientamenti delle masse popolari italiane nella prima metà del 1917', in *Rivista storica del socialismo*, vol. 6 (1963), p. 474; Spriano, *Torino operaia*, pp. 175 ff., 213–14.

[2] ibid., pp. 225–8. Lenin was at that time in hiding from arrest by the Russian provisional government, which had suppressed the Bolshevik party after a revolt in Petrograd on 16 July.

[3] The best account of the revolt is in Spriano, pp. 235–51. For an eye-witness account by a worker who took part, see Montagnana, I, pp. 44–9.

[4] The main exceptions were a few Austrophil ultra-clericals and Miglioli's pacifist unions, which continued to compete with the socialists for the support of the masses, particularly in the countryside.

lare, was 'All our duty, but no responsibility for the war'.[1] Meda was more enthusiastic. In December 1915 he told the chamber that he was a complete convert to intervention and in 1916 he joined Boselli's government. Meanwhile chaplains served with the army and navy, and high church dignitaries made patriotic speeches. As for the Roman question, most Italian Catholics were content to leave its solution to the Vatican. They were greatly heartened when, a month after Italy entered the war, Gasparri declared publicly that the Pope had no desire to embarrass the Italian government and looked to a solution of the Roman question 'not from foreign arms, but from the triumph of feelings of justice' among the Italian people.

Benedict XV never swerved from this view. Erzberger's schemes of 1915–16 for an independent Vatican State with access to the sea, or for the establishment of the temporal power in Liechtenstein, met with no response in the Vatican. Benedict instead strove hard to improve relations with Italy and insisted that the solution of the Roman question must be found 'in agreement with Italy and with Italy alone'.[2] Nevertheless he made no secret of his regret that 'his beloved Italy' was at war. The shortcomings of the Law of Guarantees had been emphasised by the withdrawal to Switzerland in May 1915 of the German and Austro-Hungarian representatives to the Holy See. Though the Italian government handled the situation with tact and allowed ecclesiastics from enemy countries to visit Rome freely, minor incidents created friction. This in itself was sufficient reason to strive to end the war. Another reason was the desire, still strong in Benedict, to rescue Austria-Hungary from disaster while there was still time. It was therefore from a mixture of motives that, after sounding the German government, he despatched his peace note of 1 August 1917 to all belligerent states. In it he urged them to accept 'a just and lasting peace' without victory and to end the 'useless struggle'. This was 'Zimmerwald language', declared *Avanti!* with enthusiasm. Only two weeks earlier the German Catholic and Socialist parties had passed a peace resolution in the Reichstag. But the Allies refused to discuss the papal note, which they interpreted as a proposal for 'a German peace',[3] while the German government proved unwilling to agree to the most crucial point of all, the restoration of Belgium. The Pope's attempt to 'throw a lifebelt to Austria' thus failed. But the phrase 'useless struggle' in the mouth of the head of the church was remembered and had a profound influence in Italy.

The year 1917 also saw a Giolittian revival. The German peace offer in

[1] De Rosa, *L'Azione Cattolica*, II, p. 423.

[2] Engel-Jánosi, II, pp. 251–3, 262–4; Epstein, pp. 144–50.

[3] Benedict XV was widely believed in Allied countries to be pro-German, mainly because he had refused to publicly condemn German oppression in Catholic Belgium.

December had heartened every neutralist. Twenty-one deputies, mostly Giolittian, urged the government to use its influence with the Allies in favour of negotiation, and withdrew their motion only after a personal appeal by Boselli and an assurance that he shared their views.[1] At the beginning of June the Mayor of Turin attracted attention by referring to Giolitti as 'greater than ever today in the hearts of Italians'. Public indignation forced him to resign.[2] But during the secret parliamentary sittings of the same month, the Giolittians, feeling safe from the interventionist press and the patriotic demagogues, spoke out aggressively. '*Giolittismo* has always been the purest expression of patriotism', the Minister for Colonies, Colosimo, declared.[3] Turati promised his support for any government that would make peace on the basis of the *parecchio* of 1915. For the first time the events of Radiant May were critically debated and the opinion freely expressed that Italy could have fulfilled all its legitimate aspirations by remaining neutral. As the summer wore on, the pressure for an Italian peace initiative increased.

On 13 August Giolitti 'launched his encyclical'[4] at Cuneo, making his first political pronouncement since 1915. After stressing the inequality of sacrifice that war involved, he dwelt on 'the profound changes in the conduct of foreign policy' and the extent of the social and economic reforms that would be needed after victory.[5] The speech was a clear bid for the post-war premiership. It thrilled his old henchmen and roused a warm response from both socialists and Catholics.[6] In October forty-seven Giolittian deputies formed a Parliamentary Union to strengthen parliament's control over the conduct of the war. Its membership soon grew to 110, including several Catholics. The defence of parliament was a favourite theme of the Giolittians, still smarting from their humiliation in 1915, and Cadorna, the proud, authoritarian general who despised politicians, was their bugbear. But the Union was far from reflecting the full strength of those who advocated an early peace. As Russia moved towards collapse and war weariness spread at home, even some interventionists lost heart. Salandra himself believed that the possibility of peace should be carefully explored.[7]

Much of this defeatism could have been cured by military success, but

[1] *Quarant' anni*, III, 242. In conversation with Malagodi on 27 January, Giolitti denied all desire for a separate peace. In his opinion, however, Italy could not stand a third year of war; it was therefore necessary to achieve a quick military success, to be followed by Allied peace negotiations from strength. Malagodi, I, p. 109.

[2] Albertini, *Venti anni*, IV, p. 517; Hautecœur, pp. 42–3.

[3] *Quarant' anni*, III, 246–7.    [4] Hautecœur, p. 42.

[5] Giolitti, *Discorsi extraparlamentari*, pp. 289–91.

[6] Giolitti's speech was made on 13 August; the papal peace note was published on the 15th; the Turin disorders began on the 22nd.

[7] Albertini, *Venti anni*, IV, pp. 576–80.

Cadorna achieved little. A second winter of preparation had greatly strengthened the army. Its margin of superiority over the enemy, though reduced, was still not far short of two to one. Sixteen new divisions had been formed, bringing the total to fifty-nine. The number of medium guns had been doubled and that of heavy guns quadrupled; the 600 machine-guns of 1915 had increased to 8,200. But Cadorna waited until 12 May before launching his tenth Isonzo offensive on the Carso. The infantry advanced over two miles, reaching the enemy's last line before Trieste. But once again bad weather, shortage of shells and formidable defences brought the attack to a standstill. On 4 June the Austrians counter-attacked and forced the Italians almost back to their starting-point. It was the first occasion on which the enemy had thus reacted, revealing a new confidence based on the knowledge that Russia was weakening and reinforcements would soon be available. Equally vigorous counter-attacks wiped out all the gains of a costly operation in the Trentino in June.

On 18 August the eleventh battle of the Isonzo began, the biggest offensive Italy had yet attempted. Cadorna concentrated 51 divisions and 5,200 guns on the fifty miles from Tolmino to the sea. Only 19 Austrian divisions opposed them. The objectives were to wipe out the Tolmino bridgehead, which the Austrians had held since 1915, to make Gorizia secure by capturing the mountains that overlooked it on the east and to push on across the Carso towards Trieste. The operation was further designed to boost morale on the home front and relieve the Russians, now showing signs of collapse after the failure of their July offensive. At Tolmino and on the Carso the Austrians held firm. But in the centre, on the Bainsizza plateau north-east of Gorizia, the Italians advanced up to seven miles on a ten-mile front in a month of concentrated fighting. It was a splendid achievement but it proved a pyrrhic victory. The Austrians were driven to the extreme limit of resistance, but Cadorna still failed to make the decisive break-through. The German High Command decided that drastic action was required to save their allies from collapse.[1] The disintegration of the Russian army gave them their chance. Cadorna, aware that Austrian reinforcements were on their way from the east, ordered his Isonzo armies to dig in and informed the Allies on 20 September that another offensive was out of the question.

Cadorna had for many months been growing alarmed at signs of sinking morale in his troops. For this he threw the entire blame on defeatist propaganda. He did his best to seal off the war zone, inside which he banned thirty newspapers and enforced a rigid censorship.[2] But inevitably the

[1] Hindenburg, *Out of My Life* (London 1920), pp. 283–5; Ludendorff, *Meine Kriegserinnerungen* (Popular edition, Berlin 1938), p. 134.
[2] Cadorna, *Pagine polemiche*, p. 28.

contagion spread from the home front to the trenches. Soldiers went on leave. At home they read *Avanti!*, they met priests who praised the Pope's efforts for peace, they noted with disgust the gay life of the cities, the profiteers and the 'shirkers' in the factories enjoying the war. The number of desertions increased significantly. More serious, units in the front line began to be affected. In June, during the Austrian counter-attack on the Carso, 'ugly incidents had occurred in some units', including unjustified surrenders. In July a mutiny of the Catanzaro Brigade had to be suppressed by force. Cadorna felt compelled to resort to frequent summary executions and death sentences by court-martial, and occasionally even to decimation. But such measures disgusted him when he reflected that it was the politicians, not the misled soldiers, who were to blame. He bombarded the government with urgent warnings and demanded an end to 'an internal policy that was ruinous for the army's discipline and morale'.[1] But the remedy was not so simple. Cadorna, a poor psychologist, refused to admit that defeatist propaganda was effective only because military factors had already depressed morale. Repeated frontal attacks, small gains and high casualties, inadequate army welfare and the prospect of a never-ending war were in themselves sufficient to undermine fighting spirit. By October 1917 the Italian army had lost over 200,000 dead in battle and had still advanced only half the twenty-five miles from the frontier to Trieste. The Bainsizza offensive had been almost the last straw.

Cadorna was not alone in his denunciation of defeatism. The interventionists, in spite of their disagreements over war aims, were still sufficiently united to fight back against the Giolittians and pacifists. All through the summer they had been agitating for an end to the 'byzantine intrigues' of parliamentary 'saboteurs' and 'internal Boches',[2] and for the formation of a small war cabinet, on the British and French models, to intensify the war effort. Their main target was the Minister of Interior, Orlando, whose

---

[1] Letters from Cadorna to Boselli of 6, 8, 13 June and 18 August. See Cadorna, *Pagine polemiche*, pp. 32–44; also Malagodi, I, pp. 215–17. Cadorna reported to the cabinet on 3 November 1917 that on 30 September there were 56,000 deserters from the army at large in Italy, the rate having risen from 650 per month (8 per 10,000 men) in the first year of the war to 5,500 per month (25 per 10,000) between July and September 1917. But over half of these were 'deserters' only in a technical sense, being soldiers who had reported back late from leave but eventually rejoined their units. R. De Felice, 'Ordine pubblico e orientamenti delle masse popolari italiane nella prima metà del 1917', in *Rivista storica del socialismo*, vol. 6 (1963), p. 470

[2] This was Mussolini's name for the socialists, 'clericals' and Giolittians. He referred to Frassati as 'the Prussian senator'. Mussolini, IX, pp. 21–2, 243–8. There was much talk at this time in extreme interventionist circles of a military *coup d'état*, but secret overtures to Cadorna met with no response. De Felice, pp. 349–50.

appeasement of the socialists and excessive concern for constitutional liberties they attributed to a petty preoccupation with vote-catching for the next election.[1] Orlando argued in reply that in a free country such episodes as the Turin riots were the inevitable price of liberty. His aim was to narrow the gulf between neutralists and interventionists and he refused to accept the latter's claim to a monopoly of patriotism. As one of his supporters, Nitti, put it, it was by persuading your opponents, not by suffocating them, that the unity necessary in war was obtained. Boselli approved of this attitude and took little notice of Cadorna's memoranda or of civilian critics. A majority of the cabinet, including Sonnino, believed no other policy was open to it, given its dependence on a parliament that was still Giolittian at heart; the neutralists were strong, so they must be humoured.

By the autumn of 1917 the patience of the interventionists was exhausted. The government's inefficiency on the home front had become intolerable. The friction with the High Command threatened to cause paralysis and relations with the Allies still fell far short of the 'sacred union' that was necessary for victory. Boselli, for all his patriotic eloquence, was too old and weak to be prime minister in war. The cabinet was divided and unwieldy. Big demonstrations in Rome and Milan in September called for a new team. The government began to stir itself. Orlando was forced to dismiss the director-general of public security and some senior officials of his ministry, for whose heads the interventionists had long been clamouring.[2] Stiffer penalties were enacted for defeatists and subversive propaganda. Turin was declared a 'war zone' and placed under tighter military control. But this was too little and too late. When the chamber met on 16 October, the neutralists and socialists pressed their demands for an early peace. The interventionists, encouraged by the Bainsizza victory, inveighed against the government's toleration of licence. Bissolati caused a tumult by shouting to his former socialist comrades, 'For the defence of the country,

[1] Orlando claimed that Italy had had fewer strikes or internal disturbances than any other belligerent country; the Turin riots were an exceptional and isolated incident. For Orlando's retrospective defence of his internal policy, see *Memorie*, pp. 15, 47–67, 507–21. He was constantly compared by his critics to Malvy, the 'defeatist' Minister of Interior in France, just as Giolitti was compared to Malvy's friend and former patron, Caillaux. Malvy resigned on 31 August 1917 and a new French government began to take the widespread defeatism in hand. Both Malvy and Caillaux were arrested. The Italian interventionists envied the French their energetic government, especially after Clemenceau became Prime Minister in November. Caillaux had visited Rome in December 1916 to promote his idea of a Latin separate peace. One of his Italian associates, the ex-deputy Cavallini, was later tried for treason.

[2] They included Orlando's own *chef de cabinet*, Camillo Corradini, who had been using his long-standing friendship with Turati not, as the interventionists alleged, to promote sedition, but to assist Turati in weaning the Socialist party from it. De Rosa, *Giolitti e i fascismo*, pp. 43 ff., 53 ff.

I would open fire even on you.' Nitti, making a bid for return to high office, appealed for national unity, an efficient war cabinet, coordination of the home and fighting fronts, and unreserved solidarity with the Allies.[1] In a conciliatory and statesmanlike speech, which marked him as Boselli's most likely successor, Orlando combined exhortation to a greater war effort with renewed concern for liberty. 'Liberty to betray, to sabotage – no never', retorted Mussolini next day.[2] On 25 October Boselli was brought down by 314 votes to 96, interventionists and Giolittians combining as in June 1916. The previous evening the Minister for War had ended a eulogy of the army with the words, 'Now let the attack come; we do not fear it.' He did not know that the enemy had already broken through.[3]

## Caporetto

The final collapse of Russia in October 1917 threatened Italy with the situation which the military conventions of 1915 had been designed to prevent: the concentration of the entire Austrian army on the Italian front. Worse than this, the German High Command had at last agreed to what Conrad had pleaded for in vain for two years. Seven picked German divisions were sent to the Isonzo, together with eight more Austrian divisions, raising the total on that front from twenty-one to thirty-six. One thousand extra guns were added. Fifteen divisions of this formidable force were concentrated on the northern Isonzo, between Plezzo and Tolmino, hitherto a quiet sector, where four Italian divisions of poor quality were thinly spread in weak defences over thirty-three miles, with only two divisions in reserve. Thus, for the first time in Italy, the enemy obtained numerical superiority on the selected sector. The aim was to break through with overwhelming force, roll back the whole front to the Tagliamento and destroy Italy's offensive power for an indefinite time.

Cadorna was not prepared for a major attack. His chief concern was the simultaneous onslaught on the Isonzo and Trentino fronts which he expected only in the spring. His defensive precautions were therefore inadequate. On 10 October he decided to reduce his forces on the Bainsizza plateau and ordered all heavy artillery back across the Isonzo, leaving only covering troops east of the river. But even these orders for a partial defensive were imperfectly carried out, thanks to the insubordination of some

---

[1] Monticone, pp. 119–32. Nitti had been a leading Giolittian in 1911–14 but supported intervention while deploring its manner. His concept of a democratic war of survival against German militarism put him closer to Bissolati than to Sonnino. During the summer of 1917 he had visited the U.S.A. as member of an official economic and financial mission, an experience which had enhanced his reputation.

[2] Mussolini, IX, p. 297.

[3] Cilibrizzi, VII, pp. 54–64; Albertini, *Venti anni*, IV, pp. 584 ff.

of his commanders who had set their hearts on a counter-offensive.[1] On
21 October Cadorna got details of the enemy's plans from deserter Rumanian and Czech officers, but even this did not induce him to change his
dispositions. As in May 1916, he was taken by surprise. The attack caught
him with thirty-seven of his divisions concentrated in the south towards
the sea.

At 2 a.m. on 24 October the artillery bombardment started and at 8 a.m.
the infantry moved forward. Fog helped to conceal the enemy's movements. Using new tactics of deep infiltration, the German assault troops
moved along the valleys, leaving Italian positions in the mountains untouched. By 4 p.m. they had smashed through four defence lines and were
in Caporetto, seventeen miles behind the original front, still driving south
and cutting the communications of the Italians left on the Isonzo as they
went. Many Italian formations on the flanks of their advance abandoned
good positions without a shot, well-placed artillery remained mysteriously
silent and troops in the rear, suddenly finding themselves in the middle of
a battle, panicked. A gap twenty miles wide divided the Italian army in
two. The enemy themselves were astonished by their low casualties and
the speed of their advance. All Italian attempts to re-establish a continuous
line failed. After two days of confusion and indecision, Cadorna ordered a
general retreat to the Tagliamento at 2.30 a.m. on the 27th. That day the
Germans reached the plains at Cividale. On the 28th Udine, till then
Cadorna's G.H.Q., fell. The Duke of Aosta's Third Army carried out a
successful disengagement on the Carso and moved back in good order.
But some units of the Second Army, withdrawing from the Bainsizza and
Gorizia, threw away their arms and surged back apathetically in an un-
disciplined mob, shouting for peace. Roads and bridges were jammed,
traffic control broke down, and 400,000 civilian refugees completed the
chaos. By 31 October the Italian army was behind the Tagliamento. But
it had been given too little time to prepare defences. On the night of 2/3
November the enemy forced the river. The Germans inspired panic where-
ever they appeared. More units of the Second Army dissolved, their one
thought being to get home. On the 4th, after another two days of indecision,
Cadorna ordered a further withdrawal to the Piave. By now some measure
of order had been restored and the second phase of the long retreat went
more smoothly. By 9 November it was complete.

[1] Notably Luigi Capello, the impulsive commander of the Second Army, who
had won fame by his Bainsizza success. Such was his prestige that Cadorna appears
to have been reluctant to give him uncongenial orders. Albertini, *Venti anni*, V,
pp. 115–16. There were also serious weaknesses in the structure of the High Command, which made it difficult for Cadorna to ensure compliance with his orders.
P. Pieri, *L'Italia nella prima guerra mondiale*, in N. Valeri (ed.), *Storia d'Italia*
(Turin 1960), IV, pp. 722–4.

Under the shock the High Command had for a time broken down and lost all touch with the battle. But Cadorna himself quickly recovered his nerve. As in June 1916, he showed himself at his best in adversity. He knew that the Piave position, Italy's main line of defence since 1866, was strong.[1] Even so, if the enemy should attack simultaneously from the Trentino and from the east, Cadorna believed that a further fifty-mile retreat to the Adige–Mincio line might be necessary.[2] Fortunately the dreaded attack from the Trentino never came. Nevertheless the military situation at the beginning of November was grim. The Italians had lost 10,000 killed, 30,000 wounded and nearly 300,000 prisoners since 24 October. In addition 350,000 men had reached the Piave without arms or simply melted away. Three thousand guns, 300,000 rifles and vast quantities of equipment had been lost. The seventy-mile retreat had presented the enemy with a whole region of Italy and a million and a half inhabitants. Venice was now only fifteen miles from the front line. Four hundred thousand refugees had to be housed and kept alive.

The gravity of the military defeat was eclipsed by the political significance it acquired. For this Cadorna himself was largely to blame. On 28 October he had issued a communiqué which started: 'The failure to resist on the part of units of the Second Army, which cravenly withdrew without fighting or ignominiously surrendered to the enemy, has allowed the Austro-German forces to break through our left flank on the Jiulian front.' The text had been previously approved by Bissolati and the Minister for War. When it reached Rome, it was at once watered down for home consumption, but it was too late to prevent its publication abroad. Whatever Cadorna's motive, and in spite of his reference later in the same communiqué to 'the valiant efforts' of other units, the phrase was interpreted as an attempt to exculpate himself at the expense of his own troops. Nor did Cadorna try to conceal his conviction that 'the internal enemy' and the civilians were the real culprits. A bitter controversy started over whether the collapse had been military or political. In fact it was both.[3] Military

---

[1] Its defences had been strengthened during 1916–17.

[2] The extent of Cadorna's pessimism is revealed by his letter of 3 November to Orlando, in the last paragraph of which he hinted that the situation was so serious that it required other than military measures. This was interpreted by some, including Orlando himself, as advice to seek a separate peace. E. Caviglia, *Le tre battaglie del Piave* (Milan 1935), pp. 4, 271–3; Orlando, *Memorie*, pp. 266–9, 501–3.

[3] Cadorna and Bissolati both used the phrase 'military strike'. All observers agree that there was no spirit of rebelliousness in the retreating mob. In the words of one eye-witness, Amendola, the soldiers gave the impression of 'people returning home at last after a long job of work, laughing and chattering, or of a festive, good-humoured strike'. Malagodi, I, pp. 179, 184, 193–4, 223–4; Orlando, *Memorie*, pp. 230–2. They naively imagined that this was the way to end the war, and there were shouts for peace, the Pope and Giolitti.

blunders helped the enemy's initial success. Once the break-through had occurred, the full extent of the Italian army's exhaustion became apparent and the strategical shape of the Italian front dictated a big retreat. The unhealthy political atmosphere and widespread defeatism turned it into a rout.[1] The unhappy state of the Italian army was not unique. If the Germans had attacked the French army in the previous summer, when it was paralysed by mutinies, France would have had its Caporetto. But the French successfully concealed their plight. Cadorna advertised his army's failings to the world and obscured the fact that the majority of his soldiers had done their duty. Defeat once again, as in 1866 and 1896, revealed Italy's political and military weakness. 'From the day that we entered the war', wrote Cadorna in retrospect, 'there was a potential state of Caporetto.'[2]

Late on 24 October Cadorna had appealed to the British military mission for assistance.[3] The immediate response was cool. The Allies had always underestimated the danger on the Italian front[4] and both Foch and Robertson, the British Chief of Staff, believed Cadorna had more than sufficient troops to hold the attack. But two days later, after more appeals, the French and British governments realised that action was necessary. On 28 October French troops began to move by rail to Italy. On the 30th Foch and Robertson arrived at Cadorna's G.H.Q.

The military crisis had meanwhile accelerated the formation of a new government under Orlando. It took office on 30 October. It was ironic that, in the moment of defeat, the man believed by many to be responsible for that defeat should be given the direction of the war. Orlando's claim to power rested on his parliamentary skill and his wide political contacts in both neutralist and interventionist camps. Nitti, who had been the Giolittian candidate for the premiership but whose appointment had been vetoed by Sonnino, became Minister of the Treasury and the government's second personality. The interventionists felt misgivings about an Orlando–Nitti cabinet, but they were comforted by the fact that it contained no pure neutralist and by the presence of Sonnino and Bissolati as guarantees of the will to victory. All in all, it seemed to them as good a government as could be expected in a deplorable parliamentary situation.

[1] Cadorna's widow and son, General Raffaele Cadorna, in their preface to the posthumous *Pagine polemiche* (p. xi), rightly compare Caporetto with the fall of France in 1940.
[2] Cadorna, *Pagine polemiche*, p. 62. See also Albertini's stern verdict on Italy's ruling class, in *Venti anni*, V, pp. 167–74.
[3] Edmonds, p. 58.
[4] When Cadorna suspended his offensive in September, the Allies immediately decided to remove almost all the guns they had lent him earlier in the year.

One of the government's first acts was to dismiss Cadorna. Orlando had made this a condition of his acceptance of the premiership. Quite apart from Cadorna's responsibility for Caporetto, Orlando insisted that harmony between the government and the High Command, which was essential for the effective conduct of the war, would never be achieved while Cadorna remained.[1] Even had Orlando wished to retain his old antagonist, Allied pressure would have been hard to resist. Foch and Robertson had been shocked by the chaotic state of the Italian G.H.Q. and Lloyd George doubted if Italian morale would ever recover without a change of command.[2] On 5 November the British, French and Italian leaders met in council at Rapallo. Orlando's resolution left nothing to be desired: he declared he would 'resist, whatever the cost, even at the cost of retreating to my own Sicily'.[3] But he demanded fifteen Allied divisions to save Italy. Wrangling followed on the question of command. Foch wanted a single Allied command, with himself as Commander-in-Chief, to cover the whole of the Western and Italian fronts. The British generals, who had long been resisting this idea in France, joined the Italians in opposing it; but they were no more anxious than the French to put divisions of their own under Italian command, as Orlando and Sonnino insisted. The Allies made their help conditional on the dismissal of Cadorna, whom it was agreed to appoint as Italian permanent military representative on the new Supreme Inter-Allied War Council at Versailles.

The Rapallo meeting left many vital questions undecided. On 8 November Victor Emmanuel summoned the French and British statesmen to Peschiera. There, in a long speech in fluent English, he removed many doubts and impressed Lloyd George by his 'calm fortitude' and his confidence that the Piave would be held.[4] In the end six French and five British divisions were sent to Italy. Their commanders received orders to collaborate with the Italians to the utmost but retained their independence, being instructed to refer to their governments if requested to carry out any operation that might 'unduly endanger the safety' of their troops.[5] Their arrival greatly boosted Italian morale, but at first, against Cadorna's wishes, they were kept back in reserve in case there should be another break-through. The credit for holding the enemy on the Piave was therefore

---

[1] Orlando, *Memorie*, pp. 227–30, 239–41, 289–90.
[2] Lloyd George, IV, pp. 2308 ff.
[3] Aldrovandi, *Guerra diplomatica*, p. 142; Lloyd George, IV, p. 2321.
[4] ibid., p. 2325. Orlando asserts (*Memorie*, p. 269) that, with the unique exception of the King, *all* had doubts, in varying degrees, about the army's capacity for resistance. Mussolini told his sister that he wanted to die. Franchetti, Sonnino's old friend and admirer, committed suicide. Even Bissolati momentarily despaired and contemplated doing the same. De Felice, pp. 365–6, 392.
[5] Edmonds, pp. 94, 425.

entirely Italian. 'Death, not retreat', Cadorna had proclaimed in his last order of the day. His army rose to the appeal.

Cadorna's successor was Armando Diaz, a general unknown to the public. He was a competent, cautious soldier, with long experience on the staff and a good record as corps commander. Less stubborn and angular than Cadorna and eleven years younger, he was able to work in complete harmony with the government. The King and Orlando had selected him with that expectation and their choice was fully justified.[1]

On 10 November, the day after Diaz assumed command, the enemy attacked with a numerical superiority greater than on the Isonzo: 50 divisions against 33, 4,500 guns against 3,200, and Diaz had virtually no reserves. The battle was long and grim. Some ground was lost in the mountains to the north and the Piave was crossed near the sea, but after ten days all bridgeheads had been wiped out. The fiercest fighting took place in the centre on Monte Grappa, the hub of the new line where it left the Piave to swing westwards into the mountains. Fortunately the Austrians and Germans also had their difficulties: rations were short, casualties had been high, some of their troops were almost in rags and communications to the rear were overstrained. Diaz reorganised shattered units and sent them back into the line, and at last, after many vain appeals,[2] he was given command of three British and three French divisions. The number of battalions in action thus grew in a month from 423 Italian to 552 Italian and 86 Allied. Confidence slowly returned. Diaz had decided from the outset that the Piave must be held, but he also ordered defences to be prepared on the Mincio–Adige line. When the enemy launched a second major attack on 4 December, for a moment he wavered and talked of withdrawal.[3] But in the critical sector the Italians, though they lost ground, held on. On Christmas Day the fighting subsided and the enemy gave up the attempt to break through. The Germans had already withdrawn three divisions in November and the other four followed early in January. Italy had survived the worst danger. But it was to be ten months before the army regained sufficient confidence to resume the offensive.

Under the shock of Caporetto the home front, too, rallied. Italian soil had been invaded. 'It is really our war now', wrote Croce. The Vatican's *Osservatore Romano* proclaimed the Italian Catholic's duty to resist. Public prayers were offered, no longer for a just peace but for victory. Even among

[1] Orlando, *Memorie*, pp. 229–30, 254, 312–13. Diaz was also recommended strongly by his fellow southerner, Nitti, who knew him personally. Monticone, pp. 142–3, 263. According to Hankey, II, p. 724, Foch and Robertson wanted the Duke of Aosta, but he was rejected 'for dynastic reasons'.

[2] Orlando, *Memorie*, pp. 244–7, 271–2.

[3] Edmonds, pp. 111–12.

the socialists, faced now, like their French and German comrades in 1914, with a conflict of duty, there were stirrings of patriotism. Moderates like Turati, Treves, Prampolini and Rigola declared that socialism was not 'a doctrine of cowardice' and preached national resistance as the essential preliminary to a just peace.[1] When parliament met on 14 November, the proceedings were limited by agreement to patriotic appeals by Orlando, Prampolini and four former prime ministers, Giolitti, Luzzatti, Salandra and Boselli. For a time national unity was almost achieved.[2]

As the immediate danger passed, however, the old disharmony crept back. In December the interventionist groups, ever vigilant, formed a Parliamentary Fascio for National Defence, to combat defeatism and keep the government from flirting with the Giolittian Parliamentary Union. From the first its democratic element was overshadowed by the nationalists. It had soon recruited 158 deputies and 92 senators, under the vigorous leadership of Pantaleoni.[3] In their turn the Giolittians exerted themselves to rescue Orlando from the 'warmongers', Bissolati and Sonnino. During secret sittings of the chamber in December, there was bitter recrimination. Meanwhile the news of the Russian Bolshevik revolution on 7 November had fired the socialist rank and file. The Caporetto crisis, like the crisis of 1914–15, found the party divided and impotent. But under pressure from below, the left wing felt impelled to intensify its opposition, if only verbal, to the imperialist war. In parliament its spokesmen extolled Lenin for his armistice of 2 December with the Germans and called for Italy to follow his example. Even the moderate Emanuele Modigliani, carried away by the news from Russia, boasted that revolution was near. The tactics of the Giolittians were more complex. After Caporetto many of the fainter-hearted interventionists looked to Giolitti with new respect. The latter had, to the joy of his friends, come to Rome for the first time since May 1915. But he had no desire to undermine the government. Nor, as he declared in parliament, had he ever favoured, nor did he intend to favour, a separate

---

[1] Cilibrizzi, VII, pp. 159–62; Malatesta, pp. 159–65.

[2] Giolitti's speech, however, with its emphasis on the government's 'fearful responsibilities' and the need for rapid, drastic action (*Discorsi parlamentari*, III, p. 1698), seemed 'sybilline and cold' to Albertini. *Venti anni*, V, pp. 36–7.

[3] It included Salandra, Martini, Enrico Corradini, Federzoni and Bonomi. Its more extreme supporters, such as Mussolini, demanded dictatorship, the 'iron fist' against saboteurs and pacifists, and the shutting down of parliament. On the fringe of the Fascio were a number of ultra-patriotic conspiratorial groups, some of them with military connexions. De Felice, pp. 370–6, 386–91, 397–400. Pantaleoni had become a nationalist by 1914, in spite of his anti-colonialist convictions in Crispi's day. He had decided that socialism was a greater evil than protectionism, though he never renounced his faith in free trade. In 1916–18 he was a regular contributor to the extreme nationalist *La Vita Italiana*, which became the mouthpiece of the Fascio. Pareto, *Lettere a Maffeo Pantaleoni*, III, pp. 174, 190.

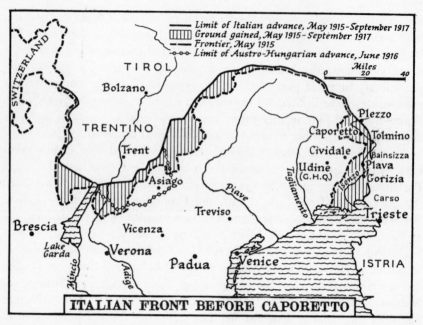

Limit of Italian advance, May 1915–September 1917
Ground gained, May 1915–September 1917
Frontier, May 1915
Limit of Austro-Hungarian advance, June 1916

Miles
0        20        40

SWITZERLAND

TIROL

Bolzano

TRENTINO

Trent

Asiago

Plezzo

Caporetto

Tolmino

Cividale

Bainsizza

Udine
(G.H.Q.)

Plava

Gorizia

Carso

Piave

Tagliamento

Isonzo

Treviso

Trieste

Brescia

Vicenza

Lake
Garda

Verona

Padua

Venice

ISTRIA

Mincio

Adige

**ITALIAN FRONT BEFORE CAPORETTO**

Frontier, May 1915
Front line, November 1917–October 1918

Miles
0        20        40

SWITZERLAND

TIROL

Bolzano

TRENTINO

Trent

Monte
Grappa

Vittorio
Veneto

Udine

Caporetto

Asiago

Montello

Piave

Tagliamento

Isonzo

Gorizia

Brescia

Vicenza

Treviso

Trieste

Lake
Garda

Verona

Padua
(G.H.Q.)

Venice

ISTRIA

Mincio

Adige

**ITALIAN FRONT AFTER CAPORETTO**

peace.[1] Nevertheless he and his supporters had serious doubts about the conduct and purpose of the war. For the moment, with the enemy on Italian soil, they held their hand and responded, though without enthusiasm, to the appeals for solidarity with the army. Orlando's policy was 'Resist, nothing but resist', and the chamber approved it on 22 December by 345 votes to 50. Orlando was not averse, however, to judicious appeasement of the neutralists. Cadorna's disgrace provided one such occasion. In January a parliamentary commission was appointed to enquire into the causes of the defeat.[2] Soon afterwards Cadorna was recalled from Versailles and placed on the retired list. Orlando was as anxious as anyone to prove that Caporetto had been a purely military collapse.

Politics thus continued. But the shock of Caporetto had a lasting effect upon the war effort. Orlando proved a good prime minister and handled his cabinet well.[3] For the first time the economic and social problems of the war were tackled systematically. The main credit for this was Nitti's. For months before his return to office he had been pressing for the mobilisation of all Italy's economic and human resources, their rational allocation between the home and fighting fronts and their unreserved commitment to the common Allied cause. He saw this as a matter of life and death; not only victory was at stake, but Italy's chances of a prosperous, democratic future. In his view it was impossible to get out of the war, because without the help of its allies Italy would be unable to live; peace could therefore be attained only by united resistance, the alternative being the Russian way of hunger, ruin and disintegration.[4] Now Nitti had his chance to put his ideas into effect. As Minister of the Treasury he set out to be the coordinator and supervisor of the whole economy, working to ensure that

[1] Giolitti, *Discorsi parlamentari*, III, p. 1699; see also Malagodi, I, pp. 188, 196–7. Not all Giolitti's supporters, however, were so clear-sighted or scrupulous. As Malagodi told him, 'You are not a Giolittian.'

[2] The commission published its report in 1919. It substantially supported the theory that the generals, not the politicians, were to blame and severely censured Cadorna and Capello. The former felt justifiably bitter at his disgrace, particularly when he compared it with the fulsome praise poured upon Diaz after victory, and resented the implication that Italy had achieved nothing between 1915 and 1917. It was not until 1925 that he received the recognition to which he was entitled, when Mussolini made him a marshal.

[3] 'At last we are a government because we have a prime minister, that is, a co-ordinator', Bissolati told Malagodi in January. Malagodi, II, pp. 247, 261.

[4] Monticone, pp. 159–60, 185; Malagodi, I, p. 206. Nitti's vision of Italy's future, which he had formed while out of office in the early years of the war, was that of a modern industrial democracy, developed by foreign and especially American capital, and fully integrated, politically and economically, in the western world. His experience with the mission to the U.S.A. in the summer of 1917 had confirmed him in these views.

victory did not compromise but strengthened Italy's economic prospects. His constant interference in his colleagues' departments was much resented[1] and in May 1918 provoked a cabinet crisis, ending in the resignation of Dallolio and Riccardo Bianchi, Ministers of Munitions and Transport. But these faults were far outweighed by his success in organising the economy for war.

The first task was to obtain an accurate picture of Italy's economic position and needs. Sinkings by submarines, shipping delays caused by the convoy system, the loss of vast stocks during the retreat and a bad harvest in 1917 combined to create an acute crisis. To feed the country it was necessary to import an absolute minimum of 250,000 tons of wheat per month; in October only 70,000 arrived, in November 136,000 and in December 140,000. The minimum monthly requirement of coal was 690,000 tons, but in November and December under 500,000 were landed. In all 1,440,000 tons of food, coal and materials were needed every month to keep the country going, and Italy had ships sufficient to carry less than one-quarter. These figures were worked out by Nitti and Silvio Crespi, a Milan cotton manufacturer whom Orlando had appointed Under-Secretary for Supplies and Consumption, and handed to the Allies.[2] For the first time the latter acquired a clear picture of Italy's needs. They found it shocking. Thanks to importunate begging and what Nitti called 'leonine courage' in telling the ugly truth, a large gift of wheat was secured from British army stocks in France, and on 22 December Crespi was proudly able to assure parliament that Italy had food for thirty days.[3] Few had realised that the margin was so narrow.

Italy now played a full part in the many inter-Allied economic organisations that came into existence. Efficient shipping control ensured Italy a fair share of transport and by the end of 1917 the convoy system had overcome the worst of the U-boat danger. Top priority was given to food. In January Crespi warned a cabinet committee that bread had run out in many parts of the south and that hunger might bring revolution within one or two months.[4] But his fears proved unfounded. The necessary supplies arrived and after February 1918 no major food shortage recurred. The fuel shortage was less easily remedied. An inter-Allied agreement in February 1918 promised delivery of the monthly minimum of 690,000 tons of coal.[5] To supplement this, Nitti promoted an ambitious development of Italy's lignite resources. But imports fell far short of promises. The coal

---

[1] 'The Minister of the Treasury can, by reason of his office, have a bit of a say in everything. And even if I did not have the right to do so, I would have the duty', Nitti wrote to Diaz on 16 December. Monticone, p. 264.

[2] Crespi, pp. 14, 27–8; Edmonds, pp. 119–20.

[3] Crespi, pp. 17–18, 21–2; Malagodi, I, p. 233.

[4] Monticone, pp. 173–6.                                      [5] Crespi, p. 54.

crisis, with consequent congestion of ports and railways and dislocation of industry, persisted until well after the end of the war.[1]

Crespi meanwhile tackled the problem of distribution. Bread and, in the large towns, meat, sugar, fats and olive oil were rationed; sweets were prohibited and two meatless days a week were instituted. Coal was reserved for war industry and civilian train services drastically cut. In a country where the standard of living was already so low, it was impossible to make much reduction in consumption.[2] But price control was tightened and heavy penalties inflicted on hoarders of grain and black marketeers. At the cost of creating a complex new bureaucracy, the state gradually established a monopoly of the purchase and distribution of the necessities of life.

On taking over the Treasury, Nitti found the financial situation to be even more critical than he had feared. In 1916–17 revenue covered less than one-quarter of expenditure.[3] He decided that shock tactics were necessary. Against the advice of the bankers, who predicted failure, he launched a fifth war loan in January 1918 with a target of 6,000 million lire and himself toured the country to publicise it in a series of patriotic appeals. It was a triumphant success, raising 6,245 millions in two months.[4] Fortified by this success, he was able to turn with greater confidence to the Allies for help with a huge and growing deficit in the balance of payments. The war had cut off most of Italy's foreign markets and forced both agriculture and industry to concentrate on domestic needs. Income from tourists and emigrants' remittances had vanished. As a consequence the proportion of Italian imports covered by exports fell from 63·8% in 1907–13 to 36·4% in 1916, 23·4% in 1917 and 20·6% in 1918.[5] Over half the deficit was accounted for by Britain and the U.S.A., the two main sources of war

---

[1] Coal imports totalled 5 million tons in 1917 and 5·8 in 1918, compared with 10·8 in 1913 and the Allied promise of 8·3. *Sommario*, p. 160.

[2] The *per capita* annual consumption of certain staple foods fell during the war as follows (Einaudi, p. 179):

|  | *1911–13* | *1913–18* |
|---|---|---|
| Wheat (kg) | 169·8 | 158 |
| Maize (kg) | 80 | 72 |
| Sugar (kg) | 4·82 | 4·66 |
| Wine (litres) | 126 | 107 |

[3] Expenditure (in millions of lire) rose from 2,501 in 1913–14 to 17,351 in 1916–1917 and 25,334 in 1917–18; the proportion covered by revenue fell from 92% in 1913–14 to 44% in 1914–15, 24% in 1916–17 and 23% in 1917–18 (the lowest previous proportion being 44% in 1866). Coppola d'Anna, p. 85.

[4] The four previous war loans, launched between January 1915 and February 1917, had together raised 9,000 million lire. Monticone, pp. 181–2. The total sum subscribed in the three years 1916–18 represented approximately 30% of the national income. Einaudi, p. 56.

[5] *Sommario*, p. 152.

supplies.[1] In November 1917 the lira fell to a record low rate of forty-three to the pound, a depreciation of 47% since 1914. Nitti was able to show that the U.S. loan of 700 million dollars, which he had himself helped to negotiate in July 1917, and the various loans granted by Britain since 1915, were totally inadequate. The Allies yielded to his persuasive pleading and provided further large credits to finance vital imports.[2] At the same time Nitti succeeded in reducing Italy's demands and imposing exchange control. Thanks to these measures the lira made a slight recovery and in the summer of 1918 was artificially pegged by inter-Allied agreement at the rate of 30·3 to the pound.[3]

While war subjected the whole economy to severe strain, it also gave a great stimulus to industrial expansion. Heavy industry boomed. New techniques of mass production were introduced. Large numbers of unskilled workmen were absorbed into the factories. To meet the demand for armaments and munitions, steel production rose by 50% and the output of electric power doubled.[4] Even more significant was the birth of a large-scale engineering industry, producing machine tools as well as war equipment. Its share of total manufacturing output rose from 21·6% to 31·8%, and at its peak it employed over 500,000 workers. By 1918 Italy was making a major contribution to Allied needs by the export of motor vehicles and aeroplanes.[5]

This expansion, carried out with little regard for cost or economic efficiency, was mainly the work of a few big firms. War greatly accelerated

[1] Monticone, p. 151. Imports (in millions of lire) from Britain and the U.S.A. respectively rose from 524 and 429 in 1907–13 to 2,666 and 6,641 in 1918. *Sommario*, pp. 155–6.

[2] According to the calculation of Crespi (p. 183) in October 1918, Italy had contracted war debts to the U.S.A., Britain and France of 14,500 million lire. This may be compared with the loan of 1,250 million (£50 million) which Italy originally asked for and obtained by the Treaty of London. In 1925–6 Italy's war debts to Britain were calculated at £370 million, and to U.S.A. at $1,648 million. *Survey of International Affairs 1926*, pp. 100–5.

[3] Einaudi, p. 354.

[4] Production of steel rose from 933,000 (1913) to 1,332,000 (1917) tons, then dropped owing to supply difficulties; output of electric power rose from 2·2 (1913) to 4·3 (1918) million Kwh. *Sommario*, pp. 129, 135. Steel's share of total industrial production rose from 5·2% to 10·8%. Romeo, p. 87. The textile industry, though fully employed throughout the war, declined in relative importance.

[5] The following production figures are taken from Romeo, p. 87; Einaudi, pp. 68–70.

|                            |         | 1915   | 1918   |
|----------------------------|---------|--------|--------|
| Machine-guns (per month)   |         | 25     | 1,200  |
| Artillery shells (per day) |         | 10,400 | 88,400 |
| Aeroplanes                 |         | 382    | 6,523  |
| Aeroplane engines          |         | 606    | 14,820 |
| Motor vehicles             | (1914)  | 9,200  | 20,000 |

the process of integration, both horizontal and vertical, which had started before 1914. Ilva became the sole proprietor of all the steelworks which it had operated since 1911 and acquired armaments works, shipyards and even a shipping line.[1] Fiat absorbed smaller firms and added the manufacture of machine-guns, railway material, submarine engines and aeroplanes to that of motor vehicles.[2] Most dramatic of all was the growth of the Ligurian shipbuilding firm of Ansaldo, which made a special leap forward after Caporetto. Between 1914 and 1918 it increased its capital from 30 million to 500 million lire and its employees from 4,000 to 56,000; it acquired iron mines and built steelworks and hydro-electric plants in the Aosta valley, and produced a total of 10,900 guns, 3,800 aeroplanes, 10 million artillery shells and 95 naval vessels, as well as a substantial number of merchant ships.[3] This, for a single firm, was a notable contribution to victory.

The emergence of these giant industrial complexes, accompanied by a tightening of the already close links between heavy industry and the banks, confronted the state with delicate problems. A giant firm, supported by a giant bank, could be tempted by the ambition to monopolise whole sectors of industry and thereby acquire commanding power in the nation's economy. Its size also made it likely to be high-handed in its dealings with governments. The latter were handicapped in their improvised attempts to direct the economy by lack of experience and technical skill. As a result war contracts were often loosely drafted and excessive profits were made.[4] Two links between industry and banking came to be of special importance: those between Ilva and the Banca Commerciale Italiana, and between Ansaldo and the Banca Italiana di Sconto. In the latter case it was the firm that controlled the bank, through the purchase of a majority of the bank's

[1] Romeo, pp. 88–9; Einaudi, p. 266. For the formation of the Ilva steel trust, see above, p. 286.

[2] Spriano, *Torino operaia*, pp. 143–5.

[3] Romeo, p. 87; Einaudi, pp. 267–8. Comparable capital increases (in millions of lire) were: Ilva from 30 (1916) to 300 (1918); Breda from 14 (1915) to 110 (1918); Fiat from 17 (1914) to 200 (1919).

[4] Industrial profits (per cent) rose during the war as follows (Romeo, p. 85):

|            | 1914 | 1917 |
|------------|------|------|
| Steel      | 6·3  | 16·5 |
| Motor-cars | 8·2  | 30·5 |
| Wool       | 5·1  | 18·7 |
| Cotton     | 0·9  | 12·8 |
| Chemicals  | 8·0  | 15·4 |
| Rubber     | 8·6  | 14·9 |

Many abuses were revealed after Nitti instituted a more effective system of audit in March 1918, but the extent of war profiteering became accurately known only after the war. Monticone, pp. 233–7.

ILF—R

shares by Pio and Mario Perrone, the proprietors of Ansaldo. A fierce struggle for power developed between the two giants. In the spring of 1918 Ansaldo made a take-over bid of an unprecedented kind for its rival, the Banca Commerciale. Had it succeeded, it would have emerged high above all competitors in industrial and financial power.[1]

Industrial battles of this magnitude had political implications which no government could overlook. In 1918 Nitti became deeply involved, mainly by virtue of his office but also through his pre-war acquaintance with the Perrone brothers. Nitti was the first to appreciate Ansaldo's importance, not only as a bulwark of national defence but also as a pioneer of that modernisation of the economy to which he looked forward in the post-war years. He therefore interfered on many occasions to secure labour or transport or materials for the firm's factories. The Perrone brothers combined the promotion of their firm's interests with the most virulent brand of chauvinism. Their take-over bid for the Banca Commerciale was presented as a patriotic attempt to liberate a key sector of the economy from German control. Ansaldo kept up a flow of memoranda on espionage, defeatism and Pangerman plots. It helped to finance the interventionists' campaign against Giolitti and parliament and branded all its opponents as traitors. When inefficiencies or bottlenecks occurred in war production, the Perrone brothers had only one explanation: the hand of the enemy.[2] A favourite target in the spring of 1918 was the Minister of Transport, Riccardo Bianchi, who was accused both of favouring Ilva against Ansaldo and of complicity with the Banca Commerciale in illegal trading with Germany. Many interpreted Bianchi's resignation as a triumph for Nitti and Ansaldo. This was an exaggeration. Bianchi was forced to resign primarily because the congestion on the railways had become intolerable. Nitti, though influenced by Ansaldo, had no personal interest in the firm and never became its tool. Instead he tried in the national interest to damp down the Ilva–Ansaldo rivalry and achieved partial success with an agreement between the leading banks in June.[3] Nevertheless his unwisely close association with the Perrone brothers gave an appearance of partiality and was to prove a political embarrassment after the war.

[1] Romeo, pp. 90–1. The two banks mentioned above, together with the Credito Italiano and the Banco di Roma, made up the 'big four'. The Banca Italiana di Sconto was founded in 1914 with capital of 15 million lire, which had grown by March 1919 to 315 million. Einaudi, p. 274.

[2] Monticone, pp. 214–19, 246–8. Orlando's comment on the Perrone brothers was apt: 'Those two are maniacs; they see the Germans, defeatism and treachery everywhere; real paranoiacs.' Malagodi, II, p. 306. Among the patriotic newspapers which Ansaldo subsidised, from the summer of 1918 onwards, was Mussolini's *Il Popolo d'Italia*. De Felice, pp. 414–18.

[3] Monticone, pp. 237–8, 242, 250–2; Einaudi, p. 272.

The army was carefully nursed over the winter. Many difficulties had been eased by the shortening of the front from 650 to 400 kilometres. This meant that there was an average of one division every 4·5 kilometres, instead of 6·8 before Caporetto. Leave and intensive training thus became easier to organise. Army rations were increased and special attention was paid to welfare and morale. A tax was imposed on those exempted from military service, in an attempt to reduce the combatant's sense of injustice. Every soldier was given a free life insurance policy. An effective information service and the first army newspapers were created. In January 1918 Bissolati took over a new Ministry of Pensions and Army Welfare. Postwar problems were studied and morale boosted by promises of the benefits that victory would bring. The most important of these was 'Land for the Peasants', which became the official post-war policy of the government. Nitti founded the National Ex-Servicemen's Organisation,[1] with a capital of 300 million lire, to purchase smallholdings for demobilised soldiers. It was generally agreed that there was no other fit reward for the humble peasant-infantryman's sacrifices.[2]

While these positive measures were taken, the negative task of suppressing defeatism was more energetically pursued. Many of the measures for which the interventionists had been agitating were now adopted. Enemy aliens were interned in January and a number of business men were arrested for trading with the enemy through Switzerland. The freedom of the socialists was drastically curtailed. The leaders of the party, whose main concern was to preserve party unity, were successful in preventing any repetition of the Turin explosion; but at the same time they rejected all appeals for national unity and severely censured Turati's reformists and the C.G.L. leaders for failing to resist the appeal of bourgeois patriotism.[3] The influence of the extremists continued to grow. They openly boasted of their share of responsibility for Caporetto, talked of sabotage and looked forward to the consummation of 'revolution by defeat' as in Russia. Angelica Balabanoff, a member of the party executive, went to Moscow to become a close collaborator of Lenin. Orlando now felt obliged to drop his pre-Caporetto scruples and to deal firmly with subversive activity. During the spring and summer of 1918 the leaders of the party in Turin

---

[1] The Opera Nazionale per i Combattenti. It started to operate in January 1919.

[2] The proportion of peasants in the army has been calculated at 50%; the proportion of war orphans from peasant families was 64%.

[3] On 23 February 1918 Turati had declared in the chamber that Orlando's 'Grappa è la nostra patria' was the sentiment 'of us all, of the whole assembly', and that 'we (socialists) too live hours of anguish'. Turati, III, p. 1557. When Orlando set up a commission to study post-war problems and nominated several socialists as members, Turati ignored his party's directive to decline the nomination.

were brought to trial on charges of organising the August riots, and a number of other prominent socialists, including Lazzari, secretary of the party, Nicola Bombacci, a leader of the revolutionary wing, and Serrati, Mussolini's successor as editor of *Avanti!*, were tried and imprisoned.

Caporetto had an important influence on inter-Allied diplomacy. It reduced the relative weight of Italy in the alliance just at the time when, under the shock of Russia's collapse, Britain and France were reviving the idea of a separate peace with Austria-Hungary. Sonnino had repeated his view on 25 October that 'Our war aims do not include the dismemberment of enemy states, nor the alteration of other people's internal systems.'[1] President Wilson expressed identical views on declaring war on Austria-Hungary in December. In that month, in spite of Italian protests,[2] Lloyd George sent General Smuts to Switzerland for talks with Mensdorff, former Austro-Hungarian ambassador in London. On 5 January 1918 he publicly disclaimed all desire to dismember Austria-Hungary, while recognising 'the legitimate claims of the Italians for union with those of their own race and tongue'. In France the conservative and Catholic-monarchist press was campaigning against national self-determination and the goverment was conducting secret diplomatic negotiations of its own. Had the Austro-Hungarian government been willing to discuss even the *parecchio* of May 1915, the British and French might have been tempted to persevere. But in their post-Caporetto mood of exaltation, the Austrians were resolved to make no concession to a beaten enemy. Italy was thus saved by Austrian intransigence from what could have been a disastrous clash of interest with lukewarm allies. By the spring of 1918 even the French and British Austrophils had realised that Austria-Hungary was now incapable of freeing itself from German domination, and hopes of a separate peace faded.[3]

---

[1] Cilibrizzi, VII, p. 331; Albertini, *Venti anni*, V, p. 235.

[2] Mamatey, p. 150. Almost simultaneously an approach was made on behalf of the Italian High Command to the Austro–Hungarian military attaché in Berne, but Sonnino appears to have prevented any serious discussion. Valiani, pp. 378, 468–9.

[3] In March Lloyd George sent Philip Kerr, his private secretary (later Lord Lothian), on another mission to Switzerland. Both the British and French negotiations were interrupted at the end of March by the German offensive in France, and the idea of a separate peace was finally wrecked in April when public recrimination broke out between Clemenceau and the Austro–Hungarian government over the earlier negotiations of Prince Sixtus.

The Vatican also was engaged between February and June 1918 in exploring the possibilities of peace on the basis of 'the *parecchio* improved in certain points'. Benedict XV declared himself willing to act as intermediary between Italy and Austria–Hungary. Nitti discussed terms with Gasparri, but made it clear that Italy

Meanwhile a new and greater danger arose. On 8 January Wilson proclaimed his Fourteen Points. The Four Principles followed on 11 February. Sonnino at once appreciated their incompatibility with the Treaty of London. To 'readjust Italy's frontiers along clearly recognisable lines of nationality', in the words of Point 9, would deprive Italy of Dalmatia and the Brenner frontier. The Allied agreements on Turkey were equally endangered. Sonnino was well aware of Wilson's detestation of secret treaties. Colonel House, Wilson's ambassador-at-large, had already sounded him in November on possible modifications of the Treaty of London and received an uncompromising refusal. Now, as American war aims took shape, the extent of Italy's isolation became apparent. Sonnino's obsession with secrecy had prevented any effective Italian propaganda in the U.S.A., such as the British and French had been quick to organise. Italy was clearly out of step with American opinion, and the two governments were incapable of talking the same political language.[1]

Italian democrats, who had repeatedly warned Sonnino of this danger, gave an enthusiastic welcome to the Fourteen Points, which reinforced their own efforts to transform the war from an imperialist dogfight into a democratic crusade. But even they felt uneasy over Point 10: the promise of 'autonomous development' to the peoples of Austria-Hungary was far from satisfying their warcry of *Delenda Austria*. The nationalists shared their concern, believing that if Austria-Hungary survived, Italy would have fought the war in vain.

In November 1917 the Bolsheviks had begun to publish the texts of all the secret Allied treaties, in order to discredit the imperialist war. On 13 February the nationalist deputy Bevione read out the text of the Treaty of London in the Italian chamber. This was the start of a long bitter controversy. Catholics protested against the ban in Article 15 on papal representation at the peace conference. The nationalists revived their charges that the Allies had double-crossed Italy over Asia Minor by failing to carry out the promise of fair shares contained in Article 9. The socialists denounced the treaty as an offence to the Slavs, Greeks and Albanians. Several Catholics and Giolittians joined the socialists in demanding immediate peace. Sonnino, unshaken by the confused clamour, stood by the treaty. It was not, he asserted, 'imperialist', but based on a compromise between ethnic principles and legitimate strategic requirements; further, it guaranteed

---

was interested in a general, not separate, peace. The Austrian June offensive put an end to these soundings. Monticone, pp. 258–62, 393–7; Engel-Jánosi, II, pp. 336–9; Valiani, pp. 379, 432 note 118.

[1] Mamatey, p. 200. Nitti had for months been pressing for the appointment of a top-rank personality as Italian high commissioner in Washington, but was unable to overcome Sonnino's veto.

that equilibrium in the eastern Mediterranean which was vital for a healthy Italy.[1] The democrats remained for the most part uneasily silent. Bissolati, though he had been a minister for nearly two years, had now learnt the truth about the Treaty of London for the first time, and it confirmed many of his fears.

Austrian and Bolshevik manœuvres, the activities of the peace party at home and the uncertainty created by Allied Austrophilia and American idealism, forced democrats and nationalists to rebuild the interventionist common front of 1915. For the first time effective pressure began to be exerted on the government for an understanding between Italy and the Yugoslavs. Albertini's *Corriere della Sera* played an important part and the Parliamentary Fascio was in the thick of the campaign. Many Italians who had despised the Mazzinian programme before Caporetto, now felt that no weapon against Austria could be safely neglected. It was a choice, wrote Mussolini later, between Mazzini and Metternich.[2] The Russian collapse not only made the Yugoslavs more conciliatory but also relieved Italian fears of militant Panslavism and Russian Adriatic bases. There was growing support for the idea that Italy, instead of clinging to the Treaty of London, should adapt its war aims to the democratic programme of the Allies and so win the leadership of the Balkan and Central European peoples.

Unofficial contacts between Italians and Yugoslavs were made in December 1917 with the help of British intermediaries, while the shock of Caporetto was still fresh.[3] At the end of January 1918 Orlando met Trumbić in London and discovered that he was a reasonable man. In February an Italian Committee for Understanding between the Oppressed Nationalities, markedly conservative in composition, was founded at the headquarters of the Trent and Trieste Society. One of its members, the liberal deputy Andrea Torre, a close collaborator of Albertini, went to London in March with Orlando's approval and reached agreement with Trumbić. On 8 April a Congress of Oppressed Nationalities assembled on the Roman Capitol. Besides the Italians and Yugoslavs, there were delegations of Serbs, Czechs, Poles and Rumanians. The Italian delegation included liberals, democrats, republicans, irredentists and nationalists.[4] The

[1] Cilibrizzi, VII, pp. 311–12.

[2] Albertini, *Venti anni*, V, p. 359; Hautecœur, p. 115; Mussolini, XI, pp. 279–81.

[3] Notably Wickham Steed, foreign editor of *The Times*, and R. W. Seton-Watson, proprietor of *The New Europe*, both of whom later became members of Lord Northcliffe's Enemy Propaganda organisation. See Steed, II, pp. 167–79; Albertini, *Venti anni*, V, pp. 252–9; Valiani, pp. 379–85. Caporetto had made Trumbić realise that Italy's defeat would mean the end of all hopes of Yugoslav independence.

[4] They included Albertini, Barzilai, Federzoni, Giuriati, Martini, Mussolini, Pantaleoni, Prezzolini and Salvemini.

Congress ended with the signing of a Pact of Rome, in which all the nationalities pledged themselves to unconditional solidarity in the struggle for liberation. In a further section the Italians and Yugoslavs expressed their mutual interest in the unification of both nations and undertook to settle frontier disputes in a spirit of friendship, according to the principles of nationality and self-determination, 'and in such manner as not to infringe vital interests of the two nations, as they will be defined at the moment of peace'.[1] Implicit in this text was Italian willingness to renounce Dalmatia and Yugoslav willingness to renounce Trieste and Istria. The pact was ceremonially presented to Orlando, who welcomed it in the name of the government. A fortnight later Orlando signed an agreement with Štefánik, the Slovak leader in exile, for the formation of a Czechoslovak Legion in Italy from prisoners taken on the Italian front.[2] Diaz's G.H.Q., which had little hope of victory in the field, eagerly set up an inter-Allied enemy propaganda organisation. Leaflets in Czech, Serbo-Croat and Rumanian were dropped over the Austrian lines, and the number of desertions increased significantly. The impact of the Rome congress upon Yugoslavs at home, hitherto resolutely anti-Italian, and upon all the subject nationalities was immense; over the next six months it played a major part in undermining the enemy's resistance. Trumbić meanwhile made a triumphal tour of the Italian front and was received by the King. Orlando told him, 'Mazzini in 1871 prophesied the alliance of Italy with the Slavs: we today are fulfilling that prophecy.'[3]

Sonnino watched all this with unrelenting disapproval. He still believed Italo-Yugoslav friendship to be a wild, impracticable dream. Albertini and Bissolati 'are mad, they are idealists', he told Sforza. He refused to attend the Rome Congress and insisted that the pact was purely unofficial.[4] He also obstructed the formation of a Yugoslav Legion, though thousands of prisoners volunteered, and made difficulties even over the Czechoslovaks. The military arguments for stimulating desertion from the Austro-Hungarian army failed to impress him. His desire in 1918 remained what it had been in 1915: to win the war with the least possible Allied help, and to hold his Allies to the Treaty of London. To renounce part of the treaty to please the Yugoslavs would be to sabotage Italy's victory and prove the neutralists right. On this subject he ceased to be open to argument.

His obstinacy won him the approval of an important group of national-

---

[1] For text see Albrecht–Carrié, pp. 347–8; Steed, II, pp. 184–5.
[2] It won its spurs in action at Dosso Alto above Lake Garda in September 1918. Beneš, pp. 286 ff.
[3] Cilibrizzi, VII, p. 342; Albertini, *Venti anni*, V, p. 353; Hautecœur, p. 112.
[4] Sforza, *Contemporary Italy*, p. 171; Mamatey, p. 246; Valiani, pp. 382, 384; DDI (6), I, 657. The Foreign Ministry was financing anti-Yugoslav propaganda through the cultural Dante Alighieri Society. Colapietra, pp. 255, 257.

ists who had refused to support the Pact of Rome and clung to their
dreams of a Roman Dalmatia. The most violent opponents of the pact
were the Istrian and Dalmatian irredentist exiles, in whose eyes the Slav
menace loomed larger as the Austrian menace faded. Brought up in a tense
atmosphere of national conflict, obsessed with the struggle between Slavs
and Italians that had dominated their native lands, they carried with them
to Italy the spirit of vendetta of the racial frontier.[1] To help the Yugoslavs,
they argued, was to help Austria; the Croats were still tools of the Habsburgs and the Yugoslav exiles were 'Austrian spies'. The Treaty of London
now became their minimum programme and those who pointed out that
Dalmatia was Slav began to be branded as 'renouncers' and traitors of
their country.[2] Many even of the supporters of the Pact of Rome had
mental reservations, including Orlando himself, who dared not quarrel
with Sonnino and was frightened of the nationalists. They accepted it as
an instrument with which to defeat Austria, without renouncing the Treaty
of London.[3] The very vagueness of the pact's text thus contained the seeds
of future discord. It was soon to prove a mere gesture of passing idealism
and goodwill.

During the summer Allied war aims rapidly crystallised. The British,
French and Americans recognised the Czechoslovaks as belligerent allies
and thus sealed the fate of Austria-Hungary. Recognition of the Yugoslavs
should logically have followed, but in every inter-Allied discussion of the
question, Sonnino imposed his veto. The British and French were astonished to find him more Austrophil than themselves. Italy became every
day more isolated. Bissolati, backed by the *Corriere della Sera*, the democratic press, the nationalist *Idea Nazionale* and Mussolini's *Popolo d'Italia*,
and privately by Diaz, still pressed his views. Early in September he at last
succeeded, after threatening resignation, in forcing the first thorough

[1] Salvemini, *Dal patto di Londra*, pp. 19, 36.
[2] Some Giolittians joined in this anti-Slav agitation, inflating Italy's war aims
in order to be able to argue that the war had been fought in vain and that they had
been right in 1915. Salvemini, *Dal patto di Londra*, p. 298; Colapietra, p. 260.
Giolitti himself 'didn't believe in Yugoslavia' and thought Sonnino right. Malagodi,
II, p. 411.
[3] This was the position of Mussolini, who was a delegate to the congress. He had
used the slogan *Delenda Austria* since August 1917. In January 1918, believing
that Austria could not be beaten by military force alone, he enthusiastically
adopted the cause of 'the peoples against Austria–Hungary', especially that of the
Czechs. But he never 'renounced' any part of the Treaty of London and expressed
strong reservations on the sacrifice of 'Fiume Italianissima'. For Mussolini, as for
the nationalists, the shame of Caporetto was a motive for inflating, not reducing,
Italy's war aims. In November 1917 he told a friend, 'On the Isonzo I was content
with Istria, Fiume and Zara; now that we are on the Piave, I want all Dalmatia.'
De Felice, p. 380; Mussolini, IX, pp. 93–6, X, pp. 243–5, 327–9, 339–41, 436–9,
XI, pp. 291–5, 309–15.

cabinet discussion of foreign policy for over two years. After a stormy debate, during which Sonnino in his turn threatened to resign, a compromise was reached on the Yugoslav question. The movement for Yugoslav unity and independence was officially recognised as being in harmony with Allied war aims. Bissolati thought he had won 'complete victory'.[1] But Sonnino continued to obstruct, yielding only inch by inch. For him the Croats and Slovenes remained enemies, with whom there could be no negotiation until the peace conference, and he continued to speak of the 'Yugoslav nationalities', thus denying their claim to be one nation. Neither Bissolati nor Sonnino was strong enough to impose his views. The end of the war found the government still paralysed and without any constructive plan for the Adriatic.[2]

## Victory

All through the spring of 1918 the reorganisation of the army continued. Diaz's deputy, Pietro Badoglio,[3] reconstructed the High Command and removed the weaknesses which had contributed to Caporetto. In January Orlando created a joint War Council of military and naval commanders and civilian ministers, for the more efficient direction of the war. Its frequent meetings, which were sometimes held near the front, promoted harmony between the government and the High Command and ensured effective political control of the army. Cadorna would never have tolerated such an institution. By June the last of the formations shattered in the great retreat had been reconstituted and losses in equipment more than made good. Each infantry regiment now had thirty-six machine-guns instead of two as in 1914. The army had started the war with 2,000 artillery weapons and now had 7,000, in spite of the loss of 3,000 after Caporetto. Large numbers of motor vehicles and aeroplanes had been acquired.[4] The Piave line had been strengthened by defences in depth and elaborate artillery plans drawn up to meet a new enemy attack. Three successful small-scale attacks, the first conducted by the French in December, had improved

---

[1] Malagodi, II, p. 384.

[2] ibid., pp. 305, 369–90, 405–7. The Rome congress and the controversy over Italian war aims are discussed at length in Albertini, *Venti anni*, V, pp. 233–78, 348–77. See also Valiani, pp. 386–99; Steed, II, pp. 209–16; Hautecœur, pp. 83–121; Colapietra, pp. 256–64, 300–1. One of the reasons for Bissolati's impatience was his fear (which later events justified) that if Italy failed to seize the leadership of the subject nationalities, France would.

[3] Badoglio had been promoted to this position in spite of his share of responsibility, as a corps commander in the critical sector, for the Caporetto break-through.

[4] Einaudi, pp. 59–60, 70–1. Between May 1915 and the end of the war, the number of motor vehicles in military use increased from 3,950 to 31,100, and that of aeroplanes from 143 to 2,693. More artillery shells were fired between January and October 1918 than in the whole period 1915–17.

morale. Though it still had little offensive spirit, the army had recovered its nerve.

Special attention was paid to the training of the shock troops known as *arditi*. These were young volunteers, drawn predominantly from the urban middle class and often straight from the universities. They were given special privileges and uniforms, which included black shirts, and much publicity. Instead of spending long periods in the trenches, they were kept in reserve, undergoing rigorous battle training, for special raids or the toughest operations. They came to despise the dull, plodding infantry, mostly recruited from the countryside, who fought with fatalistic resignation. The *arditi* 'lived in an atmosphere of bombs and flame'.[1] Close to them in temperament were the crews of the submarine-chasers[2] and the air force pilots. All Italy rang with the exploits of Commander Luigi Rizzo, who sank a battleship inside Trieste harbour in December 1917 and six months later torpedoed the *Szent Istvan*, one of Austria's four dreadnoughts, off Dalmatia, thus frustrating Admiral Horthy's attempt to break the Allied blockade across the Adriatic. Another daring raider along the Istrian and Dalmatian coasts was Costanzo Ciano.[3] Best known of all was D'Annunzio, who after returning from the trenches in 1916, conducted a private war from his comfortable base in a Venetian *palazzo*. He took part in many flights over Trieste, Trent, Pola and Kotor, losing an eye, and in August 1918 led a raid on Vienna to drop leaflets of defiant bombast. He also accompanied Ciano on some of his sea raids. Always theatrical, he became the caricature of a hero. But to the *arditi*, the pilots and the young sailors whose joy it was to 'live dangerously', he seemed the leader of the future, the personification of a more glorious and exciting Italy.

Discussion on the strategy for 1918 led to much friction between the Allies. The French and British, impressed by German numerical superiority on their front, wanted to bring their troops back from Italy where, they claimed, the Austrians were demoralised and outnumbered. Diaz challenged their figures and insisted on retaining the Allied divisions. His only concession was to send 60,000 'auxiliary troops', for whom no arms were yet available, to build roads, prepare defences and guard prisoners in France. Diaz was strongly backed by the government and especially by Nitti, who in his determination to harmonise the fighting and home fronts, kept in constant touch with the general and offered to act as his spokesman in the cabinet.[4] On 21 March the Germans launched their final offensive

---

[1] Trevelyan, *Scenes from Italy's War*, p. 87.
[2] Known as M.A.S. from their initials (*motoscafi anti-sommergibili*).
[3] The father of Galeazzo, Mussolini's future son-in-law and foreign minister.
[4] Monticone, pp. 263–9; Nitti, *Rivelazioni*, pp. 392–3.

in the west. The Allies were soon facing a desperate situation. Overruling Diaz's objections, they recalled six of their divisions from Italy, leaving only three British and two French. In compensation for the latter, two Italian divisions went to France.[1] The Italians anticipated another enemy onslaught on the scale of Caporetto as soon as the western offensive was over. Convinced that they were being shabbily treated, they looked with envy upon the American troops that were now landing in great numbers in France. Italy by contrast received a single U.S. regiment, which toured the country for propaganda purposes and saw action only in the last few days of the war.

Germany's dramatic advance in the west resolved the question of inter-Allied command, which had been shelved after Caporetto. The Italian government had continued to resist French pressure for a single command under Foch, fearing that a French commander-in-chief would starve the Italian front. Many Italians also shared Sonnino's belief that such an arrangement would be a blow to the nation's honour and morale.[2] But in April, under the threat of imminent disaster, the British accepted Foch as commander-in-chief. The Italians could hardly persist in their opposition. At a conference at Abbeville on 2 May, Orlando and Sonnino agreed that Foch should have 'powers of coordination' over the Italian front, but not direct command until Allied armies were fighting in Italy. This condition was intended to ensure that the defence of Italy would not be sacrificed to the demands of other fronts. Foch at once began to exploit his powers of coordination by urging Diaz to attack and relieve German pressure in France. Barrère pressed Foch's request in Rome. Diaz replied that the Austrians were still capable of the offensive and refused. Nitti gave him full support. While pressing in vain for the despatch of U.S. troops to Italy, he exhorted Diaz to think of only one thing, the salvation of Italy, and to attack on military grounds alone. 'Don't listen to any of us', he wrote on 15 May; 'you decide by yourself, in the light of your conscience as an Italian and a soldier.'[3] Events were to prove Diaz more nearly right than Foch, for in the middle of June the Austrians did launch a full-scale attack.

After the German offensive in France had been checked, Italy's evident weakness became the enemy's one glimmer of hope. Conrad still dreamt of a knockout blow. Italy was a drowning man clutching a lifebelt, he said; all that was required was a blow of a hatchet to chop off his fingers.[4] The

---

[1] These suffered heavy losses at Bligny during the second Battle of the Marne in July 1918, counter-attacking successfully after an initial withdrawal.

[2] National pride was also roused later in the year by proposals to appoint a non-Italian Allied naval commander-in-chief in the Mediterranean. Orlando and Sonnino, under fierce pressure from their navy, insisted on Italy retaining command of the Adriatic and successfully blocked the plan.

[3] Monticone, pp. 275–81.          [4] Albertini, *Venti anni*, V, pp. 305–6.

signing of the Peace of Brest Litovsk in January had freed more Austrian divisions for the Italian front. Fortunately for Italy, the enemy suffered from dissensions much graver than those of the Allies. The Austrians refused to contribute troops for the German offensive in France and in its turn the German High Command refused to provide German troops for an attack on Italy. The Austrians moreover were themselves divided. The two commanders in Italy, Conrad in the Trentino, Boroević on the lower Piave, both wanted to conduct the main offensive. General Arz, Conrad's successor as Chief of Staff,[1] weakly allowed them both to have their way and authorised two simultaneous attacks. In all twenty-one new divisions were transferred to Italy for the purpose, making a total of fifty-eight to the Allies' fifty-six.[2] Deserters, mainly Czech, kept Diaz well informed of enemy plans. Austrian morale was boosted by promises of easy victory and unlimited loot; army rations were increased at the expense of hungry Vienna. The objective was the Adige, beyond which the whole of northern Italy would lie open to invasion. The Austrians knew well that this was their last chance. It was a 'hunger offensive'. If it failed, collapse was inevitable.

The main attack began on 15 June along a front of ninety miles from Asiago to the sea. The Austrians won initial successes. In the mountains the brunt of the attack fell on the British and French at Asiago and on the Italians on Monte Grappa. Ground was lost, bringing the enemy perilously near the plain, but within twenty-four hours almost all had been recovered. On the Piave the enemy crossed the river on a fifteen-mile front and reached the last line of defence on the Montello. But the Italians held them. On 19 June they counter-attacked and by the 24th the Austrians had withdrawn all their troops, exhausted but in good order, back across the river. Their casualties had been double those of the Italians. This failure was, as the enemy had anticipated, decisive. Its full significance was not appreciated in Italy. But Ludendorff on hearing the news, 'had the sensation of defeat for the first time'.[3] The moral effect on the enemy's home front was disastrous. Open disaffection broke out in Hungary, strikes paralysed Vienna and the leaders of the subject nationalities abandoned their last scruples of loyalty and caution.

Foch urged Diaz to exploit his success. Diaz, knowing his troops were weary and short of munitions, confined himself to local operations. Though the British and French underestimated Austrian strength and fighting

---

[1] Conrad was dismissed from the post of Chief of Staff on the accession of Charles in 1916 and transferred to the command of the Trentino sector.
[2] 51 Italian, 3 British and 2 French. A Czech division was in process of formation.
[3] Cilibrizzi, VII, p. 369.

spirit, Diaz greatly exaggerated them.[1] Fear of repeating what he considered Cadorna's main blunder, the Bainsizza offensive, which had put an exhausted army at the enemy's mercy, made him determined to conserve his strength for the decisive battle in 1919. Not even the dramatic success of the Allied counter-attack in France, which started on 8 August, was sufficient to change his mind. At the end of August, during a visit to Paris, he asked for twenty-five U.S. divisions and the return of the 60,000 Italian auxiliary troops from France. Orlando, too, asked repeatedly for Allied reinforcements. But all these requests were refused. Diaz's outlook was wholly defensive. As late as August he was still maintaining bridging units on the Adige and the Po in case of a major retreat.[2] In spite of Sonnino's concern with the diplomatic dangers of inaction, Nitti, 'the only pessimist minister' in any Allied government, backed Diaz unreservedly and carried the cabinet with him.[3] On 22 September it was agreed to ask Foch for ten divisions from France as the indispensable minimum for an offensive.[4]

On 26 September the Allies again attacked in France, breached the Hindenburg Line and started to roll the Germans back. On the 29th the Bulgarians capitulated on the Salonika front, leaving Austria-Hungary defenceless against invasion from the south. On 4 October Germany and Austria-Hungary appealed to Wilson for an armistice and a peace based on the Fourteen Points. Orlando and several of his colleagues by now fully shared Sonnino's alarm: if the Allies won the war on distant fronts while the enemy was still entrenched on Italian soil, victory would be as bitter and inglorious as in 1866. Nitti, however, still objected to pressure upon the High Command and told Diaz on 21 October that he would resign if non-military considerations were given the least precedence over military.[5] Orlando unhappily contemplated the general's dismissal. But at last, much to Orlando's relief, Diaz set to work. Starting at the end of September with the idea of a limited operation to create a bridgehead for the spring offensive, he elaborated his plan by stages until by the middle of October he was preparing a full-scale attack. It was to be launched from the mid-Piave sector and pressed in two directions: north-eastwards across the plain and northwards into the foothills around Vittorio Veneto. A subsidiary attack was to be mounted simultaneously on Monte Grappa. The strategic aim

[1] Nitti maintained in London on 24 July that the Austrians had 71 divisions in Italy. His information appears to have come from the Italian representative on the Supreme War Council at Versailles. The British estimate of 58 or 59 was in fact very nearly correct. The two armies were roughly equal in numbers; the Allies had a marked superiority in artillery. Edmonds, pp. 244–5, 265; Crespi, p. 125.

[2] E. Caviglia, *Le tre battaglie del Piave* (Milan 1935), p. 101, note.

[3] Crespi, p. 183; Nitti, *Rivelazioni*, pp. 37–9; Malagodi, II, pp. 390–6.

[4] ibid., pp. 416–18.

[5] Monticone, pp. 293–4.

was to cut off the Austrian armies in the mountains from those on the plain and exploit success to the maximum. Bad weather and swollen rivers caused further delay, but at last the attack was fixed for 24 October, the anniversary of Caporetto.

By then Austria-Hungary was in dissolution. In the first fortnight of October the national groups in the Austrian parliament, one after the other, proclaimed their right to self-determination; first the Czechs, then the Yugoslavs, then the Italians,[1] then the Poles. Meanwhile the Yugoslav National Council, which had been formed in August in Ljubljana to work for the union of Croatia and Slovenia with Serbia, moved to Zagreb and openly challenged Hungarian authority. On 17 October the Emperor Charles tried to stop the avalanche by announcing the transformation of Austria (but not Hungary) into a federation. Next day the U.S. government declared that it was no longer prepared to make peace on the basis of the Fourteen Points; autonomy for the subject nationalities was no longer enough. This was the death knell of the Dual Monarchy.

Diaz's armies attacked early on 24 October. On Monte Grappa they met fierce resistance and reached few of their objectives, but forced the Austrians to commit most of their reserves. The main attack on the Piave also ran into difficulties. The river was in spate and carried away many of the pontoon bridges, and after three days' fighting only three small bridgeheads[2] had been won. The pessimists relapsed into gloom. 'Our troops are beaten', wrote Nitti to Orlando, 'disaster is developing. You alone are responsible.'[3] On the 29th the tide turned. Vittorio Veneto, after which the battle was later named, was entered on the 30th. Next day the enemy collapsed on Monte Grappa and the Austrian High Command ordered the evacuation of Venetia in order to 'show its good will for peace'.

The army in Italy was the last institution of the Austro-Hungarian monarchy to resist disintegration. It went on fighting partly through ignorance, partly just because it was an army. But as early as 22 October a Croat brigade had mutinied. The Italian attack momentarily galvanised resistance. But after the 27th acts of open rebellion multiplied in Hungarian, Czech and Yugoslav units, especially behind the front line. On the 29th the fleet mutinied at Pola. Two days later Károlyi, Prime Minister of the democratic revolutionary government in Budapest, ordered all Hungarian troops home to defend their native soil. The Italian advance shattered what was left of military discipline. It was Caporetto in reverse. After 30 October

---

[1] De Gasperi, leader of the Italian parliamentary group, proclaimed the right of the Trentino to self-determination on 12 October.

[2] The most important was established by Lord Cavan's Tenth Army, composed of two British and two Italian divisions.

[3] Crespi, pp. 191–2; Monticone, pp. 295–6.

the enemy soldiers were in mass flight, throwing away their arms and making for home where new national or revolutionary governments awaited them.[1] The Italians, sweeping on through Venetia in pursuit, found the bridges over the Tagliamento intact. On 3 November Udine and Trent[2] were reached and troops were landed at Trieste from the sea. The same day an Austrian military delegation signed an armistice at Villa Giusti near Padua, and at 3 p.m. on 4 November fighting ceased. In the final battle the Italians had lost 39,000 killed and wounded,[3] two-thirds of them on Monte Grappa; the Austrians had lost 30,000 killed and wounded and 427,000 prisoners. The war was over and Italian unity was complete.

The armistice terms, drawn up by the Supreme War Council in Versailles, bound the Austrians to evacuate all Italian territory and all the areas which had been promised to Italy in the Treaty of London.[4] It further bound them to facilitate Allied use of their territory and communications to continue the war against Germany. The fleet was to be surrendered. At Versailles Foch prepared a plan for forty Allied divisions under the Duke of Aosta to invade Germany from the south. By 10 November Italian troops were in contact with the Germans on the Brenner, but next day the signing of the German armistice made these plans superfluous.

In later years, after the disappointments of peace, the balance-sheet of victory seemed to most Italians meagre. Nearly 600,000 dead and half a million permanently disabled, three and a half years of social and economic exhaustion,[5] foreign trade in ruins, inflation rampant[6] and the cost of living more than doubled:[7] these were a heavy price to pay. Though the Allies seemed reluctant to recognise it, Italy's achievements, in proportion to

[1] The Czechoslovak Republic was proclaimed in Prague on 28 October. On the same day the Yugoslav National Council in Zagreb took over power from the Austro–Hungarian military command, and on the 29th Croatian independence was proclaimed. On 3 November the Polish Republic came into existence.

[2] The official historian of the British army takes delight in pointing out that two British officers entered Trent about one hour before the first Italians. The part played in the final offensive by the three British and two French divisions has been underestimated by most Italian, and overestimated by many British and French commentators. For the British military view, see Edmonds, pp. 295–6, 338–40, 355–8.

[3] Including 2,487 British and French.

[4] Though, to meet American objections, the treaty was not specifically mentioned. Orlando, *Memorie*, pp. 461–3.

[5] Total national consumption exceeded national income in 1916–20 by 14·2%. Romeo, p. 84; *Sommario*, p. 218.

[6] Note circulation rose from 3,454 million lire in 1913 to 14,465 million in 1918.

[7] The cost of living index (100 = 1913) stood in November 1918 at 264 in Italy, 220 in France, 195 in Britain, 161 in the U.S.A., 228 in Germany.

wealth, population and industrial capacity, had been as great as theirs.[1] But the aggressiveness with which Italians recited the relevant facts and figures often concealed an inner doubt as to whether they had proved themselves the equal of the French or British. Just because Italy's war effort, save minor contributions in France and the Balkans, had been confined to Italian soil,[2] it looked less spectacular than the efforts of France and Britain which had been spread over three continents. Caporetto had reopened the wounds left by Custoza and Lissa in 1866 and by Adowa in 1896. Victory had been won in the end; but how much was that victory due to Italy? Was the final success on the Italian front any more than a half-victory, as marred by previous failures as victory in Libya in 1912? A maturer, more confident people, with a longer history as a united nation, would have been less tortured by such doubts. But Italy had entered the war divided and was still divided when it ended. In no other victorious country were the wisdom or folly of the war, its gains or losses, such urgent topics of political controversy. It might be true, as Sforza boldly argues, that no country achieved its war aims more perfectly.[3] But in Italy, as in every Allied country, expectations had risen as the war dragged on. In terms of territory or colonies, economic outlets or cash compensation, Italy's rewards seemed exiguous when compared to the spoils that fell to France and Britain. The immeasurable gain of Austria-Hungary's disappearance was overlooked. What was not achieved loomed larger than what was, and more and more Italians came to believe that victory had been 'mutilated' and the war fought in vain.[4]

[1] Italy had engaged 20 to 25 enemy divisions in June 1915, 35 in 1916, 55 in October 1917 (including 8 German), 55 to 60 in 1918.

[2] A small contingent was also sent with an Allied force to Archangel in August 1918. Sonnino later favoured large-scale intervention in support of the White Russians, arguing that in view of the bolshevist threat in Italy, it was a question of self-defence. He was overruled by Orlando who agreed with Lloyd George in preferring to negotiate with the Russian bolsheviks. PPC, III, pp. 650–1. Archangel was evacuated by the Allies in the autumn of 1919.

[3] Sforza, *Contemporary Italy*, p. 187.

[4] The phrase 'mutilated victory' first appeared in an article by D'Annunzio in the *Corriere della Sera* of 24 November 1918. It quickly caught on.

# 12

# The Democratic Failure
## 1918–20

### The Anxieties of Victory

Victory was greeted with an outburst of exultation and national pride. 'It is a Roman victory', Orlando declared, for only in Roman history could another example of such a victory be found.[1] Such magnification of a victory that needed no magnification betrayed Italian sensitiveness to the suggestion that Italy had won only through Austria-Hungary's internal collapse. 'The Austrian revolution was the result, not the cause, of military defeat', Diaz told the press on 1 December.[2] There were urgent reasons for belittling the revolt of the subject nationalities, for even before the armistice had been signed, the friction between Italians and Yugoslavs had flared up into open conflict. On 29 October the Yugoslav National Council at Zagreb had proclaimed the independence of Croatia and Slovenia and their desire for union with Serbia. The Emperor Charles recognised the Council on the 31st and handed over to it the Austro-Hungarian fleet, already paralysed by mutiny. That same night two Italian officers penetrated Pola harbour and sank the enemy flagship, *Viribus Unitis*, unaware that it was already in Yugoslav hands. The Yugoslav committee in Pola thereupon appealed to the Allies for protection. Sonnino, then at Versailles for the meeting of the Supreme War Council, protested that it was monstrous that men who had been fighting Italy until the last minute of the war should now haul down one flag and hoist another, and claim to be allies.[3] Italy's case could hardly be challenged.

---

[1] Speech to people of Rome, 9 November. Orlando, *Discorsi*, p. 271.

[2] Hautecœur, pp. 130–1. In private Diaz admitted that the demoralisation of the Austro-Hungarian army had played a part, but only a minor part, in Italy's victory. Malagodi, II, p. 445.

[3] Sonnino argued that it was all 'just a new Austrian ruse'. Later, in a letter to Orlando, he referred to 'this first act of Yugoslav imperialism'. Albrecht-Carrié, pp. 52, 357–60; Mamatey, pp. 364–6; DDI (6), I, 51.

Pola was occupied by Italian forces a few days later, and after much heated inter-Allied argument the Austro-Hungarian ships were turned over to Italian, French and American crews and disarmed.[1]

The Italians quickly took advantage of the terms of the Villa Giusti armistice and occupied the parts of Dalmatia assigned to them by the Treaty of London. The Serbian representative on the Supreme War Council had accepted the armistice terms only with the reservation that the use, for purely military purposes, of the Treaty of London line must in no way prejudice the future political settlement.[2] But though Orlando urged the occupying forces to act as 'liberators', not 'oppressors',[3] relations between them and the local population were tense from the very start. The display of Yugoslav national colours was forbidden, Yugoslav newspapers were censored and suppressed, political demonstrations were banned, 'agitators' were deported to Italy and 30 out of 33 municipal councils were dissolved. Following the example set by Admiral Millo, who installed himself at Zara as military governor, the Italians behaved as if the occupied zone was already part of Italy.[4]

Italian ambitions were not confined to the Treaty of London line, but extended to the southern Adriatic also. Friction soon arose between the Italian command in Albania, which by the end of the war controlled most of that country, and the Army of the Orient, based on Salonika, which controlled the rest of the Balkans. Serbian and Greek units of the latter hoped to further their countries' long-standing designs on parts of Albania, and the Italians were determined to keep them out. Further north, Italian contingents of the Army of the Orient added to the tension by landing at Kotor and Antivari and pushing up into Montenegro. The object of this operation was to hamper the absorption of Montenegro in a united Yugoslavia.[5] The sympathies of the French navy and of General Franchet d'Esperey, commanding the Army of the Orient, lay with the Yugoslavs (and Greeks), and thus the quarrel between Italians and Yugoslavs

[1] DDI (6), I, 69, 355, 405.

[2] Aldrovandi, *Guerra diplomatica*, p. 197; Mamatey, pp. 362–3; Albrecht-Carrié, pp. 352–3.

[3] DDI (6), I, 8. The same spirit was shown in the occupied region south of the Brenner, where the military commander issued his initial proclamation in both Italian and German. Herre, pp. 59–61.

[4] See Salvemini's speech of 24 November 1920 in the chamber, in his *Dal patto di Londra*, pp. 328–33; also Temperley, IV, pp. 304–5; Alatri, *Nitti*, pp. 52–4.

[5] DDI (6), I, 7, 31, 73, 77, 89, 155, 288, 317, 758, 760, 817, 861. On 26 November a hastily and irregularly convened Montenegrin National Assembly deposed King Nicholas and voted union with Serbia. The Allies, however, declined to recognise the union and referred the Montenegrin problem to the Peace Conference.

developed into a quarrel between Italy and France. Friction between the local military and naval commanders soon caused strain between the two governments.[1]

The most serious situation arose at Fiume. On 29 October the port was evacuated by the Hungarian authorities and occupied by Yugoslav troops loyal to the Zagreb National Council. But meanwhile the Italians of Fiume had themselves set up a National Council which on the 30th proclaimed the annexation of Fiume to Italy. Next day Orlando told the Supreme War Council, 'Fiume is more Italian than Rome.'[2] Thus the acquisition of Fiume, which before the war had rarely been mentioned in even the wildest irredentist programmes, became with the disintegration of Austria-Hungary one of Italy's main aspirations. But Fiume had not been promised to Italy in the Treaty of London. Nevertheless, when news reached him of the arrival of a Serbian battalion, Orlando authorised the landing of Italian troops.[3] After a few critical days, a *modus vivendi* was reached whereby the Serbians withdrew and Italian and Allied forces took over the town under command of the Italian General Francesco Grazioli. Within hours of this agreement, the Army of the Orient announced its intention of establishing an autonomous base in the port, for the supply of its forces of occupation in the Balkans and Hungary. The Italian government agreed only under protest, foreseeing that 'the peaceful co-existence' of two large garrisons in one small town would cause trouble.[4] Its fears were soon confirmed. The French forces supported the Yugoslavs against the Fiume National Council, while the Italians behaved as if they were on Italian soil. Orlando, left to himself, would probably have given the National Council official recognition, but he was held back by Sonnino, who deprecated any action that would weaken Italy's stand on the Treaty of London.[5] Short of recognition, however, the National Council was

---

[1] Already on 9 November a disagreeable incident had been caused by a telegram from Thaon di Revel, the Italian naval commander-in-chief, to the British commanding admiral in the Adriatic, announcing that French ships would not be welcome in the northern Adriatic. Lloyd George showed the telegram to Clemenceau who exploded. Orlando and Sonnino had to apologise and rebuke Thaon di Revel. DDI (6), I, 71, 88, 101, 103, 105, 133, 135, 169. For strong comments on French hostility by Sonnino and Diaz, see also DDI (6), I, 513, 669, 676, 699. Charles-Roux, *Rome-Quirinal*, p. 340, recognises that many of the visits of French warships to Adriatic ports had a political motive. Clemenceau himself reproved Franchet d'Esperey for making a 'political, not military' plan for the occupation of Albania. Hankey, II, p. 843.

[2] Aldrovandi, *Guerra diplomatica*, p. 199. For the pre-war composition of Fiume's population, see above, pp. 353–4.

[3] DDI (6), I, 170, 183, 394.

[4] DDI (6), I, 203, 238, 377, 394, 462, 470, 519, 553, 564, 649. Barrère also protested. Charles-Roux, *Rome-Quirinal*, p. 342.

[5] DDI (6), I, 70, 134, 152, 559, 575.

given all possible support.[1] Thus Fiume, crammed with the troops of four
nationalities, became the storm centre of the Adriatic.[2]

These events magnified dissension within the government and on 28
December Bissolati resigned. President Wilson's arrival a week later on a
state visit imposed a short political truce. Every party in the country
greeted him with enthusiasm. Democrats, liberals, Catholics, nationalists,
socialists, all hoped or pretended that he was in agreement with their own
views. But with his departure controversy broke out. Bissolati had not
altered his opinions since 1916. For the sake of 'a just and durable peace',
he wished to 'renounce' Dalmatia (except for Zara), the Brenner frontier
and the Dodecanese, and so 'to free ourselves of all that is anti-Wilsonian
in our peace aims'. By virtue of the same principle of nationality, he claimed
Fiume for Italy.[3] He publicly warned Sonnino that reliance on the Treaty
of London would lead to diplomatic defeat. British and French imperialist
aims disturbed him as deeply as those of Italian nationalists. It seemed
obvious to him that Italy, being the poorest and weakest of the Great
Powers, had the greatest interest in securing a Wilsonian peace. He therefore hoped passionately that, with American support and the sympathy of
the Yugoslavs and other liberated peoples, Italy might yet fulfil Mazzini's
dream and become the leader of the new, democratic Europe.[4]

His voice of sanity was soon drowned in hysterical abuse. The nationalists argued that victory had conferred new rights on Italy. The Treaty
of London, signed on the assumption that Russia and Serbia would fight
by Italy's side, was no longer sufficient for a victorious nation that since
1917 had fought Austria-Hungary alone. Demonstrations were organised
for 'Italian Dalmatia' and the annexation of the occupied areas.[5] Beyond
the Adriatic the nationalists surveyed the great vacuum created by Russian
and Turkish collapse, and dreamt of Italian influence spreading through

[1] Caviglia, p. 92.
[2] A fair summary of the situation may be found in the report of the international
commission of enquiry, dated 9 August 1919, printed in BFP, I, 42, Appendix A.
[3] Bissolati, unlike the nationalists, would have been content with autonomy or
the status of a free city for Fiume and Zara. Nevertheless when he saw Wilson in
Rome in January at the latter's request, he recommended that Fiume should be
annexed, while accepting its physical separation from Italy by a wedge of Yugoslav territory. Malagodi, II, pp. 713–15; Valiani, p. 317, note 18.
[4] Colapietra, pp. 267–71; Malagodi, II, pp. 460–6. But even Bissolati was disgusted by Yugoslav chauvinism and forced to admit that the Italian nationalists
were right when they pointed out that there were no 'renouncers' on the Yugoslav
side. In private he described Yugoslav behaviour to Italy and to himself personally
as 'bestial'. Malagodi, II, pp. 451, 461.
[5] Federzoni asserted that of the 340,000 inhabitants of Dalmatia, 40,000 had
declared themselves Italians and 20,000 Yugoslavs; the remaining 280,000 were
peasants and 'nationally nondescript'. Alatri, *Nitti*, p. 54.

the Balkans and Asia Minor to Armenia, the Levant and, with the church's blessing, even down into Palestine.[1] But everywhere these 'just aspirations' were blocked by the British, the French and the Yugoslavs, and their tools inside Italy, the democratic 'renouncers'. When Bissolati tried to propound his programme at the Scala Opera House in Milan on 11 January, toughs organized by Mussolini broke up the meeting. D'Annunzio, in an *Epistle to the Dalmatians*, claimed Dalmatia as Italian 'by divine and human right', and instead of a pax Gallica, a pax Britannica or a pax Stelligera, imposed 'on us, the poor of Christ', called for a 'Roman peace'.[2] The old quarrel between democratic and nationalist interventionists, kept in check while the war lasted, now became a rift beyond hope of healing.

The nationalists were not numerous but their influence in the armed forces made them formidable. They enjoyed the sympathy of many highly placed generals and admirals such as the Duke of Aosta, commander of the Third Army, Admiral Millo, military governor of Dalmatia, General Giardino, who had commanded an army on Monte Grappa in the final battle, and General Grazioli, commander of the Allied forces in Fiume. Already in December 1918 anti-British and anti-French leaflets were circulating in the Third Army. *Il Popolo d'Italia* and other nationalist papers were distributed free by the army authorities. Grazioli turned a blind eye to the activities of Giovanni Host Venturi, an ultra-nationalist and ex-officer of the *arditi*, who built up an organisation of volunteers in Fiume and throughout Istria, and made its headquarters in Trieste a lively centre of military politics. D'Annunzio, besides urging the seizure of Fiume and all Dalmatia, spoke openly of the need to seize Rome as well, to put an end to the moribund parliamentary regime. There was renewed talk of a *pronunciamento*, of another 'radiant May', in which the army would back 'real' Italy against the spineless politicians. Now that the war was over, the soldiers had leisure for political conspiracy. For the first time in its sixty years of existence, the Italian army was confronted by the spirit of sedition within its ranks.[3]

A few weeks of peace were enough to show that the chamber of deputies, elected under Giolitti in 1913, was quite out of touch with the country. But it was from the chamber that Orlando's government drew such strength as it possessed. On 15 January Nitti resigned, in exasperation at his colleagues' indifference to his plans for reconversion of the economy from war

---

[1] Hautecœur, pp. 145–55, 201–2.

[2] ibid., pp. 183–4; D'Annunzio, *Lettera ai Dalmati*, reprinted in *La penultima ventura – Il sudore di sangue*, pp. 9–30.

[3] Caviglia, pp. 69–71; Bissolati, *Diario di guerra*, pp. 137–8; Bonomi, *La politica italiana dopo Vittorio Veneto*, p. 97; Alatri, *Nitti*, pp. 142–3. See also a report of June 1919 from the British ambassador in BFP, IV, pp. 7–9, note.

to peace.[1] Orlando, relieved to lose so uncomfortable a colleague, reconstructed and broadened his government, bringing in a leading Giolittian,
Facta, and a leading Salandrian, Riccio. He also took back as his *chef de
cabinet* Camillo Corradini, whom he had had to sacrifice to the ultra-
interventionists in 1917. This was a first step towards healing the rift that
the war had caused in the liberal ranks, a fact that was noted and disapproved by those who, like Albertini, wished even after victory to
exclude the neutralists from power. In spite of these changes the government remained patently weak. As Facta noted, its system was 'put off,
put off, put off'.[2] 'It's anarchy', Orlando himself admitted only half in
jest.[3] Between the two extremes of democratic renunciation and nationalist
conspiracy the mass of Italian opinion was left bewildered and the government drifted. In January Orlando and Sonnino offered Barrère and
Clemenceau unconditional support for French aspirations on the Rhine, if
France would unconditionally support Italian aspirations in the Adriatic.
Clemenceau rejected the offer, preferring to avoid the breach with Lloyd
George and Wilson which its acceptance would have caused.[4] After this
one positive initiative the Italians relapsed into inertia. Sonnino clung to
the Treaty of London and said nothing. Nationalist agitation was allowed
to continue unchallenged. Orlando was full of doubts and apprehensions.
Already in November, on his return from the Supreme War Council, he
had told Bissolati that 'Sonnino's policy had proved completely bankrupt'.
But for the moment, torn between conflicting pressures, he refused to make
a decision. The Italian peace delegation arrived in Paris without a policy,
just hoping for the best.[5]

## The Post-War Mood

Peace brought a burgeoning of blueprints for the new world. Few believed
it possible to return to 1914 and those that did kept silent. In the hour of
victory Giolitti and *Giolittismo* were the symbols of petty, discreditable
things that were gone for ever. The mass of Italians let their imaginations

[1] Monticone, pp. 324-8. Nitti's insistence on the need to bring technicians into
the cabinet, to deal efficiently with the problems of reconversion, led Orlando to
comment wearily on 'Nitti's latest mania, *tecnicismo*'. Malagodi, II, pp. 471-2.

[2] Facta to Giolitti, 20 March. *Quarant' anni*, III, 283.

[3] Charles-Roux, *Souvenirs diplomatiques. Une grande ambasse à Rome 1919-
1925*, p. 15.

[4] The offer was repeated in March. Charles-Roux, *Une grande ambasse*,
pp. 8-11, 20-1.

[5] Bissolati, *Diario di guerra*, pp. 137-8; Malagodi, II, pp. 463-5, 472-5. Luzzatti,
when asked his opinion as to what the two chief delegates would do in Paris, replied,
'Sonnino will keep silent in all the languages he knows, Orlando will talk in all the
languages he doesn't know.' Crespi, p. 242.

soar free and for a few months believed in miracles. Every party had its
prophet for the new world. The socialists offered Lenin, the democrats
offered President Wilson and his League of Nations. The nationalists
prescribed a resurrection of Imperial Rome. Even old liberals renounced
the past. 'This war is also the greatest political and social revolution
recorded by history, surpassing even the French Revolution', said
Orlando.[1] 'Yes, the war is a revolution', agreed Salandra; 'Let youth come
forward; it is the hour of youth. Let no one think that a peaceful return
to the past will be possible after this storm.'[2] Revolutions were on everyone's lips. Land for the peasants, workers' control of the factories, public
control of profits and distribution, taxation of the rich and punishment of
the war profiteers – these were the slogans of the day. Most popular of all
was the cry for a constituent assembly, to overhaul the constitution and
open the flood-gates of social reform. This was *diciannovismo*:[3] a pre-
revolutionary yearning for change and a utopian faith in a better world
to be born.

The party that should have thrived most in this atmosphere was the
Socialist party. It emerged proud and aggressive from the war which its
majority had always opposed. Since 1917 it had been looking to Moscow.
Revolution by defeat had misfired after Caporetto, but there seemed a
good chance of revolution after victory. The party elected a 'maximalist'
executive at its Rome congress in September 1918 and proclaimed the
dictatorship of the proletariat to be its goal. Turati in disgust talked of
resigning but was dissuaded by his friends. The maximalists, led by
Serrati, knew little of Russian conditions and nothing of the technique
by which Lenin had seized power. But the very word 'Soviet' had magic
properties for the flood of new recruits which was now swamping the more
experienced elements in the party. The reformists, who still held leading
posts in the trade unions and dominated the parliamentary group, wished
to intensify political and industrial action on traditional pre-war lines.
Italy was not Russia, they argued; an attempt to seize power would be
futile and merely provoke bloody reaction. But the new leaders of the
party, as Turati noted, were just 'waiting for the Soviet, and nothing else
counts'.[4] The voices of the moderates were drowned in revolutionary
bombast.

[1] Speech of 20 November 1918 in chamber of deputies. Orlando, *Discorsi*, p. 283.
[2] Quoted in Tasca, p. 16; Salvatorelli and Mira, p. 12; Salvemini, *Fascist
Dictatorship*, pp. 15–16.
[3] '1919-ism'.
[4] Turati to Kuliscioff, 27 February 1919. A month later Turati deplored the
party's 'mania for isolation and impotence' and its obsessive Byzantine disputations, and noted, 'These people prefer the contemplative life (il cenobio)' to practical political action. Turati–Kuliscioff, V, pp. 20, 59–62.

The maximalists made two decisions at the outset which were to cost them dear. The first was to intensify their onslaught on the war and on all patriots. Wherever they were in control, the tricolour was hauled down and the red flag flown in its place. They attacked not only Italy's war leaders, who were imperialist warmongers, and Turati and the reformists, who had succumbed to patriotic emotion in 1917–18, but even humble combatants who, if not suspect as reactionaries, were despised for their gullibility and often barred from party membership. This doctrinaire folly alienated thousands of 'embryo socialists' among the ex-servicemen. The second fatal decision was to have no dealings with non-socialist parties, however progressive; the party was ready to accept power, but alone. To collaborate in carrying out reforms, even though they benefited the working-class, would merely bolster the crumbling capitalist state. The greater the chaos, the sooner would revolution come. The most important task was to destroy dangerous illusions of democracy, to provoke crises and changes of government continuously till the conviction was born that only socialist power could provide a solution.[1] As events were soon to show, this was not revolution but abdication.

The socialists did not long remain unchallenged in their appeal to the masses. Early in 1919 Italy's first Catholic party was founded. Under Benedict XV the Christian democrats had emerged from the obscurity into which Pius X had driven them. Benedict's first encyclical, *Ad Beatissimi*, in November 1914 contained a clear disavowal of the witch-hunting excesses of the clerical integralists. In March 1915 Catholic Action was reorganised. A new policy-making executive was created, with Dalla Torre, President of the Unione Popolare, as chairman and Sturzo as secretary. At the same time the Unione Popolare was given supervisory and coordinating powers over the other four unions. Having thus regained the cohesion which Pius X's reforms of 1906 had destroyed, Catholic Action expanded rapidly.[2] Meanwhile the circumstances of the war had forced Italian Catholics to take an independent line in politics. While the Vatican remained neutral, Catholic Action supported the war once Italy was in it, and its leaders spoke and acted as patriots. The fact that this divergence led to so little friction was a further argument for removing the last political restrictions on Catholics. In November 1918 Sturzo obtained the approval of Cardinal Gasparri for the foundation of a political party, and on 18 January 1919 the manifesto of the Italian Popular party appeared.

[1] Tasca, p. 116; Nenni, p. 75.
[2] De Rosa, *L'Azione Cattolica*, II, pp. 435–40; Dalla Torre, pp. 58–61; Howard, pp. 94–9.

The name, borrowed from the Catholics of the Trentino, was in itself a programme. It implied that the party would be both non-confessional and politically independent of the church. This accorded with Sturzo's intentions and satisfied Gasparri's requirement that there must be no risk of the party's actions compromising the Vatican.[1] The Roman question was to be regarded as a matter for the Italian state and the Papacy, and one with which the party as such need have no special concern. Catholic Action remained in existence, under direct ecclesiastical control, but its political activity was limited to those issues that affected 'the supreme religious and moral interests' of the nation; in all other political matters the party was to enjoy autonomy. A similar distinction was made in the economic and social field. During the war the Vatican had encouraged the growth of the Catholic trade union and peasant movement, and had allowed it to relax its strict confessionalism. In March 1918, with papal approval, an Italian Confederation of Labour (C.I.L.) was founded, embracing all the 'white' Catholic trade unions and peasant leagues. It too was to be autonomous and to work closely with the Popular party, as the C.G.L. worked with the Socialist party.[2] This autonomy was not always easy to observe in practice, and it lasted only as long as the ecclesiastical authorities were prepared to tolerate it. The personnel of the party and of Catholic Action was largely identical. It was the priest who acted as the party's agent in the villages, just as he was often the key figure in the peasant unions of the C.I.L. Yet in the early post-war years the concept of a non-confessional, autonomous party was not meaningless. Both the party and the C.I.L. were to be infused with the Christian spirit, but distinguished from other parties and labour organisations not by their religious faith but by their political and social programmes.

The main themes of the party programme, which had a clear Christian democratic ring, were social legislation, reform of the tax system, land reform, decentralisation and a just peace based on Wilsonian principles and the League of Nations. As its emblem the party chose a white cross on a blue shield, inscribed with *Libertas*. Applied to current problems, this meant greater liberty in local government and the creation of a new unit, the region; greater liberty in education, through the removal of the inequalities between the state and Catholic schools; and greater liberty for the peasant and worker, through recognition of the equality of the C.I.L. with its trade union rivals. The programme reflected Catholic condemnation

[1] De Rosa, *I conservatori nazionali*, pp. 77–9, and *Storia*, pp. 42–5. Gasparri vetoed the use of either 'Catholic' or 'Christian' in the party's title. Sturzo was allowed, in spite of misgivings in the Vatican, to become secretary of the party, but forbidden to enter parliament.

[2] Dalla Torre, pp. 103–9, 116–17; Howard, pp. 106–8.

of the centralised liberal state and belief in an 'organic' state based on family, profession and local government. The immediate and basic reform which the party demanded was proportional representation, which would sweep away the corrupt personalised politics of *Giolittismo* and substitute a struggle of principle between disciplined mass parties.

In a matter of hours the new party took shape. It recruited clerical-moderates and reactionaries as well as Christian democrats.[1] Nineteen deputies declared themselves members and a large part of the Catholic press rallied to its support. Its growth was in fact too swift for stability and cohesion. At its first congress in June 1919 three groups emerged. A right wing, led by a Milanese priest, Agostino Gemelli, who had achieved fame as an army chaplain during the war, desired a confessional, clerical party. A left wing, led by Miglioli, the pacifist and 'white' trade unionist, called for a Christian proletarian party that would make capitalism its main enemy. Both wings were outnumbered by the centre, led by Sturzo, the party's secretary, and Alcide De Gasperi, formerly deputy for Trent in the Austrian parliament. They stood for a non-confessional party, drawn from all classes and united in loyalty to a comprehensive programme of reform. The triumph of these views made the Popular party predominantly the party of the small man: the peasant proprietor, small tenant and sharecropper, the artisan, the shopkeeper, the small industrialist and business man. Its main strength lay in agriculture rather than industry, and it reflected the countryside's dislike of violent change. In some areas such as Venetia it was virtually a peasant party. But nationally, just because it attracted members from all classes, it was vulnerable to dissension between conservatives and reformers in times of social tension. This was to be one of its main weaknesses, as it is the weakness of all Catholic parties.

In the atmosphere of 1919 a democratic party with an advanced political and social programme seemed to Benedict XV the surest instrument for furthering the church's interests in Italy. It was a daring break with the past. Not even the possibility of Popular collaboration with the moderate socialists alarmed him, for he was confident that the Italian Catholic movement was now sufficiently mature to be trusted with political responsibility.[2] Meanwhile he was engaged in adapting the church's international

---

[1] Among the conservatives were Giovanni Grosoli, last chairman of the Opera in 1903–4, and Carlo Santucci, only survivor of the National Conservatives of 1879, who presided over the discussions at which the Popular party's manifesto and programme were drafted. Grosoli and Santucci controlled the Catholic press trust and were able to put it at the service of the party. De Rosa, *I conservatori nazionali*, pp. 79–81 and *Storia*, p. 44.

[2] Gasparri, according to his statement ten years later, was much less enthusiastic than the Pope. He regarded the Popular party as 'the least bad of all the parties, that is, less bad than the communist, socialist, radical and liberal parties'. De Rosa, *I conservatori nazionali*, p. 78, n. 8.

position to the conditions of the post-war world. Though grieved by his exclusion from the Peace Conference, he made no attempt to exploit Italy's difficulties, even when the break between Orlando and Wilson over Fiume left Italy friendless.[1] His hope was rather to disentangle the Roman question from the tensions of international diplomacy and to end the old quarrel with Italy. Goodwill existed on both sides, thanks to the cordial relations which Orlando had established since 1914 with Benedict's closest advisers.[2] When Orlando offered to negotiate, he obtained a cautious but sympathetic response. By June 1919 he and the papal negotiator, Mgr Cerretti, had agreed on the creation of a sovereign Vatican City state, though its exact boundaries, and the question of an international guarantee, remained to be settled. The consent of parliament and the King could not be taken for granted, and in any case Orlando's fall interrupted further progress.[3] But the very fact that so much had been agreed showed that the Roman question was dead. In November Benedict XV finally cancelled the *non expedit* and next year he removed the last international inconvenience of the old quarrel by lifting the ban on visits of heads of Catholic states to the King of Italy in Rome.[4] A new confidence between church and state thus reinforced the efforts of the Popular party and was an essential element of the latter's success.

Neither the Socialist nor the Popular parties appealed to one important section of opinion, the ex-servicemen. Both socialists and Catholics had been, in varying degrees, against the war, and one of the merits of the Popular party in the eyes of the peasantry was that it was untainted by responsibility for 1915. Most ex-servicemen returned to civilian life with a hatred of war, but at the same time they resented statements that the war had been in vain. It was they who supplied the idealistic flavour of *diciannovismo*. They wanted to preserve the wartime spirit of comradeship in the trenches and distrusted the old politicians. In the first months of peace a multitude of clubs and associations sprang up to cater for their needs. Most were ultra-patriotic, but often they also reflected the radical post-war mood. Many ex-servicemen, with their hatred of capitalists and profiteers, were kept out of the Socialist party only by the folly of the maximalist leaders. Among the old politicians the most sympathetic were Bissolati and his friends, who tried to express the ex-servicemen's aspirations in terms of a democratic and Wilsonian programme. But the demo-

[1] See below, p. 529.
[2] Orlando, *Miei rapporti*, p. 63.
[3] ibid., pp. 123–38. Clearly Orlando would have secured approval for concessions of such magnitude to the Vatican only if they could have been presented as part of a general peace settlement that satisfied Italy.
[4] In the encyclical *Pacem Dei munus* of 23 May 1920.

crats, though rich in intellect and ideals, were poor in manpower, organisation and financial resources. It was the tragedy of post-war Italy that
democracy found itself crushed between revolutionary socialism on the
left and revolutionary nationalism on the right.

Among those competing for the ex-serviceman's support were two men
who were very far from being democrats: D'Annunzio and Mussolini.
D'Annunzio's role in 1915 and his spectacular exploits on sea and in the
air had made him a popular hero. In 1919 he devoted his literary and
oratorical gifts to glorification of war and denunciation of those who stood
between Italy and the 'just' rewards of victory. Though he had no
political organisation of his own, he had a devoted following among the
ex-service men. He also had his contacts with the patriotic syndicalists
of the U.I.L., which had been given a new lease of life by its creators, De
Ambris, Rossoni and Michele Bianchi, in May 1918.

Mussolini's war record had been very different from D'Annunzio's. In
May 1915, like so many of his political friends, he had tried to volunteer,
but the army would not accept him. In spite of a personal appeal to a
cabinet minister, Barzilai, he was forced to wait in frustration till his class
was called up in August.[1] After a year and a half in the front line on the
Isonzo, where he rose to the rank of corporal, he was wounded and eventually discharged. In June 1917 he returned to his *Popolo d'Italia*.

For the first two years of the war Mussolini remained a socialist, even
though dormant. After Caporetto his political views began to change. He
now preached a national, no longer a revolutionary, war. In spite of his
public support for the Rome Congress, the anti-Yugoslav tone of his articles
and his insistence on Italian Dalmatia became more strident. His relations
with the rest of the interventionist left grew cooler. In the summer of 1918
he took the fateful step of accepting subsidies for his paper from big
business, notably Ansaldo. At the same time he dropped the slogans of
Napoleon and Blanqui from the front page of *Il Popolo d'Italia* and transformed it from a 'socialist daily' into the paper of 'the combatants and
producers'.[2] This change reflected new interests. Responsive as ever to the
atmosphere around him, he sensed the significance of the vast industrial
expansion which was transforming northern Italy, and began to apply his
imagination to the problems with which that expansion would confront
post-war Italy. The experience of war had stimulated new thinking among
both industrialists and trade union leaders. There was growing recognition
of a common interest among 'producers', whether employers or workers,
in maintaining high production. Such thinking implied acceptance of the

[1] De Felice, pp. 321–2.
[2] ibid., pp. 391–406, 414–18. The word *combattenti*, used during the war to
describe front-line soldiers, was after the war transferred to ex-servicemen.

capitalist framework, abandonment of the old-fashioned Marxist insistence on class war and creation of a non-political trade union movement divorced from the Socialist party. Mussolini eagerly took up these ideas, which seemed well designed to appeal to the combatants returning without fixed political allegiances from the trenches, and he continued to elaborate them after victory.[1]

By the end of the war Mussolini had acquired a modest national reputation as ex-revolutionary, interventionist and hard-hitting patriotic journalist. He had no organisation behind him. Peace caught him unprepared; he was 'lost and searching for a road'.[2] His treachery of 1914 was an insuperable barrier between him and the Socialist party. But, like D'Annunzio, he was searching for contacts with the masses among the interventionist syndicalists and ex-service men, to whose inarticulate ideals he gave the most violent expression. He set the tone of his post-war programme in a speech of May 1918: 'We who have survived, we who are returning, demand the right to govern Italy.' In March 1919 he returned to the theme:

> A war of the masses ends with the triumph of the masses . . . The bourgeois revolution of 1789 – which was revolution and war in one – opened the gates of the world to the bourgeoisie . . . The present revolution, which is also a war, seems to open the gates of the future to the masses, who have served their hard apprenticeship of blood and death in the trenches.
> We have already made a revolution. In May 1915 . . . That was the first episode of the revolution, its beginning. The revolution continued under the name of war for forty months. It is not yet over . . .[3]

On 10 November 1918 Mussolini rode in a Milan victory parade on a lorry manned by *arditi*. 'Italy is yours', he told them. For the next few months he lived in an atmosphere of war tension and comradeship; a steel helmet, a dagger and hand grenades littered his editor's desk, and military banners with the skull and crossbones of the *arditi* hung from the walls. Ex-servicemen were his constant companions and he kept in touch with many of their clubs and societies.[4] On 23 March 1919, in a small hall

[1] ibid., pp. 406–13, 465–7, 492–7. This current of thought was not of course confined to Italy. It was strong in France and found expression in the C.G.T.'s *La bataille syndicaliste*, which Mussolini read. Mussolini's concern with industrial problems shows how far he had outgrown the rural Romagnole background of his youth; it was Milan that moulded the politics of his middle age. ibid., pp. 4, 62, 411–12.

[2] ibid., pp. 459, 465, quoting Mussolini's own words of October 1939 to his biographer, De Begnac.

[3] Speech at Bologna, 19 May 1918; *Il Popolo d'Italia*, 5 and 18 March 1919. Mussolini, XI, p. 87, XII, pp. 268, 310.

[4] Five such bodies with which Mussolini had direct contact were the Associazione fra i volontari italiani, Fascio futurista politico romano, Fascio italiano di difesa

in Piazza San Sepolcro, Milan, he founded his own national organisation, the Fasci Italiani di Combattimento. Prominent among its 119 founding members was the futurist Marinetti, whose house was at this time the headquarters of the Milanese *arditi*. The organisation soon outgrew all rivals and its members came to be generally known as *fascisti*. Its programme was soaked in *diciannovismo*. A constituent assembly, female suffrage and proportional representation, abolition of the senate, land for the peasants, a capital levy, an eight-hour day in industry and a share in factory management for the workers, more generous pensions, confiscation of ecclesiastical property and repeal of the Law of Guarantees – all these found a place beside praise of Wilson and the League of Nations, glorification of the war and insistence on the just rewards of victory. Such a mixture of nationalism and radicalism was well designed both to attract ex-servicemen and to rouse the enthusiasm of his old political allies, the futurists, the revolutionary interventionists and the syndicalists of the U.I.L.[1]

But it was not on political ideas that fascism thrived, but on the yearning for action and the opportunities it provided for satisfying this yearning. Its driving force was hatred of the Socialist party and of the democratic renouncers. On 11 January Mussolini and Marinetti organised the wrecking of Bissolati's meeting at the Scala. This was the first planned violence of post-war Italy. Thereafter the fascists systematically challenged the socialists in the streets of Milan. In April, during a local general strike, Marinetti's *arditi* disrupted a mass socialist demonstration in the centre of the city, then sacked and burnt the offices of *Avanti!* Such exploits delighted the Milanese propertied classes who began to look to extra-legal violence for the protection against bolshevism which they claimed the state was unable or unwilling to give.[2] But Mussolini did not intend to become 'the bodyguard of the bourgeoisie'. He was the enemy of the Socialist party, but the friend of the trade unions and the working-class. In March he visited the Dalmine engineering works near Milan, where the U.I.L. had organised a sit-down strike. He promised the workmen his support and praised them for striking 'creatively' without stopping production, for hoisting the tricolour, not the red flag, on their factory and for

---

nazionale, Fascio di resistenza and Associazione Arditi. The last, founded with Mussolini's blessing in November 1918, had its membership swollen to 10,000 in January after the dissolution of some of the *arditi* formations for indiscipline. In February 1919 there were 20 futurist fasci in existence. De Felice, pp. 474–83.

[1] The Fasci's programme, published in June, was drafted by De Ambris, secretary of the U.I.L. ibid., pp. 514 ff.

[2] Middle-class 'volunteers for the defence of order' had already made their appearance before the war, particularly in Emilia. See above, pp. 258, 394.

'not forgetting the nation'.[1] Mussolini claimed that his was the only truly revolutionary movement, in contrast to the sterile, reactionary Socialist party with its ruling clique of mediocre politicians, its Russian fixation and its infatuation with Lenin. He attacked all parties and stole their slogans indiscriminately. His movement was an antiparty, 'a church of all the heresies', 'a synthesis of all negations and affirmations': above all, 'an organisation not for propaganda but for battle'.[2] By October, though still confined to Milan and a few big cities, the fasci had recruited 17,000 members.[3] Their violence and exoticism attracted many of the war generation who had no political loyalties – above all, young men of the middle class who, as *arditi* or pilots or officers, had been imbued with the cult of heroism and were now finding that it was the profiteers, the 'shirkers' and the well-paid industrial working-class who enjoyed the advantages in civilian life.

Throughout 1919 a wave of social unrest swept the country. Italy, like all belligerent countries, was unprepared for the transition from war to peace. It had suffered far less material damage than France and its industry was unscathed. But war had disrupted its economy. The pattern of industry had been distorted, imports had swollen, exports had collapsed, foreign markets had been lost, emigration had ceased, the land was exhausted, the transport system had run down  British and American credits and inter-Allied control of shipping and raw materials had kept Italy going while the war lasted. But with peace came immediate pressure in Britain and the U.S.A. for the removal of all controls. The Italian delegation in Paris pleaded, to little effect, for planned distribution of vital supplies on a basis of need rather than ability to pay. A Supreme Economic Council was created for the armistice period, but it fought a losing battle. Hoover, the chief economic delegate of the U.S.A., his hands tied by home opinion, granted new credits only with the greatest reluctance and rejected all proposals for a permanent inter-Allied economic organisation.[4] In February the Council was warned that if Italy's essential needs were not quickly met, 'economic death' and revolution would inevitably follow.[5] Next month

---

[1] Mussolini, XII, pp. 314–16. See also XIII, pp. 346–9, for Mussolini's support of another syndicalist strike in September.

[2] *Il Popolo d'Italia*, 6 and 13 October; speech at first Fascist congress at Florence, 9 October; in Mussolini, XIV, pp. 43–5, 50–5, 60.

[3] Fascist statistics were highly impressionistic. The membership for October 1919 was declared at the time as 40,000, but retrospectively reduced two years later to 17,000. Even the latter figure was probably an exaggeration. Tasca, p. 55; De Felice, p. 568.

[4] Crespi, pp. 201–24, 263–9, 662–5, 682–3.

[5] PPC, X, p. 12.

inter-Allied exchange control was abandoned. The lira, which had been pegged at 30·3 to the pound in the last months of the war, dropped to 36 by mid-May. Never had Italy's economic prospects looked so bleak.

The two most vital needs were wheat and coal. Between September 1918 and March 1919 Italy received 25% less than its minimum requirements of cereals and only 52% of its requirements of other foods.[1] After March the Italians, with their scanty holdings of foreign exchange, had to compete for limited supplies against the greatly superior resources of the British and the French. But in spite of a poor harvest at home[2] and great shipping difficulties, the worst food shortages had been eliminated by the autumn. The coal problem was not solved so quickly. Before the war Italy had imported 900,000 tons a month. In February 1918 the Allies undertook to supply 690,000 but failed to keep their promise, and after the armistice deliveries dropped still further. Transport was short and strikes cut production in the British and French mines. German coal went first to those countries whose mines had been destroyed and little was left for Italy. In the first five months of 1919 only 484,000 tons per month were delivered.[3] Rail services were reduced, the ports grew congested and industry was starved. In June industrial production had still not reached the pre-war level. Exports in 1919 paid for only 36% of imports (compared with 68% in 1913).[4] Inflation was rampant. The cost of living had more than quadrupled since 1913 and was still rising. The budget deficit had grown from 214 million lire in 1913–14 to 23,345 million in 1918–19, with revenue covering only 24% of expenditure.[5]

It was the cost of living that touched off the first serious explosion. In June 1919 riots started in Emilia and spread throughout the country. In the large cities shops were sacked and 'hoarders' assaulted. Self-created citizens' committees announced 50% price reductions and assumed control of distribution, and 'every village had its Marat or its Lenin'.[6] In many places shopkeepers brought their keys to these committees and handed over their stocks in the hope of protection from the mob. Meanwhile a flood of recruits swamped the trade unions. Membership of the C.G.L. grew from 249,000 at the end of the war to 1,258,000 in October 1919 and over 2,000,000 by the autumn of 1920. The Catholic C.I.L.

---

[1] PPC, X, pp. 9–10, 59; Crespi, pp. 306–7.

[2] In 1919 Italy produced 45 million quintals of wheat and imported 21 million, compared with an annual average of 51 and 17 in 1911–13. *Sommario*, pp. 106, 159.

[3] PPC, X, pp. 226–7 350 ff. Coal imports (in millions of tons) totalled 5·8 in 1918, 6·2 in 1919 and 5·6 in 1920, compared with 10·8 in 1913. *Sommario*, p. 160.

[4] *Sommario*, p. 152; Romeo, p. 181.

[5] Coppola d'Anna, pp. 85, 88.

[6] Nenni, p. 28. See also Germanetto, pp. 137–45, for a lively communist description of the agitation in Turin.

grew even more rapidly, from 162,000 members at the end of the war to
1,160,000 in 1920 [1] The new recruits, many of them fresh from the army,
had no use for trade union discipline. Energetic and enthusiastic, and full
of the illusions of *diciannovismo*, they intended to squeeze the maximum
out of their employers – the 'profiteers' whom they had learnt to hate in
the trenches – in the shortest possible time. In the early months of 1919
strikes broke out over north Italy on a scale far surpassing that of the most
agitated pre-war years.[2] The moment was favourable. Demobilisation had
hardly begun and there was little unemployment. At first the industrialists,
impatient to restore full peace-time production, hardly resisted. In February the metal-workers' union won an eight-hour day without reduction in
wages. Workers in many other industries quickly followed their example.
New methods were devised to break down employers' resistance and
several factories in Piedmont and Lombardy were occupied by sit-down
strikers. Violence and clashes with the police were frequent and the dismal
list of 'proletarian massacres' lengthened.

In many parts of Italy the countryside was as agitated as the towns.
Wartime promises of land for the peasants had not been forgotten. The
official National Ex-Servicemen's Organisation, founded by Nitti after
Caporetto, was active in many parts of the south, acquiring land com-
pulsorily, building farmhouses and settling ex-soldiers on small plots. But
all this took time and the peasants were impatient. In August 1919 they
began to seize land in the Roman Campagna. Columns would set out at
dawn from the villages, with banners and martial music, march to the
selected estate, mark out the uncultivated land in strips or plots, and at
once begin to dig or plough, to establish ownership.[3] Often the land
selected for seizure had been the object of bitter disputes for decades and
was regarded by the peasants as rightfully theirs. Ex-servicemen were in

---

[1] Einaudi, pp. 312, 322; Serpieri, pp. 253 ff.; Neufeld, pp. 368–9. About one-
third of the C.G.L.'s membership and 80% of the C.I.L.'s was agricultural. The
U.S.I. claimed 800,000 members in 1920, the U.I.L. 200,000, and the independent
railwaymen's union another 200,000.

[2] The following figures are calculated from *ASI 1919–1921*, p. 512 and Neufeld,
p. 547:

| Year | Number of strikes | | Number of strikers involved (thousands) | |
|---|---|---|---|---|
| | Industry | Agriculture | Industry | Agriculture |
| 1901–1913 (annual average) | 1,006 | 219 | 201 | 112 |
| 1919 | 1,663 | 208 | 1,049 | 505 |
| 1920 | 1,881 | 189 | 1,268 | 1,046 |

The highest total number of strikers in any pre-war year had been 385,000 in
industry (1913) and 254,000 in agriculture (1907).

[3] Einaudi, pp. 291–2; Serpieri, pp. 212–13.

the forefront of the movement, for war had changed the mentality of the peasant soldier, making him less submissive and readier to organise and assert his rights. In September the government was forced to authorise prefects to requisition uncultivated land and distribute it to deserving claimants, provided they organised themselves in cooperatives. This encouraged the agitators and in the spring of 1920 the Sicilian *latifondi* were the scene of larger-scale seizures, organised by the Catholic peasant leagues with the encouragement of many parish priests. In April, in an attempt to damp down the agitation, the government announced that only the claims of those squatters who showed themselves capable of efficient farming would be recognised. The acreage of land which permanently changed hands by these methods was small,[1] but the movement created a great stir. Conservatives and landowners saw revolution spreading to the countryside.

Agitation was not confined to seizure of land. Peasants of every type were organising themselves, even in areas where before 1914 organisation had been unknown. Socialists and Catholics competed for their leadership. The former, though still drawing their main support from the *braccianti*, were more successful than before the war in attracting small tenants, sharecroppers and even peasant proprietors into their unions. Where the socialists were well entrenched, as in Emilia, the C.I.L. tended to represent the wealthier peasants and the Popular party the middle class, both offering an anti-socialist programme. In such cases the C.I.L. would be denounced by the C.G.L. as a strike-breaking organisation and the struggle between whites and reds would be ferocious. But elsewhere the Catholics often led the peasant agitation. In rich Tuscany, traditionally the most contented agricultural region of Italy, the *mezzadri*, with the help of the C.I.L., struggled for greater security against eviction and an increase in their share of the crop from 50% to 55% or above. Some proprietors became so disillusioned that they began replacing their *mezzadri* with cash tenants.[2] But in many areas the tenants, too, were organising and agitating for fair rents, security of tenure and compensation for improvements.[3] On the dairy farms of lower Lombardy the Catholic unions, led by Miglioli, demanded the creation of estate councils which would give the labourers a

[1] In northern Italy proprietors constituted 26% of the total agricultural population in 1911 and 36·5% in 1921. Most of this significant increase took place in 1919–21 and was the result of individual purchases of land by peasants with war-time savings. Preti, pp. 409–10. It is significant that the illegal seizure of land was very rare in the north; it was the weapon of the peasants in the centre and south who had no savings with which to buy.

[2] Preti, pp. 392–5, 401–3; Serpieri, pp. 323–8. One of the C.I.L. militants was Giovanni Gronchi, President of the Italian Republic from 1955 to 1962.

[3] Preti, pp. 403–8.

share in management and so elevate them, in accordance with Catholic doctrine, above the lowly status of wage-earner. Stubborn resistance by the proprietors led to a struggle which the unions fought with a passion and resolution that earned Miglioli the title of 'white bolshevik'.[1]

The tension was greatest, as before 1914, in the lower Po valley. Here the *braccianti* were again on the march and in the spring of 1919 they won a forty-eight-hour week. In Emilia the old, bitter struggle for work continued. In November 1918 the government, foreseeing that peace would bring at least temporary unemployment, granted official recognition and a subsidy to the labour exchanges of the socialist unions.[2] This decision had far-reaching consequences, for it greatly strengthened the power of the unions to win a monopoly of labour. They were able to extend the *turno di lavoro*[3] and to devise and enforce new methods for increasing employment. Elaborate schedules, which laid down the minimum number of men and women per hectare to be employed on each crop or agricultural operation at each season of the year, were incorporated in labour contracts.[4] The socialists also continued, as before 1914, to extract from the government public works contracts, subsidies and credits for their expanding labour and consumers' cooperatives. The aspirations of the *braccianti* were traditional; much more significant was the new ruthlessness of the means used to achieve them. Refractory proprietors were boycotted, non-union labour was black-listed and union members who disobeyed orders or failed to observe strike discipline were fined, pilloried or ostracised. Sharecroppers, peasant tenants and small proprietors were often subjected to the same form of persecution. Arson, slaughter of cattle and physical assault were not uncommon. Power went to the heads of the local union leaders who were often naive, uneducated men. They revelled in revolutionary oratory, whipped up the crudest class hatred and indulged in countless acts of petty, arbitrary tyranny. From time to time the unions would organise marches into neighbouring towns, where the *braccianti* would process through the streets, singing and shouting, in order to strike terror into the hearts of the local bourgeoisie.[5] The state authorities shrank from interference, for fear of provoking disorder, and allowed economic and even political

[1] Preti, pp. 365–7, 418–21; Serpieri, pp. 317–18. The general programme of the C.I.L. is summarised in Serpieri, pp. 310–16.

[2] Preti, pp. 373–4. Recognition was not confined to socialist labour exchanges, but in Emilia there were virtually no others.

[3] See above, p. 305.

[4] Serpieri, pp. 299–303, 417–28; Preti, pp. 385–9. This practice, tolerated by successive governments and perfected since 1945, is known as the *imponibile di mano d'opera*.

[5] Preti, pp. 421–6. Democrats no less than reactionaries were disgusted by these abuses of power. Anna Kuliscioff, for instance, wrote of 'red tyranny' at Bologna. Turati–Kuliscioff, V, pp. 412, 428.

power over wide areas to pass into the hands of the socialist unions. Never had the 'red baronies' of Emilia been so powerful.

Out of all this ferment in town and countryside a Lenin could perhaps have created a truly revolutionary movement. But there was no single leader capable of imposing his will. Behind the facade of unity and mass membership, the Socialist party and the C.G.L. were paralysed by the rivalry between maximalists and reformists, neither of whom were strong enough to get their way. The reformists were shocked by the exuberance and indiscipline of the masses. They told their supporters to take no part in the cost of living riots and tried to moderate the excesses of local leaders. The maximalists, absorbed in their blueprints for soviets and the socialisation of land, and wrangling over correct revolutionary tactics, were hardly less suspicious than the reformists of popular initiative. They condemned the land seizures as 'a demagogic, petty bourgeois movement'[1] and only when it was too late began to ponder the advantage of the slogan 'Land for the Peasants' which Lenin had used with supreme success. They too disapproved of the cost of living riots and dismissed price reductions as an absurd palliative. Even in red Emilia they missed their chance. They talked much of creating a 'second power', on which the socialist state would be built when the bourgeois state collapsed. But they failed to see that in the peasant leagues, the cooperatives, the labour exchanges and socialist local authorities a 'second power' lay ready to their hand. Instead these organisations were left to their own devices, to be discarded as soon as doctrinally reliable soviets could be established.

The most grandiose display of socialist strength was a national general strike on 20 July. Its purpose was to prevent armed intervention by Italy against the 'workers' governments' of Russia and Hungary, and to overawe the capitalists and bourgeoisie. Though incomplete, it was an imposing demonstration. But its atmosphere was that of a *festa* rather than a revolution and it led to nothing. The fears of the government and the middle class were proved false. Maximalism, like Ferri's integralism fifteen years before, was shown to have a soft core; it provided only revolutionary talk as a substitute for revolution. The moment of enthusiasm was allowed to pass and the idea of revolution grew stale. With justification Ludovico D'Aragona, secretary of the C.G.L., could say three years later, 'It is our glory and our pride that we prevented the outbreak of the revolution which the extremists desired.'[2]

There were only two genuinely revolutionary groups in Italy, both of

[1] Tasca, p. 126.
[2] Salvemini, *Fascist Dictatorship*, pp. 30–1. D'Aragona had succeeded Rigola in August 1918.

them small: the communists and the anarchists. The latter were still strong in traditionally anarchist areas such as Carrara, La Spezia, Ancona and the Marche. They also commanded much sympathy in the U.S.I. whose secretary, Armando Borghi, was an anarchist. This gave them influence wherever syndicalism still flourished: in certain sections of the Lombard engineering industry and among the railwaymen, dockers and seamen, the building labourers of Rome and Bologna, and the *braccianti* of Parma and Ferrara provinces.[1] In December 1919 Giulietti's seamen smuggled Malatesta, the greatest living Italian anarchist, out of England, where he had spent the war in exile,[2] and brought him home to Italy. He had not changed since 1872. An immediate popular insurrection was still his aim, to be achieved by incessant, intensive agitation. Italy seemed to him ripe for revolution and he set to work with fiery energy to exploit unrest and discontent wherever they could be found. The peasants were incited to seize the land, the workers to occupy the factories. Having none of the socialists' scruples about choice of allies, he was willing to accept help from anyone prepared to work for revolution. As he travelled round the country, he was hailed at mass meetings as 'the Lenin of Italy'.[3] But the socialists and C.G.L. rejected all his overtures for a united front, and by themselves the anarchists could achieve little. In vain Malatesta warned that time was precious. 'If we let the right moment slip', he wrote, 'we shall pay with tears of blood for the fright we have given the bourgeoisie.'[4]

There were two communist groups inside the Socialist party. One had been organised by Amedeo Bordiga, a young Neapolitan engineer, who at the end of 1918 founded a periodical, *Il Soviet*. In this he preached a total boycott of elections and parliament, and single-minded preparation for the violent seizure of power. Gradually he built up throughout Italy

[1] The syndicalists were, however, seriously weakened by the split between the U.I.L., to which those who had supported intervention in 1915 belonged, and the U.S.I., which had consistently opposed the war and remained anti-patriotic and anti-nationalist. The U.S.I. differed little from the C.G.L. in its attitude to the war and foreign policy, and an attempt was made in January 1919 to reunite the two organisations. It failed because the gulf between the reformist and syndicalist temperaments, which had caused the original split in 1906, was still too deep.

[2] He had been forced to leave Italy in June 1914 as a result of his leading role in Red Week.

[3] Borghi, pp. 200–11; L. Fabbri, *Malatesta. L'uomo e il pensiero* (Naples 1951), pp. 35–9, 115–16. Malatesta did not like being compared with Lenin. As he tried to convince his audiences, he believed in freedom, not the dictatorship of the proletariat, and would never consent to become a tyrant. On Lenin's death, Malatesta wrote: 'He was a tyrant, even though with the best of intentions, who strangled the Russian revolution – and we who could not love him alive, cannot mourn him dead. Lenin is dead. Long live Liberty.' E. Malatesta, *Scritti scelti* (Naples 1947), p. 170.

[4] Tasca, p. 78; Sforza, *Contemporary Italy*, p. 218.

THE DEMOCRATIC FAILURE

a network of extremist groups devoted to this programme. The second group formed in Turin around a weekly paper, *L'Ordine Nuovo*, from which it took its name. It was the product of the wartime transformation of Turin into a booming industrial city, with the most militant working-class in Italy. The leader of the group was Antonio Gramsci, a young Sardinian of humble origin, who had studied at Turin University before the war and stayed in the city ever since. Gramsci had a magnetic personality and a first-class brain. He had never travelled outside Italy, yet was capable of the effort of imagination needed to understand the Russian revolution and to adapt Lenin's theory to Italian conditions. His formula of a revolutionary alliance between the industrial workers of the north and the peasants of the south was the product of a searching Marxist analysis of the Southern question, with which his Sardinian background had made him familiar, and a shrewd appreciation of the use that Lenin had made of peasant discontent. In the huge Fiat workshops Gramsci and his friends saw the birth of the new industrial man. The factory was more than a place where men worked and earned wages: it was a social and cultural organism in which the working-class could find an outlet for its yet untapped energies, and a school in which the new proletarian élite could be trained. In particular Gramsci saw in the workshop committees (*commissioni interne*), which during the war had outgrown the traditional limits of trade union structure,[1] the germ of a native Italian version of the Russian soviets. The aim of the Ordine Nuovo group was to transform these committees into fully representative councils (*consigli di fabbrica*), through which the workers would win a share in factory management and acquire technical knowledge and experience, as a first step towards the revolutionary expropriation of industry.[2] Gramsci, like Malatesta, saw the danger of reaction if the socialists allowed the favourable moment to pass away. But he and his group were young and inexperienced and viewed with suspicion by established working-class leaders. Outside Turin they counted for little.

The maximalists continued to control the Socialist party. By their attacks on the war, their denunciation of patriots as warmongers, their fomenting of class hatred and disorder, and their endless talk of imminent revolution, they made the maximum number of enemies with the minimum of advantage. They assumed that the bourgeois state was doomed and that they would reap the harvest of its coming collapse, and did not foresee that the undermining of its defences might benefit not themselves, but a

[1] See above, p. 470.
[2] The industrialists of northern Italy had been forced during 1919 to give grudging recognition to the *commissioni interne*, but they were determined to resist any extension of their powers. Neufeld, pp. 371–4.

more ruthless enemy. When it was too late, most socialists realised what a good friend the bourgeois state had been.

## Orlando and the Peace Conference

Wilson's attention had been drawn to the Adriatic question even before he left for Europe in December 1918, but he had refused to make any premature decision. During his visit to Rome in January he was non-committal. His general policy was clear. The U.S.A. were not bound by the Treaty of London and Wilson abhorred it as he abhorred all secret treaties. He took his stand on the ninth of his Fourteen Points: 'A readjustment of the frontiers of Italy should be effected along clearly recognisable lines of nationality', and on the second of his Four Principles: 'Peoples and provinces are not to be bartered about from sovereignty to sovereignty as if they were mere chattels and pawns in a game.' The Italian view was that any 'readjustment of frontiers' must offer Italy 'the essential conditions of military security'. Though Wilson acknowledged Italian reservations on this point at the time of the armistice with Austria-Hungary, they were never officially recorded. He listened with irritated impatience to arguments about the military menace of a united Yugoslavia and vainly tried to persuade the Italians that the League of Nations would give them greater security in the Adriatic than any strategic frontier.[1]

On the question of Italy's northern frontier, Wilson's attitude was curiously different. He appears to have agreed to the Treaty of London line on the Brenner early in January.[2] But, perhaps just because he was unhappy about the consequent transfer to Italy of 230,000 Germans, 'as if they were mere chattels and pawns', he resisted any major violation of the principle of self-determination at the expense of the Yugoslavs. The maximum concession he would make was a line running north to south down the watershed of the Istrian peninsula, soon to become known as the Wilson Line. Even this left 365,000 Yugoslavs on the wrong side of the frontier; but it also left Fiume, which Wilson believed was economically

[1] Mamatey, pp. 368–71; DDI (6), I, 10, 159, 349, 406; Albrecht-Carrié, pp. 60–6, 79–81, 90, 363; Aldrovandi, *Guerra diplomatica*, pp. 190–3; Orlando, *Memorie*, pp. 404 n., 420–6. Wilson's advisers argued that in agreeing to an armistice with Germany on the basis of the Fourteen Points, Italy had consented to modify 'the pact of London in any respect in which the same is inconsistent with the Fourteen Points of the President'. Wilson himself, however, never adopted this extreme position.

[2] Malagodi, II, p. 478. The formal decision on the Brenner frontier was taken by the Peace Conference only in May, and there were moments in March and April when the issue seemed in doubt. But Wilson himself appears never to have gone back on his original decision. ibid., pp. 606, 622–5; Orlando, *Memorie*, pp. 438–9, 477.

vital to Yugoslavia, separated from Italy by fifteen miles of predominantly Slav-inhabited country.[1]

The Italian delegation was by no means united. Sonnino clung to the Treaty of London, believing that the military security which it would give far outweighed the sacrifice of Fiume. Orlando was uninterested in Dalmatia and saw all the advantages of friendship with the Yugoslavs. His views were not so different from those of Bissolati, who wished to barter Dalmatia for Fiume.[2] But he was far more responsive than Sonnino to the clamour of the nationalists. Failure to achieve a 'victorious' peace would be his certain downfall and he dared not press Sonnino too hard. His main concern was to keep his team together in the hope that, eventually, Wilson and the Allies would be induced by the strength of national feeling to recognise the justice of Italy's claim to Fiume. The first official statement of Italian demands on 7 February reflected this indecision. It claimed the Brenner frontier, Istria and central Dalmatia within the Treaty of London line on strategic grounds, and Fiume on grounds of self-determination. Orlando thus placed his delegation in an indefensible position. On the same day that the Italians presented their claims to the Conference, Wilson recognised the Yugoslav state. Greatly encouraged, the Yugoslavs offered to submit the Istrian frontier to American arbitration. The Italians refused on the ground that the Yugoslavs were ex-enemies. On 18 February Trumbić presented his demands, which included even Trieste and Gorizia. Few people in Paris took such megalomania seriously. But the Italian attitude soon forced Wilson into the position of champion of the Yugoslavs and widened the Adriatic dispute into a clash between Italy and the U.S.A.

Throughout most of April, Fiume and Dalmatia dominated the Peace Conference. Its meetings grew painful and angry and relations between Wilson and the Italians moved towards a rupture. For Wilson, Fiume had become a question of right and wrong. The Italians wrote off his moral scruples as hypocrisy and asked why national self-determination was so sacred in Dalmatia when it was cheerfully ignored in the Saar, Austria, Bohemia and the Polish Corridor.[3] The British and French, recognising

---

[1] A further reason for Italy's determination to secure Fiume was the fear that otherwise it would attract all the trade to and from central Europe. This would destroy the economy of Trieste. Barzilai, a prominent member of the peace delegation, came from Trieste. Malagodi, II, pp. 602, 628.

[2] As did Diaz. Thaon di Revel, on the other hand, had the same Dalmatian fixation as Sonnino and insisted that the possession of a naval base at Šibenik (Sebenico) was a strategic necessity for Italy. Diaz calculated that this would mean committing at least one-quarter of the Italian army to the defence of Dalmatia. Malagodi, II, pp. 464, 502–5, 524–8, 550.

[3] Wilson gave the Italians 'the impression that he wanted to retrieve his vir-

that they were bound by the Treaty of London, worked for a compromise which would relieve them of their embarrassing obligation. The most hopeful proposal was to make Fiume a free city like Danzig, under League of Nations control. Similar schemes were hatched for Zara and Šibenik, the two Dalmatian cities which had most retained their Italian character. On 4 April the Italian delegation decided to walk out of the Conference if their minimum demands were not conceded.[1] But negotiations were still in progress on the evening of 23 April when Wilson published a manifesto to the Italian people, appealing for moderation and understanding. Orlando felt bound to interpret this as an attempt to undermine his own position at home. Next day, after issuing a public protest, he left Paris for Italy, to obtain a renewed mandate from the Italian parliament.

Wilson's manifesto was a psychological blunder. He expected an outcry in Italy but deluded himself that 'opinion would probably change in the course of a week or so'. From an early age he had been an admirer of Mazzini, whose writings he regarded as the true voice of Italy. He was therefore confident that the Italian people would come to its senses once it had been given opportunity to consider the American case.[2] But the unanimous reaction in Italy was one of injured national pride. Not even Bissolati and the democrats spoke in Wilson's defence. Salvemini, one of Bissolati's most faithful supporters, upbraided Wilson for discrimination against Italy, for trying 'to impose what he considers absolute justice on the Italian people alone'.[3] The nationalists exulted. Excited crowds greeted the returning delegation at Turin and demonstrations for Fiume and Dalmatia followed it all the way to Rome. 'We are here to perform our duty, whatever that may be', declared Diaz; 'Italy can count on her sons.' Sonnino deplored the fuss, but Orlando's emotional temperament responded to the elation. 'Italy knows poverty and hunger; she does not know dishonour', he told a delirious audience on arrival in Rome.[4]

---

ginity at our expense'. Crespi, p. 459; Sforza, *Contemporary Italy*, pp. 185–6. Sonnino privately described Wilson as 'specie di clergyman'. Rodd, III, p. 377. In retrospect Orlando convinced himself that Wilson's attitude was due to some 'occult influence' (perhaps Mrs Wilson). 'It seems clear', he wrote (*Memorie*, p. 484), 'that Wilson had a personal commitment to the Yugoslavs. What it was, I don't know; but there was one.'

[1] Malagodi, II, p. 601. As early as 6 February Orlando had warned Wilson that he might be forced to take this course. ibid., pp. 536–7, 546.

[2] Albrecht-Carrié, p. 136. The idea of an appeal to the peoples against their governments had been in Wilson's mind at least as early as January. Malagodi, II, p. 476.

[3] Albrecht-Carrié, pp. 146–7; Salvemini, *Dal patto di Londra*, p. 272. For similar sentiments in Anna Kuliscioff, see Turati–Kuliscioff, V, pp. 95, 100.

[4] Hautecœur, pp. 226–7; Crespi, pp. 477–8; Salvatorelli and Mira, p. 37; Curato, II, p. 272.

Parliament gave him a victor's ovation. Police protected the American Embassy from violence. The Mayor of Rome presided over a meeting on the Capitol and demanded, in magnificent rhetoric, the Treaty of London plus Fiume plus Split. D'Annunzio and Mussolini urged a *fait accompli*: let Italy annex Fiume and Dalmatia and defy the world. 'Never have I felt so proud to be an Italian', declared D'Annunzio: Italy alone was pure, Italy alone was great, and the Conference would be powerless against 'a victorious nation, against the most victorious of nations, against the nation that had saved all nations'. Vituperation of the Allies, of the U.S.A. and of Wilson reached unsurpassed heights. Fiume became an infatuation and Rome lived again in the atmosphere of 'radiant May'.[1]

When he left Paris, Orlando had intended to obtain his mandate from parliament and return quickly, his bargaining strength restored.[2] But in the midst of the patriotic hubbub it seemed impossible that Wilson would persist in opposing a unanimous Italy's wishes. So, basking in his popularity, Orlando waited in Rome for a conciliatory gesture from Paris. This was as great a psychological error as Wilson's. The Conference carried on without the Italians, making no attempt to bring them back. The peace treaty with Germany was completed, after some of the reparation clauses had been altered to the detriment of Italy. All the mandates over Germany's African colonies were allotted to the British Empire and France. Worse still, Wilson, Clemenceau and Lloyd George showed they were determined to go ahead with the Austrian and Hungarian treaties, whether the Italians appeared or not. Furthermore, Lloyd George declared that if no Italian representatives turned up to sign the treaty with Germany, Britain and France would conclude that Italy wanted a separate peace, in which case the Treaty of London would become null and void.[3]

Lloyd George and Clemenceau had at first tried to heal the breach between Wilson and the Italians. But even they lost patience with Italy when a new dispute arose in Asia Minor. In the last days of March Sonnino had ordered the landing of two companies of Italian marines at Adalia.[4] A few weeks later two Italian warships sailed into Smyrna harbour. A battalion was also sent inland, this time with Allied approval, to Konia.

[1] Hautecœur, p. 228; Crespi, p. 251; Tasca, pp. 47–8; Aldrovandi, *Guerra diplomatica*, p. 293; D'Annunzio, *La penultima ventura – Il sudore di sangue*, pp. 83 ff.

[2] Crespi, pp. 467–71; Bonomi, *La politica italiana dopo Vittorio Veneto*, p. 37.

[3] Crespi, pp. 510, 515–16, 776–7; D. Lloyd George, *The Truth about the Peace Treaties* (London 1930), II, pp. 868–9.

[4] Sonnino had decided to carry out this operation at the end of December 1918, but suspended it owing to British opposition. DDI (6), I, 625, 633, 686, 774. The Treaty of London had promised Italy 'a just share of the Mediterranean region adjacent to the province of Adalia'.

AUSTRIA

.Tarvisio

ITALY

Udine

R. Isonzo

Gorizia

SLOVENIA

Trieste

M. Nevoso

ISTRIA

Fiume
Sušak

CROATIA

Veglia
(Krk)

Pola

Cherso

Arbe (Rab)

THE NORTH EASTERN FRONTIER
1914–1920
Miles
0    10    20    30    40    50

Lussin

———  Italo-Austrian frontier of 1914
- - -  Treaty of London line 1915
++++  Wilson Line 1919
▨▨▨  Area predominantly inhabited by Italians
o o o  Treaty of Rapallo line 1920

Sonnino's intention was clearly to stake a claim to those portions of Asia Minor which had been promised to Italy in the Treaty of London and the abortive St Jean de Maurienne Agreement. The reason for this haste was fear of the Greeks, who had their eyes not only on a wide region round Smyrna but also on the Dodecanese. But Sonnino's action precipitated exactly what he had wished to forestall and played into the hands of the Greeks. Their brilliant leader, Venizelos, was lobbying untiringly in Paris and had captivated the British and American delegations by his charm, so much more persuasive than Sonnino's dour, unyielding silence.[1] On 5 May Wilson, Clemenceau and Lloyd George sent for Venizelos and asked him if he could land troops at Smyrna forthwith. Surprised and delighted, he agreed and gave orders for the assembly of a Greek expeditionary force.

After a week of absence from the Conference, the exhilaration began to die down in Rome. Urgent messages from the Italians left in Paris warned Orlando of the perils of isolation and pleaded for immediate return.[2] Social unrest made the government highly conscious of Italy's need of reparations from Germany and credits and supplies from its allies. Orlando realised the bitter truth, that Italy counted for little and was hurting only itself by staying away. Better humiliation than isolation and bankruptcy. He therefore steeled himself to make 'the greatest personal sacrifice he had ever made for his country'. On the evening of 5 May he and Sonnino secretly boarded their special train. By the time the news was public they were back in their old seats round the Paris Conference table. They received a 'glacial' welcome. The dramatic gesture of 24 April had achieved nothing beyond inflaming Italian opinion.[3]

The wearisome negotiations on Fiume and Dalmatia started again, first with leading members of the U.S. delegation, then with Tardieu, Clemenceau's confidant, who attempted mediation. Orlando's tactics were passive

[1] Sonnino spent his few hours of relaxation in solitary walks along the Paris boulevards. He refused to lobby or make propaganda for the Italian cause, believing that, in Bonomi's words, 'to resort to such methods would be to sink to the level of the small nations which went around begging territory from world opinion'. Bonomi, La politica italiana dopo Vittorio Veneto, p. 32. He also refused overtures on 25 April from both the Greeks and the Japanese for mutual support for their unsatisfied claims against the Conference, saying 'Io non faccio porcherie'. Crespi, p. 473. See also Orlando, Memorie, pp. 386–7. Venizelos had suggested an Italo-Greek understanding as early as January. DDI (6), I, 777, 788.

[2] Crespi, pp. 509–10, 515 ff., 796–7. On the assumption that the Italians would not return in time to present the treaty to the German delegation, the conference secretariat had begun to delete all mention of Italy from the text.

[3] 'Believe me', Orlando said to Malagodi three weeks later, 'I am indeed a new Christ and must suffer my passion for the salvation of my country.' Malagodi, II, pp. 653, 685.

resistance: if Italy could hold on for another eighteen months, Wilson would be out of office and the position would be greatly improved.[1] He no longer insisted on the Treaty of London line in Dalmatia (but still asked for Zara, Šibenik and the islands), and was prepared to accept an independent state of Fiume under the League of Nations, provided it was Italian in character and the town of Fiume was territorially contiguous with Italy.[2] Wilson, however, insisted on a large, predominantly Slav buffer state and refused to move the Italian frontier east of the Wilson Line, which ruled out contiguity. Nor would he sanction any scheme unacceptable to the Yugoslavs. Wilson himself took no part in the renewed discussions, but all proposals had to be submitted to him. Though both sides made concessions, the gulf was still too wide and early in June the negotiations broke down.

Complications in Asia Minor added to the strain. The bitter pill of the Greek occupation of Smyrna was slightly sweetened for Italy by the decision to land token British, French and Italian detachments besides the Greeks. But meanwhile Sonnino, without informing even Orlando and still less the Allies, ordered the occupation of more points on the coast west of Adalia. On 15 May, the day before the Greek landing at Smyrna, Italian troops disembarked only forty miles away at the port of Scalanova. By the end of the month a clash between the Italian and Greek forces appeared imminent.

Lloyd George had previously wished to give the Italians compensation in Turkey in exchange for Fiume and Dalmatia; but he now decided that they must be cleared out of Asia Minor altogether.[3] His fertile imagination, however, inspired another scheme to satisfy Italian aspirations without conflicting with those of Britain and Greece. For several months he had been suggesting that Italian troops should replace the British in Georgia and Batum and take over the task of protecting the newly formed Transcaucasian republics.[4] On 3 June he suddenly asked Orlando to take over at once. General Enrico Caviglia, the Minister for War, Diaz and military

---

[1] Malagodi, II, pp. 670–2, 687.

[2] The National Council of Fiume had reacted to Wilson's manifesto of 23 April by inviting the Italian commander in the city, General Grazioli, to assume full powers in the name of the King. Having no authority to carry out annexation, he referred the matter to Rome and nothing came of it. Curato, II, pp. 273–9.

[3] Lloyd George had been disagreeably surprised by the opposition to Italian expansion among his own cabinet colleagues and by the strength of anti-Italian feeling among the Moslems of India, who deplored any partition of Asia Minor. Albrecht-Carrié, pp. 223–4.

[4] BFP, III, 229; Malagodi, II, pp. 563, 575. This had first been suggested in a report of the Allied Military representatives in February. R. S. Baker, *Woodrow Wilson and World Settlement* (London 1923), III, p. 6. Lloyd George wanted to reduce British commitments in order to accelerate demobilisation

experts were summoned to Paris. The Italian delegation was enthusiastic. The Caucasus would provide oil, mineral wealth, markets and outlets for emigration, and make Italy 'a dominant state'. Orlando gave orders for an expedition of 100,000 men to be prepared, two regiments of which were to embark at Taranto at the end of the month.[1]

In Africa, where their own interests were directly concerned, Britain and France were reluctant to make more than the minimum of concessions. After allotting all the African mandates to themselves in May, they agreed to set up an Anglo-Franco-Italian commission to consider Italy's colonial claims under Article 13 of the Treaty of London. The Italians hoped not only to enlarge their Libyan and east African colonies, but also to turn Ethiopia into an Italian protectorate. They therefore asked for the cession of Jarabub,[2] Kassala, Jubaland,[3] British Somaliland and Djibouti, and the sale by the French of the Djibouti–Addis Ababa railway.[4] The British and French representatives retorted that such demands went far beyond the frontier rectifications envisaged in the Treaty of London. The most that Milner, the British Colonial Secretary, would agree to cede was Jarabub and Jubaland (though within narrower boundaries than the Italians had requested). The French offered only minute adjustments of the Libyan-Tunisian frontier. The Italian representative, Crespi, declared himself dissatisfied and asked instead for a mandate over Togoland, but this too was ruled to be outside the commission's terms of reference. Once again the Italians felt slighted and frustrated.[5]

On 28 June Germany signed the Treaty of Versailles. By then the Peace Conference had done its most important work and Wilson returned to America. Orlando and Sonnino had allowed Italy to become a 'moral absentee' in all matters that did not directly concern it, and they contributed little to the German settlement.[6] Yet Italy had gained much more than public opinion was prepared to admit. It secured a share of German reparations and a permanent seat on the Council of the League of Nations.

[1] Crespi, pp. 627–32, 682.
[2] An oasis in the Egyptian western desert.
[3] See above, p. 465.
[4] Curato, II, pp. 452–67; Salata, *Il nodo di Gibuti*, pp. 277–91. These claims, which represented the minimum colonial programme of 1916–17 (see above, p. 465) with the addition of British Somaliland, had been transmitted by Sonnino to Balfour on 2 December 1918. See DDI (6), I, 436; Toscano, *Pagine di storia diplomatica contemporanea*, I, pp. 220–2.
[5] Crespi, pp. 562–6, 576–9, 615–16, 625–6; Curato, II, pp. 469–82; Toscano, *Pagine*, I, pp. 225–40; Macartney and Cremona, pp. 66–72. Lloyd George was willing to cede British Somaliland but failed to persuade his cabinet, notably Milner. D. Lloyd George, *The Truth about the Peace Treaties* (London 1930), II, pp. 897–901.
[6] Malagodi, II, pp. 524, 584–8; Orlando, *Memorie*, pp. 482–3.

By the Treaty of St Germain with Austria,[1] it acquired not only the Brenner frontier, but also a wedge of Slovene-inhabited territory round Tarvisio, beyond the Treaty of London line, which gave control of one of the main railways from Trieste to the Austrian frontier. Unlike the succession states of central and eastern Europe, Italy was asked to assume no international obligations towards its German and Slav minorities. The greater part of Austria-Hungary's merchant fleet was assigned to it. Overshadowing all else, Austria-Hungary had disintegrated into a rump Austria, a rump Hungary and four weak succession states. Italy was thus relieved of the threat to its northern frontiers that had existed since 1861 and achieved its war aims more perfectly than any other of the victor nations.[2]

But most Italians saw only the debit side of the balance-sheet. While Italy was being denied its rights in the Adriatic, Smyrna had been lost to the Greeks and Africa and the Middle East were in the exclusive grip of Britain and France. Nationalists harped on these failures and frustrations which they attributed to a conspiracy at Italy's expense. In April Britain and the U.S.A. had guaranteed France's frontier against a resurgence of German power. Why, Italians asked, had Italy not been invited to join them?[3] The Treaty of Versailles was a 'French peace', designed to rivet French hegemony on Europe; the League of Nations was an imposition by the U.S.A., France and Britain on the *gentes minores*. The nationalists hardly noticed the solid gains of the Treaty of St Germain. Encirclement by France and Yugoslavia became an obsession and innocent proposals for a Danubian customs union were at once interpreted as an anti-Italian move.[4] Italy, it was argued, could expect nothing but ingratitude from its allies; it should turn to Hungary,[5] Bulgaria, Turkey and even Germany

---

[1] The treaty was published in draft on 3 June and signed on 10 September.

[2] Sforza, *Contemporary Italy*, p. 187.

[3] See, for example, the King's hint to the British ambassador on 15 November, in BFP, IV, 126. Orlando regretted that Italy was not asked. Charles-Roux, *Une grande ambassade*, p. 47. Sonnino's view, on the other hand, was 'better isolated than in bad company'. Crespi, p. 541.

[4] In May Crespi threatened a second and final withdrawal from the Conference if a British proposal for a Danubian *Zollverein* were carried against Italy's wishes. This obsession with the possibility of a re-creation of Austria–Hungary, strengthened by memories of Allied Austrophilia during the war, blinded most Italians (but not Sonnino) to the danger of a revived Greater Germany in control of central Europe. Crespi, pp. 546–7, 567–9.

[5] Certain officers of the Italian military missions in central Europe established close relations with Bela Kun's bolshevik government, which was in power in Hungary from March to July 1919, and appear to have arranged for the sale to it of Italian arms. It is not clear whether these activities had the approval of Orlando's government. BFP, VI, 10, 29, 33, 36, 53, 62, 309. The Hungarians preferred Fiume to be Italian rather than Yugoslav, and would have liked to do a deal with Italy on this basis. Malagodi, II, pp. 588–9, 609.

for sympathy, to a bloc of proletarian nations against the plutocrats. Thus nationalist, socialist and Giolittian propaganda strangely coincided: the war had been in vain, the victory had been mutilated.[1] The truth was that the very completeness of victory had destroyed the artificial strength of Italy's pre-war international position. No longer were there two blocs with which it could bargain and between which it could oscillate. The fatal blunder of Italy's leaders was that, at a time when its economic and diplomatic weakness was most apparent, they chose the field of *Machtpolitik* on which to fight. They thus angered Wilson, lost the sympathy of the succession states and forfeited the leadership of the new European democracies. Bissolati, the despised idealist, was the true realist.

After the humiliation of the secret return to Paris, only a striking success could have saved Orlando's government. Everyone was blaming it for the economic difficulties, for the food shortages and social unrest, for the delay in demobilisation caused by the tension in the Adriatic. Orlando himself was exhausted by the nervous strain of 'fighting in a madhouse' and carried no weight in Paris.[2] A change of government and negotiators seemed indispensable if the Adriatic question was ever to be solved. The breakdown of the Paris negotiations sealed Orlando's fate. A stormy cabinet meeting was held in a railway carriage at Oulx, just inside the Italian frontier, on 21 May, at which Crespi urged resignation. He was outvoted and a precarious harmony was restored.[3] But on 19 June the government was defeated in the chamber by 259 votes to 78 and immediately resigned.

### Nitti and D'Annunzio

Orlando's successor was Nitti, who formed a government of the centre with a large Giolittian element. It differed from its predecessor in one important respect, the inclusion of two representatives of the Popular party. Nitti's instincts were democratic. He sympathised with many of the yearnings of *diciannovismo* and hoped, like Giolitti before 1914, that at least the moderate socialists could be won over by a radical programme of reform, even if the maximalists proved impervious to reason.[4] The politicians were soon saying that the Popular party might be Nitti's lawful

[1] Hautecœur, pp. 194 ff., 231 ff., 241 ff. During May Clemenceau was infuriated by speculation about an Italo–German alliance and by anti-French demonstrations in Milan and other cities. Aldrovandi, *Guerra diplomatica*, pp. 338, 354, 402, 405, 408–9.

[2] Malagodi, II, pp. 696, 700–1; Crespi, p. 544.

[3] Crespi, p. 584; Bonomi, *La politica italiana dopo Vittorio Veneto*, p. 45.

[4] The moderate socialists were like British Labour M.P.s, Nitti told the British ambassador on 22 August. BFP, V, 87; Alatri, *Nitti*, p. 494.

wife, but the Socialist party was his mistress.[1] Conservatives, nationalists and all super-patriots greeted his appointment with fury and contempt. His political past was Giolittian and even as a member of Orlando's war cabinet he had shown conspicuously little sympathy with the interventionist mystique. He was expected to be a renouncer in foreign policy and he quickly confirmed the nationalists' worst fears. Throughout his year in office, which was marked by continuous social and industrial unrest, he was attacked for appeasing the revolutionaries and destroying the authority and dignity of the state. Worst of all, in September 1919 he granted an amnesty to wartime deserters from the army. That act made him an object of implacable hatred to all who were infected by the nationalist frenzy.

Nitti's first weeks in office were full of anxiety. Riots against the cost of living in June were followed by a general strike in July. The nationalists organised hysterical demonstrations and there were even attempts to subvert the armed forces in favour of a militarist *coup d'état*.[2] Nitti kept calm. Thanks to his wartime experience and to the close connexions he had acquired in the banking and business world, he understood the realities of Italy's situation much better than most politicians. The threat of national starvation had become his obsession. For five months since resigning office he had been pondering the task of reconstruction and preparing himself to succeed Orlando. Now that the call had come, he saw himself as the saviour of his people. 'Produce more, consume less', was his comfortless prescription. During July financial and economic negotiations with the U.S.A. ran into difficulties which Nitti rightly connected with the diplomatic deadlock over the Adriatic. He recognised that Italy's foreign policy must be determined by its dependence on the U.S.A. and Britain for credits, coal and food. Beside the threat of economic disaster, Fiume mattered little. It would be folly, he argued, for Italy to persist in squabbling over a pretty garden while the house burnt down.[3] For financial reasons it was essential to accelerate demobilisation, and this meant reducing Italy's commitments, particularly in Albania, where the maintenance of a large garrison involved 'crazy expenditure' and the situation was becoming 'really disastrous'.[4] Nitti's analysis was unexceptionable and his

---

[1] Jacini, *Storia*, p. 57; Sturzo, *Italy and Fascismo*, p. 98.

[2] Alatri, *Nitti*, pp. 65–6, 78–9, 109–10, 191–3.

[3] Malagodi, II, p. 715; Giuriati, p. 131.

[4] Alatri, *Nitti*, pp. 80–1, 122, 149–50. In June 1919 most of Albania was still under Italian military occupation and the Peace Conference had reached no decision on the country's future. Orlando had demanded application of the Treaty of London, i.e. partition, with the annexation of Valona and its hinterland by Italy (see above, p. 431, note 4). Wilson opposed partition and insisted on independence for Albania within the frontiers of 1913.

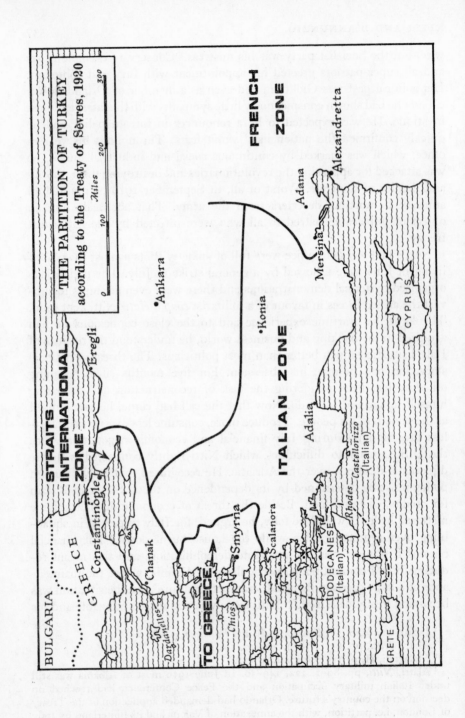

THE PARTITION OF TURKEY
according to the Treaty of Sèvres, 1920

Miles
0    100    200    300

BULGARIA

GREECE

STRAITS
INTERNATIONAL
ZONE

Constantinople

Eregli

Ankara

Chanak

Dardanelles

TO GREECE

Chios

Smyrna

Scalanora

ITALIAN ZONE

Adalia

Konia

DODECANESE
(Italian)

Rhodes

Castellorizzo
(Italian)

Adana

Mersina

Alexandretta

FRENCH
ZONE

CYPRUS

CRETE

policies were intellectually sound; but he lacked the strength of character to carry them through and in a crisis tended to vacillate and appease. His faith in the power of reason and common sense was excessive and he was more at home with statistics than with the explosive emotions of his people.[1]

Nitti found in the veteran Tittoni a Foreign Minister who shared his views. Tittoni saw that it was futile to shout for Fiume and the Treaty of London in the same breath and he was therefore ready to renounce Dalmatia. Even on Fiume he fel. less strongly than Orlando. His ambition was to negotiate a general agreement with Britain and France which would cover not only the Adriatic but also Asia Minor and Africa, gains in one area balancing losses in another. Once Britain and France had been squared, he hoped Wilson would fall into line. But he quickly discovered that Italy's position was even worse than he had expected.[2] On arrival in Paris he was presented with an Anglo-French memorandum, drafted with what its author, Balfour, admitted was 'somewhat undiplomatic candour', which argued that the Treaty of London had been rendered invalid by Italy's failure to observe all its terms during the war. This was a brutal thrust, for without the Treaty, on which the Italians had always counted in the last resort, and by which the British and French had hitherto admitted being bound, Italy's claims had no legal foundation. But Tittoni swallowed his anger, conquered the temptation to walk out of the Conference and plunged into negotiations.[3] He was rewarded by a rapid improvement in relations with his British and French colleagues, which did much to break down Italy's isolation. But Wilson still refused to make any further concession. At the end of August Nitti gloomily wrote to Tittoni, 'Time is against us . . . With our economic resources any resistance is a question of a few weeks and every delay puts us in conditions of growing inferiority.'[4]

At this point a new crisis intervened. On 6 July a petty incident started violent disturbances in Fiume, in the course of which nine French soldiers were lynched by hysterical nationalist mobs, abetted by Italian marines. The French and Italian governments kept popular indignation within bounds, but at meetings of the Council of the Peace Conference Clemenceau muttered 'Peuple d'assassins' at intervals over the next few days, loud enough for the Italian delegates to hear.[5] An Allied Commission of

---

[1] He 'preached sermons without making any decisions and without giving any orders', writes Sforza, *Contemporary Italy*, pp. 216–18. This was also Giolitti's opinion (*Memorie*, pp. 553–4).

[2] Malagodi, II, pp. 710–11.   [3] BFP, IV, 2, 4, 6; Crespi, pp. 683–5.

[4] Alatri, *Nitti*, pp. 134, 148.   [5] Crespi, pp. 702–4.

Enquiry was set up on Tittoni's suggestion and on 25 August the Conference adopted its recommendations. These included a reduction in the Italian garrison, the recall of General Grazioli, replacement of the French garrison by fresh French units, dissolution of the Fiume volunteer battalions, election of a municipal council to replace the National Council and the creation of an Allied police force and control commission. The police, most of whom would be British, were to reach Fiume on 12 September.

The order to evacuate Fiume created disaffection not only among Host Venturi's legionaries but also in certain units of the Italian garrison. A group of young officers of the Sardinian Grenadiers, led by a Major Carlo Reina, took an oath, 'Fiume or death', and sent a deputation to D'Annunzio in Venice. On 11 September D'Annunzio arrived at Ronchi, near Trieste, where the Sardinian Grenadiers were stationed, and agreed to command the mutiny. Next day he drove into Fiume at the head of 1,000 men. No resistance was offered by the Italian general in command and to avoid incidents all Allied troops were withdrawn. D'Annunzio was granted dictatorial powers by the National Council and resumed his wartime title of 'Commandant'. In defiance of his government, of the Yugoslavs and the Peace Conference, he declared he would not leave Fiume alive until it had been annexed.

The *coup* created wild enthusiasm among nationalists throughout Italy. Volunteers, including even generals, flocked to Fiume. Seven regular battalions, including two of *arditi*, deserted and by the end of the month D'Annunzio had a force of 8,000 'legionaries', together with 400 sailors and four small naval vessels.[1] It was not only the nationalists who applauded. On 28 September the chamber passed a motion reaffirming the *italianità* of Fiume. For a few weeks the interventionists of 1915 found themselves reunited in a common cause. Even Bissolati and the democrats, though they detested D'Annunzio's method, could not criticise his aim. The freemasons, the ex-servicemen's organisation and the patriotic-syndicalist U.I.L. declared their sympathy. The merchan seamen of

[1] The Trent and Trieste Society, whose president, Giuriati, was a member of the Rome Fascio, had been enrolling volunteers as early as July in anticipation of a *coup*. Host Venturi had for many months been in touch with both D'Annunzio and Mussolini. Giuriati, pp. 8–9; Alatri, *Nitti*, pp. 188–95; Valeri, *Da Giolitti a Mussolini*, pp. 44–5; De Felice, pp. 526–7. Nitti was kept well informed of these activities but seems to have underestimated the degree of complicity on the part of the military authorities. As late as 27 August he telegraphed to Tittoni in Paris, 'I have had all the volunteers making for Fiume arrested, but the movement is of no importance.' After the *coup* he told Malagodi (II, p. 718) that for two months he had been vainly warning the High Command in Venezia Giulia that something was afoot. The soldiers had 'made a fool of me', he told Turati. Turati–Kuliscioff, V, pp. 140–1.

Genoa, led by their ebullient organiser, Captain Giulietti, gave more than verbal support. During October the crews of two merchant ships mutinied on the high seas and sailed their cargoes of arms and food to Fiume. D'Annunzio had been 'the spokesman of the nation' in May 1915 and the symbol of heroism during the war. Now, for a few months, he became the idol of Italy, a second Garibaldi.

Nitti was thus faced with an explosion of 'sentimental madness' which reduced sober opinion to silence.[1] In theory three courses of action were open to him: he could annex Fiume, he could eject D'Annunzio by force or he could play for time, hoping that, when the excitement subsided, a compromise could be worked out which would satisfy home opinion, D'Annunzio and the Peace Conference. He ruled out annexation at once: it might provoke war with the Yugoslavs and it would certainly cause a rupture with the Allies and economic disaster. His first excited comment on hearing of the *coup* had been, 'We are on the eve of starvation; these events will only hasten it.'[2] Nitti's decision against annexation was approved on 25 September at a Crown Council of leading ministers, parliamentarians, party leaders and representatives of the army and navy. Annexation found only two supporters; even the nationalist Federzoni was against it.[3]

Nitti did at first consider the use of force against D'Annunzio. In his speech to the chamber on the day after the *coup*, he lamented the appearance of sedition in the army, branded D'Annunzio's volunteers as deserters and appealed to 'the workers and peasants' to support him. But there was little response. The maximalists affected to welcome 'the nationalist revolution as the precursor of the proletarian revolution'.[4] Three days later Nitti spoke again in a much more cautious tone. In the interval he had been forced to recognize that the army and navy could not be relied upon against D'Annunzio.[5] He did not dare to incur the charge of persecuting patriots at the instigation of the foreigner nor risk provoking a military *pronunciamento* which, he believed, would be followed inevitably by insurrection from the extreme left and civil war. D'Annunzio refused to negotiate with the 'anti-Italian government of Nitti' and proclaimed that it must be overthrown if Italy was to be saved. His lieutenants and

---

[1] BFP, IV, 67.

[2] Valeri, *Da Giolitti a Mussolini*, p. 40; Malagodi, II, pp. 715–22; Crespi, p. 735.

[3] Alatri, *Nitti*, pp. 239–42. All ex-Prime Ministers were invited except Pelloux, who publicly voiced his indignation at being left out. BFP, IV, 42; Charles-Roux, *Une grande ambassade*, p. 79.

[4] Nenni, p. 38; Salvatorelli and Mira, p. 49; Alatri, *Nitti*, p. 494, note. Turati commented bitterly that the socialists and workers might as well not exist, for all the resistance they offered to the rise of militarism. Turati–Kuliscioff, V, p. 147.

[5] Badoglio, p. 33; Caviglia, p. 130; Malagodi, II, p. 723.

legionaries were already saying that the march on Fiume must end at Rome. Fiume was 'an island of justice in a sea of iniquity'; it represented youth and the future, while Rome, the capital of the renouncers, represented only the corrupt past.[1] These sentiments were echoed throughout the nationalist press. Most fervent of all was Mussolini, who made himself D'Annunzio's chief spokesman in Italy. *Il Popolo d'Italia* launched a Fiume fund which raised 400,000 lire in four days, an unprecedented sum for such a cause. Captain Giulietti's seamen's union subscribed handsomely. In private Mussolini advised caution. On 7 October he made a sensational flight to Fiume by air, to warn D'Annunzio not to be rash in view of the imminent general election[2] and the uncertain state of opinion. D'Annunzio rebuked him for craven inertia.[3] But in public Mussolini allowed no doubts to appear. 'The capital of Italy is on the Carnero,[4] not on the Tiber', he wrote: 'There is "our" government which we will from now on obey.'[5]

Once annexation and the use of force had been ruled out, the government was left with the only alternative of playing for time. Nitti subjected all news from Fiume to censorship and ordered military precautions against raids or landings by legionaries on the Adriatic coast. Badoglio was appointed special military commissioner for Venezia Giulia, with orders to restore discipline in the army and avoid bloodshed. But no attempt was made to enforce a physical blockade. On the contrary, food and coal were allowed to reach Fiume in sufficient quantities,[6] supplemented by sporadic acts of piracy by Giulietti's seamen. Meanwhile Nitti set to work to negotiate a compromise with both D'Annunzio and the Allies, using what he hoped would be the most effective weapon, 'the arms of reason'.[7]

In Paris Tittoni was able to convince the Peace Conference that the government was helpless in the face of public opinion and military insubordination. His plan was to get Allied approval of a status for Fiume that would amount to annexation in all but name, then secure D'Annunzio's agreement and replace him by a royal commissioner and his volunteers by

[1] Badoglio, pp. 57, 191–2; Giuriati, pp. 36, 52–3, 94; Alatri, *Nitti*, pp. 232–3, 263–4.

[2] See below, p. 547.

[3] Pini and Susmel, II, pp. 30–5; Mussolini, XIV, pp. 475–8; De Felice, pp. 560–8.

[4] The Gulf of Carnero is the north-eastern extremity of the Adriatic, between Istria and Dalmatia, on which Fiume stands.

[5] *Il Popolo d'Italia*, 15 September. Mussolini, XIV, pp. 8–9.

[6] Some of these supplies were paid for by the government through the Red Cross. Nitti, *Rivelazioni*, p. 332.

[7] Badoglio, p. 41.

regular troops under Badoglio's command. The essential point was that the Italian town of Fiume, within the boundaries of the old *corpus separatum*, should be given autonomy inside a predominantly Slav Free State, and should have a common frontier with Italy on the west. In exchange for this concession, Italy would renounce the Treaty of London, asking only for autonomy for Zara, the cession of certain Dalmatian islands and Valona, and a mandate over the rest of Albania. Tittoni had the courage to tell the chamber on 27 September that solution along these lines was necessary. Lloyd George and Clemenceau were impressed by his conciliatory approach. Nitti backed him up with appeals to the Allies to save Italy from revolution by allowing him to make minimum concessions to nationalist opinion. But Wilson remained unmoved, even after personal appeals from Lloyd George and Clemenceau.[1] The essence of the difficulty was that Tittoni's plan was designed to keep the door open for eventual annexation; in this alone lay its limited appeal to Italian nationalists. Wilson, on the other hand, wanted a big buffer state, bounded on the west by the Wilson Line and with no special status for the town of Fiume, just in order to make annexation impossible. Thus, although the gap between the Italian and American points of view had again been narrowed, and though the British and French were keen to make 'a supreme and final effort', the negotiations broke down once more in November. Tittoni, weary and discouraged, had to admit failure and resigned.

Meanwhile tension in the Adriatic persisted. A week after the occupation of Fiume, a small body of D'Annunzio's legionaries had tried to seize the Dalmatian town of Traù, outside the Treaty of London line. A two-hour ultimatum from the commanding U.S. admiral quickly put an end to the adventure. But the Yugoslavs were justifiably anxious and, having no confidence in the ability or desire of the Italian government to prevent further *coups*, appealed repeatedly to Paris. Fortunately D'Annunzio's adventurous moods were fitful and short-lived. It was Badoglio's task to establish friendly relations with him and impress upon him the need for patience and moderation. Badoglio assured him, on Nitti's authority, that Fiume would be either Italian or independent, never Yugoslav, and by appealing to his patriotism, obtained from him a promise to place his forces under Badoglio's command, should the Yugoslavs attack.[2] At a meeting between the two men at the end of October, D'Annunzio

---

[1] Alatri, *Nitti*, pp. 287 ff.; BFP, IV, 94, 104, 105; Charles-Roux, *Une grande ambassade*, pp. 74–5.

[2] Badoglio, pp. 55, 142. Badoglio deliberately exaggerated the danger from the Yugoslavs, in order to strengthen his appeal. Alatri, *Nitti*, pp. 247–8, 347.

promised to make no further move while the negotiations in Paris continued. But on learning of Wilson's rejection of Tittoni's compromise, he broke out once again and on 14 November descended with three of his naval craft on Zara. Admiral Millo, the military governor of Dalmatia, with D'Annunzio by his side, held a joint review of the Fiume legionaries and his own troops, and declared on his sailor's oath of honour that Dalmatia would never be abandoned.[1] This provoked a sharp Allied demand for Millo's recall and a Yugoslav warning that a raid on Split, of which there were rumours, would mean war. Nitti at first agreed to recall Millo, admitting that to overlook his 'act of sedition' would ruin the discipline of the army and navy; but he soon weakened and left him in command.[2] The Zara incident took place on the eve of the Italian general election and Nitti, fearing that the extreme left might resort to violence in protest, suppressed the news until the results of the voting were known.

At the end of November Nitti, strengthened by the electoral failure of the extreme right,[3] tried again. Badoglio proposed to D'Annunzio that the government should publicly reaffirm Fiume's right to self-determination and a common frontier with Italy, then occupy the town with regular forces until the Peace Conference reached a decision. A *modus vivendi* on these lines was drafted in Rome early in December by delegates from Fiume and Sforza, Under-Secretary for Foreign Affairs. It was subsequently approved first by D'Annunzio, then by the Fiume National Council, then by 80% of the voters of Fiume in a plebiscite. But at the last minute D'Annunzio changed his mind under pressure from his extremists, annulled the plebiscite and broke off relations with Rome. Badoglio reported that, while his troops would certainly resist if attacked from Fiume, he still could not rely on them to obey an order to take the offensive.[4] Nitti therefore again shrank from force and the situation remained unchanged.

This irresponsible rupture by D'Annunzio was, however, a turning-point in the drama of Fiume. Many of his best collaborators began to desert him, realising that he was a political adventurer. Conservatives, nationalists and military and naval officers like Admiral Millo lost faith in him.[5] Giuriati, his nationalist *chef de cabinet*, resigned. Major Reina, the original instigator of the Ronchi *coup*, left Fiume in disgust. By the end of

---

[1] Giuriati, p. 78.

[2] Badoglio, pp. 118, 243, 259; BFP, IV, 138, 148; Alatri, *Nitti*, pp. 314–15, 326–30, 460. In private Nitti described Millo as a deliberate liar, 'utterly ignoble and lacking in soldierly dignity'.

[3] See below, p. 549.

[4] Alatri, *Nitti*, pp. 327, 338.

[5] A conspicuous exception was Pantaleoni, whose nationalist enthusiasm took him to Fiume in August 1920 as D'Annunzio's Minister of Finance.

December D'Annunzio's forces had dropped to 5,000. The civilian population was wearying of the legionaries, who had settled down to a delightful life of parades, patriotic songs, amorous adventure, rhetoric and café conspiracy.[1] Food shortage, unemployment, imminent bankruptcy and the ruin of the port's trade caused labour unrest and made ordinary citizens long for normalcy. In the election for the National Council, which had been held on 26 October, the annexationist National Union party had won an overwhelming victory and at once reaffirmed Fiume's desire for union with Italy. But after December the rival socialist-autonomist party, which opposed annexation for economic reasons, began to gain ground. Nitti met its leader, Riccardo Zanella, and was impressed. General Caviglia, Badoglio's successor as special commissioner in Venezia Giulia,[2] now adopted a policy of backing the National Council against D'Annunzio. This soon showed results and in April D'Annunzio was forced to surrender to the Council the internal administration of the town. By alienating the forces to which he owed the success of his original *coup*, he had ruined his chance of leading a revolution from the right. By the spring of 1920 Fiume had ceased to be a threat to the internal stability of Italy and Nitti had reasonable grounds for hoping that Caviglia's troops would soon take over.

Deserted by most of his conservative supporters, D'Annunzio turned to revolutionary politics. Giuriati's successor as *chef de cabinet* was De Ambris, one of the leaders of the U.I.L. Under his influence the syndicalist note became more marked in Fiume's public pronouncements and on 12 September 1920, the anniversary of the *coup*, D'Annunzio published his draft of a constitution for the Republic of Fiume, the Charter of the Carnero.[3] This bizarre document, a mixture of syndicalism and literary fantasy, was coolly received by the citizens of Fiume and led to the resignation of the National Council. Meanwhile D'Annunzio developed a foreign policy of his own, proclaiming the solidarity of Fiume with all oppressed peoples and proletarian nations against 'the Holy Alliance of plutocracy'. Contacts were made with the Soviet government, with Zaghlul Pasha,

---

[1] An illuminating autobiographical description of a young legionary's life at Fiume may be found in G. Comisso, *Le mie stagioni* (Milan 1951). Nitti told Turati in March 1920: 'Fiume has become a brothel, the refuge of the underworld and society prostitutes (prostitute più o meno *high life*).' Turati–Kuliscioff, V, p. 294.

[2] Badoglio handed over his command to Caviglia at the end of December on becoming army chief of staff.

[3] All citizens of Fiume were to be compelled by the constitution to belong to one of ten corporations, according to occupation and profession. The tenth corporation was 'reserved for the mysterious forces of the people in travail and ascent'. The text of the Charter is reprinted in D'Annunzio, *Per la più grande Italia*, pp. 227–64.

the Egyptian nationalist leader, and with Sean O'Kelly,[1] the representative
of Sinn Fein in Paris. A grandiose treaty was signed with disaffected
Croats and 'representatives' of Montenegro, Albania and Macedonia. Its
purpose was the disruption of Yugoslavia, with the help of arms from
Fiume, and the creation of a Dalmatian republic.[2] It was a common
belief in Fiume that Yugoslavia was 'a card castle', which would collapse
at one strong puff.[3]

   A few people in Italy hoped that D'Annunzio's revolutionary enthusiasm
was genuine and that an insurrection starting in Fiume might sweep the
left into power. One of these optimists was Malatesta, who was in contact
with Fiume through Giulietti and De Ambris.[4] When the railwaymen
struck in January 1920,[5] under mainly anarcho-syndicalist inspiration,
Malatesta thought the moment had come; but his overtures to the Socialist
party and the C.G.L. were contemptuously rejected. Soon afterwards the
'plot' was revealed in *Il Popolo d'Italia* and dismissed as an 'operetta'.
But D'Annunzio continued to play with the idea of a landing in Romagna
and a republican insurrection. In April, at a moment when Italy was again
in the grip of strikes and disorders, he approached the socialists of Trieste
with a plan for proclaiming a Soviet republic, first in Fiume, then in
Venezia Giulia. Once again the socialists spurned all contact with him and
Nitti had the affair well publicised in order to discredit him with his
conservative admirers.[6] In September a message was sent from Fiume to
the congress of oppressed nationalities which had assembled at Baku under
the wing of the Soviet government, and Lenin referred to D'Annunzio as
a revolutionary, to the shocked surprise of the maximalist Serrati who
was in Russia at the time.[7] Serrati knew D'Annunzio better than did Lenin.
Even had the maximalists been capable of rising above their anti-bourgeois
prejudices, D'Annunzio could never have made a reliable revolutionary

   [1] President of Eire and the Irish Republic from 1945 to 1959.
   [2] Giuriati, pp. 134 ff., 148 ff.; Alatri, *Nitti*, pp. 430–6.
   [3] Giuriati, p. 70. As early as April 1919 General Grazioli, the Italian commander
of Fiume, had been in touch with Croat nationalists and believed he could win
their assent to Italy's annexation of Fiume. Malagodi, II, p. 610.
   [4] Borghi, pp. 218–21. Giulietti financed Malatesta's anarchist paper, *Umanità
Nuova*. Malatesta's readiness to collaborate with Giulietti and the U.I.L. worried
many anarchists whose sympathies lay with the U.S.I. The piratical activities of
Giulietti's seamen were not inspired solely by admiration for D'Annunzio; the
*Persia* was seized and sailed to Fiume in October 1919 because it was believed that
the arms she carried were to be used against the Russian bolsheviks. Alatri, *Nitti*,
pp. 269–70.
   [5] See below, p. 552.
   [6] Valeri, *Da Giolitti a Mussolini*, pp. 51–60, 76–88; Alatri, *Nitti*, pp. 421–4;
Tasca, pp. 84–6. For a scathing criticism by Major Reina of D'Annunzio's mania
for conspiracy, see Valeri, pp. 52–3.
   [7] Tasca, p. 143.

ally. In politics he was never more than a dilettante and a theatrical show-man. No one realized this better than Mussolini, who in public continued to express 'unlimited faith in D'Annunzio's genius' and declared himself and all fascists to be 'disciplined soldiers at the Commandant's orders',[1] but behind the scenes did all he could to discourage new adventures. In September, after ignoring a pressing invitation to visit Fiume, he received from De Ambris a draft plan for an armed *coup* to make D'Annunzio dictator of an Italian republic and save the country from 'total ruin'. In his reply Mussolini made so many reservations, including the condition that no action should occur before the spring of 1921, that it is impossible to believe that he took the scheme seriously.[2] Perhaps he had already decided that if anyone was to march on Rome, it should be himself, not D'Annunzio.

## The 1919 Election

On 28 September 1919 Nitti obtained a majority of 65 on his vote of confidence in the chamber, after a wild, disorderly sitting. D'Annunzio's supporters were bitterly disappointed: Fiume had lost the first battle.[3] Next day Nitti carried out a little *coup* of his own and dissolved without warning.

An election was long overdue but had been delayed by controversy over the electoral law. Proportional representation had become the symbol of healthy political change in the eyes of all reformers. Its strongest advocates were the Popolari, the party born of the new era, the reformist socialists and two groups of pre-war anti-Giolittians, the democratic inter-ventionists and the nationalists. They were confident that it would usher in an era of mass parties and sweep away the cliques of *Giolittismo* for ever. But a few conservatives also desired it, particularly in northern con-stituencies where it seemed the only hope of retaining any seat at all in the radical mood of the post-war electorate. Orlando had successfully blocked it in the spring, but Nitti accepted it without enthusiasm and it became law in August. Italy was divided into fifty-four constituencies, with 5 to 20 members each, to be elected on party lists.[4] Giolitti remained silent, but he realised that the law was a deliberate blow against the old Italy which he had dominated. So did his opponents. In big headlines *Il Popolo d'Italia* acclaimed its passing as 'the end of a political system

---

[1] *Il Popolo d'Italia*, 19 August, 11 September. Mussolini, XV, pp. 150–1, 195–6.
[2] Mussolini, XV, pp. 313–18; De Felice, pp. 638–45.
[3] Giuriati, pp. 40, 51–2.
[4] At the same time the vote was given to all males over 21, and to those under 21 who had served in the armed forces. This increased the electorate from the 8·6 millions of 1913 to over 11·2 millions. *Compendio*, I, pp. 53–5, 106 ff.

. . . the nation's second victory over the old Giolittian chamber'.[1] The first, of course, was 'Radiant May'.

Between the dissolution of parliament and the election, the Socialist party held its congress in Bologna. It was a maximalist triumph. All reformists were ejected from the executive. The party scrapped the programme of 1892, condemned collaboration with the bourgeois state in any form and reaffirmed the dictatorship of the proletariat as its goal. The congress also declared its adherence to the Third International, founded seven months previously in Moscow by Lenin. But much of this extremism was merely verbal. Only Bordiga's small group wished to boycott the election. The majority plunged happily into the electoral campaign, preserving its revolutionary purity by demanding 'all power' for the proletariat and announcing that success at the polls would hasten the destruction of parliament and 'the organs of bourgeois domination'.[2] This combination of violent talk and electoral commitment once again revealed internal paralysis. The reformist tradition was still strong and all the maximalists could do was to neutralise it without offering any alternative.

Controversy about the past played a big part in the election. The socialists, imitating Mussolini's example of 1913, made attacks on the war and its supporters a main feature of their campaign and included two military deserters among their candidates.[3] Old wounds had recently been reopened during the parliamentary debates on the Caporetto Commission's report.[4] Against this background Giolitti launched his election manifesto, the Dronero Programme. In it he upbraided his opponents of 1915 for failing to prepare for a long war and for bungling its financial and economic problems. After deploring inflation, the burden of war debts and the perils of budget and trade deficits, he called for cuts in military expenditure, ruthless taxation of the rich and a capital levy aimed especially at the fortunes of war profiteers. A more direct challenge to the interventionists was his demand for the strengthening of parliament's powers, in order to make it impossible in future for 'reckless minorities, or governments without intelligence or conscience' to declare war.[5] The Dronero Programme was his bid for power, aimed at the Popolari and the moderate socialists as well as his faithful neutralists, and it earned him the title of 'Bolshevik of the Order of the Annunciation'. The nationalists meanwhile reviled Nitti for failing to annex Fiume and represented the election as a

[1] Salvatorelli and Mira, p. 47; see also Mussolini's article of 4 July, entitled 'First Victory', in Mussolini, XIII, pp. 221–2.
[2] Nenni, p. 41.
[3] Bonomi, *La politica italiana dopo Vittorio Veneto*, p. 108.
[4] See above, p. 485.
[5] Giolitti, *Discorsi extraparlamentari*, p. 313.

fight between themselves, the 'national' forces, and the 'anti-national' forces of the socialists, the Popolari, the democratic renouncers and the neutralists. Yet between neutralists and nationalists there were certain points of contact. Giolitti too lamented the Allies' refusal to recognise Fiume as Italian and made much of its assignment by the Treaty of London to Croatia. Moreover, while he condemned the political conduct of the war, he praised the fighting men and the military leaders who had achieved victory, and so left open a door through which ex-interventionists might pass into his camp.

The results of the voting on 16 November astonished the country. Nitti, confident of success,[1] had declined to use the government's traditional electoral weapons and had ordered his prefects to remain impartial. This made the election the freest that Italy had ever known, particularly in the south, even though it also allowed the socialists to dominate many of the northern cities and to indulge in intimidation and even violence with impunity. The result was that the old liberal and democratic groups, which had ruled Italy before 1914, found themselves in a minority and many of their leaders without a seat. Of the 508 seats, the Socialists won 156 and the Popolari, taking full advantage of the support of Catholic Action and the cancellation of the *non expedit*, won 100. With proportional representation it was mass organization and discipline that counted, the two things that the liberals and democrats conspicuously lacked.[2] Only in the south were the old groups able to maintain their hold, though even there it was weakened.[3]

The poor showing of the conservatives and nationalists, and of all interventionists, was remarkable. Mussolini's Fascio polled under 5,000 votes

[1] Two days before the poll, Nitti assured the French chargé d'affaires that 'les élections seront ministérielles et conservatrices'. Charles-Roux, *Une grande ambassade*, p. 89.

[2] The extent of the transformation is shown by the following simplified figures for 1913 and 1919:

| 1913 | | 1919 |
|---|---|---|
| | Liberals, democrats, radicals, | |
| 427 | reformists, republicans, etc. | 252 |
| 52 | Socialists | 156 |
| 29 | Catholics – Popolari | 100 |
| 508 | | 508 |

[3] 113 of the 156 Socialist deputies, and 59 of the 100 Popolari, came from constituencies north of the Apennines, and only 10 and 24 respectively from constituencies south of Rome. *Compendio*, II, p. 133. Yet, but for proportional representation, the Socialists and Popolari might have made an even cleaner sweep of the north. The working of the system in fact confirmed the calculations of its conservative rather than its radical sponsors, and prevented too sharp a divergence between north and south.

in a total of 270,000 at its birthplace, Milan, and won not a single seat. It was clear that the electorate had voted for reform and against war and adventures, both past and future.[1] 'Revolutionary Italy is born', declared *Avanti!* But the size of the Popular vote was even more significant than that of the socialists. Many middle-class voters, who before the war would have supported a liberal, had rallied to the Popolari. Most significant of all, the latter had made a breach in the socialist hold on the countryside and so built a dyke against revolution. Without the Popular party there might have been 250 socialist seats. Careful observers saw that fears of imminent revolution were misplaced. The calm, and even apathy, of the weeks of electoral campaigning had been revealing.[2] The electorate was in a radical but not a revolutionary mood, and that mood had now found constitutional, democratic expression. A military *pronunciamento* would now be much more hazardous and the appeal of revolutionary socialism had been much reduced. The prospects for democratic government were not hopeless.

But the composition of the new chamber upset all political conventions and made new parliamentary techniques necessary. Elder statesmen were tempted to write it off as ungovernable. Since the socialists and Popolari between them had won over half the seats, no liberal-democratic government could now exist without either socialist or Popular support. The socialists, loyal to the line laid down at the Bologna congress, would collaborate with no one. Most of their 156 deputies were raw newcomers, proudly ignorant of parliamentary practice and tradition, and interested only in 'sabotage'.[3] Nitti therefore became dependent on the Popolari, who found themselves in a commanding position.

In the past prime ministers had enjoyed a free choice of ministers and built up their coalition by bargains with groups and individuals. The Popolari required formal negotiations with their party. This innovation was made all the more distasteful to old parliamentary hands by the fact that Sturzo, secretary of the party and chief negotiator, was not himself a member of parliament. The Popolari, young and inexperienced, did not always use their power wisely. They made their support of successive

---

[1] In 1913 the groups which two years later formed the interventionist left (radicals, reformist and independent socialists, syndicalists and republicans) polled 21·3% of the votes; in 1919 the same groups under different titles polled only 9·1%. De Felice, pp. 431–2. In the months preceding the election Mussolini had tried without success to reconstitute a left-interventionist coalition.

[2] Only 56·6% of the electorate voted, compared with 60·4% in 1913 and 65% in 1909. *Compendio*, I, p. 2.

[3] Turati commented in March 1920: 'All they [his fellow-socialist deputies] can do is hurl insults and make uproar'; to expect them to act differently 'would be like expecting ducks to do other than quack quack'. Turati–Kuliscioff, V, p. 303.

governments conditional on the adoption of points in their own party programme and on the grant of jobs to their own members, and paid too little attention to the overriding necessity of making efficient, democratic government possible. No party not yet a year old could carry so great a responsibility without making mistakes. The Popolari were both too many to be comfortable partners in a coalition and too few to form a government of their own. Moreover they were not a cohesive party. The left wing wanted to form a coalition with the socialists. The right wing wanted to collaborate with the liberal-conservatives on an old-fashioned anti-socialist, clerical-moderate programme. The centre, which was dominant, wished to remain independent while giving Nitti strictly conditional support. Despite Sturzo's masterful efforts to moderate dissension, the party often spoke with several voices. These strains were an additional source of parliamentary confusion.

Nitti survived the election for seven troubled months. The transition to a peace-time economy was still proving difficult. There were a few hopeful signs. Some industries, notably textiles and engineering, were relatively prosperous. Savings and industrial investment were rising and a new state loan in January 1920 brought in 18,000 million lire, an unprecedented sum.[1] But the coal shortage persisted. In the first two months of 1920 barely half Italy's minimum requirement arrived from Britain, and train services had to be cut again. Rationing of bread and many other foodstuffs was reintroduced. Vigorous action was taken against profiteers, yet prices continued to rise. The lira depreciated further, from 36 to the pound in May 1919 to 50·25 in January 1920. In April the Minister of Finance, Schanzer, made another desperate appeal to Britain to avert 'national bankruptcy, and what was more, revolution'; but his plea for support for the lira and more generous supplies of coal brought nothing but sympathy. Attempts to raise loans in the City of London were unsuccessful owing to the lack of confidence of British bankers in Italy's finances.[2] In the course of 1919 the note circulation had risen from 14,465 million to 19,200 million lire.[3] The budget deficit was reduced in the 1919–20 financial year but it still remained enormous. The bread subsidy alone was costing 6,000 million lire a year. These difficulties might, in the eyes of economists and sober statesmen, constitute 'a difficult convalescence' rather than a real economic crisis;[4] but they were magnified by continuous social unrest, agitation and lawlessness, which were due only in part to economic factors.

Nitti tried to combine strength with concessions and to collaborate with

[1] Salvemini, *L'Italia economica*, pp. 279 ff.          [2] BFP, XII, 129, 141–2.
[3] *Sommario*, p. 163.                                   [4] Soleri, p. 81.

the moderate elements in the working-class movement. Important advances were made in social legislation. Unemployment insurance became compulsory in October 1919 and in February 1920 a bill for a statutory eight-hour day was presented to parliament, though not approved. The benefit of compulsory workmen's compensation, which industrial workers had enjoyed since 1898, was extended to agriculture in 1919. The voluntary old age and disability pensions schemes, which dated from 1898, were made obligatory in 1920. But these measures were received with studied indifference by the socialists. Their deputies had walked out of the chamber in November before the speech from the throne, shouting 'Long live the socialist republic'. 'Alone against all' was their slogan. The leaders of the C.G.L. and the parliamentary veterans, whose instincts were reformist, gladly collaborated with Nitti behind the scenes, helping to settle labour disputes and acquiring almost official authority. But their influence with the rank and file was small.

The first three months of 1920 were the most prolonged period of tumult that Italy had experienced since 1898. The masses were in an anarchic mood and impossible to control. In January the authority of the state was directly challenged by railway and post office strikes, led by anarcho-syndicalists. Both ended with substantial concessions by the government. They were followed by a wave of industrial sit-down strikes all over Italy. The tension was greatest in Turin, where a general strike started in April and spread to all Piedmont. Malatesta and the anarchists agitated tirelessly in the northern cities and tried to exploit their links with Fiume in the revolutionary cause.[1] The Catholics were meanwhile organizing land seizures in Sicily, agitation among the Tuscan *mezzadri* and agricultural strikes in Lombardy. There was recurrent violence: between April 1919 and September 1920, 140 clashes between police and demonstrators caused over 320 deaths.[2] The police forces, disorganized by the war, were still under strength. Troops often had to be called in, and this in turn led to strikes by railwaymen and seamen who refused to transport them, and to anti-militarist demonstrations. Fortunately for the state, these outbreaks were rarely planned or coordinated. 'This is not revolution', was Mussolini's shrewd verdict: 'it is the unconscious St Vitus' dance of maximalist epilepsy.'[3] Nitti expanded the *carabinieri* and formed a new, semi-military Guardia Regia of 25,000 men, which he did not

[1] See above, p. 546. For the strikes in Turin, see further below, p. 563.

[2] Alatri, *Origini*, p. 61.

[3] *Il Popolo d'Italia*, 4 December 1919, in Mussolini, XIV, p. 171. Turati's verdict was not dissimilar. He regarded the railway and post office strikes not as legitimate episodes of the class struggle, but as criminal, 'brigand-like acts of blackmail against the nation and the consumer, which means against the proletariat itself'. Turati–Kuliscioff, V, pp. 180–1, 188–9, 203–5.

hesitate to use. But his efforts to restore law and order earned him little credit. The left attacked him for savagery, the right for weakness. In January middle-class youths, disgusted by Nitti's appeasement of the railwaymen, volunteered to break the strike and keep the railways running. All this confusion forced Nitti to lean on the civil service and to govern largely by decree. During his frequent absences abroad parliament was kept adjourned.

## Nitti's Policy of Peace

In foreign policy Nitti achieved modest success. In January 1920 he returned to Paris and London with Tittoni's successor, Vittorio Scialoja, to resume the Adriatic negotiations. Almost at once a great step forward was taken. The British and French accepted Nitti's proposal that the Fiume *corpus separatum* should become an autonomous state under the League of Nations, linked to Italy by a narrow coastal strip, while the hinterland and the adjoining port of Sušak should go to Yugoslavia. The idea of a big buffer state was thus abandoned. They also agreed to modify the Wilson Line further in Italy's favour, in order to give a better strategic frontier east of Trieste. In return for this, Yugoslavia would acquire the district of Scutari in northern Albania and all Dalmatia (except for Zara, which would be administered by the League of Nations). But the Yugoslavs rejected this so-called Nitti Compromise and remained unmoved even by a seven-day ultimatum from Lloyd George and Clemenceau, threatening in case of refusal to enforce the Treaty of London. Nitti withdrew his proposals and formally fell back on the Treaty. Meanwhile a succession of angry notes arrived from Wilson, upbraiding the British and French for trying to present him with a *fait accompli* and for sponsoring proposals that would 'maintain injustice as against the claims of justice'. It was clear that he intended to maintain his power of veto.

Slowly, however, the problem was moving towards a solution. The British and French had now sided with Italy. Wilson remained obdurate, but his position in the U.S.A. was crumbling and his wishes no longer commanded the same respect in Europe as a year before. The Yugoslavs realised that time was against them. Nitti needed a solution more urgently than ever for domestic reasons and worked hard to get direct negotiations with the Yugoslavs under way.[1] The electoral failure of the right and the

[1] Nitti had a first unfruitful meeting with Trumbić in London in January. On 5 March they met again in Paris for five hours of discussion and made better progress. Alatri, *Nitti*, pp. 417–20. On 8 March Nitti told Turati that he had said to the Yugoslavs: 'We have got to be friends; whatever you do or say, however you insult us, you'll never succeed in making me your enemy . . . we are neighbours and have got to be good neighbours.' Turati–Kulischioff, V, pp. 270–1.

discredit into which D'Annunzio had fallen gave him greater freedom of
manœuvre. At last in May 1920 Scialoja met Pašić and Trumbić at Pallanza
on Lake Maggiore. The Yugoslavs were prepared to accept Italian sovereignty over the town of Fiume, though within a smaller area than the
*corpus separatum*; but they still insisted on the Wilson line. Scialoja held
out for the *corpus separatum* and for territorial contiguity. These talks were
interrupted by Nitti's fall.

The Adriatic dispute dominated Italy's relations with central and
eastern Europe. In a despatch to Tittoni on 6 September 1919, Nitti
wrote:[1]

> The governments of the Balkan countries, and those of the nations which
> have risen from the ruins of the Austro-Hungarian Empire, must understand
> from this moment that we have no wish to follow them in any policy of
> intrigue, rivalry or perpetual conflict: above all we must not appear as the
> instigators and inspirers of an anti-Yugoslav coalition extending its network
> of influence from the Black Sea to the Adriatic. This would be a policy of
> war, while Italy wants, and must pursue, a policy of peace.

These were sane sentiments, but Nitti did not always live up to them. In
the autumn of 1919 he made a vigorous bid for the friendship of Rumania,
at a moment when the latter was quarrelling over frontiers with Yugoslavia and defying the peacemakers in Paris. Nitti's overtures brought
exasperated accusations from the British of complicity in disloyalty to the
Peace Conference.[2] Nitti also hoped to enlist Hungary in a diplomatic bloc
with Italy and Rumania. After the collapse of Bela Kun's bolshevist
regime in August, Horthy's 'white' government looked to Italy for support
in its fight for a less harsh peace treaty and was ready in return to back
Italy's claim to Fiume.[3] But though Nitti was sympathetic to Hungarian

---

[1] Alatri, *Nitti*, p. 177.

[2] ibid., p. 248; BFP, VI, 241, 245, 277, 309, 319–20. In December both Scialoja
and Sforza denied complicity on the part of their government, but admitted that
there was ground for complaint in the activities of the Italian representative in
Bucharest. BFP, VI, 341, 381.

[3] In November 1919 the head of the Italian military mission in Budapest appears
to have offered Horthy an alliance against Yugoslavia; Italy would supply arms,
clothing and equipment, and Hungary would recover Croatia as its share of the
spoils. BFP, VI, 244, 258, 309. This may well have been private nationalist diplomacy. Nitti suffered from insubordinate officers abroad just as much as at home.
In June 1920 Curzon, the British Foreign Secretary, wrote of 'the intrigues to
which I have unfortunately good ground to believe both the French and Italian
governments have lent themselves in their relations with the Hungarians'. BFP,
XII, 169 (see also 242, 246, for similar observations in October). Curzon felt most
strongly that Britain, France and Italy should show a united front in their dealings
with their ex-enemies.

grievances,[1] his scheme failed. The Hungarians were embittered by the Rumanian occupation of their country and the Rumanians, after a change of government, accepted the Peace Conference's decision on the Rumanian-Yugoslav frontier. As the reactionary nature of Horthy's regime became apparent and the threat of a Habsburg restoration revived, Italy and Hungary drifted apart.

The slow relaxation of tension in the Adriatic allowed Italy to work out a more constructive foreign policy, less dominated by the search for allies against Yugoslavia. Relations with Austria were a significant index of the change. These were at first determined by the fate of south Tirol. In July 1919 Nitti had installed a civil administration in the liberated provinces, in place of the military government that had ruled them since the armistice. The post of civil commissioner at Trent was given to the radical Credaro, who had studied at Leipzig University and had pro-German sympathies. Nitti refused to discuss the Brenner frontier with the Austrians. He did however promise that there would be no oppression or denationalisation of the German minority, and issued instructions to this effect. His orders were ineffective, not for want of goodwill on Credaro's part, but because of obstruction from the local nationalists under Tolomei's leadership. South Tirol therefore continued to be the cause of bitterness in Austria.[2] Ill-feeling was also aroused by the behaviour of the Italian forces of occupation north of the Brenner and by the difficulties in obtaining food for starving Vienna through Trieste. At the end of 1919 Renner, the socialist Chancellor of Austria, was complaining that Italy was 'a most unpleasant neighbour with whom it is impossible to live on terms of confidence'.[3] But in April 1920 Renner paid a state visit to Rome, at Italy's invitation, and was cordially received.[4] A common dislike of Horthy and fear of the Habsburgs drew Italy and Austria together, and Nitti warmly

[1] Nitti showed his sympathy at the Allied conference in London in February and March 1920. BFP, VII, pp. 247-8, 384, 387; also *Papers and Documents relating to the Foreign Relations of Hungary* (Budapest 1939), I, 169, 177, 186, 193; Toscano, *Pagine*, I, pp. 402-4. But Scialoja stubbornly opposed suggestions of a Danubian *Zollverein* on the ground that it might lead to a political resurrection of Austria–Hungary. BFP, VII, pp. 526-7, 553-4.

[2] Alatri, *Nitti*, p. 83; BFP, VI, 62. Tolomei had installed himself after the war at Bolzano, where he founded and directed an organisation to promote the Italianisation of south Tirol. Herre, pp. 69 ff.          [3] BFP, VI, 392.

[4] According to Renner's account in *Österreich von der ersten zur zweiten Republik* (Vienna 1953), pp. 37-8, the discussions in Rome were confined to questions of finance, trade and transport, and touched on politics 'only superficially'. It would appear, however, from DDI (7), I, 306, 709, that Renner committed himself to taking no political initiative in Austria's foreign relations without prior consultation with Italy. According to Herre, pp. 148-50, the question of a special autonomous status for the Trentino and south Tirol was discussed; but nationalist pressure subsequently prevented any action by Nitti.

approved Renner's policy of reconciliation with Czechoslovakia. Italian foreign policy thus began to develop along the lines advocated by Bissolati.

One of Tittoni's first actions on reaching Paris in June 1919 was to end Sonnino's quarrel with Greece. The Tittoni–Venizelos Agreement of 29 July, to which the Peace Conference gave its blessing, reconciled Italian and Greek ambitions in both Albania and Asia Minor. In the former, Venizelos undertook to support Italian claims to Valona and a mandate over central Albania, and Tittoni to support Greek claims to northern Epirus. This confirmed the partition of Albania envisaged in the Treaty of London. In Asia Minor, by accepting a delimitation of the Italian and Greek zones which left Smyrna to Greece, Tittoni was able to regularise the position of the Italian forces whose presence the Peace Conference had hitherto refused to recognise. On the Dodecanese a compromise was reached: Italy would cede the islands to Greece, with the exception of Rhodes, the cession of which was to be subject to a plebiscite and to the cession by Britain of Cyprus. 'I have conceded only what the Conference would never have given me', reported Tittoni.[1] By ending a pointless quarrel, the Agreement did much to strengthen Italy's diplomatic position.

Nitti attached great importance to the satisfaction of Italy's reasonable aspirations in Asia Minor. This would bring economic benefits and, he hoped, provide compensation in the eyes of Italian opinion for unpalatable sacrifices in the Adriatic.[2] What Nitti asked for was a large 'zone of special interest and economic priority' in southern Anatolia and a share in the coal mines of Eregli on the shore of the Black Sea. For these he obtained Allied approval, subject to the conclusion of peace with Turkey, at the San Remo Conference in April 1920.[3] He never aimed at political annexation or permanent military occupation of any part of Turkey. Indeed he shared the view of his Turcophil Foreign Under-Secretary, Carlo Sforza, formerly Italian High Commissioner at Constantinople, that harsh treatment would only stimulate Turkish resistance.[4] This view was proved correct by the resurgence of Turkish nationalism in the interior of Asia Minor under Mustapha Kemal. By the summer of 1920 new Turkish armies were threatening all the European forces in Asia Minor, whether Greek or Italian, French or British. Venizelos, backed by Lloyd George,

[1] Alatri, Nitti, p. 111. Tittoni's judgement was proved false by Italy's subsequent success in retaining the Dodecanese. To the nationalists a bargain with a petty power like Greece represented the extreme limit of national humiliation.

[2] Alatri, Nitti, pp. 90–1, 120, 125–6.

[3] The Italian zone was virtually the same as that agreed in the St Jean de Maurienne Convention, less Smyrna which was now to be Greek.

[4] From September 1919 onwards, British representatives in Asia Minor were complaining that the Italians were 'currying favour' with the Turks and even supplying them with arms. BFP, IV, 513, 555, 561, 674.

wished to hold on to Smyrna and was unmoved by Nitti's warning against 'undertaking an unbearable burden'.[1] The French, however, began to evacuate their troops from Cilicia and in May 1920 the Italians were forced out of Konia. The power of the Allies to impose their will on Turkey was already in serious doubt.

Little progress was made towards a colonial settlement. Italian acceptance of Milner's offer of Jubaland and Jarabub[2] was confirmed by Tittoni in September 1919 and again in the Milner–Scialoja Agreement of April 1920. But the extent of the areas to be ceded remained in dispute, and Milner further insisted that the colonial agreement would become effective only 'as part of the general settlement of all the issues raised at the Peace Conference'. The effect of this reservation was to link the fates of Jubaland and Jarabub with that of the Dodecanese which, in the British view, should be ceded to Greece. The colonial negotiations therefore petered out. Few Italians felt satisfied with their Allies' interpretation of the 'equitable compensations' promised in the Treaty of London.

In Russian and German questions Nitti collaborated closely with Lloyd George.[3] One of Nitti's first acts on coming to power had been to cancel the military preparations for an expedition to the Caucasus, an adventure upon which he knew Italy was in no fit state to embark.[4] On many subsequent occasions he made it clear that he 'could not and would not make war on Russia'. Not only did he shrink from provoking disorder at home by intervention; he was also convinced that war against bolshevism was futile, because bolshevism had come to stay. Moreover Italy urgently needed normal relations with Soviet Russia in order to obtain food and raw materials. An Italian warship was therefore sent in the spring of 1920, with British approval, on a secret mission to the Black Sea, in order to establish contact with the Soviet government.[5]

[1] BFP, VIII, pp. 90–2.    [2] See above, p. 534.

[3] According to Charles-Roux, *Une grande ambassade*, p. 95, Lloyd George presented Nitti with a photograph of himself inscribed 'To my spiritual self'.

[4] Nitti, *Rivelazioni*, pp. 327–9; Alatri, *Nitti*, p. 80. The British, impatient to evacuate their troops but foreseeing that if they did, the Caucasian states would be swallowed up by the Russians, whether red or white, vented their irritation on Italy. 'As usual, it is the Italians who have got us into this mess', wrote Balfour on 9 August. BFP, III, 364. In February 1920 Nitti reluctantly agreed to contribute one battalion to an Allied force which was to be sent to Batum, for the sole purpose of maintaining order. It never in fact went, and the last British troops left Batum in July 1920. BFP, VII, pp. 253–5, 655–6, VIII, pp. 51, 98–101, 136–8, XII, pp. 553, 566, 571–2. The bolsheviks took over all three Transcaucasian republics shortly afterwards.

[5] Nitti, *Rivelazioni*, pp. 46, 195–6, and *Meditazioni*, p. 420; Alatri, *Nitti*, pp. 81–2; BFP, VII, pp. 144–7, 197–200, 211–15. The Italian troops which had been sent to Archangel in 1918 were evacuated with the remainder of the Allied force in the autumn of 1919.

Nitti also wished, like Lloyd George, to soften the economic (but not the territorial or military) clauses of the Treaty of Versailles and so strengthen German democracy. By attempting to impose a harsh settlement on Russia, Germany and Turkey simultaneously, he wrote to Lloyd George in January 1920, 'we are succeeding in uniting solidly against us three great movements of the spirit: Russian bolshevism, German patriotism and Moslem fanaticism'.[1] When the French temporarily occupied Frankfurt and four other German towns in April 1920, in retaliation for a technical breach of the peace treaty, Nitti supported the British protest, even though this caused the first open rift in the Allied united front against Germany since the war.[2] As regards reparations, he favoured a lenient policy which would make it possible for Germany to carry out the treaty. Like Lloyd George, he was ready to trust German good faith and warmly approved of the invitation to the German government to be represented, for the first time as an equal, at the reparations conference at Spa in July.[3] This revisionist policy, far-sighted and soundly proportioned to Italian strength, was marred by the lack of tact with which it was pursued. It brought him into sharp conflict with the chauvinist Millerand, who succeeded Clemenceau as French Prime Minister in January 1920, and with Millerand's admirer, Barrère. 'A fundamental divergence of ideas has emerged straight away between Millerand on the one side and Lloyd George and myself on the other', Nitti reported from the San Remo Conference in April.[4] His moderation also made him hated by the nationalists and chauvinists at home who execrated him as a renouncer, a pro-Bolshevik, a pro-German and a tool of Lloyd George and 'Anglo-Saxon plutocracy'.

In March 1920 the Popolari forced a cabinet crisis. They were dissatisfied with Nitti on two grounds: first, the delay in carrying out their

---

[1] Alatri, *Nitti*, pp. 387–8.                          [2] BFP, IX, 170, 300, 319–20.

[3] BFP, VIII, pp. 12–17, 199–204.

[4] Alatri, *Nitti*, p. 451. The French resented what they regarded as ingratitude for the support they had given Italy in the Adriatic negotiations. In March 1920 Paul Cambon, French ambassador in London, described Nitti in a letter to his brother, Jules, as 'un mélange de boche et de bolchévisme'. Paul Cambon, *Correspondence 1870–1924* (Paris 1940–6), III, p. 379. According to Nitti, Barrère had exerted all his influence in June 1919 to secure the more amenable Luzzatti as prime minister. Nitti even suspected that there was French money behind the domestic disorders of April 1920. On 22 May he asked the French government to recall Barrère, on the ground that he had been interfering in Italian internal politics. Millerand refused his request: Barrère's name, he declared, 'remains indissolubly linked with the *rapprochement* between the two Latin nations'. It was widely believed that Barrère engineered Nitti's fall in June in order to prevent his attendance at the Spa Conference next month. Nitti, *Rivelazioni*, pp. 451, 455–7; Charles-Roux, *Une grande ambassade*, pp. 118–24.

minimum programme, particularly in education and land reform; second, Nitti's discrimination against the Catholic unions in his dealings with organised labour. Catholic railwaymen and post office employees, who had stayed at work during the strikes in January, found themselves ignored by the government in the negotiations for a settlement, then treated as black-legs by their triumphant socialist fellow-workmen. This incident was not unique. The Popolari now presented Nitti with a nine-point programme, the adoption of which was their price for continued support. Liberal politicians were shocked by this attempt by a party to dictate the government's policy, which violated parliamentary tradition and revived old fears of political clericalism. Nitti therefore rejected the nine points and reformed his government, dropping the Popolari and bringing in some prominent Giolittians, among them Luzzatti.[1] Nitti still hankered after socialist support, and believed that 'future governments can go only in a socialist, labour, working-class direction'. 'Perhaps one day the socialists will see reason', he remarked to Turati. But even Turati, though moved by democratic appeals 'to collaborate to save Italy', still could not contemplate cutting himself off from his party; such action, he believed, would mean 'not our collaboration but our suicide'.[2] Nitti had therefore to be content with a precarious stopgap cabinet.

The full extent of parliament's paralysis now became clear. The right was out for Nitti's blood, the maximalists professed total indifference and neither liberals nor Popolari, divided by traditional suspicions, were alone capable of providing stable government. At their party congress at Naples in April the Popolari gave full expression to their dissatisfaction and on 11 May they joined the socialists in bringing the government down.[3] After a long crisis, Nitti formed a third government, which the Popolari consented to join; but it was virtually stillborn. On 24 May, the fifth anniversary of intervention, a demonstration for Italian Dalmatia was broken up by the police in the centre of Rome, and a student and five policemen killed. Passions rose when a large number of irredentists from Dalmatia and Fiume were arrested.[4] Nitti's bungling of the problem of the bread

[1] Nitti probably relied on the Vatican, with which he was continuing Orlando's negotiations on the Roman question, to keep the Popolari within bounds. At this time he was holding weekly secret meetings with Gasparri. Nitti, *Meditazioni*, p. 462; Howard, pp. 219, 239–40.

[2] Turati–Kuliscioff, V, pp. 279–80, 308.

[3] On this occasion Turati took the plunge and abstained, but not one of his colleagues followed him. He wrote next day to Anna Kuliscioff: 'I tell you that vote was an abomination. I tell you my comrades are criminals . . . they voted for the destruction of the state and of all moral discipline. They voted for darkness, for equivocation and, undoubtedly, for reaction.' Turati–Kuliscioff, V, pp. 332–3.

[4] Nitti, *Rivelazioni*, pp. 49–51, claims that the disorders were deliberately organised by his enemies.

subsidy proved the last straw. On 4 June, to reduce the drain on the exchequer, he raised the price of bread by decree. Provision for a state subsidy to raise the wages of the worst-paid workers failed to pacify the socialists, who organized demonstrations against so 'anti-proletarian' a measure. On 9 June Nitti withdrew the decree and announced his final resignation, amid exultation from the right and the strains of *The Red Flag* from the socialist benches.

The disappearance of Nitti marked the end of the post-war period. Frustrated by subversion on the right, the hostility of Giolitti and many liberals, and the blind refusal of the socialists to collaborate, Nitti had failed in his task. Paralysis in parliament and persistent disorder throughout the country had killed the illusions of *diciannovismo*. The democratic revolution had misfired. Gramsci optimistically compared Nitti to Kerensky, struggling against armed bands on the right but doomed, he implied, to give way to an Italian Lenin.[1] The situation had been more accurately diagnosed by Treves in March. 'This is the tragedy of the present crisis', he said; 'you can no longer impose your order on us, and we cannot yet impose ours on you.'[2]

[1] Nenni, p. 29; Alatri, *Nitti*, pp. 472–3.
[2] Tasca, p. 116; Salvatorelli and Mira, p. 70.

# 13

# The Fascist Challenge
## 1920-2

## Giolitti: Back towards Normalcy

The new Prime Minister was Giolitti, now seventy-eight years old. Most liberals, whether their past was neutralist or interventionist, Giolittian or anti-Giolittian, rallied behind him with satisfaction and relief. Wartime controversies had lost much of their sharpness. By now the middle class and most of the elder politicians looked back to the pre-war years as a golden period of prosperity and stability. Giolitti, their presiding genius, would be the *deus ex machina* who would resolve the unfamiliar perplexities of the post-war world.

At first he had the blessing of many more than the liberals. Hatred of the renouncer Nitti so obsessed the nationalists that they could look kindly and hopefully even on the 'traitor' of 1915. Mussolini supported him because his programme, especially its financial aspects, appeared 'fascist' and his cabinet included ex-interventionists. The Popolari were more cautious. Sturzo distrusted him as the evil genius of the pre-war political system. Giolitti in his turn resented Sturzo's attempts to dictate his party's policy from outside parliament and looked on him as 'an intriguing little priest'.[1] The Vatican was disappointed, realising that Giolitti would be less interested than either Orlando or Nitti in a permanent settlement of the problems of church and state.[2] But the Popular leaders had by now come to realize that unconstructive opposition on their part could wreck all

[1] Tasca, p. 107.
[2] Giolitti told Sforza at this time: 'The conversations [between Nitti and Gasparri] have been very creditable on both sides, but the best thing for the State and the Church is to continue as in the past: two parallels that get on well together without ever coming into contact.' Sforza, *Contemporary Italy*, p. 270. On another occasion Giolitti told a gathering of friends, 'No, I won't try [to reach a settlement], because if the Pope asks me for a piece of territory, even as small as a postage-stamp, I'll refuse it.' The Vatican insisted that 'a genuine territorial sovereignty, however small the territory, was an essential element of agreement'. De Rosa, *I conservatori nazionali*, p. 151.

chance of stable government. They therefore supported Giolitti, in spite of doubts, and Meda and one colleague entered the cabinet.

The socialists, as always, were divided. The maximalists showed unrelenting hostility. The reformists and trade union leaders, on the other hand, still felt drawn to Giolitti for his pre-war record, his neutralism and his progressive social and financial programme. But when Turati was offered a ministry, once again, though tempted, he refused, on the grounds that the rank and file of the party would disown him. Giolitti had to be content with Arturo Labriola, the ex-syndicalist, in the newly created post of Minister of Labour. In spite of the presence of the two Popolari, of Sforza as Foreign Minister and Bonomi, Bissolati's former colleague,[1] as Minister for War, the new cabinet was a conservative team.

Giolitti had not changed. His ultimate solution for Italy's ills was to restore the pre-war political system of which he had been undisputed master. Meanwhile he stood by his Dronero Programme of the previous year. The most urgent need, as he saw it, was to revive the Italian economy, stop the drift towards bankruptcy and repair the shaken efficiency of the administration: in short, to restore normalcy. His Minister of the Treasury, Meda, estimated the deficit for the year at 14,000 million lire, of which the bread subsidy accounted for almost half. Giolitti profited from Nitti's experience and made no immediate attempt to reduce the subsidy. Instead he obtained parliamentary approval of a capital levy, higher death duties, stiffer taxation of large incomes, expropriation of war profits and a reduction of tax evasion through compulsory registration of all stocks and shares. A commission of 15 senators and 15 deputies was set up to investigate and revise war contracts and recover excess expenditure. This was a programme calculated to please both the socialists and, with the exception of the item regarding share registration,[2] the Popolari. Two further points in his programme were clearly aimed at the Popolari: legislation to raise the status of private schools[3] and equal recognition by the state of all trade

[1] Bissolati had died in May.

[2] Many ecclesiastical bodies found it profitable and legally convenient to invest their funds in unregistered bearer shares. Giolitti's proposal therefore alarmed church circles, which feared that compulsory registration would be followed by more rigorous taxation and a consequent reduction in church income. Though these anxieties were reflected in the Popular party, it voted for the measure. For details, see Howard, pp. 253–4.

[3] A reform particularly desired by the Popolari was the institution of an impartial examining board for the state examination (*esame di stato*) in secondary schools, the equivalent of the G.C.E. This was the entry to a wide range of professional careers, and the pupils of private schools had hitherto been handicapped by the fact that the examination was conducted entirely by state school teachers. Giolitti's Minister of Education, the philosopher Croce, proposed to remove this disparity.

unions, irrespective of political colouring. On 9 July Giolitti received a vote of confidence of 264 votes to 146, and for the next month, until parliament adjourned, he enjoyed solid Popular support and almost benevolent neutrality from the socialists.

The new government was given no respite from strikes, disorder and violence. In June a regiment of Bersaglieri, about to embark for Albania, mutinied at Ancona. This set off a series of revolts in the Marche and Romagna which recalled Red Week of 1914. Malatesta and the anarchists were once again prominent. Republics were proclaimed in four towns in the Marche, railwaymen refused to transport troops and police, and Ancona itself, with its military installations, was for several days in the hands of armed civilian rebels. In July a tram strike led to clashes with students and *arditi* in Rome, followed by a general strike. In the fomenting of violence there was little to choose between socialists and nationalists, anarchists and syndicalists. Giolitti calmly tried to apply the methods which had proved successful between 1901 and 1911: minimum interference in labour disputes, provided the law was observed, but unhesitating use of the police to ensure public order.[1]

The most serious challenge came from Turin. In March the engineering and motor-car industry of that city had been paralysed by a strike of protest against the introduction of summer time in the factories, a measure which dated from the war and was detested by the workers as a symbol of wartime discipline. But the real issue was the recognition by the employers of the factory councils. The battle was led by F.I.O.M., the metal-workers' union which since the war had assumed the militant leadership of the whole labour movement. After three weeks the dispute developed into a general strike in which railwaymen, post office workers and employees of the city council joined. Soon all Piedmont was affected. Gramsci's communist group contributed an ardent insurrectionary spirit. But local enthusiasm was not enough. The socialist politicians were suspicious, trade union leaders felt their authority threatened, Milan was jealous of Turin. When the strikers were weary, the government and C.G.L. intervened and work was resumed. The factory councils survived. But the spark of Turin had failed to set Italy aflame and discouragement set in.

The strike left the industrialists bitter and revengeful. In the long wage negotiations with F.I.O.M., which began in May, they made no concessions and showed no wish to avoid another battle. On 13 August the talks broke

[1] Malatesta was arrested in October 1920. Next March, while he was still in prison, anarchists exploded a bomb in a Milan theatre, killing 20 persons. This outrage, which destroyed all public sympathy with anarchism, was followed by systematic police action and many arrests.

down. 'All discussion is pointless,' declared Edoardo Rotigliano, the employers' representative, to Bruno Buozzi, secretary of F.I.O.M. 'Ever since the war ended, the industrialists have gone on submitting to humiliation. They've had enough, and now it's your turn.'[1] Three days later an extraordinary congress of F.I.O.M. reluctantly ordered its members to work to rule. Buozzi was ready to cancel the order and reopen negotiations; but despite pressure from the government, the employers refused to budge. On 30 August the management of the Alfa Romeo works in Milan announced a lockout. To forestall this move, F.I.O.M. ordered 300 Milanese factories to be occupied. The U.S.I. and U.I.L. instructed their members to conform. Turin joined in immediately. Once again there was great revolutionary fervour. Red guards were posted at the factory gates. The factory councils sat in the managers' offices and maintained production while the supply of materials lasted. The world was to be shown that workers could run an industry as well as capitalists. In the evenings Gramsci applied his theory of the social function of the factory by organizing political and educational meetings. The aim of his revolutionary élite was the permanent occupation of the factories by the proletariat, as a first step towards the expropriation of all the means of production and the final seizure of power.

While the impact of the occupations was greatest in Milan, Genoa and Turin, the movement spread through the engineering industry to every part of Italy, until 500,000 workers were involved. Bonomi, the Minister for War, took military precautions against a revolutionary *coup*. But for a week Giolitti sat tight and waited, exactly as in 1904, declining to interrupt his Alpine holiday or to postpone a meeting in France with Millerand, the French Prime Minister. He wanted the strikers to have enough rope to hang themselves and forbade the use of force to eject them from the factories. When, however, it became known that the strikers had stocks of arms and explosives, he decided that action was required. Strong pressure was exerted on the industrialists, both directly through the prefects of Turin and Milan and indirectly through the banks, to induce them to be reasonable. The Under-Secretary of Interior, Camillo Corradini, was meanwhile urging Turati and responsible trade unionists to intervene.[2] On 10 September the leaders of the Socialist party and the C.G.L. met in Milan. Their task was to decide whether to treat the occupations as an industrial dispute or to make them a political springboard for revolution. All were conscious of the risks of passing from revolutionary talk to revolutionary action. A

---

[1] Rotigliano's actual phrase was more picturesque: 'essi [the employers] hanno continuato a calare i pantaloni'. Tasca, p. 118; Spriano, *L'occupazione delle fabbriche*, pp. 41–2.

[2] ibid., pp. 81–8, 110–12; Giolitti, *Memorie*, pp. 596–600; De Rosa, *Storia*, pp. 131–8.

majority of trade unionists favoured caution. With obvious relief the politicians acquiesced and renounced responsibility for what was agreed to be a non-political problem. The C.G.L. then made recognition of the factory councils its condition for ordering its members back to work. Negotiations were reopened with the employers and Giolitti himself presided over a joint meeting to discuss machinery for giving the workers a share in management. On 25 September the strikers sadly began to evacuate the factories.

The final settlement, which included a rise in wages and recognition in principle of the factory councils,[1] gave an appearance of victory to the workers. But in fact they had been beaten, for the second time in a year, and they knew it. They had been prepared for defence, not attack, and had failed to take the revolution out of the factories into the streets.[2] After September 1920 the Turin working-class lost heart. Outside Turin there was little revolutionary spirit. The red tide was receding in Europe since the Poles had repulsed the Russian army outside Warsaw in August. In

[1] The trade union leaders had a much more modest conception of the factory councils than Gramsci. In the C.G.L.'s view the councils' function would be to give the employees' representatives accurate knowledge of the technical and financial conditions of their firm, and so enable them to offer constructive criticism of the management's proposals, prevent 'unreasonable' wage demands and have a say in the drafting of factory regulations and the engagement and dismissal of labour. The phrase used to summarise this programme was *controllo operaio*, which means much less than 'workers' control'. Buozzi, the C.G.L. leadership, Turati and the socialist right wing, and Giolitti himself believed that the introduction of *controllo operaio* would be a turning point in capital–labour relations; it would stimulate production and could even lead to an 'economic renaissance'. For the very same reasons the Turin communists denounced the agreement as 'a clever bourgeois manœuvre'. But even the C.G.L.'s limited programme seemed presumptuous to the industrialists. See Spriano, *L'occupazione delle fabbriche*, pp. 113–15, 128; Rigola, *Storia*, p. 449; De Rosa, *Storia*, pp. 139–44. The Catholic C.I.L. drafted a much more radical scheme for co-partnership, joint management and profit-sharing, but it was generally ignored.

[2] In spite of the alarmist rumours of offensive preparations, the role of the red guards was in fact purely defensive. Even in the large and efficiently organised Fiat Centro factory in Turin, the strikers had at their disposal only 5000 rounds of machine-gun ammunition, enough for ten minutes' action. Gramsci's lieutenant, Palmiro Togliatti, told the C.G.L.'s leaders on 9 September that to try to start an insurrection in Turin alone would be disastrous; the revolution must be on a national scale. Gramsci and his colleagues feared being left in the lurch if they acted on their own. During the occupation they had become painfully aware of their alienation from the managerial and technical middle class, from the ex-servicemen and even from the agricultural unions of the Po valley, let alone the peasants in the rest of Italy. Spriano, *L'occupazione delle fabbriche*, pp. 83–6, 93–9. Perhaps the aptest comment was that of Gaetano Bensi, one of the Milan workers' representatives at the C.G.L.'s National Council: 'Revolutions are not made by first summoning an assembly in order to discuss whether one should or should not make a revolution'. ibid., p. 104.

the autumn the post-war boom collapsed. The trade unions lost members and the number of strikes dropped.[1] Soon the C.G.L. was wholly on the defensive. This was the industrialists' opportunity. Strongly organised since March 1920 in a reconstituted General Confederation of Industry (Confindustria), they obstructed all practical steps towards setting up official factory councils. As Confindustria's forceful secretary, Gino Olivetti, put it, the vital question of 'power in the factory' was involved. In February 1921 Giolitti personally drafted a bill on the subject, but it got lost in committee in an indifferent parliament. Many strike leaders and members of the factory councils were dismissed when, on the plea of economic necessity, industrial payrolls were reduced. The industrialists had seen the red flag flying over their factories in August 1920. Now they wanted revenge.

While the industrial battle was raging in Turin and Milan, many parts of the countryside were experiencing equally bitter struggles. The most important took place in the province of Bologna, where the year 1920 saw a ferocious trial of strength between the socialist Federation of Land Workers and the most militant landowners' association in Italy. Here class tension was sharper even than in industrial Turin. In October 1919 the Federation refused to negotiate collective wage agreements with the landowners' organisation and demanded separate agreements with each employer. 'The workers have the right to impose their conditions of work upon the owners', it declared, speaking in the name of not only the *braccianti* but every category of peasant labourer, sharecropper and tenant. The landowners refused and in February 1920 the *braccianti* and *mezzadri* struck. By May the entire peasant population was involved. The harvest rotted in the fields and the chamber of labour supplanted the prefect as *de facto* ruler of the province. The strike ended only on 25 October, with an agreement that gave the Federation almost all it had demanded.[2] But it proved a Pyrrhic victory.[3] Like the industrialists, the landowners of Bologna and Emilia were from that moment waiting for revenge.

There were many others who were longing for a chance to hit back at the socialists. Small peasant proprietors and tenant farmers had suffered almost as much as the larger landowners from the pressure of organised

---

[1] The membership of the C.G.L. fell from over 2,000,000 in the autumn of 1920 to just over 1,000,000 at the end of 1921. The total number of strikers in industry fell from 1,268,000 in 1920 to 645,000 in 1921. *ASI 1919–1921*, pp. 394, 512; Neufeld, p. 547.

[2] Preti, pp. 426–39; Serpieri, pp. 303–5.

[3] After the autumn of 1920 the agricultural trade unions, like the industrial, lost heart and members. The total number of agricultural strikers fell from 1,046,000 in 1920 to 79,000 in 1921. *ASI 1919–1921*, p. 512; Neufeld, p. 547. The landowners had meanwhile formed a vigorous national organisation, the General Confederation of Agriculture, in August 1920.

labour. They were frightened by the C.G.L.'s talk of nationalising the land, and if they sometimes collaborated with the socialist unions, they did so from fear rather than from conviction. In the small towns of Emilia and Lombardy, and wherever the socialists were dominant, there were elements of the population with good cause for rancour. Shopkeepers had seen their shops pillaged by the mob and their prices reduced by socialist local authorities. Small business men, retailers and contractors felt threatened by the ever-growing power of the socialist cooperatives and regarded their subsidisation by the state as a crime. House owners had lost income through rent control. Investors had responded to the patriotic appeal of war loans and now saw their savings eaten up by inflation. Minor civil servants and *fonctionnaires*, the professional classes, demobilised officers and war heroes, all felt their social and economic position threatened by organised labour and their patriotic pride insulted by the anti-militarism and revolutionary slogans of the socialists. By the end of 1920 there was ample material, in both industrial and rural areas, for a reactionary movement which could promise strong government, order and discipline.

Giolitti watched this change of political mood with satisfaction. The socialists had exhausted his patience. The reformists had given him limited support in parliament and the C.G.L. had worked with the government for industrial peace. But this was poor reward for all his efforts and far outweighed by the occupation of the factories. He therefore welcomed the stirring of the 'forces of order', just as in 1904 he had welcomed a swing to the right after the syndicalist general strike. Once the socialists had been chastened and weakened, he hoped they would at last turn to him.

Two events of the autumn of 1920 confirmed Giolitti's feeling that Italy was recovering its balance. On 4 November the second anniversary of victory was celebrated with parades, flags and speeches. A year before Nitti had held no official celebration, for fear of disturbances, but in 1920 all passed off quietly. It seemed that the quarrels between neutralists and interventionists had at last been transcended. Almost simultaneously, local elections were held throughout the country. In many cities a liberal-conservative-nationalist National Bloc was formed, with an anti-socialist programme. In Milan it received fascist support, though Mussolini confessed that he preferred to fight the socialists with revolvers rather than with votes.[1] The main issue of the elections was the 'defence of order'. The socialists, who campaigned with the slogan 'War against the state', won Milan, Bologna and most of Tuscany and Emilia, 25 out of the 69 provinces and nearly 2,200 of the 8,300 communes. But the National Bloc won not only the south but also many of the largest cities of the centre and north,

[1] Mussolini, XV, pp. 260–3, 305.

such as Rome, Florence, Genoa and Turin. It was the real victor, for it made gains while the socialists failed to hold their own.

The Popolari won 10 provinces and 1,600 communes and maintained their grip over Venetia. This was a disappointing result, which seemed to indicate that the party had already passed its peak. Internal dissension and friction with ecclesiastical authority were responsible. Strong forces within the party wished to revive pre-war clerical-moderate practice and join the National Bloc. Sturzo and the leadership opposed such a course, from fear that it would once again turn Catholics into political tools of Giolitti. But in several cities the party's official policy of independence was ignored, to the delight of much of the Catholic press. In Milan, where the Popolari were too divided to put up candidates of their own and urged their supporters to abstain, most Catholics, with the public blessing of the Archbishop, Cardinal Ferrari, and the private approval of the Vatican, voted for the Bloc. This was an important moment. The church had shown that its acceptance of the party's political autonomy was only conditional. When confronted by conflicting instructions from the party and an archbishop, many Catholic voters had obeyed the latter.[1]

The success of the National Bloc gave Giolitti confidence. Normalcy was returning and extremism was being checked by the ballot box and the common sense of the majority. The economic situation was less heartening. By the autumn of 1920 there were clear signs of depression ahead. Prices collapsed, unemployment increased, steel and motor-car output fell sharply and the whole of heavy industry came under strain. The greatest difficulties were experienced by those firms which had expanded most during the war, notably Ilva and Ansaldo. In November representatives of heavy industry and the major banks appealed urgently to Giolitti for action to check the depression of government securities, restore Italian credit abroad, discourage the flight of foreign capital, provide large credits for industry, and stimulate production through public works and state orders for ships and railway material.[2] They also pressed for relaxation of Giolitti's fiscal measures, especially the capital levy and the provisions for compulsory registration of share ownership. Their case impressed Giulio Alessio, Minister for Industry and Commerce, and Luigi Facta, Minister of Finance.[3] But Giolitti himself was less sympathetic. He was aware that with

---

[1] Howard, pp. 259–71; De Rosa, *Storia*, pp. 154–9. Meda was one of those who disapproved of the party's official policy.

[2] *Quarant' anni*, III, 320, 322.

[3] In May 1921 Facta received further representations regarding taxation of war profits. The industrialists maintained, not without justification, that Giolitti's measures were so severe as to amount to confiscation of capital; they couldn't 'pay what they hadn't got' and warned Facta that they would have to close their factories and go into liquidation. *Quarant' anni*, III, 341.

the depression came great compensating advantages. The drop in world prices brought cheaper coal and food and checked the rise in the Italian cost of living. Industrial real wages rose during 1921 to a peak 27% above the pre-war level.[1] Agriculture meanwhile was making a remarkable recovery. In 1920 there had been a disastrous crop failure; but a good harvest in 1921[2] and cheap plentiful supplies from abroad ended the food shortages. This enabled Giolitti and his Under-Secretary for Supply, Marcello Soleri, to tackle the bread subsidy and to succeed where Nitti had failed. In February 1921, against bitter socialist opposition, they started to abolish it by stages, the fall in world prices preventing the price of bread from rising too sharply. Once freed from the burden of the subsidy, Giolitti checked the rise in state expenditure and took a first decisive step towards balancing the budget.[3] Gentle deflation reduced the volume of paper money in circulation.[4] The deficit in the balance of trade was 40% smaller in 1921 than in the previous year.[5] The lira, which had fallen from 50·25 to the pound in January 1920 to 101·5 in December, rallied in the spring of 1921 and found its level slightly below 100. After 1921 Italy was able to stop borrowing from abroad.

In other fields, too, post-war chaos seemed to have been left behind. Parliament was coping efficiently with a heavy programme of legislation. Discipline in the civil service had been greatly improved, partly by persuasion, partly by the dismissal of offending officials in the post office and the Ministry of Finance. Similar pressure was applied to the railwaymen and the practice of blocking the movement of police and troops came to an end.[6] Demobilisation had reduced the three million men under arms in 1918 to half a million by the end of 1920. The reconstruction of the devastated areas of the north-east had been an outstanding success. State-subsidised land reclamation and public works had been resumed and a five-year plan for the railways drawn up. In June 1921, with the goodwill

[1] From (1913 = 100) 64·6 in 1918 to 127 in 1921. This peak was not reached again until 1949. Neufeld, p. 540; Fossati, p. 634. *Per capita* national income (1938 prices) rose to 2,499 lire in 1920, not far below the pre-war peak of 2,539 lire in 1913. *Sommario*, p. 216.

[2] Wheat production (in millions of quintals) after dropping from 51 in 1911–13 to 45 in 1919 and 37 in 1920, recovered to 51 in 1921. *Sommario*, p. 106.

[3] Salvemini, *L'Italia economica*, pp. 285–7; Coppola d'Anna, p. 85. The deficit (in millions of lire) dropped from 20,955 in 1920–1 to 17,168 in 1921–2 and 3,260 in 1922–3.

[4] Note circulation reached its peak in 1920 at 22,673 million lire, falling to 22,196 million in 1921. *Sommario*, p. 163.

[5] Exports paid for 36% of imports in 1919, 43% in 1920 and 48% in 1921. *Sommario*, p. 152; Romeo, p. 181.

[6] The extent of this practice has been greatly exaggerated by pro-fascist writers. Salvemini, *Fascist Dictatorship*, pp. 47–9, claims that there were only about 12 cases in all.

of the C.G.L., parliament approved the highest industrial tariff in Italian history. By well-used, traditional methods Giolitti was guiding Italy back to normalcy.

## Fascism Takes Root

There was one glaring exception to this general picture of returning normalcy: the growth of violence on the right. During 1920 middle-class 'defenders of order' began to take the law into their own hands. In February organisations of civilian volunteers appeared in Milan and received official encouragement from the prefect. In April Bologna followed suit. In May students and *arditi* in Rome helped to break a dustmen's strike and two months later were tearing red flags off tramcars, attacking the drivers, assaulting socialist deputies and sacking the offices of *Avanti!*. Middle-class youths, hungry for 'action', were the backbone of this movement, and the initiative in violence began to pass to the right.[1] Industrialists and land-owners quickly saw in such groups a more effective counter-revolutionary force than Giolitti, whose 'absenteeism' at the time of the factory occupations had shocked them. In the interests of order they were prepared to connive at illegality and even subversion against the incompetent liberal state.

Mussolini was the main beneficiary of this situation. After his electoral disaster in November 1919 it had seemed that his political career was at an end. Two days after the poll *Avanti!* sarcastically reported that 'a corpse in a state of putrefaction, apparently Mussolini's', had been fished out of the local canal. That same day Mussolini was arrested, at the instigation of his victorious enemies, after arms had been discovered during a search of his office by the police. Albertini intervened in his favour, on the ground that there was no point in martyrising a discredited man, and within twenty-four hours Nitti ordered his release. His movement, racked by dissension and recrimination, disintegrated. At the end of the year only 30 fasci survived, with a total membership of less than 1,000. For a while he was plunged in despair and contemplated abandoning politics and even journalism.[2]

Over the next six months his confidence slowly returned. He was one of the first to sense which way the wind was blowing. In his speeches and articles the nationalist note became more strident, while the discredit which D'Annunzio's radical experiments had brought upon Fiume increased his eligibility as an ally in conservative eyes. In July 1920, in retaliation for the assassination of two Italian naval officers at Split, youths

[1] Salvatorelli and Mira, pp. 68, 74, 84–5; De Felice, pp. 609, 616.
[2] ibid., pp. 510–11, 568, 572 ff., 587–8.

of the Trieste Fascio attacked and burnt down the headquarters of the Slovene organisations in the city. This was the first appearance of *squadristi* and Mussolini praised their action as 'the masterpiece of Trieste Fascism'. *Squadrismo* spread during the autumn to the whole of Venezia Giulia, with the active support of the military authorities. Slovene clubs and societies, trade unions and newspapers were terrorised and their premises destroyed. In February 1921 Mussolini himself paid a triumphant visit to Trieste to thank his followers and deliver an imperialist speech on foreign policy. The nationalists and fascists claimed to be fighting a war of liberation. Italian soil was being cleansed by fire and sword of its 'nests of Slav infection' and fascism was performing the role of 'advanced sentinel of the purest *italianitá*' against the reviving Austrianism of the bolshevist-Slovene *canaille*.[1]

At the end of 1920 *squadrismo* spread from its training ground in Venezia Giulia to Emilia. The first major incident occurred at Bologna. Violent passions had been aroused in that city and the surrounding countryside by the agricultural general strike which ended in October. A few weeks later the local elections returned a socialist majority, and on 21 November the new mayor, an extreme socialist, was due to be installed. The local Fascio announced its intention of using force to prevent the insult of a red flag flying over the town hall. As the mayor appeared on the balcony there were shots in the crowd thronging the *piazza* below. In the ensuing confusion bombs were thrown from the town hall, nine persons in the crowd were killed and a hundred injured, and inside the council chamber a nationalist councillor and war hero was shot dead from the public gallery.[2]

These events, for which Mussolini did not shirk responsibility,[3] inflamed passions on both sides. Fascist *squadre* sprang up all over Emilia and took the offensive, led by young ex-servicemen such as Italo Balbo of Ferrara and Dino Grandi of Bologna. Their object was to smash the socialist unions in the countryside and break their monopoly of the supply of labour. One after another, punitive expeditions made sorties from the towns: trade union offices, chambers of labour and cooperatives were attacked and burnt, leading socialists were humiliated or beaten up, dosed with castor oil or banished from the district. No distinction was made between maximalists and reformists. As the *squadre* grew in strength and boldness, they held up socialist local councils at the pistol point and forced them to resign. During the spring of 1921 they extended their operations into Tuscany, Venetia, lower Lombardy and Umbria. In April they even raided Turin, the revolutionary citadel, and burnt the People's House in the centre of the

[1] Mussolini, XV, pp. 157, 198, 226, XVI, p. 462; Tasca, pp. 160–3.
[2] Tasca, pp. 155–7; Salvatorelli and Mira, pp. 99–100; Salvemini, *Fascist Dictatorship*, pp. 63–6. [3] Mussolini, XVI, p. 27.

city. Socialists were not their only victims. Where the Popolari were strong, as in Tuscany and Lombardy, the white unions were the main target. Even syndicalists sympathetic to D'Annunzio were not spared. The *squadristi* also paid special attention to south Tirol and gave the Germans the same treatment as the Slavs of Venezia Giulia. Mussolini called for the extirpation of 'the German vipers' nest'; Alto Adige was Italian soil and must be vigorously Italianised.[1] By the middle of 1921 these expeditions had grown into systematic military operations. Large areas of northern Italy passed in the course of a few months from the fever of *diciannovismo* to a state bordering on civil war.[2]

In July 1919 Mussolini had believed that 'Fascism will always be a minority movement; it cannot spread beyond the towns.'[3] Over a year later he repeated, 'We are a minority and don't worry about our size. We prefer excellent quality to crude quantity.'[4] But now fascism underwent a startling transformation into a mass movement based on the countryside. The demoralisation of the early months of 1920 was forgotten. From 30 fasci with 870 members on 31 December 1919 the movement grew to 88 with 20,600 members a year later and to 834 with 249,000 on 31 December 1921.[5] Mussolini's ambition grew as his movement expanded. On 23 March 1921, the second anniversary of its foundation, he declared that its aim was 'to govern the nation'.[6] But growth brought new anxieties; it had been too rapid, as Mussolini himself recognised. 'Untrustworthy elements' and 'eleventh-hour profiteers' entered the fascist ranks, like 'moths round the flame', hoping to make the movement an instrument of sectional and class interests. These new recruits brought handsome contributions of cash from the agrarian middle-class of the Po valley, but they also changed the character of fascism. Many of its original members, who had come from the left, drifted away. At the second Fascist congress held in Milan in May 1920, only ten of the nineteen members of the central committee were re-

[1] Mussolini, XVI, pp. 123, 291–3, 305, 335, 346. Alto Adige is the Italian name for south Tirol.

[2] Tasca, pp. 174–5, gives the following figures, based on fascist sources, for institutions and organisations destroyed during the first six months of 1921: 17 newspapers and printing works, 59 People's Houses, 119 chambers of labour, 107 cooperatives, 83 peasant leagues, 141 socialist and communist clubs and offices. According to the Ministry of Interior's figures, between 1 January and 7 April 1921 there were 102 deaths in clashes between fascists and socialists (25 fascists, 41 socialists, 20 police and 16 others). De Rosa, *Storia*, p. 185.

[3] Mussolini, XIII, p. 220.

[4] Speech at Cremona, 5 September 1920, in Mussolini, XV, p. 183.

[5] De Felice, pp. 595, 607. The figures quoted are those of the fascist central secretariat, which may be presumed to be the most accurate. The figures published at the time (see Tasca, pp. 187, 210) were grossly inflated.

[6] Mussolini, XVI, pp. 211–13.

elected, and the eleven new members belonged predominantly to the right. In July the new committee authorised several fasci to place themselves at the disposal of the military authorities in the event of disorders provoked by the extreme left. From mid-1920 onwards the influence of the futurists, syndicalists and ex-socialists declined, while that of the reactionary middle-class elements grew.[1] Rapid growth also confronted Mussolini with difficult problems of organisation. While the movement was small, he had been able to dominate his lieutenants who were all personal friends. But now new leaders were thrown up, with impressive local followings and local sources of finance, who were less ready to accept without question instructions from a newspaper editor in distant Milan. Mussolini felt his creation escaping from his control. His anxiety was apparent in the warnings against 'violence for its own sake' which he began to issue in the spring of 1921. He foresaw that unless the exuberance of the newly joined *squadristi* was disciplined, fascism might alienate the public and create sympathy for its enemies.[2]

The fascist programme soon began to reflect the political aims of its new supporters and paymasters. The radicalism of 1919 was not yet completely abandoned. Mussolini continued to stress his preference for a republic over a monarchy, and to keep in touch with the working-class. During the occupation of the factories he deplored the portraits of Lenin which the strikers plastered on the walls and the training of a 'communist army' inside the workshops; but he also attacked the employers for refusing concessions and hailed the recognition of the factory councils as an epoch-making victory for the working-class.[3] Fascism was not the 'watchdog of capitalism'; it represented the nation, not one class or caste. Though the C.G.L. rebuffed all his overtures, he still did not despair of liberating the workers from the 'new priests' of bolshevik mystification. Nevertheless the tone of his speeches and articles began to change. There was a new emphasis on the need for 'economic demobilization' and for stripping the state of all its economic functions, even the post office and railway monopolies. Already in January 1921 he began to praise capitalism and to declare that it had 'hardly yet reached the beginning of its history'.[4]

[1] De Felice, pp. 590–8, 622–3, 626. In June 1920 the revolutionary syndicalists of Parma, De Ambris's stronghold, denounced fascism as 'anti-proletarian'. In the same month Marinetti resigned from the central committee and thereafter drifted steadily away from Mussolini, being unable to stomach the latter's appeasement of the church and the transformation of fascism into a reactionary and traditionalist (*passatista*) movement.

[2] Mussolini, XVI, pp. 112, 181–2, 219–20, 241–2.

[3] *Il Popolo d'Italia*, 5, 10, 28 September 1920, in Mussolini, XV, pp. 178–9, 192–3, 231–2; also De Felice, pp. 627–34. Mussolini had a meeting with Buozzi on 10 September, apparently in the hope of playing a mediator's role.

[4] *Il Popolo d'Italia*, 7, 14 January 1921, in Mussolini, XVI, pp. 101–3, 116–17.

Some of these apparent contradictions can be explained by the large part played in the transformation of fascism by ex-syndicalists, especially in Emilia and Tuscany. Leading fascists such as Grandi, Bianchi and Rossoni had been founders of the U.I.L. in 1914. For them, as for Mussolini, interventionism in 1915 had been the first step towards fascism and the U.I.L. was the bridge between syndicalism and patriotism. In the second half of 1920 the fascists began to shift their support from the U.I.L. to the independent 'national syndicates', which had their main following among the railwaymen, civil servants and white collar workers. In November the foundation of a national federation of *sindacati economici* received warm fascist approval. In February 1921 the first fascist agricultural labour union was founded near Ferrara, and thereafter in many areas of northern Italy fascist syndicalism followed in the steps of the *squadre*. When the socialist unions had been destroyed or terrorised into inactivity, their members would be enticed or dragooned into fascist unions and the tricolour would replace the red flag.[1] To many *braccianti* it mattered little whether socialists or fascists were in control; what did matter was to find work, and this the fascists, thanks to their close connexions with the landowners, were able to offer. The landowners looked on the *squadristi* as their private police and liked to use them to break strikes, reduce wages or enforce new labour contracts. But there were fascists who took their syndicalism seriously.[2] Having destroyed their enemies, they found themselves responsible for grappling with land hunger and unemployment, and forced to adopt many of the socialists' methods. It was now the fascists who operated minimum labour quotas and lobbied the ministries for subsidies and public works. But they were also able to promise something that the socialists couldn't. Early in 1921 Mussolini announced that fascism meant 'land for those who till it', and this proved an effective slogan for winning rural recruits.[3]

Italian socialism went down almost without fighting. From time to time *squadristi* were ambushed or assaulted, provoking savage reprisals. But communist appeals for violence in reply to violence were little heeded. The victims of the *squadre* were, for the most part, not revolutionary 'bolsheviks', but pacific, parochially minded reformists, unaware of what

---

[1] De Felice, pp. 623–4. During 1921 the membership of the socialist National Federation of Land Workers dropped from 890,000 to 294,000; that of the Catholic agricultural unions fell less steeply, from 945,000 to 749,000. Serpieri, pp. 262–3; Preti, p. 463.

[2] Tamaro, I, p. 125, writes of Grandi's 'quasi-socialist idealism' and quotes from a letter of February 1921 in which Grandi looks forward to the triumph of fascism, when 'socialism will be stronger than ever, but with different men'.

[3] Tasca, pp. 157–8, 287; Salvatorelli and Mira, pp. 130–1; *Il Popolo d'Italia*, 7, 27 January, 23, 30 March, in Mussolini, XVI, pp. 102, 130, 212–13, 229–30.

had hit them until all was over. 'Stay at home; ignore all provocation. Even silence and cowardice are sometimes heroic', was the advice of one of their leaders, Giacomo Matteotti.[1] The socialists had talked revolution for years; but when confronted with opponents who acted instead of talking, they were unprepared and helpless. In Turati's phrase, it was 'a revolution of blood against a revolution of words'.[2] The ambition of many socialists, especially in Emilia, had been to 'build socialism in one province';[3] but now the 'socialist state within the state' proved to have been built on sand.

This helplessness in the provinces was magnified by the growing disunity of the Socialist party. Having adhered to the Third International with enthusiasm in October 1919, it was now presented with Lenin's Twenty-one Conditions for continued membership. The two most difficult to swallow were the seventeenth, which required the party to take the title of 'Communist', and the seventh, which called for the immediate expulsion of the reformists, 'the accomplices of the bourgeoisie', and named Turati and Modigliani among other 'notorious opportunists'. On the subject of party unity even ardent maximalists were reluctant to obey Moscow. Serrati, for example, who was editor of *Avanti!*, felt a sense of national solidarity even with an unrepentant social democrat like Turati, and tried to convince Lenin of the differences between Italy and Russia. But many favoured unconditional acceptance, including Bordiga, Gramsci and the Socialist Youth Federation. In September 1920 the party executive adopted the Twenty-one Conditions by 7 votes to 5, but decided to refer the problem of a purge to a special congress, which met at Leghorn in January 1921. Only one question was discussed: the unity of the party. Two delegates from the Comintern, the Hungarian Rákosi and the Bulgarian Kabakchiev, derided the idea of unity – 'unity between communists and the enemies of communism';[4] Serrati defended it. Two-thirds of the delegates voted for acceptance of the Twenty-one Conditions with reservations; one-third voted for unconditional acceptance, then marched out of the congress and founded the Italian Communist party. Bordiga became its first secretary and Gramsci's *L'Ordine Nuovo* its daily newspaper. The main feature of its programme was uncompromising hostility to social democracy, the greatest enemy.

The Socialist party nevertheless reaffirmed its loyalty to the Comintern and sent a delegation led by Lazzari to its third congress in Moscow in June. Here the Russians intensified their pressure for a purge, as the essential first step towards reunion of the Socialist and Communist parties in a Communist-dominated united front. Lazzari allowed himself to be convinced, against his better judgement, but on his return to Italy still shrank

[1] Tasca, pp. 167–8; Rigola, *Storia*, p. 474.   [2] Nenni, p. 130.
[3] Tasca, pp. 184–5, 518–19.   [4] Nenni, p. 123.

from action. These internal quarrels, so entirely unrelated to the Italian crisis, demoralised the working-class movement just at the moment when the forces of reaction were building up overwhelming strength.[1]

Mussolini never ceased to boast that in 1919–20 fascism saved Italy from bolshevism. In later years this claim became a favourite item of fascist propaganda. In fact the fascist contribution to the defeat of revolution was marginal. Fascism took root only when 'bolshevism' was in full decline and incapable of revolutionary action. Mussolini recognised this last point at the time. In December 1920 he wrote of 'the death-rattle of Italian bolshevism, which is mortally stricken', and of the profound change in the psychology of the working-class since the occupation of the factories. Again in July 1921 he declared: 'To maintain that the bolshevist danger still exists in Italy is to mistake fear for reality. Bolshevism has been conquered.'[2] But in politics fear is often more potent than reality. Fascism continued to thrive on fear of bolshevism long after the danger had passed.

Fascism could never have prospered so rapidly without at least the tolerance of the state authorities. Many prefects, police and military commanders went far beyond tolerance. In Venezia Giulia the *squadre* enjoyed virtually official status. Elsewhere, particularly in Tuscany, they were supplied with lorries and arms, and serving officers joined the fasci with the approval of their superiors. Sometimes soldiers and *carabinieri* accompanied the *squadre* on punitive expeditions, fully armed and in uniform. Long-suffering policemen and state officials, after years of forced subservience to provincial socialist bosses, took little trouble to conceal their delight at the turning of the tables.[3]

This local acquiescence and even complicity did not have the government's sanction. Giolitti and his subordinates at the Ministry of Interior repeatedly instructed prefects to curb the *squadre* and punish crimes of violence. They also drew the attention of the War Ministry to the flagrant connivance of the military authorities and the discredit this brought upon the army and the nation.[4] But their exhortations were without effect. There

[1] Of the 216,327 members of the Socialist party at the end of 1920, 100,000 failed to renew their membership in either Socialist of Communist parties next year. Nenni, pp. 121, 125–8.
[2] *Il Popolo d'Italia*, 7, 31 December 1920, 2 July 1921, in Mussolini, XVI, pp. 44, 88, XVII, p. 21.
[3] Tasca, pp. 178 ff.; Salvemini, *Fascist Dictatorship*, pp. 76–84; De Felice, pp. 602–4.
[4] De Rosa, *Storia*, pp. 159–76. On 24 September 1920 a circular from the intelligence section of the army general staff praised the Fasci di Combattimento and instructed subordinate intelligence staffs to make contact with them. On 23 October Badoglio, army chief of staff, issued a further circular warning military commanders that the army must remain above politics, but did not cancel the previous instruc-

was little sense of urgency in Rome, where fascism hardly existed and the significance of what was happening in the provinces was not understood. More serious, prefects were finding it less and less easy to get their orders obeyed. Policemen and army officers refused to regard fascism as subversive and justified its illegality and violence by its patriotic aims.

Giolitti himself shared some of these feelings. He took fascist excesses no more tragically than he had taken socialist excesses in the years 1901–11, and believed they could as easily be cured by his old methods of government. Like almost all the liberal leaders, most of them much younger than himself, he failed to see that violence was the very essence of fascism or to recognise it as a movement already dedicated to the destruction of the liberal state. His tolerant attitude to fascism had no ideological basis, but was rather 'that of a father for a scapegrace son'.[1] He believed that he could master fascism and counted on time and weariness to bring moderation. Once tamed, brought into parliament and perhaps given a share of the responsibility of power, the fascists could be useful allies in the battle to restore normalcy. Events soon showed that this was a fatal miscalculation.

## The Treaty of Rapallo

In foreign as in domestic policy, Giolitti aimed at normalcy. This meant clearing up the Adriatic and Turkish questions and improving relations with France. Carlo Sforza, Giolitti's Foreign Minister, had been an interventionist and was selected for that very reason.[2] He was a democrat in the tradition of Mazzini and Bissolati, and a man of vision. Believing that the disappearance of Austria-Hungary had thrust upon Italy the leadership of central and eastern Europe, Sforza hoped to unite all the succession states in an anti-Habsburg front, pledged to preserve the peace settlement and to form a barrier against future German expansion. He therefore worked for friendship between Italy and the Slavs and for an effective League of Nations in which Italy, the natural leader of the small peoples, would play a major part. This was not starry idealism but a sensibly calculated policy for furthering essential national interests.

Giolitti and Sforza followed Nitti in backing Lloyd George's efforts for

---

tions. In 1924 Bonomi, who had been Giolitti's Minister for War, denied accusations that he had officially aided the *squadre* and tried to conceal his failure to punish pro-fascist complicity in the army. For this controversy see Bonomi, *La politica italiana dopo Vittorio Veneto*, pp. 159–60; Salvemini, *Fascist Dictatorship*, pp. 78–9; Tasca, pp. 152–5; and for a summary of the evidence and the texts of the circulars, R. Vivarelli, 'Bonomi e il fascismo', in *Rivista storica italiana*, vol. 72 (1960), pp. 147–57.

[1] De Rosa, *Giolitti e il fascismo*, pp. 71–2; De Felice, pp. 605–7.
[2] Charles-Roux, *Une grande ambassade*, p. 126.

a peace of reconciliation. Giolitti believed it was 'absolutely necessary for
Italy to have the friendship of Russia and Germany'. He therefore refused
to give arms to the Poles for their war against Soviet Russia and repeatedly
urged them to make peace.[1] The war interrupted negotiations for an Italo-
Russian commercial treaty, but a provisional agreement was signed in
December 1920 and trade representatives were exchanged next March. At
the Spa Conference on reparations in July 1920, Sforza won three successes
for Italy: representation on the Allied Rhine High Commission, an increase
in Italy's share of German reparations from $7\frac{1}{2}\%$ to 10% of the total, and
the allotment of virtually the whole Austro-Hungarian merchant fleet to
Italy. His policy was to maintain the wartime alliance with Britain and
France, but within the limits of that alliance to conciliate Germany. Thus
at Spa he opposed French intervention in the Ruhr for the purpose of extracting reparations. 'Italy would not send a single man to the Ruhr',
Giolitti told Lloyd George a month later.[2] But when, at the London Conference in March 1921, the German representatives were so intransigent
that the French proposal for sanctions secured British support, Sforza
reluctantly approved the occupation of three Ruhr towns in order to
prevent Italy's diplomatic isolation.

The first major decision of Giolitti and Sforza concerned Albania. The
Allies had still reached no decision on that country's future, but Italy's
claim to sovereignty over Valona had never been seriously challenged.
Nitti had also hoped to obtain a mandate over the rest of the country, with
the exception of northern Epirus (promised to Greece by the Tittoni–
Venizelos Agreement[3]) and possibly of Scutari (coveted by the Yugoslavs).
Wilson, however, had continued to champion the Albanians' right to self-
determination and would accept no Adriatic settlement at their expense.
Meanwhile the Albanians themselves, impatient of foreign occupation,
were beginning to take a hand. By the spring of 1920 the French and other
Allied forces had been withdrawn and only the Italians were left as a target
for Albanian xenophobia. In January a National Congress was elected and
a more resolute provisional government, whose leading spirit was Ahmed
Zogu, established itself at Tirana, out of range of the Italian fleet.[4] Its
programme was Albanian independence within the frontiers of 1913.
Irregular forces under its command gradually won control of the interior
and compelled the Italians to withdraw.

By the time that Giolitti succeeded Nitti, all the Italian forces had been
concentrated in Valona, where they were encircled by the attacking Albanians and racked by malaria. At this point mutiny broke out among troops

[1] BFP, VIII, pp. 756-7, 779.    [2] ibid., VIII, p. 757.    [3] See above, p. 556.
[4] Swire, pp. 311-13. Zogu, leader of the Moslem landowners' party, was to
emerge during 1920-2 as the outstanding figure in Albanian politics.

awaiting embarkation at Ancona, followed by widespread disorder.[1] The government decided that Albania was not worth the risk of more mutinies and insurrections. The general staff warned that Valona was untenable without an extensive hinterland, guarded by a long defensive perimeter. Giolitti believed that Italy's interest was to keep others out of Valona rather than hold it itself, and that the possession of the island of Saseno would be sufficient for this purpose.[2] He and Sforza therefore decided to abandon the claim to a mandate, hoping to preserve Italian influence by friendship with an independent Albania rather than by occupation or partition. On 22 July Sforza denounced the Tittoni–Venizelos Agreement (which committed Italy to partition) and on 2 August a treaty was signed in Tirana with the Albanian provisional government which guaranteed Albania's independence within the 1913 frontiers. Italian troops then evacuated Valona, retaining only Saseno. In December Albania was admitted to the League of Nations.

The benefits of this policy became apparent a year later, after Giolitti and Sforza had left office. With the Greeks fully occupied in Asia Minor, the main threat to Albania came from Yugoslavia, and in the autumn of 1921 Yugoslav troops made deep incursions into Albanian territory. On 9 November the Conference of Ambassadors in Paris, the successor to the Peace Conference, set up a frontier commission. At the same time the British, French, Italian and Japanese governments jointly and publicly recognised that the violation of Albania's frontiers or independence might endanger Italy's security and agreed, should Albania appeal to the League, to recommend that its defence be entrusted to Italy.[3] A few days later the Yugoslavs withdrew from Albania under strong protest, after a peremptory order from the League. Italy thus obtained what Giolitti and Sforza had aimed at: international recognition of its predominant interest in Albania and a check to Yugoslav and Greek ambitions, without the burden of a mandate or military occupation.

The evacuation of Valona in August 1920 reduced tension in the Adriatic and so helped to bring Italy and Yugoslavia together. Giolitti, like Nitti, felt he had to move cautiously, to avoid a revival of nationalist hysteria. Members of his government with his approval secretly helped D'Annunzio to obtain supplies and found him cash with which to pay Fiume's municipal employees. 'There are Italians at Fiume and we must help them', Giolitti

[1] See above, p. 563.
[2] Giolitti, *Memorie*, pp. 569–71.
[3] Macartney and Cremona, pp. 101–2; Swire, pp. 365–70; *Survey 1920–3*, pp. 343–8 and *1927*, pp. 166–7. Upholders of the League maintained that to recognise one member state as the sphere of influence of another was a violation of the Covenant.

remarked.[1] In his dealings with Yugoslavia he was no sentimentalist. In July 1920 two Italian naval officers were assassinated at Split. Giolitti not only tolerated fascist reprisals in Trieste[2] but concentrated troops along the armistice line north of Fiume. He and Sforza wanted no more than the minimum of Slavs inside Italy, realising that the welfare of Italy would not be determined by 'one island or rock more or less'.[3] They did however give high priority to good strategic frontiers, even if these involved the annexation of Slav-inhabited districts. To achieve their aim they were quite ready to use D'Annunzio's possession of Fiume as a bargaining weapon.

Sforza met Trumbić at the Spa Conference in July and Giolitti discussed the Adriatic question with both Lloyd George and Millerand during the summer. The Italians appeared to be in no hurry.[4] The Yugoslavs on the other hand were anxious to get the Italian forces of occupation out of Dalmatia. They knew that both the British and French approved of Italy's latest claims, and Wilson's sympathy by now counted for little. The Italian terms were a north-eastern frontier along the Alpine watershed and across Monte Nevoso,[5] and sovereignty over the town of Zara and four Dalmatian islands. Sforza did not ask for sovereignty over Fiume, but insisted on contiguity between the town and Italy. The final talks began at Rapallo on 7 November. The Yugoslavs made a last effort to bargain, but gave way under British and French pressure, not daring to risk the resurrection of the Treaty of London. On 12 November the Treaty of Rapallo was signed. Italy obtained its strategic frontier, Zara and the four islands, and in return renounced the rest of Dalmatia. A small Free State of Fiume was created, consisting of the *corpus separatum* together with a strip of Istrian territory which assured contiguity with Italy. Yugoslavia undertook to protect the Italian minority in Dalmatia, while Italy avoided any similar undertaking on behalf of its much larger Yugoslav minority. Giolitti and Sforza thus achieved complete success.

The treaty was a compromise, but Italy obtained much the best of the bargain. In Sforza's words, 'Italian unity had been completed within perfect

[1] Bonomi, *La politica italiana dopo Vittorio Veneto*, p. 151; Caviglia, pp. 188–91; Soleri, pp. 103–5. Soleri even arranged for the repurchase from D'Annunzio of 7,000 tons of grain seized by Giulietti's seamen.

[2] See above, pp. 570–1.

[3] Sforza to Giolitti, 17 August. *Quarant' anni*, III, 307.

[4] Giolitti, *Memorie*, pp. 571–2. Giolitti characteristically remarked to Lloyd George in August, with reference to the Russian problem, 'Questions often settle themselves if left alone and given a little time.' BFP, VIII, p. 768.

[5] This line was slightly more favourable to Italy than that of the Treaty of London. It ran well to the east of the line proposed by Italy in the Nitti Compromise of January 1920, which was itself only a minor modification of the Wilson Line and passed within ten miles of Trieste.

frontiers',[1] not by a *diktat* but by the first freely negotiated treaty since the war. In both countries the chauvinists denounced it as a betrayal of national interests. The Yugoslavs had good reason to do so, for 467,000 Croats and Slovenes were left on the wrong side of the frontier. Sforza did not underestimate their bitterness, but he hoped to neutralise it by generous treatment of the Yugoslav minority. He also had plans for an Italo-Yugoslav *consortium* to administer and develop the port and railways of Fiume. With this in mind, on the day of the treaty's signature, he gave Trumbić a secret promise that Yugoslavia should have Port Baroš[2] on the eastern edge of the port. This would be the Yugoslav contribution to the *consortium* which would help to bind the two countries' economies together. The treaty was to be, in Sforza's words, 'not only an epilogue, but the beginning of a new life for Italy'.[3]

There remained D'Annunzio. He greeted the news from Rapallo with an armed irruption into Sušak and seizure of the islands of Krk (Veglia) and Rab (Arbe), all of which the treaty assigned to Yugoslavia. There were rumours of a militarist plot to overthrow Giolitti. D'Annunzio talked of a further expedition to Šibenik, which was 'rightfully' Italian by the Treaty of London, and arranged another meeting with Millo at sea off Zara. But this time the government stood firm. Sforza forced the King to remind Millo of his sailor's oath of allegiance and the unhappy Millo told D'Annunzio he could offer no help.[4] Caviglia kept his troops firmly in hand. Among the citizens of Fiume there was much support for the treaty and little love left for heroes and adventurers. D'Annunzio however, though Caviglia promised him generous treatment, announced to the world 'I disobey'[5] and declared war on Italy. Giolitti, frustrated in his hopes of a peaceful, triumphal entry for the Italian army, reluctantly decided to use force. On Christmas Eve Caviglia's troops started to move in. After four days' fighting and the loss of fifty-three lives, D'Annunzio handed over the

[1] Despatch of 12 November 1920, the day of signature. Sforza, *Pensiero e azione*, p. 153.

[2] Before 1918 Port Baroš had been part of Croatia, not of the *corpus separatum*. Sforza's promise was to remain secret pending negotiation of the *consortium* and probably also, as his enemies later alleged, in order to facilitate ratification of the treaty by the Italian parliament.

[3] Speech in chamber of deputies, 26 November 1920. Sforza, *Pensiero e azione*, pp. 183–4.

[4] Sforza, *Contemporary Italy*, pp. 257–8; Giuriati, pp. 198–202; Giolitti, *Memorie*, p. 584.

[5] This *Disobbedisco* was a typically D'Annunzian perversion of Garibaldi's *Obbedisco* of 1866 when, in deference to the orders of the government, he evacuated the areas of the Trentino which his force of volunteers had occupied and which were to remain Austrian under the terms of the peace treaty. In the same proclamation D'Annunzio announced that 'Italy expects every man this day *not* to do his duty'.

town to the National Council which quickly negotiated surrender. The legionaries withdrew peacefully and on 18 January D'Annunzio himself left, declaring that the Italian people, absorbed in its 'Christmas gluttony' and indifferent to the fate of Fiume, was not worth dying for.[1] Abroad it seemed that at last Italy had a government worthy of the name.

Sforza intended the Adriatic settlement to be only the first stage in a much wider pacification of central Europe and the Balkans. In August 1920 Czechoslovakia had concluded a defensive alliance with Yugoslavia against Hungary. Next year Rumania adhered, so creating the Little Entente. Sforza gave it a warm welcome, recognising that its aims largely coincided with those of Italy. On the day of the signature of the Treaty of Rapallo, he and Trumbić also signed a convention to prevent the restoration of the Habsburgs or the reconstitution of Austria-Hungary. This, as Sforza intended, brought Italy closer to Czechoslovakia, which had already concluded an anti-Habsburg convention with Yugoslavia. In February 1921 Beneš, the Czechoslovak Foreign Minister, visited Rome to sign a commercial treaty. That same month the Ambassadors' Conference reaffirmed its declaration of the previous year that a Habsburg restoration would be 'neither recognised nor tolerated' by the Allied Great Powers. The ex-Emperor Charles nevertheless returned to Hungary a few weeks later. He was quickly ejected, to Italy's satisfaction. The solution of the Italo-Yugoslav quarrel had removed the basis of the Italo-Hungarian *entente* which Nitti had fostered. Hungarian hopes of Italy as a champion of treaty revision vanished and relations between the two countries worsened.[2]

With Austria, on the other hand, Italy remained on cordial terms. Sforza took the lead at successive conferences in urging international action to save it from bankruptcy. In October the Christian socialists replaced the social democrats as Austria's ruling party, but they maintained the friendly relations with Czechoslovakia that Renner had established. Sforza did not conceal his satisfaction and by conciliatory, constructive diplomacy continued to work for the consolidation of the new Europe.

[1] Tasca, pp. 141–2; Salvatorelli and Mira, p. 103. Christmas 1920 was known in later years to nationalists and fascists as 'il Natale di sangue'.

[2] Between March and September 1920 the Hungarians concentrated their hopes of revising the Treaty of Trianon (signed on 4 June but not ratified by Hungary until 13 November) on France. The French were sympathetic, hoping in return to secure Hungarian support for the Poles against Soviet Russia and a dominant position for France in the Hungarian economy. This Franco-Hungarian *entente* worried Italy and consolidated Italian links with Czechoslovakia. After September a change of personalities at the French Foreign Ministry led to a gradual reversal of French policy. *Papers and Documents relating to the Foreign Relations of Hungary* (Budapest 1939), I, 415, 563, 581, 617; Toscano, *Pagine di storia diplomatica contemporanea*, I, pp. 397–407.

He was less successful in the eastern Mediterranean. In Turkish questions, unlike German, his policy was closer to that of France than to that of Britain. Sforza was convinced that only a peace acceptable to the Turkish nationalists was worth having. This attitude brought him into sharp conflict with Britain. At the Spa Conference in July 1920 the British Foreign Secretary, Curzon, told Sforza that information had reached him from every quarter of 'Italian intrigues with the Turkish nationalists' and 'Italian attempts to make things difficult' for Britain; at Constantinople 'it was a matter of common belief that the Alliance no longer existed'. Sforza admitted serious doubts about the terms of the peace treaty with Turkey, but assured Curzon that he 'accepted the obligations of loyalty' to the common Allied policy.[1] On 10 August delegates of the Sultan's government in Constantinople signed the Treaty of Sèvres. By its terms the Straits were to be internationalised and Turkey was to be subjected to international financial control; Italy would be represented on both the Straits and the financial commissions. The limitations imposed in 1912 by the Treaty of Ouchy on Italian sovereignty in Libya were removed.[2] Turkey ceded the Dodecanese to Italy, and by the separate Bonin–Venizelos Convention[3] Italy reaffirmed the substance of the Tittoni–Venizelos Agreement with regard to the transfer of the islands to Greece.[4] At the same time

[1] Sforza subsequently assured Curzon that he had investigated the reports of Italian disloyalty in the Near and Middle East and that 'so far as he had been able to ascertain they were the result of gossip, such as was always current in the East, and had no foundation in fact'. But Curzon was not convinced and returned to the subject in November. BFP, XIII, 98, 170, 176.

[2] See above, p. 379.

[3] Bonin was Italian ambassador in Paris.

[4] The old dispute between Italy and Greece over the Dodecanese delayed the signature of the Treaty of Sèvres at the last moment. Sforza had just denounced the Tittoni–Venizelos Agreement (see above, p. 556) in order to free his hand in Albania (see above, p. 579); but this left Greece without any assurance regarding the islands. As the British Foreign Secretary, Curzon, forcefully pointed out, the Allies had agreed that Turkey should cede the Dodecanese to Italy only on the understanding that Italy would subsequently hand over the islands to Greece. When the Greeks threatened not to sign the Treaty of Sèvres, Curzon threatened not to sign the tripartite treaty on Asia Minor, and urged Sforza 'to terminate the situation in the only way that is recommended both by expediency and by justice'. Sforza duly did so by the Bonin–Venizelos Agreement. This committed Italy to hand over the Dodecanese with the exception of Rhodes, which would be ceded only if Britain ceded Cyprus and after a plebiscite. Sforza, very conscious of his vulnerability to the nationalist charge of renunciation, vainly tried to extract from Curzon a promise that Britain would not cede Cyprus without previous consultation with Italy. But Curzon set his mind at rest by declaring that 'as regards the likelihood of Cyprus being ceded to Greece, I thought that he [Sforza] need not be under any alarm in the near future'. BFP, XIII, 104–5, 107, 111–12, 115–18.

Britain, France and Italy signed a tripartite treaty confirming their previous agreement on spheres of interest in Asia Minor.[1]

Sforza had no illusions that the treaty was worth more than the paper it was written on. And so it proved. Kemal's nationalist government in Ankara rejected it outright and it was with Kemal, not with the puppet Sultan, that power now lay. Sforza did his best to dissuade Lloyd George and Venizelos from trying to enforce the treaty by Greek arms. In advising the Greeks to limit their ambitions, he claimed to be acting as their only true friend.[2] The Greek army nevertheless advanced during the summer of 1920 and occupied large areas of Thrace and western Anatolia, till halted partly by Allied warnings, partly by Turkish resistance.

In November Venizelos fell and King Constantine returned to Greece. This event destroyed what little sympathy remained in Italy for Greek aspirations. It also convinced even Lloyd George that the Treaty of Sèvres would have to be modified. In February 1921 Kemalist delegates reached Italy in an Italian ship and went on to an Allied conference in London. Sforza took the opportunity, as did the French, to negotiate behind Lloyd George's back with Kemal's Foreign Minister, Bekir Sami. In return for a promise to evacuate Italian troops from Asia Minor and to support Turkey diplomatically against Greece, he secured Turkish consent to the economic concessions in southern Anatolia and the Eregli coalfield. This convention was never ratified by the Ankara parliament, and it brought Italy nothing but accusations of sharp practice from the enraged British.[3] But Sforza persevered. When the Greeks launched a new offensive towards Ankara, he washed his hands of the whole affair. In June 1921 the last Italian troops were withdrawn from Adalia to Constantinople. Only a consular agent, vainly pressing for concessions, and a single warship remained behind to watch over the shattered dreams of Sonnino and the nationalists in Asia Minor.

Sforza's Adriatic and eastern policies were logically coherent. He aimed at friendship with Yugoslavia, to give Italy influence in the Balkans, and friendship with the new Turkey, to give Italy influence in the eastern Mediterranean. The conservatives and nationalists attacked his 'sterile Turcophilia', just as they execrated his renunciation of Dalmatia and his tough treatment of D'Annunzio. Even in its supporters the Treaty of Rapallo inspired relief or resignation rather than enthusiasm. The socialists

---

[1] See above, p. 556.

[2] Sforza, *Contemporary Italy*, p. 226, *Pensiero e azione*, pp. 298–9.

[3] Sforza pleaded in justification that the convention only obtained Turkish consent to what Britain and France had already conceded in August 1920. This was true; but it was also true that Sforza's action was a blow to the Allied unity to which Curzon attached so great importance.

approved but gave the government's foreign policy no positive support. Many Popolari thought and spoke like nationalists on Fiume and Dalmatia.[1] In June 1921 Sforza warned the chamber:

> There is no escape from this alternative. Either Italy, by becoming the friend of the smaller peoples, by making their legitimate interests her own interests and so finding a safe outlet towards the east, will assume the proud task of a Great Power – or she will have only the empty name of Great Power.[2]

Only the handful of democrats was capable of understanding such language.

## The 1921 Election and the Crisis of Fascism

Giolitti, encouraged by the results of the local elections in November 1920 and pleased with his successes at home and abroad, dissolved the chamber and held a general election on 15 May. This decision made many of his friends and colleagues unhappy.[3] It was indeed an abrupt departure from his pre-war practice of dissolving only towards the end of a parliament's term. He justified his action by the 'altered internal and external situation' and by the need to allow the liberated areas of the Trentino and Venezia Giulia to send deputies to Rome for the first time. His real aim was to weaken the socialists, now freed by the schism of their party from the pressure of their extremists, and force them at last into collaboration with himself. To abolish proportional representation was impossible, but he calculated that an election managed by himself would produce a chamber more amenable than that of 1919 and more closely resembling those of pre-war years. For this purpose he relied on a governmental National Bloc, similar to that which had been so successful in the local elections. Into this Bloc he welcomed liberals, democrats, nationalists, Catholics, even fascists, provided they seemed likely to prove useful allies in the new chamber. These tactics were successful with one major exception: in spite of pressure from its clerical-moderate wing, the Popular party stood aside, as in the previous November, and fought the election on its own.

The fascists made surprising electoral allies for Giolitti. But the evolution of Mussolini's views on the Adriatic question had already given a clue to the direction in which fascism was moving. He had been in secret contact with Giolitti since October 1920 through Lusignoli, the prefect of Milan. At the end of that month, while on a visit to Trieste, he received

---

[1] Howard, pp. 189, 208–9, 274–5.  [2] Sforza, *Pensiero e azione*, p. 277.
[3] For instance Sforza, Meda, Frassati and Nitti. *Quarant' anni*, III, 335–6, 360; Frassati, pp. 31–2; De Rosa, *Giolitti e il fascismo*, p. 72. Turati, too, tried in vain to convince Giolitti of the folly of a premature election. Turati–Kuliscioff, V, pp. 458, 460.

I L F—U

one more appeal from D'Annunzio to come to Fiume. Mussolini ignored it and returned instead to Milan for an interview with Sforza. The limits of his commitment to D'Annunzio, which had long been known to a restricted circle,[1] became public in November when, to the general astonishment, he gave a cautious welcome to the Treaty of Rapallo. It was not ideal, he agreed, and the loss of Dalmatia was anguishing: but the frontier on Monte Nevoso had been secured, Zara, 'the pearl of the Adriatic', had been saved and Fiume, thanks to D'Annunzio, was at least independent.[2] Over the next few weeks he comforted his readers with the thought that the new sovereign state of Fiume could not be forced to accept the treaty against its will. This allowed him to continue to profess loyalty to D'Annunzio. On 2 December he told a meeting of the Milan Fascio that if the government tried to coerce Fiume and act as a Yugoslav *gendarme*, he would invite the masses to 'rise as one man'.[3] But ten days earlier he had made it clear to Lusignoli that the fascists would limit their protests to words. At the beginning of December he had a cold, unhappy meeting with De Ambris in Trieste, which destroyed Fiume's last illusions of fascist help. Three weeks later, when Caviglia's troops went into action, Mussolini confined himself to denouncing Giolitti for an anti-national, fratricidal crime, in language much milder than he had used against Nitti a year before.[4]

The truth was, as he convincingly argued, that the only alternatives to submission were revolution or war, and neither was practicable. 'Only a madman or a criminal' could think of starting a new war; and revolutions were not produced out of a hat, but 'are made with the army, not against the army, with arms, not without arms', and required the sympathy of a majority of Italians. At the end of 1920 Mussolini recognised that the army was loyal to Caviglia, Millo had deserted the cause and 99% of the nation was ready to accept the treaty 'with vast sighs of satisfaction'. The Italians of Dalmatia were indeed 'the elect of the Italian people', but they would have to wait. Mussolini made it clear that his acquiescence was merely tactical: the treaty was 'a transitory document', 'a kind of truce'.[5] Even so, his arguments left many fascists frustrated and resentful. Still less did they satisfy D'Annunzio and the Dalmatian irredentists. The legionaries denounced him as a traitor and were ordered by D'Annunzio to quit the fasci and join his own Fiume Legionaries' Federation.[6] Many fascists in their

[1] De Felice, pp. 634–45.
[2] *Il Popolo d'Italia*, 12 November, in Mussolini, XV, pp. 306–8.
[3] De Felice, pp. 650–5; Mussolini, XVI, p. 39.
[4] ibid., pp. 75–85.
[5] *Il Popolo d'Italia*, 13 November, 23 December; speeches to central committee of fasci, 15 November, and at Trieste, 6 February 1921, in Mussolini, XVI, pp. 5–8, 11, 75–6, 155–7.
[6] It was widely believed that Mussolini had accepted a bribe from Giolitti, just

turn deserted D'Annunzio. The breach between the two men was never quite healed in later years.

While D'Annunzio instructed his followers to boycott the election,[1] Mussolini joined the National Bloc of D'Annunzio's arch-enemy, Giolitti. Mussolini had not forgotten the lesson of 1919, when isolation had meant impotence, and was confident that fascism was now strong enough to make tactical compromises without suffering contamination by non-fascist allies. Giolitti on his side was welcoming. As he later wrote in his *Memoirs*, he believed that 'all the forces of the country should be represented in parliament and find their outlet there'.[2] But the spirit in which Mussolini had accepted Giolitti's offer became clear during the electoral campaign. With arrogant exaggeration he declared that fascism was the dominant partner and had given a fascist imprint to the whole National Bloc. He ridiculed Giolitti's delusion that he could use fascism and promised that the youthful energies of the Vittorio Veneto generation would soon wipe out the old Italy and its effete ruling class. Fascists were destroying the bolshevik state within the state 'in preparation for the settling of accounts with the liberal state which survives'. A week before the poll he announced that 'the final goal of our impetuous march is Rome'.[3] Giolitti would have done well to take such pronouncements more seriously.

The electoral campaign was conducted with much pressure and violence. The National Bloc was primarily anti-socialist, but it was also used to root out Nitti's supporters, especially in the south, and to fight the Popolari, in spite of the fact that they had seven representatives in Giolitti's own government. In the south Giolitti used to the full all the old weapons at the government's disposal; in the north the fascists, as members of the Bloc, did his work for him.[4] Mussolini, realising that excessive violence would 'sabotage' the fascist victory, tried to impress upon the *squadre* the need for discipline and restraint; but his warnings were rarely heeded.[5] In many districts socialist and communist sympathisers were terrorised, their meetings broken up and their leaders physically assaulted or banished till the voting was over. On polling day alone, forty deaths and seventy cases of

---

as he was believed to have accepted 'French gold' at the time of his earlier 'betrayal' in 1914. Tasca, p. 191; Salvatorelli and Mira, p. 102; Répaci, I, pp. 119–20. No proof of this allegation has ever been produced and Mussolini's apologists deny it. See Pini and Susmel, II, pp. 87–9, 93–5. But there is conclusive evidence of a tacit political understanding.

[1] D'Annunzio gave his patronage to only one candidate, De Ambris.

[2] Giolitti, *Memorie*, p. 610.

[3] Mussolini, XVI, pp. 242, 272–3, 284–6, 300, 317.

[4] The only part of the south where fascism was active was Apulia, where the agrarian situation resembled that of Emilia.

[5] Mussolini, XVI, pp. 193–5, 271, 276–7, 288, 453.

serious wounding occurred.[1] Giolitti did not positively approve these excesses. In April he telegraphed to a number of prefects, 'Acts of violence during an electoral campaign are a grave crime and a disgrace to the country. A chamber elected by violence will have no moral authority'.[2] But when Sforza expressed disquiet about the electoral methods of his new allies, Giolitti replied: 'These Fascist candidacies are only fireworks; they'll make a great deal of noise, but will quickly burn out'.[3] To a questioning British official he remarked complacently, 'The Fascists are our Black and Tans.'[4] In accepting the fascists as allies, Giolitti committed the greatest blunder of his long career. In 1921 the liberal state still had strength enough to resist. But Giolitti was old and clung to his illusions. It would soon be too late to do anything but submit.

In spite of violence and intimidation the socialists and the Popolari held firm. Proportional representation this time saved the left from annihilation, just as it had saved the right in 1919. The Popolari increased their strength from 100 to 108 seats, thanks to the votes of the traditionally clerical Trentino. The socialists, in spite of their professed contempt for parliament, flocked to the polls and won 123 seats. Together with the communists, who won 15, they held only 18 seats less than the united socialists in 1919. The new chamber was thus little different from the old.[5] The only

---

[1] Salvemini, *Fascist Dictatorship*, p. 108. Salvemini regarded Giolitti's use of the *squadristi* merely as an extension of the southern *malavita* to the north. Official figures for the period of the electoral campaign (from 8 April to the eve of poll, 14 May) were 105 killed (49 'for electoral motives') and 431 wounded. De Rosa, *Giolitti e il fascismo*, p. 78. 71 more deaths (16 fascists, 31 socialists, 4 police and 20 others) occurred in the fortnight immediately following the election. De Rosa, *Storia*, p. 185.

[2] ibid., p. 172; De Felice p. 603.

[3] Sforza, *Contemporary Italy*, p. 235.

[4] C. J. S. Sprigge, *The Development of Modern Italy* (London 1943), pp. 190–1. In May 1921 the Anglo–Irish war was at its height and the Black and Tans were much in the news.

[5] The following comparative table is constructed from the figures in *Compendio*, II, pp. 130–1.

| *1919* | | | *1921* |
|---|---|---|---|
| | National Bloc | | |
| | Fascists | 35 | |
| | Nationalists | 10 | |
| — | Liberals &c. | 60* | 105 |
| — | Dissident Fascists | | 2 |
| 41 | Liberals (right wing) | | 43 |
| | Democratic Groups (left-centre, | | |
| 168* | including Radicals) | | 108* |

\* indicates the nucleus of the Giolittian centre-left majority of 1920–1.

[*continued opposite*]

novelty was the appearance of 35 fascists with Mussolini at their head. *Avanti!* claimed a great victory: 'The Italian proletariat has buried the Fascist reaction under an avalanche of red ballot-papers.'[1] But victories require to be followed up, and this the socialists failed to do. Revolution was impossible; the alternative of collaboration with non-socialists in strengthening democracy would be a betrayal of socialism. 'All that remains for us to do is to wait', declared *Avanti!*.[2] This was abdication. Their unconstructive hostility was a bitter disappointment to Giolitti. Even Turati and the parliamentary reformists, under imminent sentence of expulsion from the party, felt it morally impossible to support a man who had made himself the accomplice of fascist brutality. Weighed against this, his pre-war record, his stand against war in 1915, his programme of fiscal and social reform counted for nothing.

Giolitti's electoral failure was made more serious by the growing estrangement of the Popular party. Its main grievance was that it had loyally supported the government's economic and foreign policies, yet the reforms in which it was most interested remained still on paper. Croce's educational bill had been defeated in committee. It was true that it had reappeared in Giolitti's electoral programme, but this was not enough to remove doubts. The Popular Minister of Agriculture, Giuseppe Micheli, had obtained parliamentary approval of a bill to regulate agricultural rents and give security of tenure to small tenants; but this was only one small item in the party's agrarian programme.[3] Bad feeling had also been caused by the government's failure to treat the Catholic trade unions on an equality with their rivals. The C.I.L. had been left out of the negotiations that followed the factory occupations, and its programme of industrial co-partnership and profit-sharing had never been even discussed. As a result

| | | |
|---|---|---|
| | Republican and Democratic Left (including Republicans, | |
| 43 | Reformists, Combattenti) | 22 |
| 100 | Popolari | 108 |
| 156 | Socialists | 123 |
| — | Communists | 15 |
| — | Slavs, Germans | 9 |
| 508 | | 535 |

The ephemeral nature of many of the liberal and democratic parliamentary groups, and the frequent shifting of deputies from one to another, makes a more detailed analytical comparison impossible.

[1] Tasca, p. 189; Nenni, p. 137.

[2] Nenni, pp. 139–43.

[3] Howard, pp. 278–81, 290–4. Popular bills to break up the Sicilian *latifondi* and to create elected regional chambers of agriculture had been lost when parliament was dissolved.

of these disappointments the Popolari, on whom the government still depended for survival, were in a resentful mood, and Giolitti now paid the penalty for allowing his relations with them to deteriorate.

This was not the only cause of his insecurity. The liberals were divided and disorganised; the partisans of Nitti, Orlando and Salandra were all in varying degrees hostile. The National Bloc had little cohesion. The nationalists hated Giolitti for his foreign policy and his progressive fiscal and social programmes. Not even the fascists, who might have been expected to show gratitude for his invaluable patronage, rallied to his support. On the contrary, within a few days of the opening of the new parliament, Mussolini was making republican declarations and hinting at a fascist-socialist-Popular coalition. He had no intention of remaining just Giolitti's protégé.

Undeterred, Giolitti presented a revised edition of his 1920 programme in his old familiar style. But as soon as the new chamber met, it was clear that, as in 1904, 1909 and 1913, the election had weakened his grip. The crisis came within a fortnight during a debate on foreign affairs. Soon after Italy's ratification of the Treaty of Rapallo, the terms of Sforza's secret commitment on Port Baroš leaked out.[1] This 'mutilation' of Fiume gave the nationalists a pretext for renewing their onslaught on the government's policy of renunciation.[2] Salandra led the attack:[3] 'You have lowered our flag at Valona as at Adalia, at Castua[4] and Sebenico. The country cries "Enough". It wants peace, but not the peace of the vanquished.' Sforza retorted that the true renouncer was Salandra, who had renounced Fiume to Croatia in 1915. Tempers flared and the nationalists, fascists and a large section of the right joined Nitti's democrats, the socialists and communists in opposition. Giolitti's majority fell to 34 in a vote of 434. The Popolari too were restive and expected to abandon the government very

[1] See above, p. 581. Sforza publicly admitted his commitment for the first time during the June debate.

[2] Another point in the nationalist indictment of Sforza was his 'assassination' of Montenegro. Nitti and Giolitti had insisted at successive international conferences in 1919–20 on keeping the Montenegrin question open, mainly as a bargaining weapon, but also because of pro-Montenegrin sentiment in Italy and the King's personal concern with the deposed Montenegrin royal family. BFP, VII, pp. 172–6, 227–9, 234–7; Alatri, *Nitti*, pp. 149n., 414–15n., 419, 468. In November 1920 elections were held for a Yugoslav constituent assembly. Britain and France accepted the result of the voting in Montenegro as a free expression of the desire for incorporation in Yugoslavia. Sforza tacitly conformed and the Montenegrin question lost all international significance. After Sforza's resignation even Mussolini and the nationalists dropped the matter.

[3] Sforza, *Pensiero e azione*, p. 279.

[4] Castua was a small village between Fiume and Monte Nevoso which had been ceded to Yugoslavia after the Italian general staff had declared it of no military value.

shortly. Giolitti decided the time had come to retire and on 27 June he resigned. Thus ended a year of office in which he had displayed much of his old ability and many of his old weaknesses, but had failed to restore normalcy. This time there was to be no return to power.

The new Prime Minister was Ivanoe Bonomi, who had been Giolitti's Minister for War. The composition of his government differed little from that of its predecessor. Its weight lay slightly further to the left and the Popolari, who contributed three ministers, gave it less grudging support. On the other hand, several of Giolitti's more radical measures were dropped from its programme.[1] The main change was that Bonomi lacked Giolitti's skill and prestige. The government won a large initial vote of confidence, the socialists, communists and fascists forming the opposition. Bonomi's main aim was to reconcile fascism and socialism and end the state of incipient civil war. Though he owed his re-election at Cremona in May in part to fascist votes and had praised fascism as a new democratic force of the left,[2] he seemed ready to enforce the law more strictly than Giolitti. A striking example of the ease with which fascist lawlessness could be suppressed, given the will, occurred on 21 July at Sarzana near La Spezia. Twelve *carabinieri* opened fire on a column of 500 Tuscan *squadristi* and routed it. The enraged population, which contained a strong communist element, then joined in and hunted the demoralised *squadristi* through the countryside. Eighteen were killed. In the words of the fascist 'chief of staff' of the expedition, 'The *squadre*, so long accustomed to defeating an enemy who nearly always ran away or offered feeble resistance, could not, and did not know how to, defend themselves.'[3] The Sarzana incident was widely interpreted as a first sign that the new government intended to enforce law and order.

The incident impressed Mussolini too, and confirmed his decision to change fascist tactics. Membership of the National Bloc had made fascism respectable and election to parliament had introduced Mussolini to a fascinating new world. *Il Popolo d'Italia* began to print detailed reports of the parliamentary and party manœuvres which it had hitherto contemptuously ignored. On 1 July, during the negotiations for a new government, the King invited Mussolini to the palace for consultation. For the first time a bid for power by legal means seemed practicable. Fascism, he decided, must pass from the offensive to the constructive stage, and its

---

[1] Bonomi announced his intention of amending or suspending Giolitti's measures on war profits and the registration of bearer shares; he also dropped Giolitti's proposals with regard to *controllo operaio* in industry.

[2] Nenni, pp. 147–9; Salvemini, *Fascist Dictatorship*, p. 80.

[3] Tasca, pp. 227–8. Seven fascists were killed in a similar incident at Modena two months later.

military element give way to the political. His maiden speech in parliament on 21 June showed the direction of his thought. Its tone was fiercely anti-democratic and anti-socialist. 'The true history of capitalism is only just beginning', he declared: 'If you want to save the state, you must abolish the collectivist state that the war forced on us and return to the Manchesterian state.' It was, as Pantaleoni delightedly commented, 'the most Manchesterian speech the chamber has ever heard'. The right was gratified by his attack on Sforza's foreign policy and his arrogant references to the Germans of south Tirol. For the benefit of the Popolari (and to the disgust of his old comrade Marinetti) he spoke in favour of freedom of education and land reform, denied that fascism was anti-clerical and praised Catholicism which 'represents today Rome's Latin and imperial tradition'. Nor was the working-class forgotten. He promised to support every proposal for social legislation and declared, 'Our attitude towards the C.G.L. could change if the C.G.L. severed its links with the Socialist party.'[1]

The speech showed that Mussolini was carefully feeling his way and wanted to keep every door open. His prospects could be ruined if the *squadristi* alienated middle-class opinion and provoked organised resistance. The Sarzana incident brought home this danger. The C.G.L. and ex-service organisations were calling for an end to violence. In Rome a new organisation of *arditi del popolo*, the nucleus of anti-fascist *squadre*, had appeared. Mussolini was therefore in a mood to respond to appeals for moderation. In *Il Popolo d'Italia* he deplored the indiscipline of the *squadre*:

> In these columns it has been many times stated that our violence had to be chivalrous, aristocratic, surgical, and therefore in a certain sense humane. But it has been said in vain.
> The nation came to us when our movement meant the end of a tyranny; the nation would repudiate us if our movement were to assume the character of a new tyranny.

As Mussolini himself admitted, the fascist star had recently 'paled a little'. 'A ring of hatred' was forming round the movement and it was time to return to the original principles of Milanese fascism, which had never indulged in violence for the sake of violence.[2]

During July unofficial truce negotiations[3] between two fascist and two socialist deputies made rapid progress, with the support of Bonomi and the President of the chamber, Enrico De Nicola. On 2 August a pact of pacification was signed. Both sides undertook to end violence immediately,

---

[1] Mussolini, XVI, pp. 441–5.
[2] *Il Popolo d'Italia*, 24, 27 July, 7 August, in Mussolini, XVII, pp. 67, 74–5, 90.
[3] There had been appeals for a truce from the socialist side ever since March. Mussolini began to take the idea seriously at the end of June.

to respect each other's economic organisations and to submit violations of the pact to arbitration by special tribunals. In pursuance of this undertaking the Socialist party and C.G.L. disowned the *arditi del popolo*. For a time socialists were able to resume a normal life. They could have turned the pact into a decisive victory for themselves had they been prepared to back the government in enforcing it. But two days after approving it, the party executive again condemned collaboration with non-socialists, even against fascism. *Avanti!* declared that there had been no change in programme, but merely a 'pause' in the march towards revolution. Having sworn to destroy the bourgeois state, the party could not ask protection from it. The pact was meanwhile rejected by both anarchists and communists. The latter, too, disowned the *arditi del popolo*, on the grounds that they were 'a bourgeois manœuvre', and ordered their members to form uncontaminated *squadre comuniste*.[1] Thus working-class disunity continued while the fascist *squadristi* remained in the field and the state authorities looked on.

The pact threw the fascists into turmoil. Mussolini might think of turning his deputies into a constitutional opposition, drop hints of a coalition with the socialists and Popolari, or talk of a fascist–C.G.L. alliance independent of the socialist party. But in the north there was a storm of protest. The syndicalists and *squadristi* regarded his new respectability as a betrayal of the fascist revolutionary ideal. The agrarian reactionaries who financed the *squadristi*, though caring nothing for revolutionary ideals, were equally shocked by Mussolini's backsliding. Mussolini in fact loved parliament no better than they and his moderation was purely tactical; but it was too much for the men of action. In Emilia, Tuscany, Venetia and Umbria protest meetings condemned Mussolini and his pact. At Bologna posters appeared with the slogan 'Once a traitor, always a traitor'.[2] The fasci of Florence, Venice and other important towns dissolved their organisations in disgust and retired from the fray. 'Legality is killing us', the *squadristi* protested. 'We have come to the turning point of fascism', declared Piero Marsich, an ex-syndicalist, fascist deputy and admirer of D'Annunzio: 'Mussolini realises it, but he gives me the impression that he has lost his way. In effect there are two solutions, one parliamentary, the other national. We are for the national one, he at the moment is for the parliamentary.'[3] Faced with open rebellion in his own movement, Mussolini

[1] Tasca, p. 241; Sforza, *Contemporary Italy*, pp. 252–3.

[2] The reference was to Mussolini's 'treachery' of 1914.

[3] Tasca, p. 234. Grandi was in sympathy with Marsich at this time. Both had resented the use of the *squadre* during the electoral campaign as 'bodyguards' for the old liberals. They were tempted to regard D'Annunzio as a better leader for the 'national revolution' than Mussolini, and his Charter of the Carnero as the political model which fascism should adopt. Tamaro, I, p. 163.

hit back in *Il Popolo d'Italia*, condemning the parochialism of the *ras*[1] and the degeneration of Emilian fascism into the defence of sordid private interests. The pact was 'a historic event' and a noble service to the causes of humanity, the nation and fascism; it had shattered the united anti-fascist front, and he would therefore 'defend it with all my strength'. 'Fascism can do without me? Doubtless', he wrote on 7 August; 'but I too can do very well without fascism.' Ten days later he resigned from the national executive of the movement and seemed about to abandon fascism as he had abandoned socialism in 1914.[2]

The *ras* ignored his threats. On 10 September Balbo and Grandi organised a march by 3,000 *squadristi* on Ravenna, to show the strength of the dissidents. Mussolini was forced to recognise that they were too powerful for him and decided to compromise. His solution was to turn the movement into a party, a course that he had ridiculed as recently as July but which he now justified by arguing that fascism had already become a party in all but name. At first he intended to call it the 'Fascist Labour Party', but the final choice was 'National Fascist Party', a title that implied renunciation of any alliance with the C.G.L. By creating a party, he hoped to regain control over the movement and prepare it for the political task of governing the nation.[3] For a while he continued to talk of retiring from the leadership, but from the first it was clear that there could be no leader but himself.

The crisis was resolved at the fascist congress which assembled in Rome on 7 November. Rome was still almost untouched by fascism and its inhabitants greeted the influx of blackshirted *squadristi* with amused, sceptical surprise. This turned to disgust when brawls between delegates and workers from the Trastevere district ended in violence, loss of life and a general strike. The frigid welcome destroyed many illusions among the provincial *ras*. Both factions realised that they needed each other. Mussolini and his thirty-five deputies would count for little without the organised force of the *squadre* behind them, and the *squadre* would be insecure without a foothold inside parliament and 'legal Italy'. The congress duly decided to turn the movement into a party, and Mussolini and Grandi shelved their differences in a 'fraternal embrace'. Mussolini delivered a cautious, conservative speech in which he watered down his republicanism and declared himself a 'liberal' in economic questions. The new party's programme, published at the end of December, confirmed fascism's decisive swing to the right. All that remained of the radicalism of 1919 was a modest list of social reforms. As a political programme it was not impressive. Fascism was still without a philosophy or theory and, as far as the

---

[1] The local fascist bosses were commonly known as *ras*, a title borrowed from the feudal nobility of Ethiopia.

[2] Mussolini, XVII, pp. 80-1, 90-1, 104-5.                    [3] ibid., pp. 180-2.

rank and file was concerned, was content to remain so. Its essence was contained in two sentences of the programme: Fascism 'aspires to the supreme honour of governing the country'; and 'The *Squadre* form an integral whole with the Fasci.'[1] In Mussolini's words, the Fascist party was 'a party which very probably will resemble no other existing party: a party which is also a militia, in the most literal sense of the word'.[2] The terms of the compromise between the rival factions thus became clear. Grandi accepted the conservative political programme; Mussolini denounced the pact of pacification within a week of the Rome congress and preserved the military power of the *squadre* intact.

On the question of syndicalism, too, a compromise was reached. At the Rome congress Grandi had defined fascism as a movement of 'national democracy', based on the syndicate and the citizen-producer; its true principles were to be found in the Fiume tradition and the Charter of the Carnero, in the motto 'liberty, nation, syndicalism'.[3] Such language was not to Mussolini's taste. He did not try to stop the congress from sending a telegram of greetings to D'Annunzio. But in his opinion D'Annunzio, though 'a man of genius', was 'the man for times of emergency, not for practical, day-to-day affairs'; fascists should look to the Charter of the Carnero only as to a distant star.[4] A similar divergence of view arose over the nature of the General Confederation of Syndical Corporations, which was founded by Rossoni at Bologna in January 1922. There were many echos of the Charter of the Carnero in its programme, and some of its leading spirits wished its corporations to remain non-political and become the basic institutions of 'national democracy'.[5] Mussolini approved of the concept of 'national syndicalism', which he had preached since 1919. In his view the aim of the syndicate must be to reconcile the interests of the workers with the nation's need of higher production. They might on occasion have to employ socialist methods, but the class struggle must be the exception, class collaboration the rule.[6] Mussolini, however, regarded

---

[1] Among the main themes of the programme were glorification of the nation, a nationalist foreign policy, distrust of the League of Nations, freedom for the church within the sovereign state, reduction of the functions of the state, a balanced budget, a ban on strikes in the public services, disciplining of labour disputes and stimulation of the productive energies of the nation. For full text of the programme and statutes, see Mussolini, XVII, pp. 334–50.

[2] *Il Popolo d'Italia*, 12 November 1921, in Mussolini, XVII, p. 230. He returned to this theme repeatedly during November.

[3] Tasca, p. 249; Pini and Susmel, II, p. 150.

[4] Mussolini, XVII, pp. 220–1.

[5] The Confederation consisted of five corporations: industrial labour, agricultural labour, commerce, middle class and intellectuals, and seamen. Salvatorelli and Mira, p. 131.

[6] Mussolini, XVIII, pp. 225–9, 375–6, 385–6, 414–15.

the syndicates as only one of several instruments for the winning of political power. He was determined to keep them tightly under the control of the party and he got his way. Grandi and Rossoni submitted. The syndicates were to be fascist, not non-political; their leaders were chosen by the party, and a fascist monopoly of organised labour was accepted as the ultimate aim. This meant that when fascism attained power, the state would have absolute control of the working-class movement.[1]

The decisions of the Rome congress were a compromise between the conservative and revolutionary elements in fascism: an uneasy, ambiguous compromise which lasted for twenty years. From the first Mussolini dominated the party and only he could hold it together. Its basis was the *squadre*, which were now reorganised into a nation-wide militia under a central command. Excessive violence and local feats of prowess were henceforth discouraged, though never quite eliminated; violence was to be directed, systematically and economically, towards the conquest of the state.

An important consequence of the solution of fascism's internal crisis was the eclipse of D'Annunzio. Many legionaries now joined the fascist militia, which provided the best prospects of 'action', and accepted Mussolini's leadership. But though the Fascist party broke with D'Annunzio and Fiume radicalism, it showed that it had learnt much from the Fiume adventure. The uniforms and the black shirts, the 'Roman salute', the 'oceanic' rallies, the party hymn, *Giovinezza*; the organisation of the militia into cohorts and legions, commanded by consuls; the weird cries of *Eia Eia Alalà!*, the demagogic technique of 'dialogue' between orators and massed audiences; all the symbolism, mystique and 'style' with which the world was later to grow so familiar, were plagiarised from D'Annunzio, who in this sense too could justly claim to be one of the spiritual fathers of fascism.[2]

## The Impotence of the Liberal State

By the end of 1921 fascism, with its internal crisis resolved, had become a menace not only to the authority of the liberal state but to its very existence. From time to time Bonomi's government made attempts to assert itself. But its orders were rarely carried out. When arrests and searches for arms did take place, they were more often directed against communists or *arditi*

[1] As Salvatorelli and Mira, p. 123, point out, whereas the aim of the genuine syndicalists was *sindacalizzazione dello stato*, that of Mussolini was *statizzazione dei sindacati*.

[2] The *Giovinezza* (Youth) hymn had originally been the song of the *arditi* in the war; *Eia Eia Alalà!* had been the war-cry of D'Annunzio's air squadron.

*del popolo* than against fascists. A government circular of December 1921 ordered prefects to suppress all unofficial armed organisations, but it was a dead letter from the moment of its dispatch. A circular from the secretary of the Fascist party, Michele Bianchi, had forestalled such a step by declaring that every party member was also a member of the *squadre*. He rightly calculated that Bonomi would not dare to dissolve a party.[1] 'They can do nothing against us', boasted Mussolini in January 1922.[2]

No government, however well intentioned, could stand up to the fascist challenge unless it was solidly backed in parliament. The vital problem therefore was whether an anti-fascist coalition could be constructed from the liberal-democratic left and centre and the Popolari, with at least the benevolent support of the socialist right wing. But all attempts were frustrated by liberal dissensions, mutual suspicion between liberals, socialists and Popolari, and the inability of the right-wing socialists to break the maximalist grip over their party.

The liberals remained profoundly disunited. In November 1921 two groups of democratic deputies, Democrazia Liberale and Democrazia Sociale, with a combined membership of 150, fused in a single parliamentary organisation, the Democratic Group.[3] But their motives were mainly anti-clerical and their immediate aim was to substitute Giolitti for Bonomi, whom they regarded as too conciliatory to the Popolari. A handful of liberals, which included Alfredo Frassati,[4] Francesco Coccu-Ortu[5] and

---

[1] Salvatorelli and Mira, pp. 123–4; Tasca, pp. 253–5; Mussolini, XVII, p. 438. 'Bonomi is weak', Turati recorded after meetings with him in September and October: 'he is a man who never says no, and yields to each pressure received'. But Turati recognised his 'infinite difficulties'; pro-fascist civil servants, police and magistrates ignored the government's instructions. Turati–Kuliscioff, V, pp. 473, 477, 484, 513–14.

[2] Mussolini, XVIII, p. 8.

[3] The eclipse of the old Radical party in the 1921 election had left six liberal–democratic groupings in parliament: Liberale Democratico (Salandra); Democrazia (Giolitti, Orlando); Democrazia Liberale; Democrazia Sociale; Democrazia Italiana (Nitti); and the Riformisti, the remnants of Bissolati's old party, led since the latter's death by Bonomi. Salandra's group was the most conservative, Nitti's and Bonomi's were the most radical. The demoliberali were a conservative group led by the ex-Sonninian Giuseppe De Nava, Minister of the Treasury in Bonomi's government since July 1921. The demo-sociali were a mainly southern group, with a high proportion of Sicilians. Their leaders were Luigi Fera (Giolitti's Minister of Justice in 1920–1), Luigi Gasparotto (Bonomi's Minister for War in 1921–2) and Giovanni Colonna Di Cesarò.

[4] Frassati was a lifelong admirer of Giolitti who had been saddened by Giolitti's complacence towards fascism (*Quarant' anni*, III, 360). After December 1920, when he accepted the post of ambassador in Berlin, his personal influence on domestic politics was small; but his views found expression in his *Stampa*, the only major liberal newspaper to take a consistently critical view of fascism.

[5] Cocco-Ortu, an elder statesman from Sardinia, had started his political career

Giovanni Amendola,[1] understood the nature of fascism and the need to unite against it. But the majority of deputies shared the complacency of the elder statesmen, Salandra, Giolitti, Orlando and Nitti who, rather than combine against fascism, were more tempted, at least in private, to compete against each other for fascist support.

Further to the right, on the nationalist fringe, there were representatives of the propertied, business and professional classes whose fascist sympathies were overt and unreserved. The industrialists, unlike the landowners of the Po valley, gave few men to the fascist movement and were slow to commit themselves.[2] But by the end of 1921 Mussolini's evolution from left to right had resolved their doubts. 'The world is moving right', he declared in February 1922, and Italy must do the same; a reversion to the radicalism of 1919 would be absurd.[3] His talk of strong government and discipline, his championship of financial orthodoxy and his condemnation of 'the monopolistic, paternalist, bureaucratic state' sounded sweet to the leaders of Confindustria, embittered by the appeasement of the workers by successive liberal governments and yearning for 'new men and new methods'. Mussolini's praise of capitalism raised their hopes that he would be more sympathetic than Giolitti or Bonomi to their pleas for tax relief and subsidies from public funds. By 1922 contributions from banks and industrial firms, particularly those of Milan, were flowing into the treasury of the Fascist party and their representatives in parliament were using all their influence to block an anti-fascist coalition.[4]

---

under Cairoli and Zanardelli and held office with distinction under Giolitti in 1906-9. Now *doyen* of the chamber, he retained undimmed his Zanardellian faith in the liberal state and democratic institutions.

[1] Amendola belonged to a younger generation. A philosopher by training and inclination, he had learnt the trade of politics as Rome correspondent of the *Corriere della Sera* and became Albertini's most trusted collaborator in the battle over war aims. After the war, unlike Albertini, he moved leftwards in politics, accepted an under-secretaryship in Nitti's last government and became a leader of the Democrazia Italiana group. At first he felt sympathy for fascism which had 'spared Italy the mortal experience of Leninism' (Amendola, *La nuova democrazia*, p. 142); but by the end of 1921 he was working for a democratic-Popular-right-wing socialist coalition to restore legality and build a 'new democracy'.

[2] Guarneri, I, p. 54. A notable exception was the banker Giuseppe Volpi, governor of Tripolitania since July 1921, who joined the Fascist party in January 1922.

[3] Mussolini, XVIII, pp. 66-72; also pp. 276-8, a return to the theme in July.

[4] Rossi, *I padroni del vapore*, pp. 35-7; also Guarneri, I, p. 54. Our knowledge of fascist finances is still scanty. The most informative study is R. De Felice, 'Primi elementi sul finanziamento del fascismo dalle origini al 1924', in *Rivista storica del socialismo*, vol. 7 (1964), pp. 223-51. In its first eighteen months of existence the fascist movement had been precariously dependent upon its own members and on irregular contributions from sympathetic business men, mainly in Milan, Genoa and Turin. Many fascists 'of the first hour' found it repugnant to beg for cash from

The Popolari were by the spring of 1922 in decline: no longer the main bulwark against revolution as in 1919, but caught between socialism and fascism and showing signs of disintegration under the strain. Many of the rank and file, having experienced fascism at first hand, and some of the leaders wanted a Popular–Socialist agreement. Sturzo opposed this and carried the majority with him. In March 1922 Miglioli, the leader of the Popular extreme left, made an alliance with the socialists in his own province of Cremona, but the socialist leaders disowned it, and the Popular leaders approved only on condition that it remained strictly local. Collaboration was further hindered by the insistence of the Popolari on their schemes of educational and agrarian reform, which even moderate socialists like Turati found difficult to swallow.[1]

Relations between the Popolari and the liberals were not much more satisfactory. The main reason was liberal resentment at Popular influence inside the government. The Popolari were content with Bonomi and loyally supported him. His legislative programme was mainly inspired by them.[2] Moreover in the matter of church–state relations, his government was the most conciliatory Italy had yet known. When Benedict XV died on 22 January 1922, the Popular Minister of Justice[3] paid an official call of condolence at the Vatican, the government was represented at the funeral and flags flew at half-mast on official buildings. All this shocked liberals

---

capitalists. The sudden flowering of agrarian fascism in 1920 transformed the situation. By 1921 in large parts of rural Lombardy and Emilia a system of quasi-voluntary 'taxation' had been established, whereby the farmers' and landowners' organisations collected from their members regular contributions, assessed according to income and size of property, on behalf of the fascist movement. In some cases these funds were retained locally instead of being transmitted to Milan. Financial independence was one of the factors that allowed certain *ras* to stand up to Mussolini during the internal crisis of fascism in 1921. In the summer of 1921, however, the movement's central fund-raising machinery was overhauled and the range of its operations greatly extended, particularly towards industry. In the first six months of 1922 the number of provinces contributing regularly rose from 5 to 18 (all, with the exception of Rome, in the north). Total contributions to central funds averaged 208,000 lire per month in October–December 1921, 193,000 in January–June 1922. Bankers and industrialists, more cautious than their rural counterparts, contributed individually, not collectively; Confindustria, unlike the landowners' associations of the Po valley, avoided direct involvement.

[1] Jacini, *Storia*, pp. 130–1; Howard, pp. 348–50.

[2] Notably as regards land reform and education. In November 1921 an education bill was presented to parliament which, though it differed greatly from the abortive Croce bill, would have been of great benefit to private schools. Bonomi also pleased the Popolari (and the Vatican) by watering down Giolitti's regulations for compulsory share registration.

[3] The Ministries of Justice and Education had always been strongholds of traditional liberalism. Now, for the first time since unification, there was a Catholic in charge of the first and a Catholic under-secretary in the second.

who remained faithful to the secular tradition of the Risorgimento and led to a revival of anti-clericalism.

In its attitude to fascism, the Popular party was as divided as the liberals. Many Popolari, like many liberals, preferred to collaborate rather than resist, sometimes from hostility to socialism, sometimes from motives of self-defence in the hope of averting the assaults of the *squadristi*. The influence of the new Pope, Pius XI, was thrown behind the right wing of the party. His political conservatism, which was the product of his Lombard family background, had been strengthened by his experience in 1919–20 as nunzio in Poland, which had given him an almost physical horror of bolshevism.[1] He subsequently won Mussolini's gratitude as Archbishop of Milan by allowing fascist banners to be brought into his cathedral to be blessed. Pius XI hoped to negotiate a permanent settlement of the Roman question. He had shown his goodwill after his election by pronouncing the pontifical blessing *urbi et orbi* from the external loggia of St Peter's, for the first time since 1870. In his view a settlement might be easier to reach with a conservative, even authoritarian, government than with democrats or liberals subservient to the dogma of the secular state. There might be misgivings in the Vatican about certain aspects of fascism; but Mussolini's language had changed in recent months and some of his leading lieutenants, notably Cesare Maria De Vecchi and Dino Grandi, were known to be sympathetic to the church. Pius XI was a clerical-moderate in his politics.[2] He preferred to appease rather than antagonise. The idea of an anti-fascist coalition therefore met decisive opposition in the Vatican.

The extreme left continued to be paralysed by dissension. In March 1922 the Communist party held its second congress in Rome. The Comintern's demand for a united front with the Socialist party was rejected and the 'Rome Theses', advocating non-cooperation, were carried by a large majority. The party's slogan was to be the uncompromising 'Fascism or Communism'. The Socialist party, split into three factions, grew steadily weaker. On the left the 'Third Internationalists' pressed for full acceptance of Lenin's Twenty-One Conditions. On the right Turati and the reformists, backed by the leaders of the C.G.L., were slowly moving towards support for a coalition of 'democratic defence', though even they could still not contemplate membership of a bourgeois government. In the centre the maximalists, led by Serrati, offered their old combination of revolutionary talk and practical inaction. In October 1921 the party once again

---

[1] Jacini, *Storia*, p. 116.
[2] Even while Benedict XV was still alive, there had been indications of growing doubt in the Vatican about the 'liberalism' and non-confessionalism of the Popolari. *Quarant' anni*, III, 332; Valeri, *Da Giolitti a Mussolini*, pp. 116–19; Howard, pp. 337–8.

rejected collaboration with non-socialists at its eighteenth congress in Milan. Next month it was expelled from the Comintern for ignoring the Twenty-One Conditions and failing to purge itself. The majority of its members remained loyal to Serrati, seeing in maximalism the only formula that could avert schism. The reformists stayed in the party, still hoping that in time the maximalists would see reason. Passive resistance remained the official policy. Socialists were to wait for the fascist storm to pass over, just as they had waited for the end of the World War.[1]

But revolutionary oratory was poor comfort for trade unionists when fascist bludgeons got to work. Disgusted by the politicians, they decided to look after themselves. In February 1922 a Labour Alliance was formed by the C.G.L., U.S.I., U.I.L., and the independent railwaymen's and dockers' unions. The Socialist and Republican parties and the Anarchist Union gave their blessing; the communists, Popolari and D'Annunzian syndicalists stayed out.[2] The proclaimed object of the Alliance was to restore freedom and preserve the post-war conquests of the working-class, such as the eight-hour day. Its weapon was to be the general strike. Its very creation was a mark of despair, for to substitute direct action for political methods was no solution to the problem of fascism. This became tragically clear five months later when the strike weapon was tried and found wanting.

Bonomi's government lost ground steadily through the autumn of 1921. It was further shaken at the end of the year by a banking catastrophe. This was the culmination of the prolonged crisis of heavy industry. In May the Ilva steel and engineering cartel had been forced into liquidation.[3] Next month the situation of Ansaldo grew critical. Already in March 1920 the resources of its associate, the Banca Italiana di Sconto, had proved insufficient. In that month the Perrone brothers made a second desperate take-over bid for the assets of the Banca Commerciale Italiana, but with no more success than in 1917–18.[4] By the summer of 1921 the position

[1] Nenni, pp. 168–9. Anna Kuliscioff argued that the party unity to which Turati attached so much importance was fictitious, and urged him and his friends to 'save their souls' by asserting their independence; but she failed to convince him. Turati–Kuliscioff, V, p. 494.

[2] After losing most of its original leaders to the fascist labour movement, the U.I.L. fell under the control of its extremist republican elements which had a following especially in Rome. The railwaymen's union was led by anarcho-syndicalists. Borghi, pp. 278–9.

[3] It became the property of its chief creditors, the Banca Commerciale Italiana and the Credito Italiano, which reduced its capital from 300 million to 15 million lire and 'restored it to its strictly industrial functions'. Quarant' anni, III, 337; Einaudi, pp. 270–1.

[4] See above, p. 490.

was hopeless. Large funds were advanced by the Banca d'Italia and a consortium of the four major banks. But there was a limit to the support that Bonomi was prepared to give from public funds. On 28 December the Banca Italiana di Sconto closed its doors.[1] For several weeks there was an atmosphere of crisis and panic. Growing unemployment, aggravated by the progressive restriction of emigration to America,[2] forced Bonomi, in spite of his desire to reduce public expenditure, to launch a big programme of public works. In the spring of 1922 the economy revived. But the bank crisis had lasting political consequences. Bonomi's firmness earned him many enemies and further disillusioned big business with the liberal state.

The government's foreign policy also caused dissatisfaction. Bonomi's Foreign Minister was Pietro Della Torretta, a senior professional diplomat. Sforza had recommended him in the belief that he would ensure continuity in policy. But in office he proved unexpectedly amenable to nationalist pressure, particularly in his handling of the problems arising out of the Treaty of Rapallo.[3] In April 1921 elections in Fiume had given Zanella's autonomist party a majority, but fascists and legionaries burnt the ballot boxes and prevented the formation of a government. They also seized the disputed Port Baroš and held it for three months, only consenting to hand it over to the Yugoslavs after a personal appeal from D'Annunzio. In October the Italian government's high commissioner at last convened the constituent assembly which had been elected in April and a government was formed under Zanella. But its authority was precarious and violence increased within the Free State. Meanwhile Italian troops

[1] Einaudi, pp. 271–7; Romeo, pp. 94–6.

[2] *Sommario*, p. 65 and Neufeld, p. 521 give the following figures (in thousands) for emigrants before and after the war:

|  | Total | To countries other than European and Mediterranean |
|---|---|---|
| 1908–12 (av.) | 602 | 341 |
| 1913 | 873 | 560 |
| 1919 | 253 | 106 |
| 1920 | 615 | 409 |
| 1921 | 201 | 117 |
| 1922 | 281 | 126 |
| 1923 | 390 | 185 |
| 1924 | 365 | 125 |
| 1925 | 280 | 102 |

The U.S. Immigration Acts of 1921 and 1924 imposed an annual quota for Italians of 40,000 and 4,000 respectively. As a consequence the number of Italian emigrants to the U.S.A. fell from 377,000 in 1913 and 349,000 in 1920 to an average of 43,000 in 1921–7.

[3] *Quarant' anni*, III, 353.

evacuated two of the three zones of occupation into which Dalmatia had been divided, but remained in the third in the hinterland of Zara. This lack of resolution in pursuing Sforza's policy of friendship with Yugoslavia caused mounting irritation in Belgrade, while doing nothing to silence nationalist accusations of renunciation. As regards Turkey, Bonomi and Della Torretta continued their predecessors' efforts to reach a settlement in Asia Minor with Kemal, but with no success. In wider European matters they supported Lloyd George's efforts for reconstruction and for more normal relations with Germany and Soviet Russia.[1] This caused relations with France, which Sforza had restored to cordiality, to deteriorate almost as far as in Nitti's day. When a distinguished French military delegation visited the Italian battlefields in September 1921 at the invitation of the Minister for War, it was greeted in Venice by a hostile fascist demonstration which not even a harangue by Diaz in person was able to quell.[2] Further bad feeling arose in November from the Washington Conference, where France opposed Italy's claim to naval parity. In January 1922 a ministerial crisis in France brought Poincaré back to power in place of the moderate Briand. French policy towards Germany hardened and Bonomi became a major target of French displeasure.[3] Italian nationalists now added to their indictment of the government the accusation of subservience to Britain.

By February 1922 both right and left were ready for a change. On the 1st, on the eve of parliament's reassembly, the newly formed Democratic Group called on its friends inside the cabinet to withdraw. This irresponsible act, inspired by dislike of the Popolari, induced the government to resign without meeting the chamber, and precipitated the longest ministerial crisis that Italy had yet known. Giolitti, De Nicola and Orlando all failed to form a government. In an attempt to clarify the situation, the chamber debated and passed a democratic motion calling for the restoration of civil liberty and the rule of law. It was intended to hasten the formation of an anti-fascist coalition, preferably under Giolitti, but Mussolini brilliantly confused the issue by ordering his thirty-five followers to vote for it. The Popolari, thanks to socialist abstention, now held the key to the situation. At first they demanded a rigid coalition, with a

[1] An Italo–Russian commercial treaty was at last signed in December 1921 after nine months of negotiations.

[2] To the disgust of Barrère, who had accompanied the delegation, Della Torretta confined his apologies to a private interview, pleading that the state of public opinion made an official and public call at the French Embassy impolitic. Charles-Roux, *Une grande ambassade*, pp. 148–55.

[3] Barrère was suspected of working for the downfall of Bonomi, just as he was supposed to have had a hand in the downfall of Nitti in June 1920.

fixed proportion of portfolios for each partner, and a detailed legislative programme incorporating their own proposals for educational reform. This type of bargaining exasperated the liberals. In addition Sturzo, with the full backing of his party, exerted all his influence against Giolitti, believing that his return to power would strengthen fascism and represent the triumph of the forces which had dominated Italy before 1914. Sturzo's 'veto' proved decisive.[1] At last on 25 February a government was most reluctantly formed by Giolitti's lieutenant, Luigi Facta. Sturzo opposed even Facta but his party, largely out of weariness, overruled him. The Popolari obtained as many portfolios as in the preceding government; but with the inclusion of Salandra's lieutenant, Riccio, the new team showed a clear shift to the right. Once again the attempt to form a democratic front had proved abortive.

This crisis further undermined parliament's dwindling prestige. The country was full of rumours of military *coups*. Fascists and nationalists shouted 'We want dictatorship' outside army headquarters in the large cities. Mussolini's ideas were less crude. Though he too discussed the virtues of dictatorship in *Il Popolo d'Italia*, his plans were flexible and he was still playing for time. The very vagueness of his programme was an asset. Threats of revolutionary action, designed to keep his *squadristi* happy, were followed by statements of studied moderation, aimed at his admirers among the bankers and industrialists. He was now a parliamentary figure in his own right and had twice been consulted by the King in February. His one fear was that his opponents might unite in a coalition under Nitti or Giolitti and leave him isolated. He therefore kept in touch with the liberal leaders, rebuffing no overtures but never committing himself, flattering them and feeding their hopes that he would yet make an acceptable parliamentary ally or cabinet colleague. These tortuous manœuvres were not to the liking of the critics in his own party, who had not been completely silenced by the Rome congress. Grumblings against his 'tsarism' and the parliamentary perversion of fascism continued into the spring. Marsich, who still regarded D'Annunzio as 'the only great Italian', was the leading dissident, and Grandi and Balbo were sympathetic. The opposition became serious enough in March for Mussolini to cut short a

---

[1] Sturzo always denied exercising a 'veto'. He explained his action during the crisis as a protest against the destruction of Bonomi's government by extra-parliamentary action at a time when parliament was not sitting, and as a defence of parliament's rights and powers. This was the Popular party's line, clearly expressed at the time. Indeed if there was a 'veto', it was the party's, not Sturzo's. The party could have overruled its secretary, as it did a few days later when accepting Facta; but in Giolitti's case it chose not to do so. Sturzo, *Italy and Fascismo*, pp. 100–6; De Rosa, *Storia*, pp. 191–7; Jacini, *Storia*, pp. 122–5; Tasca, pp. 274–5, 340–1; Valeri, *Da Giolitti a Mussolini*, pp. 102–3, 119–21.

visit to Berlin and hurry back to Milan to deal with it. But on 3 April Marsich was unanimously disavowed by the National Council of the party and deserted by all his friends. Thereafter Mussolini's leadership was unchallenged.[1]

Facta's government was never more than a ghost government. The Prime Minister himself lacked the resolution and strength of character that the emergency demanded. Facta had started as a successful provincial lawyer and developed in thirty years of politics into a competent parliamentarian and a minister admirably equipped for normal times.[2] Well endowed with the Piedmontese virtues of industry and integrity, but totally lacking ambition, he was proud to call himself a gentleman and to devote himself with conscious modesty to the service of his King.[3] All his political life he had lived in the shadow of Giolitti.[4] Having accepted the burden of the premiership because his conscience would not allow him to refuse, he set himself as his main task the removal of all obstacles to Giolitti's early return to power.

His first few weeks went deceptively well. On 18 March the chamber gave him its confidence by 275 votes to 89. Parliament went on debating and legislating. The Popular Minister of Agriculture introduced a bill to regulate agricultural leases and sharecropping contracts, and another to provide funds for the expropriation of the *latifondi* and the extension of small peasant ownership. The latter was passed by the chamber, though not the senate, in August. The Popular Minister of Education presented yet another bill to benefit private schools. This was the peak of Popular legislative achievement.[5] But all these debates had an air of unreality. The future of Italy was being decided elsewhere.

Fascist violence continued. Facta spoke bravely in parliament of restoring the rule of law and exhorted his prefects, magistrates and police to do their duty. But his words had less effect even than those of his predecessors.[6]

---

[1] Tamaro, I, pp. 219–20; Pini and Susmel, II, pp. 173–7; Mussolini, XVIII, pp. 84–6. While in Berlin Mussolini had told Stresemann, the future Chancellor of Germany, 'Today there are only two persons in Italy who give orders and carry weight – his Majesty the King and I.' G. Pini, *Filo diretto con Palazzo Venezia* (Bologna 1950), p. 240.

[2] He had been Minister of Finance under Luzzatti and Giolitti in 1910–14 and 1921, and Minister of Justice under Orlando in 1919.

[3] Répaci, I, pp. 84–9; see also Facta's revealing fragment of autobiography in Répaci, II, pp. 11–22. In March 1919 he had written to Giolitti, 'Perhaps the accusation sometimes made against me, that I am excessively prudent, is true.' *Quarant' anni*, III, 283.

[4] Répaci (I, p. 585) writes of Facta's 'complesso luogotenenziale', a fair judgement.

[5] Howard, pp. 351–61, 365–72.

[6] 'Not *Facta* but *Verba*', was Scialoja's witticism. D. Varè, *Laughing Diplomat* (London 1938), p. 207.

If Turati was unfair in accusing the government of maintaining 'equi-distance between the aggressor and his victim', his accusation was fully justified as regards the government's subordinates in the provinces. On 3 March one thousand *squadristi* under the fascist deputy for Trieste, Francesco Giunta, seized Fiume, threw out Zanella's 'Austro-Croat' government, forced the 'traitor' Zanella to flee to Yugoslavia and once again proclaimed annexation to Italy. This flagrant violation of an international treaty by Italian citizens humiliated the Italian government in the eyes of the world and revealed its impotence. All Facta could do was instal a pro-visional Italian administration, under the nominal authority of the vice-president of the Fiume constituent assembly, which was in effect to con-done the *fait accompli*.

In May Balbo mobilised 50,000 labourers in a 'fascist strike', marched on Ferrara and refused to evacuate the town until the authorities had promised employment on public works. At the end of the same month 60,000 fascists were mobilised at Bologna to secure the removal of the prefect, Cesare Mori, who was insufficiently compliant to fascist wishes. The commander of the Bologna garrison negotiated a truce between the *squadristi* and the state authorities, and after a face-saving pause of three weeks, Mori was transferred to Apulia. This incident revealed the brutal fact that a large part of Italy was ruled by the Fascist party, not the government. Prefects, magistrates and local authorities either sympathised or were cowed into passivity.[1] Balbo described the Bologna mobilisation as 'a dress rehearsal for revolution'.[2] Mussolini commented on the strategy of these operations like a victorious commander-in-chief. When Rimini was occupied in July, he wrote in *Il Popolo d'Italia*: 'The situation has been transformed. Rimini in our hands gives us the pincer-grip we needed to squeeze Emilia and Romagna, and is at the same time a bridge for our penetration of the neighbouring Marche.'[3]

During the summer, however, the fascists almost overplayed their hand. Early in June the socialist right wing at last resolved to support any government that would restore law and liberty. When the maximalist majority denounced this decision as treachery, 60 of the 123 socialist deputies, under Turati's leadership, defied party discipline and set up their own independent organization.[4] The Popolari, too, were being forced

---

[1] 'The prefect [of Ferrara] has to submit to the orders I give him in the name of the Fascists', wrote Balbo in his diary. Tasca, p. 289.

[2] Tasca, p. 294.                                    [3] Mussolini, XVIII, p. 282.

[4] But as Tasca points out (pp. 302–3), mere support of a government was no longer enough. In 1921 socialist abstention would have been sufficient to give life to a liberal–democratic–Popular government; by February 1922 their votes were

by events to recognise that defence of the constitution was more important than any item in their party programme. During June and July Sturzo had a series of talks with Turati and his leading colleagues, to explore the possibility of collaboration. In mid-July all remaining doubts and reservations seemed for a moment to vanish in the storm of protest which followed yet another fascist outrage, this time in Cremona.

The province of Cremona had long been the scene of bitter enmity between the Popolari, under the militant leadership of Guido Miglioli, and the fascists commanded by Roberto Farinacci, one of the most brutal of all the *ras*. Ever since the war the labourers of the dairy farms of Soresina, organized in Miglioli's unions, had been fighting for a share in profits and management. In the violence of their language and the ruthlessness with which they conducted the class struggle, their leaders had nothing to learn from the socialists of Emilia. Twice during 1920–1 they occupied the dairies and farm buildings and hoisted the white flag of the C.I.L. In August 1921 an arbitration award (known as the Lodo Bianchi) conceded most of the unions' demands.[1] The proprietors continued to resist and turned to Farinacci's *squadre* for support. The award was never carried out, in spite of the prefect's efforts, and in May 1922 Facta acquiesced in its annulment. But the fascists were not satisfied; they intended to smash the Catholic unions as they had smashed the socialist unions elsewhere in the Po valley.[2] On 12 July 1922 *squadristi* occupied the town of Cremona, burst into the prefecture, devastated Miglioli's house and burnt the premises of trade unions and cooperatives, both Catholic and socialist.

When the news reached Rome there was an explosion of disgust and indignation. Mussolini, foreseeing a revulsion of moderate opinion, ordered Farinacci to 'suspend the operation' and evacuate the town, which he had held for five days. Miglioli and the C.I.L. stirred the Popolari into action and the democratic groups decided to join them in opposition. On

---

required, and by July nothing less than their membership of a coalition cabinet was needed. Even Turati and the reformists were always one step behind.

[1] The Lodo Bianchi was an almost unique example of the application (if only abortive) of Catholic social theory. It was economically impossible to divide large and efficient dairy farms into small peasant holdings. The aim of the C.I.L. was therefore to transform the agricultural labourer by successive stages into co-manager and co-proprietor. The landowners rightly saw in this programme a more radical threat to the rights of property than in the more conventional demands of the C.G.L. for higher wages or shorter hours. The rivalry between the red and white unions was so bitter that the former even took the side of the proprietors against the latter. Only in March 1922, when it was too late, did Miglioli and the local socialists form a united front against the fascists.

[2] Howard, pp. 313–15, 335–7, 358; Preti, pp. 365–9, 464–71; Serpieri, pp. 317–21.

19 July Facta's government was defeated by 288 votes to 103 on a clearly anti-fascist motion. Only the Giolittian liberals, Salandra's conservatives and the nationalists stood by him.[1] Deeply relieved by his unexpected 'liberation', Facta prepared to retire to the peace of rural Piedmont.[2]

Another long ministerial crisis ensued. First Orlando negotiated fruitlessly for a national government of pacification, stretching from the Popolari as far right as Salandra's conservatives and possibly even the fascists. Then Bonomi, with Turati's blessing, tried to form an anti-fascist coalition of the left and centre. But not until 28 July did the right-wing socialists take the final plunge and agree to accept cabinet office. Next day Turati overcame his socialist scruples and accepted an invitation to visit the King. By then it was too late and Bonomi had given up his attempt. In the end Giolitti's attitude was decisive. He himself took no direct part in the negotiations. In spite of appeals from Facta and other friends, he refused even to interrupt his cure at Vichy. But he made his wishes known. Like the right, he regretted Facta's fall, particularly on a motion which was 'an imperative mandate to declare war to the death on fascism'.[3] In a letter to Olindo Malagodi which the latter published on the 26th, he dismissed the idea of a Popular–socialist *connubio* as preposterous; it could only result in civil war.[4] Without his blessing no stable government could be formed. After Bonomi had failed, the King tried Meda, then Giuseppe De Nava, the leader of the demo-liberali, then Orlando for a second time, but all without success. On 30 July he summoned Facta and appealed to him, with tears in his eyes, not to abandon him like all the others. Facta dutifully sacrificed his own longing for release and consented to re-form his government.[5] Thus after eleven tense days the situation remained exactly the same as before 19 July. Giolitti's lieutenants were delighted. They had successfully wrecked the attempts at a coalition of the left and forced the Popolari and democrats back to the point of departure. Now, they believed, the situation was more than ever in the master's hands; the way lay open for him to return to power in

---

[1] Mussolini repeated his tactics of February and ordered his party to vote with the opposition. But this couldn't disguise the anti-fascist motives of the majority.

[2] Répaci, II, pp. 26–8.

[3] Giolitti to Porzio, 23 July, in Natale, pp. 749–50. See also his letters to Camillo Corradini of 21 July and to Facta of 23 July. De Rosa, *Storia*, p. 260, *Giolitti e il fascismo*, p. 17; Répaci, II, pp. 28–9. Giolitti's main preoccupation at this time was the financial crisis and the 'march towards bankruptcy'.

[4] Giolitti, *Discorsi extraparlamentari*, pp. 334–5; De Rosa, *Storia*, pp. 258–9.

[5] Répaci, I, pp. 69–70, II, pp. 31–2, 75–6. On 3 August Facta wrote to his daughter: 'I have made the most tremendous sacrifice that you can imagine; the scene that I had with the King was truly tragic . . . Believe me, no man in the world has made the sacrifice that I have made and am making. Your mother and I are both shattered by the outcome . . .'

the autumn.[1] This was the hope of Facta himself. On 26 July he had written to Giolitti, 'The only man who could put things in order is yourself.'[2]

The cabinet crisis was still unsolved when Balbo mobilised the fascists of Romagna. A 'column of fire', after terrorising the whole region, occupied Ravenna on 26 July and burnt the headquarters of its cooperatives, the pride of the Ravenna working-class.[3] On the 31st the Labour Alliance declared a general strike and delegated its powers to a secret 'action committee'. The initiative came from the rank and file, goaded to desperation by fascist attacks. No socialist or C.G.L. leader wanted the strike. Its object was to stir parliament into action in defence of constitutional liberties. In Turati's words, it was 'a strike for legality'. It proved to be an act of suicide. Except in the industrial cities the response of the workers was half-hearted. Members of the C.I.L. and the fascist syndicates remained at work. Few agricultural workers obeyed the order, and the railways and post office were scarcely affected. The sole consequence of the strike was to revive liberal and democratic terror of bolshevism and further discredit the very concept of the anti-fascist coalition which it was intended to promote.

The fascists meanwhile seized their opportunity. A manifesto of 1 August gave the state forty-eight hours 'to show proof of its authority'; if it failed, the Fascist party would 'assume full freedom of action and take the place of the state, which will once more have proved its impotence'.[4] Bianchi repeated the ultimatum in an interview with Facta and his Minister of Interior, Paolino Taddei. The threat was carried out and *squadristi* kept trains and public services running at the pistol point. On 3 August the Alliance ordered its members back to work. The fascists now passed over to the counter-offensive. In large-scale operations they took over key areas which had hitherto eluded their grasp. In Milan, Genoa, Ancona and Leghorn socialist power was broken and the town councils were forcibly ejected from office. 'In forty-eight hours of systematic, warlike violence', Mussolini boasted seven weeks later, 'we won what we would never have won in forty-eight years of preaching and propaganda.'[5] In the whole of northern Italy only two effective centres of left-wing resistance survived: Turin, where the socialists and communists held out grimly; and Parma, where in the old quarter of the city *arditi del popolo*, faithful to Parma's tradition of militant syndicalism, resisted for

---

[1] *Quarant' anni*, III, 368, 370–1. Camillo Corradini told Giolitti on 2 August: 'The union of the left never materialised because we refused to take part.'

[2] *Quarant' anni*, III, 367.

[3] Balbo's own description of these exploits is quoted in Tasca, pp. 316–17.

[4] Mussolini, XVIII, p. 329.      [5] ibid., p. 413.

five days till the attacking *squadristi* were forced to withdraw and leave the restoration of order to the army.

On 8 August the fascists demobilised. But mass rallies and mopping-up operations continued. Success brought a flood of recruits and more and more socialist unions passed over in mass to the fascist syndicates. The government was helpless. 'The state hasn't a single friend left here on which it can count', reported the prefect of Bologna on 26 August; 'For the moment my job is limited to that of an observer and routine adminis-trator.'[1] Early in October *squadristi* invaded the Trentino and south Tirol. Trent and Bolzano were occupied and 'de-Austrianised', and 'respect for the Italian flag was enforced'.[2] Once again the government capitulated, allowed the ejection of the civil commissioner, Credaro, and gave the *squadristi* a free hand against the German population. Rome, however, was still untouched. Further south, except in Apulia, Naples and a few other cities, fascism was almost unknown. Mussolini, like the Socialist party in former times, feared the 'Vendée of the south' and, ironically, it was to the backward, politically stagnant south that even many democrats looked for the salvation of Italy.[3]

The socialist rout continued. Before the end of August the Labour Alliance disintegrated. On 1 October the party assembled once again in congress at Rome and the long-postponed schism occurred. By 32,000 to 29,000 votes the maximalists expelled the reformists, who formed their own Unitary Socialist party. The rump Socialist party confirmed its adherence to the Comintern and sent a new delegation to Moscow. The C.G.L. declared its independence of both parties, hoping to save itself from the wreck. The communists, too, were torn by dissension. Now that the Socialist party had been purged, Zinoviev, President of the Comintern, intensified his pressure upon the Italian communists to conciliate Serrati's maximalist remnants and form a united front of the working masses. The right wing, led by Gramsci and Angelo Tasca, urged obedience. Bordiga's left wing distrusted Serrati, despised the maximalists, opposed fusion with the Socialist party and wished to confine the united front to the trade union field.[4]

---

[1] De Rosa, *Storia*, pp. 277–8. Between 15 August and 22 September the Minister of Justice received official notification of 369 criminal acts (including 74 homicides) committed from political motives, an average of 10 a day. *Quarant' anni*, III, 377; De Rosa, *Storia*, p. 288, note.                                    [2] Pini and Susmel, II, p. 213.

[3] For instance Amendola, who declared in a speech of 1 October: 'We [the south] still have today, as we had in the immediate post-war years, a great historic func-tion to perform, that of equilibrium and political conservatism.' Amendola, *La nuova democrazia*, p. 151. Amendola was born in Naples and represented Salerno in parliament.

[4] Bellini and Galli, pp. 60–78. Until June 1922, when he went to Russia, Gramsci

Thus, faced by the threat of total extinction, the extreme left] was incapable of joint resistance. The unitary socialists looked to parliament and were ready to collaborate with non-socialists. The maximalists still rejected collaboration with any section of the bourgeoisie, believing that it would mean 'ceasing to be ourselves',[1] and went on talking revolution. The communists, too, spurned all idea of an anti-fascist coalition. 'If the fascists destroy parliament, we shall be delighted', Bordiga declared. His party made no distinction between fascists and anti-fascists: the 'Socialist-Popular-Fascist ruling class' was its enemy and Turati, Sturzo and Mussolini were merely three names for a single 'grim tyrant'.[2] The communist programme, as divorced from reality as the revolutionary talk of the maximalists, was 'a direct and armed struggle' against fascism.[3]

These bickerings of the extreme left attracted little attention, for after August socialism as an effective political force was dead. Mussolini commented: 'If the three secretaries of the Labour Alliance had been three of the most fanatical fascists, they really could not have rendered a greater service to the cause of Italian fascism.'[4] 'Our victory', declared Grandi, 'has been shattering, absolute, superior to all our expectations.'[5] It had been as much a psychological as a physical victory. Fascists had acted as champions of law and order, and the fascist 'state of tomorrow' had proved itself stronger than the pusillanimous liberal 'state of today'. Ten days after the strike Turati, writing in the reformist newspaper, *Giustizia*, admitted defeat: 'The general strike has been our Caporetto . . . We must have the courage to recognize that today the fascists are masters of the field . . . After our Caporetto, we must find our Piave, and not despair of our Vittorio Veneto.'[6] Not even the gloomiest of them foresaw that for their Vittorio Veneto they would have to wait twenty years.

The Popolari were not as yet menaced by disintegration, but they too had their dissensions. These gave Mussolini a further opportunity to weaken anti-fascism. He cleverly combined blandishment of the Vatican with attacks on Sturzo, the 'anti-Pope', and Miglioli, 'the black demagogue' whose white bolshevism was worse than the red. The Popular party, he declared, had been infected with socialism and was now a menace

---

had been in agreement with Bordiga. While in Moscow he was converted to the Comintern line by Zinoviev. He stayed on in Russia and so was not in Italy at the time of the march on Rome.

[1] Serrati at Rome Congress, 1 October. Répaci, I, p. 210.

[2] De Rosa, *Storia*, pp. 226–8, quoting *L'Ordine Nuovo*.

[3] As the communist deputy, Repossi, told the chamber on 9 August. Répaci, I, p. 75.

[4] *Il Popolo d'Italia*, 5 August, in Mussolini, XVIII, p. 336.

[5] Tasca, p. 372.

[6] ibid., p. 338; Nenni, pp. 213–14; Répaci, II, pp. 268–9.

to Italian Catholicism. Fascists must therefore consider it a hostile party; but 'the degree of our hostility will depend on circumstances', meaning whether or not it continued to oppose fascism.[1] These tactics began to show results. In June a small group of conservative Catholics broke away to form a new political organization, confessional in character. Its leader, Carlo Ottavio Cornaggia, received an encouraging telegram from Pius XI himself.[2] On 18 September eight Popular senators, including Grosoli and Santucci, published an open letter to Sturzo condemning 'repugnant, hybrid *connubi*' with the left and calling for a purge of the party.[3] On 2 October Cardinal Gasparri declared in a confidential circular to bishops, which later leaked into the press, that the Holy See 'has always remained, and means to remain in the future, totally separate from the Popular party, as from all other political parties'. He went on to warn bishops and priests to withdraw immediately from politics.[4] Thus, though the bulk of its members stood firm behind Sturzo, the Popular party's unity and militancy was sapping away. It offered no barrier to fascism's march to power.

## The March on Rome

After August 1922 the way lay open for the final fascist challenge. Mussolini intended to govern Italy, but he had not yet decided how power was to be won. On 19 July he had spoken in the chamber of the 'internal torment' of fascism, which arose from the choice between legality and insurrection, but added that he himself preferred a legal solution.[5] On 13 August he again secured his party's approval for a policy of waiting. The next two months were spent in brilliantly neutralising all possible oppositions, by a combination of violence and political manœuvre. Insurrection, he declared, would be inevitable if his demands were not satisfied. In the forefront of his programme he now put immediate elections, to enable the fascists to obtain the representation in parliament to which their strength in the country entitled them. This was a demand with which many liberals were in sympathy.

Facta had reformed his government on a caretaker basis. On 10 August it was given a vote of confidence of 247 to 121. Parliament then adjourned. But even when free from parliamentary harassment, the cabinet soon revealed its lack of cohesion. It was expected to give way to a stronger coalition under Giolitti, Orlando or Salandra as soon as the chamber

---

[1] Mussolini, XVIII, pp. 221, 252–3, 318–20, 331.
[2] Howard, pp. 364–5.
[3] Jacini, *Storia*, pp. 303–7; Howard, p. 382.
[4] Tasca, p. 419; Binchy, pp. 137–8; Howard, pp. 382–3.
[5] Mussolini, XVIII, pp. 291–2.

reassembled in the autumn. Besides the Popolari, it contained members of all the main factions into which the liberals were divided. On the extreme right were Riccio, Salandra's representative and close friend, who had accepted office on Salandra's advice, and Schanzer, the Foreign Minister. They were convinced that the fascists would inevitably enter the government very soon and opposed coercion. Salandra, still hankering in his old age after a revival of the 'historic' Right, saw himself as a conservative prime minister with Mussolini as his junior partner. During the spring and summer he had organised meetings between his conservative friends and selected nationalists and fascists. Both personally and through Riccio he was urging Facta to reconstruct his government and to give fascism the 'stamp of legality' and the responsibilities of office.[1] A second group in the cabinet took the opposite view, that its duty was to remain in office and in the last resort to suppress fascism by force. This group was led by Amendola, Minister for the Colonies, and included Alessio, Minister of Justice, Soleri, Minister for War, and Taddei, Minister of Interior, who as prefect of Turin had won the reputation of a strong man. The third and largest group, which included Facta himself, favoured compromise and hoped that time would bring a solution. Facta's one desire was to avoid any action that might prevent Giolitti's return to power. He therefore obstructed Riccio's efforts to break up the government prematurely before Giolitti was ready. He also opposed repressive action against fascism because he knew Giolitti disapproved. Alessio submitted proposals in August for a state of siege in specially disturbed areas, and for drastic enforcement of public order; and after the fascist occupation of the Trentino in early October, Taddei threatened to resign if the cabinet failed to take strong action. But on both occasions Facta's policy of appeasement prevailed.[2]

Mussolini could not be blamed for believing that he had little to fear from Facta's government. Nor was there much danger of a more resolute government being formed. Throughout the summer the liberal and democratic politicians continued to demonstrate their ineffectualness. The disintegration of the Democratic Group in May, after only six months of existence, had increased their disunity. In August Cocco-Ortu made another attempt at reunion. Plans were discussed for launching a new democratic federation at a congress in Naples, to be followed by speeches throughout the country. It was hoped that Giolitti, Orlando, Nitti,

---

[1] Salandra, *Memorie*, pp. 14–18. Albertini agreed with Salandra. On 13 August he had declared in the senate that 'the best way to remove all pretext for violence is to invite the fascists to give proof of their capacity for directing public affairs'. Albertini, *In difesa della libertà*, p. 31.

[2] Répaci, I, pp. 171–3, 178–9.

Bonomi, De Nicola and many other prominent personalities would take part. But the Giolittians obstructed. They were convinced that their chief was now master of the political situation; a new organisation could only tie his hands and might even strengthen Nitti at his expense. Giolitti himself was as hostile as in July to any anti-fascist manœuvre. Both he and Nitti preferred to negotiate with Mussolini rather than combine against him. Within a month Cocco-Ortu's scheme was dead.[1] This democratic fiasco was followed by a vigorous manifestation by the anti-democrats. On 8 October a liberal congress assembled in Bologna to form an organised party. 'Organise or die' was the slogan and, following the current fashion, 'khaki-shirts' made their appearance. The title 'Liberal-Democratic' was rejected in favour of plain 'Liberal' by a two to one vote, to emphasise the intention to 'steer firmly to the right'. The Salandrians, nationalists and pro-fascists were dominant. It was not much of an exaggeration for Grandi to claim that Mussolini, though absent, was the real president of the congress.[2]

With the liberals half won over, the Popolari in decline and the power of the socialists shattered, there remained three potential obstacles on the fascist path to victory: the King, the army and D'Annunzio. Their combined support could still have made even Facta formidable. Victor Emmanuel himself had no love for fascism and probably looked to Giolitti to put both fascists and socialists in their places. But though several of his personal advisers, including the Minister of the Royal Household, shared such views, there were others in court circles who felt differently. The Queen Mother Margherita, who had always disliked her son playing the 'bourgeois monarch', made no secret of her sympathy for fascism. More important, the Duke of Aosta, the King's first cousin and wartime commander of the 'unbeaten' Third Army, had been since 1918 the favourite of the extreme right. He was known to be ambitious and dissatisfied.[3] In June he promised the nationalist Enrico Corradini, who visited him at Mussolini's request, that he would press the King not to oppose fascism, but added that, if he failed, he was ready to be proclaimed regent.[4] Fear of his cousin played its part in determining the King's action, and it suited the fascists that rumours of their support for the Duke should circulate. Mussolini meanwhile declared that fascism could achieve its aims without touching the monarchy, which therefore had no interest in

[1] ibid., I, pp. 242–8, II, p. 124; *Quarant' anni*, III, 371, 373.

[2] Tasca, pp. 390–2; Valeri, *Da Giolitti a Mussolini*, pp. 105–7; Répaci, I, pp. 248–56. The Giolittian delegates abstained on the critical motion.

[3] Sforza, *Contemporary Italy*, p. 258, describes how the Duke pestered him, when he was Foreign Minister, with requests to be found a minor European throne.

[4] Pini and Susmel, II, p. 187; Tamaro, I, pp. 224–5.

obstructing the fascist revolution. The threat was clear: 'The crown is not at stake, provided it keeps itself out of the stakes.'[1] It would have required courage in the King to risk his throne and face the threat of civil war in order to save the constitution. Irresolute by nature, Victor Emmanuel was not the man to welcome the responsibility of such a decision. The fascists were strong and better not antagonised. Like Facta, he preferred to appease and hope for the best.

The attitude of the army was of decisive importance, for without its aid the police and civil authorities were now incapable of suppressing a fascist insurrection. In military circles there was much sympathy with fascism, especially among the younger officers. Generals had helped to organise the *squadre* into a national militia and draft its regulations. Emilio De Bono, a general on the active reserve, was a prominent member of the party. Even the 'architects of victory', General Diaz and Admiral Thaon di Revel, had shown themselves well disposed. Soleri recognised the danger. In order to remove all doubts, he reminded army commanders of their duty to remain above politics. Special security precautions were ordered at military depots and arsenals. A few officers who had attended fascist meetings in uniform were retired and it was decided to take disciplinary action against De Bono.[2] These were modest measures but they served their purpose. Only in a few exceptional cases had sympathy with fascism as yet led to disaffection. The army still prided itself on its loyalty to King and constitution.

D'Annunzio had been progressively eclipsed by Mussolini since his ejection from Fiume, and he did not relish it. But he still dreamt of a 'national revolution', inspired by the Charter of the Carnero, and saw himself as the saviour of his country. His prestige was still high among ex-servicemen. Many of his legionaries remained devoted to him, in spite of the attraction of the fascist *squadre*.[3] He could also count on syndicalist support, particularly among the railwaymen and Giulietti's merchant seamen. The latter had no love for fascist syndicalism, as they were engaged in a bitter struggle for power in the port of Genoa with the fascist seamen's corporation, which the shipowners favoured. D'Annunzio aspired to become the patron of a united, autonomous trade union movement, standing high above the turmoil of party politics and civil war. During April and May 1922 he invited a succession of working-class leaders, including Gino Baldesi and Ludovico D'Aragona of the C.G.L., to his

---

[1] *Il Popolo d'Italia*, 23 August 1922; speech at Udine, 20 September; in Mussolini, XVIII, pp. 367, 418–19.

[2] Soleri, pp. 146–7, 156–7; Répaci, II, pp. 160–2.

[3] But many legionaries joined the fascist expedition which seized Fiume in March 1922, in spite of D'Annunzio's disapproval.

residence on Lake Garda.[1] These activities did not endear him to Mussolini, who was further incensed by D'Annunzio's description of fascism as 'agrarian slavery'.[2]

D'Annunzio's political schemes showed a fertile imagination but little realism. He was still as flighty and unreliable as he had been at Fiume. In the late summer he saw Orlando and made contact even with Nitti, his antagonist of 1919, though he would make no advances to 'the butcher' Giolitti. There were abortive attempts to arrange a meeting between himself, Nitti and Mussolini to discuss 'pacification' and the spiritual reunion of all Italians.[3] On 3 August he found himself in Milan when the *squadre* seized the town hall and consented to harangue the crowds from its balcony. But this was an act of impulsive enthusiasm. It did not mean, as Mussolini was quick to claim, that D'Annunzio had rallied to the fascist cause. When Bianchi sent him a telegram of congratulation, ending with the words *Viva il Fascismo!*, he pointedly replied that *Viva l'Italia!* was the only slogan to which he could subscribe.[4] Next month he was urging his legionaries to win over the trade unions to the principles for which they had fought at Fiume. He also promised a deputation led by De Ambris that he would mobilise the legionaries and ex-servicemen, restore civil peace with their aid, govern dictatorially for three months, then hold new elections. In this way he would save Italy from fascist tyranny.

This idea of mobilising the ex-servicemen appealed to many liberals, including the Prime Minister. Facta was a fervent patriot who had lost a son in the war; he was also a personal friend of D'Annunzio. There seemed a chance that the poet's idea could be harnessed to the government's purpose and used to force Mussolini to stick to constitutional methods. After discussions with a junior member of the government, D'Annunzio agreed to attend a mass rally of ex-servicemen in Rome on 4 November, the fourth anniversary of victory, and with Facta beside him to appeal from the Capitol for peace, order and national concord. D'Annunzio was to be

---

[1] Valeri, *D'Annunzio davanti al fascismo*, pp. 59–66. Turati approved of Baldesi's visit. D'Annunzio also received Chicherin, the Soviet Commissar for Foreign Affairs, who was attending the Genoa international conference, and surprised him by the warmth of his concern for 'the social struggles of the oppressed'.

[2] Mussolini denied that D'Annunzio had ever pronounced this phrase. But it circulated widely and it is clear, from the space Mussolini devoted to its refutation, that he regarded it as damaging.

[3] Tasca, p. 399; Nitti, *Rivelazioni*, pp. 343–7; Valeri, *D'Annunzio*, pp. 70–8. Nitti appealed to D'Annunzio to use his influence over the young to further the cause of democracy. Répaci, II, pp. 168–9. The meeting never took place owing to D'Annunzio's mysterious fall from a window of his villa on 13 August, which put him out of action for a critical month.

[4] Mussolini, XVIII, pp. 535–6.

Facta's trump card. The legionaries would forestall the *squadristi* and march legally on Rome before Mussolini.[1]

In the third week of September 1922 Mussolini and his lieutenants decided to quicken the pace. With much of Italy north of Rome in their hands, they were burdened with problems of administration, unemployment, labour unrest and the financing of a huge semi-military machine, which only control of the state would enable them to solve.[2] Time was not necessarily on their side. With the example of the Socialist party before them they knew how prolonged inaction could destroy the enthusiasm of their rank and file. At the end of September Mussolini set out on a speech-making tour of the north. 'Our programme is simple: we intend to govern Italy', he declared at a mass rally at Udine on the 20th. 'It was on the banks of the Piave that we began the march that can end only when we have reached our final goal, Rome', he told Cremona on the 24th. 'There are two governments in Italy today – one too many', he quoted with approval from the *Corriere della Sera* at Milan on 4 October.[3] It was clear that the political lull which had lasted since August was at an end.

As a new crisis approached, all eyes turned to Giolitti. Mussolini was afraid of him. He had, after all, fired on D'Annunzio and Mussolini did not wish to be his next target.[4] The great majority of liberals and democrats, even the Nittians, looked to him for leadership. Turati's Unitary Socialist party would have welcomed his return to power. Sturzo and the Popolari had dropped their 'veto'. Facta, anxious only to hand over to him at the earliest opportunity, saw that he was kept fully informed. Giolitti refused to be hurried. At the end of September he began to make leisurely soundings, using as his main intermediary the prefect of Milan, Senator Alfredo Lusignoli. In the first fortnight of October Lusignoli had four meetings with Mussolini, on which he reported fully to both Giolitti and Facta.[5] From the information with which Lusignoli and others

---

[1] Ferraris, pp. 62–4; Soleri, pp. 149–50; Tasca, pp. 397–8, 472–3; Répaci, I, pp. 390–1, II, pp. 24, 37–9, 407–8.

[2] Grandi and Bianchi were particularly frank on this point. Mussolini, XVIII, pp. 541, 559–60; *Quarant' anni*, III, 376; Répaci, II, p. 126. The fascist General Confederation of Syndical Corporations claimed 458,000 members in June (60% of them agricultural) and 800,000 by the end of October. Contributions to the party's central funds were showing a decline in the autumn of 1922.

[3] Mussolini, XVIII, pp. 416, 423, 434–5.

[4] Répaci, I, pp. 403, 434; Tasca, p. 481. According to Cesare Rossi, Mussolini remarked to him on 16 October, 'Se Giolitti torna al potere, siamo f . . . Ricordati che a Fiume ha fatto cannoneggiare D'Annunzio.'

[5] Lusignoli's reports to Facta and Giolitti are printed in Répaci, II, pp. 42 ff., 131 ff.; and those to Giolitti in Valeri, *Da Giolitti a Mussolini*, pp. 150–6. While

provided him, Giolitti's plan gradually took shape. It was to form a widely based government which would include fascists and if possible Popolari, and enjoy at least the benevolent neutrality of the unitary socialists. It would take over from Facta as soon as parliament reassembled, prepare legislation to restore the pre-war electoral system and dissolve in the spring.

Giolitti's soundings soon revealed two obstacles to his plan. The first was presented by the unitary socialists and Popolari. The former were ready to commit their eighty votes in support of a Giolitti government only if it excluded the fascists.[1] Sturzo's view was the same, though influential members of his party dissented and were ready to take office with fascist colleagues.[2] The second and much more serious obstacle arose on the fascist side. Mussolini told Lusignoli that he was willing to accept office under Giolitti, but speed was essential. He was under constant pressure from his lieutenants, particularly Bianchi, to whom the very thought of negotiation with Giolitti was distasteful.[3] To wait for a change of government until parliament met, and for an election until the spring, was out of the question. The Fascist party congress was due to open at Naples on 24 October. As soon as that was over, Mussolini impressed upon Lusignoli, the situation must be brought to a head.

On 16 October the leaders of the Fascist party and two sympathetic generals, Gustavo Fara and Sante Ceccherini, met in Milan. Mussolini announced that the moment for insurrection was near. Time was against them, he declared; the spectre of Giolitti was looming, Facta was working to reconcile Giolitti and D'Annunzio, and it was essential to forestall the patriotic rally on 4 November. De Vecchi, De Bono and the two generals pleaded for delay, protesting that the *squadre* were unprepared and un-

---

Lusignoli operated from Milan, Camillo Corradini sounded Sturzo and negotiated with Bianchi in Rome. Répaci, II, pp. 128–31, 385; Valeri, *Da Giolitti a Mussolini*, pp. 146–9.

[1] Répaci, II, p. 142; Valeri, *Da Giolitti a Mussolini*, p. 165.

[2] De Rosa, *Storia*, pp. 294–8. Frassati (pp. 41–6, 68–74) severely criticises Sturzo's attitude. It was at this moment, he argues, not in February (see above, p. 604) that Sturzo imposed a 'veto'; his 100 Popular votes would have put Giolitti rather than Mussolini into power. But as De Rosa shows, Sturzo's opposition was not decisive. Members of his party, notably Cavazzoni, would doubtless have accepted office from Giolitti, if offered, just as they accepted it from Mussolini a few weeks later. Frassati, in spite of his awareness and disapproval of Giolitti's complacence towards fascism since the 1921 election, remained convinced for the rest of his life that Giolitti would have dominated a liberal–fascist coalition and saved Italy from dictatorship. Sturzo, like many other anti-fascists, was unable to share his faith.

[3] Bianchi was pressing for immediate elections under a reconstructed Facta government in which the fascists would be represented.

armed; but Balbo and Bianchi were impatient for action and Mussolini carried the meeting.[1] A military plan for a march on Rome was approved and quadrumvirs were nominated to command the operation. Each of the latter represented a distinct tendency within the fascist movement. Balbo, ex-officer in the Alpini, who had volunteered at the age of nineteen and passed without a break from the army to the *squadre*, represented the war generation; Bianchi, general secretary of the party, a founding member of the interventionist Fascio of Milan in 1915, represented the ex-syndicalists; De Vecchi, creator of Piedmontese fascism and a firm monarchist, represented the reactionary middle class; De Bono came from the regular army. The military plan was elaborated at two further meetings of the quadrumvirs in the next four days, and commanders were appointed for the columns that were to march on Rome.

These decisions did not mean that Mussolini was committed to violence. Insurrection for its own sake had no appeal for him. Besides, he was well aware that De Vecchi and the generals were right in declaring the *squadre* unready. But it was the psychological rather than the physical effects of his military preparations to which he attached importance; they were designed to lead not to an armed clash but to a political crisis with, if possible, a peaceful solution.[2] Not only, therefore, did the negotiations with Giolitti continue; indirect contact was also maintained with Salandra, and the abortive discussions of the previous summer for a meeting between Mussolini, Nitti and D'Annunzio were revived.[3] D'Annunzio received special attention. On 16 October he, Mussolini and Giulietti signed an agreement for the suppression within thirty days of the fascist seamen's corporation in Genoa and the recognition by the shipowners of Giulietti's 'national syndicalist' organisation. The fascists of Genoa were not consulted on this act of generosity at their expense, and protested at their betrayal. But the agreement proved a successful first step towards disarming D'Annunzio and weaning him from support of Facta's patriotic rally. D'Annunzio showed his gratitude on the 19th by ordering the release of his legionaries whom he had 'mobilised' only a week before.[4] By these

[1] Répaci, I, pp. 431–5. According to Pini and Susmel, II, p. 204, Mussolini first revealed his intention to use force, if the government refused to cede power peaceably, at a private meeting on 24 August. He outlined his plans for an insurrection to ten party leaders on 29 September. Répaci, I, pp. 384–5.

[2] ibid., pp. 435–6.

[3] It was important to neutralise Nitti because his political power was considerable in the south, where fascism was extremely weak. By agreement with Mussolini, Nitti made a speech on 19 October in his constituency in which he talked of the need for elections in the near future and for the 'canalisation' of fascism into constitutional channels. In return Mussolini gave Nitti favourable coverage in the fascist press. Répaci, I, pp. 388–90, II, pp. 169–73.

[4] Tasca, pp. 406–11; Répaci, I, pp. 395–7.

persuasive means, reinforced by the threat of violence, Mussolini continued to reduce the obstacles on his road to power.

Facta was aware of the fascists' impatience and realised that his days were numbered. The suggestion put to him by Bianchi, that he should form a new government with fascist participation, failed to interest him. In spite of a growing weariness that was more moral than physical,[1] his intention was still to hold out till parliament reassembled. On 7 October the cabinet, after two days of discussions, accepted his view that an extra-parliamentary crisis must be avoided. All his hopes were pinned on the Giolitti–Lusignoli–Mussolini negotiations. If Giolitti and Mussolini could reach agreement, then he could make 'a decent exit' and disappear into the retirement for which he longed.[2] On the 12th he begged Giolitti through Malagodi to hurry because the position had become untenable, and dispatched Soleri to Piedmont in the hope of persuading him to come to Rome. But Giolitti was not yet ready.[3] On the 17th the cabinet had another tense meeting at which Riccio pressed for immediate resignation. Facta held back his colleagues only with the utmost difficulty. Soon after the meeting he again wrote to Giolitti. The position was desperate, he told him; 'one can't go on like this' with a government that everyone looked upon as dead; only Giolitti could save the situation.[4] Facta now realised that he could not survive until 7 November, the date on which the cabinet had decided parliament should reopen. He therefore began to think of engineering his fall by arranging for a substantial group of deputies to meet and pass a motion of censure; this would give his resignation a parliamentary form without the need to face the chamber. But until Giolitti was ready he had to hang on, 'treading this last step of my Calvary'; his 'high sense of duty' forbade him to 'start a crisis before knowing where it would finish'.[5]

On 21 October Lusignoli reported that 'our friend [Giolitti] is ready to do his duty'.[6] At last Facta saw light. Further messages assured him that Giolitti accepted the need for an extra-parliamentary crisis, after the

[1] Facta to his wife, 10, 20 October. Répaci, II, pp. 47, 57–8.
[2] Facta to his wife, 12, 15 October. Répaci, II, pp. 49, 53.
[3] ibid., p. 138; *Quarant' anni*, III, 379; Soleri, pp. 147–8. Giolitti insisted that before coming to Rome he must have a summons from the King or a clear invitation from a substantial section of the chamber. He was perhaps reluctant to risk another such humiliation as he had experienced in May 1915.
[4] Répaci, II, pp. 144–6; Valeri, *Da Giolitti a Mussolini*, pp. 143–9.
[5] Facta to his wife, 20 October. The self-righteous note in Facta's letters is prominent. He was comforted by press comment that he was 'the victim of duty' and assured his wife that 'my labours are universally and most highly appreciated (apprezzatissima)', above all by the King. Répaci, II, pp. 57–62.
[6] ibid., p. 59.

Fascist congress at Naples, and would form a government with the fascists if possible, without them if not. The preparations for 4 November meanwhile went ahead and a public announcement was made on the 21st. Facta hoped that the rally would create an atmosphere of patriotic enthusiasm that would give the new government an auspicious start. On the 23rd Giolitti referred in a speech at Cuneo to 'the new party which must take that place in the political life of the country to which the number of its adherents entitles it', but by legal means only.[1] On that day it seemed to Facta that Giolitti was going to pull it off and that he himself would fulfil his aim of avoiding violence and handing over 'without shocks and without uncertainties'.[2]

The government had meanwhile not overlooked the danger of fascist insurrection. On 7 October Facta consulted Diaz and Badoglio. They assured him that, in spite of undeniable sympathy with the fascists, 'the army will do its duty if it is necessary to defend Rome'.[3] Badoglio's opinion was that 'ten or twelve arrests at the most' would be enough to crush fascism.[4] Facta rejected this suggestion and opposed the call-up of two classes of reservists, on the ground that it would alarm public opinion. He nevertheless announced publicly that there would be no weakness on his part in the event of resort to illegality. Mussolini redoubled his efforts to win the army's sympathy. It was thanks to fascism, he declared, that uniforms were no longer spat upon in the streets; 'the national army won't march against the blackshirt army for the very simple reason that the fascists will never march against the national army'.[5] But he had good reason to worry. On 19 October Soleri gave orders to General Emanuele Pugliese, acting commander of the Rome garrison, to prevent the entry of fascist formations into the city, while attempting to avoid an armed clash that might precipitate civil war. Over the next few days the garrison of 2,500 men received substantial reinforcements, including five battalions of Alpini on whose loyalty Soleri, himself an ex-Alpino officer, felt certain he could rely.[6] Plans were also perfected for blocking the railways leading into Rome and establishing road blocks on the bridges and at the gates of the city. The Fascist congress seemed likely to be the critical moment.

[1] Giolitti, *Discorsi extraparlamentari*, p. 336.
[2] Répaci, II, pp. 60–3.
[3] ibid., pp. 88–9.
[4] Badoglio had resigned his post of chief of staff in February 1921 but was a leading member of the Army Council. He was widely quoted at the time as saying, 'Fascism will crumble at the first shot', but publicly denied it. V. Vailati, *Badoglio racconta* (Turin 1955), pp. 254–5; Tasca, p. 397; Pini and Susmel, II, pp. 217–18; Répaci, II, pp. 302, 380.
[5] *Il Popolo d'Italia*, 14 October. Mussolini, XVIII, pp. 443–4, 560–1.
[6] Répaci, I, pp. 466–8; Soleri, p. 150.

Facta had decided not to ban it and Riccio, as Minister for Public Works, had authorised the transport of the 30,000 delegates from every part of Italy to Naples by special trains. Police reinforcements, with troops in reserve, guarded the central and suburban stations of Rome while the delegates were passing through and made sure that they carried no arms; and in order to reduce the chances of the congress developing into insurrection, it was arranged that as many as possible of the returning trains should be routed to avoid the capital. On the 23rd Facta was able to assure the King that all precautions had been taken and that the military authorities were confident of preventing any penetration into Rome.[1]

On 24 October the fascists assembled in congress at Naples, to show the flag in the hitherto indifferent south. In a speech before the city's leading citizens in the San Carlo opera house, Mussolini praised the monarchy and the army and declared that his aim was to infuse new life, that of the war generation, into the old liberal state. Then came the threats: Facta had forced him into insurrection and now it was a question of force; fascism would not enter the government by the service door but demanded, as a minimum, five cabinet portfolios including the Foreign Ministry.[2] That evening Mussolini announced at a march past of 60,000 party members and sympathisers that it was now a matter of days, if not hours, and the blackshirts responded with shouts of 'To Rome!' The central committee of the party decided that the militia should mobilise at midnight on 27/28 October and take over public buildings in the towns. On the morning of the 28th three columns would assemble at points sixteen to forty-five miles by rail north-west, north and east of Rome and move simultaneously on the capital.[3] The quadrumvirs were to set up their headquarters at Perugia. Clashes with the army were to be avoided if possible, but all resistance was to be overcome and Rome reached at all costs. On the 25th the party leaders left Naples to organise the mobilisation, leaving Bianchi behind to wind up the now purposeless congress. Mussolini returned to Milan to watch and wait from his editor's desk.

Even now, with the military machine in motion, Mussolini kept the negotiations going. On the 25th the indefatigable Lusignoli visited D'Annunzio, hoping to secure the poet's help in bringing Giolitti and Mussolini together. This overture from 'the man of the naval gun' had a startling effect. D'Annunzio, his eyes now apparently opened to the fact that the politicians were exploiting him, that same day theatrically can-

[1] Répaci, I, pp. 438–9, 467, II, p. 63.
[2] Mussolini, XVIII, pp. 453–9.
[3] The assembly points were Santa Marinella, 45 miles north-west of Rome on the main line from Pisa; Monterotondo, 16 miles north on the main line from Florence; and Tivoli, 25 miles east on the line from Pescara.

celled his promise to attend the Rome rally and so finally abdicated leadership of the 'national revolution'.[1]

Lusignoli nevertheless persevered. On the 26th he saw Mussolini and Giolitti, and on the 27th Mussolini again. In the course of these days Mussolini received at the *Popolo d'Italia* office Silvio Crespi, Ettore Conti, Gino Olivetti, Alberto Pirelli and other leading industrialists, with whom he had been in touch for some weeks. He calmed their anxiety about the financial and economic situation and assured them that 'the aim of the imminent fascist action is the restoration of discipline, especially in the factories'.[2] He also sent a reassuring message to Nitti, kept contact with Salandra, whom he had met in Rome on his way to the Naples congress, and even authorised Bianchi to make yet another offer to Facta, which the latter immediately rejected, of fascist participation in a reconstructed Facta government.[3] Meanwhile in Rome where the political crisis was now to be precipitated, De Vecchi, Grandi and Ciano were on hand to take part in the discussions and if necessary accept a parliamentary solution.[4] All doors were to be left open until the last moment.

The first reaction of the government to the proceedings in Naples had been one of relief. All had passed off quietly, Facta reported to the King on the afternoon of the 25th, and the danger of a march on Rome seemed to be over.[5] His optimism was short-lived. The political crisis broke early next day. De Vecchi and Ciano asked Salandra to inform the King that an immediate change of government was essential if the insurrection, due to begin in two days, was to be prevented. After consulting Federzoni and Orlando, Salandra called on Facta and pressed him to resign at once. Riccio, who accompanied Salandra, threatened to bring down the government by himself if his colleagues would not act with him. Salandra's object was to pave the way for a conservative–fascist coalition which would forestall both a march on Rome and Giolitti's return to power. Facta, still hoping for a Giolitti–Mussolini agreement, telephoned to Lusignoli, but

---

[1] Répaci, I, pp. 398–400. Répaci shows that it was not the Mussolini–Giulietti seamen's pact that made D'Annunzio change his mind. But a wholly satisfactory explanation of D'Annunzio's behaviour remains to be found.

[2] Rossi, *I padroni del vapore*, pp. 37–40.

[3] Répaci, I, pp. 419–20, 475–7. Répaci convincingly demonstrates the falsity of the allegations that Facta hoped to stay in power with fascist support and deceived Giolitti in order to keep him away from Rome.

[4] As Pini and Susmel, II, pp. 233–6, point out, the behaviour of Grandi in October 1922 was in strange contrast to his behaviour a year earlier: then he had been the intransigent, anti-constitutional extremist, now he was the fervent supporter of a peaceful compromise. In their eagerness to make a march on Rome superfluous, he and De Vecchi may well have exceeded their mandate from Mussolini.

[5] Répaci, II, p. 67.

got no firm news.[1] At 4 p.m. the cabinet met. Facta proposed resignation; Alessio, Soleri, Taddei and two others objected and urged resistance to insurrection. After three hours of argument a compromise was reached: the ministers placed their portfolios at Facta's disposal and left it to him to resign or not. While Riccio kept the fascists informed through Salandra, Facta summoned the King and Giolitti urgently to Rome. Next day, the 27th, the fascists kept up the pressure by a series of private messages and press interviews. When the cabinet met in the afternoon, a majority of ministers pressed their resignations. In spite of this, military precautions were intensified. General Pugliese assured Facta of the loyalty of the troops under his command. Taddei then gave orders that if trains of fascists should attempt to reach the capital, they should be stopped at check points at a distance of fifty to seventy miles, before they reached their rendezvous, by blocking the lines if necessary and in the last resort by the use of arms.[2]

The King reached Rome at 8 p.m. on the 27th from his country estate near Pisa. He was in an irritated and impatient mood. Rather than appoint a prime minister under threat of violence, he declared, 'I'll retire into the country with my wife and son.'[3] On being informed of the defensive measures already taken, he expressed full approval. At 9 p.m. Facta went to the royal residence. He had heard on the phone from Lusignoli that the Giolitti–Mussolini negotiations were still hanging fire, and so felt obliged to offer his resignation. But after a brief conversation, he and the King agreed that Rome must be defended. On leaving, Facta ordered preparations to be made for a state of siege. The insurrection had meanwhile started prematurely. In Florence, Pisa and Cremona the *squadre* went into action before the arranged hour. During the night of 27/28 October the fascists took over most of northern and central Italy. Prefectures, town halls, railway stations and post offices were seized, usually with the complicity of prefects and local authorities. The civil power of the state crumbled away.[4]

As reports of these events flowed in to Rome, it became clear that extreme measures could not be avoided. As 12.30 a.m. on 28 October the military authorities were made responsible for public order throughout the country. Two hours later Facta paid another visit to the King. He took with him the draft of a manifesto to the Italian people in which the government announced its 'supreme duty to defend the state at all cost,

---

[1] Salandra, *Memorie*, pp. 19–21; Ferraris, pp. 79–80.

[2] ibid., pp. 94–5; Répaci, II, pp. 330–3. Five check points were established, at Civitavecchia, Viterbo, Orte, Avezzano and Sezze. In passing on Taddei's order to the commanders at these points, Pugliese was even more precise: the lines were to be blocked after exactly 300 fascists had passed through.

[3] Répaci, I, pp. 503–4.

[4] Ferraris, pp. 95–6.

by all means and against all who violate its laws'.[1] Victor Emmanuel gave it his approval. Facta then returned to the Ministry of Interior which, he declared defiantly, he would never leave alive.[2] At 5 a.m. the cabinet met. The news of insurrection had strengthened the position of the ministers who favoured resistance. Even Riccio, exasperated by the fascist resort to illegality, demanded the sternest measures. The meeting was attended by the King's A.D.C., General Cittadini, who announced that Victor Emmanuel would abdicate if a state of siege were not proclaimed. The cabinet decided unanimously that this was its duty, even though it had resigned. Facta sent a Popular colleague to sound Sturzo, who promised his party's support. Taddei instructed Pugliese to 'ensure the defence of the capital by all available means and prevent at any cost the entry of the fascist *squadre* into the city'.[3] At 7.10 prefects and military commanders were ordered to use all means to prevent the seizure of public buildings and to 'arrest immediately, without exception, the leaders and promoters of the insurrection'. At 7.50 the announcement of a state of siege from midday was telegraphed to prefectures throughout Italy and at 8.30 the government's manifesto was being posted in the streets of Rome.[4]

The government's orders for the defence of the capital were meticulously carried out. At three of the five check points, trains full of fascists attempted to pass through; they were halted and the lines blocked. Deprived of rail transport, some of the *squadristi* continued towards their rendezvous on foot; the majority waited passively in and around the stations for further orders. Four hundred policemen were sufficient to halt 20,000 men, the main body of the marchers, when they were still fifty miles or more from the capital.[5] On the morning of the 28th, at the moment when the march was intended to begin, about 9,000 men had joined the three columns; but only two of these, with 5,000 men between them, had reached their assembly points at Tivoli and Monterotondo, the third column being blocked at Civitavecchia. All were ill-armed and lacked food, shelter and motor transport; their spirits were depressed by torrential rain. The reserve column of 4,000 men at Foligno had arms for only 300 until well into the following day.[6] Communication between the

---

[1] Répaci, II, pp. 76–7.

[2] Facta, perhaps for the only time in his life, was displaying truly Piedmontese pugnacity. 'If they want to come here, they will have to carry me away in pieces', he told his *chef de cabinet*. Répaci, I, pp. 507–8; Ferraris, p. 97.

[3] ibid., p. 100; Répaci, II, p. 338.

[4] Ferraris, pp. 100–3; Répaci, II, pp. 340–4.

[5] ibid., I, pp. 527–8, 566.

[6] The estimates of the numbers involved in the march on Rome vary greatly. The above figures are taken from Répaci, I, pp. 481–7, the most thorough study of the question that has yet appeared.

columns was precarious and the quadrumvirs at Perugia never exercised
the smallest degree of control over the operation. In Rome bridges and
key points were blocked by barbed-wire barriers, the royal residence and
public buildings were guarded, public transport closed down and the
office of the Rome Fascio was occupied and searched. Pugliese had 28,000
troops and police under his command. In addition, many army reservists
applied to assist in the defence of Rome, while the nationalists, rallying to
the monarchy in spite of their pro-fascist sympathies, mobilised 4,000 of
their blueshirts and placed them at the disposal of the authorities.[1]

Outside Rome the fascist position was in few places secure. Key cities
like Turin, Genoa and Bologna were firmly under military control. In
Milan the military commander was notoriously pro-fascist and Lusignoli,
still hoping for a political solution satisfactory to Mussolini, ignored the
more drastic orders from Rome. Nevertheless the city was not in fascist
hands and Mussolini could leave the barricaded office of *Il Popolo d'Italia*
only with the tolerance of the army. In Perugia, the headquarters of the
quadrumvirs, and in Florence, where the fascists had successfully seized
key buildings during the night of the 27th/28th, the military commanders
were preparing next day to mount a counter-attack and recover control.
At midday on the 28th, even though large parts of central Italy and the Po
valley had been overrun, the prospects of the insurrection were bleak.[2]

At 9 a.m. on 28 October Facta drove to the palace to obtain the King's
formal signature to the state of siege. Victor Emmanuel refused to sign.
Between 5 a.m. and 9 a.m. he had changed his mind. His reasons are still
a subject for speculation.[3] It is likely that those whom he consulted, including senior generals, exaggerated fascist strength[4] and urged him not
to put the army's loyalty to the test.[5] It is certain that he shrank from

[1] Répaci, I, pp. 272–6, II, pp. 405–6. Loyalty to the crown came first even for
those who, like Federzoni and Raffaele Paolucci, had been assiduous advocates of
a conservative–fascist coalition. Some fascists reacted in the same way. De Vecchi
told Paolucci that if a state of siege were declared, he would join the nationalists
on the side of the King.

[2] For details of the military situation throughout the country, see Répaci, I, pp.
529–42.

[3] For a critical examination of the conflicting evidence and hypotheses regarding
the King's actions and motives, see Répaci, I, pp. 514–24, 589–97.

[4] In 1945–8 Victor Emmanuel stated that he had been told that the fascists had
100,000 men (against 5,000 to 8,000 police and troops), but had afterwards learnt
from Mussolini that there were only 30,000. Even this last figure was a gross
exaggeration. The King never enquired from Pugliese who was in command and
in the best position to know. Répaci, I, p. 515.

[5] One version (Ferraris, pp. 143–4; Répaci, II, p. 386) states that the King
asked Diaz and General Pecori Giraldi during the night what the army would do,
and received the reply: 'The army will do its duty, but it would be better not to

bloodshed; perhaps, also, he was reluctant to resort to the same extreme measures that had brought an assassin's vengeance upon his father. Nervousness about the Duke of Aosta, who had moved to the neighbour-hood of Perugia, perhaps to be near the quadrumvirs, may have played its part.[1] Whatever his motives, Facta was unable to shake him. 'One of us two must sacrifice himself', Victor Emmanuel declared; to which Facta replied, 'Your Majesty need not say which of us it must be.'[2]

At 9.30 a.m. Facta returned to his cabinet, pale and shaken.[3] One course of action only remained. At eleven he went back to the palace to place his resignation formally in the King's hands. At 11.30 an official press com-muniqué announced that the state of siege had been countermanded. The fascists drew breath again. The King went through the usual procedure of political consultations. Among those whom he saw during the day were De Nicola, president of the chamber, Cocco-Ortu, the senior crown councillor, Salandra and finally De Vecchi, hastily summoned from Perugia. De Nicola and Cocco-Ortu urged the King to wait for Giolitti to reach Rome,[4] and Cocco-Ortu exhorted him to assert his authority and save the constitution he had inherited from his great-grandfather. But it was clear to them that Victor Emmanuel had already made up his mind. At 6 p.m. he asked Salandra, his ally of May 1915, to form a government. Salandra accepted, though sceptical of his chances, on condition that Mussolini consented to serve with him.[5]

Mussolini had been kept well informed of events in Rome. In addition

---

put it to the test.' This story cannot be exactly accurate. Diaz was in Florence on the night of the 27th/28th and communications were cut; if this was his opinion, he cannot have expressed it in the critical period between 5 and 9 a.m. on the 28th.

[1] The evidence with regard to the Duke of Aosta's intentions is conflicting. Though it is difficult to believe that he would have actively abetted rebellion, it is still possible that the King was influenced by gossip or fabricated rumours. On one of the very rare occasions in later life on which Facta referred to these events, he told his daughter that at the 9 a.m. interview on the 28th the King kept repeating, 'C'è il Duca d'Aosta, c'è il Duca d'Aosta.' Répaci, II, pp. 401–2.

[2] ibid., p. 402 (evidence of Facta's daughter).

[3] Some members of the cabinet, including Soleri and Taddei, had the impression that Facta had declined to press the King, or even advised him not to sign. The evidence now available shows that their suspicions were unjustified.

[4] Giolitti had received yet another summons from Facta, in the name of the King, at 5 a.m. on the 28th. Later that day Facta and Soleri sent him a message through the prefect of Turin, greatly regretting that he was not on hand in Rome for the negotiations. Giolitti decided to take the night train on the 28th; but by that time the line had been interrupted, and he never left Turin. Répaci, II, pp. 150–2; Valeri, Da Giolitti a Mussolini, pp. 174–5.

[5] Salandra, Memorie, pp. 23–4. Victor Emmanuel told Salandra, 'I've read in an English book that men fall into two categories, parasols for the good days and umbrellas for the bad; you belong to the second, more honourable category.'

to reports from his lieutenants, De Vecchi, Grandi and Ciano, he received
telephone messages from Federzoni and from Salandra, to whom Riccio
passed on the latest inside news from the cabinet. In spite of a succession
of urgent appeals to come south, Mussolini stayed obstinately in Milan.
He preferred to remain free until the last moment. His apparent readiness
to compromise alarmed Bianchi, who twice telephoned in the night of the
26th/27th to implore him to 'say no' to all offers.[1] During the 27th and
28th Rome was skilfully kept guessing: according to one report he was
ready to clinch the negotiations with Giolitti, according to others he preferred Salandra or Orlando as colleagues. But as soon as he heard that the
state of siege had been cancelled, he raised his terms. When General
Cittadini, the King's A.D.C., begged him on the phone at 5.10 p.m. on
the 28th to come immediately to Rome, he replied that he would come
only if invited to form a government.[2] De Vecchi meanwhile spent the
rest of the day in the palace, 'a leader of the besiegers in the heart of the
fortress'.[3] At 11 p.m. he, Grandi and Ciano reached agreement with
Salandra on a coalition in which the fascists should have four cabinet
posts. But when the good news was telephoned at 1.25 a.m. to Milan,
Mussolini rejected the proposal. He agreed with Bianchi and the militant
blackshirts that it had not been worth mobilising merely for four seats in a
Salandra cabinet.[4] Nor were the fascists alone in regarding Salandra's
proposal as inadequate. Albertini was pressing for the immediate appointment of Mussolini as prime minister, believing he could be more easily
influenced in a moderate direction in Rome than in Milan. This was also
the opinion of leading Milanese business men like Crespi, Conti and
Olivetti who, gathered in the prefecture, made sure that 'the voice of the
world of industry reached the King'. The fascists, they declared, would
accept no compromise and if bloodshed was to be avoided, speed was
essential.[5] Next morning, after once again consulting his friends in Milan
on the phone, Salandra reported to the King that he had failed and that
Mussolini was the only possible prime minister. At 8.30 p.m. on 29 October
the latter caught the night train to Rome. Thirty-six hours later his
government was formed.

[1] Ferraris, pp. 87–90; Répaci, II, pp. 325–7.
[2] Ferraris, p. 115; Répaci, II, p. 346.
[3] Salandra, *Memorie*, p. 23.
[4] It has been argued that, left to himself, Mussolini might have accepted Salandra's offer. While it is not impossible that he was wavering up to the last minute,
the weight of evidence suggests that he had made up his mind to be prime minister.
On the afternoon of the 28th he had his own cabinet list ready and an uncompromising leader written for next morning's *Popolo d'Italia*. Pini and Susmel, II,
pp. 246–9; Tasca, pp. 435–7, 499.
[5] Ferraris, pp. 122–3; Salandra, *Memorie*, pp. 24–5; Rossi, *I padroni del vapore*,
pp. 37–41; Répaci, II, pp. 354, 370–1.

While the politicians negotiated, the wet and hungry blackshirt columns awaited orders. The army made no attempt, once the state of siege had been cancelled, to reoccupy the cities and buildings which the fascists had seized; but Rome remained under military control. Towards the evening of the 28th the streets filled and victory celebrations began. At 10.30 p.m. the War Ministry issued an order that bloodshed was to be avoided and only persuasion used to prevent the blackshirts' advance. On the morning of the 30th, with Mussolini already inside the city, composing his cabinet, the columns were at last allowed to march on Rome. They moved partly on foot, partly by lorry, but mostly by special trains. Fighting in the working-class district of San Lorenzo caused thirteen deaths, but the army quickly restored order. Success had swollen the blackshirt ranks to 40,000 and by the time they were ordered to evacuate the city, they numbered nearly 70,000. For six hours on the 31st they marched past the Quirinal palace, where the King took the salute between Diaz and Thaon di Revel, then on to Mussolini's hotel to acclaim the new Prime Minister. They were a disorderly rabble, dressed in a mixture of muddied uniforms, armed with rifles and shotguns, whips, daggers and bludgeons. Amongst them marched many officers and soldiers and several bemedalled generals.[1] It was a victory march, of no political significance, for power had already been won without resort to force. As Mussolini himself later commented, it had been 'a new-style revolution',[2] carried out not by the impotent high command in Perugia but from an editor's desk in Milan. With good reason an old prelate, who had watched the Italian army march in fifty-two years before, remarked as he observed the scene, 'We in 1870 defended Rome better.'[3]

[1] Soleri, p. 155, comments with disgust on the spectacle of General Capello dressed up and behaving like 'a South American general'.
[2] Pini and Susmel, II, p. 253.
[3] Salvemini, *Fascist Dictatorship*, p. 158.

# 14
# The Fascist Triumph
## 1922-5

## The Months of Illusion

Mussolini arrived in Rome at 10.50 a.m. on 30 October. 'In a few hours', he announced, 'the nation will have not just an administration; it will have a government.'[1] Twenty-five minutes later he was with the King. 'Your Majesty,' he told him, 'I bring you the Italy of Vittorio Veneto.' He worked fast. By the evening of the 31st the cabinet was complete. It was a broad-based coalition in which the extreme right predominated. Like Giolitti in his prime, Mussolini chose his ministers as individuals, not as party delegates. No one of those whom he invited declined or laid down conditions.[2] Mussolini himself took the Foreign Ministry and the Ministry of Interior. The service ministries were given to Diaz and Thaon di Revel and the philosopher Giovanni Gentile became Minister of Education. Besides these the cabinet included one nationalist (Federzoni), two right-wing Popolari, four assorted liberals and four fascists.[3]

On 16 November Mussolini addressed the reassembled chamber with a characteristic mixture of blandishment and menace. He declared:

> The revolution has its rights . . . I have refused to exploit my victory to the limit, as I could have done . . . With 300,000 young men armed to the teeth . . . I could have punished all who have defamed Fascism and tried to be-spatter it with mud. I could have turned this dingy, grey chamber into a

[1] Mussolini, XVIII, p. 471.
[2] Though Mussolini assured the Popolari that he contemplated no attack on proportional representation. Jacini, *Storia*, p. 149.
[3] The liberals consisted of one Salandrian, one Giolittian and two demo-sociali (including Di Cesarò). Seven of the fifteen under-secretaries were fascist. Mussolini had included the liberal economist, Einaudi, and Baldesi of the C.G.L. in his original list. Einaudi never received an invitation; Baldesi accepted but was later dropped because of the objections of Mussolini's big business allies. Many fascists were disgusted with the non-fascist character and tone of the cabinet. One of the fascist ministers, Giuriati, commented, 'I never thought it would take a revolution to make me buy myself a top hat.' Tamaro, I, pp. 271-4.

billet for my battalions . . . I could have closed up parliament and formed an exclusively Fascist government. I could have, but I did not wish to, at least at this early stage.

The constitution, he continued, would be respected and there would be no fascist illegality; but the chamber must adapt itself to the national conscience or disappear.[1] The deputies expressed their confidence by 306 to 116 votes and a week later gave the government one year's plenary powers, to carry out fiscal and administrative reforms and 'reduce the functions of the state'. The senate followed suit on the 29th by 196 votes to 19.

For the next eighteen months only one political issue mattered: Would fascist illegality continue or would Mussolini govern constitutionally? Would there be revolution or 'normalisation'? Outwardly there had so far been no revolution, but merely a change of ministry in which the King, the outgoing Prime Minister and the political leaders had played their accustomed part. It was true that parliament had been totally ignored, but there had been extra-parliamentary crises before 1922 and the constitution had survived. Yet behind the constitutional façade it was the threat of armed insurrection that had carried Mussolini to power. During the negotiations of October, Salandra's aim had been to legalise the fascist bid for power and to save appearances.[2] In this, together with the King and Facta, he was successful; and indeed in politics appearances can be important.[3] But little else than appearances had been saved.

For the moment, however, few Italians were willing to see this. Mussolini could count on widespread goodwill. Most of the press was benevolent. D'Annunzio generously acknowledged the fascist triumph and withdrew into melancholy solitude. Salandra and the conservatives were enthusiastic; other liberal elder statesmen were at least willing to wait and see. The King and the non-fascist ministers were regarded as sufficient guarantee of constitutional rectitude. Nitti decided that the fascist experiment must be allowed to take its course undisturbed; 'I cannot give my support, but I do not wish to oppose in any way.'[4] Albertini, speaking in the senate as 'an intransigent constitutionalist, an impenitent liberal', implored Mussolini not to abuse his victory, not to be tempted by dictatorship, but voted for him and wished him success in restoring legality and the authority of the state.[5] Giolitti might have doubts in private; but, as he wrote to Sforza, 'As regards myself, I think I ought to give an appearance of hoping for the

[1] Mussolini, XIX, pp. 17, 22, 27.

[2] Salandra, *Memorie*, p. 29.

[3] As events in 1943 showed. The King could not have removed Mussolini so smoothly from power had not some of the appearances of the constitution been preserved in 1922 and subsequent years.

[4] Nitti to Amendola, 23 April 1923. Alatri, *Origini*, pp. 34–5.

[5] Speech of 26 November 1922. Albertini, *In difesa della libertà*, pp. 39–48.

best. Who knows? Parliament may impart wisdom to Mussolini: at least he is a deputy, unlike Sturzo.'[1] He therefore publicly announced his support for 'the only government that could restore social peace', and after the speech of 16 November merely remarked that the chamber had now got the government it deserved.[2]

Mussolini meanwhile announced that his government would be 'a government of speed'. He himself set an example by working long hours in his office. Every branch of the administration was stirred into activity. Senior civil servants were charmed by his enthusiasm for administrative detail and flattered themselves that they had a promising pupil who, unlike his predecessors, would get things done. In the first months after the march on Rome the prevailing sentiment was relief that Italy once again had a government that could govern.

In February 1923 conservative opinion was gratified by the fusion of the Fascist and Nationalist parties. Immediately before and after the march on Rome there had been a sudden increase in membership of the Nationalist party, particularly in the south. To become a nationalist and profess fervent loyalty to the monarchy was the safest way of opposing fascism. For a time the old faction fights of the south took the form of rivalry, and sometimes physical violence, between fascists and nationalists. Mussolini decided to end this friction by imposing fusion, in spite of the fears of radicals like Bianchi that fascism would be adulterated by monarchist and socially reactionary influences. The future was to prove these fears justified. The gain to the Fascist party was an immediate rise in its social standing and intellectual ability and, some years later, the acquisition of a 'philosophy'.

Mussolini's deference to the church also made a most favourable impression. Within a few weeks of the march on Rome crucifixes reappeared in schools and law courts, at the Vatican's request. The next two years brought the church substantial benefits. Compulsory religious instruction in elementary schools, abolished in 1877, was restored; it was henceforth to be 'the principal foundation of public education'. The penalties for blasphemy were increased. Priests' and bishops' stipends were raised by doubling the state's contribution. Priests and theological students were exempted from military service and military chaplains were appointed. Giolitti's bill for the compulsory registration of stocks and shares, already much diluted, was dropped. Mussolini also revived his old feud with the freemasons. Though leading masons had contributed handsomely to Fascist party funds before the march on Rome, it was decided in February 1923 that membership of a masonic order was incompatible with member-

[1] Sforza, *Contemporary Italy*, p. 136. See also Ansaldo, pp. 498–500.
[2] Valeri, *Da Giolitti a Mussolini*, pp. 179–80.

ship of the party.[1] Most effective of all in winning the church's goodwill
was Gentile's educational reform of 1923, which established the single
state examination, one of the key points in the Popular party's programme,
and gave private secondary schools academic parity with state schools.
Meanwhile in January 1923 Mussolini secretly met Cardinal Gasparri in
person. The two men agreed that while the time was not ripe for a full
discussion of the Roman question, relations between the government and
the Vatican should be improved. Gasparri asked for help for the Banco di
Roma, which was facing a critical situation, and Mussolini agreed to save
it from collapse.[2] Shortly afterwards a Jesuit priest, Tacchi Venturi, became the regular intermediary between Mussolini and the Vatican. Mussolini made a good impression. He 'has assured us that he is a good Catholic,
and that the Holy See has nothing to fear from him', Gasparri told the
Belgian ambassador to the Vatican; he might have much to learn in religious matters, but he must be given time.[3]

There was no sudden, dramatic attack on the constitution; Mussolini
preferred erosion. The Fascist party tightened its grip over the civil
service, the judiciary and local government. At the end of 1922 an amnesty
was declared for 'offences committed for national ends'. The cabinet
authorised Mussolini to deal toughly with 'disturbers of the peace', which
could mean any opposition. Prefects were given greater control over
working-class organisations. In July 1923 the government gave itself
powers by decree, but for the moment kept them in reserve, to limit
freedom of the press, which now survived by grace of Mussolini alone.
'Fascism has already trampled on the more or less decomposed corpse of
the goddess Liberty', Mussolini wrote in March 1923, 'and if necessary it

[1] Many leading fascists, including Ciano, Balbo, Rossoni, De Bono, Farinacci,
Acerbo and Cesare Rossi were masons. The order to sever their masonic connexions was not, however, strictly enforced at this stage. A very few masons,
notably General Capello, resigned from the Fascist party.

[2] De Rosa, *I conservatori nazionali*, pp. 114–15. The price of the government's
help was the replacement of the bank's chairman, Senator Santucci, in whose
house Mussolini and Gasparri had met, and its managing director by nominees
of the Minister of Finance, De Stefani. De Rosa suggests (chapter 3) that De
Stefani and the Fascist party were interested in getting control of the bank, partly
because they believed, wrongly, that it financed the Popular party, partly because
of its close relationship with the network of Catholic rural banks, cooperatives
etc.

[3] Beyens, pp. 136–9. Mussolini was never 'a good Catholic', but after becoming
Prime Minister he went through some of the motions. He and Rachele Guidi had
lived as man and wife since 1910 but became legally married only in December
1915, five years after the birth of their first child. In April 1923 he had his first
three children, Edda, Vittorio and Bruno, baptised. In December 1925 he and
Rachele were married in church.

will calmly do so again.'[1] He plainly intended to stay in power, by force
if necessary. Popular consent was desirable but he could do without it.
The victory of fascism was irreversible, he declared; the old ruling class
and the old parties were finished and would be replaced by the generation
of the trenches, the new aristocracy of Italy. The revolution would develop
in stages and 'the second wave' was on its way. As for parliament, it was
reduced to almost total impotence. The government paid it less and less
attention, preferring to legislate by decree. In February 1923 Mussolini
vetoed a debate on a socialist motion of censure on the ground that 'there
is nothing to discuss in matters of internal policy; what happens, happens
by my precise, direct will and according to my explicit orders'.[2]

Two significant innovations were the creation of the Fascist Grand
Council and the permanent establishment of a militia of 300,000 men. The
Grand Council, which first met in December 1922, was Mussolini's
personal creation, responsible to himself alone. It consisted of the party
executive, the Fascist ministers and under-secretaries, the chief of police,
the leaders of the Fascist syndicates and cooperatives, the commander-in-
chief and general staff of the militia and such other party notabilities as the
Council chose to co-opt.[3] Mussolini described it as 'an essentially political
organ', thereby implying that the framing of high policy was its concern,
while the cabinet dealt merely with administration.

The militia[4] was created to give the *squadre* a military organisation and
provide for their maintenance at the public expense. Mussolini also probably hoped to reduce the power of the *ras* by centralised control. De Bono
was the first commander-in-chief. The importance of the militia was enhanced by the abolition in January 1923 of Nitti's creation, the Guardia
Regia. It was to be the main instrument of revolution, under Mussolini's
personal control, and took no oath of allegiance to the King. 'Whoever
touches the militia will get a dose of lead', Mussolini declared. If normalisation meant no militia, then there would be no normalisation.[5]

Mussolini's old tactical skill did not forsake him. Threats and brutal
frankness alternated with statesmanlike pronouncements. 'Sometimes it is
tactically necessary to make adjustments', he told the senate in June 1923;
'but political strategy – mine at least – is intransigent and absolute.'[6] He
admitted that his innovations were changing the constitution but appealed
to the example of the greatest innovator of all, Cavour.[7] Sometimes he
would talk of the militia as 'essentially Fascist'; on other occasions he would
tell his audience that the militia was a national, not a party, institution, and

---

[1] Mussolini, XIX, p. 196.     [2] ibid., p. 129.     [3] Salvatorelli and Mira, p. 185.
[4] Its official title was Milizia Volontaria per la Sicurezza Nazionale (M.V.S.N.).
Many army officers resented it as a rival and no doubt remembered that in 1861
Garibaldi's legions had been disbanded and absorbed in the regular army.
[5] Mussolini, XX, pp. 164, 175.   [6] ibid., XIX, p. 262.   [7] ibid., XIX, pp. 257–8.

invite it to recognise the 'historical and idealist continuity' between Garibaldi's legions and the blackshirts.[1] Conservatives and most liberals were at first only too ready to be reassured by such exercises of his imagination.

It was by the brilliant use of these tactics that he secured the reform of the electoral system. The fascists had won only thirty-five seats in 1921. They intended to leave nothing to chance next time. The problem was to ensure that the party remained permanently in power without alienating non-fascist sympathisers. A bill drafted by Giacomo Acerbo, one of the ablest of the fascist under-secretaries, provided the answer: the whole country would be treated as a single constituency and the electoral list that polled the greatest number of votes, provided this was over 25% of the total, would win two-thirds of the seats; the remaining one-third would be distributed among the other lists by proportional representation.

Since the King, to Mussolini's annoyance, refused to promulgate Acerbo's reform by decree, it had to be submitted to parliament. For a few weeks the chamber shook off its apathy and the government was forced to look to its majority. Mussolini argued in defence of the bill that it would replace unstable coalitions by a government resting on a solid majority. This was an argument well designed to appeal to conservatives and it made some impression even on the Popolari, the champions of proportional representation. A special commission, of which Giolitti was chairman and only two fascists were members, approved the bill by a large majority, mainly for fear of the consequences of rejection. On 10 July the parliamentary debate began. Rome was full of blackshirts, the Fascist press promised the 'second wave' if the chamber failed to do its duty and the tension recalled the days of May 1915 and October 1922. Mussolini made the most parliamentary speech of his career, welcoming amendments and appealing for cooperation.[2] The debate that followed was largely confined to technical details. This, as Mussolini had intended, divided the opposition. On 15 July the bill was carried on its second reading by 235 votes to 139 (mostly socialists and communists), with 77 abstentions (mostly Popolari). During the detailed discussion of the bill's clauses, the government's majority on one occasion dropped to 21, but the final voting was 223 to 123. There were defections from nearly all the opposition groups. As Turati observed, many were 'afraid of winning'.[3] In November the bill passed through the senate in a single sitting. It was now certain that the fascists and their allies would have at least 356 seats out of 535 in the next chamber. Mussolini had won one of his most brilliant political victories.

Meanwhile the business and industrial world was well content. On

---

[1] ibid., XIX, pp. 97, 254–5; XX, pp. 136, 164, 175.
[2] ibid., XIX, pp. 317–20.          [3] Turati–Kuliscioff, VI, p. 97.

31 October 1922 Confindustria pledged its loyal collaboration with the new government, the product of 'the youthful forces of the Nation', for 'the economic rebirth' of Italy. A fortnight later Mussolini showed his appreciation by borrowing three of the industrialists' favourite words to describe his programme: 'Economy, Work, Discipline'. Turati was justified in observing that it was the voice of Confindustria that spoke from the government benches.[1] Industrialists dismissed any fears of dictatorship that Mussolini's parliamentary manner might have aroused with the thought that strong government was needed, both at home and abroad, and that there was 'no need to be afraid of words'.[2] Mussolini repeatedly declared that the state must 'renounce its economic functions' and allow private enterprise free play. 'All this is classical liberalism of the purest and most authentic stamp', commented Einaudi.[3] Mussolini kept his word. Armed with the plenary powers voted by parliament, he set about pruning the machinery of state. The telephone system was handed over to private enterprise on highly favourable terms. The state monopoly of life insurance, created by Giolitti in 1912, was ended. Rent control was abolished, the civil service cut down and the personnel of the railways reduced by 16%. The Ministry of Labour was suppressed and the partially elected Supreme Labour Council replaced by a nominated body. A bill for compulsory unemployment insurance was dropped. All the land reforms sponsored by the Popolari were shelved. Most of Giolitti's radical fiscal measures of 1920, which Mussolini had praised at the time, were cancelled. Death duties were reduced[4] and the commission of enquiry into war profiteering, set up by Giolitti in 1920, was hurriedly wound up. The limits of Mussolini's 'classical liberalism' were also significant. Many of the tariffs of 1921 were raised and a campaign for self-sufficiency in wheat was launched. Public funds were used to reconstruct the firm of Ansaldo, to complete the liquidation of the Banca Italiana di Sconto and to rescue the Banco di Roma when it was on the verge of disaster.[5] From every point of view the business and propertied classes had reason to be grateful.

[1] Rossi, *I padroni del vapore*, pp. 40–4, 183.

[2] ibid., p. 184, quoting from the diary of Senator Ettore Conti, a magnate of the electrical industry and a past president of Confindustria.

[3] L. Einaudi, *Cronache economiche e politiche di un trentennio*, VI (Turin 1963), p. 962. But Einaudi, veteran free trader and future President of the Italian Republic, was very soon to become one of the most resolute of liberal anti-fascists.

[4] Revenue from death duties (millions of lire) fell from 305 in 1922–3 to 117 in 1924–5 and 72 in 1925–6. Rossi, *I padroni del vapore*, p. 62.

[5] Ernesto Rossi (in *I padroni del vapore*, ch. 6) justly describes this process as 'the socialisation of losses'. The Banco di Roma had greatly expanded its activities during and after the war, making risky investments in industry at home and in commercial ventures abroad, and was shaken by the crash of the Banca Italiana di Sconto in 1921. Romeo, p. 98; De Rosa, *I conservatori nazionali*, pp. 103–6, 117–20.

Before the march on Rome the leaders of industry had one cause for anxiety: the advocacy by certain sections of the Fascist party, and notably by Rossoni, secretary of the Fascist trade unions, of 'integral syndicalism'. The integral syndicalists called for the compulsory reorganisation of each branch of industry into managers', technicians' and workmen's syndicates, under a coordinating syndicate which would be responsible for preventing conflict between them. The employers did not object to the regimentation of their workers in the interests of production, but had no desire to be so regimented themselves. Mussolini soon allayed their fears. In November 1923 the Fascist Grand Council recognised Confindustria as the sole representative of the industrialists. Next month Mussolini presided over a meeting at Palazzo Chigi, the new seat of the Foreign Ministry, of leaders of the party, Confindustria and the Fascist unions. It decided to set up a permanent commission of five representatives of the employers and five of the unions to improve relations between management and labour and promote class collaboration. Rossoni was told that there was no place for integral syndicalism in industry. Olivetti, secretary of Confindustria, welcomed this formation of a 'united industrial front'. The agreement left Confindustria untouched and in return for its loyal collaboration, which was given, assured it privileges and power that would have been unthinkable in Giolitti's day.[1]

The policy of the Minister of Finance, Alberto De Stefani, was also wholly acceptable to the business world. De Stefani, formerly a liberal professor of economics, had become the Fascist party's chief economist. In the cabinet he vigorously and successfully opposed Rossoni's schemes to 'substitute the syndicate for the government'.[2] His programme of economy in expenditure and tax reduction was irreproachably orthodox. Though inflation persisted, its pace slackened.[3] The budget deficit was steadily reduced until in March 1924 De Stefani was able to announce the

[1] Rossi, *I padroni del vapore*, pp. 78–81; Guarneri, I, pp. 65–6; Mussolini, XX, pp. 132–5. The business community showed its gratitude in hard cash. Total contributions to central fascist funds, which had dropped to 169,000 lire per month in the second half of 1922, rose to 447,000 per month between the march on Rome and the end of 1924. After October 1922 there was a marked increase in large corporate contributions from banks, insurance companies and Confindustria itself. 5·8 million of the 9 million lire contributed between 1 October 1921 and 31 December 1924 came from industry, 4·1 million after October 1922. The march on Rome cost 730,000 lire (for food, transport, accommodation etc.) and it took the party a year to pay off the resulting debts. See R. De Felice, 'Primi elementi sul finanziamento del fascismo dalle origini al 1924', in *Rivista storica del socialismo*, vol. 7 (1964), pp. 241–4.

[2] Tamaro, I, p. 364.

[3] The cost of living index (1913 = 100) dropped from 416·8 in 1921 to 411·9 in 1923 but rose again to 426·4 in 1924 and 479 in 1925. Fossati, p. 631; *Sommario*, p. 172.

first surplus for sixteen years.[1] The fascists naturally made the most of this
triumph and gave no credit to their predecessors for preparing the return
to solvency.

Mussolini was fortunate in coming to power at the very moment when
throughout the world economic depression was giving way to recovery.
The major industrial countries had overcome the worst of their post-war
difficulties and trade was picking up. In 1923 Italy too entered a phase of
economic growth that ¡was to last six years.[2] The painful reorganisation of
heavy industry, which followed the disasters of 1920–1, had now been completed. Ilva and Ansaldo, pared of many of their wartime excrescences,
began to forge ahead again.[3] In 1924 steel production passed the wartime
peak of 1917 and next year reached a level almost twice as high as that
of 1922.[4] The engineering industry flourished on electrification of the railways and a growing export market for motor vehicles. The shipyards,
including those recently acquired at Trieste, were busy. The most rapid
rate of growth was achieved by the electrical, chemical and artificial silk
industries, the last being a total newcomer with a great future.[5] Italy's
foreign trade made a satisfactory recovery. Thanks in part to a series of
commercial treaties with France, Germany, Switzerland, the succession
states of central Europe and the Soviet Union, exports increased faster
than imports. The value of exports doubled between 1922 and 1925, and in
1924 exports paid for 73·7% of imports, the highest percentage (with the
exception of 1914) since 1906.[6] This favourable trend created a feeling of
buoyant confidence throughout the industrial and business world. Economic recovery was the greatest single factor in winning adherents to the
Fascist regime.

The working-class gained least from these developments. The socialist
and Catholic unions had had no chance to recover from the demoralisation
of 1920–2. The physical assaults of the *squadristi* had shattered their organisation and made strikes or effective wage pressure impossible. As a consequence the index of industrial real wages fell by 11% between 1921 and

[1] The corrected figures show that the deficit (millions of lire) fell from 17,168
in 1921–2 to 3,260 in 1922–3 and 989 in 1923–4; the surplus for 1924–5 was 439.
Coppola d'Anna, p. 85.
[2] The index of industrial production (1896–1900 = 100) rose from 180 in 1916–
1920 to 208 in 1921–5 and 282 in 1926–30. Neufeld, p. 529.
[3] Romeo, pp. 98, 102–4.
[4] *Sommario*, p. 129.
[5] Romeo, pp. 106–10; *Sommario*, p. 135. Production of electric power (millions
of kWh) increased from 4,730 in 1922 to 8,390 in 1926. By 1927 the capital invested in the electrical industry was two-and-a-half times greater than that invested
in steel and mechanical engineering combined.
[6] *Sommario*, p. 152. In 1924 Italy also achieved a surplus on its balance of payments for the first time since 1914. *Sommario*, p. 215.

1924.[1] Nevertheless even some sections of the working-class were for a time well disposed to the new government. When D'Aragona, secretary of the C.G.L., announced in the chamber that his organisation was now independent of all political parties, Mussolini interjected 'At last!' and assured him that the C.G.L. would not receive the same treatment as the Socialist party. The official enactment of the eight-hour day in March 1923 seemed fulfilment of this promise. Mussolini still liked to talk of himself as a worker and to fancy himself as the leader of a 'Fascist Workers' party'. Fascism, he repeated on many occasions, would be neither anti-proletarian nor servile to the capitalist class. In December 1922 he had discussions with Tito Zaniboni and Gino Baldesi of the C.G.L., and Baldesi, again with Turati's approval, paid a second visit to D'Annunzio. The C.G.L. was purged by its right-wing leaders of communists, who were rebuked for inciting the workers against the government and trying 'to involve them in a struggle from which they must remain absolutely aloof'.[2] There was talk of unifying the trade union movement by fusing the C.G.L., U.I.L. and D'Annunzio's unions,[3] a proposal of which D'Annunzio, who had long preached 'national syndicalism', strongly approved.[4] Nothing came of these ideas because of the resolute opposition of the Fascist syndicates to any resurrection of their defeated rivals. On 15 December the Fascist Grand Council approved Rossoni's proposal that no working-class organisations outside the fascist syndicates should be given official recognition. The fusion of the Fascist and Nationalist parties two months later put a final end to the possibility of a genuinely 'Fascist-Labour' party.

Mussolini nevertheless continued to oppose Rossoni's demand for a monopoly of the trade union movement, even though his General Confederation of Syndical Corporations added 'Fascist' to its title in December 1922. In the summer of 1923 Mussolini had further talks with D'Aragona and his colleagues, which led to rumours that they were being offered a

---

[1] From (1913 = 100) 127 in 1921 (the post-war peak) to 116 in 1923 and 112·6 in 1924. Fossati, p. 634; Neufeld, p. 540.

[2] Tasca, p. 461.

[3] ibid., pp. 474–5; Salvatorelli and Mira, pp. 171–2; Tamaro, I, pp. 296–7; De Rosa, *Storia*, pp. 310–18; Valeri, *D'Annunzio*, pp. 95–101.

[4] D'Annunzio was anxious to influence fascism in a radical, 'labour' direction. But his chief concern at this time was to protect Giulietti's seamen's union against systematic violation by the shipowners of the pact of 16 October (see above, p. 619). A long battle on this issue ended only in June 1924 with the destruction of Giulietti's union and D'Annunzio's resentful admission of defeat. Mussolini kept a close watch on D'Annunzio's activities through a special police agent, Giovanni Rizzo, who was attached to D'Annunzio's household, with the poet's consent, in March 1923. But Mussolini never had cause to fear D'Annunzio politically after the march on Rome. Pini and Susmel, II, pp. 287, 319, 326, 339, 348–9, 354–5; G. Rizzo, *D'Annunzio e Mussolini* (Milan 1960), pp. 11 ff.; Valeri, *D'Annunzio*, pp. 104–9, 143–5.

seat in the cabinet. Mussolini formally recognised the independence of the C.G.L. and in August its leaders obtained the approval of a congress for their support of the government. At about the same time Achille Grandi, secretary of the Catholic C.I.L., saw Mussolini and secured a public statement that the government was opposed to all kinds of monopoly, trade union monopoly included.[1] These assurances were deceptive. In fact the fascist unions, though still representing a small minority of workers, enjoyed a privileged position, as the Palazzo Chigi agreement showed. But on paper fascist and non-fascist unions were left free to compete. For a time it seemed that in this field also Mussolini had his extremists under control.

Yet behind the façade of moderation, illegality continued. Within three days of becoming Prime Minister, Mussolini had instructed local party bosses that 'We must preserve discipline and respect for others; in no way must we infringe personal liberties.' These orders, which were carefully publicised, shocked many fascists, as had the formation of a coalition cabinet in which the fascists were so few. The rank and file felt cheated of the fruits of victory and in northern Italy, undeterred by warnings, the *squadristi* set about mopping up the last islands of 'resistance. On 18 December 1922 twenty-two workmen were killed during fascist assaults on working-class institutions in Turin.[2] Next month there were thirteen deaths in La Spezia.

Catholics in Lombardy, Tuscany and the Trentino also suffered. The attacks on Catholic unions, newspapers and local councils continued. When the Bishop of Brescia appealed to Mussolini to stop the violence, Augusto Turati, the local *ras*, commented that there might be collaboration between fascists and Popolari in Rome, but in Brescia there was just pure fascism.[3] Another target was Molinella, a stronghold of reformist socialism near Bologna, which was terrorised into submission by punitive expeditions. In August 1923 a priest, Don Giovanni Minzoni, was murdered near Ferrara by *squadre* under Balbo's command. Independent-minded fascists were treated with special severity. In May 1923 a fascist deputy, Alfredo Misuri, criticised the power of the militia, the identification of party and state, and the irresponsible 'oligarchy' around Mussolini, and demanded the restoration of parliament and freedom of criticism. At the end of his speech Giolittian liberals, ex-nationalists and even a fascist under-secretary crowded round to congratulate him. That same evening he was beaten up

[1] Jacini, *Storia*, pp. 159–60; Pini and Susmel, II, p. 300.
[2] The fascist pretext was the killing in self-defence of two *squadristi* by a young communist. For a communist eye-witness account, see Montagnana, I, pp. 137–45. The fascist perpetrators were included in the amnesty declared five days later.
[3] Salvatorelli and Mira, p. 172.

outside parliament by Balbo's *squadristi*, none of whom were prosecuted.[1] In all it has been calculated that there were 2,000 victims of fascist violence, fifty of them deputies, between the march on Rome and the end of 1923.[2]

Some of these outrages, as was later revealed, were ordered by Mussolini personally; most were probably not, and some angered and embarrassed him. It was not easy to control a party which had swollen to a membership of 800,000 in July 1923. Provincial bosses rebelled against orders from Rome. *Ras* quarrelled with *ras* and local feuds led to violence. Mussolini occasionally took action. A few of the least disciplined were arrested and the party's organisation was overhauled. Castor oil was officially banned as a political weapon. But there were too many reservations in Mussolini's attitude. Fascist assaults were depicted as mild, justified reprisals. Illegality would cease, he declared, when anti-fascist provocation and 'criminally irresponsible opposition' ceased.[3] Mussolini did not condemn violence, but only 'stupid' or 'useless' violence; and he was the judge of its stupidity or uselessness. He was temperamentally incapable of sustained moderation. Opposition exasperated him; he wanted his opponents to live with perpetual fear over their heads. Still an avid newspaper reader, he would note the names of subscribers published in the anti-fascist press and send them to his local bosses for suitable action.[4] Such behaviour, and his frequent outbursts of intemperate language, created an atmosphere in which *squadristi* could act with good hopes of immunity. There were, moreover, men in responsible positions and intimate contact with Mussolini who lacked even Mussolini's few scruples. An organisation later known as the Cheka grew up during 1923 with the task of supplementing legal repression with individual acts of terrorism. It was recruited from young *squadristi*, many of whom had criminal records. High officials gave it protection. Mussolini knew some of the young thugs personally and sometimes joined their

---

[1] ibid., pp. 197–8. The under-secretary was reprimanded and resigned his post. In the early days of fascism, Misuri had organised the punitive expeditions of the *squadristi* of Perugia. In the spring of 1922 he was expelled from the party for indiscipline and joined the nationalists, only to become a fascist again on the fusion of the two parties a year later. Another fascist 'revisionist', Rocca, who attacked the illegalities of the *ras* and demanded revision of the constitution on syndicalist lines, was luckier than Misuri in being merely expelled from the party instead of being assaulted. Pini and Susmel, II, pp. 351–2, 365; Salvatorelli and Mira, pp. 207–8, 228.

[2] Mussolini gave details on 28 January 1924 of 15 assaults on fascists during the current month, and on 3 January 1925 announced that 11 fascists had been killed during the previous November and December. Mussolini, XX, pp. 165–6, XXI, p. 239.

[3] ibid., XX, p. 164.

[4] Salvemini, *Fascist Dictatorship*, pp. 400–1, quoting Cesare Rossi. By September 1923 it was the practice of the police to make lists of subscribers to opposition newspapers and keep a special eye on them. De Rosa, *Storia*, p. 421.

celebrations after an exploit. Toleration of this political underworld made Mussolini the accomplice, if not the direct instigator, of criminal violence.[1]

As the months passed, doubts grew. But the opposition remained ineffective and hopelessly divided. The wrangles between the communists, the maximalist Socialist party and the reformist Unitary Socialist party paralysed the extreme left. The Popolari shrank from alliance with socialists. Most liberals, even when uneasy about the trend of fascism, thought that the only alternative was reversion to the confusion of 1919–22, which would end in the victory of 'bolshevism'.

The least compromising in their opposition were the communists. At first they were not unduly pessimistic. Though they admitted that for the moment no counter-offensive was possible against such 'overwhelmingly powerful forces', they gave fascism a maximum life of five years.[2] The maximalists tended to agree with them. In any case fascists were little worse than bourgeois liberals. The latter, for their part, wasted few tears on the tribulations of the extreme left. On the very day that Mussolini became Prime Minister, the Turin police turned over the premises of *Ordine Nuovo* to the fascists. The Communist party began to lead a precarious, semi-legal existence. In February 1923, 2,000 communists and socialists were arrested, though all but 150 were released shortly afterwards. The courts still offered a measure of protection. Serrati, the maximalist leader, was prosecuted for sedition in June and four months later Bordiga, secretary of the Communist party, and several of his leading colleagues were tried for conspiracy against the state. All were acquitted. On hearing that Serrati had been released, Mussolini commented, 'The bench acquits, I shoot.'[3] Both communists and maximalists were constantly harassed and intimidated and subjected to cat and mouse arrests. Only in a few big cities did the Communist party enjoy even a minimum of security from arbitrary police action.

Persecution, however, did not heal the extreme left's dissensions. Now that the Socialist party had been purged of its reformist leaders, Moscow was pressing for a proletarian united front. Communist and maximalist delegates attended the fourth congress of the Comintern in November 1922 and a joint commission under Zinoviev's chairmanship reached agreement for fusion. But there was resistance in both parties. The majority of the communists, led by Bordiga, distrusted Serrati and preferred the policy of independence as expounded in the party's Rome Theses of March 1922.

[1] Salvatorelli and Mira, pp. 211–12; Salvemini, *Fascist Dictatorship*, pp. 406–8; Pini and Susmel, II, p. 336.
[2] Tasca, p. 460; Montagnana, I, pp. 133–4.
[3] Salvemini, *Fascist Dictatorship*, p. 389.

The maximalist opponents of fusion found a new leader in Pietro Nenni, a recent recruit to the party who had rapidly risen to the editorship of *Avanti!*[1] In April 1923 an extraordinary congress of the rump Socialist party rejected fusion and four months later, at Nenni's instigation, Serrati and his 'Third Internationalists' were expelled. The inevitable consequences of these byzantine disputations was apathy and demoralisation. Both the Communist and Socialist parties suffered heavy losses in membership during 1923.

While the maximalists continued to pour scorn on parliament and liberal institutions, even in the face of triumphant fascism, the Unitary Socialists spoke out courageously in their defence. Two deputies, Modigliani and Matteotti, interrupted Mussolini's speech on 16 November 1922 with the cry *Viva il Parlamento!* Turati compared Mussolini's handling of the chamber to that of a lion-tamer speaking with whip in hand – in this case to drugged lions.[2] Unlike the maximalists, the Unitary Socialists confined their opposition to legal methods and so were tolerated by the government, even though they were frequently targets for the *squadristi*. They hoped that by continuing to perform with dignity and patience the role of a parliamentary opposition, by waiting for the government to discredit itself and refusing to provide a target for the 'second wave', they would establish their claim to the succession when fascism eventually came to die a natural death. Turati faithfully followed these tactics during the debate on the electoral reform, in spite of growing nausea at the degradation of parliament by the sycophantic majority.[3] His party's outspokenness earned it the sympathy and collaboration of independent democrats and of many Popolari. But outside parliament its influence was small. The reformists remained what they had been since 1919, a group of generals without troops.

The Popolari, separated by deep suspicion from the extreme left, were themselves divided. Sturzo believed that fascism and Christian democracy, as he conceived it, were irreconcilable. But in spite of his opposition the party executive had approved Popular membership, on an individual basis, of Mussolini's coalition, regarding it as a lesser evil than a wholly fascist government. The party had also voted for the grant     plenary powers to the cabinet. At the same time, standing by their 1919 programme and their motto *Libertas*, its spokesmen defended the rights of parliament,

---

[1] Nenni, like Mussolini, was a native of the Romagna. He entered politics as an extreme republican. In 1911 he had demonstrated with Mussolini against the Libyan war and gone to prison with him. In 1914, like Mussolini, he became an interventionist, but broke with him after a short period in 1919 as a leading member of the Bologna Fascio. He joined the Socialist party in 1921.

[2] Salvatorelli and Mira, p. 163.

[3] Turati–Kuliscioff, VI, p. 67.

constitutional liberties and trade union freedom. This independence angered Mussolini who did his utmost to undermine the party by building up Cornaggia's independent Catholic party, the National Union, by flattering and inciting the Popular right wing and by ingratiating himself with the church direct.

The Popular party's fourth congress at Turin in April 1923 showed that, in spite of divisions among the leaders, the rank and file retained its faith in democracy. The conservative wing, now calling itself the National Right, was very active. Led by Stefano Cavazzoni, one of the two Popular members of the cabinet, it pressed for unconditional collaboration with Mussolini, 'the man sent by Providence', for a clean break with the 'demagogy' of 1919 and for the expulsion of Miglioli's left wing. Miglioli demanded total opposition. The majority was prepared to support the government on three conditions: that the fascist revolution was brought within the bounds of the constitution, that proportional representation was retained and that their own independence was respected. 'One collaborates standing, not on one's knees', Sturzo had said in March,[1] and this was the main theme of his speech at the congress. He carried an overwhelming majority with him. For a few weeks it seemed that, after a year of uncertainty and demoralisation, the party had recovered its confidence and sense of mission.

Mussolini was disagreeably surprised. He demanded more than conditional support and recognised the congress for what it was – the most formidable expression of anti-fascist feeling since the march on Rome. Sturzo's speech was 'the speech of an enemy', commented Il Popolo d'Italia, and the voting was 'equivocal and insincere'.[2] Three days after the congress ended, Mussolini summoned his Popular ministers and ordered them to clarify their party's position. Seventy Popular deputies signed a humiliating pledge of loyalty, in an effort to avert a rupture.[3] But this was not enough. On 24 April the ministers resigned. Next day a small group of conservatives broke away to form a National Popular Party, with unconditional support of Mussolini as its programme.

The Popolari now came under intense pressure from the government, the Fascist party, the pro-fascist Catholics and the church. The Vatican openly showed its benevolence to the government and the Catholic press urged Sturzo not to create difficulties. The concept of autonomy in politics was no longer in favour. Since December 1922 Pius XI's main concern had been to revive and reorganise Catholic Action, and through it to recover control over the laity, even in political questions.[4] The Popular party, it

[1] Sturzo, *Italy and Fascismo*, p. 131; De Rosa, *Storia*, p. 341.
[2] ibid., pp. 364–71.
[3] Jacini, *Storia*, p. 174; Howard, pp. 414–15; De Rosa, *Storia*, pp. 372–6.
[4] Howard, pp. 398–400, 436–7.

seemed to many clerics, had served its purpose and was now merely an obstacle to good relations between church and state: worse still, it was a standing temptation to the fascists to indulge in anti-clericalism, as the brutal language of the fascist press and the physical assaults on Catholic institutions in Lombardy showed. Sturzo's position became impossible and on 10 July he resigned from the secretaryship. Next day *L'Osservatore Romano* praised his action as a step towards pacification.

Sturzo's resignation occurred on the very day that parliament began to debate the electoral reform bill. The two events were connected. The result of the debate further demoralised the Popolari. In spite of their devotion to proportional representation, they allowed themselves to be drawn into discussion of the technical details of the bill, thus conceding the principle.[1] When it came to voting they abstained, with the exception of nine deputies of the right wing, led by the ex-minister Cavazzoni. The latter were promptly expelled from the party and during the summer several more conservatives voluntarily followed them. Though the core of the party remained solid, the Popolari now faced the threat of dissolution and could no longer count on the Vatican for support. For the rest of the year their motto was 'Neither collaboration nor opposition'; but in fact they had moved far towards the latter. On 1 August the Fascist Grand Council proclaimed Sturzo and his party to be 'enemies of the government and of fascism'.

The liberals were even more divided than the Popolari. A few had dissociated themselves at the outset from the complacent majority. Sforza, who had been ambassador in Paris since ceasing to be Foreign Minister, resigned when Mussolini formed his government[2] and became one of his boldest critics in the senate. Albertini very soon realised that 'normalisation' of fascism was an illusion. In the senate and in his paper he criticised with growing asperity the undermining of the constitution through legislation by decree. Early in 1923 the *Popolo d'Italia* was already attacking the *Corriere della Sera* as 'an enemy paper' and referring to

[1] In a discussion with Mussolini in May, De Gasperi had suggested that the party that polled a plurality of votes, provided it reached a minimum of 40%, should be given 60% of the seats. Mussolini insisted on 25% and 66%. Thirty years later as Prime Minister, De Gasperi was responsible for a law which gave 65% of the seats to the party which polled 50·01% of the votes.

[2] It was a question of conscience, not politics, he told Giolitti. *Quarant' anni*, III, 385. The reason he gave publicly was that a key post like the Paris embassy should be held by a man in sympathy with the government's foreign policy. In private he assured Mussolini that he had resigned 'out of a profound personal regard for you', and wished his government a long and happy life 'because if its life were short, that would mean disaster'. Sforza too hoped for the best, but not for long. DDI (7), I, 1–4, 10, 15, 17.

Albertini as 'the Croat senator'.[1] Frassati's *Stampa* was even more out-spoken. Frassati resigned in November 1922 from the Berlin embassy to which Giolitti had appointed him, with less publicity but from the same motives as Sforza. He now condemned the present disorder as worse than the 'bolshevism' from which Mussolini claimed to have rescued Italy. Thus the two greatest liberal papers were in opposition.

In the chamber the leading liberal critic was Amendola, who had been one of Facta's most resolute ministers before the march on Rome. He and his group of thirty, mostly from the south, were the only liberals who never voted for Mussolini's government. For the first few months they were restrained, waiting for the Prime Minister to reveal his intentions. But on 12 July Amendola spoke against the electoral reform, warning parliament that if it passed the bill, thereby sanctioning the imposition of the will of a minority upon the electorate, it would 'deny its own very nature and betray its past, its present and its future'.[2] This speech drew applause from the extreme left and marked him out as a champion of democracy. Amendola was a strong, austere man, intellectually rigorous and driven by a deeply religious conscience. Unlike his former political leader, Nitti, he refused to keep silent.[3] Though he had no illusions about an early collapse of fascism, he threw himself into the task of galvanising the opposition and bringing democrats, socialists and Popolari together. His outspokenness earned him a savage beating by *squadristi* at Christmas 1923.[4]

The most uncompromising liberals of all were the small group that gathered round the weekly *Rivoluzione Liberale* in Turin. Its leader was Piero Gobetti, a young man of only twenty-two. He attacked fascism fearlessly, but with equal ferocity rejected the whole liberal tradition since 1861. Deeply influenced by his friendship with Gramsci and by personal experience of the occupation of the factories in 1920, he believed that only the working-class could defeat fascism. He therefore set himself the long-term task of forming a new liberal élite, willing when the time came to give the masses the help they would need.[5] The greatest immediate danger, as he saw it, was the 'normalisation' for which almost all liberals, openly or secretly, longed. He found even Amendola and Turati wanting; their 'technical opposition' was merely 'collaboration by criticism'. He fought

[1] Valeri, *Da Giolitti a Mussolini*, pp. 181–3.

[2] Amendola, *La nuova democrazia*, pp. 160–2, 173–7.

[3] Nitti had abdicated from politics after the march on Rome, leaving the leader-ship of the liberal left to Amendola. His silence did not spare him from having his house sacked by *squadristi* a short time before the assault on Amendola. He went abroad in June 1924.

[4] On having the news telephoned to him in Milan, Mussolini is alleged to have commented, 'Today I'll eat with a better appetite.'

[5] Gobetti, *Opere*, I, pp. 225–6.

not 'to replace Mussolini within six months by Nitti, Orlando or Giolitti', but to destroy the roots from which fascism had sprung. Mussolini, in his view, was merely the product on a giant scale of those same vicious forces that had given birth to 'the phenomena of Depretis and Giolitti'.[1] Gobetti's intransigence drew down upon him Mussolini's special fury and was to be the inspiration of a later generation of anti-fascists. But at the time, by emphasising liberal divisions, he weakened the opposition more than the government.

Though at first the liberal anti-fascists were few, their numbers grew as disillusionment spread. By the autumn of 1923 Bonomi and his parliamentary following had joined the critics in defence of the constitution. During the winter the liberal ministers, like the Popolari six months earlier, struggled to maintain a minimum of independence. But Mussolini wanted obedience, not collaboration and his patience was becoming exhausted. In February 1924 Giovanni Colonna Di Cesarò, the Sicilian leader of the demo-sociali, resigned and one further step was taken towards a purely fascist government.

## The Assassination of Matteotti

Mussolini dissolved parliament in January 1924 and the general election followed on 6 April. The government presented a single list of 356 names. Of these about two-thirds were fascists, the remainder consisting of a variety of right-wing Catholics, liberals and conservatives, including Salandra and Orlando. These non-fascists were included in spite of the Fascist party's confidence that it could win without allies, chiefly in order to make sure of the south where fascism was still weak. Flattery of the conservatives also brought generous support from big business. Confindustria issued circulars to its members, urging them to contribute to the government's election fund. Salandra, still believing that he could influence fascism by collaborating, announced in a fulsome electoral speech that he was handing on to Mussolini 'the banner of the liberal ideal'.[2] Mussolini also tried to win over Giolitti with an offer of most of the Piedmontese seats for his friends and elevation to the senate for himself.[3] Giolitti, however, declined and presented his own independent lists in Piedmont and Liguria. He still supported the government, but only as long as it rested on consent, not force. In contrast to Salandra he declared that the

---

[1] ibid., pp. 430, 535, 544–5, 643.
[2] Pini and Susmel, II, p. 359. Salandra personally negotiated with Mussolini the inclusion of his own supporters in the government's list. Salandra, *Memorie*, pp. 42–4.
[3] Soleri, pp. 178–80.

Liberal party, 'which has so glorious a past, cannot be allowed to disappear', but 'must fight the battle alone' under its own name and flag.[1]

The election campaign pitilessly revealed the opposition's disunity. The communists invited the socialists to form a united bloc, but only Serrati's small group of 'Third Internationalists', shortly to be merged in the Communist party, consented. Turati and Nenni refused in the name of their respective parties, with the result that the extreme left faced the electors with three separate lists. The Liberal party allowed its members either to join the government list or, like Giolitti, to remain independent. Not even the democrats and opposition liberals, among whom Amendola, Bonomi and Di Cesarò were the most prominent, were able to form a single united list. The Popolari, reaffirming their belief in liberty, parliamentary government and the rule of law, ranged themselves clearly with the opposition. They conspicuously lacked sympathy from the Vatican which kept frigidly neutral. One hundred and fifty prominent Catholics issued a manifesto condemning opposition to fascism and on 24 March the Pope himself praised the government for 'restoring religious values'. Though the Popular party appeared to have retained its cohesion better than any other non-fascist party, its strength was visibly ebbing.

The electoral battle was fought by the opposition under the greatest difficulties. In addition to all the traditional pressures at the disposal of governments, open violence was practised by the militia on a scale undreamt of in Giolitti's day.[2] Both Socialist parties had to abandon public meetings a month before polling day. The Popolari were the special target of fascist fury. Cesare Forni, a dissident fascist deputy, was beaten up by the Cheka by express order of Francesco Giunta, secretary of the Fascist party. Mussolini's anonymous comment in *Il Popolo d'Italia* was 'Traitors perish'.[3] Though most of his colleagues were forced out of the battle, Forni bravely persevered. Mussolini himself hardly bothered to take part in the campaign because, as he explained, 'election games', though 'a grim necessity' for the present, were a mortifying experience and part of 'the old Italy' which he despised; besides, he added, he was busy on much more important things.[4]

As was to be expected, the government won a crushing victory. It secured the election of 374 of its supporters, 275 of them fascists. In spite of violence and intimidation, the opposition and independent groups polled 2·5

[1] Giolitti, *Discorsi extraparlamentari*, pp. 347, 352.

[2] Salvatorelli and Mira, pp. 218–21. Giolitti himself was horrified by the reports of violence which he received and 'could never have believed that such things could happen in Italy'. But the only advice he could give his friends was 'passive resistance' and Tolstoyan patience. De Rosa, *Storia*, pp. 442–6.

[3] Mussolini, XX, pp. 204–5; Salvemini, *Fascist Dictatorship*, pp. 290–1, 391–2.

[4] Mussolini, XX, pp. 161–2.

million of the 7·2 million votes. Their numbers in the new chamber were much diminished.[1] The Popolari won 39 seats instead of 108 in 1921; the socialists, almost equally split between the two parties, 46 instead of 123; the democratic groups (including the republicans), 30 instead of 124. Only the communists increased their representation, from 15 to 19.[2] It was in the north, where fascism had been born, that the opposition was strongest. In Piedmont, Liguria, Lombardy and Venetia the government list was in

[1] The following summary comparison of the 1921 and 1924 elections is based on the figures in Compendio, II, pp. 130–1.

|  | 1921 | 1924 |  |
|---|---|---|---|
| National Bloc | | | Government List |
| Fascists 35 | | 275 | Fascists |
| Nationalists 10 | | | |
| Liberals &c. | | 99 | Non-fascists |
| (incl. Giolittians) 60 | | | |
| | 105 | 374 | |
| Dissident fascists 2 | | 1 | Dissident fascist |
| Liberals (right wing) 43 | | 15 | Liberals (incl. Giolittians) |
| Democratic groups | | | |
| (left centre, incl. radicals) 108 | | | |
| | | 28 | Democratic opposition |
| Republican and Democratic Left | | | |
| (incl. Republicans, Reformists, | | | Republican and Democratic |
| Combattenti) 22 | | 9 | Left |
| Popolari 108 | | 39 | Popolari |
| | | 24 | Unitary Socialists |
| Socialists 123 | | | |
| | | 22 | Socialists (maximalist) |
| Communists 15 | | 19 | Communists |
| Slavs, Germans 9 | | 4 | Slavs, Germans |
| | 535 | 535 | |

[2] The communists, for reasons that are not clear, were left relatively undisturbed for most of 1924 and were allowed to start a new paper, L'Unità, in February. Mussolini may have welcomed a limited communist revival as a weapon to intimidate his liberal and conservative sympathisers into continued submission. His leniency may also have been connected with his diplomatic wooing of Soviet Russia (see below, p. 683). The leader of the Communist group in the chamber was Gramsci, who had with the backing of Zinoviev and the Comintern replaced Bordiga as secretary of the party. Serrati's group of 'Third Internationalists' was formally merged in the Communist party in August 1924. Carr, Socialism in One Country, III (i), p. 167.

a numerical minority. The south, in spite of intensive fascist penetration since the march on Rome, was still less fascist than the north; but its old habit of voting for the government of the day prevailed. The Fascist party vented its resentment after the results were announced in a series of assaults on Catholic institutions in Lombardy and Venetia, which delighted Farinacci but drew sentences of excommunication from the Bishop of Vicenza and a public protest from Gasparri himself.

The new chamber met on 24 May, the ninth anniversary of the declaration of war, and the speech from the throne described the election as the triumph of 'the victory generation'. The Fascist ministers appeared for the first time in party uniform and their supporters were in a boisterous mood. The debate that followed was chiefly notable for the speech of Giacomo Matteotti, which showed the qualities of a true leader. Matteotti had since 1919 represented Rovigo, near the mouth of the Po, where as a young man he had organised the *braccianti*. In the war he served as an army conscript but remained an uncompromising pacifist. After Caporetto he was interned for defeatism. Tough and reserved, indifferent to popularity, well versed in public finance and the problems of education and local government, he had few intellectual equals among his fellow-socialists. When the split came in October 1922, he followed Turati into the right-wing Unitary Socialist party and early in 1924 became its secretary. His forceful personality, organising skill and the recklessness with which he exposed fascist misdeeds had restored vitality to his shattered party, both in parliament and outside. On 30 May, for over an hour, amid a storm of fascist interruptions, he described the violence, fraud and intimidation that had dominated the election and demanded that the chamber should declare it totally invalid. As he finished he remarked to his friends, 'Now you can prepare my funeral oration.'[1]

His speech had indeed exasperated the fascists, who responded with violent abuse and threats. Mussolini himself declared in *Il Popolo d'Italia* on 1 June that the majority had been too patient and that Matteotti's monstrous provocations deserved something more concrete than a verbal reply.[2] That same day Mussolini ordered the prefect of Turin by telegram to 'make life difficult' for Gobetti.[3] On 3 June a group of opposition deputies were assaulted as they left the parliament building. But on the 7th, as if to show that fascism was still two-faced, Mussolini told the chamber he was ready to collaborate with anyone in the cause of reconstruction and

---

[1] A. Schiavi, *La vita e l'opera di Giacomo Matteotti* (Rome 1957), p. 150; Sforza, *Contemporary Italy*, p. 262; P. Nenni, *Ten Years of Tyranny in Italy* (London 1932), p. 164.

[2] Mussolini, XX, p. 303.                                        [3] ibid., p. 384.

drew a distinction between opposition, which he accepted, and the present methods of the opposition, which he condemned. It was the most conciliatory speech he had ever made in parliament. In private he even discussed the construction of a coalition wider than that of 1922.[1] Then on 10 June it became known that Matteotti had disappeared. Few doubted that fascists were responsible.

These suspicions were justified. Matteotti had been kidnapped outside his house by five ex-*squadristi* under the command of Amerigo Dumini and bundled into a car. He resisted and shouted for help, whereupon he was subjected to a brutal assault and stabbed to death. The body was buried after dark in a wood fifteen miles outside Rome, where it was discovered two months later.[2] The assassins formed part of the so-called Cheka, which was under the direct control of Cesare Rossi, head of the Prime Minister's press office,[3] and Giovanni Marinelli, treasurer of the Fascist party. Dumini drew his salary from Rossi's office and had been used for previous exploits such as the assaults on Forni, Misuri and Amendola. The car had been borrowed from Filippo Filipelli, editor of the fascist *Corriere d'Italia*. The existence of Dumini's band was well known not only to De Bono, chief of police, but also to Mussolini. The question that convulsed Italy for the next six months was how far the government should be held responsible for assassination.

Long before these facts leaked out, a wave of horror and anger swept the country. For a few critical weeks fascism was helpless and demoralised. Mussolini was isolated, his antechamber was deserted. Four cabinet ministers, Federzoni, Gentile, Aldo Oviglio and De Stefani, wavered in their loyalty.[4] Fascist deputies sounded Soleri on the chances of an undersecretary's post in a Giolitti government.[5] Party members left their badges

[1] He appears to have been considering D'Aragona and Baldesi of the C.G.L., Luzzatti, Meda and even Amendola. But it is more likely that this was just talk. Pini and Susmel, II, pp. 374–5; Tamaro, I, pp. 418–19. In any case it is certain that he was proposing not collaboration on equal terms, but submission to his direction.

[2] Dumini's own account may be found in his *17 Colpi* (Milan 1951), in which he maintains that his orders were to kidnap Matteotti and extract from him information about illegal socialist activities at home and in France. The kidnappers' failure to take the most elementary precautions does indeed suggest that the murder was unpremeditated.

[3] According to one journalist's account, Cesare Rossi had remarked, after hearing Matteotti's speech, 'The only thing with people like Matteotti is to let the revolver speak.' Salvemini, *Fascist Dictatorship*, p. 319.

[4] Pini and Susmel, II, p. 380; Tamaro, I, pp. 423–6. A substantial number of ex-nationalists urged Mussolini to resign.

[5] Soleri, p. 183. According to Mussolini's own statement to a journalist in 1945 in the last months of his life, he had himself contemplated resigning in June 1924 and recommending the King to appoint Turati as his successor.

at home and stayed away from meetings. In the militia orders were widely ignored. Initially Mussolini seems to have hoped that the crime could be hushed up and when he spoke in the chamber on 12 June he was reticent and evasive. But a casual spectator of the kidnapping had reported the number of Filipelli's car to the police. This led the investigation straight to the heart of the Fascist party. The police and judiciary still enjoyed a precarious independence.[1] Mussolini could have silenced them by an act of force and by accepting responsibility for the crime, but shrank from so revolutionary a step. After the first shock had passed, however, his determination to stay in power never weakened. He therefore played for time and resorted to his usual tactics in a crisis, a combination of concession and force.

On 13 June he again faced the chamber. 'Only an enemy, who had spent long nights in thinking up something diabolical against me, could have committed this crime', he declared; it was an anti-fascist, an anti-national crime. He promised that justice would be done. But the government's conscience was clear; let there be no political exploitation or provocation, for it would defend itself at any cost.[2] On this warning note the chamber hurriedly adjourned. In the next few days, under pressure from leading members of the Fascist Grand Council, Mussolini ordered De Bono, Cesare Rossi and Aldo Finzi, Under-Secretary at the Ministry of Interior, to resign. By the end of the month Rossi, Marinelli, Filipelli, Dumini and three of his assistants were under arrest and the judicial investigation was under way. Meanwhile Federzoni, the ex-nationalist, took over the Ministry of Interior from Mussolini, a step which pleased conservative and Catholic opinion. On the 24th Mussolini repeated his assurances in the senate and promised to restore the power and prestige of parliament. But again he warned the opposition not to exploit the tragedy. Sforza was defiant. The assassination, he declared, had been organised 'at the very heart of government'. Albertini, though more restrained, earnestly rebuked his liberal colleagues for resigning themselves to violence as a method of administration.[3] But only twenty-one senators voted against the government and six abstained. Mussolini's show of moderation persuaded two conservative liberals, Alessandro Casati and Gino Sarrocchi, and a right-wing Catholic to join the government. Casati and Sarrocchi did so with Salandra's approval. Though Giolitti's group refused a similar invitation,

---

[1] The investigating judge in charge of the case has stated that he would have arrested Mussolini had he not been a deputy and therefore subject to the jurisdiction of the senate, not the ordinary courts. M. Del Giudice, *Cronistoria del processo Matteotti* (Palermo 1954), p. 22.

[2] Mussolini, XX, pp. 327-9.

[3] Albertini, *In difesa della libertà*, pp. 68-70.

most liberals still shrank from 'a leap in the dark' into open opposition and alliance with the left.[1]

On 13 June representatives of all sections of the opposition – Amendola's and Di Cesarò's liberal-democrats, the Popolari, both socialist groups, the republicans and the communists – decided to take no further part in the proceedings of parliament 'so long as grave uncertainty persists regarding the sinister episode'. This was the beginning of 'the Aventine secession',[2] in which about one hundred deputies took part. Led by Amendola, Turati and De Gasperi, Sturzo's successor as secretary of the Popular party, they resolved to have no dealings with a government that was morally tainted, confident that when once the government's complicity had been proved, fascism would collapse amid general execration. The Aventine secession was a moral gesture, based on faith that time was on its side and justice would prevail.

This uncompromising stand, however, concealed both indecision and impotence. The opposition had no plan or organisation, and exhausted itself in hours of academic discussion. As Turati reported unhappily, it was impossible to get the groups to agree on any positive line of action; 'one makes an enormous effort, only to decide on nothing'.[3] A very few wished to act. When the storm first broke, Sforza urged the socialist and republican leaders to hurry to the Foreign Ministry and arrest Mussolini in his office. Turati, too, wished to be bold, feeling that 'every quarter of an hour lost is a betrayal' and that 'time works for the enemy'.[4] Initially at least boldness might have succeeded. But the moment was allowed to pass. Amendola and the Popolari were hesitant and moderate counsels prevailed. A communist proposal for a general strike was rejected by the two socialist parties and the C.G.L., which remembered all too well the 'legalitarian' strike of August 1922. The communists then broke away in disgust after less than a week and decided to return to the chamber as soon

[1] Soleri, pp. 183–4; Salandra, *Memorie*, pp. 49–51.

[2] A withdrawal from the chamber had been previously considered by both Amendola and the Popolari. The opposition did not physically withdraw to the Aventine Hill but remained in the parliament building. The name was taken from the several occasions in the history of ancient Rome when the *plebs* seceded from the Roman assembly and set up its rival assembly on the Aventine. The phrase was in current use. Mussolini had written on three occasions in 1921–2 of 'the socialists on the Aventine', when referring to their refusal to cooperate with other parties; Anna Kuliscioff wrote of Serrati 'retiring to the Aventine'. Mussolini, XVI, p. 393, XVII, p. 143, XVIII, p. 38; Turati–Kuliscioff, V, p. 523.

[3] ibid., VI, pp. 196, 227.

[4] Sforza, *L'Italia dal 1914 al 1944 quale io la vidi* (Rome 1946), p. 131; Turati–Kuliscioff, VI, pp. 208, 227, 230. Turati admired Sforza's courage and thought 'he is perhaps the man of tomorrow'.

as it reopened. The Aventine, clinging on Amendola's insistence to constitutional methods, reaffirmed its decision not to return to parliament until
a new government had been formed that would abolish the militia and
restore the rule of law. At the end of June that day seemed not far off. Even
Turati, for all his doubts and impatience, had many moments of optimism
in which he believed that 'the reign of Satan' was doomed.[1]

The Aventine's passivity made the King arbiter of the situation, and it
was upon the King that Amendola relied. Within a few days of Matteotti's
murder, Finzi, Rossi and Filipelli, indignant at being used as scapegoats,
had all separately composed memoranda purporting to show that, whatever
their own responsibility for the Cheka, Mussolini had approved and often
directly ordered its crimes. These memoranda found their way into the
hands of the opposition and were passed on to the King. 'I am not a judge',
was his comment; 'I should not be told such things.'[2] The King was
also urged by Stefano Jacini for the Popolari and by Sforza to free himself of responsibility for the regime.[3] But Victor Emmanuel took refuge
in the forms of constitutional monarchy. 'I am blind and deaf', he said;
'my eyes and ears are the senate and the chamber of deputies', and before
he could act, the government must be defeated in parliament.[4] In his view
the opposition had put itself in the wrong by abandoning parliament. It is
true that, as the crisis dragged on through the summer and the original
hopes of an early return to parliament faded, the Aventine began to consolidate. The Unitary Socialists and the Popolari formed joint committees
and their leaders discussed closer collaboration. Turati publicly declared
that anti-clericalism was dead in the Socialist party and De Gasperi responded warmly.[5] The Popular–Socialist coalition, which could have saved
Italian democracy in 1919–22, seemed to be taking shape at the eleventh
hour, offering the alternative government which was Amendola's aim. But
the internal dissensions were still great. Republicans and monarchists,
Catholics and socialists, reformists and revolutionaries were united only
in protest. 'Everyone feels that something ought to be done', Turati
observed on 13 July, 'but no positive decision can be reached.'[6] Victor
Emmanuel could be excused for failing to be impressed. The Aventine

---

[1] Letter of 19 June. On the 25th he wrote, 'The truth is that everything is col-
lapsing around him [Mussolini].' Turati–Kuliscioff, VI, pp. 215, 232. Sforza told
Charles-Roux on 8 July that the fascists and their chief were 'mortellement
atteints' and the Mussolini myth had been destroyed, and confidently predicted a
Giolitti–Sforza government. Charles-Roux, *Une grande ambassade*, pp. 273–4.
[2] Sforza, *Contemporary Italy*, pp. 262–3.
[3] Jacini, *Storia*, p. 227.
[4] Tamaro, I, p. 432.
[5] De Rosa, *Storia*, pp. 471–4; Howard, pp. 450–1.
[6] Turati–Kuliscioff, VI, p. 252.

therefore went on waiting for a lead from the King, the King waited for a lead from parliament and parliament was boycotted by the Aventine. The deadlock was complete.

Matteotti's murder created anti-fascism as a political movement. Thousands of Romans made a pilgrimage to the spot where Matteotti had been abducted and heaped it with flowers. Turati was cheered in the streets and former opponents paid him court.[1] The anti-fascist press boomed. Albertini, shedding the last of his inhibitions,[2] turned the *Corriere della Sera* into a formidable organ of opposition. Its circulation rose to 800,000, twice that of the entire fascist press. A new association, Italia Libera, was founded to unite all varieties of anti-fascist, including even D'Annunzians. It built up a vigorous membership, particularly among the post-war generation, and even began to recruit its own militia. The ex-servicemen, assembled in conference in July, added their voice of protest and demanded a return to legality. Even D'Annunzio briefly broke the political silence he had observed since the march on Rome and expressed in a press interview his pain and disgust at Italy's ruin.[3] The strength of anti-fascist feeling throughout the country was undeniable. But as the summer wore on and nothing happened, the moral question grew stale and apathy set in again. The initiative passed to the fascists.

While his opponents made no move, Mussolini slowly recovered confidence. The solidarity of the party reasserted itself and his ante-chamber filled up. Blackshirts demonstrated their loyalty in the provinces. Deputations journeyed to Rome to put heart into Mussolini. 'Duce, untie our hands', demanded Farinacci. Seventy-five fascist deputies urged him in a memorandum to counter-attack. Mussolini's tone became more aggressive. At the end of August he set out on a tour of speech-making in the provinces. He returned to Rome in a buoyant mood, feeling that he had renewed contact with the people and that the people were with him. At party meetings and in the Fascist Grand Council he repeated that there would be no return to the past and that he would never allow the regime to be put on trial. The motto of 'young, passionate Italian Fascism', he announced, should be 'Live dangerously'. 'A government doesn't fall when it doesn't wish to fall', he told a French journalist. As for the impotent oppositions, he

[1] ibid., pp. 205, 225, 243.

[2] Albertini wrote on 22 August, 'The experiment [of normalisation] has now been made; the conclusion has been – Matteotti.' Valeri, *Da Giolitti a Mussolini*, p. 189; Tamaro, I, p. 473.

[3] D'Annunzio's words were: 'Sono molto triste di questa fetida ruina.' They gave Mussolini a shock. But D'Annunzio, beyond discussing with his visitors how long Mussolini's government would last, made no further move. Valeri, *D'Annunzio*, pp. 116–23, 153–61.

boasted to the miners of Monte Amiata, if ever they dared to pass from talk to action, 'we shall turn them into straw for the blackshirts' encampments'.[1]

Once again his tactics and timing were masterly. Threats alternated with gestures of moderation. The decree of July 1923 limiting the freedom of the press was now put into effect, but in deference to conservative and even fascist protests, still not enforced with full rigour. Mussolini announced that the militia would be integrated in the armed forces and take an oath of allegiance to the King on 28 October, the second anniversary of the march on Rome. He created fifty-three new senators, almost all non-fascists. Blackshirt violence did not entirely cease,[2] but Federzoni instructed prefects to maintain strict order and discipline in the militia was greatly improved.[3] Even when a fascist deputy was murdered in September by a mentally deranged workman, who declared he was avenging Matteotti, there were no organised reprisals.

Such restraint caused acute frustration inside the Fascist party, but once again it won sympathisers outside. At the end of July a large gathering of financiers and industrialists at Genoa demonstrated its 'undiminished faith' in Mussolini and condemned the 'speculation' of the 'hybrid opposition'.[4] The church too remained on the government's side. The Vatican openly disapproved of the Aventine. A week after the assassination, *L'Osservatore Romano* praised Mussolini's 'resolute conduct in the face of the tragic event' and added, 'Let him who is without sin cast the first stone.' On 21 July Federzoni reaffirmed the government's intention to respect the liberty and prestige of the church. 'The overthrow of Mussolini could plunge the country in fire and blood', Gasparri told the diplomatic corps. Pius XI urged patience and calm. Not even the press decree shook Catholic complacency. For the church, fascism was 'the lesser evil'.[5] On 8 September Pius XI himself, in an address to university students, deplored the talk of a Popular–Socialist coalition and reminded Catholics that obedience was required of them even in politics when the latter 'approach the altar'.[6]

[1] Mussolini, XXI, pp. 40, 57, 86. On the comfort and strength which Mussolini clearly obtained from oratorical 'communion with the masses', see Tamaro, I, p. 332, II, p. 7; Pini and Susmel, II, pp. 309, 313.

[2] Between 29 July and 30 September 1924 fascists were responsible for 16 deaths, 36 serious woundings, 172 assaults and 146 attacks on property.

[3] Mussolini announced on 11 November that 845 fascists were in prison and a further 4,460 were awaiting trial. Mussolini, XXI, p. 139.

[4] Rossi, *I padroni del vapore*, p. 186.

[5] Rossi, *Il manganello e l'aspersorio*, pp. 133–7; Beyens, p. 237. Pius XI was particularly concerned that there should be calm during 1925, which was to be a Holy Year.

[6] Rossi, *Il manganello e l'aspersorio*, pp. 146–52. A coalition between Popolari and socialists would be a *conventio Christi ad Belial*, wrote the Jesuit *Civiltà Cattolica*.

*Il Popolo d'Italia* jubilantly published yet another circular from Gasparri to bishops, instructing them to prevent their priests from taking part in party politics. The Vatican's aim was clearly to force Catholics out of the Popular party and into Catholic Action.[1] These warnings coincided with intense pressure from the government[2] and Fascist party. In October Sturzo left Italy for exile. The Vatican had always regarded the Popular party as expendable; now it was to be discarded.

For the moment, however, the Popolari fought on in the cause of anti-fascism. In the autumn of 1924 it seemed to be making headway. Doubts were growing among the liberals who had declined to join the Aventine. Giolitti and his followers had stayed in the chamber because they believed abstention was a betrayal of the deputy's mandate.[3] But at the Liberal party congress at Leghorn in October, it was Giolitti's lieutenant, Soleri, who proposed and carried a motion calling on the two liberal ministers, Casati and Sarrochi, to resign. By a two-thirds majority the congress asserted its independence of the government and demanded the abolition of the militia and the restoration of the constitution and civil liberties. A similar appeal came from the president of the ex-servicemen's association, after fascist and anti-fascist ex-servicemen had come to blows at the Armistice Day celebration on 4 November. When parliament reassembled in November, Giolitti deplored the absence of freedom of the press, begged Mussolini not to treat the Italian people as 'unworthy of the liberties it had enjoyed in the past', and formally withdrew his support from the government.[4] Orlando followed suit a few days later and Salandra in mid-December. The government won its vote of confidence on 15 November by 315 votes to 6, with 26 abstentions. A week later, on the Ministry of Interior's estimates, the voting was 337–17–18. In the senate on 3 December 54 voted against the government and 37 abstained, compared with 21 and 6 in June. In the absence of the Aventine the liberals, often reluctantly, were assuming the role of opposition. Deputies with loyalties to the ex-servicemen were particularly restless and even some fascists pressed for concessions.

Throughout November and December tension revived. On 8 November

[1] Jacini, *Storia*, pp. 234–7; De Rosa, *Storia*, pp. 481–3; Howard, pp. 448–57; Rossi, *Il manganello e l'aspersorio*, p. 153.

[2] Prefects were instructed to give active support to the pro-fascist groups which had broken with the Popular party. De Rosa, *Storia*, p. 484. Yet another of these, the Centro Nazionale Italiano, was founded on 12 August. It was joined by a number of senators and deputies including two veterans of the Opera, Santucci and Grosoli.

[3] Frassati, pp. 50–1. Many years later Mussolini remarked, 'Giolitti on the Aventine would have been the end of us.' Y. De Begnac, *Palazzo Venezia* (Rome 1950), p. 357.

[4] Giolitti, *Discorsi parlamentari*, IV, p. 1877.

Amendola launched a new organisation, the National Union of Liberal and Democratic Forces. Its manifesto was signed by 200 leading personalities of the worlds of politics, journalism and learning. The Union's aim was to win back the middle class from fascism to democracy, to broaden the base of the old liberal state and hold out the hand of friendship to the working-class. At a great meeting of the opposition parties in Milan on 30 November, Amendola castigated the industrialists for consigning the Italian people to the fascist bludgeon and for accepting, 'from petty utilitarian calculation, a state of affairs that is the negation of morality and civilisation'. Speaking of the Aventine, he declared, 'Here we win or fall, here the freedom of Italy is conquered or lost . . . No compromise is possible between the contradictory principles that struggle today for the spiritual and political mastery of our history.'[1]

The Aventine meanwhile reaffirmed its belief on 11 November that 'parliament's salvation lies today outside the parliamentary chamber'. A new manifesto demanded a transitional government above party that would hold elections and end 'free crime in an unfree state'. The opposition leaders renewed their attempts to stir the King into action, arguing that Mussolini had broken his June promise to restore legality and ensure justice. Bonomi, on Amendola's initiative, showed the King the Filipelli and Rossi memoranda, but to no effect.[2] When Giolitti came to Rome in mid-November, there were discussions of a plan whereby the King would 'liquidate' Mussolini if the Aventine liquidated itself, then throw his weight behind a Giolitti–Salandra–Orlando coalition. The Popolari told both Giolitti and Salandra that they would not oppose it and tried to get the two men to meet. Amendola however refused to compromise. Discouraged, the three liberal ex-premiers declined to press the King. A less ambitious plan was hatched by the ex-nationalist war hero, Raffaele Paolucci, and forty-four deputies of the majority, for obtaining guarantees of normalisation, electoral reform and the return of the Aventine. This plan was discussed with Salandra and with the liberal minister, Sarrochi, but Mussolini killed the manœuvre by proposing without warning the restoration of the single-member constituency system. This hint of an early dissolution brought the dissident fascists to heel and split Salandra's group as well.[3]

The end of the year saw the climax of the Matteotti crisis. In the course

---

[1] Amendola, *La nuova democrazia*, pp. 209, 213.

[2] Salvemini, *Fascist Dictatorship*, p. 365. Bonomi had lost his seat in April 1924 but was in close touch with the Aventine. As an ex-prime minister he could expect to have influence with the King.

[3] Salandra, *Memorie*, pp. 61–4; Pini and Susmel, II, pp. 404–6. The ex-fascist Rocca offered to bring over fifty supporters of the government to the opposition if the Aventine returned to parliament. Tamaro, I, pp. 475–6.

of a libel action brought by Balbo against the newspaper *Voce Repubblicana*, documentary evidence was produced that Balbo had ordered the *ras* of Ferrara to beat up socialists recently acquitted by the courts and had promised, on high authority, that there would be no legal prosecution. He was obliged to resign his rank of general of the militia. On 3 December Albertini made the episode the basis of the sternest denunciation the senate had yet heard. It was now clear, he said, that *squadrismo* and crime were 'the inevitable product of this regime' and that Mussolini was personally responsible.[1] A few days later Giunta was forced out of the vice-presidency of the chamber when his complicity in the assault on Forni was proved, though the chamber declined to authorise his prosecution. On 6 December Giuseppe Donati, the young and reckless editor of the Popular party's *Il Popolo*, indicted De Bono before the High Court of the Senate for connivance at political crime, and the senate ordered an enquiry. Finally on 29 December Amendola's *Il Mondo* published the Rossi memorandum in full, thereby making public for the first time the allegations that Mussolini had given direct orders for acts of violence (though not for the murder of Matteotti). 'Everyone has the impression that we are very near the end', wrote Turati on the 30th, and 'rapid solutions are on the way'.[2] As the year ended it looked as if the Aventine might be within grasp of victory.

## Dictatorship

The publication of the Rossi memorandum forced Mussolini to act, for the regime was in danger. For many weeks he had been under pressure from the party. The provincial *ras* dismissed Matteotti's death as in itself a triviality but saw in it an opportunity for launching the second wave of the revolution. Why, asked Farinacci, should the party admit defeat 'just because a few fascists happen to have committed a thousandth part of what we had the right to commit in the days of our far too generous revolution'? 'Keep your bludgeons handy', he suggested, should be the party's New Year motto.[3] On 31 December thirty-three consuls of the militia called on Mussolini. In a stormy interview they warned him that there must be no more scapegoats and urged him to shoulder all the responsibilities of the revolution.[4]

In fact Mussolini had already made his decision. On the previous day the cabinet had resolved on repression, against the protests of the two liberal ministers. On the 31st the opposition press was confiscated through-

---

[1] Albertini, *In difesa della libertà*, p. 83.
[2] Turati–Kuliscioff, VI, p. 324.
[3] Salvatorelli and Mira, p. 250; Jacini, *Storia*, p. 250.
[4] Pini and Susmel, II, pp. 407–8; Tamaro, II, pp. 60–2.

out Italy and in many cities the mobilised militia raided the houses
of anti-fascists, broke up their meetings and wrecked their newspaper
offices. 'So Pisa yesterday was normalised', wrote the Bishop, Cardinal
Maffi, to Federzoni: 'as a bishop I wept, as an Italian I blushed with
shame'.[1] On 3 January Mussolini addressed the chamber. He denied the
existence of a Cheka, denied ordering assaults on anti-fascists, pointed to
'the hundreds of fascists in prison' for illegal acts of violence and defied
the chamber to impeach him. Then came the challenge.[2]

> I here declare, before this chamber and before the whole Italian people, that
> I, I alone, assume the political, moral and historical responsibility for all that
> has happened . . . If fascism has been a criminal association, I am the head of
> that association . . . If all the acts of violence have been the result of a given
> historical, political and moral climate, well then, mine is the responsibility,
> because I have created that climate by my propaganda from the days of
> intervention down till today.

The speech ended with denunciation of the Aventine as a seditious,
republican organisation.

> When two irreducible elements are in conflict, the solution is force . . . You
> may be sure that within forty-eight hours from this speech of mine, the
> situation will be clarified all alone the line.

The opposition was impotent to meet such a challenge. In a wordy
manifesto it declared that, with the dropping of the constitutional mask,
the moral battle had been won. But the political battle had been lost.
Effective resistance was impossible. Casati and Sarrochi resigned from
the government. Salandra severed his last link by resigning his post of
delegate to the League of Nations and declared that his two years of collaboration had been in vain.[3] But these gestures made little impression. Even
an idea for a joint démarche to the King by Orlando, Giolitti and Salandra,
the last two now reconciled after ten years' estrangement, fell through. As
Turati summed up the situation, 'The two main elements, the King and
the army, are still two question marks and the decision can only come from
them.'[4] But the Ministers for War and the Navy, General Di Giorgio and
Admiral Thaon di Revel, of whom the opposition had had hopes of support,
remained at their posts. From outside politics came powerful voices of
support. On 19 January the leading industrialists of Lombardy expressed
full confidence in the government, which had ensured discipline, calm and

[1] Salandra, *Memorie*, p. 74.
[2] Mussolini, XXI, pp. 235–40.
[3] But only six of the thirty members of his liberal Right followed him and the
group broke up, ending Salandra's dream 'of the rebirth of a glorious tradition'.
Salandra, *Memorie*, pp. 69–75.
[4] Letter of 2 January. Turati–Kuliscioff, VI, p. 334.

efficient production.[1] The King meanwhile dismissed the Rossi memorandum as 'a lot of nonsense' and accepted the new fascist ministers whom
Mussolini brought into the cabinet.[2] In vain Amendola warned him that
the battle for the constitution would end in 'a historic disaster' unless he
proudly took his courage in his hands and intervened.[3] Victor Emmanuel,
though resenting Mussolini's dictation, calculated that compliance was
less risky than resistance. His passivity made him the prisoner and accomplice of fascism. It also sealed the fate of the monarchy, though its destruction was delayed by twenty-one years.

Mussolini's promise to 'clarify the situation within forty-eight hours'
was not an idle one. The militia was mobilised, over one hundred members
of the opposition were arrested, hundreds of homes were searched by the
police and 'subversive' groups dissolved. Prefects received orders to deal
drastically with any expression of anti-fascism and to tighten their control over the press. Over the next two years the grip of the dictatorship
steadily tightened and individual liberty dwindled. 'We wish to make the
nation fascist (*fascistizzare la nazione*)', Mussolini declared, 'so that tomorrow Italian and Fascist will be the same thing.'[4] 'Everything in the
State, nothing outside the State, nothing against the State' was his aim.[5]

In February 1925 the extremist Farinacci was appointed secretary of
the Fascist party, to the delight of the provincial *ras*. Though Federzoni
was able, as Minister of Interior, to limit the amount of damage he could
do, periodic outbursts of *squadrismo* continued. In October Florence was
subjected to a night of systematic violence, arson, looting and terror.[6]
Meanwhile the judiciary lost the last shreds of independence. When the
*squadristi* who had purged Molinella of socialism were acquitted on charges
of murder and assault, Farinacci congratulated their judges on understanding the difference between crime and 'an episode of the revolution'. De
Bono was acquitted by the High Court 'for lack of evidence' and a week
later was appointed Governor of Tripolitania. On 31 July an amnesty was
declared for all political crimes except murder and manslaughter, and the

[1] Rossi, *I padroni del vapore*, pp. 192–3.
[2] After July 1925 the cabinet was composed entirely of fascists.
[3] After January 1925 the anarchist Amendola moved rapidly towards a republican position. On 13 November in a talk with a senior court official he bitterly
observed that the opposition had been 'abandoned to the hatred and insane violence
of the enemy. All this would not have been possible unless the King had permitted
it . . . The King has abandoned us.' Alatri, *Origini*, pp. 131–2.
[4] Speech to the fourth congress of the Fascist party in Rome, 22 June 1925. In
the same speech he launched the slogan 'Tutto il potere a tutto il fascismo'.
Mussolini, XXI, pp. 362–3.
[5] Speech of 28 October 1925. ibid., p. 425.
[6] Salvemini, *Fascist Dictatorship*, pp. 178–86.

penalties for these were reduced. In December the public prosecutor released all but five of the persons implicated in the death of Matteotti, on the grounds that it was a case of political abduction, not premeditated murder. Mussolini himself, writing in the fascist monthly *Gerarchia*, referred to 'the involuntary character of what took place' and 'a practical joke which degenerated into a horrible tragedy'.[1] In January 1926 the five accused were at last put on trial. Farinacci defended them 'in Fascist style' and turned the trial into a prosecution of Matteotti and anti-fascism. Two were acquitted; the other three were sentenced to six years' imprisonment and under the terms of the amnesty released after two months.[2]

The Aventine lingered on after January 1925. In June the Popolari, after expelling Miglioli on the left and more pro-fascists on the right, reasserted their intransigence at their fifth party congress in Rome. De Gasperi declared that fascist theory and practice were the negation of the Christian concept of the state. In the same month the National Union held its first and only congress in Rome. These were to be the last openly organised expressions of anti-fascist opinion for eighteen years. Amendola and his friends stood firm, in spite of pressure from the conservatives who founded a new National Liberal party with Scialoja as president and the support of big business. Though he carried on the fight for democracy with truly religious intensity, even Amendola now had no illusions. 'It's a matter of twenty years', he told his family; he was consciously working for future generations.[3] Turati too went on wearily fighting, no longer expecting results but in order to satisfy his own conscience.[4] But demoralisation set in during the summer of 1925. The moral campaign was stale, the public indifferent and the anti-fascist press reduced almost to silence. A growing number of deputies urged a 'descent from the Aventine' to the chamber, the only place where the opposition's voice could be heard. First the communists, then the maximalist socialists, then small groups of democrats broke away. Finally in January 1926 the Popolari decided to return to parliament. They were physically ejected and denied readmission except after unconditional submission. Only three accepted these humiliating conditions. In November the 123 opposition deputies, including the

[1] Mussolini, XXI, p. 435.
[2] A new trial was held in 1947. By then two of the five were dead. The other three were sentenced (one *in absentia*) to death, later commuted to thirty years' imprisonment.
[3] E. Amendola Kühn, *Vita con Giovanni Amendola* (Florence 1960), p. 606. Amendola had thus reached the conclusion that Gobetti had reached after the march on Rome. On 24 May 1925 Gobetti wrote: '*Rivoluzione Liberale* proclaimed the Aventine . . . in November 1922. We were the only ones to declare that we would never compromise . . . That meant renouncing all hope of results for ten years.' Gobetti, *Opere*, I, pp. 826–7.
[4] Turati–Kuliscioff, VI, p. 354.

communists, were formally deprived of their seats. This was the Aventine's inglorious end.

Trade union liberty, like political liberty, was suppressed by stages. During the second half of 1924 the fascist syndicates organised a number of strikes, both agricultural and industrial, in northern Italy. One of their motives was to outbid the non-fascist unions for working-class support. In this they were unsuccessful. The socialists and communists, in spite of their divisions, were still far stronger than the fascists in industry. In March 1925 the fascists staged a limited strike in the engineering industry of Lombardy, Piedmont and Liguria. The C.G.L. then intervened and greatly extended it, showing their power by keeping most of the strikers out for three days after the fascist syndicates had ordered a return to work. This was the last major strike in Italy for eighteen years. A month later the socialists and communists again won an overwhelming majority of the seats on the factory councils in the Turin Fiat works, and in July the Fiat management was forced to grant a wage increase. This was the last legal victory of organised labour.[1]

On 2 October 1925 representatives of Confindustria and the General Confederation of Fascist Syndical Corporations met under the chairmanship of Farinacci at the Palazzo Vidoni, the party's headquarters in Rome. An agreement was signed by which the two organisations recognised each other as the sole legitimate representatives of workers and employers in industry. Rossoni, the fascist syndicalist leader, had at last reached his goal of a monopoly of organised labour. But the price paid was heavy. Over the next six months factory councils were abolished, chambers of labour were occupied by the police, strikes and lockouts were made illegal, wage contracts were given the force of law and machinery was set up for compulsory arbitration. While Confindustria remained intact in spirit, structure and personnel,[2] the syndicates were subjected to an increasingly rigorous discipline under officials nominated by the Fascist party from above. Before long they had become mere cogs in the machinery of state. The Palazzo Vidoni pact was the death of genuine syndicalism. The non-fascist unions lingered on for a time, legally tolerated but powerless. 'The remaining red and white organisations are destined to merge themselves

[1] For conflicting versions of these events, see Salvatorelli and Mira, pp. 274–5; Montagnana, I, pp. 167–9; Mussolini, XXI, pp. 289–90; Tamaro, II, p. 91.

[2] As Guarneri, a prominent member of Confindustria, has written, the Fascist party 'always stopped at the threshold of the Confederation of Industry and never succeeded in imposing its own men'. Guarneri, I, p. 55. In December 1925 the Confederation added 'Fascist' to its title and was given a seat in the Fascist Grand Council. Mussolini ordered all his diplomatic representatives to publicise this event abroad: 'the adhesion of all the great economic forces to the regime is now complete'. DDI (7), IV, 201.

[in the fascist sydicates] or to perish', Mussolini pronounced.[1] They preferred to perish. The C.I.L. was dissolved in November 1926[2] and two
months later the C.G.L. shared its fate.

Four attempts on Mussolini's life occurred between November 1925 and
October 1926. Each was followed by violent retaliation against anti-
fascists, in spite of orders to the contrary from Mussolini. Their effect was
to create sympathy for him[3] and to give the government the pretexts it
needed for improving the machinery of dictatorship. After the plot of
November 1925 by an ex-socialist deputy, Zaniboni, of which the police
had been fully informed, the Unitary Socialist party was dissolved and the
police occupied freemasons' lodges throughout Italy. The press was
further restricted and Albertini was forced out of the editorship of the
*Corriere della Sera* which he had built up to greatness. The servile parliament passed a series of 'Fascist laws' for the defence of the regime which
left the constitutional façade threadbare. These were the brainchild of
Alfredo Rocco, ex-nationalist and leading theorist of the organic, collectivist, totalitarian state, whom Mussolini had appointed Minister of Justice
in January 1925. Every kind of association was brought under state supervision and secret societies were made illegal – a law aimed in the first place
at freemasonry. Three fascist commissioners were appointed to bring the
ex-servicemen's organisations to heel. Judges, civil servants and teachers
were subjected to a drastic purge and made liable to dismissal for activities
or opinions 'incompatible with the general political directives of the government'. Mussolini was given the new title of Head of the Government
and Prime Minister, to whom ministers were to be responsible and in whose

[1] Mussolini, XXI, p. 434.
[2] In the last years of its life the C.I.L., like the Popular party, was harassed not
only by the Fascist government but also by Catholic Action which, with the full
approval of the Vatican, wished to establish direct control over all Catholic social
and economic organisations. Catholic Action claimed to be able to provide more
effective protection against fascism than either the Popular party or an autonomous
C.I.L. In November 1925 the C.I.L. accepted the protective wing of Catholic
Action. But when in March 1926 the latter urged Catholics to join the fascist
syndicates, the C.I.L. resisted and was promptly disowned. Howard, pp. 467–9,
474–85; De Rosa, *Storia*, pp. 505–23.
[3] For the fulsome expressions of joy over Mussolini's escape by high clerics,
officials of Catholic Action and the Catholic press, see Rossi, *Il manganello e
l'aspersorio*, pp. 170–82. They made a sharp contrast to the silence with which the
church had greeted previous attempts on the lives of Italian kings and prime
ministers. Pius XI himself on 20 December 1925 spoke of 'the almost visible intervention of Divine Providence'. In April and November 1926 he sent Mussolini
warm private messages. DDI (7), IV, 293, 473. The Pope's benevolence may in
large part be explained by the fact that the prospects of a permanent settlement of
the Roman question and of church–state relations were brighter than at any
moment since 1870.

hands the executive power was concentrated. The role of parliament was further reduced by the grant to the government of power to legislate by decree. The powers of prefects were increased, all the representative institutions of local government were swept away and 7,000 *podestà* were appointed to replace elected mayors of communes. Anti-fascists in exile, whose numbers were steadily growing,[1] were made liable to loss of Italian citizenship and to confiscation of their property.[2]

The machinery of dictatorship was perfected after the fourth attempt on Mussolini's life in October 1926. On this occasion blackshirt reprisals were on a savage scale. All parties except the Fascist were suppressed and the last remnants of an opposition press disappeared. All the communist leaders then in Italy were arrested and the badly disrupted party went underground.[3] Gramsci disappeared into prison, to emerge eleven years later only to die. A thorough reorganisation of the police was carried out by its new chief, Arturo Bocchini, who was later to become one of the most powerful and efficient rulers of fascist Italy. The death penalty, abolished by Zanardelli's penal code of 1890, was reintroduced. The old penalty of banishment was revived and growing numbers of political opponents were sent to small islands or remote corners of Italy under police supervision. Emigration became illegal and passports were withdrawn. In January 1927 another law for the defence of the state made anti-fascist propaganda a treasonable offence and created a Special Tribunal for judging crimes against the state in secret. Twelve votes were cast against the law in the chamber, forty-nine in the senate. Shortly afterwards came the creation of a secret political police. The machinery of the police state was complete.

## Mussolini's First Steps in Foreign Policy

In foreign as in domestic policy Mussolini started cautiously. He came to power with little knowledge of foreign affairs, to which until the beginning of 1922 he had devoted only superficial attention. As a leading critic of

[1] The year 1925 saw the departure to France of Sforza, Salvemini, Donati, Gobetti and Amendola. The last two died early in 1926 from the injuries received at fascist hands. Turati and Nenni escaped at the end of 1926. Nitti and Sturzo had already left in 1924.

[2] Salvatorelli and Mira, pp. 267–72.

[3] Throughout 1924–5 the Italian Communist party had been torn by an internal dispute between the Bordiga and Gramsci factions. The dispute turned on the united front, which Zinoviev and the Comintern still demanded and Bordiga still opposed, and on the relationship between the Italian and Soviet Communist parties. It also reflected the struggle for power in the Soviet Union after Lenin's death. Bordiga became identified with Trotsky, Gramsci with Stalin. By the beginning of 1926 Bordiga had been defeated and Gramsci was undisputed leader, with Moscow's full blessing. Bellini and Galli, pp. 151 ff.; Carr, *Socialism in One Country*, III (i), pp. 163–8, 367–72.

renunciation, he had written much of Italy's imperial and Mediterranean destiny and its need to expand and cast off the shackles of international plutocracy. But on concrete questions such as German reparations, the League of Nations, relations with Britain and France, treaty revision in central Europe or the peace settlement with Turkey, he had expressed only vacillating and stereotyped opinions which showed few signs of serious thinking. Sensitive as always to his surroundings and eager to learn, he was soon at home in the world of diplomatic routine and protocol, and quickly developed an effective technique for impressing foreigners. In this initial period he was content to be the pupil of the secretary-general of the Foreign Ministry, Salvatore Contarini, a man of moderate nationalist views not unlike those of his fellow-Sicilian, San Giuliano. Contarini envisaged for Italy a dignified and equal share, with Britain and France, in the pacification of Europe. The key to success was collaboration with Britain, without which none of the ragged ends left by the peace settlement could be tidied up to Italy's advantage. If fascism brought a new note of toughness into Italian diplomacy, that was to be welcomed as more likely than the good manners of Mussolini's predecessors to win the African and Mediterranean concessions for which Italy had been waiting for four years. Contarini therefore set out to harness fascism to the traditional objectives of Italian diplomacy, to make it respected abroad, to neutralise the pressure from the party for innovation and sensation, and to transform Mussolini from demagogue into statesman.[1] His object was to normalise fascist foreign policy, just as Mussolini's liberal and Popular collaborators hoped to normalise its domestic policy.

Contarini's influence was apparent in one of Mussolini's first acts as Foreign Minister. The hopes of the ultra-nationalists had been raised by Mussolini's speech at Udine in September in which, to cries of *Fiume italiana!* and *Dalmazia italiana!*, he had called for an end to 'renunciation and cowardice'.[2] But on 31 October 1922 he ordered the fascists of Fiume to keep quiet and create no complications.[3] Those who hoped for a Dalmatian crusade were quickly disappointed. On 16 November he assured parliament that the peace treaties would be carried out, whether they were good or bad, adding that they were neither eternal nor incapable of improvement.[4] Faithful to this promise, he accepted the conventions for executing the Treaty of Rapallo which Facta's Foreign Minister, Schanzer, had negotiated with the Yugoslavs at Santa Margherita, and had them ratified by parliament in February 1923.[5] Subsequently Sušak (but not Port Baroš) and the third and last zone of occupation in Dalmatia were

---

[1] Guariglia, pp. 13–15; Di Nolfo, pp. 48–52.      [2] Mussolini, XVIII, p. 416.
[3] Guariglia, p. 12; DDI (7), I, 6.      [4] Mussolini, XIX, p. 18.
[5] The conventions included detailed administrative arrangements with regard

evacuated by Italian troops, and relations with Yugoslavia moved closer to normal.

The second problem that demanded Mussolini's immediate attention was the peace settlement with Turkey. During the summer of 1922 the Turks had routed the Greeks and thrown them headlong out of Asia Minor. In mid-September Kemal's armies reached the zone of Allied military occupation at the Straits. The Facta government, following the French example, promptly withdrew the Italian units to the western shore, leaving the British to face the Turks alone at Chanak. For a few tense days war seemed imminent. Schanzer tried ineffectually to mediate, while leaving no doubt that Italy would remain neutral. The crisis ended with the signing of an armistice at Mudania on 11 October and a peace conference to revise the moribund Treaty of Sèvres was called for 20 November at Lausanne.

Mussolini saw an opportunity for putting Italy once again in the forefront of the international scene. On 16 November he promised parliament that he would safeguard Italy's dignity and national interests, and force Britain and France to examine their consciences. He summed up his policy in the phrase *Do ut des* and 'the simple formula, Nothing for nothing'.[1] Two days later he showed how he intended to |safeguard Italy's dignity. On hearing that Poincaré, the French Prime Minister, and Curzon, the British Foreign Secretary, had arranged a discussion *à deux* in Paris, he peremptorily invited them to meet him on the evening before the conference opened at Territet, a few miles nearer Italy than Lausanne. Curzon and Poincaré, half amused, half irritated, went.[2] Mussolini told the press that the meeting would decide whether Italy's place in the Alliance was that of 'a servant or chambermaid' or that of a Great Power, and promised to speak out 'frankly, in fascist style'.[3] After a brief talk the three statesmen announced that they had reached agreement on all the questions to be discussed at Lausanne, 'on a basis of perfect equality' between the three allies. Foreigners and professional diplomats might raise their eyebrows at this implied admission of Italy's inequality; but the gesture exactly fulfilled Italian hopes that the new Prime Minister, the representative of the war generation, would made Italy's voice heard and secure the victorious peace to which it was entitled.[4]

After two days at Lausanne, Mussolini returned to Italy in high spirits.

---

to Fiume and Zara and guarantees for the Italians of Dalmatia. The latter were to be allowed to opt for Italian citizenship, if they so wished, and still reside permanently in Yugoslavia. Mussolini optimistically told the senate that the conventions would preserve the *italianità* of Dalmatia. Mussolini, XIX, p. 147.

[1] ibid., p. 19.    [2] DDI (7), I, 118 ff.; Nicolson, *Curzon*, pp. 288–90.
[3] Mussolini, XIX, p. 31.    [4] Guariglia, pp. 17–21.

In a private talk with Curzon he had reopened the question of the Middle Eastern mandates and thought he had secured recognition of Italy's right to an equal share with Britain and France.[1] It seemed that he had succeeded in the course of a few days where his spineless predecessors had failed in years of negotiation. But he was soon cruelly disillusioned. Curzon explained that he had agreed only to a friendly discussion of the question between allies and that he had no intention of allowing such a discussion to complicate the peace negotiations at Lausanne. Mussolini threatened to disrupt the anti-Turkish united front to which Curzon attached much importance. But Curzon, exasperated by such crude bargaining, refused to be blackmailed. On 4 December he reminded the Italian delegate at Lausanne of the disastrous consequences of Orlando's withdrawal from Paris in April 1919. Mussolini was forced to submit.[2]

Having failed to get satisfaction over mandates, Mussolini concentrated on the more important aim of securing sovereignty over the Dodecanese. The British, as reluctant as in 1912–14 to see Italy permanently established in the Aegean, were pressing for fulfilment of the promise made in 1920 to cede the islands to Greece.[3] Mussolini replied forcibly that the promise had been conditional on obtaining the benefits in Asia Minor promised to Italy by the Treaty of Sèvres; but now that Kemal's victory had made the treaty worthless, Italy's hands were free as regards the Dodecanese.[4] At the conference Mussolini gained his point: by the Treaty of Lausanne, signed in July 1923, the Dodecanese was ceded to Italy.[5] But Curzon persisted in maintaining that the question was not yet closed and told Mussolini that Britain would not cede Jubaland until Greece was satisfied.

The third major problem of 1922–3 was German reparations. Since the summer of 1922 the fascist press had been sympathising with the French in their differences with Britain over the treatment of Germany and clamouring for a Latin alliance to end Italy's subjection to Britain in the Mediterranean.[6] It was not therefore surprising that Poincaré and Barrère were

---

[1] DDI (7), I, 141, 145.

[2] DDI (7), I, 166, 200, 204–5, 211; Nicolson, *Curzon*, pp. 303–4; Di Nolfo, pp. 56–64.

[3] The Bonin–Venizelos Agreement of August 1920 (see above, p. 583).

[4] DDI (7), I, 70. This position had already been taken up by Schanzer who denounced the Bonin–Venizelos Agreement on 8 October 1922.

[5] In addition to the Dodecanese proper, Turkey also ceded to Italy the small island of Castellorizzo, 70 miles east of Rhodes and less than 2 miles off the Turkish coast, which had been occupied by Italian naval forces in March 1921 in fulfilment of the terms of the Treaty of Sèvres. Its value to Italy was nil but Mussolini set great store on its acquisition. To renounce something acquired by his 'renouncer' predecessors would have been unthinkable. Guariglia, p. 22.

[6] Salvatorelli and Mira, pp. 176–9. Mussolini had repeatedly attacked Schanzer for servility to Britain. Mussolini, XVIII, pp. 274–5, 314–15, 401–3.

delighted with the new Italian government. Mussolini proclaimed in press interviews that 'Germany can pay and can pay well, so must be forced to pay'.[1] Early in December he went to London for an Allied reparations conference to which he submitted an Italian plan, midway between the French and British points of view, for a comprehensive settlement of reparations and inter-Allied war debts. The conference failed to reach agreement, mainly owing to British opposition to Poincaré's plans for seizing 'productive pledges', should Germany default on reparations payments. Mussolini considered that insufficient attention had been paid, especially by the British, to himself and his plan, and when the conference reassembled in Paris next month, he declined to attend. A new British plan for cutting down reparations and reducing war debts proportionately was rejected both by Poincaré and the Italian delegate. Open rupture between France and Britain followed. On 9 January the Reparations Commission declared Germany in default, the Italian delegate voting with the French against the British. On the 11th the French army moved into the Ruhr.

The fascist press was jubilant: France and Italy had broken the British yoke, Germany would soon be brought to heel and a continental bloc formed. Such fantasies were not without official inspiration. Mussolini himself was intrigued by the idea of 'the so-called continental united front' and 'a continental bloc of an economic character', to be composed of Italy, France, Belgium and Germany.[2] But pressure from his diplomatic advisers and the unfavourable reaction of the foreign and non-fascist Italian press soon induced him to define the limits of his support for France. Italian engineers, he declared, went into the Ruhr mines with the French because Italy must have German coal and couldn't afford to be left out of any settlement that France might force on Germany; but this collaboration meant only 'moral and technical solidarity', not approval of military occupation. Mussolini was indeed telling the truth when he protested that he had always tried to restrain the French from resorting to extreme measures.[3] On 15 January he assured his cabinet that the proposal for an anti-British bloc 'is non-existent'.[4] In the chamber he played down the crisis so that there was little debate on it. The Italian engineers became mere observers. Mussolini did his utmost not to get involved in the conflict and reverted to an independent position, much nearer to Britain than to France. Throughout the spring and early summer of 1923 he was working for Anglo-Italian mediation between France and Germany and early evacuation of the Ruhr.

[1] ibid., XIX, pp. 39, 60.
[2] Mussolini to ambassador in Paris, 10 January. DDI (7), I, 324; Di Nolfo, pp. 72–7.
[3] DDI (7), I, 323–4, 336, 338, 340.     [4] Mussolini, XIX, p. 101.

Mussolini's first ten months were on balance reassuring to foreign governments and his own diplomatists. The Fascist government had a good press abroad and was much admired in business and industrial circles. Apart from socialists, there were few uncompromising critics. Rodd, the British ambassador, compared Mussolini's newly donned morning coat and top hat to Garibaldi's 'I obey' of 1866: the blackshirted revolutionary had been tamed, like his red-shirted predecessor.[1] Others were less complacent. 'He is a thoroughly unscrupulous and dangerous demagogue – plausible in manner but without scruple or truth in conduct', wrote Curzon to Bonar Law after his meetings in Lausanne.[2] But such thoughts were kept private. Three months later Curzon referred in public to Mussolini as 'a man of marvellous energy and a mailed fist', who had crushed internal disorder and restored Italy's prestige. Such language went straight to Mussolini's heart.[3] In May 1923 George V paid a state visit to Rome, bestowed the G.C.B. on Mussolini and publicly referred to the crisis which had been 'overcome under the wise guidance of a strong statesman'. The visit seemed to set the seal on Fascist Italy's respectability.

The summer of 1923 brought a dramatic change. Relations with Greece had been bad for many months. Greek opinion was embittered by Italy's success both in keeping the Dodecanese and in obtaining international agreement to a line for Albania's southern frontier that frustrated the Greek claim to 'northern Epirus'. Mussolini was exasperated by the hostility of the Greek press and by a succession of anti-Italian demonstrations. He decided that serious incidents were likely in August when the Treaty of Lausanne was ratified and Italian sovereignty proclaimed at Rhodes. At the end of July the Italian battle fleet was concentrated at Taranto and a plan worked out for the occupation of Corfu in the event of trouble.[4] The intention was to cow and humiliate Greece and so demonstrate Italian might.

On 27 August the Italian members of the commission which was delimiting the frontiers of Albania were assassinated on Greek soil. Mussolini decided to put into effect at once the naval plans that had been prepared.[5] On the 29th he despatched a twenty-four-hour ultimatum to Greece, in

[1] Salvatorelli and Mira, p. 178.
[2] R. Blake, *The Unknown Prime Minister* (London 1955), p. 485. See also Salvemini, *Mussolini diplomatico*, pp. 48–51, for uncomplimentary comments by Curzon, Bonar Law and Poincaré.
[3] DDI (7), I, 565, 568; Salvatorelli and Mira, p. 184.
[4] Foschini, pp. 401–2.
[5] The timing of the assassination was so convenient as to invite the suspicion that it was not fortuitous; but no evidence of any complicity on Mussolini's part has yet emerged. See Di Nolfo, pp. 82–6.

terms reminiscent of the Austro-Hungarian ultimatum of July 1914 to Serbia.[1] It demanded an indemnity of 50 million lire, an enquiry into the crime to be completed within five days 'with the assistance of the Italian military attaché', the execution of the guilty, and ceremonial apologies and funeral honours.[2] Next day the Greek government accepted some of the demands and rejected others, while denying Mussolini's assumption that it was responsible. On 31 August the Italian fleet appeared off Corfu and demanded its surrender. The Greek military commander refused, whereupon after two hours' warning the fleet shelled the Venetian citadel, killing or wounding some twenty of the Greek refugees from Turkey who were its only occupants. By nightfall 1,000 men had been put ashore and the Italian flag was flying over the town. This senseless act[3] transformed Greece in the eyes of the world into a gallant little nation resisting a big bully, and entirely obscured the initial crime of assassination.[4] Greece appealed to the League of Nations and Italy was condemned almost unanimously for an act of aggression. At Geneva it was recognised that the first major challenge to the League had occurred.

This reaction took Mussolini by surprise. He had never attached much importance to the League, which he regarded as 'an Anglo-French duet', nor shown any interest in its proceedings.[5] In the belief that Italy's dignity as a Great Power ruled out any judgement of its honour and vital interests by ill-informed, distant statelets, he announced that the League had no jurisdiction in the Corfu affair. If it insisted on meddling, he threatened to walk out. Salandra, the chief delegate at Geneva, regarded this thesis as untenable but did his best.[6] The French, angling for Italian support in the Ruhr, were ostentatiously sympathetic.[7] The British delegates, under

[1] According to Foschini, p. 404, it was modelled on the Allied ultimatum to Greece of December 1916, which followed attacks on the British and French troops which had landed at Piraeus.

[2] DDI (7), II, 188–9, 195; F. P. Walters, *History of the League of Nations* (Oxford 1952), I, p. 245; *Survey of International Affairs 1920–3*, p. 349.

[3] Fascist apologists have always argued that the bombardment was justified by the Greek commander's 'resistance'. After the evacuation of Corfu, however, Admiral Thaon di Revel, the Minister for the Navy, reprimanded the commander of the naval squadron for opening fire after merely 'verbal' resistance. DDI (7), II, 414. His orders were to use force only if the Greeks used it. In August 1926 Mussolini himself wrote privately of 'the terrible handicap of an unnecessary bombardment'. DDI (7), IV, 387.

[4] Mussolini defended his action by citing Palmerston's conduct towards Greece over the Don Pacifico affair in 1850. The comparison was apt. Mussolini, XX, p. 7.

[5] Though he had appointed Salandra as Italian delegate in December 1922 in order to increase Italy's weight in the League. Salandra, *Memorie*, p. 36.

[6] DDI (7), II, 227, 242, 248, 264, 269; Salandra, *Memorie*, pp. 105–8; Mussolini, XX, pp. 8–10.

[7] Charles-Roux, *Une grande ambassade*, pp. 236–47. The French feared that

pressure from opinion at home, acted as the League's champions, though
Curzon assured Mussolini that it was loyalty to the League, not hostility
to Italy, that prompted this policy.[1] Mussolini however won his point. The
League of Nations Council reluctantly agreed that the dispute should be
handled by the Conference of Ambassadors, to which the Albanian frontier
commission was responsible and whose decisions the Greeks had already
undertaken to accept. The Conference then pressed on them substantially
the same demands as Mussolini had made in his ultimatum, with the important difference that satisfaction was to be given to the Conference, not
to Italy alone. The ceremonial apologies were duly carried out, an international investigation into the assassination was opened and the Greek
government deposited 50 million lire in a Swiss bank pending a decision
of the Hague International Court.

As soon as the Greeks submitted to the Conference of Ambassadors, the
British pressed for evacuation of Corfu. They had not forgotten that the
'temporary' occupation of the Dodecanese in 1912 had lasted ten years and
now seemed likely to become permanent.[2] A tense confrontation followed.
The Italian battle fleet was secretly put on a war footing in case the British
attempted to interfere in the Adriatic.[3] But gradually and very reluctantly
Mussolini gave way. At first he insisted that the assassins must be punished
before Corfu could be evacuated. Then, under further pressure from the
Conference of Ambassadors, he agreed to be satisfied by the unconditional
payment to Italy of the 50 million lire as reparation. To this the Conference consented with some misgiving, provided that it was proved that
the Greek government had been negligent in its enquiries. Negligence
was duly reported by the international commission of enquiry, the 50
million lire were handed over[4] and on 27 September Corfu was evacuated.

The Corfu affair was an important event in inter-war history. Supporters
of the League of Nations deplored the League's 'abdication' in referring
the dispute to the Conference of Ambassadors and felt humiliated by the

---

League of Nations interference at Corfu might be a precedent for interfering in
the Ruhr. The Corfu crisis coincided with a critical moment in Franco–German
relations; German passive resistance to the French in the Ruhr ceased on the same
day that Corfu was evacuated.

[1] DDI (7), II, 274.

[2] It has often been suggested (e.g. Guariglia, p. 29) that Mussolini's aim was
indeed to hold on to Corfu indefinitely. While it can be assumed that he would
have missed no opportunity of doing so, the phrase used, for what it is worth, in
his report to the King on 31 August is 'a peaceful and temporary occupation'.
DDI (7), II, 216.

[3] Foschini, pp. 408–9.

[4] Mussolini donated 10 of the 50 millions to a fund for Greek refugees from
Turkey.

final injustice to Greece.[1] A Great Power had been appeased and the League's moral authority undermined. In Italy Mussolini's action was undoubtedly popular. The fascist press vilified Geneva and contrasted Mussolini's vindication of national dignity with Giolitti's spinelessness in 1920, when two Italian naval officers had been assassinated at Split. National pride had been assuaged and the world successfully defied in a righteous cause.[2] The diplomatists and the traditionalists like Salandra were less complacent, even though they felt that, contrary to all reasonable expectation, the final result had been satisfactory. In their eyes Mussolini's chief merit had been to let others clean up the mess after he had broken the windows.[3] Though under pressure from his party, he was dissuaded from walking out of the League and accepted the argument that Italy could not afford the luxury of absence.[4] Even so, the debates at Geneva and Britain's relentless pressure for evacuation had humiliated him. The final agreement, which his representative at the Conference of Ambassadors considered a diplomatic success, seemed to Mussolini 'a gratuitous and impudent mystification at the expense of Italy'.[5] But in public it was claimed as a great diplomatic victory.[6]

The explosion of Corfu was followed by a calm in Italy's foreign policy which lasted two years. Its most remarkable feature was reconciliation between Italy and Yugoslavia. In his dealings with the Yugoslavs, Mussolini showed a sanity and restraint that contrasted sharply with his brutality towards the Greeks. By the terms of the Santa Margherita conventions a mixed Italo-Yugoslav commission had been set up in Fiume to settle the frontiers and constitution of the Free State and the administration of the port. It failed to make progress. In July 1923 Mussolini lost patience and reopened direct negotiations with Belgrade. By then it was known that the

---

[1] The assassins have not been identified to this day. It may be assumed that there was connivance at the crime by the Greek local authorities on the spot, but any direct responsibility on the part of the government in Athens has never been proved.

[2] Twelve years later the same emotions were aroused by the conquest of Ethiopia. The Corfu affair is a striking foretaste of the Ethiopian crisis of 1935. The reactions of British, French and Italian opinion were identical, and Curzon and Poincaré anticipated the roles of Hoare and Laval.

[3] Guariglia, p. 31.

[4] ibid., pp. 29–30; Mussolini, XX, pp. 108–9, 323.

[5] DDI (7), II, 379. It continued to rankle. On 10 August 1940 Mussolini remarked to Ciano that 'since 1923 he has some accounts to settle, and the Greeks deceive themselves if they think that he has forgotten'. *Ciano's Diary*, ed. M. Muggeridge (London 1947), p. 282.

[6] On 24 May 1924 he told an American journalist: 'I fought for international morality; I fought for the tranquillity of the Balkan states; I fought against war; I fought for civilisation.' Mussolini, XX, p. 293.

Yugoslav government would shed no tears over the disappearance of the Fiume Free State. Mussolini wished to discover what price Italy would have to pay for its acquisition. At first the Yugoslavs proposed Zara or the island of Lagosta as compensation. Mussolini angrily rejected this suggestion. He was prepared to make large concessions over the administration of the port and railways of Fiume, to hand over Port Baroš and to modify the frontier between the Free State and Yugoslavia in the latter's favour; but in no circumstances would he permit alterations to the Italo-Yugoslav frontier as fixed by the Treaty of Rapallo.[1] On 24 August he publicly set 15 September as the time limit for the deliberations of the Fiume mixed commission. But the deadlock persisted. On 17 September, at the height of the Corfu crisis, he sent General Giardino to Fiume to take command in the name of Italy. As the Yugoslavs lamented, this was thinly disguised annexation.

For a few days there was dangerous tension. Apprehensive foreign governments expected Yugoslavia and Greece to combine in joint resistance to Italy. Mussolini even made overtures to Stresemann, the newly appointed German Chancellor and Foreign Minister, for German help in neutralising France, should war break out over Fiume. But the crisis quickly subsided. Stresemann had decided to conciliate France and made it clear that Germany would not take sides in the Adriatic.[2] To the disgust of the

[1] DDI (7), II, 126, 166, 284, 314.

[2] DDI (7), II, 360, 373. Immediately after receiving Stresemann's disappointing reply, Mussolini instructed his ambassador to get in touch with the Chancellor's nationalist critics, who were accusing him of capitulation to France. (Stresemann's government ended passive resistance in the Ruhr on 27 September.) The nationalists hoped to obtain diplomatic support and arms from Italy, overthrow Stresemann and end, by force if necessary, all forms of Allied control of their country. Private discussions on the possibility of Italo–German collaboration continued between individual Italians and German nationalist politicians and soldiers (including General von Seeckt, Commander of the Reichswehr) until March 1924. Contarini was not informed and in the later stages even the Italian ambassador was by-passed by unofficial emissaries, one of whom was General Capello. But the talks lost their main purpose on Mussolini's side when he reached agreement with Yugoslavia in January. DDI (7), II, 405, 489, III, 39, 43.

Cassels (pp. 141–2) shows that the negative reply to Mussolini's enquiry was not as final as the published Italian documents imply. In December Stresemann, having meanwhile given up the chancellorship but remaining Foreign Minister, suggested a secret meeting with an emissary of Mussolini in Switzerland; Mussolini countered with an invitation to meet himself in person in Capri. But Stresemann could not risk publicity for a meeting which might, by alarming Britain and France, delay progress towards a reparations settlement; he therefore 'regretfully declined'. The German nationalists later accused him of rejecting an Italian offer of a military alliance.

Mussolini had no scruples about exploiting resurgent German nationalism for short-term ends, regardless of the long-term consequences for European and Italian security. There is some evidence of Italian assistance for Germany's

Greeks, both Mussolini and the Yugoslavs were careful to keep Fiume and Corfu separate. The Yugoslavs were in no position to fight and therefore had little choice but to accept the *fait accompli*. There was also positive good will on their side. Pašić, the Prime Minister, and Ninčić, his Foreign Minister, were keen on agreement, as were most Serbs; the opposition came from the Croats[1] and Slovenes. King Alexander in particular brought all his influence to bear on his cabinet and, as he told an Italian diplomat some years later, 'courted the displeasure of his entire country' by his efforts to reach a settlement. In personal messages he promised Mussolini his support, expressed his admiration for the Duce's achievement and looked forward to 'a real alliance' in the future, which would stabilise central Europe and reduce its dependence on France and Britain.[2]

After more months of protracted haggling, agreement was precipitated at the end of the year by the announcement that a Franco-Czechoslovak alliance was imminent, and by the visit of Beneš, the Czechoslovak Foreign Minister, to Belgrade for a meeting of the Little Entente Council. Mussolini smelt a plot to attach Yugoslavia to France rather than to Italy, and authorised his ambassador in Belgrade to do all he could to 'paralyse' Beneš.[3] On 24 January 1924 Pašić arrived in Rome. Three days later the Treaty of Rome was signed. The town of Fiume became part of Italy.[4] The rest of the Free State, together with Port Baroš, was ceded to Yugoslavia. To this agreement was added, at Yugoslavia's request, a general treaty of friendship, to run for five years, which bound both countries to preserve the peace settlement. Mussolini thus renounced treaty revision

---

clandestine rearmament during 1923–4. Cassels, pp. 143–4; DDI (7), III, 43. For Mussolini's contemporaneous contacts with the Bavarian separatist extreme right, see below, p. 695.

[1] While opposed to any Italo-Yugoslav agreement which would perpetuate the Treaty of Rapallo frontiers, some Croat nationalists were so embittered by Serbian misgovernment of Yugoslavia that they were prepared to accept even Italian help in liberating their country from Serbian domination. In 1923–4 there were talks in Vienna between Radić, leader of the Croat Peasant party and spokesman for virtually all Croats, and Attilio Tamaro, the local representative of the Fascist party. Mussolini would doubtless have been ready to support Radić and work for the disruption of Yugoslavia if his negotiations with Belgrade had failed; but in December 1923 his response to Croat overtures was negative. 'I stick to the Serbs', he told Tamaro. DDI (7), II, 499, III, 696; Tamaro, I, p. 378.

[2] DDI (7), II, 372, 499, 536, 571; J. F. Montgomery, *Hungary the Unwilling Satellite* (New York 1949), pp. 245 ff.

[3] DDI (7), II, 546, 548, 561–2. The Franco-Czechoslovak alliance was signed on 25 January 1924.

[4] In spite of efforts to attract central European trade, it stagnated for the next twenty years. Its inhabitants were given no say in its fate. In October 1923 Giardino had reported to Mussolini that 'any expression of their wishes would be against us, almost wholly'. DDI (7), II, 441.

and committed himself to Sforza's policy. There were protests from the Croats on one side, some fascist militants and veterans of D'Annunzio's legions on the other, but Giardino kept Fiume quiet. Mussolini received the Collar of the Annunciation and D'Annunzio became the Prince of Monte Nevoso. To his cabinet Mussolini declared, in words that might have been Sforza's: 'For too long the Fiume question has been a kind of portcullis, impeding a vision of, and direct and immediate contacts with, the immense Danubian world. Italy can now move only in an easterly direction . . . her lines of pacific expansion lie towards the east.'[1]

But hardly had Fiume been removed as a bone of contention when it was replaced by Albania. Since 1920 that country had enjoyed relative stability under Ahmed Zogu. In June 1924 his rival, Fan Noli, Orthodox Bishop of Durazzo and leader of the Democratic party, staged a successful rebellion and installed himself in Tirana as Prime Minister. Zogu escaped to Yugoslavia where, with the connivance of the Yugoslav army and frontier authorities and the tolerance (if no more) of the government in Belgrade, he organised a force of Albanian exiles and White Russian mercenaries, stiffened by Albanian conscripts released from the Yugoslav army. With its help he was back in Tirana by Christmas and shortly afterwards was elected President of the Albanian Republic.[2] Fan Noli departed into exile.

Throughout these months of confusion there was popular pressure both in Yugoslavia and in Italy for full-scale intervention, in Yugoslavia on behalf of Zogu, in Italy on behalf of Fan Noli. Both governments however resisted and published a joint declaration of non-intervention on 8 June.[3] Two days later the Matteotti crisis erupted. For the rest of the year Italian policy was moulded by Contarini, who believed in non-intervention as the continuation of Italy's pre-war Albanian policy.[4] Under his guidance Mussolini kept in step with Nincic, the Yugoslav Foreign Minister, withheld recognition from Fan Noli's government, ignored its increasingly desperate appeals for help and protestations of devotion to Italy, warned it not to provoke the Yugoslavs and refused it arms.[5] He also showed patience in accepting, despite justifiable scepticism, the assurances of the

[1] Mussolini, XX, p. 181.
[2] From 1914 to 1924 Albania had been a kingdom in name, though Prince William of Wied made no attempt to recover the throne he had abandoned in 1914 (see above, p. 428). In 1928 Albania once again became a kingdom when President Zogu proclaimed himself King Zog I.                                   [3] DDI (7), III, 236 ff.
[4] Between 1897 and 1914 Italy and Austria-Hungary had agreed to keep out of Albania for the sake of harmonious mutual relations. Contarini likewise believed that only by keeping out of Albania could Italy and Yugoslavia remain friends.
[5] DDI (7), III, 305, 420, 460, 524, 625.

Yugoslav government that it was trying to restrain its subordinates on the frontier from conniving with Zogu.[1] Only in December, when it was too late to save Fan Noli, did Mussolini protest against Yugoslav violation of the non-intervention agreement. Ninčić promptly reaffirmed his intention to act in Albania 'unconditionally in agreement with Italy' in the spirit of the Treaty of Rome, and undertook to delay his recognition of Zogu until Mussolini felt able to take simultaneous action.[2] A remarkable degree of cooperation was thus maintained in difficult circumstances, thanks to King Alexander's determination, shared by his ministers, to align his country decisively with Italy.[3]

The year 1925 brought a decisive change. As soon as he was back in control in Tirana, Zogu began to make soundings for Italian financial and economic aid. They met with a wary response. Zogu's ties with the Yugoslavs were notorious and it was he who had chased the Italians out of Valona in 1920. Mussolini required convincing proof of friendliness before committing himself.[4] But at the end of January negotiations began. Mussolini had by then surmounted the crisis at home and took up the Albanian problem with new confidence and vigour. Albania could not survive without capital and technical aid. Here Italy, with its superior resources, enjoyed the advantage over Yugoslavia. Mussolini's intention was to establish a position of economic predominance. Diplomatic channels were supplemented by a secret mission in the person of a fascist deputy, Alessandro Lessona, who warmed the climate of negotiation by arranging a cash gift to relieve Zogu's personal penury.[5] The main obstacle arose not from the Yugoslavs, who in accordance with Ninčić's policy were obligingly cooperative, but from British oil interests backed by British diplomacy. This obstacle was overcome with the help of Britain's new Foreign Secretary, Austen Chamberlain.[6] On 22 February Mussolini

[1] DDI (7), III, 588, 624 ff., 634 ff.

[2] DDI (7), III, 638–9, 672, 683 ff. Mussolini recognised Zogu's government on 18 March 1925.

[3] DDI (7), III, 63, 80, 83, 316, 412, 530, 603, 671–2. 'Italy ought to put herself at the head of the Little Entente and direct its policy,' Alexander told the Italian ambassador in March 1924.

[4] DDI (7), III, 654, 660 ff., 679 ff.    [5] Lessona, pp. 81–100.

[6] DDI (7), III, 701 ff., 720 ff., 727–31; Swire, pp. 453–4. The Anglo-Persian Oil Company had a provisional concession in Albania dating from 1921. It was the threat of ratification of this concession by the Albanian national assembly that stirred Mussolini into frantic activity, in the belief that it conferred monopoly rights on the British company. He appealed to Austen Chamberlain for his personal support in a matter of vital interest to Italy, and asked him to press the Albanian government to delay ratification. Chamberlain declined and ratification occurred on 16 February. Mussolini then protested at the unfriendly action of Eyres, the British minister in Tirana, in terms that Chamberlain regarded as offensive. Eyres nevertheless appears to have been instructed to cease obstructing Italian

authorised a loan on such terms that, in the opinion of an Italian negotiator, it amounted to 'a mortgage on the whole Albanian economy, surpassing all our most optimistic expectations'.[1] A few weeks later the Italian minister in Tirana was able to boast that the foundations had been laid of Italian predominance in not only the economic, but also the political, life of Albania.[2]

During the summer of 1925 one economic prize after another was extracted from Zogu: first a commercial treaty, then oil concessions, then the foundation of an Italian Society for the Economic Development of Albania, which financed a loan of fifty million gold francs to the Albanian government, then the creation under Italian control of a National Bank which issued the first national currency. Zogu also received Italian instructors for his army and generous supplies of arms.[3] Having conceded so much in the economic field, he next pressed for political compensation, in the form of a promise of continuous Italian support against his neighbours and a guarantee 'against all possible surprises'.[4] Lessona, whom Mussolini sent to Tirana to negotiate independently of the Foreign Ministry, gladly complied with Zogu's wishes; he was convinced that Zogu was 'the winning card' and that alliance with him would give Italy that 'absolute dominion of the Adriatic' which was its due.[5] By July Mussolini was able to tell the King that Zogu was 'acquired for Italy'.[6] Next month Zogu and Lessona agreed on the draft of a secret military treaty. At the last minute Contarini, shocked by what he regarded as a reckless commitment, was able to persuade Mussolini to disown Lessona and not to sign.[7] But this victory for prudence was shortlived. Next year the negotiations were resumed, this time through diplomatic channels. Now Mussolini's goal was political domination; he intended to wipe out the shame of 1920.[8] On 27 November 1926 a pact of friendship and security was signed in

wishes, and Mussolini was able to frustrate the British company's plans. He later admitted that 'the good will and far-sighted views' of the British government had transformed 'a state of tension' into 'a state of collaboration'. DDI (7), IV, 376. The problem of the oil concessions was eventually settled by agreements between Anglo-Persian and Italian and other companies to share the spoils.

For Mussolini's relations with Chamberlain, see below, pp. 691–3.

[1] DDI (7), III, 732, 735.                           [2] DDI (7), III, 763.
[3] Swire, pp. 460–6.                                  [4] DDI (7), III, 833.
[5] Lessona, pp. 83, 94, 111–12.                      [6] DDI (7), IV, 68.
[7] DDI (7), IV, 63; Lessona, pp. 100–20; Di Nolfo, pp. 183–4. At one stage of the negotiation Zogu was in such desperate need of money to pay his army that he demanded a further loan of 6 million lire within three days. Lessona made a dramatic weekend dash back to Rome, persuaded Mussolini to provide the cash and helped him to collect it by ringing round the ministries on a Sunday morning.
[8] In July–August 1920 Mussolini had condemned Giolitti's abandonment of Albania as 'a second Caporetto'. 'Never since Adowa has Italy sunk so low,' he wrote to D'Annunzio. In 1923 he declared, 'When I heard of the evacuation of

Tirana by which Italy guaranteed Zogu's regime against external and internal subversion and established the equivalent of a protectorate over Albania.

The inevitable price of this policy was rupture with Yugoslavia. On 20 July 1925 a further series of technical conventions, dealing with Fiume, Zara and the Italian minority in Dalmatia, were signed at Nettuno. They involved big concessions by the Yugoslavs and were intended to be the final settlement of problems arising out of the Treaty of Rapallo. Ten days after their signature King Alexander declared, 'Now there can be no cloud between our two countries.'[1] His optimism was illusory. In the autumn, by a startling transformation of Yugoslavia's internal situation, Radić, leader of the Croat Peasant party, and a number of his colleagues entered Pašić's cabinet. In deference to its Croat members the new coalition decided not to present the Nettuno Conventions to parliament for ratification.[2] Hostility to Italy meanwhile increased as the Italianisation of the Slav minority across the frontier grew more rigorous. In November fascist violence against the Slavs of Trieste provoked anti-Italian riots in Zagreb and Dalmatia. Italy's penetration of Albania completed the alienation. Now the Serbs too, who had worried little over distant Fiume, felt the menace on their frontier and came to share the anti-Italian sentiments of the Croats and Slovenes.

Ninčić persevered throughout 1926 in his pursuit of Italy's friendship, but it was a losing battle. The Pact of Tirana destroyed what little was left of Yugoslav goodwill. 'The Yugoslav government could have signed a similar pact with Ahmed Zogu long ago,' Ninčić told the Italian ambassador, but had refrained from doing so in the interest of friendship with Italy; now Italy had established 'a veritable protectorate behind our backs'. 'The policy (of friendship) between our two countries,' he continued, 'is based on such deep-rooted interests that I cannot understand why you should wish to compromise it.'[3] On 6 December he resigned, in order to draw Europe's attention to an event which had 'undermined the conviction on which he had based his policy' since 1924. Four days later Pašić, the one man who might have mastered the situation, died. The pact made a lasting rift in the Balkans. But Mussolini did not care. He had achieved his first independent success in diplomacy and was proud of it. Already in October 1926 he had urged his chief of staff, Badoglio, to accelerate military preparations against Yugoslavia, adding the comment:[4] 'Fortunately the Italy of today is capable of administering to the Yugoslavs one of those lessons sufficient to correct the mental and political delinquencies

---

Valona, I wept. And that is not just a rhetorical phrase.' Mussolini, XV, pp. 89, 311, XX, p. 111.   [1] DDI (7), IV, 76.
[2] The Yugoslav parliament did not ratify the conventions until August 1928.
[3] DDI (7), IV, 512.   [4] DDI (7), IV, 446.

of any people. But once again, there is not a minute to lose.' He had
decided that Yugoslavia was an enemy.

The rift between Italy and Yugoslavia had a profound effect upon
central Europe. Sforza had intended the Treaty of Rapallo to be a step
towards a stable settlement on the Danube, and for that reason had linked
it with an anti-Habsburg convention. Italy in his view could best achieve
security on its northern frontiers by assuming the leadership of the succession states in defence of the peace treaties. The essential elements of such
a policy were friendship with Czechoslovakia and reinforcement of
Austria's independence. For almost three years after the march on Rome
it appeared that this was Mussolini's policy also. In the summer of 1922
the Austrian Republic was threatened by bankruptcy and political disintegration. By the Geneva Protocols of 4 October, Britain, France, Italy
and Czechoslovakia agreed to provide a large loan for financial reconstruction under League of Nations control. Mussolini accepted this obligation
on coming into power and assured the Austrian Chancellor, Monsignor
Seipel, that he would follow his predecessors' policy.[1] Relations with
Austria continued to be satisfactory, in spite of some weeks of tension in
the autumn of 1923, caused by Austrian irredentist agitation over south
Tirol. In Hungary, whose conservative rulers were the leading champions
in Europe of treaty revision, the march on Rome had stirred hopes of
Italian support. But Mussolini kept in step with the Little Entente. The
Hungarian irredentists received no encouragement and had their immedi-
ate hopes dashed by the Italo-Yugoslav treaty. In September 1924 the
Hungarian government was again bluntly reminded that Italy opposed
treaty revision.[2]

Towards Czechoslovakia Mussolini at first showed much goodwill. He
had not forgotten his championship of the Czech cause in 1917–18. In
August 1923 Beneš was given a cordial reception in Rome. Immediately
afterwards came the Corfu crisis. Beneš played the role of champion of
the League of Nations and took little trouble to conceal his dislike of
fascism, which he was convinced would not last. This Mussolini found
hard to forgive. He also resented Beneš's international prestige and diplomatic experience, and began to regard him as an undesirable rival. Mussolini had little use for collaborators; he wished to dominate. Beneš on his
side, like his President, Thomas Masaryk, was a dedicated democrat and
never more than lukewarm in his desire for friendship with fascist Italy.[3]

[1] DDI (7), I, 61.                          [2] DDI (7), III, 486, 490.
[3] Kybal, I, pp. 352, 358, 363, 367, II, pp. 66–76; DDI (7), II, 119, 652, III, 178.
Beneš had friends among the anti-fascist opposition and saw Amendola during
his visit to Rome in August 1923. In 1944 Beneš claimed that, unlike almost all

Nevertheless for the rest of 1923 the two countries continued to cooperate in Austrian and Hungarian matters. Beneš repeatedly expressed his approval of Mussolini's Adriatic policy and his wish to keep in step with Italy, and was able to contribute to Italo-Yugoslav reconciliation by personal intercession in Belgrade.[1] But when Beneš suggested that Czechoslovakia should adhere to the Treaty of Rome, Mussolini refused. His suspicions had been revived by the Franco-Czechoslovak treaty, widely believed in Italy to contain secret military clauses. He took it as proof that Czechoslovakia had become the tool of French 'encirclement' and was working for a Danubian Confederation that would be as detrimental to Italy as a resurrected Habsburg Monarchy. The spirit of the Treaty of Rome was therefore anti-French and anti-Czech, as his pleasure in, as he imagined, outwitting France and weakening the Little Entente revealed. When Beneš visited Rome again in May 1924, the atmosphere was cool. The sole result of the meeting was an Italo-Czechoslovak treaty of friendship which never bore fruit.

During 1925–6, as the rift between Italy and Yugoslavia widened, Italy and Czechoslovakia drew further apart. The Czechs felt close affinities with the Yugoslavs, based on common Slav sentiment and common wartime experience, and the tightening of the fascist dictatorship increased the estrangement of Czech opinion. Beneš was still ready to collaborate over Austria, which in May 1925 he declared to be 'essentially an Italo-Czechoslovak problem'.[2] But mutual trust never revived. By 1926 Mussolini had abandoned all pretence of following the policy he had inherited from Sforza. The alliance with Czechoslovakia was allowed to wither and die. The contrary policy which he now adopted was the diplomatic encirclement of Yugoslavia[3] and the drawing together of Austria and Hungary, under exclusive Italian patronage, to form a counterweight to the Little Entente. Treaties of friendship were signed with Rumania in September 1926 and with Hungary in April 1927. The latter was followed by Mussolini's public espousal of the cause of treaty revision. Renewed tension over Albania led to the signature on 11 November 1927 of a Franco-Yugoslav treaty, long postponed from Yugoslav reluctance to offend Italy.[4] Eleven

---

other European statesmen, he did not have a single word in favour of Mussolini on his conscience. Compton Mackenzie, *Dr Beneš* (London 1946), p. 335.

[1] DDI (7), I, 390, II, 46, 136, 553, 560, 595; Kybal, II, p. 68.

[2] DDI (7), IV, 6.

[3] The diplomatic encirclement of Yugoslavia was 'precisely what we want to achieve', noted Grandi, Under-Secretary for Foreign Affairs, in September 1926. DDI (7), IV, 425.

[4] The French had first proposed a pact in 1924, to complement their treaty with Czechoslovakia; the Yugoslavs proposed instead a tripartite Franco–Italo–Yugoslav pact based on the Treaty of Rome. This latter idea was revived in 1925, with

days later a new military alliance between Italy and Albania was concluded
at Tirana. This completed the division of central Europe and the Balkans
into clients of Italy and clients of France, and finally wrecked Mussolini's
most constructive piece of statesmanship, the Treaty of Rome.

In the long run only cooperation between Italy and Czechoslovakia
could ensure Austria's survival. An opportunity for strengthening the
barriers against an *Anschluss* arose during the Locarno negotiations, but
Mussolini threw it away.[1] Instead he set to work to make Austria an
exclusive dependency. This policy had two fatal flaws. First, Italy had
neither the financial nor the military resources that the task would demand,
as soon as German power revived. Second, dependence upon Italy was
unacceptable to the Austrian people. Outside the Christian Socialist party,
many of whose members, including Seipel, admired Italian fascism, there
were few Austrians who felt anything but dislike or contempt for Italy.
To the Habsburg legacy of hatred and the bitterness at Italy's betrayal in
1914 was now added rancour at the persecution of the south Tirolese. In
spite of frequent eruptions of anti-Italian feeling, Mussolini persevered.
In 1934 he appeared to have achieved success. But it was a Pyrrhic victory.
Austria was transformed into a fascist satellite, but in the process was
so weakened and demoralised as to be incapable of resisting Hitler's
onslaught when it came.

Anglo-Italian relations took several months to recover after Corfu. But
Mussolini did not wish to aggravate the quarrel. In November 1923 he
declared his opposition to any further occupation of German territory.[2]
This removed British suspicions that Italy had committed itself to France
in the German question in return for French sympathy over Corfu. Next
month Curzon made a fresh effort to settle the problems outstanding from
the peace conference. His intention was to bargain the cession by Britain
to Italy of Jubaland against the cession by Italy to Greece of at least part
of the Dodecanese.[3] The negotiations over 'the desolate waste' of Jubaland
had now dragged on for over four years. George V, just before his state
visit to Rome in May 1923, had suggested that 'we might be more generous

---

Chamberlain's blessing, in the form of a 'Balkan Locarno' to which Czechoslovakia
also might adhere. Mussolini publicly deprecated it as 'premature' and in private
expressed uncompromising opposition to 'any combination that included France'.
He wanted to exclude France from the Balkans and Adriatic, not to accept French
partnership. In February 1926 Ninčić visited Rome but achieved nothing. Disappointed, he and Briand initialled a Franco-Yugoslav treaty next month, but in
deference to Mussolini's forcibly expressed objections, postponed final signature.
DDI (7), IV, 237, 261, 269, 271, 273, 275, 280, 283.

[1] See below, pp. 689–91.                              [2] Mussolini, XX, p. 106.
[3] DDI (7), II, 512 ff., 531 ff., 542, 555–8.

to Italy, especially after all we have got out of the war': but Curzon had decided that the visit should be given no political significance.[1] Now once again the talks broke down. Mussolini claimed Jubaland in fulfilment of the Treaty of London and refused to renounce any part of the Dodecanese, the last small remnant of Italy's wartime aspirations in the eastern Mediterranean. In January 1924 the Labour party took office in Britain. Ramsay MacDonald decided, after an initial hesitation, to make the concession that Curzon had refused. Overruling the Foreign Office, he accepted the Italian view that Jubaland and the Dodecanese should be divorced. On 15 July an agreement for the transfer of Jubaland was signed in London.[2]

Apart from this one agreement, Mussolini's relations with Ramsay MacDonald were not happy. The latter had been in office less than forty-eight hours when a disagreeable incident occurred over recognition of Soviet Russia. This was a matter to which Mussolini had recently devoted much attention. Even before the march on Rome there had been persistent demands from the Fascist party for a more dynamic policy in the orient. The fact that fascism was inexorably anti-bolshevist need not, it was argued, preclude profitable contact with Russia. Priding himself on his realism, Mussolini foresaw a great future for Italian trade; Italy could be liberated from the grip of the plutocracies, from dependence on British coal and American grain. As a journalist and ex-revolutionary, Mussolini was fascinated by Lenin and the problem of Russia's future. Was not Lenin's New Economic Policy proof that Russia had turned its back on communism? Could Lenin now be starting on the same political path that he himself had taken eight years before? 'Only capitalism,' Mussolini had recently declared, 'can put Russia back on its feet.'[3] Might there not, here too, be an opening for fascist leadership and enterprise? For all these reasons Mussolini decided to improve relations. On the other side the public reaction of the Soviet leaders to fascism's rise to power had been in conspicuous contrast to that of the Italian communists, and they were ready to seize any opportunity of recruiting Italy to the German-Russian front created at Rapallo in March 1922. Within a few weeks of taking office, Mussolini infused new life into the commercial negotiations which had been dragging on since trade missions were exchanged in 1921. At Lausanne the Italian delegation, to Curzon's annoyance, went out of its way to show sympathy with the unsuccessful Soviet claim to be fully

---

[1] Nicolson, *King George V*, p. 374.

[2] DDI (7), III, 122, 143, 165, 206, 210, 388; *Survey of International Affairs 1924*, pp. 466–7. Mussolini from his side contributed to the agreement by accepting a smaller area of territory than some of his 'renouncer' predecessors had claimed.

[3] *Il Popolo d'Italia*, 15 September 1922. Mussolini, XVIII, p. 406.

represented at the conference.[1] But the results were meagre. In July 1923 the Soviet government made it clear that without *de jure* recognition there would be no trade concessions.[2] Mussolini accepted this and on 30 November announced in parliament that *de jure* recognition would accompany the signature of the commercial treaty then under negotiation. The Moscow press greeted this as the first 'breach in the old Entente united front against Soviet Russia'.[3]

When the British Labour government took office in January 1924, it was, like Mussolini, both committed to recognition and eager to reap the commercial benefits of being early in the field. Owing to George V's repugnance to receiving an ambassador from the murderers of his cousins, it was decided to exchange only chargés d'affaires.[4] Ramsay MacDonald appealed to Mussolini to do the same and the latter agreed, assuming that proposals for joint diplomatic action would follow. A few days later he read in the press that the British had forestalled him and granted unconditional recognition. Incensed at what seemed a deliberate act of bad faith, he signed an Italo-Soviet trade agreement on 7 February, formally granted *de jure* recognition and despatched a full ambassador to Moscow to arrive before his British colleague.[5] It was in part to make amends for the offence he had given that Ramsay MacDonald decided to be generous over Jubaland. But Mussolini did not easily forgive such affronts.

A more serious cause of friction was ideological. The rank and file of the Labour party had strong anti-fascist sentiments and insisted on giving public expression to them. In March 1924 an unofficial proposal to send two Labour M.P.s to observe the Italian election drew an official protest from Mussolini and an order to De Bono to expel them should they appear

[1] DDI (7), I, 172, 321, 752, II, 1, 2. Soviet delegates were admitted only to the discussions on the Straits. After an interview with Mussolini, the Soviet representative in Rome, Vorovsky, had reported to Moscow on 8 November 1922: 'It is clear that it is easier for a revolutionary government like that of Mussolini . . . to reach agreement with the Soviet government . . . He [Mussolini] regards Russia as a natural ally . . . We can count firmly on Mussolini.'

[2] DDI (7), II, 104.

[3] Mussolini, XX, pp. 120–3; Carr, *The Interregnum*, p. 249.

[4] In 1924 the diplomatic convention was still observed by which only ambassadors were accredited to heads of state. This meant that George V would not personally have to receive a chargé d'affaires. Nicolson, *King George V*, pp. 385–6.

[5] DDI (7), II, 594, 597, 605, 612 ff., 633; III, 4, 18; *Survey of International Affairs 1924*, pp. 228–30; Tamaro, I, pp. 381–4. Relations with Soviet Russia continued to be outwardly cordial and Rykov, Chairman of the Council of People's Commissars, assured Mussolini that he would allow no communist propaganda to penetrate Italy. DDI (7), II, 649. In June 1924, at the height of the Matteotti crisis, the Soviet ambassador ostentatiously entertained Mussolini at an official banquet. Four months later, in spite of a protest from the central committee of the Italian Communist party, he again invited Mussolini to his embassy

in Italy.[1] The assassination of Matteotti increased the strain. A large meeting of Labour M.P.s, at which Ramsay MacDonald and two of his cabinet colleagues were present, condemned the murder and sent greetings and sympathy to the Italian Socialist party. Mussolini refused to be placated by assurances that a party meeting could not commit the British government, and that Ramsay MacDonald had attended as a party member, not as Prime Minister.[2] These and similar incidents kept the Italian ambassador in London busy throughout 1924 making protests, investigating anti-fascist demonstrations and trying to persuade the British press to see the error of its ways. Just as Matteotti's assassination turned anti-fascism into a significant political force in Italy, so it created anti-fascism as a factor in international relations.[3] Ramsay MacDonald's personal efforts to improve Anglo-Italian relations therefore met with limited success. When the Conservatives returned to power in November 1924, Mussolini publicly rejoiced that 'another sector of the international anti-fascist front' had collapsed.[4]

Ideological antagonism had an even greater impact upon relations with France. As early as December 1922 Mussolini had officially protested against the hostile tone of the French democratic press.[5] Such protests were to become more frequent and strident as the years passed, for Mussolini remained an avid newspaper reader all his life and never lost the journalist's tendency to exaggerate the importance of what other journalists wrote.[6] Another cause of friction was the swelling stream of anti-fascist exiles to France. In February 1924 a fascist journalist and old comrade of Mussolini was assassinated by an anarchist in Paris. Tension rose in June when Poincaré's conservative government was replaced by the radical-socialist Cartel des Gauches under Herriot, only a few days before Matteotti's assassination. Feeling ran dangerously high among the French left and the chamber formally condemned the crime, though the govern-

---

to celebrate the anniversary of the Russian revolution. Mussolini attended. Carr, *Socialism in One Country*, III (i), pp. 168–9.

[1] DDI (7), III, 99, 100, 108–9. 'Italy is not a British dominion', Mussolini wired to De Bono. The British government duly quashed the plan.

[2] DDI (7), III, 280, 292, 309.

[3] The extent to which Mussolini was aware of this is shown by the prominent place which the Matteotti affair occupies in the published Italian diplomatic documents. See DDI (7), III, 270 ff.

[4] Mussolini, XXI, p. 134.

[5] DDI (7), I, 272.

[6] Mussolini paid more attention to the French press than to any other, chiefly because he read French without difficulty. It is significant that a majority of the diplomatic documents drafted in his own handwriting (as noted in the published volumes) concerned the foreign press or public opinion. He required his ambassadors to make strenuous efforts to present a favourable image of fascism.

ment was able to see that the wording of the motion was as inoffensive as possible to Italy.[1] The governments of the Cartel des Gauches, like Ramsay MacDonald's, struggled to keep the animosity within bounds. In 1925 bans were imposed on public lectures by Nitti and Sturzo in Paris, in order to appease Mussolini.[2] But these efforts could not prevent France becoming in fascist eyes the chief enemy.

No progress meanwhile was made towards a settlement of differences in Africa and the Mediterranean. The main bone of contention was Tunis. Of the approximately 100,000 Italians[3] in Tunisia, nearly half had been born in that country, yet under the 1896 convention[4] were still Italian citizens. It was therefore not surprising that French governments were under growing pressure to end this seemingly anomalous privilege and to impose French nationality. In 1918 Clemenceau had denounced the 1896 convention but agreed to leave it provisionally in force pending fresh negotiations. During the Ruhr crisis Mussolini sounded Poincaré on its renewal, as the price of Italian support against Britain and Germany in Europe. Poincaré replied that such a concession would never obtain the approval of the French parliament.[5] The dispute was brought into the open in November 1924 when Mussolini spoke in the chamber of Italy's passionate interest in Tunis and of the sword of Damocles suspended above the heads of 130,000 Italian settlers.[6] The leaders of the Cartel des Gauches were sympathetic but, like Poincaré, declared a renewal of the 1896 convention, even for a few years, to be impossible. The best they could offer was a tacit, unofficial understanding which chauvinist French opinion would not notice.[7]

A second source of friction was Tangier. Having renounced all interest in Morocco by its pre-war agreements with France, Italy had been excluded from Tangier's international administration. Mussolini now argued that times had changed: Italy's status as a Great Power entitled it to parity at Tangier, as elsewhere in the Mediterranean.[8] To this the French were inflexibly opposed; Britain, though sympathetic, was unwilling to press them. Consequently when a three-Power conference assembled in October 1923 in Paris, to draw up a statute for Tangier, Italy was refused admittance. Mussolini resentfully tried to circumvent French opposition by offering an alliance to Spain, where Primo de Rivera had just been installed as

[1] DDI (7), III, 304, 320.                [2] DDI (7), III, 782, 786, 790.
[3] They numbered 85,000 (compared with 54,000 French) according to the French census of 1921, 130,000 according to Mussolini in 1924. The census of 1931 was the first in which the French were shown as outnumbering the Italians.
[4] See above, p. 203.                [5] DDI (7), II, 134–5, 147, 152, III, 185.
[6] Mussolini, XXI, p. 159.                [7] DDI (7), III, 748, 856.
[8] These arguments had already been put forward, to no avail, by Mussolini's predecessors in 1920–2.

dictator. Mussolini expected great things of Primo, in whom he saw a kindred spirit, and Primo gladly acknowledged the kinship between his and Mussolini's governments, both of which were 'resolved to maintain their countries in an atmosphere of austere morality and strict order'.[1] On 16 November a Spanish-Italian commercial treaty was signed. Immediately afterwards King Alfonso paid a state visit to Rome, where he presented Primo as 'my little Mussolini'.[2] But in spite of the fulsome compliments that were exchanged, the Spaniards wished neither to offend France nor to be patronised by Mussolini. Italy wanted Spanish support for the expansion of Italian influence in the Mediterranean, but could offer Spain little in return. To Mussolini's disgust the negotiations for an alliance petered out[3] and he declined to accompany Victor Emmanuel on the return visit to Spain in June 1924. Italy meanwhile refused to recognise the Anglo-Franco-Spanish convention of December 1923. But not until 1928 did Mussolini succeed in securing an Italian share in the administration of Tangier.

The French were equally obstructive over adjustments to the frontiers of Libya and economic and political concessions in Ethiopia. Here their dilatoriness far surpassed even that of Britain. By 1925 Mussolini and his advisers had decided to aim at a comprehensive colonial settlement in which Italy would bargain concessions in Tunisia against compensations elsewhere. But the chances of success seemed slim. It was indeed not until the Laval–Mussolini pact of January 1935 that Italy agreed to relinquish its claims in Tunisia and France finally honoured its promise of colonial adjustments under Article 13 of the Treaty of London.[4]

In the intensive European negotiations of 1924–5 Mussolini took no initiative. His main concern was to ensure that Italy was not left out. On this point he was hyper-sensitive. The first hint of negotiations to which he was not invited brought a flow of enquiries and protests from Rome. But in general he was content to follow the British lead. One of the first acts of the new British Foreign Secretary, Austen Chamberlain, was to go to Rome in December 1924 for a meeting of the League of Nations Council. He made good use of the opportunity for private talks with Mussolini. The Matteotti crisis was then at its climax and Mussolini made sure that the meeting received maximum publicity. He was delighted with a British

---

[1] DDI (7), II, 378, 433.      [2] Pini and Susmel, II, p. 340.
[3] DDI (7), II, 510, 582, 590, 654; Guariglia, pp. 33–4, 52. A treaty of friendship between Italy and Spain was finally signed in August 1926 but was never of any significance.
[4] Except for the infinitesimal modifications of the Libyan-Tunisian frontier in Italy's favour, agreed in September 1919.

Foreign Secretary who treated him as an equal and responded warmly to Chamberlain's discreet flattery. This was the beginning of a cordial collaboration which lasted throughout the Conservative administration from 1924 to 1929.

Meanwhile in July 1924 a big step had been taken towards a sane reparations settlement at another international conference in London. De Stefani represented Italy and made a modest contribution to its success. It was followed in the autumn, to Mussolini's satisfaction, by the first stage of the evacuation of the Ruhr. In October the Geneva Protocol, designed to reinforce the League of Nations Covenant, was approved by the League Assembly. Mussolini announced that he was ready to sign if everyone else signed. But when the British Conservative government refused to ratify it, he declared his satisfaction that it had been buried with 'a first-class, or even third-class, funeral'.[1] In November he told the chamber, 'Italy needs a long period of peace', and disclaimed any intention of being 'original' in his foreign policy.[2] The assassination of Matteotti had reinforced his inclination to be prudent. While he was fighting for survival at home, he had no time for adventures abroad and was forced to be content with a passive role.

In January 1925 the long negotiations for a western security pact began. On 9 February Germany offered France a treaty covering the Franco-German and Belgo-German frontiers, to be guaranteed by Britain and Italy. Initial reactions were unfavourable. But by March the British and French governments had reached agreement on the main problems involved, and with the return of Briand to the French Foreign Ministry in April, more rapid progress was made. Mussolini welcomed the idea of a five-Power pact as an improvement on that of an Anglo-Franco-German agreement from which Italy would be excluded. But from the Italian point of view there were obvious dangers. Italy's defence lay on the Brenner, not the Rhine. Not only would the proposed pact add little to Italy's security; it might even, so it seemed to many Italians, 'indirectly, by the simple fact of its existence, diminish rather than strengthen the efficacy of the peace treaties' by introducing a distinction between first-class and second-class frontiers.[3] Did not Germany's willingness to renounce Alsace-Lorraine imply the intention to turn eastward or southward? Could France, still less Britain, be trusted not to sacrifice Austria in return for security in the west? And if Austria were absorbed by Germany, would

---

[1] Mussolini, XXI, pp. 227, 267–8; also DDI (7), III, 781.

[2] Mussolini, XXI, pp. 164–5. This speech was his only pronouncement of importance on foreign affairs between June 1924 and March 1925.

[3] Mussolini to ambassador in London, 14 March. DDI (7), III, 761 (see also 774, 780).

Italy be left to defend the Brenner alone? Such questions were also much in the minds of the French, who shared the Italian concern for Germany's other frontiers. On this question the interest of the two countries coincided. But when the French made overtures for a wider pact, offering in the words of President Doumergue to 'regard the line running from the Rhine to the Adriatic as a single frontier',[1] Mussolini made no response. The British attitude was decisive. Austen Chamberlain had made it clear that Britain's commitment would be limited to the Rhine; Britain could not participate in a pact on any other terms. But he also gave Mussolini solemn assurances that he had no thought of sacrificing Austria and that the special guarantee for the Rhine would in no way undermine the peace treaties.[2] This for the moment set Mussolini's mind at rest. While professing indifference and even hostility to the prospects of Franco-German reconciliation, he conformed to Britain's wishes and gave the proposed pact his unenthusiastic approval.

In May Mussolini suddenly shook off his passivity. In the previous month Field-Marshal Hindenburg, the candidate of the right-wing parties, had been elected President of Germany. This event stirred the hopes of all nationalists and Pangermans, and in particular heartened the Austrian partisans of union with Germany. It coincided with an unwelcome growth of interest on the part of German nationalists in south Tirol. For this the Italians had only themselves to blame. In the spring of 1923 Mussolini had adopted Italianisation as the official policy of his government and made its instigator, Tolomei, a senator. Tolomei elaborated the programme in Thirty-one Points in a speech at Bolzano in July, and since then it had been applied by the administration with growing rigour. The use of the name 'Alto Adige' became obligatory and that of 'south Tirol' or 'German Tirol' a penal offence. German towns were given Italian names and German street signs removed, the German press was harassed and the German language progressively suppressed in the law courts, administration and schools.[3]

These measures provoked a bitter anti-Italian press campaign in Germany, to which the Italian press replied with equal passion. Early in May 1925 the Italian government made an official protest in Berlin. The response of the German Foreign Minister, Stresemann, was not reassuring. German and Austrian opinion was almost unanimous in favour of an *Anschluss*, he

---

[1] Report of ambassador in Paris, 4 March. DDI (7), III, 743.
[2] Report of ambassador in London, 2 April. DDI (7), III, 787.
[3] Herre, pp. 273 ff.; *Survey of International Affairs 1927*, pp. 190–5. For a full and passionate account by one of the leaders of the Catholic Volkspartei, who was elected to the Italian parliament in 1921 and 1924 as deputy for Bolzano, see E. Reut-Nicolussi, *Tyrol under the Axe of Italian Fascism* (London 1930).

told the Italian ambassador; conditions in Austria were intolerable, and other governments were much less opposed to union than Italy.[1] Mussolini's reaction was to declare in the senate on 20 May that the annexation of Austria to Germany 'would deprive Italy's victory of all meaning' and could therefore never be tolerated. 'Not only must the Rhine frontier be guaranteed,' he continued, 'but that of the Brenner also; the Brenner frontier is irrevocable and the Italian government will defend it at any cost.'[2] Three weeks later he repeated in private his opinion that 'the union of Austria to Germany would mean almost certainly the renewal of war'.[3] This tough language had some effect. Stresemann quickly gave assurances that his government neither intended nor even wished to bring about an *Anschluss*.[4]

After this alarm Mussolini again lost interest. In June Briand repeated the offer to supplement the Rhine pact with a Franco-Italian agreement on the Brenner and Austrian independence, and undertook 'unconditionally' to give the Italians 'all the guarantees they would care to ask for'.[5] Chamberlain welcomed Briand's proposal. But Mussolini was evasive; he had decided to wait and see.[6] The fascist press campaigned against partici-

---

[1] DDI (7), III, 846; Stresemann, II, pp. 80-2.

[2] B. Mussolini, *Scritti e discorsi*, V (Milan 1934), pp. 78-9. Mussolini's warning was addressed as much to Britain as to Germany. He had been shocked by reports that the British ambassador in Berlin, Lord D'Abernon, had been suggesting to Stresemann that Germany might annex Austria as compensation for renouncing Alsace-Lorraine. DDI (7), III, 772, IV, 17, 21.

[3] Mussolini to ambassadors in London and Paris and delegate to League of Nations, 8 June. DDI (7), IV, 21.

[4] DDI (7), IV, 13, 26. Stresemann maintained that the Italian ambassador had misunderstood and exaggerated the significance of what had been a casual reference to the *Anschluss* question. Cassels, p. 153.

[5] DDI (7), IV, 17-18, 27, 32, 37.

[6] DDI (7), IV, 24, 35, 42. There is some evidence from the German side, but none as yet from the Italian, that at this time Mussolini sounded the German government on the question of a Brenner guarantee. But as Stresemann later claimed to have pointed out, a German guarantee could only be given on the assumption that Austria was one day to be united with Germany; Mussolini's enquiry had therefore been 'sent to the wrong address'. Stresemann, II, pp. 157-8, 451-2; P. Schmidt, *Statist auf diplomatischer Bühne* (Bonn 1949), p. 88.

Cassels plausibly suggests (pp. 153-4) that Stresemann and Mussolini had reached 'a tacit, self-denying understanding' over Austria: Mussolini dropped the matter from fear that discussion might bring an *Anschluss* nearer; Stresemann did the same from fear that it might provoke an international guarantee. The fact that the reference in Mussolini's senate speech of 20 May to the need for a Brenner guarantee was later omitted from the official record suggests that Stresemann had asked for and received assurances that Mussolini had no further intention of bringing up the matter for international discussion. In February 1926 Mussolini denied that he had ever asked for a German guarantee. Mussolini, XXII, p. 76.

pation in the Rhine pact and Mussolini told the King with malicious satisfaction that it was likely to come to the same inglorious end as the Geneva Protocol.[1] His studied indifference caused perplexity and disappointment in Britain and France, but the negotiations continued without him.

At this stage many of Mussolini's diplomatic advisers grew alarmed. Led by Contarini, they impressed upon him the advantages of being a co-guarantor with Britain of the frontiers of western Europe and the dangers of being left out. Their advice was reinforced by renewed and pressing invitations from Britain and France. The pact would be 'perfect' if Italy joined, said Briand on 27 August; 'Even now Italy would be welcomed with open arms.'[2] Mussolini still had his doubts but gradually thawed. As a first step he sent an Italian representative in August to the conference of legal experts in London. Though he rejected yet another French offer of a separate agreement on the Brenner,[3] at the last minute he decided to go in person to Locarno on 16 October to initial the five-Power pact.

Mussolini's presence at Locarno gave Chamberlain much gratification. On his return to London he recorded:[4] 'All my pleasant impressions of him [Mussolini] gained in Rome [in 1924] were renewed and confirmed . . . I am confident that he is a patriot and a sincere man; I trust his word when given . . .' Over the next year their personal relationship blossomed. Chamberlain did much to earn Mussolini's gratitude. Throughout 1925–6 he smoothed Italy's path to hegemony in Albania. Over Tangier he was equally compliant, even though his pressure upon France and Spain brought no immediate result. In December 1925 came two Anglo-Italian colonial agreements. The first gave Italy possession at last of Jarabub on the border of Libya and Egypt;[5] the second adjusted and amplified the Anglo-Franco-Italian agreement of 1906 on Ethiopia to the mutual advan-

---

[1] Mussolini to Victor Emmanuel, 17 July. DDI (7), IV, 68.

[2] DDI (7), IV, 111.

[3] On 27 and 28 August. DDI (7), IV, 111–12. The reason Mussolini gave the French for his rejection was unconvincing. He argued that because German aggression was more likely to occur on the Rhine than on the militarily formidable Brenner, an *Anschluss*, by strengthening Germany, would hurt France more than Italy, and therefore a guarantee would be of less value to Italy than to France. DDI (7), IV, 21, 120. His real reasons were probably four: first, a French guarantee of Italy's frontier would have a humiliating element of patronage; second, he hoped to make France pay, in Tunis, Tangier or elsewhere in Africa, for any further contribution to French security; third, he wished to stick close to Britain; and fourth, for the moment he was satisfied with Stresemann's assurances.

[4] Sir C. Petrie, *Life and Letters of Sir Austen Chamberlain* (London 1940), II, pp. 295–6.

[5] Italy's acquisition of Jarabub had been agreed in principle by the Milner–Scialoja agreement of 1920 (see above, p. 557), but subsequently delayed by the

tage of Britain and Italy.[1] Chamberlain and Mussolini met again at Rapallo at the end of 1925, and for the fourth time in September 1926 on Chamberlain's yacht in Leghorn harbour. Lady Chamberlain contributed to the success of the last occasion by wearing a prominent fascist badge for the photographers' benefit.[2] Mussolini was delighted with the frankness and cordiality of their talks, which convinced him of 'the profound value of the Anglo-Italian *entente*'.[3]

Franco-Italian relations presented a very different picture. If Yugoslavia was the main target of Mussolini's dynamism in eastern Europe, France provided the target in the west. At almost every point of Europe and the Mediterranean, French and Italian interests seemed to clash. French 'encirclement' became an Italian obsession. During 1926 the tension rose almost as high as in Crispi's heyday. In April, after a provocative visit by Balbo, Under-Secretary for Air, to the Italian community in Tunis, the French staged joint army and navy manœuvres at Bizerta. In the autumn two attempts on Mussolini's life were followed by widespread anti-French demonstrations and a serious frontier incident.[4] The fascist press abused the French government for complicity with anti-fascist criminals and Mussolini publicly called for an end to the 'scandalous and incredible tolerance' of the authorities 'across the frontier'.[5] The anti-fascist emigration, long the subject of Italian diplomatic protests, now became a public international issue. Rumours of imminent Italian attack spread through southern France, the French Mediterranean fleet was reinforced and troops were moved up to the frontier. The announcement

---

grant of independence to Egypt in 1922. Heavy British pressure was needed to make the Egyptians disgorge. In compensation the Egyptian frontier was extended a short way west of Sollum. DDI (7), III, 794, 834; Guariglia, pp. 36–42; Lord Lloyd, *Egypt since Cromer* (London 1934), II, pp. 149–50. The Italians were impatient to occupy Jarabub in order to stop its use by the still unsubdued Senussi as a base for their guerrilla campaign. The Italians did not complete their conquest of Cyrenaica until 1931.

[1] DDI (7), IV, 208. When Ethiopia was admitted to the League of Nations in 1923 on French initiative (and with Mussolini's grudging approval when he realised he couldn't stop it: DDI (7), II, 165, 169, 177, 179, 193), it was widely assumed that the 1906 agreement on spheres of influence (see above, p. 362) was dead. The sudden British proposal to reactivate it in 1925 therefore came as a pleasant surprise to Mussolini.

[2] Salvemini, *Mussolini diplomatico*, p. 410; Tamaro, II, p. 199. Mussolini noted immediately after the meeting: 'Chamberlain is, at heart, something of a sympathiser with fascism . . . They all, with the exception of the Minister [Chamberlain], gave me the Roman salute at the moment of my departure.' DDI (7), IV, 443.

[3] DDI (7), IV, 442.

[4] The first of the would-be assassins, the anarchist Lucetti, had returned from exile in France expressly in order to make his attempt. The second had no French associations.                                    [5] Mussolini, XXII, p. 201.

of the Pact of Tirana added to the tension. The crisis subsided at the end of the year, but its causes persisted. Repeated Italian demands for a curb on press comment and repressive police action against the exiles were met with the reply that the French press was free and the traditional right of asylum could not be restricted. Ideological antagonism thus continued to embitter the long-standing rivalry of the two countries in Africa, the Mediterranean, central and eastern Europe.

The persistent Franco-Italian tension caused Chamberlain much concern. His long-term aim was to bring the four Great Powers together under the aegis of the League of Nations and so lay the foundations of a lasting peace. Locarno had been the first step towards the stabilisation of Europe. Chamberlain now hoped to extend the spirit of Locarno to central Europe and the Balkans, to the Mediterranean and colonial Africa. Within the framework of this policy he was anxious to obtain maximum satisfaction for Italy's legitimate ambitions. He was therefore ready to use his influence in Albania on Italy's behalf, to 'put in a good word' with the French[1] and, even at the cost of some imperial inconvenience to Britain, to find a little more room for Italy in north and east Africa and on the Red Sea. His calculation was that sympathy and judicious flattery might win Mussolini for constructive statesmanship in the cause of peace. There were times when Mussolini seemed content to be cast in this role. But in the long run he could not be satisfied with so conservative an ambition. International normalisation was as antipathetic to him as normalisation at home. Just as Crispi had striven to give the defensive Triple Alliance an offensive point, so Mussolini tried to make his *entente* with Britain an instrument of his dynamism. There was thus a dangerous ambiguity in the Anglo-Italian relationship, which the Ethiopian crisis of 1935 finally and disastrously revealed.

The years 1925–6 do not mark so clear a turning-point in foreign policy as in internal affairs. Nevertheless, as 1924 had shattered hopes of normalisation at home, so 1925 brought growing disappointment to those who hoped for normalisation in foreign policy. The fascist militants who had clamoured since the march on Rome for a 'second wave', called also for a clean break with the diplomatic traditions of the past. Once the domestic battle had been won, the pressure upon the Foreign Ministry and upon Mussolini himself increased. In the summer of 1925 the transition from traditional to fascist diplomacy began. A first sign of yielding came in May with the transfer of Dino Grandi to the Foreign Ministry as Under-Secretary. This was approved by Contarini and many conservatives, who saw in Grandi the makings of a teachable, responsible mediator between

[1] DDI (7), IV, 461.

the diplomatists and the party.[1] But the motive behind the appointment, beside that of relieving the burden of work upon Mussolini, was to weaken the professionals.

One aspect of the foreign policy for which party militants were pressing was the promotion of fascism beyond Italy's frontiers. They included Giuseppe Bastianini, secretary-general of the organisation for fasci abroad, who wished to develop close links 'between the fascisms of different nations'.[2] Mussolini was at first extremely cautious. When in November 1922 the Hungarian Prime Minister, Bethlen, expressed anxiety about the support that the Hungarian Fascist party might receive from Italy, he was given a categorical reply: fascism was a strictly Italian phenomenon and had no concern with any party of a similar character abroad.[3]

There were occasions on which another note was sounded. At the state banquet for the King of Spain in November 1923, at which Primo de Rivera was present, Mussolini said: 'Though fascism is a typically Italian phenomenon, there is no doubt that some of its postulates are of a universal nature, seeing that many countries have suffered, and are suffering, from the degeneration of the democratic and liberal systems.' In February 1925 his personal organ, *Gerarchia*, expressed the hope that 'possibly before long a large part of Europe will have become more or less fascist'.[4] A year later at a meeting of party leaders he declared: 'We represent a new principle in the world; we represent the exact, categorical, definitive antithesis of the whole world of democracy, plutocracy, freemasonry, in short of the whole world of the immortal principles of 1789.'[5] But in spite of the growing frequency of such pronouncements, which caused strain with democratic nations like France and Czechoslovakia, Italian diplomacy remained for some time to come substantially free of ideological inspiration. Only in the decade after 1930 did the promotion of fascism in foreign countries become the policy of the Italian state.[6]

This did not mean that Mussolini's activities abroad were confined to conventional diplomacy. If the Foreign Minister was content to keep to

[1] Guariglia, pp. 47–50, 63; Di Nolfo, pp. 140–1. Events proved their judgement at least in part correct. Grandi was by no means insensitive to counsels of moderation and in later years made a competent foreign minister (Guariglia, himself a professional, says 'one of the best').          [2] DDI (7), IV, 126.

[3] DDI (7), I, 69, 115, 275. According to Kybal, I, p. 359, Mussolini refused to receive the Hungarian fascist leader, Friedrich, and forbade any direct agreement between the Italian and Hungarian parties. In January 1926 he again dissociated himself from the Hungarian Fascist party and denied that there had ever been any relations, direct or indirect, between it and the Italian government. DDI (7), IV, 219.          [4] Mussolini, XX, p. 113; Pini and Susmel, III, pp. 43–4.

[5] Mussolini, XXI, p. 109.

[6] Mussolini's much-quoted statement that 'Fascism is not an article for export' was made as late as March 1928.

orthodox methods, the leader of the Fascist party observed no such limitations. Party officials were encouraged to establish fraternal relations with foreign fascists.[1] Financial and other encouragement was given to the Corsican separatist movement.[2] Mussolini also took a personal interest in the parties of the German extreme right, particularly in Bavaria. Their antics did not impress him. Just before the abortive Munich *Putsch* of November 1923, he dismissed Hitler and his associates as 'clowns'.[3] Contacts were nevertheless maintained with the Nazi and similar movements, and unofficial emissaries continued to travel between Germany and Rome.[4]

In June 1925 Giunta, a Dalmatian by birth and hero of the 1922 fascist *coup* at Fiume, referred in the chamber to 'the policy of Count Sforza,

[1] There are a few traces of these contacts in the diplomatic documents. In February 1923 De Vecchi received an invitation to visit the fascists of Rumania. DDI (7), I, 531. In December 1926, on the morrow of a military *coup d'état* in Lithuania, Bastianini claimed credit for his previous contacts with the Lithuanian Fascist party and told Mussolini, 'This revolution, too, acknowledges in you its spiritual leader.' DDI (7), IV, 551.

[2] DDI (7), I, 427, 548, IV, 460; Salvemini, *Mussolini diplomatico*, p. 130. In conversation with the Italian ambassador in 1926, Poincaré showed that he was aware of the subsidising by Italy of the Corsican separatist newspaper. DDI (7), IV, 420.

[3] 'Buffoni'. DDI (7), II, 474. A few days after taking office Mussolini had asked the consul in Munich for an immediate report on the Bavarian situation and on 'the possibilities of action on the part of the extreme right elements'. On 17 November 1922 the Italian delegate to the Allied Rhineland Commission reported fully on the Bavarian extremists, including 'Hittler, the leader of the fascists', whose party, as he correctly noted, differed from all other sections of the German nationalist extreme right in advocating renunciation of south Tirol in order to win Italy as an ally against France. Hitler confirmed these views in October 1923, at a moment of tension between Italy and Austria over south Tirol, in a statement to the fascist *Corriere Italiano*. In February 1926, during another acute phase of the south Tirolese question, he reiterated his policy in an article which was subsequently incorporated in the second part of *Mein Kampf*. Herre, pp. 300–2; W. W. Pese, 'Hitler und Italien 1920–1926' in *Vierteljahrhefte für Zeitgeschichte*, vol. 3 (1955), pp. 121–6.

[4] The evidence regarding these unofficial contacts is fragmentary. Three prominent Nazis are known to have taken a special interest in Italy: Göring, who spent a year there in exile after the Munich *Putsch*; Hans Frank, the future ruler of occupied Poland; and General Ritter von Epp. E. Wiskemann, *The Rome–Berlin Axis* (London 1966), pp. 40-1. F. Anfuso, in *Da Palazzo Venezia al Lago di Garda* (Milan 1957), p. 34, mentions the following names: Lüdecke, de Fiori, Major Renzetti, Professor Manacorda, Prince Philip of Hesse (who in 1925 married Victor Emmanuel's daughter, Princess Mafalda).

According to his own account Lüdecke, an early associate of Hitler, went to Milan in September 1922, armed with an introduction from Ludendorff, and had a four-hour talk with Mussolini, who at that time had not heard of Hitler. During a second visit to Italy in August 1923 Mussolini, now Prime Minister, could spare him time for only a few words, and he totally failed in his main purpose of carried out by the Fascist government, that is by Contarini'. Mussolini vehemently denied that his policy had been in any way inspired by 'that liar and traitor'.[1] But his denial didn't convince his critics. The radical policy which the latter demanded was no less than the destruction of Yugoslavia and the formation of a series of small, weak states on Italy's eastern frontier. For this reason the nationalists and Dalmatian irredentists, many of whom were ex-citizens of Austria-Hungary, maintained a close interest in Croat aspirations for independence. After the march on Rome unofficial fascist contacts were maintained, with Mussolini's approval, both with Radić, leader of the disaffected Croat Peasant party, and with dissident Montenegrins, irredentist Albanians and Bulgarian and Macedonian terrorists.[2] These clandestine contacts behind the backs of the diplomatists conflicted directly with the official policy of friendship with Yugoslavia. To many of the old school, including Contarini, such a double game was intolerable. By the end of 1925 Contarini's position had become impossible. The repudiation of Lessona's treaty with Zogu and Mussolini's signature of the Locarno pact were his last successes. He now found Albanian and Yugoslav affairs increasingly handled by unofficial agents or in special departments outside his control. In March 1926 he finally resigned. With his departure one of the last restraining influences upon Mussolini was removed.[3]

---

obtaining money from the Italian government for Hitler's movement. Kurt W. Lüdecke, *I Knew Hitler* (New York 1937), pp. 68–71, 135–45. See also Pese, in *Vierteljahrhefte für Zeitgeschichte*, vol. 3, pp. 116–22. There is no doubt that Hitler was anxious to establish direct contact with the fascist government at this time and had already acquired what was to prove a life-long admiration for Mussolini. But there is as yet no evidence of any response other than non-committal sympathy from Mussolini's side.

For references in the files of the German Foreign Ministry to unofficial contacts, see Cassels, pp. 146–51. In November 1923 the German ambassador in Rome, von Neurath, acquitted Mussolini of complicity in the Munich *Putsch*, being of the opinion that he was 'too clever to compromise himself'; but in May 1925 he told Stresemann that he was convinced of Mussolini's continued liaison with fascist sympathisers in Germany. Stresemann was aware of Mussolini's undiplomatic activities, which helps to explain the persistently cool relations between the two men. DDI (7), III, 85; Cassels, p. 144; Viscount D'Abernon, *An Ambassador of Peace* (London 1929–30), II, pp. 282–3.

For Mussolini's contacts in 1922–4 with German nationalists in Berlin, see above, p. 674, note 2.                                  [1] Mussolini, XXI, pp. 350–2.

[2] See for example the proposal submitted to Mussolini in September 1924 by Roncagli, secretary of the Associazione Nazionale Dalmazia, for a secret Danubian-Balkan Committee to further 'the secret policy which Your Excellency has declared to be of great value'; and the recommendation from the naval general staff in December that the Croat Peasant party should receive secret support. DDI (7), III, 517, 615. For earlier Italian contacts with Radić, see above, p. 675, n. 1.

[3] Guariglia, p. 14; Di Nolfo, pp. 144, 184.

Mussolini had outgrown the tutelage of his professional advisers. The satisfaction with which the latter had welcomed Italy's participation in the western security pact was soon tempered. Mussolini's decision to go to Locarno had been taken reluctantly and with bad grace. He attached no more importance to the treaty than to the numerous other pacts he signed over the years; they were of interest to him only in so far as they conferred momentary prestige or provided an opportunity for publicising his own diplomatic skill. His signature of Locarno did not mean, as Chamberlain and Contarini would have liked, that he was committed to a far-sighted policy of stabilisation in Europe. On the contrary, it was exactly because Locarno was intended to stabilise and to 'crystallise' the peace settlement that he disliked it so much. He preferred a fluid Europe in which there would be scope for 'dynamic' diplomacy.

His resentment at being persuaded to be moderate, and the discomfort he felt in the peacemaker's role, soon became apparent. Within three weeks of Locarno, when celebrating the seventh anniversary of victory, he confessed his disbelief in perpetual peace and declared that Italy must have a strong army and navy and 'an air force that dominates the skies'.[1] In December he told the chamber that he considered 'the Italian nation in a permanent state of war', and announced in *Gerarchia* that 'the Fascist revolution will have in 1926 its Napoleonic year'.[2] That year started with an explosion over south Tirol. Public expressions of sympathy with the Tirolese Germans from Stresemann and the Bavarian Prime Minister provoked Mussolini to reply in the senate with a speech of extreme chauvinism which Tolomei himself could not have surpassed. Alto Adige, he declared, was 'geographically and historically Italian' and the Brenner frontier was 'a frontier traced by the infallible hand of God'; so far from lowering the Italian tricolour on the Brenner, Fascist Italy would if necessary carry it beyond.[3] In April he visited Libya. From the bridge of the battleship *Cavour* that bore him to Tripoli, he announced, 'We are Mediterraneans and our destiny, without imitating anyone, has been and always will be on the sea.' A week later, on African soil, he declared, 'We are hungry for land because we are prolific and intend to remain so.'[4] His voyage, with its accompanying fleet movements, so alarmed the Turkish government

---

[1] Mussolini, XXI, pp. 443–4.  [2] ibid., XXII, pp. 37, 67.

[3] ibid., pp. 68–73; Herre, pp. 375–6; Cassels, pp. 154–8. See also DDI (7), IV, 215, 218, for Mussolini's hysterical rage against the Germans, which his ambassador in Berlin, De Bosdari, later described as showing 'clear signs of paranoia' and a disturbed mind.

[4] Mussolini, XXII, pp. 112–14, 118. The reconquest of Libya, after the forced withdrawal to the coast in 1915–18, had begun before the march on Rome under the direction of Volpi, governor of Tripolitania from 1921 to 1925. The first success was the reoccupation of Misurata, east of Tripoli, in February 1923.

that it ordered partial mobilisation to forestall an Italian descent upon Adalia.[1] The stormy year ended with the protectorate over Albania, rupture with Yugoslavia and crisis in relations with France.

By 1926 Mussolini was displaying all the faults which later brought Italy to ruin. The foreign observers who had dismissed the Corfu affair as a momentary aberration were wrong. Mussolini might have mastered the outward forms of diplomacy, but he remained a demagogue at heart. Impetuous by nature, craving for action and incapable of patience or consistency, he indulged his momentary fancies with reckless disregard of their long-term effects. It is true that extravagant words were repeatedly belied by sober actions, and when fascist aspirations were translated into diplomatic proposals, they often surprised by their modesty. Nevertheless his flamboyant gestures and the calculated ambiguity of his pronouncements created constant tension.[2] Even in his first decade of power, Mussolini was a disrupter of the stability of Europe. On his own he could do only limited damage; Italy's weakness and the risk of isolation forced him to keep his megalomania within bounds. But he had not long to wait. After 1933 the resurgence of Germany under Hitler gave him the freedom of manœuvre to 'live dangerously' as he had always yearned.

[1] DDI (7), IV, 298, 302, 475. Italo-Turkish relations had long been uneasy. In the summer of 1924 Mussolini ordered his Minister for War, General Di Giorgio, to make a study of the problems that war with Turkey would raise. Di Giorgio reported pessimistically in December. DDI (7), III, 169, 216, 227, IV, 604. In the weeks preceding Mussolini's visit to Libya, the Italian press had been full of Italy's colonial aspirations and of the empty spaces of Adalia that awaited Italian emigrants.

[2] Arnold Toynbee in *Survey of International Affairs 1927*, p. 115, justly compared Mussolini's role on the European stage in 1922–7 with those of William II in 1894–1914 and Napoleon III in 1851–70.

# EPILOGUE

The 'fascist laws' of 1925–6 brought political life to an end and imposed a silence that was to last until 1943. In April 1926 Rocco inaugurated the corporative state with what Mussolini called 'the revolutionary law *par excellence*, destined to live in history'. The corporative structure took eight more years to complete. In its final form it consisted of a pyramid of institutions designed to represent 'the interests of production'. The base of the pyramid was provided by 160 national federations of employers' and workers' syndicates and professional associations, embracing every citizen in his occupational capacity. In the middle were 22 corporations, 16 jointly representing the employers and workers in separate branches of production, the remaining 6 representing the professions. The apex was formed by a National Council of Corporations, nominally a deliberative assembly, and a Ministry of Corporations, which was the real seat of power. The task of these institutions was to regulate all problems of production, employment, social welfare and labour relations.

The terminology of the corporative state was syndicalist, with echoes of D'Annunzio's Charter of the Carnero. Official speeches and publications extolled the 'solidarity' of the factors of production, the equality of capital and labour, and the direct participation of workers and employers in the process of government. At first such claims were taken seriously by ex-syndicalists, some of whom saw in the system the embryo of a new social order which might supersede capitalism. As late as the mid-1930s small groups of young fascist intellectuals still hoped that the corporative state might evolve into a genuine 'economic democracy'. But all such hopes proved illusory. In practice the corporations remained part of the machinery of authoritarian government. Their officers were not elected but appointed from above. Though the employers' representatives retained a limited degree of independence, those of the workers were merely bureaucratic agents of the state. The corporations served chiefly to regiment the working-class and, after the slump of 1929, to facilitate the extension of state control over the economy. The addition of a corporative façade did nothing to modify the structure of dictatorial power.

The constitution continued to be eroded. In 1928 a new electoral law was presented to parliament. It laid down three stages of election: first, the nomination by employers', workers' and professional organisations of 800 candidates; second, the elimination by the Fascist Grand Council of half this number; and third, the submission of the remaining 400 names to the electorate, in a single national constituency, for plebiscitary approval. Fifteen deputies and forty-six senators voted against the bill. In the chamber their spokesman was Giolitti, now eighty-six years of age and within four months of death. The bill, he declared, by removing every element of genuine representation and electoral choice, 'signified the decisive rupture of the fascist regime with the constitution'.[1] A new chamber was duly 'elected' in 1929 and again in 1934. It provided unanimous support for the regime. Acclamation and servile adulation replaced debate. In 1939 a further constitutional reform abolished the chamber of deputies and substituted a Chamber of Fasci and Corporations, composed of the National Council of the Fascist Party and the National Council of Corporations, both in effect nominated bodies. The last faint traces of the parliamentary system were swept away.

Two laws of December 1928 and December 1929 gave legal form to the *de facto* dictatorship. The Fascist Grand Council was given constitutional status and responsibility for submitting nominations for Head of Government to the King. Mussolini was thus made accountable to the party instead of parliament, and the King was made powerless to act, even had he wished, until the Grand Council revolted against its leader. The Council remained Mussolini's instrument, meeting only at his summons. On rare occasions it functioned as a forum of debate; but its proceedings were normally dominated by the Duce's harangues and resembled a parade more than a deliberation. The Council played no significant role until July 1943, when it turned against Mussolini and precipitated his fall. Even then it failed to nominate a successor and abdicated its responsibility to the King.

In the last months of his life Mussolini publicly reproached himself for his moderation after 1922. His mistake, he declared, had been to leave the fascist revolution half finished and accept a division of power with the crown. This was the myth of the dyarchy.[2] Mussolini's motives in creating the myth are clear: in 1944 he needed a scapegoat to blame for Italy's disasters. But the dyarchy, in the sense of a genuine division of power, was

[1] Giolitti, *Discorsi extraparlamentari*, p. 354; Salvatorelli and Mira, pp. 327–8. After Giolitti had spoken, Mussolini shouted to him, 'We'll come to you to learn how to make elections.' Giolitti replied, 'Hon. Mussolini, you are too modest. I never dreamt of having a chamber like yours.'

[2] Mussolini's apologia was published in a series of articles in the *Corriere della Sera* entitled 'The Stick and the Carrot', later translated as *Memoirs 1942–1943* (London 1949).

a fiction. For twenty years the monarchy gave fascism no trouble. In January 1925 Victor Emmanuel privately showed displeasure at Mussolini's *coup*,[1] and on several later occasions he protested against encroachments upon the royal prerogative. But in public he remained silent, passively accepting each stage of the process of constitutional erosion. In 1943 he acted only when Mussolini and his regime had already foundered in a war of their own making. The responsibility of the crown and the non-fascist partners of the dyarchy lay not, as Mussolini asserted, in their opposition to fascism, but in their acquiescence. At no stage before 1943 did the crown constitute an obstacle to fascist power.

It was nevertheless an important feature of fascist Italy that many none fascist institutions survived. As a consequence relations between party and state were complex and ambiguous. After the march on Rome the party found itself divided between conservatives hoping for the absorption of the revolution by the state, and radicals demanding the absorption of the state by the revolution. Some of the latter wished to sweep away all the institutions of the effete past, not excluding the monarchy, and renew the ruling class from top to bottom. When Farinacci, ex-socialist railwayman and *ras* of Cremona, became secretary of the party in February 1925, on the crest of the second wave, the hopes of the radicals soared. 'We shall not renounce the rights of the revolution,' Farinacci declared, and promised to extend the methods he had used at Cremona to the whole nation. Mussolini publicly commended his secretary and called for the *fascistizzazione* of the state. But suddenly in April 1926 Farinacci was dismissed. This was a decisive moment. Having used the support of the radicals to consolidate his personal power, Mussolini now abandoned their programme. Never again was the secretaryship held by a man of high standing in the party. To succeed Farinacci, Mussolini appointed Augusto Turati, the first of a line of mediocrities content to obey rather than to lead. Under their rule the process of centralisation of the party, which began at the Rome congress in November 1921, was completed. The *ras* were replaced by a paid bureaucracy of regional and provincial officials who commanded no local following. Local initiative was reduced to a minimum. *Squadrismo* too disappeared; it had become, in Mussolini's words, an anachronism. After 1926 the party turned its back decisively on its origins and ceased to be an independent force.

In the end both conservatives and radicals were disappointed. Neither did the state absorb the party nor the party absorb the state. Italy continued to be governed by two parallel hierarchies of institutions, each deeply influencing the other but remaining distinct. Mussolini stood at

[1] According to Mussolini's retrospective account, this incident was 'the first clash of the dyarchy'.

the apex of both, as Head of Government and Duce of Fascism. Beneath him the party militia coexisted with the regular armed forces, the prefect coexisted with the provincial party official. Even in the police and judiciary a certain distinction lingered on, between the royal *carabinieri* and the ordinary courts of law on the one hand, and the secret political police and the fascist Special Tribunal on the other. The parallelism was symbolised by the two anthems, the *Marcia Reale* and the *Giovinezza*, both played on official occasions. With time the process of *fascistizzazione* did diminish the independence and *esprit de corps* of the old state institutions. From 1927 the fascist prefect, the fascist diplomatist and the fascist judge became more common. In the armed forces, especially the army, a display of fascist enthusiasm could accelerate promotion.[1] The character of the senate, too, was transformed; as elder statesmen died and new fascist blood was injected, it became indistinguishable from the lower house in its black shirts and well-drilled unanimity. The schools, the press and sport were special targets for fascist penetration. Nevertheless even dedicated fascists, appointed to infuse a new spirit into old institutions, did not always escape the influence of tradition. It was also Mussolini's policy on many occasions to strengthen the authority of officials such as the prefect, even at the party's expense. If *fascistizzazione dello stato* had its successes, there was also a contrary process of *statizzazione del fascismo*. And because the crown provided a focus for traditional loyalties, Mussolini never commanded the same blind obedience as did Hitler after becoming Head of State in 1934. In this limited sense a dyarchy existed.

Though it was Mussolini himself who coined the word 'totalitarian' to describe the fascist state, the dictatorship was never truly totalitarian. Italy escaped the scale of oppression that Hitler and Stalin imposed upon their peoples. Fascist absolutism was tempered by inefficiency, by the element of anarchic individualism in the Italian character, and by the deep-seated humanitarian instincts that the Italian people has always shown in its dealings with the oppressed. It was tempered also by the national capacity for compromise and *combinazione*. The classes and interests that had ruled Italy before 1914 were forced to yield ground to the new regime, but they were never deprived of the essential bases of their power. Though fascism lasted for twenty years, it produced no new ruling class as did the Soviet system in the same period of time. With the exception of the honourable but small minority that emigrated, the personnel of the old ruling class survived, whether in the professions or in the public service. This was especially true of the south. The fusion of the Nationalist and Fascist parties in 1923, and the inclusion of non-fascists in the govern-

[1] The air force, being new and without tradition, was always the most fascist of the armed forces; the navy was the least.

mental bloc for the election of 1924, were but the first steps in a continuing process of adaptation. Radical fascists like Bianchi the Calabrian and Padovani, party secretary in Naples, had hoped to use the revolutionary force of fascism to transform the south's stagnant society. Instead the fascist regime compromised. The possessors of real power made their terms with Mussolini just as they had made their terms with Cavour and his successors after 1860. In 1924 Mussolini declared war on the Mafia in a highly publicised campaign, later proclaimed to have ended in total victory. But the Mafia, like the Neapolitan Camorra, survived. There was little change in the relations between the holders of local power and the central government in Rome. The prefect remained as much an ambassador of a distant Power as in Depretis's or Giolitti's day. The fascist regime, like the liberal, accepted in large part the political and social legacy of the past and barely stirred the surface of southern society.

Much of the credit for the relative mildness of the regime must go to Mussolini. Though a dictator, he remained a human being. He could commit brutalities in hot blood or on a reckless impulse, but he was never a systematic persecutor. Indeed he found it as hard to be consistent in oppression as in any other field of human activity. In his early years of power he even preserved a certain detachment and openness of mind. When Salvemini sent him his *Mussolini diplomate* in 1932, Mussolini read and annotated the book and even corrected a few errors.[1] He also found time to study the foreign press and on occasions was even capable of learning from it.

His mind closed, however, as the years passed. 'Mussolini is always right', proclaimed the *Perfect Fascist's Vade Mecum* of 1926.[2] Within a few years the slogan stared down from countless walls throughout Italy and the empire. Incessantly Italians were exhorted to 'Believe, Obey, Fight'. Every fascist, on admission to the party, swore 'to follow without argument the orders of the Duce'. The cult of the Duce grew into a religion. No man could long remain impervious to such adulation. In his prime Mussolini had thrived on controversy. Now, with the Italian press drilled into ever more complete uniformity, he was deprived of the stimulus as well as the restraint of opposition. Constant 'changes of the guard' in party and state accentuated his lonely eminence. Potential rivals were kept at a distance. Grandi became absorbed in foreign affairs, Balbo in the air force and later in colonial government. Having silenced his critics at home, Mussolini became increasingly resentful of criticism abroad. His visit to Locarno in October 1925 was his last to a foreign country until the fateful visit to Berlin in 1937, and he was never again to set foot on free soil.

[1] Salvemini, *Mussolini diplomatico*, pp. 497 ff.
[2] Pini and Susmel, III, p. 86.

Suggestions that he should, like other European statesmen, make a personal appearance at the League of Nations were rejected with scorn. Only in Italy, where an appropriate choreographic setting could be prepared, did he feel certain of commanding respect. Under such conditions his judgement and sense of reality rapidly declined. In the end he became the victim of his own propaganda and no independent force was left to pull him back from the brink.

There was one independent force in Italy that could have been a formidable opponent: the church. Many fascists with a socialist or futurist past yearned to de-Vaticanise Italy, to fight the church to the death and break its spiritual hold. Mussolini preferred to compromise. He found that the leaders of the church were ready to meet him halfway. Even before the march on Rome Pius XI had seen the potential advantages of a fascist victory. After 1922 Mussolini's government enjoyed ecclesiastical approbation on a scale that no liberal government had ever received. Even when the *squadre* turned on Catholic institutions in 1924–6, the restrained tone of the church's protests contrasted strikingly with the shrill denunciations of liberal usurpations after 1861. Secret overtures for a final settlement of the dispute between church and state were made from both sides in 1926. The negotiations lasted three years. On 11 February 1929 Mussolini and Gasparri signed a treaty, financial convention and concordat which together constituted the Lateran Agreements.

By the treaty Italy abrogated the Law of Guarantees and recognised the temporal power of the Papacy, in the form of a miniature, perpetually neutral Vatican City State. The treaty also reaffirmed the vague formula of Article I of the Italian constitution by which the Roman Catholic religion had been declared 'sole religion of state'. In return the Papacy declared the Roman question to be 'definitively and irrevocably resolved and therefore eliminated' and recognised 'the Kingdom of Italy under the dynasty of the House of Savoy, with Rome as capital of the Italian state'. By the financial convention Italy paid 750 million lire in cash and a further 1,000 million in Italian state bonds, as restitution for the expropriations of 1861–70. The concordat, linked with the treaty on Pius XI's personal insistence, regulated relations between church and state. Here Mussolini showed, in Pius XI's words, that he 'lacked the preconceptions of the liberal school'. Of the many concessions that he made, three in particular were such as no liberal government before 1922 could have contemplated. First, the Italian state undertook to prevent any occurrence in Rome that might 'conflict with the sacred character of the eternal city', an undertaking that could amount to a papal veto on political or religious activities of which the church disapproved. Second, apostate or censured priests were to be excluded from any position 'in immediate contact with the public', a provision that later resulted in the exclusion of the modernist Buonaiuti from his university chair. Third and most sweeping, the state recognised 'the sacrament of marriage as regulated by canon law', thus severely limiting its own power to legalise divorce.[1] Only a few voices from the liberal past protested. The long process of 'reconciliation in indifference'[2] had reached its conclusion.

The Conciliation of 1929 was one of Mussolini's greatest triumphs. In reconciling Italy and the Papacy, he could claim to have succeeded where even Cavour had failed.[3] Fascist Italy secured the blessing of the church, thereby gaining in prestige abroad and in moral force at home. In the plebiscitary election of 1929 which followed six weeks after the agreements, the president of Catholic Action urged all the faithful to cast their vote for the regime. For the next eight years the church watched the activities of the fascist state with almost uninterrupted benevolence. When Mussolini exploited that benevolence in the cause of Italian aggrandisement, the church from Pius XI downwards acquiesced. Its blessing was freely given to the conquest of Ethiopia and to the anti-communist crusade in Spain. For all but the final few years, the church must be numbered among the collaborators, not the resisters.

The church's position differed, however, from that of other collaborators in one important respect: within its own sphere its independence was never threatened. It is true that that sphere was forced under fascist pressure to contract. Already before 1929 the Catholic cooperatives, rural banks and trade unions had been abandoned. It also proved necessary to sacrifice the Catholic boy scout movement in face of the fascist claim to monopolise the physical and moral education of youth. After the conciliation Catholic Action came under renewed attack. Once again the church was forced to retreat and give assurances that Catholic Action would eschew politics and bar anti-fascists from its leadership. Nevertheless the essentials of independence were preserved. After 1925, as in 1904–14, democratic Catholics were forced to withdraw from the political to the religious sphere. But just as in the earlier period seeds germinated

[1] On this point, as Mussolini admitted to the King, 'the State retreats a long way.' Another important clause of the concordat extended compulsory religious instruction, by teachers approved by the church, from primary to secondary schools (though not, as the papal negotiators originally requested, to the universities).

[2] The phrase is Jemolo's. See above, p. 228.

[3] This claim was highly offensive to liberals who remembered that Cavour had desired a 'Free Church in a Free State' and had believed that 'the era of concordats' was over. See above, p. 9. The spirit in which Mussolini settled with the church recalled Crispi rather than Cavour; like Crispi, Mussolini hoped to make the church an *instrumentum regni*.

below the surface which bore fruit in the Popular party, so now within the ranks of Catholic Action a new generation prepared itself for the leadership of post-fascist Italy. The church outlived fascism as it had outlived the liberal nineteenth century. After the introduction of racial laws in 1938, it silently and progressively dissociated itself from the regime. The disintegration of Italy in 1943 thrust upon it a unique role as a stabilising and cohesive force; a role symbolised by that of the Pope himself who, when the King and government fled from Rome, became for a few months the city's sole protector. The church emerged from the disaster with enhanced strength and prestige, to play a dominant part in the new democratic Italy.

The fascist regime is even today still praised for its material achievements: it built the first motorways and made the trains run to time. In fact its achievements had few original features, apart from the blaze of publicity which accompanied them and the extravagant admiration they received at home and abroad. In October 1925 Mussolini declared it was one of the aims of his government 'to translate other people's pious and worthy intentions into concrete achievement'.[1] The twenty years' record shows that of all Mussolini's promises, this modest one came nearest to fulfilment. One of the sources of his popularity, at least in the early years, was the impression that he gave to reformers and technical experts that the fascists, unlike parliamentary governments, could 'get things done'. In some fields such as transport, public works and social services, Mussolini did achieve a more rapid advance than his predecessors. But the policies that he pursued differed little from the well-tried policies of the pre-fascist era. Even in those fields where fascism accomplished most, there was little innovation. Industrialisation and economic growth continued until 1929, but no faster and in no different form than could have been expected under a liberal government. After 1929 Italy's response to the slump was neither more original nor more successful than that of other nations. Despite the fascist claim to have forged a new national solidarity, class divisions widened. Land reform made as little progress as before 1914, with the exception of the settlement of ex-servicemen on small-holdings by the O.N.C., Nitti's creation. Land improvement was not neglected; but even the much-vaunted draining of the Pontine Marshes had equally admirable precedents in the lower Po valley before 1914. Italy's endemic unemployment and rural overpopulation were aggravated by Mussolini's simultaneous ban on emigration and stimulation of the birth rate. Fascist policy for the south consisted merely in increased expenditure on public works and a yet higher wheat import duty to stimulate home

[1] Mussolini, XXI, p. 409.

production. The south's basic problems were left to fester and the gap between north and south grew still wider. When fascism collapsed, none of the major problems that Mussolini had inherited were nearer solution.

Fascism reached its peak of success during the six years following the conciliation with the church. Repression continued, but the regime rested mainly on consent. The great majority of Italians, without embracing the fascist creed, acquiesced. Italy enjoyed stability, internal order and external peace. With the passage of time consciences were dulled. Many who had fought fascism suppressed their doubts or conformed. Force of habit and lack of an alternative undermined the will to resist. The conquest of Ethiopia further strengthened the regime. Sanctions revived the patriotic emotion of 1915 and 1919 and rallied the people in a battle of 'one nation against fifty'. The shame of Adowa was wiped out. But the proclamation of the empire in May 1936 was Mussolini's last triumph. From that moment the decline set in. The regime's growing subservience to Nazi Germany, symbolised by the anti-semitic laws, began the alienation of the mass of Italians which a ruinous war was to complete.[1]

After 1925 the public expression of anti-fascist opinion inside Italy was confined to the academic world. In a few learned journals, notably *La Critica*, Croce's historical, literary and philosophical review, liberal ideals were kept alive. For twenty years Croce inspired a resistance of the intellect. A few heroic individuals and groups, mainly from the professional middle class, were not content with intellectual resistance. With support from across the frontiers, they were able from time to time to circulate clandestine literature and make defiant public gestures that kept the idea of opposition alive. But none escaped the secret police for very long. The only continuous organised resistance on a national scale was provided by the Communist party. In 1926 it went underground and prepared for a long struggle. Over the next fifteen years it maintained a skeleton organisation inside Italy and kept contact with the working-class, mainly in the industrial north. It also contributed the majority of the martyrs to the prisons, penal islands and firing squads. Its fighting record won it admiration far outside the working-class; indeed one of fascism's main legacies to posterity was the prestige it conferred on communism. But in spite of the backing of the Comintern and a powerful international movement, the communists were hard put to it to hold their own in the years 1926–35. Even they could do no more than fight a holding operation while waiting for events outside Italy.

[1] There is no more damning verdict on the fascist achievement than the fact that Italy was worse prepared for war in 1940 than under the despised liberal regime in 1915.

It was therefore in exile that anti-fascism survived. The Italian presence was vigorously maintained in the socialist and communist Internationals. Men like Nitti, Sturzo, Sforza and Salvemini spoke out for Italian democracy and ensured that not the whole world equated Italy with fascism. Despite all Mussolini's efforts, the voice of the other Italy was not silenced. Life in exile was often futile and demoralising. Many did not live to see fascism fall. But their exertions were not in vain. In 1924 Amendola had spoken of 'a future that already lives in us'.[1] The exiles kept that future alive and supplied a precious thread of continuity between the Aventine of 1924–5 and the Resistance of 1943–5.

In exile and during the struggle for liberation, anti-fascists argued fiercely over the shape of the new Italy that they hoped to create. None, with the exception of a handful of liberals, wished to go back to 1922. For the communists and socialists and for the democrats of the reborn Party of Action, the Resistance was a second Risorgimento, an opportunity to complete the work that was left unfinished in 1861. They realised, like Gobetti, that this would be a far more formidable task than the mere destruction of fascism; it would involve cutting out the cancers of the old Italy from which fascism had sprung. In the event the second Risorgimento, like the first, disappointed its protagonists. Victory over fascism did not bring the sweeping political and social transformation for which so many in the Resistance fought. Nor did it more than partially renew the personnel of public life. In June 1945 a government fully representative of the Resistance was formed by Ferruccio Parri, lately chairman of the clandestine Committee of National Liberation for Northern Italy.[2] Parri's government lasted only five months and achieved little. Its resignation symbolised the failure of the hopes of the Resistance generation. In 1946, unlike in 1861, a constituent assembly was elected and a new constitution drawn up. By a narrow majority of the electorate, voting in a referendum, the monarchy was swept away. The old senate was replaced by an elected body. The principle of decentralisation was recognised and substantial powers devolved upon four peripheral regions.[3] But these were virtually the limits of the changes that occurred. After 1945 the prefects reasserted their traditional power at the expense of the Resistance's Committees of National Liberation; the regular army and police forces eliminated the

[1] Amendola, *La nuova democrazia*, p. 210.

[2] Parri's government was a coalition of the six anti-fascist parties which constituted the Committees of National Liberation (CLNs): Communist, Socialist, Action, Democratic Labour, Christian Democratic and Liberal. The CLN for Northern Italy (CLNAI) was the central political organ of the Resistance in 1943–5.

[3] Sicily, Sardinia, Val d'Aosta and Trentino–Alto Adige. A fifth region, Friuli–Venezia Giulia, was given autonomous status in 1963.

partisans just as Garibaldi's redshirts had been eliminated eighty years before; many anti-fascists, returning from prison or exile, took up high position in the democratic state,[1] but had to accept as colleagues men who had never opposed fascism. The old Italy once again showed its power of survival.

The first election after liberation showed that Italy's political face had changed surprisingly little since 1922. It was not Giolitti's Italy that re-emerged, but an Italy still in the throes of transition from liberalism to democracy. Before 1914 Giolitti had contained and in part absorbed the inevitable challenge of democracy. The First World War, while deepening the rift between 'legal' and 'real' Italy, had also accelerated the irruption of the masses into politics and strengthened their claim to power. In the ensuing conflict, fought out in a context of economic dislocation and political violence, liberal Italy had foundered. After 1945 the process of adaptation to democracy, of reconciling 'legal' and 'real' Italy, was resumed. From the outset the mass of the people declared its allegiance not to the old liberal Italy but to the two forces which since 1861 had been outside the liberal state: Catholicism and socialism. In the election of June 1946 three major parties emerged: the Christian Democratic with 207 seats, the Socialist with 115 and the Communist with 104. The Liberal party with 46 found itself a small minority, while the Action Party with only 7 suffered a mortal blow. The organised forces of 'black' and 'red' Italy now decisively outnumbered those of the liberal and democratic heirs of the first Risorgimento. The liberal heritage had passed to non-liberals.

The Catholics accepted that heritage without hesitation. The incorporation of the Lateran Agreements *in toto* in the 1948 republican constitution cancelled the last traces of Catholic hostility to the Italian state. The Christian Democratic party had meanwhile been founded clandestinely in 1942–3, in time to play a role in the Resistance. Its leaders were in part survivors from the Popular party, in part members of the new political generation moulded by Catholic Action. It differed from its precursor of 1919 in two important respects: its conservative elements were stronger

[1] The most prominent pre-fascist statesmen to play a part in post-fascist politics were: Bonomi, first civilian post-fascist Prime Minister in 1944–5; De Gasperi, Prime Minister from 1945 to 1953 and chief architect of the new Italy; Sforza, De Gasperi's Foreign Minister from 1947 to 1951; Nenni, leader of the Socialist party; and Togliatti, leader of the Communist party. Einaudi, liberal economist and collaborator of Albertini before 1925, was first President of the Italian Republic from 1948 to 1955; Gronchi, Catholic trade union leader, was the second from 1955 to 1962. Orlando, Nitti and Sturzo played the role of elder statesmen until their deaths in the 1950s.

and its political autonomy was more restricted. The dominant position that the church enjoyed in the aftermath of fascist collapse ensured that the new party's links with ecclesiastical authority and Catholic Action were very close. Thanks to the church's solid backing it emerged after the war with the confident look of a governing party.

In November 1945 De Gasperi became Italy's first Catholic Prime Minister. For the next eight years he was his country's indispensable leader. In May 1947 he ejected the communists and socialists from his coalition. This shattered what little was left of the unity of the Resistance forces and inaugurated a new phase of Italian political life. In April 1948, at the height of the 'cold war', a general election was fought on the single issue of resistance to communism. The Christian democrats, with all the material and spiritual resources of the church and Catholic Action behind them, won a majority of seats in the chamber. This massive intrusion of the church into public life filled champions of the secular state with alarm. It seemed that the prophecies of liberals like Farini at the turn of the century had been fulfilled. The destruction of the Italian monarchy had opened the road to the clerical republic of which Rampolla had dreamed; without a king in the Quirinal the Vatican had resumed its ancient sway over Rome.

Events falsified the worst of these fears. De Gasperi was a democrat, not a clerical reactionary. Like Sturzo thirty years before, he held the balance between the right and left wings of his party. For five years after 1948 Italy was in the forefront of the 'cold war', its internal divisions reflecting the cleavage in the world outside. De Gasperi aligned his country unconditionally with the West and rigorously suppressed subversion and disorder. But the anti-communist crusade was never allowed to get out of control. Like Giolitti between 1903 and 1914, De Gasperi governed from a central position, leaning sometimes to the right, more often to the left. All but two of his successive cabinets after May 1947 contained representatives of at least one of the three parties of the 'secular' centre – liberals, republicans and social democrats – even though for most of that period he was not dependent upon their votes in parliament. This preference for rule by the centre, in the tradition of Cavour's *connubio*, brought repeated denunciations of *trasformismo*. In the 1953 election De Gasperi's party lost its majority and he himself was forced to resign. But throughout the ensuing period of confusion the Christian democrats, as the largest party, continued to monopolise the office of prime minister and to shoulder the main burden of government. Though some of De Gasperi's successors leant heavily rightwards and governed in a different spirit and style, on the whole his practice prevailed. This willingness of the Christian democrats to share their power with other democrats tempered fears of monopolistic clerical rule and plainly signified Catholic acceptance of the political heritage of the Risorgimento.

The extreme left by contrast reverted to its familiar role of opposition. Disunity and intransigence, the weaknesses that had brought it to disaster in 1918–22, reappeared. Already split between the communists and socialists, it was further weakened in 1947 by a schism in the Socialist party. A minority led by Giuseppe Saragat founded a right-wing Socialist Workers' party in the social democratic tradition of Turati, and joined De Gasperi's coalition; the left-wing majority remained faithful to Nenni in the maximalist tradition of Serrati. More splits and regroupings occurred over the next four years. Under the impact of the westward thrust of the Soviet Union, the Italian extreme left was as mesmerised and divided as the previous socialist generation under the impact of the Russian revolution. After their ejection from power in 1947, the communists set out systematically to undermine democratic institutions. Successive governments were fought with every weapon of calumny, obstruction and agitation, stopping short only of insurrection. The socialists were less intransigent, but in the interests of working-class solidarity clung to their Unity of Action Pact with the communists that dated from 1934. In place of De Gasperi's policy of alignment with the West, the socialists demanded neutralism, the communists alignment with the East. The 'cold war' thus reopened and deepened the rift between 'legal' and 'real' Italy. With the communists and socialists together commanding the allegiance of over one-third of the electorate, it seemed that the alienation of the militant working class from the Italian state was as profound as ever. Communist extremism meanwhile stimulated a limited but ominous revival of the monarchist and neo-fascist extreme right. For almost a decade Italian democracy was in great danger.

With the thaw that followed Stalin's death, the rift narrowed. As the external pressures of the 'cold war' subsided, Catholic anti-communism and socialist philocommunism both lost their rigidity. In July 1953 Nenni launched the idea of an 'opening to the left' which would bring his own party into the governmental majority. Socialist disillusionment with the socialist–communist alliance was intensified in 1956 by Khrushchev's revelations to the Soviet Communist party's twentieth congress and by the Hungarian revolution. These events reinforced the advocates of a democratic 'socialist alternative'. In 1957 the Unity of Action Pact was terminated. This signified abandonment of sterile intransigence and acceptance of a constructive programme of reform designed, in Nenni's words, to 'infuse democratic principles into the laws and customs of our country' and to bring 'the working-class masses fully within the structure of the democratic and republican state'. As the Socialist party moved right, the Christian democrats moved left. The election of Pope John XXIII in

1958 accelerated this process by creating an atmosphere of conciliation and *détente*. Moderate socialists and radical Christian democrats found much common ground. In March 1962, after nearly ten years of debate and struggle within both parties, the 'opening to the left' was made. A new coalition of Christian democrats, republicans and social democrats was formed, to which the socialists gave their support. In December 1963 the coalition was renewed and strengthened. Leading socialists entered the cabinet and Nenni became vice-premier under a Christian democratic prime minister. A substantial part of the extreme left thus accepted the liberal heritage.[1] The Catholic–socialist *connubio*, which could have saved Italian democracy in 1919–22, came into being at last.

The first two post-fascist decades witnessed remarkable material progress. The 'economic miracle', starting in 1952, brought Italy an unprecedented period of prosperity and growth. In industrial and agricultural production, in literacy, welfare and standard of living, all previous peaks were left far behind. *Per capita* national income, which had increased by 53% between 1901 and 1950, rose by another 40% between 1957 and 1959.[2] Rapid industrialisation profoundly altered the balance of the economy and the face of Italian society. Between 1950 and 1960 the proportion of the population engaged in industry for the first time surpassed that engaged in agriculture. Italy entered the ranks of advanced industrial nations.

In 1967 many of the basic national problems which confronted Italy at its birth still awaited solution. The 'economic miracle' was by itself no panacea. Though it increased the nation's capacity for social and economic reconstruction, it also aggravated the old disequilibrium between industry and agriculture, town and countryside, and north and south. Italy's wealth multiplied but its distribution remained harshly unequal. Nevertheless the years after 1945 saw great progress. The 'cold war' brought compensation in the form of massive United States aid. At long last a start was made with

---

[1] Not all socialists accepted the 'opening to the left'. In December 1964 a small left-wing group broke away to form a new Socialist Party of Proletarian Unity, pledged to maintain solidarity with the communists. In October 1966 Saragat's social democrats and Nenni's socialists merged in a United Socialist party, thus reducing the number of parties of the extreme left from four to three.

[2] *Per capita* national income in lire (at 1938 prices) rose over the century as follows (see *Indagine*, p. 42; Neufeld, p. 538; Romeo, p. 149):

| 1861–70 | 1863 | 1911–20 | 2458 |
| 1871–80 | 1907 | 1921–30 | 2844 |
| 1881–90 | 1885 | 1931–40 | 3046 |
| 1891–1900 | 1913 | 1941–50 | 2684 |
| 1901–10 | 2267 | 1951–59 | 4112 |

land reform. The south received for the first time its due share of the nation's attention and resources. Instead of tinkering with the Southern question, like their pre-fascist and fascist predecessors, post-fascist governments worked out and put into execution a comprehensive long-term plan of investment and development. Housing and education were improved and the gap between Italy and the rest of western Europe in standards of social welfare was reduced. A sane and far-sighted foreign policy was an essential factor in this progress. De Gasperi and Sforza took the first steps towards membership of a united West European community of equals; their successors reaped the fruits of their efforts. Relieved of imperial burdens and cured of nationalist megalomania, Italy acquired greater security and a sounder international economic position than ever before in its history. The pace of progress slowed down during the period of political confusion that followed the election of 1953 and De Gasperi's death. But the 'opening to the left' created the opportunity for a further leap forward. The programme of the Christian democratic–socialist coalition included full implementation of the democratic constitution of 1948, especially the clauses on regional decentralisation; a large degree of planning and state control of the economy in the interests of social justice; greater equality of opportunity in education; measures to deal with rural poverty and stagnation; and a massive extension of the social services. Such a programme, if carried out, could go far towards closing the gap between 'legal' and 'real' Italy and bring the long-sought goal of national unity within reach.

In 1961 united Italy celebrated its centenary. In the perspective of those hundred years it is possible to assess the achievement of the liberal half-century. Its imprint, for good and for bad, remains plainly visible. Not even twenty years of fascism were sufficient to erase it. The catalogue of liberal Italy's failures is long. To it have contributed not only the multifarious enemies of liberalism, but also generations of impatient democratic reformers and perfectionists. Italians are their own fiercest critics and after 1861 there was material in plenty to hand. But at the end of a work on 'Italy from Liberalism to Fascism', in the perspective of 1967, it is legitimate to close on an optimistic note. In spite of the strains of 1887–1901, the crisis of 1914–25 and the cataclysm of 1940–5, Italy has enjoyed many of the blessings of slow but sure progress and continuing growth. The foundations laid by Cavour, consolidated by Depretis, strengthened and broadened by Giolitti, emerged from the fascist hurricane sufficiently strong to bear the new democratic superstructure of De Gasperi and his successors. The makers of Italy had built well.

ILF—AA

# BIBLIOGRAPHY

The following abbreviations have been used in the footnotes:

ASI: *Annuario statistico italiano.*
BD: Gooch and Temperley, *British Documents on the Origins of the War, 1898–1914.*
BFP: Woodward and Butler, *Documents on British Foreign Policy, 1919–1939.*
DDF: *Documents diplomatiques français 1871–1914.*
DDI: *I documenti diplomatici italiani.*
GP: *Die Grosse Politik.*
PPC: *Papers Relating to the Foreign Relations of the United States, The Paris Peace Conference.*
PRO: Public Record Office.

ALATRI, P., *Lotte politiche in Sicilia sotto il governo della Destra (1866–74),* Turin 1954.
    *Nitti, D'Annunzio e la questione adriatica,* Milan 1959.
    *Le origini del fascismo,* Rome 1956.
ALBERTINI, L., *In difesa della libertà,* Milan 1947.
    *The Origins of the War of 1914,* 3 vols, Oxford 1952–7.
    *Venti anni di vita politica,* 5 vols, Bologna 1950–3.
ALBRECHT-CARRIÉ, R., *Italy at the Paris Peace Conference,* New York 1938.
ALDROVANDI MARESCOTTI, L., *Guerra diplomatica,* Milan 1937.
    *Nuovi ricordi,* Milan 1938.
AMENDOLA, G., *La nuova democrazia,* Naples 1951.
*Annuario statistico italiano,* Rome 1878– .
ANSALDO, G., *Il ministro della buonavita,* Milan 1950.
ARIAS, G., *La questione meridionale,* 2 vols, Bologna 1921.
ASKEW, W. C., *Europe and Italy's Acquisition of Libya,* Durham, N.C. 1942.
BADOGLIO, P., *Rivelazioni su Fiume,* Rome 1946.
BATTAGLIA, R., *La prima guerra d'Africa,* Turin 1958.
BELLINI, F. and GALLI, G., *Storia del Partito Comunista Italiano,* Milan 1953.
BENEŠ, E., *My War Memoirs,* London 1928.
BEYENS, R., *Quatre ans à Rome 1921–1926,* Paris 1934.
BINCHY, D. A., *Church and State in Fascist Italy,* Oxford 1941.
BISSOLATI, L., *Diario di guerra,* Turin 1935.
    *La politica estera dell' Italia dal 1897 al 1920,* Milan 1923.

BONOMI, I., *La politica italiana da Porta Pia a Vittorio Veneto*, Turin 1944.
*La politica italiana dopo Vittorio Veneto*, Turin 1955.
*Leonida Bissolati e il movimento socialista in Italia*, 2nd ed., Rome 1945.
BORGHI, A., *Mezzo secolo di anarchia*, Naples 1956.
BORSA, G., *Italia e Cina nel secolo XIX*, Milan 1961.
BÜLOW, PRINCE B. VON, *Memoirs*, 4 vols, London 1931–2.
CADORNA, L., *Altre pagine sulla grande guerra*, Milan 1924.
*La guerra alla fronte italiana*, 2 vols, Milan 1921.
*Pagine polemiche*, Milan 1950.
CAIZZI, B., ed., *Antologia della questione meridionale*, Milan 1950.
CAROCCI, G., *Agostino Depretis e la politica interna italiana dal 1876 al 1887*, Turin 1956.
CARR, E. H., *A History of Soviet Russia, The Interregnum*, London 1954.
*Socialism in One Country, 1924–1926*, III, London 1964.
CASSELS, A., 'Mussolini and German Nationalism 1922–5', in *Journal of Modern History*, vol. 35 (June 1963), pp. 137–57.
CATALUCCIO, F., *Antonio di San Giuliano e la politica estera italiana dal 1900 al 1914*, Florence 1935.
CAVIGLIA, E., *Il conflitto di Fiume*, Milan 1948.
CECIL, LADY G., *Life of Robert Marquis of Salisbury*, 4 vols, London 1921–32.
CHABOD, F., *L'Italie contemporaine*, Paris 1950.
'Kulturkampf e Triplice Alleanza', in *Rivista storica italiana*, vol. 62 (1950), pp. 257–80.
*Storia della politica estera italiana dal 1870 al 1896, I, Le premesse*, Bari 1951.
CHARLES-ROUX, F., *Souvenirs diplomatiques, Rome-Quirinal février 1916–février 1919*, Paris 1958.
*Souvenirs diplomatiques, Une grande ambassade à Rome 1919–1925*, Paris 1961.
CHIALA, L., *La spedizione di Massawa*, Turin 1888.
*Pagine di storia contemporanea*, 3 vols, Turin 1892–3.
CIASCA, R., *Storia coloniale dell' Italia contemporanea*, Milan 1938.
CILIBRIZZI, S., *Storia parlamentare, politica e diplomatica d'Italia*, 8 vols, Naples 1939–52.
COLAJANNI, N., *Gli avvenimenti di Sicilia e le loro cause*, 2nd ed., Palermo 1896.
COLETTI, F., *Dell' emigrazione italiana*, in *Cinquanta anni di storia italiana*, III, Milan 1911.
*Compendio delle statistiche elettorali italiane dal 1848 al 1934*, 2 vols, Istituto Centrale di Statistica e Ministero per la Costituente, Rome 1947.
COPPOLA D'ANNA, F., *Popolazione, reddito e finanze pubbliche dell' Italia dal 1860 ad oggi*, Rome 1946.
CORBINO, E., *Annali dell' economia italiana*, 5 vols, Città di Castello 1931–8.
CORRADINI, E., *Discorsi politici*, Florence 1923.
*Il nazionalismo italiano*, Milan 1914.
*Il volere d'Italia*, Naples 1911.
*L'ora di Tripoli*, Milan 1911.
CRESPI, S., *Alla difesa d'Italia in guerra e a Versailles*, Milan 1937.

CRISPI, F., *Memoirs*, 3 vols, London 1912–14.
   *Politica interna*, Rome 1924.
   *La prima guerra d'Africa*, Milan 1914.
   *Scritti e discorsi politici*, Rome 1890.
CRISPOLTI, C. and AURELI, G., *La politica di Leone XIII*, Rome 1912.
CROCE, B., *A History of Italy 1871–1915*, Oxford 1929.
CURATO, F., *La conferenza della pace*, 2 vols, Milan 1942.
DALLA TORRE, G., *I cattolici e la vita pubblica italiana, 1866–1920*, Vatican City 1944.
D'ANNUNZIO, G., *Opere*, National edition, *La penultima ventura – Il sudore di sangue*, Verona 1932.
   *Per la più grande Italia*, Verona 1932.
DE BOSDARI, A., *Delle guerre balcaniche*, 2nd ed., Milan 1931.
DE FELICE, R., *Mussolini il rivoluzionario 1883–1920*, Turin 1965.
*Democrazia e socialismo in Italia. Carteggi di Napoleone Colajanni 1878–1898*, ed. S. M. Ganci, Milan 1959.
DE ROSA, G., *I conservatori nazionali*, Brescia 1962.
   *Giolitti e il fascismo*, Rome 1957.
   *Storia del Partito Popolare*, Bari 1958.
   *Storia politica dell' Azione Cattolica in Italia*, 2 vols, Bari 1953–4.
DI NOLFO, E., *Mussolini e la politica estera italiana 1919–1933*, Padua 1960.
*Documents diplomatiques français 1871–1914*, 1ᵉ série 1871–1900, 16 vols, 2ᵉ série 1901–1911, 14 vols, 3ᵉ série 1911–1914, 11 vols, Paris 1929–59.
*I documenti diplomatici italiani*, Terza serie 1896–1907, Quarta serie 1907–1914, Quinta serie 1914–1918, Sexta serie 1918–1922, Settima serie 1922–1935, Rome 1952–  .
EDMONDS, SIR J. E. and DAVIES, H. R., *Military Operations: Italy 1915–1919*, London 1949.
EINAUDI, L., *La condotta economica e gli effetti sociali della guerra italiana*, Bari 1933.
ENGEL-JÁNOSI, F., *Österreich und der Vatikan*, 2 vols, Graz 1958–60.
EPSTEIN, K., *Matthias Erzberger and the Dilemma of German Democracy*, Princeton 1959.
ERZBERGER, M., *Erlebnisse im Weltkrieg*, Stuttgart 1920.
*L'esercito italiano nella grande guerra 1915–1918*, I, *Le forze belligeranti*, Ministero della Guerra, Rome 1927.
EVANS-PRITCHARD, E. E., *The Sanusi of Cyrenaica*, Oxford 1949.
FARINI, D., *Diario di fine secolo*, 2 vols, Rome 1962.
FERRARIS, E., *La marcia su Roma veduta dal Viminale*, Rome 1946.
FINALI, G., *Memorie*, Faenza 1955.
FOERSTER, R. F., *The Italian Emigration of Our Times*, Cambridge, Mass., 1919.
FONZI, F., *I cattolici e la società italiana dopo l'unità*, Rome 1953.
FORTUNATO, G., *Il Mezzogiorno e lo stato italiano*, 2 vols, Bari 1911.
   *Pagine e ricordi parlamentari*, 2 vols, Florence 1926–7.
FOSCHINI, A., 'A trent' anni dall' occupazione di Corfu', in *Nuova Antologia*, vol. 459 (1953), pp. 401–12.
FOSSATI, A., *Lavoro e produzione in Italia dalla metà del secolo XVIII alla seconda guerra mondiale*, Turin 1951.

FRANCHETTI, L., *Mezzogiorno e colonie*, Florence 1950.
FRANCHETTI, L. and SONNINO, S., *La Sicilia*, 2nd ed., 2 vols, Florence 1925.
FRASSATI, A., *Giolitti*, Florence 1959.
GALLI, C., *Diarii e lettere*, Florence 1951.
GAMBASIN, A., *Il movimento sociale nell' Opera dei Congressi 1874–1904*, Rome 1958.
GAYDA, V., *L'Italia d'oltre confine*, Turin 1914.
  *Modern Austria*, London 1915.
GERMANETTO, G., *Memorie di un barbiere*, 6th ed., Rome 1950.
GERSCHENKRON, A., 'Notes on the Rate of Industrial Growth in Italy, 1881–1913', in *The Journal of Economic History*, vol. 15 (1955), pp. 360–75.
GIAMPIETRO, E., *Ricordi e riforme*, Casalbordino 1903.
GIOLITTI, G., *Discorsi extraparlamentari*, with introduction by N. Valeri, Turin 1952.
  *Discorsi parlamentari*, 4 vols, Rome 1953–6.
  *Memorie della mia vita*, 3rd ed., Milan 1945.
GIURIATI, G., *Con D'Annunzio e Millo in difesa dell' Adriatico*, Florence 1954.
GOBETTI, P., *Opere complete*, I, Turin 1960.
GOOCH, G. P. and TEMPERLEY, H. W. V., *British Documents on the Origins of the War 1898–1914*, 11 vols, London 1925–38.
GRAMSCI, A., *La questione meridionale*, Rome 1951.
GREY OF FALLODON, VISCOUNT, *Twenty-Five Years*, 2 vols, London 1925.
*Die Grosse Politik der Europäischen Kabinetten 1871–1914*, 53 vols, Berlin 1922–7.
GUARIGLIA, R., *Ricordi 1922–1946*, Naples 1950.
GUARNERI, F., *Battaglie economiche tra le due grandi guerre*, 2 vols, Milan 1953.
HALPERIN, S. W., *Italy and the Vatican at War*, Chicago 1939.
HANKEY, LORD, *The Supreme Command 1914–1918*, 2 vols, London 1961.
HAUTECŒUR, L., *L'Italie sous le ministère Orlando*, Paris 1919.
HELMREICH, E. C., *The Diplomacy of the Balkan Wars*, Cambridge, Mass., 1938.
HERRE, P., *Die Südtiroler Frage*, Munich 1927.
HOSTETTER, R., *The Italian Socialist Movement, I, Origins (1860–1882)*, Princeton 1958.
HOWARD, E. P., *Il Partito Popolare Italiano*, Florence 1957.
*Indagine statistica sullo sviluppo del reddito nazionale dell' Italia dal 1861 al 1956*, Istituto Centrale di Statistica, Rome 1957.
*L'Italia radicale. Carteggi di Felice Cavallotti 1867–1898*, ed. L. Dalle Nogare and S. Merli, Milan 1959.
JACINI, S., *Un conservatore rurale della nuova Italia*, 2 vols, Bari 1926.
  *Storia del Partito Popolare Italiano*, Milan 1951.
JEMOLO, A. C., *Chiesa e Stato in Italia negli ultimi cento anni*, Turin 1948.
JOLL, J., *Intellectuals in Politics*, London 1960.
KING, BOLTON and OKEY, T., *Italy To-day*, 2nd ed., London 1909.
KYBAL, V., 'Czechoslovakia and Italy', in *Journal of Central European Affairs*, I, vol. 13 (1953–4), pp. 352–68; II, vol. 14 (1954–5), pp. 65–76.
LABRIOLA, A., *Lettere a Engels*, Rome 1949.
LANGER, W. L., *European Alliances and Alignments*, New York 1931.
LESSONA, A., *Memorie*, Florence 1958.

LIPPARINI, L., *Andrea Costa*, Milan 1952.
LLOYD GEORGE, D., *War Memoirs*, 6 vols, London 1933-6.
LOWE, C. J., *Salisbury and the Mediterranean*, London 1965.
LUZZATTI, L., *Memorie autobiografiche e carteggi*, 2 vols, Bologna 1931-5.
*Opere*, 4 vols, Bologna 1924-52.
LUZZATTO, G., *Storia economica dell' età moderna e contemporanea*, Part II,
    Padua 1948.
MACARTNEY, M. H. H. and CREMONA, P., *Italy's Foreign and Colonial Policy
    1914-1937*, Oxford 1938.
MALAGODI, O., *Conversazioni della guerra 1914-1919*, 2 vols, Milan 1960.
MALATESTA, A., *I socialisti italiani durante la guerra*, Milan 1926.
MAMATEY, V. S., *The United States and East Central Europe 1914-1918*,
    Princeton 1957.
MARANELLI, C. and SALVEMINI, G., *La questione dell' Adriatico*, 2nd ed.,
    Rome 1919.
MARDER, A. J., *British Naval Policy 1880-1905*, London 1940.
*La marina italiana nella grande guerra*, I, *Vigilia d'armi sul mare*, Ufficio Storico
    della R. Marina, Florence 1935.
MICHELS, R., *Storia critica del movimento socialista italiano*, Florence 1926.
MONTAGNANA, M., *Ricordi di un militante*, Milan 1947.
MONTICONE, A., *Nitti e la grande guerra 1914-1918*, Milan 1961.
MORANDI, C., *Politica estera dell' Italia dopo il '70*, Florence n.d.
MOSCA, G., *Partiti e sindacati nella crisi del regime parlamentare*, Bari 1949.
MUSSOLINI, B., *Opera omnia*, ed. E. and D. Susmel, 36 vols, Florence 1951-
    63.
NATALE, G., *Giolitti e gli italiani*, Milan 1949.
NENNI, P., *Storia di quattro anni*, 2nd ed., Rome 1946.
NEUFELD, M. F., *Italy: School for Awakening Countries*, Ithaca 1961.
NICOLSON, H., *Curzon: The Last Phase 1919-1925*, London 1934.
*King George V*, London 1952.
NITTI, F. S., *Il bilancio dello Stato dal 1862 al 1896-7*, Naples 1900.
*Il capitale straniero in Italia*, Bari 1915.
*L'Italia all' alba del secolo XX*, Turin 1901.
*Meditazioni dell' esilio*, Naples 1947.
*La ricchezza d'Italia*, Naples 1904.
*Nord e Sud*, Turin 1900.
*Rivelazioni: dramatis personae*, Naples 1948.
ORLANDO, V. E., *Discorsi per la guerra e per la pace*, Foligno 1923.
*Memorie 1915-1919*, Milan 1960.
*Miei rapporti di governo con la Santa Sede*, 2nd ed., Milan 1944.
PAPAFAVA, F., *Dieci anni di vita italiana 1899-1909*, 2 vols, Bari 1913.
*Papers relating to the Foreign Relations of the United States: The Paris Peace
    Conference 1919*, 13 vols, Washington 1942-7.
PARETO, V., *Lettere a Maffeo Pantaleoni*, ed. G. De Rosa, 3 vols, Rome 1960.
PINI, G. and SUSMEL, D., *Mussolini, l'uomo e l'opera*, 4 vols, Florence 1952-5.
PIRRI, P., *Pio IX e Vittorio Emanuele II dal loro carteggio privato, III, La
    questione romana 1864-1870*, in *Miscellanea historiae pontificiae*, XXIV
    and XXV, Vatican City 1961.

PRETI, L., *Le lotte agrarie nella valle padana*, Turin 1955.

PRIBRAM, A. F., *The Secret Treaties of Austria-Hungary*, 2 vols, Cambridge, Mass. 1920–1.

PUBLIC RECORD OFFICE, F.O. 45, Italy: correspondence from British Embassy in Rome.

*Quarant' anni di politica italiana. Dalle carte di Giovanni Giolitti*, 3 vols, Milan 1962.

RÉPACI, A., *La marcia su Roma*, 2 vols, Rome 1963.

RIGOLA, R., *Il movimento operaio nel Biellese*, Bari 1930.

*Storia del movimento operaio italiano*, Milan 1947.

RIGUZZI, B., *Sindacalismo e riformismo nel Parmense*, Bari 1931.

ROCHAT, G., 'L'esercito italiano nell' estate 1914', in *Nuova rivista storica*, vol. 45 (1961), pp. 295–348.

RODD, SIR J. RENNELL, *Social and Diplomatic Memories*, 3 vols, London 1922–5.

ROMANO, S. F., *Storia dei fasci siciliani*, Bari 1959.

*Storia della questione meridionale*, Palermo 1945.

ROMEO, R., *Breve storia della grande industria in Italia*, Milan 1961.

ROSSELLI, N., *Mazzini e Bakounine*, Turin 1927.

ROSSI, E., *Il manganello e l'aspersorio*, Florence 1958.

*I padroni del vapore*, Bari, 1955.

SALANDRA, A., *L'intervento 1915*, Milan 1930.

*La neutralità italiana 1914*, Milan 1928.

*Memorie politiche 1916–1925*, Milan 1951.

SALANDRA, A. and SONNINO, S., 'Carteggio della neutralità', in *Nuova Antologia*, vol. 377 (1935), pp. 483–503.

SALATA, F., *Per la storia diplomatica della questione romana*, Milan 1929.

*Il nodo di Gibuti*, Milan 1939.

SALOMONE, A. W., *Italian Democracy in the Making*, Philadelphia 1945.

SALVATORELLI, L., *La Triplice Alleanza*, Milan 1939.

SALVATORELLI, L. and MIRA, G., *Storia del fascismo*, Rome 1952.

SALVEMINI, G., *Dal patto di Londra alla pace di Roma*, Turin 1925.

*The Fascist Dictatorship in Italy*, London 1928.

'L'Italia economica dal 1919 al 1922', in *Studi in onore di Gino Luzzatto*, III, Milan 1950.

*Mussolini diplomatico*, Bari 1952.

*La politica estera dell' Italia dal 1871 al 1914*, Florence 1944.

*Scritti sulla questione meridionale (1896–1955)*, Turin 1955.

SANDONÀ, A., *L'irredentismo nelle lotte politiche e nelle contese diplomatiche italo-austriache*, 3 vols, Bologna 1932–8.

SERENI, E., *Il capitalismo nelle campagne*, Turin 1948.

SERPIERI, A., *La guerra e le classi rurali italiane*, Bari 1930.

SERRA, E., *Camille Barrère e l'intesa italo-francese*, Milan 1950.

*L'intesa mediterranea del 1902*, Milan 1957.

SERTOLI SALIS, R., *Le isole italiane dell' Egeo*, Rome 1939.

SFORZA, C., *Contemporary Italy*, London 1946.

*Pensiero e azione di una politica estera italiana*, Bari 1924.

SODERINI, E., *Il pontificato di Leone XIII*, 3 vols, Milan 1932–3.

SOLERI, M., *Memorie.* Turin 1949.

*Sommario di statistiche storiche italiane*, Istituto Centrale di Statistica, Rome 1958.

SPADOLINI, G., *Giolitti e i cattolici*, Florence 1960.

*L'opposizione cattolica*, Florence 1954.

SPRIANO, P., *L'occupazione delle fabbriche*, Turin 1964.

*Torino operaia nella grande guerra*, Turin 1960.

STEED, H. W., *Through Thirty Years*, 2 vols, London 1924.

STRESEMANN, G., *Diaries, Letters and Papers*, ed. E. Sutton, 3 vols, London 1935–40.

STRINGHER, B., *Gli scambi con l'estero e la politica commerciale italiana dal 1860 al 1910*, in *Cinquanta anni di storia italiana*, III, Milan 1911.

STURZO, L., *I discorsi politici*, Rome 1951.

*Italy and Fascism*, London 1926.

*Survey of International Affairs 1920–3, 1924, 1926, 1927*, ed. A. J. Toynbee, London 1925–9.

SWIRE, J., *Albania, the Rise of a Kingdom*, London 1929.

TAMARO, A., *Venti anni di storia 1922–1943*, 2 vols, Rome 1954.

TASCA, A., *Nascita e avvento del fascismo*, Florence 1950.

TAYLOR, A. J. P., 'British Policy in Morocco 1886–1902', in *The English Historical Review*, vol. 66 (1951), pp. 342–74.

TEMPERLEY, H. W. V., *History of the Peace Conference of Paris*, 6 vols, London 1920–4.

TEMPERLEY, H. W. V. and PENSON, L. M., *Foundations of British Foreign Policy*, Cambridge 1938.

TITTONI, T., 'Ricordi personali di politica interna', in *Nuova Antologia*, vol. 342 (1929), pp. 304–27, 441–67.

TOMMASINI, F., *L'Italia alla vigilia della guerra*, 5 vols, Bologna 1934–41.

TOSCANO, M., *Gli accordi di San Giovanni di Moriana*, Milan 1936.

*Pagine di storia diplomatica contemporanea*, 2 vols, Milan 1963.

*Il patto di Londra*, Bologna 1934.

*La Serbia e l'intervento in guerra dell' Italia*, Milan 1939.

TREVELYAN, G. M., *Grey of Fallodon*, London 1937.

*Scenes from Italy's War*, London 1919.

TURATI, F., *Discorsi parlamentari*, 3 vols, Rome 1950.

TURATI, F. and KULISCIOFF, A., *Carteggio*, V, *Dopoguerra e fascismo 1919–1922*, Turin 1953; VI, *Il delitto Matteotti e l'Aventino*, Turin 1959.

UNDERWOOD, F. M., *United Italy*, London 1912.

VALENTI, G., *L'Italia agricola dal 1861 al 1911*, in *Cinquanta anni di storia italiana*, II, Milan 1911.

VALERI, N., *Da Giolitti a Mussolini*, Florence 1956.

*D'Annunzio davanti al fascismo*, Florence 1963.

VALIANI, L., *La dissoluzione dell' Austria-Ungheria*, Milan 1966.

VERCESI, E., *Il movimento cattolico in Italia 1870–1922*, Florence 1923.

*Tre papi*, Milan 1929.

VIGEZZI, B., *I problemi della neutralità e della guerra nel carteggio Salandra-Sonnino (1914–1917)*, Milan 1962.

'Le Radiose Giornate del maggio 1915 nei rapporti dei prefetti', in *Nuova rivista storica*, vol. 43 (1959), pp. 313–44, and vol. 44 (1960), pp. 54–111.

VÖCHTING, F., *Die italienische Südfrage*, Berlin 1951.

VOLPE, G., *Italia moderna 1815–1915*, 3 vols, Florence 1943–52.

WALTERS, E., 'Austro-Russian Relations under Goluchowski', in *The Slavonic Review*, II, vol. 31 (1952–3), pp. 503–27; III, vol. 32 (1953–4), pp. 187–214.

WOODWARD, E. L. and BUTLER, R., *Documents on British Foreign Policy 1919–1939*, First series, London 1947– .

ZAGHI, C., *P. S. Mancini, l'Africa e il problema del Mediterraneo 1884–1885*, Rome 1955.

ZINGALI, G., *Liberalismo e fascismo nel mezzogiorno d'Italia*, 2 vols, Milan 1933.

# SELECTED BOOKS IN ENGLISH

The best general histories of the liberal half-century are:

1. Dennis Mack Smith, *Italy, A Modern History*, Ann Arbor and London 1959.
   A brilliant, deeply pessimistic interpretation, emphasising the defects and weaknesses of liberal Italy.

2. B. Croce, *A History of Italy 1871–1915*, Oxford 1929.
   The philosopher's tribute to the liberal achievement. Its publication in Italian in 1928 was a major contribution to the intellectual resistance to fascism.

3. R. Albrecht-Carrié, *Italy from Napoleon to Mussolini*, New York 1950.
   Sober and dispassionate.

4. C. J. S. Sprigge, *The Development of Modern Italy*, London 1943.
   A brief but brilliant analysis reflecting the anti-Depretis anti-Giolitti democratic school of thought.

5. C. Sforza, *Contemporary Italy*, London 1946.
   Impressionistic but of value as the interpretation of a leading participant in the events of 1915–25.

Two short introductions to modern Italy deserve special mention for their perceptiveness and wide range:

6. E. Wiskemann, *Italy*, Oxford 1947.
7. H. Stuart Hughes, *The United States and Italy*, Cambridge, Mass. 1953.

An excellent study of the politics of the Giolittian period is:

8. A. W. Salomone, *Italian Democracy in the Making*, Philadelphia 1945.

On the Roman question, Church–State relations and the Catholic political movement:

9. D. A. Binchy, *Church and State in Fascist Italy*, Oxford 1941.
   A masterly study by an Irish Catholic scholar. Includes much information on the pre-fascist period.

10. A. C. Jemolo, *Church and State in Italy 1850–1960*, Oxford 1960.
    A deeply perceptive Liberal Catholic interpretation, abridged from the same author's *Chiesa e Stato in Italia negli ultimi cento anni*.

11. R. Webster, *Christian Democracy in Italy 1860–1960*, London 1961.
    A good general history.

12. S. W. Halperin, *Italy and the Vatican at War*, Chicago 1939.
    A detailed study of the crucial years 1870–8.

13. E. E. Y. Hales, *Pio Nono*, London 1954.
    A good biography by an English Catholic.

14. E. Soderini, *Leo XIII, Italy and France*, London 1935.
    A translation of vol. II of *Il pontificato di Leone XIII*.

On Italian socialism:

15. W. Hilton-Young, *The Italian Left*, London 1949.
    Slight but useful, in the absence of a fuller study, as an introduction to the subject.

16. R. Hostetter, *The Italian Socialist Movement, I, Origins (1860–1882)*, Princeton 1958.
    An excellent study based on the massive research which Italian scholars have conducted in the subject in recent years.

Memoirs and biographies are few. Italian statesmen rarely write memoirs, Italian scholars are rarely attracted to the biographical form, and the few books that do appear are rarely translated. The list is therefore parsimonious:

17. F. Crispi, *Memoirs*, 3 vols, London 1912–14.
    The second and third volumes deal with foreign policy between 1877 and 1896.

18. G. Giolitti, *Memoirs of my Life*, London 1923.
    In spite of a poor translation, the quality of Giolitti's mind and temperament comes through. The recently published selection from Giolitti's papers (*Quarant' anni di politica italiana*) shows with what care and accuracy the *Memoirs* were compiled.

On economic and social history:

19. Shepard B. Clough, *Economic History of Modern Italy*, New York 1964.
    A brave but disappointing attempt to fill a huge gap in the literature. Contains much essential information not otherwise available in English.

20. M. F. Neufeld, *Italy: A School for Awakening Countries*, Ithaca 1961.
    In spite of its misleading title, a valuable social history of Italy since unification. A mine of information, historical and statistical, on the Italian economy, labour movement, social legislation, etc.

21. R. F. Foerster, *The Italian Emigration of Our Times*, Cambridge, Mass. 1919.
    The classic work on the subject.

On foreign policy before 1914:

22. L. Albertini, *The Origins of the War of 1914*, 3 vols, Oxford 1952–7.
    A major contribution, judged by the highest standards of international

scholarship, to the study of pre-1914 Europe, as well as the most comprehensive account in English of Italian foreign policy.

23. W. C. Askew, *Europe and Italy's Acquisition of Libya*, Durham, N.C. 1942.
    A scholarly monograph.

The best-known textbooks in English on pre-1914 European diplomacy tend to pay little attention to Italy. The most notable exceptions are W. L. Langer, *European Alliances and Alignments*, New York 1931, and *The Diplomacy of Imperialism*, New York 1935, which give Italy a fair share of attention. The publication of the Italian diplomatic documents, now in progress, will make such indifference less excusable in the future.

A. J. P. Taylor, *The Struggle for Mastery in Europe 1848–1918*, Oxford 1954, shows not only indifference but anti-Italian prejudice. See p. xxiii, note 4, which excepts the Italians from the generalisation that 'all diplomatists were honest, according to their moral code'. If this is a statement that Italian diplomatists were habitual liars, Mr Taylor offers no evidence for it; and could not do so, because there is none.

On the First World War and the Peace Conference:

24. A. Salandra, *Italy and the Great War*, London 1932.
    An abridged translation of *La neutralità* and *L'intervento*.

25. W. W. Gottlieb, *Studies in Secret Diplomacy during the First World War*, London 1957.
    A meticulous analysis of the diplomacy of Italy's intervention, marred by a crude Marxist exaggeration of the influence of economic factors on foreign policies.

26. J. A. Thayer, *Italy and the Great War. Politics and Culture 1870–1915*, Madison 1964.
    A full-scale study of Italian neutrality and intervention, preceded by an analysis of selected topics and episodes from the period 1870–1914. The author's aim is to examine 'the causal relation between ideas and politics'. Especially valuable because based on exhaustive study of the press and contemporary writing. Strongly pro-Giolitti and anti-Salandra in tone; the conclusion being that Italy's intervention was 'a refutation of the whole work of the Postrisorgimento'.

27. R. Albrecht-Carrié, *Italy at the Paris Peace Conference*, New York 1938.
    The basic work, though it needs revision in the light of recent documentation and research.

28. M. H. H. Macartney and P. Cremona, *Italy's Foreign and Colonial Policy 1914–37*, Oxford 1938.
    A well-informed survey based on contemporary published material.

On Mussolini:

29. Sir Ivone Kirkpatrick, *Mussolini, Study of a Demagogue*, London 1964.
    The best comprehensive biography in English, though the pre-1922 section is the least satisfactory and contains many errors of detail.

30. G. Megaro, *Mussolini in the Making*, London 1938.
    Still by far the best work in English on Mussolini's early political career and intellectual development.

31. P. Monelli, *Mussolini, An Intimate Life*, London 1953.
    A short and highly readable biography with shrewd insights into Mussolini's character and temperament, but excessive emphasis on his private life and personal idiosyncrasies.

32. Laura Fermi, *Mussolini*, Chicago 1961.
    A straightforward and perceptive study, stronger on Mussolini's personality than on his politics.

On the fascist rise to power and the early years of fascist rule:

33. A Rossi, *The Rise of Italian Fascism*, London 1938.
    Still the best single work on the subject, even though it appeared (in English and French) as long ago as 1938. In the Italian edition of 1950 (published under the author's real name, Angelo Tasca, and the title *Nascita e avvento del fascismo*) the text was unchanged but much new material was added in extensive footnotes.

34. F. Chabod, *History of Italian Fascism*, London 1963.
    A dispassionate summing-up by a great anti-fascist historian of the fascist generation.

35. E. Nolte, *Three Faces of Fascism*, London 1965.
    Part III is a survey of Italian fascism.

Three important accounts by anti-fascist leaders, written in exile, are:

36. P. Nenni, *Ten Years of Tyranny in Italy*, London 1932.

37. G. Salvemini, *The Fascist Dictatorship in Italy*, London 1928.

38. L. Sturzo, *Italy and Fascismo*, London 1926.

On fascist government and institutions:

39. H. Finer, *Mussolini's Italy*, London 1935.

40. Dante L. Germino, *The Italian Fascist Party in Power*, Minneapolis 1959.

41. Herbert W. Schneider, *Making the Fascist State*, New York 1928.

42. H. Arthur Steiner, *Government in Fascist Italy*, New York 1938.

On anti-fascism:

43. C. F. Delzell, *Mussolini's Enemies*, Princeton 1961.

# CABINETS AND LEADING
# MINISTERS 1870-1925

| | PRIME MINISTER | MINISTER OF INTERIOR | FOREIGN MINISTER |
|---|---|---|---|
| Dec 1869–June 1873 | Lanza | Lanza | Visconti Venosta |
| July 1873–Mar 1876 | Minghetti | Cantelli | Visconti Venosta |
| Mar 1876–Mar 1878 | Depretis | Nicotera (to Dec 1877) Crispi (from Dec 1877) | Melegari (to Dec 1877) Depretis (from Dec 1877) |
| Mar 1878–Dec 1878 | Cairoli | Zanardelli | Corti |
| Dec 1878–July 1879 | Depretis | Depretis | Depretis |
| July 1879–May 1881 | Cairoli | Villa (to Nov 1879) Depretis (from Nov 1879) | Cairoli |
| May 1881–July 1887 | Depretis | Depretis (to Apr 1887) Crispi (from Apr 1887) | Mancini (to June 1885) Depretis (June–Oct 1885) Robilant (Oct 1885– Mar 1887) Depretis (from Apr 1887) |
| Aug 1887–Feb 1891 | Crispi | Crispi | Crispi |

**Note.** The list of Prime Ministers, Ministers of Interior and Foreign Ministers is complete; other ministers are included only if mentioned in the text.

| **Abbreviations** | | | | | | |
|---|---|---|---|---|---|---|
| A | Agriculture | E | Education | M | Munitions | PW PublicWorks |
| AIC | Agriculture, | I | Industry | N | Navy | T Treasury |
| | Industry and | IC | Industry & | P | Posts | Tpt Transport |
| | Commerce | | Commerce | PMW | Pensions | W War |
| C | Colonies | J | Justice | | & Military | wp without |
| | | L | Labour | | Welfare | portfolio |

| MINISTERS OF FINANCE AND TREASURY (T) | MINISTERS FOR WAR (W) AND NAVY (N) | OTHER LEADING MINISTERS |
|---|---|---|
| Sella | Ricotti (W) | |
| Minghetti | Ricotti (W) | Spaventa (PW)   Finali (A) |
| Depretis (to Dec 1877) | Brin (N) | Mancini (J) Zanardelli (PW) (to Nov 1877) |
| Magliani (from Dec 1877) | | |
| Seismit-Doda | | Baccarini (PW) |
| Magliani | | |
| Grimaldi (to Nov 1879) | | Baccarini (PW) |
| Magliani (from Nov 1879) | | |
| Magliani | Ricotti (W) (Oct 1884–Apr 1887) Bertolè-Viale (W) (from Apr 1887) Brin (N) (from Mar 1884) | Zanardelli (J) (to May 1883 and from Apr 1887) Baccarini (PW) (to May 1883) Saracco (PW) (from Apr 1887) |
| Magliani (to Dec 1888) Grimaldi (Dec 1888–Feb 1889 and from Dec 1890) Seismit-Doda (Mar 1889–Sept 1890) Giolitti (T) (Mar 1889–Dec 1890) | Bertolè-Viale (W) Brin (N) | Zanardelli (J) Saracco (PW) (to Feb 1889) Finali (PW) (from Mar 1889) Boselli (E) (from Feb 1888) |

|  | PRIME MINISTER | MINISTER OF INTERIOR | FOREIGN MINISTER |
|---|---|---|---|
| Feb 1891–May 1892 | Rudinì | Nicotera | Rudinì |
| May 1892–Nov 1893 | Giolitti | Giolitti | Brin |
| Dec 1893–Mar 1896 | Crispi | Crispi | Blanc |
| Mar 1896–June 1898 | Rudinì | Rudinì | Caetani (to July 1896) Visconti Venosta (from July 1896) |
| June 1898–June 1900 | Pelloux | Pelloux | Canevaro (to May 1899) Visconti Venosta (from May 1899) |
| June 1900–Feb 1901 | Saracco | Saracco | Visconti Venosta |
| Feb 1901–Oct 1903 | Zanardelli | Giolitti (to June 1903) Zanardelli (from June 1903) | Prinetti (to Mar 1903) Morin (from Apr 1903) |
| Nov 1903–Mar 1905 | Giolitti | Giolitti | Tittoni |
| Mar 1905–Feb 1906 | Fortis | Fortis | Tittoni (to Dec 1905) San Giuliano (from Dec 1905) |
| Feb 1906–May 1906 | Sonnino | Sonnino | Guicciardini |
| May 1906–Dec 1909 | Giolitti | Giolitti | Tittoni |

| MINISTERS OF FINANCE AND TREASURY (T) | MINISTERS FOR WAR (W) AND NAVY (N) | OTHER LEADING MINISTERS |
|---|---|---|
| Colombo<br>Luzzatti (T) | Pelloux (W) | |
| Grimaldi (T) | Pelloux (W) | Martini (E) |
| Sonnino<br>(to June 1894)<br>and (T) (to Mar 1896)<br>Boselli<br>(from June 1894) | | Saracco (PW)<br>Boselli (A)<br>(to June 1894) |
| Colombo (T)<br>(to July 1896)<br>Luzzatti (T)<br>(from July 1896) | Ricotti (W)<br>(to July 1896)<br>Pelloux (W)<br>(July 1896–Dec 1897)<br>Brin (N) | Prinetti (PW)<br>(July 1896–Dec 1897)<br>Gianturco (E)<br>(to Sept 1897)<br>(J) (Sept–Dec 1897)<br>Cocco-Ortu (A)  Zanardelli (J)<br>(from Dec 1897)   (from Dec 1897) |
| Carcano<br>(to May 1899)<br>Boselli (T)<br>(from May 1899) | Bettolo (N)<br>(from May 1899) | Nasi (P)        Fortis (AIC)<br>(to May 1899)   (to May 1899)<br>Salandra (AIC)  San Giuliano (P)<br>(from May 1899)  (from May 1899) |
| Rubini (T) | | Carcano (AIC)   Gianturco (J) |
| Wollemborg<br>(to July 1901)<br>Carcano<br>(from July 1901) | Bettolo (N)<br>(Apr–June 1903) | Cocco-Ortu (J)<br>Nasi (E) |
| Rosano<br>(Nov 1903)<br>Luzzatti<br>(from Dec 1903) | Mirabello (N) | Orlando (E) |
| Carcano (T) | Mirabello (N) | |
| Salandra<br>Luzzatti (T)<br>Carcano (T) | Mirabello (N)<br>Casana (W)<br>(Dec 1907–Apr 1909)<br>Spingardi (W)<br>(from Apr 1909)<br>Mirabello (N) | Sacchi (J)    Boselli (E)<br>Pantano (A)<br>Orlando (J)   Schanzer (P)<br>(from Mar 1907)<br>Cocco-Ortu (AIC)<br>Gianturco (PW)   Bertolini (PW)<br>(to Nov 1907)      (from Nov 1907) |

| | PRIME MINISTER | MINISTER OF INTERIOR | FOREIGN MINISTER |
| --- | --- | --- | --- |
| Dec 1909–Mar 1910 | Sonnino | Sonnino | Guicciardini |
| Mar 1910–Mar 1911 | Luzzatti | Luzzatti | San Giuliano |
| Mar 1911–Mar 1914 | Giolitti | Giolitti | San Giuliano |
| Mar 1914–June 1916 | Salandra | Salandra | San Giuliano (to Oct 1914) Sonnino (from Nov 1914) |
| June 1916–Oct 1917 | Boselli | Orlando | Sonnino |
| Oct 1917–June 1919 | Orlando | Orlando | Sonnino |
| June 1919–June 1920 | Nitti | Nitti | Tittoni (to Nov 1919) Scialoja (from Nov 1919) |
| June 1920–June 1921 | Giolitti | Giolitti | Sforza |
| July 1921–Feb 1922 | Bonomi | Bonomi | Della Torretta |
| Feb 1922–Oct 1922 | Facta | Taddei | Schanzer |

| MINISTERS OF FINANCE AND TREASURY (T) | MINISTERS FOR WAR (W) AND NAVY (N) | OTHER LEADING MINISTERS |
|---|---|---|
| Salandra (T) | Spingardi (W)<br>Bettolo (N) | Scialoja (J)   Rubini (PW)<br>Luzzatti (AIC) |
| Facta | Spingardi (W) | Credaro (E)   Sacchi (PW) |
| Facta | Spingardi (W) | Credaro (E)   Nitti (AIC)<br>Sacchi (PW)   Bertolini (C)<br>(from Nov 1912) |
| Rubini (T)<br>(to Oct 1914)<br>Carcano (T)<br>(from Oct 1914) | Porro (W)<br>(Mar 1914)<br>Grandi (W)<br>(Mar–Oct 1914)<br>Zupelli (W)<br>(Oct 1914–Apr 1916) | Martini (C)   Riccio (P)<br>Orlando (J)<br>(from Nov 1914)<br>Grippo (E)<br>(from Nov 1914)<br>Barzilai (wp)<br>(from July 1915) |
| Meda<br>Carcano (T) | Giardino (W)<br>(1917) | Bissolati (wp)   Bonomi (PW)<br>Sacchi (J)   Colosimo (C)<br>Bianchi (wp)   Scialoja (wp)<br>De Nava (IC)   Fera (P) |
| Meda<br><br>Nitti (T)<br>(to Jan 1919) | Caviglia (W)<br>(from Jan 1919) | Bissolati (PMW)   Dallolio (M)<br>(to Dec 1918)   (to May 1918)<br>Bianchi (Tpt)   Sacchi (J)<br>(to May 1918)   (to Jan 1919)<br>Crespi (wp)   Colosimo (C)<br>Facta (J)   Riccio (A)<br>(from Jan 1919)   (from Jan 1919)<br>De Nava (IC)<br>(from Jan 1919) |
| Schanzer<br>Tedesco (T)<br>(to Mar 1920)<br>Luzzatti (T)<br>(from Mar 1920) | | |
| Tedesco<br>Meda (T) | Bonomi (W)<br>(to Mar 1921) | Croce (E)   Alessio (I)<br>Labriola (L)   Micheli (A)<br>Fera (J)   Peano (PW) |
| Soleri<br>De Nava (T)<br>Peano (T) | Gasparotto (W)<br><br>Soleri (W) | Micheli (PW)<br><br>Alessio (J)   Riccio (PW)<br>(from Aug 1922)<br>Amendola (C)   Di Cesarò (P) |

|                          | PRIME MINISTER | MINISTER OF INTERIOR                              | FOREIGN MINISTER |
| ------------------------ | -------------- | ------------------------------------------------ | ---------------- |
| Oct 1922–(July 1943)     | Mussolini      | Mussolini (to June 1924) Federzoni (June 1924– Nov 1926) Mussolini (from Nov 1926) | Mussolini        |

| MINISTERS OF FINANCE AND TREASURY (T) | MINISTERS FOR WAR (W) AND NAVY (N) | OTHER LEADING MINISTERS | |
|---|---|---|---|
| De Stefani (to July 1925) | Diaz (W) (to Apr 1924) | Cavazzoni (L) (to Apr 1923) | Gentile (E) (to June 1924) |
| Volpi (from July 1925) | Di Giorgio (W) (Apr 1924–Apr 1925) | Federzoni (C) (to June 1924) | Oviglio (J) (to Jan 1925) |
| | Thaon di Revel (N) (to Apr 1925) | Di Cesarò (P) (to Jan 1924) | |
| | Mussolini (W) (N) (from Apr 1925) | Casati (E) (June 1924–Jan 1925) | |
| | | Sarrocchi (PW) (June 1924–Jan 1925) | |
| | | Rocco (J) (from Jan 1925) | |

# INDEX